ISBN 978-0-331-06783-5
PIBN 11010086

FB &c Ltd, Dalton House, 60 Windsor Avenue, London, SW19 2RR.
Company number 08720141. Registered in England and Wales.

For support please visit www.forgottenbooks.com

STATUTES AT LARGE

OF THE

STATE OF NEW YORK,

CONTAINING

THE GENERAL STATUTES PASSED IN THE YEARS

1871, 1872, 1873 AND 1874,

WITH A

REFERENCE TO ALL THE DECISIONS UPON THEM.

ALSO,

THE CONSTITUTION OF THE STATE OF NEW YORK

AS AMENDED IN 1875.

EDITED BY

JOHN W. EDMONDS

AND

WILLIAM HILDRETH FIELD.

VOLUME IX.

PUBLISHED BY
WEED, PARSONS & COMPANY,
ALBANY, N. Y.
1875.

WEED, PARSONS AND COMPANY,
PRINTERS AND STEREOTYPERS,
ALBANY, N.Y.

TITLES

OF ALL THE

LAWS PASSED BY THE LEGISLATURE OF NEW YORK

AT ITS NINETY-FOURTH SESSION,

1871.

[The titles of the acts inserted in this compilation are in this list printed in italics.]

CHAP. 1. An Act to authorize the issue of Monroe county bonds. Passed January 4, 1871; three-fifths being present.

CHAP. 2. An Act for the relief of the Free Medical and Surgical Dispensing Association of the city of Buffalo. Passed January 13, 1871; three-fifths being present.

CHAP. 3. *An Act to amend an act entitled "An act to regulate the term of office of Notaries Public." Passed January* 17, 1871.

CHAP. 4. An Act to authorize the trustees of the village of Owego to convey or otherwise dispose of the public park or square in said village, or a part thereof, for certain purposes. Passed January 20, 1871; three-fifths being present.

CHAP. 5. An Act in relation to the improvement of the Eighth and Tenth avenues in the city of New York. Passed January 20, 1871; three-fifths being present.

CHAP. 6. An Act to amend an act entitled "An act to incorporate the Presbyterian Committee of Home Missions of the General Assembly of the Presbyterian Church in the United States of America," passed April eighteenth, eighteen hundred and sixty-two. Passed January 20, 1871.

CHAP. 7. An Act authorizing the city of Albany to issue bonds for certain purposes. Passed January 20, 1871; three-fifths being present.

CHAP. 8. An Act to authorize the Board of Trustees of the town of Morrisania, in the county of Westchester, to borrow money for certain purposes upon the faith and credit of said town. Passed January 25, 1871; three-fifths being present.

CHAP. 9. An Act to amend chapter one hundred and fifty-seven of the Laws of eighteen hundred and sixty, entitled "An act relative to lands devised by Augustus Van Cortlandt, deceased," passed April third, eighteen hundred and sixty. Passed January 25, 1871.

CHAP. 10. An Act to authorize the extension of the time for the collection of taxes in the several towns and cities in this State. Passed January 26, 1871; three-fifths being present.

CHAP. 11. *An Act providing for additional compensation to deputies, clerks and assistants in the various departments of the State government. Passed January* 26, 1871; *three-fifths being present.*

CHAP. 12. *An Act supplementary to the act entitled "An act to provide for the incorporation of religious societies," passed April fifth, eighteen hundred and thirteen. Passed January* 31, 1871; *three-fifths being present.*

CHAP. 13. An Act to legalize the proceedings of the Board of Supervisors in and for the county of Chautauqua. Passed January 31, 1871; three-fifths being present.

CHAP. 14. An Act to provide for the mode and manner of electing town and other officers at annual elections, to be held in and for the several towns in the county of Richmond, and to legalize the election of town officers, elected at the annual election, held in the several towns of said county, the seventh day of June, eighteen hundred and seventy. Passed January 31, 1871; three-fifths being present.

CHAP. 15. An Act to authorize the village of Athens, in the county of Greene, to borrow money to purchase a steam fire engine and apparatus, and procure another engine house and lot. Passed January 31, 1871; three-fifths being present.

CHAP. 16. *An Act to amend section one of chapter four hundred and nine of the Laws of eighteen hundred and seventy, entitled "An act to authorize circuit courts and courts of oyer and terminer to require the attendance of additional jurors." Passed January* 31, 1871; *three-fifths being present.*

CHAP. 17. An Act to extend the time for the collection of taxes of the Tremont Fire District of the town of West Farms, of the county of Westchester. Passed February 1, 1871; three-fifths being present.

CHAP. 18. *An Act to amend chapter one hundred and ninety-four of the Laws of eighteen hundred and forty-nine, entitled "An act to vest in the Board of Supervisors certain legislative powers, and to prescribe their fees for certain services," passed April third, eighteen hundred and forty-nine. Passed February* 2, 1871; *three-fifths being present.*

CHAP. 19. An Act to authorize the Avenue C Railroad Company, of the city of New York, to extend their railroad tracks through certain streets and avenues in the city of New York. Passed February 2, 1871.

CHAP. 20. An Act to authorize the city and town of Binghamton to purchase a toll-house and land in said city. Passed February 6, 1871; three-fifths being present.

CHAP. 21. An Act to incorporate the American Home Missionary Society. Passed February 6, 1871.

CHAP. 22. An Act to amend an act entitled "An act to incorporate the Turnverein in the city of New York," passed March twenty, eighteen hundred and fifty-seven. Passed February 6, 1871.

CHAP. 23. An Act to authorize the Poughkeepsie and Eastern Railroad to cancel a portion of its first mortgage bonds, and to substitute therefor bonds of smaller denominations. Passed February 6, 1871; three-fifths being present.

CHAP. 24. An Act to amend the act entitled "An act to provide for a supply of water in the city of Albany," passed April ninth, eighteen hundred and fifty. Passed February 6, 1871; three-fifths being present.

CHAP. 25. *An Act appropriating money to pay for the publication of the official canvass, and for deficiency in public printing. Passed February* 8, 1871; *three-fifths being present.*

CHAP. 26. An Act to authorize the Board of Supervisors of the county of Suffolk to borrow moneys in addition to the amounts the law now authorizes. Passed February 8, 1871; three-fifths being present.

CHAP. 27. An Act to change the name of the Brooklyn Homœopathic Dispensary, to authorize it to sell, mortgage or lease its property, to establish and maintain an hospital, and to increase the number of trustees. Passed February 9, 1871.

CHAP. 28. An Act to authorize the County Clerk of the county of Albany to complete the index of records in said Albany county clerk's office, left unfinished by former clerks. Passed February 9, 1871; three-fifths being present.

CHAP. 29. An Act to confirm the official acts of Oliver A. Barstow, a justice of the peace of the town of Nichols, Tioga county. Passed February 10, 1871; three-fifths being present.

CHAP. 30. An Act relative to lands devised by John Tonnele, deceased. Passed February 10, 1871; three-fifths being present.

CHAP. 31. An Act to authorize the Common Council of the city of Lockport to raise, by tax, moneys to pay the present indebtedness of the city. Passed February 10, 1871; three-fifths being present.

CHAP. 32. *An Act to amend the first section of the third title of the eighth chapter of the second part of the Revised Statutes in relation to the custody of minor children. Passed February* 10, 1871; *three-fifths being present.*

CHAP. 33. An Act to release to Wilhelmine Janecke the interest of the State in certain lands in the city of Buffalo, Erie county. Passed February 14, 1871; by a two-third vote.

CHAP. 34. An Act supplemental to an act entitled "An act appointing Jesse P. Haines, Elijah C. Odell and Philetus R. Perry commissioners for draining certain lands in the town of Royalton, county of Niagara," passed April twenty-five, eighteen hundred and sixty-seven. Passed February 14, 1871; three-fifths being present.

CHAP. 35. An Act for the relief of Clark Snook. Passed February 14, 1871; three-fifths being present.

CHAP. 36. An Act for the relief of Christ's Church of West Burlington, in the county of Otsego. Passed February 14, 1871.

CHAP. 37. An Act to amend an act entitled "An act to incorporate the Ladies' Washington Association of Hempsted, Queens county," passed April twenty-two, eighteen hundred and sixty-nine. Passed February 14, 1871.

CHAP. 38. An Act in relation to commissioners appointed under special acts of the legislature for laying out avenues, roads and highways in the county of Westchester, and to regulate the payment of principal and interest on the town bonds of said county by the supervisors thereof. Passed February 15, 1871; three-fifths being present.

CHAP. 39. An Act to prevent the opening of streets or roads through the grounds of St. John's College, in the town of West Farms, county of Westchester. Passed February 15, 1871.

CHAP. 40. An Act to amend an act entitled "An act for the relief of the Cannon Street Baptist Church, of the eighteenth ward of the city of Brooklyn," passed March fifth, eighteen hundred and seventy. Passed February 15, 1871; three-fifths being present.

CHAP. 41. An Act to incorporate the Troy Masonic Hall Association. Passed February 15, 1871.

CHAP. 42. An Act relative to land devised by Gerard W. Morris, deceased. Passed February 15, 1871.

CHAP. 43. An Act to exempt the county of Westchester from the provisions of chapter eight hundred and eighty-eight of the laws of eighteen hundred and sixty-nine, entitled "An act to amend title sixteen, chapter eight, part three of the Revised Statutes, relative to proceedings for the drainage of swamps, marshes and other low or wet lands, and for draining farm lands," passed May twelve, eighteen hundred and sixty-nine. Passed February 16, 1871; three-fifths being present.

CHAP. 44. An Act to provide for the completion of the court-house for the Ninth Judicial District of the city of New York. Passed February 17, 1871; three-fifths being present.

CHAP. 45. An Act to amend an act entitled "An act fixing the time for the election of trustees, town officers and members of the board of education of the school district of the town of Morrisania, county of Westchester, and for regulating such elections," passed March twelfth, eighteen hundred and sixty-nine. Passed February 17, 1871; three-fifths being present.

CHAP. 46. An Act to authorize the Troy Cemetery Association to enlarge its cemetery. Passed February 17, 1871.

CHAP. 47. An Act to provide for the further supply of the city of Brooklyn with water, and for the payment of the expenses thereof. Passed February 18, 1871; three-fifths being present.

CHAP. 48. An Act to incorporate the Odd Fellows' Hall Association of Watertown. Passed February 18, 1871.

CHAP. 49. An Act to amend an act entitled "An act to incorporate the city of Rome," passed February twenty-third, eighteen hundred and seventy. Passed February 18, 1871; three-fifths being present.

CHAP. 50. An Act to confirm the official acts of Harvey C. Smith, a justice of the peace of the town of Clarkstown, in the county of Rockland. Passed February 18, 1871; three-fifths being present.

CHAP. 51. An Act to amend the charter of the village of Warsaw, and to authorize said village to raise money to procure water and to protect said village and the property therein against loss by fire. Passed February 18, 1871; three-fifths being present.

CHAP. 52. An Act to amend the several acts relating to taxes upon dogs so far as relates to the city and town of Lockport, in the county of Niagara, and making the funds derived from such tax in said city and town a common fund to pay for injuries upon sheep occasioned by dogs in said city and town collectively. Passed February 23, 1871; three-fifths being present.

at annual elections, to be held in and for the several towns in the county of Richmond, and to legalize the election of town officers, elected at the annual election, held in the several towns of said county, the seventh day of June, eighteen hundred and seventy. Passed January 31, 1871; three-fifths being present.

CHAP. 15. An Act to authorize the village of Athens, in the county of Greene, to borrow money to purchase a steam fire engine and apparatus, and procure another engine house and lot. Passed January 31, 1871; three-fifths being present.

CHAP. 16. *An Act to amend section one of chapter four hundred and nine of the Laws of eighteen hundred and seventy, entitled "An act to authorize circuit courts and courts of oyer and terminer to require the attendance of additional jurors." Passed January* 31, 1871; *three-fifths being present.*

CHAP. 17. An Act to extend the time for the collection of taxes of the Tremont Fire District of the town of West Farms, of the county of Westchester. Passed February 1, 1871; three-fifths being present.

CHAP. 18. *An Act to amend chapter one hundred and ninety-four of the Laws of eighteen hundred and forty-nine, entitled "An act to vest in the Board of Supervisors certain legislative powers, and to prescribe their fees for certain services," passed April third, eighteen hundred and forty-nine. Passed February* 2, 1871; *three-fifths being present.*

CHAP. 19. An Act to authorize the Avenue C Railroad Company, of the city of New York, to extend their railroad tracks through certain streets and avenues in the city of New York. Passed February 2, 1871.

CHAP. 20. An Act to authorize the city and town of Binghamton to purchase a toll-house and land in said city. Passed February 6, 1871; three-fifths being present.

CHAP. 21. An Act to incorporate the American Home Missionary Society. Passed February 6, 1871.

CHAP. 22. An Act to amend an act entitled "An act to incorporate the Turnverein in the city of New York," passed March twenty, eighteen hundred and fifty-seven. Passed February 6, 1871.

CHAP. 23. An Act to authorize the Poughkeepsie and Eastern Railroad to cancel a portion of its first mortgage bonds, and to substitute therefor bonds of smaller denominations. Passed February 6, 1871; three-fifths being present.

CHAP. 24. An Act to amend the act entitled "An act to provide for a supply of water in the city of Albany," passed April ninth, eighteen hundred and fifty. Passed February 6, 1871; three-fifths being present.

CHAP. 25. *An Act appropriating money to pay for the publication of the official canvass, and for deficiency in public printing. Passed February* 8, 1871; *three-fifths being present.*

CHAP. 26. An Act to authorize the Board of Supervisors of the county of Suffolk to borrow moneys in addition to the amounts the law now authorizes. Passed February 8, 1871; three-fifths being present.

CHAP. 27. An Act to change the name of the Brooklyn Homœopathic Dispensary, to authorize it to sell, mortgage or lease its property, to establish and maintain an hospital, and to increase the number of trustees. Passed February 9, 1871.

CHAP. 28. An Act to authorize the County Clerk of the county of Albany to complete the index of records in said Albany county clerk's office, left unfinished by former clerks. Passed February 9, 1871; three-fifths being present.

CHAP. 29. An Act to confirm the official acts of Oliver A. Barstow, a justice of the peace of the town of Nichols, Tioga county. Passed February 10, 1871; three-fifths being present.

CHAP. 30. An Act relative to lands devised by John Tonnele, deceased. Passed February 10, 1871; three-fifths being present.

CHAP. 31. An Act to authorize the Common Council of the city of Lockport to raise, by tax, moneys to pay the present indebtedness of the city. Passed February 10, 1871; three-fifths being present.

CHAP. 32. *An Act to amend the first section of the third title of the eighth chapter of the second part of the Revised Statutes in relation to the custody of minor children. Passed February* 10, 1871; *three-fifths being present.*

CHAP. 33. An Act to release to Wilhelmine Janecke the interest of the State in certain lands in the city of Buffalo, Erie county. Passed February 14, 1871; by a two-third vote.

CHAP. 74. An Act to incorporate the Cherry Valley Springs Hotel Company. Passed March 7, 1871.

CHAP. 75. An Act to amend the act entitled "An act to amend the act entitled An act to amend the act entitled 'An act in relation to the Grosvenor Library of the city of Buffalo,' passed April eleventh, one thousand eight hundred and fifty-nine, passed April eighth, eighteen hundred and sixty-one," passed April seventeenth, eighteen hundred and sixty-eight. Passed March 7, 1871; three-fifths being present.

CHAP. 76. An Act relative to the acquisition of real property by the American Society for the Prevention of Cruelty to Animals, and to amend the charter thereof. Passed March 8, 1871; three-fifths being present.

CHAP. 77. *An Act to punish mortgagors of personal property who shall fraudulently sell, assign, exchange, secrete or otherwise dispose of personal property mortgaged by them. Passed March* 8, 1871; *three-fifths being present.*

CHAP. 78. An Act to incorporate the Eastchester Savings Bank. Passed March 8, 1871.

CHAP. 79. An Act to authorize the town of Pelham, in the county of Westchester, to raise money for the purpose of constructing a town dock on City Island, in said town. Passed March 8, 1871; three-fifths being present.

CHAP. 80. An Act for the election of a receiver of taxes and assessments for the town of Rye and village of Port Chester. Passed March 8, 1871; three-fifths being present.

CHAP. 81. An Act in relation to the collection of water rents in the city of Brooklyn Passed March 8, 1871; three-fifths being present.

CHAP. 82. An Act to further amend the charter of the village of Medina, in the county of Orleans. Passed March 8, 1871; three-fifths being present.

CHAP. 83. An Act to amend an act entitled "An act to incorporate 'The Society for the Protection of Destitute Roman Catholic Children in the city of New York,'" passed May fifth, eighteen hundred and sixty-three. Passed March 8, 1871.

CHAP. 84. *An Act to authorize the owners and holders of certain railroad mortgage bonds, made payable to bearer, to render the same payable to order only. Passed March* 9, 1871.

CHAP. 85. An Act in relation to the Warrensburgh and Chester Plank-road Company. Passed March 9, 1871.

CHAP. 86. An Act to amend the charter of "The Sisters of Charity of St. Vincent de Paul," a corporation created and organized under and pursuant to the laws of this State. Passed March 10, 1871.

CHAP. 87. An Act to authorize the Common Council of the city of Binghamton to borrow money for the purpose of enlarging the county grounds surrounding the court-house in said city. Passed March 10, 1871; three-fifths being present.

CHAP. 88. An Act to incorporate the Grand Lodge of the Benevolent and Protective Order of Elks. Passed March 10, 1871.

CHAP. 89. An Act to amend an act entitled "An act to incorporate the Port Chester Savings Bank," passed March fourteenth, eighteen hundred and sixty-five, amended by act passed April twentieth, eighteen hundred and sixty-seven, also by act passed May sixth, eighteen hundred and sixty-nine. Passed March 10, 1871.

CHAP. 90. An Act to authorize the construction and maintaining of a free bridge over the Chenango river in the city of Binghamton, and to borrow money therefor. Passed March 13, 1871; three-fifths being present.

CHAP. 91. An Act to incorporate the "Bund Sorgenfrei," of the city of New York. Passed March 13, 1871.

CHAP. 92. An Act authorizing the construction of a railroad from Clinton square to Wolf street, in the city of Syracuse. Passed March 13, 1871.

CHAP. 93. An Act to amend and consolidate the several acts relating to the public schools of the city of Auburn. Passed March 14, 1871; three-fifths being present.

CHAP. 94. An Act to amend chapter five hundred and eighty-one of the Laws of eighteen hundred and sixty-six, relative to the City Sunday School and Missionary Society of the Methodist Episcopal Church. Passed March 14, 1871.

CHAP. 95. *An Act to amend an act entitled "An act to authorize the formation of gas-light companies," passed February sixteenth, eighteen hundred and forty-eight. Passed March* 14, 1871.

CHAP. 96. An Act to provide for the completion of the town hall at Saratoga Springs. Passed March 14, 1871; three-fifths being present.

Chap. 53. An Act relative to lands in the city of New York devised by Robert Swift Livingston, deceased. Passed February 23, 1871.

Chap. 54. An Act to incorporate the Barrett Bridge Company. Passed February 25, 1871; three-fifths being present.

Chap. 55. An Act to provide for the completion of the court-house in the third judicial district in the city of New York. Passed February 27, 1871; three-fifths being present.

Chap. 56. An Act to provide a further supply of pure and wholesome water for the city of New York. Passed February 27, 1871; three-fifths being present.

Chap. 57. An Act in relation to the widening and straightening of Broadway, in the city of New York, and to regulate the practice in that proceeding. Passed February 27, 1871; three-fifths being present.

Chap. 58. An Act to amend an act entitled "An act to incorporate the Oriental Savings Bank of the city of New York," passed May first, eighteen hundred and sixty-nine. Passed February 28, 1871.

Chap. 59. An Act to extend the time for the collection of taxes in the city of Oswego. Passed March 2, 1871; three-fifths being present.

Chap. 60. An Act to amend an act for supplying the village of Plattsburgh with pure and wholesome water, passed April seventeenth, one thousand eight hundred and sixty-eight. Passed March 2, 1871; three-fifths being present.

Chap. 61. An Act to legalize the acts of Joshua Brown, a justice of the peace, in the county of Tompkins. Passed March 3, 1871; three-fifths being present.

Chap. 62. An Act in relation to "The Ladies' Union Aid Society of the Methodist Episcopal Church in the city of New York." Passed March 3, 1871; three-fifths being present.

Chap. 63. An Act to amend the act entitled "An act to incorporate the Canandaigua Driving Park Association for the improvement of horses and to encourage the breeding of horses," passed April nineteenth, eighteen hundred and seventy. Passed March 3, 1871.

Chap. 64. An Act extending the provisions of certain laws permitting municipal corporations to aid in the construction of railroads to certain towns in the county of Erie. Passed March 3, 1871; three-fifths being present.

Chap. 65. An Act to revise and consolidate the laws in relation to the village of Geneva, in the county of Ontario. Passed March 3, 1871; three-fifths being present.

Chap. 66. An Act to release to Mary Darcy Mahar, sister to Stephen Darcy, deceased, all the estate, right and title of the people of the State of New York in and to certain lands in the city of Syracuse, in the county of Onondaga. Passed March 6, 1871, by a two-third vote.

Chap. 67. An Act to amend an act entitled "An act to incorporate the Oswego Falls Agricultural Society," passed April twenty-ninth, eighteen hundred and sixty-eight. Passed March 6, 1871.

Chap. 68. *An Act to amend "An act for the incorporation of private and family cemeteries," passed April first, eighteen hundred and fifty-four. Passed March* 6, 1871.

Chap. 69. An Act to confirm the official acts of James M. Pulver, a justice of the peace of the town of Gorham, in the county of Ontario. Passed March 6, 1871; three-fifths being present.

Chap. 70. An Act to amend an act entitled "An act to amend the charter of the village of Dunkirk," passed April twentieth, eighteen hundred and sixty-seven, and amendments thereto passed February eighteenth, eighteen hundred and seventy. Passed March 6, 1871; three-fifths being present.

Chap. 71. An Act to amend chapter eighty-five of the Laws of eighteen hundred and sixty-three, entitled "An act in relation to the Troy and Cohoes Railroad Company," passed April seventh, eighteen hundred and sixty-three. Passed March 7, 1871.

Chap. 72. An Act to extend the time for the collection of taxes in the town of Newtown, in the county of Queens. Passed March 7, 1871; three-fifths being present.

Chap. 73. An Act authorizing the extension of the time for the collection of taxes in the town of Pendleton, in the county of Niagara. Passed March 7, 1871; three-fifths being present.

CHAP. 74. An Act to incorporate the Cherry Valley Springs Hotel Company. Passed March 7, 1871.

CHAP. 75. An Act to amend the act entitled "An act to amend the act entitled An act to amend the act entitled 'An act in relation to the Grosvenor Library of the city of Buffalo,' passed April eleventh, one thousand eight hundred and fifty-nine, passed April eighth, eighteen hundred and sixty-one," passed April seventeenth, eighteen hundred and sixty-eight. Passed March 7, 1871; three-fifths being present.

CHAP. 76. An Act relative to the acquisition of real property by the American Society for the Prevention of Cruelty to Animals, and to amend the charter thereof. Passed March 8, 1871; three-fifths being present.

CHAP. 77. *An Act to punish mortgagors of personal property who shall fraudulently sell, assign, exchange, secrete or otherwise dispose of personal property mortgaged by them. Passed March* 8, 1871; *three-fifths being present.*

CHAP. 78. An Act to incorporate the Eastchester Savings Bank. Passed March 8, 1871.

CHAP. 79. An Act to authorize the town of Pelham, in the county of Westchester, to raise money for the purpose of constructing a town dock on City Island, in said town. Passed March 8, 1871; three-fifths being present.

CHAP. 80. An Act for the election of a receiver of taxes and assessments for the town of Rye and village of Port Chester. Passed March 8, 1871; three-fifths being present.

CHAP. 81. An Act in relation to the collection of water rents in the city of Brooklyn Passed March 8, 1871; three-fifths being present.

CHAP. 82. An Act to further amend the charter of the village of Medina, in the county of Orleans. Passed March 8, 1871; three-fifths being present.

CHAP. 83. An Act to amend an act entitled "An act to incorporate 'The Society for the Protection of Destitute Roman Catholic Children in the city of New York,'" passed May fifth, eighteen hundred and sixty-three. Passed March 8, 1871.

CHAP. 84. *An Act to authorize the owners and holders of certain railroad mortgage bonds, made payable to bearer, to render the same payable to order only. Passed March* 9, 1871.

CHAP. 85. An Act in relation to the Warrensburgh and Chester Plank-road Company. Passed March 9, 1871.

CHAP. 86. An Act to amend the charter of "The Sisters of Charity of St. Vincent de Paul," a corporation created and organized under and pursuant to the laws of this State. Passed March 10, 1871.

CHAP. 87. An Act to authorize the Common Council of the city of Binghamton to borrow money for the purpose of enlarging the county grounds surrounding the court-house in said city. Passed March 10, 1871; three-fifths being present.

CHAP. 88. An Act to incorporate the Grand Lodge of the Benevolent and Protective Order of Elks. Passed March 10, 1871.

CHAP. 89. An Act to amend an act entitled "An act to incorporate the Port Chester Savings Bank," passed March fourteenth, eighteen hundred and sixty-five, amended by act passed April twentieth, eighteen hundred and sixty-seven, also by act passed May sixth, eighteen hundred and sixty-nine. Passed March 10, 1871.

CHAP. 90. An Act to authorize the construction and maintaining of a free bridge over the Chenango river in the city of Binghamton, and to borrow money therefor. Passed March 13, 1871; three-fifths being present.

CHAP. 91. An Act to incorporate the "Bund Sorgenfrei," of the city of New York. Passed March 13, 1871.

CHAP. 92. An Act authorizing the construction of a railroad from Clinton square to Wolf street, in the city of Syracuse. Passed March 13, 1871.

CHAP. 93. An Act to amend and consolidate the several acts relating to the public schools of the city of Auburn. Passed March 14, 1871; three-fifths being present.

CHAP. 94. An Act to amend chapter five hundred and eighty-one of the Laws of eighteen hundred and sixty-six, relative to the City Sunday School and Missionary Society of the Methodist Episcopal Church. Passed March 14, 1871.

CHAP. 95. *An Act to amend an act entitled "An act to authorize the formation of gas-light companies," passed February sixteenth, eighteen hundred and forty-eight. Passed March* 14, 1871.

CHAP. 96. An Act to provide for the completion of the town hall at Saratoga Springs. Passed March 14, 1871; three-fifths being present.

CHAP. 97. An Act to authorize the trustees of Cortland Academy to remove the bodies buried on lands owned by the said trustees in Homer village, Cortland county. Passed March 14, 1871; three-fifths being present.

CHAP. 98. An Act authorizing the surrogate of Queens county to adopt a new seal. Passed March 14, 1871; three-fifths being present.

CHAP. 99. An Act in relation to the running of ferry boats by the Union Ferry Company across the East river. Passed March 14, 1871.

CHAP. 100. An Act to amend an act entitled "An act to authorize the town of Bainbridge to purchase the bridge over the Susquehanna river in said town, and the property and franchise appertaining thereto, of the existing Bainbridge Bridge Company, and to maintain the same as a free bridge, and to borrow money therefor," passed March sixteen, eighteen hundred and sixty-nine. Passed March 14, 1871; three-fifths being present.

CHAP. 101. An Act to incorporate the Trustees of the Corning Foundation for Educational and other Christian Work, under the control of the Protestant Episcopal Church, in the diocese of Albany. Passed March 14, 1871.

CHAP. 102. An Act to amend an act entitled "An act to incorporate the village of Oneonta, Otsego county," passed April twentieth, eighteen hundred and seventy. Passed March 14, 1871; three-fifths being present.

CHAP. 103. An Act to amend an act entitled "An act to incorporate the Oswego County Savings Bank." Passed March 14, 1871.

CHAP. 104. An Act to amend the charter of the Savings Bank of Utica. Passed March 14, 1871.

CHAP. 105. An Act authorizing the Board of Supervisors of the county of Broome to acquire and hold for public use certain land in the city of Binghamton. Passed March 14, 1871; three-fifths being present.

CHAP. 106. An Act in relation to filing certain maps relating to lands in the county of Westchester. Passed March 14, 1871; three-fifths being present.

CHAP. 107. An Act to provide for the erection of a town hall in the town of Madrid, in the county of St. Lawrence. Passed March 14, 1871; three-fifths being present.

CHAP. 108. An Act to legalize and confirm the official acts of Charles C. Barrett and John H. Bell as overseers of the poor of the town of Lenox, Madison county. Passed March 15, 1871; three-fifths being present.

CHAP. 109. An Act to revise and amend an act entitled "An act to authorize the Town Board of the town of Amity, in the county of Allegany, to purchase a public cemetery," passed March twenty-six, eighteen hundred and sixty-six, and to authorize the construction of a public vault therein. Passed March 15, 1871; three-fifths being present.

CHAP. 110. *An Act to amend an act entitled "An act in relation to the fees of county treasurers," passed May eleven, eighteen hundred and forty-six. Passed March* 15, 1871; *three-fifths being present.*

CHAP. 111. An Act relative to the American Congregational Union, in the city of New York. Passed March 15, 1871.

CHAP. 112. An Act to confirm a certain indenture of lease made by the Mayor, Aldermen and Commonalty of the city of New York to the Foundling Asylum of the Sisters of Charity of the city of New York. Passed March 15, 1871; three-fifths being present.

CHAP. 113. An Act in relation to the Normal School bonds, issued by the village of Cortland. Passed March 15, 1871; three-fifths being present.

CHAP. 114. An Act to amend section four of chapter one hundred and twenty-three, of the Laws of eighteen hundred and sixty-four, entitled "An act to incorporate the New Brooklyn Turnverein," passed April fifth, eighteen hundred and sixty-four. Passed March 15, 1871.

CHAP. 115. An Act to provide for the election of a supervisor at large for Kings county, and prescribing his powers and duties. Passed March 16, 1871; three-fifths being present.

CHAP. 116. An Act in relation to the Fire Department of the city of Brooklyn. Passed March 16, 1871; three-fifths being present.

CHAP. 117. An Act to amend an act entitled "An act to authorize the levying of a tax upon the town of Gouverneur, in the county of St. Lawrence, for the benefit of the Gouverneur Wesleyan Seminary, and to increase the capital stock of said Seminary," passed April twenty-third, eighteen hundred and sixty-nine. Passed March 16, 1871; three-fifths being present.

CHAP. 118. An Act to release the interest of the State in certain lands, of which John Frost died possessed, to Elizabeth Ann Frost, his widow. Passed March 16, 1871, by a two-third vote.

CHAP. 119. An Act to amend the charter of the village of Potsdam. Passed March 16, 1871; three-fifths being present.

CHAP. 120. *An Act authorizing the Comptroller to pay over certain moneys appropriated by chapter eight hundred and twenty-two of the Laws of eighteen hundred and sixty-nine, for the construction of a bridge in the town of Carrolton. Passed March* 16, 1871, *by a two-third vote.*

CHAP. 121. An Act to amend chapter eleven of the Laws of eighteen hundred and seventy, entitled "An act authorizing the Utica Mechanics' Association to borrow money for the purpose of building a hall, and to sell certain real estate, and amending its charter. Passed March 16, 1871.

CHAP. 122. An Act to provide for supplying the village of Canandaigua with water, and submitting to the tax-payers of said village the question of the construction of water-works, and of bonding said village for the purpose of such construction. Passed March 17, 1871; three-fifths being present.

CHAP. 123. An Act to amend an act entitled "An act to incorporate the Excelsior Savings Bank in the city of New York," passed May eleventh, eighteen hundred and sixty-nine. Passed March 17, 1871.

CHAP. 124. An Act to extend the time for the collection of taxes in the town of Southfield, Richmond county. Passed March 17, 1871; three-fifths being present.

CHAP. 125. An Act to confirm the title of Martin Phelan to certain real estate conveyed to him by Zelley Schwartz, an alien. Passed March 17, 1871, by a two-third vote.

CHAP. 126. An Act concerning "The Police Life Insurance Fund" and the powers and duties of the police department of the city of New York. Passed March 17, 1871.

CHAP. 127. An Act to facilitate the construction of the Lake Ontario Shore Railroad, and to amend the several acts in relation thereto. Passed March 17, 1871; three-fifths being present.

CHAP. 128. An Act to authorize the city of Brooklyn to borrow money, and also to raise money by tax to meet certain deficiencies and liabilities. Passed March 17, 1871; three-fifths being present.

CHAP. 129. An Act to amend an act entitled "An act to consolidate and amend the several acts relating to the village of Peekskill, to alter the bounds and to enlarge the powers of the corporation of said village," passed March twenty-fifth, eighteen hundred and fifty-nine. Passed March 17, 1871; three-fifths being present.

CHAP. 130. An Act authorizing the town of Friendship, Allegany county, to issue bonds for the use and benefit of Friendship Academy. Passed March 20, 1871; three-fifths being present.

CHAP. 131. An Act to renew the charter of the New York State Agricultural Society. Passed March 20, 1871.

CHAP. 132. An Act to amend an act entitled "An act to erect the village of Middleburgh into a separate road district," passed April seventh, eighteen hundred and fifty-nine, and the act amendatory thereof, passed February fifteenth, eighteen hundred and sixty-seven. Passed March 20, 1871; three-fifths being present.

CHAP. 133. An Act to authorize and empower the Hackensack and New York Extension Railroad Company to build a bridge over the Minnisceongo creek. Passed March 20, 1871.

CHAP. 134. An Act to amend an act entitled "An act to incorporate the College of Pharmacy of the city of New York," passed March twentieth, eighteen hundred and fifty-six. Passed March 20, 1871.

CHAP. 135. An Act to repeal chapter seven hundred and seven of the Laws of eighteen hundred and sixty-eight, entitled "An act to define the powers and duties of commissioners of highways in the town of Cortlandt, in the county of Westchester, in relation to laying out and constructing new roads, and the construction of bridges in said town, and prescribing the mode of assessing and paying the costs and damages therefor," passed May seventh, eighteen hundred and sixty-eight. Passed March 20, 1871; three-fifths being present.

CHAP. 136. An Act to repeal chapter five hundred and forty-eight of the Laws of eighteen hundred and sixty-five, being an act entitled "An act to authorize the election of commissioner of highways for a term of three years, in the town of Lenox, Madison county," passed April twenty-second, eighteen hundred and sixty-five. Passed March 20, 1871; three-fifths being present.

CHAP 137. An Act to amend an act entitled "An act to incorporate the village of Holley," passed April third, eighteen hundred and sixty-seven. Passed March 20, 1871; three-fifths being present.

CHAP. 138. *An Act making an appropriation for the Antietam National Cemetery for a memorial of the patriotic dead of Antietam, South Mountain and Monocacy. Passed March* 20, 1871, *by a two-third vote.*

CHAP. 139. An Act to authorize the Common Council of the city of Brooklyn to open, grade, pave and complete certain streets in said city. Passed March 20, 1871; three-fifths being present.

CHAP. 140. An Act to amend chapter six hundred and thirty-two of the Laws of eighteen hundred and sixty-eight, entitled "An act to amend an act entitled 'An act to establish fire limits, and for the more effectual prevention of fires in the city of Brooklyn,'" passed April thirty, eighteen hundred and sixty-six. Passed March 20, 1871; three-fifths being present.

CHAP. 141. An Act to abolish tolls on certain roads and bridges in the towns of Newtown and Flushing, in the county of Queens, and provide compensation therefor. Passed March 21, 1871; three-fifths being present.

CHAP. 142. An Act to incorporate the Matteawan Savings Bank. Passed March 21, 1871.

CHAP. 143. An Act to incorporate the American Peat Fuel Company. Passed March 21, 1871.

CHAP. 144. An Act to amend an act entitled "An act to create a Board of Trustees for the town of Morrisania, in the county of Westchester, and to define their powers," passed April twenty-second, eighteen hundred and sixty-four, as amended by subsequent acts. Passed March 21, 1871; three-fifths being present.

CHAP. 145. An Act to incorporate the Eighth Ward Savings Bank of the city of New York. Passed March 22, 1871.

CHAP. 146. *An Act extending the provisions of certain laws, permitting municipal corporations to aid in the construction of railroads to the counties of Albany and Greene. Passed March* 21, 1871; *three-fifths being present, without the approval of the governor.*

CHAP. 147. An Act releasing certain real estate in the city of Brooklyn, whereof William Geen died seized, to Bridget Geen, of said city. Passed March 22, 1871, by a two-third vote.

CHAP. 148. An Act authorizing the Commissioners of Highways of the town of Stony Point, in the county of Rockland, to build a drawbridge over Minisceongo creek, in said town, and authorizing said town to aid therein. Passed March 22, 1871; three-fifths being present.

CHAP. 149. An Act to amend an act entitled "An act to enable the several highway districts in the town of Greenburgh, in Westchester county, west of, or through which the highway known as the late Highland Turnpike runs, to macadamize and otherwise improve public highways within their respective districts," passed April twenty-second, eighteen hundred and sixty-seven. Passed March 22, 1871; three-fifths being present.

CHAP. 150. An Act to change the corporate name and title of the religious corporation known as "The Second Methodist Episcopal Church of White Plains," in the county of Westchester, to "The Memorial Methodist Episcopal Church of White Plains," and for the re-organization thereof. Passed March 22, 1871.

CHAP. 151. An Act to incorporate the Port Jervis Driving Park Association. Passed March 22, 1871.

CHAP. 152. An Act to amend chapter four hundred and ninety-seven, of the Laws of eighteen hundred and sixty-nine, entitled "An act to establish a receiver of taxes and to authorize the sale of lands for non-payment of taxes, and for the collection of unpaid taxes in the town of Flushing, Queens county." Passed March 22, 1871; three-fifths being present.

CHAP. 153. An Act to release the interest of the People of this State in certain lands heretofore conveyed to Jane Suggett, an alien, and to confirm conveyances made by her. Passed March 22, 1871, by a two-third vote.

CHAP. 154. An Act to amend the charter of the Buffalo City Cemetery, and to restore the exemption of cemeteries in said city from local assessment. Passed March 22, 1871; three-fifths being present.

CHAP. 155. An Act to extend the time for the collection of taxes in the city of Elmira. Passed March 22, 1871; three-fifths being present.

CHAP. 156. An Act in relation to "The Long Island Club." Passed March 22, 1871.

CHAP. 157. An Act to amend an act entitled "An act to incorporate the Williamsburgh Sharpshooters Society, of the city of Brooklyn," passed May ninth, eighteen hundred and sixty-eight. Passed March 22, 1871.

CHAP. 158. An Act to incorporate the New Paltz Savings Bank. Passed March 22, 1871.

CHAP. 159. An Act to repeal an act entitled "An act to incorporate the Tarrytown Fire Department," passed May fifth, eighteen hundred and seventy, so far as the same affects the town of Greenburgh, in the county of Westchester. Passed March 22, 1871; three-fifths being present.

CHAP. 160. An Act to extend the time for the collection of taxes in the several towns in the county of Richmond, and to authorize the collectors of taxes in said towns to proceed with the collection thereof. Passed March 23, 1871; three-fifths being present.

CHAP. 161. An Act to confirm the title of John M. Clark to certain lands in the city of Syracuse, county of Onondaga. Passed March 24, 1871, by a two-third vote.

CHAP. 162. An Act to amend the charter of the village of Pulaski. Passed March 24, 1871; three-fifths being present.

CHAP. 163. An Act in aid of the Nursery and Child's Hospital of the city of New York, and to re-appropriate certain moneys for the benefit thereof. Passed March 24, 1871, by a two-third vote.

CHAP. 164. *An Act to amend an act passed April fourteen, eighteen hundred and fifty-two, entitled "An act further to amend an act entitled 'An act authorizing the incorporation of Rural Cemetery Associations,' passed April twenty-seven, eighteen hundred and forty-seven." Passed March* 24, 1871.

CHAP. 165. An Act for the relief of William Reed, Emery M. Lyon and Benjamin L. Woodruff. Passed March 24, 1871; three-fifths being present.

CHAP. 166. An Act to amend chapter one hundred and sixty-six of the Laws of eighteen hundred and seventy, passed April nine, eighteen hundred and seventy, entitled "An act to amend an act entitled 'An act to continue in force an act to incorporate the New York Institution for the Blind,' passed April twenty-first, eighteen hundred and thirty-one, and to extend the benefits of said institution," passed April sixteenth, eighteen hundred and fifty-two. Passed March 24, 1871; three-fifths being present.

CHAP. 167. An Act to provide for the appointment of an additional number of notaries public for the county of New York. Passed March 24, 1871; three-fifths being present.

CHAP. 168. An Act to prohibit burials in the cemetery at the corner of Delaware and North streets, in the city of Buffalo. Passed March 24, 1871; three-fifths being present.

CHAP. 169. An Act to authorize the Trustees of the New Paltz Academy to sell the real estate belonging to such academy, and to purchase a new site for the same. Passed March 24, 1871; three-fifths being present.

CHAP. 170. An Act to authorize the Trustees of McLean Cemetery Association to remove and re-inter bodies in said cemetery, and to assess lot holders for the improvement of the grounds. Passed March 24, 1871.

CHAP. 171. *An Act in relation to assessment of highway labor in certain cases. Passed March* 24, 1871; *three-fifths being present.*

CHAP. 172. An Act to authorize the town of Yonkers to issue bonds for the improvement of South Broadway, in the village of Yonkers, from Main street to the south line of the village. Passed March 24, 1871; three-fifths being present.

CHAP. 173. An Act to amend an act entitled "An act for the benefit of the Union School in Hamilton, New York, passed eighteen hundred and sixty-two," passed April twenty-seventh, eighteen hundred and sixty-nine. Passed March 27, 1871; three-fifths being present.

CHAP. 174. An Act to amend an act entitled "An act relating to schools in the town of

Seneca Falls," passed April sixteenth, eighteen hundred and sixty-seven. Passed March 27, 1871; three-fifths being present.

CHAP. 175. An Act to extend and continue the incorporation known as "The President and Directors of the Fort Miller Bridge Company." Passed March 27, 1873.

CHAP. 176. An Act to legalize certain acts and proceedings of the commissioners of construction and commissioners of appraisal appointed under and by virtue of an act of the legislature, entitled "An act to provide for laying out and improving roads and avenues in the village and town of Saratoga Springs," passed May fifth, eighteen hundred and seventy. Passed March 27, 1871; three-fifths being present.

CHAP. 177. An Act to authorize a special election of Trustees of Hillside Cemetery Association. Passed March 27, 1873.

CHAP. 178. An Act to incorporate the Haverstraw Savings Bank of the town Haverstraw in the county of Rockland. Passed March 27, 1871.

CHAP. 179. An Act to encourage the construction of sidewalks in the village of Unadilla, Otsego county, and to repeal chapter three hundred and forty-two, Laws of eighteen hundred and sixty, and chapter four hundred and twenty, Laws of eighteen hundred and sixty-nine, and all acts heretofore passed in relation thereto. Passed March 27, 1871; three-fifths being present.

CHAP. 180. An Act in aid of the Boys' and Girls' Lodging-houses of the Children's Aid Society of the city of New York. Passed March 27, 1871, by a two-third vote.

CHAP. 181. An Act to extend the time for the collection of taxes in the town of Jamaica, Queens county. Passed March 27, 1871; three-fifths being present.

CHAP. 182. An Act to amend an act entitled "An act to incorporate the Trustees of the Church Erection Fund of the General Assembly of the Presbyterian Church in the United States of America," passed March thirty-first, eighteen hundred and fifty-five. Passed March 27, 1871.

CHAP. 183. An Act to amend an act entitled "An act to incorporate the village of Cobleskill, Schoharie county," passed April three, eighteen hundred and sixty-eight. Passed March 27, 1871; three-fifths being present.

CHAP. 184. *An Act in relation to the publication of the laws of the State. Passed March* 27, 1871; *three-fifths being present.*

CHAP. 185. An Act to incorporate the National Eclectic Medical Association. Passed March 27, 1871.

CHAP. 186. An Act to amend an act entitled "An act in relation to academies and schools in the village of Ogdensburgh," passed April thirteen, eighteen hundred and fifty-seven, and the acts amendatory thereof. Passed March 27, 1871; three-fifths being present.

CHAP. 187. An Act providing for the division of the town of Newtown, in Queens county, and the apportionment of the town property and town debts. Passed March 27, 1871; three-fifths being present.

CHAP. 188. *An Act to amend chapter four hundred and two of the Laws of eighteen hundred and fifty-four, being "An act for the better security of mechanics and others erecting building in the counties of Westchester, Oneida, Cortland, Broome, Putnam, Rockland, Orleans, Niagara, Livingston, Otsego, Lewis, Orange and Dutchess," passed April seventeen, eighteen hundred and fifty-four. Passed March* 27, 1871; *three-fifths being present.*

CHAP. 189. An Act authorizing the city of Syracuse to raise money for purchasing a steam fire-engine, to be located in the first ward of said city. Passed March 27, 1871; three-fifths being present.

CHAP. 190. An Act to amend an act entitled "An act to revise and consolidate the laws in relation to the village of Ithaca, in the county of Tompkins," passed April twenty-one, eighteen hundred and sixty-four. Passed March 27, 1871; three-fifths being present.

CHAP. 191. An Act to amend an act entitled "An act to incorporate the village of Goshen," passed April eighteenth, eighteen hundred and forty-three, so as to enable the inhabitants of said village to obtain a supply of water for public and private uses. Passed March 27, 1871; three-fifths being present.

CHAP. 192. An Act to extend the time for the collection of taxes in the towns of Hempstead, North Hempstead and Oyster Bay, county of Queens. Passed March 27, 1871; three-fifths being present.

CHAP. 193. An Act to legalize the call for charter election, to be held in the village of

Oneida, Madison county, on the fourth day of April, eighteen hundred and seventy-one. Passed March 27, 1871; three-fifths being present.

CHAP. 194. An Act to amend an act entitled "An act to establish a police department in and for the city of Brooklyn, and to define its powers and duties," passed April fifth, eighteen hundred and seventy, being chapter one hundred and thirty-six of the Laws of eighteen hundred and seventy. Passed March 28, 1871; three-fifths being present.

CHAP. 195. An Act to amend an act entitled "An act to incorporate the Bowling Green Savings Bank of the city of New York," passed May nineteen, eighteen hundred and sixty-eight. Passed March 28, 1871.

CHAP. 196. An Act to incorporate the Troy Security and Trust Company. Passed March 28, 1871.

CHAP. 197. An Act to authorize the West Utica Presbyterian Chapel to dispose of its real estate. Passed March 28, 1871.

CHAP. 198. An Act releasing the interests of the State in certain lands, of which Frederick Staudt died possessed, to Jacobina Wilhelmina Fussel. Passed March 28, 1871, by a two-third vote.

CHAP. 199. An Act to amend an act entitled "An act to amend the charter of Saratoga Springs, passed March twenty-sixth, eighteen hundred and sixty-six, and for the purpose of securing a supply of pure and wholesome water for the use of said village," passed May fourth, eighteen hundred and sixty-eight. Passed March 28, 1871; three-fifths being present.

CHAP. 200. An Act to change the name of "The First Universalist Society and Church, in the city of Hudson," and to authorize said society to take and hold by gift, grant, devise, purchase or otherwise, real and personal estate. Passed March 28, 1871.

CHAP. 201. An Act to incorporate "The St. Patrick's Literary and Benevolent Association," of the city of Rochester. Passed March 28, 1871.

CHAP. 202. An Act to establish a board for the examination of and licensing druggist and prescription clerks in the city of New York. Passed March 28, 1871; three-fifths being present.

CHAP. 203. An Act to enable the city of Rochester to raise five thousand dollars to furnish rooms in the State arsenal, in said city, for the use of the Fifty-fourth regiment of the New York State National Guard. Passed March 28, 1871; three-fifths being present.

CHAP. 204. An Act releasing the interests of the State in certain lands, of which James Jackson died seized and possessed, to Hannah Jackson, his widow. Passed March 29, 1871, by a two-third vote.

CHAP. 205. An Act relative to the collection of Harbor Master's fees in the city of New York. Passed March 29, 1871; three-fifths being present.

CHAP. 206. An Act to incorporate the Fulton Savings Bank, in the county of Oswego. Passed March 29, 1871.

CHAP. 207. An Act to amend an act entitled "An act relating to certain non-resident highway taxes in Franklin county," passed May first, eighteen hundred and sixty-nine. Passed March 29, 1871; three-fifths being present.

CHAP. 208. *An Act in relation to the duties and liabilities of sheriffs in certain cases. Passed March* 29, 1871; *three-fifths being present.*

CHAP. 209. An Act to authorize the extension of the Cherry Valley, Sharon and Albany Railroad into or through any town in the counties of Otsego or Herkimer, and to facilitate the construction thereof. Passed March 29, 1871; three-fifths being present.

CHAP. 210. An Act to amend an act entitled "An act to amend the Revised Statutes in relation to laying out of public roads, and of the alteration thereof, in the town of Greenburgh," passed April fifteenth, eighteen hundred and fifty-four, and in addition thereto. Passed March 29, 1871; three-fifths being present.

CHAP. 211. An Act to repeal an act entitled "An act to provide for an additional justice of the peace in the town of Pomfret, in the county of Chautauqua," passed February thirteenth, eighteen hundred and fifty-two. Passed March 29, 1871; three-fifths being present.

CHAP. 212. An Act for the relief of the Rector, Churchwardens and Vestrymen of the Holy Trinity Church of Harlem, in the city and county of New York. Passed March 29, 1871.

CHAP. 213. An Act to extend the distribution of Croton water through the city of New

York, and to lay the necessary mains to deliver it at higher elevations; and also to provide for the expense of water-meters. Passed March 29, 1871; three-fifths being present.

Chap. 214. An Act to repeal chapter seven hundred and eighty-one of the Laws of eighteen hundred and sixty-six, entitled "An act in relation to draining certain land in the town of Fishkill, in the county of Dutchess, passed April twenty-four, eighteen hundred and sixty-six. Passed March 29, 1871; three-fifths being present.

Chap. 215. An Act to amend an act entitled "An act to supply the city of Binghamton with pure and wholesome water," passed April twenty-five, eighteen hundred and sixty-seven, and the acts amendatory thereof. Passed March 29, 1871; three-fifths being present.

Chap. 216. An Act to amend an act entitled "An act to designate the place of holding the meetings of the Board of Supervisors of Oswego county, and to regulate the compensation of the members thereof," passed April six, eighteen hundred and sixty-nine. Passed March 29, 1871; three-fifths being present.

Chap. 217. An Act to incorporate the Harlem Library. Passed March 29, 1871.

Chap. 218. An Act to amend an act entitled "An act to correct abuses in the city of New York, in the relaying of pavement by the property owners and others, whenever a portion of the pavement is temporarily removed," passed April nineteen, eighteen hundred and sixty-two. Passed March 29, 1871; three-fifths being present.

Chap. 219. *An Act to provide redress for words imputing unchastity to a female. Passed March* 29, 1871.

Chap. 220. An Act to further provide for the rebuilding and repairing of sewers in the city of New York. Passed March 29, 1871; three-fifths being present.

Chap. 221. An Act to repeal so much of chapter eight hundred and six of the Laws of eighteen hundred and seventy, being an act entitled "An act in relation to certain streets in the city of New York," as relates to the extension of Madison avenue. Passed March 29, 1871; three-fifths being present.

Chap. 222. An Act to enable the Laflin and Rand Powder Company to take stock in other companies. Passed March 29, 1871.

Chap. 223. An Act to release the estate, title and interest of the People of the State of New York in and to the real estate of which William Gray, late of the town of Hempstead, in Queens county, died seized, to Catherine Demott. Passed March 29, 1871, by a two-third vote.

Chap. 224. An Act to authorize the extension of the track of the East New York and Jamaica Railroad Company, and the consolidation of the Jamaica and Brooklyn Plank-road Company and the East New York and Jamaica Railroad Company, and with any other railroad company running in the county of Kings. Passed March 30, 1871.

Chap. 225. An Act to amend chapter eight hundred and eighty of the Laws of eighteen hundred and sixty-seven, entitled "An act for the protection of persons traveling upon Fourth avenue, in the city of New York." Passed March 30, 1871; three-fifths being present.

Chap. 226. An Act in relation to changing the grades and grading a portion of the Ninth avenue, and of certain other streets and avenues in the city of New York. Passed March 30, 1871; three-fifths being present.

Chap. 227. An Act to provide for the regulating, grading, curbing, guttering and flagging of certain streets in the city of New York. Passed March 30, 1871; three-fifths being present.

Chap. 228. An Act to amend the charter of the Employment and Indemnity Company, in the city of New York. Passed March 30, 1871.

Chap. 229. An Act to amend chapter two hundred and ninety-seven of the Laws of eighteen hundred and sixty-five, entitled "An act to amend the charter of the city of Rochester, so as to provide police commissioners for said city. Passed March 30, 1871; three-fifths being present.

Chap. 230. An Act to amend an act entitled "An act to amend an act entitled 'An act to provide for the incorporation of villages,' passed December seven, one thousand eight hundred and forty-seven, and the several acts amendatory thereof, so far as the same relate to the village of Mount Vernon, in the county of Westchester, and to declare, enlarge and define the powers and duties of the officers of said village, and to confirm and extend the powers of the corporation of said village," passed May ten, eighteen hundred and seventy. Passed March 30, 1871; three-fifths being present.

CHAP. 231. An Act to amend an act entitled "An act to authorize the improvement and sale of certain portions of Prospect Park, in the city of Brooklyn," passed April twenty-third, eighteen hundred and seventy. Passed March 31, 1871; three-fifths being present.

CHAP. 232. An Act to amend "An act supplementary to an act in relation to a public park in the city of Albany," passed April twenty-three, eighteen hundred and seventy. Passed March 31, 1871; three-fifths being present.

CHAP. 233. An Act to authorise the supervisor of the town of German Flats to convey certain real estate. Passed March 31, 1871; three-fifths being present.

CHAP. 234. An Act to amend the revised charter of the city of Syracuse. Passed March 31, 1871; three-fifths being present.

CHAP. 235. An Act supplementary to an act entitled "An act to amend the charter of the Sisters of Charity of St. Vincent de Paul," passed March ten, eighteen hundred and seventy. Passed March 31, 1871.

CHAP. 236. An Act to amend chapter six hundred and eighty-eight of the Laws of eighteen hundred and seventy, entitled "An act to amend an act entitled an act to enable the town of New Rochelle, in Westchester county, to raise money to build a town hall, passed March thirtieth, eighteen hundred and sixty-eight." Passed March 31, 1871; three-fifths being present.

CHAP. 237. An Act to amend an act entitled "An act to establish a Homœopathic Asylum for the Insane at Middletown, New York," passed April twenty-eight, eighteen hundred and seventy. Passed March 31, 1871; three-fifths being present.

CHAP. 238. *An Act to provide for the payment of the crier and attendants of the court of appeals. Passed March* 31, 1871; *three-fifths being present.*

CHAP. 239. *An Act to amend the Revised Statutes in regard to surrogate's bonds. Passed March* 31, 1871.

CHAP. 240. An Act to organize and establish a police for the town and village of Yonkers. Passed March 31, 1871; three-fifths being present.

CHAP. 241. An Act to amend the charter of the Excelsior Life Insurance Company. Passed March 31, 1871.

CHAP. 242. *An Act to authorise the Canal Commissioners to construct a road bridge over the Erie canal, near the Cowasselon creek, in the county of Madison. Passed April* 4, 1871; *three-fifths being present.*

CHAP. 243. An Act to authorize Union School District No. 2, in the village of Weedsport, to borrow money for the purpose of rebuilding the school-house in said district. Passed April 1, 1871; three-fifths being present.

CHAP. 244. An Act to incorporate the Ithaca Fire Department. Passed April 1, 1871; three-fifths being present.

CHAP. 245. *An Act relating to military exemptions. Passed April* 1, 1871; *three-fifths being present.*

CHAP. 246. An Act to amend an act entitled "An act to revise and consolidate the laws in relation to Amsterdam village, in Montgomery county," passed April seventeen, eighteen hundred and fifty-four, and acts amendatory thereof. Passed April 1, 1871; three-fifths being present.

CHAP. 247. An Act to authorise the supervisor of the town of Locke, in the county of Cayuga, to convey the cemetery in the village of Milan, on lot twenty-two, to the Trustees of Milan Cemetery Association. Passed April 1, 1871; three-fifths being present.

CHAP. 248. An Act authorizing the Common Council of the city of Lockport to raise, by tax, three thousand dollars to rebuild the fire-engine house in the second ward of said city. Passed April 1, 1871; three-fifths being present.

CHAP. 249. An Act to exempt the real estate of the trustees of the Masonic Hall and Asylum Fund from taxation. Passed April 1, 1871; three-fifths being present.

CHAP. 250. An Act to repeal "An act to establish a Capital Police District, and to provide for the government thereof," passed April twenty-second, eighteen hundred and sixty-five, and the several acts amendatory thereof and supplementary thereto, and to provide for settling up the affairs of the Capital Police District, and distributing the surplus funds thereof, and to dispose of the Capital Police Life Insurance Fund. Passed April 1, 1871; three-fifths being present.

CHAP. 251. An Act to amend an act entitled "An act to amend and consolidate the several acts in relation to the charter of the city of Hudson," passed April tenth, eighteen hundred and fifty-four, as amended by acts passed April fifteenth, eighteen hundred and fifty-seven, February sixteenth, eighteen hundred and fifty-eight, April thirteenth, eighteen hundred and sixty-one, April twenty-second, eighteen hundred and sixty-four, and March twenty-fifth, eighteen hundred and sixty-eight. Passed April 1, 1871; three-fifths being present.

CHAP. 252. An Act to amend the charter of the village of Geddes, in the county of Onondaga. Passed April 1, 1871; three-fifths being present.

CHAP. 253. *An Act to protect the harbors adjoining Long Island Sound, in the county of Suffolk. Passed April* 1, 1871; *three-fifths being present.*

CHAP. 254. An Act to legalize the acts of the inhabitants of school districts number one, two, five and nine, in the town of Wilson, in the county of Niagara, in forming a Union Free School District, and the official acts of the Board of Education therein. Passed April 1, 1871; three-fifths being present.

CHAP. 255. An Act to amend an act entitled "An act to incorporate the Association for the benefit of colored orphans in the city of New York," passed April sixteenth, eighteen hundred and thirty-eight. Passed April 1, 1871.

CHAP. 256. An Act to release the title and interest of the people of the State of New York, in and to certain real estate, to Elizabeth Hale, John Hale, Helena Hale, Charles Hale and Alexander Hale, children of John Hale, deceased, and to Elizabeth Hale, his widow. Passed April 1, 1871, by a two-third vote.

CHAP. 257. An Act to incorporate Touissant L'Ouverture College. Passed April 3, 1871.

CHAP. 258. An Act to extend the time for the completion, and to facilitate the construction of, the New York and Albany Railroad. Passed April 3, 1871; three-fifths being present.

CHAP. 259. *An Act in relation to acrobatic exhibitions. Passed April* 3, 1871; *three-fifths being present.*

CHAP. 260. *An Act to amend an act entitled "An act to authorize the formation of railroad corporations and to regulate the same," passed April two, eighteen hundred and fifty, so as to permit municipal corporations to aid in the construction of railroads, passed May eighteen, eighteen hundred and sixty-nine. Passed April* 3, 1871; *three-fifths being present.*

CHAP. 261. An Act to incorporate the Greenwich Railroad Equipment Company. Passed April 3, 1871.

CHAP. 262. An Act to incorporate the Progress Club in the city of New York. Passed April 3, 1871.

CHAP. 263. *An Act to repeal chapter one hundred and forty-five of the Laws of eighteen hundred and twenty-three, entitled "An act declaring part of the river Conhocton a public highway." Passed April* 3, 1871; *three-fifths being present.*

CHAP. 264. An Act to amend the charter of the Loaners' Bank, of the city of New York. Passed April 4, 1871.

CHAP. 265. An Act to repeal chapter five hundred and twenty-one of the Laws of eighteen hundred and sixty-nine, entitled "An act to incorporate the Fort Ann Water Works Company." Passed April 4, 1871.

CHAP. 266. An Act authorizing the election of a Police Justice in the village of New Rochelle. Passed April 4, 1871; three-fifths being present.

CHAP. 267. An Act in relation to the Hudson River Turnpike Company. Passed April 4, 1871.

CHAP. 268. An Act for the relief of the towns of Warrensburgh and Thurman, in the county of Warren, and to contribute toward the building of a bridge across the Hudson river, between said towns, at or near the mouth of the Schroon river. Passed April 4, 1871, by a two-third vote.

CHAP. 269. An Act authorizing the trustees of the society known as "The Shepherd's Fold of the Protestant Episcopal Church, in the State of New York," to place for adoption, or to bind out children committed to the care of said society in certain cases, and authorizing the Board of Supervisors of the county of New York to appropriate money thereto. Passed April 4, 1871.

CHAP. 270. An Act for the relief of John Graff. Passed April 4, 1871; three-fifths being present.

CHAP. 271. An Act to amend an act to incorporate the village of Warwick, passed April fifteenth, eighteen hundred and sixty-seven, so as to enable the inhabitants of said village to obtain a supply of water for public and private uses. Passed April 4, 1871; three-fifths being present.

CHAP. 272. An Act to amend the act entitled "An act to revise the charter of the city of Auburn," passed April twenty-second, eighteen hundred and sixty-nine. Passed April 4, 1871; three-fifths being present.

CHAP. 273. An Act to increase the powers of the Rochester St. Mary's Hospital of the Sisters of Charity, a corporation. Passed April 4, 1871.

CHAP. 274. *An Act to amend chapter four hundred and thirty-two of the Laws of eighteen hundred and seventy, entitled "An act to amend section six of chapter eight hundred and fifty-five of the Laws of eighteen hundred and sixty-nine, entitled 'An act to extend the powers of Boards of Supervisors, except in the counties of New York and Kings,'" passed April twenty-seven, eighteen hundred and seventy. Passed April* 4, 1871; *three-fifths being present.*

CHAP. 275. An Act authorizing the laying out and opening a public highway, less than three rods wide, in the town of Portville, county of Cattaraugus. Passed April 4, 1871; three-fifths being present.

CHAP. 276. An Act to provide for the better support of the poor in the city and town of Newburgh, in the county of Orange. Passed April 4, 1871; three-fifths being present.

CHAP. 277. *An Act to protect the buoys moored in the Niagara river. Passed April* 4, 1871; *three-fifths being present.*

CHAP. 278. An Act to amend the charter of the Commercial Warehouse Company of New York, and to authorize said company to accept and execute certain trusts. Passed April 4, 1871.

CHAP. 279. An Act to change the name of the village of Wellsville, Allegany county, to that of Genesee. Passed April 4, 1871; three-fifths being present.

CHAP. 280. An Act to incorporate the Society of the Sisters of St. Joseph, of the city of Troy. Passed April 4, 1871.

CHAP. 281. An Act to authorize Thomas H. Knickerbocker, William Parrott and H. Clay Root and their associates to construct a railway in the village of Schoharie. Passed April 4, 1871.

CHAP. 282. An Act to amend an act entitled "An act to increase the number of judges of the city court of Brooklyn, and to regulate the civil and criminal jurisdiction thereof," passed April twenty-eighth, eighteen hundred and seventy. Passed April 4, 1871; three-fifths being present.

CHAP. 283. *An Act to amend an act entitled "An act to amend chapter nine hundred and seven of the Laws of eighteen hundred and sixty-nine, entitled 'An act to amend an act entitled an act to authorize the formation of railroad corporations, and to regulate the same,' passed April two, eighteen hundred and fifty, so as to permit municipal corporations to aid in the construction of railroads," passed May eighteen, eighteen hundred and sixty-nine, passed May eighteen, eighteen hundred and seventy. Passed April* 4, 1871; *three-fifths being present.*

CHAP. 284. An Act to amend an act entitled "An act to incorporate the Mutual Savings Bank of Troy," passed April fifteen, eighteen hundred and fifty-seven. Passed April 4, 1871.

CHAP. 285. An Act to provide for the erection of a town hall in the village of Mount Vernon, town of East Chester, county of Westchester. Passed April 4, 1871; three-fifths being present.

CHAP. 286. An Act to amend an act entitled "An act to revise and amend the act to incorporate the Orphan Asylum Society, in the city of Utica," passed March twenty-six, eighteen hundred and fifty-six. Passed April 4, 1871.

CHAP. 287. *An Act to amend the law for the assessment and collection of taxes in cases where farms or lots are divided by county lines. Passed April* 4, 1871; *three-fifths being present.*

CHAP. 288. An Act to provide for the payment of the expenses incurred under chapter six hundred and fourteen of the Laws of eighteen hundred and seventy, entitled "An act to authorize the Common Council of the city of Brooklyn to open, grade, pave and complete Willoughby avenue, in the city of Brooklyn, from Grand avenue to Classon avenue," passed May third, eighteen hundred and seventy. Passed April 5, 1871; three-fifths being present.

CHAP. 289. An Act confirming the official acts of trustees in school district number eleven, of the town of Urbana, Steuben county. Passed April 5, 1871; three-fifths being present.

CHAP. 290. An Act in relation to the powers and duties of the Board of Commissioners of the Department of Public Parks, including provision for the several public parks, squares and places, and other works under the jurisdiction and direction of said department, in the city of New York. Passed April 5, 1871; three-fifths being present.

CHAP. 291. An Act to amend an act entitled "An act to improve certain water rights in the town of Pawling and elsewhere, in the county of Dutchess," passed May ninth, eighteen hundred and sixty-seven. Passed April 5, 1871; three-fifths being present.

CHAP. 292. An Act to amend section three of chapter two hundred and two of the Laws of eighteen hundred and seventy, relative to the police court-house, in the third judicial district in the city of New York. Passed April 5, 1871; three-fifths being present.

CHAP. 293. *An Act to amend an act entitled "An act concerning pilots of the channel of the East river, commonly called Hell Gate," passed April fifteen, eighteen hundred and forty-seven, and the various acts amendatory thereof, passed March twelve, eighteen hundred and sixty, March fourteen, eighteen hundred and sixty-five, and April sixteen, eighteen hundred and sixty-eight. Passed April* 5, 1871; *three-fifths being present.*

CHAP. 294. An Act to change the name of "The Wadsworth Normal and Training School," making an appropriation to pay off the debt incurred for the construction of the building, and to enable the commissioners appointed by the act entitled "An act in relation to the establishment of a normal and training school in the village of Geneseo, to be called 'The Wadsworth Normal and Training School,'" to complete said building so as to allow the State to accept the building and the grounds appurtenant thereto, and to legalize the acts of the board of trustees of the village of Geneseo in issuing bonds pursuant to chapter six hundred and one of the Laws of eighteen hundred and sixty-eight, and the act amendatory thereof. Passed April 5, 1871; three-fifths being present.

CHAP. 295. An Act to amend chapter one hundred and five of the Laws of eighteen hundred and sixty-eight, passed April first, eighteen hundred and sixty-eight, entitled "An act to provide for draining certain swamp lands in the town of New Rochelle, in the county of Westchester, and also to amend the act, chapter five hundred and forty-seven of the Laws of eighteen hundred and seventy," passed May second, eighteen hundred and seventy, being an amendment to said act. Passed April 5, 1871; three-fifths being present.

CHAP. 296. An Act making provision for the payment of a portion of the bonded debt of the town of Sterling, Cayuga county. Passed April 5, 1871; three-fifths being present.

CHAP. 297. An Act to release to Margaret Mulligan the interest of the State in certain lands in the city of Brooklyn, Kings county. Passed April 5, 1871, by a two-third vote.

CHAP. 298. An Act to authorize the New York and Oswego Midland Railroad Company to extend its road, and to facilitate the construction thereof. Passed April 5, 1871; three-fifths being present.

CHAP. 299. An Act to incorporate the Clairmont Library Association of the city of New York. Passed April 5, 1871; three-fifths being present.

CHAP. 300. An Act to incorporate the New York Railway Company, for the purpose of providing rapid transit through the city and county of New York and Westchester county, and to provide for the construction and operation of railways therefor. Passed April 5, 1871; three-fifths being present.

CHAP. 301. An Act increasing the corporate powers of "The Havens Relief Fund Society." Passed April 5, 1871.

CHAP. 302. An Act in relation to the punishment of offenses tried in the court of special sessions of the peace in and for the city and county of New York. Passed April 5, 1871; three-fifths being present.

CHAP. 303. *An Act to amend an act entitled "An act to amend title sixteen, chapter eight, part three of the Revised Statutes, relative to proceedings for the draining of swamps, marshes or other low and wet lands," passed May twelve, eighteen hundred and sixty-nine. Passed April* 5, 1871; *three-fifths being present.*

CHAP. 304. An Act to release the title and interest of the people of the State of New York, in and to certain real estate, of which Alfred Webb, late of the city of New York, died seized, to Edwin Webb. Passed April 6, 1871, by a two-third vote.

CHAP. 305. An Act providing for the disposal of excise moneys in the county of Niagara. Passed April 6, 1871; three-fifths being present.

CHAP. 306. An Act to amend an act entitled "An act to revise and amend an act entitled

'An act to incorporate the village of Canton,' passed May thirteenth, eighteen hundred and forty-five, and the several acts amendatory thereof," passed April twenty-second, eighteen hundred and sixty-five. Passed April 6, 1871; three-fifths being present.

CHAP. 307. An Act to levy a tax upon the town of Stockholm, in the county of St. Lawrence, to reimburse Jason Bicknell for expenses incurred in defending several suits brought for alleged misapplication of bounty moneys, while acting as a war finance committee in said town. Passed April 6, 1871; three-fifths being present.

CHAP. 308. An Act to enable lodges of Knights of Pythias to take, hold and convey real and personal property. Passed April 6, 1871.

CHAP. 309. An Act to provide for the construction of a main and lateral drain or sewer in Navy street, Johnson street and Hudson avenue, and other streets and avenues in the city of Brooklyn. Passed April 6, 1871; three-fifths being present.

CHAP. 310. An Act to amend an act entitled "An act amending the charter of the village of Glens Falls, and empowering the trustees thereof to supply said village with pure and wholesome water," passed May fifth, eighteen hundred and sixty-three. Passed April 6, 1871; three-fifths being present.

CHAP. 311. An Act to amend an act entitled "An act to organize and establish a police for the village of West Troy," passed April twenty-eighth, eighteen hundred and seventy. Passed April 6, 1871; three-fifths being present.

CHAP. 312. An Act to enable the Fulsome Landing Bridge Company to complete their bridge across the Hudson river, between the towns of Chester and Johnsburgh, and to legalize the acts of the tax payers of the town of Schroon in relation to their subscription to the capital stock of said company. Passed April 6, 1871; three-fifths being present.

CHAP. 313. An Act to authorize the Empire Mutual Life Insurance Company to increase its capital stock. Passed April 6, 1871.

CHAP. 314. An Act to amend the act entitled "An act incorporating the New York Northern Railroad Company," passed April twenty-eighth, eighteen hundred and sixty-six. Passed April 6, 1871.

CHAP. 315. An Act enlarging the powers of the Lordville and Equinunk Bridge Company. Passed April 6, 1871.

CHAP. 316. An Act relative to the Institute of St. Paul the Apostle. Passed April 6, 1871; three-fifths being present.

CHAP. 317. An Act repealing chapter seven hundred and twenty-eight of the Laws of eighteen hundred and sixty-seven, entitled "An act authorizing the assessment of highway labor upon the Westerlo Turnpike road, in the county of Albany, and regulating the tolls thereon." Passed April 6, 1871; three-fifths being present.

CHAP. 318. An Act to authorize the city of Rochester to borrow moneys to pay off its present floating debt, and to issue its bonds for the payment thereof. Passed April 6, 1871; three-fifths being present.

CHAP. 319. An Act to release the interest of the people of the State of New York, to certain lands, to David Duane. Passed April 6, 1871, by a two-third vote.

CHAP. 320. An Act to repeal an act passed April twenty-eighth, eighteen hundred and sixty-nine, entitled "An act to amend the Revised Statutes in relation to laying out public roads, and the alteration thereof, in the county of Putnam." Passed April 6, 1871; three-fifths being present.

CHAP. 321. An Act declaring a certain road, in the town of Westport, Essex county, a public highway. Passed April 6, 1871; three-fifths being present.

CHAP. 322. An Act for the consolidation of the debt of the city of New York. Passed April 6, 1871; three-fifths being present.

CHAP. 323. An Act for the consolidation of the debt of the county of New York. Passed April 6, 1871; three-fifths being present.

CHAP. 324. An Act to incorporate "The Sisterhood of Grey Nuns," in the State of New York. Passed April 6, 1871.

CHAP. 325. An Act to further amend an act entitled "An act to provide for the widening and improvement of Union street, in the city of Brooklyn," passed April twenty-seventh, eighteen hundred and sixty-six. Passed April 6, 1871; three-fifths being present.

CHAP. 326. *An Act giving the consent of the State of New York to the purchase by, and ceding jurisdiction to, the United States over certain lands, within this State, to be occupied as sites for light-houses and keepers' dwellings. Passed April* 6, 1871, *by a two-third vote.*

CHAP. 327. An Act to amend an act entitled "An act to incorporate the Father Matthew United Benevolent Total Abstinence Benefit Society," passed May five, eighteen hundred and sixty-three. Passed April 6, 1871; three-fifths being present.

CHAP. 328. An Act to re-enact and amend an act entitled "An act to provide a further supply of pure and wholesome water for the city of New York," passed February twenty-seven, eighteen hundred and seventy-one. Passed April 6, 1871; three-fifths being present.

CHAP. 329. *An Act to amend chapter eight hundred of the Session Laws of eighteen hundred and sixty-six, relative to the taking of lands for the erection of school-houses or making additions thereto. Passed April 6, 1871; three-fifths being present.*

CHAP. 330. An Act to incorporate the "Westchester Club," in the county of Westchester. Passed April 6, 1871.

CHAP. 331. An Act providing for the appointment of an interpreter for the justices' courts of the fourth and fifth districts of the city of Brooklyn. Passed April 6, 1871; three-fifths being present.

CHAP. 332. An Act for the relief of the Bath Library Association. Passed April 6, 1871; three-fifths being present.

CHAP. 333. An Act to amend an act entitled "An act to authorize the laying out and constructing a road from Pitcairn, St. Lawrence county, to Diana, Lewis county, and apply the tax on certain lands along the line of said road, to pay the expenses of laying out and constructing the same," passed May sixth, eighteen hundred and sixty-nine. Passed April 6, 1871; three-fifths being present.

CHAP. 334. An Act to facilitate the construction of the Syracuse and Chenango Valley Railroad. Passed April 6, 1871; three-fifths being present.

CHAP. 335. An Act to authorize the appointment of a person to be public administrator in the county of Kings, and to determine the powers and duties of such officer. Passed April 6, 1871; three-fifths being present.

CHAP. 336. An Act further to amend an act entitled "An act to authorize the towns of Yonkers and East Chester to widen, make, extend and improve several highways in said towns," passed April twenty-second, eighteen hundred and sixty-nine. Passed April 6, 1871; three-fifths being present.

CHAP. 337. An Act in relation to the police justices and justices of the justices' court of the city of Albany. Passed April 6, 1871; three-fifths being present.

CHAP. 338. An Act to incorporate the Saugerties Savings Bank of the village of Saugerties, Ulster county, New York. Passed April 6, 1871.

CHAP. 339. An Act to amend "An act to incorporate the Clinton County Savings Bank," passed May fifth, eighteen hundred and sixty-nine. Passed April 6, 1871.

CHAP. 340. An Act to incorporate the Putnam County Savings Bank. Passed April 6, 1871.

CHAP. 341. An Act to incorporate the Westchester County Trust Company. Passed April 6, 1871.

CHAP. 342. An Act authorizing the Reformed Protestant Dutch Church, of New Hackensack, to convey lands for cemetery purposes. Passed April 6, 1871; three-fifths being present.

CHAP. 343. An Act to create a separate road district in the village of Starkville, Herkimer county. Passed April 6, 1871; three-fifths being present.

CHAP. 344. An Act authorizing the construction of a carriage and passenger bridge over the outlet of Lake George, a navigable stream, in the town of Ticonderoga, Essex county. Passed April 6, 1871; three-fifths being present.

CHAP. 345. An Act to incorporate the Clinton Driving Park Association for the improvement of the breed of horses and cattle, and to encourage improvements in agriculture and mechanics. Passed April 6, 1871.

CHAP. 346. An Act to lay out, open and grade Sixtieth street, in the city of Brooklyn and towns of New Utrecht and Gravesend, in the county of Kings. Passed April 6, 1871; three-fifths being present.

CHAP. 347. An Act to provide for the establishment of one or more public parks in and adjoining the city of Syracuse. Passed April 7, 1871; three-fifths being present.

CHAP. 348. *An Act to authorize the Canal Commissioners to construct a swing bridge over the Erie canal, on Buffalo street, in the city of Rochester, and to use the materials of the old bridge in constructing a bridge over said canal to connect Munger and Averill street, in said city. Passed April* 7, 1871; *three-fifths being present.*

CHAP. 349. An Act to amend an act entitled "An act to incorporate the Lower California Company," passed May tenth, eighteen hundred and sixty-seven. Passed April 7, 1871.

CHAP. 350. An Act to authorize the Utica, Clinton and Binghamton Railroad Company to construct, maintain and operate a swing bridge over the Erie canal, in the second ward in the city of Utica. Passed April 7, 1871.

CHAP 351. *An Act in relation to canal bridges, in the village of Norwich, and making an appropriation therefor. Passed April* 7, 1871; *three-fifths being present.*

CHAP. 352. *An Act to authorize the construction of a bridge over the Chenango canal, in the city of Binghamton, at the intersection with Chenango street, in said city. Passed April* 7, 1871; *three-fifths being present.*

CHAP. 353. An Act to authorize the Syracuse Northern Railroad Company to construct and maintain a swing bridge over the Oswego canal, in the first ward of the city of Syracuse. Passed April 7, 1871.

CHAP. 354. An Act to release to Christina Getrost, the interest of the State in certain lands, in the city of Buffalo. Passed April 7, 1871, by a two-thirds vote.

CHAP. 355. An Act to amend chapter one hundred and seventeen of the Laws of eighteen hundred and seventy-one, entitled "An act to amend an act entitled 'An act to authorize the levying of a tax upon the town of Gouverneur, in the county of St. Lawrence, for the benefit of the Gouverneur Wesleyan Seminary, and to increase the capital stock of said seminary,'" passed March sixteenth, eighteen hundred and seventy-one. Passed April 7, 1871; three-fifths being present.

CHAP. 356. An Act to amend an act entitled "An act to regulate, grade, widen, gravel and improve a public highway in the towns of East Chester, Scarsdale and White Plains, in the county of Westchester, commonly called the Old White Plains Post Road, and also a portion of Fourth avenue, in the village of Central Mount Vernon," passed May eighteenth, eighteen hundred and sixty-nine; and also to amend the act amendatory of and supplementary to said original act, passed May fifth, eighteen hundred and seventy, and to extend the provisions of said acts. Passed April 7, 1871; three-fifths being present.

CHAP. 357. An Act to amend the charter of the Commonwealth Life Insurance Company. Passed April 7, 1871.

CHAP. 358. An Act to amend an act entitled "An act to incorporate the city of Binghamton," passed April ninth, eighteen hundred and sixty-seven, and the several acts amending the same. Passed April 7, 1871; three-fifths being present.

CHAP. 359. *An Act to amend an act entitled "An act to revise and consolidate the general act relating to public instruction." Passed April* 7, 1871; *three-fifths being present.*

CHAP. 360. An Act to amend an act entitled "An act to provide for the promotion of public health and for draining and reclaiming overflowed and wet lands adjoining Black lake and its tributaries, in the counties of St. Lawrence and Jefferson, and for improving the hydraulic power at Ogdensburgh," passed May fourth, eighteen hundred and sixty-four, being chapter five hundred and seventy-seven of the Laws of eighteen hundred and sixty-four, as amended by chapter one hundred and eighty of the Laws of eighteen hundred and sixty-eight. Passed April 7, 1871; three-fifths being present.

CHAP. 361. *An Act to facilitate the admission of certain wills as evidence in courts of justice. Passed April* 7, 1871.

CHAP. 362. An Act to release to Mary Tilman the interest of the people of this State to lands in the city of Brooklyn, whereof Robert Tilman died seized. Passed April 7, 1871, by a two-third vote.

CHAP. 363. An Act to amend an act entitled "An act to incorporate the village of Alden, in Erie county, New York," passed May seventh, eighteen hundred and sixty-nine. Passed April 7, 1871; three-fifths being present.

CHAP. 364. An Act to provide for the purchase of a new school-house site, and for the erection of a school-house thereon, in school district number three, at Whitestone, in the town of Flushing, in Queens county, and for the sale of the present school-house and site in said district. Passed April 7, 1871; three-fifths being present.

CHAP. 365. An Act to incorporate the New York Cotton Exchange. Passed April 8, 1871.

CHAP. 366. An Act to amend an act entitled "An act to incorporate the village of Frankfort," passed May fourth, one thousand eight hundred and sixty-three. Passed April 8, 1871; three-fifths being present.

CHAP. 367. An Act to prevent the taking of fish from lake Salubria, in the town of Bath, Steuben county. Passed April 8, 1871; three-fifths being present.

CHAP. 368. An Act to amend the act entitled "An act to amend an act passed March twenty-eight, eighteen hundred and fifty-five, entitled 'An act to amend an act entitled an act to incorporate the firemen of the village of Brooklyn,' passed April sixteenth, eighteen hundred and twenty-three," passed April twenty-fifth, eighteen hundred and sixty-four. Passed April 8, 1871; three-fifths being present.

CHAP. 369. An Act to amend an act passed April second, eighteen hundred and sixty-nine, entitled "An act to reorganize the Board of Water and Sewerage Commissioners of the city of Brooklyn, and to provide for the repaving, repairing and cleaning the streets of said city by said board," as the same is amended by chapter six hundred and fifty-two of the Laws of eighteen hundred and seventy. Passed April 8, 1871; three-fifths being present.

CHAP. 370. An Act to authorize the Common Council of the city of Rochester to raise money for the purpose of continuing and completing the survey and map of said city already commenced and now in progress. Passed April 8, 1871; three-fifths being present.

CHAP. 371. An Act to amend "An act to authorize the construction of a lock-up in the town hall, located at Brewsters, in the town of Southeast, Putnam county, and to enable the Board of Commissioners for building the town hall to raise moneys to pay for and complete the same," passed March sixteenth, eighteen hundred and seventy. Passed April 8, 1871; three-fifths being present.

CHAP. 372. An Act authorizing "The Syracuse Northern Railroad Company" to mortgage its real estate and personal property. Passed April 8, 1871.

CHAP. 373. An Act in relation to the American Geographical and Statistical Society. Passed April 8, 1871.

CHAP. 374. An Act in relation to the fees of the clerk of the county of Kings. Passed April 8, 1871; three-fifths being present.

CHAP. 375. An Act to authorize the construction of a railroad in and through certain streets and avenues in the counties of Madison and Oneida. Passed April 8, 1871.

CHAP. 376. An Act to authorize the city of Buffalo to issue its bonds for the purpose of extending the supply of water to the city and its inhabitants. Passed April 8, 1871; three-fifths being present.

CHAP. 377. An Act in relation to a bridge across the Allegany river, on the Indian Reservation, in the town of Red House, in the county of Cattaraugus, and making an appropriation for the same. Passed April 8, 1871, by a two-third vote.

CHAP. 378. *An Act to amend an act entitled "An act authorizing the incorporation of Rural Cemetery Associations," passed April twenty-seven, eighteen hundred and forty-seven, and all supplementary acts appertaining thereto. Passed April* 8, 1871.

CHAP. 379. An Act to amend an act entitled "An act to incorporate the Binghamton and Port Dickinson Railroad Company," passed May first, eighteen hundred and sixty-eight. Passed April 8, 1871.

CHAP. 380. An Act providing for the disposal of excise moneys, in the county of Allegany. Passed April 8, 1871; three-fifths being present.

CHAP. 381. An Act for the collection of taxes and assessments and Croton water rents in the city of New York, and to amend the several acts in relation thereto. Passed April 8, 1871; three-fifths being present.

CHAP. 382. An Act to authorize the Hope Mutual Life Insurance Company of New York to increase its capital stock. Passed April 11, 1871.

CHAP. 383. An Act to provide for the election of a receiver of taxes for the town and village of Greenbush, county of Rensselaer. Passed April 11, 1871; three-fifths being present.

CHAP. 384. An Act to authorize the Commissioners of the Land Office to convey the interest of the State in certain lands in Black Rock. Passed April 11, 1871, by a two-third vote.

CHAP. 385. An Act to establish a receiver of taxes, and to authorize the sale of lands for non-payment of taxes and for the collection of unpaid taxes in the town of Newtown, Queens county. Passed April 11, 1871; three-fifths being present.

CHAP. 386. An Act to incorporate "The Hemlock Lake Union Agricultural Society." Passed April 11, 1871.

CHAP. 387. An Act to amend chapter one hundred and forty-one of the Laws of eighteen hundred and seventy-one, entitled "An act to abolish tolls on certain roads and bridges in the towns of Newtown and Flushing, in the county of Queens, and provide compensation therefor," passed March twenty-one, eighteen hundred and seventy-one, and supplemental thereto. Passed April 11, 1871; three-fifths being present.

CHAP. 388. An Act extending the provisions of certain laws, permitting municipal corporations to aid in the construction of railroads in the county of Niagara, excepting the town of Royalton, in said county. Passed April 11, 1871; three-fifths being present.

CHAP. 389. An Act to alter the commissioners' map of the city of Brooklyn, and to provide for certain expenses incurred in opening a street hereby closed. Passed April 11, 1871.

CHAP. 390. An Act to amend an act entitled "An act to incorporate the International Bridge Company," passed April seventeenth, eighteen hundred and fifty-seven. Passed April 11, 1871.

CHAP. 391. An Act to amend the charter of the city of Utica. Passed April 11, 1871; three-fifths being present.

CHAP. 392. An Act to incorporate the Southern New York Baptist Association. Passed April 11, 1871.

CHAP. 393. An Act to authorize the board of trustees of the village of Yonkers, in the county of Westchester, to widen, straighten, macadamize, gravel, pave, curb, gutter, drain, make and improve Main street. Passed April 11, 1871; three-fifths being present.

CHAP. 394. An Act to authorize the Avon, Geneseo and Mount Morris Railroad Company to extend and alter its tract, to increase its capital stock and to avail itself of the act passed May tenth, eighteen hundred and sixty-nine, permitting municipal corporations to aid in the construction of railroads. Passed April 11, 1871; three-fifths being present.

CHAP. 395. An Act in relation to persons who abandon or threaten to abandon their families in the county of Kings. Passed April 11, 1871; three-fifths being present.

CHAP. 396. An Act to amend chapter three hundred and thirteen of the Laws of eighteen hundred and thirty, entitled "An act to vest certain privileges in the freeholders and inhabitants of the village of Monticello, in the county of Sullivan," passed April twentieth, eighteen hundred and thirty. Passed April 11, 1871; three-fifths being present.

CHAP. 397. An Act to authorize the construction of a swing bridge over the Chenango canal in the village of Hamilton, at the point where Pleasant street crosses said canal. Passed April 11, 1871; three-fifths being present.

CHAP. 398. An Act in relation to the improvement of the First avenue, in the city of New York. Passed April 11, 1871; three-fifths being present.

CHAP. 399. An Act to authorize the village of Corning, Steuben county, to borrow money to construct water-works for said village. Passed April 11, 1871; three-fifths being present.

CHAP. 400. An Act to release to the sister, nephew and niece of Jacob Schlegel, deceased, all the right, title and interest of the people of the State of New York, in and to a certain house and lot of land in the city of New York, in the county of New York, and also a certain lot of land in the town of East Chester, in the county of Westchester. Passed April 11, 1871, by a two-third vote.

CHAP. 401. An Act to incorporate the Synod of Western New York. Passed April 11, 1871.

CHAP. 402. An Act to incorporate the Goshen Savings Bank, Goshen, Orange county, New York. Passed April 11, 1871.

CHAP. 403. An Act to incorporate the Dickinson Hotel Company. Passed April 11, 1871.

CHAP. 404. An Act to amend, and supplementary to an act entitled "An act relative to the widening, straightening, laying out and opening of St. Ann's avenue and Carr avenue, in the town of Morrisania, in the county of Westchester," passed May seventh, eighteen hundred and sixty-nine, as amended May fifth, eighteen hundred and seventy. Passed April 11, 1871; three-fifths being present.

CHAP. 405. An Act to amend an act entitled "An act for the incorporation of the village of Oxford, and for other purposes," passed April six, eighteen hundred and eight, and to amend the several acts amendatory thereof, and to increase the powers of the trustees of said village. Passed April 11, 1871; three-fifths being present.

CHAP. 406. An Act to authorize the construction and maintaining of a free bridge over the Susquehanna river, in the city of Binghamton, and to borrow money therefor. Passed April 11, 1871; three-fifths being present.

CHAP. 407. An Act to incorporate "Our Home Hygienic Institute of Dansville, New York." Passed April 11, 1871.

CHAP. 408. An Act to incorporate the Society of the Friars Minor of the Order of St. Francis. Passed April 11, 1871.

CHAP. 409. An Act to authorize the conveyance to the Place College of the interest of the people of the State of New York, in certain premises at Binghamton, Broome county; and to credit on the lien of the amount due the Place College for rent of the premises. Passed April 11, 1871, by a two-third vote.

CHAP. 410. An Act to amend an act entitled "An act to establish and maintain a police force in the city of Troy," passed April twenty-ninth, eighteen hundred and seventy. Passed April 11, 1871; three-fifths being present.

CHAP. 411. An Act to amend an act entitled "An act to incorporate the National Savings Institution of the city of New York," passed April twentieth, eighteen hundred and sixty-seven. Passed April 12, 1871; three-fifths being present.

CHAP. 412. An Act amending chapter three hundred and twenty-eight of the Laws of eighteen hundred and sixty-six, entitled "An act to provide for the completion of a public highway in the counties of Essex and Franklin, and applying the non-resident highway taxes upon certain lands in the said county of Essex for that purpose." Passed April 12, 1871; three-fifths being present.

CHAP. 413. An Act to provide for the improvement of Newtown creek, between Maspeth avenue and Metropolitan avenue. Passed April 12, 1871; three-fifths being present.

CHAP. 414. An Act to incorporate the Lutheran Emigrants' House Association of New York. Passed April 12, 1871.

CHAP. 415. *An Act in relation to the fees of sheriffs, except in the counties of New York, Kings and Westchester. Passed April* 12, 1871; *three-fifths being present.*

CHAP. 416. An Act to incorporate the St. George's Brotherhood of the town of Flushing, Queens county. Passed April 12, 1871.

CHAP. 417. An Act to amend an act entitled "An act to incorporate the Schenectady Water Company," passed April thirteen, eighteen hundred and sixty-five. Passed April 12, 1871.

CHAP. 418. An Act to incorporate "The Oblate Missionaries of the Immaculate Conception," in the State of New York. Passed April 12, 1871.

CHAP. 419. *An Act to authorize the sale of unoccupied lands of burial-ground and rural cemetery associations. Passed April* 12, 1871; *three-fifths being present.*

CHAP. 420. An Act to release to Thomas Shortall, Richard Shortall, Mary Leury, Christopher Shortall, Ellen Shortall, and Eliza J. Shortall, children of James Shortall, deceased, certain lands in the town of Attica, in the county of Wyoming. Passed April 12, 1871, by a two-third vote.

CHAP. 421. An Act to extend the time for the organization of the New York Loan and Indemnity Company. Passed April 12, 1871.

CHAP. 422. An Act to amend an act authorizing the purchase of right of way, laying out and constructing a public road in the town of Little Falls, county of Herkimer, passed April nineteenth, eighteen hundred and sixty-seven. Passed April 12, 1871; three-fifths being present.

CHAP. 423. An Act to amend an act entitled "An act to amend and consolidate the several acts relating to the village of Lansingburgh." Passed April 12, 1871; three-fifths being present.

CHAP. 424. An Act in relation to the records and papers of the surrogate's court of the county of Rensselaer. Passed April 12, 1871; three-fifths being present.

CHAP. 425. An Act in relation to unpaid taxes in the county of Monroe. Passed April 12, 1871; three-fifths being present.

CHAP. 426. An Act to amend an act entitled "An act to incorporate the Columbian Fire Engine Company No. One of Spring Valley, Ramapo, Rockland County, State of New York," passed April four, eighteen hundred and sixty-two. Passed April 12, 1871; three-fifths being present.

CHAP. 427. An Act to incorporate the "New York Free Medical College for Women." Passed April 12, 1871.

CHAP. 428. An Act to authorize George Wade, of Fishkill, Dutchess county, and Erastus B. Rudd, of the city and county of New York, to establish and continue a ferry across the Hudson river from Cornwall Landing, in the county of Orange, to the opposite side of the river in Dutchess county. Passed April 12, 1871.

CHAP. 429. An Act to change the name of the Buffalo and Washington Railway Company. Passed April 12, 1871.

CHAP. 430. An Act to amend an act entitled "An act requiring the highway tax of the New York Central Railroad Company through the town of Mentz, to be applied to the repairs of certain highways in the said town," passed April second, one thousand eight hundred and sixty-two. Passed April 12, 1871; three-fifths being present.

CHAP. 431. An Act to authorize Trinity Church, Buffalo, and Christ Church, Buffalo, to consolidate. Passed April 12, 1871.

CHAP. 432. An Act to incorporate the Union Hotel Company in the city of Buffalo. Passed April 12, 1871.

CHAP. 433. An Act to repeal "An act to create a Metropolitan Sanitary District and Board of Health therein, for the preservation of life and health, and to prevent the spread of disease," so far as relates to the county of Westchester, and to provide for the appointment of boards of health in the several towns and villages in said county, and defining their powers and duties. Passed April 12, 1871; three-fifths being present.

CHAP. 434. An Act to amend an act entitled "An act to incorporate the Clairmont Savings Bank of the city of New York," passed April twenty-second, eighteen hundred and seventy. Passed April 12, 1871.

CHAP. 435. An Act to incorporate the Fish Creek Improvement Company. Passed April 12, 1871.

CHAP. 436. An Act to incorporate the Norwich Water-works Company, and to authorize the trustees of the village of Norwich to take and lease lands and water for the purposes of said company. Passed April 12, 1871; three-fifths being present.

CHAP. 437. An Act to amend an act entitled "An act to incorporate the New York and Long Island Bridge Company, for the purpose of constructing and maintaining a bridge over the East river, between the city of New York and Queens county," passed April sixteen, eighteen hundred and sixty-seven. Passed April 12, 1871; three-fifths being present.

CHAP. 438. An Act to amend an act entitled "An act in relation to the punishment of offenses tried in the court of special sessions of the peace in and for the city and county of New York," passed April fifth, eighteen hundred and seventy-one. Passed April 12, 1871; three-fifths being present.

CHAP. 439. An Act to authorize The Watkins Sanitarium Company to borrow money for the purposes of its business, and to secure the payment of the same by mortgage of the lands and other property of said corporation. Passed April 12, 1871.

CHAP. 440. An Act making an appropriation for the construction of a bridge over French creek. Passed April 12, 1871, by a two-third vote.

CHAP. 441. An Act to authorize the laying out and construction of an avenue from the village of Ballston Spa, half way to the village of Saratoga Springs. Passed April 12, 1871; three-fifths being present.

CHAP. 442. An Act further to amend and revise an act entitled "An act to authorize the construction of a railroad from the village of Horseheads to the city of Elmira, in the county of Chemung, through the streets of said village and city," passed April eighteen, eighteen hundred and sixty-six. Passed April 12, 1871.

CHAP. 443. An Act to repeal chapter one hundred and seventeen of the Laws of eighteen hundred and sixty-nine, entitled "An act to authorize Danforth Mott to establish and maintain a ferry across Lake Champlain at Rouse's Point, in the town of Champlain, in the county of Clinton." Passed April 12, 1871.

CHAP. 444. An Act relative to lands in the town of Greenburgh, county of Westchester, devised by Alexander Fowler, deceased, to Elizabeth Tompkins and her descendants. Passed April 12, 1871, by a two-third vote.

CHAP. 445. An Act to amend an act entitled "An act to authorize the lighting of public streets and avenues in the town of West Farms, in the county of Westchester," passed May second, eighteen hundred and seventy. Passed April 12, 1871; three-fifths being present.

CHAP. 446. An Act to repeal chapter eight hundred and ninety-nine of the Laws of eighteen hundred and sixty-nine, being "An act for the construction of an avenue in the town of Gravesend, in the county of Kings." Passed April 12, 1871; three-fifths being present.

CHAP. 447. An Act to amend the charter of the village of Cortland, and to regulate the sale of merchandise at auction in said village. Passed April 12, 1871; three-fifths being present.

CHAP. 448. An Act to incorporate the Oxford Hotel Company. Passed April 12, 1871.

CHAP. 449. An Act authorizing the trustees of the village of College Point to issue bonds and borrow money for the erection of a school-house in said village and to increase the school tax in said village. Passed April 12, 1871; three-fifths being present.

CHAP. 450. An Act to incorporate the Troy Commercial College. Passed April 12, 1871.

CHAP. 451. An Act to amend the charter of "The Odd Fellows' Asylum of the State of New York." Passed April 12, 1871.

CHAP. 452. An Act to legalize and confirm the proceedings of the board of trustees of the village of Silver Creek, re-incorporating said village, and the election by the inhabitants thereof, held on the twenty-eighth day of February, eighteen hundred and seventy-one, under and in pursuance of an act for the incorporation of villages, passed April twentieth, eighteen hundred and seventy Passed April 12, 1871; three-fifths being present.

CHAP. 453. An Act in relation to the Middletown and Crawford Railroad Company. Passed April 12, 1871.

CHAP. 454. An Act to extend the time for the Staten Island and Elizabethport Ferry Company to put their ferry in operation. Passed April 12, 1871.

CHAP. 455. An Act to provide for the purchase of a steam fire-engine in the village of Castleton, Rensselaer county, and for the more effectual protection of said village against fire. Passed April 12, 1871; three-fifths being present.

CHAP. 456. *An Act to amend the banking laws of this State. Passed April* 13, 1871.

CHAP. 457. *An Act to establish the southerly bounds of the State lands at Clinton prison. Passed April* 13, 1871, *by a two-third vote.*

CHAP. 458. An Act to provide for the extension of the Rondout and Oswego Railroad to the east bank of the Hudson river, and to establish a ferry over said river. Passed April 13, 1871, by a two-third vote.

CHAP. 459. An Act to incorporate the Mechanics' Savings Bank of Brooklyn. Passed April 13, 1871.

CHAP. 460. An Act to enable the Mayor and Common Council of Long Island City to borrow money. Passed April 13, 1871; three-fifths being present.

CHAP. 461. An Act to revise the charter of Long Island City. Passed April 13, 1871; three-fifths being present.

CHAP. 462. An Act to regulate coroners' inquests in the city and county of New York, and to authorize the appointment of a clerk to the board of coroners. Passed April 13, 1871; three-fifths being present.

CHAP. 463. An Act for the relief of William H. Baker. Passed April 13, 1871; three-fifths being present.

CHAP. 464. An Act to authorize school district number three, of the town of Castleton, in the county of Richmond, to borrow money for the purpose of completing a school building in said district, and to provide for the payment thereof. Passed April 13, 1871; three-fifths being present.

CHAP. 465. An Act in relation to the fire-alarm telegraph in the city of New York. Passed April 13, 1871; three-fifths being present.

CHAP. 466. An Act to incorporate the Elmira Park Association. Passed April 13, 1871.

CHAP. 467. An Act to authorize a public cemetery in the town of Williamstown, Oswego county. Passed April 13, 1871; three-fifths being present.

CHAP. 468. An Act requiring owners, agents and drivers of loaded vehicles upon wheels, running upon the Buffalo and Williamsville McAdam road with rims or tires less than five inches in width, to permit their vehicles and loads to be weighed. Passed April 13, 1871.

CHAP. 469. An Act to protect, improve and keep in repair the west part of the road formerly known as the Buffalo Plank-road, in the county of Erie. Passed April 13, 1871; three-fifths being present.

CHAP. 470. An Act in relation to receivers or collectors of taxes in the town of East Chester, county of Westchester. Passed April 13, 1871; three-fifths being present.

CHAP. 471. An Act to amend an act entitled "An act to incorporate the Chehocton Bridge Company, in Delaware county," passed April thirtieth, eighteen hundred and sixty-nine. Passed April 13, 1871.

CHAP. 472 An Act to incorporate the Capital City Medical College. Passed April 13, 1871; three-fifths being present.

CHAP 473. An Act to amend an act entitled "An act to incorporate the Colored Home of the city of New York," passed May eighth, eighteen hundred and forty-five. Passed April 13, 1871.

CHAP. 474. An Act to incorporate the Chautauqua Lake Camp Meeting Association of the Erie Conference of the Methodist Episcopal Church. Passed April 13, 1871.

CHAP. 475. *An Act to amend an act entitled "An act to amend the several acts relating to the power of the Commissioners of Immigration and for the regulation of the Marine Hospital," passed April thirteenth, eighteen hundred and fifty-three. Passed April* 13, 1871; *three-fifths being present.*

CHAP. 476. An Act authorizing and empowering the city of Rochester to extend its drainage and sewerage beyond the city limits. Passed April 13, 1871; three-fifths being present.

CHAP. 477. An Act for the relief of the corporation styled "The Rector and Members of Saint Peter's Church, in the Manor of Cortlandt, near Peekskill." Passed April 13, 1871.

CHAP. 478. An Act to further amend, and supplementary to an act entitled "An act to regulate, grade, widen, macadamize and improve a public highway in the towns of East Chester and Westchester, in the county of Westchester, commonly called the Old White Plains Road, and also a portion of First street, in the village of Mount Vernon," passed May fourteenth, eighteen hundred and sixty-eight, and as amended by act passed May eighteenth, eighteen hundred and sixty-nine, and further amended by act passed May fifth, eighteen hundred and seventy. Passed April 13, 1871; three-fifths being present.

CHAP. 479. An Act to incorporate the Pamelia, Orleans and Clayton Macadamized Road Company. Passed April 13, 1871; three-fifths being present.

CHAP. 480. An Act to authorize the Common Council of the city of Oswego to sell certain real estate in said city. Passed April 13, 1871; three-fifths being present.

CHAP. 481. *An Act to amend an act passed May two, eighteen hundred and sixty-four, and entitled "An act to amend an act entitled 'An act to authorize the formation of corporations for manufacturing, mining, mechanical or chemical purposes,'" passed February seventeenth, eighteen hundred and forty-eight. Passed April* 13, 1871.

CHAP. 482. *An Act to amend an act entitled "An act in relation to the powers and jurisdiction of surrogate's courts," passed April twenty-fifth, eighteen hundred and sixty-seven." Passed April* 13, 1871.

CHAP. 483. An Act relative to proceedings to vacate assessments in the city of Brooklyn. Passed April 13, 1871; three-fifths being present.

CHAP. 484. An Act to authorize the Board of Trustees of the town of Morrisania to lay out and open One Hundred and Fifty-sixth street, from St. Ann's avenue to the Third avenue, in the town of Morrisania, county of Westchester. Passed April 13, 1871; three-fifths being present.

CHAP. 485. An Act to authorize the village of Dunkirk to issue bonds for the purpose of supplying said village with water, and to create a board of water commissioners. Passed April 13, 1871; three-fifths being present.

CHAP. 486. *An Act in relation to the qualifications of persons to be admitted to practice in the courts of this State as attorneys, solicitors and counselors. Passed April* 13, 1871.

CHAP. 487. An Act to release the interest of the State in and to certain lands owned by Alice Jennings, an alien, deceased, and vest the same in James Jennings, her surviving husband. Passed April 13, 1871, by a two-third vote.

CHAP. 488. An Act to provide for the completion of the repavement of Atlantic avenue, between Flatbush avenue and Classon avenue, in the city of Brooklyn. Passed April 14, 1871; three-fifths being present.

CHAP. 489. An Act to amend an act entitled "An act to incorporate the village of Tottenville, in the town of Westfield, county of Richmond," passed April twenty-eighth, eighteen hundred and sixty-nine. Passed April 14, 1871; three-fifths being present.

CHAP. 490. An Act to incorporate the Ocean Hill Association for the improvement of the eastern portion of the ninth and twenty-first wards of the city of Brooklyn. Passed April 14, 1871.

CHAP. 491. An Act to provide for the relief and support of the poor of the county of Kings, and to change the name of the office of the superintendents of the poor therein to the office of the commissioners of charities. Passed April 14, 1871; three-fifths being present.

CHAP. 492. An Act relative to courts of civil and criminal jurisdiction in the city of Brooklyn. Passed April 14, 1871.

CHAP. 493. An Act for the relief of Richard Platt. Passed April 14, 1871; three-fifths being present.

CHAP. 494. An Act to give the Board of Town Auditors, of the town of Ava, Oneida county, power to audit certain accounts. Passed April 14, 1871; three-fifths being present.

CHAP. 495. An Act establishing a ferry from Barber's Point, in the county of Essex, across Lake Champlain. Passed April 14, 1871; three-fifths being present.

CHAP. 496. An Act to amend the charter of the Odd Fellows' Asylum of the State of New York. Passed April 14, 1871.

CHAP. 497. An Act to improve and enlarge the Lancaster Rural Cemetery, situated in the town of Lancaster, Erie county. Passed April 14, 1871; three-fifths being present.

CHAP. 498. An Act to amend an act passed April seventeenth, eighteen hundred and fifty-seven, entitled an act to amend an act passed May second, eighteen hundred and thirty-four, incorporating the village of Camden. Passed April 14, 1871; three-fifths being present.

CHAP. 499. An Act to repeal the act entitled "An act to incorporate the Waterville Volunteer Fire Company," passed April twenty-fourth, eighteen hundred and twenty-nine, and also to repeal the acts amendatory thereof. Passed April 14, 1871.

CHAP. 500. An Act to authorize the Yates County Agricultural Society to sell and convey its real estate and to purchase other real estate. Passed April 14, 1871.

CHAP. 501. An Act authorizing the village of Charlotte to take control of the cemetery in said village, also to purchase additional grounds for the burial of their dead, and to provide for the election of three commissioners to take supervision of the same. Passed April 14, 1871; three-fifths being present.

CHAP. 502. An Act to amend an act declaring the village of Adams a valid corporation, to enlarge its powers and to make said village a separate road district, passed May twenty-sixth, eighteen hundred and fifty-three. Passed April 14, 1871; three-fifths being present.

CHAP. 503. An Act to change the day of holding the annual election for directors of the Agricultural Insurance Company, from the second to the third Wednesday of January in each year. Passed April 14, 1871.

CHAP. 504. An Act to amend "An act to incorporate the National Savings Bank in the city of Albany," passed May sixth, eighteen hundred and sixty-eight. Passed April 14, 1871.

CHAP. 505. An Act to amend an act entitled "An act to incorporate the city of Ogdensburgh," passed April twenty-seventh, eighteen hundred and sixty-eight, also the act amendatory thereof, passed April fifteenth, eighteen hundred and sixty-nine. Passed April 14, 1871; three-fifths being present.

CHAP. 506. An Act to incorporate the Real Estate Trust Company of the city of New York. Passed April 14, 1871.

CHAP. 507. An Act to amend chapter seven hundred and seventy-nine of the Laws of eighteen hundred and seventy, entitled "An act to incorporate the Farmers and Mechanics' Savings Bank of the city of Lockport." Passed April 14, 1871.

CHAP. 508. An Act to incorporate the Rockland Savings Bank. Passed April 14, 1871.

CHAP. 509. An Act to incorporate the "Security Deposit Company of the city of New York." Passed April 14, 1871.

CHAP. 510. An Act to incorporate "The Excelsior Safe Deposit Company," to be located in the city of New York. Passed April 14, 1871.

CHAP. 511. An Act to incorporate the Milton Savings Bank, in the county of Ulster. Passed April 14, 1871.

CHAP. 512. An Act to amend the charter of the village of Yonkers. Passed April 14, 1871; three-fifths being present.

CHAP. 513. An Act to authorize the Newtown and Flushing Railroad Company ot build a drawbridge over Flushing creek, in the county of Queens. Passed April 15, 1871.

CHAP. 514. An Act to amend an act entitled "An act to incorporate the Inebriates' Home for Kings county," passed May ninth, eighteen hundred and sixty-seven, and the act amendatory thereof, passed April thirtieth, eighteen hundred and sixty-eight. Passed April 15, 1871; three-fifths being present.

CHAP. 515. An Act to prevent frauds in auction sales, and fraudulent conduct on the part of auctioneers in the cities of New York and Brooklyn. Passed April 15, 1871.

CHAP. 516. An Act to incorporate the University Railway of Syracuse. Passed April 15, 1871.

CHAP. 517. An Act to authorize the construction of a railroad from the South Side railroad of Long Island, at a point in the village of Babylon, Suffolk county, to the steamboat dock, at the southern part of said village. Passed April 15, 1871.

CHAP. 518. An Act for the removal of certain old burial grounds in the town of Wilson, Niagara county. Passed April 15, 1871; three-fifths being present.

CHAP. 519. An Act to authorize the widening of that portion of Park street lying between Elm and Glen streets, in the village of Glen's Falls, county of Warren. Passed April 15, 1871; three-fifths being present.

CHAP. 520. An Act to improve certain water powers upon the Wappinger's creek. Passed April 15, 1871.

CHAP. 521. An Act to incorporate the Kingston Water-works Company. Passed April 15, 1871; three-fifths being present.

CHAP. 522. An Act to legalize and confirm the official acts of the commissioners of highways of the town of Irondequoit, Monroe county, and authorizing the opening of highways, of not less than forty feet wide, in said town. Passed April 15, 1871; three-fifths being present.

CHAP. 523. An Act to enlarge the jail limits of the county of Schuyler. Passed April 15, 1871.

CHAP. 524. An Act to authorize the trustees of the Penfield Seminary to sell the property of that corporation and to dispose of the proceeds of the sale. Passed April 15, 1871; three-fifths being present.

CHAP. 525. An Act to amend an act entitled "An act to incorporate the Central Park Savings Bank in the city of New York," passed April nineteenth, eighteen hundred and sixty-seven, and the act amendatory thereof, passed April twenty-second, eighteen hundred and sixty-eight. Passed April 15, 1871.

CHAP. 526. An Act legalizing the acts of the members of the Congregational Church of Edinburgh in changing the name of said church. Passed April 15, 1871.

CHAP. 527. An Act to authorize the construction of a street railroad in the city of Auburn. Passed April 15, 1871.

CHAP. 528. An Act to authorize the construction of a street railroad in the city of Auburn, and from thence to the Owasco lake. Passed April 15, 1871.

CHAP. 529. An Act to incorporate the Superintendents of the Fair Ground of the Town of Oswegatchie. Passed April 15, 1871; three-fifths being present.

CHAP. 530. An Act authorizing the commissioners of highways of the town of Cortlandt county of Westchester, to build a bridge over the small creek emptying into the Hudson river at Lent's Cove. Passed April 15, 1871; three-fifths being present.

CHAP. 531. An Act to authorize the construction of a swing bridge across the Chenango canal, in the village of Sherburne, in the county of Chenango. Passed April 15, 1871; three-fifths being present.

CHAP. 532. An Act for the relief of the town of Pompey, in the county of Onondaga. Passed April 15, 1871; three-fifths being present.

CHAP. 533. An Act to repeal section two of chapter four hundred and fifty of the Laws of eighteen hundred and seventy, entitled "An act to amend an act entitled 'An act to amend the charter of the village of Johnstown, and the several acts amendatory thereof, and to extend the boundary of said village,'" passed March thirtieth, eighteen hundred and sixty-seven; and further to amend an act entitled "An act to amend the charter of the village of Johnstown and the several acts amendatory thereof, and to extend the boundary of said village," passed March thirtieth, eighteen hundred and sixty-seven. Passed April 15, 1871; three-fifths being present.

CHAP. 534. An Act relative to the improvement of certain portions of the counties of Westchester and New York, including provisions for communication between said counties, and for improving the navigation of Harlem river and Spuyten Duyvil creek. Passed April 15, 1871; three-fifths being present.

CHAP. 535. *An Act to extend the operation and effect of the act passed February* 17, 1848, *entitled "An act to authorize the formation of corporations for manufacturing, mining, mechanical or chemical purposes." Passed April* 15, 1871.

CHAP. 536. An Act to amend the act entitled "An act to amend the act to combine into one act the several acts relating to the city of Albany, passed April twelfth, eighteen hundred and forty-two, and the several acts amendatory thereof; and also to repeal the act establishing a Capital Police District, and to provide for the government thereof, passed April twenty-second, eighteen hundred and sixty-five, and the several acts amendatory thereof in so far as they relate to the city of Albany," passed March sixteenth, eighteen hundred and seventy. Passed April 15, 1871; three-fifths being present.

CHAP. 537. *An Act requiring commissioners of towns, cities and villages, appointed under the several acts to facilitate the construction of railroads in this State, to present bonds and coupons paid by them before the boards of auditors in towns, cities and villages, and providing for the cancellation and preservation of the same. Passed April* 17, 1871; *three-fifths being present.*

CHAP. 538. An Act to amend an act entitled "An act for the incorporation of cities and villages," passed December seventh, eighteen hundred and forty-seven, so far as the same relates to the village of North Tonawanda, Niagara county. Passed April 17, 1871; three-fifths being present.

CHAP. 539. An Act for the relief of Thomas Brazelle. Passed April 18, 1871; three-fifths being present, without the approval of the Governor.

CHAP. 540. An Act to amend an act entitled "An act to incorporate the New York Loan and Improvement Company," passed May sixth, eighteen hundred and seventy. Passed April 18, 1871.

CHAP. 541. An Act to discontinue and close a portion of Bedford street in the city of Troy. Passed April 18, 1871; three-fifths being present.

CHAP. 542. An Act to provide for the payment of certain claims growing out of the widening and improvement of Fourth avenue in the city of Brooklyn. Passed April 18, 1871; three-fifths being present.

CHAP. 543. An Act to alter the commissioners' map of the city of Brooklyn. Passed April 19, 1871, three-fifths being present.

CHAP. 544. An Act to incorporate "The New York Maennerchor." Passed April 19, 1871.

CHAP. 545. An Act to authorize the common council of the city of Buffalo to abate a nuisance in the Main and Hamburgh canal in said city. Passed April 19, 1871; three-fifths being present.

CHAP. 546. An Act authorizing the trustees of Union Free School District Number Nine, of the town of Oyster Bay, Queens county, to issue bonds and borrow money for the erection of a new school-house in said district. Passed April 19, 1871; three-fifths being present.

CHAP. 547. An Act for the better preservation of the records of the surrogate's court in the county of Schoharie, and fixing the place of keeping the surrogate's office in said county. Passed April 19, 1871; three-fifths being present.

CHAP. 548. *An Act to amend an act entitled "An act relative to the care and education of deaf-mutes, passed April twelfth, eighteen hundred and seventy, and amendatory of an act to provide for the care and education of indigent deaf-mutes under the age of twelve years," passed April twenty-fifth, eighteen hundred and sixty-three. Passed April* 19, 1871; *three-fifths being present.*

CHAP. 549. An Act in relation to passenger fare on the Rochester and Pine Creek Railroad. Passed April 19, 1871.

CHAP. 550. An Act to amend the act to incorporate the Attica Water-works Company, passed May sixth, eighteen hundred and seventy. Passed April 19, 1871; three-fifths being present.

CHAP. 551. *An Act to amend an act entitled "An act to legalize orders made by county judges in certain cases," passed April thirteenth, eighteen hundred and sixty-five. Passed April* 19, 1871; *three-fifths being present.*

CHAP. 552. An Act authorizing Susanna Newbould to hold and convey real estate. Passed April 19, 1871, by a two-third vote.

CHAP. 553. An Act in relation to extending Third street in the city of Troy from Madison street to Ida street, and constructing certain bridges over the Poestenkill creek in said city. Passed April 19, 1871; three-fifths being present.

CHAP. 554. An Act to amend an act entitled "An act to amend an act incorporating the village of Sing Sing in the county of Westchester," passed April ninth, eighteen hundred and fifty-three, and the act supplementary thereto and amendatory thereof, passed April eighteenth, eighteen hundred and fifty-nine, and also the act supplementary thereto and amendatory thereof, passed March third, eighteen hundred and sixty-six, passed April sixteenth, eighteen hundred and sixty-nine. Passed April 19, 1871; three-fifths being present.

CHAP. 555. An Act to incorporate the Enterprise Savings Bank in the village of College Point. Passed April 19, 1871.

CHAP. 556. An Act relating to Queens County Railway Company. Passed April 19, 1871.

CHAP. 557. An Act to amend an act entitled "An act to amend and consolidate the several acts in relation to the charter of the city of Rochester," passed April eighth, eighteen hundred and sixty-one, and the several acts amendatory thereof, as hereinafter designated. Passed April 19, 1871; three-fifths being present.

CHAP. 558. An Act to release the interest of the people of this State in certain real estate, of which Paul Pontan, late of the city of Brooklyn, county of Kings, died seized, to Nannette Johnson. Passed April 19, 1871, by a two-third vote.

CHAP. 559. An Act to widen and improve North Second street, in the city of Brooklyn. Passed April 19, 1871; three-fifths being present.

CHAP. 560. *An Act to amend an act entitled "An act to authorize the formation of railroad corporations and to regulate the same," passed April second, eighteen hundred and fifty. Passed April* 19, 1871.

CHAP. 561. An Act to amend the charter of the city of Brooklyn. Passed April 19, 1871; three-fifths being present.

CHAP. 562. An Act in relation to the taxes to be annually raised in the city of Brooklyn, and county of Kings. Passed April 19, 1871; three-fifths being present.

CHAP. 563 An Act to incorporate the Citizens' Savings Bank of Syracuse. Passed April 19, 1871.

CHAP. 564. An Act to incorporate the Bay Ridge Athenaeum. Passed April 19, 1871.

CHAP. 565. An Act to authorize "The Brooklyn Children's Aid Society," to acquire and hold additional real estate. Passed April 19, 1871.

CHAP. 566. An Act to provide for the proper drainage of lands within the corporate limits of the city and county of New York. Passed April 19, 1871; three-fifths being present.

CHAP. 567. An Act providing for the opening and improvement of new roads and avenues, and closing old highways in the town of Flatbush, in Kings county. Passed April 19, 1871; three-fifths being present.

CHAP. 568. An Act to enable and authorize the inhabitants of the town of Galen, Wayne county, to raise money by tax, to pay John Thomas, George H. Pidge and Robert Tillow, for damages sustained by them by the blowing down of a portion of town hall in Clyde, Wayne county. Passed April 19, 1871; three-fifths being present.

CHAP. 569. An Act to repeal chapter one hundred and eighteen of the laws of eighteen hundred and sixty-nine, entitled "An act to amend an act entitled 'An act to authorize a tax to be levied in the town of Constable, to build or purchase a town house,' passed April twenty-first, eighteen hundred and forty-six," passed April sixth, eighteen hundred and sixty-nine. Passed April 19, 1871; three-fifths being present.

CHAP. 570. An Act in relation to changing the present grades and establishing new grades for certain streets in the city of New York. Passed April 19, 1871; three-fifths being present.

CHAP. 571. An Act to provide the funds for the purchase of hose and other property required for the use of the Flatbush Fire Company, in the town of Flatbush, in Kings county, and for keeping its property in order. Passed April 19, 1871; three-fifths being present.

CHAP. 572. An Act to amend an act entitled "An act in relation to elections in the city and county of New York," passed April fifth, eighteen hundred and seventy. Passed April 19, 1871; three-fifths being present.

CHAP. 573. An Act relative to the local government of the county of New York. Passed April 19, 1871; three-fifths being present.

CHAP. 574. An Act to amend an act entitled "An act to reorganize the local government of the city of New York," passed April fifth, eighteen hundred and seventy. Passed April 18, 1871; three-fifths being present.

CHAP. 575. An Act to amend an act entitled "An act to promote the public health in the town of New Utrecht, in the county of Kings," passed April thirteenth, eighteen hundred and fifty-nine. Passed April 18, 1871; three-fifths being present.

CHAP. 576. *An Act re-appropriating a certain portion of the income of the United States Deposit Fund for the benefit of academies. Passed April* 19, 1871; *three-fifths being present.*

CHAP. 577. An Act authorizing the comptroller to settle and adjust claims against William J. Moses. Passed April 19, 1871.

CHAP. 578. An Act to authorize the village of Yonkers to issue bonds for the purpose of raising money to construct bridges over the Nepperhan river. Passed April 19, 1871; three-fifths being present.

CHAP. 579. An Act to lay out, open, construct and keep in repair Ocean avenue, in the county of Kings." Passed April 19, 1871; three-fifths being present.

CHAP. 580. *An Act to amend an act entitled "An act giving the consent of the State of New York to the purchase by, and ceding jurisdiction to, the United States over certain lands within this State, to be occupied as sites for light-houses and keepers' dwellings," passed April sixth, eighteen hundred and seventy-one, and supplemental thereto. Passed April* 19, 1871, *by a two-third vote.*

CHAP. 581. An Act to authorize the commissioners appointed by chapter two hundred and seventy-two of the Laws of eighteen hundred and sixty-nine, to change the route of Mosholu avenue, in the town of Yonkers. Passed April 19, 1871; three-fifths being present.

CHAP. 582. An Act to provide for the payment of certain assessments on property of the Roman Catholic Orphan Asylum of the city of Brooklyn. Passed April 19, 1871; three-fifths being present.

CHAP. 583. An Act to make provision for the local governments of the city and county of New York. Passed April 19, 1871; three-fifths being present.

CHAP. 584. An Act to provide for the better prevention of fires in the city of New York, and to prescribe the powers and duties of the city fire marshal in relation thereto. Passed April 19, 1871; three-fifths being present.

CHAP. 585. An Act for the relief of John Hand. Passed April 19, 1871; three-fifths being present, without the approval of the Governor.

CHAP. 586. An Act for the relief of Charles P. Skinner. Passed April 19, 1871; three-fifths being present, without the approval of the Governor.

CHAP. 587. An Act for the relief of Hulburt E. Brown. Passed April 19, 1871; three-fifths being present, without the approval of the Governor.

CHAP. 588. An Act to authorize the construction of a bridge over the Chenango canal, at the village of Bouckville, in the county of Madison. Passed April 19, 1871; three-fifths being present.

CHAP. 589. An Act to amend an act entitled "An act to lay out, extend and grade Fairmount avenue, in the town of West Farms, in the county of Westchester," passed May eleventh, eighteen hundred and sixty-nine. Passed April 19, 1871; three-fifths being present.

CHAP. 590. An Act for the relief of Mary Dahomy. Passed April 19, 1871, by a two-third vote.

CHAP. 591. An Act in relation to the bonded debt of the town of East Chester, county of Westchester. Passed April 19, 1871; three-fifths being present.

CHAP. 592. An Act to incorporate the People's Savings Bank of Poughkeepsie, New York. Passed April 19, 1871.

CHAP. 593. An Act for the relief of A. Bryant Campbell, of the town of Lebanon and county of Madison. Passed April 19, 1871, by a two-third vote.

CHAP. 594. An Act to amend an act entitled "An act to provide for a supply of water in the city of Poughkeepsie, and for sewers therein," passed April twelfth, eighteen hundred and sixty-seven. Passed April 19, 1871; three-fifths being present.

CHAP. 595. An Act to authorize the city of Troy to fund its floating debt. Passed April 19, 1871; three-fifths being present.

CHAP. 596. An Act for the relief of Mary Megarr, the widow, and the heirs of William Megarr, deceased. Passed April 19, 1871, by a two-third vote.

CHAP. 597. An Act to authorize the Fulton Bank of Brooklyn to increase its capital stock. Passed April 19, 1871.

CHAP. 598. An Act to confirm the official acts of Peter C. Wyckoff, a justice of the peace, in the town of Fleming, in the county of Cayuga. Passed April 19, 1871; three-fifths being present.

CHAP. 599. An Act to amend an act to incorporate the Young Men's Association for Mutual Improvement in the city of Albany, passed March twelfth, eighteen hundred and thirty-five. Passed April 19, 1871.

CHAP. 600. An Act to authorize the city of Elmira to borrow money and issue bonds of the city therefor, for the purpose of liquidating its present indebtedness. Passed April 19, 1871; three-fifths being present.

CHAP. 601. An Act to amend the charter of the Merchants' Life Insurance Company. Passed April 19, 1871.

CHAP. 602. An Act to authorize the construction of a bridge, for railroad purposes, over the Erie canal, in the city of Utica. Passed April 19, 1871.

CHAP. 603. *An Act in relation to appeals from Surrogate's Courts. Passed April* 19, 1871; *three-fifths being present.*

CHAP. 604. An Act to incorporate the Traders' Deposit Company. Passed April 19, 1871.

CHAP. 605. An Act to amend the charter of the Harlem River and Port Chester Railroad Company. Passed April 19, 1871.

CHAP. 606. An Act to authorize the trustees of the village of White Plains, in the county of Westchester, to regulate, grade, macadamize or pave Railroad avenue, in said village. Passed April 19, 1871; three-fifths being present.

CHAP. 607. An Act to authorize the Commissioners of Public Charities and Correction of the city of New York to commit persons committed to their care by police magistrates, and to commit persons asking for commitments as vagrants. Passed April 19, 1871; three-fifths being present

CHAP. 608. *An Act to amend an act entitled "An act to provide for the incorporation of fire insurance companies," passed June twenty-fifth, eighteen hundred and fifty-three. Passed April* 19, 1873.

CHAP. 609. An Act to regulate the construction and protection of railway crossings in the county of Kings. Passed April 19, 1871.

CHAP. 610. *An Act to legalize executions issued by the county clerk of the several counties of this State upon judgments rendered by justices of the peace and docketed in their respective offices, and the sales of property on such executions. Passed April* 19, 1871; *three-fifths being present.*

CHAP. 611. An Act to authorize the board of trustees of the village of Middletown to issue semi-annual interest bonds in the place of annual interest bonds unsold, and to destroy such annual interest bonds. Passed April 19, 1871; three-fifths being present.

CHAP. 612. An Act to regulate the storing and keeping of crude petroleum, earth or rock oil, or any of its products, within the corporate limits of the village of Middletown. Passed April 19, 1871; three-fifths being present.

CHAP. 613. An Act to legalize the official acts of Henry M. McQuoid as notary public. Passed April 19, 1871; three-fifths being present.

CHAP. 614. An Act to authorize the city of Newburgh to borrow moneys and issue bonds therefor, for the payment of the existing contingent debt of said city, and to provide for the payment of said bonds and the interest thereon by levy and collection of taxes. Passed April 19, 1871; three-fifths being present.

CHAP. 615. An Act to authorize the New York and Rockaway Railroad Company to construct a drawbridge over Foster's Meadow canal. Passed April 19, 1871.

CHAP. 616. An Act to incorporate the Mutual Benefit Life Policy, Loan and Trust Company of New York. Passed April 19, 1871.

CHAP. 617. An Act to authorize and empower the Comptroller of this State to settle and adjust the claims of Willis S. Barnum against the State, and the claims of the State against said Willis S. Barnum. Passed April 19, 1871; three-fifths being present.

CHAP. 618. An Act to amend chapter one hundred and twenty-two, Laws of eighteen hundred and seventy-one, being an act entitled "An act to provide for supplying the village of Canandaigua with water, and submitting to the tax payers of said village the question of the construction of water-works, and of bonding said village for the purpose of such construction," passed March seventeenth, eighteen hundred and seventy-one. Passed April 19, 1871; three-fifths being present.

CHAP. 619. An Act to determine settlement of the claim of the State of New York against the county of Westchester, for arrears of State tax. Passed April 20, 1871; three-fifths being present.

CHAP. 620. An Act to enable "The Permanent Committee on Education for the Ministry of the General Assembly of the Presbyterian Church in the United States of America," to transfer its property to the new board created by the General Assembly, when the same shall have been incorporated, and to vest in such new incorporation the rights, franchises and privileges of the former body. Passed April 20, 1871.

CHAP. 621. An Act to incorporate The American Acclimatization Society. Passed April 20, 1871.

CHAP. 622. An Act for the relief of the Brooklyn, Winfield & Newtown Railway Company. Passed April 20, 1871.

CHAP. 623. An Act to amend the act entitled "An act to incorporate the American Trust Company of the city of New York," passed May eleventh, eighteen hundred and sixty-nine. Passed April 20, 1871; three-fifths being present.

CHAP. 624. An Act further to amend the act entitled "An act to incorporate the American Trust Company of the city of New York," passed May eleventh, eighteen hundred and sixty-nine. Passed April 20, 1871.

CHAP. 625. An Act to amend and reduce to one act the several acts relating to buildings in the city of New York, passed May fourth, eighteen hundred and sixty-six, May seventeenth, eighteen hundred and sixty-seven, and May sixth, eighteen hundred and sixty-eight. Passed April 20, 1871; three-fifths being present.

CHAP. 626. An Act to enable the St. Lawrence Valley Agricultural and Horticultural Society of Fort Covington to hold real and personal estate sufficient for the purposes of their incorporation, and raise money for the same. Passed April 20, 1871.

CHAP. 627. An Act to authorize the late trustees of the West Lowville Burying-ground to convey the lands owned by said West Lowville Burying-ground to West Lowville Rural Cemetery Association in the town of Lowville. Passed April 20, 1871.

CHAP. 628. An Act to alter the map or plan of the city of New York, by laying out thereon a public place for a parade ground, and to authorize the taking of the same. Passed April 20, 1871; three-fifths being present.

CHAP. 629. An Act to authorize William Hilliker to establish and maintain a ferry across the Cayuga lake at Cayuga Bridge. Passed April 20, 1871; three-fifths being present.

CHAP. 630. An Act in regard to assessments for street improvements in the city of Cohoes. Passed April 20, 1871; three-fifths being present.

CHAP. 631. An Act to amend an act entitled "An act to amend the charter of the village of Westfield," passed April nineteenth, eighteen hundred and sixty-seven. Passed April 20, 1871; three-fifths being present.

CHAP. 632. An Act to amend an act entitled "An act to incorporate the village of Wurtsboro," passed February nineteenth, eighteen hundred and sixty-six. Passed April 20, 1871.

CHAP. 633. An Act to change the name of Eugene E. Lagrave to Eugene Mickell Beals. Passed April 20, 1871.

CHAP. 634. An Act to establish the perfect legitimacy of Eugene Mickell Beals, in reference to his mother, and his right to inherit real and personal property from or through his mother, the same as her lawful issue. Passed April 20, 1871.

CHAP. 635. *An Act to amend article four of title four of chapter eleven of part first of the Revised Statutes, "of division and other fences." Passed April 20, 1871; three-fifths being present.*

CHAP. 636. An Act to incorporate the Fire Department of the village of Middletown. Passed April 20, 1871.

CHAP. 637. An Act to provide for the appointment of police commissioners in the village of Green Island, Albany county, and to establish a police force therein. Passed April 20, 1871; three-fifths being present.

CHAP. 638. An Act to incorporate the Farmers and Mechanics' Savings Bank of Schenectady. Passed April 20, 1871.

CHAP. 639. An Act to regulate and protect the planting of oysters in the public waters of the towns of Jamaica and Hempstead, in the county of Queens. Passed April 20, 1871; three-fifths being present.

CHAP. 640. An Act to release the interest of the State in the real estate of which Daniel Collins, late of the town of Geneseo, Livingston county, New York, died seized, to Margaret Collins. Passed April 20, 1871, by a two-third vote.

CHAP. 641. An Act to release the interest of the people of this State in certain real estate in the city of Buffalo, to Frederick Scott. Passed April 20, 1871, by a two-third vote.

CHAP. 642. An Act relative to lands bequeathed by the last will and testament of Thomas Murphy, deceased, to William E. Murphy, for and during his natural life. Passed April 20, 1871, by a two-third vote.

CHAP. 643. An Act to amend section forty-six of chapter seven hundred and ninety-three of the Laws of the State of New York, entitled "An act to revise, amend and consolidate the charter of, and the several acts relating to, the village of Geneseo, in the county of Livingston, and to enlarge the boundaries of said village, and to extend the powers of the corporation," passed May nineteenth, eighteen hundred and seventy. Passed April 20, 1871; three-fifths being present.

CHAP. 644. An Act to amend an act incorporating the village of Plattsburgh, passed April thirteenth, eighteen hundred and fifty-nine. Passed April 20, 1871; three-fifths being present.

CHAP. 645. An Act to incorporate the East Side Savings Bank for Sailors in the city of New York. Passed April 20, 1871.

CHAP. 646. An Act to amend an act entitled "An act to amend an act entitled 'An act in relation to draining certain lands in the town of Cicero, in the county of Onondaga,' passed April sixteenth, eighteen hundred and fifty-eight," passed April tenth, eighteen hundred and sixty. Passed April 20, 1871; three-fifths being present.

CHAP. 647. An Act confirming former appropriations made in relation to the manual labor school upon the Tonawanda Reservation, and to require the trustees of the Tonawanda Manual Labor School to give additional security. Passed April 20, 1871, by a two-third vote.

CHAP. 648. An Act to authorize the town of Pelham, in the county of Westchester, to raise money for the purpose of constructing a town dock at Shoal Harbor, in said town. Passed April 20, 1871; three-fifths being present.

CHAP. 649. An Act authorizing the town of Springwater, in the county of Livingston, to raise money by tax for the purpose of erecting a town and soldiers' Memorial Hall. Passed April 20, 1871: three-fifths being present.

CHAP. 650. An Act repealing chapter three hundred and forty-five of the Laws of eighteen hundred and sixty-seven, passed April twelfth, eighteen hundred and sixty-seven, chapter seven hundred and ninety-seven of the Laws of eighteen hundred and sixty-eight, passed May ninth, eighteen hundred and sixty-eight, and chapter eight hundred and eighty of the Laws of eighteen hundred and sixty-eight, passed July twenty-eighth, eighteen hundred and sixty-eight, relating to draining lands in the town of Amherst, Erie county. Passed April 20, 1871; three-fifths being present.

CHAP. 651. *An Act to make a contribution toward the completion of the Washington National Monument. Passed April 20, 1871, by a two-third vote.*

CHAP. 652. *An Act in relation to the refiling of certain certificates of incorporation in the office of the Secretary of State.* *Passed April* 20, 1871; *three-fifths being present.*

CHAP. 653. *An Act making an appropriation to pay the expenses of the collection of tolls, superintendence, ordinary repairs and maintenance of the canal for the fiscal year, commencing on the first day of October, eighteen hundred and seventy, to supply deficiencies in former appropriations and to confirm the action of the Commissioners of the Canal Fund in providing funds for the above purposes.* *Passed April* 20, 1871; *three-fifths being present.*

CHAP. 654. *An Act making an appropriation to pay the expenses of the collection of tolls, superintendence, ordinary repairs and maintenance of the canals for the fiscal year, commencing on the first day of October, eighteen hundred and seventy-one.* *Passed April* 20, 1871; *three-fifths being present.*

CHAP. 655. *An Act making appropriations for the payment of the principal and interest on the canal debt, commencing on the first day of October, eighteen huudred and seventy-one, and to provide for the payment of the debt contracted under section twelve, article seven of the Constitution.* *Passed April* 20, 1871; *three-fifths being present.*

CHAP. 656. An Act to amend an act entitled "An act empowering certain towns, in the counties of Cattaraugus and Erie, to purchase and convey the right of way for railroad purposes," passed April twenty-third, eighteen hundred and sixty-four. Passed April 20, 1871; three-fifths being present.

CHAP. 657. *An Act to amend the act passed February seventeenth, eighteen hundred and forty-eight, entitled "An act to authorize the formation of corporations for manufacturing, mining, mechanical or chemical purposes."* *Passed April* 20, 1871; *three-fifths being present.*

CHAP. 658. An Act to amend an act entitled "An act to authorize the construction of a railway and tracks in the towns of West Farms and Morrisania," passed May second, eighteen hundred and sixty-three. Passed April 20, 1871.

CHAP. 659. An Act to amend an act entitled "An act to authorize the closing of that portion of the Jamaica and Brooklyn plank-road lying within the limits of the city of Brooklyn," passed April twenty-fourth, eighteen hundred and sixty-nine. Passed April 21, 1871; three-fifths being present

CHAP. 660. An Act to facilitate mortgage loans on land, authorized to be sold, forming a portion of Prospect Park, in the city of Brooklyn. Passed April 21, 1871.

CHAP. 661. An Act to enable the Board of Education, of the city of Brooklyn, to sell certain lands. Passed April 21, 1871,

CHAP. 662. An Act in relation to the pay of firemen in the city of Brooklyn. Passed April 21, 1871; three-fifths being present.

CHAP. 663. An Act further to amend the charter of the Brooklyn Improvement Company. Passed April 21, 1871.

CHAP. 664. An Act to amend an act entitled "An act to incorporate the Market Savings Bank of the city of New York," passed May fifth, eighteen hundred and sixty-three. Passed April 21, 1871.

CHAP. 665. An Act to incorporate the New York Botanical Club. Passed April 21, 1871.

CHAP. 666. *An Act to authorize judicial inquiry as to the sanity af persons indicted for capital offenses.* *Passed April* 21, 1871; *three-fifths being present.*

CHAP. 667. An Act to amend chapter six hundred and thirty-one of the Laws of eighteen hundred and sixty-six, entitled "An act to provide for the drainage of lands in the town of Flushing, Queens county." Passed April 21, 1871; three-fifths being present.

CHAP. 668. *An Act to provide for the payment of counsel required to be employed on behalf of the State, in pursuance of the provisions of section two of chapter three hundred and twenty-one of the Laws of eighteen hundred and seventy.* *Passed April* 21, 1871; *three-fifths being present.*

CHAP. 669. *An Act to amend an act entitled "An act to authorize the formation of railroad corporations, and to regulate the same," passed April second, eighteen hnndred and fifty.* *Passed April* 21, 1871.

CHAP. 670. An Act to authorize the making and opening of a road or avenue from the intersection of the highway running east of Rockland lake with the highway running from the lake to Rockland Lake Landing, in the county of Rockland, to intersect the highway running from Upper Piermont to Orangeburgh. Passed April 21, 1871; three-fifths being present.

CHAP. 671. An Act to authorize the making and opening of a road or avenue from Main street, in the village of Nyack, in the county of Rockland, to the Hook mountain. Passed April 21, 1871; three-fifths being present.

CHAP. 672. *An Act for the removal of obstructions in the Big Chazy river and for the improvement of the same. Passed April 21, 1871, by a two-third vote.*

CHAP. 673. An Act to authorize the construction of sewers in the village and town of Saratoga Springs. Passed April 21, 1871; three-fifths being present.

CHAP. 674. An Act to amend an act entitled "An act to provide for laying out and improving roads and avenues in the village and town of Saratoga Springs." Passed April 21, 1871; three-fifths being present.

CHAP. 675. An Act to grade, pave, curb, gutter, flag and regulate Little Nassau street, in the city of Brooklyn. Passed April 21, 1871; three-fifths being present.

CHAP. 676. An Act to lay down a new street upon commissioner's map of the city of Brooklyn, and to provide for the improvement of the same. Passed April 21, 1871; three-fifths being present.

CHAP. 677. An Act to authorize the Common Council of the city of Brooklyn to open, grade and pave Van Brunt street in said city. Passed April 21, 1871; three-fifths being present.

CHAP. 678. An Act to amend section one of chapter two hundred and twenty-six of the Laws of eighteen hundred and seventy, entitled "An act to authorize the construction of a swing bridge over the Erie canal in the village of Albion, in the county of Orleans." Passed April 22, 1871; three-fifths being present, without the approval of the governor.

CHAP. 679. An Act to amend an act entitled "An act to supply the village of Watertown with pure and wholesome water, and for other purposes," passed March twenty-second, eighteen hundred and fifty-three, and the several acts amendatory thereto. Passed April 21, 1871; three-fifths being present.

CHAP. 680. An Act in relation to the location and erection of public buildings for the use of Erie county and the city of Buffalo. Passed April 21, 1871; three-fifths being present.

CHAP. 681. An Act to incorporate the Long Island City and Calvary Cemetery Railroad Company. Passed April 21, 1871.

CHAP. 682. An Act to amend an act entitled "An act to authorize certain towns in the counties of Ulster, Delaware, Greene and Schoharie, to issue bonds and take stock in the Rondout and Oswego Railroad," passed April seventeenth, eighteen hundred and sixty-six. Passed April 25, 1871; three-fifths being present.

CHAP. 683. An Act amending, revising and consolidating the several acts in relation to the village of Greenbush, passed March twenty-second, eighteen hundred and fifty-four, and April twenty-ninth, eighteen hundred and sixty-three. Passed April 25, 1871; three-fifths being present.

CHAP. 684. *An Act to provide for the improvement of the hydraulic power of the North branch of the Saranac river, and to improve the navigation of said North branch. Passed April 25, 1871; three-fifths being present.*

CHAP. 685. An Act to incorporate the Saranac River Improvement and Lumber Company. Passed April 25, 1871; three-fifths being present.

CHAP. 686. An Act to repeal section two of chapter six hundred and eighty-two of the Laws of eighteen hundred and sixty-nine, entitled "An act to authorize the Whitehall and Plattsburgh Railroad Company to take increased fare, and to establish a ferry." Passed April 25, 1871.

CHAP. 687. An Act for the relief of the Brooklyn Central Dispensary. Passed April 25, 1871, by a two-third vote.

CHAP. 688. *An Act to amend an act entitled "An act for the incorporation of villages," passed April twentieth, eighteen hundred and seventy. Passed April 25, 1871; three-fifths being present.*

CHAP. 689. An Act for the relief of Jonas Rivenburgh. Passed April 25, 1871, by a two-third vote.

CHAP. 690. An Act for the relief of Henry Rankin and Henry Livingston. Passed April 25, 1871; three-fifths being present.

CHAP. 691. *An Act appropriating moneys for the Hudson River State Hospital for the Insane. Passed April 25, 1871; three-fifths being present.*

CHAP. 692. An Act to provide for the erection of school-houses, and a building for the Normal College, in the city of New York. Passed April 25, 1871; three-fifths being present.

CHAP. 693. *An Act to amend "An act in relation to Savings Banks," passed March twentieth, eighteen hundred and fifty-seven, and to confer additional powers upon the superintendent of the Banking Department in relation to Savings Banks in this State. Passed April 25, 1871; three-fifths being present.*

CHAP. 694. An Act for the relief of the owners of real estate situate on the Allegany river in McKean county, Pennsylvania, above the feeder dam, for the Genesee Valley canal, at Millgrove, Cattaraugus county. Passed April 25, 1871; three-fifths being present.

CHAP. 695. *An Act to amend an act entitled "An act to extend the powers of Boards of Supervisors, except in the counties of New York and Kings," passed May eleventh, eighteen hundred and sixty-nine. Passed April 25, 1871; three-fifths being present.*

CHAP. 696. *An Act to amend an act entitled "An act to amend chapter seven hundred and twenty-seven of the Laws of eighteen hundred and sixty-nine, entitled 'An act authorizing cities and villages to acquire title to property for burial purposes and to levy taxes for the payment of the same,' passed May eighth, eighteen hundred and sixty-nine, passed May ninth, eighteen hundred and seventy. Passed April 25, 1871; three-fifths being present.*

CHAP. 697. *An Act to amend an act entitled "An act to authorize the formation of gas-light companies," passed February sixteen, eighteen hundred and forty-eight. Passed April 25, 1871; three-fifths being present.*

CHAP. 698. *An Act to provide for building a bridge across the Tonawanda creek, on the Tonawanda Indian Reservation, and making an appropriation for the same. Passed April 25, 1871, by a two-third vote.*

CHAP. 699. *An Act to provide for taking testimony in certain matters relating to State charitable institutions. Passed April 25, 1871; three-fifths being present.*

CHAP. 700. *An Act in relation to stenographers in the circuit courts, courts of oyer and terminer and special terms of the supreme court, in the sixth, seventh and eighth judicial districts. Passed April 25, 1871; three-fifths being present.*

CHAP. 701. An Act authorizing the sale, by their guardian, of the real estate of the infant children of Charles H. Mann, deceased. Passed April 25, 1871; three-fifths being present.

CHAP. 702. *An Act relative to contracts for advertisements in newspapers published on Sunday. Passed April 25, 1871; three-fifths being present.*

CHAP. 703. *An Act further to amend the acts for the protection and improvement of the Seneca Nation of Indians, residing on the Cattaraugus and Allegany Reservations in this State. Passed April 25, 1871; three-fifths being present.*

CHAP. 704. An Act to amend an act entitled "An act relative to a bridge over the Chenango river, at Oxford," passed April fifth, eighteen hundred and twenty-two. Passed April 25, 1871; three-fifths being present.

CHAP. 705. *An Act to amend chapter three hundred and sixty-eight of the Laws of eighteen hundred and sixty-five, entitled "An act for the incorporation of societies or clubs for certain social and recreative purposes." Passed April 25, 1871.*

CHAP. 706. An Act to release the interest of the people of State of New York in certain real estate to Catharine McCabe. Passed April 25, 1871, by a two-third vote.

CHAP. 707. An Act to enable Lucy Robins to take and hold real estate, and to release to her the interest and title in lands escheated to the State. Passed April 25, 1871, by a two-third vote.

CHAP. 708. *An Act to amend the sixth section of title three, chapter eight, part second of the Revised Statutes, relating to guardians and wards. Passed April 25, 1871; three-fifths being present.*

CHAP. 709. *An Act to amend an act entitled "An act to establish an Insurance Department," passed April fifteenth, eighteen hundred and fifty-nine. Passed April 25, 1871.*

CHAP. 710. *An Act to authorize the clerks of certain counties to appoint additional special deputies. Passed April 25, 1871; three-fifths being present.*

CHAP. 711. *An Act to amend an act entitled "An act in relation to the State Cabinet of Natural History," passed May second, eighteen hundred and seventy. Passed April 25, 1871; three-fifths being present.*

CHAP. 712. *An Act in relation to the election of representatives in congress, senators and members of assembly. Passed April 25, 1871; three-fifths being present.*

CHAP. 713. *An Act in relation to the chronic pauper insane. Passed April 25, 1871; three-fifths being present.*

CHAP. 714. An Act to amend chapter one hundred and forty-one of the Laws of eighteen hundred and seventy-one, entitled "An act to abolish tolls on certain roads and bridges in the towns of Newtown and Flushing, in the county of Queens, and provide compensation therefor." Passed April 25, 1871; three-fifths being present.

CHAP. 715. *An Act making appropriations for certain expenses of government, and for supplying deficiencies in former appropriations. Passed April 26, 1871, by a two-third vote.*

CHAP. 716. An Act to amend an act entitled "An act to authorize the formation of a railroad company from the village of Hempstead to the village of Jamaica, in the county of Queens," passed April twenty-first, eighteen hundred and sixty-six. Passed April 25, 1871; three-fifths being present.

CHAP. 717. *An Act to provide ways and means for the support of government. Passed April 26, 1871; three-fifths being present.*

CHAP. 718. *An Act making appropriations for the support of government. Passed April 26, 1871; three-fifths being present.*

CHAP. 719. An Act to amend an act entitled "An act to revise the charter of the city of Buffalo," passed April twenty-eight, eighteen hundred and seventy. Passed April 25, 1871; three-fifths being present.

CHAP. 720. An Act to establish a department of police in the city of Buffalo, and to provide for the government thereof. Passed April 26, 1871; three-fifths being present.

CHAP. 721. *An Act to amend and consolidate the several acts relating to the preservation of moose, wild deer, birds and fish. Passed April 26, 1871; three-fifths being present.*

CHAP. 722. *An Act amendatory of, and supplemental to the following acts, namely, an act entitled "An act establishing a quarantine and defining the qualifications, duties and powers of the health officer for the harbor and port of New York," passed April twenty-ninth, eighteen hundred and sixty-three; an act entitled "An act in relation to quarantine in the port of New York, and providing for the construction of the permanent quarantine establishment," passed April twenty-one, eighteen hundred and sixty-six; an act entitled "An act in relation to quarantine in the port of New York, and to amend existing acts relative thereto," passed April twenty-two, eighteen hundred and sixty-nine, and an act entitled "An act in relation to the sale of the Marine Hospital grounds," passed May nineteenth, eighteen hundred and sixty-eight. Passed April 26, 1871; three-fifths being present.*

CHAP. 723. An Act to authorize the supervisor of the town of Phelps, Ontario county, to refund certain tax moneys heretofore collected in said town. Passed April 26, 1871; three-fifths being present.

CHAP. 724. An Act to define the powers of the corporation attorney of the city of New York, in suits for fines and penalties. Passed April 26, 1871; three-fifths being present.

CHAP. 725. *An Act for the relief of the surviving members of the First Regiment of New York Volunteers who served in the war with Mexico. Passed April 26, 1871; by a two-third vote.*

CHAP. 726. An Act to amend chapter one hundred and forty-eight of the Laws of eighteen hundred and seventy-one, entitled "An act authorizing the commissioners of highways of the town of Stony Point, in the county of Rockland, to build a drawbridge over Minnisceongo creek, in said town, and authorizing said town to aid them," passed March twenty-second, eighteen hundred and seventy-one. Passed April 26, 1871, three-fifths being present.

CHAP. 727. An Act to amend section six of chapter one hundred and thirty-nine of the Laws of eighteen hundred and seventy, entitled "An act to annex parts of the towns of Bethlehem and Watervliet, in the county of Albany, to the city of Albany, and to exempt such parts thereof from certain taxes, and to annex a part of the city of Albany to the town of Watervliet." Passed April 26, 1871; three-fifths being present.

CHAP. 728. An Act to confirm and extend the right of William Mason to maintain a ferry across Chautauqua lake. Passed April 26, 1871; three-fifths being present.

CHAP. 729. An Act authorizing the Board of Supervisors of the county of Essex to levy and assess certain taxes on certain lands in the town of Minerva, in said county. Passed April 26, 1871; three-fifths being present.

CHAP. 730. An Act in relation to highways in the county of Rockland. Passed April 26, 1871; three-fifths being present.

CHAP. 731. An Act to authorize Abram B. Conger to construct and maintain a bridge across the Minnisceongo creek, in the town of Stony Point, in the county of Rockland. Passed April 26, 1871.

CHAP. 732. An Act to amend section three of chapter seven hundred and sixty-six of the Laws of eighteen hundred and seventy, entitled "An act to improve and keep in repair the highway from Wilmington to North Elba, in the county of Essex. Passed April 26, 1871; three-fifths being present.

CHAP. 733. *An Act in relation to actions against sheriffs. Passed April* 26, 1871.

CHAP. 734. An Act authorizing the commissioners of highway of the town of Bethlehem, in the county of Albany, to lay out and open a highway two rods wide. Passed April 26, 1871; three-fifths being present.

CHAP. 735. An Act making an appropriation and authorizing a loan on the credit of the county of Wayne, and the levying a tax for paying the same, for the purpose of building a bridge across Great Sodus bay, in the county of Wayne. Passed April 26, 1871, by a two-third vote.

CHAP. 736. An Act to provide for the better support of the poor in the city of Poughkeepsie, in the county of Dutchess. Passed April 26, 1871; three-fifths being present.

CHAP. 737. An Act to provide for the election of an auditor of the county of Kings, and prescribing his powers and duties. Passed April 26, 1871; three-fifths being present.

CHAP. 738. An Act to amend an act entitled "An act to establish the office of receiver of taxes in the town of Westchester." Passed April 26, 1871; three-fifths being present.

CHAP. 739. An Act to amend an act entitled "An act to provide for the better support of the poor in the city and town of Newburgh, in the county of Orange," passed April fourth, eighteen hundred and seventy-one. Passed April 26, 1871; three-fifths being present.

CHAP. 740. An Act to provide for the manner and time for election of chief engineer and assistants, in the village of Rhinebeck, by the fire department of said village. Passed April 26, 1871; three-fifths being present.

CHAP. 741. An Act to confirm and legalize the official acts of the president and board of trustees of the village of Carthage, in the county of Jefferson, during the years eighteen hundred and sixty-nine and eighteen hundred and seventy. Passed April 26, 1871; three-fifths being present.

CHAP. 742. An Act in relation to storage and the keeping of combustible material in the city of New York, the use and control of the fire alarm telegraph, the incumbrance of hydrants, and other purposes connected with the prevention and extinguishment of fires therein, and imposing certain powers and duties upon the board of fire commissioners of the said city. Passed April 26, 1871; three-fifths being present.

CHAP. 743. An Act to amend an act entitled "An act for the relief of the Grand Street, Prospect Park and Flatbush Railroad Company," passed May second, eighteen hundred and seventy. Passed April 26, 1871.

CHAP. 744. An Act to amend an act passed April twenty-eighth, eighteen hundred and sixty-six, entitled "An act to amend an act entitled an act in relation to jurors and the appointment and duties of a commissioner of jurors in the county of Kings, passed April seventeenth, eighteen hundred and fifty-eight." Passed April 26, 1871; three-fifths being present.

CHAP. 745. An Act to protect and keep in repair the Southern boulevard in the towns of West Farms and Morrisania, in the county of Westchester. Passed April 26, 1871; three-fifths being present.

CHAP. 746. *An Act to amend an act entitled "An act to revise and consolidate the general act relating to public instruction," passed May second, eighteen hundred and sixty-four. Passed April* 26, 1871; *three-fifths being present.*

CHAP. 747. *An Act to amend an act entitled "An act to establish a law library for the eighth judicial district in the city of Buffalo," passed May fourth, eighteen hundred and sixty-three. Passed April* 26, 1871; *three-fifths being present.*

CHAP. 748. An Act to amend the act incorporating the Exempt Firemen's Association of the City of Albany, passed April seventeenth, eighteen hundred and sixty-eight. Passed April 26, 1871.

CHAP. 749. An Act to provide for improving Mount Vernon avenue in the village of West Mount Vernon, county of Westchester. Passed April 26, 1871; three-fifths being present.

CHAP. 750. An Act to incorporate "The Trustees of the Estate belonging to the Diocese of Long Island," and to authorize said corporation to acquire and hold land for religious, charitable and benevolent purposes. Passed April 26, 1871.

CHAP. 751. An Act to repeal chapter one hundred and sixty-one of the Laws of eighteen hundred and sixty-three, entitled "An act to amend chapter one hundred and one of the Laws of eighteen hundred and sixty-two, entitled 'An act in relation to the support and custody of indigent and insane persons of the county of Genesee.'" Passed April 26, 1871; three-fifths being present.

CHAP. 752. An Act to authorize a change in the line of Second avenue in the town of New Utrecht. Passed April 26, 1871; three-fifths being present.

CHAP. 753. An Act to legalize the election of trustees and other corporation officers of the village of Gowanda. Passed April 26, 1871; three-fifths being present.

CHAP. 754. An Act in relation to the distribution of moneys reimbursed the several townships of Rensselaer county for excess of years, provided by chapter twenty-nine, Laws of eighteen hundred and sixty-five. Passed April 26, 1871; three-fifths being present.

CHAP. 755. An Act to enlarge the burying ground at Flat Brook, in the town of Canaan, Columbia county. Passed April 26; 1871; three-fifths being present.

CHAP. 756. *An Act to prevent the deposit of carrion, offal, or dead animals, in the North and East rivers, or in the bay of New York or Raritan bay, within the jurisdiction of the State of New York. Passed April* 26, 1871; *three-fifths being present.*

CHAP. 757. An Act amending and enlarging the powers, privileges and franchises of the Geddes and Syracuse Gas-light Company. Passed April 26, 1871; three-fifths being present.

CHAP. 758. An Act to authorize the city of Troy to take water from the Hudson river, and from other sources, and to facilitate the acquisition of land for the construction of works, reservoirs, and laying pipes or other means to conduct said water to said city. Passed April 26, 1871; three-fifths being present.

CHAP. 759. An Act concerning the Brooklyn and Rockaway Beach Railroad Company. Passed April 26, 1871.

CHAP. 760. An Act to amend an act entitled "An act to amend the charter of the village of Saratoga Springs," passed March twenty-sixth, eighteen hundred and sixty-six. Passed April 26, 1871; three-fifths being present.

CHAP. 761. An Act to amend section thirteen of the act entitled "An act to consolidate school districts nnmbers five, eight, eleven and fifteen of the town of Kingston, Ulster county, into one school district, passed April twenty-ninth, eighteen hundred and sixty-three." Passed April 26, 1871; three-fifths being present.

CHAP. 762. An Act to amend "An act to incorporate the village of Mount Morris," passed May second, eighteen hundred and thirty-five, and the several acts subsequent amending the same. Passed April 26, 1871; three-fifths being present.

CHAP. 763. An Act to amend the act entitled "An act to revise, amend and consolidate the laws in relation to the village of Norwich, in the county of Chenango," passed March twenty-third, eighteen hundred and fifty-seven, and the act amendatory thereto, passed April third, eighteen hundred and sixty-seven. Passed April 26, 1871; three-fifths being present.

CHAP. 764. An Act to prevent obstruction to travel in the city of Brooklyn. Passed April 26, 1871.

CHAP. 765. An Act to provide for the laying out of streets, avenues, roads and parks in Long Island City. Passed April 26, 1871; three-fifths being present.

CHAP. 766. *An Act to allow the justices of the Supreme Court assigned to hold the General Terms thereof in the several judicial d partments of this State, to fix the time and places of holding the same. Passed April* 27, 1871; *three-fifths being present.*

CHAP. 767. An Act to amend chapter five hundred and thirty-six of the Laws of eighteen hundred and seventy-one, entitled "An act to amend the act entitled 'An act to amend the act to combine into one act the several acts relating to the city of Albany, passed April twelfth, eighteen hundred and forty-two, and the several acts amendatory thereof, and also to repeal the act establishing a capital police district, and to provide for the government thereof, passed April twenty-second, eighteen hundred and sixty-five, and the several acts amendatory thereof, in so far as they relate to the city of Albany," passed April fifteenth, eighteen hundred and seventy one. Passed April 27, 1871; three-fifths being present.

CHAP. 768. An Act to authorize the construction of an addition to the armory in the city of Syracuse. Passed April 27, 1871; three-fifths being present.

Chap. 769. An Act to provide for a re-assessment and re-award to pay for the lands taken by Mamaroneck avenue, in the county of Westchester, and to finish and complete the said avenue. Passed April 27, 1871; three-fifths being present.

Chap. 770. An Act to provide for the completion of Westchester avenue, in the county of Westchester. Passed April 27, 1871; three-fifths being present.

Chap. 771. An Act to preserve the public documents in the clerk's office of the town of Westchester. Passed April 27, 1871; three-fifths being present.

Chap. 772. An Act to provide for the discharge of the commissioners appointed under chapter four hundred of the Laws of eighteen hundred and sixty-seven, entitled "An act to authorize the extension of Central road or avenue in the county of Westchester, at or near Woodlawn cemetery, in the town of Yonkers, to a point at or near the village of White Plains," passed April sixteenth, eighteen hundred and sixty-seven, and their successors in office. Passed April 27, 1871; three-fifths being present.

Chap. 773. An Act to amend an act entitled "An act to amend an act entitled 'An act to create a board of trustees for the town of Morrisania, in the county of Westchester, and to define their powers,'" passed April twenty-second, eighteen hundred and sixty-four, as amended by subsequent acts, passed March twenty-first, eighteen hundred and seventy-one. Passed April 27, 1871; three-fifths being present.

Chap. 774. An Act supplementary to an act entitled "An act to authorize the laying of sidewalks in the highways, streets and avenues in the town of West Farms, in the county of Westchester," passed April twenty-eighth, eighteen hundred and sixty-four. Passed April 27, 1871; three-fifths being present.

Chap. 775. An Act to authorize the board of trustees of the town of Morrisania, and the board of town officers of the town of West Farms, to appoint commissioners to survey the water-shed of Millbrook, in said towns, in the county of Westchester. Passed April 27, 1871; three-fifths being present.

Chap. 776. *An Act to authorize religious corporations created by special charter to exercise the same powers as are given to religious societies incorporated under the general act to provide for the incorporation of religious societies, passed April fifth, eighteen hundred and thirteen, and the acts amendatory thereof or supplementary thereto. Passed April 27, 1871; three-fifths being present.*

Chap. 777. An Act incorporating the New York Produce Commission Company. Passed April 27, 1871.

Chap. 778. *An Act to re-appropriate moneys for construction of new work upon and extraordinary repairs of the canals of this State. Passed April 27, 1871; three-fifths being present.*

Chap. 779. An act to provide for the election of a separate officer in each of the counties of Otsego and Saratoga, to be surrogate. Passed April 27, 1871; three-fifths being present.

Chap. 780. An Act supplementary to an act entitled "An act to widen and improve Franklin avenue, in the town of Flatbush," passed May tenth, eighteen hundred and sixty-nine. Passed April 27, 1871; three-fifths being present.

Chap. 781. An Act to provide for the construction of a fishway in the Mohawk river, at the upper aqueduct, near the city of Schenectady. Passed April 27, 1871, by a two-third vote.

Chap. 782. An Act to authorize William R. Norris to construct and use a tram road in the public highway in the town of Fort Ann, in the county of Washington. Passed April 27, 1871; three-fifths being present.

Chap. 783. An Act relating to building bridges in the village of Niagara Falls. Passed April 27, 1871; three-fifths being present.

Chap. 784. An Act authorizing the city of Buffalo to build a bridge over Buffalo river, and to issue bonds for the purpose of paying the expense of building such bridge. Passed April 27, 1871; three-fifths being present.

Chap. 785. An Act to amend an act entitled "An act to authorize the selection and location of certain grounds for public parks in the city of Buffalo, and to provide for the maintenance and embellishment thereof," passed April fourteenth, eighteen hundred and sixty-nine. Passed April 27, 1871.

Chap. 786. An Act to legalize the election of corporation officers in the village of Weedsport, and to amend the charter of said village. Passed April 27, 1871; three-fifths being present.

CHAP. 787. An Act to amend the charter of the Niagara Fire Insurance Company. Passed April 27, 1871.

CHAP. 788. An Act to extend the time for organization of "The Staten Island Bridge Company." Passed April 27, 1871.

CHAP. 789. An Act to amend an act entitled "An act to authorize certain towns and villages in the counties of Onondaga, Madison and Chenango to issue bonds to take stock in the Syracuse and Chenango Valley Railroad Company," passed May fourth, eighteen hundred and sixty-eight. Passed April 27, 1871; three-fifths being present.

CHAP. 790. An Act to amend the charter of the Ogdensburgh and Lake Champlain Railroad Company. Passed April 27, 1871.

CHAP. 791. An Act to amend an act entitled "An act to incorporate the village of New Brighton," passed April twenty-sixth, eighteen hundred and sixty-six, and an act amending the same, passed April twenty-second, eighteen hundred and sixty-seven. Passed April 27, 1871; three-fifths being present.

CHAP. 792. An Act to incorporate the National Prison Association of the United States of America. Passed April 27, 1871.

CHAP. 793. An Act to incorporate the Salmon River Improvement Company. Passed April 27, 1871.

CHAP. 794. An Act to further amend the charter of the village of Albion, in the county of Orleans. Passed April 27, 1871; three-fifths being present.

CHAP. 795. An Act to incorporate the Western New York Poultry Society. Passed April 27, 1871.

CHAP. 796. An Act to amend an act entitled "An act to incorporate the American Missionary Association," passed April nineteenth, eighteen hundred and sixty-two. Passed April 27, 1871.

CHAP. 797. An Act to incorporate the singing society Germania of the city of Poughkeepsie. Passed April 27, 1871.

CHAP. 798. An Act to incorporate the Young Men's Catholic Association of the city of Buffalo. Passed April 27, 1871.

CHAP. 799. *An Act in relation to the Marine court of the city of New York and to amend an act entitled "An act to reduce the several acts in relation to the Marine court of the city of New York, into one act, and to extend the jurisdiction of said court," passed May second, eighteen hundred and seventy. Passed April* 27, 1871; *three-fifths being present.*

CHAP. 800. An Act for the relief of John and William Rothery. Passed April 27, 1871, by a two-third vote.

CHAP. 801. *An Act to prevent the spread of contagious diseases in the city of New York, and to provide for the proper care and treatment of persons afflicted with such disease. Passed April* 27, 1871; *three-fifths being present.*

CHAP. 802. *An Act to amend chapter six hundred and seventy-seven of the Laws of eighteen hundred and sixty-seven, entitled "An act to prevent fraud and fraudulent practices upon or by hotel keepers and innkeepers," passed April twenty-third, eighteen hundred and sixty-seven. Passed April* 27, 1871.

CHAP. 803. An Act for the appointment of commissioners to manage the real estate of the Mechanics' Institute of the city of Buffalo. Passed April 28, 1871; three-fifths being present.

CHAP. 804. An Act in regard to the term of office of marshal in the city of New York. Passed April 28, 1871; three-fifths being present.

CHAP. 805. An Act to amend the charter of the village of White Plains, in the county of Westchester. Passed April 28, 1871; three-fifths being present.

CHAP. 806. An Act to incorporate the "Gramercy Boat Club," of the city of New York. Passed April 28, 1871.

CHAP. 807. An Act to incorporate the Nautilus Club, of the city of New York. Passed April 28, 1871.

CHAP. 808. An Act supplementary to chapter three hundred of the Laws of eighteen hundred and seventy-one, entitled "An act to incorporate the New York Railway Company for the purpose of providing rapid transit through the city and county of New York and Westchester county, and to provide for the construction and operation of railways therefor," and to amend the same. Passed April 28, 1871; three-fifths being present.

CHAP. 809. An Act to legalize and confirm the acts of the commissioners of the towns of Thompson and Forestburgh, in the county of Sullivan, and of Deerpark, in the county of Orange, in issuing and disposing of the bonds of their respective towns, to build a railroad from the village of Monticello, in the county of Sullivan, to the village of Port Jervis, in the county of Orange, under chapter five hundred and fifty-three of the Laws of eighteen hundred and sixty-eight, and to legalize and confirm all bonds heretofore issued by such commissioners, under said chapter of laws now held by or owned by bona fide purchasers. Passed April 28, 1871; three-fifths being present.

CHAP. 810. An Act to amend an act entitled "An act to incorporate the city of Watertown," passed May eighth, eighteen hundred and sixty-nine, and to confirm the acts of the common council in reference to local assessments for local improvements. Passed April 28, 1871; three-fifths being present.

CHAP. 811. An Act for the relief of Elisha H. Powell. Passed April 28, 1871; three-fifths being present.

CHAP. 812. An Act to incorporate the Zimmerman's Verein, Number One, of the city of New York. Passed April 28, 1871.

CHAP. 813. An Act to amend an act entitled "An act to incorporate the village of Mechanicville, in the county of Saratoga, New York," passed May fourteenth, eighteen hundred and seventy. Passed April 28, 1871; three-fifths being present.

CHAP. 814. An Act to amend an act entitled "An act to amend the charter of the village of Horseheads, in Chemung county," passed April fourteenth, eighteen hundred and fifty-five, and also the several acts amendatory thereof. Passed April 28, 1871; three-fifths being present.

CHAP. 815. *An Act declaring a portion of Swiss creek, in the town of Croghan, Lewis county, a public highway. Passed April* 28, 1871.

CHAP. 816. An Act to incorporate the St. Patrick's Hall Association of the city of New York. Passed April 28, 1871.

CHAP. 817. An Act to authorize the Smith and Parmelee Gold Company to issue a preferred stock. Passed April 28, 1871.

CHAP. 818. An Act to provide for the erection and repair of bridges over the Wallkill river, on the dividing line between the towns of Hamptonburgh and Wallkill, in the county of Orange. Passed April 28, 1871; three-fifths being present.

CHAP. 819. An Act to incorporate "The Association of the Bar of the city of New York." Passed April 28, 1871.

CHAP. 820. An Act to authorize the formation of associations to carry on the business of marketing in the city of New York. Passed April 28, 1871.

CHAP. 821. An Act to supply the village of Gloversville with pure and wholesome water. Passed April 28, 1871; three-fifths being present.

CHAP. 822. An Act to incorporate the Breslau Central Union Building Association of New York. Passed April 28, 1871.

CHAP. 823. An Act to incorporate the People's Safe Deposit Company of the city of New York. Passed April 28, 1871.

CHAP. 824. *An Act for the improvement of the navigation of the tributaries of the Great South Bay. Passed April* 28, 1871, *by a two-third vote.*

CHAP. 825. An Act to incorporate the Oswego Driving Park Association. Passed April 28, 1871.

CHAP. 826. An Act to authorize the Black River and St. Lawrence Railway Company to carry freight and passengers and charge fare. Passed April 28, 1871.

CHAP. 827. An Act to authorize the New York Guaranty and Indemnity Company to accept and execute certain trusts.. Passed April 28, 1871.

CHAP. 828. An Act changing the time for the annual election of directors of the Glens Falls Insurance Company. Passed April 28, 1871.

CHAP. 829. An Act to authorize the Genesee and Water Street Railroad Company to extend its track. Passed April 28, 1871.

CHAP. 830. An Act to amend an act entitled "An act to incorporate the Hudson and Harlem River Canal Company," passed May second, eighteen hundred and sixty-three, and the amendment thereto, passed April twenty-first, eighteen hundred and sixty-four, and the amendment thereto, passed April tenth, eighteen hundred and sixty-six. Passed April 28, 1871.

CHAP. 831. *An Act for the protection of private parks and grounds, and to encourage the propagation of fish and game. Passed April 28, 1871.*

CHAP. 832. An Act to incorporate the Excelsior Hotel Company. Passed April 28, 1871.

CHAP. 833. An Act to provide for the opening and extending of North Thirteenth street, in the city of Brooklyn, from its present westerly terminus to the East river, and to the permanent bulkhead line. Passed April 28, 1871; three-fifths being present.

CHAP. 834. *An Act to amend an act entitled "An act to extend the jurisdiction of surrogate's courts," passed April twenty-third, eighteen hundred and sixty-seven. Passed April 28, 1871; three-fifths being present.*

CHAP. 835. An Act to change the name of "The Hope Union Mission School, Brooklyn," and to exempt the property of the same from taxation. Passed April 28, 1871; three-fifths being present.

CHAP. 836. *An Act for the removal of obstructions in Indian river, and for the improvement of the navigation of said river. Passed April 28, 1871, by a two-third vote.*

CHAP. 837. An Act to repeal an act entitled "An act to enable the American and Foreign Bible Society to unite and consolidate with the American Baptist Publication Society," passed March eleventh, eighteen hundred and seventy. Passed April 28, 1871.

CHAP. 838. An Act to amend an act entitled "An act to provide for the construction of a railroad from the city of Poughkeepsie to the Connecticut or Massachusetts line, and to authorize towns to subscribe to the capital stock thereof," passed April thirteenth, eighteen hundred and sixty-six. Passed April 28, 1871.

CHAP. 839. An Act to provide for the assessment and collection of the cost of the improvement of the Gowanus canal in the city of Brooklyn, and for the reconstruction of docks in said improvement which have sunk or become unfit for use. Passed April 28, 1871; three-fifths being present.

CHAP. 840. An Act in relation to the Buffalo City Insurance Company. Passed April 28, 1871.

CHAP. 841. An Act making provision for the support of certain dispensaries in the city of Albany. Passed April 28, 1871; three-fifths being present.

CHAP. 842. An Act to authorize the formation of a mutual insurance company in the towns of Ellisburgh, Henderson, Adams and Lorraine, in the county of Jefferson, and the towns of Boylston and Sandy Creek, in the county of Oswego. Passed April 28, 1871.

CHAP. 843. An Act to close and discontinue Stewart's alley, in the city of Brooklyn. Passed April 28, 1871; three-fifths being present.

CHAP. 844. An Act to amend an act entitled "An act to facilitate the construction of the Whitehall and Plattsburgh Railroad," passed March twentieth, eighteen hundred and sixty-seven, and to renew the appropriation made thereby. Passed April 28, 1871; three-fifths being present.

CHAP. 845. An Act to amend chapter fifty-nine of the Laws of eighteen hundred and sixty-three, entitled "An act for the incorporation of the trustees of the Parochial Fund of the Protestant Episcopal Church, in the diocese of Western New York," passed March twenty-sixth, eighteen hundred and sixty-three. Passed April 28, 1871; three-fifths being present.

CHAP. 846. An Act to open, grade and pave Sherman street, in the city of Brooklyn. Passed April 28, 1871; three-fifths being present.

CHAP. 847. An Act to incorporate the Slate Dock Company of Rhinebeck, in the county of Dutchess. Passed April 28, 1871.

CHAP. 848. *An Act for the improvement of the navigation of the Bouquet river. Passed April 28, 1871; three-fifths being present.*

CHAP. 849. An Act to alter the commissioners' map of the city of Brooklyn. Passed April 28, 1871; three-fifths being present.

CHAP. 850. An Act to authorize the Common Council of the city of Brooklyn to open and improve Steuben street and Schenck street, from Flushing avenue to Lafayette avenue. Passed April 28, 1871; three-fifths being present.

CHAP. 851. An Act authorizing the Rochester Orphan Asylum to have three additional trustees. Passed April 28, 1871.

CHAP. 852. An Act to amend an act entitled "An act to incorporate the Cohoes Company." Passed April 28, 1871.

CHAP. 853. An Act to amend an act entitled "An act to enable the Fulsome Landing

Bridge Company to complete their bridge across the Hudson river, between the towns of Chester and Johnsburgh, and to legalize the acts of the tax payers of the town of Schroon in relation to their subscription to the capital stock of said company," passed April sixth, eighteen hundred and seventy-one. Passed April 28, 1871; three-fifths being present.

CHAP. 854. An Act to authorize the South Side Railroad Company of Long Island to alter the par value of the shares of its capital stock. Passed April 28, 1871.

CHAP. 855. *An Act for the improvement of the east and west branches of the St. Regis river. Passed April* 28, 1871, *by a two-third vote.*

CHAP. 856. An Act for the relief of Rufus L. Howard. Passed April 28, 1871; three-fifths being present.

CHAP. 857. An Act to amend an act entitled "An act to amend an act to encourage and facilitate the construction of a railroad along the valley of the upper Hudson into the wilderness in the northern part of this State, and the development of the resources thereof," passed April twenty-seventh, eighteen hundred and sixty-three, and for the relief of the Adirondack Company, formed under said act, passed May eighth, eighteen hundred and sixty-eight. Passed April 28, 1871; three-fifths being present.

CHAP. 858. *An Act making an appropriation for the removal of obstructions from Chautauqua lake and outlet. Passed April* 28, 1871, *by a two-third vote.*

CHAP. 859. *An Act to provide for the election of certain judicial and other officers, and to fix their terms of office. Passed April* 28, 1871; *three-fifths being present.*

CHAP. 860. An Act to incorporate the Grand Commandery of the State of New York. Passed April 28, 1871.

CHAP. 861. An Act to amend an act entitled "An act in relation to common schools, in the village of Elmira," passed April fourth, eighteen hundred and fifty-nine. Passed April 28, 1871; three-fifths being present.

CHAP. 862. An Act relating to the New York and White Plains Railroad Company. Passed April 28, 1871.

CHAP. 863. An Act to incorporate the Long Island Market Company. Passed April 28, 1871.

CHAP. 864. An Act to incorporate Thomas Wildey Encampment, number thirty-nine, Independent Order of Odd Fellows, of the State of New York. Passed April 28, 1871.

CHAP. 865. An Act to incorporate the Young Men's Christian Association of the city of Schenectady. Passed April 28, 1871.

CHAP. 866. An Act in relation to filling in sunken lots in the city of Brooklyn, and the filling in, regulating, grading and paving opened streets, through certain low grounds in said city. Passed April 28, 1871; three-fifths being present.

CHAP. 867. An Act to supply the village of Fort Ann with pure and wholesome water. Passed April 28, 1871; three-fifths being present.

CHAP. 868 *An Act to foster and develop the internal commerce of the State by inviting and rewarding the practical and profitable introduction upon the canals of steam, caloric, electricity or any motor other than animal power for the propulsion of boats. Passed April* 28, 1871; *three-fifths being present.*

CHAP. 869. *An Act making appropriations for certain public and charitable institutions. Passed April* 28, 1871, *by a two-third vote.*

CHAP. 870. *An Act to amend an act entitled "An act for the incorporation of villages," passed April twentieth, eighteen hundred and seventy. Passed April* 29, 1871; *three-fifths being present.*

CHAP. 871. An Act to amend, extend and continue an act entitled "An act to incorporate the Bankers' Life Insurance and Trust Company of New York," passed May sixth, eighteen hundred and seventy, and to ratify and confirm the acts and proceedings of the corporators of the said company. Passed April 29, 1871; three-fifths being present.

CHAP. 872. *An Act to amend an act entitled "An act for the better security of mechanics and others erecting buildings and furnishing materials therefor in the several cities of this State (except the city of New York), and in the villages of Syracuse, Williamsburgh, Geneva, Canandaigua, Oswego and Auburn," passed May seventh, eighteen hundred and forty-four. Passed April* 29, 1871; *three-fifths being present.*

CHAP. 873. An Act to allow the Mutual Protection Life Assurance Society to increase its capital. Passed April 29, 1871.

CHAP. 874. *An Act authorizing surrogates, in the several counties, to employ stenographers. Passed May* 1, 1871; *three-fifths being present.*

CHAP. 875. An Act for the incorporation of Trades Unions and Societies of Workingmen. Passed May 1, 1871.

CHAP. 876. An Act to incorporate the Saugerties Landing Tramroad Company. Passed May 1, 1871; three-fifths being present.

CHAP. 877. An Act to amend the charter of the city of Brooklyn. Passed May 1, 1871; three-fifths being present.

CHAP. 878. An Act to authorize the consolidation of certain Gas-light Companies in the city of Brooklyn. Passed May 2, 1871; three-fifths being present.

CHAP. 879. *An Act in relation to certain work on section five of the Erie canal. Passed May* 2, 1871; *three-fifths being present.*

CHAP. 880. An Act to provide for the construction of a swing bridge over city ship canal, in the city of Buffalo. Passed May 2, 1871; three-fifths being present.

CHAP. 881. An Act to incorporate the Sparkhill Creek Canal Company. Passed May 2, 1871, by a two-third vote.

CHAP. 882. An Act to provide for the drainage of the swamp, bog and other low and wet lands in the town of East Chester, county of Westchester. Passed May 2, 1871; three-fifths being present.

CHAP. 883. *An Act to amend title four of chapter eighteen of part first of the Revised Statutes, entitled "Special provisions relating to certain corporations." Passed May* 2, 1871.

CHAP. 884. An Act to provide for the drainage of the swamp, bog and other low and wet lands in the village of White Plains and adjacent thereto. Passed May 2, 1871; three-fifths being present.

CHAP. 885. An Act for the relief of George Dinsmore. Passed May 2, 1871; three-fifths being present

CHAP. 886. An Act to amend an act entitled "An act to incorporate the Buffalo East Side Street Railway Company," passed May tenth, eighteen hundred and seventy. Passed May 2, 1871.

CHAP. 887. An Act in relation to the salary of the supervisors of Albany county. Passed May 3, 1871; three-fifths being present.

CHAP. 888. *An Act in relation to insurance companies, corporations, associations, partnerships and individuals of foreign governments, doing fire insurance business in this State. Passed May* 3, 1871; *three-fifths being present.*

CHAP. 889. An Act to amend chapter one hundred and sixty of the Laws of eighteen hundred and sixty-six, entitled "An act to facilitate the construction of the Schoharie Valley Railroad," also chapter six hundred and sixteen of the Laws of eighteen hundred and sixty-seven, entitled "An act to reduce the number of directors of the Schoharie Valley Railroad." Passed May 3, 1871; three-fifths being present.

CHAP. 890. An Act in relation to the Seventy-ninth Regiment, National Guard, State of New York. Passed May 10, 1871, by a two-third vote.

CHAP. 891. An Act for the relief of E. B. Van Dusen. Passed May 10, 1871; three-fifths being present.

CHAP. 892. An Act in relation to the contracts of Ambrose Clark and William H. Douglas, for repairing the towing-path and rebuilding the towing-path on construction section number three hundred and sixty-eight of the Erie canal, and the work connected therewith. Passed May 10, 1871; three-fifths being present.

CHAP. 893. An Act in relation to the Sixth Regiment, National Guard, of the State of New York. Passed May 10, 1871, by a two-third vote.

CHAP. 894. An Act to change the corporate name of the Clifton Springs Water Cure Company. Passed May 10, 1871.

CHAP. 895. *An Act for the erection of a swing bridge across the Chemung canal feeder, on Franklin street, in the village of Horseheads. Passed May* 10, 1871; *three-fifths being present.*

CHAP. 896. An Act for the relief of Alexander Barkley. Passed May 10, 1871; three-fifths being present.

CHAP. 897 An Act to incorporate the Poughkeepsie Bridge Company for the purpose of constructing and maintaining a bridge, appurtenances and approaches to the same over the Hudson river, at a point or points between the city of Poughkeepsie and the town of Lyod, Ulster county, on said river. Passed May 10, 1871.

CHAP. 898. An Act for the relief of Gardner Welles, assignee in trust for the benefit of the creditors of Pringle and Claffy. Passed May 10, 1871; three-fifths being present.

CHAP. 899. An Act for the relief of N. Stanton Gere. Passed May 10, 1871; three-fifths being present.

CHAP. 900. An Act for the relief of Joseph Scoville and Lewis H. Eaton. Passed May 10, 1871; three-fifths being present.

CHAP. 901. An Act to authorize the Oakwood Street Railroad, in and adjacent to the city of Syracuse, and in the county of Onondaga, to change the route of its road. Passed May 10, 1871.

CHAP. 902. An Act for the relief of W. T. Dennison. Passed May 10, 1871; three-fifths being present.

CHAP. 903. *An Act to amend section four of chapter six hundred and fifty-five of the Laws of eighteen hundred and seventy, entitled "An act to provide for the introduction of an improved system of towage upon the canals of this State." Passed May* 10, 1871; *three-fifths being present.*

CHAP. 904. An Act for the relief of R. Nelson Gere and Charles W. Steves. Passed May 10, 1871; three-fifths being present.

CHAP. 905. An Act for the relief of William H. Douglass. Passed May 10, 1871; three-fifths being present.

CHAP. 906. An Act to incorporate the Weehawken Transportation Company. Passed May 10, 1871.

CHAP. 907. *An Act relative to savings banks. Passed May* 10, 1871.

CHAP. 908. An Act for the relief of George W. Hunt. Passed May 10, 1871; three-fifths being present.

CHAP. 909. An Act to incorporate the Glens Falls Water-works Company. Passed May 10, 1871; three-fifths being present.

CHAP. 910. An Act to amend an act entitled "An act to incorporate the Tontine Mutual Savings Bank of the city of New York," passed May eleventh, eighteen hundred and sixty-nine. Passed May 10, 1871.

CHAP. 911. *An act to provide for the introduction of the American system of cable towage upon the canals of this State. Passed May* 10, 1871; *three-fifths being present.*

CHAP. 912. *An Act for the construction of a swing bridge over the Cayuga inlet. Passed May* 10, 1871; *three-fifths being present.*

CHAP. 913. An Act for the relief of W. B. Birdseye. Passed May 10, 1871; three-fifths being present.

CHAP. 914. An Act to incorporate the Cornwall Savings Bank of Orange county. Passed May 10, 1871.

CHAP. 915. An Act to incorporate "The Sixth Ward Savings Bank of the city of Albany." Passed May 10, 1871.

CHAP. 916. An Act to supply the village of Yonkers with pure and wholesome water. Passed May 10, 1871; three-fifths being present.

CHAP. 917. An Act to extend and improve Fourth street, in the city of Brooklyn. Passed April 10, 1871; three-fifths being present.

CHAP. 918. An Act to amend the charter of the city of Cohoes. Passed May 11, 1871; three-fifths being present.

CHAP. 919. An Act to enlarge the boundaries of the city of Auburn. Passed May 11, 1871; three-fifths being present.

CHAP. 920. An Act for the relief of the National Fiber Company. Passed May 11, 1871; three-fifths being present.

CHAP. 921. An Act to authorize the Central Railroad Company of Long Island to construct a draw-bridge over Flushing creek, in the county of Queens. Passed May 11, 1871; three-fifths being present.

CHAP. 922. An Act to lay out, open and grade Forty-ninth street in the town of New Utrecht in the county of Kings, from Franklin avenue to the New Utrecht road in said town. Passed May 12, 1871; three-fifths being present.

CHAP. 923. An Act to incorporate the American Mortgage and Trust Company in the city of New York. Passed May 12, 1871.

CHAP. 924. An Act to incorporate the United States Mortgage Company. Passed May 12, 1871.

CHAP. 925. *An Act to amend chapter nine hundred and seven of the Laws of eighteen hundred and sixty-nine, entitled "An act to amend an act entitled 'An act to authorize the formation of railroad corporations and to regulate the same,'" passed April second, eighteen hundred and fifty, so as to permit municipal corporations to aid in the construction of railroads; and also to amend chapter five hundred and seven of the Laws of eighteen hundred and seventy, entitled "An act to define the powers of commissioners appointed under chapter nine hundred and seven of Laws of eighteen hundred and sixty-nine, bonding municipalities to aid in the construction of railroads." Passed May* 12, 1871; *three-fifths being present.*

CHAP. 926. An Act to lay out and improve a public highway in the town of Flatbush, on the easterly side of Prospect Park. Passed May 12, 1871; three-fifths being present.

CHAP. 927. An Act to fix the compensation of assessors in the town of West Farms, in Westchester county. Passed May 13, 1871; three-fifths being present.

CHAP. 928. An Act in relation to the laying out, opening and constructing of a public highway in the town of Hempstead, Queens county. Passed May 23, 1871; three-fifths being present.

CHAP. 929. An Act to authorize the widening and straightening of the public highway or street laid down and designated on the map of Woodsburgh, made by Stephen Mosher, June, eighteen hundred and seventy, and filed in the office of the clerk of Queens county by Samuel Wood. Passed May 23, 1871; three-fifths being present.

CHAP. 930. *An Act to authorize a tax of one-third mill per dollar of valuation of the year eighteen hundred and seventy-one for construction of new work upon extraordinary repairs of the canals of this State. Passed May* 23, 1871; *three-fifths being present.*

CHAP. 931. An Act to amend an act entitled "An act to incorporate the 'Bond Deposit Company of the City of New York,'" passed April twentieth, eighteen hundred and sixty-six. Passed May 24, 1871; three-fifths being present.

CHAP. 932. An Act to provide for a plan for filling in low lands adjoining Fourth avenue in the tenth, twenty-second and eighth wards, in the city of Brooklyn. Passed May 26, 1871; three-fifths being present.

CHAP. 933. An Act to provide for ascertaining and paying the amount of certain claims growing out of the execution of orders of the late Metropolitan Board of Health, and of the present board of health of the city of Brooklyn. Passed May 26, 1871; three-fifths being present.

CHAP. 934. *An Act in reference to apprentices and employers. Passed May* 27, 1871.

CHAP. 935. *An Act to amend an act entitled "An act to incorporate the United States Inebriate Asylum for the reformation of the poor and destitute inebriate," passed April fifth, eighteen hundred and fifty-four, and the act amending the same, passed April twenty-third, eighteen hundred and fifty-five, and the act amending the same, passed March twenty-seventh, eighteen hundred and fifty-seven, and to amend the several acts in relation to the New York State Inebriate Asylum, and to change the number of its trustees and the mode of their appointment, and directing the management of said asylum. Passed May* 29, 1871; *three-fifths being present.*

CHAP. 936. *An Act to allow further costs in suits brought by working-women. Passed May* 29, 1871.

CHAP. 937. An Act to provide for the construction of a swing bridge over Buffalo river, in the city of Buffalo. Passed May 29, 1871; three-fifths being present.

CHAP. 938. An Act to authorize the Malden Turnpike Company to construct tramways on their turnpike road, to fix the rates of tolls thereon, and to change the location of their toll-gate. Passed June 1, 1871.

CHAP. 939. An Act to appropriate money to repair the road injured by the Genesee Valley canal, in the town of Olean, county of Cattaraugus. Passed June 2, 1871, by a two-third vote.

CHAP. 940. An Act to incorporate the Brooklyn Steam Transit Company. Passed June 2, 1871.

CHAP. 941. An Act for the relief of George Saunders. Passed June 3, 1871; three-fifths being present.

CHAP. 942. An Act for the relief of Henry D. Denison. Passed June 3, 1871. three-fifths being present.

Chap. 943. An Act to prevent the flooding of lands by reason of the construction of the State dam across the Tonawanda creek, at the village of Tonawanda. Passed June 5, 1871; three-fifths being present.

Chap. 944. An Act to authorize the construction of gas-works and the manufacture and sale of gas for the purpose of lighting a portion of the city of New York, and the streets, avenues, squares and buildings therein, and to lay pipes for that purpose. Passed June 12, 1871; three-fifths being present.

Chap. 945. An Act to authorize the rebuilding and repairing of certain wharves and piers in the city of Brooklyn. Passed June 12, 1871; three-fifths bejng present.

Chap. 946. An Act to incorporate the Lake George Baptist Association. Passed July 14, 1871.

NEW TOWNS, ETC.

Oneida County — Remsen divided and Forestport erected. December 9, 1869.

Schoharie County — Line of Carlysle settled. November 5, 1870.

Essex County — Part of Schroon annexed to Minerva. November 17, 1870.
Town line between West Port and Elizabethtown settled. March 17 1871.

CONCURRENT RESOLUTIONS.

Relative to Allegany Reservation. January 25, 1871.
Relative to disaster at Wappinger's Creek. February 14, 1871.
Relative to Income Tax. February 28, 1871.
Relative to Brevet Commissions. March 14, 1871.
Relative to Rate of Toll upon the Canals. March 22, 1871.
Relative to Claims against the United States. March 30, 1871.
Relative to Superintendent of Public Instruction. April 4, 1871.
Relative to Bribery. April 19, 1871.
Relative to Commission of Appeals. April 19, 1871.
Relative to American Institute. April 21, 1871.
Relative to State Agricultural Society. April 21, 1871.
Relative to Regents of the University. April 21, 1871.
Relative to Medical Societies. April 21, 1871.
Relative to Centennial Celebration. April 21, 1871.

NAMES CHANGED.

In New York County — Charles Edwins Cady to Charles Cady Edwins. February 1, 1870.

Joseph Gunzenhausen to Joseph Alexander Gunsen. April 1, 1870.

Joseph Taussig to Joseph Seligman Taussig. April 20, 1870.

Gustav Fredirick Focke to Gustav Frederick Folke. April 17, 1870.

Albrecht Gustav Focke to Albrecht Gustav Folke. April 17, 1870.

Joseph W. Trust to Trust Felix Gourand. June 1, 1870.

Antonio Vissani to Charles da Nazzans. July 17, 1870.

Jacob Rathgeber Rathbon to Jacob Rathgeber. September 6, 1870.

Lewis B. Peterson to Lewis R. Post. November 1, 1870.

Burritt Fitch Shephard to Robert Norsworthy Shephard. December 21, 1870.

The Sullivan Street Methodist Episcopal Church to the Washington Methodist Episcopal Church. November 12, 1870.

The Consistory of the North-west Protestant Reformed Dutch Church, in the city of New York, to Madison Avenue Reformed Church. January 1, 1871.

In Kings County — Rector, Churchwardens and Vestrymen of St. Barnabas Church, in the city of Brooklyn, county of Kings and State of New York, to Rector, Churchwardens and Vestrymen of Zion's Church, in the city of Brooklyn, county of Kings and State of New York. February 24, 1870.

John Henry Carragher to John Henry Clayton. March 20, 1870.

Lucy Elvira Carragher to Lucy Elvira Clayton. March 20, 1870.

The Wallabout Presbyterian Church of Brooklyn to the Franklin Avenue Presbyterian Church of the city of Brooklyn. April 19, 1870.

In Kings County—William Wilson to William White Wilson. September 14, 1870.

Rensselaer County—Frank Burt Wilber to Frank Willie Washburn. April 5, 1869.

Onondaga County—Henry Gustavus Best to Henry Gustavus Guy. August 5, 1870.

APPENDIX.

Rules of Court of Appeals as to the admission of Attorneys, Solicitors and Counselors. May 1, 1871.

GENERAL STATUTES

OF THE

STATE OF NEW YORK.

PASSED AT THE

94TH SESSION, 1871.

CHAP. 3.

AN ACT to amend an act entitled "An act to regulate the term of office of notaries public."

PASSED January 17, 1871.

The People of the State of New York, represented in Senate and Assembly, do enact as follows:

SECTION 1. The first section of chapter four hundred and forty-eight of the laws of eighteen hundred and sixty-nine, is hereby amended by adding, at the end thereof, the words, "and all notaries public appointed by the governor, during the recess of the Senate, except those appointed to fill vacancies occurring by death, resignation, change of residence or removal, shall, if their appointment be subsequently confirmed by the Senate, hold office from the time of their original appointment until the thirtieth day of March in the year next after the year in which their appointment shall be confirmed by the Senate." Terms of office of certain notaries defined.

Ante, vol. 6, 226; vol. 7, 451.

§ 2. This act shall take effect immediately.

CHAP. 11.

AN ACT providing for additional compensation to deputies, clerks and assistants, in the various departments of the State government.

PASSED January 26, 1871; three-fifths being present.

The People of the State of New York, represented in Senate and Assembly, do enact as follows:

SECTION 1. The treasurer shall pay, upon the warrant of the comptroller, from the general fund, additional compensation for the calendar year commencing January first, eighteen Additional compensation for year 1871.

hundred and seventy-one, to the deputies, assistants, clerks and messengers permanently employed in the office of the secretary of state, comptroller, treasurer, clerk of the court of appeals, attorney-general, department of public instruction, state engineer and surveyor, insurance department, to the librarians and their assistants and janitors in the state library, the private secretary of the governor, and clerks and messengers of the executive departments, to the secretary and assistant secretary of the regents of the university, to the curator of the state cabinet of natural history, and to the superintendent of the capitol and state hall, and the state geological hall, at the following rates of advance on the salaries received by them, or a proportionate amount for a less term of service: On all salaries of fifteen hundred dollars and under, an increase of thirty-five per cent; on all salaries over fifteen hundred and less than two thousand dollars, an increase of twenty-five per cent; on all salaries of two thousand dollars, an increase of fifteen per cent. The sum of thirty thousand dollars, or as much thereof as may be necessary, is hereby appropriated from the general fund to pay the advances provided for by this section.

Percentage of increase.

Appropriation.

Increase in railroad and insurance departments how repaid.

§ 2. The increased compensation hereinbefore given to the deputy and clerks in the railroad department, in the office of the engineer and surveyor, and to the deputy and clerks in the insurance department, shall be repaid by the several railroad and insurance companies, pursuant to chapter five hundred and twenty-six of the laws of eighteen hundred and fifty-five, and chapter three hundred and sixty-six of the laws of eighteen hundred and fifty-nine.

Additional compensation in canal department and canal offices.

§ 3. The treasurer shall pay from the canal fund, upon the warrant of the auditor of the canal department, additional compensation to the deputy and each of the clerks of the canal department, and to each of the clerks of the canal commissioners and canal appraisers, and to the clerk of the contracting board, for the calendar year commencing January first, eighteen hundred and seventy-one, at the following rates of advance on salaries received by them: On all salaries of fifteen hundred dollars and under, an increase of thirty-five per cent; on all salaries over fifteen hundred and less than two thousand dollars, an increase of twenty-five per cent, or a proportionate amount for a less term of service. The sum of five thousand dollars, or so much thereof as may be necessary, is hereby appropriated from the canal fund, not otherwise appropriated, to pay the advance provided for in this section.

Percentage.

Appropriation.

Increased pay to employees in military departments.

§ 4. The treasurer shall pay, on the warrant of the comptroller, out of any fund appropriated for military purposes, for the calendar year commencing January first, eighteen hundred and seventy-one, additional compensation to the assistants, clerks, messengers and janitors permanently employed in the office of the adjutant-general, inspector-general, quartermaster-general, paymaster-general, surgeon-general and commissary-general, at the rates of advance on the salaries received by them (or apportionate amount for less term of service, as provided for the assistants, clerks and messengers named in the first section of this act.

§ 5. This act shall take effect immediately.*

*Ante, vol. 1, p. 190, 191; vol. 3, p. 27, 30, 37, 71, 140, 141, 159; vol. 4, p. 252, 556; vol. 6, p. 305; vol. 7, p. 334, 358, 580.

CHAP. 12.

AN ACT supplementary to the act entitled "An act to provide for the incorporation of religious societies," passed April fifth, eighteen hundred and thirteen.

Ante, vol. 3, p. 687.

PASSED January 31, 1871; three-fifths being present.

The People of the State of New York, represented in Senate and Assembly, do enact as follows:

SECTION 1. The act entitled "An act to provide for the incorporation of religious societies," passed April fifth, eighteen hundred and thirteen, is hereby amended by adding thereto the following provisions:

1. It shall be lawful for any church or congregation, of the "Christian Orthodox Catholic Church of the Eastern Confession," now or hereafter existing in this state, to be incorporated according to the provisions of this act. The envoy extraordinary and minister plenipotentiary of Russia to the United States, and the consul-general of Russia to the United States, then acknowledged and received as such by the government of the United States, may sign a certificate in duplicates, showing the name or title by which they and their successors shall be known and distinguished as a body corporate by virtue of this act, which certificate shall be duly acknowledged or proved, in the same manner as conveyances of real estate: and one of such certificates shall be filed in the office of the secretary of state, and the other in the office of the clerk of the county in which such church may be erected or intended so to be; and thereupon such church or congregation shall be a body corporate, by the name or title expressed in such certificate, and the persons so signing the same shall be the trustees thereof. The successors in office of such envoy extraordinary and minister plenipotentiary and consul-general, for the time being acknowledged and received as aforesaid, shall by virtue of their office be the trustees of such church, in place of their predecessors.

Incorporation of Greek churches.

Duplicate certificate, how made and filed.

Who to act as trustees.

2. The trustees of every such church or congregation, and their successors, shall have all the powers and authority granted to the trustee or trustees of any church, congregation or society, by the fourth section of the act entitled "An act to provide for the incorporation of religious societies," passed April fifth, eighteen hundred and thirteen, and shall also have power to fix or ascertain the salary to be paid to any pastor or assistant pastor of such church appointed or commissioned, according to the rules and regulations of such church, but the whole real

Power of trustees.

and personal estate of any such church, exclusive of the church edifice, parsonage and school-houses, together with the land on which the same may be erected, and burying places, shall not exceed the annual value or income of three thousand dollars; but nothing herein contained shall be held or taken to repeal, alter or impair the effect of chapter three hundred and sixty of the laws of eighteen hundred and sixty.

Churches. Statute of wills, how applicable.

Inventory of church property, when and how filed. 3. The trustees of any church incorporated under this act are required to exhibit, upon oath, to the supreme court in the judicial district in which the church is situated, once in three years, an inventory of all the estate, real and personal, belonging to such church, and of the annual income thereof, which inventory shall be filed in the office of the clerk of the county in which such building is situated.

Re-incorporation of churches after dissolution. 4. Whenever any church incorporated under this act shall be dissolved, by means of any nonuser or neglect to exercise any of the powers necessary for its preservation or otherwise, the same may be re-incorporated in the mode prescribed in this act, within six years from the date of such dissolution, and thereupon all the property, real and personal, belonging to such dissolved corporation, at the time of its dissolution, shall vest in such new corporation.

Conveyances made to churches, confirmed. 5. All conveyances to any church incorporated under this act, of any real estate heretofore appropriated to the use of such church or the congregation thereof, or intended so to be, are hereby confirmed and declared valid and effectual, but

Proviso. nothing herein shall affect any suit or proceeding now pending involving the right or title to any property so conveyed.

Id. § 2. The legislature may at any time modify, alter or repeal this act.

§ 3. This act shall take effect immediately.

CHAP. 16.

AN ACT to amend section one of chapter four hundred and nine of the laws of eighteen hundred and seventy, entitled "An act to authorize circuit courts, and courts of oyer and terminer, to require the attendance of additional jurors."

Ante, vol. 7, p. 782.

PASSED January 31, 1871; three-fifths being present.

The People of the State of New York, represented in Senate and Assembly, do enact as follows:

SECTION 1. Section one of chapter four hundred and nine of the laws of eighteen hundred and seventy, is hereby amended so as to read as follows:

Court may require county clerk to draw additional petit jurors. § 1. Whenever any circuit court, or court of oyer and terminer, shall be satisfied that the public interest requires the attendance at such court, or at any adjourned term thereof, of a greater number of petit jurors than is now required to be drawn and summoned for such court, then said court may, by order entered in its minutes, require the clerk of the county to draw, and the sheriff to summon, such additional number of petit jurors as it shall deem necessary, which number shall be specified in said order. The clerk of the county in which such court is held shall forthwith bring into said court the box containing the names of the petit jurors from which jurors from said county are required to be drawn, and the said clerk shall, in the presence of said court, proceed publicly to draw the number of jurors specified in said order of such court, and when such drawing is complete the said clerk shall make two lists of the persons so drawn, each of which shall be certified by him to be a correct list of the names of the persons so drawn by him, one of which he shall file in his office and the other he shall deliver to the sheriff. The sheriff shall thereupon immediately proceed to summon the persons mentioned in such list to appear in the court in which the order requiring the attendance of such jurors shall have been made, on the day designated in such order, and the persons so summoned shall appear in obedience to such summons, and all the provisions of law relating to the summoning and the swearing in of jurors, and their punishment for non-attendance, not inconsistent with this act, shall apply to the swearing in, summoning and punishment of the jurors drawn and summoned under this act.

Manner of drawing.

Clerk to certify two lists of persons drawn

Sheriff to summon persons drawn.

Provisions of law applicable.

§ 2. This act shall take effect immediately.

CHAP. 18.

AN ACT to amend chapter one hundred and ninety-four of the Laws of eighteen hundred and forty-nine, entitled "An act to vest in the board of supervisors certain legislative powers, and to prescribe their fees for certain services," passed April third, eighteen hundred and forty-nine.

Ante, vol. 8, p. 331.

PASSED February 2, 1871; three-fifths being present.

The People of the State of New York, represented in Senate and Assembly, do enact as follows:

SECTION 1. Section first of chapter one hundred and ninety-four of the laws of eighteen hundred and forty-nine, entitled "An act to vest in the boards of supervisors certain legislative powers, and to prescribe their fees for certain services," is hereby amended so as to read as follows:

§ 1. The boards of supervisors of the several counties in the State, the county of New York excepted, at their annual meeting shall have power, within their respective counties, by a vote of two-thirds of all the members elected, to divide or alter in its bounds any town, or erect a new town, but they shall not make any alterations that shall place parts of the same

Power of board to alter boundaries or erect new towns.

Assent of majority of tax payers necessary on division of towns. town in more than one assembly district, nor where it is proposed to divide a town into two or more towns, unless the assent thereto of at least a majority of the tax payers whose names appear on the assessment roll of the town to be affected thereby for the year then next preceding, shall be given in writing to such division, upon application to the board as hereinafter provided, of at least twelve freeholders of each of the towns to be affected by the division, and upon being furnished with said assent in writing, and with a map and survey of the towns to be affected, showing the proposed alterations; and, if the application be granted, a copy of said map, with a certified statement of the action of said board thereunto annexed, shall be filed in the office of the Secretary of State, and it shall be the duty of the Secretary to cause the same to be printed with the laws of the next legislature after such division takes place, and cause the same to be published in the same manner as other laws are published.

Application and map to be presented.

Action of board, with map, to be filed with Secretary of State and be printed with session laws.

§ 2. This act shall take effect immediately.

CHAP. 25.

AN ACT appropriating money to pay for the publication of the official canvass, and for deficiency in public printing.

PASSED February 8, 1871; three-fifths being present.

The People of the State of New York, represented in Senate and Assembly, do enact as follows:

SECTION 1. The sum of one hundred thousand dollars, or so much thereof as may be necessary, is hereby appropriated out of any moneys in the treasury not heretofore appropriated, for payment for the publication of the official canvass, and also for deficiency in public printing for the year ending September thirty, eighteen hundred and seventy-one.

§ 2. This act shall take effect immediately.

CHAP. 32.

AN ACT to amend the first section of the third title of the eighth chapter of the second part of the Revised Statutes, in relation to the custody of minor children.

Ante, vol. 2, p. 156.

PASSED February 10, 1871; three-fifths being present.

The People of the State of New York, represented in Senate and Assembly, do enact as follows:

SECTION 1. The first section of the third title of the eighth chapter of the second part of the Revised Statutes, is hereby amended so as to read as follows:

§ 1. Every father, whether of full age or a minor, of a child likely to be born, or of any living child under the age of twenty-one years, and unmarried, may, by his deed or last will duly executed, or, in case such father shall be dead, and shall not have exercised his said right of appointment, then the mother, whether of full age or a minor, of every such child, may, by her deed or last will duly executed, dispose of the custody and tuition of such child during its minority, or for any less time, to any person or persons in possession or remainder.

§ 2. This act shall take effect immediately.

CHAP. 68.

AN ACT to amend "An act for the incorporation of private and family cemeteries," passed April first, eighteen hundred and fifty-four.

Ante, vol. 3, p. 754.

PASSED March 6, 1871.

The People of the State of New York, represented in Senate and Assembly, do enact as follows:

SECTION 1. The act entitled "An act for the incorporation of private and family cemeteries," passed April first, eighteen hundred and fifty-four, is hereby amended by striking out section seven, and adding after section six of said act the following:

§ 7. It shall be lawful for any person to set apart or dedicate by deed, or to devise by will, land to be used exclusively for a family cemetery or burial place for the dead, to appoint trustees to manage the affairs of such cemetery, to direct and prescribe the manner of appointment of such successors in such trusteeship, to set apart and grant to such trustees and their successors personal property or money, to constitute a fund to be used, either the principal or the interest thereof, or both, for the purpose of improving, maintaining in good order and condition, and adorning such cemetery or burial place, subject to and in accordance with the directions of the grantor or testator in such deed or will; but the lands so set apart, dedicated or devised, shall not in any case exceed the quantity limited by this act, nor shall the fund, so set apart and granted as aforesaid by will, exceed ten per cent of the clear value in excess of the debts and liabilities, other than legacies, of the estate of the testator; nor shall the land, property or money set apart and devoted by deed or otherwise under this act to the purposes of a cemetery, as in this and the subsequent section provided, be exempt from levy and sale under execution, except as now or hereafter exempt by law.

Family cemetery, may be set apart by deed or will.

Trustees to manage affairs.

Fund to maintain and adorn grounds.

Limitation of fund and quantity of ground.

Proviso as to exemptions.

§ 8. The executors, administrators or trustees of the estate

Executors, when to set apart or purchase burial place.

of any deceased person may, upon the written authorization and direction thereto of all the surviving heirs, legatees, devisees and next of kin of the testator or intestate, executed in person or by their lawful attorneys or general guardians, set apart, to be used exclusively as a family cemetery or burial place for the dead, suitable lands of the testator or intestate, or purchase with funds of the estate under their control suitable lands for such purpose, appoint trustees to manage the same, and direct and prescribe the manner of appointment of their successors, set apart and pay to the trustees so appointed by them, from the funds of the estate under their control, personal property or money, or both, of the value and to an amount limited in the authorization and direction aforesaid, to constitute a fund to be used, either the principal or the interest thereof, or both, for the purpose of improving, maintaining in good order and condition, and adorning such cemetery or burial place, subject to and in accordance with the rules and directions contained in the written authorization and direction aforesaid; but the quantity of land so set apart shall not exceed the limit prescribed in the foregoing section.

May set apart fund and direct management thereof.

Trustees to file acceptance, and copy of will and deed.

§ 9. The trustees appointed in accordance with the provisions of section seven, or of section eight, of this act, shall, before entering upon their duties as such trustees, file in the office of the clerk of the county in which the land set apart and dedicated for cemetery and burial purposes under section seven or section eight of this act is situated, their written acceptance of their appointment as such trustees, together with a copy of the deed or will, or written authorization and direction under which their appointment shall have been made, and together with a certificate signed by all the trustees who shall accept and agree to serve, and acknowledged before an officer authorized to take the acknowledgment of deeds, containing a description of the land so set apart, the title of the corporation thus proposed to be organized under this act, and the names of the trustees thereof; thereupon the said trustees and their successors shall be deemed legally incorporated, with all the rights and powers and subject to the liabilities of other corporations under this act; a certified copy of such certificate shall be evidence in all courts and places of the formation of such corporation. Said trustees and all successors thereof shall, before receiving the property, money and fund as herein provided for improving, maintaining and adorning the cemetery under their charge, execute to the surrogate of the county in which it is situated a bond, with sureties approved by the surrogate, in the penal sum of twice the principal sum of the fund placed in their charge, conditioned for the faithful preservation and application thereof, according to the rules, directions or by-laws prescribed in the instrument under which their appointment shall have been made, and from time to time renew their bond or execute a new bond whenever required so to do by said surrogate; they shall, also, at least once in each year, and oftener if required by the surrogate, file with him their account of receipt and expenditures on

Certificate, what to set forth.

Rights as a corporation.

Trustees to execute bond to surrogate.

To account to surrogate.

account or the fund in their hands, together with vouchers for all disbursements by them; they shall have the general care and management of the cemetery under their charge, subject to the rules and directions contained in the instrument or instruments by or under which their appointment shall have been made, and shall be subject to removal for neglect of duty or malfeasance in office in the same manner as trustees of other corporations.

§ 2. This act shall take effect immediately.

CHAP. 77.

AN ACT to punish mortgagors of personal property who shall fraudulently sell, assign, exchange, secrete or otherwise dispose of personal property mortgaged by them.

PASSED March 8, 1871; three-fifths being present.

The People of the State of New York, represented in Senate and Assembly, do enact as follows:

SECTION 1. Any mortgagor of personal property who shall hereafter, with intent to defraud a mortgagee or purchaser of such property, sell, assign, exchange, secrete or otherwise dispose of any personal property upon which he shall have given or executed a mortgage, or any instrument intended to operate as a mortgage, which at the time is a lien thereon, shall be deemed guilty of a misdemeanor, and, upon conviction thereof, shall be punished by a fine not exceeding three times the value of such property so sold, assigned, exchanged, secreted or otherwise disposed of, or by imprisonment in the county jail of the county in which such offense is committed not exceeding one year, or by both such fine and imprisonment.

Ante, vol. 4, p. 485.

§ 2. This act shall take effect immediately.

CHAP. 84.

AN ACT to authorize the owners and holders of certain railroad mortgage bonds made payable to bearer, to render the same payable to order only.

PASSED March 9, 1871.

The People of the State of New York, represented in Senate and Assembly, do enact as follows:

SECTION 1. It shall be lawful for any person or persons owning and holding any railroad mortgage bonds or other corporate bonds (for which a registry is not by law provided) heretofore issued or which may be hereafter issued and made payable in this State, and which are made payable to bearer, Railroad and other corporate bonds, how made non-negotiable.

to render the same non-negotiable by the owner and holder indorsing upon the same and subscribing a statement that said bond is the property of such owner. And thereupon the principal sum of money mentioned in said bond shall only be payable to such owner or his legal representatives or assigns.

Transfers, how made. § 2. The bonds described and referred to in the first section of this act may be transferred by an indorsement in blank, giving name and residence of assignor, or they may be transferred by an indorsement payable to bearer or to the order of the purchaser (naming him), subscribed by the assignor, giving name and place of residence.

See vol. 3, p. 650.

§ 3. This act shall take effect immediately.

CHAP. 95.

AN ACT to amend an act entitled "An act to authorize the formation of Gas-light Companies," passed February sixteen, eighteen hundred and forty-eight.

Ante, vol. 3, p. 849.

PASSED March 14, 1871.

The People of the State of New York, represented in Senate and Assembly, do enact as follows:

SECTION 1. The first section of the act entitled "An act to authorize the formation of gas-light companies," passed February sixteenth, one thousand eight hundred and forty-eight, is hereby amended, so as to read as follows:

Companies, how formed. § 1. Any three or more persons who may desire to form a company for the purpose of manufacturing and supplying gas for lighting the streets and public and private buildings of any city, village or town, or two or more villages or towns, not over five miles distant from each other, in this State, may make, sign and acknowledge before some officer competent to take the acknowledgment of deeds, and file in the office of the clerk of the county in which the business of the company shall be carried on, and a duplicate thereof in the office of the Secretary of State, a certificate in writing, in which shall be stated the corporate name of the said company, and the objects for which the company shall be formed, the amount of the capital stock of the said company, the term of its existence, not to exceed fifty years, the number of shares of which the stock shall consist, the number of directors, and their names, who shall manage the concerns of said company for the first year, and the name of the town and county in which the operations of the said company are to be carried on. (Certificates of incorporation, how filed.)

§ 2. The eighteenth section of said act is hereby amended so as to read as follows:

Companies may manufacture and sell gas. § 18. Any corporation formed under this act shall have full power to manufacture and sell and to furnish such quantities of gas as may be required in the city, town or village where the same shall be located, or said two or more villages or towns, not over five miles distant from each other, named in the certificate of incorporation, filed for lighting the streets and public and private buildings or for other purposes; and such corporation shall have power to lay conductors for conducting gas through the streets, lanes, alleys, squares and highways, in such city, villages or towns, with the consent of the municipal authorities of said city, villages or towns, and under such reasonable regulations as they may prescribe; and the said municipal authorities shall have power to exempt any corporation formed under the provisions of this act from taxation on their personal property for a period not exceeding three years from the organization of said corporation.

May lay conductors in streets, with consent of municipal authorities.

Personal property may be exempted from taxation.

§ 3. This act shall take effect immediately.

CHAP. 110.

AN ACT to amend an act entitled "An act in relation to the fees of county treasurers," passed May eleventh, eighteen hundred and forty-six.

PASSED March 15, 1871; three-fifths being present.

Ante, vol. 3, p. 339.

The People of the State of New York, represented in Senate and Assembly, do enact as follows:

SECTION 1. The first section of an act entitled "An act in relation to the fees of county treasurers," passed May eleventh, eighteen hundred and forty-six, is hereby amended so as to read as follows:

§ 1. The several county treasurers of this state shall hereafter receive for their services, instead of the fees now allowed by law, such compensation as shall be fixed by the respective boards of supervisors of their respective counties, not exceeding the half of one per cent for receiving, and the half of one per cent for disbursing all moneys belonging to their said counties respectively. In addition to such compensation so fixed as aforesaid, they shall be entitled to retain a commission of one per centum on every dollar belonging to the state which they shall receive and pay over, to wit: one-half of one per centum for receiving, and one-half of one per centum for disbursing, but in no case to exceed the sum of five hundred dollars. This act shall not apply to the counties of New York, Kings, Albany, Otsego, Onondaga, Erie and Westchester.

Boards of supervisors to fix compensation.

Limitation of percentage.

Commission upon state tax paid over.

Limitation of sum to be received therefor.

Act not to apply to certain counties.

§ 2. This act shall take effect immediately.

CHAP. 138.

AN ACT making an appropriation for the Antietam national cemetery for a memorial of the patriotic dead of Antietam, South Mountain and Monocacy.

PASSED March 20, 1871; by a two-thirds vote.

The People of the State of New York, represented in Senate and Assembly, do enact as follows:

SECTION 1. The treasurer shall pay on the warrant of the comptroller, out of any moneys in the treasury not otherwise appropriated, to the order of the board of trustees of the national cemetery at Antietam, the sum of seven thousand two hundred and eighty-one dollars, to be applied and expended by them as the complement of the quota of the state of New York, for the completion of the said national cemetery and of a monument to the memory of the patriotic dead of Antietam, South Mountain and Monocacy, who fell there in the late civil war.

CHAP. 164.

AN ACT to amend an act passed April fourteenth, eighteen hundred and fifty-two, entitled "An act further to amend an act entitled 'An act authorizing the incorporation of rural cemetery associations,' passed April twenty-seventh, eighteen hundred and forty-seven."

PASSED March 24, 1871.

Ante, vol. 3, p. 745.

The People of the State of New York, represented in Senate and Assembly, do enact as follows:

SECTION 1. Section four of an act passed April fourteenth, eighteen hundred and fifty-two, entitled "An act further to amend an act entitled 'An act authorizing the incorporation of rural cemetery associations,'" passed April twenty-seventh, eighteen hundred and forty-seven, is hereby amended so as to read as follows:

Notice of intention to apply for consent to purchase lands.

§ 4. Any such incorporation desiring to use any lands for cemetery purposes, or take a conveyance thereof, shall cause notice to be published once a week for six weeks, in the two newspapers published in said county nearest to the location of said proposed cemetery, of their intention to apply to the board of supervisors of such county, stating the time at which such application will be made, for the consent mentioned in the first section of this act.

Notice, what to contain.

Such notice shall contain a brief description of the land for which such consent is asked, and also their location and the number of acres. At such meeting, upon due proof of the publication of the notice above mentioned, the applicants and remonstrants, if any, may be heard in person or by counsel, and thereupon, if such board shall grant consent, it shall be lawful for such incorporation to take and hold the lands designated in such consent, not exceeding two hundred and fifty acres in any county.

Hearing before board of supervisors.

Associations may take, not exceeding 250 acres, upon consent.

§ 2. This act shall take effect immediately.

CHAP. 171.

AN ACT in relation to assessment of highway labor in certain cases.

PASSED March 24, 1871; three-fifths being present.

The People of the State of New York, represented in Senate and Assembly, do enact as follows:

SECTION 1. In all cases where there is an incorporated village or city within the limits of any town, which is by law a separate road district, and there shall be any real estate, owned by any person or corporation, situated partly within the limits of such village or city and partly without said village or city, it shall be the duty of the assessors of such town, after fixing the valuation of the whole of such real estate as now by law required, to determine what proportion of such valuation is on account of that part of said real estate lying without the limits of said city or village, and designate the same upon their assessment list.

Assessors to make separate valuation, of town and village or city lands.

§ 2. The valuation of the real estate lying without the limits of any city or village, so fixed and determined by the assessor, shall be the valuation on which the commissioners of highways of towns shall assess highway labor against the owner or owners of such real estate; and in no case shall the commissioners of highways assess any highway labor on property situated within the limits of any incorporated city or village which is by law a separate road district.

Highway commissioners, to assess labor for part lying in towns only.

§ 3. This act shall take effect immediately.

Ante, vol. 1, p. 464.

CHAP. 184.

AN ACT in relation to the publication of the laws of this state.

PASSED March 27, 1871; three-fifths being present.

The People of the State of New York, represented in Senate and Assembly, do enact as follows:

SECTION 1. Chapter three hundred and forty-five of the act entitled "An act for the publication of the session laws in two newspapers in each county of the state," passed April twenty-seven, eighteen hundred and sixty-eight, is hereby amended so as to read as follows:

Ratio per folio for publication. The publisher of each of the newspapers so designated as aforesaid, shall be entitled to receive for such publication of all laws above specified, a sum of fifty cents for each folio.

Ante, vol. 7, p. 808.

§ 2. This act shall take effect immediately.

CHAP. 188.

AN ACT to amend chapter four hundred and two of the Laws of eighteen hundred and fifty-four, being "An act for the better security of mechanics and others erecting buildings in the counties of Westchester, Oneida, Cortland, Broome, Putnam, Rockland, Orleans, Niagara, Livingston, Otsego, Lewis, Orange and Dutchess," passed April seventeenth, eighteen hundred and fifty-four.

Ante, vol. 4, p. 673.

PASSED March 27, 1871; three-fifths being present.

The People of the State of New York, represented in Senate and Assembly, do enact as follows:

SECTION 1. Section twenty of chapter four hundred and two of the Laws of eighteen hundred and fifty-four, entitled "An act for the better security of mechanics and others erecting buildings in the counties of Westchester, Oneida, Cortland, Broome, Putnam, Rockland, Orleans, Niagara, Livingston, Otsego, Lewis, Orange and Dutchess," passed April seventeenth, eighteen hundred and fifty-four, is hereby amended so as to read as follows:

Liens, how long to continue. § 20. Every lien created under the provisions of this act shall continue until the expiration of one year, unless sooner discharged by the court, or some legal act of the claimant in the proceedings; but if within such year proceedings are commenced under this act to enforce or foreclose such lien, then such lien shall continue until judgment is rendered therein, and for one year thereafter. Such lien shall also continue during the pendency of any appeal, and for one year after the determination thereof. Where a judgment is rendered, as aforesaid, it may be docketed in any county of this State, and enforced as if obtained in an action in a court of record.

Judgments, how doc[keted].

§ 2. This act shall take effect immediately.

CHAP. 208.

AN ACT in relation to the duties and liabilities of sheriffs in certain cases.

PASSED March 29, 1871; three-fifths being present.

The People of the State of New York, represented in Senate and Assembly, do enact as follows:

SECTION 1. Whenever any person, who may be indicted for any criminal offense, shall be held by any sheriff upon or by virtue of any order, writ or process issued in any civil action or proceeding, the court in which such indictment may be pending may, upon habeas corpus, or by order, take such person out of the custody of such sheriff and make such disposition of the prisoner as such court shall see fit. And it shall be the duty of such sheriff to obey such writ or order and to make such disposition of such prisoner as the court may direct; and such disposition of such prisoner shall not be deemed an escape, and no suit, action or proceeding shall be allowed or maintained against such sheriff for or by reason of his having obeyed any such writ or order.

§ 2. This act shall take effect immediately.

CHAP. 219.

AN ACT to provide redress for words imputing unchastity to a female.

PASSED March 29, 1871.

The People of the State of New York, represented in Senate and Assembly, do enact as follows:

SECTION 1. An action may be maintained by a female, whether married or single, to recover damages for words hereafter spoken imputing unchastity to her, and it shall not be necessary to allege or prove special damages in order to maintain such action. In such actions a married woman may sue alone, and any recovery therein shall be her sole and separate property.

§ 2. This act shall take effect immediately.

CHAP. 238.

AN ACT to provide for the payment of the crier and attendant of the Court of Appeals.

PASSED March 31, 1871; three-fifths being present.

The People of the State of New York, represented in Senate and Assembly, do enact as follows:

Salary of crier.

SECTION 1. From and after the passage of this act, the crief of the Court of Appeals shall receive an annual salary or fifteen hundred dollars, to be paid monthly, and the Comptroller is hereby directed to draw his warrant upon the Treasurer therefor; and the attendants of said court shall each receive five dollars for each and every day of their attendance on said court, to be paid, upon the certificate of the Clerk of said court of the number of days' attendance, by the Comptroller upon the presentation of such certificate.

Attendants to receive per diem allowance.

§ 2. This act shall take effect immediately.

CHAP. 239.

AN ACT to amend the Revised Statutes in regard to surrogates' bonds.

PASSED March 31, 1871.

The People of the State of New York, represented in Senate and Assembly, do enact as follows:

Surrogates to execute official bond.

SECTION 1. Section eighty-seven, article sixth, title two, chapter twelve, part one of the Revised Statutes, is hereby amended so as to read as follows:

§ 87. Every person hereafter appointed or elected to the office of surrogate of any county, shall, within twenty days after receiving notice of such appointment or election, execute to the people of this State, with two or more sufficient sureties, being resident freeholders, a joint and several bond, conditioned for the faithful performance of his duties, and for the application and payment of all moneys and effects that may come into his hands as such surrogate in the execution of his office. The bond of the surrogate of the city and county of New York shall be in the penal sum of fifty thousand dollars, and of the county of Kings shall be in the penal sum of twenty-five thousand dollars; and the bond of every other surrogate, of the other counties of the State, shall be in the penal sum of ten thousand dollars. Every surrogate's bond shall be properly acknowledged by all the persons who execute the same, and the sureties therein shall justify, in the aggregate, in double the penalty of the bond. Every such bond shall be recorded by the clerk of the county in whose office the same is filed, in the record of deeds in his office, and such record, or a certified copy thereof, shall be evidence

Penalty of bond.

How executed and recorded.

of the same force and effect as the original bond, in any action or proceeding against such surrogate or his sureties. Within thirty days after the passage of this act, and after his receipt of a copy of this act as provided for in the next section, every surrogate now in office shall execute a bond in conformity with the provisions of this section, and file the same with the clerk of his county, and in default thereof his office shall be deemed vacant.

New bonds, when to be filed.

Failure to file same to create vacancy.

§ 2. The Secretary of State forthwith, upon the passage of this act, shall send to each of the surrogates in this State a copy of this act.

Duty of Secretary of State.

§ 3. This act shall take effect immediately.

Ante, vol. 1, p. 854.

CHAP. 242.

AN ACT to authorize the Canal Commissioners to construct a road bridge over the Erie canal, near the Cowasselon creek, in the county of Madison.

PASSED April 1, 1871; three-fifths being present.

The People of the State of New York, represented in Senate and Assembly, do enact as follows:

SECTION 1. The Canal Commissioners are hereby authorized and directed to construct, or cause to be constructed and maintained, at the expense of the State, over the Erie canal, easterly of the Çowasselon creek, in the town of Lenox, in county of Madison, a road bridge, in such manner as they may deem advisable, and the expense of the same may be paid from any money appropriated, or to be appropriated, for extraordinary repairs of the Erie canal; provided that, after investigation and examination into all the facts in relation to the application for said bridge, the board of Canal Commissioners shall be of opinion that the State is under legal or equitable obligation to build said bridge. And, provided further that, before proceeding to the construction of any such bridge, the Canal Commissioners shall require and receive a full and sufficient release, legally executed, acknowledged and delivered free of expense to the State, of all claims for damages in consequence of the construction of said bridge, or of the approaches and embankments of the same, and also a good and sufficient license, or permission to the State, duly executed, acknowledged and delivered as aforesaid, to alter, raise or change such bridge approaches or embankments whenever necessary, which necessity is to be determined by the Canal Commissioners, from all persons whose property, rights or interest may be affected by such bridge, approaches or embankments. The said Canal Commissioners shall enter, or cause to be entered, in a book of records, to be kept in their office, all the testimony and facts appearing upon the investigation and examination above referred to, whether such determination be favorable or adverse to such application.

Construction of road bridge authorized.

Expenses, how paid.

Conditions upon which bridge is to be constructed.

Record of testimony.

§ 2. This act shall take effect immediately.

CHAP. 245.

AN ACT relating to military exemptions.

PASSED April 1, 1871; three-fifths being present.

The People of the State of New York, represented in Senate and Assembly, do enact as follows:

Exemption from jury duty.

SECTION 1. Every general and staff officer, every field officer and every commissioned and non-commissioned officer, musician and private, of the military forces of this State, who enlisted or accepted office during any of the time from April seventeenth, eighteen hundred and fifty-four, to April twenty-ninth, eighteen hundred and sixty-five, and was or may be honorably discharged after serving for seven years, shall forever after, so long as he remains a citizen of this State, be exempt from jury duty, and from the payment of highway taxes, not exceeding six days in any one year; and every such person, now assessed for highway taxes, shall be entitled to a deduction in the assessment of his real and personal property to the amount of five hundred dollars each year; the exemption and deduction herein provided for to be allowed only on the production to the assessor or assessors of the town, ward or city in which he resides, of a certificate of his honorable discharge after a service of seven years; and the same shall only be allowed during the time in which the books of the assessors are open for review and correction.

Deduction for highway tax or for property assessed.

Certificate of discharge to be produced.

§ 2. This act shall take effect immediately.

CHAP. 253.

AN ACT to protect the harbors adjoining Long Island Sound, in the county of Suffolk.

PASSED April 1, 1871; three-fifths being present.

The People of the State of New York, represented in Senate and Assembly, do enact as follows:

Removal of sand, gravel, etc., prohibited.

SECTION 1. No person shall take, or carry away, any sand, gravel or stones from the beach or shore of Long Island Sound, between Old Field Point and Mount Misery Point, in the town of Brookhaven, county of Suffolk, or from the beaches or shores separating said sound from Setauket or Port Jefferson harbors, in said town, or from either of them or from the outer bar or any of the bars or flats adjoining the channel or entrance to Smithtown harbor in said sound, or from either of them.

Landing with intent to remove sand, etc., prohibited.

§ 2. No person shall land or go upon said beaches, bars, flats or shores, or either of them, with intent to remove, or take or carry away, or to assist in removing or taking or carrying away, any gravel, sand or stones from said beaches, bars, flats or shores, or either of them.

§ 3. No person shall have, on board his boat or vessel, or on a boat or vessel in his possession, any sand, gravel or stones taken from said beaches, bars, flats or shores, or either of them, with intent to carry the same away. Removal of sand upon vessels prohibited.

§ 4. Whoever shall violate any of the provisions of this act shall forfeit the sum of two hundred dollars for each offense. Penalty for violation.

§ 5. Any person may, in his own name, or in the name of himself and the overseers of the poor of the town of Brookhaven (or of Smithtown, if the offense shall be alleged to have been committed on the bars or flats adjoining the entrance to Smithtown harbor), prosecute and recover the penalty provided in the next preceding section, for himself and the said overseers of the poor of said town, and, on a recovery, shall be entitled to retain one-half of said penalty, and the other half, after deducting one-half the expenses of the prosecution, shall be paid to the overseers of the poor of said town, for the support of the poor thereof. Prosecutions for penalties. Penalty, how applied on recovery.

§ 6. This act shall take effect immediately.

CHAP. 259.

AN ACT in relation to acrobatic exhibitions.

PASSED April 8, 1871; three-fifths being present.

The People of the State of New York, represented in Senate and Assembly, do enact as follows:

SECTION 1. It shall not be lawful for the proprietor, lessee or occupant of any hall, assembly room, or other place where acrobatic exhibitions are had, to suffer or permit any acrobat, rope-walker or other performer, to perform on any trapeze, tight-rope, wire, pole or other acrobatic contrivance, without net-work or other sufficient means of protection from danger by falling or other accident. Net work or protection from falling to be used.

§ 2. Each and every proprietor, lessee or occupant of such hall, assembly room or other place where acrobatic exhibitions are had, and every other person violating any of the provisions of this act shall be deemed guilty of a misdemeanor, and shall on conviction pay a fine of two hundred and fifty dollars for the first offense, and two hundred and fifty dollars for each subsequent offense, and in addition, imprisonment for not less than three months, nor exceeding one year; and in addition shall be held liable for all injuries occurring to any acrobat or other performer as aforesaid, resulting from any violation of this act. Penalty for violation of act. Liability for injuries to performers.

§ 3. Policemen, constables, marshals, sheriffs and their deputies, superintendents of public buildings, and inspectors of buildings, learning or knowing of any such violation, shall immediately arrest or cause to be arrested, all persons so violating the provisions of this act. Right to make arrests for violation hereof.

§ 4. This act shall take effect immediately.

CHAP. 260.

AN ACT to amend an act entitled "An act to authorize the formation of railroad corporations, and to regulate the same," passed April second, eighteen hundred and fifty, so as to permit municipal corporations to aid in the construction of railroads, passed May eighteen, eighteen hundred and sixty-nine.

Ante, vol. 8, p. 617; vol. 7, p. 517.

PASSED April 8, 1871; three-fifths being present.

The People of the State of New York, represented in Senate and Assembly, do enact as follows:

Proviso of bonding act as to competing railroads, not to apply to Cayuga and Tompkins counties.

SECTION 1. The provisions of section ten, of chapter nine hundred and seven, of the laws of eighteen hundred and sixty-nine, shall not apply to any city, town, village, or municipality in the counties of Cayuga and Tompkins.

§ 2. This act shall take effect immediately.

CHAP. 263.

AN ACT to repeal chapter one hundred and forty-five of the laws of eighteen hundred and twenty-three, entitled "An act declaring part of the river Conhocton a public highway."

PASSED April 8, 1871; three-fifths being present.

The People of the State of New York, represented in Senate and Assembly, do enact as follows:

SECTION 1. Chapter one hundred and forty-five of the laws of eighteen hundred and twenty-three, entitled "An act declaring part of the river Conhocton a public highway," is hereby repealed.

§ 2. This act shall take effect immediately.

CHAP. 274.

AN ACT to amend chapter four hundred and thirty-two of the laws of eighteen hundred and seventy, entitled "An act to amend section six of chapter eight hundred and fifty-five of the laws of eighteen hundred and sixty-nine, entitled 'An act to extend the powers of boards of supervisors, except in the counties of New York and Kings,'" passed April twenty-seventh, eighteen hundred and seventy.

Ante, vol. 7, pp. 485, 741.

PASSED April 4, 1871; three-fifths being present.

The People of the State of New York, represented in Senate and Assembly, do enact as follows:

SECTION 1. Section one of chapter four hundred and thirty-two of the laws of eighteen hundred and seventy, is hereby amended so as to read as follows:

§ 1. Section six of chapter eight hundred and fifty-five of the laws of eighteen hundred and sixty-nine, is hereby amended so as to read as follows:

Bills of justices of peace in criminal proceedings, what to contain.

§ 6. The bills rendered by justices of the peace for services in criminal proceedings shall, in all cases, contain the name and residence of the complainant, the offenses charged, the action of the justice on such complainant, the constable or officer to whom any warrant on such complaint was delivered, and whether the person charged was or was not arrested, and whether an examination was waived or had, and witnesses sworn thereon; and the account shall also show the final action of the justice in the premises. At any time within fifteen days after the board of town auditors of any town shall have filed with the town clerk thereof the certificate of accounts audited as required by law, any tax payer of said town may appeal from the action of said board of town auditors, in auditing the account of any justice of the peace, to the board of supervisors of the county. Said appeal shall be made by serving notice thereof, in writing, on the town clerk of the town, and on the clerk of the board of supervisors within the time above limited. The said supervisors shall, thereupon, audit the accounts of such justices of the peace, and their decision in the auditing and allowing of said account shall be final.

Appeals from action of town auditors in auditing justices' bills.

Decision of board of supervisors to be final.

§ 2. This act shall take effect immediately.

CHAP. 277.

AN ACT to protect the buoys moored in the Niagara river.

PASSED April 4, 1871; three-fifths being present.

The People of the State of New York, represented in Senate and Assembly, do enact as follows:

Penalty for fastening vessel, etc., to buoy.

SECTION 1. Any person mooring any vessel, scow or raft to any buoy placed by the United States in the Niagara river, or who shall in any manner make fast thereto any vessel, scow or raft, shall be liable to a penalty of fifty dollars for each and every offense.

Removal of willful destruction of buoy, how punished.

§ 2. Any person who shall remove or destroy any such buoy, by accident or otherwise, and shall not report such removal or accident to the collector of the port next entered after such removal or destruction, shall be liable to a penalty of one hundred dollars for each and every offense.

Penalties, how recovered.

§ 3. Said penalties may be recovered by complaint before any court competent to try the same.

Disposition of penalties, when recovered.

§ 4. In case penalties shall be collected for violation of this act, one-half shall be paid to the informer. The remainder of said penalties shall be paid to the collector of the port of Buffalo, to be used in maintaining and restoring said buoys.

When to sue for penalties.

§ 5. The collector of the port of Buffalo is hereby authorized to sue for and collect the penalties mentioned in this act.

§ 6. This act shall take effect immediately.

CHAP. 283.

AN ACT to amend an act entitled "An act to amend chapter nine hundred and seven, of the laws of eighteen hundred and sixty-nine, entitled 'An act to amend an act entitled An act to authorize the formation of railroad corporations, and to regulate the same,' passed April second, eighteen hundred and fifty, so as to permit municipal corporations to aid in the construction of railroads," passed May eighteen, eighteen hundred and sixty-nine, passed May eighteen, eighteen hundred and seventy.

Ante, vol. 7, pp. 517, 781; vol. 8, p. 617.

PASSED April 4, 1871; three-fifths being present.

The People of the State of New York, represented in Senate and Assembly, do enact as follows:

SECTION 1. Section four of chapter seven hundred and eighty-nine, of the laws of eighteen hundred and seventy, is hereby amended so as to read as follows:

§ 4. It shall be the duty of such commissioner, with all reasonable dispatch, to cause to be made and executed, the bonds of such municipal corporation, attested by the seal of such corporation affixed thereto, if such corporation has a common seal, and, if not, then by their individual seals, and signed and certified by said commissioners, who are hereby authorized and empowered to fix such common seal thereto, and to sign and certify such bonds. Such bonds shall become due and payable at the expiration of thirty years from their date, and shall bear interest at the rate of seven per cent per annum, payable semi-annually, and shall not exceed in amount twenty per cent of the entire taxable property within the bounds of said municipal corporation, as shown by said tax list, nor shall they exceed in amount the amount set forth in such petition. The said bonds shall also bear interest warrants, corresponding in number and amounts with the several payments of interest to become due thereon, but the commissioners may agree with any holders to register any such bonds, in which case the interest warrants on the registered bonds shall be surrendered, and the interest shall be payable only on the production of the registered bonds, which shall then be transferable only on the commissioners' records. The savings banks of this state are authorized to invest in said bonds, not to exceed ten per cent of their deposits. All taxes, except school and road taxes, collected for the next thirty years, or so much thereof as may be necessary, in any town, village or city, on the assessed valuation of any railroad in said town, village or city, for which said town, village or city has issued or shall issue bonds to aid in the construction of said railroad, shall be paid over to the treasurer of the county in which said town, city or village lies. It shall be the duty of said treasurer, with the money arising from taxes levied and collected as aforesaid, which has heretofore been, or shall hereafter be paid to him (including the interest thereon), to purchase the bonds of said town, issued by said town, to aid in the construction of any railroad or railroads, when the same can be purchased at or below par; the bonds so purchased, to be immediately canceled by said treasurer and the county judge, and deposited with the board of supervisors. In case said bonds so issued cannot be purchased at or below the par value thereof, then it shall be the duty of said treasurer, and he is hereby directed, to invest said money so paid to him as above mentioned, with the accumulated interest thereon, in the bonds of this state, or of any city, county, town or village thereof, issued pursuant to the laws of this state, or in bonds of the United States. The bonds so purchased, with the accumulated interest thereon, shall be held by said county treasurer as a sinking fund for the redemption and payment of the bonds issued or to be issued by said town, village or city in aid of the construction of said railroad or railroads. In case any county treasurer shall unreasonably refuse or neglect to comply with the provisions of this act, any tax payer in any town, village or city theretofore having issued

Railroad commissioners to issue bonds.

How executed.

Rate of interest, and when payable.

Limitation of amount.

Bonds to bear interest warrants, or to be registered.

Savings banks may invest therein.

Taxes upon railroad valuations to be paid to county treasurer.

Treasurer to purchase bonds of town therewith, and cancel same.

Investments by treasurer in other bonds.

Bonds purchased to be held as a sinking fund.

Proceedings in case of neglect of

duty by county treasurer. bonds in aid of the construction of any railroad or railroads, is hereby authorized to apply to the county judge, on petition, for an order compelling said treasurer to execute the provisions of this act. And it shall be the duty of said county judge, upon a proper case being made, to issue an order directing said county treasurer to execute the provisions of this act. All provisions of law now in force relating to the enforcement of the decrees or orders of the supreme court, are hereby declared to apply to and devolve upon said county judge in the enforcement of said order. The county treasurers of the several counties of this state, in which one or more towns are situated, which have issued bonds for railroad purposes, shall execute a bond, with two sufficient sureties to be approved by the county judge of the counties respectively, to the people of the state of New York, in such penal sum as may be prescribed by the board of supervisors of the respective counties, conditioned for the faithful performance of the duties devolving upon him, in pursuance of the provisions of this act.

Orders of county judge, how enforced.

County treasurers to execute additional official bonds.

§ 2. This act shall take effect immdiately.

CHAP. 287.

AN ACT to amend the law for the assessment and collection of taxes in cases where farms or lots are divided by county lines.

PASSED April 4, 1871*; three-fifths being present.

The People of the State of New York, represented in Senate and Assembly, do enact as follows:

SECTION 1. Section four, title two, chapter thirteen of the Revised Statutes, in relation to the assessment and collection of taxes, is hereby amended so as to read as follows:

Farms divided by town and county lines, how assessed.

§ 4. When the line between two towns or wards divides a farm or lot, the same shall be taxed, if occupied, in the town or ward where the occupant resides; except when such town line shall be also a county line, in which case each part shall be assessed in the town in which the same shall be situated, in the same manner as unoccupied lands are now assessed.

§ 2. This act shall take effect immediately.

* Ante, vol. 1, p. 362. Repealed, *post*, p.

CHAP. 293.

AN ACT to amend an act entitled "An act concerning pilots of the channel of the East river, commonly called Hell Gate," passed April fifteenth, eighteen hundred and forty-seven, and the various acts amendatory thereof, passed March twelfth, eighteen hundred and sixty, March fourteenth, eighteen hundred and sixty-five, and April sixteenth, eighteen hundred and sixty-eight.

Ante, vol. 4, p. 73; vol. 6, p. 446; vol. 7, p. 303.

PASSED April 5, 1871; three-fifths being present.

The People of the State of New York, represented in Senate and Assembly, do enact as follows:

SECTION 1. Section twelve of an act entitled "An act concerning pilots of the channel of the East river, commonly called Hell Gate," passed April fifteenth, eighteen hundred and forty-seven, is hereby amended so as to read as follows:

Rates of pilotage of 1865, extended to 1876.

§ 12. The provisions of section six of this act, as amended by chapter one hundred and fifteen of the laws of eighteen hundred and sixty-five, and chapter nine hundred and thirty-six of the laws of eighteen hundred and sixty-seven, are hereby continued in full force and effect until the first day of July, eighteen hundred and seventy-six. From and after the first day of March, eighteen hundred and seventy-one, it shall not be lawful for any Hell Gate pilot to take any apprentice in his said trade or profession of Hell Gate pilot.

Taking of apprentices prohibited.

§ 2. Section seven of the act concerning pilots of the channel of the East river, commonly called Hell Gate, passed April fifteenth, eighteen hundred and forty-seven, as amended by act passed March fourteenth, eighteen hundred and sixty-five; and again amended by act passed April sixteenth, eighteen hundred and sixty-eight, is hereby amended so as to read as follows:

Pilots first tendering services, if refused, to receive one-half pilotage.

§ 7. Any of said Hell Gate pilots, who shall first tender his services, may demand and receive from the master, owner or consignee of any vessel, of the burden of one hundred tons and upward, navigating the said channel of Hell Gate, to whom he shall have tendered his services as a pilot, and by whom the same shall have been refused, whether outward or inward bound, one-half pilotage for every foot of water such vessel may draw; which half-pilotage shall be the one-half of the rates of compensation established by the first section of this act. But such half-pilotage shall not be chargeable to any vessel under one hundred tons burden, sailing under coastwise license, and shall not be chargeable more than once for the same passage to any vessel; and in case any such vessel under one hundred tons burden navigating the said channel to or from the port of New York, shall make the usual signal for a pilot and shall refuse to receive on board or employ such pilot when he shall have tendered his services,

Not to be chargeable more than once.

When to apply to certain vessels under coastwise license.

then the master, owner or consignee of such vessel shall pay to such Hell Gate pilot such half-pilotage from the place at which such pilot shall have so offered his services. Any pilot who Proviso as to government vessels. shall pilot any government vessel through the said channel, shall be entitled to receive the same compensation therefor as is now provided by law for like services in piloting such vessel to or from the port of New York by the way of Sandy Hook.

§ 3. This act shall take effect immediately.

CHAP. 303.

AN ACT to amend "An act entitled an act to amend title sixteen, chapter eight, part three of the Revised Statutes relative to proceedings for the draining of swamps, marshes and other low or wet lands," passed May twelfth, eighteen hundred and sixty-nine.

Ante, vol. 7, p. 497; vol. 2, p. 568.

PASSED April 5, 1871; three-fifths being present.

The People of the State of New York, represented in Senate and Assembly, do enact as follows:

SECTION 1. Section six of "An act entitled an act to amend title sixteen, chapter eight, part three of the Revised Statutes relative to proceedings for the draining of swamps, marshes and other low or wet lands, and for draining farm lands," passed May twelfth, eighteen hundred and sixty-nine, is hereby amended so as to read as follows:

Commissioners to have survey and map of lands made. § 6. If it shall be adjudged and determined either by the said commissioners or by the said county judge, on appeal, that for the benefit of the public health such ditches, drains or channels should be opened, or that such lands should be drained, it shall be their duty (unless the same shall be done by the petitioner and owners of such lands to their satisfaction), to cause an accurate survey of all the lands to be made, Scale of map. and a map thereof to be made on a scale of three hundred and Map to show lands to be drained, and names of owners. thirty feet to one inch, showing all the lands that are proposed to be drained, the number of acres in each separate tract to be benefited by such drainage, the names of the owners and occupants thereof, so far as can be ascertained, Also levels, size and course of ditches. and relative levels of each tract and the width, depth, slope of sides, shape and course of such ditch or ditches or channels for the passage of water, as they shall determine to be necessary for the drainage of such lands. Employment of surveyor. And for the purposes of this act such commissioners are empowered to employ a competent civil engineer or surveyor, or to authorize such com- May enter lands to survey same and take levels. missioner as may be a civil engineer or surveyor to act as such, and to enter upon any and all the lands named in the petition or deemed necessary by such commissioners, and survey the same, and take levels thereof, and by themselves, their servants and agents to do all things necessary to the preparation for the construction and necessary for the construction and completion of all such ditches and channels for the passage of water as they shall deem to be necessary for the complete drainage of the said swamps, bog, meadow or other low lands.

§ 2. Section ten of said act is hereby amended so as to read as follows:

Commissioners to make statement of costs, land damages, etc.

§ 10. The said commissioners shall, as soon as said costs, expenses, land damages and compensation hereinbefore provided for, can be determined and ascertained, make a complete and detailed statement thereof, including all the claims of said commissioners, which statement shall be duly verified by such commissioners, or by a majority of them. They shall also, in case they have decided that the public health requires that such lands shall be drained, determine whether any, and if so, how much of the said sum shall be assessed to and paid by the incorporated village or villages, town or towns, or county in which the lands are situated, and they shall apportion all of the said sum, except so much thereof as they shall determine shall be paid by said village or villages, town or towns, or county among the several owners or occupants of such of the lands included in the said map, or adjacent thereto, as they shall deem to be directly benefited by the said drainage, in proportion to the amount of benefit which each receives therefrom; and the several amounts so adjudged shall constitute liens upon the respective tracts until paid or otherwise removed, with interest from the service of notice on such decision of the said commissioners, as hereinafter provided. Provided, that no portion of the cost, expenses, land damages and compensation provided for in and by said act, as hereby amended, shall be assessed to or be paid by any incorporated village or villages, town or towns, or county, in which the lands so to be drained shall be situated, unless a majority of the board of trustees in case of a village, a majority of the town board in case of a town, and a majority of the board of supervisors in case of a county, shall have joined in the petition required by the first section of said act, as hereby amended. The said commissioners shall file in the said office of the clerk of said county a copy of the said statement and of the said determination as to the village, or town, or county, in case there be any such, and of the said apportionment certified by them, which, or a duly authenticated copy of which, may be received in evidence in any suit or proceeding in this state. They shall also cause each person whose lands are assessed by them to pay any part of such sum, to be notified in writing of such statement, and also the supervisor of any town, or the president of any village that may be assessed, and the chairman of the board of supervisors of any county that may be assessed. A copy of such notice, with the affidavit of the person who served the same, that he delivered the original to the person to whom it was addressed, shall be evidence to show such service. Any person deeming himself aggrieved thereby,

To decide amount to be borne by town or village, when public health requires drainage.

To apportion residue upon lands benefited.

Assessments to be liens upon lands.

Towns, villages, etc., when to bear part of expense.

Statement of cost and determination as to villages, towns, etc. how filed.

Notice of filing, to whom given.

Proof of service.

Appeals to county judge, for correction of assessments. or any such officer deeming his village or town, or county aggrieved, may appeal from the decision of the said commissioners to the said county judge for the correction of such assessment, provided he serves upon said commissioners notice of said appeal within ten days after the service upon him of the notice of filing of such statement, and the party making the appeal shall, within ten days from the service of notice thereof on the commissioners, make a full statement of the grounds of his appeal, setting forth the points on which he feels aggrieved by the determination of said commissioners, and file a certified copy thereof in the office of the county clerk, and present the said statement to the county judge, and the county judge shall thereupon proceed without further delay than such as is necessary to give proper notice to the parties interested, to hear and finally determine the appeal. The county judge to whom any such appeal shall have been made, may, in his discretion, associate with him on the hearing of any such appeal the justices of sessions of such county. The county judge may award costs, on such appeal, to the successful party, not exceeding fifteen dollars besides his necessary disbursements, to be taxed by such county judge.

Notice thereof, how served.

Statement of grounds of appeal.

Duty of judge thereon.

May associate justices of sessions with him.

Costs on appeals limited.

§ 3. Section sixteen of said act is hereby amended so as to read as follows:

Water commissioners of towns and villages.

§ 16. The supervisor and commissioners of highways of the several towns, and the president of any incorporated village, as to lands in such village, shall be water commissioners of their respective towns, and, in addition to the powers now conferred by law upon them, they shall have the general charge and supervision of all dams, drains, ditches and channels made, completed or constructed in said towns under this act. Whenever it shall be necessary to open, deepen, repair, change, or do any work to maintain and keep in repair any such dams, ditches, drains or channels, and disputes shall arise between the owners of the lands on which such dams, drains, ditches or channels are situate, regarding the same, the said water commissioners, or a majority of them, shall take proceedings similar to those authorized hereby to be taken and had for the construction of such works; and the said water commissioners are hereby invested for such purpose, with the powers conferred upon original commissioners by this act. And where improvements of a nature and character similar to those hereby authorized shall have been made under the provisions of any special act, it shall be lawful for the county court of the county to cause the same to be hereafter kept in repair and improved by the said water commissioners of the town or towns under the provisions of this act; and the said water commissioner shall have like power and authority in all cases of subsoil or tile draining, when such subsoil or tile draining shall be, in their judgment, absolutely necessary for public or sanitary purposes, and the owner or occupant of any lands which such owner or occupant shall be desirous of so draining for such purposes, shall have to cross the lands of another in order to get an outlet, and the owner of such lands shall not be able to agree

To have general charge of drains, dams, etc.

Proceedings to deepen, repair or change same, in case of disputes between land owners.

To maintain improvements made under special acts.

Powers to extend to subsoil draining for sanitary purposes.

in regard thereto; and the said water commissioners shall have power and authority to make all such needful rules and orders in regard to subsoil or tile draining, as shall be necessary to promote and secure the proper drainage of all farming lands by the owners thereof, who shall desire to drain the same for public or sanitary purposes, without doing unnecessary injury to others or to the public highways in which such drain may be discharged; provided, that in all cases where an easement for such drains shall be procured upon the lands of another, the said drains shall be neatly, safely and expeditiously put down and covered, and the surface restored as nearly as may be to its original appearance. And no drains, ditches or other channels for the free passage of water authorized by this act, shall be put across any door-yard, inclosed garden, orchard or vineyard, nor shall any tree in such door-yards, inclosed garden, orchard or vineyard, or building, be removed without the owner's consent.

To make rules in regard to such subsoil or tile drainage.

Highways not to be injured thereby.

Drains to be covered

Not to cross gardens, vineyards, etc., without consent.

§ 4. Said act is hereby further amended by adding thereto the following section:

§ 20. All the powers and jurisdiction vested by this act, in the county judge, or in the county judge and justices of the sessions when associated with such officer, are hereby vested in the county court of the county in which such swamp lands or some portion of them are situated, and all proceedings heretofore commenced before the county judge, or county judge and justices of sessions when associated with such officer and now pending and undetermined, are transferred to and vested in the county court of the county in which such proceedings were so commenced and pending, with full power and jurisdiction in such court to conduct such proceedings to a final determination subject to the provisions of the act hereby amended. And in case the county judge of any county where such proceedings are or shall heretofore be pending shall be personally interested in such proceedings, it shall be his duty to require the county judge of some other county to hold county courts for the purpose of this act.

Jurisdiction under act vested in county court.

Pending proceedings vested in county court.

Proceeding, when county judge is an interested party.

§ 5. This act shall take effect immediately.

CHAP. 326.

AN ACT giving the consent of the state of New York to the purchase by and ceding jurisdiction to the United States over certain lands within this state, to be occupied as sites for light-houses and keepers' dwellings.

PASSED April 6, 1871; by a two-thirds vote.

The People of the State of New York, represented in Senate and Assembly, do enact as follows:

SECTION 1. Jurisdiction is hereby ceded to the United States over so much land as may be necessary for the construction

Jurisdiction of lands

ceded to United States. Limitation of quantity. Land, how selected. Boundaries and map, how filed.

and maintenance of light-houses and keepers' dwellings, and their appurtenances, within this state, as the United States may now or hereafter become owners of by purchase or otherwise, not to exceed eleven acres for each site, the same to be selected by an authorized officer of the United States, approved by the governor; and the boundaries of the land selected, with such approval indorsed thereon, and a map thereof filed in the office of the secretary of state and by him recorded; provided always, and the assent aforesaid is granted upon this condition, that this state shall retain a concurrent jurisdiction with the United States in and over the lands aforesaid, so far that all civil and such criminal process as may issue under authority of this state, against any person or persons charged with crimes committed within the bounds of this state, may be executed therein in the same manner as though this assent had not been granted.

State to retain concurrent jurisdiction of lands, for execution of process, etc.

Lands to be selected for certain light houses and keepers' dwellings.

§ 2. The foregoing shall be applicable only to the lands selected, approved and owned as aforesaid, and a survey thereof, filed and recorded as above provided, for the construction of the following light-houses and keepers' dwellings, namely: On Fisher's Island, eastern end of Long Island sound, New York, ten and three-tenths acres, more or less. On Barber's Point, Lake Champlain, New York, nine acres, more or less. On Bluff Point, Valcour Island, Lake Champlain, New York, two acres, more or less. On the west bank of Orchard creek, near its mouth, in Orleans county, purchased from Abram V. Clark of the same county, one-half acre, more or less.

Title to lands, how acquired, in case of inability to purchase same.

§ 3. In case the United States shall desire to purchase any portion of the lands selected in pursuance of the provisions of the first section of this act, and shall be unable to agree for the purchase of the same, it shall have the right to acquire title in the manner prescribed in the act entitled "An act ceding jurisdiction to the United States over land to be occupied as sites for light-houses and keepers' dwellings within this state," passed April twenty-four, eighteen hundred and sixty-seven.

§ 4. This act shall take effect immediately.

CHAP. 348.

AN ACT to authorize the canal commissioners to construct a swing bridge over the Erie canal on Buffalo street, in the city of Rochester, and to use the materials of the old bridge in constructing a bridge over said canal to connect Munger and Averill streets in said city.

PASSED April 7, 1871; three-fifths being present.

The People of the State of New York, represented in Senate and Assembly, do enact as follows:

SECTION 1. The canal commissioners are hereby authorized and required to construct a swing or turn-table bridge over the Erie canal, in the city of Rochester, at a point where said canal is intersected by Buffalo street, in place of the bridge now over said canal at the point aforesaid. Said swing bridge shall be located as near as practicable on the line of the present bridge, and to be wholly within the lines of Buffalo street. Swing bridge at Rochester. Location thereof.

§ 2. The said commissioners are hereby authorized to use so much of the materials in the abutments and superstructures of the old bridge as may be necessary in the construction of a bridge over the Erie canal, to connect Averill and Munger streets, in said city. Materials of old bridge, how used.

§ 3. This act shall take effect immediately.

CHAP. 351.

AN ACT in relation to canal bridges in the village of Norwich, and making an appropriation therefor.

PASSED April 7, 1871; three-fifths being present.

The People of the State of New York, represented in Senate and Assembly, do enact as follows:

SECTION 1. The canal commissioner in charge on the middle division of the canals is hereby authorized and directed to take down and remove the iron bridge across the Chenango canal on East Main street in the village of Norwich, and to re-erect the same across said canal on Rexford street in said village, in place of the dilapidated and unsafe wooden bridge at present existing across said canal on Rexford street, or at such other point or place on any of the canals in his division, as he may deem most beneficial to the state. Canal commissioner to remove East Main street bridge. To re-erect bridge at Rexford street.

§ 2. The canal commissioner in charge of the middle division of the canals is further authorized and directed to cause to be constructed across the Chenango canal on East Main street, in the village of Norwich, a swing or turn-table bridge, To construct swing bridge at East Main street.

of such plan or pattern as he shall deem most advisable, but of sufficient size and capacity to accommodate the public, at an expense of not more than four thousand five hundred dollars to the state.

Cost thereof limited.

Payment for work.

§ 3. The treasurer shall pay on the warrant of the auditor of the canal department, out of any money appropriated for ordinary or extraordinary repairs of the canals, such sum, not exceeding four thousand five hundred dollars, as may be necessary to defray the cost of removing the iron bridge and constructing the swing or turn-table bridge, as provided in the first and second sections of this act.

§ 4. This act shall take effect immediately.

CHAP. 352.

AN ACT to authorize the construction of a bridge over the Chenango canal in the city of Binghamton, at its intersection with Chenango street, in said city.

PASSED April 7, 1871; three-fifths being present.

The People of the State of New York, represented in Senate and Assembly, do enact as follows:

Canal commissioner to construct swing bridge.

SECTION 1. The canal commissioner in charge on the middle divison of the canals is hereby authorized and directed to construct, or cause to be constructed, a swing bridge, in place of the old and decayed bridge, at the intersection of Chenango street with the Chenango canal, in the city of Binghamton, at the expense of the state, which expense shall not exceed the sum of four thousand dollars over and above the amount of material in the old bridge, its foundations and approaches, which shall be, so far as practicable, used in the construction of said swing bridge, and preparing its foundations and approaches. The swing bridge hereby directed to be constructed shall be of the plan to be approved by said commissioner, and the expense of building said swing bridge over and above the material of the old bridge, to be used as by this act prescribed, shall be paid out of any moneys appropriated or to be appropriated for ordinary or extraordinary repairs on the middle division of the canals.

Expense limited.

Use of materials of old bridge.

Payment of expenses.

Payment for work.

§ 2. The treasurer shall pay on the warrant of the auditor of the canal department, out of any moneys appropriated for ordinary or extraordinary repairs of the canal, such sum, not exceeding four thousand dollars, as may be necessary to defray the cost of removing the old bridge, and constructing the swing bridge, as provided in the first section of this act.

§ 3. This act shall take effect immediately.

CHAP. 359.

AN ACT to amend an act entitled "An act to revise and consolidate the general acts relating to public instruction.

Ante, vol. 6, p. 304.

PASSED April 7, 1871; three-fifths being present.

The People of the State of New York, represented in Senate and Assembly, do enact as follows:

SECTION 1. Section fifty, article six, of an act entitled "An act to revise and consolidate the general acts relating to public instruction," passed May second, eighteen hundred and sixty-four, is hereby amended so as to read as follows:

§ 50. The trustees may expend in necessary and proper repairs of each school-house under their charge a sum not exceeding twenty dollars in any one year; they may also expend a sum not exceeding fifty dollars in the erection of necessary out buildings, where the district is wholly unprovided with such buildings; they may also make any repairs and abate any nuisances pursuant to the direction of the school commissioners hereinbefore provided; they may also purchase globes, maps and other apparatus such as in their judgment the interest and welfare of the school requires, but the aggregate cost thereof, estimating and including the value of school apparatus now owned by any school district, shall not exceed the sum of fifty dollars, unless authorized by the vote of a district meeting duly called; they may also provide fuel, pails, brooms and other implements necessary to keep the school-house or houses clean, and make them reasonably comfortable for use, and not provided for by a vote of the district; and may also provide for building fires and cleaning the school room by arrangement with the teacher or otherwise. They shall provide the bound blank books for the entering of their accounts, and the keeping of the school lists, the records of the district, and the proceedings of district and trustee meetings. Whenever it shall be necessary for the due accommodation of the children of the district they may hire, temporarily, any room or rooms for the keeping of schools therein. Any expenditure made or liability incurred in pursuance of this section shall be a charge upon the district, and the trustees or trustee may assess and collect the same in the same manner as other school taxes are collected. When, under the provisions of this act, any liability be incurred, the trustees or trustee may draw an order on the collector of the school district for the same, making it payable at such time as may be agreed upon, but not less than forty days from the date of the order, unless the funds are already provided for the same, and, having drawn the order in the manner as above, it shall be the duty of the trustee or trustees to provide for the payment of the same.

Expenditures by trustees, for repairs of school-house and for out-buildings.

Abatement of nuisances.

Purchase of globes and apparatus.

Fuel, brooms, etc.

Building fires and cleaning rooms.

Account and record books.

Hiring school-houses.

Expenditures by trustees, how assessed.

Orders, how drawn upon district collector.

Ante, vol. 6, p. 337.

Collector to give notice of receiving taxes.

§ 2. Section eighty-four of said act is hereby amended so as to read as follows:

§ 84. The collector, on the receipt of a warrant for the collection of taxes, shall give notice to the tax payers of the district by publicly posting, written or printed, or partly written and partly printed, notices, in at least three public places in such district; one of which shall be on the outside of the front door of the school-house, stating that he has received such warrant, and will receive all such taxes as may be voluntarily paid to him within two weeks from the time of posting said notice; and in case the whole amount shall not be so paid in, the collector shall forthwith proceed to collect the same. He shall receive for his services, on all sums paid in as aforesaid, one per cent, and upon all sums collected by him after the expiration of the time mentioned, five per cent; and in case a levy and sale shall be necessarily made by such collector he shall be entitled to traveling fees, at the rate of ten cents per mile, to be computed from the school-house in such district.

Collection of unpaid taxes.

Collection fees.

Ante, vol. 6, p. 344.

CHAP. 361.

AN ACT to facilitate the admission of certain wills, as evidence in courts of justice.

PASSED April 7, 1871.

The People of the State of New York, represented in Senate and Assembly, do enact as follows:

SECTION 1. An exemplified copy of the last will and testament of any deceased person, which shall have been admitted to probate and recorded in the office of the surrogate of any county in this state, before the first day of January, in the year one thousand eight hundred and thirty, shall be admitted in evidence, in any of the courts of this state, without the proofs and examinations taken on the probate thereof, and whether such proofs and examinations shall have been recorded or not, with like effect as if the original of such will had been produced and proven in such court. And the recording of such will shall be deemed evidence that the same was duly admitted to probate.

§ 2. This act shall take effect immediately.

CHAP. 378.

AN ACT to amend an act entitled "An act authorizing the incorporation of rural cemetery associations," passed April twenty-seventh, eighteen hundred and forty-seven, and all supplementary acts appertaining thereto.

Ante, vol. 3, p. 745.

PASSED April 8, 1871.

The People of the State of New York, represented in Senate and Assembly, do enact as follows:

Trustees may enter upon and improve lots, on removal of dead.

SECTION 1. Whenever any person or person owning or having in possession a burial lot in any incorporated cemetery shall have vacated the same by a removal of all the dead buried on said lot, and shall have left said lot in a broken and uncultivated condition for the period of one month, or more, from the date of such removal, it shall then be lawful for the trustees of such incorporated cemetery to enter on said vacated lot for the purpose of improving and beautifying the same, and grade, cut, fill or otherwise change the surface of the same, as shall, in their judgment, be for the improvement of said lot and the general improvement of such cemetery grounds, not reducing, however, the area of said lot. The cost and expense thereof shall be chargeable to said lot, in a sum not exceeding ten dollars, and not against the late owners or persons having had in possession said lot.

Expense, how charged.

Trustees may sell lots for default, in payment of such expense.

§ 2. If the person or persons owning said vacant lot shall not, within six months after such expense shall have been incurred, as provided by the first section of this act, repay to said trustees the sum so expended and authorized, it shall then be lawful for such trustees to sell said lot to pay the cost of such improvement, at public vendue, on said cemetery grounds, previous notice of such sale having been posted at the main entrance of said cemetery, at least ten days prior to the day of such sale, and shall pay any surplus arising from such sale, on demand, to the person or persons, or either of them, last in occupation of said lot.

Notice of sale.

Disposition of surplus from sale.

§ 3. This act shall take effect immediately.

CHAP. 415.

AN ACT in relation to the fees of sheriffs, except in the counties of New York, Kings and Westchester.

PASSED April 12, 1871; three-fifths being present.

The People of the State of New York, represented in Senate and Assembly, do enact as follows:

Sheriff's fees, except in

SECTION 1. For the following service hereafter done and performed by the sheriffs of the counties of this state, except certain counties. the counties of New York, Kings and Westchester, the following fees shall be allowed:

For serving summons or complaint. 1. For serving a summons, complaint or any other paper issued in any action, the sum of one dollar; and for necessary travel in making such service, the sum of six cents per mile to and from the place of service, to be computed in all cases from the court-house of the county, and if there are two or more court-houses, to be computed from that nearest to the place of service. Travel fees, and how computed.

Taking bonds. 2. For taking a bond of a plaintiff in proceedings for the claim and delivery of personal property or for taking a bond from either the plaintiff or defendant, or any other party, in any case where he is authorized to take the same, the sum of fifty cents.

Copy of bond. 3. For a certified copy of every such bond, twenty-five cents.

Serving attachment, executions or warrants. 4. For serving an attachment for the payment of money, or an execution for the collection of money, or a warrant for the same purpose issued by the comptroller or by any county treasurer, for collecting the sum of two hundred and fifty dollars or less, three cents per dollar; and for every dollar collected more than two hundred and fifty, the sum of two cents. Percentage. Mileage upon executions. For mileage on every execution, the sum of ten cents per mile for going only, to be computed from the court-house. Entering execution, etc. For receiving and entering such execution on their books and searching for property, the sum of fifty cents; How chargeable. which sum shall be a charge against, and to be collected of, the person by whom the said execution was issued, except when he is a county clerk, or of the person in whose favor the judgment was rendered, except as is otherwise hereinafter provided. How taxed in case of judgments. The said sum of fifty cents in the case of judgments, hereafter recovered, shall be one of the disbursements to be included in the bill of costs taxed in favor of the party entitled thereto. In cases where judgment has been already obtained, the said sum shall be collected by the sheriff from the defendant in the execution in the same manner as his other fees are now collected. Fees for advertising sale of real estate, how paid. The fees allowed by law and paid by such sheriff to any printer for publishing an advertisement of the sale of real estate, for not more than six weeks, and for continuing such advertisement more than six weeks, or for publishing the postponement of any such sale, the expense of such continuance or postponement shall be paid by the party requiring the same. Fees for serving executions, and for advertising, how collected. The fees herein allowed for the service of an execution, and for advertising thereon, shall be collected by virtue of such execution in the same manner as the sum therein directed to be levied; but when there shall be several executions against the defendant at the time of advertising his property in the hands of the same sheriff, there shall be but one advertising fee charged on the whole, and the sheriff shall elect on which execution he will receive the same.

Sheriff's deed. 5. For drawing and executing a deed pursuant to a sale of real estate, two dollars, to be paid by the grantee in such deed.

6. For serving a writ of possession, assistance or of restitution; putting any person entitled into the possession of premises, and removing the tenant, one dollar and fifty cents; and the same compensation for traveling to serve such writ, as is herein allowed on the service of a summons. Writ of possession, restitution, etc. Removal of tenants.

7. For taking a bond for the liberties of the jail, one dollar. Summoning a jury upon a writ of inquiry, or in any case where it shall become necessary to try the title to any personal property, attending such jury and making and returning the inquisition, two dollars and fifty cents. For summoning a jury in pursuance of the warrant or precept of commissioners appointed to inquire concerning the lunacy, idiocy or habitual drunkenness of any person, for each juror summoned the sum of twenty-five cents; for attending such jury when required, one dollar. For summoning a jury in any case not hereinbefore mentioned, one dollar; and for attending such jury when required, one dollar. Bond for jail liberties. Summoning of juries.

8. Attending before any officer with a prisoner for the purpose of having him surrendered in exoneration of his bail, or attending to receive a prisoner so surrendered, who was not committed at the time, and receiving such prisoner into his custody in either case, one dollar. Receiving or attending prisoners.

9. For attending a view, two dollars per day, and for going and returning, eight cents for each mile actually traveled. Attending view.

10. For serving an attachment against the property of a debtor under the provisions of chapter five of the second part of the Revised Statutes, or against a ship or vessel under the provisions of the eighth title of chapter eight of part third thereof, one dollar, with such additional compensation for his trouble and expenses in taking possession of and preserving the property attached as the officer issuing the warrant shall certify to be reasonable; and when the property so attached shall afterward be sold to the sheriff, he shall be entitled to the same poundage on the sum collected as if the sale had been made under an execution. For making and returning an inventory and appraisal such compensation to the appraisers, not exceeding one dollar to each per day, for each day actually employed, as the officer issuing the attachment shall allow, and twenty-five cents per folio for drafting, and twelve and a-half cents per folio for copying the inventory. For selling any property so attached, and for advertising such sale, the same allowance as for sales on execution. Attachment against debtors, or vessels. Preserving property attached. Poundage. Inventory and appraisal. Sale of property attached.

11. Attending any term of the supreme court or of the county court of any county, per day, three dollars. Attendance upon courts.

§ 2. All provisions of former acts fixing compensation for above services, and inconsistent with the provisions hereof, are hereby repealed. Repeal.

§ 3. This act shall take effect immediately.

Ante, vol. 2, pp. 668, 778; vol. 3, pp. 71, 859; vol. 4, pp. 657, 698; vol. 6, p. 551; vol. 7, p. 459.

CHAP. 419.

AN ACT to authorize the sale of unoccupied lands of burial ground and rural cemetery associations.

PASSED April 12, 1871; three-fifths being present.

The People of the State of New York, represented in Senate and Assembly, do enact as follows:

Supreme court may order sale of lands. SECTION. 1. It shall be lawful for the supreme court of this state, upon the application of the trustees of any burial ground or rural cemetery association, in case such court shall deem it proper, to make an order for the sale of any real estate belonging to such burial ground or rural cemetery association, May direct application of moneys therefrom. and to direct the application of the moneys arising therefrom by such trustees to such uses as such trustees, by the consent and approbation of such court, shall conceive to be most for the interest of the association to which the real estate so sold did belong. Grounds used for interments not to be sold. Provided, that no part or portion of the real estate of any burial ground or rural cemetery association which has been, now is, or hereafter may be used for actual interments, shall be sold in pursuance of the provisions of this act.

Proviso as to sales of real estate. § 2. No real estate of any rural cemetery or rural cemetery association shall be sold otherwise than in pursuance of the act or acts under which such cemetery or association was incorporated, nor for any other than cemetery purposes except as provided by section one of this act; and all acts and parts Repeal. of acts inconsistent with the provisions of this act are hereby repealed.

§ 3. This act shall take effect immediately.

Ante, vol. 8, pp. 745, 754; vol. 7, pp. 468, 777.

CHAP. 456.

AN ACT to amend the banking laws of this state.

PASSED April 13, 1871.

The People of the State of New York, represented in Senate and Assembly, do enact as follows:

SECTION 1. The provisions of section three of chapter four hundred and seventy-five, laws of eighteen hundred and sixty-seven, relating to the deposit of securities by banking associations and individual bankers with the superintendent of the banking Deposit of securities by banking associations and individual bankers. department, are hereby construed as follows, to wit: That after the passage of the said act, banking associations or individual banks organized pursuant to the provisions of that act, or of the banking laws of this state, either before or subsequent to the passage thereof, and not issuing circulating notes, shall, before commencing business, deposit with the superintendent, five thousand dollars in the stocks of this state or of the United States, bearing not less than six per cent interest, to be held by him as therein provided and for the purposes therein enumerated, the same to be in lieu of the deposit of one hundred thousand dollars required of banking associations, and of fifty thousand dollars required of individual bankers issuing circulating notes.

Ante, vol. 7, p. 107.

Deposits on discontinuing banking, without giving notice of intention.

§ 2. Whenever any banking association or individual banker has made a final deposit of cash or securities with the superintendent of the banking department for the purpose of redeeming its circulating notes, without giving notice of intention to discontinue the business of banking, and in pursuance thereof the superintendent has published the required notice that the notes of such bank will be redeemed by him for six years; and whenever the said six years shall have expired, and the banking association or individual banker shall be authorized to withdraw the cash or securities so deposited, such banking association or individual banker shall deposit with the superintendent of the banking department five thousand dollars in the stocks of this state or of the United States, bearing not less than six per cent interest, in like manner and for the like purposes that newly organized banks are required by the last preceding section to do. But such deposit need not be made when prior to the expiration of the term of redemption, such banking association or individual banker shall have given notice of intention to discontinue, and shall in fact have discontinued the business of banking under the laws of this state.

Bank superintendent to make examination of capital, before banks commence business.

§ 3. Whenever any banking association or individual banker shall file with the superintendent of the banking department the requisite certificate prior to commencing the business of banking under the laws of this state, it shall be the duty of the superintendent, and he shall have power before such bank shall be authorized to commence business, to examine or cause an examination to be made in order to ascertain whether the requisite capital of such bank has been paid in cash; and when upon such examination, or upon the presentation of evidence satisfactory to him it shall appear that the requisite capital has been in good faith subscribed and paid in, in cash, he shall issue his certificate to that effect in form duly authorizing such bank to commence business; and it shall be unlawful for any banking association or individual banker to commence the business of banking until such certificate and authority have been granted. The expense of making such examination shall be certified by the superintendent in such sum as he shall deem just and reasonable, and shall be paid by the institution so examined.

To issue certificate of authority.

Expense of examination, how paid.

Bank superintendent to require banks to make up deficiency when

§ 4. Whenever it shall appear from any report of any banking association or individual banker, or the superintendent shall have reason to believe that the capital of such bank is reduced, by impairment or otherwise, below the amount required by law, or by its certificate or articles of association, capital is impaired. it shall be the duty of the superintendent, and he shall have power to require such banking association or individual banker to make good the deficiency so appearing; and to give effect to such requisition, he shall have power to examine, or cause to be examined any such bank, to ascertain the amount of such impairment or reduction of capital, and whether the deficiency has been made good in compliance with his requisition; and if any such banking association or individual banker shall neglect for ninety days after such requisition has been made, to make good the deficiency so appearing or found to exist, it shall be the duty of the superintendent to refer the same to the attorney-general, whose duty it shall then become to institute such proceedings against such banking association or individual banker as are now authorized in the case of insolvent corporations. The expense of any examinations that shall be made pursuant to the provisions of this section, shall be paid by the bank so examined, in such sum as the superintendent shall certify to be just and reasonable.

May cause examination of capital to be made. To report neglect to make good deficiency to attorney-general. Attorney-general to institute proceedings. Expense, how paid.

§ 5. This act shall take effect immediately.

CHAP. 457.

AN ACT to establish the southerly bounds of the state lands at Clinton prison.

PASSED April 13, 1871; by a two-thirds vote.

The People of the State of New York, represented in Senate and Assembly, do enact as follows:

SECTION 1. The southerly bounds of the two hundred acres of land conveyed to the state of New York by St. John B. L. Skinner and others, in eighteen hundred and forty-four, for a prison site at Dannemora, is hereby fixed and determined as and at the center of Cook street in the said village of Dannemora, and it is hereby declared that the said two hundred acres do not extend, and the state has no right or title south of the said center of Cook street aforesaid.

§ 2. This act shall take effect immediately.

CHAP. 475.

AN ACT to amend an act entitled "An act to amend the several acts relating to the powers of the commis sioners of emigration, and for the regulation of the marine hospital," passed April thirteenth, eighteen hundred and fifty-three.

PASSED April 13, 1871; three-fifths being present.

The People of the State of New York, represented in Senate and Assembly, do enact as follows:

SECTION 1. Section thirteen of the act entitled "An act to amed the several acts relating to the powers of the commissioners of emigration, and for the regulation of the marine hospital," passed April thirteenth, eighteen hundred and fifty-three, is hereby amended so as to read as follows:

§ 13. The amount for which the master, owner or owners, consignee or consignees of any such ship or vessel bringing emigrants or passengers to the city of New York, may commute for any bond or bonds authorized or required by or pursuant to the seventh section of chapter five hundred and twenty-three of the laws of eighteen hundred and fifty-one, shall from and after the passage of this act be one dollar and fifty cents for each and every such passenger. Rates of commutation payable by ship-masters, etc., on account of emigrants, etc.

§ 2. All acts and parts of acts inconsistent with this act are hereby repealed. Repeal.

§ 3. This act act shall take effect immediately.

Ante, vol. 4, p. 883.

CHAP. 481.

AN ACT to amend an act passed May second, eighteen hundred and sixty-four, and entitled "An act to amend an act entitled 'An act to authorize the formation of corporations for manufacturing, mining, mechanical or chemical purposes,'" passed February seventeenth, eighteen hundred and forty-eight.

Ante, vol. 6, p. 299; vol. 8, p. 733.

PASSED April 13, 1871.

The People of the State of New York, represented in Senate and Assembly, do enact as follows:

SECTION 1. The second section of the act entitled "An act to amend an act entitled 'An act to authorize the formation of corporations for manufacturing, mining, mechanical or chemical purposes,'" passed February seventeenth, eighteen hundred and forty-eight, passed May second, eighteen hundred and sixty-four, is hereby amended so as to read as follows:

Mortgaging of real or personal estate, to secure debts.

§ 2. Any corporation formed under the said act, passed February seventeenth, eighteen hundred and forty-eight, or of the acts amending or extending the said act, may secure the payment of any debt heretofore contracted, or which may be contracted by it, in the business for which it was incorporated, by mortgaging all or any part of the real or personal estate of such corporation; and every mortgage so made shall be as valid to all intents and purposes, as if executed by an individual owning such real or personal estate, provided, that the written assent of the stockholders, owning at least two-thirds of the capital stock of such corporation, shall first be filed in the office of the clerk of the county where the mortgaged property is situated.

Validity of mortgage.

Assent of two-thirds of capital requisite.

§ 2. This act shall take effect immediately.

CHAP. 482.

AN ACT to amend an act entitled "An act in relation to the powers and jurisdiction of surrogates' courts," passed April twenty-fifth, eighteen hundred and sixty-seven.

Ante, vol. 7, p. 167.

PASSED April 13, 1871.

The People of the State of New York, represented in Senate and Assembly, do enact as follows:

SECTION 1. Section one of chapter seven hundred and eighty-two of the laws of eighteen hundred and sixty-seven, entitled "An act in relation to the powers and jurisdiction of surrogates' courts," passed April twenty-fifth, eighteen hundred and sixty-seven, is hereby amended so as to read as follows:

Accounting by testamentary trustees or guardians.

§ 1. The surrogate shall have power and jurisdiction to compel testamentary trustees or guardians to render accounts of their proceedings in the same manner as executors, administrators and guardians appointed by such surrogate are now required to account (and may require security therefrom or remove such testamentary trustees or guardians in the same manner as now provided for the giving of security by, or the removal of executors, administrators or guardians.

May require security.

§ 2. This act shall take effect immediately.

CHAP. 486.

AN ACT in relation to the qualifications of persons to be admitted to practice in the courts of this state as attorneys, solicitors and counselors.

PASSED April 18, 1871.

The People of the State of New York, represented in Senate and Assembly, do enact as follows:

SECTION 1. It shall be the duty of the judges of the court of appeals, or a majority of them, within twenty days after the passage of this act, to establish such rules and regulations as they may deem proper, in relation to the admission of persons hereafter applying to be admitted as attorneys, solicitors and counselors in all the courts of this state, a copy of which said rule, within five days after the adoption thereof, shall be filed in the office of the secretary of state, and shall be published by him in the session laws of eighteen hundred and seventy-one; * and he shall transmit a printed copy of such rules to the clerk of each of the counties of this state, and also to the chief justice of each of the general terms in this state. **Rules, when to be adopted. How filed and published by secretary of state. How distributed.**

§ 2. The rules established as above provided shall not be changed or amended, except by a vote majority of the judges of the court of appeals. **Rules, how amended.**

§ 3. Every male citizen of the age of twenty-one years hereafter applying to be admitted to practice as attorney, solicitor or counselor in the courts of record of this state, shall be examined by the justices of the supreme court, or a committee appointed by said court at a general term thereof, and if such persons so applying shall be found to have complied with such rules and regulations as may be prescribed by the court of appeals and shall be approved by said justice of the supreme court for his good character and learning, the court shall direct an order to be entered by the clerk thereof stating that such person has been so examined and found to possess the requisite qualifications required by the constitution, and the rules established by the court of appeals, and thereupon such person shall be entitled to practice as an attorney, solicitor and counselor in all the courts of record of this state until he shall be suspended from such practice for cause as provided in sections eighty-one, eighty-two and eighty-three of part one, chapter five, title four of the Revised Statutes, entitled "Of judicial officers." Nothing in this act contained shall be taken or construed to affect the provision of chapter two hundred and sixty-seven of the laws of eighteen hundred and fifty-nine, or chapter two hundred and two of the laws of eighteen hundred and sixty. **Examination of applicants for admission. Requisites for admission. Order of general term, how entered. Effect thereof. Albany and Columbia college law schools excepted.**

§ 4. This act shall take effect immediately.

* See Appendix for rules adopted by Court of Appeals.

CHAP. 535.

AN ACT to extend the operation and effect of the act passed February seventeenth, one thousand eight hundred and forty-eight, entitled "An act to authorize the formation of corporations for manufacturing, mining, mechanical or chemical purposes."

PASSED April 15, 1871.

The People of the State of New York, represented in Senate and Assembly, do enact as follows:

Act extended to purchasing lands for homesteads, etc. SECTION 1. Any three or more persons may organize themselves into a corporation in the manner specified and required in and by the act entitled "An act to authorize the formation of corporations for manufacturing, mining, mechanical or chemical purposes," passed February seventeenth, eighteen hundred and forty-eight, for the purpose of purchasing, acquiring and improving real estate for residences and homesteads, and apportioning and distributing the same among the stockholders and members of such corporation. Powers of corporation. The corporation so formed shall be subject to all the provisions and obligations of the act aforesaid, and the acts amendatory thereof, and it shall have power to take and hold, by purchase, contract, or lease, and convey such real estate as shall be necessary to carry out the objects of said corporation, and it may distribute and apportion the same among its members and stockholders in such manner as shall be determined by its by-laws; Limitation of value of real estate. provided, however, that it shall not be lawful for said corporation to hold at any one time real estate, the market value of which shall exceed the sum of five hundred thousand dollars.

§ 2. This act shall take effect immediately.

Ante, vol. 6, p. 299; vol. 8, p. 738.

CHAP. 537.

AN ACT requiring commissioners of towns, cities and villages, appointed under the several acts to facilitate the construction of railroads in this state, to present bonds and coupons paid by them before the boards of auditors in towns, cities and villages, and providing for the cancellation and preservation of the same.

PASSED April 17, 1871; three-fifths being present.

The People of the State of New York, represented in Senate and Assembly, do enact as follows:

Railroad commissioners to SECTION 1. The commissioners appointed under and by virtue of the several acts to facilitate the construction of railroads in this state, and who have been duly authorized under said laws to issue bonds of any town, city or village therein, are hereby required to present before the board of auditors of their respective towns, cities or villages, whose duty it is annually, to examine and audit the receipts and disbursements of either town, city or village officers at each annual meeting of said boards of town auditors, or the auditing board in any city or village, all such bonds and coupons thereof which have been paid by them respectively during the year then ending; also to render a written statement or report annually to said board showing in items all their receipts and expenditures, with vouchers. It shall be the further duty of said commissioners to loan on proper security or collaterals, or deposit in some solvent bank or banking institution, at the best rate of interest they may be able to obtain (not exceeding seven per cent), all moneys that shall come into their hands by virtue of their office, and not needed for current liabilities, and all interest or earning accruing from such loans or deposits shall be credited to their respective towns, cities or villages, and accounted for in their annual settlements with the said boards of auditors.

Present bonds and coupons, when paid, to board of auditors

To render account of receipts and disbursements.

To loan moneys on hand, on proper security.

Interest therefrom, how credited.

§ 2. It shall be the duty of the several boards of town auditors or any auditing board in the cities or villages of this state, before whom such bonds or coupons thereof may be presented, in pursuance of section one of this act, to cancel the same, by cutting out a portion of each bond or coupon so presented, in such manner as to effectually prevent the repayment of the same.

Cancellation of bonds and coupons.

§ 3. All bonds and coupons so presented and canceled shall be deposited for safe-keeping and future reference in the office of the clerk of the county in which such towns, cities or villages are respectively situated, and said boards of town auditors or auditing boards in any city or village, shall prepare and sign a certificate, showing a full description of all bonds or coupons so canceled and deposited by them, and shall file said certificate in the office of the clerk of their respective towns and villages, and in cities in the office of the clerk of the city.

Canceled bonds and coupons, how filed.

Certificate thereof, how filed.

§ 4. This act shall take effect immediately.

CHAP. 548.

AN ACT to amend an act entitled "An act relative to the care and education of deaf mutes, passed April twelfth, eighteen hundred and seventy, and amendatory of an act to provide for the care and education of indigent deaf mutes under the age of twelve years," passed April twenty-fifth, eighteen hundred and sixty-three.

PASSED April 19, 1871; three-fifths being present.

Ante, vol. 7, p. 669; vol. 6, p. 105.

The People of the State of New York, represented in Senate and Assembly, do enact as follows:

Care of indigent deaf mutes, in institution at Buffalo.

SECTION 1. Sections one and two of an act entitled "An act to provide for the care and education of indigent deaf mutes under the age of twelve years," passed April twenty-fifth, eighteen hundred and sixty-three, and amended by section one of an act entitled "An act relative to the care and education of deaf mutes," passed April twelfth, eighteen hundred and seventy, are severally hereby amended by adding to, and inserting therein, after the words "or in the Institution for the Improved Instruction of Deaf Mutes," wherever the same occur in said sections respectively, the words following: "or in the Lecouteulx St. Mary's Institution for the Improved Instruction of Deaf Mutes in the city of Buffalo."

§ 2. This act shall take effect immediately.

CHAP. 551.

AN ACT to amend an act entitled "An act to legalize orders made by county judges in certain cases," passed April thirteenth, eighteen hundred and sixty-five.

Ante, vol. 6, p. 481.

PASSED April 19, 1871; three-fifths being present.

The People of the State of New York, represented in Senate and Assembly, do enact as follows:

SECTION 1. "An act to legalize orders made by county judges in certain cases," passed April thirteenth, eighteen hundred and sixty-five, is hereby amended so as to read as follows:

Every order for the service of a summons, in a civil action, by publication, made by a county judge prior to the first day of January, eighteen hundred and seventy, shall have the same force and effect as though such order had been made by the court in which the action was commenced, or by a justice of the supreme court.

§ 2. This act shall take effect immediately.

CHAP. 560.

AN ACT to amend an act entitled "An act to authorize the formation of railroad corporations and to regulate the same," passed April second, eighteen hundred and fifty.

Ante, vol. 3, p. 625.

PASSED April 19, 1871.

The People of the State of New York, represented in Senate and Assembly, do enact as follows:

SECTION 1. The twenty-second section of an act entitled "An act to authorize the formation of railroad corporations and to regulate the same," passed April second, eighteen hundred and fifty, is hereby amended so as to read as follows:

§ 22. Every company formed under this act, before constructing any part of their road into or through any county named in their articles of association, shall make a map and profile of the route intended to be adopted by such company in such county, which shall be certified by the president and engineer of the company, or a majority of the directors, and filed in the office of the clerk of the county in which the road is to be made, or in the office of the register in counties where there is a register's office. The company shall give written notice to all actual occupants of the land over which the route of the road is so designated, and which has not been purchased by or given to the company, of the time and place such map and profile were filed, and that the route designated thereby passes over the land of such occupant. Any occupant or owner of land over which such route passes, feeling aggrieved by the proposed location, may, within fifteen days after receiving written notice, as aforesaid, give ten days' notice, in writing, to such company and to the owners or occupants of lands to be affected by any proposed alteration, of the time and place of an application to a justice of the supreme court, in the judicial district where said lands are situated, by petition duly verified, for the appointment of commissioners to examine the said route. Such petition shall set forth the petitioner's objections to the route designated by the company, shall designate the route to which it is proposed to alter the same, and shall be accompanied by a survey, map and profile of the route as designated by the company and of the proposed alteration thereof, copies of which petition, map, survey and profile shall be served upon the company and said owners or occupants, with the notice of the application. If the said justice shall consider sufficient cause therefor to exist, he may, after hearing such parties as shall appear, appoint three disinterested persons, one of whom must be a practical civil engineer, commissioners to examine the route proposed by the company and the route to which it is proposed to alter the same, and, after hearing the parties, to affirm the route originally designated, or adopt the proposed alteration thereof, as may be consistent with the just rights of all parties and the public, including the

Map of route of railroad to be filed, before construction.

Notice to occupants of lands.

Objections to route, how made.

Application to supreme court.

To be accompanied with map of proposed alteration

Court to appoint commissioners to examine same.

Commissioners may affirm or alter route.

owners or occupants of lands upon the proposed alteration;

Engineer on commission, to concur.

but no alteration of the route shall be made except by the concurrence of the commissioner who is a practical civil engineer, nor shall an alteration be made which will cause greater damage or injury to lands, or materially greater length of road, than the route designated by the company would cause, nor which shall substantially change the general line adopted by the company.

Determination, map and testimony, how filed.

The determination of the commissioners shall, within thirty days after their appointment, be made and certified by them, and the certificate, with the petition, map, survey and profile, and any testimony taken before them, be filed in the office of the register of the county, in counties where there is a register, otherwise in that of the county clerk.

Appeals.

Within twenty days after the filing of such certificate any party may, by notice in writing to the others, appeal to the supreme court from the decision of the commissioners, which appeal shall be heard and decided at the next general term of the court held in any judicial district in which the lands of the petitioners or any of them are situated, for which the same can be noticed according to the rules and practice of said court.

Court may affirm route or adopt alteration.

On the hearing of such appeal the court may affirm the route proposed by the company or may adopt that proposed by the petitioner.

Commissioners, how paid.

Said commissioners shall each be entitled to three dollars per day for their expenses and services, to be paid by the person who applied for their appointment; and if the route of the road as designated by the company is altered by the commissioners, and their decision is affirmed on appeal (if an appeal be taken), the company shall refund to the applicant the amount so paid.

Change of terminus of intersecting roads.

§ 2. Whenever any railroad company shall have located its road so as to terminate at any railroad previously constructed or located, whereby communication might be had with any incorporated city of this state, and any other railroad company shall subsequently locate its road so as to intersect the road of said first mentioned company, and thereby, by itself or its connections, afford communication with such city, then and in such case said first mentioned company may alter and amend its articles of association so as to have its road terminate at the point of intersection with said road so subsequently located,

Consent of stockholders requisite.

provided the consent of the stockholders representing or holding two-thirds of the stock of said company shall have been first obtained thereto.

Maps, surveys, etc., when to be filed or recorded in register's office.

§ 3. Whenever in said act any map, survey, profile, report, certificate or other paper is directed to be filed or recorded in the office of the county clerk, the same shall be filed or recorded in the office of the register of the county, provided there be a register's office in said county; and all maps, profiles, surveys, reports, certificates or other papers which have, pursuant to the provisions of said act, been heretofore filed or recorded in the office of the clerk of any county in which there is a register,

Transfer and refiling authorized.

shall be, within thirty days after the passage of this act, transferred to the office of such register, and shall be by him refiled or recorded as of the date of the original filing or record.

§ 4. Section forty-one of an act entitled "An act to authorize the formation of railroad companies and to regulate the same," passed April second, eighteen hundred and fifty, is hereby amended so as to read as follows:

Ante, vol. 8, p. 685.

§ 41. If any person employed, or who shall be employed, upon the railroad of any such corporation as engineer, conductor, baggagemaster, brakeman, switchman, fireman, bridge-tender, flagman, signalman, or having charge of the regulating or running of trains upon said railroad in any manner whatsoever, be intoxicated while engaged in the discharge of such duties, he shall, upon conviction thereof, be deemed guilty of a misdemeanor, and shall be punishable for each offense by a fine not exceeding one hundred dollars, or by imprisonment in a county jail for a term not exceeding six months, in the discretion of the court having cognizance of the offense. And if any person so employed as aforesaid by any such corporation shall, by reason of such intoxication, do any act or neglect any duty, which act or neglect shall cause the death or injury to any person or persons, he shall, upon conviction thereof, be punishable by imprisonment in the county jail for a term of not less than six months, or in the state prison for a term not exceeding five years, in the discretion of the court having cognizance of the offense.

Punishment of railroad employees for intoxication.

Punishment in case of death or injury of persons by neglect therefrom.

§ 5. Corporations may be formed under the act entitled "An act to authorize the formation of railroad corporations and to regulate the same," passed April second, eighteen hundred and fifty, for the purpose of constructing and operating railroads for public use in transporting persons and property of the gauge of three feet and six inches or less, but not less than thirty inches within the rails, whenever capital stock of said corporation to the amount of five thousand dollars, for every mile of such railroad proposed to be constructed and operated, has been in good faith subscribed; and whenever five thousand dollars or more for every mile of such railroad proposed to be constructed shall be in like manner subscribed, and ten per cent thereon in good faith actually paid in cash to the directors named in the articles of association, and an affidavit made by at least three of said directors, and indorsed on or annexed to said articles, that the amount of stock hereby required has been so subscribed as aforesaid, and ten per cent thereon paid as aforesaid, and that it is intended in good faith to construct and operate such railroad, then said articles, with such affidavit, may be filed and recorded in the office of secretary of state; provided said articles contain all the other facts required by law to be stated in articles of association made for organizing railroad corporations, under said act, entitled "An act to authorize the formation of railroad corporations and to regulate the same," passed April second, eighteen hundred and fifty; and all of the provisions of said last-mentioned act shall apply to corporations formed for the construction and operating of rail-

Narrow gauge railroads, authorized.

Capital stock required to be subscribed.

Affidavit of directors.

General railroad act, how applicable.

roads of the gauge hereinabove mentioned, except as herein provided or otherwise provided by law.

Amount of subscription required before taking lands.

§ 6. Any railroad company duly organized according to law, when the gauge of its proposed railroad shall be three feet and six inches or less, but not less than thirty inches, within the rails, may, whenever six thousand dollars for every mile of its railroad proposed to be constructed in this state is in good faith subscribed toward its capital stock, and ten per cent thereof paid in good faith in cash, apply to the supreme court in the manner provided by law for the appointment of commissioners, and all subsequent proceedings may be had to obtain the title of lands necessary for the construction and maintenance and operating said railroad, to the same extent and in the same manner as if the whole amount of the capital stock specified in its articles of association was in like manner subscribed, and ten per cent thereof in like manner paid in cash, and may lay upon such road iron of a weight not less than forty pounds to the lineal yard, and may use in switches and turn-outs irons of not less than thirty pounds to the lineal yard.

Weight of iron rails.

Existing corporations may construct narrow gauge road.

§ 7. Any railroad corporation, now duly organized and legally kept in existence, which has not constructed its railroad, may construct a railroad of the gauge hereinbefore mentioned, and may acquire title to lands necessary for the construction, maintenance and operating of such railroad on complying with the provisions of this act, and of all other provisions of law not inconsistent herewith.

§ 8. This act shall take effect immediately.

CHAP. 576.

AN ACT reappropriating a certain portion of the income of the United States Deposit Fund for the benefit of academies.

PASSED April 19, 1871; three-fifths being present.

The People of the State of New York, represented in Senate and Assembly, do enact as follows:

Application of balances of appropriation.

SECTION 1. The regents of the university are hereby authorized to apply one thousand dollars of the unexpended balance of the appropriation made by chapter two hundred and eighty-one of the laws of eighteen hundred and seventy, for the instruction of teachers of common schools, to the purchase of books and apparatus for the benefit of academies, pursuant to chapter five hundred and thirty-six of the laws of eighteen hundred and fifty-one.

Report on metric

§ 2. The regents are hereby authorized to apply a part of the said sum, not exceeding three hundred dollars, in procuring copies of the report of the committee of the university convocation of eighteen hundred and seventy, on the metric system, with the accompanying documents, to be placed in the libraries of the colleges, academies, normal and union schools of the state.

System to be placed in libraries.

§ 3. This act shall take effect immediately.

CHAP. 580.

AN ACT to amend an act entitled "An act giving the consent of the state of New York to the purchase by, and ceding jurisdiction to, the United States over certain lands within this state, to be occupied as sites for light-houses and keepers' dwellings," passed April six, eighteen hundred and seventy-one, and supplemental thereto.

Ante, p.

PASSED April 19, 1871, by a two-third vote.

The People of the State of New York, represented in Senate and Assembly, do enact as follows:

SECTION 1. Section two of an act entitled "An act giving consent of the state of New York to the purchase by, and ceding jurisdiction to, the United States over certain lands within this state, to be occupied as sites for light-houses and keepers' dwellings," is hereby amended so as to read as follows:

§ 2. The foregoing shall be applicable only to the lands selected, approved and owned as aforesaid, and a survey thereof filed and recorded as above provided, for the construction of the following light-houses and keepers' dwellings, namely: on Fisher's island, eastern end of Long Island Sound, New York, ten and three-tenth acres, more or less. On Barber's Point, Lake Champlain, New York, nine acres, more or less. On Bluff Point, Valcour island, Lake Champlain, New York, two acres or less. On the west bank of Oak Orchard creek, near its mouth, in Orleans county, purchased from Abram V. Clark, of the same county, one-half acre, more or less; and at Fair Haven, Cayuga county, New York, five acres or less.

Lands for U. S. light-houses, etc.

§ 2. This act shall take effect immediately.

CHAP. 603.

AN ACT in relation to appeals from surrogates' courts.

PASSED April 19, 1871; three-fifths being present.

The People of the State of New York, represented in Senate and Assembly, do enact as follows:

Discretionary power of surrogate, in case of appeals as to issue of letters testamentary. SECTION 1. Appeals when taken from the decree or decision of a surrogates' court, declaring the validity of a will and admitting the same to probate, shall not stay the issuing of letters testamentary to the executors, if in the opinion of the surrogate the protection and preservation of the estate of the deceased require the issuing of such letters, but such letters shall not confer power upon the executor or executors named in the will to sell real estate, pay legacies or distribute the effects of the testator until the final determination of such appeal.

Appeals to have preference. § 2. Such appeals shall have preference for hearing in the supreme court and in the court of appeals in the same order as is now prescribed by law in cases where the issuing of letters testamentary is stayed.

Repeal. § 3. All acts or parts of acts inconsistent with this act are hereby repealed.

§ 4. This act shall take effect immediately.

CHAP. 608.

AN ACT to amend an act to provide for the incorporation of fire insurance companies, passed June twenty-fifth, eighteen hundred and fifty-three.

Ante, vol. 4, p. 226.

PASSED April 19, 1871.

The People of the State of New York, represented in Senate and Assembly, do enact as follows:

SECTION 1. Section eight of chapter four hundred and sixty-six of the laws of eighteen hundred and fifty-three, entitled "An act to provide for the incorporation of fire insurance companies," is hereby amended to read as follows:

Investment of capital on loans upon real estate. § 8. It shall be lawful for any fire insurance company organized under this act, or incorporated under any law of this state, to invest its capital, and the funds accumulated in the course of its business, or any part thereof, in bonds and mortgages on unincumbered and improved real estate within the state of New York, worth fifty per cent more than the sum loaned thereon, exclusive of buildings, unless such buildings are insured and the policy transferred to said company, In public stocks or bonds. and also in the stocks of this state, or stocks or treasury notes of the United States, and also in the stocks and bonds of any county or incorporated city in this state, authorized to be issued by the legislature, and to lend the same, or any part thereof, in the security of such stocks or bonds or treasury notes, or upon bonds and mortgages as aforesaid, and to change and reinvest the same as occasion may from time to time require; but any surplus money over and above the capital stock of any such fire and inland navigation insurance companies, or any fire insurance companies incorporated under any law of this state, may be invested in or loaned upon the pledge of the public stock or the bonds of the United States, or any one of the states, or the stocks, bonds or other evidence of indebtedness of any solvent dividend paying institutions incorporated under the laws of this state or of the United States, except their own stock, and any amount not exceeding one-half the annual premium receipts of any company upon its outstanding policies in any other state of the United States, may be invested upon bond and mortgage security upon real estate in such state, which shall be certified by the superintendent of the insurance department of this state to be unincumbered, improved and worth double the sum loaned thereon, or in the stocks or bonds of any foreign country to the extent which may be provided under the laws thereof as the condition of such company doing business therein; provided that such investment in such foreign stocks or bonds shall be made only from funds which constitute a surplus over and above capital and liabilities, and subject to the approval of the superintendent of the insurance department. **Surplus over capital, how invested or loaned.**

§ 2. This act shall take effect immediately.

CHAP. 610.

AN ACT to legalize executions issued by the county clerks of the several counties of this state, upon judgments rendered by justices of the peace and docketed in their respective offices, and the sales of property on such executions.

PASSED April 19, 1871; three-fifths being present.

The People of the State of New York, represented in Senate and Assembly, do enact as follows:

SECTION 1. Executions issued by the county clerks of the several counties of this state, between the twelfth day of May, in the year one thousand eight hundred and sixty-nine, and the sixth day of May, in the year one thousand eight hundred and seventy, on judgments of justices of the peace, docketed in their respective offices, and the issuing of all such executions, and the sales of property on all such executions, are hereby made and declared legal and valid; but nothing herein contained shall affect any action or proceeding now pending to set aside, or have declared void, any such execution or sale.

§ 2. This act shall take effect immediately.

CHAP. 635.

AN ACT to amend article four, of title four, of chapter eleven, of part first of the Revised Statutes, "Of division and other fences."

Ante, vol. 1, p. 826.

PASSED April 20, 1871; three-fifths being present.

The People of the State of New York, represented in Senate and Assembly, do enact as follows:

SECTION 1. Section thirty, article four, title four, chapter eleven, part first of the Revised Statutes is hereby amended so as to read as follows:

Division fences, how maintained between improved lands.

§ 30. Where two or more persons shall have lands adjoining, each of them shall make and maintain a just and equal proportion of the division fence between them in all cases where each of such adjoining lands shall be cleared or improved. And where such adjoining lands shall border upon any of the navigable lakes, streams, or rivers within this state, it shall be and it is hereby made the duty of the owners thereof, to maintain such division fence down to the line of low-water mark in such lakes, streams and rivers.

How maintained, when lands border upon navigable lakes or rivers.

§ 2. Section thirty-one of said article is hereby amended so as to read as follows:

Fences in other cases, how maintained, unless lands are left to lie open.

§ 31. Where two or more persons shall have lands adjoining, and not within the provisions of section thirty, as hereby amended, each of them shall make and maintain a just and equal proportion of the division fence between them, except the owner or owners of either of the adjoining lands shall choose to let such lands lie open. If he shall afterward inclose it, he shall refund to the owner of the adjoining land a just proportion of the value, at that time, of any division fence that shall have been made and maintained by such adjoining owner, or he shall build his proportion of such division fence.

Refunding of value of existing fence or inclosure of lands.

§ 3. Section thirty-two of said article is hereby amended so as to read as follows:

Proviso, as to refunding value of existing fence or building proportion of fence.

§ 32. Where a person shall have cleared or improved lands lying open, he shall refund to the owner of adjoining land which is also cleared or improved, a just proportion of the value, at the time this act shall take effect, of any division fence that shall have been made and maintained by such adjoining owner between such cleared or improved lands, or he shall build his proportion of such division fence. Whenever a subdivision or new apportionment of any division fence shall become necessary by reason of the transfer of the title of either of the adjoining owners to the whole or any portion of the adjoining lands by conveyance, devise, or descent, such subdivision or new apportionment shall thereupon be made by the adjoining owners affected thereby; and either adjoining owner shall refund to the other a just proportion of the value, at the time of such transfer of title, of any division fence that

Subdivision of proportion of fence, to be made in case of change of title.

Refunding of value of existing fence.

shall theretofore have been made and maintained by such other adjoining owner, or the person from whom he derived his title, or he shall build his proportion of such division fence. The value of any fence, and the proportion thereof to be paid by any person, and the proportion to be built by him, shall be determined by any two of the fenceviewers of the town. Value of proportion of fence, how determined.

§ 4. Section thirty-nine of said article is hereby amended so as to read as follows:

§ 39. If any person who shall have made his proportion of a division fence shall be disposed to remove his fence and suffer his lands to lie open, he may do so, provided such lands are not cleared or improved, at any time between the first day of November in any one year and the first day of April following, but at no other time, giving ten days' notice to the owner or occupant of the adjoining land of his intention to apply to the fenceviewers of the town for permission to remove his fence; and if, at the time specified in such notice, any two of such fenceviewers, to be selected as aforesaid, shall determine that such fence may, with propriety, be removed, he may remove the same. Rights of persons to remove certain fences, and permit lands to be open. Notice to adjoining owner. Fence-viewers to determine propriety of removal.

§ 5. This act shall take effect immediately.

CHAP. 651.

AN ACT to make a contribution toward the completion of the Washington national monument.

PASSED April 30, 1871, by a two-thirds vote.

The People of the State of New York, represented in Senate and Assembly, do enact as follows:

SECTION 1. The sum of ten thousand dollars is hereby appropriated as the contribution of the state of New York, to be paid by the treasurer, on the warrant of the comptroller, to the treasurer of the National Washington Monument Society, whenever the governor shall certify that he is satisfied a sufficient sum has been subscribed from other sources to enable said society to resume work with a reasonable prospect of completing the obelisk or shaft. Conditional appropriation.

§ 2. A copy of the foregoing shall be transmitted by the governor to the governors of other states of the union, with a request that they communicate the same to the legislatures of their respective states. Governor to forward copy of act to other states.

CHAP. 652.

AN ACT in relation to the refiling of certain certificates of incorporation in the office of the secretary of state.

PASSED April 20, 1871; three-fifths being present.

Preamble, reciting destruction of certain certificates, by fire.

WHEREAS, The certificates of incorporation of certain corporations filed in the office of the secretary of state in the months of January, February and March, eighteen hundred and seventy-one, under chapter forty, laws of eighteen hundred and forty-eight, entitled "An act to authorize the formation of corporations for manufacturing, mining, mechanical, or chemical purposes," and the acts supplementary thereto or amendatory thereof, were destroyed by fire on the seventh day of April, eighteen hundred and seventy-one; and,

WHEREAS, Duplicate certificates of incorporation of said certificates of incorporation are filed in the offices of the clerk of the counties in which the principal places of business of said corporations are located; therefore,

The People of the State of New York, represented in Senate and Assembly, do enact as follows:

Secretary of state to file certified copies.

SECTION 1. The secretary of state is hereby authorized to procure and receive from the county clerks of the counties in this state in which the said original certificates of incorporation have been filed, a certified copy of each of such certificates, certified by the county clerk of the county in which the original certificate is filed to be a true and correct transcript of such original certificate, and of the whole thereof. And upon procuring the same the secretary of state shall indorse thereon the fact that the said certified copies are filed in pursuance of this act, and shall in addition thereto note thereon the date of the original filing. The secretary of state is also authorized to file copies of such certificate of incorporation which may have been procured from his office, and which are certified under his official seal to be true copies of such original certificates; such certified copies when so filed shall be indorsed as hereinbefore provided in reference to copies certified by county clerks.

Indorsement of filing thereon.

Certified copies, when refiled, how read in evidence.

§ 2. Copies of certificates of incorporation thus refiled in the office of the secretary of state in pursuance of this act, when certified by the secretary of state, may be read in evidence in all courts and places whatsoever, in like manner as certified copies of duplicate original certificates filed in the office of the secretary of state, and shall in all respects have the same force and effect as though they were respectively the copies of certificates of incorporation originally filed in the office of the secretary of state.

Force and effect thereof.

§ 3. This act shall take effect immediately.

CHAP. 653.

AN ACT making an appropriation to pay the expenses of the collection of tolls, superintendence, ordinary repairs and maintenance of the canals for the fiscal year commencing on the first day of October, one thousand eight hundred and seventy; to supply deficiencies in former appropriations, and to confirm the action of the commissioners of the canal fund in providing funds for the above purposes.

PASSED April 20, 1871; three-fifths being present.

The People of the State of New York, represented in Senate and Assembly, do enact as follows:

SECTION 1. The following sums are hereby appropriated out of the revenues of the state canals for the fiscal year, commencing on the first day of October, eighteen hundred and seventy: Appropriations.

For paying the expenses of the collection of tolls, the superintendence and ordinary repairs of the public works, the salaries, traveling expenses and clerk hire of the canal commissioners, the state engineer and surveyor, the canal appraisers, the salary of the auditor of the canal department, the clerk hire therein, and the incidental charges and expenses thereof, the sum of one million nine hundred and seventy-five thousand seven hundred and fifty dollars, or so much thereof as may be necessary to be expended during the fiscal year, to be distributed, applied, apportioned and disposed of as follows: For collection of tolls, superintendence, salaries, etc.

For salaries, traveling expenses and clerk hire of the canal commissioners, the sum of ten thousand and eight hundred dollars; and for the salary of the clerk of the board of canal commissioners, the sum of fifteen hundred dollars, or so much thereof as may be necessary. Canal commissioners. Clerk of board.

For the salary and traveling expenses of the state engineer and surveyor, two thousand and seven hundred dollars. State engineer.

For the salaries and traveling expenses of the superintendents of the repairs of the canals the sum of forty-three thousand dollars, or so much thereof as may be necessary. Superintendents of repairs.

For the salaries and traveling expenses of the canal appraisers, and for clerk hire in their office, the sum of eleven thousand two hundred and fifty dollars, or so much thereof as may be necessary. Canal appraisers.

For the salary of the auditor of the canal department, two thousand and five hundred dollars; and for clerk hire in the said department, the sum of thirteen thousand dollars or so much thereof as may be necessary. And the auditor may designate one of his clerks to act as secretary of the canal board, in case of sickness or inability of the auditor to perform that duty. Auditor of canal department. Designation of clerk as secretary of canal board.

Engineers on ordinary repairs. For the salaries and compensation of the engineers employed on the ordinary repairs of the canals, including the incidental expenses of such engineers, the sum of twenty-four thousand dollars, or so much thereof as may be necessary.

Collectors of canal tolls. Weighmasters and assistants. Boat inspectors. For the salaries and compensation of the collectors of canal tolls and their clerks, and for the salaries and compensation of weighmasters and their assistants, including the incidental expenses of said collectors and weighmasters, and the compensation of inspectors of boats and their cargoes, the sum of one hundred and ten thousand dollars, or so much thereof as may be necessary.

Incidentals. For the payment of such incidental and miscellaneous charges and expenses as are authorized by existing statutes to be paid out of the canal revenues, and charged in the accounts of the Erie and Champlain canal fund, the sum of sixty thousand dollars, or so much thereof as may be necessary.

Ordinary repairs. Expense of repairing breaches, etc. Issue of drafts therefor. Conditions requisite. For the payment of the expenses of the ordinary repairs of the completed canals of this state, and for the sums that may become due to the contractors for repairs, and for moneys and interest thereon heretofore expended in reparation of breaches or casualties, deducted from the aggregate expenditures, an account of the same, as certified to by the engineers, and retained from the amount of said accounts, the canal commissioners are required to issue their drafts therefor on the auditor of the canal department, in cases where and only where the money has been actually expended, as shown by the records thereof in the canal department, and where an account for the same has heretofore been filed in the canal department by the parties making such expenditures, under their contracts, and for no other object and purpose whatever, the sum of one million seven hundred thousand dollars, or so much thereof as may be necessary, to be distributed, assigned and apportioned in the first instance to the three divisions of the canals as now constituted, as follows: Amount how apportioned.

Eastern division. To the eastern division of the canals, the sum of eight hundred and fifty thousand dollars.

Middle division. To the middle division of the canals, the sum of four hundred and fifty thousand dollars.

Western division. To the western division of the canals, the sum of four hundred thousand dollars.

Payments of deficiencies to superintendents for ordinary repairs. Also to repair contractors. The further sum of five hundred and ninety-one thousand five hundred and twenty-eight dollars and thirty-seven cents is hereby appropriated from the revenues of the canals to supply deficiencies in appropriations by act chapter thirty-two of the laws of eighteen hundred and seventy, for payments to superintendents for the ordinary repairs of the completed canals of the state, and to contractors for repairs under their respective contracts, which have been advanced by the banks in accordance with resolutions of the commissioners of the canal fund, adopted July first and September sixth, eighteen hundred and seventy.

Preamble and resolution confirmed.

The following preamble and resolution of the commissioners of the canal fund, adopted October sixth, eighteen hundred and seventy, are hereby approved and confirmed:

Preamble.

"WHEREAS, No provision by law has been made to pay the expenses of the collection of the tolls, superintendence, ordinary repairs and maintenance of the canals for the fiscal year commencing on the first day of October, eighteen hundred and seventy,

Resolution as to advance of moneys.

"*Resolved*, That the comptroller be and he is hereby authorized and empowered to make arrangements with either or all of the deposit banks to advance such moneys as may be necessary for the payment of such expenses of the collection of tolls, superintendence, ordinary repairs and maintenance of the canals for the fiscal year commencing October first, eighteen hundred and seventy, until the legislature may supply such omission, upon such vouchers and drafts as shall be examined and certified by the auditor; such advance to be repaid when the legislature shall make the necessary appropriation therefor."

Restriction as to expenditures by canal commissioners.

The canal commissioners shall not expend any more money on their respective divisions, nor incur any charge against the state for the repairs of the canals during the fiscal year, than is above appropriated and apportioned to the said divisions by this act, unless the canal board, by resolution to be entered on the minutes of said board, and by the concurring votes of five members thereof, shall otherwise order and direct. And the said canal board, in case of breaks or breaches, or other extraordinary occurrences happening on any one of said divisions, causing or tending to a suspension or interruption of navigation upon such division, shall, and the said board is hereby authorized to, direct in manner above provided, the transfer of such portion of the unexpended balance of one or both the other divisions, to the division requiring the same, to keep and sustain navigation, and the commissioner in charge of the division to which such transfer or appropriation shall be made, shall expend the same in the amendment and reparation of the canals under his charge, designated in the resolution of the canal board authorizing such transfer.

Repair of breaks.

Transfer of balances therefor.

How expended.

Auditor to reserve moneys for repair contractors.

§ 2. The auditor of the canal department shall notify the canal commissioners of the sum of money that will be needed to pay the drafts, during the fiscal year, to the contractors for repairs under their contracts upon their respective divisions, and he shall reserve such sums out of the appropriations made by this act for the purpose of paying the monthly drafts to contractors, and no part of the sums so reserved shall be paid or applied to any other object or purpose, and no drafts shall be drawn on the auditor in favor of any contractor, unless upon a certificate from the canal commissioner in charge that the contractor has fulfilled his contract during the preceding month.

Payments to be made on certificate of fulfillment.

§ 3. This act shall take effect immediately.

CHAP. 654.

AN ACT making an appropriation to pay the expenses of the collection of tolls, superintendence, ordinary repairs and maintenance of the canals for the fiscal year commencing on the first day of October, one thousand eight hundred and seventy-one.

PASSED April 20, 1871; three-fifths being present.

The People of the State of New York, represented in Senate and Assembly, do enact as follows:

Appropriation. SECTION 1. The following sums are hereby appropriated out of the revenues of the state canals for the fiscal year commencing on the first day of October, eighteen hundred and seventy-one:

For collection of tolls, superintendence, salaries, etc. For paying the expenses of the collection of tolls, the superintendence and ordinary repairs of the public works, the salaries, traveling expenses and clerk hire of the canal commissioners, the state engineer and surveyor, the canal appraisers, the salary of the auditor of the canal department, the clerk hire therein, and the incidental charges and expenses thereof, the sum of one million two hundred seventy-five thousand seven hundred and fifty dollars, or so much thereof as may be necessary to be expended during the fiscal year, to be distributed, applied, appropriated and disposed of as follows:

Canal commissioners. Clerk of board. For salaries, traveling expenses and clerk hire of the canal commissioners, ten thousand eight hundred dollars, and the clerk of the board of canal commissioners, fifteen hundred dollars.

State engineer. For the salary and traveling expenses of the state engineer and surveyor, two thousand seven hundred dollars.

Superintendents of repairs. For the salaries and traveling expenses of the superintendents of repairs of the canals, the sum of forty-three thousand dollars, or so much thereof as may be necessary.

Canal appraisers. For the salaries and traveling expenses of the canal appraisers and for clerk hire in their office, the sum of eleven thousand two hundred and fifty dollars, or so much thereof as may be necessary.

Auditor of canal department. For the salary of the auditor of the canal department, two thousand five hundred dollars; and for clerk hire in the said department, the sum of thirteen thousand dollars, or so much thereof as may be necessary.

Engineers on ordinary repairs. For the salaries and compensation of the engineers employed on the ordinary repairs of the canal, including the incidental expenses of such engineers, the sum of twenty-four thousand dollars, or so much thereof as may be necessary.

Collectors of canal tolls. Weighmasters and assistants. For the salaries and compensation of the collectors of canal tolls, and their clerks, and for salaries and compensation of weighmasters, and their assistants, including the incidental expenses of said collectors and weighmasters, and the compensation of inspectors of boats and their cargoes, the sum of one hundred and ten thousand dollars, or so much thereof as may be necessary. Boat inspectors.

For the payment of such incidental and miscellaneous charges and expenses as are authorized by existing statutes to be paid out of the canal revenues, and charged in the account of the Erie and Champlain canal fund and the canal debt sinking fund, under section one of article seven of the constitution, the sum of sixty thousand dollars, or so much thereof as may be necessary. Incidentals.

For the payment of the expenses of the ordinary repairs of the completed canals of the state, and for the sums that may become due to the contractors for repairs under their contracts, and for no other object and purpose whatever, the sum of one million dollars, or so much thereof as may be necessary, to be distributed, assigned and apportioned, in the first instance, to the three divisions of the canals, as now constituted, as follows: Ordinary repairs. How apportioned.

To the eastern division of the canals, the sum of four hundred thousand dollars. Eastern division.

To the middle division of the canals, the sum of three hundred thousand dollars. Middle division.

To the western division of the canals, the sum of three hundred thousand dollars. Western division.

The canal commissioners shall not expend any more money on their respective divisions, nor incur any charge against the state for the repairs of the canals during the fiscal year, than is above appropriated and apportioned to the said division by this act, unless the canal board, by resolution, to be entered on the minutes of said board, and by the concurring votes of five members thereof, shall otherwise order and direct. And the said canal board, in case of breaks or breaches, or other extraordinary occurrences happening on any one of said divisions, causing or tending to a suspension or interruption of navigation upon such division, shall, and the said board is hereby authorized to, direct in manner above provided, the transfer of such portion of the unexpended balance of one or both the other divisions, to the division requiring the same, to keep and sustain the navigation, and the commissioner in charge of the division to which such transfer or appropriation shall be made shall expend the same in the amendment and reparation of the canals under his charge, designated in the resolution of the canal board authorizing such transfer. Restrictions as to expenditures. Repair of breaks. Transfer of balances therefor. How expended.

§ 2. The auditor of the canal department shall notify the canal commissioners of the sum of money that will be needed to pay the drafts, during the fiscal year, to the contractors for repairs under their contracts upon their respective divisions, and he shall reserve such sums out of the appropriations made by this act, for the purpose of paying the monthly drafts to contractors, and no part of the sums so reserved shall be paid or applied to any other object or purpose, and no drafts shall be drawn on the auditor in favor of any contractor, Auditor to reserve moneys for repair contractors. Payments to be made on certificate of fulfillment.

unless upon a certificate from the canal commissioner in charge, that the contractor has fulfilled his contract during the preceding month.

§ 3. This act shall take effect immediately.

CHAP. 655.

AN ACT making appropriations for the payment of the principal and interest on the canal debt, commencing on the first day of October, one thousand eight hundred and seventy-one, and to provide for the payment of the debt contracted under section twelve of article seven of the constitution.

PASSED April 20, 1871; three-fifths being present.

The People of the State of New York, represented in Senate and Assembly, do enact as follows:

Appropriation. SECTION 1. The following sums are hereby appropriated out of the canal revenues of the state canals for the fiscal year commencing on the first day of October, eighteen hundred and seventy-one:

For general fund debt sinking fund. For payment toward the sinking fund for the extinguishment of the general fund debt, the sum of fifteen hundred thousand dollars.

Payment of interest in coin, and principal of canal enlargement loan. For the payment of the interest, in coin, and reimbursement of the principal of the loans made under the constitution for the enlargement and completion of the canals, the sum of two millions three hundred and forty thousand dollars, or so much thereof as may be necessary.

Expenses of state government. To pay the general fund to defray the necessary expenses of the state government, the sum of two hundred thousand dollars.

Payment in coin, of interest on canal sinking fund debt. § 2. The sum of seventy-five thousand dollars, or so much thereof as may be necessary, is hereby appropriated from the sinking fund, under section one of article seven of the constitution, for payment of interest, in coin, on the canal debt, for which said sinking fund has been provided.

Appropriation for interest and principal on floating debt loan. § 3. The following sums are hereby appropriated, out of the proceeds of any tax to be levied and collected under the provisions of the act (chapter two hundred and seventy-one of the laws of eighteen hundred and fifty-nine), to pay the interest and reimburse the principal of the loan of two million five hundred thousand dollars to provide for the payment of the floating debt of the state:

Payment of interest thereon, in coin. To pay the interest, in coin, on said loan for the fiscal year commencing on the first day of October next, one hundred and ten thousand dollars, or so much thereof as may be necessary.

To provide for the sinking fund to pay the principal of said loan, one hundred and thirty-eight thousand eight hundred and eighty-eight dollars, being for one year's contribution to said fund, as provided for by the act aforesaid. Sinking fund, to pay principal thereof

CHAP. 657.

AN ACT to amend the act passed February seventeenth, eighteen hundred and forty-eight, entitled "An act to authorize the formation of corporations for manufacturing, mining, mechanical or chemical purposes."

Ante, vol. 3, p. 733.

PASSED April 20, 1871; three-fifths being present.

The People of the State of New York, represented in Senate and Assembly, do enact as follows:

SECTION 1. The first section of the "Act to authorize the formation of corporations for manufacturing, mining, mechanical or chemical purposes," passed February seventeenth, eighteen hundred and forty-eight, as said section was amended by chapter seven hundred and ninety-nine of the laws of eighteen hundred and sixty-six, is hereby further amended by substituting for the words "or the business of building and keeping a hotel," the words following, viz.: "or the business of erecting buildings for hotel purposes or keeping a hotel or either or both of such purposes." The provisions of this section shall apply to all corporations formed for either of the above purposes, since the first day of January, eighteen hundred and sixty-nine. Act extended to building or keeping hotels. How to apply.

§ 2. Said section one of the said act, passed February seventeenth, eighteen hundred and forty-eight, as amended by section one of chapter two hundred and sixty-two of the laws of eighteen hundred and fifty-seven, is hereby amended by inserting after the words "or the business of printing and publishing books, pamphlets and newpapers," in the first section of the last-mentioned act, the words, "or the business of preserving and dealing in meats." Extension of act, to preserving and dealing in meats

§ 3. Section twelve of the said act, passed February seventeenth, eighteen hundred and forty-eight, is hereby amended by adding thereto the following: "but whenever under this section a judgment shall be recovered against a trustee severally, all the trustees of the company shall contribute a ratable share of the amount paid by such trustee on such judgment, and such trustee shall have a right of action against his cotrustees, jointly or severally, to recover from them their proportion of the amount so paid on such judgment." Judgments against any trustee, to be binding on all trustees.

§ 4. This act shall take effect immediately.

CHAP. 666.

AN ACT to authorize judicial inquiry as to the sanity of persons indicted for capital offenses.

PASSED April 21, 1871 three-fifths being present.

The People of the State of New York, represented in Senate and Assembly, do enact as follows:

Powers of oyer and terminer to inquire as to sanity. SECTION 1. The court of oyer and terminer, in which any indictment may be pending against any person for any offense, the punishment of which is death, shall have power, with the concurrence of the presiding judge of such court, summarily to inquire into the sanity of such person, and the degree of mental capacity possessed by him, and for that purpose may appoint a commission to examine such person and inquire into the facts of his case, and report thereon to the court; and if the said court shall find such person insane or not of sufficient mental capacity to undertake his defense, they may by order remand such person to such lunatic or other asylum as, in their judgment, shall be meet, subject as to the future disposition of the person to all the provisions of chapter twenty, part first, article second, title third of the Revised Statutes.

May appoint commission to examine and report. Prisoner, how remanded, if insane.

Ante, vol. 1, p. 586

Powers of governor, after conviction. § 2. The governor shall possess the same powers conferred upon courts of oyer and terminer in the case of persons confined under conviction for offenses for which the punishment is death.

§ 3. This act shall take effect immediately.

CHAP. 668.

AN ACT to provide for the payment of counsel required to be employed on behalf of the state, in pursuance of the provisions of section two of chapter three hundred and twenty-one of the laws of eighteen hundred and seventy.

PASSED April 21, 1871; three-fifths being present.

The People of the State of New York, represented in Senate and Assembly, do enact as follows:

Services of counsel for state, to be audited and paid by auditor. SECTION 1. The services of counsel employed on behalf of the state, in pursuance of the provisions of section two, chapter three hundred and twenty-one of laws of eighteen hundred and seventy, shall be adjusted, audited and paid by the auditor of the canal department from the canal fund on production to him of an account therefor, containing the items

Account for service, how made and

therein duly verified with the certificate of the canal appraisers, that such service has been rendered, with their opinion as to the value thereof. Verified by canal appraisers.

§ 2. This act shall take effect immediately.

Ante, vol. 7, p. 711.

CHAP. 669.

AN ACT to amend an act entitled "An act to authorize the formation of railroad corporations and to regulate the same," passed April second, eighteen hundred and fifty.

Ante, vol. 3, p. 617.

PASSED April 21, 1871.

The People of the State of New York, represented in Senate and Assembly, do enact as follows:

SECTION 1. The twenty-seventh section of an act entitled "An act to authorize the formation of railroad corporations and to regulate the ame," passed April second, eighteen hundred and fifty, is hereby amended so as to read as follows:

Ante, vol. 3, p. 627.

§ 27. No company formed under this act shall lay down or use in the construction of their road any iron rail of less weight than fifty-six pounds to the lineal yard on grades of one hundred and ten feet to the mile or under, and not less than seventy pounds to the lineal yard on grades of over one hundred and ten feet to the mile, except for turn-outs, sidings and switches, provided this section shall apply only to roads now being constructed or hereafter to be constructed, when the gauge of said road exceeds four feet or over. Weight of iron rail on grades, etc. Act, how to apply.

§ 2. Section twelve of chapter one hundred and forty of the laws of eighteen hundred and fifty, is hereby amended so as to read as follows:

Ante, vol. 3, p. 620.

§ 12. As often as any contractor for the construction of any part of a railroad, which is in progress of construction, shall be indebted to any laborer for thirty or any less number of days' labor performed in constructing said road, such laborer may give notice of such indebtedness to said company in the manner herein provided; and said company shall thereupon become liable to pay such laborer the amount so due him for such labor, and an action may be maintained against said company therefor. Such notice shall be given by said laborer to said company within twenty days after the performance of the number of days' labor for which the claim is made. Such notice shall be in writing, and shall state the month and particular days of the month upon which labor was performed and remains unpaid for, the price per day, the amount due, Payment of laborers' wages. Liability of railroad company. Notice of claim to be given to company by laborers. Notice, what to state.

with the name of the contractor from whom due, the section of the road performed, and shall be signed by such laborer or his attorney, to which notice an affidavit shall be annexed, made by such laborer or his attorney, to the effect that of his own knowledge the statements contained in such notice are in all respects true. Such notice so verified, shall be served on an engineer, agent or superintendent employed by said company, having charge of the section of the road on which such labor was performed, personally or by leaving the same at the office or usual place of business of such engineer, agent or superintendent, with some person of suitable age. But no action shall be maintained against any company, under the provisions of this section, unless the same is commenced after ten and within thirty days after notice is given to the company by such laborer as above provided.

How verified and served.

Actions, when to be commenced.

§ 3. This act shall take effect immediately.

CHAP. 672.

AN ACT for the removal of obstructions in the Big Chazy river, and for the improvement of the same.

PASSED April 21, 1871, by a two-thirds vote.

The People of the State of New York, represented in Senate and Assembly, do enact as follows:

Appropriation for removing obstructions.

SECTION 1. The sum of ten thousand dollars, for public purposes, is hereby appropriated out of the moneys in the treasury belonging to the general fund, not otherwise appropriated, for the purpose of removing, and paying for the removal of obstructions from, and improving the Big Chazy river, in the county of Clinton, for the running of logs and timber down the same; which sum of money shall be disbursed by and under the direction of William Graham, of Champlain, New York, James Fitch, of Moores, and William C. Rhodes, of Dannemora, all of Clinton county, commissioners hereby appointed for that purpose.

Commissioners to disburse same.

Commissioners to execute bond.

§ 2. The said commissioners, before entering upon the duties of the office, shall execute and file in the office of the comptroller, a bond in the penal sum of twenty thousand dollars for the faithful performance of their duties, which bond shall be subject to the approval of the comptroller.

§ 3. This act shall take effect immediately.

CHAP. 684.

AN ACT to provide for the improvement of the hydraulic power of the north branch of the Saranac river, and to improve the navigation of said north branch.

PASSED April 25, 1871; three-fifths being present.

The People of the State of New York, represented in Senate and Assembly, do enact as follows:

SECTION 1. For the purpose of improving the hydraulic power of the north branch of the Saranac river, and to improve the navigation of said branch, a board of commissioners is hereby constituted to be termed and known as commissioners for the improvement of the North Branch of the Saranac river. Commissioners of improvement.

§ 2. The said board shall consist of three commissioners, of whom a majority shall constitute a quorum for the transaction of business; the first commissioners shall be Jeremiah D. Merrill, Patrick McKillip and Louis L. Smith; and in case of death, resignation, refusal to serve or other disqualification of the said commissioners or any of them, the county judge of the county of Franklin shall appoint a successor or successors. The said county judge shall also have power of removal for cause, to be specified in the order of removal. First commissioners. Vacancies, how filled. Removals for cause.

§ 3. Each commissioner, before entering upon the duties of his office, shall file in the office of the clerk of the county of Franklin, the official oath required by law, and a bond to the people of the state of New York, with sureties to be approved by the judge of Franklin county, in the penal sum of one thousand dollars, conditioned for the faithful performance of the duties of said office. Oath of office and official bonds.

§ 4. The commissioners under this act are hereby authorized and empowered to make, establish and improve Round pond, Lillypad pond and Rainbow pond, and the waters connecting the same, in township ten, in the town of Franklin, and township eighteen, in the town of Brighton, both in the county of Franklin, as a reservoir for water for the purposes specified in the first section of this act, and for that purpose to erect and maintain a dam at or near the outlet of Round pond aforesaid, of such height as they shall deem necessary, and with gates whereby the waters of said reservoir may be retained and discharged, at such times as may benefit the hydraulic power of the river and the passage of timber and logs down its channel, provided, however, that before overflowing any lands above the outlet of Round pond by the erection of such dam, the said commissioners shall acquire title to such lands by purchase or gift, if they can agree with the owners therefor; and if they are unable to agree with the owners of said lands liable to be overflowed, or any of them, and shall pay all damages to lands injured by the raising of water in said ponds or outlet, the said commissioners may, and they are Commissioners to make certain ponds a reservoir. To maintain a dam and gates for hydraulic purposes. To acquire titles to lands, before overflowing.

hereby authorized to acquire title to the same, in the manner and by proceedings similar to those prescribed in chapter one hundred and forty of the laws of eighteen hundred and fifty, entitled "An act to authorize the formation of railroad companies, and to regulate the same." The said commissioners shall not overflow said lands until the amount awarded as compensation to be made to the owner shall have been paid or deposited as required by the provisions of said chapter one hundred and forty.

Awards to be paid before overflow.

Willful injury to gates or structures a misdemeanor.

§ 5. Any and every person who shall willfully interfere with or injure any of the works, gates or structures made or erected under the provisions of this act shall be deemed guilty of a misdemeanor; and the said board of commissioners or their assigns may also maintain an action for any damage to such works, gates or structures.

Action for damages.

State not to be liable to damage, by erecting dam and reservoir.

§ 6. Nothing in this act contained shall be deemed or construed to render the state liable for any expense which may be incurred under any of the provisions thereof, nor for damage which may result from the erection, use or maintenance of the dam or reservoir authorized to be erected and constructed by this act.

§ 7. This act shall take effect immediately.

CHAP. 688.

AN ACT to amend an act entitled "An act for the incorporation of villages," passed April twenty, eighteen hundred and seventy.

Ante, vol. 7, p. 681.

PASSED April 26, 1871; three-fifths being present.

The People of the State of New York, represented in Senate and Assembly, do enact as follows:

SECTION 1. Section one of title one of the act entitled "An act for the incorporation of villages," passed April twenty, eighteen hundred and seventy, is hereby amended so as to read as follows:

Population and territory requisite for village incorporations.

§ 1. Any town or part of a town or towns not in any incorporated village, containing a resident population of not less than four hundred persons, and if it shall include in its boundaries a territory of more than one square mile in extent, containing a resident population of at the rate of not less than three hundred persons to every square mile of territory included within such boundaries, may be incorporated as a village under the provisions of this act by complying therewith.

Provisions as to survey and census not to apply to a whole town.

§ 2. The provisions of sections two, three, four, five and six of title one of said act shall not be deemed to apply in any case where the whole of any town is proposed to be incorporated.

§ 3. Section seven of title one of said act is hereby amended so as to read as follows:

§ 7. After the compliance with the preceding provisions, in case of the proposed incorporation of any part of a town or towns, or after a vote in favor of such incorporation of the whole town, at a regular or special town meeting of the voters thereof, in case of the proposed incorporation of the whole of such town as a village, a notice shall be prepared, stating that between the hours of ten A. M. and three P. M., on a specified day in said notice, at some public place within the bounds of the proposed village, designating such place, such day to be at least five weeks from the time of leaving the survey, map, description of boundaries and census for examination as hereinbefore provided, or in cases of the proposed incorporation of a whole town, not less than six weeks from the time of posting the notice hereinafter provided, an election will be held to determine whether the proposed territory shall be incorporated as a village. Such notice shall also state the proposed name of such village, set out the verbal description of its bounds, and give the amount proposed to be expended the first year of the incorporation for ordinary expenditures, as defined in this act, and shall be signed by at least twenty of the electors, resident within the bounds of said proposed village, who shall be liable to be assessed for the ordinary and extraordinary expenditures of said village. If the territorial limits of such village shall comprise parts of two or more towns, then of such twenty electors there shall be at least five from each of said towns who shall reside in the part of the town to be taken for such village. Such notice, so signed, shall be published in a newspaper, if there shall be one within the proposed bounds of said village, and copies of the same shall be posted in ten public places within said bounds at least thirty days before the day of election specified in said notice.

Notice of holding election to vote as to incorporation.

Notice to state name, boundaries, and proposed expenditures, for first year.

Notice, how signed.

Publication thereof.

§ 4. Title three of chapter two hundred and ninety-one, laws of eighteen hundred and seventy, is hereby amended by the addition of the following sections:

§ 17. The trustees of any village incorporated under this act, containing a population of three thousand and upward, may, whenever in their opinion the public interest demands it, at any time not less than thirty days preceding the next annual election for village officers, direct that at such election, and at every fourth annual election thereafter, there shall be elected a police justice, who shall be a resident of the village in which he shall be elected, and who shall hold office for four years, and shall have the same power and jurisdiction in criminal cases which justices of the peace now by law have or which may hereafter be conferred on justices of the peace by law, and shall be subject to the same duties and liabilities as the justices of the peace of the several towns of this state, and shall have jurisdiction in all cases of violation of village ordinances. When the whole of any town shall have been duly organized as a village, the electors of such village may, if they so elect at a meeting duly called for that purpose, provide for the

Trustees of certain villages may direct election of police justice

Term of office.

powers, jurisdiction and liabilities.

Election of trustees by districts, in case a

village comprises a whole town. division of such village into districts, and for the election of the trustees of such village within the several districts which shall be established therein.

Vacancies, how filled. § 18. Whenever any vacancy, by death, resignation, removal from the village or inability to discharge the duties of the office, shall occur in the said office, the trustees shall order an election to fill such vacancy at the next annual election for village officers, and in the meantime may fill the vacancy by appointment, or may designate any one of the justices of the peace of the town in which said village is situated to perform the duties of police justice until such election shall have been held.

Designation of town justice to act during vacancy.

Fees of police justice. § 19. The fees of the police justices elected or appointed as hereinbefore provided, and also of any justice of the peace while acting as police justice under designation of the trustees as provided in the last section, shall be a charge upon the village, and shall be audited and allowed in the same manner as other village charges.

How audited and allowed.

Oath of office, how filed. § 20. Every police justice elected or appointed under this act shall, within ten days after his election and before entering upon the duties of his office, take and subscribe the constitutional oath of office and file the same in the office of the town clerk of the town in which he resides.

Proviso. § 21. Any provision of title two of this act, inconsistent with the provisions hereinbefore contained, relating to police justices, shall not be held to apply to said office of police justice.

CHAP. 691.

AN ACT appropriating moneys for the Hudson River State Hospital for the Insane.

PASSED April 25, 1871; three-fifths being present.

The People of the State of New York, represented in Senate and Assembly, do enact as follows:

Appropriations for buildings, water-works, maintenance, etc. SECTION 1 The treasurer of the state is hereby authorized and directed to pay to the managers of the Hudson River State Hospital for the Insane, on the warrant of the comptroller, out of moneys in the treasury not otherwise appropriated, the sum of two hundred and fifty thousand dollars, in such sums as shall be approved of by the comptroller, to be applied toward the completion of the hospital buildings and appurtenances, the completion of the water-works and sewers, the finishing of the present sections and the maintenance of patients for the first six months, and for the purchase of a piece of land adjoining the hospital grounds, if such purchase shall be approved by the governor, comptroller and secretary of state. The expenditure of such moneys shall be duly and fully accounted for to the comptroller, with the vouchers and full details of the items and purposes, under each payment, before any other sum shall be advanced.

Purchase of adjoining lands, if approved.

Expenditures, how accounted for.

§ 2. This act shall take effect immediately.

CHAP. 693.

AN ACT to amend "An act in relation to saving banks," passed March twentieth, eighteen hundred and fifty-seven, and to confer additional powers upon the superintendent of the banking department, in relation to savings banks in this state.

Ante, vol. 4, p. 196.

PASSED April 25, 1871; three-fifths being present.

The People of the State of New York, represented in Senate and Assembly, do enact as follows:

SECTION 1. Section three of chapter one hundred and thirty-six of the laws of eighteen hundred and fifty-seven is hereby amended so as to read as follows:

§ 3. It shall be the duty of the superintendent of the banking department, as often as once in two years, either in person or by one or more competent persons by him appointed for that purpose, to visit and thoroughly examine every savings bank or institution for savings that shall be organized and doing business in this state, and the results of such examination shall be embodied in his annual report concerning savings banks, required by this act to be submitted to the legislature. And whenever any savings bank or institution for savings shall fail to make a report in compliance with this act, or whenever the superintendent shall have reason to believe that any savings bank or institution for savings is loaning or investing money in violation of its charter or of law, or is conducting business in an unsafe manner, it shall likewise be his duty, either in person or by one or more competent persons by him appointed, to visit and thoroughly examine the affairs and transactions of such institution; and whenever it shall appear to the superintendent from any examination made pursuant to the provisions of this section that any savings bank or institution for savings has been guilty of a violation of its charter or of law, or is conducting business in an unsafe manner, he shall, by an order under his hand and seal of office, addressed to the institution so offending, direct discontinuance of such illegal or unsafe practices, and a conformity with the requirements of its charter and of law, and with safety and security in its transactions; and whenever any savings bank or institution for savings shall refuse or neglect to comply with such order, or whenever it shall appear to the superintendent that it is unsafe or inexpedient for any savings bank or institution for savings to continue to transact business, he shall communicate that fact to the attorney-general, whose duty it shall then be to institute such proceedings against such savings bank or institution for savings as are now or may be hereafter authorized by law in case of insolvent corporations. The superintendent of the banking department,

Superintendent of banking department to examine savings banks.

To report thereon to legislature.

To examine savings banks failing to report or making improper investments, etc.

To direct discontinuance of unsafe or illegal practices.

To report savings banks failing to comply with orders to attorney-general.

His duty.

Power of person making examinations to administer oaths. May compel attendance of persons with books and papers. and the person or persons who may be appointed by him to examine the affairs of any savings bank shall have power to administer oaths to any person whose testimony may be required on any such examination, and to compel the appearance and attendance of any such person for the purpose of such examination, by summons, subpœna or attachment in the manner now authorized in respect to the attendance of persons as witnesses in the courts of this state; and all books and papers which may be deemed necessary to examine by the superintendent or the examiners so appointed, shall be produced, and their production may be compelled in like manner. Expenses of examination, how paid. The expense of any examination made in pursuance of the provisions of this act shall be paid by the savings bank or institution for savings so examined, in such amount as the superintendent shall certify to be just und reasonable; but Proviso. not oftener than once in two years shall any savings bank be liable to be so examined except at the expense of the state.

§ 2. This act shall take effect immediately.

CHAP. 695.

AN ACT to amend an act entitled "An act to extend the powers of boards of supervisors, except in the counties of New York and Kings," passed May eleventh, eighteen hundred and sixty-nine.

Ante, vol. 7, p. 485.

PASSED April 25, 1871; three-fifths being present.

The People of the State of New York, represented in Senate and Assembly, do enact as follows:

SECTION 1. Section five of "An act to extend the powers of boards of supervisors, except in the counties of New York and Kings," passed May eleventh, eighteen hundred and sixty-nine, is hereby amended so as to read as follows:

Informal action of town meetings, and of town officers, how legalized. § 5. The board of supervisors of any county, except New York and Kings, may, by a vote of two-thirds of all the members elected thereto, legalize the informal acts of any town meeting in raising money for any purpose for which such money is authorized to be raised by law, and by a like vote to legalize the irregular acts of any town officer, performed in County court to recommend same. good faith, and within the scope of his authority, provided such legalization shall be recommended by the county court of such county; and also, on like recommendation, to correct Correction of error in assessments, etc. any manifest, clerical or other error in any assessment or returns made by any town officer to such board of supervisors, or which shall properly come before such board for their Court may order refunding of taxes. action, confirmation or review; and upon the order of such court, made on application of the person aggrieved, and notice thereof, to such board, it shall refund to such person the amount collected from him of any tax illegally or improperly assessed or levied. An appeal may be taken from such order, as from a judgment of said court in an action. In raising the amount so refunded, such board shall adjust and apportion the same upon the property of the several towns of the county as shall be just, taking into consideration the portion of state, county and town tax included therein, and the extent to which each town has been benefited thereby.

Appeals. Taxes so refunded, how apportioned.

§ 2. This act shall take effect immediately.

CHAP. 696.

AN ACT to amend an act entitled "An act to amend chapter seven hundred and twenty-seven of the laws of eighteen hundred and sixty-nine, entitled 'An act authorizing cities and villages to acquire title to property for burial purposes, and to levy taxes for the payment of the same,' passed May eighth, eighteen hundred and sixty-nine," passed May ninth, eighteen hundred and seventy.

Ante, vol. 7, pp. 469, 760.

PASSED April 25, 1871; three-fifths being present.

The People of the State of New York, represented in Senate and Assembly, do enact as follows:

SECTION 1. The trustees of any village are hereby authorized to appoint a cemetery commission of not less than five, nor more than nine resident freeholders of said village, who shall, during their term of office, have exclusive control and management of the laying out, beautifying and improving of any lands which may be purchased by said trustees as provided by section one of the act hereby amended. The members of such commission shall hold their office for five years from and after their appointment, and when vacancies occur in such commission the same shall be filled by said trustees from the resident freeholders of said villages. All moneys appropriated by said trustees for the improvement of such lands, shall be placed in the hands of said commission to be expended by them in such laying out, beautifying and improving; and said commission shall, on the first day of March in each year during their term of office, make a report by items of their expenditures, and stating the objects thereof, to said trustees, which report shall be in writing, signed by a majority of the members of such commission and verified by their oaths.

Village cemetery commissioners. Their duties. Terms of office. Vacancies, how filled. To expend moneys raised for cemetery improvements. Annual financial report.

§ 2. This act shall take effect immediately.

CHAP. 697.

AN ACT to amend an act entitled "An act to authorize the formation of gas-light companies," passed February sixteen, eighteen hundred and forty-eight.

Ante, vol. 3, p. 849.

PASSED April 25, 1871; three-fifths being present.

The People of the State of New York, represented in Senate and Assembly, do enact as follows:

Powers of gas-light companies

SECTION 1. Section two of the act entitled "An act to authorize the formation of gas-light companies," passed February sixteen, eighteen hundred and forty-eight, is hereby amended so as to read as follows:

§ 2. When the certificate shall have been filed as aforesaid, the person who shall have signed and ackowledged the same, and their successors, shall be a body politic and corporate in fact and in name by the name stated in such certificate, and by that name have succession, and shall be capable of suing and being sued in any court of law or equity in this state; and they and their successors may have a common seal, and may make and alter the same at pleasure; and they shall, by their corporate name, be capable in law of purchasing, holding, and conveying any real and personal estate whatever, which may be necessary to enable the said company to carry on the operations named in such certificate, but shall not mortgage the same or give any lien thereon. The trustees of such company may purchase mines, manufactories and other property necessary for their business, and issue stock to the amount of the value thereof in payment therefor; and the stock so issued shall be declared and taken to be full stock, and not liable to any further calls; neither shall the holders thereof be liable for any further payments under the provisions of the tenth section of the said act; but in all statements and reports of the company to be published, this stock shall not be stated or reported as being issued for cash paid into the company, but shall be reported in this respect according to the fact.

Purchase of mines, manufactories, etc., authorized. Issue of stock therefor. Stock, how reported.

§ 3. This act shall take effect immediately.

CHAP. 698.

AN ACT to provide for building a bridge across the Tonawanda creek, on the Tonawanda Indian reservation, and making an appropriation for the same.

PASSED April 25, 1871, by a two-thirds vote.

The People of the State of New York, represented in Senate and Assembly, do enact as follows:

SECTION 1. Joseph W. Holmes, Garry K. Lester and Jeremiah Freeman are hereby appointed commissioners for the purpose of building a bridge, constructed of wood, stone and iron, across the Tonawanda creek, on the Tonawanda Indian reservation, at that point where said creek is crossed by the Akron road (so called), leading from the county of Erie into the county of Genesee. It shall be the duty of said commissioners to build, or cause to be built of the materials aforesaid, as soon as may be, after the passage of this act, a substantial wagon bridge at the point aforesaid, which shall not exceed in cost the sum of four thousand dollars. Each of said commissioners, before entering upon the duties of his office, shall give a bond to the people of the state of New York, with two or more sufficient sureties, to be approved by the comptroller, in the penalty of three thousand dollars, that he will well and faithfully discharge the duties of the commission aforesaid, and pay over and account for all moneys coming into his hands as such commissioner. Commissioners to build bridge. Materials therefor. Expenditure limited. Official bond of commissioners, how approved.

§ 2. The sum of four thousand dollars, or so much of that amount as shall be necessary, is hereby appropriated out of the general fund for the purposes of this act, and shall be paid by the treasurer on the warrant of the comptroller, to the order of said commissioners in such installments as shall be required for work actually performed or material furnished for the same. Appropriation.

§ 3. It shall be lawful for the above-named commissioners to take the stone and timber necessary for the construction of said bridge from the lands of the said Tonawanda Indian reservation, but no greater amount of stone or timber than is absolutely necessary for its construction. Use of stone and timber from Indian reservation.

§ 4. In case any of the commissioners named in the first section of this act shall decline to act, or shall die or resign, after having qualified as herein provided, the county judge of the county in which the person so declining, dying or resigning shall reside at the time of the passage of this act, is authorized, and it shall be his duty to fill such vacancy by appointment; and the person so appointed shall qualify and give bail, in the same manner as provided in the first section of this act. Vacancies in commission how filled. Appointee to execute bond.

§ 5. This act shall take effect immediately.

CHAP. 699.

AN ACT to provide for taking testimony in certain matters relating to state charitable institutions.

PASSED April 25, 1871; three-fifths being present.

The People of the State of New York, represented in Senate and Assembly, do enact as follows:

Investigation of complaints, etc.

SECTION 1. Whenever the state board of commissioners of public charities, or the managers, directors or trustees of any asylum, hospital, or other charitable institution, the managers, directors or trustees of which are appointed by the governor and senate, or by the legislature, shall deem it necessary or proper to investigate and ascertain the truth of any charge or complaint made or circulated respecting the conduct of the superintendent, assistants, subordinate officers or servants, in whatever capacity or duty employed by or under the official control of any such board, managers, directors or trustees, it shall be lawful for the presiding officer for the time being of any such board, managers, directors or trustees, to administer oaths to all witnesses coming before them respectively for examination, and to issue compulsory process for the attendance of any witness within the state whom they may respectively desire to examine, and for the production of all papers that any such witness may possess, or have in his power, touching the matter of such complaint or investigation; and willful false swearing by any witness who may be so examined is hereby declared to be perjury.

Power to administer oaths and compel attendance of witnesses. Production of papers.

Fees of witnesses.

§ 2. All persons examined as witnesses under the first section of this act shall be paid the same fees as are now paid to witnesses in the supreme court by the said board, managers, directors or trustees, authorizing the issuing of such compulsory process.

Penalty for disobeying subpœna.

§ 3. Any person willfully neglecting to obey any subpœna or citation to testify or produce papers, as provided in this act, shall be liable to a penalty of one hundred dollars, to be recovered, with costs of suit, before any court having cognizance thereof.

CHAP. 700.

AN ACT in relation to stenographers in the circuit courts, courts of oyer and terminer and special terms of the supreme court in the sixth, seventh and eighth judicial districts.

PASSED April 25, 1871; three-fifths being present.

The People of the State of New York, represented in Senate and Assembly, do enact as follows:

SECTION 1. The justices of the supreme court in the sixth, seventh and eighth judicial districts shall appoint a stenographer for their respective districts, who shall be a person skilled in his profession, and who shall continue in such employment during the pleasure of the court, and he shall receive an annual salary of two thousand five hundred dollars, to be paid as hereinafter provided. And said stenographer shall also receive his actual necessary expenses while attending said courts, and ten cents per mile for his actual travel to and from said courts and his place of residence, to be certified by the presiding justice of such courts, and such necessary sum for stationery as such justice shall certify; and the same shall be paid by the treasurer of the county from the court fund or fund from which the jurors are paid, upon such certificate. Appointment of stenographers. Salary, expenses, mileage and stationery. How certified and paid

§ 2. It shall be the duty of said stenographer to take full stenographic minutes of the testimony and other proceedings upon trials in such courts, under the direction of the presiding justice, and to furnish copies thereof, or of such portions as shall be required, on payment on behalf of the party ordering the same, of six cents for each hundred words of the copy so furnished. Stenographer to take minutes of testimony, etc. Payment for copies.

§ 3. It shall be the duty of the clerk of each of said courts to furnish said stenographer with a certificate, under his hand and seal, of the number of days such courts shall have been in session; and, upon such certificate, the court at special term shall, by an order, apportion to each county in such district such proportion of the salary hereinbefore mentioned as the number of days such court shall have been held in such county shall bear to the whole number of days such courts shall have been held in such district; and, upon such order, the county treasurer shall semi-annually pay to said stenographer the amounts so apportioned to their respective counties; and the boards of supervisors of such counties shall provide for the payment of the same. Certificate of attendance by clerk of courts. Court to proportion salary. Semi-annual payments. How provided for.

§ 4. Whenever two of such courts shall be appointed to be held at the same time, in either of said districts, it shall be lawful for the justices assigned to hold the same, to designate the court at which said stenographer shall attend, and to employ an additional stenographer to attend such other court, Designation, in case of appointment of two courts at same time.

CHAP. 708.

AN ACT to amend the sixth section of title three, chapter eight, part second of the Revised Statutes, relating to guardians and wards.

Ante, vol. 2, p. 157.

PASSED April 25, 1871; three-fifths being present.

The People of the State of New York, represented in Senate and Assembly, do enact as follows:

SECTION 1. The sixth section of title three, chapter eight, part second of the Revised Statutes, is hereby amended so as to read as follows:

Surrogates may appoint guardians for minors in certain cases. Notice to father, if living. Surrogate to inquire as to property of minor, etc.

§ 6. The surrogate, to whom application may be made under either of the preceding sections, shall have the same power to allow and appoint guardians as is possessed by the supreme court, and may appoint a guardian for a minor whose father is living, upon personal service of notice of the application for such appointment upon such father, at least ten days prior thereto; and in all cases the surrogate shall inquire into the circumstances of the minor and ascertain the amount of his personal property, and the value of the rents and profits of his real estate, and for that purpose may compel any person to appear before him and testify in relation thereto.

§ 2. This act shall take effect immediately.

CHAP. 709.

AN ACT to amend an act entitled "An act to establish an insurance department," passed April fifteenth, eighteen hundred and fifty-nine.

Ante, vol. 4, p. 252.

PASSED April 25, 1871.

The People of the State of New York, represented in Senate and Assembly, do enact as follows:

SECTION. 1. The seventh section of an act entitled "An act to establish an insurance department," passed April fifteenth, eighteen hundred and fifty-nine, is hereby amended so as tc read as follows:

Fees payable to insurance department.

§ 7. There shall be paid by every company, association, person or persons, or agent, to whom this act shall apply, the following fees toward paying the expenses of executing this act: For filing the declaration now required by law, or the certified copy of a charter also now required, the sum of thirty dollars; for filing the annual statement now required, twenty dollars; for each certificate of authority and certified copy thereof such sum not exceeding five dollars as shall be fixed from time to time by the said superintendent; for every copy of paper filed in his office, the sum of ten cents per folio, and for affixing the seal of said office to such copy and certifying the same, one dollar. In case the expenses of said department shall exceed the amount of fees collected under this act, and paid into the state treasury (exclusive of the tax upon marine premiums), the excess of such expenses shall be annually assessed by the superintendent, pro rata, upon all the insurance companies of this state; and the said superintendent is hereby empowered to collect such assessments and pay the same into the state treasury. Expenses of department above fees collected, how assessed and collected.

§ 2. This act shall take effect immediately.

CHAP. 710.

AN ACT to authorize the clerks of certain counties to appoint additional special deputies.

PASSED April 25, 1871; three-fifths being present.

The People of the State of New York, represented in Senate and Assembly, do enact as follows:

SECTION 1. The clerk of every county in this state having a population of one hundred thousand inhabitants is hereby authorized to designate one or more of the persons employed in his office to attend upon the courts of which he is clerk, and the persons so designated shall severally possess the same power and authority as the said clerk, to attend and do all the things in and about the courts for which they are severally designated. Designation of person to attend courts, in certain counties.

§ 2. Such appointment shall be in writing and shall be filed in the clerk's office of the county, and every person appointed for this duty shall, before he enters upon it, take the oath required of all officers by the constitution and laws of this state, and shall hold his appointment during the pleasure of such clerk. Appointments, how made and filed. Oath of office and term.

§ 3. This act shall take effect immediately.

CHAP. 711.

AN ACT to amend an act entitled "An act in relation to the State Cabinet of Natural History," passed May second, eighteen hundred and seventy.

Ante, vol. 7, p. 757.

PASSED April 25, 1871; three-fifths being present.

The People of the State of New York, represented in Senate and Assembly, do enact as follows:

Assistants and curators, how appointed. SECTION 1. The assistants and curators of departments provided for by the second section of the act entitled "An act in relation to the State Cabinet of Natural History," passed May second, eighteen hundred and seventy, shall be appointed by the director of the State Museum of Natural History, with the concurrence of the board of regents of the university.

Course of lectures, how organized. § 2. The annual course of free scientific lectures authorized by the third section of said act shall be organized under the direction of the board of regents and the director of the state museum.

Moneys appropriated, how expended. § 3. The moneys appropriated by the fourth section of the act above named shall be expended by the director of the state museum of natural history, with the approval of the board of regents of the university.

§ 4. This act shall take effect immediately.

CHAP. 712.

AN ACT in relation to the election of representatives in congress, senators and members of assembly.

PASSED April 25, 1871; three-fifths being present.

The People of the State of New York, represented in Senate and Assembly, do enact as follows:

Separate ballot boxes for congress, senate and assembly. SECTION 1. At each annual or special election at which a representative in congress, senator or member of assembly is hereafter to be elected, the inspectors in the several election districts in this state shall provide and keep a separate box in which all ballots for representatives in congress, to be indorsed Form of ballots. "Congress," shall be deposited; also a separate box in which all ballots for senator, to be indorsed "Senate," shall be deposited; and also a separate box in which all ballots for member of assembly, to be indorsed "Assembly," shall be Order of canvass. deposited; and the ballots deposited in said several boxes shall be estimated and canvassed in the order named above, respectively, and immediately following the estimate and canvass of the ballots indorsed "State."

Repeal. § 2. All acts and parts of acts inconsistent with the provisions of this act are hereby repealed.

§ 3. This act shall take effect immediately.

CHAP. 713.

AN ACT in relation to the chronic pauper insane.

PASSED April 25, 1871; three-fifths being present.

The People of the State of New York, represented in Senate and Assembly, do enact as follows:

SECTION 1. The board of state commissioners of public charities are hereby authorized to hear and determine all applications which may be made to them in writing, by the county superintendents of the poor of the several counties of this state, for exemption from the operation of the tenth section of the act entitled "An act to authorize the establishment of a state asylum for the chronic insane, and for the better care of the insane poor," to be known as "The Willard Asylum for the Insane," passed April eighth, eighteen hundred and sixty-five. And whenever said board on such application shall determine that the buildings and means employed to take care of the chronic pauper insane of such county are sufficient and proper for the time being for such purpose, and shall file the same in the office of the clerk of the county making such application, then and in that case, and until such determination shall be revoked as hereinafter mentioned and provided, the county superintendents of the poor of such county shall be relieved from sending the chronic pauper insane of such county to the Willard Asylum for the Insane, as now provided by law. Said board may at any time revoke such determination, but such revocation must be made in writing, and filed in the county clerk's office of the county making such application, and notice thereof shall be given in writing to the county superintendents of the poor of such county, and upon the filing of the same the said county superintendents of the poor of such county shall from thenceforward be again subject to the provisions and operations of the said act.

Board of state charities to hear and determine certain applications.

May file determination relieving counties from sending pauper insane to Willard asylum.

May revoke determination.

How filed.

Notice to superintendents of poor.

§ 2. The board of state commissioners of public charities are hereby authorized and required, whenever they shall be satisfied that the provisions made for the chronic insane in any county poor-house is inadequate and unsuitable, to direct the superintendents of the poor of such county to remove the chronic insane of that county to the Willard Asylum for the Insane within ten days after receiving a written or printed notice to make such removal.

Commissioners may direct removal of chronic pauper insane to asylum.

§ 3. This act shall take effect immediately.

CHAP. 715.

AN ACT making appropriations for certain expenses of government, and for supplying deficiencies in former appropriations.

PASSED April 26, 1871, by a two-third vote.

The People of the State of New York, represented in Senate and Assembly, do enact as follows:

Payments by treasurer. Comptroller to audit certain claims. Vouchers to be presented.

SECTION 1. The treasurer shall pay, on the warrant of the comptroller, from the several funds specified, to the persons indicated in this act, the amounts named, or such parts of those amounts as shall be sufficient to accomplish in full the purpose designed by the appropriations; but no warrant shall be issued, except in cases of salaries or extra compensation for official services, until the amounts claimed shall have been audited by the comptroller. The persons demanding payment shall present to him, if required, a detailed statement in items, verified by affidavit; and if such account shall be for services, it must show when, where and under what authority they were rendered; if for expenditures, when, where, for what and under what authority they were made; if for articles furnished, when and where they were furnished, to whom they were delivered, and under what authority; and if the demand shall be for traveling expenses, the accounts must also specify the distance traveled, the places of starting and destination, the duty or business, the date and items of expenditure. On all accounts for transportation, furniture, blank and other books furnished for use of office, binding, blanks, printing, stationery and postage, a bill, duly certified, must also be furnished; but, whenever an appropriation shall have been made for the same purpose, or the amount shall have been provided otherwise, the sums here directed to be paid shall not be considered as an addition to such appropriation, unless it shall be expressly so declared in this act.

Appropriations.

§ 2. The following amounts are hereby appropriated for the several objects specified, namely:

FROM THE GENERAL FUND.

For chaplain of the legislature.

For the clergymen officiating as chaplains of the senate and assembly during the present session of the legislature, for compensation, to be paid one-half to the clerk of the senate and one-half to the clerk of the assembly, for distribution by them to those clergymen, at the rate of three dollars for every day of attendance, six hundred dollars.

Clerks of the senate and assembly.

For the clerk of the senate, seven hundred dollars, and for the clerk of the assembly, fifteen hundred dollars, for compensation for extra clerical services and engrossing; for indexing the journals, bills and documents of the senate and assembly, in addition, to each of them, one thousand dollars; and to each of the said clerks, in addition to the foregoing, for extra compensation, eight hundred dollars.

For Charles R. Dayton, the journal clerk of the senate; for Frank B. Brown, assistant journal clerk of the senate; Charles J. Gaylord, assistant clerk of the senate; Charles E. Johnson, engrossing clerk of the senate; Edward C. Gillespie, assistant engrossing clerk of the senate; George Breck, executive clerk of the senate; Walter A. Cook, the journal clerk of the assembly; Lyman B. Smith, assistant clerk of the assembly; Andrew D. Soverhill, Charles N. Dayton, Burnet Forbes, Daniel S. Lamont, James A. Fassett, Addison S. Burdick, Edward M. Johnson, additional deputy clerks of the assembly, to each of them for compensation, nine hundred dollars; and for William J. Wilson, clerk of the engrossing committee, Henry D. Keller, speaker's clerk, and Edwin E. Coventry, clerk's secretary, to each of them for compensation, six hundred dollars. Assistant clerks of the senate and assembly. Speaker's clerk.

And for the several deputy clerks of the senate and assembly, and the clerk of the engrossing committee of the assembly, for additional compensation, to each of them, four hundred dollars, and the same allowance for mileage as is allowed to members of the legislature; and, in addition thereto, for Charles R. Dayton and Walter A. Cook, journal clerks of the senate and assembly, for extra services, to each of them, three hundred dollars. Deputy clerks of senate and assembly.

For the clerks and journal clerks of the sub-committee of the whole of the senate and assembly, to each of them, three hundred dollars. Clerks of sub-committees.

For the clerk of the senate, for advances for contingent expenses, two thousand dollars; and for the clerk of the assembly, for advances for contingent expenses, twenty-five thousand dollars. Contingent expenses of clerks of legislature.

For Isaac Rosepaugh, for carting the document mails from the capitol to the post-office during the present session, one hundred and fifty dollars. Carting document.

For A. J. Myer, for fourteen days' service as postmaster after the adjournment of the legislature of eighteen hundred and seventy, eighty-four dollars. Postmaster of 1870.

For the officers of the legislature employed, in addition to those authorized by statute, namely, John M. Sigourney, librarian of the senate; R. P. Cormack, assistant librarian of the senate; Charles S. Biddlecom, assistant postmaster of the senate for the first half of the session, and L. S. Simpson, assistant postmaster of the senate for the last half of the session; Edward Donahoe, keeper of the senate chamber; Myer Stark, janitor of the senate; James C. Huston, librarian of the assembly; William H. Lee, assistant librarian of the assembly; James M. Chase, assistant sergeant-at-arms of the assembly; Thomas Ackerson, postmaster of the assembly; Addison Seymour and Lyman S. Coleman, assistant postmasters of the assembly; John Mulville, janitor of the assembly; Thomas Dermody, keeper of the assembly chamber; Felix Riley, assistant keeper of the assembly chamber; Matthew D. Sherrill, superintendent of the documents of the assembly; Frederick Andes, superintendent of ventilation of Additional officers of the legislature.

the assembly chamber; James R. Agnew, superintendent of the wrapping department of the assembly; Michael Jordan and Parley B. Rhoades, messengers of the sub-committee of the whole; and for John W. Lawyer, superintendent of the cloak room of the assembly, to each of them for every day of actual service during the session, three dollars, and the same allowance for mileage which is made to members and officers of the legislature; for the assistant door-keepers, janitors, keepers and assistant keepers, and for the superintendent of the wrapping department, superintendent of ventilation, superintendent of the cloak room of the assembly, and superintendent of documents of the assembly, to each of them, for additional compensation for every day of service, two dollars; and for the sergeant-at-arms and the assistant sergeant-at-arms, door-keeper, and librarians and assistant librarians of the senate and assembly, and the postmaster of the assembly, assistant postmasters of the senate and assembly, to each of them, for additional compensation for every day of service, three dollars.

Per diem allowance and mileage. Additional compensation for officers of legislature.

Assistant door-keeper. For William Fonda, for compensation as assistant door-keeper of the senate, two hundred dollars.

Messengers of the senate and assembly. For the messengers employed by authority of the senate and assembly, to be paid on the certificate of the respective presiding officers, namely: Robert D. Evans, clerk and bank messenger of the senate; Lewis C. Holmes, messenger of the president of the senate; John W. Hannan and Charles H. Tracy, messengers of the sergeant-at-arms of the senate; Edgar Myer and James J. Hart, messengers of the postmaster of the senate; William Van Camp, messenger of the librarian of the senate; Leopold Stark, Peter G. Galvin and Eugene Wood, special messengers of the senate; Charles Stuart, bank messenger of the clerk of the assembly; Joseph Zeiser, messenger of the librarian of the assembly; Charles L. Keyes, messenger of the engrossing room of the assembly; Charles H. Walters, James McDonald, George H. Price, Thomas O'Brien, Thomas A. Dwyer, Peter Riley, Hugh Riley and Phillip Riley, Charles H. Williams, Willie K. Stevens, Frank McSpedon and Charles S. Drummond, messengers of the sergeant-at-arms; John McCann, Frank Grey, Dava Dean, Byron Andrus, John K. Hoyt, Joseph Jennings, William S. Pratt, George Palmer, James S. Brown and James Goff, general messengers of the assembly; Edward H. Vrooman, William Rothschild, John P. Flynn, Frank Chester, James McDermott, Richard O'Grady, Victor B. Lobdell, Myer Litchtentritt and Henry D. Carpenter, messengers to the postmaster of the assembly, to each of them, three dollars and fifty cents for every day of the session.

Clerks of committees. For the clerks of the committees of the senate, namely: of the committee on judiciary, finance, literature, municipal affairs, railroads, canals, claims, internal affairs of towns and counties, affairs of villages, public health, engrossed bills, charitable and religious societies, banks and salt, jointly, and the committees on commerce and navigation and roads and bridges, jointly, to each of them for every day of the session, four dollars, and one hundred dollars in addition; and for the clerks of committees of the assembly named in the rules, to each of them four dollars per day, and one hundred dollars in addition; and for the clerks of the committees not authorized by the rules, to each of them four dollars per day, to be paid on the certificate of the chairman of each committee, and the presiding officer of each house in which such committee has such clerk, and no clerk shall receive pay except for service on at least one committee.

For William H. Bogart, clerk to committee on engrossed bills of the senate, for extra compensation, three hundred dollars. Wm. H. Bogart.

For the door-keepers, librarians and postmasters of the assembly, acting as such under the authority of the presiding officer and clerk of said body, prior to the appointment of such officers for the present session, to each of them for every day of their service, three dollars, and for additional compensation for each day, two dollars, and the mileage allowed by law. Door-keepers and officers acting at beginning of session.

To Thomas Driffill, stenographer for the assembly, for compensation, fifteen hundred dollars. Assembly stenographer.

For Geo. H. E. Lynch, deputy assistant engrossing clerk of the assembly, the same compensation as allowed clerks of committees authorized by the rules. Geo. H. E. Lynch.

For Michael Cassidy, for compensation for additional services imposed on him by the trustees of the capitol and state officers in taking charge of the state property and buildings adjoining the capitol, six hundred dollars. Michael Cassidy.

For the women employed in cleaning the chambers and rooms adjoining the senate and assembly, for compensation, to each of them, for every day of service, to be certified by the superintendent of the capitol, two dollars; and for women employed in cleaning the geological hall, and Jane Gray and Sarah Moran, employed in cleaning the state library rooms adjoining, to each of them, for additional compensation, seventy-five dollars. Women for cleaning rooms of capitol, etc. Jane Gray and Sarah Moran.

For the pages of the senate and assembly, for compensation, to each of them, two dollars for each day of the session; and for the messengers of the committees named in the rules, to each of them, three dollars for every day of the session; and for the messengers of committees not named in the rules, to each of them, for every day of the session, two dollars and fifty cents; the messengers of the two houses shall be paid upon the certificate of the presiding officers, respectively, and the messengers of committees upon the certificate of the respective chairmen of said committees, and of the presiding officers of the two houses, respectively. Pages of the senate and assembly.

For George Graham, sergeant-at-arms of the senate, for fees and traveling expenses in subpœnaing witnesses and services in attending upon committees while investigating subjects before them, pursuant to order of the senate, three hundred and ninty-four dollars. Sergeant-at-arms of senate.

Sergeant of assembly. For the sergeant-at-arms of the assembly, for services and personal expenses in subpœnaing witnesses for various standing and special committees of the assembly, nine hundred and ninety-four dollars and eighty-three cents.

Postage on documents. For payment of postage and expenses on documents sent out by members, officers and reporters of the legislature, eight thousand dollars, or so much thereof as may be necessary.

Senate stenographer. For Andrew Devine, the stenographer of the senate, for compensation, one thousand five hundred dollars.

James C. Huston. For James C. Huston, for preparing statistical list of members and officers of the assembly, for the year eighteen hundred and seventy-one, thirty dollars.

A. J. Meyer. For A. J. Meyer, assistant sergeant-at-arms of the senate, for preparing statistical list of senate, for the year eighteen hundred and seventy-one, twenty-five dollars, and for extra compensation, one hundred dollars.

Peter Stephens. H. W. Aiken. Victor Lobdell. To Peter Stephens, for services and expenses as postmaster of the assembly, after the close of the session of eighteen hundred and seventy, while he remained as such postmaster, under the order of the house, and for H. W. Aiken, assistant postmaster of the senate, at the commencement of the session of eighteen hundred and seventy, eighty-four dollars each; and for Victor Lobdell, as messenger of the postmaster during the same period, twenty-five dollars.

D. C. McMillan. For D. C. McMillan, for attending three sessions of committee on commerce and navigation of the senate, reporting testimony therein, and transcribing the same, on the first and second days of March, ninety dollars.

Miss Jennie Stanton. For Miss Jennie Stanton, for transcribing notes of the stenographer of the assembly, three hundred and fifty dollars.

Edward Donohoe. To Edward Donohoe, keeper of senate chamber, for extra services, two hundred dollars.

Refitting of senate chamber. For the clerk of the senate, for refitting senate chamber, and fitting up and furnishing four committees' rooms, pursuant to resolution of the senate, three thousand nine hundred and sixteen dollars and twelve cents.

Felix Riley and John Mulville. To Felix Riley and John Mulville, acting keepers of assembly chamber during the illness of Patrick Durmody, one hundred dollars, in addition to the allowance already made, the same being for extra services.

James C. Huston. Wm. H. Lee. To James C. Huston, librarian of the assembly, and William H. Lee, assistant librarian of the assembly, for reading proof of the journal for eighteen hundred and seventy and eighteen hundred and seventy-one, and for other clerical services rendered by them, to each of them, three hundred dollars.

J. P. Mulligan. To John P. Mulligan, two hundred and fifty dollars, for services rendered in eighteen hundred and seventy-one.

R. D. Evans. To Robert D. Evans, two hundred and fifty dollars, for services during the summer, overseeing of work done in senate chamber.

To Daniel Witter, Michael McCann, Augustus Baker, James Lamberson, Robert E. Harvey. John L. Hughes and John Simonton, additional assistant door-keepers of the assembly, five hundred dollars each for compensation. Assistant door-keepers of assembly.

For the clerks of the committees on finance of the senate and ways and means in the assembly, as extra compensation, five hundred dollars each. Clerks of finance committee.

For the messenger of the committee of ways and means, as additional compensation, one hundred and fifty dollars. Messenger.

To Joseph Zieser, for extra services in assembly, one hundred and fifty dollars. Joseph Zieser.

For Henry D. Keller, speaker's clerk, Edwin E. Coventry, clerk's secretary, and Charles H. Walters, sergeant-at-arms' messenger, to each of them, two hundred dollars, as additional compensation. H. D. Keller and others.

For Albert S. Brawley, Edward P. Staats, Louis Barile, Edward Taylor, John Brady, Charles E. Warren, John Williams, Charles Krauschah, William Henry, M. H. Northrup, George Willys, Horace J. Haviland, John Hopkins and David Burke, messengers of the assembly, to each of them, for compensation, the same pay as is allowed committee messengers authorized by the rules. Messengers of assembly.

To Henry Williams, for services rendered the committee on the judiciary of the assembly, three hundred dollars. Henry Williams.

For Lyman B. Smith, the assistant clerk of the assembly, as extra compensation, three hundred dollars. L. B. Smith.

For Walter A. Cook, for services rendered the committee of ways and means during the present session, three hundred dollars. W. A. Cook.

For Adam W. Smith, for carriages furnished the sergeant-at-arms of the assembly in the performance of official duties, one hundred dollars. A. W. Smith.

For adjutant Francis, late of seventy-first regiment, New York State National Guard, one thousand dollars, for injuries sustained by him while in the service of the state. Adjutant Francis.

For William Rothschilds and Charles D. Hunter, general messengers, as additional compensation, one hundred dollars each. General messengers.

To Calvin E. Pratt, executor of the estate of Henry E. Ruggles, to pay a judgment recovered by him against the state of New York, December twenty-seven, eighteen hundred and fifty-eight, including interest, three thousand dollars. Calvin E. Pratt.

The contract for printing and publishing the reports of the court of appeals shall be extended for five years, provided the secretary of state shall deem it for the interests of the state. Court of appeals reports.

To Thomas Driffill, for transcribing stenographic notes of testimony taken before the special committee of investigation into the conduct of Messrs. Irving and Weed, seventy-five dollars. Thomas Driffill.

For the clerk of the senate, for books purchased for the senate library, and rebinding old volumes, ninety-three dollars. Senate library.

Hiram Calkins. For Hiram Calkins, for preparing general index to Session Laws for last five years, pursuant to resolution of senate, passed April twenty-six, eighteen hundred and seventy, twenty-seven hundred dollars.

Digest of claims. For preparing continuation of the Digest of Claims, pursuant to resolution of senate, passed April twenty-five, eighteen hundred and seventy, fifteen hundred dollars.

Index to senate papers. For arranging papers on file in senate, and preparing index to the same, pursuant to resolution of senate, passed January nineteen, eighteen hundred and seventy-one, twelve hundred dollars.

Index of senate bills. For preparing classified index of bills introduced in senate, during session of eighteen hundred and seventy, seven hundred and fifty dollars.

C. W. Armstrong, arranging files. To Cornelius W. Armstrong, for arranging the files of the assembly in such a manner that papers when wanted can be readily found, under the resolution of the assembly, passed April thirteenth, eighteen hundred and seventy, six hundred dollars.

Labeling papers. For separating and labeling papers relating to bills passed, under resolution of the assembly, passed April thirteenth, eigteen hundred and seventy, six hundred dollars.

Index of bills. For preparing an index of the bills introduced during the session of eighteen hundred and seventy, under resolution of the assembly, passed April thirteenth, eighteen hundred and seventy, seven hundred and fifty dollars.

Classified index of bills for ten years. For preparing, properly classified, and under appropriate headings, for the use of the legislature, an index to all bills printed from eighteen hundred and sixty up to and including the year eighteen hundred and seventy, and arranging the same for printing, under resolution of the assembly, passed April thirteenth, eighteen hundred and seventy, two thousand dollars.

Digest of claims of 1871. For preparing a continuation of the Digest of Claims, down to and including the present session, under resolution of the assembly, passed April thirteenth, eighteen hundred and seventy, fifteen hundred dollars.

Arrangement of petitions, papers, etc. For arranging, alphabetically, all petitions and papers connected with the bills which have been under consideration within the past five years, and have not been passed into laws, and preparing a catalogue of the same for printing, under resolution of the assembly, passed April thirteenth, eighteen hundred and seventy, twelve hundred dollars.

Horton Tidd. For Horton Tidd, clerk of the committees on banks and agriculture, jointly, for the session of eighteen hundred and seventy, the sum of five hundred and forty-eight dollars, or so much thereof as was due.

Clerk's manual. For the clerk of the assembly, for revising, mailing and sending to members of the assembly previous to the organization of the next house, the Clerk's Manual, two hundred and fifty dollars.

For Nicholas Benner, for services as clerk of the committee on public printing, in the assembly, for the session of eighteen hundred and seventy, the same having been omitted in the appropriation for that year, four hundred and sixty-eight dollars, or so much thereof as was due. Nicholas Benner.

For Robert D. Evans, bank clerk of the senate, Lewis C. Holmes, messenger of the president of the senate, John W. Hannan and Charles H. Tracy, messengers of the sergeant-at-arms of the senate, George Breck, executive clerk of the senate, and James McDonald, express messenger, for additional compensation to each of them, two hundred dollars; and for Leopold Stark and Eugene Wood, as special messengers of the senate, for extra compensation, one hundred and fifty dollars. Messengers and clerks of senate for extra compensation.

To Matthew Hawe, jr., for opening and attending the assembly library at the commencement of the session, twenty-five dollars. M. Hawe, jr.

To pay Amariah Holbrook, for witness fees attending the court of impeachment against Robert C. Dorn, canal commissioner, on presentation of the certificate of the president of said court duly verified, twenty-six dollars and seventy cents. A. Holbrook.

For Michael Delehanty, for heating and ventilating senate chamber, under the direction of the clerk of the senate, pursuant to a resolution of the senate, passed April twenty-six, eighteen hundred and seventy, and repairing ceiling of library and cloak room of the senate, four thousand one hundred and fifteen dollars. Michael Delehanty.

For Taylor and Waterman, for carpets for senate chamber and senate library, and upholstery work in senate, two thousand five hundred and twenty-eight dollars and twenty-seven cents. Taylor and Waterman.

For Charles F. Bell, for services in constitutional convention, as provided by laws of eighteen hundred and sixty-nine, page one thousand nine hundred and ten, two hundred and fifty-six dollars and fifty cents, or so much thereof as the comptroller may find to be due him. Chas. F. Bell.

For Taylor and Waterman, for carpeting, oil-cloth, upholstering, et cetera, in the engrossing and committee rooms of the assembly, and geological hall, seven hundred and forty-eight dollars and sixty-seven cents; for carpets, oil-cloths and materials furnished for the capitol, two thousand three hundred and sixty-six dollars and ninety-three cents. Taylor and Waterman.

To James Cottrell, Sandford Murray, Henry Hillman, William M. Bull, James J. Norton, William J. Nolan and Jeremiah Blauvelt, assistant door-keepers of the assembly, to each of them for compensation, five hundred dollars. Assistant door-keepers of assembly.

For Ira Porter, for painting, graining and varnishing, under direction of the clerk of the senate, one thousand and two dollars and eighty-two cents. Ira Porter.

For the legislature, for postage, express of committees, compensation of witnesses, the legislative manual, the clerk's and Croswell's manuals, and other contingent expenditures, eight thousand dollars. Postage, witness' fees, manuals, etc.

Firemen and watchmen. For the firemen employed about the capitol, state hall and geological hall, and for the watchmen, also employed during the session of the legislature for the year eighteen hundred and seventy-one, for compensation, to each of them for every day of service, to be certified by the respective superintendents, four dollars.

John Decker. For John Decker, for expenses of witnesses, witness fees and mileage in contested election case of eighteen hundred and sixty-nine, to which he was a party, six hundred and seventy-two dollars and seventy-five cents.

M. Delehanty. For M. Delehanty, for plumbing and materials furnished for assembly chamber, six hundred and nine dollars and eighty-five cents.

Tucker and Crawford. For Tucker and Crawford, for furnishing heating apparatus for committee rooms, ninety-five dollars.

Joseph McCann. For Joseph McCann, for pipes, heating apparatus, gas fixtures and other materials supplied to the state capitol, one hundred and thirty-five dollars and thirty cents.

Ira Porter. For Ira Porter, for painting, graining, lettering, et cetera, assembly post-office room, clerk's rooms, committee rooms and library ceilings, six hundred and twenty-two dollars and seventy-five cents.

Thos. B. Franklin. For Thomas B. Franklin, for labor and materials furnished in the construction of committee rooms in rear of Congress hall, one hundred and seventy-five dollars and fifty cents.

Clemshire and Bryce. For Clemshire and Bryce, for labor and materials furnished in building committee rooms at Albany, six hundred and seventy-four dollars and seventy-five cents.

P. Allanson. To P. Allanson, for carpenter work and materials furnished under order of the clerk of the assembly, one hundred and ninety dollars and twelve cents.

Lumber, hardware, etc. For lumber, moldings, hardware, et cetera, for assembly chamber, under resolution of the assembly, passed March third, eighteen hundred and seventy-one, two hundred and sixty-six dollars and seventy-one cents.

Ibid. For lumber, merchandise and labor supplied to assembly under resolution of January seventeenth, eighteen hundred and seventy-one, four hundred and ten dollars and thirty-six cents.

Jas. Allen. For James Allen, for furniture, upholstering and repairing desks, in the assembly chamber, two hundred and ninety-six dollars, and for furniture supplied committee rooms, two hundred and eight dollars.

A. Lovie. For A. Lovie, for labor performed and materials furnished for repairs to desks, et cetera, in the assembly chamber, one hundred and forty dollars and sixty-one cents.

Isaac D. Colman. For Isaac D. Colman, for services as civil engineer and surveyor, in making surveys, maps and plans, and attending the meetings of the standing committee of the senate while investigating the railroad disaster at New Hamburgh, pursuant to a resolution of the senate, adopted February nine, eighteen hundred and seventy-one, one thousand dollars.

For Adam Blake, for heating, lighting and taking care of the five committee rooms in Congress hall, two hundred and fifty dollars. Adam Blake.

For Thomas F. Gilroy, for services as clerk to joint committee on railroads in investing the New Hamburgh disaster, one hundred and fifty dollars. Thomas F. Gilroy.

For William V. Smith, for service as engineer and surveyor, in making maps and plans for the use of the committee on railroads during the investigation of the New Hamburgh disaster, and for the attendance at the meetings of said committee, five hundred dollars. Wm. V. Smith.

For Charles E. Leland, for board for witnesses and others employed by the standing committee on railroads while the investigation of the railroad disaster at New Hamburgh was being had, one hundred and fifty-six dollars and fifty cents. Chas. E. Leland.

For the proprietors of the Mansion house at Albany, for the board of witnesses called by the committee investigating the railroad disaster at New Hamburgh, fifty-six dollars. Mansion house, Albany.

For the messenger of the engrossing room of the assembly, for additional compensation, two hundred and fifty dollars. Messenger, assembly.

For James A. Curry, assistant engrossing clerk of the assembly, three hundred dollars. Jas. A. Curry.

For John A. Whalen, assistant clerk to the committee on engrossed bills, the same compensation as is paid clerks of committees authorized by the rules. John A. Whalen.

For Dennis Cummings, for services as messenger of the joint committee on railroads in the New Hamburgh investigation, fifty dollars. D. Cummings.

To Levi Cohn, for compensation, expenses, and witness fee, as agent and commissioned officer of the state of New York, while held in custody by the military authorities of the United States, from October twenty-fifth, eighteen hundred and sixty-four, to February fourteenth, eighteen hundred and sixty-five, two thousand five hundred dollars. Levi Cohn.

To Edward Donahoe, jr., for services and money expended while in city prison, Baltimore, Maryland, from October seventeenth, eighteen hundred and sixty-four, to June twenty-third, eighteen hundred and sixty-five, two thousand two hundred sixty-five dollars. Ed. Donahoe, jr.

For Robert Gray, for services as messenger, the sum of two hundred dollars, and for James Casey, for like services, the sum of two hundred dollars. R. Gray and James Casey.

For Stephen Springsteed, for expenses in contesting the seat of W. D. Murphy, in assembly of eighteen hundred and seventy, the sum of four hundred dollars. S. Springsteed.

To Hand, Hale and Swartz, for services as attorneys and counsel rendered in eighteen hundred and seventy and eighteen hundred and seventy-one, for the select committee relative to Ogdensburgh and Lake Champlain railroad investigation, five hundred dollars, to be audited and allowed by the comptroller. Hand, Hale and Swartz.

Clerk of select committee. For the clerk of the select committee appointed by resolution of the senate to investigate certain acts of the Ogdensburgh and Lake Champlain railroad company, three hundred dollars, to be paid on the certificate of the chairman of said committee.

John Parkhurst. To John Parkhurst, for services and expenses in subpœnaing witnesses for select committee to investigate the leasing of Ogdensburgh and Lake Champlain railroad, fifty dollars.

Andrew Devine. For Andrew Devine, for services in taking testimony before the committee to investigate certain acts of the Ogdensburgh and Lake Champlain railroad company, fifty dollars.

Thomas Driffill. For Thomas Driffill, for compensation due him for extra services, appropriated by chapter four hundred and ninety-two of the laws of eighteen hundred and seventy, and being a re-appropriation of money not drawn by him, two hundred and eighty-four dollars and seventy-five cents; and for Miss M. A. Dowd, for services as stenographer in transcribing notes of debates in senate and assembly, and testimony taken before senate and assembly committees, fifteen weeks at thirty-five dollars a week, five hundred and twenty-five dollars.

Miss M. A. Dowd.

Thos. E. Stewart and E. Durnin. For Thomas E. Stewart and Eugene Durnin, for counsel fees and disbursements in the case of the contested election in the seventh assembly district of New York city, one thousand dollars each.

St. Mary's Parish, Rondout. For St. Mary's parish at Rondout, five hundred dollars, being the sum appropriated to that parish under the name of St. Mary's Institute at Rondout, for the maintenance and education of destitute children, by chapter seven hundred and four, laws of eighteen hundred and seventy.

Samuel Hank. For Samuel Hank, for balance due as per bill of March thirtieth, eighteen hundred and sixty-nine, five hundred and sixteen dollars and ninety-five cents.

William Prendergast. To William Prendergast, attorney for Alice Cahill, heir and next of kin of Timothy Mulcahy, deceased, being the amount paid into the treasury by the treasurer of Ulster county to the credit of the legal claimants thereof, on the settlement of the estate of said Mulcahy, eight hundred and forty-seven dollars and eighty-two hundredths dollars.

Stephen Van Dresar. For Stephen Van Dresar, to pay an award made in pursuance of chapter six hundred and fifty-nine, laws of eighteen hundred and sixty-eight, twenty-one hundred dollars, to be audited and allowed by the comptroller.

Wm. D. Murphy. For William D. Murphy, for actual expenses and balance of counsel fees in defending his right to a seat in the assembly of eighteen hundred and seventy, four hundred and eighty-nine dollars.

Anson S. Wood. For Anson S. Wood, for actual expenses in defending his right to a seat in the assembly of eighteen hundred and seventy, fifty dollars.

Comptroller's office. For the office of the comptroller, for the compensation of the clerks, three thousand dollars, and for the furniture, blank and other books necessary for the use of the office, binding, blanks, printing and other necessary incidental expenses, one thousand dollars.

For postage for the public offices, five hundred dollars. Postage.

For the regents of the university, for deficiency in the salary of the botanist, five hundred and seventy-eight dollars and eight cents, and for deficiency in appropriation for expenses, five hundred dollars. Regents of university.

For the office of the attorney-general, for furniture, blank and other books necessary for the use of the office, binding, blanks, printing and other necessary incidental expenses, five hundred dollars. Attorney-general's office.

For the land office, for compensation and mileage of the lieutenant-governor, and speaker of the assembly, for their attendance at the meetings of the commissioners, and for assessments and other expenses of public lands, two thousand dollars. Land office.

For Amasa J. Parker, for compensation for his services as counsel, rendered on the request of the secretary of state, in attending before the supreme court to resist an application for a mandamus to compel the secretary of state to file an unauthorized certificate of incorporation, two hundred and fifty dollars. Amasa J. Parker.

For the hall of the State Cabinet of Natural History and the Agricultural Museum, for repairs, cleaning, labor, gas, fuel, compensation of keeper, and other necessary expenses, three thousand five hundred dollars. Geological hall.

For the state hall, for expenses for repairs, cleaning, labor, gas, and other necessary expenses, six thousand five hundred dollars. State hall.

For the capitol, governor's mansion, and state library, for expenses for repairs, cleaning, labor, gas, fuel, and other necessary expenses, two thousand five hundred dollars. Capitol, state library and governor's mansion.

For the office of the state engineer and surveyor, for furniture, blank and other books necessary for the use of the office, binding, blanks, printing, and other necessary expenses, two hundred and fifty dollars. State engineer's office.

For the inspector of state prisons, for traveling expenses, in addition to the amount provided by law, for the current fiscal year, to each of them, eight hundred dollars. Inspectors of state prisons.

For the janitor of the state hall, and for the keeper of the geological hall and agricultural museum, to each of them, two hundred dollars. Janitor of state hall.

For the purpose of carrying out the provisions of chapter four hundred and twenty-seven of the laws of eighteen hundred and seventy, for the erection of "The State Reformatory," at Elmira, the sum of two hundred thousand dollars is hereby appropriated, and the said commissioners are authorized to pay the balance of the purchase price of the land, for the site of the same, not to exceed the sum of four thousand dollars. State reformatory at Elmira.

For the secretary of state, for furniture, blank and other books necessary for the use of the office, binding, blanks, printing, and other necessary incidental expenses, five hundred dollars. Office of secretary of state.

John Gebhard, conditional appropriation. For John Gebhard, for the purchase by the state of his collection of minerals and fossils, the sum of three thousand five hundred dollars, to be paid on the certificate of James Hall, John V. L. Pruyn and Isaac W. Jackson that the collection is worth that sum, and should be purchased by the state.

Commissioners of public accounts. For the commissioners of public accounts, Benjamin Nott, R. H. Shankland and Gilson A. Dayton, for the year ending April first, eighteen hundred and seventy-one, the usual compensation for the examination of military, bounty, and other accounts, to each of them, one thousand dollars.

Monroe county insane asylum. For the Monroe county insane asylum, to pay the expenses of introducing water, bathing and steam apparatus, and generally perfecting the accommodations for the insane, so that they may be as fully and well provided for as in a state institution, twenty thousand dollars, to be expended under the direction of the trustees of said asylum, who shall report expenditures, with vouchers therefor, to the comptroller.

State lunatic asylum. For the State Lunatic Asylum at Utica, to refund advances made from the ordinary funds of the asylum for improvements and repairs of the asylum building, forty thousand dollars.

Ibid. For the State Lunatic Asylum at Utica, for grading, paving and laying sidewalks in front of the asylum grounds, on Court and York streets, twelve thousand nine hundred and seventy-six dollars.

Hudson River State Hospital. For the Hudson River State Hospital for the Insane, for salaries of officers, eight thousand dollars, or so much thereof as may be necessary, and for furniture and extra help to prepare for reception of patients and for their accommodation, and for repairs to buildings on the property, thirteen thousand dollars, or so much thereof as may be deemed necessary by the managers of said hospital.

J. Moreau Smith. To J. Moreau Smith, for interest upon moneys paid for land purchased of the state, upon Grand Island, possession of which was withheld during certain legal proceedings, the sum of two thousand and fifty-nine and thirty-nine hundredths dollars, to be paid from moneys already appropriated by chapter four hundred and ninety-two, laws of eighteen hundred and seventy, for the purpose of refunding to purchasers, when title to land conveyed by the state shall fail.

Wm. A. Russell and M. Hale. To William A. Russell and Matthew Hale, five thousand six hundred dollars, or so much thereof as the comptroller may determine to be just and proper, to pay an award made by the commissioners of the land office under chapter four hundred and twenty-eight of the laws of eighteen hundred and sixty-nine.

Hamilton county claim. For the comptroller to pay the county of Hamilton the amount ascertained to be due said county, upon a statement of the account, in pursuance of chapter three hundred and fifty-five, laws of eighteen hundred and sixty-eight, and chapter four hundred and eighty-seven, laws of eighteen hundred and seventy, the sum of fifty-four thousand and sixty-eight dollars and twenty-three cents.

To John W. Havens, Charles Richardson and Ebenezer McMurray, appraisers appointed under chapter one hundred and thirty-two of the laws of eighteen hundred and seventy, for services and expenses, five hundred dollars, or so much thereof as the comptroller may determine to be just and proper. Appraisers of lands.

To William A. Russell, for time and expenses in subpœnaing witnesses before the appraisers appointed under chapter one hundred and thirty-two of the laws of eighteen hundred and seventy, in pursuance of a resolution of the commissioners of the land office, six hundred and seven dollars, or so much thereof as the comptroller may determine to be just and proper. Wm. A. Russell.

To S. B. Woolworth, secretary of the board of regents, for services in charge of matters appertaining to the compilation and publishing of the natural history of the state, from eighteen hundred and fifty-six to the present time, one thousand five hundred dollars in full of all demands for extra services to date. S. B. Woolworth.

For Norman S. Curtiss, assistant librarian in the state library, two hundred dollars for additional compensation. N. S. Curtiss.

For the janitor of the state library, for additional compensation, two hundred dollars. Janitor.

For the compensation of a secretary, rendered necessary by the illness of the private secretary of the governor, seven hundred and fifty dollars; and to Albert V. V. Dodge, messenger in the executive department, and to George Tunnicliff, executive clerk, for extra services, one hundred dollars. Executive department.

For the insurance department, for compensation of clerks, furniture, books, printing, stationery, and other incidental expenses, twenty-five thousand dollars. The aforesaid sum to be repaid to the treasury by the insurance companies, pursu ant to chapter three hundred and sixty-six of laws of eighteen hundred and sixty-nine, and amendments thereto. Insurance department. Repayment.

For Robert B. Nichols, for balance due for moneys expended by him while superintendent on the Black River canal, one hundred and three dollars and twelve cents. R. B. Nichols.

To John A. Patterson, for extra services in the New York state insurance department, in preparation of valuation tables for life insurance for the past four years, to be paid out of the fund of the insurance department on the certificate of the superintendent, three thousand dollars. John A. Patterson.

To C. L. Skeels and Charles W. Ward, clerks employed in the insurance department from September thirtieth, eighteen hundred and sixty-four, to April first and June first, eighteen hundred and sixty-five respectively, the same percentage on their respective salaries, during the time so employed, as was paid to the deputy and other clerks in said department, who were so employed on the said thirtieth of September, and who continued so employed on the thirty-first December, eighteen hundred and sixty-six, under the provisions of chap- C. L. Skeels and C. W. Ward.

ter ninety-seven, laws of eighteen hundred and sixty-seven, section one.

Deputy secretary of state. For the deputy secretary of state as clerk to the commissioners of the land office, five hundred dollars.

Indexing session laws. For the office of the secretary of state, for indexing the session laws of eighteen hundred and seventy-one, five hundred dollars.

Clerk hire of secretary of state. For the office of the secretary of state, for deficiency in appropriation for clerk hire, one thousand two hundred dollars.

Treasurer for interest on mortgage. To the treasurer, to be by him applied on account of interest due on the mortgage of Peggy Smith to the state, being the amount paid June fifteenth, eighteen hundred and fifty-seven, to the then attorney-general, in foreclosure proceeding thereon, and not credited in the account, one hundred and thirty-seven dollars and sixty-nine cents, provided the balance due on the same is paid into the treasury.

Treasurer's office. For the office of the treasurer, for furniture, blank and other books necessary for the use of the office, binding, blanks, printing and other necessary expenses, one thousand five hundred dollars; and for expenses heretofore incurred in repairing and furnishing said office, one thousand dollars.

Ibid. For extra services performed in the office of the treasurer, and expenses incurred in paying the money to the soldiers of the war of eighteen hundred and twelve, in pursuance of chapter five hundred and twenty-four, laws of eighteen hundred and seventy, twelve hundred dollars, or so much thereof as may be necessary, to be paid on the certificate of the treasurer.

State engineer's office. For the office of the state engineer and surveyor, to be repaid to the treasury by the several railroad corporations of this state in proportion to their respective gross receipts, pursuant to chapter five hundred and twenty six, laws of eighteen hundred and fifty-five, as follows: Deputy. Railroad laws. For the deputy state engineer and surveyor, for preparation of the annual report of the state engineer and surveyor on railroads for the year eighteen hundred and seventy, and for compiling and indexing the railroad laws of the state, one thousand five hundred dollars; Argus Company. to the Argus Company, for printing and binding the said reports for the year eighteen hundred and seventy, five thousand eight hundred and forty-three dollars.

Traveling expenses. For the state engineer and surveyor, for extra traveling expenses during the year eighteen hundred and seventy, three hundred dollars.

Jas. Hall. For James Hall, as state geologist, for the use of working rooms, fuel, lights and other expenses incurred for the preparation of the palæontology of New York, and for the distribution of duplicate fossils, as provided by law, to the first of January, eighteen hundred and seventy-one, one thousand dollars; Commission to examine work on palæontology. and it shall be the duty of the lieutenant-governor, the comptroller and secretary of state, to examine the condition of the work on the palæontology of the state and the distribution of duplicate collections of fossils and minerals, as ordered by law, and they are authorized to fix a proper compensation for authorship, the superintendence of drawings and engravings; for clerk hire and the use of working rooms; for the arranging, labeling and distribution of the duplicate fossils and minerals, provided that the entire sum shall not exceed twenty-five hundred dollars per annum, which sum is hereby appropriated.

For compilation of the general and special laws of the state relating to the support of the poor, with notes, forms and instructions adapted thereto, in pursuance to chapter four hundred and seventy, and for superintendence of the publication thereof, the sum of fifteen hundred dollars, payable upon the certificate of the secretary of state. Poor laws.

For Morven M. Jones, for extra services in supervision of the printing of the session laws of eighteen hundred and seventy, and legislative manual, five hundred dollars. M. M. Jones.

For superintendent of public instruction, for additional compensation, two thousand five hundred dollars. Superintendent of public instruction.

For the State Normal School at Fredonia, for repairs and improving grounds and fencing, five thousand dollars, to be expended under the direction of the local board of said school, the accounts of the expenditure of said money to be audited by the superintendent of public instruction. Fredonia Normal school.

For the State Normal School at Brockport, for repairs and improving grounds and fencing, five thousand dollars, to be expended under the direction of the local board of said school, the accounts of the expenditure of said money to be audited by the superintendent of public instruction. Brockport Normal school.

For the State Normal School at Potsdam, for inproving grounds and fencing, three thousand dollars, to be expended under the direction of the local board of said school, the accounts of the expenditure of said money to be audited by the superintendent of public instruction. Potsdam Normal school.

The local board of the State Normal and Training School at Potsdam is hereby authorized to use and expend from and out of the academic fund of said school such sum as shall be necessary, not to exceed one thousand dollars in any one year, nor five thousand dollars in all, to procure a residence for the use of the principal of said school; the property to be purchased to be conveyed to and held by the state in the same manner and to the same extent as the real estate and buildings of said school. Residence for principal of Potsdam school.

For Edward Danforth, for additional compensation for services as deputy superintendent of public instruction, one thousand dollars. E. Danforth.

For James C. Brown, for extra services in the department of public instruction, seven hundred and fifty dollars. J. C. Brown.

For Daniel Shaw, for services in the department of public instruction during the years eighteen hundred and sixty-eight, sixty-nine and seventy, five hundred dollars. Daniel Shaw.

To James Bell, for witness and traveling fees for himself, Robert Sherman, Lewis Kenyon and Albert Bell, witnesses Witness fees.

before the committee on privileges and elections of the assembly in February, eighteen hundred and seventy, forty-three dollars and sixty cents.

Darius Lyon. To Darius Lyon, for witness and traveling fees before the committee on privileges and elections of the assembly of eighteen hundred and seventy, in February of that year, fifty dollars.

Israel Nusbaum. For Israel Nusbaum, for compensation for additional services imposed upon him by the commissioners of the land office as custodian of the Geological Hall, in pursuance of a resolution of the assembly, the sum of three hundred dollars.

Comptroller's office for examining soldiers' claims. For extra services performed in the comptroller's office, in preparing and examining the claims and apportioning and paying the money to the soldiers of the war of eighteen hundred and twelve, in pursuance of chapter five hundred and twenty-four, laws of eighteen hundred and seventy, one thousand five hundred dollars, or so much thereof as may be necessary, to be paid on the certificate of the comptroller.

Blind institution at Batavia. Twenty-five thousand dollars, or so much thereof as may be necessary, is hereby appropriated for the purchase of land to enlarge the grounds of the New York State Institution for the Blind at Batavia, to be paid to George Bowen and Henry I. Glowaski, who are hereby appointed commissioners on behalf of the state to make such purchase.

Ibid. To the New York State Institution for the Blind at Batavia for furnishing, repairs and other necessary expenses, three thousand dollars.

State library, shelving, etc. For the trustees of the state library, for boxes for British patents, two hundred dollars, and for additional shelving, five hundred dollars.

Binding of U. S. census returns. The trustees of the state library are hereby authorized to apply the unexpended balance of the appropriation of five hundred dollars made in chapter four hundred and ninety-two of the laws of eighteen hundred and seventy, for binding returns of the United States census of eighteen hundred and sixty, to the binding of any other books which they may deem necessary.

Charles Peck. To Charles Peck, botanist, for traveling and incidental expenses, one hundred and twenty-six dollars and seventy-five cents.

Settlement of suit of Catharine A. Fowler. The attorney-general and auditor of the canal department, if in their judgment the interest of the state require, are hereby authorized to settle and adjust the suit of Catharine A. Fowler against Franklin A. Alberger, late canal commissioner, for the recovery of the value of a canal boat destroyed by order of said commissioner while repairing a break in the canal near Palmyra in the year eighteen hundred and sixty-six; and the sum of fifteen hundred dollars, or so much thereof as may be necessary, is hereby appropriated for the purpose, to be paid to the parties entitled thereto on the certificate of the auditor.

To William A. Beach, two thousand dollars; to Matthew Hale, two thousand dollars, and to William Odell, one thousand dollars, for counsel and services on behalf of the people on the indictment against William Whitbeck and others, for murder, including the trial and proceedings preliminary thereto; the said sums when paid to be in full of all demands on account of said case. Counsel at Whitbeck murder trial.

For the employees of the adjutant-general's office, for additional compensation for services performed under chapter four hundred and seventy, laws of eighteen hundred and sixty-nine, and chapter five hundred and twenty-four, laws of eighteen hundred and seventy, fifteen hundred dollars, to be paid on the certificate of the adjutant-general. Adjutant-general's office.

For Stephen H. Hammond, deputy attorney-general, for extra services, one thousand dollars. Deputy-attorney-general.

To the comptroller for compensation of the clerk in his department, performing the duties of deputy comptroller from July first, eighteen hundred and sixty-eight, to January first, eighteen hundred and seventy, one thousand dollars, or so much thereof as the comptroller shall deem just and equitable. Deputy comptroller.

For the judges of the court of appeals, the commissioners of appeals, and the justices of the supreme court, for deficiency in appropriations for their salaries, for the current fiscal year, fifty-three thousand and five dollars and eighty-four cents. Judges of court of appeals and supreme court.

For the judges of the court of appeals, the commissioners of appeals, and the justices of the supreme court, for their per diem allowance, as provided by law, to the close of the current fiscal year, thirty thousand dollars. Per diem allowance for judges.

For the expenses of the general terms of the supreme court, as provided in section twelve, chapter four hundred and eight, laws of eighteen hundred and seventy, to the close of the current fiscal year, twenty thousand dollars. Expenses of general terms.

For the commissioners to revise the statutes, for deficiency in the appropriation for their salaries, to the close of the current fiscal year, eleven thousand two hundred and fifty dollars, and for their expenses during the same period, as provided in chapter thirty-three, laws of eighteen hundred and seventy, two thousand two hundred and fifty-dollars, and each commissioner shall be entitled to receive his actual expenditures, under section six of said act, to an amount not exceeding two thousand dollars in any one year. Commissioners to revise statutes.

For fees of surrogates, twenty-five dollars. Surrogates

For the clerk of the court of appeals, for furniture, blank and other books necessary for the use of the office, binding, blanks, printing and other necessary expenses, one thousand five hundred dollars. Office of clerk to court of appeals.

For the clerk of the commission of appeals, for his salary to the close of the present fiscal year, four thousand three hundred and twenty-seven dollars and forty-five cents, and for the necessary expenses of his office, including printing of calendar, five hundred dollars. Clerk of commission of appeals.

State reporter. For the state reporter for deficiency in salary, pursuant to chapter six hundred and ninety-eight, laws of eighteen hundred and sixty-nine, one thousand and ninety-one dollars and sixty-seven cents.

Clerk of court of appeals. For the clerk of the court of appeals for deficiency in salary, pursuant to chapter six hundred and ninety-eight, laws of eighteen hundred and sixty-nine, one thousand eight hundred and seventy-five dollars.

Crier and attendants of courts. For the crier and attendants of the court of appeals and commission of appeals, for their compensation, one thousand dollars, or so much thereof as may be necessary.

B. Curtin. For Bartholomew Curtin, for five days' services as attendant at the meetings of the judges of the supreme court, fifteen dollars.

Attendants of court of appeals. For each of the attendants of the court of appeals, an additional compensation of one dollar and fifty cents per day, from the tenth day of October last up to April first, eighteen hundred and seventy-one.

H. H. Burhans. For H. H. Burhans, for services as messenger of the office of the commission of appeals, from July first, eighteen hundred and seventy, to October first, eighteen hundred and seventy-one, two hundred dollars.

Crier and attendants of commission of appeals. For the clerk of the commissioners of appeals, for the usual additional compensation of criers, attendants and clerk for the May term of the commission which is to be held in the city of New York, four hundred dollars.

Stenographer of second judicial district. For the stenographers of the supreme court of the second judicial district, to be paid only from the moneys received into the treasury pursuant to chapter seven hundred and sixty-five of the laws of eighteen hundred and sixty-five, of the laws of eighteen hundred and sixty-eight, the appointment of such stenographers to be duly certified by the justices making the same, five thousand dollars.

Wm. F. Bonynge. For William F. Bonynge, stenographer for the eighth judicial district, one thousand dollars.

Stenographer of executive department. For the compensation of a stenographer for the executive department, to be paid on the certificate of the governor, as may be necessary, two thousand dollars.

Andrew Devine. For Andrew Devine, for services for transcribing nine hundred and eighty folios of testimony in the New Hamburgh disaster, two hundred and forty-five dollars.

Cornelius Ten Broeck. For Cornelius Ten Broeck, for compensation for extra work done as clerk in and about the organization of the court and commission of appeals, seven hundred and fifty dollars.

Private secretary. For additional compensation to the private secretary of the governor, for the calendar year, eighteen hundred and seventy-one, one thousand dollars.

G. J. Raynor. To Gilbert J. Raynor, for compensation for services as temporary clerk of the commission and court of appeals in July, eighteen hundred and seventy, one hundred dollars.

J. McFarlane, H. F. Dunn. To James McFarlane and Hugh F. Dunn, for attendance upon the court of appeals during the July term thereof, eighteen hundred and seventy, to each of them, the sum of twenty-five dollars.

For additional compensation for Richard Barber, as assistant to the clerk of the commission of appeals, from July first, eighteen hundred and seventy, to October first, eighteen hundred and seventy-one, six hundred dollars. R. Barber.

For Banks Brothers, for law books supplied to the offices of the secretary of state and attorney-general, regents of the university, senate of the state of New York, for the libraries of the court of appeals at Rochester and Syracuse, the Schenectady law library, for the state reporter, and for the court of appeals library, and the clerk of the assembly, and the committees of the legislature, eleven thousand nine hundred and eighteen dollars and eighty-five cents. Banks Brothers, for law books.

For the board of commissioners constituted by the act entitled "An act in relation to quarantine and providing for the construction of the permanent quarantine establishment," passed April twenty-first, eighteen hundred and sixty-six, the sum of two hundred thousand dollars to be applied by said board to the payment of the existing obligations of said board for work done under its authority, to the payment of the rent which shall become due upon the lease entered into by said board pursuant to chapter four hundred and ninety-two of the laws of eighteen hundred and seventy, to the payment of such amount as the health officer of the port of New York shall certify to be due to any person for labor and services performed, or materials furnished, in fitting up and furnishing the residence of the health officer and his deputies, with their appurtenances, to the completion of the island on West Bank for a boarding station, and for the erection and equipment of suitable buildings on said island, for the reception of passengers who may have been exposed to disease, and who may be sent there by the health officer; provided, however, that such buildings shall be erected upon plans approved by the health officer, and under a contract to be entered into therefor in the manner prescribed in the fourth section of the act aforesaid, except that said board may, in its discretion, reject any bid which it may not deem for the interest of the state to accept, and it may also enter into separate contracts for separate portions of said work. Quarantine. Appropriation how applied. Fitting up on residence. Completion of island on West Bank, buildings, etc. Plans, how approved and contracted for.

For the commissioners of quarantine, for the care and maintenance of the quarantine establishment, the payment of the employees therein, and to enable the said commissioners to pay such expenses as shall be necessarily incurred by them in the discharge of their official duties during the current year, the sum of sixty thousand dollars, and said commissioners shall also therefrom pay the running expenses of a steamboat for boarding vessels and transporting the sick and burying the dead. Maintenance of quarantine. Running of steamboat.

For the said commissioners of quarantine, for the purpose of repairing and providing new boilers for the steamboats Andrew Fletcher and Governor Fenton, the sum of ten thousand four hundred dollars. Boilers for steamboats.

William Gould & Son. For William Gould & Son, for law books and stationery supplied to attorney-general's office, seventy-five dollars and seventy cents.

Publishing rules of practice. For publishing rules of practice, adopted by convention of justices and judges, one hundred and twenty-six dollars.

Thomas J. Bishop. For Thomas J. Bishop, for services rendered in making up the calendar of the commission of appeals for the year eighteen hundred and seventy-one, one hundred dollars.

Law libraries. For the law libraries in each of the judicial districts of the state, to each of them, one thousand dollars, and in addition to the law library in the eighth judicial district, at Buffalo, the sum of twenty-five hundred dollars

Quarantine. For fitting up the "Illinois," at quarantine, fifteen thousand dollars.

Police at quarantine. For the health officer of the port of New York, the sum of five thousand dollars, or so much thereof as may be necessary, to pay the salaries of not exceeding five policemen at quarantine; such policemen may be appointed, and may at pleasure be dismissed by him; and they shall perform patrol and police duty under his direction in connection with the quarantine establishment and upon the waters of the bay of New York; and they shall possess all the powers possessed by policemen in the cities of New York and Brooklyn. And any person arrested by either of said policemen for violating any law relating to quarantine, in said port, may be taken by him before any court of criminal jurisdiction, or any magistrate or police justice, within the county of Richmond, and, thereupon, the court, magistrate or police justice, before whom such offender shall be brought, shall have jurisdiction to hear, try and punish the offense committed by him, in the same manner and with the like effect as if the same had been committed within the limits over which such court, magistrate or police justice has jurisdiction to punish offenses under existing laws.

How appointed, their duties and powers.

Trial of persons arrested by them.

Thos. H. Farron. To Thomas H. Farron, for materials furnished and labor paid for in the improvement of the quarantine grounds at Staten Island, the alteration, refitting and furnishing of the residence of the health officer and his assistants, twelve thousand five hundred and ninety-six dollars and fifty-three cents, to be paid on the certificate of the health officer, and for the personal services of the said Thomas H. Farron, five thousand dollars.

Rent of part of quarantine establishment. For the said board of commissioners, twelve thousand dollars, for rent and keeping in order of that portion of the quarantine establishment leased by said commissioners, under the provisions of chapter four hundred and ninety-two of the laws of eighteen hundred and seventy; to be paid only upon statements and estimates being first submitted to and approved by the comptroller.

Shore inspectors. For the shore inspectors, under the bill to prevent the throwing of offal and dead animals in the North and East rivers and New York and Raritan bays, now in the hands of the governor, six hundred and twenty-five dollars, for salary until the first of October next, if the bill become a law.

For the Buffalo State Asylum for the insane, for the construction of buildings, one hundred and fifty thousand dollars. Buffalo state asylum.

For the institution for the improved instruction of deaf mutes in New York city, twenty-five thousand dollars, to be used in the care and education of said deaf mutes, and payable on the order of the treasurer of said institution. Instruction of deaf mutes.

To Willis H. Adsit, Hamilton N. Towner and Artemus H. Whitney, for costs and expenses incurred as commissioners, under chapter eight hundred and eighty of the laws of eighteen hundred and sixty-nine, in legal proceedings instituted under said act against the comptroller, seven hundred and fifty dollars; to be audited and allowed by the comptroller.

For Mrs. David S. Jones, the daughter of De Witt Clinton, for purchase of a portrait of Governor De Witt Clinton, by Ingham, now in her possession, to be paid upon the certificate of John V. L. Pruyn, chancellor of the university, that the said portrait has been placed in the state library as the property of the state, the sum of five thousand dollars. Mrs. David S. Jones for portrait of Ex-Gov. Clinton.

For work done and being done with the approval of the commissioners of the land office, in repairing and improving the executive mansion, geological hall and other buildings belonging to the state, and for fitting up committee rooms for the senate and assembly, the sum of twenty-eight thousand three hundred and ninety-four dollars and twenty-five cents, or so much thereof as may be necessary, said expenses to be paid by the comptroller, upon vouchers approved by the commissioners of the land office. Hereafter the lessee of Congress hall shall pay an annual rental for said building of not less than six thousand dollars, in the discretion of the commissioners of the land office. Repairs and improvements of state buildings. Rent of Congress hall.

For William Hastings, for advertising general orders of the adjutant-general, nine hundred and seventeen dollars and eighty-five cents. William Hastings.

For the care and support of sick disabled soldiers, one hundred and twenty-one dollars and twenty-one cents, being unexpended balance of fifty thousand dollars appropriated by chapter eight hundred and twenty-two, laws of eighteen hundred and sixty-nine, which is hereby reappropriated, and two thousand nine hundred and fifty-one dollars and thirteen cents, being proceeds of sale of property at Soldiers' home, at Albany, returned to comptroller, November thirtieth, eighteen hundred and sixty-nine, or so much thereof as may be necessary, is hereby appropriated for the same purpose, the same to be paid on the certificate of the governor, in like manner as payments were made on account of the Soldiers' home. Support of disabled soldiers.

To James B. Swain and Francis B. Fisher, for damages sustained prior to the abrogation by the state of the contract made with them by the inspectors of state prisons, and for costs and disbursements incurred by them in pursuance of the provisions of chapter six hundred and thirty-three, laws of eighteen hundred and sixty-eight, two thousand five hundred dollars, to be paid by the comptroller out of any moneys in the treasury not otherwise appropriated, upon the receipt J. B. Swain and F. B. Fisher.

in full of said Swain and Fisher of all claims of any nature growing out of said contract, to be audited and allowed by the comptroller.

S. McKeel and B. A. Yeomans. For Stephen McKeel and Byron A. Yeomans, for payment in full to them for damages sustained by reason of the non-fulfillment of a contract made with Henry C. Nelson, acting as the warden of Sing Sing prison, four thousand five hundred dollars.

Richmond county agricultural society. To the Richmond County Agricultural Society, the same being the amount appropriated for the year eighteen hundred and sixty-eight, and now remaining in the treasury and being hereby reappropriated, eighty-two dollars and eighty-eight cents.

Survey of state line. To reimburse the county of Chautauqua for expenses incurred in making the survey of the state line, pursuant to the resolution of the senate of April nineteen, eighteen hundred and sixty-seven, and the direction of the regents of the university, to be paid to the county treasurer of said county, three hundred and ninety-six dollars and fifty-five cents.

Claim of James M. Smith. How certified. The comptroller is hereby authorized and directed to pay to James M. Smith, upon the certificate of the attorney-general to the comptroller, certifying that the judgment for costs hereinafter referred to were obtained in suits or proceedings which were duly instituted and prosecuted as by law required, fifty-four thousand five hundred and eighty-five dollars and thirty-seven cents, for judgments for costs in sundry suits commenced by the district attorney for the county of New York, in the name of the people of this state, for a violation of section twenty-one of an act entitled "An act to establish a metropolitan police district," passed April fifteenth, eighteen hundred and fifty-seven, in which judgments have been given for the defendants, with costs, against the people of this state, Filing of stipulation and release. upon said James M. Smith filing with the comptroller a consent or stipulation in writing that all suits in which he is attorney or counsel, now pending, and in which judgments have not been obtained, may be discontinued, without costs to defendants or the people of this state; and also upon said Smith's executing and delivering to the comptroller a release in full satisfaction of all claims or demands which he, the said Smith, now has, or may hereafter have, against the people of this state, for or by reason of any matter or thing growing out of or arising from, by or in any suits or prosecutions against any person or persons, for a violation of said section twenty-one of the above mentioned act.

Elizabeth Craft. The sum of eight hundred and forty-five dollars is hereby reappropriated for the purposes named in chapter two hundred and fifty-one, laws of eighteen hundred and sixty-nine, being an act entitled "An act for the relief of Elizabeth Craft, the widow of Edwin Craft."

Agent of Onondaga Indians. For the agent of the Onondaga Indians, for deficiency in compensation, pursuant to chapter six hundred and thirty-five, laws of eighteen hundred and sixty-nine, thirty dollars.

For fees of county clerks, one hundred and fifty dollars. County clerks.

For R. H. Gardner, for additional compensation for services as agent of the Onondaga Indians, one hundred dollars. R. H. Gardner.

For R. H. Shankland, for additional compensation as agent of the Onondaga Indians, five hundred dollars. R. H. Shankland.

To the Ithaca Calendar Clock Company, fifty dollars for a calendar clock for the executive chamber. Ithaca Calendar Clock Co.

For deficiency in the regular appropriation for the current fiscal year to meet the expense of re-uniforming and re-equipping the national guard, fifty-five thousand dollars. National guard.

For Charles Vandervoort for money advanced by him to equip and fit for the field the fifty-fifth regiment of the national guard, the sum of forty-eight hundred and thirty dollars, and interest thereon from January first, eighteen hundred and sixty-four. Charles Vandervoort.

For Thomas Colgan, assignee of Louis Kazinskie, for services rendered in the recruiting service under the order of the governor, dated twenty-fourth day of August, eighteen hundred and sixty-one, fifteen hundred dollars. Thomas Colgan.

For repairing the arsenals and armories belonging to the state, ten thousand dollars. Arsenals and armories.

For heating apparatus in state armory at Rochester, and completing said building as recommended by the adjutant-general, five thousand dollars. Rochester armory.

To Gersline and Aldridge, for balance due them for work and material in building state armory at Rochester, six thousand seven hundred and thirty-eight dollars. Gersline and Aldridge.

For finishing the work and improvements at the head of Cayuga lake, in accordance with the recommendations of the state engineer and the canal commissioners, twelve thousand five hundred dollars. The said sum to be expended under the direction of William W. Wright, commissioner in charge. Work at head of Cayuga lake.

For the payment of taxes and assessments on the state arsenal at Brooklyn, N. Y., five hundred and forty-three dollars and thirty-two cents. Taxes on Brooklyn arsenal.

For David Smiley, payable to his wife, for injuries received by the premature discharge of a gun while in the service of the state, two hundred dollars, upon the certificate of the adjutant-general that said Smiley was in the service of the state at the time of the accident, and received injuries justifying the payment of the amount hereby appropriated. David Smiley.

For the New York State Poultry Society, to be paid upon the order of Thomas B. Kingsland, as president, the sum of one thousand five hundred dollars. N. Y. state poultry society.

For Henry M. Williams, for expenses and services under the appointment of Governor Fenton, as commissioner at French Universal Exposition at Paris, in eighteen hundred and sixty-seven, ten thousand dollars. H. M. Williams.

For Reverend William McClellan, for clerical and other services rendered to the convicts at Sing Sing prison, nine hundred dollars. Rev. Wm. McClellan

For Bernard Casserly, for expenses incurred by him in defraying the expenses of the delegates to the National B. Casserly.

Emigration Convention, at Indianapolis, and for moneys paid by him to the secretary of said delegates as compensation for services rendered, one thousand two hundred and fifty dollars.

Danforth Briggs. To Danforth Briggs, for personal injuries received at the hands of one of the convicts while in the discharge of his duty as keeper in Clinton prison, and to reimburse him for expenses of medical attendance thereupon, five hundred dollars.

Geo. W. Wilson. For George W. Wilson, lessee of docks at Coney Island, for expenses incurred by him in consequence of the proceedings to take a part of Coney Island for quarantine purposes, under chapter seven hundred and seventeen of the laws of eighteen hundred and sixty-eight, three thousand dollars.

New capitol. New capitol commissioners. The sum of six hundred and fifty thousand dollars is hereby appropriated toward the erection of a new capitol; and Hamilton Harris, William C. Kingsley, William A. Rice, Chauncey M. Depew, Delos De Wolf, and Edwin A. Merritt, are hereby appointed commissioners for the purpose of erecting the new capitol, in the place of the present board. No percentage or compensation shall be paid to contractors or other persons upon the value or amount of any day labor performed on said building, or any labor which shall be done and be paid for by the day, week, or month, under the pretense of superintending such labor or otherwise, except final and entire compensation to necessary foremen or superintendents, for their services by the day, week, or month. Foremen, etc., not to be interested. And said commissioners shall not employ as superintendent or foremen upon such building any person or persons who, during the time of such employment, are or may be engaged or interested in the construction of any other building, or in carrying on any other work. Preference to be given to state mechanics, etc. And the mechanics and laborers of this state shall have the preference in doing the work on said building, provided it shall not increase the cost of said work, and the labor to be performed by day's work and not by contract.

M. J. Ferrey. For Moses J. Ferrey, for arrears of compensation as state agent at Baltimore, Md., for the relief of the sick and wounded soldiers of New York in the United States service, pursuant to chapter two hundred and twenty-four of the laws of eighteen hundred and sixty-three, twenty-seven hundred thirty-two and seventy-three one hundredths dollars.

Commissioners to report tax code. For David A. Wells, George W. Cuyler and Edwin Dodge, commissioners appointed to report upon the tax and assessment law of the state, for expenses and compensation, to be adjusted and apportioned among themselves, the sum of nine thousand dollars; and the said commissioners are directed to report, for the consideration of the legislature at its next session, a draft of a tax code or law, with estimates of expenses and collections thereunder.

New armory at Auburn. Commissioners. The sum of twenty-five thousand dollars is hereby appropriated for the purchase of site for and the erection of a new armory in the city of Auburn, N. Y.; and James McQuade, Elmore P. Ross, John H. Chedell, Clinton McDougall and Charles W. Pomeroy are hereby appointed commissioners for the purpose of selecting site and superintending the construction of said armory; and said commissioners shall, before entering upon said work, execute a bond to the people of the state of New York, conditioned that they will faithfully discharge their duties as such commissioners, and will truly account to the comptroller of the state for all moneys received by them for the purpose aforesaid, which bond shall be approved by the comptroller of the state. Official bond.

For the reimbursement of Charles H. Lee, Nehemiah Case and George W. Tew, for moneys advanced and paid by them to contractors as commissioners appointed under chapter seven hundred and seventeen, laws of eighteen hundred and sixty-eight, for the building of the bridge across Cattaraugus creek, on the Indian reservation, and the costs of the litigation, the sum of six thousand four hundred and ninety-five dollars and seventy-five cents. Bridge across Cattaraugus creek.

For the reimbursement of Erie county, to be paid to the treasurer thereof, for moneys advanced and paid by said county for the building of said bridge across Cattaraugus creek, on the Indian reservation, the sum of five hundred dollars. Payment to Erie county.

For the canal fund, for the payment of interest on deferred payments of the state tax levied for canal purposes in the years eighteen hundred and sixty-seven, eighteen hundred and sixty-eight and eighteen hundred and sixty-nine, twenty-seven thousand five hundred and thirty-two dollars and eighty-five cents. Interest on deferred payment of state tax.

For B. and D. Hughes, for compensation in full for the dredge built on their plan and patent, the sum of fifteen thousand dollars. On the payment of this appropriation, the state shall become the sole owner of said dredge, and shall forever have the right to build and use as many dredges on the said plan and patent as may be necessary for the use of the state. B. and D. Hughes. Right to use dredges.

To pay for lands taken for the purposes of a new capitol, ten thousand dollars, or so much thereof as may be necessary. New capitol lands.

For Solomon Scheu, for compensation for extra services as inspector of state prisons, one thousand dollars. Solomon Scheu.

For William C. Rhodes, as compensation for services as superintendent in manufacturing department of Clinton prison, to be paid upon the certificate of state prison inspectors, showing the necessity therefor, two thousand dollars. Wm. C. Rhodes.

For H. S. Van Etten, as compensation for services as superintendent in manufacturing department of Sing Sing prison, to be paid upon the certificate of inspectors of state prisons, certifying to the necessity therefor, two thousand dollars. H. S. Van Etten.

For the port wardens of the port of New York, for the purchase of a safe or the construction of a vault for the preservation of the state records of that board, three thousand five hundred dollars. Safe and vault for port wardens.

For the Willard Asylum, for the extension of the north wing of the asylum building, sixty-five thousand dollars; for Willard Asylum.

the purchase of the docks and premises connected therewith, belonging to John H. Hoster, which purchase the trustees of said asylum are hereby authorized and directed to make, the sum of fifteen thousand dollars, provided the same can be purchased for that sum, and the further sum of three thousand dollars for repairing and improving the same; for group of detached buildings, forty thousand dollars; for water supply, including enlargement of reservoirs and extraordinary expenditures during the years of eighteen hundred and seventy and seventy-one, eight thousand dollars; for roads, fences, buildings, trees, grading, stock, et cetera, for farm, seven thousand dollars; for finishing and furnishing chapel, two thousand five hundred dollars; for fuel, ten thousand dollars; for printing, stationery and medical books, one thousand five hundred dollars; for ventilating buildings, two thousand dollars; for contingencies to cover extraordinary purposes, such as lack of water, failure of crops, altering or perfecting rooms for use of patients, three thousand five hundred dollars; for unsettled bills and interest of Clark and Allen, due them in full for claims, growing out of contract with them for boilers, and so forth, for the Willard Asylum, two thousand dollars; for portico and stairs for main building, five thousand dollars; for furniture for north wing and detached buildings, five thousand dollars; and the sum of one thousand dollars to allow the trustees to settle in full with the foreman of labor on the farm and buildings.

State prisons. For the support and maintenance of the state prisons for the residue of the current year, including expenses of manufacturing at Clinton prison, three hundred and twenty-five thousand dollars.

Auburn prison. For the Auburn prison, for repairs, improvements and support of works, as follows, namely: for hose, three thousand dollars; for repairs to main building and wings, one thousand dollars; for ordinary building and repairs, two thousand dollars; for paint and oil, five hundred dollars; for bathing tubs, and so forth, one thousand dollars; for new doors, casements and locks, for north wing, ten thousand dollars; for shoe-shop roof, two thousand dollars; for bibles and library books, two hundred and fifty dollars; for the completion of cells, seven thousand dollars.

Clinton prison. For the Clinton prison, for new state shop, five hundred dollars; for plank for prison inclosure, five hundred dollars; for repairs to plank-road, one thousand five hundred dollars; for library books, two hundred and fifty dollars; for new coal kilns, one thousand five hundred dollars.

Sing Sing prison. For the Sing Sing prison, for building and repairs, five thousand dollars; for bibles and hymn books, two hundred and fifty dollars; for the erection of a storehouse, two thousand five hundred dollars.

Asylum for insane convicts. For the asylum for insane convicts, for support and maintenance for the residue of the current fiscal year, four thousand five hundred dollars; for general repairs, one thousand dollars; for fire hose, eight hundred dollars; for surgical instruments, one hundred dollars; and for library books, one hundred dollars.

To Mrs. Lewis W. Washington, of Halltown, West Virginia, the sum of twenty thousand dollars, or so much thereof as may be necessary, for the purchase of certain relics of General George Washington, offered by her to the state, to be paid only upon the certificate of Martin Grover, and the chancellor of the university, and J. Carson Brevoort, that said relics are, in their opinion, genuine, and that it is desirable, in their judgment, that they should be placed in the museum of the state library. Mrs. Lewis W. Washington, for relics. How paid.

To the auditor of the canal department, to make good a deficiency in the canal fund, on account of the robbing of the safe in the collector's office in the city of New York, in the year eighteen hundred and sixty-four, to settle the account of the late collector, two thousand four hundred and fifty dollars, or so much thereof as may be necessary, the same having been heretofore appropriated by chapter seven hundred and seventeen of the laws of eighteen hundred and sixty-eight. Settlement with canal collector, New York city.

For Henry E. Baker, in compliance with a resolution of the canal board, passed December thirtieth, eighteen hundred and fifty-nine, one hundred dollars, the same to be paid from the canal fund. H. E. Baker.

For the purchase of books and philosophical and chemical apparatus for the normal and training school at Cortland village, the sum of five thousand dollars, to be expended by the local board, with the consent of the state superintendent of public instruction; the accounts of the expenditures of said money to be audited by the superintendent of public instruction. Cortland normal school.

For Michael S. Meyers, to reimburse him for expenses incurred as prison commissioner under resolution of April twenty-sixth, eighteen hundred and seventy, three hundred and forty-seven dollars and forty-six cents. Michael S. Meyers.

For Thomas Fencer, for expenses incurred by him as prison commissioner under resolution of April twenty-sixth, eighteen hundred and seventy, four hundred dollars and fifty cents. Thomas Fencer.

For payment of balance of counsel fees of the assembly committee on savings banks, authorized by chapter four hundred and ninety-two of the laws of eighteen hundred and seventy, six hundred and fifty dollars. Savings banks investigation.

For E. C. Wines, for expenses as commissioner on prison labor commission, under resolution of the legislature of April twenty-sixth, eighteen hundred and seventy, nine hundred and twenty-five dollars and six cents. E. C. Wines.

For Thomas Fencer, Michael S. Myers and E. C. Wines, for services on prison labor commission, authorized by joint resolution of the legislature of eighteen hundred and seventy, the sum of one thousand dollars each, and said commission is hereby discontinued. Prison labor commission.

For Henry Storms, for arrears of compensation for repayment of amounts due him as commissary-general, for supplies of arms and military stores and accoutrements to arsenals, Henry Storms.

members of the militia and brigades, pursuant to act of the legislature, passed April twenty-sixth, eighteen hundred and twenty-three, and for services as agent for settling the demands of this state against the United States, in pursuance of laws passed February tenth, eighteen hundred and eighteen, and April twenty-fourth, eighteen hundred and twenty-three, ten thousand dollars, or such part of that amount as is found to be equitably due and unpaid; and the adjutant-general, the comptroller and the attorney-general are hereby authorized and directed to make an immediate and fair examination of all charges, accounts and payments made to and by him, and to award to him whatever amount they shall find to be equitably due.

Examinations of claims and awards.

Miss Sarah Starr. For Miss Sarah Starr, formerly matron of the state lunatic asylum at Utica, for injuries sustained in the discharge of such duty, the sum of one thousand dollars.

Andrew Smith. For Andrew Smith, for injuries received while at work on the new capitol, and expense of medical attendance, one hundred dollars.

Joseph N. Greene. For Joseph N. Greene, in full for payment for brick manufactured by said Greene and used in the construction of Willard asylum, and for brick yards and fixtures thereon, erected by said Greene, and used by the commissioner in the construction of said asylum, three thousand six hundred and sixty-seven dollars.

John P. Gray. For John P. Gray, for examination, by request of the governor, of Powell of Lewis county, and Michael Ferguson, of Tompkins county, under sentence of death, to ascertain and report their mental condition to the governor, one hundred dollars.

John J. White. For John J. White, for extra services rendered as county clerk of Kings county, ninety-six dollars and twenty-five cents.

Legislative printing. For printing for the legislature, including wrapping and binding, also for the publication of the official canvass and other official printing, and for printing and binding the session laws of eighteen hundred and seventy-one, thirty thousand dollars.

Murray and Goodwin. For Murray and Goodwin, for lithographing, engraving and printing (under direction of the clerk of the assembly), pursuant to resolution adopted April first, eighteen hundred and seventy, twenty-two hundred and twenty-five dollars.

Commissioners of fisheries. For the commissioners of fisheries, fifteen thousand dollars; to be expended as they may deem proper for the purpose of replenishing the lakes and rivers of this state with fish.

City of Newburgh. For the city of Newburgh, for money expended in and about Washington's headquarters, at Newburgh, one thousand six hundred and forty-three dollars and seventy-eight cents.

Argus Company. For the Argus Company, for printing and binding (under direction of the clerk of the assembly), five thousand copies of the report of the committee on Indian affairs, pursuant to resolution adopted April twenty-second, eighteen hundred and seventy; seven hundred copies of the report of savings banks in relation to unclaimed deposits, pursuant to resolution adopted April fourteenth, eighteen hundred and seventy; eight hundred copies of catalogue of petitions and papers on the files of the assembly, pursuant to resolution adopted April thirteenth, eighteen hundred and seventy; eight hundred copies classified index of bills introduced into the assembly, pursuant to resolution adopted April thirteenth, eighteen hundred and seventy; five hundred copies of index to assembly bills on file, pursuant to resolution adopted April thirteenth, eighteen hundred and seventy; to printing and binding (under direction of the clerk of the senate), five hundred copies digest of claims, pursuant to resolution adopted April twenty-sixth, eighteen hundred and seventy; five hundred copies of classified index of bills introduced into the senate, pursuant to resolution; five hundred copies catalogue of petitions and papers on the files of the senate, pursuant to resolution adopted, and five hundred copies of index to laws of the state of New York, pursuant to resolution adopted April twenty-sixth, eighteen hundred and seventy, nine thousand eight hundred and twenty-seven dollars; and for printing eleven hundred and eighty copies of report and testimony of the joint committee on railroads to investigate the cause of the railroad disaster at New Hamburgh, nine hundred and eighty-five dollars.

For printing reports, blanks and labels for state cabinet of natural history, for the years eighteen hundred and sixty-nine and eighteen hundred and seventy, five hundred and eight dollars and fifteen cents, and for printing on fine paper and binding in cloth, under resolution of the assembly, adopted February five, eighteen hundred and sixty-nine, two thousand copies of volume one, and two thousand copies of volume two, of the report of the adjutant-general for eighteen hundred and sixty-eight, eight thousand one hundred and sixty dollars, or so much thereof of the several sums as the comptroller, upon an investigation of their claims and accounts, shall determine to be justly then due, taking into consideration the quantities furnished and prices charged therefor. Ibid.

For Charles Van Benthuysen and Sons, for printing, et cetera, ordered by the assembly, the sum of forty-three thousand five hundred and ninety-eight dollars, or so much thereof of the amounts claimed as the comptroller, upon an investigation of their claims and accounts, shall determine to be justly their due, taking into consideration the quantities furnished and prices charged therefor. Chas. Van Benthuysen and Sons.

To Weed, Parsons and Company, for deficiency in appropriation of eighteen hundred and seventy, for printing the manual of the regents of the university, per resolution of senate, passed April twenty-ninth, eighteen hundred and sixty-nine, three hundred and fifteen dollars. For civil lists for the assembly for eighteen hundred and seventy, per resolution of assembly, passed April seventeen, eighteen hundred and seventy, three thousand and forty-five dollars; and for Weed, Parsons and Co. Regents' manual. Civil lists.

civil list of eighteen hundred and seventy, for the senate, state officers and regents of the university, pursuant to a resolution of the senate, passed April seventh, eighteen hundred and seventy, four thousand two hundred and sixty dollars. For lithographing five thousand six hundred railroad maps and five thousand five hundred railroad title pages, for railroad report of eighteen hundred and seventy, eighteen hundred and fifty-six dollars, to be paid upon the certificate of the state engineer and surveyor; the treasury to be reimbursed by collections from the railroad companies, in pursuance of the provisions of law. For printing and binding thirteen thousand seven hundred and ninety-five school registers for the department of public instruction, thirteen thousand seven hundred and ninety-five dollars, to be paid upon the certificate of the superintendent of public instruction. For printing and binding five hundred copies proceedings of the university convocation, pursuant to resolution of assembly, passed March ninth, eighteen hundred and seventy, one thousand three hundred and twenty dollars and thirty cents. For seventy-two copies legislative manual of eighteen hundred and seventy, for new members of assembly, pursuant to resolution of assembly, passed January fourth, eighteen hundred and seventy-one, seventy-two dollars.

Railroad maps.

School registers.

University convocation proceedings.

Legislative manual.

For thirty-two copies legislative manual of eighteen hundred and seventy, and thirty-two New York civil lists of eighteen hundred and seventy, pursuant to resolution of senate, passed January fourth, eighteen hundred and seventy-one, one hundred and twenty-eight dollars. For five hundred copies of the annual report of eighteen hundred and sixty-nine, and five hundred copies of the annual report of eighteen hundred and seventy, of the superintendent of insurance, three thousand dollars, to be paid upon the certificate of the superintendent of insurance department, the treasury to be reimbursed by collections from the insurance companies, in pursuance of the provisions of law. For printing and binding, under the directions of the regents, one thousand copies of the meteorological observations made since eighteen hundred and fifty, pursuant to resolution of assembly, passed April first, eighteen hundred and seventy, and for compiling and superintending the printing of the same, eleven thousand nine hundred and eighty-five dollars. For printing and binding eighty copies index to volumes one, two and three of translations of Dutch manuscripts of the office of the secretary of state, four hundred and thirty-four dollars and eighty cents. For two thousand five hundred and twenty volumes of Barnes' condensed New York insurance reports, pursuant to resolution of assembly, passed April sixteenth, eighteen hundred and seventy, fourteen thousand nine hundred and twenty dollars, to be paid on the certificate of the secretary of state of the delivery of the work at the secretary's office for distribution to members of the legislature, or so much thereof as may be certified by the superintendent of the insurance department to be the value thereof upon their delivery to the secre-

Manual and civil lists.

Insurance report.

Meteorological observations.

Index of Dutch manuscripts.

Barnes' condensed insurance reports.

How paid.

tary of state for distribution, such sum to be reimbursed to the treasury out of the insurance fund.

Printing for Prison labor commission. For printing for the state commission on prison labor, appointed under concurrent resolution, passed April twenty-sixth, eighteen hundred and seventy, seven hundred and ninety-five dollars and eighty cents. Legislative manuals. For three hundred and seventy legislative manuals of eighteen hundred and seventy-one, furnished to the clerks and messengers of the senate committees, and the messenger of the senate, pursuant to resolution of the senate passed March tenth, eighteen hundred and seventy-one, three hundred and seventy dollars. Wade's Poor Laws. For Wade's Code of Poor Laws of the state of New York, furnished pursuant to resolution of assembly, passed March fifteenth, eighteen hundred and seventy-one, and resolution of the senate, passed March twenty-two, eighteen hundred and seventy-one, twelve thousand seven hundred and fifty-four dollars. Auditor's financial report. For printing and binding one thousand copies auditor's financial report for eighteen hundred and seventy, for canal department, to be paid on the certificate of auditor, eight hundred and sixty-nine dollars and fifty-nine cents. Legislative manuals. For legislative manuals, lettering and diagrams, furnished to senators, members of assembly, officers of the legislature and state officers, pursuant to concurrent resolution, passed March, eighteen hundred and seventy-one, to be paid on the certificate of the clerk of the senate for the senate, the clerk of the assembly for the assembly, and the secretary of state for the state officers, thirty-six thousand nine hundred and forty-nine dollars, or so much thereof of the several sums as the comptroller, upon an investigation of the claims and accounts, shall find to be justly due, taking into consideration the quantities furnished and prices charged therefor.

Accounts of Weed, Parsons and Co., how adjusted. In adjusting the account between the said Weed, Parsons and Company, and the state, the comptroller shall allow and pay them for all completed work which they have notified the secretary of state or other officers who were to receive them, was ready for delivery, and was actually destroyed by fire in their printing establishment, on the morning of the seventh of April, eighteen hundred and seventy-one, the same as though it had been delivered to the state. Duplicating of state work. And the said Weed, Parsons and Company are hereby authorized and directed to duplicate all state work arrested or destroyed and not delivered, and the comptroller shall allow in full therefor; and shall pay on account thereof so much of the moneys herein appropriated to be paid the said Weed, Parsons and Company, as shall remain after the settlement, as hereinbefore provided. How paid. And the account therefor shall be settled, adjusted and paid in the same manner above prescribed, and the means necessary to pay the same shall be taken from any appropriation made or to be made for legislative printing.

Weed, Parsons and Co. To Weed, Parsons and Company, in liquidation of the deduction made on their account by the state printer, for the year eighteen hundred and sixty-nine, for extra composition, extra corrections, stereotyping and lithographing, the sum of

twenty-seven thousand six hundred and eighty dollars, said deductions to be presented to the comptroller in detail, with affidavit of one of said firm, and like affidavit of one of the state printers.

J. D. Parsons, Jr. John D. Parsons, jr., for furnishing one thousand nine hundred and eighty-eight copies supervisors' manual, and one thousand nine hundred and eighty-eight copies, assessors, collectors and town clerks' manual, pursuant to resolution of the assembly, passed April twenty-third, eighteen hundred and seventy, eleven thousand nine hundred and thirty-four dollars. For furnishing two thousand nine hundred and eighty-five copies of Cook's Highway Laws, pursuant to resolution of assembly, passed April twenty-fifth, eighteen hundred and seventy, eleven thousand four hundred and forty-seven dollars and fifty cents.

For supervisors' manual and assessors' manual.

Highway laws.

Ibid. For furnishing one thousand nine hundred and eighty-eight copies of assessors, collectors and town clerks' manual, and one thousand nine hundred and eighty-eight copies supervisors' manual, pursuant to resolution of the assembly, passed March eight, eighteen hundred and seventy-one, eleven thousand nine hundred and thirty-four dollars.

Ibid. For furnishing one thousand nine hundred and eighty-eight copies Cook's Highway Laws, pursuant to resolution of the assembly, passed March, eighteen hundred and seventy-one, seven thousand nine hundred and fifty-eight dollars, or so much thereof of the several sums as the comptroller, upon an investigation of the claims and accounts, shall find to be justly due, taking into consideration the quantities furnished and prices charged therefor.

Proviso as to payment for printing. Hereafter, no moneys appropriated for printing shall be paid, in cases where such printing has been made in contravention of law.

Oswego armory. The sum of twenty thousand dollars in addition to the appropriation made by chapter four hundred and fifty-nine of the laws of eighteen hundred and seventy, for the construction of the armory or arsenal in the city of Oswego, the expenditures to be made by the commissioners named in said act, and paid as therein provided.

John Callahan. To John Callahan, for services as state agent for the relief of sick and wounded soldiers at Alexandria, Va., during the months of January and February, eighteen hundred and sixty-five, two hundred dollars.

Niagara county. For the county of Niagara, to reimburse the same for money paid out in the support of Susan Green, an insane Indian woman, in the state lunatic asylum, three hundred dollars.

New Jersey commissioners. For the commissioners appointed to confer with the state of New Jersey, in regard to quarantine jurisdiction, boundary line, et cetera, pursuant to section seven of chapter six hundred and thirteen, of the laws of eighteen hundred and sixty-five, for compensation and expenses, three thousand dollars.

Cattaraugus reservation bridge. For the bridge on the Cattaraugus reservation, near Versailles, the money to be paid on the order of Asher Wright, five hundred dollars; and the said bridge shall hereafter be kept in repair by the commissioners of highways of the towns of Perrysburgh and Collins.

For John McGroaty, for money advanced to the St. Joseph's school, in the city of Brooklyn, two thousand three hundred and fifty dollars, that being the amount to which said school was entitled under chapter seven hundred and four of the laws of eighteen hundred and seventy, but which amount was not drawn. John McGroarty.

The sum of sixteen hundred dollars appropriated by chapter seven hundred and seventeen of the laws of eighteen hundred and sixty-eight, unexpended balance, made for similar objects, is hereby appropriated to paying the expenses of the litigation of the state with the Central railroad company of New Jersey, and the same objects therein mentioned. Litigation with Central Railroad Company of New Jersey.

For Richard Dunn, for compensation for unpaid services while lieutenant in the one hundred and seventy-fifth regiment, New York state volunteers, two hundred and seventy-five dollars and sixteen cents. Richard Dunn.

For Peter I. McAvoy, for rations furnished to the fifth regiment of New York volunteers from February fourteenth, eighteen hundred and sixty-two, eight hundred dollars. Peter I. McAvoy.

For William L. Michaels, for damage done to his property by the one hundred and thirty-fourth regiment, New York volunteers, six hundred dollars, or so much thereof as the adjutant-general may decide to be justly his due. Wm. L. Michaels.

For the state prison and asylum for insane convicts at Auburn, for deficiency of appropriation for the supply of water, one hundred and twenty-five dollars. Water at Auburn prison.

For the Western House of Refuge, to pay deficiencies in former appropriations, twenty thousand dollars. The further sum of ten thousand dollars is also hereby appropriated to said institution to pay the expenses of entrance and gate lodge, sewerage and other improvements, as recommended by the board of managers in their annual report for eighteen hundred and seventy-one. Western House of Refuge.

For the New York asylum for idiots at Syracuse, for additional buildings, thirty thousand dollars. Idiot asylum.

For compensation and expenses of the commissioners to locate an asylum for the insane in western New York, in pursuance of chapter four hundred and fourteen, laws of eighteen hundred and sixty-nine, such unpaid balance of the sum of one thousand five hundred dollars as remains unexpended for the purpose mentioned in chapter four hundred and ninety-two, laws of eighteen hundred and seventy. Insane asylum of western New York.

Asher P. Nichols, Marshall B. Champlain, Homer A. Nelson, Albert Haight and Norman M. Allen are hereby appointed commissioners to examine the subject of the taxation of lands upon the Buffalo creek, Allegany and Cattaraugus Indian reservations in the counties of Erie and Cattaraugus under chapter two hundred and fifty-four of the laws of eighteen hundred and forty, and chapter one hundred and sixty-six of the laws of eighteen hundred and forty-one, or other laws, and report to the next legislature a proper and equitable plan for Commission to examine as to taxation of lands on Indian reservation. Report thereon.

the adjustment and settlement of the same as between the state, the said counties and individuals.

FROM THE CANAL FUND.

Canal auditor. For the auditor of the canal department, for addition to his salary for the year one thousand eight hundred and seventy-one, the sum of fifteen hundred dollars.

Additional payment to late auditor. For the late auditor of the canal department, for addition to his salary for the years one thousand eight hundred and seventy, and one thousand eight hundred and seventy-one, the sum of two thousand dollars.

E. H. Crocker. For E. H. Crocker, division engineer, for services rendered outside of his duties in the fall of eighteen hundred and sixty-nine, in preparing the annual report of Oliver Bascom, canal commissioner, deceased, and for extra services rendered in eighteen hundred and sixty-eight, during the four months' suspension of Robert C. Dorn, in the performance of the duties of canal commissioner, the sum of six hundred dollars.

James G. Grindlay. For James G. Grindlay, from the canal fund, the sum of one hundred and twenty-five dollars, the same being the amount appropriated in eighteen hundred and seventy, but which could not be drawn by reason of a clerical error in the act appropriating the same.

Clerk hire of canal appraisers. For clerk hire in the office of the canal appraisers, in addition to the amount now allowed by law, the sum of eight thousand dollars, or so much thereof as shall be found necessary, to be paid by the auditor of the canal department, on the certificate of the chairman of the board of canal appraisers, the same to be paid from the canal fund.

Additional pay of appraisers. For the canal appraisers, for additional compensation to each of them, three thousand dollars.

Cornelius Glen and S. C. Murray. For Cornelius Glen and S. Cady Murray, to each of them, for extra services in the office of the canal appraisers, five hundred dollars.

PAYABLE FROM THE GENERAL FUND DEBT SINKING FUND.

Coin to pay Indian annuities. For premium for the purchase of coin to pay Indian annuities, seven hundred dollars.

Coin to pay interest on state debt. For premium for the purchase of coin to pay the interest on the general fund state debt, twenty thousand dollars.

FROM THE FREE SCHOOL FUND.

School department for delinquent school districts. For an additional contingent fund, for the department of public instruction, to pay equitable allowances to delinquent school districts, two thousand five hundred dollars.

§ 3. This act shall take effect immediately.

CHAP. 717.

AN ACT to provide ways and means for the support of government.

PASSED April 26, 1871; three-fifths being present.

The People of the State of New York, represented in Senate and Assembly, do enact as follows:

SECTION 1. There shall be imposed for the fiscal year, beginning on the first day of October, eighteen hundred and seventy-one, on each dollar of real and personal property of this state subject to taxation, taxes for state purposes hereinafter mentioned, which taxes shall be assessed, levied and collected by the annual assessment and collection of taxes for that year, in the manner prescribed by law, and shall be paid by the several county treasurers into the treasury of this state, to be held by the treasurer for application to the purposes specified; that is to say, for the general fund, and for the payment of those claims and demands which shall constitute a lawful charge upon that fund during the fiscal year commencing October first, eighteen hundred and seventy-one, one mill; and to provide for deficiency in that fund for fiscal year ending on the thirtieth day of September, one thousand eight hundred and seventy, three-eighths of one mill. For the free school fund for the maintenance of common schools in this state, one mill and one-fourth of one mill, as directed by chapter four hundred and six, laws of eighteen hundred and sixty-seven. For the payment of the interest and redemption of the principal of the state debt of two and one-half million dollars, as provided in chapter two hundred and seventy-one, laws of eighteen hundred and fifty-nine, one-eighth of one mill. For the payment of the interest, and to provide for the redemption of the principal of the state bounty debt, as authorized by chapter three hundred and twenty-five, laws of eighteen hundred and sixty-five, two mills. And an additional tax of three-eighths of one mill on each dollar of valuation of real and personal property subject to taxation, for the purposes of the new capitol.

State tax. One and three-eighth mills for general fund. One and one-fourth mills for common schools. One-eighth mill for floating debt. Two mills for bounty debt. Three-eighth mill for new capitol.

CHAP. 718.

AN ACT making appropriations for the support of government.

PASSED April 26, 1871; three-fifths being present.

The People of the State of New York, represented in Senate and Assembly, do enact as follows:

SECTION 1. The several amounts named in this act are hereby appropriated and authorized to be paid, from the several funds

Appropriation.

indicated, to the respective public officers, and for the several purposes specified, for the fiscal year beginning on the first day of October, in the year eighteen hundred and seventy-one, namely:

FROM THE GENERAL FUND.

EXECUTIVE DEPARTMENT.

Governor. For the governor, for salary, four thousand dollars.

Private secretary. For the private secretary of the governor, for salary, two thousand dollars.

Clerks and messengers. For the clerks and messengers in the executive department, for compensation, six thousand dollars.

Furniture, printing and incidentals. For the executive department, for furniture, blank and other books necessary for the use of the department, binding, blanks, printing, stationery, telegraphing and other incidental expenses, two thousand five hundred dollars.

Apprehension of criminals. For the executive department for the apprehension of criminals, pursuant to part one, chapter nine, title one, section fifteen of the Revised Statutes, two thousand dollars; Fugitives from justice. for the apprehension of fugitives from justice, pursuant to part four, chapter two, title seven, section forty-five of the Revised Statutes, and chapter one hundred and forty-seven of the laws of eighteen hundred and forty-six, one thousand dollars.

JUDICIARY.

Judges and commissioners of appeals. Justices of supreme court. Additional compensation of justices and stenographers in second judicial district. For the judges of the court of appeals, for salaries, forty-nine thousand five hundred dollars; for the commissioners of appeals, for salaries, thirty-five thousand dollars; for the justices of the supreme court, for salaries, one hundred and ninety-eight thousand dollars; for the justices of the supreme court in the second judicial district, not residing in the county of Kings, for additional compensation, pursuant to chapter seven hundred and sixty-five of the laws of eighteen hundred and sixty-eight, five thousand dollars; and for the stenographers, appointed under the said act, five thousand dollars. Said amounts to be paid only from the moneys which shall be paid into the treasury for taxes levied for the purposes of said act, and in pursuance thereof. State reporter. For the state reporter, for salary, three thousand five hundred dollars, which is hereby declared to be the salary of said officer. Expenses of chief and associate judges of court of appeals. The chief judge and associate judges of the court of appeals shall each receive the sum of two thousand dollars, annually, from the time they entered upon the duties of their offices, respectively, in lieu of expenses now allowed by law.

Per diem expenses of justices of supreme court. To pay the per diem expenses of the justices of the supreme court, pursuant to section nine of chapter four hundred and eight of the laws of eighteen hundred and seventy, fifty thousand dollars, or so much thereof as may be necessary.

Law libraries. To purchase, for the judges of the court of appeals, additional law libraries, which, with the law libraries now owned by the state for the judges thereof, shall be and remain the law libraries for them, and to furnish the book-cases therefor, twenty thousand dollars, or so much thereof as may be necessary therefor. The said sum shall be expended under the direction of the chief judges of the said court, and the order of the chief judge shall be a voucher therefor. And the income of the fund in the control and custody of the said court, heretofore used and applied to the replenishing of the law libraries of the said judges, shall continue to be applied to the replenishing of the said libraries, and those hereby provided for; said income to be expended under the like direction and order. Appropriation, how expended. Income of fund, how applied.

For the per diem allowance of commissioners of appeals and justices of the supreme court, eighteen thousand dollars, and for the expenses of the general terms of the supreme court, twelve thousand dollars. Commissioners of appeals and justices of supreme court.

For the crier and attendants of the court of appeals, and the commissioners of appeals, five thousand dollars. Crier and attendants of courts.

For salaries of the commissioners to revise the statutes, fifteen thousand dollars, and for reasonable expenses of clerical service and other incidental matters for said commissioners, three thousand dollars. Commissioners to revise statutes.

OFFICE OF THE CLERK OF THE COURT OF APPEALS.

For the clerk of the court of appeals, for salary, five thousand dollars, which is hereby fixed as his annual salary from the date of his appointment. Clerk of the court of appeals.

For the deputy clerk of the court of appeals, for salary, two thousand dollars, which is hereby declared to be the salary of said officer. Deputy clerk.

For the clerk of the court of appeals, for compensation of clerks employed in his office, three thousand five hundred dollars; and for furniture, blank and other books necessary for the use of the office, binding, blanks, printing and other necessary incidental expenses, seven hundred dollars. Clerk hire in office. Furniture, printing, etc.

OFFICE OF CLERK OF COMMISSIONERS OF APPEALS.

For clerk of the commission of appeals, for salary, three thousand five hundred dollars. Clerk of commission of appeals.

For clerk of the commission of appeals, for compensation of clerk employed in his office, one thousand four hundred dollars; and for pay of messenger for commission, two hundred dollars; and for furniture, blank and other books necessary for the use of the office, binding, blanks, printing and other necessary expenses, five hundred dollars. Clerk hire and messenger. Furniture, printing, etc.

OFFICE OF THE ATTORNEY-GENERAL.

For the attorney-general, for salary, two thousand dollars. Attorney-general.

For the deputy attorney-general, for salary, two thousand dollars. Deputy attorney-general.

For the attorney-general, for compensation, pursuant to part one, chapter eight, title five, section six of the Revised Additional compensation.

Pay of counsel to assist. Statutes, two thousand dollars; for counsel to assist him, pursuant to chapter three hundred and fifty-seven of the laws of eighteen hundred and forty-eight, three thousand dollars; for compensation of clerks and messengers employed in his office, one thousand six hundred dollars; for furniture, blank and other books necessary for the use of the office, binding, blanks, printing and other necessary incidental expenses, five hundred dollars; for costs of suits, fees of sheriffs, compensation of witnesses, and for expenditures and disbursements necessarily incurred by him, in or about the prosecution or defense of any action or claim in which the people of this state may be interested, pursuant to part three, chapter ten, title three, section fifty-one of the Revised Statutes, two thousand dollars.

Clerks and messengers. Furniture, books, etc. Costs, fees of sheriffs, witnesses, etc.

Expenses of medical commissioners. For defraying the expenses of medical commissioners appointed by the governor or courts of oyer and terminer to inquire into the mental condition of persons under indictment or conviction for offenses, the punishment of which is death, two thousand dollars.

OFFICE OF THE SECRETARY OF STATE.

Secretary of state. For the secretary of state, for salary, two thousand five hundred dollars.

Deputy secretary. For the deputy secretary of state, for salary, two thousand dollars.

Clerk hire For the secretary of state, for compensation of clerks employed in his office, ten thousand dollars.

Historical and ancient record department. For compensation of the translator in the secretary of state's office, pursuant to chapter five hundred and thirty-nine of the laws of eighteen hundred and sixty-five, one thousand five hundred dollars; for compensation of messenger, eight hundred dollars; and for furniture, blank and other books necessary for the use of the office, binding, blanks, printing and other necessary incidental expenses, one thousand two hundred dollars.

Messenger. Printing, furniture, binding, etc.

COMPTROLLER'S OFFICE.

Comptroller. For the comptroller, for salary, two thousand five hundred dollars.

Deputy comptroller. For the deputy comptroller, for salary, two thousand dollars.

Accountant. For the comptroller, for compensation of the accountant and transfer officer of his office, two thousand dollars.

Second deputy. For compensation of the chief clerk and auditor, acting as second deputy comptroller, to continue only during the illness of the present deputy comptroller, two thousand dollars; for compensation of the clerks employed in the office, eighteen thousand dollars; and for furniture, blank and other books necessary for the use of the office, binding, blanks, printing, and other necessary incidental expenses, one thousand two hundred dollars; and for compensation of messenger, five hundred dollars.

Clerk hire. Furniture, blank books, etc. Messenger.

For the comptroller, for advances to county treasurers on account of taxes on property of non-residents, which may be returned to his office, pursuant to chapter four hundred and twenty-seven, title one, section ten of the laws of eighteen hundred and fifty-five, sixty thousand dollars; for payments to commissioners of moneys received into the treasury for taxes on lands of non-residents, and appropriated to the construction of roads, six thousand dollars; for compensation of the agents designated by him to examine the accounts of auctioneers, one thousand two hundred dollars; for the payment of expenses of books and stationery for the transfer office, at the bank of the Manhattan company, in the city of New York, two hundred and fifty dollars; for compensation of the agent employed in the city of New York to superintend the issue and transfer of state stocks, pursuant to chapter two hundred and nine of the laws of eighteen hundred and sixty-six, seven hundred and fifty dollars; for repayment of money to purchasers for redemption of lands sold for taxes, fifty thousand dollars; for repayment of money erroneously paid into the treasury for taxes, ten thousand dollars; for repayment of money in cases of failure of title to lands sold by the state, three hundred dollars; to J. Moreau Smith to re-imburse him for interest money paid to the state, and taxes upon lands purchased by him at a re-sale held by the state engineer and surveyor in eighteen hundred and fifty-eight, during the pendency of an action to obtain possession thereof, and which was determined in his favor by the court of appeals in October, eighteen hundred and sixty-eight, the sum of two thousand and fifty-nine dollars and thirty-five cents; and for money paid into the treasury, through mistake, pursuant to part one, chapter eight, title three, section fifteen of the Revised Statutes, five hundred dollars.

Advances for non-resident taxes. Non-resident road taxes. Auction agents. Manhattan company. Agent for transfer of state stocks. Redemption, and erroneous tax payments. Failure of title. J. Moreau Smith, for payment of interest moneys.

TREASURER'S OFFICE.

For the treasurer, for salary, one thousand five hundred dollars, and for compensation for countersigning transfer and assignments of securities made in the banking department, pursuant to chapter one hundred and three of the laws of eighteen hundred and fifty-seven, one thousand dollars. Treasurer.

For the deputy treasurer, for salary, two thousand dollars. Deputy.

For the treasurer, for compensation of the clerks employed in his office, five thousand dollars; and for furniture, blank and other books necessary for the use of the office, binding, blanks, printing and other necessary incidental expenses, eight hundred dollars. Clerk hire. Furniture and incidentals.

DEPARTMENT OF PUBLIC INSTRUCTION.

For the superintendent of public instruction, for salary, two thousand five hundred dollars. Superintendent of public instruction.

For the deputy superintendent of public instruction, for salary, one thousand five hundred dollars. Deputy.

Clerk hire. Expenses. For the department of public instruction, for compensation of clerks, six thousand dollars; for expenses, pursuant to part one, chapter fifteen, title two, section eleven of the Revised Statutes, and chapter five hundred and fifty-five, title one, section thirteen of the laws of eighteen hundred and sixty-four, five hundred dollars; and for furniture, blank and other books necessary for the use of the department, binding, blanks, printing and other necessary incidental expenses, one thousand dollars. Furniture and incidentals.

OFFICE OF THE STATE ENGINEER AND SURVEYOR.

Deputy state engineer. Clerks to prepare railroad reports. Printing and binding thereof. For the deputy state engineer and surveyor, for salary, two thousand dollars; for compensation of clerks employed to assist in preparation of the report of the state engineer and surveyor on railroads, two thousand two hundred dollars; and for expenses of printing and binding said report, five thousand dollars. The aforesaid salary, compensation and expenses of printing and binding, whether ordered by the legislature or otherwise, shall be paid to the treasury by the several railroad companies of this state, in proportion to their gross receipts, pursuant to chapter five hundred and twenty-six of the laws of eighteen hundred and fifty-five. Repayment by railroad companies.

Clerk hire in office. For the state engineer and surveyor, for compensation of clerks employed in his office, two thousand eight hundred and fifty dollars; and for furniture, blank and other books necessary for the use of the office, binding, blanks, printing, and other necessary incidental expenses, five hundred dollars. Furniture and incidentals.

BANKING DEPARTMENT.

Superintendent of banking dept. Deputy. For the superintendent of the banking department, for salary, five thousand dollars; for compensation of the deputy superintendent and clerks employed in the department, and for furniture, blank and other books necessary for the use of the department, binding, blanks, printing and other necessary incidental expenses, fifteen thousand dollars. The aforesaid salary, compensation and other expenses here indicated shall be repaid to the treasury by the several banks and banking associations of this state, pursuant to chapter one hundred and sixty-four of the laws of eighteen hundred and fifty-one. Furniture, printing, blanks, etc. Expenses, how repaid by banks.

INSURANCE DEPARTMENT.

Supt. of ins. dept. Deputy and clerks. Furniture, blanks, etc. For the superintendent of the insurance department, for salary, seven thousand dollars; for compensation of the deputy superintendent and clerks employed in the department, and for furniture, blank and other books necessary for the use of the department, binding, blanks, printing and other necessary incidental expenses, fifty-three thousand dollars. The aforesaid salary, compensation and other expenses here indicated shall be repaid to the treasury by the several insurance companies, associations, persons and agents, pursuant Expense, how repaid by insurance companies.

to chapter three hundred and sixty-six of the laws of eighteen hundred and fifty-nine.

INSPECTOR OF GAS-METERS.

For the inspector of gas-meters, for salary and contingent expenses, pursuant to chapter one hundred and sixteen of the laws of eighteen hundred and sixty, and to the conditions and requirements imposed by chapter one hundred and thirty-five of the laws of eighteen hundred and sixty-three, two thousand five hundred dollars; which amount shall be repaid to the treasury by the several gas-light companies, pursuant to chapter three hundred and eleven of the laws of eighteen hundred and fifty-nine; but no payment shall be made by the comptroller upon such salary till an amount equal to such payment shall be received by him from the gas companies, or some of them.

Inspector of gas-meters. Expenses, how repaid by gas companies. Payments when to be made.

INSPECTION OF STEAM BOILERS.

For inspector-in-chief of steam boilers, created by chapter nine hundred and sixty-nine of the laws of eighteen hundred and sixty-seven, for salary of chief and assistants, office, clerk hire, printing, traveling and contingent expenses, ten thousand dollars.

Chief and assistant inspectors of boilers. Clerk hire and expenses.

STATE ASSESSORS.

For the state assessors, for compensation and traveling expenses, pursuant to chapter three hundred and twelve of the laws of eighteen hundred and fifty-nine, to each of them, one thousand five hundred dollars.

State assessors.

COMMISSIONERS OF PUBLIC ACCOUNTS.

For the commissioners of public accounts, for compensation and traveling expenses, pursuant to chapter two hundred and twenty-three of the laws of eighteen hundred and sixty-two, to each of them, five hundred dollars.

Commissioners of public accounts.

WEIGHTS AND MEASURES.

For the superintendent of weights and measures, for salary, three hundred dollars.

Weights and measures.

QUARANTINE.

For the commissioners of quarantine, salaries, to each of them, two thousand five hundred dollars.

Commissioners of quarantine.

OFFAL INSPECTION.

For the shore inspector, under the bill passed by the legislature in regard to offal, et cetera, thrown in the water of the

Shore inspector.

East and North rivers and New York and Raritan bays, now in the hands of the governor, for salary, fifteen hundred dollars, if the said bill shall become a law.

PUBLIC OFFICES.

Mileage of lieut.-gov. and speaker. Expenses of lands. For the land office, for compensation and mileage of the lieutenant-governor and of the speaker of the assembly, for their attendance at the meeting of the commissioners, and for assessments and other expenses of public lands, two thousand dollars.

Postage for public officers. Stationery. For the several departments and public offices, for postage on official letters, documents and for other matters sent by mail, of the governor, clerk of the court of appeals, attorney-general, secretary of state, comptroller, treasurer, superintendent of public instruction, state engineer and surveyor, adjutant-general and inspector-general, pursuant to chapter four hundred and seventy-seven of the laws of eighteen hundred and sixty-two, five thousand dollars; and for stationery for the aforesaid offices and departments, five thousand dollars.

REGENTS OF THE UNIVERSITY.

Secretary and assistant regents. Botanist. Messengers, printing and expenses. For the regents of the university, for salary of the secretary, two thousand dollars; for salary of the assistant secretary, one thousand dollars; for compensation of a botanist for arranging the herbarium in the state cabinet of natural history, one thousand five hundred dollars; for postage, printing, stationery, compensation of messengers, expenses of regents in attending meetings of the board, and other necessary purposes, three thousand dollars.

CAPITOL, EXECUTIVE MANSION, STATE HALL, STATE LIBRARY AND STATE CABINET.

Superintendent of capitol. Repairs, gas cleaning, etc. For the capitol and state library, for compensation of superintendent, nine hundred dollars; and for expenses for repairs, cleaning, labor, gas and other necessary purposes, ten thousand dollars.

Superintendent of state hall. Repairs, gas, labor, etc. For the state hall, for compensation of superintendent, nine hundred dollars; and for expenses for repairs, cleaning, labor, gas and other necessary purposes, five thousand dollars; and for expenses, repairs, cleaning, labor, gas and other necessary expenses of the executive mansion, four thousand dollars.

Fuel. For the capitol, executive mansion, state hall and state library, for fuel, five thousand dollars.

Librarians and janitor of state library. Books, binding and transportation. For the state library, for salaries of the librarians and assistant librarians, four thousand five hundred dollars; for compensation of janitor, seven hundred dollars; to the trustees of the state library, for purchase of books, four thousand dollars; for binding, lettering and marking books, one thousand seven hundred dollars; for transportation of books and other necessary expenses of the library, one thousand dollars.

Keeper of old state hall, repairs, gas, fuel, etc.

For the hall of the state cabinet of natural history and the agricultural museum, for repairs, cleaning, labor, gas, fuel, compensation of keeper and other necessary expenses, three thousand five hundred dollars.

Drawings for natural history.

For the persons employed in preparing drawings for the natural history of the state, for compensation, two thousand five hundred dollars.

State museum of natural history. Assistants. Increase of collection. Expenditures, how approved.

For the state museum of natural history, for the salary of the directors, as established in the appropriation bill of eighteen hundred and seventy, for three assistants, as now employed by him, and for the general increase and preservation of the collection, pursuant to chapter five hundred and fifty-seven of the laws of eighteen hundred and seventy, ten thousand dollars; all the expenditures to be made by the director, with the approval of the board of regents of the university.

LEGISLATURE.

Legislature mileage and compensation, etc. Postage, committees, witnesses, manuals, etc.

For the legislature, for compensation and mileage of the members and officers, ninety thousand dollars; for advances for contingent expenses to the clerk of the senate and the clerk of the assembly, twenty thousand dollars; and for postage, expenses of committees, compensation of witnesses, the Legislative manual, the Clerk's and Croswell's manuals, and other contingent expenditures, eighteen thousand dollars.

Legislative printing. Official canvass, session laws and natural history.

For printing for the legislature, including mapping, binding and engraving, also for publication of the official canvass and other official notices, for printing and binding the session laws of eighteen hundred and seventy, and for printing the natural history of the state, one hundred and seventy-five thousand dollars.

Transportation of books, expense of boxes, etc. Law reports for other states.

For the transportation of public documents by express, the session laws, the journals and documents of the legislature, reports, books and packages for the public offices, and the expenses of boxes pursuant to chapter two hundred and fifty-four of the laws of eighteen hundred and forty-seven, five thousand dollars, and for supplying other states with reports of the court of appeals and the supreme court, pursuant to chapter five hundred and thirty-six of the laws of eighteen hundred and thirty-six, five hundred dollars.

STATE PRISONS, ETC.

Inspectors of state prisons.

For inspectors of state prisons, for salaries to each of them, one thousand and six hundred dollars; and for traveling expenses, to each of them, six hundred dollars.

State prisons, for maintenance and supply of water.

For the state prisons, for maintenance, four hundred thousand dollars; and for the supplying of Croton water to the prison at Sing Sing, pursuant to chapter two hundred and eighty-two of the laws of eighteen hundred and sixty-one, one thousand five hundred dollars; and for supply of water to the prison asylum at Auburn, fifteen hundred dollars.

Repayment to contractors. For repayment to contractors at the state prisons of deposits made by them, pursuant to chapter four hundred and sixty-five of the laws of eighteen hundred and sixty-three, two thousand dollars.

Penitentiaries, for maintenance. For the penitentiaries of this state, for maintenance of convicts incarcerated in them, pursuant to chapter one hundred and fifty-eight of the laws of eighteen hundred and fifty-six, chapter five hundred and eighty-four of the laws of eighteen hundred and sixty-five, and chapter six hundred and sixty-seven of the laws of eighteen hundred and sixty-six, ten thousand dollars.

Sheriffs, for transporting convicts. For the sheriffs of the several counties of this state, for compensation for transportation of convicts to the state prisons, houses of refuge and penitentiaries of this state pursuant to chapter one hundred and twenty-three of the laws of eighteen hundred and forty-nine, and chapter one hundred and fifty-eight of the laws of eighteen hundred and fifty-six, twenty thousand dollars.

ASYLUM FOR INSANE CONVICTS.

Asylum for insane convicts. For the asylum for insane convicts, for maintenance, pursuant to chapter one hundred and thirty of the laws of eighteen hundred and fifty-eight, sixteen thousand dollars.

STATE LUNATIC ASYLUMS.

State lunatic asylum. Mark Jack and female convicts. For the state lunatic asylum, for salaries of officers, eleven thousand dollars, and for the maintenance of Mark Jack, an insane Indian, two hundred and fifty dollars; and for the maintenance of female convicts, six hundred dollars.

HOUSES OF REFUGE FOR JUVENILE CONVICTS.

Juvenile delinquents. For the society for the reformation of juvenile delinquents in the city of New York, forty thousand dollars.

Western house of refuge. For house of refuge for western New York, forty thousand dollars.

PUBLIC CHARITIES.

Deaf and dumb institution. For the institution for the deaf and dumb, for the instruction and maintenance of three hundred and fifty state pupils for one year, pursuant to chapter five hundred and fifty-five of the laws of eighteen hundred and sixty-four, or a proportionate amount for a shorter period of time, or a smaller number of pupils, as shall be duly verified, one hundred and five thousand dollars, and this sum is in full of all demands upon the state in behalf of said institution during the next fiscal year.

N. Y. institution for the blind. For the New York institution for the blind, for the instruction and maintenance of one hundred and fifty state pupils for one year, pursuant to chapter five hundred and fifty-five of the laws of eighteen hundred and sixty-four, or a proportionate amount for a shorter period of time, or a smaller number of pupils, as shall be duly verified, forty-five thousand dollars.

For the New York state institution for the blind, at Batavia, for the support and maintenance of the institution, thirty-five thousand dollars. N. Y. state institution at Batavia.

For the Willard asylum for the insane, at Ovid, for the support and maintenance of the institution, twenty thousand dollars, and for salaries of officers, eight thousand dollars. Willard asylum for insane.

For the state asylum for idiots, twenty-five thousand dollars. Idiot asylum.

For the state commissioners of public charities, for the salary of the secretary, twenty-five hundred dollars; for traveling expenses of the commissioners and secretary, for office rent, clerk hire, stationery, lights, fuel and contingencies, three thousand dollars. State commissioners of public charities.

MILITIA.

For the national guard of the state of New York, for salaries, pay of officers and privates, purchase of arms, uniforms, equipments and military supplies, and other authorized expenditures, two hundred thousand dollars; but no muster rolls for volunteers shall be printed. National guard, for salaries, arms, uniforms, etc.

For services and expenses in the bureau of military statistics, three thousand dollars, payable out of the military record fund. Bureau of military statistics.

For altering the small arms of the national guard to, or exchanging them for breech-loaders, under the direction of the governor, two hundred and fifty thousand dollars, or so much thereof as necessary, payable after the first of October, eighteen hundred and seventy-two. Alteration of small arms to breech-loaders.

ONONDAGA SALT SPRINGS.

For the salt springs of Onondaga, for salary of superintendent, compensation of clerks and other persons employed, and for other necessary expenses, pursuant to chapter three hundred and forty-six of the laws of eighteen hundred and fifty-nine, fifty thousand dollars. Superintendent of salt springs, clerks and expenses.

AGRICULTURE.

For the state society for the promotion of agriculture, and for the agricultural societies of the several counties of this state, for donations, twenty thousand dollars; and for salary of the entomologist of the state society, one thousand dollars. State and county agricultural societies. Entomologist.

INTEREST ON STATE INDEBTEDNESS.

For interest on the debt of thirty-six thousand dollars, created for the benefit of the Stockbridge Indians, pursuant to chapter two hundred and eight of the laws of eighteen hundred and forty-eight, and chapter thirty-seven of the laws of eighteen hundred and fifty, two thousand one hundred and sixty dollars. Stockbridge Indian debt.

INDIAN AFFAIRS.

Onondaga Indians. For the Onondaga Indians, for relief, pursuant to chapter two hundred and six of the laws of eighteen hundred and fifty-eight, three hundred dollars.

Attorney of Tonawanda Senecas. For the compensation of the attorney of the Tonawanda band of Seneca Indians, pursuant to chapter one hundred and thirty-nine of the laws of eighteen hundred and sixty-seven, three hundred dollars.

Agent of Onondagas. For the agent of the Onondaga Indians, for compensation, pursuant to chapter three hundred and seventy-six of the laws of eighteen hundred and fifty-one, two hundred dollars.

Ibid. For the agent of the Onondaga Indians, for compensation, pursuant to chapter one hundred and seventy-eight of the laws of eighteen hundred and forty-seven, sixty-five dollars.

Agent for taking census and paying annuities. For the agent for taking the census of Onondaga Indians on the Allegany, Cattaraugus, Tuscarora and Tonawanda reservations, and paying their annuities for compensation pursuant to chapter seventy-three of the laws of eighteen hundred and fifty-eight, one hundred and fifty dollars.

Attorney of St. Regis. For the attorney of the St. Regis Indians, for compensation, pursuant to chapter three hundred and twenty-five of the laws of eighteen hundred and sixty-one, one hundred and fifty dollars.

Attorney of Senecas. For the attorney of the Seneca Indians, for compensation, pursuant to chapter one hundred and fifty of the laws of eighteen hundred and forty-five, one hundred and fifty dollars.

Removal of intruders from Indian land. For the expense of removing intruders on Indian lands, pursuant to chapter two hundred and four of the laws of eighteen hundred and twenty-one, two hundred dollars.

Commissioners of pilots. For commissioners of pilots, for payment of the expenses necessarily incurred by them in executing the several laws relating to the harbor of New York, four thousand five hundred dollars.

Washington headquarters. For Washington's Headquarters at Newburgh, for compensation of the keeper, two hundred dollars.

FROM THE GENERAL FUND DEBT SINKING FUND.

INTEREST ON STATE INDEBTEDNESS.

Interest on general fund debt. For interest on three million eight hundred and twenty-nine thousand eight hundred and thirty-one dollars and fifty-three cents of state indebtedness, known and designated as the general fund debt, one hundred and ninety-nine thousand one hundred and ninety dollars and fifty-two cents.

INDIAN ANNUITIES.

Payment to Onondagas. Cayugas. Senecas. For the several Indian nations, for the payment of their annuities, as follows, namely: to the Onondagas, two thousand four hundred and thirty dollars; to the Cayugas, two thousand three hundred dollars; to the Senecas, five hundred dollars; and to the St. Regis Indians, two thousand one hundred and thirty-one dollars and sixty-seven cents. St. Regis.

FROM THE BOUNTY DEBT SINKING FUND.

INTEREST, ETC.

For interest on state indebtedness incurred for the payment and reimbursement of counties, pursuant to chapters two hundred and twenty-six, and three hundred and twenty-five of the laws of eighteen hundred and sixty-five, henceforth to be known and designated as the "bounty debt," and for the investment of contributions to the bounty debt sinking fund, four million dollars. Interest on bounty debt, and for sinking fund.

FROM THE FREE SCHOOL FUND.

DIVIDENDS TO COMMON SCHOOLS.

For the common schools of this state, for their maintenance, two million five hundred thousand dollars, or such part of that amount as shall be received from the proceeds of the tax of one mill and one-quarter of one mill, on each dollar of taxable property of this state, levied for the support of common schools, to be divided and apportioned, pursuant to title three of chapter five hundred and fifty-five of the laws of eighteen hundred and sixty-four. One and one-fourth mill tax for common schools.

For the state normal and training school, at Brockport, for its maintenance, eighteen thousand dollars. Hereafter the number of members of the local board of said school, as recommended by the superintendent of public instruction, shall not exceed nine, and the following named persons, now members of said board, shall constitute the local board for said school, namely: Jerome Fuller, M. B. Anderson, Daniel Holmes, Eliphalet Whitney, Joseph Toizier, J. Durware Decker, Augustus F. Brainerd, Henry W. Seymour, John A. Latta. Normal School at Brockport. Local board, how recommended. Names of board.

For the state normal and training school, at Fredonia, for its maintenance, eighteen thousand dollars. Fredonia Normal School.

For the state normal and training school, at Potsdam, for its maintenance, eighteen thousand dollars. Potsdam.

For the state normal and training school, at Cortland, for its maintenance, eighteen thousand dollars. Cortland.

For the state normal school at Albany, for its maintenance, sixteen thousand dollars. Albany.

For the state normal and training school at Geneseo, for its maintenance, eighteen thousand dollars. Geneseo.

For the state normal and training school at Oswego, for its maintenance, eighteen thousand dollars; and for the construction of the proper heating apparatus for warming the building, the sum of ten thousand dollars, or so much thereof as may be necessary, to be expended under the direction of the local board of trustees. Oswego. Heating apparatus.

FROM THE ELMIRA FEMALE COLLEGE EDUCATIONAL FUND.

Elmira Female College. For the Elmira Female College, under chapter six hundred and forty-three, laws of eighteen hundred and sixty-seven, three thousand five hundred dollars.

Appropriations, how paid. § 2. The amounts herein appropriated shall be paid by the treasurer from the respective funds as specified, and the salaries named shall be established and fixed by this act for the several officers for whom they are designated; but the comptroller shall not draw his warrant for payment of the several amounts heretofore named, except for salaries and other expenditures and appropriations, the amounts of which are duly established and fixed by law, till the persons demanding them shall present to him a detailed statement in items of the same; and if such account shall be for services, it must show when, where, and under what authority they were rendered; if for expenditures, when, where, and under what authority they were made; if for articles furnished, when and where they were furnished, to whom they were delivered, and under what authority; and if the demand shall be for traveling expenses, the account must also specify the distance traveled, the place of starting and destination, the duty or business, the date and items of expenditures. All accounts, in discretion of the comptroller, must be verified by an affidavit, to the effect that the account is true, just and correct, and that no part of it has been paid, but is actually and justly due and owing; on all accounts for transportation, furniture, blank and other books purchased for the use of office, binding, blanks, printing, stationery, postage, cleaning and other necessary incidental expenses, a bill, duly receipted, must also be furnished; and it shall be the duty of the treasurer to report annually to the legislature the detail of these several expenditures.

Drawing of warrants by comptroller. Detailed statement, in items. Accounts to be receipted, etc. Treasurer to report annually to legislature.

Annual reports of certain institutions. § 3. All institutions and societies entitled by this act to receive money from the state, shall make an annual report to the legislature, on or before the fifteenth day of January in each year, and no such money shall be paid in any such case until such report is made therein.

he has sent the said papers, and shall, in said affidavits, specify the names and places of residence of the persons to whom the said papers were sent.

FROM THE UNITED STATES DEPOSIT FUND.

CAPITAL, DIVIDENDS TO SCHOOLS AND ACADEMIES, INSTRUCTION OF TEACHERS.

For investment as capital of the United States deposit fund, pursuant to chapter one hundred and fifty of the laws of eighteen hundred and thirty-seven, one hundred thousand dollars. Capital of U. S. deposit fund

For the common schools of this state, for their maintenance, and including the salaries of the school commissioners of the several counties, pursuant to title three of chapter five hundred and fifty-five of the laws of eighteen hundred and sixty-four, and chapter two hundred and thirty-seven of the laws of eighteen hundred and thirty-eight, one hundred and sixty-five thousand dollars. Common schools and school commissioners.

For the academies of this state, for their maintenance, pursuant to chapter two hundred and thirty-seven of the laws of eighteen hundred and thirty-eight, twenty-eight thousand dollars. Academies.

For the common school fund, to be added to its capital, pursuant to the ninth article of the constitution, twenty-five thousand dollars. Capital of common school fund.

For the teachers of common schools, for their instruction in those academies which the regents of the university shall designate for that purpose, pursuant to chapter two hundred and thirty-five of the laws of eighteen hundred and fifty-two, as amended by chapter four hundred and ten of the laws of eighteen hundred and fifty-five, eighteen thousand dollars. Instruction of teachers in academies.

For the repayment of money erroneously paid into the treasury, pursuant to part one, chapter eight, title three, section fifteen of the Revised Statutes, five hundred dollars. Repayment of moneys.

FROM THE COLLEGE LAND SCRIP FUND.

THE CORNELL UNIVERSITY.

For the Cornell University, pursuant to chapter five hundred and eighty-five of the laws of eighteen hundred and sixty-five, thirty-five thousand dollars. Cornell University

FROM THE CORNELL ENDOWMENT FUND.

CORNELL UNIVERSITY.

For the Cornell University, pursuant to chapter five hundred and fifty-four of the laws of eighteen hundred and sixty-eight, ten thousand dollars. Ibid.

Use of swivel gun prohibited. § 3. No person shall at any time kill any wild duck, goose or brant, with any device or instrument known as a swivel or punt gun, or with any gun other than such guns as are habitually raised at arms' length and fired from the shoulder, or shall use any net, device or instrument, or gun other than such gun as aforesaid, with intent to capture or kill any such wild duck, goose or brant, under a penalty of one hundred dollars.

Shooting at wild geese, etc., from vessels, prohibited. § 4. No person shall sail for any wild fowl, or shoot at any wild goose, brant or duck, from any vessel propelled by steam or sails, or from any boat or other structure attached to the same, under a penalty of ten dollars.

Use of floating battery prohibited. § 5. No person shall use any floating battery or machine for the purpose of killing wild fowl, or shoot out of any such floating battery or machine at any wild goose, brant or duck, under a penalty of one hundred dollars for each offense.

Woodcock. § 6. No person shall kill or expose for sale, or have in his or her possession after the same has been killed, any woodcock, between the first day of February and the fifteenth day of July, under a penalty of fifty dollars for each bird.

Quail. § 7. No person shall kill or expose for sale, or have in his or her possession after the same has been killed, any quail, between the first day of January and the twentieth day of October, under penalty of twenty-five dollars for each bird.

Partridges or prairie chickens. § 8. No person shall kill or expose for sale, or have in his or her possession after the same has been killed, any ruffed grouse, commonly called partridge; or pinnated grouse, commonly called prairie chicken, between the first day of January and the first day of September, under a penalty of twenty-five dollars for each bird.

Eagles, sparrows, oriole and other song birds. § 9. No person shall at any time within this state, kill or expose for sale, or have in his or her possession after the same is killed, any eagle, woodpecker, night-hawk, sparrow, yellow-bird, wren, martin, oriole or bobolink or other song-bird, under a penalty of five dollars for each bird.

Robins, starlings, etc. § 10. No person shall kill or expose for sale, or have in his possession after the same has been killed, any robin, brown thrasher, meadow lark or starling, save only during the months of August, September, October, November and December, under a penalty of five dollars for each bird.

Ornithologists protected. § 11. The last two sections shall not apply to any person who shall kill any bird for the purpose of studying its habits or history, or having the same stuffed and set up as a specimen; or to any person who shall kill on his own premises any robins in the act of destroying fruits or grapes. Protection of fruits.

Robbing nests prohibited. § 12. No person shall destroy or rob the nest of any wild birds whatever under a penalty of twenty-five dollars for each offense.

Protection of wild pigeons on nesting ground. § 13. No person shall kill, catch or discharge any fire arms at any wild pigeon while on its nesting ground, or break up, or in any manner disturb such nesting ground, or the birds therein, or discharge any fire-arm at any distance within one-fourth of a mile of such nesting place at any pigeon, under a penalty of twenty-five dollars for each offense.

§ 14. No person shall, at any time or place within this state, take any ruffed grouse, commonly called partridge, or any quail, with any trap or snare, under a penalty of twenty-five dollars for each bird, except upon his own grounds. Penalty for taking partridge or quail in traps.

§ 15. There shall be no shooting or hunting, or having in possession in the open air the implements for shooting, on the first day of the week called Sunday, and any person violating the provision of this section shall be liable to a penalty of not more than twenty-five dollars, nor less than ten dollars for each offense. Hunting or shooting on Sunday prohibited.

§ 16. Any person who shall knowingly trespass upon lands for the purpose of shooting, hunting or fishing thereon, after public notice by the owner or occupant thereof, as provided in the following section, shall be liable to such owner or occupant in exemplary damages to an amount not exceeding one hundred dollars, and shall also be liable to such owner or occupant for the value of the game killed or taken. The possession of implements of shooting or fishing shall be presumptive evidence of the purpose of the trespass. Penalty for trespass upon lands, after notice.

§ 17. The notice referred to in the preceding section shall be given by erecting and maintaining sign-boards, at least one foot square, in at least two conspicuous places on the premises; such notices to have appended thereto the name of the owner or occupant, and any person who shall tear down, or in any way deface or injure any such sign-board, shall be liable to a penalty of one hundred dollars. Notice, how given by land owners.

§ 18. No person or corporation shall throw or deposit, or permit the same to be thrown or deposited, any coal tar, refuse from gas-houses, or other deleterious substance, or cause the same to run or flow into or upon any of the rivers, lakes, ponds, or streams of this state, under a penalty of fifty dollars for each offense, in addition to liability for all damage he may have done; but this section shall not apply to streams of flowing water which constitutes the motive power of the machinery of manufacturing establishments, where it is necessary for the manufacturing purposes carried on in such establishment, to throw from, or run the refuse matter and material thereof into such stream. Proviso as to deposit of coal tar, etc., in certain streams.

§ 19. No person shall at any time catch any speckled trout with any device save with a hook and line, except for the purpose of propagation, as hereinafter provided, or place any set lines in waters inhabited by them, under a penalty of fifty dollars for each offense. Speckled trout.

§ 20. No person shall kill or expose for sale, or have in his or her possession after the same has been killed, any speckled trout, save only from the fifteenth day of March to the fifteenth day of September, under a penalty of twenty-five dollars for each fish. But this section shall not prevent any person from catching trout with nets in waters owned by them, to stock other waters. Period of time for taking or selling trout.

§ 21. No person shall kill or expose for sale, or have in his or her possession, after the same has been killed, any salmon trout, or lake trout, in the months of October, November, Salmon or lake trout.

December, January and February, under a penalty of ten dollars for each fish, except that in Otsego lake fish may be caught or killed by hook and line only, but they may be had alive for artificial propagation, or the stocking of other waters. Nor shall fish be taken from the lakes in Westchester and Putnam, from the first day of November to the first day of April.

Proviso as to Otsego lake, and lakes of Putnam and Westchester counties.

Black or Oswego bass.

§ 22. No person shall kill or expose for sale, or have in his or her possession after the same has been killed, any black bass, Oswego bass, or muscalonge, between the first day of January and the twentieth day of May, except alive, for artificial propagation or the stocking of other waters, under a penalty of ten dollars for each offense.

Catching fish by draining off waters, or dragging seines prohibited.

§ 23. No person shall catch any bass, trout or other fish, in any of the waters of this state, by shutting or drawing off any portion of said waters, or by dragging or drawing small nets or seines therein, when the water shall be wholly or in part drawn off in any of the ponds, lakes, rivers, streams and the waters surrounding Staten Island, under a penalty of twenty-five dollars for each offense.

Proviso as to Oneida, Onondaga and Keuka lakes.

§ 24. No person shall set or use, or assist in setting or using, any pound, weir, seine, trap-net or set-net in the waters of Oneida and Onondaga lakes, or Keuka, commonly called Crooked lake, or in any of their outlets, inlets or tributaries, at any time during the term of ten years from the passage of this act, under a penalty of fifty dollars for each offense.

Use of traps, dams, weirs, etc., in certain streams, prohibited

§ 25. No person shall kill or catch any fish in the Mohawk or Clyde rivers, Irondequoit bay, in the county of Monroe, or in the inlets thereof, or the lakes in the counties of Westchester, Rockland, Wyoming, Columbia, Ulster, Genesee, Orange, Putnam, Herkimer, Rensselaer, Sullivan, Tioga, Cortland, Broome and Livingston, by any trap, dam, weir, net, seine, or by any device whatever, other than that of angling with hook and line or with a spear, under a penalty of twenty-five dollars for each offense.

Fishing in Oil creek reservoir.

§ 26. It shall not be lawful for any person or persons to take or catch fish of any kind or in any manner, after the passage of this act, in the waters of the Oil creek reservoir, in the counties of Allegany and Cattaraugus, or from the streams tributary thereto, at any place within the distance of one mile from the inlet of such streams into said reservoir at high-water mark, under a penalty of ten dollars for each fish so caught or taken, but such fish may be caught and taken after the expiration of two years from the passage of this act in any other manner than by nets, baskets or seines.

Fishing with purse nets in Suffolk county waters.

§ 27. It shall be unlawful for any person to use any purse net for the catching of fish in any of the waters within the jurisdiction of this state, lying easterly of the boundary line between the counties of Queens and Suffolk, excepting the waters of Long Island sound, Garner's bay and little Peconic bay, under a penalty of two hundred dollars for each offense.

Fishing in canals, etc., with

§ 28. No person shall at any time take any fish with a net, spear or trap of any kind, or set any trap, net, weir or pot with intent to catch fish in any of the fresh waters or canals of this state, except as hereinbefore or hereinafter provided; nor shall it be lawful at any time, to draw any seine or net for the taking of fish in any portion of Flushing bay or its branches, nor in Lake Canandaigua, Cayuga, Champlain or the inlets thereof; and any person violating the provisions of this section shall be deemed guilty of a misdemeanor, and shall likewise be liable to a penalty of twenty-five dollars for each offense; but suckers, catfish, bullheads, bony fish, or moss bunkers, eels, white fish, shad, herring and minnows are exempted from the operation of this section, also pike, in all waters save those lying in Columbia county and Cayuga lake; provided, however, that nothing in this section shall be so construed as to legalize the use of gill nets in any of the inland waters or canals of this state, nor seines or nets of any kind in the waters of Otsego lake, except from the first day of March to the last day of August, and no gill nets except during the months of July and August. But no such seine or net shall have meshes less than two inches in size, and, in the Hudson river, the meshes of all gill nets and set nets shall not be less than four and one-half inches in size each, and those of fykes set in any of the waters surrounding Long Island, Fire Island, Staten Island, and the bays and salt water estuaries and rivers approaching thereto, to be not less than four and one-half inches in size; and any person who shall willfully injure or destroy, by grappling or otherwise, any nets used in the Hudson or East rivers for the purpose of catching shad, shall be liable to a penalty of twenty-five dollars for each offense, and, in default of payment thereof, shall be imprisoned in the county jail of the county within whose jurisdiction the offense may be committed for not more than thirty days. All drawing of seines in the Susquehanna river is prohibited.

traps and nets prohibited. Uses of nets in Flushing bay, Lakes Champlain, Cayuga and Canandaigua prohibited. Proviso as to suckers, moss bunkers, etc. Use of gill nets in inland waters prohibited. Size of meshes of nets and fykes in Hudson river, etc. Injury of shad nets by grappling prohibited. Susquehanna river.

§ 29. It shall be unlawful for any person or persons to take, catch or procure in or from Conesus lake, Hemlock lake and Silver lake, or the inlets or outlets thereof lying within the counties of Livingston, Ontario and Wyoming, any fish, except minnows, with or by any means or device other than a hook and line. And no person shall, in any manner whatever, take or catch from the waters of said lakes, or the inlets or outlets thereof, any pike, pickerel, muscalonge, salmon trout, black bass or rock bass between the first day of January and the first day of May. No person shall knowingly sell, or offer for sale, any fish caught from said lakes, or the inlets or outlets thereof, contrary to the provisions of this section; and it shall be unlawful for any person knowingly to purchase any fish so taken in or from said lakes, or inlets or outlets. Whoever shall violate any foregoing provisions of this section shall be deemed guilty of misdemeanor, and shall also be subject to a penalty for each offense of not less than fifteen nor more than fifty dollars, to be recovered in a civil action with costs, as hereinafter provided. All fines or penalties imposed under the provisions of this section may be recovered, with

Fishing in Conesus, Hemlock and Silver lakes. Penalty for violation hereof. How recovered and applied. costs of suit, by any person or persons, in his or their own names, by an action of the supreme court or any court of record of this state, which action shall be governed by the same rules as other actions in said supreme court or other court of record, except that, in a recovery by the plaintiff or plaintiffs in such suits in said court of less than fifty dollars, the plaintiff shall be entitled to costs not exceeding the amount of such recovery. On the non-payment of any judgment recovered in pursuance hereof, the defendant shall be committed to the common jail of the county in which such action shall be brought, for the period which shall be computed at the rate of one day for each dollar of the amount of judgment, not to exceed thirty days. Any penalties, when collected, shall be paid by the court before which recovery shall be had, one-half to the commissioners of fisheries of the state of New York, and the remainder to the plaintiff or plaintiffs.

Dams upon fluvial waters to have sluice-way and apron.

§ 30. Every person building or maintaining a dam upon any of the fluvial waters of this state, which dam is higher than two feet, shall likewise build and maintain during the months of March, April, May, September, October and November, for the purpose of the passage of fish, a sluice-way in the said channel at least one foot in depth at the edge of the dam and of proper width, with four inch square cross pieces upon the bottom of the sluice-way three feet apart, which sluice-way shall be placed at an angle of not more than seven degrees, and extending entirely to the running water below the dam, and which sluice-way shall be protected on each side by an apron at least one foot in height, to confine the water therein. Every person violating the provisions of this section shall, for each month's violation thereof, forfeit the sum of twenty-five dollars, to be recovered by and in the name of the overseer of the poor of any town adjoining the stream upon which such neglect shall happen.

Penalty for violation hereof.

Boards of supervisors may authorize election of game constable.

§ 31. It shall be lawful for the boards of supervisors of the several counties of the state, by the affirmative vote of a majority of the members elected, at a regular meeting of such boards respectively, to authorize the election in each or any of the towns of their respective counties, of an officer to be designated the game constable, who shall be chosen at town-meetings as other town officers are chosen, and hold office for the term of one year; and he shall take the oath of office the same, and be vested with, and have the same powers in serving process under this act, that town constables now possess in serving civil process. It shall be the duty of the game constable, after reliable information, to prosecute all violations of this act, and he shall receive such compensation for his services as is allowed by law for like services to constables of towns, and also one-half of all penalties recovered by him for violations of this act. In case of neglect or refusal of any game constable to prosecute any such violation, he shall forfeit the penalty of twenty-five dollars, to be sued for and recovered as specified in this act. Whenever any game constable shall fail to recover the penalty in any prosecution commenced by him pursuant to

How elected, his powers and duties.

this section, the costs of suit incurred by him shall be a charge against the county, and it shall be the duty of the board of supervisors of the county to audit and allow the same, as other county charges are audited and allowed.

§ 32. It shall be lawful for the board of supervisors of any county to make any regulations protecting other birds, fish or game than those mentioned in this act, and such ordinance shall be published in the papers in such county in which the Session Laws are published, and in the state paper before going into effect. Supervisors may pass ordinance to protect game.

§ 33. Any person may sell or have in his or her possession any pinnated grouse, commonly called prairie chicken, ruffed grouse, commonly called partridge, or quail, from the first day of January to the first day of March, and shall not be liable to any penalty under this act, provided he proves that such birds or game were killed within the period provided by this act, or were killed outside the limits of this state, at some place where the law did not prohibit such killing. Sale of prairie chickens, partridge, etc., during certain months.

§ 34. Nothing in this act contained shall apply to fish caught or to the taking of fish in the waters of Lake Ontario, or any of its bays or estuaries within the counties of Oswego, Wayne, Jefferson and St. Lawrence, nor to the catching of fish in any way in the St. Lawrence river. Act not to apply to Lake Ontario, St. Lawrence river and certain counties.

§ 35. In all prosecutions under this act, against common carriers or express companies, it shall be competent for them to show that the prohibited article in his or her possession, came into such possession in another state, or from beyond the United States, at some place where the law did not prohibit the possession; and such evidence shall be a valid defense to the prosecution. Proof by express companies, as to possession of game from beyond state.

§ 36. Any justice of the marine or district court of the city of New York, or any justice of the peace, police or other magistrate, upon receiving sufficient security for costs on the part of the complainant, and sufficient proof by affidavit that any of the provisions of this act have been violated by any person being temporarily within his jurisdiction, but not residing there permanently, or by any person whose name and residence are unknown, is hereby authorized to issue his warrant for the arrest of such offender, and to cause him to be committed or held to bail to answer the charge against him; and any such justice or magistrate, upon receiving proof of probable cause for believing in the concealment of any game or fish mentioned in this act during any of the periods prohibited, shall issue his search warrant and cause search to be made in any house, market, boat, car or other building, and for that end may cause any apartment, chest, box, locker, crate or basket to be broken open and the contents examined. Any court of special sessions is hereby invested with jurisdiction to try and dispose of all and any of the offenses against the provisions of this act occurring in the same county. Issue of warrants for arrest of persons violating act. Right of search.

§ 37. In case of failure by any person to pay the penalty imposed upon him pursuant to this act, he shall be committed to the common jail of the county for a period of not less than Imprisonment for non-payment of fines.

five days, and at the rate of one day for every dollar of the judgment when the same exceeds five dollars.

Penalties under this act, how recovered.

§ 38. All penalties imposed by this act may be recovered, with costs of suit, by any person in his own name, before a justice of the peace, in the county where the offense was committed, or where the defendant resides, where the amount recovered does not exceed the jurisdiction of such justice, or when such suit shall be brought in the city of New York, before any justice of the district court or of the marine court of said city; and such penalties may be recovered in the like manner in any court of record in the state, but on a recovery by the plaintiff in such case for a less sum than fifty dollars, the plaintiff shall only be entitled to costs to an amount equal to the amount of such recovery; and it shall be the duty of any district attorney in this state, and he is hereby required, to commence actions for the recovery of the penalties allowed hereby, upon receiving proper information, and in all actions brought by such district attorney, one-half of the penalty recovered shall belong to the person giving information on which the action is brought, and the other half shall be paid to the treasurer of the county for the support of the poor.

In N. Y. city.

Actions, how brought by district attorney.

State bounty for killing wolves and panthers.

§ 39. A state bounty of thirty dollars for a grown wolf, fifteen dollars for a pup wolf, and twenty dollars for a panther, shall be paid to any person or persons who shall kill any of said animals within the boundaries of this state. The person or persons claiming said bounty shall prove the death of the animal so killed by him or them, by producing satisfactory affidavits and the skull and skin of said animal, before the supervisor and one of the justices of the peace of the town within the boundaries of which the said animal was killed. Whereupon said supervisor and justice of the peace, in the presence of each other, shall burn and destroy the said skull, and brand the said skin so that it may be thereafter identified, and issue to the person or persons claiming and entitled to the same, an order on the treasurer of the county to which said town belongs, stating the kind of animal killed, the date of the killing of the same, and the amount of the bounty to be paid in virtue of the within section of this act; and the county treasurers of this state are hereby authorized and directed to pay all orders issued as aforesaid; and all orders issued in the manner aforesaid, and paid by the treasurer of any county in this state, shall be a charge of said county against the state, the amount of which charge, on delivery of the proper vouchers, the comptroller is hereby authorized and directed to allow in the settlement of taxes due from said county to the state.

Proof to be presented.

How paid.

Penalty for keeping snares, nets, etc., on banks of certain waters.

§ 40. Any person having in his or her possession on the shores of any lake, or on the banks of, or upon any waters inhabited by salmon, salmon-trout, lake-trout, or book-trout, black or Oswego bass or muscalonge, during the closed season, without the permission of the commissioners of fisheries, any snares, nets, stake poles or other devices used in unlawfully taking such fish, shall be liable to a penalty of fifty dollars, but nothing herein contained shall apply to that portion of the Hudson river south of the dam at Troy.

§ 41. No person shall place in any fresh water stream, lake or pond, without the consent of the owner, any lime or other deleterious substance, or any drug or medicated bait, with intent thereby to injure, poison or catch fish, nor place in any pond or lake stocked with or inhabited by trout, bass, pike, pickerel or sunfish, any drug or other deleterious substance, with intent to destroy such trout or other fish. Any person violating the provisions of this section shall be deemed guilty of a misdemeanor, and shall, in addition thereto, and in addition to any damage he may have done, be liable to a penalty of one hundred dollars. Placing of lime or drugs in streams; prohibited. Penalty

§ 42. All acts and parts of acts, the provisions of which are superseded by this act, or related to the same subject, or which are inconsistent with the same, are hereby repealed. Repeal.

§ 43. The counties of Delaware and Chenango are exempted from the operation of sections sixteen, seventeen and thirty-one. Exemption.

§ 44. The fourth section of chapter five hundred and sixty-seven of the laws of eighteen hundred and seventy, entitled "An act to amend act entitled 'An act to appoint commissioners of fisheries for the state of New York,'" passed April twenty-second, eighteen hundred and sixty-eight, is hereby amended by adding thereto the words or the waters of Gravesend bay and those lying easterly from the line drawn from the extreme west point of Coney Island to Fort Lafayette, nor to the county of Suffolk. Proviso as to size of meshes, etc., of pounds or weirs in certain waters.

§ 45. Nothing in chapter five hundred and sixty-seven of the laws of eighteen hundred and seventy shall apply to or affect the setting or using of any pound, weir, set or fly-net, by any person in any of the salt waters within the jurisdiction of this state, lying easterly of the boundary line between the counties of Queens and Suffolk. Use of pounds or weirs, etc. in Suffolk county waters.

§ 46. It shall not be lawful for any person to take eels in fikes or pots at any time between the first day of October and the first day of March in any year, in the waters of Jamaica bay. Taking of eels in Jamaica bay regulated.

§ 47. This act shall take effect on the first day of May, eighteen hundred and seventy-one, except as herein otherwise provided. Act, when to take effect.

Ante, vol. 4, p. 108; vol. 6, pp. 158, 299, 852; vol. 7, pp. 199, 297, 808, 839, 522.

CHAP. 722.

AN ACT amendatory of and supplemental to the following acts, namely: An act entitled "An act establishing a quarantine, and defining the qualifications, duties, and powers of the health officer for the harbor and port of New York," passed April twenty-ninth, eighteen hundred and sixty-three; an act entitled "An act in relation to quarantine in the port of New York, and providing for the construction of the permanent quarantine establishment," passed April twenty-one, eighteen hundred and sixty-six; an act entitled "An act in relation to quarantine in the port of New York, and to amend existing acts relative thereto," passed April twenty-two, eighteen hundred and sixty-nine; and an act entitled "An act in relation to the sale of the Marine Hospital grounds," passed May nineteenth, eighteen hundred and sixty-eight.

PASSED April 26, 1871; three-fifths being present.

Preamble. WHEREAS, in the year eighteen hundred and fifty-two, the commissioners of emigration of the state of New York held in fee certain lands and buildings on Ward's Island, comprising the state emigrant hospital and refuge establishment, and, in trust for the people of this state, certain other lands and buildings on Staten Island, comprising the marine hospital and quarantine establishment, of which the said commissioners then had control; and,

WHEREAS, the expenses incurred in the management of the said marine hospital were so great as to compel the said commissioners to mortgage the said lands on Staten Island and Ward's Island for the sum of two hundred thousand dollars, which mortgage was given with the express consent of the governor, attorney-general and comptroller of the state, as required by law; and,

WHEREAS, by an act passed March six, eighteen hundred and fifty-seven, chapter eighteen, the control of the quarantine establishment was taken from the said commissioners of emigration and vested in a board of quarantine commissioners; and, by a further act passed April twenty-nine, eighteen hundred and sixty-three, chapter three hundred and fifty-eight, the said commissioners of emigration were directed to execute and acknowledge a suitable and proper conveyance to the state of all their right, title and interest in the said lands on Staten Island as held by them in trust, and by an amendment to the said last-mentioned act, passed April twenty-five, eighteen hundred and sixty-four, chapter three hundred and ninety-eight, confirmed by an act passed April twenty-second, eighteen hundred and sixty-seven, chapter five hundred and forty-three, "the sum" required and directed to be furnished by the commissioners of emigration toward the payment of said mortgage "is fixed at fifty thousand dollars, that sum being deemed the fair proportion thereof which should be paid by them as a condition of having the lands held by them on Ward's Island, and covered by said mortgage, released from the lien thereof;" and,

WHEREAS, notwithstanding said apportionment, and although since the appointment of the quarantine commissioners in eighteen hundred and fifty-seven, the said commissioners of emigration have derived no benefit from the said quarantine lands on Staten Island, and have been relieved of the duties connected therewith formerly imposed on them, they have nevertheless been required to pay out of the fund supplied by emigrants, in accordance with law, the interest on the whole amount of said mortgage of two hundred thousand dollars, of which one hundred and fifty thousand dollars was debt incurred in support of the marine hospital at quarantine and acknowledged as such by the legislature of eighteen hundred and sixty-four; and,

WHEREAS, considerations of justice and public policy alike require that the interest so paid on said sum of one hundred and fifty thousand dollars should be refunded by the state to the commissioners of emigration in order that the money thus temporarily diverted from the commutation fund may be applied to the legitimate purposes contemplated in the establishment of such fund; therefore,

The People of the State of New York, represented in Senate and Assembly, do enact as follows:

SECTION 1. The lieutenant-governor, attorney-general, and comptroller are hereby authorized and directed to examine into the validity and legality of the claim against the state for the payment of interest by the commissioners of emigration, as set forth in the foregoing preamble, and to report to the next legislature whether in their judgment said claim is a legal and valid claim against the state.

Commissioners to examine into claim of commissioners of emigration. To report thereon to legislature.

§ 2. This act shall take effect immediately.

CHAP. 733.

AN ACT in relation to actions against sheriffs.

PASSED April 26, 1871.

The People of the State of New York, represented in Senate and Assembly, do enact as follows:

SECTION 1. Any action heretofore commenced, or which may hereafter be commenced, against any sheriff, in his official capacity, in any court of record, shall be entitled to precedence, after issue joined, over any and all other cases at issue in such court, not now entitled to preference by law, and shall be so placed on the trial calendar of such court.

Actions against sheriffs to have precedence.

Actions, when to be commenced. § 2. No action shall be brought against any sheriff upon a liability incurred by the doing of an act in his official capacity and in virtue of his office, or by the omission of an official duty, not including the non-payment of money collected upon an execution, unless the same shall be commenced within one year from the time when the cause of action shall have accrued.

§ 3. This act shall take effect immediately.

CHAP. 746.

AN ACT to amend an act entitled "An act to revise and consolidate the general act relating to public instruction," passed May second, eighteen hundred and sixty-four.

Ante, vol. 6, p. 304.

PASSED April 26, 1871; three-fifths being present.

The People of the State of New York, represented in Senate and Assembly, do enact as follows:

SECTION 1. Section nine of title thirteen of the act entitled "An act to revise and consolidate the general act relating to public instruction," passed May second, eighteen hundred and sixty-four, is hereby amended so as to read as follows:

Ante, vol. 6, p. 362.

Appeals of school officers to county judge in case of refusal of district to pay expenses of actions. § 9. Whenever an officer or officers mentioned in the last preceding section of this act shall have complied with the provisions of said section, and the inhabitants shall have refused to direct the trustees to levy a tax for the payment of the costs, charges and expenses therein mentioned, it shall be lawful for him or them then and there to give notice orally and publicly, that he will appeal to the county judge of the county, and in case of his disability to act in the matter by reason of being disqualified or otherwise, then to the district attorney of the county in which the school-house of said district is located; from the refusal of said meeting to vote a tax for the payment of said claim, and the inhabitants may then and there, or at any subsequent district meeting, appoint one or more of the inhabitants of the district to protect the rights and interests of the district upon said appeal; and the officer or officers before mentioned shall thereupon, within ten days, serve upon the clerk of said district (or if there be no such clerk, upon the town clerk of the town), a copy of the aforesaid account so sworn to, together with a notice in writing, that on a certain day therein specified he or they intend to present such account to the county judge or to the district attorney, as the case may be, for settlement. And the clerk shall record such notice, together with the copy of the account, and the same shall be subject to the inspection of the inhabitants of the district. And it shall be the duty of the person or persons appointed by any district meeting for that purpose, to appear before the county judge, or the district attorney, as the case may be, on

District may appoint inhabitant to protect its interests.

Notice of presenting accounts to judge.

Account to be subject to inspection.

the day mentioned in the notice aforesaid, and to protect the rights of the district upon such settlement; and the expenses incurred in the performance of this duty shall be a charge upon said district, and the trustees, upon presentation of the account of such expenses, with the proper voucher therefor, may levy a tax therefor, or add the same to any other tax to be levied by them; and their refusal to levy said tax for the payment of said expenses shall be subject to an appeal to the superintendent of public instruction.

§ 2. Section ten of title thirteen of said act is hereby amended so as to read:

Ante, vol. 6, p. 862.

County judge to hear proofs.

§ 10. Upon the appearance of the parties, or upon due proof of service of the notice and copy of the account, the county judge or the district attorney, as the case may be, shall examine into the matter, and hear the proofs and allegations propounded by the parties, and decide by order whether or not the account, or any and what portion thereof ought justly to be charged upon the district, and his decision shall be final; but no portion of such account shall be so ordered to be paid, which shall appear to the county judge or to the district attorney, as the case may be, to have arisen from the willful neglect or misconduct of the claimant. The account, with the oath of the party claiming the same, shall be prima facie evidence of the correctness thereof. The county judge or district attorney, as the case may be, may adjourn the hearing, from time to time, as justice shall seem to require.

To decide upon account presented.

§ 3. This act shall take effect immediately.

CHAP. 747.

AN ACT to amend an act entitled "An act to establish a law library for the eighth judicial district in the city of Buffalo, passed May four, eighteen hundred and sixty-three."

Ante, vol. 6, p. 143.

PASSED April 26, 1871; three-fifths being present.

The People of the State of New York, represented in Senate and Assembly, do enact as follows:

SECTION 1. Section two of an act entitled "An act to establish a law library for the eighth judicial district in the city of Buffalo, passed May four, eighteen hundred and sixty-three," is hereby amended so as to read as follows:

Trustees of law library.

§ 2. The said library shall be under the care and management of Charles Daniels and Dennis Bowen, and the person succeeding to the office of judge of the superior court of Buffalo, in the place of Joseph G. Masten, deceased, and their successors in office, who shall be known as the trustees of the law library of the eighth judicial district. In case of a vacancy

Vacancies, how filled. in said board of trustees it shall be filled at a general term of the supreme court of the fourth judicial department by the judges thereof, subject, however, to such orders, rules and regulations touching the same as may be made from time to time by a majority of the justices of the supreme court residing in said district. Appropriations, how disbursed. All appropriations made for said library shall be paid to the said trustees, to be by them disbursed in the purchase of books for said library. Rules for management of library. The said trustees may make rules and regulations for the management and protection of said library, and prescribe penalties for the violation thereof; Penalties for violation and for injuries. and may sue for and recover such penalties, and may maintain actions for injuries to said library; Rooms, furniture, etc. they may procure proper furniture for said library, hire suitable rooms, employ a librarian, provide fuel and lights, and defray all the incidental expenses of the care and management of said library; Annual county tax therefor. they shall yearly ascertain the amount necessary for the aforesaid purposes and certify it to the board of supervisors of Erie county, who shall pay the same. Report to regents. They shall yearly make a report to the regents of the university of the state of said library.

§ 2. This act shall take effect immediately.

CHAP. 756.

AN ACT to prevent the deposit of carrion, offal, or dead animals in the North and East rivers, or the bay of New York, or Raritan bay, within the jurisdiction of the state of New York.

PASSED April 26, 1871; three-fifths being present.

The People of the State of New York, represented in Senate and Assembly, do enact as follows:

Unlawful to cast dead animals in waters of state. SECTION 1. It shall not be lawful for any person or persons to throw or cast any dead animal, carrion, offal, or other putrid or offensive matter in the waters of the North and East rivers, adjoining the counties of New York, Kings, Westchester and Richmond, or in the bay of New York, or in Raritan bay, within the jurisdiction of this state.

Unlawful to move or aid in moving such material on bay with intent to cast into the ocean without permit. § 2. It shall not be lawful for any person or persons to sail, navigate, or move, or to aid, direct, or assist in sailing, navigating, or moving, or to be employed upon, or to accompany, any boat or vessel containing any such animal or material as aforesaid, through or upon the waters of that part of New York bay known as the Narrows, and lying between Forts Wadsworth and Hamilton, or any part of said bay south of said Narrows, with the intent or for the purpose of throwing or casting such animal or material, or any portion thereof, into the ocean, or sea, or in any portion of the waters mentioned in this act, without a permit in writing, first obtained therefor from the inspector to be appointed under this act, who shall have the power of granting such permits from time to time, as he shall deem proper, and which shall not be inconsistent with the provisions of the first section of this act, and having such regard to the course and condition of the then existing winds and tides as, in his judgment, shall best tend to prevent the subsequent return or deposit of any of such contents of said boat or vessel within the waters of this state, if cast upon the waters beyond the jurisdiction thereof.

§ 3. Any person offending against the provisions of this act shall be deemed guilty of a misdemeanor, and liable to imprisonment for a term of not less than six months, and to a fine of not less than five hundred dollars, in the discretion of the court, for each and every offense, and may be arrested by the authorities of either of the counties of New York, Kings, Westchester or Richmond. The courts in said counties, respectively, shall have power and jurisdiction to try said offender, whether the offense be committed within the respective counties or not. Out of any moneys received for fines under this act, such sum or sums shall be allowed and paid for the expenses and disbursements attending the arrest as the court or magistrate may deem reasonable and proper. *Offenders guilty of misdemeanor.* *Courts to have jurisdiction if offense committed out of county.*

§ 4. Immediately after the passage of this act, and within one month preceding the first day of May in each third year hereafter, the governor, by and with the consent of the senate, shall appoint one respectable citizen of said county of Kings, who shall be known and designated as the "shore inspector" of the counties of New York, Kings, Westchester, and Richmond, and who, during the term of his office, shall reside within one-half mile of the shore, at that part of the bay known as the Narrows, as the same is defined in the second section of this act, and he shall, within ten days after his said appointment, take the constitutional oath of office, and file the same with the secretary of state. The term of office of the inspector first appointed under this act shall be for three years, ending on the first day of May, eighteen hundred and seventy-four, and the terms of his successors in office, respectively, shall expire on the first day of May in every third year thereafter. In case of any vacancy in such office by death, resignation, refusal to serve, failure to take the oath within said ten days, or disqualification as to residence, as aforesaid, or otherwise, the said vacancy shall forthwith be filled by appointment by the governor, who is also authorized to accept any such resignation; and such appointment shall be only for the unexpired portion of the term in which the vacancy exists. Each inspector to be appointed under this act shall serve as herein provided, and until his successor shall have been duly appointed and qualified as aforesaid, and shall receive an annual salary of fifteen hundred dollars, which shall be in lieu of all other compensation for his services under this act, and shall be paid by the comptroller of the state quarterly out of any moneys in the treasury not otherwise appropriated. *Appointment of shore inspector.* *Residence.* *Oath of office.* *Term.* *In case of vacancy, governor to appoint.* *Salary.*

§ 5. It shall be the duty of the said inspector diligently to investigate, and report without delay to the proper magistrate *Duty of inspector.*

or court, any and all violations of any of the provisions of this act, that the offender may be duly arrested and punished therefor, and to aid, in all proper ways, in the enforcement thereof, and he shall have power to arrest in any of the said counties any person or persons who may be found by him actually engaged in violating any of the provisions of this act, and to take such person or persons before such magistrate or court, whose duty it shall be to require such inspector to make complaint, under oath, of such person or persons so arrested, as to such violation, when the allegations of such complaint shall be duly heard and disposed of as herein provided.

Power to arrest.

Unlawful to transport offensive matter on water except by steam power.

§ 6. It shall not be lawful for any person or persons to sail, navigate, or move, or to aid, direct, or assist in sailing, navigating, or moving, or to be employed upon or accompany any boat or vessel engaged in transporting any dead animals, carrion, offal, or other putrid or offensive matter upon the waters aforesaid, unless the same be propelled by steam power, under the penalties provided for in section three of this act.

§ 7. This act shall take effect immediately.

CHAP. 766.

AN ACT to allow the justices of the supreme court, assigned to hold the general terms thereof in the several judicial departments of this state, to fix the times and places of holding the same.

PASSED April 27, 1871; three-fifths being present.

The People of the State of New York, represented in Senate and Assembly, do enact as follows:

Justices to designate times and places for holding terms.

SECTION 1. Within twenty days after the passage of this act, the several justices of the supreme court who have been assigned to hold the general terms thereof in the several judicial departments of this state, shall, by appointment in writing, designate the times and places for holding the general terms of said court, within their respective judicial departments, for two years from January first, eighteen hundred and seventy-one; provided, that at least one term in each year shall be designated to be held in each of the judicial districts composing the several judicial departments of this state; but in appointing such general terms, one shall be held in Elmira, one in Oswego, and one in Binghamton.

Proviso.

Appointment to be signed and filed.

§ 2. Such appointment in writing shall be signed by the justices so designating them, or by a majority of them, and filed in the office of the secretary of state, who shall immediately cause such appointments to be published in the state paper for one month.

Justices to make like appointments every two years.

§ 3. On or before the first day of December, in the year eighteen hundred and seventy-two, and thereafter every two years, the justices aforesaid, shall make like appointments for the holding of the general terms of the supreme court, within their respective departments, which appointments shall also, on or before the fifteenth of December, in such year, be filed in the office of the secretary of state, and immediately thereafter be, by him, published in the state paper for one month.

§ 4. When the time now appointed for the holding of any general term shall come within twenty days after the passage of this act, the same shall be held pursuant to such appointment, but after that time no general term shall be held, except in pursuance of an appointment as in this act specified. Appointments to be in pursuance of.

§ 5. All acts and parts of acts inconsistent with the provisions of this act are hereby repealed.

§ 6. This act shall take effect immediately.

CHAP. 776.

AN ACT to authorize religious corporations, created by special charter, to exercise the same powers as are given to religious societies incorporated under the general act to provide for the incorporation of religious societies, passed April fifth, eighteen hundred and thirteen, and the acts amendatory thereof and supplementary thereto.

PASSED April 27, 1871; three-fifths being present.

The People of the State of New York, represented in Senate and Assembly, do enact as follows:

SECTION 1. Any religious corporation within this state, created by any special charter, shall, notwithstanding such charter, have all the powers and authority given to any trustees, congregations, or societies incorporated under the act entitled "An act to provide for the incorporation of religious societies," passed April fifth, eighteen hundred and thirteen, or any act amendatory thereof or supplementary thereto, and the property acquired for any school-house or dwelling-house for the use of a minister, shall not be included in the estimate of the value of the property to the possession of which such corporation may be restricted.

Ante, vol. 3, pp. 687, 696, 697, 698, 701, 702; vol. 4, pp. 54, 783; vol. 7, p. 140.

CHAP. 778.

AN ACT to re-appropriate moneys for construction of new work upon and extraordinary repairs of the canals of this state.

PASSED April 27, 1871; three-fifths being present.

The People of the State of New York, represented in Senate and Assembly, do enact as follows:

Unexpended balance under chapter 877 of 1869 re-appropriated.

SECTION 1. The unexpended balance of one million eight hundred and seven thousand six hundred and sixty-five dollars and two cents, appropriated by the act entitled "An act to authorize a tax of three-quarters of a mill per dollar for the year eighteen hundred and sixty-nine, for constructing new work upon and extraordinary repairs of the canals of this state," passed May twelfth, eighteen hundred and sixty-nine, being the sum of five hundred and thirty-one thousand seven hundred and fifty-one dollars, is hereby re-appropriated to the same objects specified in said act, in the manner following, namely:

Eastern division.

For the eastern division of the canals, the sum of four hundred and sixty-eight thousand seven hundred and fifty-one dollars of said amount, to be expended in such a manner as the canal board shall direct, subject only to all the conditions and restrictions for the expenditures of appropriations for extraordinary repairs of canals contained in chapter seven hundred and sixty-seven, laws of eighteen hundred and seventy. The sum of twenty-seven thousand dollars, appropriated by chapter eight hundred and seventy-seven, laws of eighteen hundred and sixty-nine, to pay the difference in cost between a stone dam and a dam of wood across the Hudson river at Fort Miller bridge, is hereby re-appropriated for the same purpose, the said dam to be built on a line parallel with the old structure, and not exceeding twenty feet below the same. The remainder of said unexpended balance of appropriations made by said act, being the sum of sixty-three thousand dollars, together with the unexpended balance of appropriations made by act chapter seven hundred and sixty-seven, laws of eighteen hundred and seventy, for constructing new work upon and extraordinary repairs of the canals on the middle division, amounting to the sum of ninety-eight thousand dollars, are hereby re-appropriated and appropriated to the same objects and purposes, to be expended in such manner as the board of canal commissioners shall direct. But in case any balance remains unexpended of said appropriation for any such object, by reason of change of plan reducing the cost of the same, or for any object which may be considered unnecessary by the commissioner in charge, then any and all such sums so remaining unexpended are hereby appropriated for the following specified objects (or so much thereof as may be necessary), namely:

Dam at Fort Miller bridge.

Middle division.

For removing old and inserting new feed pipes and building waste-weir and spillway to Madison brook reservoir, fifteen thousand dollars. Madison brook reservoir.

For improving side cuts at Salina, ten thousand dollars. Side cuts at Salina.

For completing and raising and strengthening of berme bank of Erie canal east of lock fifty, four thousand dollars. Berme bank, lock fifty.

For relaying walls in cement at Syracuse, five thousand dollars. Syracuse.

For vertical wall at Seneca Falls, five thousand dollars. Seneca Falls.

For rebuilding state dredge, four thousand dollars. State dredge.

For reconstructing race and feeder on Owasco outlet, ten thousand dollars. Owasco outlet.

For removing bench walls and building slope, pavement and vertical wall on the Erie and Oswego canals within the city of Syracuse, ten thousand dollars. Syracuse.

For iron bridge over creek at Havana, two thousand dollars. Havana.

For iron bridge over creek at Watkins, two thousand dollars. Watkins.

For new dam at Waterloo, ten thousand dollars. Waterloo.

For sluice at Montezuma, one thousand five hundred dollars. Montezuma.

For refunding moneys paid by Thomas W. Amsbury, for protecting banks of Mill creek at Watkins, two thousand and ninety dollars. T. W. Amsbury.

For refunding money advanced by P. H. Field in completing certain work at Geneva on the Cayuga and Seneca canal, one thousand three hundred and ten dollars. P. H. Field.

For flood gates at Elmira, six hundred dollars. Elmira.

For paying for brush and stone protection, banks of the Crooked lake canal, two thousand eight hundred dollars. Crooked lake.

For amount due the heirs of David B. Smith, for lot at Port Byron, one thousand and seventy dollars. The unexpended sum of twenty-five hundred dollars appropriated by act chapter eight hundred and seventy-seven, laws of eighteen hundred and sixty-nine, to construct a bridge on the Erie canal on the farm of Arsino B. Warner, in the town of Greece, county of Monroe, is re-appropriated to changing plan of bridges on the western division of the canals. Heirs of D. B. Smith. Bridge on farm of A. B. Warner.

§ 2. The unexpended balance of the sum of one hundred and fifty-seven thousand nine hundred and twenty-seven dollars and sixty-nine cents, re-appropriated by section one of the act entitled "An act to re-appropriate moneys for paying awards made by the canal appraisers in eighteen hundred and sixty-six, for paying the expense of sundry improvements upon the canals, and for rebuilding the Oneida lake canal," passed May tenth, eighteen hundred and sixty-nine, being the sum of sixty-three thousand six hundred and ninety dollars and forty-five cents, is hereby re-appropriated to the same objects and purposes mentioned and provided in said act. Balance, under chapter 815 of 1869, § 1.

§ 3. The unexpended balance of the sum of two hundred and sixty-four thousand four hundred and ninety-eight dollars and twenty-six cents, re-appropriated by section two of the act aforesaid, to "secure the navigation of the Oneida lake canal," being the sum of twenty-four thousand five hundred and nine dollars and forty-seven cents, is hereby re-appropriated for the same object and purpose. Sec. 2 of same act.

State dam at Troy to be re-let. § 4. The canal board are hereby authorized and required, within thirty days after the passage of this act, to re-let the building of the state dam at Troy, on such plan as they may deem for the best interests of the state, in case the existing contract for said work shall be surrendered without claim for damages from the state.

CHAP. 801.

AN ACT to prevent the spread of contagious diseases in the city of New York, and to provide for the proper care and treatment of persons afflicted with such disease.

PASSED April 27, 1871; three-fifths being present.

The People of the State of New York, represented in Senate and Assembly, do enact as follows:

May borrow money on credit of city for public charities. SECTION 1. The comptroller of the city of New York is hereby authorized and directed to borrow, on the credit of the city, from time to time, such sum and sums of money as the commissioners of public charities and correction of said city shall, by resolution, declare to be necessary, not exceeding in all the sum of one hundred thousand dollars, and to pay over such moneys to said board. Said board is hereby authorized to hire, purchase or construct, proper places for the care and treatment of persons sick with contagious disease, and shall provide proper care and attendance for such persons so sick when removed to such place or places, and shall defray the expense thereof out of the moneys so borrowed, which moneys shall be included in and raised and collected as part of the taxes for the year one thousand eight hundred and seventy-one.

Contagious diseases, may provide proper care and attention to sick.

§ 2. This act shall take effect immediately.

CHAP. 802.

AN ACT to amend chapter six hundred and seventy-seven of the laws of eighteen hundred and sixty-seven, entitled "An act to prevent fraud and fraudulent practices upon or by hotel-keepers and inn-keepers," passed April twenty-third, eighteen hundred and sixty-seven.

Ante, vol. 7, p. 143.

PASSED April 27, 1871.

The People of the State of New York, represented in Senate and Assembly, do enact as follows:

SECTION 1. Section two of the act passed April twenty-third, eighteen hundred and sixty-seven, entitled "An act to prevent fraud and fraudulent practices upon and by hotel-keepers and inn-keepers," is hereby amended so as to read as follows:

§ 2. Every keeper of a hotel or inn shall post in a public and conspicuous place, in the office or public room and in every bed-room in said house, a printed copy of this act, and a statement of the charges or rate of charges by the day, and for meals furnished and for lodging. No charge or sum shall be collected or received by any such person, for any service not actually delivered, or for a longer time than the person so charged actually remained at such place. For any violation of this section, or of any provision herein contained, the offender shall forfeit to the injured party three times the amount so charged, and shall not be entitled to receive any money for the meals, services or time charged. Duty of hotel-keepers, etc. Penalty for violation of.

§ 2. This act shall take effect immediately.

CHAP. 815.

AN ACT declaring a portion of Swiss creek, in the town of Croghan, Lewis county, a public highway.

PASSED April 28, 1871.

The People of the State of New York, represented in Senate and Assembly, do enact as follows:

SECTION 1. So much of the stream known as Swiss creek, in the town of Croghan, Lewis county, as runs southerly and south-westerly from the lands of Solomon J. Young in said town to the Black river, is hereby declared and constituted a public highway for the purpose of floating logs, timber or lumber down the same. Declared a highway.

§ 2. Any and all damages sustained by the owners of lands bordering upon said Swiss creek, or through whose lands the same flows, to be paid by the persons causing such damage. Damages caused to be paid for.

CHAP. 824.

AN ACT for the improvement of the navigation of the tributaries of the Great South bay.

PASSED April 28, 1871, by a two-thirds vote.

The People of the State of New York, represented in Senate and Assembly, do enact as follows:

SECTION 1. The sum of five thousand dollars is hereby appropriated out of any moneys in the treasury belonging to the general fund, not otherwise appropriated, for the purpose of improving the navigation of the tributaries of the Great South bay; which sum of money shall be expended by and under the direction of James H. Doxsee, of the town of Islip, James B. Duff, of the town of Brookhaven, and Alfred C. Mott, of the town of Brookhaven, all of the county of Suffolk, commissioners hereby appointed for that purpose. Amount of appropriation. How expended. Commissioners.

The said sum of five thousand dollars is to be paid upon the presentation of proper vouchers to the comptroller.

Official bond of commissioners. § 2. The said commissioners, before entering upon the duties of their office, shall execute and file in the office of the comptroller a bond to the people of the state of New York in the penal sum of ten thousand dollars, conditioned for the faithful performance of their duties, with sufficient sureties, to be approved of by the comptroller; and the comptroller, upon the filing of said bond, shall draw his warrant upon the treasurer for the said sum of five thousand dollars in favor of the said commissioners, and the treasurer shall pay the same out of the said fund.

Doxsee's and Patchoque creeks. § 3. The said commissioners shall expend the said sum of money upon the improvement of the navigation of Doxsee's creek and Patchoque creek and such other tributaries of the Great South bay as they shall deem most desirable.

To make annual report. § 4. The said commissioners shall annually report their proceedings, on or before the first day of December in each year, verified by their oath, to the comptroller. The said commissioners shall receive no compensation for their services out of the moneys hereby appropriated.

Vacancies, how filled. § 5. The comptroller shall have power to fill vacancies that may occur in said board of commissioners.

§ 6. This act shall take effect immediately.

CHAP. 831.

AN ACT for the protection of private parks and grounds, and to encourage the propagation of fish and game.

PASSED April 28, 1871.

The People of the State of New York, represented in Senate and Assembly, do enact as follows:

Notice to be published. SECTION 1. Any owner, lessee or occupant of lands desiring to lay out or devote the same for the purposes of a private park or grounds, or the propagating of fish or game, shall publish at least once a week for three months, in a paper of general circulation, printed in the county or counties within which such lands are situated, a notice describing the same, and that they will be used for a private park.

To be posted up along entire boundary. § 2. It shall be the duty of such owner, lessee or occupant, within six months after the final publication of said notice, to post or put up notices or signboards warning all persons against trespassing upon such private park or grounds, which notices shall not be less than a foot square, and placed not more than forty rods apart along the entire boundary of said lands, but when the said lands shall be inclosed by fences not less than six feet high, then said notices or signboards shall be placed not more than one-half a mile apart.

Punishment for injuries to § 3. Any person who shall cut, break or destroy any fence or inclosure, or any tree, branch, shrub or underwood, or shall put on said grounds, or in the waters thereon, any poisonous or other deleterious substance, or who shall trespass upon said park or grounds, shall, in addition to treble damages to be recovered in a civil action to be brought by said owner, lessee or occupant, be proceeded against under the provisions of article one, title three, chapter two of the fourth part of the Revised Statutes.

premises or waters.

Treble damages.

§ 4. Any person who shall willfully and maliciously deface or destroy any sign or notice posted or put up as aforesaid, or who shall place any object against or near such fence or inclosure, so that dogs or other animals can gain access or get into said park or grounds, or so that animals kept therein can escape therefrom, or who shall put or take into said park or grounds any dog or other destructive animal, or who shall kill or attempt to kill, destroy or attempt to destroy any game or fish without first obtaining permission of such owner, lessee or occupant, shall, in addition to treble damages to be recovered in a civil action to be brought by said owner, lessee or occupant, be liable to a penalty not exceeding twenty-five dollars, or imprisonment in the county jail not exceeding thirty days, or both.

Destroying or defacing signs.

Dogs.

Killing or destroying game or fish.

§ 5. One-half of any penalty recovered under sections three and four of this act shall go to the superintendent of the poor of the county wherein the offense shall be committed, and the other half shall go to the informer, except when such informer is in the employ of the owner, lessee or occupant aforesaid, in which case the whole of the said penalty shall be paid to the said superintendent of the poor.

Half of penalty to the poor.

Half to informer.

Exceptions.

§ 6. Upon complaint made on oath to any justice of the peace in the county wherein such land or any part thereof is situated, that any person has committed any of the offenses specified in the fourth section of this act, such justice shall issue his warrant for the apprehension of the offender, and cause him or her to be brought before him for examination.

Proceedings before justice.

§ 7. If such justice be satisfied by the confession of the offender or by other competent testimony that such person has committed any of the offenses referred to in sections three and four of this act, he shall make up and sign a record of conviction thereof, which shall be filed in the office of the clerk of the county, and shall fine such offender in a penalty not exceeding twenty-five dollars, or by warrant under his hand, commit such offender to the county jail not exceeding thirty days, there to remain until such fine be paid, or such offender be discharged according to law.

Record of conviction.

Fine.

Commitment.

§ 8. Any person who shall be convicted of a second or any subsequent offense may, in addition to the penalty provided therefor, be imprisoned in the county jail for a period of not more than one year.

Second offense.

§ 9. No conviction or sentence shall be had under the provisions of this act without trial by jury of the party arrested, if requested, according to the law in cases of trial for other misdemeanors.

Jury trial, if requested.

§ 10. This act shall take effect immediately.

Appointment of commissioners. which money shall be expended by and under the direction of Daniel Shaw, George Plumb and Orson Richards, commissioners hereby appointed for that purpose.

How to be expended. § 2. The said sum of ten thousand dollars is hereby appropriated for the purposes aforesaid, and shall be expended by said commissioners in clearing and improving the channel of the east and west branches of said river, and for the construction of such piers, booms and dams as may be necessary for the passage of logs and other lumber over and through such channels.

Commissioners to file bonds for performance of duties. § 3. The said commissioners shall, before entering upon the duties of their office, execute and file, in the office of the comptroller of this state, a bond, with sufficient sureties, to be approved of by the comptroller, in the penal sum of twenty thousand dollars, for the faithful performance of their duties.

No compensation for services. § 4. The said commissioners shall receive no compensation for their services out of the moneys hereby appropriated; they shall make a report of their proceedings on oath to the comptroller, on the first day of December in each year, of all their expenditures under this act; and thereupon the comptroller shall draw his warrant upon the treasurer for the amount of such expenditures, payable to the order of said commissioners, not exceeding the amount hereby appropriated. Commissioners to report.

CHAP. 858.

AN ACT making an appropriation for the removal of obstructions from Chautauqua lake and outlet.

PASSED April 28, 1871, by a two-third vote.

The People of the State of New York, represented in Senate and Assembly, do enact as follows:

Appropriations to remove obstructions. SECTION 1. The treasurer shall pay on the warrant of the comptroller, out of any moneys in the treasury not otherwise appropriated, the sum of five thousand dollars, on the presentation of proper vouchers to the supervisors of the towns of Busti, Chautauqua, Ellery, Ellicott and Harmony, which sum shall be or have been expended by them for the removal of obstructions from Chautauqua lake and outlet, as prescribed by chapter four hundred and ninety-two of the laws of eighteen hundred and seventy. Provided, however, that nothing herein contained shall be construed as allowing any dredging in the outlet of Chautauqua lake, and provided that the work shall be let to the lowest responsible bidder; and provided, also, that the discharge of water at the outlet shall not be increased in quantity beyond its natural capacity. Provided, however, that no money shall be paid in pursuance of this act, except upon the written certificate of the state engineer, that the work provided to be done herein has been performed in a manner approved by him. To be let to lowest bidder. Money to be paid on certificate of state engineer only.

§ 2. This act shall take effect immediately.

CHAP. 859.

AN ACT to provide for the election of certain judicial and other officers, and to fix their terms of office.

PASSED April 28, 1871; three-fifths being present.

The People of the State of New York, represented in Senate and Assembly, do enact as follows:

SECTION 1. There shall be elected at the next general election a county judge, in the respective counties of this state, where the term of the present county judge shall expire on the first day of January, one thousand eight hundred and seventy-two, and in the counties in which the term of the present county judge does not expire on that day, then at the general election preceding the date on which such term shall expire (except in the counties of New York and Kings), who shall hold office for six years, and shall perform all the duties, possess all the powers now conferred upon county judges, or which may hereafter be conferred, and shall perform all of the duties which are now or may be hereafter imposed by the laws of this state; provided, however, that nothing in this act contained shall affect the election of county judge of the county of Greene, had at the general election in the year eighteen hundred and seventy, and the said election of said county judge is hereby legalized and confirmed for the full term of six years from the first day of January, eighteen hundred and seventy-one. Time of holding election. Powers and duties. Not to affect election of county judge of Greene county. Legalized and confirmed.

§ 2. There shall be elected at the next general election a separate officer to perform the duties of the office of surrogate in each of the counties of this state, where the term of the present surrogate shall expire on the first day of January, one thousand eight hundred and seventy-two, and in counties in which the term of the present surrogate does not expire on that day, then at the general election preceding the date on which such term shall expire, and in counties having a population exceeding forty thousand, in which such separate officer shall be determined upon as hereinafter provided. Time for election of surrogate. Population to exceed forty thousand.

§ 3. In all cases where any county in this state (except the counties of New York and Kings) shall have a population exceeding forty thousand, the board of supervisors therein, at any meeting of such board, special or regular, called in the usual form, may by resolution thereof provide for the election, at the following general election, of an officer other than the county judge who shall perform the duties of surrogate therein. May by resolution provide for election of a person to perform duty of surrogate.

§ 4. Such resolution shall be immediately delivered by the clerk of the board of supervisors to the county clerk, whose duty it shall be to file the same in the office of the clerk of said county, and keep the same as a part of the records thereof. Within ten days after such resolution shall be filed in the office of such county clerk, he shall transmit to the office of the sec- Resolution to be filed. Copy of resolution to be transmitted to secretary of state. retary of state, to be filed and kept in his office, a copy of such resolution duly certified by him. Supervisors to fix salary of county judge and surrogate. The board of supervisors in the several counties of this state (except New York and Kings) shall, at the annual meeting in the year eighteen hundred and seventy-one, fix the salary of the county judge, in those counties where the salary has not been fixed since the adoption of the sixth article of the constitution, and in counties in which surrogates shall be elected, they shall fix the salary of the surrogate, which salaries shall not be less than the salaries now paid such officers, respectively.

When to enter upon their duties. § 5. The separate officer elected and performing the duties of the office of surrogate, and the legal officer discharging the duties of county judge and of surrogate, and elected at the election provided for in this act, shall enter upon their duties on the first day of January next after such election, and shall hold their office for the term of six years from said first day of January; but where such officer shall be elected to fill a vacancy, then they shall enter upon the discharge of the duties of the office to which they have been elected, immediately upon the receipt of the certificate of such election.

Vacancies. § 6. Whenever the office of county judge shall be vacant in a county having a population exceeding forty thousand, the board of supervisors of that county, if there be a separate officer to perform the duties of the office of surrogate of said county, may resolve that there shall be no such officer in said county, and thereupon the office of such officers shall be deemed vacant and abolished from the time the office of county judge shall be filled; and if there be no such officer, such board may resolve that there shall be such officer in such county, in which case such officer shall be elected at the time and in the manner in all respects that the county judge in said county shall be elected. To be abolished or filled by supervisors.

To be surrogates of counties. § 7. The separate officers elected to perform the duties of the office of surrogate, under the fifteenth and sixteenth sections, article six of the constitution of this state, shall be denominated surrogates of the respective counties.

District attorney to act in case of disability of surrogate or county judge. § 8. Whenever any surrogate in a county shall be precluded from acting as such in any case by reason of interest, relationship by consanguinity or affinity to any party interested therein, so that he would be excluded from being a juror, or by reason of being a witness of any will, or having acted as counsel in such case, and there are no legal officers in such county to discharge the duties of such surrogate, or where such officer shall also be incapacitated from acting as such surrogate by reason of the foregoing disabilities in the case of the surrogate, the county judge of such county, or in case of his disability for like causes, then the district attorney shall possess the power and exercise jurisdiction in all respects in such case as the surrogate of such county would be authorized to possess and exercise were it not for such disability. To receive pro rata compensation. The district attorney of such county, while acting as surrogate in such case, shall be entitled to receive the same compensation, pro rata, as the officer acting as county judge and surrogate of such county is entitled to receive, to be audited by the board of supervisors, and to be paid by the county treasurer in the same manner as the salary of the county judge and surrogate shall be paid; and in counties where there is a separate officer to perform the duties of the office of surrogate, then the district attorney of such county shall receive the same compensation, pro rata, as such surrogate shall be entitled to receive in such county for the time said district attorney shall be acting as surrogate in such cases of disability, which shall be authorized by the board of supervisors, and paid as the salary of such separate officer elected to perform the duties of the office of surrogate is paid.

Supervisors to audit. County treasurer to pay. Amount of salary entitled to receive. How paid.

§ 9. This act shall take effect immediately.

CHAP. 868.

AN ACT to foster and develop the internal commerce of the state by inviting and rewarding the practical and profitable introduction upon the canals, of steam, caloric, electricity, or any motor other than animal power, for the propulsion of boats.

PASSED April 28, 1871; three-fifths being present.

The People of the State of New York, represented in Senate and Assembly, do enact as follows:

SECTION 1. George B. McClellan, Horatio Seymour, Erastus S. Prosser, David Dows, George Geddes, Van R. Richmond, Willis S. Nelson, George W. Chapman, William W. Wright and John D. Fay are hereby appointed a commission to practically test and examine inventions, or any and all devises which may be submitted to them for that purpose, by which steam, caloric, electricity, or any other motor than animal power, may be practically and profitably used and applied in the propulsion of boats upon the canals; said examination and tests shall be had by the said commissioners at such time or times during the season of canal navigation, for the year eighteen hundred and seventy-one and seventy-two, as they may order and direct; said commissioners shall have the right, and they are hereby expressly required to reject all such inventions or devices, if in their opinion none of the said inventions or devices shall fully and satisfactorily meet the requirements of this act; but said commissioners shall demand and require: *First.* The inventions and devices to be tested and tried at their own proper costs and charges of the parties offering the same for trial. *Second.* That the boat shall, in addition to the weight of the machinery and fuel reasonably necessary for the propulsion of said boat, be enabled to transport, and shall actually transport, on the Erie canal on a test or trial exhibition, under the rules and regulations now govern-

Commissioners to test motor power other than animal, on canals. How and when examination shall take place. May reject inventions. Parties owning inventions to pay cost of testing. Boats to carry two hundred tons.

ing the boats now navigating the canals at least two hundred tons of cargo. *Third.* That the rate of speed made by said boat shall not be less than an average of three miles per hour, without injury to the canals or their structures. *Fourth.* That the boat can be readily and easily stopped or backed by the use and power of its own machinery. *Fifth.* That the simplicity, economy and durability of the invention or device must be elements of its worth and usefulness. *Sixth.* That the invention, device or improvement can be readily adapted to the present canal boats; and, lastly, that the commissioners shall be fully satisfied that the invention or device will lessen the cost of canal transportation and increase the capacity of the canals. Any means of propulsion or towage other than by a direct application of power upon the boat which does not interfere in any manner with the present method of towage on the canals, and complying in all other respects with the provisions of this act, may be entitled to the benefits thereof; but this shall not be construed to apply to the system known as the Belgian system, or to any mode of propulsion by steam engines or otherwise upon either bank of the canals.

Rate of speed. Requirements. Simplicity, etc., an element of worth. Must be adapted. Must satisfy commissioners. Requirements to entitle to benefits. Not to apply to Belgian system, nor to power on banks of canals.

Manner of testing. § 2. No such test shall be made if the same shall in any manner retard, hinder or delay the passage of boats navigating the canals under the present system.

Duty and privileges of commissioners. § 3. If the commissioners herein appointed shall, upon such examination and test, as is provided for in the first section of this act, conclude and determine at any time that one or more inventions or devices aforesaid, but not to exceed three in number, shall be in all respects a full and satisfactory, practicable and profitable adaptation to the wants of the canals by reason of a new, useful and economical means of propulsion for boats within the meaning of this act, it shall then, and not otherwise, be their duty to grant unto the owner or owners of such inventions or devices, his or their attorney, their certificate or certificates under their hands as such commissioners, that they have so determined and adjudged to the owner or owners of the invention or device which, in the judgment of said commissioners, possesses in the greatest degree of perfection the requisites mentioned in the first section, they shall grant a certificate which shall be known as certificate No. one; and to the owner or owners of the next best invention or device they shall grant a certificate as aforesaid, which shall be known as certificate No. two; and to the owner or owners of the third best invention or device they shall grant a certificate as aforesaid, which shall be known as certificate No. three.

May grant certificates of perfection. Number of certificates.

Commissioners to take oath of office. § 4. Before entering upon the duties of his office each commissioner herein named shall take and subscribe an official oath, which shall be filed at once in the office of the secretary of state. Any vacancy arising from any cause in said commission, may be filled, on the application of the remaining commissioners, by the governor.

Governor to fill vacancies.

Expense of commissioners to be paid out of sum § 5. The reasonable expenses of the said commission, not exceeding in all the sum of five thousand dollars, to be determined by the said board, shall be paid out of any sum which may be awarded to the person or persons receiving the certificates mentioned in the third section of this act, in proportion to the amount awarded to the holders of said certificates, provided such certificates shall be granted; and if no such certificates shall be granted, then the same shall be paid by the treasurer on the warrant of the comptroller out of any moneys in the treasury not otherwise appropriated.

Awarded to persons receiving certificates

Treasurer to pay on warrant of comptroller.

§ 6. Upon the production by the owner or owners, or his or their attorney, of such certificate or certificates as may be granted under the provisions of this act, to the comptroller, he shall draw his warrant upon the treasurer of the state of New York for the sum of fifty thousand dollars, payable to the said owner or owners of said invention, device, his or their attorney, out of any money in the treasury not otherwise appropriated, in case but one certificate shall have been granted by said commissioners. If two certificates shall have been granted, and no more, then the said comptroller shall draw his said warrant upon the said treasurer for the sum of thirty-five thousand dollars, payable to the owner or owners of certificate No. one; and said comptroller shall also draw his said warrant upon the said treasurer for the sum of fifteen thousand dollars, payable to the owner or owners of certificate No. two. If three certificates shall be granted by said commissioners, then and in that case the said comptroller shall draw his said warrant upon the said treasurer for the sum of thirty thousand dollars, payable to the owner or owners of certificate No. one; and one of fifteen thousand dollars, payable to the owner or owners of certificate No. two; and one of five thousand dollars payable to the owner or owners of certificate No. three.

Comptroller to draw warrant for payment of certificates.

Warrants for each certificate.

How payments shall be apportioned.

§ 7. If, on or before the first day of November, eighteen hundred and seventy-three, the commissioners hereinbefore named shall, upon due examination, find and determine that the said invention or device has been successfully operated upon the canals, and has been or will be largely adopted as a motor on said canals by reason of its superiority over any other known method of propulsion, then and in such case they shall grant a further certificate of that fact, and the comptroller, upon its presentation to him, shall draw his warrant upon the treasurer of the state for the further sum of fifty thousand dollars, payable to the said owner or owners of the said device, his or their attorney, out of any money in the treasury not otherwise appropriated; but in case of the granting by said commissioners of more than one certificate, as stated in section six of this act, then and in that case the sum of fifty thousand dollars, mentioned in this section, shall be divided among and paid to the owners of the said certificates in the proportion, and in the manner as stated in section six of this act.

Appropriation to be made by comptroller, on successfully operating.

CHAP. 869.

AN ACT making appropriations for certain public and charitable institutions.

PASSED April 28, 1871, by a two-third vote.

The People of the State of New York, represented in Senate and Assembly, do enact as follows:

Conditions upon which comptroller shall pay appropriations. SECTION 1. The treasurer shall pay, on a warrant of the comptroller, out of any moneys in the treasury not otherwise appropriated, the several amounts specified in this act to the persons duly authorized to receive the same; but no sum here indicated shall be paid to any hospital, asylum, home for the friendless or educational institution, till the president, secretary or managers of the same shall have made to him a report of their operations, pursuant to chapter four hundred and nineteen of the laws of eighteen hundred and sixty-four, entitled "An act requiring officers of scientific and eleemosynary institutions to make annual reports," unless such requirement shall have been expressly waived in this act. Requirement to entitle to participate.

Appropriations. § 2. The following amounts are hereby appropriated for the several purposes specified, namely:

For Orphan Asylums and Homes for Friendless. For orphan asylums, homes for the friendless, and other charitable institutions of like character, for their maintenance, one hundred and fifty thousand dollars, to be paid as follows, namely: The said amount shall be divided among the several counties in proportion to their respective valuations, as the same are established by law; and the sums thus awarded to each county shall be paid to the following incorporated orphan asylums and institutions, in proportion to the number of orphans and homeless persons maintained in them during the present fiscal year, namely: Division among counties according to taxable valuation.

Names of charitable institutions. The Albany Orphan Asylum; the Albany Guardian Society and Home for the Friendless; American Female Guardian Society and Home for the Friendless of the city of New York; the Association for the Relief of Respectable Aged Indigent Females, New York; the Society of Our Lady of Refuge, Buffalo; the Brooklyn Industrial School Association and Home for Destitute Children; the Brooklyn Industrial School Association, eastern district; the Buffalo Orphan Asylum; the Cayuga Asylum for Destitute Children; the Chapin Home for the Aged and Indigent, New York; the Charity Foundation of the Protestant Episcopal Church, Buffalo; the Children's Aid Society, New York; the Children's Friend Society, Albany; the Children's Home Society (day home), Troy; the Church Charity Foundation of Long Island; the Colored Home, New York; the Colored Orphan Asylum, New York; the Convent of the Sisters of Mercy, Brooklyn; the Davenport Female Orphan Asylum; the Evangelical Lutheran St. John's Orphan Home, Buffalo; Five Points House of Industry; the Five Points Mission, New York; the Free School Academy of the

Sacred Heart, Manhattanville; the Hebrew Benevolent and Orphan Asylum Society; Home for Homeless Girls, New York; the Home for the Friendless, Auburn; the Home for the Friendless, Buffalo; the Home for the Friendless, Newburgh; the Home for the Friendless, Rochester; the Home for the Friendless, Schenectady; the Home for the Aged of the Little Sisters of the Poor, Brooklyn; the House of the Good Shepherd, Brooklyn; the House of the Good Shepherd, New York; the House of Mercy, New York; the House of Reception, Mariner's Harbor; Howard Colored Orphan Asylum, Brooklyn; the Hudson Orphan and Relief Association; Institution of Mercy, East Houston staeet, New York; the Institution of Mercy (orphan asylum), Eighty-first street, New York; the Jefferson County Orphan Asylum; the Ladies' Union Relief Association, New York; the Roman Catholic Reformatory at Buffalo; the Ingleside Home at Buffalo; the Ladies' Union Aid Society of the Methodist Episcopal Church, New York city; Ladies' Benovelent Society, Schenectady; Le Couteulx St. Mary's Deaf and Dumb Asylum, Buffalo; Ladies' Union Benevolent Society, Ithaca; Nursery and Child's Hospital, New York; New York Magdalen Benevolent Society; New York Juvenile Guardian Society; Orphan Asylum Society, Brooklyn; Orphan Asylum Society, New York; Orphan Asylum Society of the Holy Trinity Church, Brooklyn, eastern division; Orphan Home and Asylum of the Protestant Episcopal Church, New York; Orphans' Home St. Peter's Church, Albany; the House of Shelter, Albany; Onondaga County Orphan Asylum; Ontario County Orphan Asylum; Oswego Orphan Asylum; Orphan House of the Holy Saviour, Cooperstown; Patriot Orphan Home; Poughkeepsie Orphan House and Home for the Friendless; Protestant Episcopal Church Home, Rochester; Providence Lunatic Asylum, Buffalo; Rochester Industrial School; Rochester Orphan Asylum; Roman Catholic Orphan Asylum, Brooklyn; Roman Catholic Orphan Asylum, New York; Sheltering Arms, New York; Sisters of the Order of St. Dominick (asylum), New York; Society for the Relief of Destitute Children of Seamen; Society for the Relief of Half-orphan and Destitute Children, New York; Society for the protection of Destitute Children, Buffalo; Society of the Sisters of Saint Joseph, of the city of Troy; Society for the protection of Destitute Roman Catholic Children, New York; Southern Tier Orphan Asylum; St. Barnabas' House, New York; St. Joseph's Orphan Asylum, New York; St. Joseph's German Roman Catholic Asylum, Rochester; New St. Joseph's Male Orphan Asylum, Buffalo; St. John's Female Orphan Asylum, Utica; St. Luke's Home for Indigent Christian Females, New York; St. Mary's Boys' Orphan Asylum, Rochester; St. Mary's German Orphan Asylum, Buffalo; St. Mary's Orphan Asylum, Canandaigua; St. Mary's Orphan Asylum, Clifton; St. Mary's Orphan Asylum, Dunkirk; St. Patrick's Female Orphan Asylum, Rochester; St. Patrick's Orphan Asylum for Destitute Children, Newburgh; St. Peter's German Roman Catholic Orphan Asylum, Rondout; St. Stephen's Catholic Orphan Asylum, New York; St. Thomas' Orphan Asylum, Batavia; St. Vincent de Paul Orphan Asylum, Syracuse; St. Vincent Female Orphan Asylum, Albany; St. Vincent Female Orphan Asylum, Buffalo; the Rochester House for Idle and Truant Children; St. Vincent Female Orphan Asylum, Troy; St. Vincent Infant Orphan Asylum, Buffalo; St. Vincent Male Orphan Asylum, Albany; St. Vincent Male Orphan Asylum, Utica; Susquehanna Valley Home and Industrial School for Indigent Children; Syracuse Home Association; Thomas Orphan Asylum for Destitute Indian Children; Troy Catholic Male Orphan Asylum; Troy Orphan Asylum; Utica Orphan Asylum; Union Home and School for Children of our Volunteers, New York; Male Orphan Asylum of the Church Charity foundation, Buffalo; Female Orphan Asylum of the Church Charity Foundation, Buffalo; by whatever name said institutions are known; and to the other orphan asylums and homes for friendless and destitute persons in this state, except Leake and Watts Orphan Asylum in the city of New York. In the counties having no asylum or institution for the maintenance and education of indigent orphans and homeless persons, the aforesaid dividend shall be paid to the order of the treasurer of each of such counties.

County treasurers to receive dividends.

Donations to charitable institutions.

For the Thomas Asylum for Orphan and Destitute Indian Children, for the education and maintenance of one hundred children, at the rate of eighty-five dollars per capita, eight thousand five hundred dollars. And to the Indian Mission School, on the Allegany reservation, on the order of its principal, three hundred dollars.

For the Home of the Friendless, Schenectady, one thousand eight hundred and seventy-five dollars. For the Syracuse Home Association, one thousand five hundred dollars.

For the Sisters of Mercy, Brooklyn, five thousand dollars.

For the St. Vincent Female Orphan Asylum, Buffalo, five thousand dollars.

For the St. Mary's Boys' Orphan Asylum, Rochester, seven thousand five hundred dollars. For the Home of the Friendless at Albany, one thousand five hundred dollars.

For the St. Vincent de Paul Asylum of Syracuse, two thousand two hundred and twenty-five dollars.

For the Providence Lunatic Asylum, Buffalo, one thousand one hundred and twenty-five dollars.

For the Sisters of St. Ursula, of East Morrisania, three thousand dollars.

For the Asylum of Our Lady of Refuge, Buffalo, seven hundred and fifty dollars.

For the Rochester Female Charitable Society, seven hundred and fifty dollars.

For the Ontario Orphan Asylum, Canandaigua, three thousand dollars.

For the Onondaga County Orphan Asylum, two thousand two hundred and twenty-five dollars.

Donations to charitable institutions.

For the St. Patrick's Orphan Asylum, Newburgh, five thousand dollars in addition to the amount in the general appropriation.

For the Chapin Home for the Aged and Infirm, New York city, ten thousand dollars.

For the Women's Aid Society and Home for Training Girls in New York city, three thousand seven hundred and fifty dollars; to be paid when the managers of said societies shall have filed with the comptroller a report of its operations, financial condition and management since its incorporation; such report to be in lieu of the report required by the first section of this act and the law therein mentioned.

For the Dispensary and Hospital Society of the Women's Institute of the city of New York, seven thousand five hundred dollars, to be paid when the managers of the said society shall have filed with the comptroller are port of its operations, financial condition and management since its incorporation, such report to be in lieu of the report required by the first section of this act and the law therein mentioned.

For the House of the Good Shepherd, Rockland county, fifteen thousand dollars.

For the Home of the Friendless, Auburn, two thousand dollars.

For the Oswego Orphan Asylum, at Oswego, five thousand dollars.

For the St. Mary's Orphan Asylum at Dunkirk, three thousand seven hundred and fifty dollars.

For St. Michael's Female Free School, Flushing, Queens county, eighteen hundred and seventy-five dollars.

For St. Michael's Male Free School, Flushing, Queens county, eighteen hundred and seventy-five dollars.

For the Southern Tier Orphan Home at Elmira, five thousand dollars.

For the Evangelical Luthern St. John's Orphan Home, Buffalo, five thousand dollars.

For the Le Couteulx St. Mary's Deaf and Dumb Asylum, Buffalo, in addition to the amount due them in the general appropriation, fifteen hundred dollars.

For the Orphan Asylum Society of the city of Brooklyn, seven thousand five hundred dollars, in addition to the appropriation of the same amount in the year eighteen hundred and seventy, which is hereby re-appropriated.

For the Buffalo Hospital of the Sisters of Charity, seven thousand five hundred dollars.

For the Ingleside Home of Buffalo, seven thousand five hun dred dollars.

For the S. R. Smith Infirmary of Richmond county, seven hundred and fifty dollars.

For the Troy Orphan Asylum, three thousand seven hundred and fifty dollars.

For the Roman Catholic Orphan Asylum of the city of Brooklyn, ten thousand dollars.

Donations to charitable institutions.

For the Roman Catholic Orphan Asylum of the city of New York, ten thousand dollars.

For the Society for the Aid of Friendless Women and Children, Brooklyn, ten thousand dollars.

For the Hebrew Benevolent Society of the city of Albany, five hundred dollars.

For the Hebrew Benevolent Society of the city of Brooklyn, E. D., five hundred dollars.

For the Mariner's Family Industrial Society of the port of New York, seven thousand five hundred dollars.

For the Hudson Orphan and Relief Association, five thousand dollars.

For the Orphan Asylum connected with St. Patrick's church, corner Prince and Mott streets, New York city, seven thousand five hundred dollars.

For the Ladies Union Benevolent Society of Ithaca, for the charitable purposes of the institution, ten thousand dollars, to be paid on affidavit of the president and treasurer of said society, presented to the comptroller, that a like sum of ten thousand dollars has been raised by subscription and paid into the treasury of the society.

For the Working Women's Protective Union, for the equipment of a building for its use, the sum of eleven thousand two hundred and fifty dollars, when the sum of fifteen thousand dollars shall have been raised by private subscription to the same object, and upon satisfactory proof to the comptroller that said sum of fifteen thousand dollars has been actually paid to said Union.

For the Troy Catholic Male Orphan Asylum Association, five thousand dollars.

For the St. Vincent's Female Orphan Asylum, Troy, one thousand dollars.

For the Rochester Home for Idle and Truant Children, three thousand dollars.

For the Rochester Orphan Asylum, seven thousand five hundred dollars.

For the St. Joseph's Orphan Asylum, Rochester, one thousand dollars.

For the Rochester Home for the Friendless, one thousand dollars.

For the St. Patrick's Female Orphan Asylum, Rochester, one thousand dollars.

For the New York Female Magdalen Benevolent Society, three thousand dollars.

For the Sisters of the Order of St. Dominick, New York, five thousand dollars.

For the Sisters of Charity at Rondout, for aid to build an orphan asylum, six thousand dollars.

For the Jefferson County Orphan Asylum, fifteen hundred dollars.

For the Society for the Relief of Destitute Children of Seamen, one thousand five hundred dollars.

For the Sailors' Home, Tonawanda, five hundred dollars.

Donations to charitable institutions.

For the Poughkeepsie Orphan House and Home for the Friendless, three thousand dollars.

For the St. Joseph's Institute, on Fourth street, New York city, in charge of Sister Mary Cleophas, two thousand two hundred and fifty dollars.

For the House of the Good Shepherd, Brooklyn, eleven thousand two hundred and fifty dollars.

For the St. Peter's Institute on Barclay street, New York city, in charge of Mother Jerome, one thousand five hundred dollars.

For the De La Salle Institute, New York city, one thousand five hundred dollars.

For the Pitts Street Industrial School in the city of New York, for the care and maintenance of destitute children, two thousand two hundred and fifty dollars.

For Institute for Destitute Children of the village of Greenbush, five hundred dollars.

For the New York House of Mercy, Eighty-second street, New York, ten thousand dollars.

For the St. Vincent Male Orphan Asylum, Utica, eleven thousand two hundred and fifty dollars.

For the Utica Orphan Asylum, three thousand dollars.

For the Home for the Homeless at Utica, three thousand dollars.

For the St. Luke's Home at Utica, three thousand dollars.

For the St. Elizabeth Hospital and Home at Utica, three thousand dollars.

For the Homœopathic Lying-in Asylum in the city of Brooklyn, two thousand two hundred and fifty dollars, to be paid when the managers of the said asylum shall have filed with the comptroller a report of its operations, financial condition and management since its incorporation, such report to be in lieu of the report required by the first section of this act.

For the charity week-day schools of the state, to be paid on the warrant of the comptroller pro rata, according to the number of scholars instructed in them without charge during the last fical year, to be divided by the comptroller on the first day of July next, on certificates duly verified by affidavit, seventy-five thousand dollars.

For the Industrial School for Children, situated on South Third, near Fourth street, in the eastern district of the city of Brooklyn, seven hundred and fifty dollars.

For the St. Bonaventure's College and Sisters of Charity, Allegany, seven thousand five hundred dollars.

For the Susquehanna Valley Home and Industrial School for Indigent Children, twenty thousand dollars.

For the St. Mary's Orphan Asylum and Academy, Canandaigua, three thousand seven hundred and fifty dollars.

For the Catholic Reformatory of Buffalo, five thousand dollars.

For the Union Home and School in the city of New York, for the care and maintenance of the orphan children of volunteer soldiers and sailors, seven thousand five hundred dollars.

Donations to charitable institutions.

For the Twenty-first Ward Mission and Industrial School Association of the city of New York, to aid in the erection of buildings, payable on the order of the treasurer, fifteen thousand dollars.

For the St. Joseph's Home for Old and Indigent Ladies, Fifteenth street and Seventh avenue, in the city of New York, three thousand dollars.

For the St. Joseph's German American Industrial School, located on the corner of One Hundred and Twenty-ninth street and Ninth avenue, Manhattanville, in the city of New York, three thousand dollars.

For the House of the Good Shepherd, in the city of New York, ten thousand dollars.

For the Christian Brothers' Academy at Albany, three thousand seven hundred and fifty dollars.

For the Female Academy of the Sacred Heart, Albany county, for the purpose of providing accommodation for free scholars, five thousand dollars.

For the Juvenile Guardian Society of New York, ten thousand dollars.

For the James Street Industrial School, in the city of New York, five thousand dollars.

For the Young Ladies Institute at Auburn, New York, three thousand dollars, to be paid to Sylvester Willard, president of the board of trustees thereof, and expended under the direction of said board, in the purchase of a library and apparatus for said institute.

For the Cayuga Asylum for Destitute Children, one thousand five hundred dollars.

For the St. Mary's Reformatory School, Court street, Brooklyn, two thousand two hundred and fifty dollars.

For the Day Home, Troy, five thousand dollars.

For the Rochester Industrial School, three thousand dollars.

For the Society for the Protection of Destitute Roman Catholic Children, New York, five thousand dollars.

For the Patriot Orphan Home of New York, two thousand dollars.

For the Association of the Old Ladies' Home of the city of Poughkeepsie, eighteen hundred and seventy-five dollars.

For the St. Mary's School for Girls, Albany, seven hundred and fifty dollars.

For the Cary Collegiate Seminary, Oakfield, three thousand seven hundred and fifty dollars.

For the St. Ann's Reformatory School of the fifth ward of the city of Brooklyn, five thousand dollars.

For the hospitals of the State, except the New York hospital, Bellevue hospital and St. Luke's hospital, in the city of New York, to be divided among them in proportion to the number of beneficiary patients in them, and the time that such patients shall have been under treatment during the present fiscal year, for which no other provision has been made, seventy-five thousand dollars.

For the House of Shelter of the city of Albany, three thousand seven hundred and fifty dollars, for the enlargement of their house or the purchase of a new building.

Donations to charitable institutions.

For the German Charity School, in charge of the Sisters of St. Francis, corner of Sherman and Robin streets, Albany, twenty-two hundred and fifty dollars.

For the St. John's College, Brooklyn, for the education of Destitute Children, two thousand five hundred dollars.

For the Mount Sinai Hospital in the city of New York, five thousand dollars.

For St. Mary's Widows and Lying-in Women's Hospital, Buffalo, eighteen hundred and seventy-five dollars.

For the St. John's Riverside Hospital of Yonkers, five thousand two hundred and fifty dollars.

For the New York Dispensary for Diseases of the Throat and Chest, two thousand two hundred and fifty dollars.

For the Dispensary located at Manhattanville, in the city of New York, one thousand five hundred dollars.

For the German American Dispensary of the city of New York, six hundred dollars.

For the St. Peter's Hospital, Brooklyn, three thousand dollars.

For the New York State Hospital for Diseases of the Nervous System, three thousand dollars.

For the New York Society for the Relief of the Ruptured and Crippled, three thousand seven hundred and fifty dollars.

For the Northeastern Homœopathic Dispensary, New York city, two thousand two hundred and fifty dollars.

For the Hahnemann Hospital of the city and state of New York, twenty-two thousand five hundred dollars, to aid in the construction of building.

For the Northeastern Homœopathic Medical and Surgical Dispensary of the city of New York, eleven hundred and twenty-five dollars.

For the Rensselaer Polytechnic Institute at Troy, three thousand seven hundred and fifty dollars.

For the infirmary of the New York College of Dentistry, three thousand seven hundred and fifty dollars.

For the Cancer Hospital of the city of New York, one thousand one hundred and twenty-five dollars.

For the Hoffman Dispensary of the city of New York, one thousand five hundred dollars.

For the New York Eye and Ear Infirmary, New York city, one thousand five hundred dollars.

For the New York Ophthalmic and Aural Institute, two thousand dollars.

For the New York Dispensary, New York city, ten thousand dollars.

For the Women's Hospital of the state of New York, three thousand seven hundred and fifty dollars.

For the St. Barnabas Hospital, Poughkeepsie, eight hundred dollars.

Donations to charitable institutions.

For the St. Francis Hospital of the Sisters of the Poor in the city of New York, seven thousand five hundred dollars.

For the Dorcas Society of Peekskill, county of Westchester, payable on the order of the treasurer, one thousand dollars.

For the Albany city Homœopathic Dispensary, to be paid on the certificate of one of the trustees, five thousand dollars.

For the St. Joseph's Hospital at Syracuse, seven thousand five hundred dollars.

For the Albany City Hospital, five thousand dollars.

For the Nursery and Child's Hospital, in the county of Richmond, eighteen thousand seven hundred and fifty dollars.

For the Central Dispensary, New York city, three thousand seven hundred and fifty dollars.

For the Brooklyn Orthopœdic Infirmary, three hundred and seventy-five dollars.

For the Parochial School attached to the church of St. Peter and St. Paul, situate on Second street, near South Third street, in the city of Brooklyn, seven hundred and fifty dollars.

For the Parochial School attached to the church, situate on North Sixth street, between Fifth and Sixth streets in the city of Brooklyn, under charge of Reverend Doctor Mullane, seven hundred and fifty dollars.

For the Parochial School attached to St. Joseph's church, in the city of Brooklyn, under charge of Reverend Doctor Corcoran, five thousand dollars.

For St. Patrick's Parochial School, Kent avenue, Brooklyn, three hundred and seventy-five dollars.

For Long Island College Hospital, thirty-seven hundred and fifty dollars.

For the Brooklyn Eclectic Dispensary, J. P. Powers, president, seven hundred and fifty dollars.

For New York Seamen's Association, ten thousand dollars.

For the Morrisania Homœopathic Dispensary, five hundred dollars.

For the St. Peter's Hospital, Albany, five thousand dollars.

For the Western Dispensary for Women and Children, New York city, seven hundred and fifty dollars.

For the Sisters of Charity of the Troy Hospital, ten thousand dollars.

For the St. Mary's Hospital, Rochester, seven thousand five hundred dollars.

For the Rochester City Hospital, fifteen thousand dollars.

For the Northern Dispensary of the city of New York (Eighth avenue), five thousand dollars.

For the New York Dispensary for Diseases of the Skin, five thousand dollars.

For the Buffalo Homœopathic Dispensary, five hundred and sixty-five dollars.

For the Buffalo Free Medical and Surgical Dispensary, three hundred and seventy-five dollars.

For the Brooklyn Dispensary, seven hundred and fifty dollars.

For the General Hospital, Buffalo, seven thousand five hundred dollars.

Donations to charitable institutions.

For the House of Rest for Consumptives, Tremont, Westchester county, two thousand five hundred dollars.

For the Home of the Aged and Orphan of the Church Charity Foundation of Long Island, in the city of Brooklyn, five thousand dollars.

For the Orthopœdic Dispensary of the city of New York, five thousand dollars.

For the Western Homœopathic Dispensary, one thousand eight hundred and seventy-five dollars.

For the Western Homœopathic Dispensary for Women and Children, three hundred and seventy-five dollars.

For the Wayside Industrial Home, one thousand dollars.

For the Children's Fold, New York city, one thousand dollars.

For the St. Vincent Hospital, New York city, five thousand dollars.

For the Brooklyn Homœopathic Hospital, ten thousand dollars; to be paid when the managers of the said asylum hospital shall have filed with the comptroller a report of its operations, financial condition and management since its incorporation, such report to be in lieu of the report required by the first section of this act and the law therein mentioned.

For the St. Mary's Female Hospital, Brooklyn, five thousand dollars.

For the Home for the Aged, under the care of the Little Sisters of the Poor, in the city of Brooklyn, ten thousand dollars.

For the New York Ophthalmic Hospital, two thousand five hundred dollars; for the New York Dispensary for the Treatment of Cancer, one thousand dollars; for the Northeastern Dispensary of the city of New York, one thousand and five hundred dollars; for the Bond Street Homœopathic Dispensary, one thousand five hundred dollars; for the Eclectic Medical Dispensary, in the city of New York, two thousand five hundred dollars; for the Demilt Dispensary, two thousand five hundred dollars; for the Homœopathic Medical College Dispensary, one thousand dollars; for the Dispensary of the New York Medical College for Women, five hundred dollars; for the German Dispensary of the city of New York, six hundred dollars; for the New York Homœopathic Dispensary, two thousand dollars; for the Eastern Dispensary of the city of New York, one thousand dollars; for the New York Infirmary Dispensary, five hundred dollars; for the Dispensary at Poughkeepsie, eight hundred dollars; for the Albany City Homœopathic Dispensary, one thousand dollars; for the Dispensary of the Troy Hospital, five hundred dollars; for the Buffalo City Dispensary, five hundred dollars; for the Yorkville Dispensary, in the city of New York, one thousand dollars; for the Harlem Dispensary in the city of New York, one thousand dollars; for the Branch Tompkins Square Homœopathic Dispensary, one thousand dollars; for the Brooklyn City Dispensary, seven hundred dollars; the Williamsburgh

Dispensary, one thousand dollars, and the Dispensary of the Brooklyn Homœopathic Hospital, one thousand dollars; Long Island College Hospital Dispensary, five hundred dollars; Albany Hospital Dispensary, one thousand dollars; for the St. Peter's Hospital Dispensary, Albany, seven hundred and fifty dollars; for the Gates Avenue Homœopathic Dispensary, Brooklyn, five hundred dollars; for the German Medical Society of Williamsburgh, to be applied to the purchase of medicines and surgical appliances for indigent patients, gratuitously treated by said society, and the members thereof, two hundred and twenty-five dollars; for St. Peter's Dispensary, Brooklyn, five hundred dollars; for the Manhattan Dispensary of New York, three thousand dollars; for the Association for Befriending Children, five thousand dollars; for the Buffalo Orphan Asylum, two thousand dollars.

Purchase of medicines and surgical appliances

§ 3. This act shall take effect immediately.

CHAP. 870.

AN ACT to amend an act entitled "An act for the incorporation of villages," passed April twenty, eighteen hundred and seventy.

Ante, vol. 7, p. 681.

PASSED April 29, 1871; three-fifths being present.

The People of the State of New York, represented in Senate and Assembly, do enact as follows:

SECTION 1. Section one of the act entitled "An act for the incorporation of villages," passed April twenty, eighteen hundred and seventy, is hereby amended so as to read as follows:

Population and territory requisite for incorporation.

§ 1. Any part of any town or towns not in any incorporated village, containing a resident population of not less than three hundred persons, and if it shall include in its boundaries a territory of at least one square mile in extent, containing a resident population of at the rate of not less than three hundred persons to every square mile of territory included within such boundaries, may be incorporated as a village under the provisions of this act, by complying therewith.

§ 2. Section six of title four of said act is hereby amended so as to read as follows:

Ante, vol. 7, p. 698.

Highway tax.

§ 6. In addition to the amount raised by the trustees for "ordinary expenditures," the trustees shall have power, in any one year, in addition to the poll tax, to raise by tax such sum as they may deem necessary, not exceeding in any one year the amount of one per cent on the assessed valuation of such village, to be denominated a highway tax, to work and improve the roads, avenues, streets, public squares and parks, lanes and crosswalks of said village, and all persons and incorporated companies owning property and estate, real and personal, in said village, to be assessed and collected as all other taxes are, by the provisions of this act. The money so raised, with the proceeds of the poll tax, shall be devoted to the purposes expressed in this section, and kept apart as a separate and distinct fund by the treasurer.

Highway moneys to be kept separate.

§ 3. Section one of title seven of the said act is hereby amended so as to read as follows:

Ante, vol. 7, p. 698.

§ 1. A village incorporated under this act shall constitute a separate highway district within its corporate limits, exempt from the superintendence of any one, except the board of trustees, who shall be commissioners of highways in and for such village, and shall have all the powers of commissioners of highways of towns in this state, subject to this act, and, as such, they shall have power to discontinue, lay out, open, widen, alter, change the grade, or otherwise improve roads, avenues, streets, public parks or squares, lanes, crosswalks and sidewalks; and for that purpose may take and appropriate any land in said village; but no road, avenue, street, lane or sidewalk, shall be opened or altered, unless all claims for damages on account of such opening or altering shall be released without remuneration, except on the written petition of at least ten freeholders residing in said village, which petition shall specify the improvement to be made, describe the land to be taken, state the owner or owners thereof, when known, and shall be filed in the office of the clerk of the village. On the presentation of such petition the trustees shall and must meet and examine the same; and, if they decide the improvement shall be made, they shall so decide by resolution, to be entered in the minutes of the board; and they shall thereupon put up, in five public places in said village, a correct description of the lands to be taken to make such improvement, and a notice that the trustees, at a place and on a day, and at an hour therein specified, not less than five days from the date and posting thereof, will meet and hear any objections that may be made to the taking of such land, or making such improvement; a copy of which notice must be served on the owner or owners of such land, at least five days before said meeting, unless said owner is a non-resident of such village; in which case, said notice and description must be deposited in the said village post-office, directed to said owner, at least twenty days before such meeting. Any person interested may be heard, and introduce testimony before the board of trustees as to the matter, on the day specified in the notice, or on such other days as the board may appoint. After such hearing, the trustees may deny the petition, or approve and declare by resolution, to be entered in their minutes, their intention to make the said improvements, and proceed to obtain possession of the lands described, in the manner provided by this act.

Village to be separate highway district.

Trustees to have power of highway commissioners therein.

Proceedings for street improvements when damages are claimed.

Petition of freeholders.

Trustees to decide thereon.

Description of lands to be taken, how posted.

Service of notice of hearing upon land owners.

Hearing of interested persons.

Decision of trustees as to making improvements.

§ 4. Section two of title seven of the said act is hereby amended so as to read as follows:

Ante, vol. 7, p. 699.

§ 2. Whenever any road, avenue, street, square or park, lane or sidewalk is opened or altered, the damages claimed by reason thereof may be determined by agreement between the board of trustees and the persons claiming such damages; but in case the damages are not so determined or released, the board shall, on being notified by the president, as in case of a special meeting, or at a regular meeting, meet and cause a jury of six freeholders to be summoned to determine and award said damages. Five days' notice of the time and place of such meeting shall be given to the owner or owners of such lands, if residents of the village, and if not such residents, then notice shall be sent ten days before such meeting, by mail, directed to the place of residence, if known, of each of such non-residents. The jury shall be sworn to faithfully and impartially execute their duty; shall examine the premises, hear the proofs and allegations of the parties, and reduce the testimony to writing, if any is taken; and they shall determine and award to the owner or owners of such lands such damages as they will sustain by the proposed alteration or improvement, after making allowance for any benefit which the said owner or owners may derive therefrom. The determination and award of the jury shall be signed by them and filed in the office of the village clerk, and a copy served on the persons entitled to such award. If no appeal is made within twenty days from the time of such service, the determination and award of such jury shall be final and conclusive on all persons interested. A copy of such award, certified by the clerk under the seal of the village, shall be evidence of the same in all courts and places and all actions and proceedings.

Trustees to summon jury to assess damages.

Service of notice of meeting.

Jury to be sworn, examine premises and hear proofs.

To award damages.

Award, how filed and served

Appeals, when to be made.

Copy of award evidence.

§ 5. Section thirty-three of title eight of the said act is hereby amended so as to read as follows:

Ante, vol. 7, p. 707.

§ 33. The boards of supervisors of the several counties are hereby authorized and empowered to extend the boundaries of any incorporated village within their respective counties, upon the petition of the president and board of trustees of such village, by a vote of a majority of all the supervisors elected, to be taken by yeas and nays, provided that no act, ordinance or resolution for such purpose shall be valid and operative, unless it shall receive the affirmative vote of the supervisors of the town or towns from which the additional territory is to be taken, in which such village is situated, and of the supervisor or supervisors, if any, of such village. And the said boards of supervisors are also authorized and empowered to diminish the boundaries of any incorporated village within their respective counties, so as to exclude from such incorporation any portion of the territory embraced therein, upon the petition of two-thirds of the electors resident within the portion of territory sought to be so excluded, who shall be liable to be as-

Boards of supervisors may extend boundaries of villages, on petition.

Affirmative vote of supervisor of town or towns requisite.

May diminish the boundaries.

sessed for the ordinary and extraordinary expenditures of such village, by a vote of a majority of all the supervisors elected, to be taken by yeas and nays, provided that no act, ordinance or resolution for such purpose shall be valid and operative, unless it shall receive the affirmative vote of the supervisor or supervisors, if any, of such village. Proviso.

§ 6. This act shall take effect immediately.

CHAP. 874.

AN ACT authorizing the surrogates in the several counties to employ stenographers.

PASSED May 1, 1871; three-fifths being present.

The People of the State of New York, represented in Senate and Assembly, do enact as follows:

SECTION 1. The surrogate of any county of this state may, in his discretion, employ a stenographer, who shall be skilled in the practice of his art, and who shall be sworn to the faithful discharge of his duties, and who shall be paid a reasonable compensation, to be certified by the surrogate as a part of the costs of the proceedings, and who shall, under the direction of such surrogate, take full stenographic notes of all proceedings in the court of said surrogate in which oral proofs shall be given, which notes shall be fairly transcribed, and, after being signed by the witnesses, deponent or affiant, shall be filed in the office of said surrogate. By consent of the parties to the proceedings in which said proof shall be taken, and said surrogate, the signing of such record of proof by the witness, deponent or affiant may be waived, in which case such record, after being authenticated by the certificate of said stenographer, or of said surrogate, shall be deemed to be the record of any proofs or proceedings so taken, and this section shall apply to all cases where such oral proofs shall have been taken by a stenographer under the direction of such surrogate. Surrogates may employ stenographers. Duties, compensation, etc. Notes to be authenticated and filed.

§ 2. This act shall not apply to the surrogates' courts of the counties in this state now employing stenographers under any provision of law heretofore enacted. Shall not apply to certain counties.

See vol. 5, pp. 71, 141; vol. 6, pp. 135, 552, 553; vol. 7, p. 495.

§ 3. This act shall take effect immediately.

CHAP. 879.

AN ACT in relation to certain work on section five of the Erie canal.

PASSED May 2, 1871; three-fifths being present.

The People of the State of New York, represented in Senate and Assembly, do enact as follows:

Canal board to make examination, etc. If work not embraced in contract.

SECTION 1. The canal board is hereby authorized and required to make an examination as to certain work performed by Edwin H. French on superintendent's section five of the Erie canal, in the winter and spring of eighteen hundred and sixty-five, and if said board shall find that said work was not embraced in the special notice of letting under which he entered into contract with the state, nor contemplated at the time of the letting, the said board shall award him such amount as they may find he is legally entitled to receive.

§ 2. This act shall take effect immediately.

CHAP. 883.

AN ACT to amend title four of chapter eighteen of part first of the Revised Statutes, entitled "Special provisions relating to certain corporations."

Ante, vol. 1, p. 562.

PASSED May 2, 1871.

The People of the State of New York, represented in Senate and Assembly, do enact as follows:

Amendment to Revised Statutes relating to certain corporations.

SECTION 1. The eleventh section of the fourth title of chapter eighteen of the first part of the Revised Statutes, is hereby amended so as to read as follows: "The provisions of this title shall not apply to any religious society, nor to any moneyed corporation, which shall have been or shall be created, or whose charter shall be renewed or extended after the first day of January, one thousand eight hundred and twenty-eight, and which shall be subject to the provisions of the second title of this chapter.

§ 2. This act shall take effect immediately.

CHAP. 888.

AN ACT in relation to insurance companies, corporations, associations, partnerships and individuals of foreign governments, doing fire insurance business in this state.

PASSED May 3, 1871; three-fifths being present.

The People of the State of New York, represented in Senate and Assembly, do enact as follows:

SECTION 1. No foreign insurance company shall make any contract of insurance of any kind or description against loss or damage by fire or inland navigation risks, nor expose themselves to any such loss by any one risk or hazard for any greater amount in proportion to its capital, as determined by the provisions of this act, than companies organized under the laws of this state may do.

Restrictions as to taking risks.

§ 2. The capital of such foreign insurance company, doing fire insurance business in this state, or any such company hereafter admitted to such business in this state, shall, for all the purposes of this act and of the general insurance laws of this state, be the aggregate value of such sums or securities, as such company shall have on deposit in the insurance and other departments of this state and of the other states of the United States, for the benefit of policyholders in any of such states or in the United States, and all bonds and mortgages for money loaned on real estate in this state, or any state of the United States, provided such loans have been made in conformity with the laws of such state providing for the incorporation of insurance companies therein, and the investment of their capital, and all other assets and property in the United States in which fire insurance companies, organized under the laws of this state, may by the laws thereof invest, provided such bonds and mortgages, assets and property, shall be vested in and held in the United States by trustees approved by the superintendent of the insurance department of this state, and citizens of the United States for the general benefit and security of all its policyholders and creditors in the United States, after taking from such aggregate value the same deductions for losses, debts and liabilities in this and the other states of the United States, and for premiums upon risks therein not yet expired, as is authorized or required by the laws of this state or the regulations of its insurance department with respect to fire insurance companies, organized under the laws of this state. The said trustees are hereby authorized to invest in and hold and convey real estate to the same extent and subject to the same restrictions, rules and regulations to which companies incorporated in this state are subject.

Capital stock aggregate value of securities deposited.

Must be vested in and held in the United States by trustees.

Shall conform to rules of insurance department of this state.

§ 3. To determine the amount of such capital, the agent or attorney of such foreign insurance company, doing fire insurance business in this state, shall, within four months after the passage of this act, and in the month of January of every year

Must render statement of items making up capital.

Superintendent may make examinations, and issue certificate of compliance with requirements.

thereafter, render to him a detailed statement of the items making up the said capital, and of the deductions to be made therefrom, subscribed and verified by the oath of such agent or attorney, and said superintendent shall have authority to make such examination in respect to such assets and liabilities as he shall deem proper, and upon compliance with the requirements of this act, it shall be his duty thereupon, and from year to year thereafter, to issue to such foreign insurance company a certificate of the amount of its so determined capital, and that the requirements of this act have been complied with, upon which capital it may transact business in this state, but subject to all the restrictions and limitations of the laws regulating fire insurance companies, incorporated under the laws of this state.

Trustees to be appointed by board of managers. Must file vote or resolution of appointment with superintendent. Superintendent to have power to examine trustees, etc., under oath, also books, etc.

§ 4. The trustees, referred to in the second section of this act, shall be appointed directly by the board of managers or directors of such foreign insurance company, and a duly certified copy of the vote or resolution by which they were appointed, shall, together with a certified copy of the trust deed or instrument under which they are to act, be filed in the office of the superintendent of the insurance department; and the said superintendent shall have the same power to examine such trustees, or the agent or attorney of such company, under oath, and their assets, books and accounts, either in person or by one or more persons to be appointed by him, as by law he has as to the officers, agents, assets, books and accounts of any company, authorized to do the fire insurance business in this state. And if, by such examination, it shall appear that the net capital, for which the last certificate shall be outstanding, has been materially reduced, the superintendent may call in such certificate and issue another corresponding with such reduced capital.

May call in certificate.

Foreign companies must comply with provisions of this act.

§ 5. No foreign insurance company, or any agent or attorney thereof, shall be admitted to transact the business of fire insurance in this state, to take risks until, in addition to all other requirements of the laws now in force in this state, such company shall comply with the provisions of this act, and receive the certificate of the superintendent of the insurance department mentioned in the third section of this act.

Restrictions as to reinsurance.

§ 6. It shall not be lawful for any such foreign insurance company, their agent or attorney, directly or indirectly, to contract for or effect any reinsurance of any risk on property in this state, with any insurance company, corporation, associations, partnership or individual other than such as companies, chartered by the state of New York, may lawfully make reinsurance in.

Capital subject to taxation.

§ 7. The capital of any foreign insurance company, so determined and certified, shall be subject to taxation the same as the capital of fire insurance companies, organized under the laws of this state, to be levied, assessed and collected, as prescribed by the laws of this state, at such place in this state as such foreign insurance company shall have its principal office.

§ 8. The affairs of every foreign insurance company, doing fire insurance business in this state, shall be subject to the same supervision and examination by the superintendent of the insurance department, as those of fire insurance companies organized under the laws of this state, as to the examination of its books, assets, accounts and general condition; and every foreign insurance company, doing fire insurance business in this state, and its agents and trustees, shall at all times be subject to, and be required to make the same statements, and to answer the same inquiries, and be subject to the same examinations, and in case of default therein, to the same penalties and liabilities as fire insurance companies organized under the laws of this state, or any of the officers thereof, are or may be liable to by the laws of this state or the regulations of its insurance department; and the said superintendent is hereby authorized whenever he shall deem it necessary, either in person or persons by him appointed, to repair to the general office of any such foreign insurance company wherever the same may be, and make an investigation and examination of the affairs and condition of such company. The said superintendent is hereby authorized to cancel and revoke the certificate of any foreign insurance company, refusing or unreasonably neglecting to comply with any of the provisions of this act, or to allow the examination herein provided for to be made, and to prevent such company from doing business in this state.

Affairs subject to laws regulating fire insurance companies in this state.

In default of compliance with requirements, to be subject to penalties.

Superintendent authorized to examine affairs.

Superintendent may cancel certificate.

§ 9. Any violation of any of the provisions of this act shall subject the party so violating to a penalty of five hundred dollars for each violation, which shall be sued for and recovered in the manner provided for in section twenty-five of "An act to provide for the incorporation of fire insurance companies," passed June twenty-five, eighteen hundred and fifty-three, and the amendments thereto, with the same liability to imprisonment in case of non-payment as therein provided.

Penalty for violating provisions of act.

Ante, vol. 4, p. 241.

§ 10. The term foreign insurance company, as used in this act, includes any company, corporation, association, partnership or individual of any foreign government doing fire insurance business in this state, whether incorporated or not.

What included in this act.

§ 11. This act shall take effect immediately.

CHAP. 895.

AN ACT for the erection of a swing bridge across the Chemung canal feeder on Franklin street, in the village of Horseheads.

PASSED May 10, 1871; three-fifths being present.

The People of the State of New York, represented in Senate and Assembly, do enact as follows:

Canal commissioners to construct bridge. SECTION 1. The canal commissioners are hereby authorized and directed to remove the present bridge across the Chemung canal feeder, on Franklin street, in the village of Horseheads, county of Chemung, and construct, in the place thereof, a swing bridge.

Material to be used. § 2. The materials of said bridge directed to be removed, are to be used, so far as the same may be suitable, in the construction of said swing bridge, and the expenses of such removal and construction to be paid out of any moneys appropriated for the extraordinary repairs or improvements of the middle division of the canals.

§ 3. This act shall take effect immediately.

CHAP. 903.

AN ACT to amend section four of chapter six hundred and fifty-five of the laws of eighteen hundred and seventy, entitled "An act to provide for the introduction of an improved system of steam towage upon the canals of this state."

Ante, vol. 7, p. 767.

PASSED May 10, 1871; three-fifths being present.

The People of the State of New York, represented in Senate and Assembly, do enact as follows:

SECTION 1. Section four of chapter six hundred and fifty-five of the laws of eighteen hundred and seventy, is hereby amended so as to read as follows:

Right to cease after three years. § 4. In case the said Norman W. Kingsley, Charles H. Gardner, their associates and successors, or corporation aforesaid, shall neglect or fail to introduce said system of towing on the Erie canal within three years after the passage of this act, all rights and privileges herein granted shall cease.

§ 2. This act shall take effect immediately.

CHAP. 907.

AN ACT relative to savings banks.

PASSED May 10, 1871.

The People of the State of New York, represented in Senate and Assembly, do enact as follows:

SECTION 1. It shall be lawful for the directors or trustees of any savings bank or institution for savings, located in the county of New York, to keep their available fund or any part thereof on deposit in any bank or banking association organized under any law or laws of this state, or of the United States, or in any trust company incorporated by the laws of this state, and receive interest thereon at such rate as may be agreed upon. The bank or trust company in which the deposits of the available fund shall be kept shall be designated by a vote of the majority of all the trustees, exclusive of any who are at the time directors of any bank of discount or trustee of any trust company in which the deposits of such savings bank are authorized by the provisions of this section to be kept; but the sum so kept on deposit in any one bank or trust company shall not exceed twenty per cent of the capital of such bank or trust company, and shall not exceed twenty-five thousand dollars, or ten per cent of the whole amount of deposits with the said savings bank or institution for savings; but nothing in this section shall be construed to relieve any savings bank or institution for savings from investing their deposits or funds, over and above the reserve or available fund, as required by their several charters and the laws relatimg to savings banks.

In New York county, may deposit funds and receive interest thereon.

Place of deposit to be designated by vote of trustees.

Deposits not to exceed 20 per cent of capital.

Not relieved from general laws.

§ 2. It shall be lawful for the trustees of any savings bank to designate by their by-laws the number necessary to constitute a quorum. In all cases where less than a majority is designated, it shall require, to constitute a quorum, the presence of the president and the secretary or the recording officer, or of a vice-president and the secretary or the recording officer; but in no case shall a quorum be constituted less than seven, and the several charters of the savings banks or institutions for savings, located in the city and county of New York, are hereby so amended as to conform to this section, except that this section shall not apply to those savings banks which are now allowed by law to have a quorum less than seven.

Quorum, how designated.

Charters amended to conform to this act.

Exception.

§ 3. It shall be lawful for the directors or trustees of any savings bank or institution for savings in this state, by a resolution to be incorporated in their by-laws, and a copy to be filed with the superintendent of the banking department, to reduce the number of directors or trustees, as provided for in the charter of said bank, to a number not less than fifteen; and thereafter as vacancies occur the same shall not be filled

Power to reduce number of directors.

until the number is reduced to fifteen, or to such greater number as the board in such resolution shall designate.

Repeal. § 4. All acts or parts of acts inconsistent with this act are hereby repealed.

§ 5. This act shall take effect immediately.

CHAP. 911.

AN ACT to provide for the introduction of the American system of cable towage upon the canals of this state.

PASSED May 10, 1871; three-fifths being present.

The People of the State of New York, represented in Senate and Assembly, do enact as follows:

SECTION 1. Permission is hereby granted to James Richmond and William S. Farnell, of the city of Lockport, New York, their associates and successors, who may organize a corporation under the act entitled "An act to authorize the formation of corporations, for manufacturing, mining, mechanical and chemical purposes," passed February seventeenth, eighteen hundred and forty-eight, and any act or acts amendatory thereof, to introduce upon the canals of this state an improved system of cable towage, under a patent or patents to be held or acquired by said corporation, with the exclusive right to use the said system thereon, during the full term for which the said corporation may be organized.

May introduce on canal improved system of towage.

§ 2. The said James Richmond, William S. Farnell, their associates and successors, as heretofore specified, are hereby authorized and empowered to transport cargoes, and to tow boats and floats, loaded or unloaded, for hire, upon the canals of this state, at a rate of speed not exceeding four miles per hour, and which shall not work unusual or permanent injury thereto; and for such purpose may purchase, construct, erect and use thereon, such boats, boilers, engines, apparatus, chains, cables, structures and machinery, as shall be necessary to apply and operate said improved system of cable towage, in such manner as shall not interfere with navigation on said canal. Nothing, however, in this section contained, shall be construed as excluding other parties from the rights or privileges of propelling or towing any boats or floats upon the canals of this state, by the agency of steamboats, propellers, tugs, chains, cables, elevated railways, engines or animal power, but simply to vest in the said James Richmond and William S. Farnell, their associates and successors, or corporation organized as aforesaid, the exclusive right to apply and operate the said improved system of cable towage.

May transport cargoes, etc. Rate of speed. What motor may be used. Not to obstruct navigation. May not exclude others from towing, etc. Exclusive right to improved system.

Necessary machinery exempt from tolls. § 3. The machinery, engines and boilers, used in pursuance of this act, the boats carrying the same, and the fuel and materials necessarily used in propelling the necessary boats and machinery to operate said towage system, shall be exempt from the payment of tolls upon all the canals of this state, but in no case shall fuel or material be exempt from payment of tolls, except when on boats actually using the same.

§ 4. In case the said James Richmond, William S. Farnell, their associates and successors, or corporation aforesaid, shall neglect or fail to introduce said system of towage on the Erie canal, within eighteen months after the passage of this act, all rights and privileges herein granted shall cease. On neglect or failure, privilege to cease.

§ 5. Nothing herein contained shall be construed to exclude the system of towage hereby authorized from the supervision and control of the canal board, but the same shall be subject to all the rules and regulations established, and to be established, by the canal board for the navigation of the canals. System of towing to be under control of canal board.

§ 6. The legislature may, at any other time, repeal, alter or modify the provisions of this act. Legislature may repeal or modify.

§ 7. This act shall take effect immediately.

CHAP. 912.

AN ACT for the construction of a swing bridge over the Cayuga inlet.

PASSED May 10, 1871; three-fifths being present.

The People of the State of New York, represented in Senate and Assembly, do enact as follows:

SECTION 1. The commissioner in charge of the middle division of the canals is hereby authorized and directed to construct an iron swing bridge over the Cayuga inlet, on State street, in the village of Ithaca, in place of the present old structure, heretofore constructed and paid for by the state. Commissioner of middle division of canals shall construct bridge.

§ 2. The sum of two thousand dollars is hereby appropriated out of any moneys in the treasury not otherwise appropriated, for the purposes of this act, and the payments for the construction of the bridge hereby authorized, shall be made upon the certificate of the canal commissioner in charge of the middle division of the canals of this state. Sum appropriated. Payment to be made upon certificate of commissioner.

§ 3. This act shall take effect immediately.

CHAP. 925.

AN ACT to amend chapter nine hundred and seven of the laws of eighteen hundred and sixty-nine, entitled "An act to amend an act entitled 'An act to authorize the formation of railroad corporations and to regulate the same,'" passed April second, eighteen hundred and fifty, so as to permit municipal corporations to aid in the construction of railroads, and also to amend chapter five hundred and seven of the laws of eighteen hundred and seventy, entitled "An act to define the powers of commissioners appointed under chapter nine hundred and seven of laws of eighteen hundred and sixty-nine, bonding municipalities to aid in the construction of railroads."

Ante, vol. 7, p. 517.

PASSED May 12, 1871; three-fifths being present.

The People of the State of New York, represented in Senate and Assembly, do enact as follows:

SECTION 1. Section first of chapter nine hundred and seven of the laws of eighteen hundred and sixty-nine is hereby amended so as to read as follows:

Tax payers may make application to county judge.

§ 1. Whenever a majority of the tax payers of any municipal corporation in this state who are taxed or assessed for property, not including those taxed for dogs or highway tax only, upon the last preceding assessment roll or tax list of said corporation, and who are assessed or taxed, or represent a majority of the taxable property, upon said last assessment roll or tax list, shall make application to the county judge of the county in which such municipal corporation is situate, by petition, verified by one of the petitioners, setting forth that they are such majority of tax payers, and are taxed or assessed for or represent such a majority of taxable property, and that they desire that such municipal corporation shall create and issue its bonds to an amount named in such petition, and invest the same, or the proceeds thereof, in the stock or bonds (as said petition may direct) of such railroad company in this state as may be named in said petition, it shall be the duty of said county judge to order that a notice shall be forthwith published in some newspaper in such county, or, if there be no newspaper published in said county, then in some newspaper printed in an adjoining county, directed to whom it may concern, setting forth that on a day therein named, which shall not be less than ten days nor more than thirty days from the date of such publication, he will proceed to take proof of the facts set forth in said petition as to the number of tax payers joining in such petition, and as to the amount of taxable property represented by them. Any solvent corporation or company assessed or taxed on said last assessment roll or

That town issue bond, and invest same in railroad companies.

Judge to order notice of taking proof of facts.

Solvent corporations may

tax list may join in such petition, and shall have all the rights and privileges under this act as other tax payers. Any person, partnership or corporation upon whom it shall have been intended to levy a tax by virtue of said last assessment list and tax roll, under whatever name, and who shall have paid or are liable to pay such tax thus intended to be assessed and levied, shall be a tax payer, entitled to represent the property thus taxed, and as such entitled to all the rights and privileges of this act. The petition authorized by this section may be absolute or conditional; and if the same be conditional the acceptance of a subscription founded on such petition shall bind the railroad company accepting the same to the observance of the condition or conditions specified in such petition; provided, however, that non-compliance with any condition inserted in such petition shall not in any manner invalidate the bonds created and issued in pursuance of such petition. No municipal corporation shall issue its bonds under the provisions of this act for a greater amount than twenty per centum of the taxable property thereof as appears on its said last assessment list or tax roll. The words "municipal corporation" when used in this act shall be construed to mean any city, town or incorporated village in this state, and the word "taxpayer" shall mean any incorporation or person assessed or taxed for property, either individually or as agent, trustee, guardian, executor or administrator, or who shall have been intended to have been thus taxed and shall have paid or are liable to pay the tax as hereinbefore provided, or the owner of any non-resident lands, taxed as such, not including those taxed for dogs or highway tax only, and the words "tax list or assessment roll" when used in this act shall mean the tax list or assessment roll of said municipal corporation last completed before the first presentation of such petition to the judge. But nothing herein contained shall be construed so as to include the city of New York or the counties of New York, Kings, Erie, Westchester, Onondaga, and the town of Royalton in the county of Niagara, within the provisions of this act.

Join in such petition. Any person, partnership or firm entitled to represent property, and enjoy rights, etc. Petition may be absolute or conditional, and shall be binding on company accepting it. Rate of percentage at which bonds may be issued. Construction of the words "municipal corporation," "tax payer," etc. City and counties excluded from provisions of act.

§ 2. Section two of chapter nine hundred and seven of the laws of eighteen hundred and sixty-nine is hereby amended so as to read as follows:

Ante, vol. 7, p. 518.

§ 2. It shall be the duty of the said judge at the time and place named in the said notice to proceed and take proof as to the said allegations in said petition, and if it shall appear satisfactorily to him that the said petitioners, or the said petitioners and such other tax payers of said municipal corporation as may then and there appear before him and express a desire to join as petioners in said petition, do represent a majority of the tax payers of said municipal corporation as shown by the last preceding tax list or assessment roll, and do represent a majority of the taxable property upon said list or roll, he shall so adjudge and determine, and cause the same to be entered of record in the office of the clerk of the county in which said municipal corporation is situated, and such

Judge to take proof. May adjudge and cause same to be entered in county clerk's office. judgment and the record thereof shall have the same force and effect as other judgments and records in courts of record in this state; and in case any county judge, to whom any such petitions may have been presented, shall be declared incompetent or ineligible, or in any manner disqualified to hear the same, by any court on certiorari from any determination of such county judge in any proceeding under this act had before him, the original petitions, filed with the county clerk in such proceeding and on such determination, may be taken from file and presented to a judge of an adjoining county or a justice of the supreme court; and in all such cases the same proceedings may be had before such county judge or justice of the supreme court as are required by the provisions of this act. The judge shall file the petition as part of the judgment roll, and on making his final determination in any case, he shall forthwith publish notice thereof for three weeks, at least once in each week, in the same newspaper in which notice of such hearing was published as ordered.

Proceedings in case of incompetency of judge to act.

Filing of judgment roll, and notice of final determination.

§ 3. Section ten of chapter nine hundred and seven of the laws of eighteen hundred and sixty-nine is hereby amended so as to read as follows:

Ante, vol. 7, p. 521.

General provisions. § 10. Nothing herein contained shall be construed as permitting any municipal corporation, in or through which a railroad has already been constructed and is in operation, to aid in the construction of any other railroad under the provisions of this act, unless the railroad already built is assessed or taxed upon the assessment roll specified in this act; provided, however, that this section shall not apply to any railroad exempted from taxation by any law of this state.

How act may apply.

Review of proceedings to be by certiorari. § 4. Review of proceedings under the acts hereby amended shall be by certiorari, and no writ of certiorari shall be allowed unless said writ shall be allowed within sixty days after the last publication of notice of the judge's final determination, as provided in section two of this act, and where such judgment is so entered prior to the passage of this act, unless said writ is allowed within sixty days after the passage of this act. On the return of the certiorari the court out of which the same issued shall proceed to consider the matter brought up thereby, and shall review all questions of law and of fact determined for or against either party by the county judge. And the said courts or court of appeals in appeals now pending, and in all future proceedings, may reverse or affirm or modify, in all questions of law or fact, his final determination, or may remand the whole matter back to said county judge to be again heard and determined by him. And it may by order direct that he proceed thereon *de novo*, in the same manner and with the same effect as if he had taken no action therein, or it may by such order specify how and in what particulars he shall hear and determine the same on such remanding thereof. Applications for certiorari shall be on notice. On review, persons taxed for dogs or highway tax only shall not be counted as tax payers unless that claim

When writ may be allowed.

Proceedings on return of writ.

Court of appeals may reverse or affirm, or remand back to county judge.

May direct to proceed *de novo* thereon.

was made before the county judge. The county judge shall forthwith proceed to carry into effect all orders of any court on review under this act.

County judge to carry into effect all orders.

§ 5. Chapter five hundred and seven of the laws of one thousand eight hundred and seventy is hereby amended by adding to the end of section first as follows: But in case such commissioners and such railroad corporation cannot agree, or in case said commissioners refuse to make any agreement, then in either case the supreme court at general term may, on motion and after hearing all parties interested, determine upon what terms and conditions said bonds should be delivered to said railroad corporations, having due regard to the public good, the rights of said municipal corporation, whose bonds are authorized to be issued and the rights of said railroad corporation, and shall have power to compel the delivery of said bonds on such terms and conditions, and in such manner as it shall thus determine upon, by the usual process of the court. Said court shall also, by the usual process of said court in like cases, have power at any time to prevent by injunction the issue of said bonds or any portion thereof, on notice and for good cause shown. And any justice of said court may grant a temporary injunction until such motion can be heard.

On disagreement of commissioners, supreme court to determine conditions for delivering bonds.

Court may, by injunction, prevent issuing of bonds.

Injunction

Ante, vol. 7, p. 751.

§ 6. Section four of chapter nine hundred and seven of laws of eighteen hundred and sixty-nine, as amended by chapter two hundred and eighty-three of the laws of eighteen hundred and seventy-one, is hereby amended by adding at the end thereof as follows: In case of a vacancy in the office of commissioners, or in case all commissioners are notified of any meeting, a majority of the commissioners shall have and exercise all the powers and duties of the three commissioners. The said commissioners may issue the said bonds payable at any time they may elect, less than thirty years, any law heretofore passed to the contrary, but they shall not so issue said bonds that more than ten per cent of the principal of the whole amount of bonds issued shall become due or payable in any one year.

Vacancies. Majority of commissioners may exercise powers.

Bonds when payable.

Ante, vol. 7, p. 518.

§ 7. This act shall take effect immediately.

CHAP. 930.

AN ACT to authorize a tax of one-third mill per dollar of valuation, of the year eighteen hundred and seventy-one, for construction of new work upon, and extraordinary repairs of, the canals of this state.

PASSED May 23, 1871; three-fifths being present.

The People of the State of New York, represented in Senate and Assembly, do enact as follows:

One-third mill tax for new work and extraordinary repairs.

SECTION 1. There shall be imposed for the fiscal year beginning on the first day of October, eighteen hundred and seventy-one, a state tax of one-third mill on each dollar of the real and personal property in this state subject to taxation, which tax shall be assessed, levied and collected by the annual assessment and collection of taxes for that year, in the manner prescribed by law, and shall be paid by the several county treasurers into the treasury of this state, to be held by the treasurer for application to the following purposes, to wit:

EASTERN DIVISION — ERIE CANAL.

Removal of slope wall and wall benches.

For removing slope wall and wall bench, and constructing slope pavement and vertical walls, the sum of seventy-five thousand dollars, thirty-seven thousand five hundred dollars of which shall be appropriated to removing wall benches and constructing slope pavement and vertical wall between Port Schuyler and Lower Mohawk aqueduct.

Construction of slope and vertical wall at Utica.

For removing old slope wall and docking, and constructing vertical wall in cement on the berme side of the Erie canal, in the city of Utica, from the guard-lock eastward one thousand feet, the sum of six thousand five hundred dollars.

Utilizing feed-water.

For utilizing the feed-water at lock thirty-seven, Erie canal, as authorized by resolution of the canal board, bearing date the eighth of December, eighteen hundred and seventy, the sum of four thousand dollars, or so much thereof as may be necessary.

CHAMPLAIN CANAL.

Constructing stop gates at Glens Falls feeder.

For constructing the stop gates near the mouth of the Glens Falls feeder, on the twelve mile level, the sum of two thousand five hundred dollars, or so much thereof as may be necessary. This work to be done by the canal commissioner in charge, by contract or otherwise, as he may deem for the best interest of the state, and to be ready for navigation this spring.

Constructing two locks north of Waterford.

For the construction of two locks on the enlarged plan, and section work connected at the "Three Locks" just north of the village of Waterford, the sum of forty thousand dollars, or so much thereof as may be necessary. This appropriation to be applied to pay the excess over the cost of rebuilding the "Three Locks" on the old plan. The Fort Miller dam shall be built in a line parallel with the old structure, and not exceeding twenty feet below the same. To build Fort Miller dam.

For dredging of points of elbow and other points of Whitehall basin, and paying percentage retained under existing contracts, as may be directed by the commissioner in charge, the sum of ten thousand dollars, or so much thereof as may be necessary. Dredging at Whitehall basin.

In addition to the appropriation made by chapter seven hundred and sixty-seven, laws of eighteen hundred and seventy, for vertical wall on the Glens Falls feeder at Sandy Hill, now under contract and in process of construction, the further sum of seven thousand dollars, or so much thereof as may be necessary, is appropriated for the same object, and to protect and make secure the tow-path bank adjacent to and above the said work. Additional appropriation for vertical wall on Glens Falls feeder.

BLACK RIVER CANAL.

To pay the balance on final account on the work of enlarging, widening and deepening the first level of the Black river canal, as authorized by chapter five hundred and seventy-nine, laws of eighteen hundred and sixty-seven, the sum of twenty-five hundred dollars, and to pay the balance on final account for building a wooden bridge over the Black river canal, as authorized by chapter eight hundred and seventy-seven, laws of eighteen hundred and sixty-nine, the sum of three hundred and five dollars and sixty-three cents. To pay balance on enlarging, etc., first level. To pay balance for wooden bridge.

For changing plans of bridges on the eastern division, the sum of fifteen thousand dollars. Changing plans of bridges.

MISCELLANEOUS.

For removing wall benches and constructing vertical wall from a point on the berme bank of the Erie canal, where the second bridge west of the Utica guard-lock intersects said canal, to a point eight hundred feet easterly thereof; and for the construction of a road bridge over the Erie canal at Jason street, in the city of Utica, the sum of nine thousand five hundred dollars. For removing wall benches and constructing vertical wall at Utica. For road bridge in Utica.

For removing wall benches and constructing six hundred feet of vertical wall on the berme bank of the Erie canal between Madison street and a point one hundred and fifty feet easterly of Washington street, and for removing wall benches and constructing five hundred feet of vertical wall on the berme bank of the Erie canal easterly of Lynch street, in the city of Rome, the sum of eight thousand dollars, or so much thereof as may be necessary. Removing wall benches and constructing vertical wall. Removing wall benches, constructing vertical wall at Rome.

MIDDLE DIVISION — ERIE CANAL.

For completing Cowasselon aqueduct, the sum of two thousand dollars. Completing Cowasselon aqueduct.

Protecting lands at head of Onondaga lake.

For the payment of amount to be expended in protecting the land lying at the head of Onondaga lake, in the county of Onondaga, from high-water rise in said lake, pursuant to act chapter one hundred and forty-two of the laws of eighteen hundred and seventy, the sum of seventy-five hundred dollars, or so much thereof as may be necessary.

Completing excavation at bottom of canal, between lock 47 and Limestone creek feeder.

For continuing and completing the excavating bottom of the Erie canal, between lock forty-seven and Limestone creek feeder the sum of five thousand dollars, or so much thereof as may be necessary. This appropriation shall be applied to pay the repair contractor the difference only between the cost of excavating the same to the uniform original depth as required by the original terms of his contract, and the necessary depth, as recommended by the state and division engineer.

Completing culvert

For completing culvert near Burdick's bridge, the sum of six hundred dollars.

OSWEGO CANAL.

Rebuilding high dam.

For prosecuting the rebuilding of high dam, the sum of twenty-two thousand dollars.

For removing dam and cribs, and protecting berme bank.

How work shall be done.

Repair contractor to execute bond for performance.

For removing the Horse Shoe dam and cribs above, and protecting berme bank near said dam, the sum of five thousand five hundred dollars, or so much thereof as may be necessary. The remainder of the cost, if any, shall be paid from any money appropriated for ordinary repairs of the canals. This work shall be done by the repair contractor, under the direction of the canal commissioner in charge. Provided, however, that before commencing the said work said repair contractor shall execute and deliver to said commissioner a good and sufficient bond, conditioned that he will perform such portion of work in removing said dam as may belong to him to do under his repair contract, without making any claim upon the state for the same, and no portion of this appropriation shall be expended until such bond has been so executed.

To pay heirs of Geo. W. Humphrey

To pay the heirs of George W. Humphrey, a final estimate for work done on enlargement of sections nineteen and twenty, according to the final estimate on file in the auditor's office, the sum of two thousand dollars.

Raising low banks.

For raising the low banks on the river levels, now in progress, the sum of fifteen thousand dollars.

CAYUGA AND SENECA CANAL.

Protecting berme bank at Seneca lake.

For protecting the berme bank of the canal along the shore of Seneca lake from damage in time of high water, the sum of ten thousand dollars.

Bottoming out original material.

For bottoming out original material between Cayuga free bridge, left undone under the stop law of eighteen hundred and sixty-two, the sum of five hundred dollars.

CROOKED LAKE CANAL.

For reconstructing feeder and lengthening lake lock, the sum of three thousand dollars. *Reconstructing feeder, etc.*

GENERAL.

For changing plan of bridges on the middle division of the canals, the sum of twenty thousand dollars. *Changing plan of bridges.*

To pay for construction of road bridge on the Chemung canal feeder, authorized by chapter five hundred and seventy-eight, laws of eighteen hundred and seventy, for which no appropriation has been made, the sum of forty-seven hundred and seventy-nine dollars. *Constructing road bridge on Chemung canal feeder.*

For construction of a culvert or sewer under and across the Cayuga and Seneca canal at Waterloo, the sum of thirty-five hundred dollars. *Constructing culvert at Waterloo.*

For constructing a road bridge over the Erie canal, just easterly of the Cowaselon creek, in the town of Lenox, authorized by law, for which no appropriation has been made, the sum of four thousand dollars, or so much thereof as may be necessary. *Road bridge east of Cowaselon creek, in town of Lenox.*

For construction of a swing bridge across the Chenango canal, on East Main street, in the village of Norwich, and removing the present bridge across said canal on East Main street to Rexford street in said village, the sum of forty-five hundred dollars, or so much thereof as may be necessary. *Swing bridge across Chenango canal, at Norwich.*

For the construction of a bridge over the Chenango canal at the village of Bouckville, in the county of Madison, the sum of two thousand one hundred and fifty dollars, or so much thereof as may be necessary, in accordance with chapter five hundred and eighty-eight of laws of eighteen hundred and seventy-one. *Bridge over Chenango canal, at Bouckville.*

For the construction of a swing bridge over the Chenango canal in the village of Sherburne, in place of the old bridge at that point, the sum of three thousand dollars, to carry out the provisions of chapter five hundred and thirty-one of the laws of eighteen hundred and seventy-one, or so much thereof as may be necessary. *Swing bridge over Chenango canal at Sherburne.*

For the construction of a swing bridge over the Chenango canal, in the village of Hamilton, the sum of four thousand five hundred dollars, or so much thereof as may be necessary, in accordance with chapter three hundred and ninety-seven of the laws of eighteen hundred and seventy-one. *Swing bridge over Chenango canal at Hamilton.*

To pay the late repair contractor for superintendent's section number one, Chenango canal, for permanent improvements, twenty-five thousand eight hundred and thirty-five dollars, and the canal commissioner shall issue his draft for the same on his approval of the certificate of the assistant engineer in charge of said section at the time of the surrender of his contract. *To pay late repair contractor of section number one, Chenango canal.*

For construction of a swing bridge across the Chenango canal, in the city of Binghamton, at a point where said canal *Swing bridge over*

Chenango canal at Binghamton. intersects Chenango street in said city, the sum of four thousand dollars, or so much thereof as may be necessary.

To raise and repair approaches at Warren st. bridge, Syracuse. To raise and repair the approaches to the Warren street bridge, at the intersection of Warren and James streets, in the city of Syracuse, with wood pavement, nine thousand dollars, or so much thereof as may be necessary.

To clean out and put in repair drain in Big Flats and Painted Post. The sum of seven thousand dollars is hereby appropriated to clean out and put in proper repair the drain made by the state upon the lands of Thomas Noyes, Reuben Mundy and others in the towns of Big Flats, county of Chemung, and of Painted Post, in the county of Steuben, authorized by chapter seven hundred and forty-seven of laws of eighteen hundred and seventy.

For bulkhead or other structure in outlet of Owasco lake by direction of canal commissioners. The sum of fifteen hundred dollars is hereby appropriated for the construction of a bulkhead or other adequate structure in or upon the outlet of the Owasco lake, for the purpose of storing water in the Owasco lake for canal purposes, said sum, or so much thereof as may be necessary, to be expended by and under the direction of the canal commissioner in charge of the middle division of the Erie canal.

Extending breakwater, etc., at Watkins. For extending breakwater and dredging out and other improvements of the harbor at Watkins, on the Chemung canal, the sum of fifteen thousand dollars, or so much thereof as may be necessary.

Vertical wall at Weedsport. To pay for excavation and vertical wall of wood or stone on the berme bank of the Erie canal in or near the village of Weedsport, the sum of five thousand dollars, or so much thereof as is necessary.

Stone pier or breakwater at Seneca Falls, conditions of appropriation, etc. For a stone pier or breakwater in the Seneca river at Seneca Falls, the sum of eight thousand dollars, or so much thereof as may be necessary, if, in the opinion of the board of canal commissioners, the same is necessary to protect the state against all claims for damages; provided, however, and upon the express condition, that all persons affected thereby shall execute to the board of canal commissioners a good and suffcient release in writing, free of expense to the state, of all claims for damages which they have existing against the state, and which may hereafter arise in consequence of the construction of said work.

For ditch near Canastota. For ditch on berme side Erie canal, near Canastota, three hundred and seventy-five dollars, or so much thereof as may be necessary.

For completing extension of Chenango canal. For completing the Chenango canal extension from the point of its commencement, near Binghamton, to Owego, and opening the same for navigation, the sum of one hundred and seventy-five thousand dollars, or so much thereof as may be necessary; said sum, or any part thereof, to be used for no other purpose whatever.

For completing Oneida lake canal. For completing the Oneida lake canal, the sum of twenty-five thousand dollars, or so much thereof as may be necessary; said sum, or any part thereof, to be used for no other purpose whatever.

WESTERN DIVISION — ERIE CANAL.

For reconstructing docking along the channel leading to Niagara river, below ship lock at Black Rock, the sum of six hundred dollars. For constructing docking at Black Rock.

For constructing guard piers, and protecting and securing swing bridge at Ferry street in Black Rock harbor, the sum of five thousand dollars. For guard piers, etc., in Black Rock harbor.

For constructing a pipe sewer at Tonawanda, under the Erie canal, the sum of three thousand five hundred dollars. For pipe sewer at Tonawanda.

For constructing a stop gate at Holley, the sum of three thousand dollars. Stop gate at Holley.

To pay for vertical wall at Macedon, authorized by act chapter two hundred and eighty-one, laws of eighteen hundred and sixty-nine, and for constructing a bridge across State ditch, and improving grade of main road bridge approach leading to New York Central depot at that place, the sum of five thousand four hundred dollars. For vertical wall and bridge across State ditch, at Macedon.

For continuing and completing the work now under contract for deepening, improving and protecting channel leading from waste-weir at Newark, the sum of two thousand dollars. Completing work at waste-weir, at Newark.

For reducing bottom of canal through rock cuts on construction sections numbers two hundred and seventy-seven, two hundred and seventy-eight, two hundred and eighty-two, two hundred and eighty-three, two hundred and eighty-five, and two hundred and eighty-six, long level, the sum of fifteen thousand dollars. Reducing bottom of canal on construction sections, etc.

For sidewalks on Fulton street bridge in the city of Buffalo, five hundred dollars. Sidewalks at Buffalo.

For vertical wall on the north side of the Main and Hamburgh street canal between Louisiana and Hamburgh streets, the sum of ten thousand dollars, or so much thereof as may be necessary. Vertical wall on Main and Hamburgh street canal.

To re-imburse Benjamin F. Sherman for expense incurred in procuring and inserting tile drain in and filling up a large ditch constructed and left open by the state through his lots in the village of Clyde, and leading to a culvert under the Erie canal in said village, the sum of four hundred dollars, or so much thereof as may be necessary. To re-imburse Benj. F. Sherman for tile drain at Clyde.

For constructing iron Whipple arch truss bridge over Erie canal, at Black Rock, first bridge below Black Rock lock, the sum of five thousand dollars, or so much thereof as may be necessary; the canal commissioner in charge of the western division shall issue his draft to the repair contractor therefor when completed. Iron bridge over Erie canal at Black Rock.

For the construction of a swing bridge at Rochester, and bridge connecting Munger and Averill streets in said city, authorized by chapter three hundred and forty-eight, laws of eighteen hundred and seventy-one, twenty thousand dollars, or so much thereof as may be necessary. Bridges at Rochester.

The item "for opening channel for surplus waters from culvert and waste-weir on Erie canal, near Mabies, in the town of Royalton, county of Niagara, three thousand dollars," raised For opening channel on Erie canal, at Royalton. Re-appropriation. and appropriated by act chapter seven hundred and sixty-seven of the laws of eighteen hundred and seventy, not having been expended by reason of the non-compliance with the conditions of said appropriation, the same is hereby re-appropriated, to be expended in the completion of unfinished work, in the manner authorized and provided for by act, chapter five hundred and eighty-one of the laws of eighteen hundred and seventy.

Completing work authorized by chapter 581, laws of 1870. For completing unfinished work authorized for by act chapter five hundred and eighty-one of the laws of eighteen hundred and seventy, to be expended in the manner prescribed by said act, the sum of three thousand dollars, or so much thereof as may be necessary.

Removing material from prism of Erie canal. For removing original material from the prism of the Erie canal on construction sections numbers two hundred and seven, two hundred and eight, two hundred and nine, and two hundred and twelve, to improve the navigation on the same, the sum of five thousand five hundred dollars.

Stone abutment at Mount Morris. For constructing a stone abutment and docking at east end of dam across Genesee river at Mount Morris, thirteen thousand dollars, or so much thereof as may be necessary.

Work under contract for Genesee Valley canal. To pay for work now under contract, and for protecting Genesee Valley canal against the encroachments of the Genesee river, twelve thousand dollars, or so much thereof as may be necessary.

For moving lock at Nunda. For moving lock at Nunda on the Genesee Valley canal, the sum of ten thousand dollars, or so much thereof as may be necessary. This amount to be paid from any money appropriated or to be appropriated for extraordinary repairs of the canals.

MISCELLANEOUS.

Bridges, change of plan. Two road bridges over Erie canal. For changing plan of bridges constructed and to be constructed on western division, including the building of two road bridges over the Erie canal, one on construction section number two hundred and sixty-seven, at the town line between Gates and Greece, and one on construction section number two hundred and seventy-five, in the town of Ogden, forty-five thousand dollars, or so much thereof as may be necessary.

Vertical walls at Bushnell's basin and Cartersville. For constructing vertical walls at Bushnell's basin and Cartersville, the sum of three thousand dollars, or so much thereof as may be necessary.

Vertical wall at Fairport. For vertical wall at Fairport, commencing at the east end of the vertical wall on the berme side of the Erie canal, the sum of one thousand dollars.

To pay allowances made by canal board in previous year. For the payment of the allowances made by the canal board during the year eighteen hundred and seventy, with interest thereon as allowed by law, the sum of thirty-eight thousand four hundred and ten dollars and sixty-five cents.

Powers of canal commissioners In order to remove all doubts in respect to the authority of the canal commissioners to commence the new works for which appropriations are herein made, and no legislative direction is otherwise given by special laws, it is hereby declared that the said canal commissioners are hereby authorized to construct or cause to be constructed all such new works for which appropriations are herein made, subject, however, to all restrictions, provisions and conditions contained in this act. No part or portion of the moneys herein appropriated for new work shall be expended or paid, nor shall any contract involving such expenditure and payment be made on behalf of this state, until the maps, plans and estimates for such new work shall have been submitted to and approved by the canal board. All contracts for work or material on any canal (other than ordinary repairs) which shall be directed by the canal board to be advertised and let, shall be made with the persons who shall offer to do or provide the same at the lowest price with adequate security for their performance, which letting shall be under regulations to be made by the board of canal commissioners as to the form, regularity and validity of all bids, securities and contracts. And the canal commissioners may require the deposit by the proposer for said work or materials of such a sum in money, United States bonds or stocks of the state of New York, not exceeding twenty nor less than eight per cent of the aggregate estimate of the work to be let, as they may deem necessary to secure the entering into said contract.

to perform work under this act.

Canal board to approve plan and estimates.

Restrictions upon making contracts.

Canal commissioners may require deposits.

And in case the proposer, to whom such work shall be awarded, shall neglect or refuse to enter into said contract, the sum so deposited shall be forfeited to the state, and the commissioners shall pay the same into the state treasury, and it shall become a part of the canal fund. And upon the entering into said contract, the sum of money, bonds or stocks required by the commissioners as security for the entering into said contract, together with such other additional securities as they may require, may be held as security for the completion of the work; and shall be paid into the treasury of the state, and be invested by the commissioners of the canal fund, as they shall deem advisable, until the said contract shall be fully completed, and final settlement thereof made, at which time the said sum, with the accumulated interest thereon, shall be repaid to the said contractor by the treasurer, upon the warrant of the auditor.

Proposer to forfeit sum deposited on a failure to fulfill contract.

Money, bonds, etc. required as security — how invested.

But in case he shall enter into said contract and fail in the performance thereof, the same shall be declared abandoned by said commissioners, pursuant to the terms of the contract, then the sum of money so deposited shall be forfeited to the state, and paid into the treasury and become a part of the canal fund.

On failure in performance, forfeiture and disposition of sums deposited.

The canal board may, in the resolution authorizing any work to be let, prescribe the length of time of advertising not less than ten days. No more money shall be expended on the works hereinbefore enumerated than is above appropriated, and it shall not be lawful for the officers having in charge the execution of the said works to make any contracts whereby an expenditure in excess of the appropriation will be incurred, or any further appropriation for the same rendered necessary.

Canal board may prescribe time for advertising.

Restrictions upon making contracts in excess of appropriations.

Investment of surplus moneys of sinking fund to meet tax.

To meet the appropriations made in this act of the moneys to be collected by and upon the said tax with as little delay as practicable, the commissioners of the canal fund or comptroller may, from time to time, invest in the said tax any surplus moneys of the principal of the sinking funds under article seven of the constitution, a sum or sums not exceeding in all the amount to be realized from said tax hereby authorized; and the moneys so invested shall be applied to pay the appropriation under this act; and so much of the moneys arising from the said tax as may be necessary, when paid into the treasury, is hereby pledged, and shall be applied in the first instance, to reimburse the said sinking funds for the amount invested in said tax, and for the interest on the same, at a rate not exceeding six per cent per annum, from the time of investment to the day of payment. The final account for any new work authorized by the provisions of this act, or any previous acts, or for which money has been or is hereby appropriated, may be subject to revision by the canal board.

Reimbursement thereof.

Final accounts for new work to be subject to revision by canal board.

§ 2. This act shall take effect immediately.

CHAP. 934.

AN ACT in reference to apprentices and employers.

PASSED May 27, 1871.

The People of the State of New York, represented in Senate and Assembly, do enact as follows:

Consent of legal guardian before taking a minor as apprentice.

SECTION 1. On and after the passage of this act, it shall not be lawful for any person or persons in this state to employ or take as an apprentice any minor person to learn the art or mystery of any trade or craft without first having obtained the consent of such person's legal guardian or guardians; nor shall any minor person be taken as an apprentice aforesaid unless an agreement or indenture be drawn up in writing, in accordance with the provisions of this act, and duly executed under seal by the person or persons employing said apprentice, and also by the parents or parent, if any be living, or by the guardian or guardians of said apprentice, and likewise by said minor person so becoming an apprentice.

Indentures in writing.

By whom executed.

Contents of indentures.

§ 2. Said agreement or indenture, in order to make the law valid, shall contain the following covenants and provisions:

Must be bound for a term of years.

1. That said minor person shall be bound to serve his employer or employers for a term of not less than three nor more than five years.

Shall not leave during term of apprenticeship.

2. That said minor person so indentured shall not leave his said employer or employers during the term for which he shall be indentured, and if any said apprentice so indentured as aforesaid shall leave his said employer or employers, except as hereinafter provided, the said employer or employ-

May compel return

ers may compel the return of the said apprentice under the penalties of this act. of apprentice.

3. That said employer or employers shall covenant and agree in said indenture to provide at all times during the continuance of the same, suitable and proper board, lodging and medical attendance for said apprentice, and said employer or employers shall also further covenant and agree to teach or cause to be carefully and skillfully taught to his or their said apprentice every branch of his or their business to which said apprentice may be indentured, and said employer or employers shall be further bound, at the expiration of said apprenticeship, to give to said apprentice a certificate in writing, stating that said apprentice has served a full term of apprenticeship of not less than three nor more than five years, at such trade or craft as may be specified in said indenture. Agreement of employer in indentures. Must give certificate in writing stating full service of apprenticeship.

§ 3. Any person or persons taking an apprentice without complying with the provisions of this act shall be deemed guilty of a misdemeanor, and on conviction thereof in the court of sessions of general or special sessions, held in and for the county in which the business of said employer or employers may be conducted, shall be subject to a fine of not less than five hundred dollars, the fine to be paid to the treasurer of said county for the use and benefit of said county. Non-compliance deemed a misdemeanor. Penalty.

§ 4. Any and all indentures made under and in pursuance of the provisions of this act shall not be canceled or anulled before the expiration of the term of said indentures, except in case of death; or, by the order of or judgment of the county or supreme court of this state for good cause, and any apprentice so indentured who shall leave his employer or employers without his or their consent or without sufficient cause, and shall refuse to return, may be arrested upon the complaint of said employer or employers, and taken before any magistrate having jurisdiction of misdemeanors, who may cancel said indentures, and on conviction commit said apprentice to the house of correction, house of refuge, or county jail, in and for said county, for such length of time as such magistrage may deem just, or until said apprentice shall have attained the age of twenty-one years, and in case said apprentice so indentured shall willfully neglect or refuse to perform his portion of the contract as specified in said indenture, then said indenture may be canceled in the manner aforesaid, and said apprentice so violating said indentures shall forfeit all back pay and all claims against said employer or employers, and said indentures shall be canceled. Indentures, how canceled. Proceedings in case of violation on part of apprentice. Punishment for leaving employer. On neglect of apprentice to perform his part of contract, indenture may be canceled.

§ 5. Should any employer or employers neglect or refuse to teach or cause to be taught to said apprentice the art or mystery of the trade or craft to which said apprentice has been indentured, or fail at any time to provide suitable or proper board, lodging and medical attendance, said apprentice individually, or his parent or parents, guardian or guardians, may bring an action against said employer or employers, to recover damages sustained by reason of said neglect or refusal; and, if proved to the satisfaction of the court, said court shall May bring action on failure of employer to provide for and teach apprentices. And if proven, indentures to be canceled, and fine imposed. direct said indentures to be canceled, and may impose a fine on said employer or employers, not exceeding one thousand and not less than one hundred dollars, and said fine shall be collected and paid over to said apprentice or his parent or guardian for his sole use and benefit.

Indentures conflicting with this act invalid. § 6. Any indentures made and executed, wherein parts conflict with or are not in accordance with the provisions of this act, shall be invalid and without any binding effect.

Repeal. § 7. All acts or parts of acts inconsistent herewith are hereby repealed.

§ 8. This act shall take effect immediately.

CHAP. 935.

AN ACT to amend an act entitled "An act to incorporate the United States Inebriate Asylum for the reformation of the poor and destitute inebriate," passed April fifth, eighteen hundred and fifty-four, and the act amending the same, passed April twenty-third, eighteen hundred and fifty-five, and the act amending the same, passed March twenty-seven, eighteen hundred and fifty-seven, and to amend the several acts in relation to the New York State Inebriate Asylum and to change the number of its trustees and the mode of their appointment, and directing the management of said asylum.

PASSED May 29, 1871; three-fifths being present.

The People of the State of New York, represented in Senate and Assembly, do enact as follows:

Governor to appoint fifteen trustees. SECTION 1. The governor is hereby authorized to appoint fifteen trustees of the New York State Inebriate Asylum, designating at the time of such appointment their respective Classification of trustees. terms of office with reference to the following classification, to wit: five of said trustees shall serve for four years, five for five years, and five for six years, from the time of their appointment, and they shall hold their offices until others are Subject to removal, for cause, by senate. appointed in their stead, and shall be subject to be removed for cause, at any time, by the senate, upon the recommendation of the governor. Their successors shall be appointed by the governor, by and with the advice and consent of the senate, and shall hold their offices for six years, and until others are appointed in their stead, and subject to be removed in the manner aforesaid. Property of asylum vested in. The property, affairs and concerns of the New York State Inebriate Asylum shall be vested in, managed and conducted by, the said board of trustees. Board to appoint officers. And said trustees shall have power to fix and appoint the officers of said asylum, and determine their compensation respectively.

§ 2. The said trustees, as such, shall receive no compensation for their services, but may receive their actual and reasonable traveling expenses, and said trustees and other officers shall have no interest, direct or indirect, in the furnishing of any building materials, supplies or thing, or on any contract for labor, for said asylum. No compensation for services.

§ 3. The aforesaid acts, and the several acts in relation to said asylum, are repealed so far only as to give this act full force and effect. Repeal of former acts.

Ante, vol. 240, p. 464.

§ 4. This act shall take effect immediately.

CHAP. 936.

AN ACT to allow further costs in suits brought by working women.

PASSED May 29, 1871.

The People of the State of New York, represented in Senate and Assembly, do enact as follows:

SECTION 1. In any action hereafter brought in the district court for any judicial district in the city of New York, or in any justice's court in the city of Brooklyn, by or in behalf of any female employee, or by the parent or guardian of any such female employee, for the recovery of any sum of money for wages earned, or materials furnished, by such employee to any person or persons, there shall be allowed to the plaintiff, in addition to the costs now allowed by law, the sum of five dollars in addition to the amount recovered in said action; and in case the amount recovered by the plaintiff shall exceed ten dollars, there shall be allowed the plaintiff, in addition to the costs now allowed by law, the sum of ten dollars. If any action brought by any female employee shall be settled, the plaintiff shall be entitled to the sums above mentioned, in addition to the costs, the same as though such action had been tried; but this act shall not be construed so as to apply to any action brought by any person employed as a domestic or servant. Additional costs to be allowed in New York and Brooklyn. When action is settled. How act to be construed.

§ 2. The clerks of said several courts shall tax said sums as costs, and shall thereupon insert the same in the judgment. Said sums to be taxed as costs.

§ 3. This act shall take effect immediately.

CONCURRENT RESOLUTIONS

OF THE

SENATE AND ASSEMBLY.

CONCURRENT RESOLUTIONS relative to a portion of the Allegany reservation occupied by the Seneca nation of Indians, becoming populated by white people and asking for a sale of the whole or a part of said reservation.

WHEREAS, A portion of the Allegany reservation occupied by the Seneca nation of Indians has become populated by the white people; and

WHEREAS, They have been induced to make settlements thereon, especially in the town of Salamanca, on account of the natural business location of the place and a ratification by the legislature of the state of New York, of leases made by them with the Seneca nation of Indians; and

WHEREAS, The sale of this reservation was recommended by the Indian agent in eighteen hundred and sixty-eight; and

WHEREAS, It has become a matter of importance to the white settlers who have made improvements and invested their means in business pursuits thereon; therefore

Resolved (if the senate concur), That the senators from this state in congress be instructed and the representatives be requested to procure the passage of some act or the formation of a treaty with the Seneca nation of Indians, whereby title may be obtained to the whole or a portion of the Allegany reservation, or such relief secured for white settlers as the circumstances demand.

Resolved (if the senate concur), That the governor of the state of New York be authorized at any time to appoint a commissioner on behalf of the state to act in conjunction with a commissioner appointed by the United States for the purpose of carrying out the foregoing object.

Resolved (if the senate concur), That the governor be requested to transmit a copy of the foregoing preamble and resolutions to each of the senators and representatives in the congress of the United States from this state.

STATE OF NEW YORK,
In Assembly, *January* 18, 1871.

The foregoing resolutions were duly passed.
By order of the assembly.
C. W. ARMSTRONG,
Clerk.

STATE OF NEW YORK,
In Senate, *January* 25, 1871.

The foregoing resolutions were duly concurred in.
By order of the senate.
HIRAM CALKINS,
Clerk.

CONCURRENT RESOLUTION relative to investigation of the causes for the disaster on the Hudson River Railroad, at Wappinger's creek.

WHEREAS, The senate did, on the ninth day of February, eighteen hundred and seventy-one, adopt a resolution authorizing and directing the standing committee on railroads of that body to inquire into and ascertain the causes of the recent terrible disaster on the Hudson River Railroad at Wappinger's creek, and also to inquire into other matters relating to the safety of the public; and

WHEREAS, On the same day, the assembly adopted a similar resolution; and

WHEREAS, The subpœnaing and examination of witnesses from various parts of the state upon the same subject before different committees and at different times, entails a double expense upon the state and a great annoyance to the witnesses themselves; therefore,

Resolved (if the senate concur), That the standing committees of each branch of the legislature be authorized and directed to act in joint session under the resolution of the senate, and to report thereunder to both the senate and assembly.

STATE OF NEW YORK,
In Assembly, *February* 14, 1871.

The foregoing resolution was duly passed.
By order of the assembly.
C. W. ARMSTRONG,
Clerk.

STATE OF NEW YORK,
In Senate, *February* 14, 1871.

The foregoing resolution was duly passed.
By order of the senate.
HIRAM CALKINS,
Clerk.

STATE OF NEW YORK,
In Senate, Albany, *February* 28, 1871.

Resolved (if the assembly concur), That the senators and representatives in congress from this state be respectfully requested to use every exertion before the adjournment of the present congress to repeal the income tax.

Resolved (if the assembly concur), That a copy of this resolution be transmitted to our representatives in congress.

By order.

HIRAM CALKINS,
Clerk.

STATE OF NEW YORK,
In Assembly, *February* 28, 1871.

The foregoing resolutions were duly concurred in.

By order.

C. W. ARMSTRONG,
Clerk.

CONCURRENT RESOLUTION authorizing the governor to confer brevet commissions upon officers of the national guard, in certain cases.

Resolved (if the senate concur), That the governor be and is hereby authorized to confer upon any officer of the national guard of the state of New York, who has been or may hereafter be honorably discharged from the military service of this state, and has re-entered or may hereafter re-enter said service as an officer, a brevet commission, corresponding in rank with the commission highest in grade, which such officer may have received from the governor of this state.

STATE OF NEW YORK,
In Assembly, *March* 1, 1871.

The above resolution was duly passed.

By order of the assembly.

C. W. ARMSTRONG,
Clerk.

STATE OF NEW YORK,
In Senate, *March* 14, 1871.

The above resolution was duly passed.

By order of the senate.

HIRAM CALKINS,
Clerk.

CONCURRENT RESOLUTION relative to rate of toll upon the canals.

Resolved (if the assembly concur), That the canal board be respectfully requested to reduce the rates of toll upon apples, potatoes, and all esculent roots, to one mill per thousand pounds per mile, being the rate imposed until the toll sheet of eighteen hundred and fifty-two.

STATE OF NEW YORK,
In Senate, *March* 1, 1871.

The foregoing resolution was duly passed.

By order.

HIRAM CALKINS,
Clerk.

STATE OF NEW YORK,
In Assembly, *March* 22, 1871.

Concurred in without amendment.

By order.

C. W. ARMSTRONG,
Clerk.

CONCURRENT RESOLUTION for the appointment of an agent to collect claims due the state from the United States.

WHEREAS, There is believed to be due to the state of New York, by the United States, an amount of indebtedness for expenditures made by the state for the suppression of the late rebellion, which can be collected by supplying deficient testimony and proper explanations; therefore,

Resolved (if the assembly concur), That the governor be authorized to appoint a special agent to prepare and collect such claims from the United States, on behalf of the State; the said agent to receive as compensation for the services thus rendered, such a percentage of the amount collected as the governor may deem proper to be allowed.

STATE OF NEW YORK,
In Senate, *March* 27, 1871.

The foregoing resolution was duly passed.

By order.

HIRAM CALKINS,
Clerk.

STATE OF NEW YORK,
In Assembly, *March* 30, 1871.

Concurred in.

By order.

C. W. ARMSTRONG,
Clerk.

ELECTION of superintendent of public instruction.

STATE OF NEW YORK,
ALBANY, *April* 4, 1871.

We certify, that at a joint convention of the senate and assembly, held in the assembly chamber, on the fourth day of April, one thousand eight hundred and seventy-one, pursuant to law, and a concurrent resolution of both houses, Abram B. Weaver, of the county of Oneida, having received a majority of all the votes cast, was duly elected superintendent of public instruction for the term of three years, from the first Tuesday of April, one thousand eight hundred and seventy-one.

Witness our hands and the seals of the senate and assembly, this fourth day of April, one thousand eight hundred and seventy-one.

[L. S.] ALLEN C. BEACH,
President Senate.
HIRAM CALKINS,
Clerk Senate.

[L. S.] WILLIAM HITCHMAN,
Speaker Assembly.
C. W. ARMSTRONG,
Clerk Assembly.

CONCURRENT RESOLUTIONS proposing an amendment of the constitution relative to bribery.

Resolved (if the assembly concur), That section two of article two of the constitution be amended so that it shall read as follows: "Laws may be passed excluding from the right of suffrage all persons who have been or may be convicted of bribery or larceny, or of any infamous crime, and for depriving every person who shall make or become directly or indirectly interested in any bet or wager depending upon the result of any election, or who shall pay, give or receive, or promise to pay or give money or other property, or valuable consideration, with intent to influence any elector in giving his vote, or to deter any elector from voting, from the right to vote at such election, or from holding any office voted for at such election.

Resolved (if the assembly concur), That said amendment to said section two be referred to the legislature, to be chosen at the next general election of senators, and that pursuant to section one of article thirteen of the constitution, it be published for three months previous to the time of such election.

STATE OF NEW YORK,
In Senate, *April* 4, 1871.

The foregoing resolutions were duly passed.

By order.

HIRAM CALKINS,
Clerk.

STATE OF NEW YORK,
In Assembly, *April* 19, 1871.

The foregoing resolutions were duly passed.
By order.

C. W. ARMSTRONG,
Clerk.

CONCURRENT RESOLUTION relative to the court of appeals, and for the extension of the term of service of the commissioners of appeals.

Resolved (if the assembly concur), That the sixth article of the constitution of this state be amended by adding thereto the following section:

§ 28. The court of appeals may order any of the causes, not exceeding five hundred in number, pending in that court at the time of the adoption of this provision, to be heard and determined by the commissioners of appeals, and the legislature may extend the term of service of the commissioners of appeals for a period not exceeding two years.

Resolved (if the assembly concur), That the foregoing amendment be referred to the legislature to be chosen at the next general election of senators; and that in conformity to section one of article thirteen of the constitution, it be published for three months previous to the time of such election.

STATE OF NEW YORK,
In Senate, *April* 4, 1871.

The foregoing resolutions were duly passed.
By order.

HIRAM CALKINS,
Clerk.

STATE OF NEW YORK,
In Assembly, *April* 19, 1871.

The foregoing resolutions were duly concurred in.
By order.

C. W. ARMSTRONG,
Clerk.

CONCURRENT RESOLUTION relative to printing the Transactions of the American Institute of the city of New York.

Resolved (if the senate concur), That twenty copies of the [illegible] report of the Transactions of the American Institute of the city of New York, for the year ending in April, eighteen hundred and seventy, be printed for each member, officer and reporter of the legislature, fifteen hundred copies for the use of said institute; twenty copies for each agricultural society in counties electing one member of assembly; and a proportionate number in counties electing more than one member of assembly; ten copies for each town or union agricultural society; and fifty copies for the regents of the university; and that the said report be bound in the same manner as last year, and distributed as designated without delay.

STATE OF NEW YORK,
In Assembly, *April* 5, 1871.

The foregoing resolution was duly passed.
By order of the assembly.
C. W. ARMSTRONG,
Clerk.

STATE OF NEW YORK,
In Senate, *April* 21, 1871.

The foregoing resolution was duly passed.
By order of the senate.
HIRAM CALKINS,
Clerk.

CONCURRENT RESOLUTION relative to printing the transactions of the New York State Agricultural Society for the year eighteen hundred and seventy.

Resolved (if the senate concur), That fifteen copies of the transactions of the New York State Agricultural Society for the year eighteen hundred and seventy, be printed for each member, officer and reporter, of the legislature; fifteen hundred copies for the use of the society; twenty copies for the county agricultural society in each county electing one member of assembly, and a proportionate number in counties electing more than one member of assembly; fifteen copies for each town and union agricultural society; four hundred and twenty copies for the American Institute in the city of New York, and one hundred copies for the regents of the university; and that the said report be bound in the same manner as last year, and distributed as above provided without delay.

STATE OF NEW YORK,
In Assembly, *April* 7, 1871.

The foregoing resolution was duly passed.
By order of the assembly.
C. W. ARMSTRONG,
Clerk.

STATE OF NEW YORK,
In Senate, *April* 21, 1871.

The foregoing resolution was duly passed.
By order of the senate.
HIRAM CALKINS,
Clerk.

CONCURRENT RESOLUTION relative to furnishing copies of the reports of the regents of the university.

Resolved (if the assembly concur), That fifteen hundred copies of the report of the regents of the university on the State Museum of Natural History be printed in the usual form for the use of the regents, and three hundred for the use of the curator.

STATE OF NEW YORK,
In Senate, *April* 20, 1871.

This resolution was duly passed.
By order.
HIRAM CALKINS,
Clerk.

STATE OF NEW YORK,
In Assembly, *April* 21, 1871.

Concurred in.
By order.
C. W. ARMSTRONG,
Clerk.

CONCURRENT RESOLUTION relative to furnishing copies of the State Homœopathic and Eclectic Medical Societies.

Resolved (if the assembly concur), That there be printed for each senator, officer and reporter of the senate, ten copies each of the transactions of the State Homœopathic Medical Society and the State Eclectic Medical Society, and five hundred copies of the State Medical Society, and of the State Homœopathic Medical Society, for the use of the State Homœopathic Medical Society, and five hundred extra copies of the State Eclectic Medical Society, for the use of said society.

STATE OF NEW YORK,
In Senate, *April* 20, 1871.

This resolution was passed.
By order.
HIRAM CALKINS,
Clerk.

STATE OF NEW YORK,
In Assembly, *April* 21, 1871.

Concurred in.

By order.
C. W. ARMSTRONG,
Clerk.

CONCURRENT RESOLUTION relative to centennial celebration of the independence of the United States, at the city of Philadelphia.

Resolved (if the senate concur), That John T. Hoffman, governor of this state, and three persons to be appointed by him, the Hon. Allen C. Beach, lieutenant-governor, and five members of the senate to be appointed by him, the Hon. William Hitchman (the speaker of this house), and seven members of the assembly to be appointed by him, shall be a committee of the state of New York to co-operate with committees of other states upon the subject of the centennial celebration of the independence of the United States, to be held at the city of Philadelphia in the year eighteen hundred and seventy-six; and said committee thus appointed to act until the end of such celebration. They are hereby required to report to each intervening legislature and make such recommendations and suggestions to the legislature, from time to time, as they may think proper and expedient in reference to said centennial celebration. The said committee thus appointed shall bear and pay its own expenses, so that no charge for the same shall be made against the state.

STATE OF NEW YORK,
In Assembly, *April* 21, 1871.

The foregoing resolution was duly passed.
By order of the assembly.
C. W. ARMSTRONG,
Clerk.

STATE OF NEW YORK,
In Senate, *April* 21, 1871.

The foregoing resolution was duly passed.
By order of the senate.
HIRAM CALKINS,
Clerk.

APPENDIX.

RULES AND REGULATIONS established by the judges of the court of appeals, in relation to admission of attorneys, solicitors and counselors in the courts of this state.

STATE OF NEW YORK, *ss:*

The judges of the court of appeals, pursuant to the provisions of chapter 486 of the laws of 1871, ordain and establish the following rules and regulations in relation to the admission of persons hereafter applying to be admitted as attorneys, solicitors and counselors in the courts of this state.

I.

No person shall be permitted to practice as an attorney, solicitor or counselor in any court of record of this state, without a regular admission and license by the supreme court at a general term thereof. To obtain such admission and license, except in cases otherwise provided for by said act, the person applying must be examined under the direction of the court. The time for the examination of persons applying to be admitted as attorneys, solicitors and counselors, shall be Thursday of the first week of each general term, in the several departments; and the time for taking the oath of office shall be on such day thereafter as the court may direct.

The examinations shall in all cases be public, and unless conducted by the judges of the court, shall be by not less than three practicing lawyers of at least seven years standing at the bar, to be appointed by the court.

II.

To entitle an applicant to an examination, he must prove to the court:

1. That he is a citizen of the United States, and that he is twenty-one years of age, and a resident of the department within which the application is made, and that he has not been examined in any other department for admission to practice and been refused admission and license, within three months immediately preceding, which proof may be made by his own affidavit of the facts.

2. That he is a person of good moral character, by the certificate of the attorneys with whom he has passed his clerkship, but which certificate shall not be deemed conclusive evidence, and the court must be satisfied on this point after a full examination and inquiry.

3. That he has served the clerkship or pursued the substituted course of study prescribed by the rules as requisite to an examination. The clerkship may be proved by the certificate of the attorneys with whom the same was served, or, in case of their death or removal from the state, by such other evidence as shall be satisfactory to the court.

The proof of any time of study allowed as a substitute for any part of the clerkship required by these rules, shall be by the certificate of the teacher or president of the faculty, under whose instructions the person has studied, together with the affidavit of the applicant; the proof must be satisfactory to the presiding judge of the court, who alone shall make the order allowing a reduction from the regular term of clerkship by reason of such studies.

III.

No person shall be admitted to examination as an attorney, solicitor or counselor, unless he shall have served a regular clerkship of three years in the office of a practicing attorney of the supreme court, after the age of seventeen years.

IV.

It shall be the duty of the attorney with whom the clerkship shall be commenced, to file a certificate in the office of the clerk of the court of appeals, certifying that the person has commenced a clerkship with him, and the clerkship shall be deemed to have commenced on the day of the filing of the certificate. A copy of the certificate, certified by the clerk of the court of appeals, with the date of the filing thereof, shall be produced to the court at the time of an application for examination.

V.

When a clerkship has already commenced, or shall have commenced before these rules shall take effect, the certificate required by the preceding rule, verified by the affidavit of the attorney, stating the time of the actual commencement of such clerkship, may be filed at any time before the first day of November next.

VI.

It shall be the duty of an attorney to give to a clerk, when he shall leave his office, a certificate stating his moral character, the time of clerkship which he has passed with him, and the period which has been allowed him for vacation.

Not more than three months shall be allowed for vacations in any year.

The term of clerkship will be computed by the calendar year, and any person applying for admission, whose period of clerkship shall expire during the term at which the application shall be made, will be admitted to examination at the customary day of the same term.

VII.

Any portion of time, not exceeding one year, actually spent in regular attendance upon the law lectures in the university of New York, Cambridge university, or the law school connected with Yale college, or a law school connected with any college or university of this state, having a department organised with competent professors and teachers, in which instruction in the science of law is regularly given, shall be allowed in lieu of an equal period of clerkship in the office of a practicing attorney of the supreme court.

VIII.

Persons who have been admitted and have practiced three years as attorneys in the highest court of law in another state, may be admitted without examination, to practice as attorneys, solicitors and counselors in the courts of this state. But such persons must have become residents of this state before applying for admission, and must bring a letter of recommendation from one of the judges of the highest court of law in the state from which they came.

IX.

These rules shall take effect on the first day of June, 1871.

Dated ALBANY, *May* 1, 1871.

S. E. CHURCH,
W. F. ALLEN,
M. GROVER,
R. W. PECKHAM,
CHAS. A. RAPALLO,
CHAS. J. FOLGER,
CHAS. ANDREWS.

Indorsed, "Filed May 4, 1871."

D. WILLERS, Jr., *Dep. Secretary of State.*

AMENDMENTS to rules and regulations for admission of attorneys and counselors.

STATE OF NEW YORK, *ss:*

The judges of the court of appeals, pursuant to the provisions of chapter 486 of the laws of 1871, make the following amendments to the rules established by them May 1, 1871, in relation to the admission of attorneys and counselors in the courts of this state:

As to persons who had been, during one year or more, immediately preceding the first of May, 1871, engaged in the study of the law in the office of a practicing lawyer, or in any law school, or in the law department of any college or university, with the view of applying for admission to practice in the courts of this state, the said rules, adopted May 1, 1871, shall not take effect until June 1, 1872, but on proof of the facts to the satisfaction of the presiding justice of the general term at which such persons may apply for admission, they shall, at any time before June 1, 1872, be entitled to admission according to the laws and practice existing at the time of the adoption of said rules.

Graduates of the university of the city of New York, who shall have commenced their course of study in the law department of that university at any time prior to May 1, 1872, shall, on complying with the requirements of chapter 187 of the laws of 1870, be entitled to admission upon the examination and in the manner provided in that act.

But the proofs of citizenship, age, residence and good moral character required by said rules, adopted May 1, 1871, must be made by all applicants for admission referred to in this amendment.

ALBANY, *June* 14, 1871.

S. E. CHURCH,
W. F. ALLEN,
CHAS. A. RAPALLO,
CHAS. ANDREWS.

Indorsed, "Filed June 16, 1871."

D. WILLERS, JR., *Dep. Secretary of State.*

TITLES

OF ALL THE

LAWS OF THE STATE OF NEW YORK,

PASSED AT THE

NINETY-FIFTH SESSION OF THE LEGISLATURE.

1872.

[The titles of the acts included in this compilation are in this list printed in italics.]

CHAP. 1. An Act to provide for the payment of certain bonds of the city and county of New York. Passed January 10, 1872; three-fifths being present.

CHAP. 2. An Act to amend an act entitled "An act to revise the charter of the city of [illegible]," passed April twenty-eighth, eighteen hundred and seventy. Passed January [illegible], 1872; three-fifths being present.

CHAP. 3. An Act to authorize the Poughkeepsie and Eastern Railroad Company to cancel a portion of its first mortgage bonds and to substitute therefor bonds of a larger denomination. Passed January 18, 1872.

CHAP. 4. An Act to amend an act passed April twenty-sixth, eighteen hundred and sixty-nine, entitled "An act for the election of a receiver of taxes and assessments for the town of Cortlandt and village of Peekskill." Passed January 23, 1872; three-fifths being present.

CHAP. 5. An Act to legalize the acts of Robert H. Hill, a justice of the peace of the town of Kingston, Ulster county. Passed January 24, 1872; three-fifths being present.

CHAP. 6. An Act to legalize the official acts and proceedings of Cyrillo S. Lincoln, a justice of the peace of the town of Naples, county of Ontario. Passed January 24, 1872; three-fifths being present.

CHAP. 7. An Act to confirm orders of the court of general sessions of the peace in and for the city and county of New York, continuing the last November term thereof; and to define the construction of chapter ten of the laws of eighteen hundred and sixty-two, entitled "An act to empower the court of the general sessions of the peace, in and for the city and county of New York, to extend its terms and to authorize its adjournments." Passed January 24, 1872; three-fifths being present.

CHAP. 8. An Act to incorporate "The Association of the Bar of Oneida county." Passed January [illegible], 1872.

CHAP. 9. An Act relating to appropriations and deficiencies in the city and county of New York, and the audit and payment of salaries and claims in said city and county. Passed January [illegible], 1872; three-fifths being present.

CHAP. 10. *An Act to authorize the extension of the time for the collection of taxes in the several towns of this state. Passed January* 30, 1872; *three-fifths being present.*

CHAP. 11. An Act in relation to filling vacancies in the board of public instruction in the city of [illegible]. Passed January 31, 1872; three-fifths being present.

CHAP. 12. *An Act prescribing the officers and employees that may be elected, appointed or employed by the senate and assembly, fixing the salary and compensation thereof, and regulating the proceedings of investigating committees and providing for the payment of the expenses thereof. Passed February 1, 1872; three-fifths being present.*

CHAP. 13. An Act to legalize and confirm the acts and proceedings of Henry C. Duryea, as special surrogate of the county of Orange. Passed February 2, 1872; three-fifths being present.

CHAP. 14. An Act to authorize the railroad commissioners of the town of Lowville, in Lewis county, to issue bonds on said town in place of others now falling due, and otherwise amending chapter four hundred and twenty-six of the laws of eighteen hundred and sixty-six. Passed February 2, 1872; three-fifths being present.

CHAP. 15. An Act to confirm the title of Horace T. Cook to the office of a justice of the peace, and to legalize his official acts as such justice of the peace. Passed February 2, 1872; three-fifths being present.

CHAP. 16. An Act to extend and define the jail liberties of the city and county of Albany Passed February 5, 1872; three-fifths being present.

CHAP. 17. *An Act to increase the duties of clerks of boards of supervisors. Passed February 6, 1872.*

CHAP. 18. An Act to repeal section two of an act entitled "An act to further amend the charter of the village of Albion, in the county of Orleans," passed April twenty-seventh, eighteen hundred and seventy-one. Passed February 7, 1872.

CHAP. 19. An Act to legalize the vote of the town of Mount Morris, in the county of Livingston, at the town meeting of said town held on the seventh day of March, eighteen hundred and seventy-one, by which certain moneys were voted to be paid to the estate of McNiel Seymour, deceased, and to Noble Denison, and authorizing the board of town auditors of said town to audit and allow, and the board of supervisors of said county to levy and collect the same. Passed February 7, 1872; three-fifths being present.

CHAP. 20. An Act to amend an act entitled "An act to widen and improve a portion of Washington avenue in the city of Brooklyn, and extend the same into the town of Flatbush," passed April twenty-third, eighteen hundred and seventy. Passed February 7, 1872; three-fifths being present.

CHAP. 21. An Act to provide for the establishment of fire limits in the village of Tonawanda, Erie county, N. Y. Passed February 7, 1872; three fifths being present.

CHAP. 22. An Act for the relief of Patrick Mullins, by providing for the release of his real estate from the lien of a certain bond executed by him. Passed February 7, 1872; three-fifths being present.

CHAP. 23. An Act relative to lands in the city of Brooklyn, county of Kings, devised in and by the last will and testament of Leffert Lefferts, deceased, to Elizabeth Dorothea Brevoort for and during her natural life. Passed February 8, 1872.

CHAP. 24. An Act to authorize the board of education of district number nine, in the town of Perrinton, to construct a school building, and provide means for payment therefor. Passed February 8, 1872; three-fifths being present.

CHAP. 25. An Act to incorporate the Lockport Driving Park Association. Passed February 8, 1872; three-fifths being present.

CHAP. 26. *An Act to amend an act entitled "An act in relation to the fees of sheriffs except in the counties of New York, Kings and Westchester," passed April twelve, eighteen hundred and seventy-one. Passed February 8, 1872; three-fifths being present.*

CHAP. 27. An Act to authorize the town of Herkimer, Herkimer county, to issue bonds upon its credit for the purpose of raising money to be contributed toward building a new court-house for said county in said town. Passed February 8, 1872; three-fifths being present.

CHAP. 28. An Act to amend an act entitled "An act in relation to the bonded debt of the town of East Chester, county of Westchester," passed April nineteenth, eighteen hundred and seventy-one. Passed February 8, 1872; three-fifths being present.

CHAP. 29. An Act to amend an act entitled "An act relating to appropriations and deficiencies in the city and county of New York, and the audit and payment of salaries and claims in said city and county," passed January thirtieth, eighteen hundred and seventy-two. Passed February 9, 1872; three-fifths being present.

CHAP. 30. An Act to amend an act entitled "An act to amend the act incorporating the village of Plattsburgh, passed April thirteenth, eighteen hundred and fifty-nine," passed April twenty, eighteen hundred and seventy-one. Passed February 10, 1872; three-fifths being present.

CHAP. 31. An Act to amend an act entitled "An act to incorporate the village of Port Richmond," passed April twenty-fourth, eighteen hundred and sixty-six. Passed February 10, 1872; three-fifths being present.

CHAP. 32. An Act relative to lands held in trust by Harry G. Moore for the benefit of Nehemiah Denton and his descendants. Passed February 10, 1872.

CHAP. 33. An Act to amend an act entitled "An act to incorporate the Manhattan Dispensary of the city of New York," passed May sixth, eighteen hundred and seventy; and authorizing a change in the name thereof. Passed February 12, 1872; three-fifths being present.

CHAP. 34. An Act authorizing and requiring the town of Naples, Ontario county, to raise a further sum of money to provide for the completion and furnishing of the Town and Soldiers' Memorial Hall, in said town. Passed February 12, 1872; three-fifths being present.

CHAP. 35. An Act to authorize the county treasurer of Kings county to designate one of his assistants to act as deputy in his absence. Passed February 13, 1872; three-fifths being present.

CHAP. 36. An Act to change the name of the Mutual Protection Life Assurance Society and provide for an increase of its capital. Passed February 13, 1872.

CHAP. 37. An Act to change the name of Flatbush Avenue Industrial School and Nursery. Passed February 15, 1872.

CHAP. 38. *An Act providing for appeals from the decisions of county superintendents of the poor. Passed February* 15, 1872; *three-fifths being present.*

CHAP. 39. An Act to amend an act passed April twenty-second, eighteen hundred and sixty-two, entitled "An act to incorporate the Union Home and School for the education and maintenance of the children of volunteers," and the act amendatory thereof, passed March thirtieth, eighteen hundred and sixty-six. Passed February 15, 1872.

CHAP. 40. An Act to provide for supplying the village of Flushing, Queens county, with pure and wholesome water. Passed February 15, 1872; three-fifths being present.

CHAP. 41. An Act to authorize the trustees of the village of Clyde, Wayne county, New York, to raise by tax the sum of twelve hundred dollars, wherewith to pay the indebtedness existing against said village. Passed February 15, 1872; three-fifths being present.

CHAP. 42. An Act to authorize the election of a police justice in and for the village of Flushing, Queens county, and to prescribe his duties and compensation, and regulating charges in criminal proceedings in said village. Passed February 16, 1872; three-fifths being present.

CHAP. 43. An Act to incorporate the Little Falls Water-works Company. Passed February 16, 1872; three-fifths being present.

CHAP. 44. An Act in relation to the filing of the certificate of incorporation of "The Keating Lumber Company." Passed February 16, 1872.

CHAP. 45. An Act supplementary to, and amendatory of, "An act in relation to a public park in the city of Albany, passed May fifth, eighteen hundred and sixty-nine, and the acts supplementary and amendatory thereof. Passed February 16, 1872; three-fifths being present.

CHAP. 46. An Act to amend an act entitled "An act to amend and consolidate the charter of the village of Middletown," passed March thirty-one, eighteen hundred and sixty-six. Passed February 17, 1872; three-fifths being present.

CHAP. 47. An Act to amend an act entitled "An act to reorganize the fire department of the city of Albany," passed March twenty-nine, eighteen hundred and sixty-seven. Passed February 19, 1872; three-fifths being present.

CHAP. 48. *An Act in relation to superintendents of the poor. Passed February* 19, 1872; *three-fifths being present.*

CHAP. 49. An Act to amend the certificate of incorporation, or charter, of the Midnight Mission. Passed February 19, 1872.

CHAP. 50. An Act to authorize the village of Flushing, Queens county, to borrow money and issue bonds therefor, for the purpose of paying the floating indebtedness of said village, and for the general improvement thereof. Passed February 19, 1872; three-fifths being present.

CHAP. 51. An act to authorize the election of an additional justice of the peace in the town of Manlius, in the county of Onondaga. Passed February 19, 1872; three-fifths being present.

CHAP. 52. An Act to incorporate the Delhi Water Company. Passed February 19, 1872; three-fifths being present.

CHAP. 53. An Act to confirm the conveyance of real and personal estate by the "Beth El" congregation of Jews of the city of New York, to the congregation "Shaaray Tefila," of the city of New York. Passed February 23, 1872.

CHAP. 54. An Act to extend to the towns of Skaneateles and Spafford, of the county of Onondaga, the provisions of the act entitled "An act to amend an act entitled 'An act to authorize the formation of railroad corporations, and to regulate the same,' passed April second, eighteen hundred and fifty, so as to permit municipal corporations to aid in the construction of railroads, passed May the fifteenth, eighteen hundred and sixty-nine," and of acts amendatory thereof. Passed February 23, 1872; three-fifths being present.

CHAP. 55. An Act to establish the tenth ward in the city of Utica. Passed February 27, 1872; three-fifths being present.

CHAP. 56. *An Act relating to the settling, signing and sealing of bills of exceptions in criminal cases. Passed February 27, 1872.*

CHAP. 57. An Act for the relief of John N. Dunn and Eliphalet J. Swain. Passed February 27, 1872; three-fifths being present.

CHAP. 58. An act to authorize Orson Richards and Eber Richards to construct and maintain a swing bridge over the Glens Falls feeder, in the village of Sandy Hill. Passed February 27, 1872.

CHAP. 59. An Act to amend chapter five hundred and thirty-nine of the laws of eighteen hundred and seventy, entitled "An act in relation to jurors in the city and county of New York." Passed February 28, 1872; three-fifths being present.

CHAP. 60. An Act to amend an act entitled "An Act to amend the several acts incorporating the village of Weedsport, in the county of Cayuga," passed April seventh, eighteen hundred and fifty-seven. Passed February 28, 1872; three-fifths being present.

CHAP. 61. An Act to authorize the extension of the time for the collection of taxes in the town of Moriah, Essex county. Passed February 28, 1872; three-fifths being present.

CHAP. 62. An Act extending the provisions of certain laws permitting municipal corporations to aid in the construction of railroads, in the towns of Salina and Clay and the village of Liverpool, in the county of Onondaga. Passed February 28, 1872; three-fifths being present.

CHAP. 63. An Act to extend the time for the collection of taxes in the city of Oswego. Passed February 28, 1872; three-fifths being present.

CHAP. 64. An Act to amend chapter one hundred and forty-eight of the laws of eighteen hundred and sixty-seven, entitled "An act to amend an act entitled 'An act to condense and amend the several acts incorporating or relating to the village of Skaneateles,'" passed April sixteenth, eighteen hundred and fifty-seven, passed March twenty-fifth, eighteen hundred and sixty-seven. Passed February 29, 1872; three-fifths being present.

CHAP. 65. *An Act to repeal section forty-three of chapter seven hundred and twenty-one, of the laws of eighteen hundred and seventy-one, entitled "An act to amend and consolidate the several acts relating to the preservation of moose, wild deer, birds and fish," passed April twenty-sixth, eighteen hundred and seventy-one. Passed February 29, 1872; three-fifths being present.*

CHAP. 66. An Act to amend an act entitled "An act requiring the highway tax of the New York Central Railroad Company through the town of Mentz, to be applied to the repairs of certain highways in the said town," passed April second, one thousand eight hundred and sixty-two. Passed February 29, 1872; three-fifths being present.

CHAP. 67. An Act to authorize the city of Oswego to convey by deed certain land in said city. Passed February 29, 1872; three-fifths being present.

CHAP. 68. An act to authorize the Harlem and New York Navigation Company to issue bonds and to mortgage its real estate to secure the payment of the same. Passed February 29, 1872.

CHAP. 69. An Act to amend an act entitled "An act to authorize the trustees of the village of Ellenville to borrow money for the purpose of introducing water into the village, and to control and regulate the use of the same," passed April fifth, eighteen hundred and sixty-six, and supplemental thereto. Passed February 29, 1872; three-fifths being present.

CHAP. 70. *An Act for the erection of an iron bridge over the Champlain canal at Comstock's Landing, in the county of Washington. Passed February* 29, 1872; *three-fifths being present.*

CHAP. 71. An Act to amend an act entitled "An act to authorize the Watervliet Turnpike Company to construct and maintain a railroad on their present road, and to extend the same into and through the village of West Troy and Cohoes and the town of Watervliet and the city of Albany, to increase the capital stock and to alter their corporate name," passed April fifteenth, eighteen hundred and sixty-two, by increasing the capital stock of the company for the purpose of paying the outstanding bonds thereof. Passed February 29, 1872.

CHAP. 72. An Act to amend chapter one hundred and fifty-six of the laws of eighteen hundred and sixty-eight, entitled "An act to incorporate the village of Greenport, Suffolk county." Passed March 1, 1872; three-fifths being present.

CHAP. 73. An Act to extend the time for the collection of taxes in Richmond county. Passed March 1, 1872; three-fifths being present.

CHAP. 74. An Act to authorize the extension of the time for the collection of taxes in the town of Liberty, Sullivan county. Passed March 1, 1872; three-fifths being present.

CHAP. 75. An Act to extend, widen, alter and improve Banker street, to close a portion of the same, and to improve Union avenue, in the city of Brooklyn. Passed March 2, 1872; three-fifths being present.

CHAP. 76. An Act legalizing the conveyance of the fair grounds of the Cattaraugus County Agricultural Society. Passed March 4, 1872.

CHAP. 77. An Act to amend an act entitled "An act to amend an act entitled 'An act to revise the charter of the city of Utica,' passed February twenty-eight, eighteen hundred and sixty-two," passed February twenty-fifth, eighteen hundred and seventy. Passed March 4, 1872.

CHAP. 78. An Act to authorize the city of Watertown to borrow money and issue bonds of the city therefor, for the purpose of liquidating its present indebtedness. Passed March 4, 1872; three-fifths being present.

CHAP. 79. An Act to amend an act entitled "An act to incorporate the city of Cohoes," passed May nineteenth, eighteen hundred and sixty-nine, and the act amendatory of the same, passed May eleventh, eighteen hundred and seventy-one. Passed March 4, 1872; three-fifths being present.

CHAP. 80. An Act to amend an act entitled "An act to renew and amend an act entitled 'An act relative to the General Society of Mechanics and Tradesmen of the city of New York,'" passed April first, eighteen hundred and fifty-six. Passed March 4, 1872.

CHAP. 81. *An Act to amend an act passed April nineteenth, eighteen hundred and seventy-one, entitled "An act to amend an act entitled 'An act to authorize the formation of railroad corporations and to regulate the same,'" passed April second, eighteen hundred and fifty. Passed March* 5, 1872; *three-fifths being present.*

CHAP. 82. *An Act to prevent the cutting or taking of ice from Chautauqua lake at certain points therein. Passed March* 6, 1872; *three-fifths being present.*

CHAP. 83. An Act to repeal chapter three hundred and thirty-seven of the laws of eighteen hundred and sixty-five, entitled "An act to prevent manufacturers of fish guano and oil from emptying their refuse waters into the harbors and bays of Suffolk county," passed April eight, eighteen hundred and sixty-five. Passed March 6, 1872.

CHAP. 84. An Act to amend the charter of the village of Potsdam. Passed March 6, 1872; three-fifths being present.

CHAP. 85. An Act to establish the rates of toll on the Western plank-road, in the counties of Franklin and Clinton. Passed March 7, 1872; three-fifths being present.

CHAP. 86. An Act authorizing the canal commissioner of the eastern division to raise a certain road-bed in the town of Kingsbury, county of Washington. Passed March 7, 1872; three-fifths being present.

CHAP. 87. An Act to extend the time for beginning the construction of the road of the Cattaraugus Railway Company. Passed March 7, 1872; three-fifths being present.

Chap. 88. An Act to authorize the electors of the town of Lodi, in the county of Seneca, to vote at their annual town meeting for or against levying a tax of one thousand dollars upon the taxable property of said town, to secure the use and occupation of a town hall for the public purposes of said town. Passed March 7, 1872; three-fifths being present.

Chap. 89. An Act to legalize the acts of Stafford Wade, Leverett Spring and Aaron A. Spencer, commissioners of the town of Arcade, in purchasing certain bonds and coupons of said town with moneys arising from the sale of certain railroad stock belonging to said town, and to authorize said commissioners to cancel the same. Passed March 7, 1872; three-fifths being present.

Chap. 90. An Act to release the interest of the people of the state of New York in and to certain lands in Oneida county to George A. Reynolds. Passed March 7, 1872, by a two-third vote.

Chap. 91. *An Act supplementary to and amendatory of chapter eighty of the laws of eighteen hundred and seventy, entitled "An act to provide for the enrollment of the militia, for the organization of the national guard of the state of New York and for the public defense, and entitled the military code." Passed March 7, 1872; three-fifths being present.*

Chap. 92. *An Act to amend an act entitled "An act to amend an act passed March twenty-three, eighteen hundred and fifty, entitled "An act for the protection of purchasers of real estate upon sales by order of surrogates;" passed April twenty, eighteen hundred and sixty-nine. Passed March 7, 1872; three-fifths being present.*

Chap. 93. An Act to confer additional powers upon the New York Steam Cable Towing Company, a corporation organized pursuant to the requirements of chapter five hundred and seventy-six of the laws of eighteen hundred and seventy, and to authorize said company to issue the preferred stock and bonds thereof. Passed March 8, 1872; three-fifths being present.

Chap. 94. An Act to incorporate the Moose River Improvement Company. Passed March 8, 1872.

Chap. 95. An Act to legalize certain obligations incurred by the city of Brooklyn. Passed March 8, 1872; three-fifths being present.

Chap. 96. An Act in relation to Columbia College, in the city of New York. Passed March 8, 1872; three-fifths being present.

Chap. 97. An Act to authorize the Bruynswick Rural Cemetery Association, in the county of Ulster, to acquire title to property for burial purposes. Passed March 8, 1872.

Chap. 98. An Act to divide the county of Sullivan into two school commissioner districts. Passed March 8, 1872; three-fifths being present.

Chap. 99. An Act to enable the Shepherd Fold of the Protestant Episcopal church in the state of New York to take by grant and hold real estate to the amount of one hundred thousand dollars in value. Passed March 9, 1872; three-fifths being present.

Chap. 100. *An Act in relation to the dividends of life insurance companies. Passed March 9, 1872.*

Chap. 101. An Act to amend an act entitled "An act to amend an act entitled 'An act to incorporate the village of Port Byron,'" passed May twelfth, eighteen hundred and sixty-nine. Passed March 9, 1872; three-fifths being present.

Chap. 102. An Act to incorporate the Onondaga County Milk Association. Passed March 12, 1872.

Chap. 103. An Act to authorize the city of Buffalo to raise money to extend the supply of water to the city and its inhabitants, and for that purpose to issue its bonds. Passed March 12, 1872; three-fifths being present.

Chap. 104. *An Act in relation to trustees and directors of charitable and benevolent institutions. Passed March 12, 1872.*

Chap. 105. An Act for the division of the town of Huntington, in the county of Suffolk, and the erection of a new town from the southern part of said town, and for the apportionment of the town property and town debts. Passed March 13, 1872; three-fifths being present.

Chap. 106. An Act to authorize the extension of the time for the collection of taxes in the town of Plattsburgh, in the county of Clinton. Passed March 13, 1872; three-fifths being present.

CHAP. 107. An Act to extend the time for the collection of taxes in the towns of Jamaica, Hempstead, North Hempstead and Oyster Bay, county of Queens. Passed March 15, 1872; three-fifths being present.

CHAP. 108. An Act to authorize Dodge and Stevenson Manufacturing Company to issue preferred stock. Passed March 15, 1872.

CHAP. 109. An Act to authorize the village of Silver Creek, in the county of Chautauqua, to purchase, hold, use and convey certain real estate, and to legalize proceedings relative thereto. Passed March 15, 1872; three-fifths being present.

CHAP. 110. An Act releasing the interests of the state in certain lands, of which Hannah Jane Butcher died possessed, to William Butcher, her surviving husband. Passed March 15, 1872, by a two-third vote.

CHAP. 111. An Act granting jurisdiction to the United States over a certain piece of land, within this state, to be occupied as a site for offices and storehouses in the construction, repair and maintenance of a pier for the formation of a harbor, at Oswego, New York. Passed March 15, 1872, by a two-third vote.

CHAP. 112. An Act to release the interest of the people of the state of New York in and to certain lands in Sullivan county to Harry Eisner. Passed March 15, 1872, by a two-third vote.

CHAP. 113. *An Act to relieve juvenile delinquents from certain disqualifications. Passed March 18, 1872.*

CHAP. 114. *An Act in relation to limited partnerships. Passed March* 18, 1872.

CHAP. 115. *An Act to supply the deficiency in the appropriation to pay the expenses of the superintendence, ordinary repairs and maintenance of the canals for the remainder of the fiscal year, which commenced on the first day of October, eighteen hundred and seventy-one, and to regulate the manner of drawing warrants by the auditor of the canal department upon the treasurer. Passed March* 19, 1872; *three-fifths being present.*

CHAP. 116. *An Act to amend an act entitled "An act to facilitate the forming of agricultural and horticultural societies," passed April thirteenth, eighteen hundred and fifty-five. Passed March* 19, 1872.

CHAP. 117. An Act relating to the Erie Railway Company, repealing chapter nine hundred and sixteen of the laws of eighteen hundred and sixty-nine, so far as relates to the classification of directors of the Erie Railway Company and the prolongation thereby of their terms of office, and vacating the offices of directors of said company had thereunder and ordering a new election for a full board of directors of said company, and providing regulations relating to the elections of directors of said company and the transfer of its stock. Passed March 20, 1872.

CHAP. 118. An Act to amend an act entitled "An act to incorporate the village of Chateaugay, in the county of Franklin," chapter four hundred and thirteen, laws of eighteen hundred and sixty-nine, and an act amendatory thereof. Passed March 20, 1872; three-fifths being present.

CHAP. 119. An Act to release to Mary Wheleleam the real estate of which John Wheleleam died seized, in the town of Canandaigua, county of Ontario. Passed March 20, 1872, by a two-third vote.

CHAP. 120. *An Act to authorize the descent of real estate to female citizens of the United States and their descendants, notwithstanding their marriage with aliens. Passed March* 20, 1872, *by a two-third vote.*

CHAP. 121. An Act to incorporate the "New Rochelle Mænnerchor." Passed March 20, 1872.

CHAP. 122. An Act to authorize the Cazenovia and De Ruyter Railroad Company to take increased fare on their road. Passed March 21, 1872.

CHAP. 123. An Act to amend chapter five hundred and fifteen of the laws of eighteen hundred and sixty-nine, entitled "An act for the incorporation of the Grand Lodge of the Independent Order of Good Templars of the State of New York," passed May third, eighteen hundred and sixty-nine. Passed March 21, 1872.

CHAP. 124. An Act authorizing the Syracuse Northern Railroad Company to extend its road and make certain connections, and mortgage its real estate and personal property; and certain towns in Onondaga, Oswego and Jefferson counties to issue bonds in aid thereof. Passed March 21, 1872; three-fifths being present.

CHAP. 125. An Act to amend an act entitled "An act to incorporate the city of Lockport," passed April eleventh, eighteen hundred and sixty-five, and the acts amendatory thereof. Passed March 22, 1872; three-fifths being present.

CHAP. 126. An Act to amend an act entitled "An act to revise the charter of Long Island city." Passed March 22, 1872; three-fifths being present.

CHAP. 127. An Act to provide for the purchase of a steam fire-engine, in the village of Tonawanda, Erie county, and for the more effectual protection of said village against fires. Passed March 23, 1872; three-fifths being present.

CHAP. 128. *An Act to amend an act entitled "An act to amend an act, passed July twenty-first, eighteen hundred and fifty-three, entitled 'An act to amend an act to provide for the incorporation of companies to construct plank-roads,' passed May seventh, eighteen hundred and forty-seven," and the acts amendatory thereof, passed April fourteen, eighteen hundred and fifty-five. Passed March* 23, 1872; *three-fifths being present.*

CHAP. 129. An Act to amend an act passed May third, eighteen hundred and seventy, entitled "An act to amend an act to incorporate the city of Troy," passed April twelfth, eighteen hundred and sixteen, and the several acts amendatory thereof, and also to amend other acts relating to the city of Troy. Passed March 23, 1872; three-fifths being present.

CHAP. 130. An Act to amend an act entitled "An act to incorporate the Haverstraw Savings Bank, of the town of Haverstraw, in the county of Rockland," passed April twenty-seventh, eighteen hundred and seventy-one. Passed March 23, 1872; three-fifths being present.

CHAP. 131. An Act to amend an act entitled "An act incorporating the Goshen Savings Bank," passed April eleven, eighteen hundred and seventy-one. Passed March 23, 1872.

CHAP. 132. An Act to amend "An act to provide for a supply of water in the city of Poughkeepsie, and for sewers therein," passed April twelfth, eighteen hundred and sixty-seven; and also to amend an act entitled "An act to amend an act entitled 'An act to provide for a supply of water in the city of Poughkeepsie, and for sewers therein,'" passed April twelfth, eighteen hundred and sixty-seven, passed April ninth, eighteen hundred and seventy; and also to amend an act entitled "An act to amend an act entitled 'An act to provide for a supply of water in the city of Poughkeepsie, and for sewers therein,'" passed April twelfth, eighteen hundred and sixty-seven, passed April nineteenth, eighteen hundred and seventy-one. Passed March 23, 1872; three-fifths being present.

CHAP. 133. An Act to amend an act entitled "An act in relation to the establishment of a normal and training school in the village of Plattsburgh," to be called "The Plattsburgh Normal and Training School," passed May seventh, eighteen hundred and sixty-nine. Passed March 23, 1872; three fifths being present.

CHAP. 134. An Act to authorize the surrogate of Albany county to issue letters of administration of the personal estate which was of Charles D. Mills, deceased, to his widow, Elizabeth P. Mills. Passed March 25, 1872.

CHAP. 135. An Act to authorize the city of Buffalo to borrow money, and to subscribe to the capital stock of the Buffalo and Jamestown Railroad Company. Passed March 25, 1872; three fifths being present.

CHAP 136. An Act relating to the New York and Long Island Ferry Company. Passed March 26, 1872; three-fifths being present.

CHAP. 137. An Act to amend an act entitled "An act to incorporate the superintendents of the fair grounds of the town of Oswegatchie, passed April fifteen, eighteen hundred and seventy-one. Passed March 27, 1872; three-fifths being present.

CHAP. 138. An Act to authorize the Buffalo and Springville Railroad Company to change the terminus of their road. Passed March 27, 1872; three-fifths being present.

CHAP. 139. *An Act to amend an act entitled "An act in relation to stenographers in the circuit courts, courts of oyer and terminer, and special terms of the supreme court in the sixth, seventh and eighth judicial districts, and to repeal chapter forty-one of the laws of eighteen hundred and sixty-seven, and chapter six hundred and seventy-two of the laws of eighteen hundred and sixty-nine." Passed March* 27, 1872; *three-fifths being present.*

CHAP. 140. An Act to amend an act entitled "An act to incorporate the village of New Brighton," passed April twenty-six, eighteen hundred and sixty-six, and an act amending the same, passed April twenty-second, eighteen hundred and sixty-seven; and also an act amending the same, passed April twenty-seventh, eighteen hundred and seventy-one. Passed March 27, 1872; three-fifths being present.

CHAP. 141. *An Act to confirm the title of certain persons to real estate questioned by reason of alienage of former owners. Passed March* 27, 1872, *by a two-third vote.*

CHAP. 142. *An Act to authorize the extension of the time for the collection of taxes in the several towns and cities in this state. Passed March 27, 1872; three-fifths being present.*

CHAP. 143. *An Act to authorize the various towns throughout the state which shall have an excess of money accruing from the excise law to expend the same. Passed March 27, 1872; three-fifths being present.*

CHAP. 144. An Act to amend the charter of the city of Albany, passed March sixteenth, eighteen hundred and seventy, and the several acts amendatory thereof. Passed March 28, 1872; three-fifths being present.

CHAP. 145. An Act to amend an act entitled "An act to incorporate the village of Goshen, passed April eighteenth, eighteen hundred and forty-three," and passed March twenty-six, eighteen hundred and sixty-six. Passed March 28, 1872; three-fifths being present.

CHAP. 146. *An Act to authorize corporations to hold and convey real estate for business purposes in other states with the consent thereof. Passed March 28, 1872.*

CHAP. 147. *An Act to extend the provisions of chapter one hundred and thirteen of the laws of the year eighteen hundred and fifty-three, entitled "An act declaring Indian river a public highway." Passed March 28, 1872; three-fifths being present.*

CHAP. 148. *An Act providing for additional compensation to deputies, clerks and assistants in the various departments in the state government. Passed March 28, 1872; three-fifths being present.*

CHAP. 149. An Act to incorporate the Importers and Grocers' Board of Trade in the city of New York. Passed March 28, 1872; three-fifths being present.

CHAP. 150. An Act to incorporate the city of Kingston. Passed March 29, 1872; three-fifths being present.

CHAP. 151. An Act to extend the time for organizing the Niagara Water-works Company and to amend the charter thereof. Passed March 29, 1872; three-fifths being present.

CHAP. 152. An Act to enable the Board of Education of the village of Salem to borrow or raise, by tax, money for school purposes, and to provide for the payment thereof, with interest, if borrowed, by tax on said village. Passed March 29, 1872; three-fifths being present.

CHAP. 153. An Act to provide an armory in the city of Brooklyn, county of Kings, for the use of the twenty-third regiment of the national guard of the state of New York. Passed April 1, 1872; three-fifths being present.

CHAP. 154. An Act to amend an act entitled "An act to amend and consolidate the several acts relating to the village of Hornellsville," passed April ninth, eighteen hundred and sixty-seven. Passed April 1, 1872; three-fifths being present.

CHAP. 155. An Act for the relief of Cornelia Townsend. Passed April 1, 1872; three-fifths being present.

CHAP. 156. An Act for the relief of Simon DeGraff, James Conway and George W. Phelps, and to authorize the board of supervisors of the county of Livingston to audit and allow the claims of Simon DeGraff, James Conway and George W. Phelps for constructing and repairing a bridge over the Genesee river in the county of Livingston, and to levy a tax for the amount allowed. Passed April 1, 1872; three-fifths being present.

CHAP. 157. An Act to incorporate the Little Valley Water-works Company. Passed April 1, 1872.

CHAP. 158. An Act authorizing the Cattaraugus County Agricultural Society to borrow money, to be used in improving its fair grounds. Passed April 1, 1872.

CHAP. 159. An Act to amend an act entitled "An act to revise and amend an act entitled 'An act to incorporate the village of Canton,' passed May thirteenth, eighteen hundred and forty-five, and the several acts amendatory thereof," passed April twenty-second, eighteen hundred and sixty-five, and amended April sixth, eighteen hundred and seventy-one. Passed April 2, 1872; three-fifths being present.

CHAP. 160. An Act to establish a Board of Health and of Vital Statistics in the county of Richmond, and to define its powers and duties. Passed April 2, 1872; three-fifths being present.

CHAP. 161. *An Act for the protection of tax payers against the frauds, embezzlements and wrongful acts of public officers and agents. Passed April 7, 1872; three-fifths being present.*

CHAP. 162. An Act to confirm and make valid the title of the Evangelical Lutheran St. John's Church, Unaltered Augsberg Confession, in the city and county of New York, to certain real estate occupied by it in said city. Passed April 2, 1872.

CHAP. 163. An Act to extend the time for the completion of the Erie and New York City Railroad. Passed April 2, 1872.

CHAP. 164. *An Act to provide for the completion of lock number two on the Erie canal, and to make an appropriation for said object. Passed April* 2, 1872; *three-fifths being present.*

CHAP. 165. An Act in relation to the Brooklyn City and Newtown Railroad Company. Passed April 2, 1872.

CHAP. 166. An Act authorizing the city of Rochester to issue its bonds to an amount not to exceed seventy-five thousand dollars, for the purpose of building a free academy. Passed April 3, 1872; three-fifths being present.

CHAP. 167. An Act to legalize the vote of the legal voters of the town of Greece, in the county of Monroe, held March fifth, eighteen hundred and seventy-two, to raise money in aid of the Lake Ontario Shore Railroad Company, and to authorize the board of supervisors to levy a tax to raise the same. Passed April 3, 1872; three-fifths being present.

CHAP. 168. An Act to authorize the village of Greenbush to issue bonds for the purpose of raising money. Passed April 3, 1872; three-fifths being present.

CHAP. 169. An Act to facilitate the construction of the New York and Canada Railroad, and extending thereto the provisions of certain laws relating to the Whitehall and Plattsburgh Railroad Company. Passed April 3, 1872; three-fifths being present.

CHAP. 170. An Act to amend the act entitled "An act to amend the several acts incorporating the village of Owego, in the county of Tioga," passed April ninth, eighteen hundred and fifty-one. Passed April 3, 1872; three-fifths being present.

CHAP. 171. An Act to authorize the Brooklyn City Railroad Company to extend their road along Putnam and Nostrand avenues and Halsey street to Broadway in the city of Brooklyn. Passed April 4, 1872.

CHAP. 172. An Act to release the title and interest of the people of this state in certain real estate in the town of Frankfort, Herkimer county, to Owen Salisbury. Passed April 6, 1872, by a two-third vote.

CHAP. 173. An Act to release and convey the interest of the people of the state of New York in certain real estate in the city of Utica, of which Owen J. Owens died possessed, to Owen Griffiths, his nephew. Passed April 6, 1872, by a two-third vote.

CHAP. 174. An Act to amend chapter ninety-two, laws of eighteen hundred and sixty-nine, entitled "An act to provide for the compensation of members of the board of supervisors of the county of Oneida." Passed April 6, 1872; three-fifths being present.

CHAP. 175. An Act to amend an act entitled "An act to amend an act to incorporate the Savings Bank of the city of Utica," passed April twenty-sixth, eighteen hundred and thirty-nine, passed April eleventh, eighteen hundred and seventy. Passed April 6, 1872.

CHAP. 176. An Act in relation to the village of Canandaigua, and to provide a police justice and police constable in said village, and defining their jurisdiction, power and duties. Passed April 6, 1872; three-fifths being present.

CHAP. 177. An Act in relation to the establishment and care of a cemetery by the village of Geneva, Ontario county, and to provide means for the same. Passed April 6, 1872; three-fifths being present.

CHAP. 178. An Act empowering commissioners of certain municipal corporations to subscribe for bonds of "The Rochester and State Line Railway Company," in place of stock. Passed April 6, 1872; three-fifths being present.

CHAP. 179. An Act to provide for supplying the city of Hudson, Columbia county, New York, with pure and wholesome water. Passed April 6, 1872; three-fifths being present.

CHAP. 180. An Act to incorporate the Citizens' Plate Glass Insurance Company. Passed April 6, 1872.

CHAP. 181. *An Act for the better prevention of the procurement of abortions and other like offenses, and to amend the laws relative thereto. Passed April* 6, 1872; *three-fifths being present.*

CHAP. 182. An Act to authorize the city of Rochester to issue its bonds in aid of the Lake Ontario Shore Railroad Company, and to take the bonds or stock of that company therefor. Passed April 6, 1872; three-fifths being present.

CHAP. 183. An Act to authorize the city of Rochester to issue its bonds in aid of the Rochester, Nunda and Pennsylvania Railroad Company, and to take the bonds of that company therefor. Passed April 6, 1872; three-fifths being present.

CHAP. 184. An Act authorizing the town of Little Valley, Cattaraugus county, to issue bonds to pay its indebtedness incurred in the building of the court-house and jail in said town. Passed April 6, 1872; three-fifths being present.

CHAP. 185. An Act to authorise the city of Rochester to issue its bonds in aid of the Rochester and State Line Railway Company, and to take bonds of that company therefor. Passed April 6, 1872; three-fifths being present.

CHAP. 186. An Act to amend title twelve of the charter of the city of Albany, entitled "The police department," passed March sixteenth, eighteen hundred and seventy. Passed April 6, 1872; notwithstanding the objections of the governor.

CHAP. 187. An Act to repeal chapter eight hundred and seventy-seven of the laws of eighteen hundred and seventy-one, and to provide for the transfer of the duties of the registrar of arrears of taxes to the collector of taxes and assessments of the city of Brooklyn. Passed April 8, 1872; three-fifths being present.

CHAP. 188. An Act to regulate the ferries running from the foot of Tenth street and Twenty-third street, in the city of New York, across the East river to Green Point, in the city of Brooklyn. Passed April 8, 1872.

CHAP. 189. An Act to amend chapter sixty-five of the laws of eighteen hundred and seventy-one, entitled "An act to revise and consolidate the laws in relation to the village of Geneva, in the county of Ontario, passed March third, eighteen hundred and seventy-one. Passed April 8, 1872; three-fifths being present.

CHAP. 190. An Act to amend chapter one hundred and seventeen of the laws of eighteen hundred and fifty, entitled "An act to amend an act to provide for the better repairing certain roads in the town of Coeymans," passed December fourteenth, eighteen hundred and forty-seven. Passed April 8, 1872; three-fifths being present.

CHAP. 191. An Act to confirm the official acts of the trustees of the village of Phelps. Passed April 9, 1872; three-fifths being present.

CHAP. 192. An Act to amend an act entitled "An act to authorize the village of Dunkirk to issue bonds for the purpose of supplying said village with water, and to create a board of water commissioners," passed April thirteenth, eighteen hundred and seventy-one. Passed April 9, 1872; three-fifths being present.

CHAP. 193. An Act to incorporate the Psi Chapter of the Psi Upsilon Fraternity in the village of Clinton, in the county of Oneida, in the state of New York. Passed April 10, 1872.

CHAP. 194. An Act to amend an act entitled "An act to consolidate and amend the several acts relating to the village of Warsaw, and to enlarge the powers of the corporation of said village," passed March seventeenth, eighteen hundred and sixty. Passed April 10, 1872; three-fifths being present.

CHAP. 195. An Act to amend an act entitled "An act to change the name of the First Universalist Society and Church in the city of Hudson, and to authorize said society to take and hold by gift, grant, devise, purchase or otherwise, real and personal estate," passed March twenty-eighth, eighteen hundred and seventy-one. Passed April 10, 1872.

CHAP. 196. An Act for the relief of the heirs of Daniel Early, deceased, late of the city of New York. Passed April 10, 1872, by a two-third vote.

CHAP. 197. An Act to incorporate the Society of St. Vincent de Paul, in the city of New York. Passed April 10, 1872.

CHAP. 198. An Act to authorize the city of Rochester to borrow money to pay off its debt incurred in the purchase of a site for a free academy, and to issue its bonds for the payment thereof. Passed April 10, 1872; three-fifths being present.

CHAP. 199. An Act to authorise the city Rochester to borrow money to pay off the deficiencies arising from non-payment of taxes and assessments, and to issue its bonds for the payment thereof. Passed April 10, 1872; three-fifths being present.

CHAP. 200. An Act to authorize the making of an extension or branch of the Gowanus canal, in the city of Brooklyn. Passed April 10, 1872; three-fifths being present.

CHAP. 201. An Act to amend an act entitled "An act to amend the charter of the village of Warsaw, and to authorise said village to raise money to procure water and to protect said village and the property therein against loss by fire, passed February eighteenth, eighteen hundred and seventy-one. Passed April 10, 1872; three-fifths being

CHAP. 202. An Act to legalize the issue of certain bonds by the city of Rochester for the purpose of raising money for the relief of sufferers by the Chicago fire. Passed April 10, 1872; three-fifths being present.

CHAP. 203. An Act to amend the charter of the village of Perry, county of Wyoming. Passed April 10, 1872; three-fifths being present.

CHAP. 204. An Act in relation to a board of health for the town and village of Saratoga Springs, Saratoga county. Passed April 10, 1872; three-fifths being present.

CHAP. 205. An Act to amend an act entitled "An act giving permission to the United States to remove a portion of the public work known as the Erie Basin breakwater, in or near Buffalo harbor," passed April twenty-seventh, eighteen hundred and sixty-eight." Passed April 10, 1872; three-fifths being present.

CHAP. 206. An Act to extend the time for the collection of taxes in the city of Elmira. Passed April 10, 1872; three-fifths being present.

CHAP. 207. An Act to legalize the acts of Sherman B. Daboll, as notary public of Madison county. Passed April 10, 1872.

CHAP. 208. An Act to incorporate the South Worcester Cemetery Association. Passed April 10, 1872; three-fifths being present.

CHAP. 209. *An Act to amend an act entitled "An act for the incorporation of benevolent, charitable, scientific and missionary societies," passed April twelfth, eighteen hundred and forty-eight. Passed April* 10, 1872.

CHAP. 210. An Act authorizing and directing the surrogate of the county of Cattaraugus to distribute to the collateral next of kin of Sarah Denman her legacy under the last will and testament of her father, Ashbel Freeman, deceased, and also her distributive share as one of the next of kin of the estate of her deceased sister, Catharine Freeman. Passed April 10, 1872; three-fifths being present.

CHAP. 211. An Act to authorize the town auditors of the town of Saratoga Springs, to issue bonds for the completion of and furnishing the town hall at Saratoga Springs. Passed April 10, 1872; three-fifths being present.

CHAP. 212. An Act to provide for fair grounds in the county of Chemung. Passed April 10, 1872; three-fifths being present.

CHAP. 213. An Act to amend "An act to enable Ezra Cornell to found a public library and literary institution in the village of Ithaca, and to incorporate the same," passed April fifth, eighteen hundred and sixty-four. Passed April 11, 1872; three-fifths being present.

CHAP. 214. An Act to amend "An Act to provide for the construction of a main and lateral drain or sewer in Navy street, Johnson street and Hudson avenue, and other streets and avenues in the city of Brooklyn," passed April sixth, eighteen hundred and seventy-one. Passed April 11, 1872; three-fifths being present.

CHAP. 215. An Act to authorize the trustees of the Black River Annual Conference to pay and transfer to the trustees of Central New York Conference, certain funds and property. Passed April 11, 1872.

CHAP. 216. An Act to dissolve the New York and Richmond Granite Company. Passed April 11, 1872.

CHAP. 217. An Act to change and fix the number of trustees of the Attica Union Free School and Academy. Passed April 11, 1872.

CHAP. 218. An Act for the erection of an iron bridge over the Erie canal at West Troy, in the county of Albany. Passed April 11, 1872; three-fifths being present.

CHAP. 219. An Act in relation to the erection of public buildings for the use of the city of Rochester. Passed April 12, 1872; three-fifths being present.

CHAP. 220. An Act relative to the laying out and opening of Madison avenue, north of One Hundred and Twentieth street, in the city of New York. Passed April 12, 1872; three-fifths being present.

CHAP. 221. An Act to amend an act entitled "An act to authorize the common council of the city of Binghamton to borrow money for the purpose of purchasing a site for a high school and erecting and furnishing a building thereon." Passed April 12, 1872; three-fifths being present.

CHAP. 222. An Act authorizing the city of Albany to close a part of Quackenbush street, and to permit the erection of bridges over certain streets in said city. Passed April 12, 1872; three-fifths being present.

CHAP. 223. An Act for the relief of the devisees and heirs at law of Louis Planer and Josephine Planer, deceased. Passed April 12, 1872, by a two-third vote.

CHAP. 224. An Act to amend an act entitled "An act to consolidate and amend the several acts relating to the village of Watkins, and to enlarge the powers of the corporation of said village," passed April third, eighteen hundred and sixty-one. Passed April 12, 1872; three-fifths being present.

CHAP. 225. An Act to authorize the board of education of school district number ten, in the town of Warsaw, to erect a school building, and to provide means for payment thereof. Passed April 12, 1872; three-fifths being present.

CHAP. 226. An Act to amend an act entitled "An act in relation to the village of Canandaigua, and to provide a police justice and police constables in said village, and defining their jurisdiction, powers and duties," passed April sixth, A. D. eighteen hundred and seventy-two. Passed April 12, 1872; three-fifths being present.

CHAP. 227. An Act to amend an act passed May ninth, eighteen hundred and sixty-eight, entitled "An act to amend section three of chapter eight hundred and seventeen of the laws of eighteen hundred and sixty-six, entitled 'An act to lay out and construct a road from the river road in township number fourteen, in the town of Johnsburgh, to the Carthage road, near the head of Long lake, in the county of Hamilton.'" Passed April 12, 1872; three-fifths being present.

CHAP. 228. An Act to regulate a ferry between the cities of New York and Brooklyn. Passed April 13, 1872.

CHAP. 229. An Act for the relief of Sarah Wyatt, widow of Samuel Wyatt. Passed April 13, 1872; three-fifths being present.

CHAP. 230. An Act to limit the amount of money to be paid to the Hornell Library Association to five hundred dollars, and to amend chapter five hundred and forty-nine of the laws of eighteen hundred and sixty-nine. Passed April 13, 1872; three-fifths being present.

CHAP. 231. An Act to provide for supplying the village of Peekskill with water, and authorizing the issue of bonds therefor, and to create a board of water commissioners. Passed April 16, 1872; three-fifths being present.

CHAP. 232. An Act to authorize the rebuilding and repairing of certain wharves and piers in the city of Brooklyn. Passed April 16, 1872; three-fifths being present.

CHAP. 233. An Act to confer upon Horace O. Tracy and Peter Fish the right to establish a ferry across Cayuga lake, and to extend in their behalf an act to establish such ferry, passed April fifth, eighteen hundred and forty-four, and extended by chapter thirty-one, laws of eighteen hundred and fifty-eight, to Horace O. Tracy and Isaac A. Brokaw, for the term of fourteen years from the fifth day of April, eighteen hundred and fifty-eight. Passed April 16, 1872.

CHAP. 234. An Act to amend chapter eight hundred and fifty-three of the laws of eighteen hundred and sixty-seven, entitled "An act to incorporate St. Agnes Cemetery," passed May ninth, eighteen hundred and sixty-seven. Passed April 16, 1872; three-fifths being present.

CHAP. 235. *An Act to amend section ten of chapter seven hundred and thirty-nine of the laws of eighteen hundred and fifty-seven, entitled "An act to authorize the formation of town insurance companies." Passed April* 16, 1872.

CHAP. 236. An Act to incorporate the Soldiers' Monument Society of Niagara county. Passed April 16, 1872; three-fifths being present.

CHAP. 237. An Act revising, amending and consolidating the charter of, and the several acts relating to, the village of Geneseo, in the county of Livingston, modifying the powers of the corporation, and the duties of its officers. Passed April 16, 1872; three-fifths being present.

CHAP. 238. An Act to release the interest of the people of the state of New York in certain lands to Charles O. Jones. Passed April 16, 1872, by a two-third vote.

CHAP. 239. An Act to lay out, open and grade Bay Ridge avenue, in the town of New Utrecht, in the county of Kings. Passed April 16, 1872; three-fifths being present.

CHAP. 240. An Act to authorize the Second Avenue Railroad Company in the city of New York to extend their tracks and operate the same. Passed April 16, 1872; three-fifths being present.

CHAP. 241. An Act in relation to the Chemung Railroad Company. Passed April 16, 1872; three-fifths being present.

Chap. 242. An Act confirming certain proceedings of the common council of the city of Buffalo, and authorizing the issue of the bonds of said city for the purpose of aiding the people of the city of Chicago. Passed April 16, 1872; three-fifths being present.

Chap. 243. An Act in relation to the First Baptist Church and Society in Ogdensburgh. Passed April 16, 1872.

Chap. 244. An Act to change the name of the Sixth Ward Savings Bank of the city of Albany. Passed April 16, 1872.

Chap. 245. An Act to allow the town of Bethany, Genesee county, to raise an increased amount of money for the construction and repair of roads and bridges in said town, and to legalize and confirm the action of the last annual town meeting in relation to raising moneys for said purpose. Passed April 16, 1872; three-fifths being present.

Chap. 246. An act to amend an act entitled "An act to supply the village of Middletown with water for public and private purposes," passed April third, eighteen hundred and sixty-six, and of the amendments thereto, passed May fourteenth, eighteen hundred and sixty-seven. Passed April 16, 1872; three-fifths being present.

Chap. 247. An Act relative to certain lands in the city of Brooklyn in Kings county, which, in and by the last will and testament of Thomas Poole, deceased, were devised by him to the executors therein named, in trust, for the use and benefit of said testator's daughter Eliza, for and during her natural life. Passed April 16, 1872.

Chap. 248. *An Act to authorize the formation, establishing and maintaining of driving parks and park associations. Passed April* 16, 1872; *three-fifths being present.*

Chap. 249. An Act to confirm the title of Francis Melvin to certain land in the city of Buffalo. Passed April 16, 1872.

Chap. 250. An Act releasing the interest of the state in certain lands and premises of which Maurice Roche, late of Coxsackie, in the county of Greene, died seized, and authorizing his heirs at law to hold and convey the same. Passed April 16, 1872, by a two-third vote.

Chap. 251. An Act to enable Mary Conlan to take and hold real estate, and to release to her the interest and title in lands escheated to the state. Passed April 16, 1872, by a two-third vote.

Chap. 252. An Act to legalize the election of trustees and other corporative officers of the village of Fonda. Passed April 16, 1872; two-thirds being present.

Chap. 253. An Act to authorize the Clifton Mining Company to succeed to the rights of the Clifton Iron Company. Passed April 17, 1872.

Chap. 254. An Act for the appropriation of fifteen hundred dollars to repair a road across the Onondaga Indian reservation. Passed April 17, 1872; three-fifths being present.

Chap. 255. An Act relative to Sandford street and the Wallabout Bridge road in the city of Brooklyn. Passed April 17, 1872; three-fifths being present.

Chap. 256. An Act to compel the commissioners appointed to build a town hall in the town of New Rochelle, under chapter eighty-eight of the laws of eighteen hundred and sixty-eight, and all acts amendatory thereof, to account. Passed April 17, 1872; three-fifths being present.

Chap. 257. An Act to prolong the time for the payment of the capital stock of the Coxsackie Malleable and Grey Iron Company, and for the execution and recording of the certificate thereof, and to legalize the acts of said company. Passed April 17, 1872.

Chap. 258. An Act releasing the interest of the people of the state of New York in certain real estate to the Five Points House of Industry. Passed April 17, 1872, by a two-third vote.

Chap. 259. An Act to repeal chapter two hundred and eighty-five of the laws of eighteen hundred and seventy-one, entitled "An act to provide for the erection of a town hall in the village of Mount Vernon, town of East Chester, county of Westchester," passed April fourth, eighteen hundred and seventy-one. Passed April 17, 1872; three-fifths being present.

Chap. 260. *An Act to amend the act entitled "An act in relation to the qualifications of persons to be admitted to practice in the courts of this state as attorneys, solicitors and counselors," passed April thirteen, eighteen hundred and seventy-one. Passed April* 17, 1872.

Chap. 261. An Act to incorporate the Ulster General Hospital. Passed April 18, 1872; three-fifths being present.

CHAP. 262. An Act for the relief of the inhabitants of the union school district number one, in the town of Moreau, in the county of Saratoga. Passed April 18, 1872; three-fifths being present.

CHAP. 263. An Act to amend an act entitled "An act to incorporate the New York Infant Asylum," passed March eleventh, eighteen hundred and sixty-five. Passed April 18, 1872; three-fifths being present.

CHAP. 264. An Act to authorize the board of supervisors of the county of Warren to raise and levy the sum of five thousand dollars on the town of Caldwell, in the county of Warren. Passed April 18, 1872; three-fifths being present.

CHAP. 265. An Act to amend an act entitled "An act to facilitate the construction of the New York and Canada Railroad, and extending thereto the provisions of certain laws relating to the Whitehall and Plattsburgh Railroad Company," passed April third, eighteen hundred and seventy-two. Passed April 18, 1872.

CHAP. 266. An Act to repeal so much of chapter six hundred and forty, laws of eighteen hundred and seventy, as relate to non-resident lands in the county of Franklin. Passed April 18, 1872; three-fifths being present.

CHAP. 267. An Act to amend chapter one hundred and seventy-seven of the laws of eighteen hundred and seventy, entitled "An act to incorporate the village of Pittsford, county of Monroe, state of New York," passed April eleventh, eighteen hundred and seventy. Passed April 18, 1872; three-fifths being present.

CHAP. 268. An Act to provide for the improvement of the hydraulic power of the Little Salmon river, in Franklin county, and to check freshets therein. Passed April 18, 1872; three-fifths being present.

CHAP. 269. An Act authorizing the construction of a bridge across the Hudson river at the city of Albany, and incorporating the "Albany and Greenbush Bridge Company." Passed April 18, 1872; three-fifths being present.

CHAP. 270. An Act to erect the village of Greenville into a separate road district. Passed April 18, 1872; three-fifths being present.

CHAP. 271. An Act to authorize the town of Kingsbury, in the county of Washington, to issue bonds to raise the necessary money to rebuild the court-house in said town. Passed April 18, 1872; three-fifths being present.

CHAP. 272. An Act to regulate the compensation of the special county judge and special surrogate of Chautauqua county. Passed April 18, 1872; three-fifths being present.

CHAP. 273. An Act to declare Otter creek and its tributaries, in Lewis and Herkimer counties, a public highway. Passed April 18, 1872; three-fifths being present.

CHAP. 274. *An Act to amend an act entitled "An act for the erection and maintenance of watering troughs in the public highways," passed April seven, eighteen hundred and sixty-[illegible]. Passed April 18, 1872; three-fifths being present.*

CHAP. 275. An Act to authorize the trustees of the village of Flushing to issue bonds and [illegible] money for the purchase of a steam fire-engine, and for the mapping and establishment of lines and grades for the streets and public places in said village. Passed April 18, 1872; three-fifths being present.

CHAP. 276. An Act to incorporate the trustees of the Home for the Destitute Children [illegible] county. Passed April 18, 1872; three-fifths being present.

CHAP. 277. An Act to authorize the laying out, opening and working of a public highway in the village of Canandaigua, Ontario county, and raising money to defray the expenses [illegible] said highway. Passed April 18, 1872; three-fifths being present.

CHAP. 278. An Act making further provision as to the police department of the city of Albany. Passed April 18, 1872; three-fifths being present.

CHAP. 279. An Act relative to the streets, avenues, wharves, piers and bulkheads of the village of College Point, in the county of Queens. Passed April 18, 1872; three-fifths being present.

CHAP. 280. An Act to repeal chapter nine hundred and twenty-eight of the laws of eighteen hundred and seventy-one, entitled "An act in relation to the laying out, opening and constructing of a public highway in the town of Hempstead, Queens county." Passed April 18, 1872; three-fifths being present.

CHAP. 281. An Act to provide for the erection of a town house in the town of New Lots, Kings county. Passed April 18, 1872; three-fifths being present.

CHAP. 282. An Act to amend an act entitled "An act to authorize the Syracuse Northern Railroad Company to construct and maintain a swing-bridge over the Oswego canal, in the first ward of the city of Syracuse," passed April seven, eighteen hundred and seventy-one, so as to include the Erie canal, the second, third and other wards of said city. Passed April 18, 1872; three-fifths being present.

CHAP. 283. *An Act to authorize plank-road and turnpike companies, formed under and by virtue of part first, chapter eighteen, title one, article five of the Revised Statutes, to extend their charter or corporate existence. Passed April 18, 1872; three-fifths being present.*

CHAP. 284. An Act to establish a court of special sessions in and for the city of Albany, and to confer further judicial powers upon the recorder of said city. Passed April 19, 1872; three-fifths being present.

CHAP. 285. *An Act to amend an act entitled "An act to extend the powers of boards of supervisors, except in the counties of New York and Kings," passed May eleventh, eighteen hundred and sixty-nine. Passed April 19, 1872; three-fifths being present.*

CHAP. 286. An Act to incorporate Smyrna Lodge Number One Hundred and Sixteen, Independent Order of Odd Fellows of the state of New York. Passed April 19, 1872.

CHAP. 287. An Act to incorporate the Board of Home Missions of the Presbyterian church in the United States of America, and to enable the Presbyterian Board of Home Missions, formerly the Presbyterian Committee of Home Missions, to transfer its property to said new corporation, and to vest in such new corporation the corporate rights, franchises and privileges of the former body, and also to enable said new corporation to accept a transfer of the property of the trustees of the Board of Domestic Missions of the general assembly of the Presbyterian church in the United States of America, and to become the legal successor of the said last-mentioned corporation. Passed April 19, 1872.

CHAP. 288. An Act to authorize the village of Herkimer to improve the public road leading from said village to Middleville, in Herkimer county, by repairing and macadamizing the same, and to raise money to make such improvement. Passed April 19, 1872; three-fifths being present.

CHAP. 289. An Act to amend an act entitled "An act to amend an act to incorporate the village of Goshen, passed April eighteenth, eighteen hundred and forty-three, so as to enable the inhabitants of said village to obtain a supply of water for public and private uses," passed March twenty-seventh, eighteen hundred and seventy-one. Passed April 19, 1872; three-fifths being present.

CHAP. 290. An Act to authorize the Blossburg Coal Company, the successors and assigns of the "Bloss Coal Mining and Railroad Company," a corporation organized and existing under the laws of the commonwealth of Pennsylvania, to hold real estate for the purposes of its business. Passed April 19, 1872.

CHAP. 291. An Act to incorporate the Catskill Water Company. Passed April 19, 1872.

CHAP. 292. An Act to amend an act entitled "An act to authorize the construction of a street railroad in the city of Auburn, and from thence to the Owasco lake," passed April fifteenth, eighteen hundred and seventy-one. Passed April 19, 1872; three-fifths being present.

CHAP. 293. An Act to amend the act entitled "An act to provide for laying out and improving roads and avenues in the village and town of Saratoga Springs," passed May fifth, eighteen hundred and seventy.. Passed April 22, 1872; three-fifths being present.

CHAP. 294. An Act to authorize the construction of a bridge over Sing Sing kill, in the village of Sing Sing. Passed April 22, 1872; three-fifths being present.

CHAP. 295. An Act to repeal chapter nine hundred and six of the laws of eighteen hundred and sixty-nine, and chapter six hundred and forty-nine of the laws of eighteen hundred and seventy, and chapter three hundred and fifty-six of the laws of eighteen hundred and seventy-one, so far as the same relate to the town of Pelham, in Westchester county, and the supervisor thereof, and to enable said town to construct part of the road in said acts referred to. Passed April 22, 1872; three-fifths being present.

CHAP. 296. An Act concerning the Sodus Bay, Corning and New York Railroad Company, and providing for a change in its corporate name. Passed April 22, 1872.

CHAP. 297. An Act to amend an act entitled "An act to alter the map or plan of the city of New York," passed April fifteenth, eighteen hundred and fifty-nine, relative to the Seventh avenue in the city of New York. Passed April 22, 1872; three-fifths being present.

CHAP. 298. An Act in relation to The First Baptist Church and Society in Ogdensburgh. Passed April 22, 1872; three-fifths being present.

CHAP. 299. An Act to amend an act passed April twenty-fourth, eighteen hundred and sixty-five, entitled "An act for the improvement of part of the city of New York between One Hundred and Tenth street and Harlem river." Passed April 22, 1872; three-fifths being present.

CHAP. 300. An Act to repeal chapter five hundred and forty-nine of the laws of one thousand eight hundred and sixty-eight, entitled "An act to regulate, grade, and macadamize the highway known as the Westchester turnpike and post road, commencing at a point in said road on the line dividing the towns of West Farms and Morrisania," and the acts amendatory thereof to discharge the commissioners appointed by such act or acts amendatory thereof, and to empower the town officers of the various towns and the president and trustees of the village of Rochelle, through which said turnpike and post road passes to perform certain duties. Passed April 22, 1872; three-fifths being present.

CHAP. 301. An Act to legalize and confirm the official acts of Gaylord S. Graves, a justice of the peace of the town of Bainbridge, in the county of Chenango. Passed April 22, 1872.

CHAP. 302. An Act to amend chapter seventy-seven of the laws of eighteen hundred and seventy, and chapter five hundred and thirty-six of the laws of eighteen hundred and seventy-one, passed respectively, March sixteenth, eighteen hundred and seventy, and April fifteenth, eighteen hundred and seventy-one, entitled "An act to amend the act, to combine into one act the several acts relating to the city of Albany, passed April twelve, eighteen hundred and forty-two, and the several acts amendatory thereof, in so far as they relate to the city of Albany." Passed April 22, 1872; three-fifths being present.

CHAP. 303. An Act to amend section one of chapter seven hundred and thirty of the laws of eighteen hundred and seventy-one, entitled "An act in relation to highways in the county of Rockland." Passed April 22, 1872; three-fifths being present.

CHAP. 304. An Act to release the title and interest of the people of the state of New York in and to certain real estate in the city of Brooklyn, to Sarah Groom. Passed April 22, 1872, by a two-third vote.

CHAP. 305. An Act to authorize the Pelham and Portchester Railroad Company to cross such arms of the sea, bays, inlets or navigable streams as may be found necessary to build said road, and to build draw-bridges over the same. Passed April 22, 1872; three-fifths being present.

CHAP. 306. An Act to amend an act entitled "An act to amend an act entitled 'An act to incorporate the association for the benefit of colored orphans in the city of New York,' passed April sixteen, eighteen hundred and thirty-eight," passed April one, eighteen hundred and seventy-one. Passed April 22, 1872.

CHAP. 307. An Act extending the provisions of certain laws permitting municipal corporations to aid in the construction of railroads, to the village of Middleport in the county of Niagara. Passed April 22, 1872; three-fifths being present.

CHAP. 308. An Act to amend an act entitled "An act to establish a department of police in the city of Buffalo, and to provide for the government thereof," passed April twenty-sixth, eighteen hundred and seventy-one. Passed April 23, 1872; three-fifths being present.

CHAP. 309. An Act to provide for regulating, grading and graveling the White Plains road, commonly called North street, lying wholly in the town of New Rochelle and partly in the village of New Rochelle, in the county of Westchester. Passed April 23, 1872; three-fifths being present.

CHAP. 310. An Act authorizing the construction of a bridge across the Hudson river at the city of Troy. Passed April 23, 1872; three-fifths being present.

CHAP. 311. An Act to amend an act entitled "An act to vest certain real estate belonging to the state, in the town of Marlborough, Ulster county, and to establish a public highway," passed May ninth, eighteen hundred and sixty-eight. Passed April 23, 1872, by a two-third vote.

CHAP. 312. An Act to authorize the lighting of public streets and avenues in the town of Fishkill, in the county of Dutchess. Passed April 23, 1872; three-fifths being present.

CHAP. 313. An Act to amend chapter two hundred and forty-seven of the laws of eighteen hundred and sixty-eight, entitled "An act to incorporate the Metropolitan Boat Club of the city of New York." Passed April 23, 1872.

Chap. 314. An Act confirming a conveyance of real estate to Dennis Murphy and authoizing him to hold real estate. Passed April 23, 1872, by a two-third vote.

Chap. 315. *An Act to amend an act entitled "An act to amend an act entitled 'An act to reduce the number of town officers and town and county expenses, and to prevent abuses in auditing town and county accounts,' passed May tenth, eighteen hundred and forty-five," passed December fourteen, eighteen hundred and forty-seven. Passed April* 23, 1872 ; *three-fifths being present.*

Chap. 316. An Act to prevent the taking of fish from Loon lake in the town of Wayland, Steuben county. Passed April 23, 1872; three-fifths being present.

Chap. 317. An Act to authorize the county clerk of Montgomery county to sign the certificates of record of deeds and mortgages and other records, or of filing papers recorded or filed in Montgomery county clerk's office, which were not signed by the former clerk of said county of Montgomery. Passed April 23, 1872; three-fifths being present.

Chap. 318. An Act to erect an armory in Greenpoint, Seventeenth ward, in the city of Brooklyn. Passed April 23, 1872; three-fifths being present.

Chap. 319. *An Act to amend an act entitled "An act to amend chapter one hundred and ninety-four of the laws of eighteen hundred and forty-nine, entitled 'An act to vest in the boards of supervisors certain legislative powers and to prescribe their fees for certain services,' passed April three, eighteen hundred and forty-nine,'" passed February two, eighteen hundred and seventy-one. Passed April* 23, 1872 ; *three-fifths being present.*

Chap. 320. An Act to amend an act in relation to the rates of wharfage, and to regulate piers, wharves, bulkheads and slips, in the cities of New York and Brooklyn, passed May sixth, eighteen hundred and seventy. Passed April 23, 1872.

Chap. 321. An Act to incorporate the Troy, Lansingburgh and Cohoes Bridge Company, for the purpose of constructing and maintaining a bridge, appurtenances and approaches to the same, over the Hudson river from some point on Van Schaick's island, in the city of Cohoes, to some point in the village of Lansingburgh, south of Bolton's brewery, on said river. Passed April 23, 1872; three-fifths being present.

Chap. 322. An Act to discharge William Hoffman from the debtors' jail in the city of New York, commonly called the "Ludlow street jail," and to discharge him from arrest and imprisonment under the orders of arrest, by virtue of which he is now imprisoned in said jail, and to exonerate his person from any existing or future arrest or imprisonment on any civil process in any civil action issuing out of any court of law, or on any execution issuing on any judgment rendered or to be rendered in any such action, in every case in which the cause of action arose since January first, eighteen hundred and seventy-one, and existed at the time of the passage of this act. Passed April 24, 1872.

Chap. 323. An Act authorizing the election of a receiver of taxes and assessments for the town and village of Saratoga Springs. Passed April 24, 1872; three-fifths being present.

Chap. 324. An Act entitled "An act to amend an act entitled 'An act to authorize the making and opening of a road or avenue from the intersection of the highway running east of Rockland lake, with the highway running from the lake to Rockland lake landing, in the county of Rockland, to intersect the highway running from Upper Piermont to Orangetown," passed April twenty-first, eighteen hundred and seventy-one, and to extend said Highland avenue south to the state line. Passed April 24, 1872; three-fifths being present.

Chap. 325. An Act to provide for the improvement of the highways extending from Lansing street, Genesee street and Caroline avenue, in the village of West Troy, to the Loudon road, in the town of Watervliet (highways lying in part in the town of Watervliet and in part in the village of West Troy), and to authorize the board of supervisors of the county of Albany to assess the expense thereof upon the said town. Passed April 24, 1872; three-fifths being present.

Chap. 326. An Act for the removal of bodies and remains of bodies from a certain burial ground connected with the Second Reformed Church of Bethlehem, to the Bethlehem cemetery. Passed April 24, 1872.

Chap. 327. An Act to amend an act entitled "An act to amend the act entitled 'An act to incorporate the village of Bath, in the county of Steuben,' passed June twentieth, eighteen hundred and fifty-one, and the act amendatory thereof, passed April twenty-fifth, eighteen hundred and sixty-six." Passed April 24, 1872; three-fifths being present.

CHAP. 328. An Act to authorize the trustees of the village of Andes, in Delaware county, to proceed to protect said village from the effects of high water, and to raise money to pay for the same; also to amend chapter seven hundred and thirty-one of laws of eighteen hundred and sixty-five, in relation thereto. Passed April 24, 1872; three-fifths being present.

CHAP. 329. An Act to amend an act entitled "An act to incorporate the Elmira Park Association," passed April thirteenth, eighteen hundred and seventy-one. Passed April 24, 1872; three-fifths being present.

CHAP. 330. An Act relative to the Hudson Suspension Bridge and New England Railway Company, and authorizing the extension of its road. Passed April 24, 1872; three-fifths being present.

CHAP. 331. An Act supplemental to an act entitled "An act for the appointment of commissioners to lay out a plan for roads and streets in the towns of Kings county," passed May seventh, eighteen hundred and sixty-nine. Passed April 24, 1872; three-fifths being present.

CHAP. 332. An Act to incorporate the Holy Sepulchre Cemetery, in the city of Rochester. Passed April 24, 1872; three-fifths being present.

CHAP. 333. An Act authorizing the construction and maintenance of a highway from the north line of the township of Hollywood, in the county of St. Lawrence, into township number twenty-five in Franklin county. Passed April 24, 1872; three-fifths being present.

CHAP. 334. *An Act making an appropriation to pay the expenses of the collection of tolls, superintendence, ordinary repairs and maintenance of the canals for the fiscal year commencing on the first day of October, eighteen hundred and seventy-two. Passed April 24, 1872; three-fifths being present.*

CHAP. 335. An Act to authorize the election of an additional justice of the peace in the town of Sodus, in the county of Wayne. Passed April 24, 1872; three-fifths being present.

CHAP. [illegible]. An Act to amend chapter one hundred and ninety of the laws of eighteen hun-[illegible] sixty, entitled "An act extending to Oliver A. Field the right to establish and [illegible] a ferry across the Hudson river," passed April sixth, eighteen hundred and [illegible]. Passed April 24, 1872; three-fifths being present.

CHAP. [illegible]. An Act to authorise the Ira Union Cemetery Association to acquire title to [illegible] lands or lots, number twelve and number twenty four, of the original town-[illegible] Cato, now Ira, in the county of Cayuga. Passed April 24, 1872; three-fifths [illegible] present.

[illegible] An Act to authorise the Rondout and Kingston Gas-light Company to issue [illegible] purposes. Passed April 24, 1872; three-fifths being present.

CHAP. 339. An Act to amend an act entitled "An act to organize a fire department and board of fire commissioners in and for the city of Troy," passed April thirteenth, eighteen hundred and sixty-one. Passed April 24, 1872; three-fifths being present.

CHAP. 340. An Act requiring the highway tax of the New York Central Railroad Company through the town of Macedon, Wayne county, to be applied to the repairs of certain highways in said town. Passed April 24, 1872; three-fifths being present.

CHAP. 341. An Act in reference to the Young Men's Association for Mutual Improvement in the city of Albany. Passed April 24, 1872; three-fifths being present.

CHAP. 342. An Act to provide for the building of iron bridges across the Chemung river, in the city of Elmira, and bonding said city to pay the expenses thereof. Passed April 24, 1872; three-fifths being present.

CHAP. 343. *An Act to amend the act chapter seven hundred and seventy-eight of the laws of eighteen hundred and seventy-one, reappropriating certain moneys for the construction of new work upon and extraordinary repairs of the canals of this state. Passed April 24, 1872; three-fifths being present.*

CHAP. 344. An Act to amend an act entitled "An act in relation to the receiver of taxes of Morrisania," passed April twenty-eighth, eighteen hundred and seventy. 24, 1872; three-fifths being present.

Act to provide for the election of a fifth justice of the peace in the town of Richland, in and for the county of Oswego, and for the future election of five justices of the peace of said town. Passed April 24, 1872; three-fifths being present.

CHAP. 346. *An Act for the improvement of the navigation of the Hudson river, and to make an appropriation therefor. Passed April* 24, 1872; *three-fifths being present.*

CHAP. 347. An Act to authorize the Montour Cemetery Association of the village of Havana, Schuyler county, New York, to remove the bodies buried in the old burial ground in said village to the new cemetery of said association, and to vest the title of said old burial ground in the said association. Passed April 24, 1872.

CHAP. 348. An Act to confirm and legalize the action of the board of supervisors of Cayuga county, in relation to the number of superintendents of the poor of said county. Passed April 24, 1872; three-fifths being present.

CHAP. 349. An Act to authorize the appointment of commissioners to fix the grade and improve sidewalks, and open and improve streets in the town of New Lots, Kings county. Passed April 24, 1872; three-fifths being present.

CHAP. 350. *An Act to amend an act entitled "An act to authorize the formation of railroad corporations and to regulate the same," passed April second, eighteen hundred and fifty. Passed April* 24, 1872.

CHAP. 351. An Act for the extension of the Utica, Chenago and Cortland railroad. Passed April 24, 1872; three-fifths being present.

CHAP. 352. An Act to amend an act entitled "An act to incorporate the city of Rome," passed February twenty-third, eighteen hundred and seventy. Passed April 24, 1872; three-fifths being present.

CHAP. 353. An Act to amend an act entitled "An act to incorporate the New Brighton Fire Engine Company Number Four," passed April nineteenth, eighteen hundred and fifty-nine. Passed April 24, 1872; three-fifths being present.

CHAP. 354. An Act to authorize the common council of the city of Brooklyn to open, grade, pave and complete Douglass street and other streets in said city. Passed April 24, 1872; three-fifths being present.

CHAP. 355. *An Act to repeal chapter two hundred and eighty-seven of the laws of eighteen hundred and seventy-one, passed April four, eighteen hundred and seventy-one, entitled "An act to amend the law for the assessment and collection of taxes in cases where farms or lots are divided by county lines." Passed April* 24, 1872; *three-fifths being present.*

CHAP. 356. An Act to prohibit catching speckled trout in the county of Madison for the period of three years. Passed April 24, 1872; three-fifths being present.

CHAP. 357. *An Act to amend an act entitled "An act for the incorporation of villages," passed April twentieth, eighteen hundred and seventy. Passed April* 24, 1872; *three-fifths being present.*

CHAP. 358. *An Act to confirm the title of citizens of this state to lands for which they have heretofore taken conveyances from aliens. Passed April* 24, 1872, *by a two-third vote.*

CHAP. 359. An Act to authorize the common council of the city of Utica to borrow and disburse money for city purposes, and to levy and collect a tax to pay the same. Passed April 24, 1872; three-fifths being present.

CHAP. 360. An Act to amend the charter of the American Bible Society. Passed April 24, 1872.

CHAP. 361. An Act in relation to the Sea Cliff Grove and Metropolitan Camp Ground Association. Passed April 24, 1872; three-fifths being present.

CHAP. 362. An Act to incorporate the Mutual Trust Institution of the city of New York. Passed April 24, 1872.

CHAP. 363. An Act to amend an act entitled "An act to establish a police department in and for the city of Brooklyn, and to define its powers and duties," passed April fifth, eighteen hundred and seventy, and the acts amendatory thereof, passed March twenty-eight, eighteen hundred and seventy-one. Passed April 25, 1872; three-fifths being present.

CHAP. 364. An Act to create a department of city works in the city of Brooklyn, and to supersede and abolish the "Permanent Board of Water and Sewerage Commissioners, and the office of street commissioner," in said city. Passed April 25, 1872; three-fifths being present.

CHAP. 365. An Act for the relief of the Coney Island and Brooklyn Railroad Company. Passed April 25, 1872.

CHAP. 366. An Act to incorporate the Walden Savings Bank. Passed April 25, 1872.

CHAP. 367. An Act to authorize a double session of the court of general sessions of the peace in and for the city and county of New York, and confirming a resolution of the board of supervisors of said county relative to the judges thereof. Passed April 25, 1872; three-fifths being present.

CHAP. 368. An Act to amend an act entitled "An act to amend an act to enable the several highway districts in the town of Greenburgh, Westchester county, west of and through which the highway known as the late Highland turnpike runs, to macadamize and otherwise improve the public highways within their respective districts," passed April twenty-second, eighteen hundred and sixty-seven. Passed April 25, 1872; three-fifths being present.

CHAP. 369. *An Act giving the consent of the state of New York to the purchase by and ceding jurisdiction to the United States over certain land on Cumberland head, Clinton county, within this state, to be occupied as site of light-house and keepers' dwellings." Passed April 25, 1872, by a two-third vote.*

CHAP. 370. An Act to amend an act entitled "An act to incorporate the Buffalo East Side Street Railway Company," passed May tenth, eighteen hundred and seventy. Passed April 25, 1872.

CHAP. 371. An Act to amend an act entitled "An act for the incorporation of cities and villages, passed December seventh, eighteen hundred and forty-seven," so far as the same relates to the village of North Tonawanda, Niagara county, passed April seventeenth, eighteen hundred and seventy-one. Passed April 25, 1872; three-fifths being present.

CHAP. 372. An Act to amend the charter of the Orphan Asylum Society in the city of New York. Passed April 25, 1872; three-fifths being present.

CHAP. 373. An Act in relation to the appointment of clerk, deputy clerk and other officers of the court of special sessions of the peace in and for the city and county of New York. Passed April 25, 1872; three-fifths being present.

CHAP. 374. *An Act to amend the act entitled "An act to authorize the formation of gas-light companies, passed February sixteen, eighteen hundred and forty-eight." Passed April* 25, 1872.

[illegible]. An Act to amend section two of chapter nine of the laws of eighteen hundred [illegible]-two, entitled "An act relating to appropriations and deficiencies in the city [illegible] of New York, and the audit and payment of salaries and claims in said city [illegible]," passed January thirty, eighteen hundred and seventy-two. Passed April [illegible]; three-fifths being present.

[illegible]. An Act to provide for a vote of the inhabitants of the towns of Little Falls, [illegible] and Danube, in the county of Herkimer, upon the question of the completion of the bridge over the Mohawk river at Fink's basin, in the county of Herkimer, and to [illegible] for the payment of the indebtedness incurred by the commissioners appointed [illegible] chapter nine hundred and three of the laws of eighteen hundred and sixty-nine [illegible] towns on account of said bridge. Passed April 25, 1872; three-fifths being [illegible].

[illegible]. *An Act to amend an act entitled "An act to amend article four of title four, [illegible], of part first of the Revised Statutes, 'of division and other fences.'" Passed* [illegible] 1872.

[illegible]. An Act to amend an act entitled "An act to supply the city of Binghamton [illegible] pure and wholesome water," passed April twenty-fifth, eighteen hundred and [illegible], and the acts amendatory thereof. Passed April 25, 1872; three-fifths being [illegible].

[illegible]. An Act to extend and define the limits of the village of Hornellsville. Passed [illegible], 1872; three-fifths being present.

[illegible]. An Act granting to the West Shore Land and Improvement Company further [illegible]. Passed April 26, 1872; three-fifths being present.

[illegible]. An Act to provide for the adjusting of certain accounts of the city of Brooklyn. [illegible] April 26, 1872; three-fifths being present.

[illegible]. An Act for the relief of the town of Perrinton in the county of Monroe. [illegible] April [illegible], 1872; three-fifths being present.

[illegible]. An Act to legalize certain proceedings of the common council of the city of [illegible] for the relief of Frederick Haake. Passed April 26, 1872; three-fifths [illegible]

[illegible]

CHAP. 384. An Act to authorize the common council of the city of Albany to issue the bonds of said city to provide for the taking of property for an United States building at the said city, and to provide for compensating the owners of the property so taken therefor. Passed April 26, 1872; three-fifths being present.

CHAP. 385. An Act to provide for the payment of certain indebtedness of the city of Elmira. Passed April 26, 1872; three-fifths being present.

CHAP. 386. An Act to extend Monhagen avenue in the town of Walkill, Orange county. Passed April 26, 1872; three-fifths being present.

CHAP. 387. An Act to supply the city of Rochester with pure and wholesome water. Passed April 27, 1872; three-fifths being present.

CHAP. 388. An Act to amend an act entitled "An act to incorporate the city of Kingston," passed March twenty-ninth, eighteen hundred and seventy-two. Passed April 26, 1872; three-fifths being present.

CHAP. 389. An Act to establish a receiver of taxes and to authorize the sale of lands for non-payment of taxes, and for the collection of unpaid taxes in the town of Hempstead, in the county of Queens. Passed April 26, 1872; three-fifths being present.

CHAP. 390. An Act to amend chapter three hundred and ten of the laws of eighteen hundred and sixty-four, being an act to incorporate the Farmers' Protective Union. Passed April 26, 1872.

CHAP. 391. An Act to confirm a deed from the consistory of the Reformed Dutch Church of Poughkeepsie, to the consistory of the Second Reformed Dutch Church of Poughkeepsie. Passed April 26, 1872.

CHAP. 392. *An Act in relation to the Supreme Court Library at Binghamton. Passed April 26, 1872.*

CHAP. 393. An Act in relation to the highway in the town of Yonkers, known as Central road or avenue. Passed April 26, 1872; three-fifths being present.

CHAP. 394. An Act to prevent the obstruction of highways in the county of Chautauqua by the accumulation of snows therein. Passed April 26, 1872; three-fifths being present.

CHAP. 395. An Act to incorporate The Society of Members of the New York Stock Exchange for Mutual Relief, in the city and county and state of New York. Passed April 26, 1872; three-fifths being present.

CHAP. 396. An Act to incorporate the Mamaroneck and Rye Neck Fire Department. Passed April 26, 1872; three-fifths being present.

CHAP. 397. An Act to amend an act entitled "An act to amend and consolidate the several acts relating to the village of Lansingburgh," passed April sixteenth, eighteen hundred and sixty-four. Passed April 27, 1872; three-fifths being present.

CHAP. 398. An Act to incorporate the Batavia Literary Association, and appropriating certain money thereto. Passed April 27, 1872; three-fifths being present.

CHAP. 399. An Act to incorporate the Oswego Railroad Bridge Company, for the purpose of constructing and maintaining a railroad bridge across the Oswego river, in the city of Oswego. Passed April 27, 1872.

CHAP. 400. An Act to incorporate the Oswegatchie Bridge Company. Passed April 27, 1872.

CHAP. 401. An Act to incorporate the Young Men's Universalist Association of the city of New York. Passed April 27, 1872.

CHAP. 402. An Act to release the interest of the people of the state of New York in certain real estate to Elizabeth Handley. Passed April 27, 1872, by a two-third vote.

CHAP. 403. An Act to authorize the construction of a bridge over Tunison's creek in Richmond county. Passed April 27, 1872; three-fifths being present.

CHAP. 404. An Act to amend chapter three hundred and forty-eight of the laws of eighteen hundred and sixty-seven, being an act to amend an act entitled "An act to incorporate the Young Men's Christian Association of the city of Poughkeepsie," passed April twelfth, eighteen hundred and sixty-seven. Passed April 27, 1872.

CHAP. 405. An Act to amend an act entitled "An act to incorporate the city of Ogdensburgh," passed April twenty-seventh, eighteen hundred and sixty-eight. Passed April 27, 1872; three-fifths being present.

CHAP. 406. An Act to authorize the construction of a lock-up in the village of Lima, Livingston county, and the assessment of the expense thereof as a tax upon the village of Lima and the town of Lima, in said county. Passed April 27, 1872; three-fifths being present.

CHAP. 407. An Act to amend an act entitled "An act to provide for the appointment of police commissioners in the village of Green Island, Albany county, and to establish a police force therein," passed April twenty, eighteen hundred and seventy-one. Passed April 27, 1872; three-fifths being present.

CHAP. 408. An Act to provide for the erection of a town hall in the town of Rhinebeck, county of Dutchess. Passed April 27, 1872; three-fifths being present.

CHAP. 409. *An Act to amend an act entitled "An act to establish regulations for the Port of New York," passed April sixteen, eighteen hundred and fifty-seven. Passed April 27, 1872; three-fifths being present.*

CHAP. 410. *An Act making appropriations for the payment of the principal and interest on the canal debt, commencing on the first day of October, eighteen hundred and seventy-two, and to provide for the payment of the debt contracted under section twelve of article seven of the constitution. Passed April 27, 1872; three-fifths being present.*

CHAP. 411. *An Act to prevent and punish certain fraudulent practices in relation to altering counterfeit money or coin. Passed April 27, 1872; three-fifths being present.*

CHAP. 412. *An Act to amend an act entitled "An act to provide for the improvement of Grass river and of the water power thereon, and to check freshets therein." Passed April 27, 1872; three-fifths being present.*

CHAP. 413. An Act to legalize and confirm the official acts of William H. Ireland, a justice of the peace of the town of Coventry, in the county of Chenango. Passed April 27, 1872; three-fifths being present.

CHAP. 414. An Act to legalize and provide for the election of trustees of Sleepy Hollow Cemetery at Tarrytown, and to confirm their official acts. Passed April 27, 1872.

CHAP. 415. An Act to incorporate the Riverhead Savings Bank. Passed April 27, 1872.

CHAP. 416. An Act to provide for the rehearing by the comptroller of the appeal in the matter of the town of Floyd, in the county of Oneida, against the board of supervisors of said county. Passed April 29, 1872; three-fifths being present.

CHAP. 417. An Act in relation to a part of Mamaroneck avenue in the town of Mamaroneck, in the county of Westchester. Passed April 27, 1872; three-fifths being present.

CHAP. 418. An Act in relation to Union avenue in the towns of Mamaroneck and Rye, in the county of Westchester. Passed April 27, 1872; three-fifths being present.

CHAP. 419. An Act to authorize the board of education of Union Free School District Number Nine of the town of Mount Pleasant to borrow money. Passed April 27, 1872; three-fifths being present.

CHAP. 420. An Act in relation to the East and West Martinsburgh burial grounds. Passed April 27, 1872; three-fifths being present.

CHAP. 421. An Act to legalize the action of the town meeting of the town of West Turin, Lewis county, held on the twentieth day of February, eighteen hundred and seventy-two. Passed April 27, 1872.

CHAP. 422. An Act to repeal so much of chapter eight hundred and sixty-eight, of the laws of eighteen hundred and sixty-seven, being an act relating to certain non-resident highway taxes in Clinton county, and the old military tract, as relate to non-resident lands in Franklin county, and the payment of the taxes assessed and collected from the same. Passed April 27, 1872; three-fifths being present.

CHAP. 423. An Act to authorize the town of Canton to aid in the construction of a reservoir upon the head-waters of Grass river, and to legalize the action of the special town meeting of the town of Canton, held February twenty-fourth, eighteen hundred and seventy-two. Passed April 27, 1872; three-fifths being present.

CHAP. 424. *An Act to provide for the dissolution of religious societies, except in the city and county of New York, and for the sale and disposition of the proceeds of the property of said societies. Passed April 27, 1872; three-fifths being present.*

CHAP. 425. An Act to authorize the common council of the city of Brooklyn to open, grade, pave and complete certain streets in said city. Passed April 27, 1872; three-fifths

CHAP. 426. *An Act to amend chapter six hundred and thirty-seven of the laws of eighteen hundred and seventy-one, entitled "An act to amend the act passed February seventeen, eighteen hundred and forty-eight, entitled 'An act to authorize the formation of corporations for manufacturing, mining, mechanical or chemical purposes,'" passed April twentieth, eighteen hundred and seventy-one. Passed April* 27, 1872; *three-fifths being present.*

CHAP. 427. An Act to amend an act entitled "An act to provide for the opening and improvement of Park avenue, between Bridge street and Hudson avenue and Clinton avenue and Broadway, in the city of Brooklyn," passed April seventeenth, eighteen hundred and sixty-eight. Passed April 27, 1872; three-fifths being present.

CHAP. 428. An Act to authorize the taking of certain lands in the city of Buffalo, for the purposes of an avenue leading from the Parade park southerly to Seneca street. Passed April 27, 1872; three-fifths being present.

CHAP. 429. An Act to authorize the city of Buffalo and the board of supervisors of Erie county to grant and convey certain lands in the city of Buffalo. Passed April 27, 1872; three-fifths being present.

CHAP. 430. An Act to amend "An act relating to building bridges in the village of Niagara Falls," passed April twenty-seventh, eighteen hundred and seventy-one. Passed April 25, 1872; three-fifths being present.

CHAP. 431. An Act to authorize the board of supervisors of Franklin county to assess upon the town of Fort Covington five hundred dollars for the purpose of building sidewalks in that town. Passed April 27, 1872; three-fifths being present.

CHAP. 432. *An Act to amend chapter ninety, laws of eighteen hundred and sixty-nine, being an act entitled "An act to provide for the improvement of the navigation of the Racket river and of the hydraulic power thereon, and to check freshets therein," passed April two, eighteen hundred and sixty-nine. Passed April* 29, 1872; *three-fifths being present.*

CHAP. 433. *An Act to amend chapter seven hundred and twenty-one of the laws of eighteen hundred and seventy-one, entitled "An act to amend and consolidate the several acts relating to the preservation of moose, wild deer, birds and fish," passed April twenty-sixth, eighteen hundred and seventy-one, also to repeal section thirty of said act. Passed April* 29, 1872; *three-fifths being present.*

CHAP. 434. An Act to repeal chapter one hundred, laws of eighteen hundred and fifty-eight, entitled "An act to construct a highway from the old state road, in Essex county, to the Port Kent and Hopkinton turnpike, in Franklin county." Passed April 29, 1872; three-fifths being present.

CHAP. 435. An Act to amend an act entitled "An act to incorporate the New York Botanical Club," passed April twenty-one, one thousand eight hundred and seventy-one. Passed April 29, 1872; three-fifths being present.

CHAP. 436. *An Act relative to the setting of fykes and other nets in Harlem and East rivers. Passed April* 22, 1872.

CHAP. 437. An Act to constitute a separate road district in the town of Palatine, in the county of Montgomery. Passed April 29, 1872; three-fifths being present.

CHAP. 438. An Act relating to courts of record and other courts in the city and county of New York. Passed April 29, 1872; three-fifths being present.

CHAP. 439. An Act to change the grade of One Hundred and Thirty-sixth and One Hundred and Thirty-seventh streets, between St. Ann's avenue and Cypress avenue, in the town of Morrisania, county of Westchester. Passed April 29, 1872; three-fifths being present.

CHAP. 440. An Act to amend an act entitled "An act to provide for the incorporation of villages, passed December seventh, eighteen hundred and forty-seven, and the several acts amendatory thereof so far as the same relates to the village of New Rochelle, in the county of Westchester," passed April twenty, eighteen hundred and sixty-four. Passed April 30, 1872; three-fifths being present.

CHAP. 441. An Act to amend chapter five hundred and thirty-four of the laws of eighteen hundred and seventy-one, entitled "An act relative to the improvement of certain portions of the counties of Westchester and New York, including provisions for communication between said counties, and for improving the navigation of Harlem river and Spuyten Duyvil creek. Passed April 30, 1872; three-fifths being present.

CHAP. 442. An Act to release the interest of the state in certain lands of which Thomas Breen died seized, to Margaret Breen, his widow. Passed April 30, 1872, by a two-third vote.

CHAP. 443. An Act to incorporate the Brooklyn City Safe Deposit Company. Passed April 30, 1872.

CHAP. 444. An Act to amend an act entitled "An act to make provisions for the local government of the city of New York," passed April nineteenth, eighteen hundred and seventy-one, and to make further provision therefor, for the year eighteen hundred and seventy-two. Passed April 30, 1872; three-fifths being present.

CHAP. 445. An Act to provide for the speedy construction of sewers in a certain portion of the city of Brooklyn. Passed April 30, 1872; three-fifths being present.

CHAP. 446. An Act to release the interest of the people of the state of New York in certain land to Mary M. Imhorst. Passed April 30, 1872, by a two-third vote.

CHAP. 447. An Act to release to Mary McGarrity the right, title and interest of the people of the state of New York in and to certain real estate in the city of Brooklyn. Passed April 30, 1872, by a two-third vote.

CHAP. 448. An Act to revise and amend an act entitled "An act to construct a road from Carthage, in Jefferson county, to Lake Champlain, in the county of Essex," passed April fourteenth, eighteen hundred and forty-one. Passed April 30, 1872; three-fifths being present.

CHAP. 449. An Act to enable the board of education of the city of Brooklyn to sell certain lands. Passed April 30, 1872; three-fifths being present.

CHAP. 450. An Act to legalize the action of the common council of the city of Syracuse in borrowing and donating money to aid the sufferers by fire at Chicago. Passed April 30. 1872; three-fifths being present.

CHAP. 451. An Act to incorporate the St. Patrick's Temperance and Benevolent Society of Kingsbridgeville, in the county of Westchester. Passed April 30, 1872.

CHAP. 452. An Act for the relief of Thomas O'Brien. Passed April 30, 1872; three-fifths being present.

CHAP. 453. An Act to change the name of the Brooklyn City, Hunter's Point and Prospect Park Railroad Company, to the Brooklyn Crosstown Railroad Company. Passed April 30, 1872.

CHAP. 454. An Act to regulate the rate of charges for carrying passengers on the Gloversville and Northville Railroad. Passed April 30, 1872.

CHAP. 455. An Act to appropriate money for the building of a bridge over the Cayuga Inlet, in the village of Ithaca. Passed May 1, 1872; three-fifths being present.

CHAP. 456. An Act to authorize the canal commissioners to construct a road bridge over the Chemung canal in the village of Watkins, in Schuyler county. Passed May 1, 1872; three-fifths being present.

CHAP. 457. An Act to provide for the payment of certain officers and employees of the senate and assembly for their services. Passed May 1, 1872; three-fifths being present.

CHAP. 458. *An Act to provide for the formation of free public libraries. Passed May* 1, 1872; *three-fifths being present.*

CHAP. 459. An Act to amend, extend and continue an act entitled "An act to incorporate the Bankers' Life Insurance and Trust Company of New York, passed May sixth, eighteen hundred and seventy." Passed May 1, 1872.

CHAP. 460. An Act to establish a ferry from Barber's Point, in the town of Westport, in the county of Essex, across Lake Champlain, and to repeal chapter four hundred and ninety-five of the laws of eighteen hundred and seventy-one. Passed May 1, 1872.

CHAP. 461. An Act to incorporate "St. Agnes Cemetery," of Syracuse, New York. Passed May 1, 1872; three-fifths being present.

CHAP. 462. An Act to amend an act entitled "An act to authorize the village of Yonkers to issue bonds for the purpose of raising money to construct bridges over the Nepperhan river," passed April nineteenth, one thousand eight hundred and seventy-one. Passed May 1, 1872; three-fifths being present.

CHAP. 463. An Act to amend "An act entitled 'An act to authorize the supervisors of Monroe county to raise money to pay for the site of the State Armory in the city of Rochester, and to pay for the use of rooms therein," passed April nineteenth, eighteen hundred and sixty-seven. Passed May 1, 1872; three-fifths being present.

CHAP. 464 An Act legalizing the action of the town of Norfolk, St. Lawrence county, New York, in the purchase of a town hall and site. Passed May 1, 1872; three-fifths being present.

CHAP. 465. An Act to authorize the common council of the city of Brooklyn to open Eighth avenue from Tenth avenue to Greenwood cemetery. Passed May 1, 1872; three-fifths being present.

CHAP. 466. An Act to amend an act entitled "An act to incorporate the village of Savannah, Wayne county, New York," passed April fifteenth, eighteen hundred and sixty-seven. Passed May 1, 1872; three-fifths being present.

CHAP. 467. An Act concerning the Syracuse branch of the New York, Utica and Ogdensburg Railroad Company, and providing for a change in its corporate name. Passed May 1, 1872; three-fifths being present.

CHAP. 468. An Act to revise, amend and consolidate the several acts in relation to the charter of the city of Hudson. Passed May 1, 1872; three-fifths being present.

CHAP. 469. An Act to authorize Isabella Isler, wife of John Isler, Adelle Isler, wife of Charles Isler, and Josefa Isler, wife of Alfred Isler, to hold, devise and convey certain real estate in the city of New York. Passed May 1, 1872.

CHAP. 470. An Act to amend section two of chapter eight hundred and ninety of the laws of eighteen hundred and sixty-eight, entitled "An act to authorize Louis Runyon to establish and maintain a ferry across Seneca lake at Lodi landing. Passed May 1, 1872.

CHAP. 471. An Act amending chapter six hundred and thirty-seven of the laws of eighteen hundred and sixty-six, entitled "An act in relation to the College of the City of New York," passed April seventeenth, eighteen hundred and sixty-six. Passed May 1, 1872; three-fifths being present.

CHAP. 472. An Act placing that portion of the Skaneateles and Elbridge plank-road, lying between the village of Elbridge and Skaneateles junction, under the jurisdiction of the commissioners of highways of the town of Elbridge. Passed May 1, 1872; three-fifths being present.

CHAP. 473. An Act to amend chapter five hundred and eighty-three of the laws of eighteen hundred and seventy-one, entitled "An act to make provision for the local government of the city and county of New York," passed April nineteenth, eighteen hundred and seventy-one. Passed May 1, 1872; three-fifths being present.

CHAP. 474. An Act empowering the Buffalo Street Railroad Company to make certain advances to and contracts with the Buffalo East Side Street Railway Company. Passed May 3, 1872.

CHAP. 475. *An Act in relation to challenges of jurors in criminal cases. Passed May* 3, 1872; *three-fifths being present.*

CHAP. 476. An Act to amend section one of chapter one hundred and twenty-four of the laws of eighteen hundred and seventy-two, and to authorize the Syracuse Northern Railroad Company to continue its road to the New York Central and Hudson River Railroad and to the Syracuse and Chenango Valley Railroad. Passed May 3, 1872.

CHAP. 477. An Act extending the jurisdiction of the park commissioners of the city of Buffalo. Passed May 3, 1872; three-fifths being present.

CHAP. 478. An Act to provide for increased penalties for riding or driving any animal or animals across bridges or over rivers in the town of Brasher, St. Lawrence county Passed May 3, 1872; three-fifths being present.

CHAP. 479. An Act relative to lands bequeathed by the last will and testament of Joseph Cudlipp, deceased, to Joseph Cudlipp, Anna M. Walsh, Sarah C. Cudlipp and Elizabeth A. O'Keefe, for and during their natural lives. Passed May 3, 1872.

CHAP. 480. An Act to incorporate the St. Lawrence Bridge Company. Passed May 3, 1872.

CHAP. 481. An Act to amend an act entitled "An act to incorporate the village of Warwick," passed April fifteenth, eighteen hundred and sixty-seven. Passed May 3, 1872; three-fifths being present.

CHAP. 482. An Act to authorize the United States Contracting Company to change its name. Passed May 3, 1872.

CHAP. 483. *An Act to amend an act entitled "An act to prevent the unlawful taking of oysters planted within the waters of the state of New York," passed April twenty-first, eighteen hundred and sixty-six. Passed May 3, 1872; three-fifths being present.*

CHAP. 484. An Act to provide for the endowment of the Unadilla academy. Passed May 3, 1872; three-fifths being present.

CHAP. 485. *An Act to amend chapter twelve of the laws of eighteen hundred and seventy-two, entitled "An act prescribing the officers and employees that may be elected, appointed or employed by the senate or assembly, fixing the salary and compensation thereof and regulating the proceedings of investigating committees, and providing for the payment of the expenses thereof." Passed May 3, 1872; three-fifths being present.*

CHAP. 486. An Act to release the interest of the people of the state of New York in certain land to John Lietz. Passed May 3, 1872, by a two-third vote.

CHAP. 487. An Act to amend an act entitled "An act to provide for the erection of wharves and piers in the Harlem river, below the Second avenue," passed April fourth, eighteen hundred and sixty-eight. Passed May 3, 1872; three-fifths being present.

CHAP. 488. An act to confirm the oath of Henderson Harger, collector of taxes of the town of Carrolton, in the county of Cattaraugus, to his return for the non-payment of non-resident taxes of the year eighteen hundred and seventy-one. Passed May 3, 1872; three-fifths being present.

CHAP. 489. An Act to provide for the exchange of first mortgage bonds of the Poughkeepsie and Eastern Railroad Company for second mortgage bonds of the said company, by the commissioners appointed to issue the bonds of the city of Poughkeepsie, in aid of the construction of the Poughkeepsie and Eastern Railroad, and to invest the same or the avails thereof in the first mortgage bonds of the said railroad company. Passed May 3, 1872; three-fifths being present.

CHAP. 490. An Act to authorize the city of Rochester to borrow money to pay off its present debt for Arsenal square improvement, and to issue its bonds for the payment of the same. Passed May 3, 1872; three-fifths being present.

CHAP. 491. An Act authorizing John Rosekrans, of Wayland, in the county of Steuben, to remove the remains of certain persons buried on his premises to the Wayland cemetery in said town. Passed May 3, 1872.

CHAP. 492. An Act to abolish the office of the trustees of the freeholders and commonalty of the town of Huntington, in the town of Huntington, county of Suffolk, and to create their successors. Passed May 3, 1872; three-fifths being present.

CHAP. 493. An Act to provide for the improvement of a portion of the Coney Island plank-road, as recently widened. Passed May 3, 1872; three-fifths being present.

CHAP. 494. An Act to amend an act entitled "An act to incorporate the Erie Basin Dock Company, in the city of Brooklyn," passed April eleven, eighteen hundred and sixty-[illegible]. Passed May 3, 1872.

CHAP. 495. An Act to amend an act entitled "An act to incorporate the Lewiston Suspension Bridge Company," passed March twenty-sixth, eighteen hundred and forty-nine. Passed May 3, 1872.

CHAP. 496. An Act to authorize the common council of the city of Syracuse to construct a [illegible] sewer in Harrison street, and to raise money to pay for the same. Passed May 3, 1872; three-fifths being present.

CHAP. 497. An Act to amend chapter three hundred and twenty-three of the laws of eighteen hundred and fifty-nine, entitled "An act to define the powers and duties of the superintendents of the poor in the county of Monroe." Passed May 3, 1872; three-fifths being present.

CHAP. 498. *An Act for the protection of livery stable keepers and other persons keeping horses at livery or pasture. Passed May* 3, 1872.

CHAP. 499. An Act in relation to petit jurors for the county courts and courts of sessions, in the county of Westchester. Passed May 3, 1872; three-fifths being present.

CHAP. 500. An Act to amend an act entitled "An act to amend the act entitled 'An act to provide for laying out and improving roads and avenues in the village and town of Saratoga Springs,'" passed May fifth, eighteen hundred and seventy, passed April twenty-second, eighteen hundred and seventy-two. Passed May 3, 1872; three-fifths being present.

CHAP. 501. An Act for the relief of the Lake Champlain and Moriah Railroad Company. Passed May 3, 1872; three-fifths being present.

CHAP. 502. *An Act declaring Cold brook, in the county of Clinton, and Alder brook in the counties of Clinton and Franklin, tributaries of the Saranac river and emptying into the north branch of that river, public highways. Passed May* 3, 1872.

CHAP. 503. An Act to incorporate the Whitestone Savings Bank. Passed May 3, 1872; three-fifths being present.

CHAP. 504. An Act to incorporate the College Point Savings Bank. Passed May 3, 1872; three-fifths being present.

CHAP. 505. An Act to incorporate the New York and Canada Bridge and Tunnel Company. Passed May 4, 1872.

CHAP. 506. An Act to legalize the acts of the railroad commissioners of the town of Hammond, St. Lawrence county. Passed May 4, 1872; three-fifths being present.

CHAP. 507. An Act to incorporate the Fire Island Hotel, and establish ferries across Fire Island or Great South Bay, in Suffolk county. Passed May 4, 1872; three-fifths being present.

CHAP. 508. An Act to provide for the audit and payment of certain claims and expenses incurred by the direction of the governor and attorney-general in the city of New York. Passed May 4, 1872; three-fifths being present.

CHAP. 509. *An Act to appropriate moneys for construction of new work upon and extraordinary repairs of the canals of this state, and for the payment of awards made by the canal appraisers. Passed May* 4, 1872; *three-fifths being present.*

CHAP. 510. An Act authorizing the board of supervisors of the county of Westchester to investigate the acts and proceedings of certain boards of commissioners for making or extending highways. Passed May 4, 1872; three-fifths being present.

CHAP. 511. An Act to repeal an act entitled "An act to provide for a police court-house in the ninth judicial district in the city of New York," passed April twenty-seven, eighteen hundred and seventy; also to repeal an act entitled "An act to provide for the completion of the court-house for the ninth judicial district of the city of New York," passed February seventeenth, eighteen hundred and seventy-one. Passed May 4, 1872; three-fifths being present.

CHAP. 512. An Act to provide for the improvement of part of One Hundred and Fifty-fifth street, in the city of New York. Passed May 4, 1872; three-fifths being present.

CHAP. 513. *An Act to provide for the erection of houses of detention or lock-ups in the several towns in this state. Passed May* 4, 1872; *three-fifths being present.*

CHAP. 514. An Act to define section five of chapter five hundred and eighty-three of the laws of eighteen hundred and seventy-one, relating to the entry of judgments. Passed May 4, 1872; three-fifths being present.

CHAP. 515. An Act to amend and in addition to an act entitled "An act to incorporate the New England Society, in the city of New York," passed April fifteenth, one thousand eight hundred and thirty-three. Passed May 4, 1872.

CHAP. 516. An Act extending the provisions of certain laws permitting municipal corporations to aid in the construction of railroads, to the county of Erie. Passed May 4, 1872; three-fifths being present.

CHAP. 517. *An Act in relation to the unadjusted claims of the soldiers in the war of eighteen hundred and twelve. Passed May* 4, 1872; *three-fifths being present.*

CHAP. 518. *An Act in relation to the mounted batteries of artillery of the National Guard. Passed May* 4, 1872; *three-fifths being present.*

CHAP. 519. *An Act to repeal chapter two hundred and forty-five of the laws of eighteen hundred and seventy-one, entitled "An act relating to military exemptions." Passed May* 4, 1872; *three-fifths being present.*

CHAP. 520. An Act to amend an act entitled "An act to incorporate the village of Lima, Livingston county, passed April twenty-fifth, eighteen hundred and sixty-seven. Passed May 6, 1872; three-fifths being present.

CHAP. 521. An Act to amend an act entitled "An act to authorize the construction of a railroad through Twenty-third street, in the city of New York, passed May tenth, eighteen hundred and sixty nine," so as to authorize the comptroller of the city of New York to carry into effect the powers conferred by the first section of the above act upon the commissioners of the sinking fund of the city of New York, in relation to the advertising and sale of the franchise for building such railroad to the highest bidder, on paying the amount of such bid or giving security for such payment satisfactory to said comptroller, to issue the certificate of title to such grant mentioned in said first section of said act to Sidney A. Yeomans or to his assigns, and granting all the rights, privileges, powers and benefits conferred and prescribed in the second, third and fourth sections of said act to Sidney A. Yeomans and his assigns, and requiring him or his assigns to finish, complete and equip said road within eight months from the time of receiving such certificate. Passed May 6, 1872.

Chap. 522. An Act to revive and amend the act to incorporate the Wyoming Benevolent Institute, passed April twenty-eighth, eighteen hundred and seventy. Passed May 6, 1872.

Chap. 523. An Act to incorporate Addison Spring Water Company. Passed May 6, 1872.

Chap. 524. *An Act to protect purchasers on sales of real estate of infants by special guardians prior to January first, eighteen hundred and fifty-two. Passed May 6, 1872.*

Chap. 525. An Act to amend an act passed April ninth, eighteen hundred and sixty-seven, entitled "An act to amend and consolidate the several acts relating to the village of Hornellsville." Passed May 6, 1872; three-fifths being present.

Chap. 526. An Act to provide for the repair, improvement, construction and protection of bridges on the Cattaraugus Indian Reservation, in the counties of Erie and Cattaraugus. Passed May 6, 1872; three fifths being present.

Chap. 527. An Act to incorporate a railroad company to construct a street railroad in the city and town of Oswego, in the county of Oswego. Passed May 6, 1872.

Chap. 528. An Act to amend an act entitled "An act to incorporate the Sisterhood of Grey Nuns in the state of New York," passed April sixth, A. D. eighteen hundred and seventy-one. Passed May 6, 1872.

Chap. 529. An Act for the relief of the German United Evangelical St. John's Church of the city of Buffalo. Passed May 6, 1872.

Chap. 530. *An Act increasing the powers and duties of courts of special sessions except in the city and county of New York and the city of Albany. Passed May 6,* 1872; *three-fifths being present.*

Chap. 531. An Act to amend the charter of the Young Men's Christian Association of the city of New York. Passed May 6, 1872.

Chap. 532. An Act to amend an act entitled "An act requiring the district attorney of the county of Erie to give a bond to pay over all moneys received by him as such district attorney, and to provide for the appointment of an assistant district attorney for that county," passed April thirteenth, eighteen hundred and fifty-seven. Passed May 6, 1872; three-fifths being present.

Chap. 533. An Act granting the consent of the state of New York to the purchase by the United States of certain lands for the purpose of the erection of a public building at Utica and ceding jurisdiction over the same. Passed May 6, 1872, by a two-third vote.

Chap. 534. An Act for the relief of certain religious societies in the county of Kings. Passed May 6, 1872.

Chap. 535. An Act to amend chapter five hundred and thirty-nine of the laws of eighteen hundred and seventy, entitled "An act in relation to jurors in the city and county of New York," passed May second, eighteen hundred and seventy. Passed May 6, 1872; three-fifths being present.

Chap. 536. An Act for the lighting of the streets in the town of New Lots, in the county of Kings. Passed May 6, 1872; three-fifths being present.

Chap. 537. *An Act to provide for furnishing two statues of eminent deceased citizens of this state, to be placed in the capitol in Washington in compliance with the invitation of the President of the United States. Passed May* 6, 1873; *three-fifths being present.*

Chap. 538. An Act to define the jail limits of the county of Jefferson. Passed May 6, 1872.

Chap. 539. An Act to amend "An act to incorporate the village of Mount Morris," passed May second, eighteen hundred and thirty-five, and the several acts subsequent amending the same. Passed May 6, 1872; three-fifths being present.

Chap. 540. An Act to amend "An act authorizing the trustees of the village of Mount Morris to subscribe to the capital stock of the Mount Morris Water-works Company," passed May third, eighteen hundred and sixty-nine. Passed May 6, 1872; three-fifths being present.

CHAP. 541. *An Act making appropriations for the support of government. Passed May 6, 1872; three-fifths being present.*

CHAP. 542. An Act in relation to making and repairing highways and bridges in the town of Flatlands, in Kings county. Passed May 6, 1872; three-fifths being present.

CHAP. 543. An Act conferring jurisdiction upon the canal appraisers to hear and determine the claim of Joshua W. Ketchum. Passed May 6, 1872; three-fifths being present.

CHAP. 544. *An Act to declare the day for holding the general state election a public holiday. Passed May 6, 1872; three-fifths being present.*

CHAP. 545. An Act to open, widen, straighten, work and grade Third avenue in the town of Morrisania. Passed May 6, 1872; three-fifths being present.

CHAP. 546. An Act to incorporate the Mechanicville Bridge Company, for the purpose of constructing and maintaining a bridge over the Hudson river between the village of Mechanicville and the town of Schaghticoke. Passed May 6, 1872; three-fifths being present.

CHAP. 547. An Act to incorporate the Otselic Reservoir Company in the counties of Madison and Chenango. Passed May 6, 1872; three-fifths being present.

CHAP. 548. An Act to incorporate "The National American University of Music and other liberal arts," in the city of New York. Passed May 6, 1872.

CHAP. 549. An Act to authorize the water commissioners of the city of Watertown to borrow money for the construction of a reservoir, and for other purposes. Passed May 6, 1872; three-fifths being present.

CHAP. 550. *An Act to encourage steam towage upon the canals of this state. Passed May 6, 1872.*

CHAP. 551. An Act to amend an act entitled "An act to incorporate the city of Newburgh," passed April twenty-second, eighteen hundred and sixty-five, and the several acts amendatory thereof. Passed May 6, 1872; three-fifths being present.

CHAP. 552. An Act to amend an act entitled "An act to authorize the construction and use of a railroad from the southerly side of Newtown creek, in the city of Brooklyn, to the village of Astoria, and through certain streets of said village," passed May fifth, eighteen hundred and sixty-three. Passed May 6, 1872.

CHAP. 553. An Act to authorize the Ridgefield and New York Railroad Company to extend their road through the towns of Lewisboro, Poundridge and Rye, in the county of Westchester. Passed May 6, 1872.

CHAP. 554. An Act to amend an act entitled "An act to lay out, open and grade Sixtieth street in the city of Brooklyn, and towns of New Utrecht and Gravesend, in the county of Kings," passed April sixth, eighteen hundred and seventy-one. Passed May 6, 1872; three-fifths being present.

CHAP. 555. An Act to provide for the election of a police justice in and for the village of Cayuga, and defining its powers and duties. Passed May 6, 1872; three-fifths being present.

CHAP. 556. An Act to amend the charter of the New York Produce Exchange Company, and to confer powers upon said company. Passed May 6, 1872.

CHAP. 557. An Act to provide for supplying the village of College Point, in the county of Queens, with pure and wholesome water. Passed May 6, 1872; three-fifths being present.

CHAP. 558. An Act to provide for supplying the village of Whitestone, in the county of Queens, with pure and wholesome water. Passed May 6, 1872; three-fifths being present.

CHAP. 559. An Act to authorize the city of Oswego to borrow and disburse moneys for city purposes. Passed May 6, 1872.

CHAP. 560. An Act to provide for the rebuilding of the bridge over the Oneida river, between the towns of Clay, in the county of Onondaga, and Hastings, in the county of Oswego, at Caughdenoy. Passed May 6, 1872; three-fifths being present.

CHAP. 561. An Act to authorize the construction of a railroad from the village of Watkins to the village of Havana, in the county of Schuyler, and in and through the streets of said villages. Passed May 6, 1872; three-fifths being present.

CHAP. 562. An Act to amend the charter of the Society of St. John Land, in the county of Suffolk, incorporated under the provisions of the act entitled "An act for the incorporation of benevolent, charitable, scientific and missionary societies," passed April twelfth, eighteen hundred and forty-eight. Passed May 6, 1872; three-fifths being present.

CHAP. 563. An Act to amend an act entitled "An act in relation to the custody and disposition of the money arising from the sale of the plain or common lands of the town of Hempstead, Queens county, New York," passed May third, eighteen hundred and seventy. Passed May 6, 1872; three-fifths being present.

CHAP. 564. An Act to amend the charter of the village of Carthage, Jefferson county. Passed May 6, 1872; three-fifths being present.

CHAP. 565. An Act to amend an act entitled "An act to incorporate the Amsterdam Waterworks Company," passed March seventeenth, eighteen hundred and sixty-five. Passed May 6, 1872; three-fifths being present.

CHAP. 566. An Act to incorporate the New York Deposit and Loan Company. Passed May 7, 1872.

CHAP. 567. An Act conferring additional power upon the trustees of the village of Batavia. Passed May 6, 1872; three-fifths being present.

CHAP. 568. An Act to amend an act entitled "An act in relation to the location and erection of public buildings for the use of Erie county and the city of Buffalo," passed April twenty-one, eighteen hundred and seventy-one. Passed May 7, 1872; three-fifths being present.

CHAP. 569. An Act to amend chapter one hundred and sixty-five of the laws of eighteen hundred and sixty-nine, entitled "An act to authorize the selection and location of certain grounds for public parks, in the city of Buffalo, and to provide for the maintenance and embellishment thereof," passed April fourteenth, eighteen hundred and sixty-nine; and also to authorize the city of Buffalo to issue bonds for laying out, improving and embellishing the same. Passed May 7, 1872; three-fifths being present.

CHAP. 570. *An Act to ascertain by proper proofs the citizens who shall be entitled to the right of suffrage in the state of New York, except in the city and county of New York and the city of Brooklyn, and to repeal chapter five hundred and seventy of the laws of eighteen hundred and seventy-one, entitled "An act to amend an act entitled 'An act in relation to elections in the city and county of New York.'" Passed May* 7, 1872; *three-fifths being present.*

CHAP. 571. An Act to legalize the vote of the electors of the town of Booneville, Oneida county, to raise money to improve certain roads in said town. Passed May 7, 1872; three-fifths being present.

CHAP. 572. An Act to change the time of the appointment of overseers of highways and to define their duties in the county of Suffolk. Passed May 7, 1872; three-fifths being present.

CHAP. 573. An Act in relation to the alteration of town boundaries in the county of Franklin. Passed May 7, 1872; three-fifths being present.

CHAP. 574. *An Act further to amend chapter eight hundred and sixty-four of the laws of eighteen hundred and sixty-eight, entitled "An act to authorize the drainage of marsh land." Passed May* 7, 1872; *three-fifths being present.*

CHAP. 575. An Act to regulate elections in the city of Brooklyn. Passed May 7, 1872.

CHAP. 576. An Act for the relief of the Rochester and State Line Railway Company. Passed May 7, 1872; three-fifths being present.

CHAP. 577. An Act to release to Mary Ann Black certain real estate in the city of Auburn, in the county of Cayuga, of which Archibald Black, her late husband, died seized. Passed May 7, 1872, by a two-third vote.

CHAP. 578. An Act to facilitate the construction by the New York and Albany Railroad Company of a railroad on the west side of the Hudson river, by authorizing the city of Albany to issue its bonds and the Delaware and Hudson Canal Company to guaranty the same for the purpose of aiding in such construction. Passed May 7, 1872; three-fifths being present.

CHAP. 579. An Act in relation to the clerks of the marine court of the city of New York. Passed May 7, 1872; three-fifths being present.

CHAP. 580. An Act in relation to certain local improvements in the city of New York. Passed [illegible]; three-fifths being present.

Chap. 581. An Act supplementary to and amendatory of an act entitled "An act to amend and consolidate the charter of the village of Middletown," passed February seventeenth, eighteen hundred and seventy-two. Passed May 7, 1872; three-fifths being present.

Chap. 582. An Act to incorporate the Union Stock Yard and Market Company. Passed May 7, 1872.

Chap. 583. *An Act to re-appropriate certain money for the enlargement of the Champlain canal, and also to re-appropriate the sum of forty-four thousand dollars, a portion of the unexpended balance appropriated by chapter seven hundred and sixty-eight of the laws of eighteen hundred and seventy, to pay awards by the canal appraisers and the canal board for the years eighteen hundred and sixty-eight and eighteen hundred and sixty-nine, and further, to re-appropriate the sum of ten thousand dollars for the purpose of rebuilding, of stone, the state dam at Troy. Passed May* 7, 1872; *three-fifths being present.*

Chap. 584. An Act in relation to certain lands in the twelfth ward of the city of New York, belonging to the mayor, aldermen and commonalty of said city. Passed May 7, 1872; three-fifths being present.

Chap. 585. *An Act to authorize the agent and warden of the Auburn prison to sell certain lands belonging to the state. Passed May* 7, 1872; *three-fifths being present.*

Chap. 586. An Act relating to lands in the city of New York, devised by Frances Wiener, deceased. Passed May 7, 1872.

Chap. 587. *An Act to authorize the appointment of assistant district attorney in certain counties in this state. Passed May* 7, 1872; *three-fifths being present.*

Chap. 588. An Act to amend the act entitled "An act to amend and make additions to an act entitled 'An act to revise the charter of the city of Oswego,'" passed April sixteen, eighteen hundred and sixty, and the acts amendatory thereto as amended April fifteen, eighteen hundred and seventy. Passed May 7, 1872; three-fifths being present.

Chap. 589. An Act in relation to the Board of Trustees of the General Convention of Universalists in the United States of America. Passed May 7, 1872.

Chap. 590. An Act to regulate processions and parades in the cities of the state of New York. Passed May 7, 1872.

Chap. 591. An Act to authorize the Pennsylvania and Sodus Bay Railroad, the Sodus Bay and Corning Railroad Company, and the Sodus Point and Southern Railroad Company to connect their respective railroads by branches therefrom. Passed May 7, 1872.

Chap. 592. An act making provision for the support of the Albany City Dispensary. Passed May 7,1872; three-fifths being present.

Chap. 593. An Act to extend the distribution of Croton water through the city of New York, and to lay the necessary mains to deliver it at higher elevations. Passed May 7, 1872; three-fifths being present.

Chap. 594. An Act to authorize the Utica, Ithaca and Elmira Railroad Company to extend their road, and to confirm their purchase of a portion of the road-bed of the Lake Ontario, Auburn and New York Railroad, and for other purposes. Passed May 8, 1872.

Chap. 595. An Act to amend as to the county of Kings an act entitled "An act to amend and consolidate the several acts relating to the preservation of moose, wild deer, birds and fish," passed April twenty-sixth, eighteen hundred and seventy-one, and repealing section forty-six of said act. Passed May 8, 1872; three-fifths being present.

Chap. 596. An Act to amend an act entitled "An act to incorporate the New Paltz Savings Bank," passed March twenty-second, eighteen hundred and seventy-one. Passed May 8, 1872.

Chap. 597. An Act to extend the time for the completion of the Rondout and Port Jervis Railroad Company. Passed May 8, 1872.

Chap. 598. *An Act for the better preservation of horse records. Passed May* 8, 1872; *three-fifths being present.*

Chap. 599. *An Act to amend chapter three hundred and forty-six of the laws of eighteen hundred and fifty-nine, entitled "An act concerning the salt springs and the manufacture of salt," passed April fifteenth, eighteen hundred and fifty-nine. Passed May* 8, 1872; *three-fifths being present.*

Chap. 600. An Act relating to lands devised by David Stanley, deceased. Passed May 8, 1872.

Chap. 601. An Act to authorize the Buffalo, New York and Philadelphia Railway Company to guarantee the bonds of other railway companies. Passed May 8, 1872.

CHAP. 602. An Act to authorize the removal of the remains of all persons interred in Monroe street cemetery, in the city of Rochester, to Mount Hope or other cemeteries in the city, and the taking of the lands included within the bounds of said Monroe street cemetery by the city of Rochester for public school and park purposes; also the issue of bonds by said city to defray the expenses thereof. Passed May 8, 1872; three-fifths being present.

CHAP. 603. An Act to legalize the official acts and proceedings of John R. Williams, a justice of the peace of the town of Knox, in the county of Albany. Passed May 8, 1872.

CHAP. 604. An Act to authorize the Roundout and Oswego Railroad Company to extend its road and change its corporate name. Passed May 9, 1872; three-fifths being present.

CHAP. 605. An Act to amend an act entitled "An act to revise the charter of the city of Auburn," passed April twenty-second, eighteen hundred and sixty-nine. Passed May 9, 1872; three-fifths being present.

CHAP. 606. An Act to provide for the adjustment and payment for services and disbursements made and rendered for the Seneca Nation of Indians, by Frank A. Newell, while attorney for said nation. Passed May 9, 1872; three-fifths being present.

CHAP. 607. An Act to amend an act entitled "An act to amend and consolidate the several acts relative to the village of Ballston Spa," passed April twelfth, eighteen hundred and fifty-five, as amended by "An act to amend an act entitled 'An act to amend and consolidate the several acts relative to the village of Ballston Spa,'" passed May ninth, eighteen hundred and sixty-eight, and for the purpose of securing an additional supply of water for the use of said village. Passed May 9, 1872; three-fifths being present.

CHAP. 608. An Act for the preservation of fish in the waters of Steele's creek and McGowan's creek in the county of Herkimer. Passed May 9, 1872; three-fifths being present.

CHAP. 609. *An Act to amend an act entitled "An act to authorize the formation, establishing and maintaining of driving park and park associations," passed April seventeenth, eighteen hundred and seventy-two. Passed May* 9, 1872; *three-fifths being present.*

CHAP. 610. An act to amend the charter of the New York Bond Deposit Company of the city of New York. Passed May 9, 1872.

CHAP. 611. *An Act in relation to the capital stock of corporations. Passed May* 9, 1872.

CHAP. 612. An Act to amend an act entitled "An act to incorporate the Utica and Mohawk Street Railroad Company," passed May seventeenth, eighteen hundred and sixty-nine. Passed May 9, 1872.

CHAP. 613. *An Act re-appropriating a certain portion of the income of the United States Deposit Fund for the benefit of academies. Passed May* 9, 1872; *three-fifths being present.*

CHAP. 614. An Act to extend the time for the collection of assessments for the improvement of Atlantic avenue in the town of New Lots, Kings county. Passed May 9, 1872; three-fifths being present.

CHAP. 615. An Act to establish St. Paul's American Protestant Episcopal Church, Rome, Italy, by a board of trustees in New York city. Passed May 9, 1872.

CHAP. 616. *An Act to amend chapter seven hundred and forty-four of the laws of eighteen hundred and sixty-seven, entitled "An act to define the objects of the New York State Institution for the Blind, and to provide for its management," passed April twenty-four, eighteen hundred and sixty-seven. Passed May* 9, 1872; *three-fifths being present.*

CHAP. 617. An Act to provide for the purchase of a fire apparatus for the village of Canajoharie, and for the more effectual protection of said village against fire. Passed May 9, 1872; three-fifths being present.

CHAP. 618. An Act to authorize the Brooklyn Improvement Company to issue preferred and special stock. Passed May 9, 1872.

CHAP. 619. *An Act dividing the state into congressional districts. Passed May* 6, 1872, *notwithstanding the objections of the governor.*

CHAP. 620. An Act to restrict the power of the city of Brooklyn to issue bonds or loan its credit for local improvements. Passed May 10, 1872; three-fifths being present.

CHAP. 621. An Act to amend an act entitled "An act for establishing a turnpike road between the cities of Albany and Schenectady," passed March thirtieth, eighteen hundred and two, and authorizing the president, directors and company of said turnpike road to abandon a part of their road. Passed May 10, 1872; three-fifths being present.

CHAP. 622. An Act to provide for examining and auditing the accounts of certain commissioners for making, improving or extending certain roads in the town of Yonkers. Passed May 10, 1872; three-fifths being present.

CHAP. 623. An Act to amend the charter of the Agricultural Insurance Company of Watertown, Jefferson county, New York. Passed May 10, 1872.

CHAP. 624. An Act to amend the charter of the United States Life Insurance Company in the city of New York. Passed May 10, 1872.

CHAP. 625. An Act to amend an act entitled "An act to revise the charter of the city of Utica," passed February twenty-eight, eighteen hundred and sixty-two, passed February twenty-fifth, eighteen hundred and seventy. Passed May 10, 1872; three-fifths being present.

CHAP. 626. An Act to amend section fourteen of an act entitled "An act to incorporate the Sidney and Unadilla Bridge Company," passed April twenty-seventh, eighteen hundred and sixty-six. Passed May 10, 1872.

CHAP. 627. *An Act in the relation to the court for the trial of impeachments. Passed May* 10, 1872.

CHAP. 628. An act to supply the village of Warren, in the county of Rockland, with pure and wholesome water. Passed May 10, 1872; three-fifths being present.

CHAP. 629. An Act relating to the marine court in the city of New York, declaring and defining its jurisdiction and practice, and consolidating the several acts affecting the said court. Passed May 10, 1872; three-fifths being present.

CHAP. 630. An Act to amend an act entitled "An act to incorporate the New York Life Insurance and Trust Company," passed March ninth, eighteen hundred and thirty, and the act amendatory thereof, passed May second, eighteen hundred and thirty-four. Passed May 10, 1872.

CHAP. 631. An Act in relation to the college of the city of New York. Passed May 10, 1872.

CHAP. 632. An Act in relation to the Brooklyn Club. Passed May 10, 1872.

CHAP. 633. An Act relating to the Queens County Railway Company. Passed May 10, 1872; three-fifths being present.

CHAP. 634. An Act relating to the Pacific Mail Steamers Company, authorizing the reduction of its capital stock and prescribing the qualification of directors. Passed May 11, 1872.

CHAP. 635. An Act to amend the charter of the Foundling Asylum of the Sisters of Charity in the city of New York. Passed May 11, 1872; three-fifths being present.

CHAP. 636. An Act in relation to the incorporation of the village of Whitney's Point. Passed May 11, 1872; three-fifths being present.

CHAP. 637. An Act to amend an act entitled "An act to provide for the election of police commissioners for the city of Oswego, and to organize a police department therein, and to amend the charter of said city," passed April sixteenth, eighteen hundred and seventy. Passed May 11, 1872; three-fifths being present.

CHAP. 638. An Act to amend an act entitled "An act to authorize the board of trustees of the town of Morrisania to lay out and open One Hundred and Fifty-sixth street, from St. Ann's avenue to the Third avenue, in the town of Morrisania, county of Westchester," passed April thirteenth, eighteen hundred and seventy-one. Passed May 11, 1872; three-fifths being present.

CHAP. 639. An Act to amend an act entitled "An act to provide for the drainage of the swamp, bog and other low and wet lands in the village of White Plains and adjacent thereto," passed May second, eighteen hundred and seventy-one. Passed May 11, 1872; three-fifths being present.

CHAP. 640. An Act to amend the charter of the Lutheran Cemetery at Middle Village, Long Island. Passed May 11, 1872; three-fifths being present.

CHAP. 641. An Act to incorporate the Auburn City Hospital. Passed May 11, 1872; three-fifths being present.

CHAP. 642. An Act to open and extend South Eleventh street, in the city of Brooklyn, from its present termination to Third street. Passed May 11, 1872; three-fifths being present.

CHAP. 643. An Act to empower the levying of a tax on Union School District Number One in the town of Clarence, county of Erie, for the purpose of creating a permanent fund for the employment of teachers, and to regulate the investment and management of said fund; also to create the office of loan commissioner for said district, and to provide for the exemption of said district from taxes for the payment of teachers' wages. Passed May 11, 1872; three-fifths being present.

Chap. 644. An Act to incorporate the Trustees of the Presbytery of Westchester. Passed May 11, 1872.

Chap. 645. An Act to release the interests of the people of this state in certain lands, to Sarah Mann, and to authorize her to hold and convey the same. Passed May 11, 1872; three-fifths being present.

Chap. 646. An Act to incorporate the Port Richmond Savings Bank. Passed May 11, 1872.

Chap. 647. An Act to incorporate "The Shelter Island Grove and Camp-meeting Association of the Methodist Episcopal Church." Passed May 11, 1872.

Chap. 648. An Act repealing the act entitled "An act to incorporate the Port Jervis Driving Park Association," passed March twenty-second, eighteen hundred and seventy-one. Passed May 11, 1872.

Chap. 649. *An Act further to amend chapter three hundred and nineteen of the laws of eighteen hundred and forty-eight, entitled "An act for the incorporation of benevolent, charitable, scientific and missionary societies," and the several acts amendatory thereof. Passed May* 11, 1872.

Chap. 650. An Act authorizing the trustees of the village of Tonawanda to raise money, by tax, to pay the indebtedness of said village. Passed May 11, 1872; three-fifths being present.

Chap. 651. *An Act to provide for the construction of a canal bridge over the Erie canal at Madison street, in the city of Rome. Passed May* 13, 1872; *three-fifths being present.*

Chap. 652. *An Act to authorize the construction of a draw or swing bridge over the Erie canal in the city of Utica. Passed May* 13, 1872; *three-fifths being present.*

Chap. 653. *An Act to amend an act entitled "An act authorizing the canal commissioners to construct a swing bridge over the Erie canal, on Buffalo street, in the city of Rochester, and to use the materials of the old bridge in constructing a bridge over said canal to connect Munger and Averill streets in said city," passed April seven, eighteen hundred and seventy-one. Passed May* 13, 1872; *three-fifths being present.*

Chap. 654. An Act to amend chapter five hundred and eighty-five of laws of eighteen hundred and sixty-five, entitled "An act to establish Cornell University and to appropriate to it the income of the sale of public lands granted to this state by congress on the second day of July, eighteen hundred and sixty-two, also to restrict the operation of chapter five hundred and eleven of the laws of eighteen hundred and sixty-three. Passed May 13, 1872.

Chap. 655. An Act to authorize the sale of the state armory at Ballston Spa. Passed May 13, 1872; three-fifths being present.

Chap. 656. An Act to incorporate the Mechanics' and Traders' Exchange of the city of Brooklyn. Passed May 13, 1872.

Chap. 657. An Act to enable the commissioners of the land office to convey a school-house lot to the trustees of school district number three, in the town of Dannemora. Passed May 13, 1872, by a two-third vote.

Chap. 658. An Act to extend the time of beginning the construction of the Newburgh and [illegible] Railway, and expending ten per cent of the amount of its capital stock thereon. Passed May 13, 1872; three-fifths being present.

Chap. 659. An Act for the preservation of shell fish in the town of North Hempstead, in Queens county. Passed May 13, 1872; three-fifths being present.

Chap. 660. An Act to authorize the president and trustees of the village of West Troy to raise by tax upon the taxable property within said village, the sum of four thousand [illegible] hundred and forty-six dollars and seventy-three cents, to pay the outstanding indebtedness of said village. Passed May 13, 1872; three-fifths being present.

Chap. 661. An Act to authorize the New York Loan and Indemnity Company to accept and execute certain [illegible]. Passed May 13, 1872.

Chap. 662. An Act to extend the time for the collection of taxes in the village of Richfield Springs, in the county of Otsego. Passed May 13, 1872.

CHAP. 663. An Act for the completion of Westchester avenue, in the towns of White Plains, Harrison and Rye, in the county of Westchester. Passed May 13, 1872; three-fifths being present.

CHAP. 664. An Act to authorize the rebuilding and repairing of certain wharves and piers in the city of Brooklyn, New York. Passed May 13, 1872; three-fifths being present.

CHAP. 665. An Act to extend the time for the organization of the Mutual Fire Insurance Company. Passed May 13, 1872; three-fifths being present.

CHAP. 666. An Act to amend an act entitled "An act for the protection of the planting of oysters, in the towns of Islip and Huntington, in the county of Suffolk, New York," passed March thirty-one, eighteen hundred and sixty-six. Passed May 13, 1872, by a two-third vote.

CHAP. 667. An Act supplementary to an act entitled "An act to regulate and protect the planting of oysters in the public waters of the towns of Jamaica and Hempstead, in the county of Queens," passed April twenty, eighteen hundred and seventy-one. Passed May 13, 1872; three-fifths being present.

CHAP. 668. An Act to amend an act entitled "An act to authorize the trustees of the village of White Plains, in the county of Westchester, to regulate, grade and macadamize or pave Railroad avenue in said village," passed April nineteenth, eighteen hundred and seventy-one, and for the protection of the pavement on the said street or avenue. Passed May 13, 1872; three-fifths being present.

CHAP. 669. *An Act in relation to mechanics' liens. Passed May* 13, 1872; *three-fifths being present.*

CHAP. 670. *An Act relative to the care and education of deaf mutes. Passed May* 13, 1872; *three-fifths being present.*

CHAP. 671. An Act to amend an act entitled "An act to incorporate the Journeymen's Ship Joiners' Benevolent Association of the city of New York," passed April thirteenth, eighteen hundred and forty. Passed May 13, 1872.

CHAP. 672. An Act to amend "An act to incorporate the New York City Sunday School and Missionary Society of the Methodist Episcopal Church," passed April fourteen, eighteen hundred and sixty-six. Passed May 13, 1872; three-fifths being present.

CHAP. 673. An Act to amend an act entitled "An act to incorporate the Troy Young Men's Association," passed April twentieth, eighteen hundred and thirty-five. Passed May 13, 1872.

CHAP. 674. An Act to extend the time within which the taxes to be raised in the city and county of New York, and the general fund of the said city and county, for the year eighteen hundred and seventy-two, may be fixed, set apart and apportioned, and provide further regulations in respect thereto. Passed May 13, 1872; three-fifths being present.

CHAP. 675. An Act in relation to the elections in the city and county of New York, and to provide for ascertaining, by proper proofs, the citizens who shall be entitled to the right of suffrage thereat. Passed May 14, 1872; three-fifths being present.

CHAP. 676. An Act to amend chapter nine of the laws of eighteen hundred and seventy-two, entitled "An act relating to appropriations and deficiencies in the city and county of New York, and the audit and payment of salaries and claims in said city and county," by providing for the audit and payment of additional claims. Passed May 14, 1872; three-fifths being present.

CHAP. 677. An Act in relation to the cleaning of the streets, avenues, lanes, alleys, gutters, wharves, piers and heads of slips in the city of New York, and the removal of all ashes, garbage, rubbish, and sweepings, and all dead animals, blood, offal and other refuse matter, and all bones, fish not fit for human food, and all diseased, tainted and impure meats, and other like matters in said city, therefrom, and in relation to the supervision and enforcement of and the cancellation of existing contracts and arrangements in respect thereto. Passed May 14, 1872; three-fifths being present.

CHAP. 678. An Act to legalize the proceedings of the Quincy Rural Cemetery Association, held December first and second, eighteen hundred and seventy-one, in the town of Ripley, county of Chautauqua, New York. Passed May 14, 1872.

CHAP. 679. An Act authorizing the commissioners of public charities and correction in the city of New York, to acquire title to portions of Ward's Island, and the water rights surrounding the same. Passed May 14, 1872; three-fifths being present.

CHAP. 680. *An Act to amend an act entitled "An act in relation to wills," passed April twenty-third, eighteen hundred and sixty-four. Passed May* 14, 1872; *three-fifths being present.*

Chap. 681. An Act in relation to the filing of certain claims of Nicholas Shaub, Charles Shultz, William Hilman, John Kretzel, Christian Deidrich, Jacob Nagle, George Goodnough, Betts and Ayer, Joseph Hermon, John Kippert, Frederick Rodenz, Charles Deidrich, Jr., Frederick Deidrich, John Rahberg, Theodore Hartlavan, John Henning, John Brensing, Charles Deidrich, Sr., Joseph Bliss and Thomas J. Collins. Passed May 14, 1872; three-fifths being present.

Chap. 682. An Act to amend section three of chapter three hundred and sixty-four of the laws of eighteen hundred and seventy-one, entitled "An act to provide for the purchase of a new school-house site, and for the erection of a school-house thereon, in school district number three, at Whitestone, in the town of Flushing, in Queens county, and for the sale of the present school-house and site in said district." Passed May 14, 1872; three-fifths being present.

Chap. 683. An Act to provide the village of Lansingburgh, in the county of Rensselaer, with a supply of pure and wholesome water. Passed May 14, 1872; three-fifths being present.

Chap. 684. An Act to amend section two of chapter two hundred and three of laws of eighteen hundred and sixty-three, relating to the village of Niagara City, in the county of Niagara. Passed May 14, 1872; three-fifths being present.

Chap. 685. An Act to extend the provisions of chapter fifty-seven of the laws of eighteen hundred and sixty, entitled "An act conferring additional powers and duties on courts of special sessions in the county of Monroe," and chapter forty-seven of the laws of eighteen hundred and seventy, being an act amendatory thereof, to the county of Wayne. Passed May 14, 1872; three-fifths being present.

Chap. 686. An Act to amend an act entitled "An act to erect the village of Middleburgh into a separate road district," passed April seventh, eighteen hundred and fifty-nine, and the acts amendatory thereof, passed February fifteenth, eighteen hundred and sixty-seven, and March twentieth, eighteen hundred and seventy-one. Passed May 14, 1872; three-fifths being present.

Chap. 687. An Act to provide means for the support of the Inebriates' Home for Kings county, and the better government thereof. Passed May 14, 1872; three-fifths being present.

Chap. 688. An Act to amend an act entitled "An act to increase the number of judges of the city court of Brooklyn, and to regulate the civil and criminal jurisdiction thereof," passed April twenty-eighth, eighteen hundred and seventy. Passed May 14, 1872; three-fifths being present.

Chap. 689. An Act extending the provisions of certain laws permitting municipal corporations to aid in the construction of railroads to the town of Marcellus, in the county of Onondaga. Passed May 14, 1873; three-fifths being present.

Chap. [illegible]. An Act to amend an act entitled "An act to incorporate the Industrial Exhibition Company, and to authorize said company to purchase real estate in the city of New York, and to erect a building or buildings which shall be used as an industrial exhibition," passed April twenty-first, eighteen hundred and seventy. Passed May 14, [illegible]; three-fifths being present.

[illegible]. An Act to amend chapter four hundred and two of the laws of eighteen hundred and fifty-four, being "An act for the better security of mechanics and others erecting buildings in the counties of Westchester, Oneida, Cortland, Broome, Putnam, [illegible], Orleans, Niagara, Livingston, Otsego, Lewis, Orange and Dutchess," passed [illegible] seventeenth, eighteen hundred and fifty-four, extending the provisions thereof, [illegible] all acts amendatory thereof, to the county of Erie, excepting the city of Buffalo. Passed May 14, 1872; three-fifths being present.

[illegible]. An Act to amend section three of chapter nineteen of the laws of eighteen hundred and twenty-one, to perpetuate certain testimony respecting the title of the [illegible] estate in this state. Passed May 14, 1872.

[illegible]. *An Act in relation to the service of citations on lunatics and idiots. Passed May [illegible], 1872; three-fifths being present.*

Chap. 694. An Act making an appropriation for the improvement of the wagon road [illegible] westerly from the Adirondack railroad depot, in the town of Hadley, Saratoga county, to [illegible]'s Hollow, in the town of Edingburgh, in said county, a distance of [illegible] miles. Passed May 14, 1872, by a two-third vote.

[illegible]. An Act to incorporate the New York Homoeopathic Surgical Hospital, in the city of New York. Passed May 14, 1872; three-fifths being present.

CHAP. 696. *An Act to amend chapter two hundred and nine of the laws of eighteen hundred and forty-seven, entitled "An act in relation to cemeteries in incorporated villages." Passed May 14, 1872; three-fifths being present.*

CHAP. 697. An Act to incorporate the Genesee Valley Water Works Company. Passed May 14, 1872; three-fifths being present.

CHAP 698. *An Act to amend an act entitled "An act respecting elections other than for militia and town officers," passed April fifth, eighteen hundred and forty-two. Passed May 14, 1872.*

CHAP. 699. *An Act to establish a rifle range and to promote skill in marksmanship among the national guard. Passed May 14, 1872; three-fifths being present.*

CHAP. 700. *An Act to supply deficiencies in former appropriations, and to pay the indebtedness of the state on account of the canals, which deficiencies and indebtedness have been changed into liabilities for money borrowed to pay them, or into certificates of indebtedness on which the state is now paying interest, and to pay the floating indebtedness of the state and the estimated liabilities for the present fiscal year not yet provided for by law, and to raise money therefor by an issue of the bonds of the state, and to provide for submitting the question thereon to the people. Passed May 15, 1872; three-fifths being present.*

CHAP. 701. An Act to incorporate the German American Mutual Warehousing and Security Company. Passed May 14, 1872.

CHAP. 702. An Act to improve and regulate the use of the Fourth avenue in the city of New York. Passed May 14, 1872; three-fifths being present.

CHAH. 703. An Act to extend the powers of notaries public in the city and county of New York, and in the county of Kings. Passed May 14, 1872; three-fifths being present.

CHAP. 704. An Act to provide for the collection of the expenses of constructing certain sewers in the city of Brooklyn, and to confirm the construction of said sewers. Passed May 14, 1872; three-fifths being present.

CHAP. 705. An Act requiring the Brooklyn, Winfield and Newtown Railway Company to close a portion of its route, and granting additional privileges to said company. Passed May 14, 1872.

CHAP. 706. An Act to authorize the Morrisania Steamboat Company to issue bonds, and to change the place of their principal office. Passed May 14, 1872.

CHAP. 707. An Act to authorize the supervisors of the town of New Utrecht, county of Kings, to pay over certain money to the commissioners for grading Fourth avenue, in said town. Passed May 14, 1872; three-fifths being present.

CHAP. 708. An Act relative to the North Park Railroad Company. Passed May 14, 1872.

CHAP. 709. An Act to amend an act entitled "An act to amend the charter of the Buffalo Orphan Asylum," passed April two, eighteen hundred and thirty-nine. Passed May 14, 1872.

CHAP. 710. An Act to amend an act entitled "An act to open and widen portions of Sackett, Douglas and President streets, and otherwise alter the commissioners' map of the city of Brooklyn," passed May sixth, eighteen hundred and sixty-eight. Passed May 14, 1872; three-fifths being present.

CHAP. 711. An Act to provide for the collection of assessments against Prospect park and the parade grounds, in the county of Kings. Passed May 14, 1872; three-fifths being present.

CHAP. 712. An Act to incorporate the Rochester Trust Company. Passed May 14, 1872.

CHAP. 713. An Act to regulate taxation for road purposes in the village of Tarrytown, Westchester county. Passed May 14, 1872; three-fifths being present.

CHAP. 714. An Act to amend an act entitled "An act to extend and improve Fourth street in the city of Brooklyn," passed April tenth, eighteen hundred and seventy-one, and to confirm certain proceedings had thereunder. Passed May 14, 1872; three-fifths being present.

CHAP. 715. An Act to amend an act entitled "An act for the further extension of Prospect park, in the city of Brooklyn," passed April twenty-fourth, one thousand eight hundred and sixty-eight. Passed May 14, 1872; three-fifths being present.

CHAP. 716. An Act to authorize the construction of a street railroad from the city of Auburn to Willow Brook, in the town of Owasco. Passed May 14, 1872.

CHAP. 717. An Act to reimburse the commissioners named in chapter six hundred and fifty-three of laws of eighteen hundred and sixty-nine, for moneys expended by them in the discharge of their trust conferred by the provisions of said act. Passed May 14, 1872, by a two-third vote.

CHAP. 718. An Act to re-enact and amend chapter one hundred and twenty-five of the laws of eighteen hundred and fifty-one, entitled "An act to incorporate the Minisceongo Ferry Company, in the county of Rockland." Passed May 14, 1872; three-fifths being present.

CHAP. 719. An Act to incorporate "The Palette of the city of New York." Passed May 14, 1872.

CHAP. 720. An Act to alter the commissioners' map of the city of Brooklyn. Passed May 14, 1872; three-fifths being present.

CHAP. 721. An Act to amend chapter three hundred and sixty-six of the laws of eighteen hundred and seventy, entitled "An act in regard to public libraries incorporated in the state of New York." Passed May 14, 1872; three-fifths being present.

CHAP. 722. An Act to authorize the common council of the city of Brooklyn to open and grade, pave and complete certain streets in said city. Passed May 14, 1872; three-fifths being present.

CHAP. 723. An Act to amend an act entitled "An act to provide for the improvement of Newtown Creek, between Maspeth avenue and Metropolitan avenue," passed April twelfth, eighteen hundred and seventy-one. Passed May 14, 1872; three-fifths being present.

CHAP. 724. An Act to provide for increased penalties for riding or driving any animal or animals across the bridges over the streams in the town of Ellisburgh, in the county of Jefferson. Passed May 14, 1872; three-fifths being present.

CHAP. 725. An Act to amend an act entitled "An act to incorporate the National Trust Company of the city of New York," passed April nineteenth, eighteen hundred and sixty-seven. Passed May 14, 1872.

CHAP. 726. An Act to amend an act passed May eleventh, eighteen hundred and sixty-six, entitled "An act to lay out and improve a public highway or avenue from Prospect Park, in the city of Brooklyn, toward Coney Island, in the county of Kings." Passed May 14, 1872; three-fifths being present.

CHAP. 727. An Act to authorize the board of supervisors of Queens county to issue a warrant for the collection of the taxes of the town of Newtown, Queens county, for the year eighteen hundred and seventy-one. Passed May 14, 1872; three-fifths being present.

CHAP. 728. An Act to amend an act entitled "An act to incorporate the city of Elmira," passed April seventh, eighteen hundred and sixty-four, and the several acts amendatory thereof. Passed May 15, 1872; three-fifths being present.

CHAP. 729. An Act in relation to the improvement of the Eighth avenue, in the city of New York. Passed May 15, 1872; three-fifths being present.

CHAP. 730. An Act for the relief of the Standard Life Insurance Company. Passed May 15, 1872.

CHAP. 731. An Act to establish the seventh ward in the city of Elmira. Passed May 15, 1872.

CHAP. 732. An Act to amend an act in relation to the cleaning of the streets, avenues, lanes, alleys, gutters, wharves, piers and heads of slips in the city of New York, and the removal of all ashes, garbage, rubbish and sweepings, and all dead animals, blood, offal and other refuse matter, and all bones, fish not fit for human food, and all diseased, tainted and impure meats, and other like matters in said city therefrom, and in relation to the supervision and enforcement of and the cancellation of existing contracts and arrangements in respect thereto, passed May fourteenth, eighteen hundred and seventy-two. Passed May 15, 1872.

CHAP. 733. An Act making appropriations for certain expenses of government, and for supplying deficiencies in former appropriations. Passed May 15, 1872; three-fifths being present.

CHAP. 734. An Act to provide means to pay the canal and general fund deficiencies directed to be paid by the act chapter seven hundred of the laws of eighteen hundred and seventy-two. Passed May 15, 1872; three-fifths being present.

CHAP. 735. An Act to confirm proceedings under chapter nine hundred and five of the laws of eighteen hundred and sixty-nine, and chapter seven hundred and fifty of the laws of eighteen hundred and seventy, relative to laying out a public highway in the towns of Jamaica and Newtown, Queens county. Passed May 15, 1872; three-fifths being present.

CHAP. 736. *An Act to provide ways and means for the support of government. Passed May* 15, 1872; *three-fifths being present.*

CHAP. 737. An Act to alter the commissioner's map of the city of Brooklyn. Passed May 15, 1872; three-fifths being present.

CHAP. 738. An Act to amend certain provisions of law relating to wharves, piers and bulkheads in the city of New York. Passed May 16, 1872.

CHAP. 739. An Act to make provision for the improvement of the several parks, squares and places in the city of New York. Passed May 16, 1872; three-fifths being present.

CHAP. 740. An Act in relation to completing certain work in Black Rock Harbor, and at Lower Black Rock, Buffalo. Passed May 16, 1872; three-fifths being present.

CHAP. 741. An Act to confirm an assessment for the expense of paving Broad street in the city of Utica. Passed May 16, 1872; three-fifths being present.

CHAP. 742. An Act for the relief of Cornelia G. Fuller and Annie E. Fitzhugh, devisees and legatees under the last will and testament of Charles H. Carrol, deceased. Passed May 16, 1872; three-fifths being present.

CHAP. 743. An Act to repeal chapter eight hundred and eighty-nine of the laws of eighteen hundred and seventy-one, entitled "An act to amend chapter one hundred and sixty of the laws of eighteen hundred and sixty-six, entitled 'An act to facilitate the construction of the Schoharie Valley Railroad,'" also chapter six hundred and sixteen of the laws of eighteen hundred and sixty-seven, entitled "An act to reduce the number of directors of the Schoharie Valley Railroad Company; to re-enact the portions of the chapter so amended, and other acts which were repealed by said chapter eight hundred and eighty-nine of the laws of eighteen hundred and seventy-one, and for the election of directors of said railroad company;" also relative to the stock of said railroad company held or owned by the town of Schoharie. Passed May 16, 1872; three-fifths being present.

CHAP. 744. An Act for the relief of Rosa Abba Boughton and Addie E. Boughton. Passed May 16, 1872; three-fifths being present.

CHAP. 745. An Act to amend "An act authorizing the confinement of convicts from Dutchess county, in the Albany Penitentiary," et cetera, passed April fifteenth, one thousand eight hundred and fifty-four. Passed May 16, 1872; three-fifths being present.

CHAP. 746. *An Act relating to the examination of candidates for the degree of doctor of medicine. Passed May* 16, 1872.

CHAP. 747. *An Act for the suppression of the trade in and circulation of obscene literature, illustrations, advertisements and articles of indecent or immoral use, and obscene advertisements of patent medicines and articles for producing abortion, and to repeal chapter four hundred and thirty of the laws of eighteen hundred and sixty-eight. Passed May* 16, 1872; *three-fifths being present.*

CHAP. 748. An Act for the relief of J. Rowe Fanning. Passed May 16, 1872.

CHAP. 749. An Act to amend an act entitled "An act to authorize the employment of a stenographer for the county court and court of sessions in the county of Monroe," being chapter forty-six of the laws of eighteen hundred and sixty-four. Passed May 16, 1872; three-fifths being present.

CHAP. 750. An Act to amend chapter five hundred and eleven of the laws of eighteen hundred and seventy, relative to a railroad from Syracuse to Onondaga Hill. Passed May 16, 1872; three-fifths being present.

CHAP. 751. An Act to legalize the official acts and proceedings of Samuel F. Powell, a justice of the peace of the town of Coeymans, in the county of Albany. Passed May 16, 1872.

CHAP. 752. An Act to amend an act entitled "An act to authorize the construction of a railroad from the village of Olean to the Erie railway depot at Olean," passed May seventh, eighteen hundred and sixty-eight. Passed May 16, 1872; three-fifths being present.

CHAP. 753. An Act to incorporate the French Emigration Society of New York. Passed May 11, 1872; three-fifths being present.

CHAP. 754. An Act for the relief of the American Female Guardian Society and Home for the Friendless, of the city of New York, in aid of its industrial schools and other departments of charity. Passed May 17, 1872; three-fifths being present.

CHAP. 755. An Act to amend an act entitled "An act to incorporate the New York Loan and Improvement Company," passed May sixth, eighteen hundred and seventy. Passed May 17, 1872.

CHAP. 756. An Act to provide for laying out and opening a public road or highway in the town of Geddes, Onondaga county. Passed May 17, 1872; three-fifths being present.

CHAP. 757. *An Act to perfect an amendment to the constitution relative to the court of appeals and for the extension of the services of the commissioners of appeals. Passed May* 17, 1872; *three-fifths being present.*

CHAP. 758. An Act to release to John Shafer the right, title and interest of the people of the state of New York in and to certain real estate in the city of New York. Passed May 17, 1872, by a two-third vote.

CHAP. 759. An Act to amend an act entitled "An act to incorporate the East Side Association of the city of New York," passed May ninth, eighteen hundred and sixty-eight. Passed May 17, 1872; three-fifths being present.

CHAP. 760. An Act to provide for the improvement of a certain highway in the town of Newtown, Queens county, and the city of Brooklyn, Kings county, and for the payment of property taken for such improvement. Passed May 17, 1872; three-fifths being present.

CHAP. 761. *An Act to amend chapter eighty of the laws of eighteen hundred and seventy, entitled "An act to provide for the enrollment of the militia for the organization of the national guard of the state of New York and for the public defense, and entitled the military code." Passed May* 17, 1872; *three-fifths being present.*

CHAP. 762. An Act to incorporate the German United Evangelical Synod of the East. Passed May 17, 1872.

CHAP. 763. An Act to amend an act entitled "An act to amend the charter of the village of Saratoga Springs," passed March twenty-sixth, eighteen hundred and sixty-six, and the acts amendatory thereof. Passed May 17, 1872; three-fifths being present.

CHAP. 764. An Act to authorize the consolidation of the Rochester, Nunda and Pennsylvania Railroad with certain other railroads, and to ratify and confirm the action of said railroads heretofore had relating to the consolidation thereof. Passed May 17, 1872.

CHAP. 765. *An Act to legalize payments made by the comptroller to justices of the supreme court in the second judicial district, and to authorize further payments by said comptroller to said justices. Passed May* 17, 1872; *three-fifths being present.*

CHAP. 766. An Act to amend chapter seven hundred and fifty of the laws of eighteen hundred and seventy-one, entitled "An act to incorporate the trustees of the estate belonging to the diocese of Long Island," and to authorize said corporation to acquire and hold land for religious, charitable and benevolent purposes. Passed May 17, 1872.

CHAP. 767. *An Act to establish the compensation of county judges and surrogates, pursuant to the fifteenth section of the amended sixth article of the constitution. Passed May* 17, 1872; *three-fifths being present.*

CHAP. 768. An Act in relation to the salary of the surrogate of the city and county of New York. Passed May 17, 1872; three-fifths being present.

CHAP. 769. An Act to release to Frederick Schleuter all the right, title and interest of the people of the state of New York in and to certain premises in the town of Northfield, in the county of Richmond, and to confirm the title to said premises. Passed May 17, 1872, by a two-third vote.

CHAP. 770. An Act to amend an act entitled "An act to amend and consolidate the several acts in relation to the charter of the city of Rochester," passed April eighth, eighteen hundred and sixty-one. Passed May 20, 1872.

CHAP. 771. An Act to amend the several acts in relation to the city of Rochester. Passed May 20, 1872; three-fifths being present.

Chap. 772. *An Act to authorize the canal commissioners to construct a road bridge over the Erie canal in the town of Gates, in the county of Monroe. Passed May* 20, 1872; *three-fifths being present.*

Chap. 773. An Act to release the interest of the people of the state of New York in the real estate of which William Long, late of Minerva, Essex county, died seized to Isaac Hagan. Passed May 20. 1872, by a two-third vote.

Chap. 774. An Act to incorporate the Fire Department of the village of Watkins. Passed May 20, 1872; three-fifths being present.

Chap. 775. An Act to release the interest of the people of the state of New York in certain real estate to Alicia C. O'Brien. Passed May 20, 1872, by a two-third vote.

Chap. 776. *An Act further to amend an act entitled "An act to amend an act to prevent animals from running at large in the public highways," passed April twenty-third, eighteen hundred and thirty-two, passed May ninth, eighteen hundred and sixty-seven, passed April twenty-ninth, eighteen hundred and sixty-nine. Passed May* 2, 1872; *three-fifths being present.*

Chap. 777. An Act in relation to the filing of certain claims of Ann Egbert, Mrs. C. T. Hill and Ann Egbert, John G. Wormley, Charles H. Hammond, D. L. McNulty, Martin Hammond, George W. Lovell and Lorenzo D. Hughson. Passed May 20, 1872; three-fifths being present.

Chap. 778. *An Act to amend chapter seven hundred and sixty-six of the laws of eighteen hundred and seventy-one, entitled "An act to allow the justices of the supreme court assigned to hold the general terms thereof in the several judicial departments of this state, to fix the times and places of holding the same," passed April twenty-seventh, eighteen hundred and seventy-one. Passed May* 20, 1872; *three-fifths being present.*

Chap. 779. *An Act requiring commissioners of highways to act as inspectors of plank-roads and turnpikes. Passed May* 20, 1872.

Chap. 780. *An Act in relation to plank-roads. Passed May* 20, 1872.

Chap. 781. An Act to amend an act entitled "An act for the removal of obstructions from the outlet of Cayuga lake and the channel of the Seneca river," passed April thirteenth, eighteen hundred and fifty-eight, and the several acts amendatory thereof, being chapter four hundred and sixty-five of the laws of eighteen hundred and sixty-two, and chapter three hundred and four of the laws of eighteen hundred and sixty-eight. Passed May 20, 1872; three-fifths being present.

Chap. 782. *An Act to amend section one hundred and fifty-six of article four of chapter three of title two of part four of the Revised Statutes, in relation to bodies of deceased convicts at Auburn State prison. Passed May* 20, 1872.

Chap. 783. *An Act to authorize the canal commissioners to construct a road bridge over the Tonawanda creek, western division of the Erie canal, at or near Bush's place, connecting the Bush road with Sawyer's creek road at Martinsville. Passed May* 20, 1872; *three-fifths being present.*

Chap. 784. *An Act to provide for the care and maintenance by the canal commissioners of certain bridges over a portion of the Black river used for canal purposes. Passed May* 20, 1872; *three-fifths being present.*

Chap. 785. An Act authorizing the city of Elmira to use a portion of the Chemung canal for a public street, and for other purposes. Passed May 20, 1872; three-fifths being present.

Chap. 786. An Act for the relief of Pratt and Company. Passed May 20, 1872; three-fifths being present.

Chap. 787. An Act authorizing the city of Binghamton to use a portion of the Chenango canal for a public street. Passed May 20, 1872.

Chap. 788. *An Act to amend part one, chapter eleven, title three, article two, section forty-three of the Revised Statutes in relation to constables. Passed May* 20, 1872; *three-fifths being present.*

Chap. 789. An Act to enable the Astoria and Hunter's Point Railroad Company to extend their road. Passed May 21, 1872.

Chap. 790. An Act to establish a special road district and appropriate the highway taxes on the non-resident lands therein for the constructing of a road from Blood's hotel to Tupper's lake, Franklin county. Passed May 21, 1872; three-fifths being present.

Chap. 791. An Act to enable the mayor and common council of Long Island City to borrow money. Passed May 21, 1872; three-fifths being present.

Chap. 792. An Act to authorize "The United Petroleum Farms Association," to dispose of the proceeds of its real estate. Passed May 21, 1872.

CHAP. 793. An Act in relation to the debts of the town of Newtown, Queens county. Passed May 21, 1872; three-fifths being present.

CHAP. 794. An Act to confirm the election of game constable in the several towns of Lewis county. Passed May 21, 1872; three-fifths being present.

CHAP. 795. An Act authorizing the formation of a separate road district in the county of Essex. Passed May 21, 1872; three-fifths being present.

CHAP. 796. An Act to incorporate the New York and South American Contract Company. Passed May 21, 1872.

CHAP. 797. An Act to amend an act entitled "An act to incorporate the Poughkeepsie Female Guardian Society," passed April fifteenth, eighteen hundred and fifty-two. Passed May 21, 1872; three-fifths being present.

CHAP. 798. An Act to provide for the improvement of Pleasant street, in the city of Utica, and town of New Hartford, Oneida county, between Oneida street and Seymour avenue. Passed May 21, 1872; three-fifths being present.

CHAP. 799. An Act to incorporate the New York Construction Company of the city of New York. Passed May 21, 1872.

CHAP. 800. *An Act making an appropriation for the improvement of the navigation of Peconic river in the county of Suffolk. Passed May* 21, 1872, *by a two-third vote.*

CHAP. 801. *An Act for the improvement of the main, middle and north branches of Grass river. Passed May* 21, 1872, *by a two-third vote.*

CHAP. 802. An Act to incorporate the New York Coal Exchange and to confer certain powers upon it. Passed May 21, 1872.

CHAP. 803. An Act to amend an act entitled "An act to incorporate a seminary of education under the name of the Tracy Female Institute," passed April seventeenth, eighteen hundred and fifty-seven. Passed May 21, 1872.

CHAP. 804. An Act to remove the county site of Queens county, to procure a new county site, to appoint commissioners to erect a court-house and jail, and to provide for expenses of the same. Passed May 21, 1872; three-fifths being present.

CHAP. 805. An Act to incorporate the Bay Ridge Contracting Company. Passed May 21, 1872.

[illegible]. An Act to amend an act entitled "An act to incorporate the House of the [illegible] in the city of New York," passed May sixth, eighteen hundred and seventy. [illegible] May 21, 1872.

[illegible]. An Act to amend an act entitled "An act to incorporate the Brevoort Savings [illegible] city of New York," passed May twelfth, eighteen hundred and sixty-nine. [illegible] 21, 1872.

[illegible]. An Act to amend an act entitled "An act in relation to the Troy Water-[illegible]" [illegible] March ninth, eighteen hundred and fifty-five. Passed May 21, 1872; [illegible] being present.

[illegible]. An Act to authorise the construction of a sewer in the county of Kings, from [illegible] buildings at Flatbush in said county. Passed May 21, 1872; three-fifths [illegible] present.

[illegible]. An Act in relation to the Williamsburgh Dispensary, to change the corporate [illegible], and to define and enlarge its powers. Passed May 21, 1872; three-fifths being present.

CHAP. 811. An Act for the improvement of First street and Franklin street, in the city of Brooklyn. Passed May 21, 1872; three-fifths being present.

CHAP. 812. An Act to confirm, reduce and levy certain assessments on the city of Brooklyn. Passed May 21, 1872; three-fifths being presnt.

CHAP. 813. An Act for the relief of the Grand Street, Prospect Park and Flatbush Railroad Company. Passed May 21, 1872; three-fifths being present.

CHAP. 814. An Act to amend an act entitled "An act to incorporate the Real Estate Trust Company of the city of New York," passed April fourteenth, eighteen hundred and seventy-one. [illegible] May 21, 1872.

CHAP. 815. An A[illegible] the improvement of Myrtle avenue in the city of Brooklyn. Passed May 21, 1872; [illegible] being present.

Chap. 816. An Act to amend an act entitled "An act to create a board of trustees for the town of Morrisania, in the county of Westchester, and to define their powers," passed April twenty-second, eighteen hundred and sixty-four, and the acts amending the same. Passed May 21, 1872; three-fifths being present.

Chap. 817. An Act to regulate the practice of pharmacy and the sale of poisons in the city and county of New York. Passed May 22, 1872.

Chap. 818. An Act to incorporate "The German American Loan and Mortgage Company." Passed May 22, 1872.

Chap. 819. *An Act supplemental to an act entitled "An act for the improvement of the navigation of the tributaries of the Great South Bay," passed April twenty-eighth, eighteen hundred and seventy-one. Passed May 22, 1872, by a two-third vote.*

Chap. 820. *An Act to authorize the formation of corporations to provide the members thereof with lots of land suitable for homesteads. Passed May 22, 1872.*

Chap. 821. An Act to authorize the city of Newburgh to borrow money and issue bonds therefor for the payment of the existing contingent debt of said city, and to provide for the payment of said bonds and the interest thereon by levy and collection of taxes. Passed May 22, 1872; three-fifths being present.

Chap. 822. An Act to lay out, construct and keep in repair Flatbush avenue, in the county of Kings. Passed May 22, 1872; three-fifths being present.

Chap. 823. An Act to amend an act entitled "An act to facilitate the construction of the New York and Oswego Midland Railroad, and to amend the several acts in relation thereto," passed March twenty-sixth, eighteen hundred and sixty-eight. Passed May 22, 1872; three-fifths being present..

Chap. 824. An Act to amend chapter nine hundred and seven of the laws of eighteen hundred and sixty-nine, entitled "An act to amend an act entitled 'An act to authorize the formation of railroad corporations and to regulate the same,' passed April second, eighteen hundred and fifty, so as to permit municipal corporations to aid in the construction of railroads," as amended by chapter nine hundred and twenty-five of the laws of eighteen hundred and seventy-one, so far as the same is applicable to the Sodus Bay and Corning Railroad Company under its present or former corporate name. Passed May 22, 1872; three-fifths being present.

Chap. 825. An Act to authorize and require the New York and Harlem Railroad Company to extend their tracks through certain streets and avenues of the city of New York, for the use of their small cars only. Passed May 22, 1872.

Chap. 826. *An Act to repeal chapter chapter six hundred and sixty-eight of the laws of eighteen hundred and seventy-one, entitled "An act to provide for the payment of counsel required to be employed on behalf of the state in pursuance of the provisions of section two of chapter three hundred and twenty-one of the laws of eighteen hundred and seventy. Passed May 22, 1872; three-fifths being present.*

Chap. 827. An Act to improve the navigation of the Baldwinsville canal. Passed May 22, 1872; three-fifths being present.

Chap. 828. An Act to amend an act entitled "An act to revise the charter of the city of Buffalo," passed April twenty-eighth, eighteen hundred and seventy; amended April twenty-fifth, eighteen hundred and seventy-one; amended January twelfth, eighteen hundred and seventy-two, and to amend section forty-five of chapter seven hundred and nineteen of the laws of eighteen hundred and seventy-one. Passed May 22, 1872; three-fifths being present.

Chap. 829. *An Act in relation to the formation of railroad companies. Passed May 22,* 1872.

Chap. 830. An Act to amend an act entitled "An act to incorporate the Binghamton and Port Dickinson Railroad Company. Passed May 22, 1872.

Chap. 831. An Act to authorize the board of canal commissioners to settle with James H. Sherrill for constructing a stone dam across the Mohawk river, at Cohoes, for the Erie and Champlain canals, at prices equal to the cost of such work as found by the canal board under chapter five hundred and forty-three of the laws of eighteen hundred and seventy. Passed May 22, 1872; three-fifths being present.

Chap. 832. An Act to authorize the Peekskill Iron Company to construct and operate a narrow gauge railroad in the towns of Cortlandt, Westchester county, and Phillipstown, Putnam county. Passed May 22, 1872; three-fifths being present.

CHAP. 833. An Act to authorise the Metropolitan Transit Company to construct and operate certain railroads in the city of New York, and to construct and use for railroad purposes two bridges across the Harlem river. Passed May 22, 1872.

CHAP. 834. An Act to incorporate the New York City Rapid Transit Company, and to authorize the said company to construct and operate an underground railway in the city of New York. Passed May 22, 1872.

CHAP. 835. An Act relating to the New York Society for the relief of the ruptured and crippled. Passed May 22, 1872.

CHAP. 836. An Act to regulate places of public amusement in the city of New York. Passed May 22, 1872; three-fifths being present.

CHAP. 837. An Act to incorporate the Hunter's Point and Flushing Railroad Company. Passed May 22, 1872.

CHAP. 838. *An Act to amend "An act to secure to creditors a just division of the estates of debtors who convey to assignees for the benefit of creditors," passed April thirteenth, eighteen hundred and sixty. Passed May* 20, 1872.

CHAP. 839. An Act to incorporate the Queens Railway Company. Passed May 23, 1872; three-fifths being present.

CHAP. 840. An Act to confirm the acts of Hezekiah W. Whitney, administrator, with the will annexed, of the estate of Melvin S. Whitney, deceased. Passed May 23, 1872.

CHAP. 841. An Act to enable the supervisors of the city and county of New York to raise money, by tax, to pay money appropriated by George H. E. Lynch, late clerk of the superior court of the city of New York. Passed May 23, 1872; three-fifths being present.

CHAP. 842. An Act in relation to the improvement of streets in the city of New York, between Sixth and Seventh avenues, and north of the southerly line of One Hundred and Tenth street. Passed May 23, 1872; three-fifths being present.

CHAP. 843. *An Act to amend an act entitled "An act supplementary to the act entitled "An Act to authorize the formation of railroad corporations, and to regulate the same," passed April second, eighteen hundred and fifty. Passed May* 23, 1872; *three-fifths being present.*

CHAP. 844. An Act to compensate William S. Copland for services rendered in examining and making copies of certain accounts of the county of New York. Passed May 23, 1872; three-fifths being present.

CHAP. 845. An Act concerning certain female habitual drunkards, vagrants and prostitutes, in the city of Brooklyn and county of Kings. Passed May 23, 1872; three-fifths being present.

CHAP. 846. An Act to establish a rapid transit steam ferry between Westchester county and New York city. Passed May 23, 1872.

CHAP. 847. An Act to amend an act entitled "An act to amend an act entitled 'An act to amend an act entitled An act to incorporate the village of Flushing, passed April fifteenth, eighteen hundred and thirty-seven, and the several acts amendatory thereof, passed March twentieth, eighteen hundred and fifty-seven, passed May third, eighteen hundred and sixty-nine," passed May seventh, eighteen hundred and seventy. Passed May 23, 1872; three-fifths being present.

CHAP. 848. *An Act to appoint commissioners of parks for the state of New York. Passed May* 23, 1872.

CHAP. 849. An Act to incorporate "The Buffalo Catholic Institute." Passed May 23, 1872.

CHAP. 850. *An Act to authorize a tax of seven-tenths of a mill per dollar of valuation of the year eighteen hundred and seventy-two, for the construction of new work upon and extraordinary repairs of the canals of this state. Passed May* 23, 1872; *three-fifths being present.*

CHAP. 851. An Act to amend an act entitled "An act to amend an act entitled 'An Act to incorporate the Tontine Mutual Savings Bank of the city of New York, passed May [illegible], eighteen hundred and sixty-nine,'" passed May tenth, eighteen hundred and seventy-one. Passed May 23, 1872.

CHAP. 852. An Act to alter the map or plan of the city of New York. Passed May 24, 1872; three-fifths being present.

CHAP. 853. An Act to incorporate the Mosholu Division, number two hundred and eight, Sons of Temperance. Passed May 24, 1872.

CHAP. 854. An Act to authorize the city of Brooklyn to borrow money, and levy and collect a tax for the repayment of the same, to cover expenditures made by the authorities of said city during the year eighteen hundred and seventy-one, and to provide for certain extraordinary expenses in said city. Passed May 24, 1872; three-fifths being present.

CHAP. 855. An Act to reduce the rates of ferriage on certain ferry routes between the cities of New York and Brooklyn and to establish rates of ferriage thereon, and to regulate the running of said ferries. Passed May 25, 1872.

CHAP. 856. An Act to legalize and confirm the acts of the railroad commissioners of the town of Morristown in issuing and delivering the bonds of said town in aid of the Black River and Morristown Railroad. Passed May 25, 1872; three-fifths being present.

CHAP. 857. An Act to amend an act entitled "An act to incorporate the Poughkeepsie Bridge Company, for the purpose of constructing and maintaining a bridge, appurtenances and approaches to the same, over the Hudson river at a point or points between the city of Poughkeepsie and the town of Lloyd, Ulster county, on said river," passed May tenth, eighteen hundred and seventy-one. Passed May 25, 1872.

CHAP. 858. An Act to amend an act entitled "An act to enable the mayor and common council of Long Island City to borrow money," passed April thirteenth, eighteen hundred and seventy-one. Passed May 25, 1872.

CHAP. 859. An Act to amend an act entitled "An act to provide for the laying out of streets, avenues, roads and parks in Long Island City," passed April twenty-sixth, eighteen hundred and seventy-one. Passed May 25, 1872; three-fifths being present.

CHAP. 860. An Act to amend chapter one hundred and ninety of the laws of eighteen hundred and seventy, in relation to supervisors of the county of New York. Passed May 31, 1872; three-fifths being present.

CHAP. 861. An Act to amend the charter of the Reserve Mutual Life Insurance Company. Passed May 31, 1872.

CHAP. 862. An Act to amend the charter of the National Burglar Insurance Company of the city of New York, passed May eighth, eighteen hundred and sixty-eight. Passed May 31, 1872.

CHAP. 863. An Act to authorize the South Side Railroad Company of Long Island to build or purchase branches, extend its main line, and to purchase the stock of the New York and Flushing Railroad Company, the Far Rockaway Branch Railroad Company and Rockaway Railway Company of Queens county, New York, and of the Hunter's Point and South Side Railway Company, also of Queens county, New York, and to consolidate the said companies, or any two or more of them, into one corporation, and also to use steam dummies. Passed May 31, 1872.

CHAP. 864. An Act to authorize the Adirondack Company to construct and operate a branch of its railroad from its main line to the north bounds of the state. Passed May 31, 1872.

CHAP. 865. An Act in relation to certain suits and proceedings by and against the late metropolitan fire department. Passed May 31, 1872; three-fifths being present.

CHAP. 866. An Act to incorporate the city of Yonkers. Passed June 1, 1872; three-fifths being present.

CHAP. 867. An Act to provide for the repavement and improvement of Henry street, between Pierrepont street and Fulton street, in the city of Brooklyn. Passed June 1, 1872; three-fifths being present.

CHAP. 868. An Act to incorporate the United States Loan and Security Company. Passed June 1, 1872.

CHAP. 869. An Act to incorporate the proprietors of the Shinnecock Hills and lands in the town of Southampton, Suffolk county. Passed June 1, 1872; three-fifths being present.

CHAP. 870. An Act to incorporate the Peekskill Ferry, Dock and Transportation Company. Passed June 1, 1872; three-fifths being present.

CHAP. 871. An Act to incorporate the Ramapo Hunting and Village Park Association, in the county of Rockland. Passed June 1, 1872; three-fifths being present.

CHAP. 872. An Act in relation to the Croton aqueduct and other public works in the city of New York. Passed June 3, 1872; three-fifths being present.

CHAP. 873. *An Act to establish and maintain an institution for the relief of indigent and disabled soldiers and sailors of the state of New York. Passed June 3, 1872; three-fifths being present.*

CHAP. 874. An Act in regard to Union Free School, district number one, in the town of Milton, and to enlarge its boundaries and authorize the board of education thereof to raise money to purchase sites and to build or purchase school-houses. Passed June 3, 1872; three-fifths being present.

CHAP. 875. An Act to encourage and facilitate the construction of a railroad from the town of Edinburgh, Saratoga county, to the Mohawk valley, and the preparation of the natural products of the soil for market. Passed June 8, 1872; three-fifths being present.

CHAP. 876. An Act to authorize the towns of Portland, Chautauqua, Sherman, Clymer, or adjoining towns in the county of Chautauqua, to issue bonds in aid of the Buffalo, Corry and Pittsburgh Railroad Company, and to take the bonds of said company therefor. Passed June 8, 1872; three-fifths being present.

CHAP. 877. An Act to incorporate the Fresco Painters' Benevolent and Protective Union of the city and county of New York. Passed June 8, 1872; three-fifths being present.

CHAP. 878. An Act to repeal an act entitled "An act relative to the improvement of certain portions of the county of Westchester and New York, including provisions for communication between said counties, and for the improving of the navigation of Harlem river and Spuyten Duyvil creek," passed April fifteenth, eighteen hundred and seventy-one, so far as relates to the survey of the towns of East Chester and Westchester, in the county of Westchester, and to amend the same in other respects. Passed June 9, 1872; three-fifths being present.

CHAP. 879. An Act to amend an act entitled "An act to amend, consolidate and re-enact an act entitled 'An act to incorporate the village of Edgewater,'" passed March twenty-second, eighteen hundred and sixty-six, and an act amending the same, passed April twenty-second, eighteen hundred and sixty-seven, and to extend the powers of the corporation, passed May fifth, eighteen hundred and seventy. Passed June 8, 1872; three-fifths being present.

CHAP. 880. An Act to incorporate the New York and Queens County Bridge Company for the purpose of constructing and maintaining a bridge over the East river, between the city of New York and the county of Queens. Passed June 8, 1872; three-fifths being present.

CHAP. 881. An Act to incorporate the Manhattan Mercantile Association of New York. Passed June 11, 1872.

CHAP. 882. An Act to amend an act entitled "An act to consolidate the cities of Brooklyn and Williamsburgh and the town of Bushwick into one municipal government, and to incorporate the same," passed April seventeenth, eighteen hundred and fifty-four. Passed June 11, 1872; three-fifths being present.

CHAP. 883. *An Act to confer jurisdiction on the supreme court or the judges thereof, in proceedings under chapter nine hundred and seven of the laws of eighteen hundred and sixty-nine, entitled "An act to authorize the formation of railroad corporations and to regulate the same," passed April second, eighteen hundred and fifty, so as to permit municipal corporations to aid in the construction of railroads, as amended by chapter nine hundred and twenty-five of the laws of eighteen hundred and seventy-one, and to repeal section ten of said act as thus amended. Passed June 15, 1872.*

CHAP. 884. *An Act to provide for a commission to propose amendments to the constitution. Passed June 15, 1872; three-fifths being present.*

CHAP. 885. An Act to incorporate "The Gilbert Elevated Railway Company," and to provide a feasible, safe and speedy system of rapid transit through the city of New York. Passed June 17, 1872; three-fifths being present.

CHAP. 886. An Act to legalize the proceedings of certain commissioners appointed for the drainage of wet lands in Onondaga county. Passed June 20, 1872; three-fifths being present.

CHAP. 887. An Act repealing the act entitled "An act for the appointment of commissioners of records for the city and county of New York," passed April thirteenth, eighteen hundred and fifty-five, and providing for the sale and disposition of the indices, records, documents and property held by said commissioners under said act. Passed June 20, 1872; three-fifths being present.

CHAP. 888. An Act concerning a separate officer as surrogate of Rensselaer county. Passed October 20, 1871.

CONCURRENT RESOLUTIONS.

As to Fifteenth Amendment United States Constitution. Passed February 8, 1872.
As to pay of members of the Legislature. Passed April 4, 1872.
As to pier and bulkhead lines in the Harbor of New York. Passed April 6, 1872.
As to Albany as a Port of Entry. Passed April 17, 1872.
As to the Court of Appeals. Passed April 26, 1872.
As to bribery. Passed May 2, 1872.
As to State Prisons. Passed May 3, 1872.
As to printing house for the blind. Passed May 10, 1872.

NAMES CHANGED.

Albany County — Alexander Tugaw to Alexander Tugaw Adams. March 6, 1871.
St. Lawrence County — George W. Jackson to George W. Boodey. January 13, 1872.
New York County — Joseph Sattig to John Sattig. February 18, 1871.
Diederich Schackenberg to Richard Berg. March 18, 1871.
George Ress to George Michel. May 8, 1871.
The American Baptist Missionary Convention to The Consolidated American Baptist Missionary Convention. June 3, 1871.
Lillian Isabella Mooney to Lillian Isabella Edwards. June 15, 1871.
Joseph Bemelmans to Joseph Bemel. June 20, 1871.
Francis Duffy to Frank Duffy. June 30, 1871.
Mary Tracy to Mary Robinson. June 27, 1871.
Henry M. Levy to Henry M. Lewis. June 30, 1871.
The Church of St. Charles to The Church of St. Elizabeth. May 1, 1872.
Charlotte E. Smith to Charlotte E. Adams. September 5, 1871.
Isaac H. Hart to Henry J. Hart. November 10, 1871.
Eleventh Presbyterian Church in the city of New York to the Presbyterian Memorial Church of New York city. November 16, 1871.
William Rossiter Chadwick to William Sidney Rossiter. January 1, 1872.
Joseph Kettner to Francis Joseph Kettner. December 22, 1871.
Charles T. Morrison to Charles T. Sohampain. January 9, 1872.
Albany County — The Bott and Johnson Manufacturing Company to the Albany Card and Paper Company. January 2, 1872.
The Trustees of the Pearl Street Baptist Society of the city of Albany to the Emanuel Baptist Church. January 2, 1872.
Monroe County — Charles Woollard to Charles Briggs. April 10, 1871.
John Woollard to John Briggs. April 10, 1871.
First Reformed Lutheran Society of Brockport to the First Church of the Evangelical Association of the village of Brockport. January 20, 1872.
Kings County — Ferdinand O'Reilly to Edwin Ferdinand Marsden. March 1, 1871.
Martin Schnackenberg to Martin Berg. March 18, 1871.
Charles Edward Low to Chauncey Edward Low. January 20, 1872.

GENERAL STATUTES

OF THE

STATE OF NEW YORK,

PASSED AT THE

95TH SESSION, 1872.

CHAP. 10.

AN ACT to authorize the extension of the time for the collection of taxes in the several towns of this state.

PASSED January 30, 1872; three-fifths being present.

The People of the State of New York, represented in Senate and Assembly, do enact as follows:

SECTION 1. If any collector of taxes in any town of this state shall, within fifteen days after the passage of this act, pay over all moneys collected by him, and shall renew his bond as is herein provided, the time for the collection of taxes and for making return thereof by him shall be as is herein provided, extended to a day not later than the fifteenth day of March, eighteen hundred and seventy-two. Such bond shall be renewed with such sureties as in any town shall be approved by the supervisor thereof, or in case of his inability to act, by the town clerk thereof. The penalty thereof in any case shall be double the amount of the taxes in that case remaining uncollected. The bond shall be approved in writing and filed as required by law, and have all the effect of a collector's bond. A copy of the bond, and the approval thereof, shall within fifteen days after the passage of this act, be delivered to the county treasurer of the county in which is said town. The time, not later than the said fifteenth day of March, eighteen hundred and seventy-two, to which the collection of said taxes, and the making returns thereof may be extended, shall in any

Collector to renew official bonds.

Bonds, how renewed.

Limit of extension.

town be fixed and limited in writing, and indorsed on the warrant of the collector by the supervisor of the town, or in case of his inability to act, by the town clerk thereof.

Secretary of state to distribute printed copies. § 2. It shall be the duty of the secretary of state, at once, after the passage of this act, to cause it to be printed upon slips of paper, and to deliver to each county treasurer a sufficient number thereof, to supply one to each collector of taxes in said county, and it shall be the duty of said county treasurer to deliver one thereof to each collector of taxes in his county.

§ 3. This act shall not extend to any of the cities of this state.

§ 4. This act shall take effect immediately.

CHAP. 12.

AN ACT prescribing the officers and employees that may be elected, appointed or employed by the senate and assembly, fixing the salary and compensation thereof, and regulating the proceedings of investigating committees, and providing for the payment of the expenses thereof.

PASSED February 1, 1872; three-fifths being present.

The People of the State of New York, represented in Senate and Assembly, do enact as follows:

Senate may elect or appoint certain officers. SECTION 1. The senate may elect or appoint a clerk, a stenographer, a sergeant-at-arms, and an assistant, who shall act as postmaster, an assistant postmaster, a door-keeper and six assistants, one person who shall act as a janitor and keeper of the senate chamber and its ante rooms, and one assistant; not more than sixteen persons to serve as clerks of committees, and not more than eighteen pages, including those who serve as messengers and pages to committees. Other officers, how appointed. The president of the senate may appoint a clerk and a messenger, and the clerk of the senate may appoint an assistant clerk, a journal clerk, four deputy clerks, one of whom shall act as clerk of the committee on engrossed bills, a librarian, an assistant librarian, a superintendent of documents and three messengers.

Assembly may elect or appoint certain officers. § 2. The assembly may elect or appoint a clerk, a stenographer, a sergeant-at-arms and an assistant, a postmaster and an assistant, a superintendent of documents, a door-keeper and ten assistants, one person who shall perform the duties of janitor and keeper of the assembly chamber and its ante rooms, and an assistant, a mail carrier, who shall carry the mails for both the senate and assembly, not more than sixteen persons to serve as clerks of committees, not more than six general messengers, and not more than thirty pages, to be in employ and drawing pay at one time, including pages who shall act as messengers to committees. The speaker may appoint a clerk and messenger, and the clerk of the assembly may appoint an assistant clerk, a journal clerk, and not more than nine deputies, one of whom shall be clerk to the committee on engrossed bills, a librarian and an assistant, and not more than five messengers.

Other officers, how appointed.

§ 3. The following salaries shall be paid for the annual session of the legislature.

To the clerks of each house, three thousand dollars; to the assistant clerks and journal clerks, each fifteen hundred dollars.

To the deputy clerks, each twelve hundred dollars, except to the clerks assigned to the committees on engrossed bills, to them, to the clerk of the president of the senate and to the speaker's clerk, six hundred dollars.

Salaries of clerks, assistant clerks, journal clerks, deputy clerks, etc.

To the sergeants-at-arms, the assistant sergeant-at-arms, the librarians, the assistant librarians, the postmaster of the assembly, the assistant postmasters of the senate and assembly, and the door-keepers to each of them six dollars per day; to the assistant door-keepers, the keepers and janitors, the assistant-keepers and janitors and superintendent of documents of the senate and assembly, each five dollars per day; and each of the officers in this section above named shall receive the same mileage as is now allowed by law to the members of the legislature.

Salaries of other officers.

To the stenographers, fifteen hundred dollars each.

To the clerks of the committees, each five dollars per day.

To the mail carrier, three dollars per day.

To the messengers, each three dollars per day.

To the pages, each two dollars per day.

And no extra allowance shall be made to the officers and employees above named on any pretense whatever.

No extra allowance to be made.

The mileage, salary and per diem allowance in this section provided for shall be paid on the warrant of the comptroller, upon the certificate of the president of the senate for the officers and employees of the senate, and on the certificate of the speaker for the officers and employees of the assembly.

Salaries and mileage, how paid.

§ 4. No other person not a member of the legislature shall be appointed to any position, or employed for any purpose, in either house, other than such as are hereinbefore provided for, except that whenever, in the judgment of either house, an emergency shall arise in which additional employees or assistants shall be required, such additional persons may be temporarily appointed or employed, as either house may deem actually necessary, but no such person shall be appointed, employed or paid, unless a resolution of such house authorizing it shall be first adopted, by the affirmative vote of a majority of all the members elected to such house, and on such vote the ayes and noes shall be taken and entered at large upon the journal of such house, which resolution shall distinctly and fully specify the emergency that has rendered the employment of such additional assistants necessary, the name of the person proposed to be appointed or employed,

No person to be appointed or employed except in case of emergency, to be determined by a vote of either house.

Ayes and nays to be taken.

the rate of compensation to be allowed him, and the duration of such employment; and such employment shall cease at the time specified in such resolution, or sooner, if the purposes of such employment shall have been accomplished.

Standing committee charged with duty of making investigation, may appoint sub-committee.

§ 5. Whenever any standing committee of either house shall be charged with the duty of making any inquiry or investigation, such committee shall have power to appoint a sub-committee to consist of not less than three of its own members to make such inquiry or investigation, and to take testimony in relation thereto; and such committee or sub-committee shall have all the power and authority that is now conferred by law upon any committee, which, by the terms of its appointment, is authorized to send for persons and papers; and the chairman of any committee or sub-committee shall have all the power and authority that is now conferred by law upon the chairman of any committee which by the terms of its appointment is authorized to send for persons and papers, and the chairman of such committee and of such sub-committee shall be authorized to administer oaths to all witnesses coming before such committee or sub-committee for examination. Every witness attending as such before any such committee or sub-committee shall be entitled to the same fees as are allowed witnesses in civil suits in courts of record. Such fees need not be prepaid, but the comptroller shall draw his warrant for the payment of the amount thereof, when the same shall have been certified to by the chairman of such committee, and duly proved, by affidavit or otherwise, to the satisfaction of the said comptroller. Whenever, by resolution of either house, a committee shall be directed to conduct an investigation, or take testimony in any other place than the city of Albany, the comptroller shall draw his warrant for the payment of the actual and necessary expenses incurred thereby by such committee or the sub-committee having in charge such investigation, inquiry or taking of testimony, together with the actual and necessary expenses of such officers and employees as shall be authorized to accompany them; but no such expenses shall be paid until a bill of the items thereof, in detail, shall be rendered to the comptroller, and the correctness thereof shall be certified by the chairman of such committee, and duly approved by the president of the senate in the case of a committee of the senate, and by the speaker of the assembly in the case of a committee of the assembly, and duly proved, by affidavit or otherwise, to the satisfaction of the comptroller.

Chairman of sub-committee may administer oaths.

Witnesses to receive per diem and mileage.

Expenses, how paid.

Bills to be certified and proved to satisfaction of the comptroller.

§ 6. All laws and parts of laws inconsistent with this act are hereby repealed.

§ 7. This act shall take effect immediately.

CHAP. 17.

AN ACT to increase the duties of clerks of boards of supervisors.

PASSED February 6, 1872.

The People of the State of New York, represented in Senate and Assembly, do enact as follows:

SECTION 1. The clerks of the boards of supervisors of the several counties in this state shall, on or before the second Monday in December in each year, transmit to the comptroller, by mail, in the form which shall be prescribed by the comptroller, a certificate or return of all the indebtedness of their respective counties, and of each town, village and ward therein. Clerks of boards of supervisors to report indebtedness of counties, villages and towns to comptroller.

§ 2. The clerk who shall refuse or neglect to make such return shall forfeit to the people of this state the sum of fifty dollars.

§ 3. This act shall take effect immediately.

Ante, vol. 1, pp. 840, 584.

CHAP. 26.

AN ACT to amend an act entitled "An act in relation to the fees of sheriffs, except in the counties of New York, Kings and Westchester," passed April twelfth, eighteen hundred and seventy-one.

Ante,

PASSED February 8, 1872; three-fifths being present.

The People of the State of New York, represented in Senate and Assembly, do enact as follows:

SECTION 1. Subdivision one of section one of the act entitled "An act in relation to the fees of sheriffs except in the counties of New York, Kings and Westchester," passed April twelve, eighteen hundred and seventy-one, is hereby amended so as to read as follows:

1. For serving a summons or summons and complaint, or summons and notice of object of action, or any other paper issued in any action, the sum of one dollar, and for necessary travel in making such service the sum of six cents per mile to and from the place of service, to be computed in all cases from the court-house of the county; and if there are two or more court-houses, to be computed from the nearest to the place of service. Sheriff's fees for service and travel.

§ 2. This act shall take effect immediately.

CHAP. 38.

AN ACT providing for appeals from the decisions of county superintendents of the poor.

PASSED February 15, 1872; three-fifths being present.

The People of the State of New York, represented in Senate and Assembly, do enact as follows:

Either party may appeal to county court.

SECTION 1. Upon the decision hereafter by the superintendent or superintendents of the poor of any county in this state, of any dispute that shall arise or has arisen, concerning the settlement of any poor person, either or any of the parties interested in such decision may appeal therefrom to the county court of the county in which such decision shall be made.

Notice of appeal to be served within thirty days.

§ 2. Such appeal shall be made by the service, by the party appealing, upon the other parties interested in such decision, within thirty days after notice of the same, of a notice of appeal, which shall be signed by the appellant, and which shall specify the grounds of the appeal.

§ 3. The hearing of such appeal may be brought on by either party in or out of term, upon notice of fourteen days.

Decision on appeal to be final.

§ 4. Upon such appeal a new trial of such matters in dispute shall be had before the county court, and its decision thereon shall be final and conclusive, and the same costs shall be awarded upon such appeal as are now allowed on appeals from courts of justice of the peace to the county courts.

§ 5. All laws and parts of laws now in force, and which are inconsistent or in conflict with the provisions of this act, are hereby repealed.

§ 6. This act shall take effect immediately.

Ante, vol. 1, p. 575.

CHAP. 48.

AN ACT in relation to superintendents of the poor.

PASSED February 19, 1872; three-fifths being present.

The People of the State of New York, represented in Senate and Assembly, do enact as follows:

Persons who have been elected superintendents of the poor, and have failed to file official bond, may file

SECTION 1. Every person who has been duly elected superintendent of the poor of any county in this state previous to the passage of this act, and who has neglected to take the oath of office, or to execute his official bond as required by law, may, within thirty days after the passage of this act, execute and file in the office of the county clerk his official bond with such sureties and conditions for the payment of such an amount as shall be approved and prescribed by the county judge in and for such county, and within the said thirty days, may take and subscribe the oath of office required by law; and when he shall have so filed his said bond, and taken his oath of office, he is hereby invested with all the powers and duties of the said office. And all the official acts of any such person, done and performed by him previous to the passage of this act are hereby confirmed and declared valid, and of as full force and effect as if the statute in such case made and provided had been fully complied with by such person; and he is also hereby released from any penalties imposed by law to which he may have been liable previous to the passage of this act, by reason of his neglect to execute and file his official bond and take his oath of office within the time provided by law; but nothing in this act contained shall in any way affect any proceedings under any existing law already instituted or in progress against any such person.

same within 30 days after passage of this act.

Previous official acts confirmed.

Not to affect proceedings already instituted

§ 2. This act shall take effect immediately.

Ante, vol. 3, p. 330; vol. 4, p. 915.

CHAP. 56.

AN ACT relating to the settling, signing and sealing of bills of exceptions in criminal cases.

PASSED February 27, 1872.

The People of the State of New York, represented in Senate and Assembly, do enact as follows:

SECTION 1. It shall be the duty of the several justices of the supreme court of this state, and of the county judges and justices of sessions in the several counties therein to settle, sign and seal bills of exceptions in criminal cases tried before them at any court of oyer and terminer or courts of sessions held in any county in this state, in the same manner and with like effect after the expiration of their term of office as if done before. And in case any such justice, judge or justice of sessions, who has sat on the trial of any criminal case in either of said courts, shall die before the settling, signing and sealing of such bill of exceptions, then the surviving member or members of said court shall settle, sign and seal the same.

Judges, etc., to settle bills of exceptions in criminal cases after expiration of term of office.

In case of death, survivor to settle same.

§ 2. This act shall take effect immediately.

CHAP. 65.

AN ACT to repeal section forty-three of chapter seven hundred and twenty-one of the laws of eighteen hundred and seventy-one, entitled "An act to amend and consolidate the several acts relating to the preservation of moose, wild deer, birds and fish," passed April twenty-sixth, eighteen hundred and seventy-one.

PASSED February 29, 1872; three-fifths being present.

The People of the State of New York, represented in Senate and Assembly, do enact as follows:

Repeal. SECTION 1. Section forty-three of chapter seven hundred and twenty-one of the laws of eighteen hundred and seventy-one, entitled "An act to amend and consolidate the several acts relating to the preservation of moose, wild deer, birds and fish," passed April twenty-sixth, eighteen hundred and seventy-one, which reads as follows:

§ 43. "The counties of Delaware and Chenango are exempted from the operation of section sixteen, seventeen and thirty-one," is hereby repealed.

Ante, vol.

§ 2. This act shall take effect immediately.

CHAP. 70.

AN ACT for the erection of an iron bridge over the Champlain canal at Comstock's Landing, in the county of Washington.

PASSED February 29, 1872; three-fifths being present.

The People of the State of New York, represented in Senate and Assembly, do enact as follows:

Commissioners to cause to be rebuilt of iron the bridge at Comstock's Landing. SECTION 1. The canal commissioners are hereby authorized and directed to cause to be rebuilt of iron, the bridge now standing across the Champlain canal at Comstock's Landing, in the county of Washington, whenever in their judgment it shall be necessary to rebuild the same. The cost of said iron bridge not to exceed three thousand dollars.

§ 2. The expense of such new bridge shall be paid out of any moneys appropriated, or to be appropriated, for the extraordinary repairs of the eastern division of the canals.

§ 3. This act shall take effect immediately.

CHAP. 81.

AN ACT to amend an act passed April nineteenth, eighteen hundred and seventy-one, entitled "An act to amend an act entitled 'An act to authorize the formation of railroad corporations and to regulate the same,'" passed April second, eighteen hundred and fifty.

PASSED March 5, 1872; three-fifths being present.

The People of the State of New York, represented in Senate and Assembly, do enact as follows:

SECTION 1. Section fifth of the act passed April nineteenth, eighteen hundred and seventy-one, entitled "An act to amend an act entitled 'An act to authorize the formation of railroad corporations and to regulate the same,' passed April second, eighteen hundred and fifty," is hereby amended so as to read as follows:

Corporations may be formed for operating railroads with gauge of three feet six inches, or less, but not less than thirty inches within the rails.

§ 5. Corporations may be formed under the act entitled "An act to authorize the formation of railroad corporations and to regulate the same," passed April second, eighteen hundred and fifty, for the purpose of constructing and operating railroads for public use in transporting persons and property, of the gauge of three feet and six inches or less, but not less than thirty inches within the rails; whenever capital stock of said corporation to the amount of one thousand dollars for every mile of such railroad proposed to be constructed and operated has been in good faith subscribed, and whenever one thousand dollars or more for every mile of such railroad proposed to be constructed shall be in like manner subscribed, and ten per cent thereon in good faith actually paid in cash to the directors named in the articles of association, and an affidavit made by at least three of said directors, and indorsed on or annexed to said articles that the amount of stock hereby required has been so subscribed as aforesaid, and ten per cent thereon paid as aforesaid, and that it is intended in good faith to construct and operate such railroad, then said articles with such affidavit may be filed and recorded in the office of secretary of state, provided said articles contain all the other facts required by law to be stated in articles of association made for organizing railroad corporations under said act entitled "An act to authorize the formation of railroad corporations and to regulate the same," passed April second, eighteen hundred and fifty; and all the provisions of said last-mentioned act shall apply to corporations formed for the construction and operating of railroads of the gauge herein above mentioned, except as herein provided, or otherwise provided by law.

§ 2. This act shall take effect immediately.

Ante, p. , vol. 3, p. 617.

CHAP. 82.

AN ACT to prevent the cutting or taking of ice from Chautauqua lake at certain points therein.

PASSED March 6, 1872; three-fifths being present.

The People of the State of New York, represented in Senate and Assembly, do enact as follows:

Ice not to be cut or removed from Chautauqua lake within certain distances of the highway.

SECTION 1. It shall be unlawful for any person to cut or remove, or cause to be cut or removed, any ice from Chautauqua lake within five rods on the southeast side and fifteen rods on the northeast side of a direct line running from the center of the highway, on the south shore of said lake, on lot fifty-eight, in the town of Ellicott, in the county of Chautauqua, where said highway abuts on said lake, to the center of the highway on the north shore of said lake between the lands of Isaac Noble and M. C. Martin, on lot fifty-nine, in said town, where said highway abuts on said lake.

Penalty.

§ 2. For every violation of the provisions of section one of this act, the person guilty of such violation shall be subject to a penalty of twenty-five dollars, to be sued for and recovered before any justice of the peace of the town of Ellicott, by the supervisor of said town, for the benefit of the poor of said town.

§ 3. This act shall take effect immediately.

CHAP. 91.

AN ACT supplementary to and amendatory of chapter eighty, of the laws of eighteen hundred and seventy, entitled "An act to provide for the enrollment of the militia, for the organization of the national guard of the state of New York, and for the public defense, and entitled the military code."

PASSED March 7, 1872; three-fifths being present.

The People of the State of New York, represented in Senate and Assembly, do enact as follows:

Word "white" stricken out of military code.

SECTION 1. Section one of the act entitled "An act to provide for the enrollment of the militia, for the organization of the national guard of the state of New York, and for the public defense, and entitled the military code," passed March seventeen, eighteen hundred and seventy, is hereby amended by striking out the word "white" in the first line of the aforesaid first section.

§ 2. This act shall take effect immediately.

Ante, vol. 8, p. 240; vol. 7, p. 112.

CHAP. 92.

AN ACT to amend an act entitled "An act to amend an act passed March twenty-three, eighteen hundred and fifty, entitled 'An act for the protection of purchasers of real estate upon sales by order of surrogates,'" passed April twenty, eighteen hundred and sixty-nine.

Ante, vol. 7, p. 433.

PASSED March 7, 1872; three-fifths being present.

The People of the State of New York, represented in Senate and Assembly, do enact as follows:

SECTION 1. Section one of an act entitled "An act to amend an act passed March twenty-three, eighteen hundred and fifty, entitled 'An act for the protection of purchasers of real estate upon sales by order of surrogates,'" passed April twenty, eighteen hundred and sixty-nine, is hereby amended so as to read as follows:

§ 1. Section three of the act entitled "An act for the protection of purchasers of real estate upon sales by order of surrogates, passed March twenty-three, eighteen hundred and fifty, is hereby amended so as to read as follows:

§ 3. Nor shall any such sale be invalidated nor in any wise impeached, by reason that any such petition was or shall be presented by less than the whole number of executors or of administrators; nor by reason that, after the filing of any such petition, any bond required by law has been, or shall be, given by less than the whole number of the executors or administrators petitioning; nor by reason that any further proceeding, notice, sale, deed, or return has been, or shall be had or made, by less than the whole number of executors or administrators petitioning; nor by reason of any omission to serve upon any minor, heir, or devisee, personally, or by publication, a copy of the order to show cause required by the fifth section of the fourth title of chapter six, part second, of the Revised Statutes; provided such order shall have been duly served on the general guardian of the minor, or the guardian appointed in such proceeding; nor by reason of any irregularity in any matter or proceeding after the presenting of any petition and the giving notice of the order to show cause why the authority or direction applied for should not be granted, and before the order confirming such sale; nor after a lapse of five years from the time of such sale, where the notice of such sale has been published for six weeks successively before the day of such sale, although such publication may not have been for the full period of forty-two days; and in all cases where the records of the office of the surrogate, before whom such proceedings were taken, have been removed from the house, office, or other building in which such proceedings were taken, to another house, office or other building, after such

Sales of real estate by order of surrogate not to be impeached for irregularity.

proceedings were taken, and the full period of twenty-five years has elapsed since said sale, it shall be presumed that guardians have been duly appointed for all minor devisees of the real estate sought to be sold in such proceeding, such presumption to be rebutted only by record evidence in such office showing affirmatively that such guardian or guardians were not appointed; provided, that nothing in this act contained shall be construed to affect in any manner any suit or proceeding already commenced for the recovery of any lands or the proceeds thereof, sold under or by virtue of any order of any surrogate's court.

Not to affect suits and proceedings already commenced.

§ 2. This act shall take effect immediately.

CHAP. 100.

AN ACT in relation to the dividends of life insurance companies.

PASSED March 9, 1872.

The People of the State of New York, represented in Senate and Assembly, do enact as follows:

Life insurance companies may ascertain and distribute proportion of surplus accruing to each policy.

SECTION 1. It shall be lawful for any life insurance company organized under the laws of this state, to ascertain at any given time, and from time to time, the proportion of surplus accruing to each policy from the date of the last to the date of the next succeeding premium payment, and to distribute the proportion found to be equitable either in cash, in reduction of premium, or in reversionary insurance, payable with the policy, and upon the same conditions as therein expressed at the next succeeding date of such payment; any thing in the charter of any such company to the contrary notwithstanding.

Ante, vol. 6, p. 782; vol. 7, p. 299.

§ 2. This act shall take effect immediately.

CHAP. 104.

AN ACT in relation to trustees and directors of charitable and benevolent institutions.

PASSED March 12, 1872.

The People of the State of New York, represented in Senate and Assembly, do enact as follows:

No director or trustee to receive compensation.

SECTION 1. No trustee or director of any charitable or benevolent institution, organized either under the laws of this state or by virtue of a special charter, shall receive, directly or indirectly, any salary or emolument from said institution, nor shall any salary or compensation whatever be voted or allowed by the trustees or directors of any institutions organized for charitable or benevolent purposes, to any trustee or director of said institution for services, either as trustee or director, or in any other capacity.

Ante, vol. 3, p. 505.

CHAP. 113.

AN ACT to relieve juvenile delinquents from certain disqualifications.

PASSED March 18, 1872.

The People of the State of New York, represented in Senate and Assembly, do enact as follows:

Disqualification to vote, etc., not to apply to persons committed to house of refuge, etc.

SECTION 1. The disqualification to testify created by section twenty-three (original number) of title seven, chapter first of part fourth of the Revised Statutes, and the prohibition to vote at any election contained in section fifteen of chapter two hundred and forty of the laws of eighteen hundred and forty-seven, shall not apply to a person heretofore convicted, or hereafter to be convicted of felony, or of any infamous crime, and in consequence thereof committed to one of the houses of refuge, or other reformatories organized under the laws of this state.

Ante, vol. 1, p. 724.

§ 2. This act shall take effect immediately.

CHAP. 114.

AN ACT in relation to limited partnerships.

PASSED March 18, 1872.

The People of the State of New York, represented in Senate and Assembly, do enact as follows:

Special partners may lease to general partners lands, etc.

SECTION 1. It shall be lawful for a special partner in any limited partnership to lease to the general partner or partners any lands, tenements or other property for the purposes of the partnership, at such rents and upon such terms as may be agreed upon between them.

Ante, vol. 1, p. 719.

§ 2. This act shall take effect immediately.

CHAP. 115.

AN ACT to supply the deficiency in the appropriation to pay the expenses of the superintendence, ordinary repairs and maintenance of the canals for the remainder of the fiscal year which commenced on the first day of October, eighteen hundred and seventy-one, and to regulate the manner of drawing warrants by the auditor of the canal department upon the treasurer.

PASSED March 19, 1872; three-fifths being present.

The People of the State of New York, represented in Senate and Assembly, do enact as follows:

SECTION 1. Whereas, by act chapter six hundred and fifty-four of the laws of eighteen hundred and seventy-one, entitled "An act making an appropriation to pay the expenses of the collection of tolls, superintendence, ordinary repairs and maintenance of the canals for the fiscal year commencing on the first day of October, eighteen hundred and seventy-one, passed April twenty, eighteen hundred and seventy-one, the following, among other, appropriations were made, to wit: For the payment of the expenses of the ordinary repairs of the completed canals of this state, and for the sums that may be due to the contractors for repairs under their contracts, and for no other object and purpose whatever, the sum of one million dollars, or so much thereof as may be necessary to be distributed, assigned and apportioned in the first instance to the three divisions of the canals, as now constituted, as follows: To the eastern division of the canals, the sum of four hundred thousand dollars; to the middle division of the canals, the sum of three hundred thousand dollars; to the western division of the canals, the sum of three hundred thousand dollars. And whereas, there remains now unexpended in the treasury but ninety-five thousand seven hundred and sixty-nine dollars and sixty-three cents balance of one million dollars so as above appropriated; therefore, the sum of seven hundred thousand dollars, or so much thereof as may be necessary, is hereby appropriated out of the revenues of the state canals for the fiscal year commencing on the first day of October, eighteen hundred and seventy-one, for the payments of the ordinary repairs of the completed canals of the state, and for the sums that may become due to the contractors for repairs under their contracts, and for no other object and purpose whatever, to be distributed, assigned and apportioned in the first instance to the three divisions of the canals as now constituted, as follows: To the eastern division of the canals, the sum of three hundred and fifty thousand dollars; to the middle division of the canals, the sum of one hundred and fifty thousand dollars; to the western division of the canals, the sum of two hundred thousand dollars.

$700,000 appropriated for payment of ordinary repairs of completed canals and for sums due contractors.

How apportioned.

§ 2. The auditor of the canal department shall notify the canal commissioners of the sums of money that will be needed to pay the drafts during the fiscal year to the contractors for repairs under their contracts upon their respective divisions, and he shall reserve such sums out of the appropriations made by this act, for the purpose of paying the monthly drafts to contractors, and no part of the sums so reserved shall be paid or applied to any other object or purpose, and no draft shall be drawn on the auditor in favor of any contractor, unless upon a certificate from the canal commissioner in charge that the contractor has fulfilled his contract during the preceding month. Auditor must notify commissioners of amount required during fiscal year and must reserve same.

§ 3. The commissioners of the canal fund are hereby authorized and required to borrow, on the credit of the state, reimbursable out of the revenues of the state canals within this fiscal year, and in anticipation of such revenues, such sum or sums of money, not exceeding in all the sum of seven hundred thousand dollars, as may from time to time be necessary to pay the expenses of the superintendence, ordinary repairs and maintenance of the canals during the remainder of this fiscal year, as provided for in this act. Commissioners of the canal fund authorized to borrow $700,000 to pay expenses of repairs, etc.

§ 4. Hereafter each warrant that may be drawn by the auditor of the canal department upon the treasurer for the payment of any moneys heretofore or hereafter appropriated by law, shall particularly specify the chapter and date of the passage of such law, and when more than one item of appropriation is contained in any such law, then the said warrant shall also specifically state the item of appropriation out of the sum of which the amount of such warrant shall be paid. All warrants drawn by auditor to specify the chapter and date of passage of law, etc.

§ 5. This act shall take effect immediately.

CHAP 116.

AN ACT to amend an act entitled "An act to facilitate the forming of agricultural and horticultural societies," passed April thirteenth, eighteen hundred and fifty-five.

PASSED March 19, 1872.

The People of the State of New York, represented in Senate and Assembly, do enact as follows:

SECTION 1. Section five of an act entitled "An act to facilitate the forming of agricultural and horticultural societies," passed April thirteenth, eighteen hundred and fifty-five, is hereby amended so as to read as follows:

§ 5. The officers of said society shall consist of a president, and at least one vice-president, a secretary, a treasurer, and six directors. The president and vice-president, secretary and Officers.

treasurer shall be elected annually, and the first year there shall be elected six directors; they shall be divided by lot into three classes: the first class to serve one year, the second class two years, and the third class three years; and at the expiration of each term there shall be elected two directors to serve three years, and all vacancies that may occur to be filled only for the term made vacant. The election of all officers shall be by ballot of the stockholders or members, who shall have been such not less than thirty days prior to such election. The board of managers shall consist of the president, the first vice-president, secretary, treasurer, and six directors, a majority of whom shall constitute a quorum for the transaction of business; and it shall be the duty of said officers to so manage the property and concerns of the said society, as will best promote the interests of agriculture, horticulture and the mechanic arts; and they shall hold annual fairs and exhibitions, and distribute premiums to the best and most meritorious exhibitors in their several departments.

Directors classified. Election. Board of managers. Duty of officers.

§ 2. This act shall take effect on the first day of May, eighteen hundred and seventy-two.

CHAP. 120.

AN ACT to authorize the descent of real estate to female citizens of the United States, and their descendants, notwithstanding their marriage with aliens.

Ante, vol. 4, p. 301.

PASSED March 20, 1872, by a two-third vote.

The People of the State of New York, represented in Senate and Assembly, do enact as follows:

Marriage by a woman who is a citizen, with an alien, not to affect descent of her real property.

SECTION 1. Real estate in this state now belonging to, or hereafter coming or descending to, any woman born in the United States, or who has been otherwise a citizen thereof, shall, upon her death, notwithstanding her marriage with an alien and residence in a foreign country, descend to her lawful children of such marriage, if any, and their descendants, in like manner, and with like effect, as if such children or their descendants were native born or naturalized citizens of the United States. Nor shall the title to any real estate now owned by, or which shall descend, be devised or otherwise conveyed to such woman, or to her lawful children, or to their descendants, be impaired or affected by reason of her marriage with an alien, or the alienage of such children or their descendants.

§ 2. This act shall take effect immediately.

CHAP. 128.

AN ACT to amend an act entitled "An act to amend an act, passed July twenty-first, eighteen hundred and fifty-three, entitled 'An act to amend an act to provide for the incorporation of companies to construct plank-roads,' passed May seventh, eighteen hundred and forty-seven," and the acts amendatory thereof, passed April fourteen, eighteen hundred and fifty-five.

PASSED March 23, 1872; three-fifths being present.

The People of the State of New York, represented in Senate and Assembly, do enact as follows:

Certain persons liable to perform highway labor may be assessed upon the line of plank-road.

SECTION 1. Section first of an act entitled "An act to amend an act, passed July twenty-first, eighteen hundred and fifty-three, entitled 'An act to amend an act to provide for the incorporation of companies to construct plank-roads,' passed May seventh, eighteen hundred and forty-seven," and the acts amendatory thereof, passed April fourteenth, eighteen hundred and fifty-five, is hereby amended so as to read as follows:

§ 1. Every person liable to do highway labor, living or owning property on the line of any plank-road of this state, may, on making application in writing to the commissioner or commissioners of their respective towns, on or any day previous to the time of making the highway warrants by such commissioners, be assessed the apportionment of highway labor for such property upon such plank-road, and the commissioner or commissioners may, in their discretion, assess such person for the land or property owned by him in or upon the line of said plank-road as a separate road district.

§ 2. This act shall take effect immediately.

Ante, vol. 3, p. 581.

CHAP. 139.

AN ACT to amend an act entitled an act in relation to stenographers in the circuit courts, courts of oyer and terminer and special terms of the supreme court, in the sixth, seventh and eighth judicial districts, and to repeal chapter forty-one of the laws of eighteen hundred and sixty-seven, and chapter six hundred and seventy-two of the laws of eighteen hundred and sixty-nine.

PASSED March 27, 1872; three-fifths being present.

The People of the State of New York, represented in Senate and Assembly, do enact as follows:

Act of 1871 extended to third, fourth and fifth judicial districts.

SECTION 1. The act in relation to stenographers in the circuit courts, court of oyer and terminer, and special terms of the supreme court, in the sixth, seventh and eighth judicial districts, passed April twenty-fifth, eighteen hundred and seventy-one, is hereby amended so as to include the third, fourth and fifth judicial districts, in addition to those above named; and in the third judicial district the justices of the supreme court may, in their discretion, appoint two stenographers.

§ 2. Chapter forty-one of the laws of eighteen hundred and sixty-seven, and six hundred and seventy-two of the laws of eighteen hundred and sixty-nine, are hereby repealed.

§ 3. This act shall take effect immediately.

CHAP. 141.

AN ACT to confirm the title of certain persons to real estate, questioned by reason of alienage of former owners.

PASSED March 27, 1872, by a two-third vote.

The People of the State of New York, represented in Senate and Assembly, do enact as follows;

Titles not to be impeached by reason of alienage.

SECTION 1. The title of any citizen or citizens of this state to any lands within this state shall not be questioned or impeached by reason of the alienage of any person or persons, from or through whom such title may have been derived. Provided, however, that nothing in this act shall affect the rights of the state in any case in which proceedings for escheat have been instituted.

Ante, vol. 3, p. 242.

§ 2. Nothing in this act shall affect or impair the right of any heir, devisee, mortgagee or creditor, by judgment or otherwise.

§ 3. This act shall take effect immediately.

CHAP. 142.

AN ACT to authorize the extension of the time for the collection of taxes in the several towns and cities in this state.

PASSED March 27, 1872; three-fifths being present.

The People of the State of New York, represented in Senate and Assembly, do enact as follows:

SECTION 1. If any collector of taxes in any town or city in this state shall, within fifteen days after the passage of this act, pay over all moneys collected by him, and shall renew his bond as is herein provided, the time for the collection of taxes and for making returns thereof by him shall be as is herein provided, extended to a day not later than the fifteenth day of April, eighteen hundred and seventy-two. Such bond shall be renewed with such sureties as in any town shall be approved by the supervisor thereof, or, in case of his inability to act, by the town clerk thereof, and in any city shall be approved by such officer or board therein as is authorized by law to approve of collector's bonds. The penalty expressed in such bond, in every case, shall be double the amount of the taxes in that case remaining uncollected. The bond shall be approved in writing and filed as required by law, and have all the effect of a collector's bond. A copy of the bond and the approval thereof. shall, within fifteen days after the passage of this act, if it is the bond of a collector of taxes in any town, be delivered to the county treasurer of the county in which is located said town, and if it is the bond of a collector of taxes in any city, it shall be delivered to the officer or board in said city authorized to receive taxes from said collector. The time, not later than the said fifteenth day of April, eighteen hundred and seventy-two, to which the collection of said taxes and the making returns thereof may be extended, shall, in any town, be fixed and limited in writing and indorsed on the warrant of the collector by the supervisor of the town, or, in case of his inability to act, by the town clerk thereof, and in any city by the common council thereof.

Collectors to pay over moneys and renew bonds.

Bonds, how renewed.

Penalty.

To be filed.

Time extended till April 15th.

§ 2. It shall be the duty of the secretary of state, at once, after its passage, to cause this act to be printed upon slips of paper, and to deliver to each county treasurer and to the mayor of each city, a sufficient number thereof to supply one to each collector of taxes in said county and city, and it shall be the duty of said county treasurer and of said mayor to deliver one thereof to each collector of taxes in his city or county respectively.

Duty of secretary of state, treasurers and mayors.

§ 3. This act shall not extend to the cities of New York, Albany, Brooklyn, Troy, Buffalo, Rochester and Binghamton, or to any city of this state wherein taxes are collected under special laws.

Not to extend to certain cities.

§ 4. This act shall take effect immediately.

CHAP. 143.

AN ACT to authorize the various towns throughout the state, which shall have an excess of money accruing from the excise law, to expend the same.

PASSED March 27, 1872; three-fifths being present.

The People of the State of New York, represented in Senate and Assembly, do enact as follows:

Town board may expend money for town purposes.

SECTION 1. It shall be lawful for the town board of any town, whose yearly receipts from the excise board are in excess of the amount required to maintain the poor of said town, to expend the balance of the same on other ordinary town expenses.

§ 2. All acts and parts of acts inconsistent with this act are hereby repealed.

§ 3. This act shall take effect immediately.

CHAP. 146.

AN ACT to authorize corporations to hold and convey real estate, for business purposes, in other states, with the consent thereof.

PASSED March 28, 1872.

The People of the State of New York, represented in Senate and Assembly, do enact as follows:

Corporations may hold real estate in other states.

SECTION 1. It shall be lawful for any corporation organized under the laws of this state, and transacting business in several states, to acquire, hold and convey, in such states, with the consent thereof, such real estate as shall be requisite for such corporation in the convenient transaction of its business.

§ 2. This act shall take effect immediately.

Ante, vol. 1, p. 556.

CHAP. 147.

AN ACT to extend the provisions of chapter one hundred and thirteen of the laws of the year one thousand eight hundred and fifty-three, entitled "An act declaring Indian river a public highway."

PASSED March 28, 1872; three-fifths being present.

The People of the State of New York, represented in Senate and Assembly, do enact as follows:

SECTION 1. The act of the year one thousand eight hundred and fifty-three, chapter one hundred and thirteen, declaring Indian river a public highway, is hereby amended so as to extend its provisions to that part of said river running through the town of Wilna in the county of Jefferson, and the town of Diana in the county of Lewis, from a point of said river known as the Natural Bridge, in said town of Wilna. Provided that any and all parties before using said river as a public highway shall execute a bond, approved by a majority of the town boards of the towns of Antwerp and Wilna in Jefferson county and Diana in Lewis county, and deliver the same at the town clerk's office of the respective aforesaid towns, and to be there filed as a good and sufficient security against any and all damages that may be done to any and all property, public or private, such as bridges, booms, dams, mills, machinery, etc., etc., that are now or may hereafter be erected on said river, by using it as a public highway.

Act making Indian river a public highway extended.

Parties using river to give bond.

§ 2. This act shall take effect immediately.

Ante, vol. 3, p. 600.

CHAP. 148.

AN ACT providing for additional compensation to deputies, clerks and assistants in the various departments in the state government.

PASSED March 28, 1872; three-fifths being present.

The People of the State of New York, represented in Senate and Assembly, do enact as follows:

SECTION 1. The treasurer shall pay, upon the warrant of the comptroller, from the general fund, additional compensation for the balance of the fiscal year, commencing January first, eighteen hundred and seventy-two, and closing on the first day of October, eighteen hundred and seventy-two, to the deputies, assistants, clerks and messengers permanently employed in the office of the secretary of state, comptroller, treasurer, attorney-general, department of public instruction, state engineer and surveyor, insurance department, to the

Additional compensation for balance of fiscal year.

librarians and their assistants and janitors in the state library, the private secretary of the governor, and clerks and messengers of the executive departments, to the secretary and assistant secretary of the regents of the university, to the curator of the state cabinet of natural history, and to the superintendent of the capitol and state hall, and the state geological hall, to the clerks of the court of appeals, and of the commission of appeals at the following rates of advance on the salaries received by them, or a proportionate amount for a less term of services: on all salaries of fifteen hundred dollars and under, an increase at the rate of thirty-five per cent; on all salaries over fifteen hundred and less than two thousand dollars, an increase at the rate of twenty-five per cent; on all salaries of two thousand dollars, an increase at the rate of fifteen per cent. The sum of twenty-two thousand five hundred dollars, or as much thereof as may be necessary, is hereby appropriated from the general fund to pay the advances provided for by this section.

Percentage of increase.

Increase in railroad and insurance departments, how paid.

§ 2. The increased compensation hereinbefore given to the deputy and clerks in the railroad department, in the office of the engineer and surveyor, and to the deputy and clerks in the insurance department, shall be paid by the several railroad and insurance companies, pursuant to chapter five hundred and twenty-six of the laws of eighteen hundred and fifty-five, and chapter three hundred and sixty-six of the laws of eighteen hundred and fifty-nine.

Additional compensation in canal department and canal offices.

§ 3. The treasurer shall pay from the canal fund, upon the warrant of the auditor of the canal department, additional compensation to the deputy and each of the clerks of the canal department, and to each of the clerks of the canal commissioners and canal appraisers, and to the clerk and assistant clerk of the board of canal commissioners for the balance of the present fiscal year commencing January first, eighteen hundred and seventy-two, and closing October first, eighteen hundred and seventy-two, at the following rates of advance on salaries received by them: On all salaries of fifteen hundred dollars and under, an increase at the rate of thirty-five per cent; on all salaries over fifteen hundred and less than two thousand dollars, an increase at the rate of twenty-five per cent; or a proportionate amount for a less term of service. The sum of four thousand four hundred dollars, or so much thereof as may be necessary, is hereby appropriated from the canal fund, not otherwise appropriated, to pay the advance provided for in this section.

Percentage.

Increased pay in military departments.

§ 4. The treasurer shall pay, on the warrant of the comptroller, out of any money appropriated for military purposes, for the balance of the present fiscal year commencing January first, eighteen hundred and seventy-two, and closing October first, eighteen hundred and seventy-two, additional compensation to the assistants, clerks, messengers and janitors permanently employed in the office of the adjutant-general, inspector-general, quartermaster-general, paymaster-general, surgeon-general, and commissary-general, at the rates of advance on the salaries received by them (or a proportionate amount for a less term of service), as provided for the assistants, clerks and messengers named in the first section of this act.

§ 5. This act shall take effect immediately.

CHAP. 161.

AN ACT for the protection of tax payers against the frauds, embezzlements and wrongful acts of public officers and agents.

PASSED April 2, 1872; three-fifths being present.

The People of the State of New York, represented in Senate and Assembly, do enact as follows:

Tax-payers may maintain action against municipal officer to prevent waste.

SECTION 1. All officers, agents, commissioners and other persons acting for and on behalf of any county, town or municipal corporation in this state, and each and every of them, may be prosecuted, and an action or actions may be maintained against them to prevent waste or injury to any property, funds or estate of such county, town or municipal corporation by any person residing in such county, town or municipal corporation assessed for and liable to pay taxes therein, or who has paid taxes therein within one year previous to the commencement of any such action or actions. This act shall not be so construed as to take away any right of action from any county, town or municipal corporation, or from any public officer, or as affecting actions now pending brought by them or any of them.

§ 2. This act shall take effect immediately.

CHAP. 164.

AN ACT to provide for the completion of lock number two on the Erie canal, and to make an appropriation for said object.

PASSED April 2, 1872; three-fifths being present.

The People of the State of New York, represented in Senate and Assembly, do enact as follows:

Lock to be completed.

SECTION 1. The canal board is hereby directed to complete the construction of lock number two on the Erie canal, and the sum of twenty thousand dollars, or so much thereof as is necessary under the existing contract, is appropriated for that purpose, to be paid out of the forty thousand dollars appropriated by act, chapter nine hundred and thirty of the laws of eighteen hundred and seventy-one for the construction of two locks on the enlarged plan, and section work connected at the three locks just north of the village of Waterford, provided, that, if the contractor for any reason should fail to comply with his contract, the canal board may complete said work in such manner as they may think best for the interest of the state, and may apply said sum of twenty thousand dollars, or so much thereof as may be necessary for said purpose.

§ 2. This act shall take effect immediately.

CHAP. 181.

AN ACT for the better prevention of the procurement of abortions and other like offenses, and to amend the laws relative thereto.

PASSED April 6, 1872; three-fifths being present.

The People of the State of New York, represented in Senate and Assembly, do enact as follows:

Punishment for causing miscarriage.

SECTION 1. Any person who shall hereafter willfully administer to any woman with child, or prescribe for any such woman, or advise or procure her to take any medicine, drug, substance or thing whatever, or shall use or employ, or advise or procure her to submit to the use or employment of any instrument or other means whatever, with intent thereby to produce the miscarriage of any such woman, unless the same shall have been necessary to preserve her life or that of such child, shall, in case the death of such child or of such woman be thereby produced, be deemed guilty of a felony, and upon conviction shall be punished by imprisonment in a state prison for a term not less than four years or more than twenty years.

Punishment for taking medicine to cause miscarriage.

§ 2. Any woman pregnant with child who shall take any medicine, drug, substance or thing whatever, or shall use or employ, or suffer any other person to use or employ, or submit to the use or employment of any instrument or other means whatever, with the intent thereby to produce the miscarriage of the child of which she is so pregnant, unless the same shall have been necessary to preserve her life or that of such child, shall, in case the death of such child shall be thereby produced, be deemed guilty of a felony, and upon conviction shall be punished by imprisonment in the state prison for a term not less than four years or more than ten years.

Punishment for advertis-

§ 3. Every person who shall administer to any pregnant woman, or prescribe for any such woman, or advise or procure any such woman to take any medicine, drug, substance or thing whatever, or manufacture, advertise, or sell any such medicine, drug, substance or thing whatever, or shall use or employ any instrument or other means whatever, with intent thereby to procure the miscarriage of any such woman, shall upon conviction be punished by imprisonment in a county jail, or in a state prison, not less than one nor more than three years, in the discretion of the court.

ing, etc., medicine or thing with intent to cause miscarriage.

§ 4. Whosoever shall unlawfully supply or procure any advice, instruction, medicine, drug, substance or thing whatever, knowing that the same is intended to be unlawfully used or employed, with intent to procure the miscarriage of any woman, whether she be or be not pregnant, shall be deemed guilty of a misdemeanor, and shall upon conviction be punished by imprisonment in a county jail, not less than three months nor more than one year, or by a fine not exceeding one thousand dollars, or by both such fine and imprisonment.

Punishment for supplying medicine, etc., knowing the same is intended to cause miscarriage.

§ 5. All acts and parts of acts inconsistent with this act are hereby repealed.

Ante, vol. 5, pp. 145, 146; vol. 7, pp. 810, 464.

§ 6. This act shall take effect immediately.

CHAP. 209.

AN ACT to amend an act entitled "An act for the incorporation of benevolent, charitable, scientific and missionary societies," passed April twelfth, eighteen hundred and forty-eight.

PASSED April 10, 1872.

The People of the State of New York, represented in Senate and Assembly, do enact as follows:

SECTION 1. Section one of an act entitled "An act for the incorporation of benevolent, charitable, scientific and missionary societies," passed April twelfth, eighteen hundred and forty-eight, is hereby amended by adding to said section after the word "charitable," in the fourth line thereof, the word "religious," so that said act shall authorize the incorporation of religious societies in the same manner as in case of organization of societies "for benevolent, charitable, scientific or missionary purposes."

Religious societies, how incorporated.

Ante, vol. 3, p. 705.

§ 2. This act shall take effect immediately.

CHAP. 235.

AN ACT to amend section ten of chapter seven hundred and thirty-nine of the laws of eighteen hundred and fifty-seven, entitled "An act to authorize the formation of town insurance companies."

Ante, vol. 6, p. 866; vol. 7, p. 103.

PASSED April 16, 1872.

The People of the State of New York, represented in Senate and Assembly, do enact as follows:

SECTION 1. Section ten of chapter seven hundred and thirty-nine of the laws of eighteen hundred and fifty-seven, entitled "An act to authorize the formation of town insurance companies," is hereby amended so as to read as follows:

Powers limited. § 10. No company formed under this act shall insure any property out of the limits of the town in which the office of the company is located, nor shall they insure any property other than detached dwellings and their contents, farm buildings and their contents, and such stores, hotels, churches, school-houses and other public buildings, together with their contents, as the directors of any company formed under this act shall deem proper; nor shall they insure any property within the limits of any incorporated city or village in this state.

§ 2. This act shall take effect immediately.

CHAP. 248.

AN ACT to authorize the formation, establishing and maintaining of driving park and park associations.

PASSED April 16, 1872; three-fifths being present.

The People of the State of New York, represented in Senate and Assembly, do enact as follows:

Corporations, how formed. SECTION 1. Any six or more persons of full age, citizens of this state, who shall desire to form a driving park, or park association in this state may make, sign and acknowledge, before any officer authorized to take the acknowledgment of deeds in this state, and file in the office of the secretary of state, and also in the clerk's office of the county in which the business of such association is to be conducted, a certificate in writing wherein shall be stated the name and title whereby such association shall be known in law, the amount of its capital stock, the number of shares into which such capital stock is divided, the location, particular business and objects of such associations, the number of trustees, directors or managers to manage the same and the names of such trustees, directors or managers for the first year of its existence. Such articles of association shall not be filed as aforesaid until one-twentieth part of the amount of stock fixed as aforesaid shall have been actually paid in to the directors in cash, nor until there shall be indorsed thereon, or annexed thereto, an affidavit made by at least three of the directors named in such articles of association, that the amount of stock required in the first section of this act to be subscribed has been subscribed, and that one-twentieth part of the amount has been actually paid in as aforesaid.

§ 2. Upon filing a certificate as aforesaid, the persons who shall have signed and acknowledged such certificate and their associates and successors, shall thereupon by virtue of this act be a body politic and corporate by the name stated in such certificate, and by that name they and their successors shall and may have succession, and shall be persons in law capable of suing and being sued, and they and their successors may have and use a common seal, and may change and alter the same at pleasure; and they and their successors, by their corporate name, shall in law be capable of taking and receiving, purchasing and holding real estate for the purpose of their incorporation, and for no other purpose, to a sum not exceeding one hundred thousand dollars in value, and personal estate for like purpose to an amount not exceeding one hundred thousand dollars, and make by-laws for the management of its affairs not inconsistent with the laws of this state or of the United States. When to become bodies corporate.

§ 3. The capital stock of any such association shall be divided into shares of not less than ten dollars nor more than one hundred dollars each, as the by-laws of said association shall require, to be paid in cash by the stockholders at such time, and in such manner, and in such installments as the directors or managers of the association may require, and under such penalties for neglecting the payment of installments as may be prescribed by the by-laws of such association; provided, that at least thirty days' notice, printed or in writing, shall be given by the treasurer of such association of the time when the shares are required to be paid; such shares shall be deemed personal property, transferable only on the books of said association, in such manner as prescribed by its by-laws. Capital stock.

All the stockholders of every association, organized under this act, shall be severally and individually liable to an amount equal to the capital stock held by them respectively, to the creditors of such association, for all debts contracted by the directors or agents of such association for its use, until the whole amount of capital stock, fixed and limited by said association, is paid in, and a certificate thereof filed in the office aforesaid. Liability of stockholders.

§ 4. The officers of any such association shall consist of a president, and at least one vice-president, a secretary, a treasurer, and any number of directors which is divisible by three, but not more than fifteen in all. The president and vice-president, secretary, and treasurer, shall be elected annually, and Officers.

the first year the whole number of electors shall be elected; they shall be divided by lot into three classes; the first class to serve one year, the second class two years, and the third class three years; and at the expiration of each term a sufficient number of directors shall be elected to fill each class, and to serve three years; and all vacancies that may occur shall be filled only for the term made vacant. The election of all officers shall be by ballot of the stockholders or members, and no person who is not a stockholder shall be eligible to any office. The board of managers shall consist of the president, the first vice-president, secretary, treasurer and directors a majority of whom shall constitute a quorum for the transaction of business; and it shall be the duty of said officers to so manage the property and concerns of the said society as will best promote the objects of such associations as set forth in the certificate of incorporation.

Election of.

Managers.

Racing prohibited.

§ 5. Nothing in this act contained shall be construed to allow the racing, running, trotting or pacing of horses for any bet or wager, contrary to the provisions of article fifth, chapter twenty, title eight, and part first of the Revised Statutes.

Real estate of, how sold.

§ 6. Any such association may, in case the uses and convenience thereof so require, upon application to the supreme court of the district wherein said association at the time of such application shall be situated, or the county court of the county wherein such association is organized, obtain the requisite order and power to sell, from time to time, the whole or any part or parts of its real estate, the granting of such order to be in the discretion of the court, and such application to be made only when authorized by said association at any annual meeting thereof, by a vote in person or by proxy of not less than two-thirds in amount of all stockholders voting, and printed or written notice of the intention to vote for such application having been served on every stockholder by the secretary of such association by depositing the same in the post-office where such association is located, properly folded and directed to him at the post-office nearest his place of residence, as shall appear from the books of the association kept for this purpose, with the postage paid thereon, at least twenty days prior to the time of said meeting.

Increase of capital stock.

§ 7. The said association may increase its capital stock to any amount, not exceeding the amount as provided in section two of this act, at any annual meeting thereof, by a vote in person or by proxy, of not less than two-thirds in amount of all the stockholders, notice of such intention to increase its capital stock having been given as prescribed in the preceding section of this act; and such notice must state the time and place of the meeting, and to what amount it is proposed to increase the capital stock. The proceedings of such meeting must be entered on the minutes of the proceedings of the association, and thereupon the amount sanctioned, not exceeding the limit hereinbefore provided, by a vote of two-thirds of all said stockholders, shall be deemed the amount of the capital stock of said association.

§ 8. The officers of any association organized under the provisions of this act shall be jointly and severally liable for all debts due from said association, contracted while they are officers thereof, provided a suit for the collection of the same be brought within one year after the debt shall become due and payable. Liability of officers

§ 9. During any public exhibition held on the ground of such association, the sheriffs of counties within which the same are situated are hereby authorized, at the request of the officers of the association, to appoint so many special policemen as may be deemed necessary to aid in preserving order and enforcing the rules of the association, provided, that the compensation for the services of such special policemen shall in no event be a charge upon any county, city, town or village. Sheriffs to appoint policemen.

§ 10. The president, secretary and treasurer of every such association shall annually prepare a full statement of the receipts and expenditures of such association during the year preceding the day of the annual election, with a schedule of its property, debts and obligations, which statement and schedule shall be verified by the affidavits of two of said officers, and shall be filed in the county clerk's office of the county in which such association shall be located within one week after such annual election, and otherwise published as the by-laws of the association shall or may prescribe. Financial statement

§ 11. Every association formed under this act shall possess the powers and be subject to the provisions and restrictions contained in the third article of the eighteenth chapter of the Revised Statutes. General powers.

§ 12. All associations for the purposes specified in this act, which have been formed under any special act, may reorganize under this law at any time.

§ 13. This act shall take effect immediately.

CHAP. 260.

AN ACT to amend the act entitled "An act in relation to the qualification of persons to be admitted to practice in the courts of this state, as attorneys, solicitors and counselors," passed April thirteen, eighteen hundred and seventy-one.

PASSED April 17, 1872.

The People of the State of New York, represented in Senate and Assembly, do enact as follows:

SECTION 1. The last paragraph of section three of chapter four hundred and eighty-six of the laws of eighteen hundred and seventy-one is hereby amended so as to read as follows: Nothing in this act contained shall be taken or construed to affect the provisions of chapter three hundred and ten of the laws of eighteen hundred and fifty-five, or of chapter two Act of 1871 amended.

hundred and sixty-seven of the laws of eighteen hundred and fifty-nine, or of chapter one hundred and eighty-seven of the laws of eighteen hundred and sixty, or of chapter two hundred and two of the laws of eighteen hundred and sixty.

Ante, p. 95.

§ 2. This act shall take effect immediately.

CHAP. 274.

AN ACT to amend an act entitled "An act for the erection and maintenance of watering troughs in the public highways," passed April seventh, eighteen hundred and sixty-nine.

PASSED April 18, 1872; three-fifths being present.

The People of the State of New York, represented in Senate and Assembly, do enact as follows:

SECTION 1. The first section of an act entitled "An act for the erection and maintenance of watering troughs in the public highways," passed April seventh, eighteen hundred and sixty-nine, is hereby amended so as to read as follows:

Abatement of tax for watering troughs.

§ 1. The commissioners of highways in the several towns of this state shall annually abate three dollars from the highway tax of any inhabitant of a road district, who shall construct on his own land, and keep in repair, a watering trough beside the public highway, well supplied with fresh water, the surface of which shall be two or more feet above the level of the ground, and easily accessible for horses with vehicles; but the said commissioners of highways respectively may designate the number necessary for the public convenience in each district, and no others than those designated shall be allowed this abatement of tax.

§ 2. The two following sections shall be added to said act, and shall be the second and third sections thereof:

Abatement of toll on plank-roads for watering troughs.

§ 2. The directors of the several plank-road and turnpike road companies in this state shall annually abate three dollars from the toll of any inhabitant, not an innkeeper, or all of it if in the aggregate not exceeding that sum, who shall construct on his own land, and keep in repair, a watering trough beside the plank-road or turnpike road as the case may be, well supplied with fresh water, the surface of which shall be two or more feet above the level of the ground, and easily accessible for horses with vehicles; but the commissioners of highways of the towns respectively shall, and they are hereby invested with full power and authority to designate those necessary for the public convenience along said plank-road or turnpike road, as the case may be, and no others than those designated shall be allowed both such abatement of toll and highway labor.

§ 3. In case the directors of any plank-road or turnpike road company in this state shall refuse or neglect to abate the toll as aforesaid, in compliance with the provisions of the preceding section, any inhabitant having constructed a watering trough in compliance therewith may notify the commissioner or commissioners of highways, as the case may be, of the town in which the same had been erected, of such neglect or refusal on the part of the directors aforesaid, whose duty it shall be, and who are hereby invested with full power and authority to proceed, without delay, to an examination of said watering trough; and if, upon a full examination of the same, the said commissioner or commissioners, as the case may be, or a majority of them, shall deem it necessary for the convenience of the public that such watering trough ought to be maintained, he or they, as the case may be, shall forthwith notify the said directors accordingly, by serving a written notice on the president of the company, to that effect, in which the necessity of its maintenance shall be clearly expressed; and if the said directors shall still refuse or neglect to abate the toll as aforesaid, and shall demand and take toll, on application for such abatement, in violation of the provisions of the preceding section, for the space of thirty days after the service of such notice, they shall be liable to a penalty of twenty dollars, to be recovered in an action at law at the suit of the person having constructed said watering trough. Duty of commissioners in case of refusal of directors to abate toll. Penalty.

§ 3. This act shall take effect immediately.

Ante, vol. 7, p. 424.

CHAP. 283.

AN ACT to authorize plank-road and turnpike companies formed under and by virtue of part first, chapter eighteen, title one, article five of the Revised Statutes, to extend their charter or corporate existence.*

PASSED April 18, 1872; three-fifths being present.

The People of the State of New York, represented in Senate and Assembly, do enact as follows:

SECTION 1. Any plank-road company or turnpike company which shall have been formed under and by virtue of part first, chapter eighteen, title one, article five of the Revised Statutes, and the several acts amendatory thereto, and which shall have been managed and carried on any plank-road or turnpike road for twenty years, and whose entire dividends have not exceeded fifty per cent of the original capital stock, may continue their corporate existence for a period not exceeding thirty Corporate existence of certain plank-roads continued.

* There is no such article in the Revised Statutes. Such a law was passed in 1847, and will be found ante, vol. 8, p. 549.

years in addition to the time specified in the original articles of association, by complying with the following requirements: Consent shall be obtained in writing from two-thirds of the supervisors of the towns or wards which said road passes through or into; and which shall be acknowledged before some officer authorized to take acknowledgments by the laws of the state of New York; consent shall also be obtained in writing from the persons owning two-thirds of the capital stock of such company, and in which shall also be stated the number of years which they shall desire such corporate existence extended; which shall also be so acknowledged, and to which shall be attached the affidavit or affidavits of some officer or officers of the said company, in which shall be stated the name of each town or ward through or into which such road passes; the number of years which such company has already existed; and that the aggregate amount of dividends have not exceeded one-half of the original capital stock.

Consent of supervisors and stockholders to be obtained.

Consent and affidavit to be filed.

§ 2. Such consent of said supervisors and stockholders, together with the said affidavit, shall be filed in the office of the secretary of state, and thereupon the corporate existence of said plank-road or turnpike company shall be extended for the period of time so specified in such consent of such stockholders.

Evidence.

§ 3. A copy of the consent of such supervisors and stockholders, together with a copy of such affidavit annexed thereto and certified to be a copy by the secretary of state, or his deputy, shall in all courts and places be presumptive evidence of the corporate existence of such company for the time therein specified, and of the facts therein stated.

CHAP. 285.

AN ACT to amend an act entitled "An act to extend the powers of boards of supervisors, except in the counties of New York and Kings," passed May eleventh, eighteen hundred and sixty-nine.

PASSED April 19, 1872; three-fifths being present.

The People of the State of New York, represented in Senate and Assembly, do enact as follows:

SECTION 1. An act entitled "An act to extend the powers of boards of supervisors, except in the counties of New York and Kings," passed May eleventh, eighteen hundred and sixty-nine, is hereby amended by adding at the end thereof an additional section as follows:

On written application of town offi-

§ 9. The board of supervisors of Queens county, in addition to the powers conferred by the first section of this act, shall have power at any meeting of which notice is given as hereinafter provided, to authorize the supervisors of any town or towns in such county, on written applications of the supervisor, town clerk, justices of the peace and commissioners of highways, or a majority of them, of such town, or if more than one town is affected thereby, then of said officers or a majority of them of each of such towns, to borrow such sum of money for and on the credit of such town or towns, as the said town officer may deem necessary to lay out, build, widen, grade, macadamize or repair any road or roads, or to purchase for public use, any plank-road, turnpike or toll road or toll bridge in such town or towns, or to pay any existing debt incurred in good faith by or on behalf of such town, for such purpose, before the passage of this act; and the said board of supervisors shall have power to prescribe the form of obligation to be issued on any such loan, and the time and place of payment, the time not to exceed ten years from the date of such obligation, and the rate of interest thereon not exceeding seven per cent per annum. And the said board of supervisors shall have power, and it shall be their duty from time to time, as the said obligations shall become due and payable, to impose upon the taxable property of such town sufficient tax to pay the said principal and interest of such obligations according to the terms and conditions thereof. In case the bridge or road so laid out, built, widened, graded, macadamized or repaired shall be situated in two or more towns in said county, then the said board of supervisors shall have the power to apportion the expense thereof, among such towns in such proportions as may be just. If in the case of the building, widening or improving of any road, or of the purchase for public use of any toll road or toll bridge, the supervisors of the town or towns in which such road is located shall not be able to agree with the owners of the land required for such improvement or of such toll road or toll bridge, as to the price to be paid therefor, then the board of supervisors of the county shall have power to apply to the supreme court of the judicial district, in which said county is situated, for the appointment of three commissioners to appraise and determine the value of the land so required, or of such toll road or toll bridge. Such application and appointment shall be made as in proceedings by railroad corporations to acquire title to real estate under existing statute, and the commissioners so appointed shall act and make report, and the owners of such lands or roads or bridges shall have similar right of appeal, and all incidental proceeding shall be conducted as in such railroad proceeding. When the value of said lands or roads or bridges shall in such manner have been finally determined, the said lands or roads or bridges shall vest in the town or towns in which they are respectively located, upon payment by said town or towns of said determined value, to the owners thereof, within six months after such final determination. Upon receiving the written application of town officers hereinbefore mentioned, the said board of supervisors shall publish a notice in every newspaper published in the town or towns affected by such

Queens county board of supervisors may authorize supervisor of town to borrow money to lay out, etc., roads.

Tax to be imposed to pay principal and interest as it falls due.

Proceedings to purchase toll roads, etc.

Notice to be published.

application, which notice shall contain a copy of such application, and shall name a time and place when and where said board will meet to consider such application.

Ante, vol. 7, p. 485.

CHAP. 315.

AN ACT to amend an act entitled "An act to amend an act entitled 'An act to reduce the number of town officers and town and county expenses, and to prevent abuses in auditing town and county accounts, passed May tenth, eighteen hundred and forty-five,' passed December fourteen, eighteen hundred and forty-seven."

PASSED April 23, 1872; three-fifths being present.

The People of the State of New York, represented in Senate and Assembly, do enact as follows:

SECTION 1. Section two of the act entitled "An act to amend an act entitled 'An act to reduce the number of town officers and town and county expenses, and to prevent abuses in auditing town and county accounts, passed May tenth, eighteen hundred and forty-five,' passed December fourteenth, eighteen hundred and forty-seven," is hereby amended so as to read as follows:

§ 2. The fifth section of said act is hereby amended so as to read as follows:

Damages upon laying out roads, how assessed.

§ 5. Whenever any damages are now allowed to be assessed by law, when any road or highway shall be laid out, altered or discontinued, in whole or in part, such damages shall be assessed by not less than three commissioners, to be appointed by the county court of the county in which such road shall be, on the application of the commissioner or commissioners of highways of the town; or in case the said commissioners of highways should neglect or refuse to make such application for the space of thirty days after having been requested so to do, it shall be lawful for the said county court to appoint such commissioners on the application of any of the owners of the land through which such road shall have been laid out; and the commissioners so appointed shall take the oath of office prescribed by the constitution, and shall proceed, on receiving at least six days' notice of the time and place, to meet the commissioners of highways, and to take a view of the premises, hear the parties and such witnesses as may be offered before them; and they shall all meet and act, and shall assess all damages which may be required to be assessed for the said highway, and shall be authorized to administer oaths to witnesses who may be produced before them under this section: and when they shall all have met and acted, the assessment agreed to by a majority of them shall be valid; and when such

Official oath.

assessment shall be so made, it shall be delivered to one of the commissioners of highways of the town, who, within ten days after receiving the same, shall file it in the town clerk's office in the said town. Assessment to be filed.

§ 2. This act shall take effect immediately.

Ante, vol. 8, pp. 804, 811.

CHAP. 319.

AN ACT to amend an act entitled "An act to amend chapter one hundred and ninety-four of the laws of eighteen hundred and forty-nine, entitled 'An act to vest in the board of supervisors certain legislative powers, and to prescribe their fees for certain services,'" passed April third, eighteen hundred and forty-nine, passed February second, eighteen hundred and seventy-one.

PASSED April 23, 1872; three-fifths being present.

The People of the State of New York, represented in Senate and Assembly, do enact as follows:

SECTION 1. Section one of chapter eighteen of the laws of eighteen hundred and seventy-one, entitled "An act to amend an act entitled 'An act to amend chapter one hundred and ninety-four of the laws of eighteen hundred and forty-nine, entitled 'An act to vest in the boards of supervisors certain legislative powers, and to prescribe their fees for certain services,'" passed April third, eighteen hundred and forty-nine, passed February second, eighteen hundred and seventy-one, is hereby amended so as to read as follows:

§ 1. The board of supervisors of the several counties in this state, the county of New York excepted, at their annual meeting, shall have power within their respective counties, by vote of two-thirds of all the members elected, to divide or alter in its bounds, any town, or erect a new town; but they shall not make any alterations that shall place parts of the same town in more than one assembly district, nor where it is proposed to divide towns into two or more towns, unless upon application to the board as hereinafter provided, of at least twelve freeholders of each of the towns to be affected by the division, and upon being furnished with a map and survey of the towns to be affected, showing the proposed alterations, and if the application be granted, a copy of said map, with a certified statement of the action of said board thereunto annexed shall be filed in the office of the secretary of state, and it shall be the duty of the secretary to cause the same to be Supervisors may, by a two-third vote, divide towns.

printed with the laws of the next legislature after such divisio takes place, and cause the same to be published in the same manner as other laws are published.

§ 2. This act shall take effect immediately.

CHAP. 334.

AN ACT making an appropriation to pay the expenses of the collection of tolls, superintendence, ordinary repairs and maintenance of the canals for the fiscal year commencing on the first day of October, one thousand eight hundred and seventy-two.

PASSED April 24, 1872; three-fifths being present.

The People of the State of New York, represented in Senate and Assembly, do enact as follows:

Appropriations. SECTION 1. The following sums are hereby appropriated out of the revenue of the state canals for the fiscal year, commencing on the first day of October, eighteen hundred and seventy-two: For paying the expenses of the collection of tolls, the superintendence and ordinary repairs of the public works, the salaries, traveling expenses and clerk hire of the canal commissioners, the state engineer and surveyor, the canal appraisers, the salary of the auditor of the canal department, the clerk hire therein and the incidental charges and expenses thereof, the sum of one million three hundred and ten thousand four hundred and eighty-five dollars, or so much thereof as may be necessary to be expended during the fiscal year, to be distributed, applied, apportioned and disposed of as follows: (For collection of tolls, superintendence, salaries, etc.)

Canal commissioners and clerk. For salaries, traveling expenses and clerk hire of the canal commissioners, twelve thousand and sixty dollars, and the clerk of the board of canal commissioners, two thousand and twenty-five dollars.

State engineer. For the salary and traveling expenses of the state engineer and surveyor, two thousand seven hundred dollars.

Superintendent of repairs. For the salaries and clerk hire of the superintendent of repairs of the canals, the sum of seventy thousand dollars, or so much thereof as may be necessary.

Canal appraisers. For the salaries and traveling expenses of the canal appraisers, and for clerk hire in their office, the sum of twelve thousand two hundred dollars, or so much thereof as may be necessary.

Auditor of canal department. For the salary of the auditor of the canal department, two thousand five hundred dollars, and for clerk hire in the said department, the sum of fifteen thousand dollars, or so much thereof as may be necessary.

Engineers on ordi- For the salaries and compensation of the engineers employed on the ordinary repairs of the canals, including the incidental nses of such engineers, the sum of twenty-four thousand ars, or so much thereof as may be necessary. nary repairs.

For the salaries and compensation of the collectors of canal tolls, and their clerks, and for salaries and compensation of weigh-masters and their assistants, including the incidental expenses of said collectors and weigh-masters, and the compensation of inspectors of boats and their cargoes, the sum of one hundred and ten thousand dollars, or so much thereof as may be necessary. Collectors of tolls, clerks, weigh-masters, etc.

For the payment of such incidental and miscellaneous charges and expenses as are authorized by existing statutes to be paid out of the canal revenues, and charged to the account of the Erie and Champlain canal fund and the canal debt sinking fund, under section one of article seven of the constitution, the sum of sixty thousand dollars, or so much thereof as may be necessary. Incidental expenses.

For the payment of the expenses of the ordinary repairs of the completed canals of the state, and for the sums that may become due to the contractors for repairs under their contracts, and for no other object and purpose whatever, the sum of one million dollars, or so much thereof as may be necessary to be distributed, assigned and apportioned in the first instance to the three divisions of the canals as now constituted, as follows: Expenses of ordinary repairs.

To the eastern division of the canals, the sum of four hundred thousand dollars. Eastern division.

To the middle division of the canals, the sum of three hundred thousand dollars. Middle division.

To the western division of the canals, the sum of three hundred thousand dollars. Western division.

The canal commissioners shall not expend any more money on their respective divisions, nor incur any charge against the state for the repairs of the canals during the fiscal year than is above appropriated and apportioned to the said division by this act, unless the canal board, by resolution to be entered on the minutes of said board, and by the concurring votes of five members thereof, shall otherwise order and direct. And the said canal board, in case of breaks or breaches, or other extraordinary occurrences happening on any one of said divisions, causing or tending to a suspension or interruption of navigation upon such division, shall, and the said board is hereby authorized to, direct in manner above provided, the transfer of such portion of the unexpended balance of one or both the other divisions, to the division requiring the same, to keep and sustain navigation, and the commissioner in charge of the division to which such transfer of appropriation shall be made, shall expend the same in the amendment and reparation of the canals under his charge, designated in the resolution of the canal board authorizing such transfer. Restrictions as to expenditures by commissioners.

§ 2. The auditor of the canal department shall notify the canal commissioners of the sum of money that will be needed to pay the drafts, during the fiscal year, to the contractors for repairs under their contracts upon their respective divisions, Auditor to reserve moneys for repair contractors.

and he shall reserve such sums out of the appropriations made by this act for the purpose of paying the monthly drafts to contractors, and no part of the sums so reserved shall be paid or applied to any other object or purpose, and no drafts shall be drawn on the auditor in favor of any contractor, unless upon a certificate of the canal commissioner in charge that the contractor has fulfilled his contract during the preceding month.

§ 3. This act shall take effect immediately.

CHAP. 343.

AN ACT to amend the act chapter seven hundred and seventy-eight of the laws of eighteen hundred and seventy-one, re-appropriating certain moneys for the construction of new work upon and extraordinary repairs of the canals of this state.

PASSED April 24, 1872; three-fifths being present.

The People of the State of New York, represented in Senate and Assembly, do enact as follows:

Appropriation to improve Madison Brook reservoir. SECTION 1. The sum of ten thousand dollars appropriated by act chapter seven hundred and seventy-eight of the laws of eighteen hundred and seventy-one, for reconstructing race and feeder on the Owasco outlet, may be applied in the discretion of the board of canal commissioners to the completion and further improvements of Madison Brook reservoir for the purpose of affording an additional supply of water to the Erie canal.

Canal commissioners may expend certain sums for certain purposes. In addition to the objects enumerated in said act chapter seven hundred and seventy-eight, laws of eighteen hundred and seventy-one, and to which certain specific sums therein named may be lawfully applied, the board of canal commissioners are hereby authorized to expend the following sums, and for the following purposes, to wit:

Refunding moneys to John Lang. For refunding moneys to John Lang, treasurer, which were expended in protecting banks of Mill creek and repairing swing bridge at Watkins and dredging the harbor at Dresden, the sum of eleven hundred and fifty-five dollars and forty-two cents.

Waste-weir at Horseheads. For building a new waste-weir on the Chemung canal at or near Horseheads, six hundred dollars, or so much thereof as may be necessary.

Crooked Lake canal. For paying for brush and stone protection to the banks and locks of the Crooked Lake canal, the sum of three thousand dollars, or so much thereof as may be necessary.

John Leahey for dams on Gibson creek. For payment of John Leahey for constructing two dams on Gibson creek, Chemung canal feeder, such sum as shall appear to be due to said Leahey, according to the estimate of D.

Whitford, assistant engineer, not exceeding four thousand one hundred and eighty dollars and forty cents, provided that the sums appropriated to John L[illegible]g and for building a waste-weir near Horseheads, for brush and stone on the Crooked Lake canal, and to John Leahey for building dam at Gibson's creek, shall be paid by the commissioners in charge of the middle division of the canals, on the approval of the estimates and vouchers therefor by the state engineer.

State dredge.

For expense of the state dredge of the middle division in excavating Geneva harbor and basin during the winter and spring months, two thousand five hundred dollars, or so much thereof as may be necessary.

For building a dump boat for state dredge, eight hundred dollars, or so much thereof as may be necessary.

Cayuga and Seneca canal.

For completing the improvements of the berme bank of the Cayuga and Seneca canal, near Geneva, two thousand dollars, or so much thereof as may be necessary.

State dam at Waterloo.

Fifteen thousand dollars in lieu of the sum of ten thousand dollars, provided by chapter seven hundred and seventy-eight of the laws of one thousand eight hundred and seventy-one, for building such dam, bulkheads and other works at or near the site of the present state dam at Waterloo, as the canal board may deem necessary for the uniform maintenance of navigation, having due regard to the rights of the owners and occupants of hydraulic privileges on the Seneca outlet. Said dam shall be built in such manner and of such materials as shall be approved by the canal board, and sufficient to restore and maintain the waters of Seneca lake to their original natural height but not above said natural height; and the said canal commissioners shall construct such other works and erections as may be necessary for such purpose and to carry into effect chapter four hundred and seventy-nine of the laws of eighteen hundred and fifty-seven, to such extent as they shall deem meet, and also remove all bars and obstructions in the channel of the Seneca outlet or river and the canal above the upper locks at Waterloo, to the depth required by said act so far as they shall deem meet. The whole expense not to exceed fifteen thousand dollars.

Additional supply of water at Rome level.

Provided, however, that the unexpended balance of the sum of one hundred thousand dollars appropriated by chapter eight hundred and seventy-seven, laws of eighteen hundred and sixty-nine, for the construction of Fish creek feeder, and re-appropriated by the act hereby amended, may, in the discretion of the board of canal commissioners, be applied and expended as they shall direct in the construction of any feeders or reservoirs which will furnish an additional supply of water on the Rome level.

§ 2. This act shall take effect immediately.

CHAP. 346.

AN ACT for the improvement of the navigation of the Hudson river, and to make an appropriation therefor.

PASSED April 24, 1872; three-fifths being present.

The People of the State of New York, represented in Senate and Assembly, do enact as follows:

Appropriation to improve navigation on Hudson river. SECTION 1. The sum of fifty thousand dollars is hereby appropriated out of any moneys in the treasury not otherwise appropriated, for the purpose of removing obstructions in and improving the navigation of the Hudson river between the city of Troy and the village of Coxsackie, and for dredging, deepening and widening the channel of said river where it is necessary between the said city of Troy and the said village of Coxsackie, and five thousand dollars of said moneys, or so much thereof as may be necessary to complete said channel, shall be used in completing the west channel of said river between Roah Hook and Barren Island.

Commissioners to expend money. § 2. The state engineer and surveyor, Samuel Schuyler, Alfred Van Santvoord, William H. Taylor and Thomas McManus, are hereby appointed commissioners, and are hereby authorized and empowered to superintend and control the expenditure of the said sum so appropriated by the first section of this act.

After expenditure is verified, comptroller to draw warrant on treasurer for amount. § 3. The comptroller of the state is hereby authorized to draw his warrant on the treasurer of this state for the payment of any money expended by the said commissioners, not exceeding the amount appropriated by this act, provided the expenditure of the same is verified in due form by the oath of said commissioners, or a majority of them, to the effect that such moneys have been expended for the purpose of improving the navigation of the Hudson river, as herein provided, or that the labor, material or machinery has been either duly performed, or furnished, and provided further, that the said commissioners shall receive no compensation for their services in the discharge of the duties created by this act, beyond their actual expenses. Not to receive compensation.

Commissioners to give bond. § 4. The commissioners appointed by this act shall, before they are authorized to draw upon the comptroller for any of the moneys appropriated by this act, execute to the people of the state of New York, a bond in the penal sum of fifty thousand dollars, with satisfactory sureties, conditioned that they will faithfully discharge their duties as such commissioners and truly account to the comptroller of the state for the expenditure of all moneys received by them under this act, which bond shall be approved by the comptroller and the treasurer of this state, and such accounting shall take place within thirty days after the payment of such moneys to said commissioners.

§ 5. The commissioners hereby appointed shall also have the power to prescribe rules and regulations relative to the dumping of earth, stone, gravel, sand or any other materials in or near the said river which, in their opinion, would have a tendency to obstruct navigation; and any person or persons who shall, by themselves or their agents, violate such rules and regulations, shall be liable to a penalty of one hundred dollars, to be recovered in any court of competent jurisdiction in the name of said commissioners or any one of them; and they shall have the further power to remove any and all obstructions to navigation in the Hudson river, between the said city of Troy and the said village of Coxsackie, or to lighter, or cause to be lightered, any boat or vessel which may be aground by reason of drawing a greater depth of water than the channel affords, or which from any other cause whatever may be obstructing the navigation of said river; and they, or either of them, or their agents, are hereby authorized to remove such boat or vessel so aground and obstructing the navigation as aforesaid, and to assess the expense of such lightering or removing on such vessel and cargo, and said expenses incurred shall be a lien on such cargo, boat or vessel as aforesaid, and shall be enforced and collected as hereinbefore provided.

To prescribe rules for dumping of earth, etc., near river.

Penalty.

May lighter or remove vessels aground.

Expense to be assessed on vessels.

§ 6. The said commissioners shall not be directly or indirectly interested in any contract made under this act.

§ 7. All acts and parts of acts inconsistent with this act are hereby repealed.

§ 8. This act shall take effect immediately.

CHAP. 350.

AN ACT to amend an act entitled "An act to authorize the formation of railroad corporations, and to regulate the same," passed April second, eighteen hundred and fifty.

PASSED April 24, 1872.

The People of the State of New York, represented in Senate and Assembly, do enact as follows:

SECTION 1. Paragraph six of section twenty-eight of the act entitled "An act to authorize the formation of railroad corporations, and to regulate the same," passed April second, eighteen hundred and fifty, is hereby amended by adding thereto the following: And all companies whose railroads are or shall hereafter be crossed, intersected or joined as aforesaid, shall receive from each other and forward to their destination all goods, merchandise and other property intended for points on their respective roads, with the same dispatch and at a rate of freight not exceeding the local tariff rate charged for sim-

Companies to receive and carry freight from connecting companies at same rate as from individuals. ilar goods, merchandise and other property ... forwarded from the same points for individuals and other corporations.

§ 2. This act shall take effect immediately.

CHAP. 355.

AN ACT to repeal chapter two hundred and eighty-seven of the laws of eighteen hundred and seventy-one, passed April fourth, eighteen hundred and seventy-one, entitled "An act to amend the law for the assessment and collection of taxes in cases where farms or lots are divided by county lines."

PASSED April 24, 1872; three-fifths being present.

The People of the State of New York, represented in Senate and Assembly, do enact as follows:

Chap. 28, laws of 1871, repealed. SECTION 1. Chapter two hundred and eighty-seven of the laws of eighteen hundred and seventy-one, entitled "An act to amend the law for the assessment and collection of taxes in cases where farms or lots are divided by county lines," is hereby repealed.

§ 2. This act shall take effect immediately.

Ante, p. 76.

CHAP. 357.

AN ACT to amend an act entitled "An act for the incorporation of villages," passed April twentieth, eighteen hundred and seventy.

PASSED April 24, 1872; three-fifths being present.

The People of the State of New York, represented in Senate and Assembly, do enact as follows:

SECTION 1. Section ten of title three of an act entitled "An act for the incorporation of villages," passed April twentieth, eighteen hundred and seventy, is hereby amended so as to read as follows:

No account to be audited unless made out in items and verified. § 10. No such account or claim shall be allowed by the trustees unless it shall be made out in items and accompanied by the affidavit of the person claiming to have rendered the services or furnished the materials or made the disbursements therein charged, that the items of such account or claim are correct as to the service, materials and disbursements men-

[illegible] such services and materials were rendered and furnished and disbursements made for the corporation, and no part of such claim has been paid. The claimant may be examined on oath by the trustees in relation to said claim and the items thereof. The affidavit and oath herein mentioned may be taken before the president of the village, or any of the trustees or the clerk of the village, and when certified by either of them may be read in evidence in any court of this state in the same manner as oaths and affidavits taken and certified by a justice of the peace; but no fee shall be charged or received by any president or trustee for any oath or affidavit taken before them or either of them. Nothing herein shall be construed as preventing the trustees from disallowing any account or claim in whole or in part when so made out and verified, nor from requiring other or further evidence of the correctness and reasonableness thereof. Any person willfully swearing false in reference to any matter herein contained shall be guilty of perjury.

Claimant may be examined on oath.

Ante, vol. 7, p. 681.

CHAP. 358.

AN ACT to confirm the title of citizens of this state to lands for which they have heretofore taken conveyances from aliens.

PASSED April 24, 1872, by a two-third vote.

The People of the State of New York, represented in Senate and Assembly, do enact as follows:

SECTION 1. The title of any citizen or citizens of this state to any land or lands within this state, which may have heretofore been purchased by any such citizen or citizens from any alien or aliens, and for which a conveyance has been heretofore taken by any such citizen or citizens from any alien or aliens, shall not in any manner be questioned or impeached by reason or on account of the alienage of the person or persons from whom such conveyance shall have been taken, or by reason of any devise of any such land or lands to any such person or persons, in any last will and testament being inoperative or void on account of the alienage of such person or persons; but all devises of land or lands heretofore made by any last will and testament to any alien or aliens from whom a conveyance of such land or lands so devised shall heretofore have been taken by any citizen or citizens of this state, are hereby declared to be valid and effectual, so far that the title of such citizen or citizens to such land or lands shall not be affected by any invalidity of any such devise; provided, however, that nothing in this act contained shall affect the rights of this state in any case in which proceedings for escheat have

Title of citizens not to be impeached by alienage of grantors.

Not to affect rights of state in cases pending.

been already instituted prior to the first day of January, one thousand eight hundred and seventy-two.

§ 2. This act shall take effect immediately.

Ante, vol. 8, p.

CHAP. 369.

AN ACT giving the consent of the state of New York to the purchase by and ceding jurisdiction to the United States over certain land on Cumberland Head, Clinton county, within this state, to be occupied as site of light-house keeper's dwelling.

PASSED April 25, 1872, by a two-third vote.

The People of the State of New York, represented in Senate and Assembly, do enact as follows:

Consent given to United States to purchase land on Cumberland Head.

SECTION 1. The consent of the state of New York is hereby given to the purchase by the United States, at any time, of a piece or parcel of land on Cumberland Head, in the county of Clinton, within this state, and adjoining the present light-house site of that name, not to exeed ten acres, to be used for the purposes of a light-house site and keeper's dwelling; and the owner or owners of said land are authorized to sell and convey the same to the United States for the purposes aforesaid.

Jurisdiction ceded to United States.

§ 2. The jurisdiction of the state of New York in and over the said land is hereby ceded to the United States, subject to the restrictions hereinafter mentioned.

State to retain concurrent jurisdiction for service of process.

§ 3. The said consent is given and the said jurisdiction ceded upon the express condition that the state of New York shall retain a concurrent jurisdiction with the United States in and to said land, so far as that all civil, criminal and other process which may issue under the laws or authority of the state of New York may be executed thereon in the same manner as if such consent had not been given, or jurisdiction ceded, except so far as such process may affect the real or personal property of the United States.

Jurisdiction, when to vest.

§ 4. The jurisdiction hereby ceded shall not vest in any respect to said land, until the United States shall have acquired the title by purchase or otherwise.

Survey and map to be made.

§ 5. A survey and map of the land hereinbefore mentioned, with a description with metes and bounds, shall be presented to the governor for approval, and when by him approved, and his approval indorsed thereon, they shall be forwarded to the secretary of state to be by him recorded.

How title to land may be acquired in case of non-agreement

§ 6. In case the United States shall desire to purchase the land mentioned in the first section of this act, and shall be unable to agree with the owner or owners of the same for the purchase, it shall have the right to acquire title in the manner prescibed in the act entitled "An act ceding jurisdiction to the

United States [illegible] land to be occupied as sites for light-houses and keepers' dwellings within this state," passed April twenty-four, eighteen hundred and sixty-seven. with owners.

§ 7. This act shall take effect immediately.

CHAP. 37[illegible].

AN ACT to amend the act entitled "An act to authorize the formation of gas-light companies," passed February sixteenth, eighteen hundred and forty-eight.

PASSED April 25, 1872.

The People of the State of New York, represented in Senate and Assembly, do enact as follows:

SECTION 1. Section second of the act entitled "An act to authorize the formation of gas-light companies," passed February sixteenth, one thousand eight hundred and forty-eight, is hereby amended so as to read as follows:

§ 2. When the certificate shall have been filed as aforesaid, the persons who shall have signed and acknowledged the same, and their successors, shall be a body politic and corporate, in fact and in name, by the name stated in such certificate, and by that name have succession, and shall be capable of suing and being sued in any court of law or equity in this state; and they and their successors may have a common seal, and make and alter the same at pleasure; and they shall, by their corporate name, be capable in law of purchasing, holding and conveying any real and personal estate whatever, which may be necessary to enable the said company to carry on the operations named in such certificate; and said company may, from time to time, borrow such sums of money as may be necessary for carrying on said operations, not exceeding one-half the capital stock of said company, and may issue and dispose of its bonds for any amount so borrowed, and mortgage the corporate property and franchises of said company to secure the payment of any debt contracted by it for the purposes aforesaid.

When to be a body corporate.

Corporate seal.

May borrow money and mortgage corporate property.

§ 2. Section three of said act is hereby so amended, that the stockholders of any such company may elect not to exceed thirteen, instead of nine directors, to manage the affairs of such company.

Number of directors.

§ 3. This act shall take effect immediately.

Ante, vol. 3, pp. 849, 855; vol. 7, p. 100.

CHAP. 377.

AN ACT to amend an act entitled "An act to amend article four of title four, chapter eleven of part first of the Revised Statutes, of division and other fences."

Ante, vol. 1, p. 826.

PASSED April 25, 1872.

The People of the State of New York, represented in Senate and Assembly, do enact as follows:

SECTION 1. Section thirty of article four of title four of chapter eleven of part first of Revised Statutes is hereby amended by adding at the end of the section as follows:

Fence viewers to direct location of division fence. And, wherever such adjoining lands one-half or more of which are improved, shall be bounded by or upon either bank of a stream of water not navigable, the fence viewers of the town, in which the same are situated, shall direct in the manner hereinafter mentioned, upon which bank of such stream, and where upon such bank, the division fence shall be located, and the portion thereof to be kept and maintained by each of such adjoining owners.

§ 2. This act shall take effect immediately.

CHAP. 392.

AN ACT in relation to the supreme court library at Bing hamton.

PASSED April 26, 1872.

The People of the State of New York, represented in Senate and Assembly, do enact as follows:

Librarian, how appointed. SECTION 1. The librarian of the supreme court library at Binghamton shall be appointed by a majority of the justices of the supreme court of the sixth judicial district, and shall hold his office during the pleasure of said justices.

Salary. § 2. The salary of said librarian shall be paid on the first day of January in each year; and the amount thereof shall be fixed in the month of December in each year, for that year, by a majority of said justices of the supreme court; but such salary shall not exceed three hundred dollars in any year; one-half of which shall be paid out of the fund belonging to said library, and the other half shall be paid by the county of Broome.

Librarian subject to directions of justices. § 3. Said librarian shall be subject to the directions of said justices, and shall be governed by such rules and regulations as they shall make from time to time.

Contingent expenses to be paid by Broome county.

§ 4. The contingent expenses of said library, except for the purchase of books, shall be paid as heretofore by the county of Broome; which contingent expenses must be first certified to be correct by one of said justices or by the county judge of said county.

Clerk not to have any charge of library.

§ 5. The clerk of said county shall not hereafter have any charge, care or control of said library. But the librarian, to be appointed by virtue of this act, shall perform all acts and duties, in respect to said library, heretofore required of said clerk.

§ 6. All laws inconsistent with this act are hereby repealed, and this act shall take effect immediately.

CHAP. 409.

AN ACT to amend an act entitled "An act to establish regulations for the port of New York," passed April sixteenth, eighteen hundred and fifty-seven.

PASSED April 27, 1872; three-fifths being present.

The People of the State of New York, represented in Senate and Assembly, do enact as follows:

SECTION 1. Section one of an act entitled "An act to establish regulations for the port of New York," passed April sixteen, eighteen hundred and fifty-seven, is hereby amended so as to read as follows:

Steamboats not to discharge ashes, etc., in certain waters.

Penalty.

§ 1. It shall not be lawful to throw or cause to be thrown into the waters of the port of New York, below Spuyten Duyvil creek, on Hudson river, or below Throg's Point, on the East river, nor in the bay inside of Sandy Hook, any cinders or ashes from any steamboat under the penalty of fifty dollars for each and every offense, recoverable by the commissioners hereinafter named; and for such penalty, the steamboat from which such cinders or ashes were thrown, its master and owner, shall be liable; and any steamboat using or having any pipe or opening so constructed as to admit of putting ashes or cinders through the same into the water shall be liable to a fine of fifty dollars for each and every time such pipe or opening shall be used for such purpose within the limits aforesaid, after service on the master or owner of said steamboat of a notice by said commissioners not to use the same, to be recoverable by the said commissioners in an action against the owners of such steamboat, and such steamboat shall also be liable therefor. It shall be lawful for either of said commissioners of pilots, or the agent of said board of commissioners of pilots, at any time, in the day time, to go on board of and examine any steamboat in the harbor of New York,

Commissioners of pilots may examine boats, etc.

for the purpose of ascertaining whether any such pipe or opening exists on such steamboat.

§ 2. This act shall take effect immediately.

CHAP. 410.

AN ACT making appropriations for the payment of the principal and interest on the canal debt, commencing on the first day of October, one thousand eight hundred and seventy-two, and to provide for the payment of the debt contracted under section twelve of article seven of the constitution.

PASSED April 27, 1872; three-fifths being present.

The People of the State of New York, represented in Senate and Assembly, do enact as follows:

Appropriations. SECTION 1. The following sums are hereby appropriated out of the revenues of the state canals for the fiscal year commencing on the first day of October, eighteen hundred and seventy-two:

Sinking fund. For payment toward the sinking fund for the extinguishment of the general fund debt, the sum of fifteen hundred thousand dollars.

Canal enlargement loan. For the payment of the interest in coin, and reimbursement of the principal of the loans made under the constitution for the enlargement and completion of the canals, the sum of two millions three hundred and forty thousand dollars, or so much thereof as may be necessary.

State government. To pay the general fund, to defray the necessary expenses of the state government, the sum of two hundred thousand dollars.

Interest on canal debt. § 2. The sum of sixty-five thousand dollars, or so much thereof as may be necessary, is hereby appropriated from the sinking fund under section one of article seven of the constitution, for payment of interest in coin, on the canal debt for which said sinking fund has been provided.

Interest and principal of floating debt loan. § 3. The following sums are hereby appropriated out of the proceeds of any tax to be levied and collected under the provisions of the act (chapter two hundred and seventy-one of the laws of eighteen hundred and fifty-nine), to pay the interest and reimburse the principal of the loan of two million five hundred thousand dollars, to provide for the payment of the floating debt of the state.

Interest in coin. To pay the interest, in coin, on said loan for the fiscal year, commencing on the first day of October next, sixty thousand dollars, or so much thereof as may be necessary.

Sinking fund to pay principal. To provide for the sinking fund to pay the principal of said loan, one hundred and thirty-eight thousand eight hundred and eighty-eight dollars, being for one year's contribution to said fund, as provided by the act aforesaid.

CHAP. 411.

AN ACT to prevent and punish certain fraudulent practices in relation to altering counterfeit money or coin.

PASSED April 27, 1872; three-fifths being present.

The People of the State of New York, represented in Senate and Assembly, do enact as follows:

SECTION 1. Any person who shall [illegible] for distribution or circulation, or cause to be printed for distribution or circulation, any circular, letter, card, pamphlet, handbill or other publication, offering or purporting to offer for sale, exchange, or as a gift, any counterfeit paper money or coin, or any so-called fac-similes of United States notes or coin, or of national or other bank notes; and any persons who shall distribute, with intent to commit any fraud, any such circular, letter, card, pamphlet, handbill or other publication, shall be deemed guilty of a misdemeanor, and, upon conviction thereof, shall be imprisoned in the county jail not less than six months, and not more than one year, or shall be fined not less than five hundred, and not more than one thousand dollars, or both in the discretion of the court.

Circulars, etc., offering, etc., counterfeit money not to be printed or distributed.

Penalty.

§ 2. This act shall take effect immediately.

CHAP. 412.

AN ACT to amend an act entitled "An act to provide for the improvement of Grass river, and of the water power thereon, and to check freshets therein."

PASSED April 27, 1871; three-fifths being present.

The People of the State of New York, represented in Senate and Assembly, do enact as follows:

SECTION 1. Section two of chapter eighty-three of the laws of eighteen hundred and sixty-nine, is hereby amended so as to read as follows:

§ 2. The said board shall consist of five commissioners, a majority of whom shall constitute a quorum for the transaction of business. Benjamin Squire, David M. Jones, Burziller Hodskin, William M. Stevenson and James Miller of St. Lawrence county, shall be such commissioners, and in case of death, refusal to serve, removal from the county or other disqualifications, the county court of St. Lawrence county shall, by appointment in writing, to be filed in the clerk's office of said county, fill such vacancy; the person so appointed to fill a vacancy to be a resident of the same town as his predecessor in office, and said commissioners, or any of them, may be removed from office by the county court of said county, or by the supreme court for malfeasance or inefficiency in office.

Commissioners.

Vacancies, how filled.

§ 2. Section five of said chapter is hereby amended by striking out the words "t[illegible]" wherever they occur in said section, and inserting [illegible] the words "one-half."

§ 3. All water [illegible] situate on Grass river, in the town of Russell, is [illegible]t from the provisions of this act, and also from the [illegible]s of the original act to which this act is an amendment, but this shall not affect the regularity or validity of any assessment heretofore made for the purpose of said reservoir upon any water power property not situate in said town of Russell, but the amount already assessed upon water power property in said town of Russell shall be added to and included by the assessors under said act in the assessment next hereafter to be made upon the other water power property on said river not within the limits of said town of Russell.

§ 4. This act shall take effect immediately.

CHAP. 424.

AN ACT to provide for the dissolution of religious societies, except in the city and county of New York, and for the sale and disposition of the proceeds of the property of such societies.

PASSED April 27, 1872; three-fifths being present.

The People of the State of New York, represented in Senate and Assembly, do enact as follows:

When and how religious society may be dissolved and property sold.

SECTION 1. Whenever any religious society incorporated by law shall cease to act in its corporate capacity and keep up the religious services, it shall be lawful for the supreme court of this state, upon the application of a majority of the trustees thereof incorporated by law, except in the city and county of New York, in case said court shall deem it proper so to do, to order and decree a dissolution of such religious society, and for that purpose to order and direct a sale and conveyance of any and all property belonging to such society, and after providing for the ascertaining and payment of the debts of such society, and the necessary costs and expenses of such sale and proceedings for dissolution, so far as the proceeds of such sale shall be sufficient to pay the same; such court may order and direct any surplus of such proceeds remaining after paying such debts, costs and expenses, to be devoted and applied to any such religious, benevolent, or charitable objects or purposes as the said trustees may indicate by their petition and the said court may approve.

Proceeds, how disposed of.

Petition, what to contain.

§ 2. Such application to the said court shall be made by petition, duly verified by said trustees, which petition shall state the particular reason or causes why such sale and dissolution are sought; the situation, condition, and estimated value of the property of said society or corporation, and the particular object or purpose to which it is proposed to devote any surplus of the proceeds of such property; and such petition shall, in all cases, be accompanied with proof that notice of the time and place of such intended application to said court, has been duly published once in each week for at least four weeks successively, next preceding such application, in a newspaper published in the county where such society is located.

§ 3. In case there shall be no trustees of such religious society residing in the county in which such society is located, such application may be made, and such proceedings taken, by a majority of the members of such religious society residing in such county. When members may make the application.

§ 4. This act shall take effect immediately.

Ante, vol. 3, p. 694.

CHAP. 426.

AN ACT to amend chapter six hundred and fifty-seven of the laws of eighteen hundred and seventy-one, entitled "An act to amend the act passed February seventeen, eighteen hundred and forty-eight, entitled 'An act to authorize the formation of corporations for manufacturing, mining, mechanical or chemical purposes,'" passed April twentieth, eighteen hundred and seventy-one.

Ante, p. 115.

PASSED April 27, 1872; three-fifths being present.

The People of the State of New York, represented in Senate and Assembly, do enact as follows:

SECTION 1. Section two of chapter six hundred and fifty-seven of the laws of eighteen hundred and seventy-one, entitled "An act to amend the act passed February seventeenth, eighteen hundred and forty-eight, entitled 'An act to authorize the formation of corporations for manufacturing, mining, mechanical or chemical purposes,'" is hereby amended so as to read as follows:

§ 2. Said section one of the said act, passed February seventeenth, eighteen hundred and forty-eight, as amended by section one of chapter two hundred and sixty-two of the laws of eighteen hundred and fifty-seven, is hereby amended by inserting after the words "or the business of printing and publishing books, pamphlets and newspapers," in the first section of the last-mentioned act, the words "or the business of preserving and dealing in meats, or the business of making butter, cheese, concentrated or condensed milk, or any other products of the dairy; or the business of erecting buildings for church sheds or laundry purposes, and the carrying on of laundry business." Companies may organize to deal in meats, butter, to build church sheds, etc.

§ 2. This act shall take effect immediately.

CHAP. 432.

AN ACT to amend chapter ninety, laws of eighteen hundred and sixty-nine, being an act entitled "An act to provide for the improvement of the navigation of the Racket river, and of the hydraulic power thereon, and to check freshets therein," passed April second, eighteen hundred and sixty-nine.

PASSED April 29, 1872; three-fifths being present.

The People of the State of New York, represented in Senate and Assembly, do enact as follows:

Commissioners to have one year in which to make and file surveys and maps.

SECTION 1. The commissioners appointed under and in pursuance of chapter ninety, laws of eighteen hundred and sixty-nine, being an act entitled "An act to provide for the improvement of the navigation of the Racket river, and of the hydraulic power thereon, and to check freshets therein," shall have one year from and after the passage of this act in which to make and file the surveys and maps contemplated and required by the sixth section of said act; and in case any part or portion of the river, or of the lakes, ponds or lands mentioned in said sixth section shall be situate outside of the boundaries of St. Lawrence county, then the maps and surveys of such part and portion shall be filed also in the office of the clerk of the county where the same shall be located.

Schedules and descriptions to what lots to apply.

§ 2. The schedules and descriptions authorized and provided for in and by the seventh section of said act, shall apply to the lots and parcels of land on which there is a hydraulic power dependent upon the waters of Racket river, situate in the towns of Potsdam and Pierrepont in said county of St. Lawrence, and to no other; and nothing in said act contained shall authorize the assessment of any water powers heretofore used or occupied, or the owners of such water powers, on account of the dam or works heretofore constructed or rebuilt, or the works authorized by said act, except such as are situate in the towns aforesaid; and the schedules heretofore made by the appraisers under said act shall be in nowise invalidated or affected by reason of the omission therefrom of lots and parcels of land or water powers not within the towns aforesaid, or either of them.

Certain owners of water power not to be assessed.

What expenses, etc., to be included in appraisement.

§ 3. Any assessment which may be made by the appraisers under or in pursuance of said act may, in the discretion of the appraisers making the same, include expenses for building or rebuilding of the dams and works heretofore constructed and rebuilt, together with the cost or price of land, timber or other property taken or to be taken under this act; and any other costs and expenses of protecting, managing, maintaining or improving the dams, reservoirs and works authorized or contemplated by said act, and any and all proper costs and expenses of carrying out and enforcing the provisions of said act; and any one assessment may, in the discretion of the [illegible] the same include any part or portion of such [illegible], damages, costs and expenses.

§ 4. In case the commissioners appointed or authorized by said act shall acquire title thereunder to any lands not situate in said county of St. Lawrence, that survey or description of the same, with a written statement or notice that such commissioners have acquired title thereto shall, within one month after such commissioners shall have perfected title to the same, be filed in the office of the clerk of the county where such land shall be located. Written statement, etc., to be filed in county clerk's office.

§ 5. This act shall take effect immediately.

CHAP. 433.

AN ACT to amend chapter seven hundred and twenty-one of the laws of eighteen hundred and seventy-one, entitled "An act to amend and consolidate the several acts relating to the preservation of moose, wild deer, birds and fish," passed April twenty-six, eighteen hundred and seventy-one, also to repeal section thirty of said act.

PASSED April 29, 1872; three-fifths being present.

The People of the State of New York, represented in Senate and Assembly, do enact as follows:

SECTION 1. Section one of the act entitled "An act to amend and consolidate the several acts relating to the preservation of moose, or wild deer, birds and fish," passed April twenty-six, eighteen hundred and seventy one, is hereby amended so as to read as follows:

§ 2. No person or persons shall pursue or cause to be killed, any moose, elk, cariboo or wild deer, in any part or place within this state, except in the months of September and October, and in the first ten days of the month of November in any year; but it shall not be lawful at any season of the year to pursue deer with dogs in the county of Steuben. Any person violating the provisions of this section, by pursuing with dogs, or ensnaring or entrapping, any moose, elk, cariboo or wild deer, or by killing any of said animals contrary to the provisions herein, shall be deemed guilty of a misdemeanor, and upon conviction thereof shall be subject to a fine of fifty dollars, or be imprisoned in the county jail not exceeding three months, or both, at the discretion of the court, for each and every offense. The possession by any person of a carcass or green hide of any such animal, except during the time herein provided for killing the same, shall be deemed prima facie evidence that the person in whose possession such carcass or green hide is found, killed the animal to which said carcass or green hide belonged; and it shall be unlawful to sell, transport or Killing of deer prohibited except in certain months. Penalty. Possession of carcass or green hide evidence of killing.

Express companies, etc., not to carry carcass or green hide.

carry the carcass and hide, or carcass alone, after being killed, of any moose, elk, cariboo or wild deer, except during the months of time herein specified in which such animals may be killed, and the owner or owners, or corporations owning or running any line of stages, steamboats or railroads, and the owner or owners of any private conveyance upon which any carcass or green hide of such animals shall be found or conveyed, shall be subject to a penalty of fifty dollars for each and every offense.

Penalty.

§ 2. Section twenty-one of said act is hereby amended so as to read as follows:

When salmon or lake trout may be caught.

§ 21. No person shall kill or expose for sale, or have in his or her possession after the same has been killed, any salmon-trout or lake-trout, in the months of October, November, December, January and February, under a penalty of ten dollars for each fish, except that in Otsego lake; fish may be caught or killed by hook and line only, but they may be had alive for artificial propagation or the stocking of other waters.

Not to apply to certain waters.

§ 3. Nothing in this act contained shall in any manner affect or apply to the waters of the River St. Lawrence, the lakes in Jefferson county, or the waters of Lake Ontario, except Irondequoit bay.

Section fifth of act amended limited.

§ 4. Section fifth of said act is hereby repealed, except as it applies to that portion of the Great South bay, in the county of Suffolk, lying between Smith's Point and Quoque, and to the bays lying upon the southern portion of the county of Queens and Kings.

§ 5. Section six of said act is hereby amended so as to read as follows:

When woodcock may be killed.

§ 6. No person shall kill or expose for sale, or have in his or her possession after the same has been killed, any woodcock between February first and July third, under a penalty of fifty dollars for each bird.

§ 6. The twenty-seventh section of said act is hereby stricken out and the following substituted therefor:

Certain nets not to be used.

§ 27. No person shall use any purse or pound net for the catching of fish in Port Washington or Manhassett bays in the county of Queens, under a penalty of fifty dollars.

§ 7. Section twenty-eight of said act is hereby amended so as to read as follows:

Fish not to be taken with nets, spears, etc.

§ 28. No person shall at any time take any fish with a net, spear or trap of any kind, or set any trap, net, weir or pot with intent to catch fish in any of the fresh waters or canals in this state, except as hereinbefore or hereinafter provided; nor shall it be lawful at any time to draw any seine or net for the taking of fish in any portion of Flushing bay or its branches, nor in lakes Canandaigua, Cayuga, Oneida, Champlain, Great Sodus bay, in the county of Wayne, or the inlets thereof; and any person violating the provisions of this section shall be deemed guilty of a misdemeanor, and shall likewise be liable to a penalty of twenty-five dollars for each offense; but suckers, catfish, bullheads, bony fish, or moss-bunkers, eels, white fish, shad, herring and minnows, are exempted from the oper-

Penalty.

Certain fish exempted.

ation of this section, also pike, in all waters save those lying in Columbia county and Oneida and Cayuga lakes and their inlets, provided, however, that nothing in this section shall be so construed as to legalize the use of gill-nets in any of the inland waters or canals in this state; nor seines or nets of any kind in the waters of Otsego lake, except from the first day of March to the last day of August, and no gill-nets, except during the months of July and August. But no such seine or net shall have meshes less than two inches in size, and in the Hudson river, the meshes of all gill-nets shall not be less than four and one-half inches in size each, and those of fykes set in any of the waters surrounding Long Island, Fire Island, Staten Island and the bays and salt water estuaries and rivers approaching thereto, to be not less than four and one-half inches in size; and any person who shall willfully injure or destroy, by grappling or otherwise, any nets used in the Hudson or East rivers for the purpose of catching shad, shall be liable to a penalty of twenty-five dollars for each offense, and, in default of payment thereof, shall be imprisoned in the county jail of the county within whose jurisdiction the offense may be committed, for not more than thirty days. All drawing of seines in the Susquehanna river is prohibited.

Gill-net not to be used. When nets may be used in Otsego lake. Size of meshes. Injuries to shad nets by grappling, etc. Drawing seines prohibited.

§ 8. The thirtieth section of said act is hereby repealed.

§ 9. No person shall catch with a hook and line, or otherwise, any pickerel, perch or bass from the Goodhue or Cranberry lakes, situate in the towns of Addison and Thurston, county of Steuben, from the first day of December to the twentieth day of May in each year, under a penalty of ten dollars for each fish so taken or had in possession, the penalty to be recovered as already provided for in chapter seven hundred and twenty-one of laws of eighteen hundred and seventy-one.

Fishing with hook and line.

§ 10. This act shall take effect immediately.

CHAP. 436.

AN ACT relative to the setting of fykes and other nets in Harlem and East rivers.

PASSED April 29, 1872.

The People of the State of New York, represented in Senate and Assembly, do enact as follows:

SECTION 1. It shall not be lawful for any person to set, or use for the purpose of taking or capturing fish, a fyke or set net, or other net, in the waters of the Harlem river, or of the East river, or of confluent brooks within three miles in any direction from middle gate, so called, in said East river, or take up or draw the same within the said three miles.

Fykes not to be used in Harlem or East rivers, etc.

Penalty. § 2. Any person violating the provisions of the foregoing section shall be deemed guilty of a misdemeanor, and shall, on conviction, be subject to a fine of not less than twenty-five dollars or more than one hundred dollars, or imprisonment for not less than ten days or more than thirty days, to be sued for and recovered with costs in any court held by a civil justice, or in any other court of law in the county in which such offense may be committed, in the name of any party suing for the same, one-half of which shall belong to such party, the other half to the town officers of any town, for the benefit of said town, that such suit may be commenced in.

§ 3. This act shall take effect immediately.

CHAP. 458.

AN ACT to provide for the formation of free public libraries.

PASSED May 1, 1872; three-fifths being present.

The People of the State of New York, represented in Senate and Assembly, do enact as follows:

Towns and villages may establish and maintain free public libraries. SECTION 1. Each town and city and village in this state may, by resolution duly adopted by their common council, board of trustees and town auditors, respectively, establish and maintain a free public library therein, with or without branches, for the use of the inhabitants thereof, and provide suitable rooms therefor, under such regulations for its government as may from time to time be prescribed by the board of town auditors of the town, or the city council, or the board of trustees of the village. Proviso as to villages. Provided, nevertheless, when any village shall establish a library under this act it shall be exempt from any charge for the establishment or maintenance of any library in the town in which it is situated.

Amount that may be appropriated. § 2. Any town, or city, or village, may appropriate money for suitable buildings or rooms, and for the foundation of such library a sum not exceeding one dollar for each of its legal voters who voted at the next preceding annual election therein, in the year next preceding that in which such appropriation is made; and may also appropriate annually for the maintenance and increase thereof, or of any public library duly organized under the laws of this state in said town, city or village, a sum not exceeding fifty cents for each of its legal voters as aforesaid, in the year next preceding that in which such appropriation is made, and may receive, hold and manage any devise, bequest or donation for the establishment, increase or maintenance of a free public library within the same. Amount, how audited, levied and collected. The moneys herein authorized to be appropriated shall be audited, assessed, levied and collected as other town, village or city charges are now audited, assessed, levied and collocated; provided, that no such money shall be appropriated unless a majority of all the taxable inhabitants of said town, city or village where said library is to be located, petitioned to the board, mentioned in the first section, in writing, for the establishment of such library. In obtaining signatures or consents to such petition for said library, reference shall be had only to the last preceding assessment roll of such town, city or village, and when the genuineness of such signatures to such petitions or consent, and the fact that said signatures constitute a majority of the tax payers as aforesaid shall be proven to the satisfaction of the judge of the county in which said library is to be located, the sufficiency of which proof shall be certified by such county judge, said petition or consent, together with said certificate of said county judge, shall be filed by the clerk of such town, city or village, in the county clerk's office of the county in which such library is to be established. Petition to contain names of a majority of tax payers. To be proved and filed.

§ 3. This act shall take effect immediately.

CHAP. 475.

AN ACT in relation to challenges of jurors in criminal cases.

PASSED May 8, 1872; three-fifths being present.

The People of the State of New York, represented in Senate and Assembly, do enact as follows:

SECTION 1. The previous formation or expression of an opinion or impression in reference to the circumstances upon which any criminal action at law is based, or in reference to the guilt or innocence of the prisoner, or a present opinion or impression in reference thereto, shall not be a sufficient ground of challenge for principal cause to any person who is otherwise legally qualified to serve as a juror upon the trial of such action; provided, the person proposed as a juror who may have formed or expressed or has such opinion or impression as aforesaid, shall declare on oath that he verily believes that he can render an impartial verdict according to the evidence submitted to the jury on such trial, and that such previously formed opinion or impression will not bias or influence his verdict, and provided the court shall be satisfied that the person so proposed as a juror does not entertain such a present opinion as would influence his verdict as a juror. Expression of opinion or present opinion not ground of challenge for principal cause. Proviso.

§ 2. The people and the accused, in all capital cases, shall also be entitled to thirty peremptory challenges. Peremptory challenges.

§ 3. All existing acts conflicting with the provisions of the foregoing sections are hereby repealed.

§ 4. This act shall take effect immediately.

CHAP. 483.

AN ACT to amend an act entitled "An act to prevent the unlawful taking of oysters planted within the waters of the state of New York," passed April twenty-one, eighteen hundred and sixty-six.

PASSED May 3, 1872; three-fifths being present.

The People of the State of New York, represented in Senate and Assembly, do enact as follows:

SECTION 1. Section one of the act entitled "An act to prevent the unlawful taking of oysters planted within the waters of the state of New York," passed April twenty-one, eighteen hundred and sixty-six, is hereby amended so as to read as follows:

Penalty for unlawfully disturbing or taking oysters.

§ 1. Any person who shall unlawfully take up, or take and carry away by any means, or who shall by means of dredges, drags, rakes, tongs or other implements, or in any manner, catch, interfere with, or disturb the oysters of another now or hereafter lawfully planted upon the bed of any of the rivers, bays, sounds or other waters within the jurisdiction of this state, shall be deemed guilty of a misdemeanor, and upon conviction shall be punished by a fine not exceeding two hundred and fifty dollars, or by imprisonment in the common jail of the county, where the offense was committed, for a period not exceeding six months, or by both such fine and imprisonment.

§ 2. Section two of said act is hereby amended so as to read as follows:

Special sessions to try and punish offenders.

§ 2. The court of special sessions of this state, in and for the county where any offense shall be committed under the provisions of this act, shall have jurisdiction to hear, try and determine the same, and, upon conviction, to punish the offender as provided in the first section of this act.

§ 3. This act shall take effect immediately.

Ante, vol. 6, p. 835.

CHAP. 485.

AN ACT to amend chapter twelve of the laws of eighteen hundred and seventy-two, entitled "An act prescribing the officers and employees that may be elected, appointed or employed by the senate and assembly, fixing the salary and compensation thereof, and regulating the proceedings of investigating committees, and providing for the payments of the expense thereof."

PASSED May 3, 1872; three-fifths being present.

The People of the State of New York, represented in Senate and Assembly, do enact as follows:

SECTION 1. Sections one, two and three of an act entitled "An act prescribing the officers and employees that may be elected, appointed or employed by the senate and assembly, fixing the salary and compensation thereof and regulating the proceedings of investigating committees, and providing for the payment of the expenses thereof," passed February first, eighteen hundred and seventy-two, are hereby amended so as to read as follows:

Officers to be elected or appointed by the senate.

§ 1. The senate may elect or appoint a clerk, a stenographer, a sergeant-at-arms and an assistant, who shall act as postmaster, an assistant-postmaster, a door-keeper and six assistants, one person who shall act as janitor and keeper of the senate chamber and its ante-rooms, and one assistant; not more than sixteen persons to serve as clerks of committees, and not more than eight pages, and not more than ten messengers to committees. The president of the senate may appoint a clerk and messenger, and the clerk of the senate may appoint an assistant clerk, a journal clerk, four deputy clerks, one of whom shall act as clerk of the committee on engrossed bills; a librarian, an assistant librarian, a superintendent of documents and three messengers.

By the president. By the clerk.

Officers to be elected or appointed by the assembly.

§ 2. The assembly may elect or appoint a clerk, a stenographer, a sergeant-at-arms and an assistant, a postmaster and an assistant, a superintendent of documents, a door-keeper and ten assistants, one person who shall perform the duties of janitor and keeper of the assembly chamber and its ante-rooms, and an assistant; a mail carrier, who shall carry the mails for both the senate and assembly; not more than sixteen persons to serve as clerks of committees, not more than six general messengers, not more than seventeen messengers to committees, one of whom shall serve as messenger to the committee on engrossed bills, and not more than twenty pages to be in employ and drawing pay at one time. The speaker may appoint a clerk and messenger, and the clerk of the assembly may appoint an assistant clerk, a journal clerk, and not more than nine deputies, one of whom shall be clerk to the commit-

By the speaker. By the clerk.

tee on engrossed bills, a librarian and an assistant, and no more than five messengers.

Salaries. § 3. The following salaries shall be paid for the annual session of the legislature: To the clerks of each house, three thousand dollars; to the assistant clerks and journal clerks, each fifteen hundred dollars; to the deputy clerks, each twelve hundred dollars, except to the clerks assigned to the committees on engrossed bills to them; to the clerk of the president of the senate and to the speaker's clerk, six hundred dollars; to the sergeant-at-arms, the assistant sergeant-at-arms, the librarian, the assistant librarians, the postmaster of the assembly, the assistant postmasters of the senate and assembly, and the door-keepers, to each of them, six dollars per day; to the assistant door-keepers, the keepers and janitors, the assistant keepers and janitors and superintendents of documents of the senate and assembly, each five dollars per day; and each of the officers in this section above named shall receive the same mileage as is now allowed by law to the members of the legislature. To the stenographers, fifteen hundred dollars each; to the clerks of the committees, each five dollars per day; to the mail carriers, three dollars per day; to the pages, each, two dollars per day. No extra allowance. And no extra allowance shall be made to the officers and employees above named on any pretense whatever. Salary, etc. how paid. The mileage, salary and per diem allowance in this section provided for shall be paid on the warrant of the comptroller, upon the certificate of the president of the senate for the officers and employees of the senate, and on the certificate of the speaker for the officers and employees of the assembly. All appointments made under this act shall be entered on the journal of the house wherein they are so made; such entry shall specify the date of the appointment and the length of time the same is to be continued.

§ 4. This act shall take effect immediately.

CHAP. 498.

AN ACT for the protection of livery-stable keepers and other persons keeping horses at livery or pasture.

PASSED May 3, 1872.

The People of the State of New York, represented in Senate and Assembly, do enact as follows:

Livery-stable keepers, etc., to have lien for keep of horses. SECTION 1. It shall be lawful for all livery-stable keepers and other persons keeping any horse or horses at livery or pasture, or boarding the same for hire under any agreement with the owner thereof, to detain such horse or horses until all charges under such agreement for the care, keep, pasture or Proviso. board of such horses shall have been paid; provided, how-

[illegible]er, that notice in writing shall first be given to such owner in person or at his last-known place of residence, of the amount of such charges, and the intention to detain such horse or horses until such charges be paid.

§ 2. From the time of giving such notice and while such horse or horses are so detained and no longer, such livery-stable keeper or other person shall have a lien upon such horse or horses for the purpose of satisfying any execution which may be issued upon a judgment obtained for such charges. When lien to be effective.

§ 3. This act shall take effect immediately.

CHAP. 502.

AN ACT declaring Cold brook, in the county of Clinton, and Alder brook, in the counties of Clinton and Franklin, tributaries of the Saranac river, and emptying into the north branch of that river, public highways.

PASSED May 8, 1872.

The People of the State of New York, represented in Senate and Assembly, do enact as follows:

SECTION 1. That Cold brook, in the county of Clinton, and Alder brook, in the counties of Clinton and Franklin, tributaries of the Saranac river, and emptying into the north branch of said Saranac river, are, and each of said brooks is hereby declared a public highway at the point of confluence of each with said Saranac river. Cold brook and Alder brook made public highways.

§ 2. All the provisions of the act entitled "An act declaring the river Saranac a public highway," passed May thirteenth, eighteen hundred and forty-six, as amended by the act entitled "An act to amend an act declaring the river Saranac a public highway," passed April thirteenth, eighteen hundred and fifty-three, are hereby made applicable to the said Cold brook and Alder brook, and each of them.

§ 3. This act shall take effect immediately.

CHAP. 509.

AN ACT to re-appropriate moneys for construction of new work upon, and extraordinary repairs of, the canals of this state, and for payment of awards made by the canal appraisers.

PASSED May 4, 1872; three-fifths being present.

The People of the State of New York, represented in Senate and Assembly, do enact as follows:

Re-appropriation. SECTION 1. The unexpended balance of two millions one hundred and eighty thousand six hundred and forty-six dollars appropriated by the act entitled "An act to authorize a tax of one mill per dollar of valuation of the year eighteen hundred and seventy, for construction of new work upon, and extraordinary repairs of, the canals of this state," passed May ninth, eighteen hundred and seventy, being the sum of eight hundred and fifty thousand nine hundred and forty-three dollars and ninety-one cents, or so much thereof as shall remain unexpended on the ninth day of May, eighteen hundred and seventy-two, is hereby re-appropriated to the same objects, except as otherwise provided by section one of act chapter seven hundred and seventy-eight of the laws of eighteen hundred and seventy-one; and the unexpended balance of one million eleven thousand one hundred and thirty-eight dollars and forty-two cents, appropriated by the act entitled "An act to authorize a tax of seven-eighths of a mill per dollar of valuation for the payment of the awards of the canal appraisers, and for supplying deficiencies in appropriations of eighteen hundred and sixty-eight and eighteen hundred and sixty-nine," passed May ninth, eighteen hundred and seventy, being the sum of four hundred and sixty-five thousand one hundred and seventy-three dollars and forty-six cents, except the sum of forty-four thousand re-appropriated from said funds by senate bill number four hundred and seven, and entitled "An act to re-appropriate certain money for the enlargement of the Champlain canal, and to also re-appropriate the sum of forty-four thousand dollars, a portion of the unexpended balance appropriated by chapter seven hundred and sixty-eight of the laws of eighteen hundred and seventy, to pay awards by canal appraisers and the canal board for the years eighteen hundred and sixty-eight and eighteen hundred and sixty-nine, or so much thereof as shall remain unexpended on the ninth day of May, eighteen hundred and seventy-two, is hereby re-appropriated to the same object.

Act of 1870. Amount. To what objects. Amount. Act of 1870.

§ 2. This act shall take effect immediately.

CHAP. 513.

AN ACT to provide for the erection of houses of detention or lock-ups in the several towns in this state.

PASSED May 4, 1872; three-fifths being present.

The People of the State of New York, represented in Senate and Assembly, do enact as follows:

SECTION 1. The electors of each town in this state shall have power, at their annual town meeting, to direct the erection of one or more houses of detention or lock-ups for the detention of persons committed by the magistrates thereof, and to direct such sums to be raised in such town by tax for the expense of building or of maintaining the same, as they may deem necessary. Electors may direct erection of lock-ups.

§ 2. Said houses of detention or lock-ups may be used for the purpose of keeping and confining all persons temporarily arrested by any constable or officer in said towns, or committed by any magistrate of said towns, and may be used for keeping and confining any and all persons arrested or committed for any crime in said towns the same as in any county jail, except that no person shall be confined therein after final commitment to serve out any sentence of the court after he shall be found guilty of any offense. Lock-ups, for what purpose to be used.

§ 3. This act shall take effect immediately.

CHAP. 517.

AN ACT in relation to the unadjusted claims of the soldiers in the war of eighteen hundred and twelve.

PASSED May 4, 1872; three-fifths being present.

The People of the State of New York, represented in Senate and Assembly, do enact as follows:

SECTION 1. The adjutant-general is hereby authorized and required to hear and determine the claim of any soldier of the war of eighteen hundred and twelve, and upon proof that would have entitled him to a certificate under the act, chapter five hundred and ninety-seven of the laws of eighteen hundred and fifty-seven, shall issue to said soldier a certificate such as provided for in said act for the amount due, which certificate shall have the same force and effect as if issued under said law, but no obligation to pay the same is hereby created against the people of this state. Adjutant-general to hear and adjust claims.

CHAP. 518.

AN ACT in relation to the mounted batteries of artillery of the national guard.

PASSED May 4, 1872; three-fifths being present.

The People of the State of New York, represented in Senate and Assembly, do enact as follows:

Amount to be paid mounted batteries annually.

SECTION 1. In lieu of the annual allowance to mounted batteries of artillery of the national guard prescribed in section one hundred and seventy-eight of chapter eighty of the laws of eighteen hundred and seventy, known as the military code, there shall, for the current year, and each year hereafter, be paid to each mounted battery the sum of one thousand dollars, for the purpose of aiding such batteries in defraying the expenses of the drills and parades required by law; which sums, and also those paid in like manner by the state, in lieu of furnishing uniforms, as provided in section one hundred and thirteen of chapter eighty of laws of eighteen hundred and seventy, together with the fines collected from delinquent officers, non-commissioned officers, musicians and privates, shall constitute the military funds of such mounted batteries.

How paid.

§ 2. The comptroller shall annually draw his warrant upon the treasurer in favor of the county treasurer of each county in which said mounted battery or batteries of artillery are organized, for each mounted battery the said sum of one thousand dollars, in the same manner and form as prescribed by section one hundred and seventy-eight of chapter eighty, laws of eighteen hundred and seventy; provided, always, that each mounted battery, claiming the said appropriation, shall furnish satisfactory evidence to the adjutant-general that such mounted battery has made the number of drills and parades required by law, fully mounted and equipped, and the certificate of the adjutant-general to that effect shall be necessary to be given to the comptroller before he shall draw his warrant, as above prescribed.

§ 3. This act shall take effect immediately.

CHAP. 519.

AN ACT to repeal chapter two hundred and forty-five of the laws of eighteen hundred and seventy-one, entitled "An act relating to military exemptions."

Ante, p. 70.

PASSED May 4, 18[illegible] three-fifths being present.

The People of the State of New York, represented in Senate and Assembly, do enact as follows:

SECTION 1. Chapter two hundred and forty-five of the laws of eighteen hundred and seventy-one, entitled "An act relating to military exemptions," is hereby repealed. Chapter 245, laws of 1871, repealed.

§ 2. This act shall take effect immediately.

CHAP. 524.

AN ACT to protect purchasers on sales of real estate of infants, by special guardian, prior to January first, eighteen hundred and fifty-two.

PASSED May 6, 1872.

The People of the State of New York, represented in Senate and Assembly, do enact as follows:

SECTION 1. All sales of real estate belonging to infant owners, made by special guardians under the orders of the supreme court, county court or late court of chancery, prior to January first, eighteen hundred and fifty-two, and the conveyances therefor executed by said special guardian, are hereby ratified and confirmed, notwithstanding the omission by any such special guardian, to affix to his or her signature, his or her title as special guardian, or to sign the name of the infant or infants whose real estate was thus conveyed to such deed of conveyance; provided, that the person who executed such conveyance was the duly appointed special guardian of such infant or infants, and such conveyance was in other respects executed in conformity to the order of the court in which the proceedings for such sale were had. Sales of infants' real estate made prior to June 1, 1852, ratified and confirmed

§ 2. This act shall not affect the right of any party to any suit or legal proceeding, commenced before the passage thereof, in consequence of the irregularity of any proceeding, or the invalidity of any deed which by the foregoing section is legalized and made valid. Not to affect existing suits and proceedings.

§ 3. This act shall take effect immediately.

Ante, vol. 2, p. 202.

CHAP. 530.

AN ACT increasing the powers and duties of courts of special sessions, except in the city and county of New York, and the city of Albany.

Ante, vol. 5, p. 248.

PASSED May 6, 1872; three-fifths being present.

The People of the State of New York, represented in Senate and Assembly, do enact as follows:

Jurisdiction of court of special sessions.

SECTION 1. The second section of the act entitled "An act defining the powers and duties of courts of special sessions except in the city and county of New York and the city of Albany and courts of sessions, and regulating appeals in criminal cases," passed April seventeenth, eighteen hundred and fifty-seven, is hereby amended by adding to said section, at the end thereof, as follows: Charges for offenses against the provisions of chapter three hundred and seventy-five of the laws of eighteen hundred and sixty-seven, entitled "An act for the more effectual prevention of cruelty to animals," also for offenses against the provisions of chapter six hundred and eighty-two of the laws of eighteen hundred and sixty-six, entitled "An act better to prevent cruelty to animals."

§ 2. This act shall take effect immediately.

CHAP. 537.

AN ACT to provide for furnishing two statues of eminent deceased citizens of this state to be placed in the capitol at Washington, in compliance with the invitation of the president of the United States.

PASSED May 6, 1872; three-fifths being present.

The People of the State of New York, represented in Senate and Assembly, do enact as follows:

Governor, secretary of state, and Erastus D. Palmer to contract for statue of George Clinton to be placed in the capitol at Washington.

SECTION 1. The governor, the secretary of state, and Erastus D. Palmer, of Albany, are hereby appointed commissioners for the purpose of making a contract, in behalf of the state, for furnishing annd delivering a marble statue of George Clinton, the first governor of the state, the same to be one of two statues, which, when completed, are to be handed over, on the part of this state, to the president of the United States, to be placed in the capitol at Washington. The subject of the other of said statues to be designated, and the statue provided for, by the next legislature.

§ 2. This act shall take effect immediately.

CHAP. 541.

AN ACT making appropriations for the support of government.

PASSED May 6, 1872; three-fifths being present.

The People of the State of New York, represented in Senate and Assembly, do enact as follows:

Appropriation for fiscal year.

SECTION 1. The several amounts named in this act are hereby appropriated and authorized to be paid, from the several funds indicated, to the respective public officers, and for the several purposes specified, for the fiscal year beginning on the first day of October in the year eighteen hundred and seventy-two, namely:

FROM THE GENERAL FUND — EXECUTIVE DEPARTMENT.

Expenses of the executive department.

For the governor, for salary, four thousand dollars.

For the private secretary of the governor, for salary, two thousand five hundred dollars.

For the clerks and messengers in the executive department, for compensation, seven thousand seven hundred dollars.

For expenses of the house occupied by the governor, five thousand dollars.

For the executive department, for furniture, blank and other books necessary for the use of the department, binding, blanks, printing, stationery, telegraphing, and other incidental expenses, two thousand five hundred dollars.

For the executive department for the apprehension of criminals, pursuant to part one, chapter nine, title one, section fifteen of the Revised Statutes, one thousand dollars; for the apprehension of fugitives from justice, pursuant to part four, chapter two, title seven, section forty-five of the Revised Statutes, one thousand dollars.

JUDICIARY — COURT OF APPEALS.

Expenses of the court of appeals.

For judges of the court of appeals, for salaries and expenses, pursuant to chapter two hundred and three of the laws of eighteen hundred and seventy, and chapter seven hundred and eighteen of the laws of eighteen hundred and seventy-one, sixty-three thousand five hundred dollars.

For the commissioners of appeals, for salaries, pursuant to chapter two hundred and three of the laws of eighteen hundred and seventy, thirty-five thousand dollars.

For state reporter, for salary, pursuant to chapter six hundred and ninety-eight of the laws of eighteen hundred and sixty-nine, and chapter seven hundred and eighteen of the laws of eighteen hundred and seventy-one, five thousand dollars, which shall be his annual salary from and after February fourteenth, eighteen hundred and seventy-two, and for clerical help to the state reporter, two thousand dollars.

Expenses of the court of appeals.

For the clerk of the court of appeals, for salary, pursuant to chapter seven hundred and eighteen of the laws of eighteen hundred and seventy-one, five thousand dollars.

For the deputy clerk of the court of appeals, for salary, pursuant to chapter two hundred and eighty-one of the laws of eighteen hundred and seventy, three thousand dollars.

For the messenger to the clerk of the court of appeals and the state engineer and surveyor (the same messenger) for his annual salary, from October first, eighteen hundred and seventy-two, six hundred dollars.

For clerks in the office of the clerk of the court of appeals, for salaries, pursuant to chapter six hundred and forty-five of the laws of eighteen hundred and sixty-nine, forty-five hundred dollars.

For furniture, books, binding, printing calendar, and other necessary expenses of the office of the clerk of the court of appeals, pursuant to chapter six hundred and forty-five of the laws of eighteen hundred and sixty-nine, twenty-five hundred dollars.

For compensation of criers and attendants for the court of appeals and commission of appeals, pursuant to chapter ninety-five of the laws of eighteen hundred and sixty-four, and chapter two hundred and three of the laws of eighteen hundred and seventy, and chapter two hundred and thirty-eight of the laws of eighteen hundred and seventy-one, five thousand dollars.

For clerk of the commission of appeals, for salary, pursuant to chapter two hundred and three of the laws of eighteen hundred and seventy, thirty-five hundred dollars.

For compensation of the clerk and messenger and office expenses in the office of the clerk of the commission of appeals, twenty-one hundred dollars.

SUPREME COURT.

Expenses of the supreme court.

For justices of the supreme court, for salaries and expenses, pursuant to chapter four hundred and eight of the laws of eighteen hundred and seventy, two hundred and thirty-seven thousand six hundred dollars.

The said justices of the supreme court, except in the first judicial district, shall each receive the sum of twelve hundred dollars, annually, from the first day of January, eighteen hundred and seventy-two, in lieu of and in full of all expenses now allowed by law. This subdivision shall not increase the pay of any judge except the justices of the supreme court.

For compensation of stenographers, pursuant to chapter seven hundred and sixty-five of the laws of eighteen hundred and sixty-eight, five thousand dollars.

For the expenses of the commissioners of appeals, pursuant to chapter four hundred and eight of the laws of eighteen hundred and seventy, seven thousand six hundred dollars.

For the expenses of the general terms of the supreme court, pursuant to chapter four hundred and eight of the laws of eighteen hundred and seventy, ten thousand dollars.

For the attorney-general, for salary, two thousand dollars.

For the deputy attorney-general, for salary, three thousand five hundred dollars.

For clerk and messenger in the office of the attorney-general, for salaries, two thousand dollars.

For furniture, books, binding, blanks, printing, and other necessary expenses of the office of the attorney-general, five hundred dollars.

For costs of suits, fees of sheriffs, compensation of witnesses and for expenses and disbursements by the attorney-general, pursuant to part three, chapter ten, title three, section fifty-one of the Revised Statutes, two thousand dollars.

For sheriff's fees, for the removal of convicts, five hundred dollars.

For compensation of counsel employed to assist the attorney-general, pursuant to chapter three hundred and fifty-seven of the laws of eighteen hundred and forty-eight, three thousand dollars.

For services and expenses of medical commissioners, appointed pursuant to chapter six hundred and sixty-six of laws of eighteen hundred and seventy-one, by the governor or courts of oyer and terminer, to inquire into the mental condition of persons under indictment or conviction for offenses, the punishment of which is death, three thousand dollars; the amount to be paid in each case to be certified by the governor.

For compensation and expenses of the attorney-general, pursuant to part one, chapter eight, title five, section six of the Revised Statutes, and to counsel designated by him to represent him, two thousand dollars, or so much thereof as may be proper, the amount to be certified by the governor, and the appropriation made for this purpose by act, chapter seven hundred and eighteen of the laws of eighteen hundred and seventy-one, is hereby made applicable to the payment of counsel designated by the attorney-general to represent him in such duties. All costs adjudged to the people of this state, in actions prosecuted or defended by the attorney-general, may be applied by him in his discretion to any of the purposes for which appropriations are hereinbefore made in relation to his office, and this shall apply to the costs aforesaid received during the present fiscal year, and the attorney-general shall, at the close of such fiscal year, render to the comptroller an account of such costs received, with vouchers of such expenditures.

Costs adjudged to the people, how applied.

OFFICE OF THE SECRETARY OF STATE.

Expenses of office of secretary of state.

For the secretary of state, for salary, two thousand five hundred dollars.

For the deputy secretary of state and clerk of the commissioners of the land office, for salary, and for indexing and making marginal notes of the session laws, thirty-five hundred dollars, and no other or further compensation shall hereafter be allowed in the supply bill or by the commissioners of the land office to such officer.

For clerks in the office of the secretary of state, for salaries, sixteen thousand five hundred dollars.

For messenger in the office of secretary of state, for salary, one thousand dollars.

The office of translator in the office of secretary of state is hereby abolished, to take effect on the first day of October, eighteen hundred and seventy-two.

For furniture, blank and other books, binding, blanks, printing and other necessary expenses of the secretary of state's office, two thousand dollars.

COMPTROLLER'S OFFICE.

Expenses of office of the comptroller.

For the comptroller, for salary, two thousand five hundred dollars.

For the deputy comptroller, for salary, two thousand dollars.

For the second deputy comptroller, for salary, three thousand dollars.

For clerks in the office of the comptroller, for salaries, twenty-four thousand dollars.

For messenger in the office of the comptroller, for salary, five hundred dollars.

For furniture, books, binding, blanks, printing and other necessary expenses of the office of the eomptroller, pursuant to chapter two hundred and eighty of the laws of eighteen hundred and sixty-four, one thousand five hundred dollars.

TREASURER'S OFFICE.

Expenses of office of the treasurer.

For the treasurer, for salary, one thousand five hundred dollars, and for compensation for countersigning transfers and assignments of securities, made in the banking department, to be refunded to the treasury, pursuant to chapter one hundred and three of the laws of eighteen hundred and fifty-seven, one thousand dollars.

For the deputy treasurer, for salary, three thousand dollars.

For clerks in the office of the treasurer, for salaries, pursuant to chapter six hundred and forty-five of the laws of eighteen hundred and sixty-nine, six thousand dollars.

For furniture, books, binding, printing, extra clerk hire, and other necessary expenses of the office of the treasurer, pursuant to chapter six hundred and forty-five of the laws of eighteen hundred and sixty-nine, fifteen hundred dollars.

DEPARTMENT OF PUBLIC INSTRUCTION.

Expenses of department of public instruction.

For the superintendent of public instruction, for salary, five thousand dollars.

For the deputy superintendent of public instruction, for salary, three thousand dollars.

For the clerks in the office of the superintendent of public instruction, for salaries, pursuant to chapter six hundred and forty-five of the laws of eighteen hundred and sixty-nine, eight thousand six hundred and seventy-five dollars.

For furniture, books, binding, blanks, printing and other necessary expenses in the office of the superintendent of public instruction, pursuant to chapter two hundred and eighty of the laws of eighteen hundred and sixty-four, two thousand dollars.

STATE ENGINEER'S AND SURVEYOR'S OFFICE.

For the deputy state engineer and surveyor, for salary, two thousand dollars. Expenses of state engineer's and surveyor's office.

For compensation of clerks to assist in the preparation of railroad reports, twenty-two hundred dollars, and for the expenses of printing and binding said reports, five thousand dollars (to be refunded by the several railroad companies), pursuant to chapter five hundred and twenty-six of the laws of eighteen hundred and fifty-five.

For clerks in the office of the state engineer and surveyor, for salaries, pursuant to chapter two hundred and eighty of the laws of eighteen hundred and sixty-four, thirty-five hundred dollars.

For furniture, books, binding, blanks, printing and other necessary expenses of the office of the state engineer and surveyor, pursuant to chapter two hundred and eighty of the laws of eighteen hundred and sixty-four, five hundred dollars.

For James Hall, as state geologist, as compensation for authorship, the superintendence of drawings and engravings, for clerk hire, and the use of working rooms, for the arranging, labeling and distribution of the duplicate fossils and minerals, as fixed by the lieutenant-governor, comptroller and secretary of state, pursuant to chapter seven hundred and fifteen of the laws of eighteen hundred and seventy-one, two thousand five hundred dollars. State geologist.

BANKING DEPARTMENT.

For the superintendent of the banking department, for salary, five thousand dollars. Revised Statutes, volume second, page five hundred and ninety. Expenses of banking department.

For clerk hire, furniture, books, binding, blanks, printing and other necessary expenses of the office of the superintendent of the banking department, fifteen thousand dollars.

The aforesaid salary, clerk hire and other expenses above indicated, shall be refunded to the treasury, by the several banks and banking associations of this state, pursuant to chapter one hundred and sixty-four of the laws of eighteen hundred and fifty-one.

INSURANCE DEPARTMENT.

Expenses of insurance department. For the superintendent of insurance department, for salary, seven thousand dollars, pursuant to chapter three hundred and twenty-six of the laws of eighteen hundred and sixty-one, and chapter seven hundred and thirty-two of the laws of eighteen hundred and sixty-eight.

For clerk hire, furniture, books, binding, blanks, printing and other necessary expenses of the insurance department, fifty-three thousand dollars.

The aforesaid salary, clerk hire and other expenses above indicated shall be refunded to the treasury, by the several insurance companies, associations, persons and agents, pursuant to chapter three hundred and sixty-six of the laws of eighteen hundred and fifty-nine.

All fees and perquisites of every name and nature, charged, received and collected by the insurance department, or any officer thereof (taking therefrom only actual traveling and other necessary expenses, to be audited and allowed by the comptroller), shall be immediately paid into the state treasury.

STATE ASSESSORS.

Assessors. For the state assessors, for compensation and traveling expenses, pursuant to chapter three hundred and twelve of the laws of eighteen hundred and fifty-nine, the sum of four thousand dollars, or so much thereof as may be necessary.

Commissioners of public accounts abolished. The office of the commissioners of public accounts is hereby abolished, to take effect on the first day of October, eighteen hundred and seventy-two.

INSPECTORS OF GAS-METERS.

Inspectors of gas-meters. For the inspectors of gas-meters, for salary and contingent expenses, pursuant to chapter one hundred and sixteen of the laws of eighteen hundred and sixty, and to the conditions and requirements imposed by chapter one hundred and thirty-five of the laws of eighteen hundred and sixty-three, two thousand five hundred dollars; which amount shall be refunded to the treasury by the several gas-light companies, pursuant to chapter three hundred and eleven of the laws of eighteen hundred and fifty-nine. But no payment shall be made by the comptroller upon such salary and expenses till an amount equal to such payment shall be received by him from the gas companies, or some of them.

To be repaid by gas companies.

QUARANTINE COMMISSIONERS.

Commissioners of quarantine. For the commissioners of quarantine, for salaries, to each of them, two thousand five hundred dollars, pursuant to chapter three hundred and fifty-eight of the laws of eighteen hundred and sixty-three.

AUCTIONEERS' ACCOUNTS.

For compensation of the agent to examine the accounts of auctioneers (Revised Statutes, volume second, page four hundred and sixty-seven, and chapter five hundred and forty-seven of the laws of eighteen hundred and sixty-six), one thousand two hundred dollars, or so much thereof as may be necessary. Agent to examine auctioneers' accounts.

WEIGHTS AND MEASURES.

For superintendent of weights and measures, for salary, three hundred dollars, pursuant to chapter one hundred and thirty-four of the laws of eighteen hundred and fifty-one. Superintendent.

LAND OFFICE.

For assessments and other expenses of public lands, and for the compensation and mileage of the lieutenant-governor and the speaker of the assembly, for attendance as commissioners of the land office, two thousand dollars. Land office.

PUBLIC OFFICES.

For postage on official letters, documents and other matter, sent by mail, of the governor, secretary of state, comptroller, treasurer, superintendent of public instruction, attorney-general, state engineer and surveyor, adjutant-general, inspector-general and clerks of the court and commission of appeals, pursuant to chapter four hundred and thirty-five of the laws of eighteen hundred and sixty-two, five thousand dollars; and for stationery for the aforesaid public officers and departments (R. S., vol. 1, p. 480), five thousand dollars. Postage, etc.

CAPITOL.

For repairs, cleaning, labor, gas and other necessary expenses of the capitol, ten thousand dollars. Repairs, etc.

For the superintendent of the capitol, for salary, nine hundred dollars. Superintendent.

STATE HALL.

For repairs, cleaning, labor, gas and other necessary expenses of the state hall, five thousand dollars. Repairs, etc.

For superintendent of state hall, for salary, nine hundred dollars. Superintendent.

REGENTS OF THE UNIVERSITY.

For secretary of the regents of the university, for salary, two thousand five hundred dollars. Expenses of regents of the university.

For assistant secretary of the regents of the university, for salary, two thousand dollars.

For compensation of a botanist, for arranging the herbarium in the museum of natural history, fifteen hundred dollars.

Postage, etc. For expense of postage, expressage, printing, stationery, visitation, compensation of a messenger, expenses of regents in attending meetings of the board and other necessary expenses, two thousand five hundred dollars.

STATE LIBRARY.

Expenses of the state library For the purchase of books for the state library, four thousand dollars.

For binding, lettering and marking books for the state library, one thousand seven hundred dollars.

For repairs, cleaning, gas, transportation of books and other necessary expenses of the state library, one thousand dollars.

For the salaries of the librarians and assistants, and janitor of the state library, six thousand eight hundred dollars.

HALL FOR THE STATE CABINET OF NATURAL HISTORY, AND THE AGRICULTURAL MUSEUM.

Expenses of hall for the state cabinet of natural history, etc. For the state cabinet of natural history, pursuant to chapter five hundred and fifty-seven of the laws of eighteen hundred and seventy, ten thousand dollars.

For the special increase of the zoological collection of the museum of natural history, one thousand dollars.

For repairs, cleaning, labor, gas, fuel and other necessary expenses, including the compensation of the keeper of the hall for the state cabinet of natural history, three thousand five hundred dollars.

For the persons employed in preparing drawings for the natural history of the state, for compensation, two thousand five hundred dollars. Syracuse university to share in distribution of fossils. The Syracuse university is hereby included in the provisions specified in chapter one hundred and seventy-nine of the laws of eighteen hundred and sixty-eight, in regard to the distribution of duplicate fossils and minerals to the Cornell university.

FUEL.

Fuel. For fuel for the capitol, the state hall, and the state library, five thousand dollars.

AGRICULTURAL.

Agricultural societies. For donations to the societies in the several counties of the state, and to the state society, for the promotion of agriculture, twenty thousand dollars.

Entomologist abolished. The office of state entomologist is hereby abolished, to take effect on the first day of October, eighteen hundred and seventy-two.

LEGISLATURE.

Expenses of the legislature. For compensation and mileage of members and officers of the legislature, ninety thousand dollars.

For advances to the clerks of the senate and assembly, for contingent expenses, twenty thousand dollars.

For postage, expenses of committees, compensation of witnesses, legislative manual, Croswell's manual and clerk's manual and other contingent expenses of the legislature, eighteen thousand dollars. Postage, etc.

STATE PRINTING.

For the legislative printing for the state, including binding, mapping, engraving, publication of the official canvas and other official notices, pursuant to chapter twenty-four of the laws of eighteen hundred and forty-six, and chapter two hundred and fifty-four of the laws of eighteen hundred and forty-seven, one hundred and twenty-five thousand dollars. Legislative printing.

STATE PRISONS, ETC.

For the inspectors of state prisons, for salaries, to each of them, one thousand six hundred dollars; and for traveling expenses to each of them, six hundred dollars. Inspectors.

For the support and maintenance of the several state prisons, and for material and expense of manufacturing, pursuant to chapter two hundred and forty of the laws of eighteen hundred and fifty-four, and chapter forty-three of the laws of eighteen hundred and sixty-five, six hundred thousand dollars. Support and maintenance of state prisons.

For compensation of sheriffs for the transportation of convicts to the prisons, asylum for insane convicts, house of refuge and penitentiaries, pursuant to chapter one hundred and twenty-three of the laws of eighteen hundred and forty-six, of chapter one hundred and fifty-eight of the laws of eighteen hundred and fifty-six, and chapter six hundred and sixty-five of the laws of eighteen hundred and seventy-one, twenty thousand dollars. Sheriffs, for transportation of convicts.

For supplying Croton water to the Sing Sing prison, pursuant to chapter two hundred and eighty-two of the laws of eighteen hundred and sixty-one, one thousand five hundred dollars. Croton water at Sing Sing prison.

For supplying of water for Auburn prison and asylum for insane convicts, one thousand five hundred dollars. Water at Auburn.

For the maintenance of convicts sentenced to penitentiaries, pursuant to chapter one hundred and fifty-eight of the laws of eighteen hundred and fifty-six, of chapter five hundred and eighty four of the laws of eighteen hundred and sixty-five, and of chapter six hundred and sixty-seven of the laws of eighteen hundred and sixty-six, ten thousand dollars. Maintenance of convicts at penitentiaries.

For refunding deposits to prison contractors, pursuant to chapter four hundred and sixty-five of the laws of eighteen hundred and sixty-three, two thousand dollars. Refunding deposits to contractors.

ASYLUM FOR INSANE CONVICTS.

For the support and maintenance of the asylum for insane convicts, pursuant to chapter one hundred and thirty of the laws of eighteen hundred and fifty-eight, sixteen thousand dollars.

STATE LUNATIC ASYLUM.

Salaries. For salaries of the officers of the state asylum for lunatics, pursuant to chapter one hundred and forty-two, and chapter five hundred and ninety-five of the laws of eighteen hundred and sixty-seven, and chapter two hundred and ninety-five of the laws of eighteen hundred and seventy, eleven thousand dollars.

Mark Jack. For the support of Mark Jack, an insane Indian at the asylum, two hundred and fifty dollars.

Insane female convicts. For the support of insane female convicts at the state lunatic asylum, six hundred dollars.

HUDSON RIVER STATE HOSPITAL FOR THE INSANE.

Salaries. For salaries of the officers of the Hudson River State Hospital for the insane, eight thousand dollars, or so much thereof as may be necessary.

INDIAN AFFAIRS.

Onondaga Indians. For the relief of the Onondaga Indians, pursuant to chapter two hundred and six of the laws of eighteen hundred and fifty-eight, three hundred dollars.

Compensation of agent. For compensation of the agent of the Onondaga Indians, pursuant to chapter two hundred and twenty-eight of the laws of eighteen hundred and forty-three, of chapter three hundred and seventy-six of the laws of eighteen hundred and fifty-one, and of chapter two hundred and eighty-one of the laws of eighteen hundred and seventy, two hundred dollars.

For compensation of the agent of the Onondaga Indians, pursuant to chapter one hundred and seventy-eight of the laws of eighteen hundred and forty-seven, and chapter six hundred and thirty-five of the laws of eighteen hundred and sixty-nine, sixty-five dollars, or so much thereof as may be necessary.

For compensation of the agent of the Onondaga Indians, on the Allegany and Cattaraugus reservations, pursuant to chapter two hundred and thirty-three of the laws of eighteen hundred and fifty-seven, and chapter seventy-three of the laws of eighteen hundred and fifty-eight, one hundred and fifty dollars.

Attorney of the St. Regis Indians. For compensation of the attorney of the St. Regis Indians, pursuant to chapter three hundred and twenty-five of the laws of eighteen hundred and sixty-one, one hundred and fifty dollars.

Attorney of Seneca Indians. For compensation of the attorney of the Seneca Indians, pursuant to chapter one hundred and fifty of the laws of eighteen hundred and forty-five, one hundred and fifty dollars.

Attorney of Tonawanda For compensation of the attorney for the Tonawanda band of Seneca Indians, pursuant to chapter eight hundred and thirty-nine of the laws of eighteen hundred and sixty-seven, three hundred dollars. band of Indians.

For the county of Niagara, to re-imburse the same for moneys paid out in support of Susan Green, an insane Indian woman, in the state lunatic asylum and the Willard asylum, two hundred and fifty dollars; and hereafter said Indian shall be supported in the Willard asylum, at the expense of the state, so long as she shall remain insane. Niagara county, for support of Susan Green.

ONONDAGA SALT SPRINGS.

For salary of the superintendent, compensation of clerks and other persons employed, and other necessary expenses of the Onondaga salt springs, pursuant to chapter three hundred and forty-six, section thirty-six, of the laws of eighteen hundred and fifty-nine, fifty-six thousand dollars. Salary, etc.

MILITIA OF THE STATE.

For expenses of the National Guard of the state of New York, pursuant to chapter eighty of the laws of eighteen hundred and seventy, two hundred thousand dollars. Expenses of National Guard.

So much, and not exceeding seventy-five thousand dollars, of the appropriation of two hundred and fifty-thousand dollars for "altering the small arms of the National Guard to, or exchanging them for, breech-loaders," provided for in chapter seven hundred and eighteen of the laws of eighteen hundred and seventy-one, as may not be required for that purpose, may, in the discretion of the governor, be used for the general purposes of the National Guard as specified above. Appropriation for altering small arms may be used for general purposes.

ROADS.

For payments to commissioners, of moneys received into the treasury for taxes on lands of non-residents, appropriated to the construction of roads, six thousand dollars. Payments to commissioners.

INTEREST ON STATE INDEBTEDNESS.

For interest on the debt of thirty-six thousand dollars, created for the benefit of the Stockbridge Indians, pursuant to chapter two hundred and eight of the laws of eighteen hundred and forty-eight, and chapter thirty-seven of the laws of eighteen hundred and fifty, two thousand one hundred and sixty dollars. Interest on state debt.

COUNTY TREASURERS.

For advances to county treasurers, on account of taxes on property of non-residents, which may be returned to the comptroller's office, sixty thousand dollars. Advances to county treasurers.

TRANSPORTATION.

For expenses of transportation of the session laws, journals and documents of the legislature, reports, books, etc., and Transportation of session laws, etc. packages by express for the public offices, and for expenses of boxes, pursuant to chapter two hundred and fifty-four of the laws of eighteen hundred and forty-seven, five thousand dollars.

REPAYMENT OF MONEYS.

Redemption of lands sold for taxes. For repayment of money to purchasers for redemption of land sold for taxes, fifty thousand dollars.

Erroneous payments. For repayment of money erroneously paid into the treasury for taxes, ten thousand dollars.

Repayments to purchasers in case of failure of title. For repayment of money in cases of failure of title to lands sold by the state (Revised Statutes, volume one, page five hundred and forty-one), three hundred dollars.

For repayment of money paid into the treasury through mistake (Revised Statutes, page four hundred and seventy-nine), five hundred dollars.

MISCELLANEOUS.

Court of appeals reports. For supplying other states with reports of the court of appeals, and of the supreme court, pursuant to chapter five hundred and thirty-six of the laws of eighteen hundred and thirty-six, five hundred dollars.

Books, etc. For expenses of books and stationery for the transfer office, at the Manhattan company, New York, two hundred and fifty dollars.

For compensation of agent in the city of New York, to superintend the issue and transfer of state stock, pursuant to chapter two hundred of the laws of eighteen hundred and sixty-six, seven hundred and fifty dollars.

For supplying the "Mexico Independent" to the deaf and dumb persons of this state, in the same manner and upon the same terms as the "Radii" was required to do under and pursuant to chapter three hundred and twenty-nine of the laws of eighteen hundred and thirty-nine, five hundred dollars.

For the compensation of the keeping of Washington's headquarters, one hundred dollars.

For expense of the board of harbor commissioners, New York, five thousand dollars.

For the commissioners to revise the statutes of the state, appointed under chapter thirty-three of the laws of eighteen hundred and seventy, for their services, fifteen thousand dollars; and for their expenditures for clerical services and other incidental matters, six thousand dollars. The said commissioners' terms of office and time to complete their work is hereby extended two years.

DEAF AND DUMB.

Donations to charitable institutions. For the support and instruction of three hundred and fifty pupils at the Institution for Deaf and Dumb in New York, pursuant to chapter ninety-seven of the laws of eighteen hundred and fifty-two, or a proportionate amount for a shorter period of time than one year, or for a smaller number of pupils, as shall be duly verified by affidavits of the president and secretary of the institution, one hundred and five thousand dollars; and this sum is in full of all demands upon the state in behalf of said institution during the next fiscal year. Donations to charitable institutions.

For the support and instruction of one hundred and fifty pupils for one year at the Institution for the Blind in New York, or a proportionate amount for a shorter period of time than one year, or for a smaller number of pupils, as shall be duly verified by affidavits of the president and secretary of the institution, forty-five thousand dollars.

JUVENILE DELINQUENTS.

For the Society for the Reformation of Juvenile Delinquents in the city of New York, forty thousand dollars.

HOUSE OF REFUGE.

For the House of Refuge for western New York, forty thousand dollars.

IDIOT ASYLUM.

For the State Asylum for Idiots, at Syracuse, thirty-two thousand dollars.

WILLARD'S ASYLUM FOR THE INSANE.

For the salaries of officers of the Willard Asylum for the Insane, nine thousand dollars. Salaries.

So much of section nine, chapter three hundred and forty-two of the laws of eighteen hundred and sixty-five, relating to the Willard asylum, as reads as follows: "Said trustees shall also fix the rate per week, not exceeding two dollars, for the board of patients," is hereby repealed, and the said trustees of the Willard asylum shall hereafter annually fix the price per week, not to exceed the actual cost of support and attendance exclusive of officers' salaries, as provided in relation to the State asylums at Utica and Poughkeepsie. Price per week, how fixed.

The successors to the trustees of said asylum, who shall be appointed pursuant to the provisions of chapter eight hundred and twenty-two of the laws of eighteen hundred and sixty-nine, shall hold their offices respectively for the term of eight years; except that the term of office of such trustees as are or shall be appointed to succeed Samuel R. Wells and Francis O. Mason shall be computed from the date at which their terms of office terminated, to wit: the ninth day of May, eighteen hundred and seventy-one. Terms of office.

INSTITUTION FOR THE BLIND, BATAVIA.

For the maintenance of the Institution for the Blind, at Batavia, thirty-five thousand dollars.

STATE COMMISSIONERS OF PUBLIC CHARITIES.

Salaries, etc. For the salary of the secretary of the commissioners of public charities, twenty-five hundred dollars, and for the traveling expenses of the commissioners and the secretary, and for office expenses, clerk hire and contingencies of the state commissioners of public charities, two thousand five hundred dollars.

Appropriations to educational institutions. From the free school fund for the State Normal School at Albany, for its maintenance, eighteen thousand dollars.

For the State Normal and Training School at Brockport, for its maintenance, eighteen thousand dollars.

Hereafter, the number of members of the local board of said school, as recommended by the superintendent of public instruction, shall not exceed eleven, and, in addition to the present board, Arnold N. Braman and Elijah Chriswell shall be members of said board.

For the State Normal and Training School at Buffalo, for its maintenance, eighteen thousand dollars.

For the State Normal and Training School at Cortland, for its maintenance, eighteen thousand dollars.

For the State Normal and Training School at Fredonia, for its maintenance, eighteen thousand dollars.

For the State Normal and Training School at Geneseo, for its maintenance, eighteen thousand dollars.

For the State Normal and Training School at Oswego, for its maintenance, eighteen thousand dollars.

For the State Normal and Training School at Potsdam, for its maintenance, eighteen thousand dollars.

Teachers' institutes. For the maintenance of the teachers' institutes, pursuant to chapter five hundred and fifty-five, title eleven of the laws of eighteen hundred and sixty-four, eighteen thousand dollars.

Common schools. For the support of the common schools of this state, two millions five hundred and sixty thousand dollars, or so much thereof as shall remain of the proceeds of the tax of one and one-fourth mills upon each dollar of the taxable property in the state, levied for the support of common schools, after deducting from the proceeds of said tax the several sums appropriated in the last nine items above mentioned.

Academies, etc. For the benefit of the academies and academical departments of the union schools, the sum of one hundred and twenty-five thousand dollars, or so much thereof as may be derived from a tax of one-sixteenth of one mill upon each dollar of the taxable property of the state; the sum thus arising to be divided as the literature fund is now divided, which is hereby ordered to be levied for each and every year.

PAYABLE FROM THE GENERAL FUND DEBT SINKING FUND.

Interest on general fund debt. For interest on the sum of three millions eight hundred and twenty-nine thousand, eight hundred and thirty-one dollars and fifty-three cents, of the general fund state debt, one hundred and ninety-nine thousand one hundred and ninety dollars and fifty-two cents.

For the payment of the annuities to the several Indian tribes, viz.: Indian annuities.

Onondagas, two thousand four hundred and thirty dollars.

Cayugas, two thousand three hundred dollars.

Senecas, five hundred dollars.

St. Regis, two thousand one hundred and thirty-one dollars and sixty-seven cents.

PAYABLE FROM SCHOOL FUND—CAPITAL.

For investment, for loans to towns and counties, pursuant to chapter one hundred and ninety-four of the laws of eighteen hundred and forty-nine, fifty thousand dollars, or so much thereof as may be necessary. Loans to town and counties.

REVENUE.

For dividends to common schools (R. S., vol. 1, p. 538), one hundred and seventy thousand dollars. To common schools.

For support of Indian schools, pursuant to chapter seventy-one of the laws of eighteen hundred and fifty-six, four thousand dollars. Indian schools.

For refunding money paid into the treasury for redemption of lands sold for arrears of consideration, pursuant to chapter four hundred and fifty-seven of the laws of eighteen hundred and thirty-six, five hundred dollars. Refunding moneys for redemption of lands.

For refunding surplus moneys received on re-sales of land (R. S., vol. 1, p. 496), five hundred dollars. Surplus moneys.

For expenses of lands (R. S., vol. 1, p. 554), two hundred dollars. Expenses.

PAYABLE FROM THE LITERATURE FUND.

For dividends to the academies, pursuant to chapter two hundred and thirty-seven of the laws of eighteen hundred and thirty-eight, twelve thousand dollars. Dividends to academies.

For the purchase of text-books, maps and globes, philosophical and chemical apparatus for the academies (R. S., vol. 2, p. 72), three thousand dollars. Text-books, etc.

PAYABLE FROM THE UNITED STATES DEPOSIT FUND.

For investment as capital of the United States deposit fund, pursuant to chapter one hundred and fifty of the laws of eighteen hundred and thirty-seven, one hundred thousand dollars, or so much thereof as may be necessary. U. S. deposit fund.

REVENUE.

For dividends to common schools, pursuant to chapter two hundred and thirty-seven of the laws of eighteen hundred and thirty-eight, including the salaries of the county school commissioners, pursuant to chapter one hundred and seventy-nine Dividends to common schools.

of the laws of eighteen hundred and fifty-six, one hundred and sixty-five thousand dollars.

Academies. For dividends to academies, pursuant to chapter two hundred and thirty-seven of the laws of eighteen hundred and thirty-eight, twenty-eight thousand dollars.

Capital of common school fund. For amount to be added to the capital of the school fund (article nine of the constitution), twenty-five thousand dollars.

Instruction of common school teachers. For instruction of common school teachers in the academies designated by the Regents of the University, pursuant to chapter two hundred and thirty-five of the laws of eighteen hundred and fifty-two, eighteen thousand dollars.

PAYABLE FROM THE BOUNTY DEBT SINKING FUND.

Contributions to sinking fund. For investment of contributions to the sinking fund and payment of interest on the state indebtedness, incurred pursuant to chapters two hundred and twenty-six and three hundred and twenty-five of the laws of eighteen hundred and sixty-five, known and designated as the bounty debt, four millions one hundred thousand dollars, or so much thereof as may be necessary.

PAYABLE FROM THE COLLEGE LAND SCRIP FUND REVENUE.

Cornell university. For the Cornell university, pursuant to chapter five hundred and eighty-five of the laws of eighteen hundred and sixty-five, thirty-five thousand dollars.

PAYABLE FROM THE CORNELL ENDOWMENT FUND REVENUE.

Ibid. For the Cornell university, pursuant to chapter five hundred and fifty-four of the laws of eighteen hundred and sixty-eight, ten thousand dollars.

PAYABLE FROM THE MILITARY RECORD FUND REVENUE.

For expenses of the Bureau of Military Statistics, three thousand dollars.

PAYABLE FROM THE ELMIRA FEMALE COLLEGE EDUCATIONAL FUND REVENUE.

Elmira Female college. For the Elmira Female college, pursuant to chapter six hundred and forty-three of the laws of eighteen hundred and sixty-seven, three thousand five hundred dollars.

Appropriations, how paid. § 2. The amounts herein appropriated shall be paid by the treasurer from the respective funds as specified, and the salaries named shall be established and fixed by this act for the several officers for whom they are designated; but the comptroller shall not draw his warrant for the payment of the several amounts heretofore named, except for salaries and other expenditures and appropriations, the amounts of which are duly established and fixed by law, till the persons demanding them shall present to him a detailed statement in items of the same; and if such account shall be for services, it must show

Warrants by comptroller.

when, where and under what authority they were rendered; if for expenditures, when, where and under what authority they were made; if for articles furnished, when and where they were furnished, to whom they were delivered, and under what authority; and if the demand shall be for traveling expenses, the account must also specify the distance traveled, the place of starting and destination, the duty or business, and the date and items of expenditures. All accounts must be verified by an affidavit to the effect that the account is true, just and correct, and that no part of it has been paid, but is actually and justly due and owing; on all accounts for transportation, furniture, blank and other books purchased for the use of office, binding, blanks, printing, stationery, postage, cleaning and other necessary and incidental expenses, a bill duly receipted must also be furnished; and it shall also be the duty of the treasurer to report annually to the legislature the detail of these several expenditures. No officer, clerk or employee, whose salary is fixed or provided for by this bill, or whose employment by the head of a department is authorized herein, shall, under any pretext whatever, receive any other or additional compensation by any appropriation in the supply bill or otherwise, for any performance of official, clerical or other duty required by law to be performed in the department in which he is such officer, clerk or employee.

Accounts to be verified.

No additional compensation.

§ 3. All institutions and societies, entitled under the provisions of this act to receive money from the state, shall make an annual report to the legislature, which report shall be presented on or before the fifteenth day of January in each year, and no money hereby appropriated shall be paid to any institution or association which has neglected to make such report, unless a report of its condition be filed with the comptroller within ten days after notice by the comptroller to such institution or association to make and file the same.

Certain institutions to report annually.

CHAP. 544.

AN ACT to declare the day for holding the general state election a public holiday.

PASSED May 6, 1872; three-fifths being present.

The People of the State of New York, represented in Senate and Assembly, do enact as follows:

SECTION 1. The day for holding the general state election in each year shall be a public holiday, for the purpose and with the effect provided in and by chapter three hundred and seventy of the laws of eighteen hundred and seventy, entitled "An act to amend an act entitled 'An act to designate the holidays to be observed in the acceptance and payment of bills of exchange and promissory notes, passed April fourth, eighteen hundred and forty-nine,' passed April twenty-third, eighteen hundred and seventy."

Day for holding general election a holiday.

CHAP. 550.

AN ACT to encourage steam towage upon the canals of this State.

PASSED May 6, 1872.

The People of the State of New York, represented in Senate and Assembly, do enact as follows:

Portion of canal to be allotted for experimenting with road steam towage.

SECTION 1. The canal commissioners are hereby authorized and directed to allot and set out to D. O. Williamson a distance on the Erie canal of not less than five miles, at such point as may be most convenient and suitable, for the purpose of experimenting with his road steam engine for the towage of boats, said experiments being made under the direction of said commissioners.

§ 2. This act shall take effect immediately.

CHAP. 570.

AN ACT to ascertain, by proper proofs, the citizens who shall be entitled to the right of suffrage in the state of New York, except in the city and county of New York and the city of Brooklyn, and to repeal chapter five hundred and seventy-two of the laws of eighteen hundred and seventy-one, entitled "An act to amend an act entitled 'An act in relation to elections in the city and county of New York.'"

See Laws, 1871, p. 1227.

PASSED May 7, 1872; three-fifths being present.

The People of the State of New York, represented in Senate and Assembly, do enact as follows:

Board of registry of elections.

SECTION 1. The several inspectors who now are or who may be hereafter elected or appointed inspectors of election, for the several election districts in the towns and cities of this state, except in the city and county of New York and the city of Brooklyn, for the year eighteen hundred and seventy-two, are hereby declared to be a board of registry of elections under this act; and for the purposes herein named, the said inspectors, and their successors in office, shall meet annually, on Tuesday, three weeks previous to the general election, at nine o'clock, A. M., at the place designated for holding the poll of said election, and organize themselves as a board for the purpose of registering the names of the legal voters of such district, and shall sit until nine o'clock, P. M., of each day; and for this purpose they shall appoint one of their number chair-

When board to meet.

Chairman.

man of the board, who shall administer to the other inspectors the oath of office, as by the constitution, and the same oath shall then be administered to the chairman by one of the other inspectors. The said board shall then proceed to make a list of all persons qualified and entitled to vote at the ensuing election, in the election district of which they are inspectors. Said list, when completed, shall constitute and be known as the register of electors of said district. The said inspectors, at their first meeting on Tuesday, three weeks preceding the general election, shall have power, if necessary, to sit two days for the purpose of making said list, provided that at the annual election next prior to said meeting, the number of votes in the district of which they are inspectors exceeded four hundred. List of voters. Number of days to sit.

§ 2. Said registers shall each contain a list of persons so qualified and entitled to vote in said election district, alphabetically arranged according to their respective surnames, so as to show in one column the name at full length and in another column in cities and incorporated villages, the residences by the number of the dwelling, if there be a number, or if the person be an occupant of a tenement house occupied by several persons, or a lodging place, then they shall also enter the number of the room, if any, and the floor or story of said tenement or lodging-house occupied by said person, and the name of the street on which said dwelling-house, tenement or lodging place is located. It shall be the duty of said inspectors to enter in said lists the names of all persons residing in their election districts whose names appear on the poll-list kept in said district at the last preceding general election, and for this purpose said inspectors are authorized to take from the office in which they are filed, the poll list made and filed by the inspectors of such district at the general election held next prior to the making of such register. In case a new election district shall be formed, the said inspectors shall enter in the list the names of such persons entitled to vote in the new election district, whose names appear upon the poll-list of the last general election, kept in the district or districts from which said new election district is formed. The said inspectors shall complete, as far as practicable, the said register on the day or days of their meeting aforesaid, and shall make four copies thereof, and certify the register and each of the copies to be a true list of the voters in their district, so far as the same are known to them, within two days thereafter. The said original list, with the list taken from the office as aforesaid, shall be filed in the office of the town clerk of the town or city clerk of the city in which said election district may be, and one copy of said list shall be kept by each of said inspectors, and be carefully preserved by him for their use on the day or days hereafter mentioned for revision and correction of the same. One copy of said list shall, immediately after its completion, be posted in some conspicuous place in the room in which such meeting shall be held, and be accessible to any elector who may desire to examine the same or make copies thereof. What registers to contain. What names to be entered. In case of new election district. Four copies to be made. Original list to be filed. Each inspector to keep a copy. One copy to be posted.

Second meeting.

§ 3. The said boards of inspectors shall meet on Friday of the week preceding the day of the general election, at the places designated for holding the polls of election, for the purpose of revising and correcting said list; and for this purpose, in cities, they shall meet at eight o'clock in the morning, and remain in session until nine o'clock, P. M., of that day and the day following, and in other districts they shall meet at nine o'clock in the morning and remain in session until nine of that day. And they shall then revise, correct, add to and subtract from, and complete the said lists, and shall on that day add to the said list the name of any person who would, on the first Tuesday succeeding the first Monday of November, be entitled, under the provisions of the constitution and laws of this state, to exercise the right of suffrage in their respective election districts. But in making such addition on that day, or on any prior day, they shall not place on the said list the name of any person, except in strict compliance with the provisions of section two and section four hereof, and the other provisions of this act.

Length of session.

Lists to be revised and corrected and names added.

What names to be added.

Proceedings to be open and voters to be heard.

§ 4. The proceedings of said board of inspection shall be open, and all persons residing and entitled to vote in said district shall be entitled to be heard by said inspectors, in relation to corrections or additions to said register. One of the lists so kept by said inspectors as aforesaid, shall be used by them on the day or days for making corrections or additions for the purpose of completing the registers for such district. No addition shall be made to the said register of the name of any person, nor shall the name of any person be placed thereon, except one who shall have appeared in person before said board; and any person not born in the United States, on applying to have his name placed on the registry, shall prove that he is a citizen of the United States, by producing a certificate of naturalization from a court of competent jurisdiction; nor shall any other proof of his being a citizen be received, unless he shall first show to the satisfaction of the board of registry, that said certificate has been issued to him and that he is unable to produce such certificate, by reason of loss or destruction thereof.

One list to be used for making corrections.

Naturalized citizens to produce certificate.

Names to be erased.

§ 5. It shall be the duty of said inspectors, at their meetings for revising and correcting said lists, to erase therefrom the name of any person inserted therein who shall be proved, to the satisfaction of said inspectors, to be a non-resident of said district, or otherwise not entitled to vote in said district, at the election then next to be held. Any elector residing in said district, and entitled to vote therein, may appear before said board of inspectors and require his name to be recorded on said alphabetical list, and upon complying with the requirements of this act, the same shall be recorded. Any person so requiring his name to be entered on said list shall make the same statement as to street or number thereof, and where he resides, required by the provisions of this act of persons offering their votes at the election, and shall be subject to the same pains and penalties for refusing to give such information, or

Electors may appear and require their names to be entered.

Statements to be made.

for falsely giving the same, and shall also be subject to challenge, either by the inspectors, or either of them, or by any elector whose name appears upon said alphabetical list, and the same oath may be administered by the inspectors, as may by law be administered to persons offering to vote at an election. At such meeting for revision and correction, it shall be the right of any elector of the district to examine said registry, and if upon oath he shall declare that he has reason to believe that any person on said list is not a qualified elector, the said inspectors shall place the words "to be challenged" opposite the name of such person, to whom, while offering his vote, the general oath as to qualifications shall be administered, and if he shall refuse to take such oath, he shall not be permitted to vote.

If any elector declares on oath that any person is not a voter, the words "to be challenged" to be entered opposite.

§ 6. After said list shall have been fully completed, the said inspectors shall cause four copies of the same to be made, each of which shall be certified by them to be a correct list of the voters of their district, one of which shall be filed in the office of the town clerk of towns, and in cities, in the office of the city clerk, and one of which copies shall be retained by each of the said inspectors. It shall be the duty of the said inspectors carefully to preserve the said list for their use on election day, and to designate one of their number or one of the clerks, at the opening of the polls, to check the name of every voter voting in such district whose name is on the register; and no vote shall be received at any annual election in this state unless the name of the person offering to vote be on the said registry, made and completed as hereinbefore provided, preceding the election; and any person whose name is on the registry may be challenged, and the same oaths shall be put as are now prescribed by law. This section shall be taken and held by every judicial or other tribunal as mandatory and not directory. And any vote which shall be received by the said inspectors of election in contravention of this section shall be void, and shall be rejected from the count in any legislative or judicial scrutiny into any result of the election.

Four copies corrected list to be made

How disposed of.

Names to be checked.

No person to vote whose name is not on registry.

This section to be taken as mandatory

§ 7. The clerks at each poll, in addition to the duties now prescribed by law, shall enter on the poll lists kept by them, in the columns prepared for that purpose, opposite the name of each person voting, the same statement or minute hereinbefore required of inspectors in making the registry, but such entry is not to be made by them, if the registry contains correctly the name and residence of such voter. Every elector at the time of offering his vote shall, if required, truly state the street in which he resides, and if the house, lodging or tenement in which he resides is numbered, the number thereof, and if a tenement or lodging-house, the number of the room, if any, and the floor or story of such tenement or lodging-house; and the clerks of the poll shall truly enter in the appropriate column of the poll list, opposite the name of the elector, the street in which the elector resides, and the number, in case the house, tenement or lodging-house is numbered, and if a tenement or lodging-house the number of the room, if any, and the floor or story of such tenement or lodging-house; and

Duties of poll clerks.

Statement to be made if required, by elector, at time of offering his vote.

if such house, tenement, lodging or room is not numbered, then the clerk shall enter "not numbered" in the column of the poll list set apart for that purpose; and in case of refusal to make the statement as aforesaid, the vote of such elector shall not be received. Any person who shall willfully make any false statement in relation thereto shall be deemed guilty of a misdemeanor, and shall, upon conviction, be punished with a fine of fifty dollars, or by imprisonment in the county jail of the county, or the city prison of the city, where such voter offers to vote for a period of thirty days, or by both such fine and imprisonment.

Penalty for willful false statement.

Any qualified voter may contest right of any person to register or to vote.

§ 8. Any person who is a qualified voter in any city shall have the right in any and all election districts in such city to challenge and contest the right of any person to be placed on any register, or to vote at any poll within said city, with the same effect as though the party making the challenge was a qualified voter in the district where he makes the challenge.

Poll lists and registers to be kept together and filed.

§ 9. After the canvass of the votes, the said poll list and said register so kept and checked as aforesaid, shall be attached together, and shall, on the following day, be filed in the town clerk's office in the town in which said district shall be, and in case the district is in a city, in the city clerk's office of said city, to be used by the inspectors in making the list of voters at the next general election,

Board may appoint clerk.

§ 10. The said board may, if necessary, on the day or days of making such lists, and the correction of the same, appoint a clerk to assist them in the discharge of the duties required by this act; and the same oath shall be taken by such clerk as is required by law of clerks of the polls and of elections.

Registers to be open to inspection.

§ 11. The registers shall at all times be open to public inspection at the office of the authorities, in which they shall be deposited, without charge.

Compensation of inspectors and clerks.

§ 12. The members of the board of registration and their clerks shall each receive the same compensation as is now allowed by law for inspectors of election for each day actually employed in the making and the completion of the registry, to be paid to them at the time and in the manner in which they are paid their other fees. The necessary blanks and instructions, and other incidental expenses incurred in executing the provisions of this act, shall be provided and paid for in the manner now provided for the payment of incidental expenses of election of the like character.

Expenses for blanks, etc., how paid.

General powers.

§ 13. The said board shall have and exercise the same powers in preserving order at their meetings under this act as are given to inspectors of election for preserving order on election day.

Penalties for violation of this act.

§ 14. Any person who shall cause his name to be registered in more than one election district, or who shall cause his name to be registered, knowing that he is not a qualified voter in the ward or district where said registry is made, or who shall falsely personate any registered voter, and any person causing any such act, or aiding, abetting, inducing or procuring any person to be fraudulently registered as a voter, in any election district in which such person is not at the time a legally qualified voter, or who shall cause or procure or be in any manner instrumental in procuring any person to vote or to offer to vote in any election district in which such person is not at the time a legally qualified voter therein, or who shall advise or in any manner incite any person to vote or offer to vote at any such election in an assumed or fictitious name, shall be adjudged guilty of a felony, and shall, upon conviction thereof, be imprisoned in the state prison for a term of not less than one nor more than three years. Any person who shall swear falsely before said board of registration shall be deemed guilty of willful and corrupt perjury, and on conviction punished as such. If any member or officer of said board shall, knowingly, permit any person to register his name as a voter, or willfully violate any of the provisions of this act, or be guilty of any fraud in the execution of the duties of his office, he shall be punished, upon conviction thereof, for each and every offense, by imprisonment in the state prison for a term of not less than two nor more than five years.

§ 15. The same list required to be made and perfected at general elections shall, in the same manner, be made and perfected by the inspectors at all elections for charter officers in the several cities of this state, and at such elections for charter officers the said board shall hold the first meeting provided for in this act, three weeks prior to such charter election. *Same lists to be made for city as for general elections.*

§ 16. In cities and incorporated villages no building or part of a building shall be designated as a registry or polling place in which, or any part of which, spirituous or intoxicating liquors are sold. *Where liquors are sold not to be polling place.*

§ 17. The secretary of state shall cause this law to be printed, and a sufficient number of copies thereof to be sent to the county clerks of the several counties to supply each of the officers named in this act with a copy; and it shall be the duty of said county clerks, immediately, to transmit a copy of the same to each of the inspectors of election in each city and town of such county. *Secretary of state to print and transmit copies of this law.*

§ 18. Chapter five hundred and seventy-two of the laws of this state, passed April nineteen, eighteen hundred and seventy-one, entitled "An act to amend an act entitled 'An act in relation to elections in the city and county of New York,'" passed April five, eighteen hundred and seventy, be and the same is hereby repealed. *Chapter 572, laws of 1871, repealed.*

§ 19. This act shall not apply except in incorporated cities and villages containing over ten thousand inhabitants each, as determined by the last census. *Where this act to apply.*

§ 20. This act shall take effect immediately.

CHAP. 583.

AN ACT to re-appropriate certain money for the enlargement of the Champlain canal, and also to re-appropriate the sum of forty-four thousand dollars, a portion of the unexpended balance appropriated by chapter seven hundred and sixty-eight of the laws of eighteen hundred and seventy, to pay awards by the canal appraisers and the canal board for the years eighteen hundred and sixty-eight and eighteen hundred and sixty-nine; and further, to re-appropriate the sum of ten thousand dollars, for the purpose of rebuilding of stone the state dam at Troy.

PASSED May 7, 1872; three-fifths being present.

The People of the State of New York, represented in Senate and Assembly, do enact as follows:

Re-appropriation to enlarge Champlain canal. SECTION 1. The sum of three hundred and forty-seven thousand six hundred and twenty-five dollars, being the unexpended balance of four hundred thousand dollars, appropriated by the act entitled "An act to provide and making an appropriation to enlarge the Champlain canal," passed May eighteenth, eighteen hundred and seventy, is hereby re-appropriated to the same object.

Re-appropriation. § 2. The sum of forty-four thousand dollars, being a portion of the unexpended balance of one million and eleven thousand one hundred and thirty-eight dollars and forty-two cents, appropriated by chapter seven hundred and sixty-eight of the laws of eighteen hundred and seventy, to pay awards by the canal appraisers and the canal board, for the years eighteen hundred and sixty-eight and eighteen hundred and sixty-nine, which sum of forty-four thousand dollars being in excess of the amount required for that purpose, is hereby re-appropriated for the following purposes, to be expended under the direction of the canal commissioners:

For dam and guard-lock at Binghamton. For completing the work and paying arrearages due to the contractor on the dam and guard-lock now being constructed in the Susquehanna river at Binghamton, and the section connected therewith, for the canal extension, thirty thousand dollars.

Chenango canal. For commutation money on two bridges discontinued on the Chenango canal extension, two thousand dollars.

Owasco feeder. For the purpose of improving the Owasco feeder at and above the dam now used by the Auburn water-works company, two thousand dollars, or so much thereof as may be necessary to be expended, by and under the direction of the canal commissioners, for the present year.

Miscellaneous. For the payment of damages to certain claimants arising from the temporary diversion of the water of the outlet of

Skaneateles lake, the sum of four thousand dollars, to be settled and paid by the canal commissioners, it being expressly provided that no one claim shall be settled and paid exceeding the sum of six hundred dollars. For the payment of George Heath, for the construction of two of "Heath's patent tumble gates," in locks forty-seven and forty-eight at Syracuse, now being widened, the sum of four thousand dollars, or so much thereof as may be necessary. For the payment of certain expenses incurred in defending the state on trial of claims before the canal appraisers on the Chenango canal extension, two thousand dollars, or so much thereof as may be necessary.

State dam at Troy.

§ 3. The sum of ten thousand dollars appropriated by section one of the act entitled "An act to authorize the tax of one mill per dollar of valuation of the year eighteen hundred and seventy, for construction of new work upon and extraordinary repairs of the canals of this state, passed May ninth, eighteen hundred and seventy," for the purpose of rebuilding of stone the state dam at Troy, is hereby re-appropriated for the same purpose, subject to all of the provisions and requirements of said act.

§ 4. This act shall take effect immediately.

CHAP. 585.

AN ACT to authorize the agent and warden of the Auburn prison to sell certain lands belonging to the state.

PASSED May 7, 1872; three-fifths being present.

The People of the State of New York, represented in Senate and Assembly, do enact as follows:

Agent and warden, under direction of commissioners of the land office, to sell land.

Description of land.

Sale, how made.

SECTION 1. The agent and warden of the Auburn prison, with the approval and under the direction of the commissioners of the land office, is hereby authorized and directed to sell the piece of land belonging to the state, in the city of Auburn, lying south of the lands leading from State street, to the prison dam, being a strip of land thirteen feet and three inches on said State street, and running to a point on said lane, reserving at all times the right of way through the lane on the north side of said land to the prison dam, for the purpose of repairing or reconstructing the same: and also the right at any time of occupying so much of said land as may be necessary for the purposes of placing material for such repairs or reconstruction. Such sale to be made at public auction on said lands, upon the same notice required by law of sheriffs, in case of sale of real estate on execution, and for cash on the day of such sale.

Proceeds, to whom paid.

§ 2. The said agent and warden is directed to pay from the proceeds of said sale, if they are sufficient for that purpose, after paying the expenses thereof, to John W. Farmer, of the town of Fleming, in the county of Cayuga, the sum of one hundred and seven dollars, with interest thereon from the seventh day of April, eighteen hundred and sixty, or so much thereof as the proceeds of said sale will pay of the same.

§ 3. Any surplus moneys not paid pursuant to section two of this act, shall be paid into the treasury of the state.

§ 4. This act shall take effect immediately.

CHAP. 587.

AN ACT to authorize the appointment of assistant district attorneys in certain counties in this state.

PASSED May 7, 1872; three-fifths being present.

The People of the State of New York, represented in Senate and Assembly, do enact as follows:

Supervisors may authorize appointment of assistant district attorney.

SECTION 1. It shall be lawful for the supervisors of any county in this state having at its last census a population exceeding seventy thousand, to authorize the district attorney of such county to appoint a suitable person to be the assistant of such district attorney. Every such appointee must be a counselor at law and a citizen and resident of the county in which he is appointed. Every such appointment shall be in writing, under the hand and seal of the district attorney, and shall be filed in the clerk's office of the county in which such appointment is made. Every such person before he enters upon the duties of his office, shall take and subscribe the constitutional oath of office. Every such appointment may be revoked by the district attorney making the same, which revocation shall be in writing, and shall be filed in the said county clerk's office.

Qualification of appointee. Appointment by district attorney. Official oath. Revocation.

Powers and duties of.

§ 2. It shall be lawful for every such assistant to attend all the criminal courts which may be held in his county, and to assist in conducting all prosecutions for crimes and offenses cognizable therein. It shall also be lawful for every such assistant to attend and appear before any grand jury in his said county, and to perform the same duties before such jury as are by law imposed upon or required by the district attorney.

Compensation.

§ 3. Every such assistant district attorney shall be compensated for his services at and after such annual rate as shall be determined by the board of supervisors of the county in and for which he shall be appointed.

Not to apply to certain counties.

§ 4. The provisions of this act shall not apply to any county where the appointment of an assistant district attorney is now authorized by law.

§ 5. This act shall take effect immediately.

CHAP. 598.

AN ACT for the better preservation of horse records.

PASSED May 8, 1872; three-fifths being present.

The People of the State of New York, represented in Senate and Assembly, do enact as follows:

SECTION 1. Any person or persons owning or keeping a stallion for breeding purposes shall be required, before advertising the services of said stallion, to file a certificate, under oath, with the county clerk of the county where said stallion is owned or kept, stating name, color, age, size, together with the pedigree of said stallion as full as attainable, and the name of the person by whom said stallion was bred. Any person who shall neglect to make and file a certificate required by the provisions of this act, or who shall willfully make and file a false certificate of the statements aforesaid, shall forfeit the sum of one hundred dollars, to be recovered in any court of competent jurisdiction. It shall be the duty of the district attorney of the county wherein said stallion is owned or kept to commence an action for the recovery of the forfeiture hereby allowed upon his receiving satisfactory evidence that such advertisement has been made and that the certificate has not been filed as herein required, or that a false certificate has been so filed, said action to be brought in the name of the people of this state; in all actions wherein the penalty prescribed by this act shall be recovered and collected, one-half thereof shall be paid to the person furnishing the proof upon which such recovery was procured, and one-half shall be paid to the treasurer of the county for the support of the poor.

Owners and keepers of stallions for breeding purposes to file certificate. Certificate, what to contain. Penalty. Duty of district attorney to prosecute. Penalty recovered, to whom paid.

§ 2. This act shall take effect immediately.

CHAP. 599.

AN ACT to amend chapter three hundred and forty-six of the laws of eighteen hundred and fifty-nine, entitled "An act concerning the salt springs and the manufacture of salt," passed April fifteenth, eighteen hundred and fifty-nine.

PASSED May 8, 1872; three-fifths being present.

The People of the State of New York, represented in Senate and Assembly, do enact as follows:

SECTION 1. Section thirty-three of chapter three hundred and forty-six of the laws of eighteen hundred and fifty-nine, entitled "An act concerning the salt springs and the manufacture of salt," passed April fifteenth, eighteen hundred and fifty-nine, is hereby amended by adding thereto at the end thereof,

Property taken, how paid for.

town of Fleming, in the county of Cayuga, the sum of one hundred and seven dollars, with interest thereon from the seventh day of April, eighteen hundred and sixty, or so much thereof as the proceeds of said sale will pay of the same.

§ 3. Any surplus moneys not paid pursuant to section two of this act, shall be paid into the treasury of the state.

§ 4. This act shall take effect immediately.

CHAP. 587.

AN ACT to authorize the appointment of assistant district attorneys in certain counties in this state.

PASSED May 7, 1872; three-fifths being present.

The People of the State of New York, represented in Senate and Assembly, do enact as follows:

Supervisors may authorize appointment of assistant district attorney. Qualifications of appointee. Appointment by district attorney. Official oath. Revocation.

SECTION 1. It shall be lawful for the supervisors of any county in this state having at its last census a population exceeding seventy thousand, to authorize the district attorney of such county to appoint a suitable person to be the assistant of such district attorney. Every such appointee must be a counselor at law and a citizen and resident of the county in which he is appointed. Every such appointment shall be in writing, under the hand and seal of the district attorney, and shall be filed in the clerk's office of the county in which such appointment is made. Every such person before he enters upon the duties of his office, shall take and subscribe the constitutional oath of office. Every such appointment may be revoked by the district attorney making the same, which revocation shall be in writing, and shall be filed in the said county clerk's office.

Powers and duties of.

§ 2. It shall be lawful for every such assistant to attend all the criminal courts which may be held in his county, and to assist in conducting all prosecutions for crimes and offenses cognizable therein. It shall also be lawful for every such assistant to attend and appear before any grand jury in his said county, and to perform the same duties before such jury as are by law imposed upon or required by the district attorney.

Compensation.

§ 3. Every such assistant district attorney shall be compensated for his services at and after such annual rate as shall be determined by the board of supervisors of the county in and for which he shall be appointed.

Not to apply to certain counties.

§ 4. The provisions of this act shall not apply to any county where the appointment of an assistant district attorney is now authorized by law.

§ 5. This act shall take effect immediately.

CHAP. 598.

AN ACT for the better preservation of horse records.

PASSED May 8, 1872; three-fifths being present.

The People of the State of New York, represented in Senate and Assembly, do enact as follows:

SECTION 1. Any person or persons owning or keeping a stallion for breeding purposes shall be required, before advertising the services of said stallion, to file a certificate, under oath, with the county clerk of the county where said stallion is owned or kept, stating name, color, age, size, together with the pedigree of said stallion as full as attainable, and the name of the person by whom said stallion was bred. Any person who shall neglect to make and file a certificate required by the provisions of this act, or who shall willfully make and file a false certificate of the statements aforesaid, shall forfeit the sum of one hundred dollars, to be recovered in any court of competent jurisdiction. It shall be the duty of the district attorney of the county wherein said stallion is owned or kept to commence an action for the recovery of the forfeiture hereby allowed upon his receiving satisfactory evidence that such advertisement has been made and that the certificate has not been filed as herein required, or that a false certificate has been so filed, said action to be brought in the name of the people of this state; in all actions wherein the penalty prescribed by this act shall be recovered and collected, one-half thereof shall be paid to the person furnishing the proof upon which such recovery was procured, and one-half shall be paid to the treasurer of the county for the support of the poor.

Owners and keepers of stallions for breeding purposes to file certificate.

Certificate, what to contain.

Penalty.

Duty of district attorney to prosecute.

Penalty recovered, to whom paid.

§ 2. This act shall take effect immediately.

CHAP. 599.

AN ACT to amend chapter three hundred and forty-six of the laws of eighteen hundred and fifty-nine, entitled "An act concerning the salt springs and the manufacture of salt," passed April fifteenth, eighteen hundred and fifty-nine.

PASSED May 8, 1872; three-fifths being present.

The People of the State of New York, represented in Senate and Assembly, do enact as follows:

SECTION 1. Section thirty-three of chapter three hundred and forty-six of the laws of eighteen hundred and fifty-nine, entitled "An act concerning the salt springs and the manufacture of salt," passed April fifteenth, eighteen hundred and fifty-nine, is hereby amended by adding thereto at the end thereof,

Property taken, how paid for.

the following: "Any property taken by virtue of this section shall be paid for by agreement or appraisement, in the manner provided for in the thirty-first section of this act."

Ante, vol. 3, p. 217.

To what water act to apply. § 2. This act shall only apply to water taken from the nine mile creek during the period of suspended navigation of the Erie canal, for the purpose of working the state pumps on the salt springs reservation.

§ 3. This act shall take effect immediately.

CHAP. 609.

AN ACT to amend an act entitled "An act to authorize the formation, establishing and maintaining of driving park and park associations," passed April seventeenth, eighteen hundred and seventy-two.

Ante, p. 342.

PASSED May 9, 1872; three-fifths being present.

The People of the State of New York, represented in Senate and Assembly, do enact as follows:

SECTION 1. Section one of an act entitled "An act to authorize the formation, establishing and maintaining of driving park and park associations," is hereby amended so as to read as follows:

Associations, how formed. § 1. Any six or more persons of full age, citizens of this state, who shall desire to form a driving park, park or agricultural association in this state, may make, sign and acknowledge, before any officer authorized to take the acknowledgment of deeds in this state, and file in the office of the secretary of state, and also in the clerk's office of the county in which the business of such association is to be conducted, a certificate in writing, wherein shall be stated the name and title whereby such association shall be known in law, the amount of its capital stock, the number of shares into which such capital stock is divided, the location, particular business and objects of such association, the number of trustees, directors or managers to manage the same, and the names of such trustees, directors or managers for the first year of its existence. Such articles of association shall not be filed as aforesaid until one-twentieth part of the amount of stock, fixed as aforesaid, shall have been actually paid in to the directors in cash, and until there shall be indorsed thereon or annexed thereto an affidavit made by at least three of the directors named in such articles of association, that the amount of stock required in the first section of this act to be subscribed has been subscribed and that one-twentieth part of the amount has been actually paid in as aforesaid.

(Margin notes: Certificates to be filed. What to contain. When articles may be filed.)

§ 2. Section four of said act is hereby amended so as to read as follows:

§ 4. The officers of any such association shall consist of a president, and at least one vice-president, a secretary, a treasurer, and any number of directors which is divisible by three, but not more than fifteen in all. The president and vice-president, secretary and treasurer shall be elected annually; and the first year the whole number of directors shall be elected, they shall be divided by lot into three classes; the first class to serve one year, the second class two years and the third class three years; and at the expiration of each term a sufficient number of directors shall be elected to fill each class, and to serve three years; and all vacancies that may occur shall be filled only for the term made vacant. The election of all officers shall be by ballot of the stockholders or members, who shall have been such not less than thirty days prior to such election, and no person who is not a stockholder shall be eligible to any office. The board of managers shall consist of the president, the first vice-president, secretary, treasurer and directors, a majority of whom shall constitute a quorum for the transaction of business; and it shall be the duty of said officers to so manage the property and concerns of the said society as will best promote the objects of such association as set forth in the certificate of incorporation, and they may hold one or more fairs and exhibitions annually, and distribute premiums to the best and most meritorious exhibitors in their several departments, and may charge for admission to its grounds, also for the use of them or any part thereof.

Officers.

Directors to be classified.

Election to be by ballot.

Board of managers, of whom to consist.

Exhibitions.

§ 3. The title of said act is hereby amended so as to read as follows: To authorize the formation, establishing and maintaining of driving park, park, and agricultural associations.

Title.

§ 4. This act shall take effect immediately.

CHAP. 611.

AN ACT in relation to the capital stock of corporations.

PASSED May 9, 1872.

The People of the State of New York, represented in Senate and Assembly, do enact as follows:

SECTION 1. An incorporation, incorporated company, society or association formed under the laws of this state, excepting banks, banking associations, trust companies, life, health, accident, marine and fire insurance companies, railroad and navigation and gas companies, may increase its capital stock, as provided by section twentieth of "An act to authorize the formation of corporations for manufacturing, mining, mechanical or chemical purposes," passed February seventeenth, eighteen hundred and forty-eight; provided that this act shall not apply to corporations created by special act of incorpora-

Capital stock, how increased.

Amount limited. tion, the capital stock of which originally exceeded two hundred thousand dollars, and that such increase shall not exceed in the aggregate the amount of capital stock specified in the said act of incorporation, and any such corporation the capital of which shall be increased under the provisions of this act, and the stockholders thereof shall be subject to all the liabilities as regards such additional capital as is provided in the original act or charter in relation to its capital.

§ 2. This act shall take effect immediately.

Ante, vol. 8, pp. 726, 733.

CHAP. 613.

AN ACT re-appropriating a certain portion of the income of the United States deposit fund for the benefit of academies.

PASSED May 9, 1872; three-fifths being present.

The People of the State of New York, represented in Senate and Assembly, do enact as follows:

Regents of the university may expend balance of appropriation in purchase of books, etc. SECTION 1. The Regents of the University are hereby authorized to apply one thousand and five hundred dollars, of the unexpended balance of the appropriation made by chapter seven hundred and eighteen of the laws of eighteen hundred and seventy-one, for the instruction of teachers of common schools, to the purchase of books and apparatus pursuant to chapter five hundred and thirty-six of the laws of eighteen hundred and fifty-one.

Ante, vol. 3 p. 426.

§ 2. This act shall take effect immediately.

CHAP. 616.

AN ACT to amend chapter seven hundred and forty-four of the laws of eighteen hundred and sixty-seven, entitled "An act to define the objects of the New York State Institution for the Blind and to provide for its management," passed April twenty-fourth, eighteen hundred and sixty-seven.

Ante, vol. 7, p. 154.

PASSED May 9, 1872; three-fifths being present.

The People of the State of New York, represented in Senate and Assembly, do enact as follows:

SECTION 1. Section three of chapter seven hundred and forty-four of the laws of eighteen hundred and sixty-seven, entitled "An act to define the objects of the New York State Institution for the Blind, and to provide for its management," passed April twenty-fourth, eighteen hundred and sixty-seven, is hereby amended so as to read as follows:

§ 3. Applications for admission into the institution shall be made to the board of trustees in such manner as they may direct, but the board shall require such application to be accompanied by a certificate from the county judge or county clerk of the county or the supervisor or town clerk of the town or the mayor of the city where the applicant resides, setting forth that the applicant is a legal resident of the town, county and state claimed as his or her residence. Applications for admission, how made. Certificate required.

§ 2. This act shall take effect immediately.

CHAP. 619.

AN ACT dividing the state into congressional districts.

PASSED May 6, 1872; notwithstanding the objections of the governor.

The People of the State of New York, represented in Senate and Assembly, do enact as follows:

SECTION 1. For the election of representatives in congress of the United States, this state shall be and is hereby divided into thirty-two districts, namely: Congressional districts.

The counties of Suffolk, Queens and Richmond shall compose the first district. 1st district.

The first, second, fifth, sixth, eighth, tenth, twelfth and twenty-second wards of the city of Brooklyn shall compose the second district. 2d district.

The third, fourth, seventh, eleventh, thirteenth, nineteenth and twentieth wards of the city of Brooklyn, and the twenty-first ward of said city, as bounded by section two of chapter eight hundred and fourteen of the laws of eighteen hundred and sixty-eight, shall compose the third district. 3d district.

The ninth ward of the city of Brooklyn, as bounded by section one of chapter eight hundred and fourteen of the laws of eighteen hundred and sixty-eight, the fourteenth, fifteenth, sixteenth, seventeenth and eighteenth wards of said city, and the towns of Flatbush, Flatlands, Gravesend, New Lots and New Utrecht, in the county of Kings, shall compose the fourth district. 4th district.

The first, second, third, fourth, fifth, sixth, seventh, eighth and fourteenth wards of the city of New York and Governor's Island shall compose the fifth district. 5th district.

The eleventh and thirteenth wards of the city of New York, and that portion of the eighteenth and twenty first wards of said city lying east of Third avenue, shall compose the sixth district. 6th district.

The tenth and seventeenth wards of the city of New York, and that portion of the eighteenth ward of said city lying west of Third avenue, shall compose the seventh district. 7th district.

The ninth, fifteenth and sixteenth wards of the city of New York, and that portion of the twenty-first ward of said city 8th district.

lying west of Third avenue, shall compose the eighth district.

9th district. The twentieth and twenty-second wards of the city of New York shall compose the ninth district.

10th district. The twelfth and nineteenth wards of the city of New York, and Blackwell's, Ward's and Randall's Islands shall compose the tenth district.

11th district. The counties of Westchester, Rockland and Putnam shall compose the eleventh district.

12th district. The counties of Orange and Sullivan shall compose the twelfth district.

13th district. The counties of Dutchess and Columbia shall compose the thirteenth district.

14th district. The counties of Ulster and Greene shall compose the fourteenth district.

15th district. The counties of Albany and Schoharie shall compose the fifteenth district.

16th district. The counties of Rensselaer and Washington shall compose the sixteenth district.

17th district. The counties of Warren, Essex and Clinton shall compose the seventeenth district.

18th district. The counties of St. Lawrence and Franklin shall compose the eighteenth district.

19th district. The counties of Fulton, Hamilton, Montgomery, Saratoga and Schenectady shall compose the nineteenth district.

20th district. The counties of Delaware, Otsego and Chenango shall compose the twentieth district.

21st district. The counties of Jefferson, Lewis and Herkimer shall compose the twenty-first district.

22d district. The county of Oneida shall compose the twenty-second district.

23d district. The counties of Madison and Oswego shall compose the twenty-third district.

24th district. The counties of Onondaga and Cortland shall compose the twenty-fourth district.

25th district. The counties of Cayuga, Wayne and Seneca shall compose the twenty-fifth district.

26th district. The counties of Ontario, Livingston and Yates shall compose the twenty-sixth district.

27th district. The counties of Tioga, Tompkins, Broome and Schuyler shall compose the twenty-seventh district.

28th district. The counties of Chemung, Steuben and Allegany shall compose the twenty-eighth district.

29th district. The counties of Monroe and Orleans shall compose the twenty-ninth district.

30th district. The counties of Genesee, Niagara and Wyoming shall compose the thirtieth district.

31st district. The county of Erie shall compose the thirty-first district.

32d district. The counties of Chautauqua and Cattaraugus shall compose the thirty-second district.

CHAP. 627.

AN ACT in relation to the court for the trial of impeachment.

PASSED May 10, 1872.

The People of the State of New York, represented in Senate and Assembly, do enact as follows:

SECTION 1. The court for the trial of impeachment shall be a court of record, and when summoned shall meet at the capitol in the city of Albany. After the defendant shall have appeared, the court shall appoint a time and place in the city of Albany or elsewhere, for the further proceedings and trial of the impeachment. The clerk and officers of the senate shall be the clerk and officers of said court and the president of the senate shall preside therein, and in his absence the chief judge of the court of appeals shall preside, and in the absence of the president of the senate and the chief judge, such other member shall preside as the court shall elect. A court of record. Court to appoint time and place for trial. Clerk and officers.

§ 2. The seal of the court for the trial of impeachments heretofore procured and now deposited and recorded in the office of the secretary of state shall continue to be the seal of the court for the trial of impeachments organized under this act. Seal.

§ 3. All laws relating to the court for the trial of impeachments, the jurisdiction, powers and duties thereof, the proceedings therein, and the officers thereof, and their powers and duties shall be applicable to the court for the trial of impeachments organized by this act, the jurisdiction, powers and duties thereof, the proceedings therein, and the officers thereof, and their powers and duties so far as the same can be so applied, and are consistent with the constitution and the provisions of this act. Jurisdiction, powers and duties as prescribed by existing laws.

§ 4. This act shall take effect immediately.

CHAP. 649.

AN ACT further to amend chapter three hundred and nineteen of the laws of eighteen hundred and forty-eight, entitled "An act for the incorporation of benevolent, charitable, scientific and missionary societies," and the several acts amendatory thereof.

PASSED May 11, 1872.

The People of the State of New York, represented in Senate and Assembly, do enact as follows:

SECTION 1. Section one of chapter three hundred and nineteen of the laws of eighteen hundred and forty-eight, entitled

"An act for the incorporation of benevolent, charitable, scientific and missionary societies," is hereby amended so as to read as follows:

Societies, how formed. § 1. Any five or more persons of full age, a majority of whom shall be citizens of and residents within the state, who shall desire to associate themselves together for benevolent, charitable, literary, scientific, missionary, or mission or other Sunday school purposes, or for the purpose of mutual improvement in religious knowledge or the furtherance of religious opinion, or for any two or more of such objects combined, may make, sign, and acknowledge, before any person authorized to take the acknowledgment of deeds in this state, and file in the office of the clerk of the county in which the business of such society is to be conducted, certificates in writing, in which shall be stated the name or title by which such society shall be known in law, the particular business and objects of such society, the number of trustees, directors or managers to manage the same, and the names of the trustees, directors or managers of such society for the first year of its existence; Certificate not to be filed unless by consent of a justice of the supreme court. but such certificate shall not be filed, unless by the written consent and approbation of one of the justices of the supreme court of the district in which the place of business or principal office of such society shall be located, to be indorsed on such certificate.

Certain words stricken section 2 of act amended, and others substituted in their places. § 2. The second section of said act is hereby amended by striking out the words "fifty thousand dollars" where they occur in said section, and inserting in lieu thereof the words "one hundred and fifty-thousand dollars;" by striking out the words "seventy-five thousand dollars" where they occur in said section, and inserting in lieu thereof the words "one hundred and fifty thousand dollars," and by striking out the words "ten thousand dollars" where they occur in said section, and inserting in lieu thereof the words "thirty thousand dollars," so that the associations which may be incorporated under the acts hereby amended shall be capable of taking, receiving, purchasing and holding for the purposes of their incorporation, and for no other purpose, real estate to an amount not exceeding one hundred and fifty thousand dollars, and personal estate to an amount not exceeding one hundred and fifty thousand dollars, provided that the clear annual income of such real and personal estate shall not exceed thirty thousand dollars.

§ 3. This act shall take effect immediately.

Ante, vol. 3, pp. 705, 708, 709.

CHAP. 651.

AN ACT to provide for the construction of a canal bridge over the Erie canal at Madison street, in the city of Rome.

PASSED May 18, 1872; three-fifths being present.

The People of the State of New York, represented in Senate and Assembly, do enact as follows:

SECTION 1. The canal commissioners are hereby authorized and directed to construct a suitable iron bridge with roadway nineteen feet clear, and two sidewalks each six and a half feet clear, over the Erie canal at Madison street in the city of Rome, Oneida county, New York, provided, however, that before proceeding to the construction of any such bridge, the canal commissioners shall require and receive a full and sufficient release, executed, acknowledged and delivered free of expense to the state, of all claims for damages in consequence of the construction of said bridge or of the approaches and embankments of the same, and also a good and sufficient license or permission to the state duly executed, acknowledged and delivered as aforesaid, to alter, raise or change such bridge, approaches or embankments whenever necessary, which necessity is to be determined by the canal commissioners, from all persons whose property, rights or interests may be affected by such bridge approaches or embankments. Canal commissioners to construct iron bridge in the city of Rome. Proviso as to releases to the state.

§ 2. The treasurer shall pay, on the warrant of the auditor of the canal department, out of any money appropriated for extraordinary repairs of the eastern division of the canals, such sum not exceeding the sum of five thousand dollars, as shall be necessary to defray the expenses of the performance of the work authorized by the first section of this act. Treasurer to pay on warrant of auditor, not exceeding $5,000, to defray expense of bridge.

§ 3. This act shall take effect immediately.

CHAP. 652.

AN ACT to authorize the construction of a draw or swing bridge over the Erie canal in the city of Utica.

PASSED May 18, 1872; three-fifths being present.

The People of the State of New York, represented in Senate and Assembly, do enact as follows:

SECTION 1. The canal commissioners are hereby authorized to construct a draw or swing bridge over the Erie canal at its junction with Hotel street in the city of Utica, and the expense thereof shall be paid from any appropriation made for extra- Canal commissioners to construct swing bridge over Erie canal, in Utica. City to convey to state land necessary to be used. Releases to be executed to state. City to provide for expense of care of bridge.

ordinary repairs on the eastern division of the canals, provided that the pier or abutment on which said bridge shall swing shall not be erected or placed in the prism of the canal; and provided further, that before proceeding to the construction of such bridge the city of Utica shall purchase and convey to the state, without cost, the land necessary to be used for the purposes of said bridge, and that the canal commissioners shall require and receive a full and sufficient release, legally executed, acknowledged and delivered free of expense to the state, of all claims for damages in consequence of the construction of said bridge, or of the approaches and embankments of the same, and also a good and sufficient license or permission to the state, duly executed, acknowledged and delivered as aforesaid, to alter, raise or change such bridge, approaches or embankments, when necessary, which necessity is to be determined by the canal commissioners, from all persons whose property, rights or interests may be affected by such bridge, approaches or embankments, and further, that said city shall provide for the expense of attending to and care of said bridge, in opening of the same for the passage of boats without cost to the state.

§ 2. This act shall take effect immediately.

CHAP. 653.

AN ACT to amend an act entitled "An act to authorize the canal commissioners to construct a swing bridge over the Erie canal on Buffalo street in the city of Rochester, and to use the materials of the old bridge in constructing a bridge over said canal, to connect Munger and Averill streets in said city," passed April seventh, eighteen hundred and seventy-one.

PASSED May 18, 1872; three-fifths being present.

The People of the State of New York, represented in Senate and Assembly, do enact as follows:

SECTION 1. Section one of an act entitled "An act to authorize the canal commissioners to construct a swing bridge over the Erie canal on Buffalo street, in the city of Rochester, and to use the materials of the old bridge in constructing a bridge over said canal, to connect Munger and Averill streets in said city," passed April seventh, eighteen hundred and seventy-one, is hereby amended so as to read as follows:

Canal commissioners to construct swing bridge over Erie canal, at

§ 1. The canal commissioners are hereby authorized and required to construct a swing or turn-table bridge over the Erie canal, in the city of Rochester, at a point where said canal is intersected by Buffalo street, in place of the bridge now over said canal at the point aforesaid; said swing bridge shall be located on such a line as shall be most practicable, and in the opinion of the state engineer most conducive, to the best interests of the state and the citizens using the same. Buffalo street, Rochester.

§ 2. This act shall take effect immediately.

CHAP. 669.

AN ACT in relation to mechanics' liens.

PASSED May 18, 1872; three-fifths being present.

The People of the State of New York, represented in Senate and Assembly, do enact as follows:

SECTION 1. All the provisions of the laws relating to mechanics' liens heretofore passed shall apply to wharves, piers, bulkheads and bridges and materials furnished therefor, and labor performed in constructing said wharves, piers, bulkheads and bridges and other structures connected therewith, and the time within which said liens may be filed shall be thirty days from the time when the last work shall have been performed on said wharves, piers, bulkheads and bridges and structures connected therewith, or the time from which said materials shall have been delivered. This act shall apply to all incomplete work commenced previous to the passage of this act. Provisions of law relative to mechanics' liens to apply to wharves, piers, etc. To apply to incomplete work

§ 2. This act shall take effect immediately.

Ante, vol. 4, p. 669; vol. 7, p. 456.

CHAP. 670.

AN ACT relative to the care and education of deaf mutes.

PASSED May 18, 1872; three-fifths being present.

The People of the State of New York, represented in Senate and Assembly, do enact as follows:

SECTION 1. Sections nine and ten of title one of an act entitled "An act to revise and consolidate the general acts relating to the public instruction," passed May second, eighteen hundred and sixty-four, are hereby amended so that the same shall extend and apply to The Le Couteulx St. Mary's Institution for the improved instruction of deaf mutes in the city of Buffalo, in the like maner and with the like effect as if said institution had originally been named in the said sections respectively. Provisions of existing law to apply to The Le Couteulx St. Mary's Institution of Buffalo.

§ 2. This act shall take effect immediately.

Ante, vol. 6, p. 365.

CHAP. 680.

AN ACT to amend an act entitled "An act in relation to wills," passed April twenty-third, eighteen hundred and sixty-four.

PASSED May 14, 1872; three-fifths being present.

The People of the State of New York, represented in Senate and Assembly, do enact as follows:

SECTION 1. The first section of the act entitled "An act in relation to wills," passed April twenty-third, eighteen hundred and sixty-four, is hereby amended so as to read as follows:

Ante, vol. 6, p. 254

Wills probated in other states, exemplified copies and the proofs thereof may be recorded in this state.

§ 1. Where any real estate situate in this state has been, or shall hereafter be, devised by any person residing out of this state, and within any other state or territory of the United States, and the last will and testament of such person shall have been finally admitted to probate in such other state or territory, and filed or recorded in the office or court where the same shall have been admitted to probate, an exemplified copy of said last will and testament, or of such record thereof, and of the proofs, may be recorded in the office of the surrogate of any county in this state where any real estate so devised is situated, which record in said surrogate's office, or an exemplified copy thereof, shall be, in cases where the original cannot be produced, presumptive evidence of said will and of the due execution thereof, in all actions or proceedings relating to the lands so devised.

Evidence.

§ 2. This act shall take effect immediately.

CHAP. 693.

AN ACT in relation to the service of citations on lunatics and idiots.

PASSED May 14, 1872; three-fifths being present.

The People of the State of New York, represented in Senate and Assembly, do enact as follows:

Service of citations on idiots, lunatics, etc.

SECTION 1. In proceedings for the proof of any last will and testament, or on any accounting or other proceeding in the surrogates' court, where any party entitled to be served with a citation shall be insane or an idiot, the citation shall be served on the lunatic or idiot and on the committee of the person and estate, or of either, of such lunatic or idiot; and in case there shall not be any committee of the person and estate, or of either, then the citation shall be served on the lunatic or idiot personally, and also on the person in whose care and custody said lunatic or idiot shall be.

§ 2. Whenever a citation shall have been served on any lunatic or idiot, the surrogate shall appoint a special guardian for said lunatic or idiot, whose duty it shall be to take the care and charge of the interest of said lunatic or idiot on the proceedings for which he shall be cited. Special guardians to be appointed.

CHAP. 696.

AN ACT to amend chapter two hundred and nine of the laws of eighteen hundred and forty-seven, entitled "An act in relation to cemeteries in incorporated villages."

PASSED May 14, 1872; three-fifths being present.

The People of the State of New York, represented in Senate and Assembly, do enact as follows:

SECTION 1. Section one of chapter two hundred and nine of the laws of eighteen hundred and forty-seven, entitled "An act in relation to cemeteries in incorporated villages," as amended by chapter one hundred and seventeen of the laws of eighteen hundred and sixty-four, is hereby amended so as to read as follows:

§ 1. The tax payers of any incorporated village, at any meeting thereof lawfully convened, may, by resolution, direct the trustees of such village to purchase suitable lands for a burying ground for such village, or lands in addition to any burying ground now owned by said village, upon such terms and conditions, not inconsistent with this act, as such meeting shall prescribe; but the whole expense of purchasing such ground or additional lands in any village, fencing the same, and putting it in proper condition to be used as a burying ground, shall not exceed ten thousand dollars, unless the population of the village shall exceed four thousand persons, nor more than twenty thousand dollars in any case. And the title of such burying ground, when so purchased, shall be vested in such village by its corporate name, and shall be inalienable, except in the manner and for the purposes hereinafter mentioned. Tax payers of any village may direct trustees to purchase suitable lands for a cemetery. Expense limited. Title to vest in village.

§ 2. This act shall take effect immediately.

Ante, vol. 3, p. 749.

CHAP. 698.

AN ACT to amend an act entitled "An act respecting elections other than for militia and town officers," passed April fifth, eighteen hundred and forty-two.

PASSED May 14, 1872.

The People of the State of New York, represented in Senate and Assembly, do enact as follows:

SECTION 1. The third subdivision of the sixth section of the second title of chapter one hundred and thirty of the laws of eighteen hundred and forty-two, is amended so as to read as follows:

Vacancies in office of senator or member of assembly, how filled.

§ 3. When a vacancy exists in the office of any senator or member of assembly occurring after the first day of January in any year, the same shall be filled at the first election held thereafter in any such district where such vacancy may occur, or at a special election to be called by the governor for that purpose; provided such vacancy occurs during the first year of the term of any senator, or before the first day of March, in the second year of the term of any senator. But no vacancy shall be filled for the office of member of assembly, unless the same shall occur on or before the first day of April, in any year, unless the legislature is in session at the time such vacancy and election shall take place.

§ 2. This act shall take effect immediately.

CHAP. 699.

AN ACT to establish a rifle range and to promote skill in marksmanship among the national guard.

PASSED May 14, 1872; three-fifths being present.

The People of the State of New York, represented in Senate and Assembly, do enact as follows:

When sum of $25,000, appropriated by this act, to be expended.

SECTION 1. Whenever the national rifle association shall raise the sum of five thousand dollars, for the purpose of securing, by lease or purchase, of a rifle range for the use of first and second divisions of the national guard of the state of New York, and of such association, and for the purchase and erection of the necessary buildings and appurtenances to fit up and equip the same, and shall, by resolution of its board of directors, appropriate the same to such purpose, the sum of twenty-five thousand dollars, which is hereby appropriated out of any funds in the treasury not otherwise appropriated, shall be expended for the same purpose, as hereinafter provided.

Grounds to be selected

§ 2. The grounds for such range shall be selected by the board of directors of said national rifle association, and their location, together with the price to be paid therefor, shall be approved by the adjutant-general of the state, and also by the officers then commanding the first and second divisions of the said national guard, or by a majority of such officers, which approval shall be in writing, and shall be filed with the comptroller before any of the moneys hereby appropriated shall be expended for the payment hereof.

By board of directors and approved by adjutant-general, etc.

§ 3. The fitting up, equipping and managing of such range shall be done by the board of directors of said national rifle association, of which board the person holding the office of adjutant-general of the state and those commanding the first and second divisions of said national guard shall hereafter always be ex-officio members; and no moneys in excess of one hundred dollars shall be expended for such purpose without a two-third vote of such directors, and without the approval of at least two of such ex-officio members.

Fitting up, etc., to be done by board of managers.

Ex-officio members.

§ 4. The comptroller of the state is hereby authorized and directed to draw his warrant upon the treasury of the state for the payment of the moneys expended by said board of directors for the purposes aforesaid, as the same shall be drawn upon by them from time to time, but no drafts shall be drawn by said board upon the funds hereby appropriated, except for an expenditure authorized and approved as provided in the preceding section.

When and how money appropriated to be drawn from treasury.

§ 5. All such drafts shall specify upon their face the purpose for which they are drawn, and shall be drawn by the treasurer of said association and countersigned by another of the officers thereof, and by at least one of such ex-officio members of the said board of directors, and shall, in case such draft exceed the sum of one hundred dollars, be accompanied with the vouchers therefor, approved by two of such ex-officio members, and by the oath of the treasurer of said association, certifying that the sum or sums so ordered to be paid have been expended for the purpose of leasing or purchasing such range, or fitting up the same, or that the labor and materials have been duly performed or furnished thereon. It shall also be the duty of the treasurer of said association to file with said comptroller, every six months a detailed account of all expenditures of said association during said period, verified by him under oath.

Drafts, how drawn and countersigned.

Vouchers.

Detailed account of expenditure to be filed with comptroller.

§ 6. No officer or member of said board of directors of said national rifle association, nor any of the officers named herein as ex-officio members of such board, shall be in any way interested, directly or indirectly, in any of the contracts made by said association for the purposes aforesaid, or in any of the purchases or expenditures made under the provisions of this act; neither shall they, or any of them, receive any salary or compensation for any services they may render in and about the purchase or fitting up of such range, or the management thereof.

No officer or member of board of directors to be interested in any contract made under provisions of this act nor receive any salary for services.

§ 7. The said board of directors of said national rifle association are hereby authorized, from time to time, to establish regulations for the use and management of such range, and

Rules and regulations.

shall have power to employ the necessary markers and assistants, which regulations shall be in writing, and shall be approved by said adjutant-general and the officers then commanding the first and second divisions of said national guard, or a majority of them, before becoming operative.

Persons employed thereon invested with powers of constables.

§ 8. For the purpose of preserving the property of the state, and of said National Rifle Association upon said range, and of preventing accidents, the persons employed thereon by said rifle association are hereby vested with the powers of constables when in the performance of their duties, and wearing such badge of office as shall be prescribed by said association, and all persons trespassing upon such range, or injuring any of the targets or other property situate thereon, or willfully violating any of the regulations established to secure safety thereon, shall be deemed guilty of a misdemeanor.

Commanding officer may direct any regiment to use said range.

§ 9. The commanding officer of either of the first or second divisions of said national guard is hereby authorized to direct the use of said range by any of the regiments of his command without compensation for practice, field drill or any military purpose, whenever, and for such time, as he shall deem it proper or necessary.

Military stores for practice upon such range.

§ 10. The commander-in-chief is hereby authorized to direct the issuing of such ammunition and military equipments from the stores of the state for use upon said range by the national guard, or for rifle practice elsewhere by them, at such times and under such regulations as he shall prescribe.

"State prize" for greatest proficiency in marksmanship.

§ 11. The said commander-in-chief is also authorized to offer annually, on behalf of the state of New York, a prize not exceeding one hundred dollars in value, to be known as the "State prize," to that regiment or battalion in each division throughout the state, which shall display the greatest proficiency in marksmanship during each year, and a similar prize, not to exceed the sum of five hundred dollars in value, to the regiment or battalion which shall surpass in that respect all other regiments throughout the state during each year. Such prizes to be competed for under regulations to be established by said National Rifle Association, and approved by the commander-in-chief. And the comptroller is hereby authorized to draw his warrant in favor of the adjutant-general for the costs of such prizes, not to exceed the sum of fifteen hundred dollars in any one year, out of any moneys appropriated for military purposes.

Supervisors may appropriate for purposes provided in first section.

§ 12. The boards of supervisors of the counties of New York and Kings may each, in their discretion, appropriate an amount not to exceed the sum of five thousand dollars, in any one year, for the purposes provided in the first section of this act; and they are hereby authorized to levy a tax for such purpose upon the real and personal property of said county or counties, to be levied and collected as other moneys authorized by law are by them levied and collected.

§ 13. This act shall take effect immediately.

CHAP. 700.

AN ACT to supply deficiencies in former appropriations and to pay the indebtedness of the state on account of the canals, which deficiencies and indebtedness have been changed into liabilities for money borrowed to pay them, or into certificates of indebtedness on which the state is now paying interest, and to pay the floating indebtedness of the state, and the estimated liabilities for the present fiscal year not yet provided for by law, and to raise money therefor, by an issue of the bonds of the state, and to provide for submitting the question thereon to the people.

PASSED May 15, 1872; three-fifths being present.

The People of the State of New York, represented in Senate and Assembly, do enact as follows:

Appropriation for deficiencies and indebtedness.

SECTION 1. To supply deficiencies in former appropriations, and to pay the indebtedness of the state on account of the canals, which deficiencies and indebtedness have been changed into liabilities for money borrowed to pay them, or into certificates of indebtedness on which the state is now paying interest, and to pay the floating indebtedness of the state, and the estimated liabilities for the present fiscal year not yet provided for by law, the following amounts are hereby appropriated:

Deficiencies under act of 1870.

The sum of fifty-five thousand eight hundred and one dollars and ninety-five cents, to pay for deficiencies unprovided for in full, by act chapter seven hundred and sixty-eight of the laws of eighteen hundred and seventy.

Ibid.

The sum of two hundred and sixty-nine thousand two hundred and thirty-four dollars and eighty-four cents, to pay for deficiencies in appropriations under act chapter seven hundred and sixty-seven of the laws of eighteen hundred and seventy.

Under act of 1871.

The sum of one hundred and forty-four thousand three hundred and fifty-nine dollars and fifty-seven cents, to pay for deficiencies in appropriations under act chapter nine hundred and thirty of the laws of eighteen hundred and seventy-one.

Interest on foregoing.

The sum of sixty-five thousand dollars, or so much thereof as may be necessary to meet and pay the interest on the money borrowed, or certificates of indebtedness issued, to meet the deficiencies enumerated in the three foregoing items of deficiencies.

Awards of 1871.

The sum of three hundred and ninety-three thousand seven hundred and fifty-five dollars and fifty-one cents, for outstanding certificates of awards of canal damages made by and expenses attending cases heard before the canal appraisers in the year eighteen hundred and seventy-one, now on interest.

Interest thereon. The sum of fifty thousand dollars, or so much thereof as may be necessary to meet and pay the interest on the certificates in the last foregoing item mentioned.

Erie canal. The sum of twenty-five thousand four hundred and thirty-one dollars and ninety-nine cents, the amount of certificates on interest now outstanding for work done on the eastern division of the Erie canal in excess of any appropriation therefor.

Champlain The sum of sixty-one thousand six hundred and eleven dollars and thirty-one cents, the amount of certificates on interest now outstanding for work done on the Champlain canal improvement in excess of any appropriation therefor.

Black river. The sum of two thousand five hundred and sixty dollars, the amount of certificates on interest now outstanding for work done on the Black River canal in excess of any appropriation therefor.

Chenango canal extension. The sum of one hundred and twenty thousand dollars, or so much thereof as may be necessary, to pay the amount of certificates on interest now outstanding and for work done on the Chenango canal extension in excess of any appropriation therefor, a portion of which was specially excepted from payment out of the appropriation of such Chenango canal extension made by chapter nine hundred and thirty of the laws of eighteen hundred and seventy-one.

Oneida lake canal. The sum of twenty thousand dollars, or so much thereof as may be necessary, and now due and unpaid for work done and performed on the Oneida Lake canal, in excess of any appropriation therefor.

Interest on foregoing. The sum of forty-five thousand dollars, or so much thereof as may be necessary, to meet and pay the interest on the last four foregoing items.

Awards by canal board. The sum of two hundred and thirty-one thousand four hundred and thirty-four dollars and forty-six cents, to pay the sum of awards for damages and extra compensation made by the canal board in the year eighteen hundred and seventy-one.

Awards by canal commissioners The sum of seventy-one thousand nine hundred and sixty-four dollars and sixty-eight cents, to pay the sum of awards for damages and extra compensation and expenses attending the same, made by the board of canal commissioners in the year eighteen hundred and seventy-one.

Interest on foregoing. The sum of twenty-five thousand dollars, or so much thereof as may be necessary to pay the interest on the last two foregoing items.

Interest on canal debt, 1871. The sum of three hundred and fifty-six thousand seven hundred and sixty-six dollars and sixty-five cents, to supply the deficiency in the canal debt sinking fund, to meet the requirements of section three, article seven of the constitution of the state, for interest and the canal debt, which was due September thirty, eighteen hundred and seventy-one.

The sum of five hundred and fifty-seven thousand one hundred dollars, to supply the canal debt sinking fund with means to pay interest on the thirtieth day of September, eighteen hundred and seventy-two, as required by section three, article seven of the constitution of the state. Interest on canal debt 1872.

The sum of one hundred and twenty-four thousand four hundred and fifteen dollars, or so much thereof as may be necessary, due and to be paid on final settlement of contracts for moneys heretofore retained by the state to secure the performance of contracts. Final settlement of contracts.

The sum of four millions fifty-one thousand one hundred and fifty-nine dollars for the present acknowledged deficiency, and the estimated liabilities of the general fund up to the thirtieth day of September, eighteen hundred and seventy-two, for the payment of which no appropriations have been made, but which such indebtedness has been incurred and such liabilities created, according to the report of the late comptroller, transmitted to the legislature January second, eighteen hundred and seventy-two. Deficiencies and liabilities.

§ 2. To provide the means of paying the said appropriation for the canals under the provisions of this act, and to pay the floating indebtedness of the state and the estimated liabilities for the present fiscal year not yet provided by law, a debt of this state is hereby authorized, which debt shall be for the single object of raising the money to pay the appropriation herein named. Debt authorized to pay appropriation.

§ 3. The debt hereby created shall not exceed the sum of six millions six hundred thousand dollars, and there shall be imposed, levied and assessed upon the taxable property of this state a direct annual tax to pay the interest on said debt as such interest falls due, which said direct annual tax shall be sufficient to pay such interest as it falls due. And there shall also be imposed, levied and assessed upon the taxable property of this state a direct annual tax to pay, and sufficient to pay in the space of twelve years from the time of the passage of this act, the whole of the debt created under and by the provisions of this act. Of the debt to be created under and by virtue of the provisions of this act, the principal of one-third part thereof shall be paid in four years from the passage of this act, the principal of one-third part thereof shall be paid in eight years from the passage of this act, and the principal of one-third part thereof shall be paid in twelve years from the passage of this act. Limit. Annual tax for interest. Tax for debt. Debt, when to be paid.

§ 4. To obtain the money necessary for the purposes contemplated by this act, the comptroller is authorized to issue the bonds of the state in such sums each as shall seem meet to him, with coupons thereto attached, for the payment of the interest on such bonds, at a rate not exceeding six per centum per annum, half yearly, on the first days of July and January in each year until the principal is payable, at such place in the city of New York as shall seem meet to him. One-third part of such bonds shall be payable in four years from the passage of this act, one-third part of such bonds shall be pay- Comptroller to issue state bonds. Bonds, when payable.

able in eight years from the passage of this act, one-third part of such bonds shall be payable in twelve years from the passage of this act, and the whole principal shall be payable in such place in New York city as the comptroller shall deem meet. The comptroller shall, before disposing of said bonds or any of them, advertise the proposals for the same, and shall open the proposals, and award the same to the highest bidder at a rate not less than par, which advertising and disposition shall be according to the provisions of law now existing.

Comptroller to advertise for proposals.

Act to be submitted to the people.

§ 5. This act shall be submitted to the people at the next general election to be held in this state. The inspectors of election in the different election districts in the state, shall provide at each poll on said election day, a box in the usual form for the reception of the ballots herein provided; and each and every elector of this state may present a ballot which shall be a paper ticket, on which shall be printed or written, or partly written and partly printed, one of the following forms, namely: "For the act to create a state debt to pay the canal and general fund deficiencies," or "Against the act to create a state debt to pay the canal and general fund deficiencies." The said ballots shall be so folded as to conceal the contents of the ballots, and shall be indorsed "Act in relation to canal and general fund deficiencies."

Vote, how to be taken.

Inspectors to canvass vote.

§ 6. After finally closing the polls of such election, the inspectors thereof shall immediately and without adjournment proceed to count and canvass the ballots given in relation to the proposed act, in the same manner as they are by law required to canvass the ballots given for governor, and thereupon shall set down in writing and in words at full length, the whole number of votes given "For the act to create a state debt;" and the whole number of votes given "Against the act to create a state debt," and certify and subscribe the same, and cause the copies thereof to be made, certified and delivered, as prescribed by law in respect to the canvass of votes given at an election for governor; and all the provisions of law in relation to elections, other than for military and town officers, shall apply to the submission to the people herein provided for.

Election laws to apply.

Secretary of state to have the law printed and circulated.

§ 7. The secretary of state shall, with all convenient dispatch, after this act shall receive the approval of the governor, cause the same to be struck off and printed upon slips in such numbers as shall be sufficient to supply the different officers of this state concerned in notifying or holding elections, or in canvassing the votes, and shall transmit the same to such officers.

Act, when to take effect.

§ 8. Sections five, six and seven of this act shall take effect immediately upon its passage, but the second, third and fourth sections thereof shall not become a law until it is ratified by the people in pursuance of the constitution and the provisions thereof.

Chapter 700.

§ 9. This act shall be chapter seven hundred of the laws of eighteen hundred and seventy-two.

CHAP. 721.

AN ACT to amend chapter three hundred and sixty-six of the laws of eighteen hundred and seventy, entitled "An act in regard to public libraries incorporated in the state of New York."

PASSED May 14, 1872; three-fifths being present.

The People of the State of New York, represented in Senate and Assembly, do enact as follows:

SECTION 1. Section one of chapter three hundred and sixty-six of the laws of eighteen hundred and seventy is hereby amended so as to read as follows:

Penalty for injuries to books, etc., by officers, clerks, agents or members or other persons.

§ 1. If any officer, clerk, agent or member of any public library, duly incorporated under the laws of the state of New York, or any other person whatever, shall thereafter willfully cut, mark, mutilate, or otherwise injure any book, volume, map, chart, magazine, newspaper, painting or engraving, belonging to or deposited in any public library so incorporated as aforesaid, or shall procure such injury te be done as herein stated, every such person shall be deemed to be guilty of a misdemeanor, and, upon conviction thereof by any court of competent jurisdiction, shall be liable for each offense to a fine of not more than one hundred dollars, at the discretion of the court; provided, however, that no prosecution shall be maintained under this act, unless the library prosecuting shall have at least two printed copies of this act conspicuously placed upon its premises.

§ 2. This act shall take effect immediately.

Ante, vol. 7, p. 717.

CHAP. 733.

AN ACT making appropriations for certain expenses of government, and for supplying deficiencies in former appropriations.

PASSED May 15, 1872, by a two-third vote.

The People of the State of New York, represented in Senate and Assembly, do enact as follows:

Payments by treasurer.

SECTION 1. The treasurer shall pay, on the warrant of the comptroller, from the several funds specified, to the persons indicated in this act, the amounts named, or such parts of those amounts as shall be sufficient to accomplish in full the purposes designated by the appropriations; but no warrant shall be issued except in cases of salaries or extra compensation for official services until the amounts claimed shall have been audited and allowed by the comptroller, who is hereby authorized to determine the same. The persons demanding payment shall present to him, if required, a detailed statement

Comptroller to audit certain claims.

Vouchers to be presented.

in items verified by affidavit, and if such account shall be for services it must show when, where, and under what authority they were rendered; if for expenditures, when, where, and for what, and under what authority they were made; if for articles furnished, when and where they were furnished, to whom they were delivered, and under what authority; and if the demand shall be for traveling expenses the accounts must also specify the distance traveled, the places of starting and destination, the duty or business, the date and items of expenditure. On all accounts for transportation, furniture, blank and other books furnished for use of office, binding, blanks, printing, stationery and postage, a bill duly certified must also be furnished; but, whenever an appropriation shall have been made for the same purpose, or the amount shall have been provided otherwise, the sums herein directed to be paid shall not be considered as an addition to such appropriation unless it shall be expressly so declared in this act. For the purpose of a full and perfect examination into the items of any bill herein allowed, the comptroller is further authorized to examine, under oath to be administered by him, any person applying for any appropriation herein named.

Appropriations. § 2. The following amounts are hereby appropriated for the several objects specified, namely:

FROM THE GENERAL FUND.

For chaplains of the legislature. For the clergymen officiating as chaplains of the senate and assembly during the present session of the legislature, for compensation, to be paid, one-half to the clerk of the senate and one-half to the clerk of the assembly, for distribution by them to those clergymen, at the rate of three dollars for every day of attendance, six hundred dollars.

Clerk of the assembly. For the clerk of the assembly for revising, mailing, sending to members of the assembly, previous to the organization of the next house, the clerk's manual, two hundred and fifty dollars.

Clerk of the senate. For the clerk of the senate, five hundred dollars, and for the clerk of the assembly, seven hundred and fifty dollars, for indexing the journals, bills and documents of the senate and assembly; for the clerk of the senate, four hundred dollars, and for the clerk of the assembly, seven hundred and fifty dollars for compensation for extra clerical services and engrossing; and for the clerks and journal clerks of the subcommittees of the whole of the senate and assembly, to each of them, three hundred dollars.

Clerk of the assembly for funeral of William M. Ely. For the clerk of the assembly, for advances for expenses in relation to the funeral of Honorable William M. Ely, including drapery in rear of the speaker's chair, the engrossing and framing of the resolutions of the assembly, and the expenses of the assembly committee in attending the funeral, three hundred and seventeen dollars and fifty-three cents; for Of Peter G. Peck. advances for expenses of the funeral of Honorable Peter G. Peck, late member of assembly, three hundred and eight dollars and forty cents; for advances for expenses in relation to the funeral of Professor Morse, two hundred and thirty dollars; and for advances for expenses attending the funeral of Honorable Erastus Corning, one hundred and twenty-five dollars; and for advances for carrying the mails of the assembly from the commencement of the session until the fifth of February, eighteen hundred and seventy-two, the sum of twenty-two dollars. Of Professor Morse. Of Erastus Corning.

To the clerk of the senate, for advances for expenses attending the funeral of Honorable Jacob Hardenbergh, the sum of one hundred and thirty-five dollars and fifty cents. Of Jacob Hardenbergh.

For the clerk of the senate, for advances for carrying the mails of the senate from the commencement of the session until the fifth day of February, eighteen hundred and seventy-two, the sum of thirty-five dollars. Carrying mails.

To the clerk of the assembly, for advances for carriages and other expenses for governor, court of appeals and committees from senate and assembly, for funeral of the late Senator Hardenbergh, at Kingston, one hundred and fifty-eight dollars. Late Senator Hardenbergh.

For the clerks, and the journal, assistant and deputy clerks, and stenographers of the senate and assembly, for compensation for clerical and stenographic services from and after the tenth day of April, until the close of the present session, to each of them, the same per diem compensation respectively as their respective salaries as now established by law would give per day for a session of one hundred days. And to the clerks of the president of the senate and speaker of the assembly, and the clerks of the committees on engrossed bill, to each of them six dollars per day, for services from and after the tenth day of April until the close of the present session, such service to be certified by the presiding officers of the respective houses of the legislature. Clerks, etc., of senate and assembly.

For the clerk of the committee on ways and means of the assembly, for additional compensation, five hundred dollars; for the clerks of the committees on the affairs of cities of the senate and assembly, to each of them for additional compensation, three hundred dollars; for the clerk of the committee on finance of the senate, and the clerks of the committees on judiciary of the senate and assembly, to each of them, for additional compensation, two hundred and fifty dollars; and for the clerks of the committees on railroads, commerce and navigation and on canals, of the senate and assembly, to each of them, for additional compensation, one hundred and fifty dollars. Clerks of committees, for additional compensation.

For the clerk of the special committee appointed by resolution of the senate to investigate and report upon the charges against James Terwilliger, clerk of the senate, one hundred dollars. Case of James Terwilliger.

For A. S. Burdick, clerk of the committee on apportionment, thirty-five dollars. A. S. Burdick.

For John N. Parker, for repairs in the assembly chamber and clerk's rooms, the sum of thirty-eight dollars and forty-one cents. John N. Parker.

J. & W. J. Blackall. For J. & W. J. Blackall, for locks, keys, etc., and repairs in clerk's desk, clerk's rooms, assembly library and committee rooms, the sum of sixty-four dollars and forty cents.

Private secretary. For the private secretary of the governor, for additional compensation for the calendar year eighteen hundred and seventy-two, one thousand dollars.

S. B. Griswold. For Stephen B. Griswold, for preparing catalogues of the library of the court of appeals and for unpacking, arranging, labeling and shelving the same, one hundred dollars.

Messenger of clerk of court of appeals. For the messenger to the clerk of the court of appeals and the state engineer and surveyor (one and the same messenger), from April first, eighteen hundred and seventy-one, to October first, eighteen hundred and seventy-two, nine hundred dollars.

S. H. Sweet. For Sylvanus H. Sweet, late deputy state engineer and surveyor, for work and clerk hire in preparation of the annual report on railroads for the year eighteen hundred and seventy-one, one thousand five hundred dollars, to be refunded to the treasury by the several railroad corporations of this state, in proportion to their respective gross receipts, pursuant to chapter five hundred and twenty-six of the laws of eighteen hundred and fifty-five.

A. J. Chester. For A. J. Chester, for services for thirteen months in posting accounts in the "School fund loan," and making an index to "Bond books," in the comptroller's office, during the administration of William F. Allen, late comptroller, five hundred and seventy dollars.

Hugh F. Dunn and James McFarlane. For Hugh F. Dunn and James McFarlane, for extra compensation as attendants on the commission of appeals during the years eighteen hundred and seventy and eighteen hundred and seventy-one, to each of them, one hundred and twenty-six dollars.

M. M. Jones. For M. M. Jones, late chief clerk to the secretary of state, for extra services in supervision of the printing of the session laws of eighteen hundred and seventy-one, and legislative manual, five hundred dollars.

Thomas Willard. For Thomas Willard, for transcribing one thousand forty-two pages of the assembly journal of eighteen hundred and seventy-one, pursuant to a resolution of the house of assembly, dated April twenty, eighteen hundred and seventy-one, the sum of five hundred dollars; and hereafter no person other than the clerks of the assembly shall be assigned to such duty.

Charlotte B. Briggs, widow of Gilman P. Briggs. For Charlotte B. Briggs, of Canandaigua, widow of Gilman P. Briggs, who at the time of his death, on the twenty-first day of February last, was, and for several months previously had been, a clerk in the department of public instruction, the sum of one hundred and seventy dollars, being his salary for the month of February, and his extra compensation for the months of January and February, eighteen hundred and seventy-two, in full of all compensation and extra compensation allowed him by law.

James Barnes. For James Barnes, late deputy state engineer and surveyor, for preparation of the annual report of the state engineer and surveyor on railroads for the year eighteen hundred and sixty-six, and for compiling and indexing the laws of the state, to be refunded to the treasury by the several railroad corporations of this state in proportion to their respective gross receipts, pursuant to chapter five hundred and twenty-six of the laws of eighteen hundred and fifty-five, the sum of one thousand dollars.

To comptroller, to pay clerks for extra labor.

For the comptroller, to be distributed by him among the persons entitled thereto, for extra labor performed by the clerks in his office in preparing for and making a sale of lands in eighteen hundred and seventy-one, for arrears of taxes for the years eighteen hundred and sixty-one, eighteen hundred and sixty-two, eighteen hundred and sixty-three, eighteen hundred and sixty-four and eighteen hundred and sixty-five; stating accounts to purchasers and issuing fourteen thousand certificates of sale, the sum of twenty-four hundred dollars.

Clerk of commission of appeals.

For the clerk of the commission of appeals for additional compensation and expenses of crier, attendants and clerks for the May term of the commission to be held in t
York, five hundred dollars, to be paid to the cl
mission upon his certificate of the service of the various parties among whom he shall distribute the same.

A. G. Hawley.

To A. G. Hawley, for services as clerk to the committees of agriculture and militia of the senate, during the session of eighteen hundred and seventy-one, the sum of five hundred and thirty-six dollars, the same having been omitted by mistake from the supply bill of eighteen hundred and seventy-one by an error in engrossing the same.

Office of secretary of state.

For the office of the secretary of state, for deficiency in clerk hire from January first to October first, eighteen hundred and seventy-two, two thousand dollars.

Anson S. Wood.

For Anson S. Wood, deputy secretary of state, for indexing the session laws of eighteen hundred and seventy-two, and for preparing marginal notes to the same, and for services as clerk of the commissioners of the land office from January first to October first, eighteen hundred and seventy-two, and for extra compensation for the last three-quarters of the current fiscal year, the sum of eleven hundred and twenty-five dollars; provided that said deputy secretary of state shall not be entitled to receive the extra compensation given by the act of the legislature of eighteen hundred and seventy-two, entitled "An act providing for additional compensation to deputies, clerks and assistants in the various departments of the state government."

Edward P. Gould.

For Edward P. Gould, chief clerk in the office of the secretary of state, for the last three-quarters of the present fiscal year, the sum of three hundred and seventy-five dollars; but no extra compensation shall hereafter be allowed him for the supervision of the printing of the session laws and legislative manual of eighteen hundred and seventy-two.

Deputy treasurer.

For the deputy treasurer, for extra compensation for the last three-quarters of the current fiscal year, the sum of seven hundred and fifty dollars; provided, that said deputy treasurer shall not be entitled to receive the extra compensation given by the act of the legislature of eighteen hundred and seventy-two, entitled "An act providing for additional compensation to deputies, clerks and assistants in the various departments of the state government."

State reporter. To the state reporter, for deficiency in salary for balance of fiscal year, nine hundred and forty-one dollars, sixty-seven cents.

John W. Dickson. For John W. Dickson, for expenses incurred by him in attending as a witness on the eighth day of March, eighteen hundred and seventy-one, at Albany, under and by virtue of a subpœna summoning him to attend as such on the first day of March before the committee on insurance, the sum of twenty-five dollars.

Mary Moquin. For Mrs. Mary Moquin, mother of Charles D. Moquin, for his services as messenger to the committee on claims of the senate during the session of eighteen hundred and seventy, the sum of two hundred dollars, the same being a re-appropriation of the amount appropriated to C. D. Moquin.

Robert Richards. For Robert Richards, as messenger of the committee on insurance, from January second to February fifteenth, eighteen hundred and seventy-two, the sum of one hundred and thirty-five dollars.

H. B. Baxter. For H. B. Baxter, for services as clerk of the committee on internal affairs of the assembly, from the commencement of the session of eighteen hnndred and seventy-two until the eighth day of February, the sum of one hundred and ninety dollars.

Wm. H. Stevens. For William H. Stevens, for two days' service in reporting senate debates and transcribing the same, thirty dollars.

H. Rulison. For H. Rulison, for making a statistical list of the senators and officers of the senate and their boarding places, twenty-five dollars.

Hiram Calkins. For Hiram Calkins, for preparing an index of the papers on the files of the senate, and also a classified index of the bills introduced into the senate, pursuant to a resolution of the senate adopted April twenty-first, eighteen hundred and seventy-one, five hundred dollars.

A. J. Myers. For A. J. Myers, postmaster of the senate of eighteen hundred and seventy-one, for fourteen days' service after the adjournment, and for four days' service at the opening of the present session, and mileage, ninety-nine dollars.

Leopold Stark. For Leopold Stark, postmaster's messenger of the senate of eighteen hundred and seventy-one, forty-two dollars, for fourteen days' service after the adjournment.

H. A. Homes. For Henry A. Homes, for two years extra labor in preparing condensed catalogue of the state library, in accordance with the instructions of the board of regents, the sum of five hundred dollars.

Jennie Stanton. For Jennie Stanton, for services as engrossing clerk for the assembly in the year eighteen hundred and seventy-one, the sum of two hundred dollars.

For Verplanck Colvin, of Albany, N. Y., ten hundred dollars, to aid in completing survey of the Adirondack wilderness of New York, and a map thereof; and he shall render to the legislature, within thirty days after the opening of the next annual session thereof, a full report of his explorations and survey. Verplanck Colvin.

For George W. Chapman, late canal commissioner, for his compensation in making his final report after the expiration of his term of office, the sum of three hundred dollars. Geo. W. Chapman.

For Charles H. Peck, for disbursements in the field, as state botanist, one hundred and forty-five dollars and six cents. Charles H. Peck.

For Cornelius Ten Broeck, deputy clerk of the court of appeals, for extra compensation for the last three-quarters of the current fiscal year, provided, that said deputy clerk shall not be entitled to receive the extra compensation given by the act of the legislature of eighteen hundred and seventy-two, entitled "An act providing for additional compensation to deputies, clerks, and assistants in the various departments of the state government," seven hundred and fifty dollars. Cornelius Ten Broeck.

For George Tunnecliff and Edwin C. Shafer, for extra services in the executive department, to each of them the sum of two hundred dollars, and to Edward Miggael, for extra services as military messenger, one hundred dollars. Executive clerks.

For Albert V. V. Dodge, the governor's messenger, for extra compensation, one hundred dollars. A. V. V. Dodge.

For the trustees of the state library, for additional shelving, one thousand dollars. Trustees of state library.

For William Wasson, late canal appraiser, for extra compensation for services, the sum of seven thousand and seventy-seven dollars and seventy-eight cents. William Wasson.

For Joseph N. Green, one hundred and ninety-seven dollars for the balance of his claim as allowed in the supply bill of eighteen hundred and seventy-one. Joseph N. Green.

The sum of twenty-five thousand dollars is hereby appropriated for the completion of the new armory in the city of Auburn, and the inspector-general of the state, Elmore P. Ross, John S. Clark, John H. Chedell, Clinton D. McDougall and Charles W. Pomeroy are hereby appointed commissioners for such purpose; but no part of said sum shall be paid over to said commissioners until the last-named five commissioners shall execute a bond to the people of the state of New York, to be approved by the comptroller, conditioned that they will faithfully discharge their duties as such commissioners, and truly account to the comptroller for all moneys received by them for the purpose aforesaid; but said commission shall not receive any compensation for any service, or either of them, directly or indirectly, in any contract for materials or labor. New armory at Auburn. Commissioners.

For the state armory at Oswego, for completing the same and for necessary heating apparatus, according to architect's estimate and the recommendation of the inspector-general and quartermaster-general, the sum of nine thousand two hundred and fifty dollars. State armory at Oswego.

At Schenectady. For the completion of the state armory at Schenectady, for firing platform and cannon house, five thousand dollars.

Fencing arsenal grounds at Rochester. For the purpose of building a fence to inclose the arsenal grounds in the city of Rochester, and to repay the sums already necessarily expended in fitting up and furnishing the rooms in the arsenal, the sum of eighteen thousand dollars.

State armory at Syracuse. The sum of ten thousand dollars is hereby appropriated, out of any moneys in the treasury not otherwise appropriated, in addition to the sum of twenty thousand dollars appropriated by chapter seven hundred and sixty-eight of the laws of eighteen hundred and seventy-one, which sum is hereby re-appropriated for the purpose of enlarging and completing the state armory at Syracuse, for the use of the twenty-fourth brigade, national guard of the state of New York, and for the housing and protection of the park of artillery attached thereto, to be expended under the direction of the inspector-general of the state of New York, the chief of ordnance of the state of New York, brigadier-general John A. Green, of the twenty-fourth brigade, national guard, Henry L. Duguid and Thomas B. Fitch, of the city of Syracuse, are hereby appointed commissioners for that purpose, and shall serve as such without compensation. The said John A. Green, Henry L. Duguid and Thomas B. Fitch shall, before entering upon the execution of this commission, execute to the people of this state a bond in the penal sum of sixty thousand dollars, with satisfactory securities, to be approved by the comptroller and treasurer of the state, conditioned for the faithful discharge of their duties as such commissioners. All vouchers for expenditures under this appropriation are to be subject to the approval of the comptroller.

Commissioners.

Commissioners of land office to sell arsenal at Batavia. The commissioners of the land office are hereby authorized pursuant to law, to sell the state arsenal at Batavia, and the grounds thereof, if, in their opinion, they deem such sale advisable.

J. L. Snow. For J. L. Snow, for services and disbursements as clerk to the commission appointed by chapter seven hundred and fifteen, laws of eighteen hundred and seventy-one, the sum of one hundred and fifty dollars.

Late state engineer. For the late state engineer and surveyor, for extra traveling expenses during the year eighteen hundred and seventy-one, four hundred dollars.

James C. Brown. For James C. Brown, for extra services in the department of public instruction from the first of January to the first of October, eighteen hundred and seventy-two, five hundred and sixty-two dollars and fifty cents.

Expenses of prosecuting war claims against U. S. For services and expenses in the preparation and prosecution of the war claims of the state against the United States, thirteen thousand dollars, or so much thereof as may be necessary, to be paid on the certificate of the governor of this state, provided that such allowance shall not exceed in all two per cent upon the amount which has been allowed and passed to the credit of the state since January first, eighteen hundred and sixty-nine, and the same percentage on the amount of any further settlement and allowance which may be made before the first day of January next.

For the expenses of the officers of the United States service appointed by the president of the United States to revise the exterior lines of the harbor of New York, to be paid upon vouchers to be furnished to and audited by the comptroller of this state, the sum of five thousand dollars, or so much thereof as may be necessary. Expenses of officers of the U. S. to revise exterior lines of harbor of New York.

For the city of Albany, for amount apportioned and assessed by the authorities of said city upon the lot on the west side of Eagle street and north side of State street, between Maiden lane and Hawk street in said city, designated on the map returned to the common council of said city as Capitol park, etc., for the benefit derived by said lot in consequence of a drain constructed by order of said city authorities, the sum of four thousand six hundred and fifty-six dollars and twenty-eight cents, to be paid on the certificate of the attorney-general. City of Albany for street assessments.

For the city of Utica, for the amount apportioned and assessed by the authorities of said city upon the property belonging to the state in said city, connected with the New York State Lunatic Asylum, for constructing sewer in Warren street in said city; for grading York street and for iron well at the south-west corner of Court and York streets, the sum of three hundred and twenty-two dollars and seventy-eight cents, to be paid on the certificate of the attorney-general. City of Utica, for street assessments.

For the city of Rochester, for the amount apportioned and assessed by the authorities of said city upon the property belonging to the state known as the Western House of Refuge, for sewer constructed in Lake avenue and Varnum street in said city, the sum of three thousand two hundred and forty-one dollars. City of Rochester, for sewer assessments.

For the re-imbursement of Erie county, to be paid to the treasurer thereof, for moneys advanced and paid by said county, interest being reckoned to date, for building a bridge across Cattaraugus creek, on the Indian reservation, the sum of six thousand one hundred and ninety-two dollars and eighty-two cents; and the paragraph of chapter seven hundred and fifteen of the laws of eighteen hundred and seventy-one, page one thousand five hundred and seventy-nine, appropriating five hundred dollars for that purpose, is hereby repealed. Erie county for bridge across Cattaraugus creek, on Indian reservation.

For O. B. Latham, late capitol commissioner, for his expenses in the preparation of the memorial to the legislature, in the matter of the new capitol, assembly document number one hundred and sixty-five, April tenth, eighteen hundred and sixty-nine, the sum of one hundred dollars. O. B. Latham.

For the legal representatives of the Hon. William M. Ely, late a member of the assembly, for his per diem allowance during the present session, three hundred dollars, and for mileage, twenty-eight dollars and forty cents. Legal representatives of William M. Ely.

For the legal representatives of the Hon. Peter G. Peck, deceased, late a member of the assembly, the sum of one hun- Of Peter G. Peck.

dred and twenty-three dollars, for the balance of his per diem allowance during the present session.

Of Jacob Hardenbergh. The legal representatives of the late Hon. Jacob Hardenbergh, late state senator, are hereby authorized to draw his per diem allowance during the present session, three hundred dollars, and the mileage allowed by law, twelve dollars.

Office of comptroller, for furniture, books, etc. For the office of the comptroller, for furniture, blank and other books necessary for the use of the office, binding, blanks, printing, and other necessary expenses, three thousand five hundred dollars.

Postage. For postage for the public offices, one thousand eight hundred dollars.

Office of attorney-general, for books, etc. For the office of the attorney-general, for furniture, blank and other books necessary for the use of the office, binding, blanks, printing, and other necessary incidental expenses, five hundred dollars.

Land office, for lieutenant-governor, and speaker. For the land office, for compensation and mileage of the lieutenant-governor and speaker of the assembly, for their attendance at the meetings of the commissioners of the land office, and for assessments and other expenses of public lands, six thousand dollars.

State cabinet of natural history, for repairs, etc. For the hall of the state cabinet of natural history and the agricultural museum, for repairs, cleaning, labor, gas, fuel, compensation of keeper, and other necessary expenses, three thousand dollars.

For books. The unexpended remainder of one hundred and sixty-five dollars and five cents of the appropriation made by chapter seven hundred and seventeen of the laws of eighteen hundred and sixty-eight, and chapter four hundred and ninety-two, laws of eighteen hundred and seventy, to the state cabinet of natural history for the purchase and binding of books, is hereby reappropriated in the terms therein stated for the same purpose. Lectures may be discontinued. The course of lectures required by chapter five hundred and fifty-seven, laws of eighteen hundred and seventy, and chapter seven hundred and eleven, laws of eighteen hundred and seventy-one, may be discontinued in the discretion of the regents of the university; and the resolution of the legislature of eighteen hundred and sixty-nine, requiring the opening and lighting of the rooms of the state cabinet of natural history, is hereby rescinded.

Agents to examine auctioneers' accounts. For compensation of the agents designated by the comptroller to examine the accounts of auctioneers, five hundred dollars.

State hall. For the state hall, for expenses for repairs, cleaning, labor, gas, and other necessary expenses, five thousand five hundred dollars.

Capitol. For the capitol, for expenses for repairs, cleaning, labor, gas, and other necessary expenses, five thousand dollars.

Office of state engineer, for books, etc. For the office of the state engineer and surveyor, for furniture, blank and other books necessary for the use of the office, binding, blanks, printing, and other necessary expenses, one thousand five hundred dollars.

For the office of the secretary of state, for furniture, blank and other books necessary for the use of the office, binding, blanks, printing, and other necessary expenses, one thousand five hundred dollars. Office of secretary of state, for books, etc.

For the office of the state treasurer, for furniture, blank and other books necessary for the use of the office, binding, blanks, printing, and other necessary expenses, two hundred dollars. Office of state treasurer, for books, etc.

For printing for the legislature, including wrapping and binding; also for the publication of the official canvass and other official printing, and for printing and binding the session laws of eighteen hundred and seventy-two, one hundred and twenty-five thousand dollars. Printing for legislature, official canvass, etc.

For the electors of president and vice-president, and for special messenger, for compensation, three thousand dollars. Electors of president and vice-president.

For the compensation of sheriffs, for transportation of persons indicted for capital offenses, who have been, or may be, delivered to the superintendent of the state lunatic asylum for insane convicts at Auburn, in pursuance of chapter six hundred and sixty-six of the laws of eighteen hundred and seventy-one, five hundred dollars. Sheriff, for transportation of convicts.

For the sheriffs of the several counties of this state, for compensation for transportation of convicts to the state prisons, houses of refuge and penitentiaries of this state, two thousand dollars.

For stationery for the public offices and departments, five hundred dollars. Stationery for public offices.

For the clerk of the court of appeals, for deficiency in his salary for the last fiscal year, in pursuance of chapter seven hundred and eighteen, laws of eighteen hundred and seventy-one, one thousand one hundred and four dollars and sixty-two cents. Clerk of court of appeals.

For the criers and attendants of the court of appeals and commission of appeals, three thousand dollars. Criers and attendants.

For the office of the clerk of the court of appeals, for furniture, blank and other books necessary for the use of the office, binding, blanks, printing, and other necessary expenses, one thousand dollars. Office of clerk of court of appeals, for furniture, etc.

For the office of the superintendent of public instruction, for furniture, blank and other books necessary for the use of the office, binding, blanks, printing, and other necessary expenses, two thousand five hundred dollars. Superintendent of public instruction.

For refunding moneys paid into the state treasury by railroad companies by mistake, the sum of fifteen hundred dollars, or so much thereof as may be necessary. Refunding moneys paid by mistake.

For advertising, printing and services of auctioneer in connection with tax sale held by the comptroller, in September, eighteen hundred and seventy-one, seven thousand one hundred and forty-five dollars and fifty-one cents. Tax sale, expenses of.

For the legislature for advances for contingent expenses of the clerk of the senate and the clerk of the assembly, six thousand dollars; and for postage, expenses of committees, compensation of witnesses, the legislative manual, the Clerk's Contingent expenses of legislature, etc.

and Croswell's manual and other contingent expenses, eight thousand dollars.

Purchase of coin for interest on debt.

For the purchase of coin for the payment of the interest on the general fund debt, including the Indian annuities, seven thousand five hundred dollars, or so much thereof as may be necessary.

Payment of bounties.

For the payment of bounties, in pursuance of section thirty-nine, chapter seven hundred and twenty-one of the laws of eighteen hundred and seventy-one, eight hundred dollars.

Second deputy comptroller.

For the second deputy comptroller, in order to make his compensation in all equal to three thousand dollars per annum for the years eighteen hundred and seventy-one and eighteen hundred and seventy-two, the sum of one thousand three hundred and fifty dollars, or so much thereof as may be necessary.

Comptroller's office.

For providing additional room for the comptroller's office and paying the expense incident thereto, the sum of three thousand dollars, or so much thereof as may be necessary.

Counsel to assist attorney-general.

For counsel to assist the attorney-general, pursuant to chapter three hundred and fifty-seven of the laws of eighteen hundred and forty-eight, and to supply deficiency in the present condition of that fund for the balance of the current fiscal year, the sum of sixteen hundred and ten dollars.

Deputy attorney-general.

For the deputy attorney-general, for extra compensation for the last three quarters of the current fiscal year, the sum of eleven hundred and twenty-five dollars; provided, that said deputy attorney-general shall not be entitled to receive the extra compensation given by the act of the legislature of eighteen hundred and seventy-two, entitled "An act providing for additional compensation to deputies, clerks and assistants in the various departments of the state government."

Refunding money to purchasers, etc.

For refunding to purchasers of lands from the state in case the patents have been canceled by the commissioners of the land office, the sum of one thousand dollars, or so much thereof as may be necessary, to be paid on the order of said commissioners and audit of the comptroller.

Warburton, Bonynge and Underhill.

For Warburton, Bonynge and Underhill, stenographers, for reporting and transcribing the testimony taken before the assembly committee on commerce and navigation, in the matter of investigation into the charges against the Pacific Mail Steamship Company, the sum of eighty-three dollars.

Treasurer of port-wardens of the port of N. Y.

The comptroller of this state is hereby authorized out of the unexpended balance remaining in the treasury of the sum appropriated to the port-wardens of the port of New York, by chapter seven hundred and fifteen of the laws of eighteen hundred and seventy-one, page five hundred and eighty, to pay to the treasurer of the said port-wardens the sum of six hundred and twenty-eight dollars and sixty-four cents, for books and stationery furnished them.

Binding the U. S. census.

For binding the United States census of eighteen hundred and seventy, as transmitted to the office of the secretary of state of this state from the census bureau at Washington, the sum of two hundred dollars, or so much thereof as may be necessary.

For the New York State Poultry Society, the sum of fifteen hundred dollars, to be paid upon the order of Thomas B. Kingsland, as president. N. Y. S. poultry society.

For Richard H. Mapes, to re-imburse him for costs and expenses incurred by him in defending his title to lands purchased from the state, and to refund to him the consideration money paid for the same, the sum of five hundred dollars, or so much thereof as shall be certified by the attorney-general and the state engineer and surveyor to be a just and legal claim against the state, in case the state was an individual or corporation. Richard H. Mapes.

For M. R. Patrick, of Manlius, New York, late cattle commissioner, for expenses incurred in the years eighteen hundred and seventy and eighteen hundred and seventy-one by the commissioners, with the approval of the governor and late comptroller, and to re-imburse him for advances made by him in paying such expenses, the sum of one thousand dollars or so much thereof as may be necessary, to be audited by the comptroller. M. R. Patrick.

For David A. Wells, George W. Cuyler and Edwin Dodge, commissioners appointed to report upon the tax and assessment laws of the state, for expenses and compensation to February, eighteen hundred and seventy-two, when they closed their labors, the sum of six thousand dollars, to be adjusted and apportioned as follows: three thousand dollars thereof to David A. Wells, and the balance thereof to be divided equally between the other two commissioners. Commissioners to report upon tax and assessment laws.

For the commissioners to revise the statutes of the state, appointed under chapter thirty-three of the laws of eighteen hundred and seventy, for deficiency in the appropriation for their expenditures for clerical services and other incidental matters, for the fiscal year commencing October one, eighteen hundred and seventy-one, the sum of three thousand dollars. Commissioners to revise the statutes.

For the board of commissioners on steam navigation on the canal, appointed under chapter eight hundred and sixty-eight of the laws of eighteen hundred and seventy-one, for their reasonable expenses in the discharge of their duty, the sum of five thousand dollars, or so much thereof as may be necessary, to be determined by said board of commissioners. Commissioners on steam navigation on the canals.

For Van R. Richmond, John T. Agnew and Henry O. Chesebro, for compensation for services as commissioners appointed under chapter eight hundred and sixty-four of the laws of eighteen hundred and sixty-eight, to appraise the value of the lands under water belonging to the state, mentioned in said act, to each of them the sum of five hundred dollars. Commissioners under ch. 864, laws of 1868.

For services and expenses of medical commissioners appointed by the governor and courts of oyer and terminer, pursuant to chapter six hundred and sixty-six, laws of eighteen Commissioners under ch. 666, laws of 1871.

hundred and seventy-one, to inquire into the medical condition of persons under indictment or conviction for offenses, the punishment of which is death, two thousand dollars, the amount to be paid in each case to be certified by the governor.

Commissioners under ch. 613, laws of 1865. For the commissioners appointed to confer with the state of New Jersey, in regard to quarantine jurisdiction, boundary line, etc., pursuant to section seven, chapter six hundred and thirteen, laws of eighteen hundred and sixty-five, for compensation and expenses, three thousand dollars.

Commissioners of fisheries. For the commissioners of fisheries, to be expended as they may deem proper, upon vouchers to be approved by the comptroller, for the purpose of replenishing the lakes and rivers of this state with fish, the sum of fifteen thousand dollars.

Dwight King. For Dwight King, for services as the secretary of the Ruloff lunacy commission, the sum of one hundred and fifty dollars.

Checks of late paymaster-general. To pay certain checks drawn by John D. Van Buren, George Bliss, junior, and Selden E. Marvin, late paymaster-general, to the order of enlisted men for bounty due to them respectively, paid into the treasury under chapter seven hundred and fifty-six of the laws of eighteen hundred and sixty-nine, the sum of five thousand dollars, or so much thereof as may be necessary.

Certificates issued to soldiers of war of 1812. The sum of two thousand nine hundred and eighty-four dollars and forty-nine cents, being the balance in the treasury appropriated by the acts chapter four hundred and seventy, laws of eighteen hundred and sixty-nine, and chapter five hundred and twenty-four, laws of eighteen hundred and seventy, is hereby re-appropriated to the payment of certain certificates issued to the militia of this state for services in the war of eighteen hundred and twelve, as provided in said acts.

School-house on Onondaga reservation. For erecting a school-house on the Onondaga reservation, for the use of the Onondaga Indians, the sum of five hundred dollars, to be paid to and expended under the direction of the Honorable Horatio Seymour, of Utica, and the Reverend F. D. Huntington, bishop of the diocese of central New York, if the same shall be deemed advisable by the superintendent of public instruction, and which school is to be subject to the visitation and control of the superintendent of public instruction.

School-house for St. Regis tribe of Indians. For erecting a school-house for the use of the St. Regis tribe of Indians, the sum of two hundred and fifty dollars, if the same shall be considered necessary by the superintendent of public instruction, to be paid to and expended under the direction of said superintendent, and which school is to be subject to his visitation and control.

Niagara county, for support of Susan Green. For the county of Niagara, to re-imburse the same for money paid out in the support of Susan Green, an insane Indian woman, and an inmate of Niagara county alms-house, three hundred dollars, or so much thereof as may be necessary.

Ordnance department, for For the ordnance department, payable to Samuel W. Johnson of that department, for its use, on the certificate of the adjutant-general, the sum of forty dollars for a United States flag (ensign 10x19) for the use of the St. Regis Indians. Flag for St. Regis Indians.

Dolly Johnson.

For Dolly Johnson, an Oneida Indian, to re-imburse her for all sums of money, including attorneys' and counsel fees, which have been actually and reasonably expended by her or for which she is liable, in and about procuring the passage of the act, chapter five hundred and twenty-nine of the laws of eighteen hundred and sixty-nine, and in and about proceedings before the commissioners of the land office, for the purpose of vacating the patent for the lands mentioned in said act of eighteen hundred and sixty-nine, the sum of six hundred dollars, or so much thereof as may be necessary. The comptroller is hereby authorized to require the production of vouchers, upon oath, specifying the items of such expenditures and liabilities.

Annuities to Stockbridge Indians.

For Nelson K. Hopkins, comptroller, to pay balance of annuities to nine Stockbridge Indians, one hundred and forty-two dollars, with interest at six per cent per annum, transferred from the credit of Sanford E. Church, late comptroller, to the general fund deposit, December first, eighteen hundred and seventy.

Taylor and Waterman, for carpets, etc.

For Taylor and Waterman, for carpets, shades, webbing and other materials supplied for the capitol, and for labor performed on the same, two thousand one hundred and thirteen dollars and thirteen cents; and for oil cloth supplied for the executive chamber, and for labor performed therein, seventeen dollars and seventeen cents; and for carpets supplied for the adjutant-general's office, and for labor performed therein, five hundred and eight dollars and twenty-five cents.

Henry Smith.

For Henry Smith, employed by the late attorney-general for attending Fulton county oyer and terminer, upon the designation of the attorney-general, to aid the district attorney on the trial of the people against John Lucas, indicted for murder, and for attending an adjourned term when said cause was tried, the sum of one thousand dollars.

Amasa J. Parker.

For Amasa J. Parker, for compensation for his services as counsel, rendered on the request of the late secretary of state, in attending and arguing twice before the supreme court, and once before the court of appeals, to resist an application for a mandamus to compel the secretary of state to file an unauthorized certificate of incorporation, the sum of six hundred dollars.

Joseph Potter.

For Joseph Potter, for costs and expenses incurred in defense of a suit brought against him by the people on the relation of Samuel W. Jackson, to test his right to the office of justice of the supreme court under the election of November, eighteen hundred and seventy-one, to be verified by oath, and to be certified by a justice of the supreme court to be just and reasonable, the sum of fifteen hundred and fifty-nine dollars and fifty cents, or so much thereof as may be necessary.

Samuel Jackson.

For Samuel W. Jackson, for costs and expenses incurred in the suit brought to test the right to the office of justice of the supreme court under the election of November, eighteen hundred and seventy-one, as between Samuel W. Jackson and Joseph Potter, to be verified by oath, and certified by a justice of the supreme court to be just and reasonable, the sum of nine hundred and fifty-seven dollars and seventy-five cents, or so much thereof as may be necessary.

R. W. Peckham, Jr. For Rufus W. Peckham, Junior, employed by the late attorney-general, two thousand dollars for counsel and services in behalf of the people on the trial of the indictment for murder against David Montgomery, at Rochester, including his services on the preliminary issue of insanity, the trial and all proceedings preliminary thereto; the said sum when paid to be in full of all demands on account of said case.

Robert E. Andrews. For Robert E. Andrews, of Hudson, New York, employed by the late attorney-general, the sum of one thousand dollars for counsel and services in behalf of the people on the trial of the indictment for murder against Aratus F. Pierce, at Lockport, and for expenses in going to and returning from the place of trial.

Lorenzo Morris. For Lorenzo Morris, of Fredonia, New York, employed by the late attorney-general, the sum of five hundred dollars for counsel and services in behalf of the people on the trial of the indictment for murder against Charles Marlow, in Chautauqua county, and for all his expenses and charges in that case.

Rollin Tracy. For Rollin Tracy, of Auburn, for his costs and expenses in the several courts in defending the interest of the state in the suit brought by Hall and Lewis against Morgan Augsbury as agent of the state prison at Auburn, and the parties composing the firm of Sheldon and company as contractors therein, six hundred and seven dollars and fifty cents; and to re-imburse him for moneys paid by him for printing cases and briefs in said case in supreme court and court of appeals, two hundred and sixty-six dollars and twenty-five cents; to re-imburse him for moneys paid by him to engineers for surveys and maps used on the trial of said case, two hundred dollars; and for his counsel fee on the trial thereof, two hundred and fifty dollars.

David Wight. For David Wight, of Auburn, for the costs taxed in the suit brought by Hall and Lewis against Morgan Augsbury as agent of the Auburn State Prison, and the parties composing the firm of Sheldon and company as contractors therein, the sum of three hundred and sixty-eight dollars and forty-eight cents, and the further sum of seventy-seven dollars and thirty-seven cents as interest thereon from the seventeenth day of March, eighteen hundred and sixty-nine; and also the sum of one hundred and twelve dollars and eighty-eight cents for the costs taxed in said suit on appeal to the general term, and the further sum of fifteen dollars and eighty cents as interest on said last-named sum from March twelve, eighteen hundred and seventy.

Charles B. Sedgwick. For Charles B. Sedgwick, for counsel fee for argument in the court of appeals and subsequently in attending before a judge of the court on settling the modified judgment in the case of Hall and Lewis against Morgan Augsbury and Sheldon and company, as the representatives of the interest of the state, the sum of five hundred dollars.

For Frederick L. Westbrook, upon the designation of the late attorney-general, for preparing brief and arguing cause at the general term at Albany in the January term, eighteen hundred and seventy-two, and subsequently in the court of appeals in March, eighteen hundred and seventy-two, and expenses in attending courts on the trial of the indictment of the people against Thomas Bennett, indicted for murder, the sum of five hundred and fifty dollars. Frederick L. Westbrook.

For Amasa J. Parker, for counsel fees and expenses incurred on the retainer of the late attorney-general in the suit of the people against the Central Railroad Company of New Jersey, the sum of nine hundred and eighty-one dollars and six cents, or so much thereof as shall be certified by the governor to be fair and reasonable. Amasa J. Parker.

For Lorenzo Morris, for compensation for assisting district attorney of Chautauqua county, on the trial of the capital case of the people against Marlow, upon the requisition of the governor, the sum of one thousand dollars. Lorenzo Morris.

For Elbridge G. Lapham, for compensation for assisting the district attorney of Oneida county, on the trial of the capital case of the people against McGee, upon a requisition of a justice of the supreme court, and for compensation for assisting said district attorney in the capital case of the people against Josephine McCarthy, upon a like requisition, the sum of six hundred dollars, or so much thereof as shall be certified by the governor to be fair and reasonable. Elbridge G. Lapham.

For Peter S. Palmer, for services as counsel in the Black river canal claims before the canal appraisers, for traveling expenses in attending meetings of the board of canal appraisers, and visiting and examining the reservoir, and in taking testimony, one thousand four hundred and seventy-nine dollars and twenty-six cents. Peter S. Palmer.

For David P. Loomis, for services and expenses as counsel for the state in seventy-four canal claim cases, upon the certificate of the canal appraisers, the sum of four hundred and forty-eight dollars and one cent. David P. Loomis.

From and after the passage of this act the district attorney for any county in which an important criminal case is to be tried, with the approval in writing of the county judge of the county, which shall be filed in the county clerk's office, may employ counsel to assist him in such trial, and the cost and expense thereof to be certified by the judge presiding on such trial shall be a charge upon the county in which the indictment in the case is found, and shall be assessed, levied and collected by the board of supervisors of such county at its next annual assessment, levy and collection of county taxes after such services shall have been performed, and thereupon be paid over to the party entitled to the same. District attorney may employ counsel in criminal cases.

For compensation to the members of the court for the trial of impeachments, other than the judges of the court of appeals, which members shall receive for their services while Compensation of members of the court for the trial of impeachments and of managers.

actually attending said court, when summoned, the same rate of compensation as the judges of the court of appeals (other than the chief judge) are entitled by law to receive for their services and expenses for the same time, and for compensation of the managers on the part of the assembly, who shall receive the same rate of compensation as the members of said court of impeachment (other than the said chief judge) are entitled to receive for services and expenses for the same time, thirty-five thousand dollars, or so much thereof as shall be necessary; and for the per diem and mileage of the officers of said court at the same rate as the same officers are allowed by law for attendance upon the legislature, and for the expenses of necessary stenographic assistants and printing, service of subpœnas (where not served by an officer of the court) and for fees of witnesses to be paid on the certificate of the president of the court, fifteen thousand dollars, or so much thereof as shall be necessary; and for the necessary expenses of the managers and of counsel employed by them during the trial, not above provided for, to be paid on the certificate of the chairman of said board of managers, six thousand dollars, or so much thereof as may be necessary; and the comptroller is hereby authorized to pay the expenses of printing the testimony heretofore taken by the judiciary committee of the assembly in the judicial investigation in the city of New York, and authorized by resolution of the assembly, and the sum of six thousand dollars, or so much thereof as shall be necessary, is hereby appropriated for that purpose.

Of officers of the court.

Expenses of managers and counsel employed by them.

Comptroller to adjust accounts of H. C. Tanner, and treasurer to pay same.

The comptroller is hereby authorized and directed to adjust the account of Hudson C. Tanner, stenographer, for reporting the Black river claims, so called, and when so adjusted the treasurer shall pay him at the same rate, proportionately for actual service, and when actually subject to the direction of the state attorney in those cases, less the amount already paid, as the assembly stenographer is entitled to receive for reporting and transcribing, and to reimburse him for moneys expended by him for assistant stenographers and other necessary disbursements, and for that purpose the sum of nine thousand two hundred and seven dollars, or so much thereof as may be necessary, is hereby appropriated.

Law libraries of the 5th and 8th judicial districts.

For the law library of the eighth judical district, fifteen hundred dollars, and for the law library of the fifth judicial district, four thousand dollars for the purchase of books.

Superintendent of public instruction.

For the superintendent of public instruction, additional compensation for the year ending April first, eighteen hundred and seventy-two, the sum of twenty-five hundred dollars; and for the fractional part of the year, ending September thirtieth, eighteen hundred and seventy-two, the sum of twelve hundred and fifty dollars; and hereafter the said superintendent shall receive no other compensation than that allowed by law.

State prison at Sing Sing.

For the state prison at Sing Sing, for the support of the quarry works, to be paid from moneys received from the income of said works, seven thousand dollars per month, and any part of this appropriation not used in any one month can be drawn and used in any succeeding month, if required; and all receipts derived from said quarry works shall be reported monthly to the comptroller, and the moneys derived therefrom shall be paid monthly into the treasury of the state; and for the purchase of testaments and books for the library of said prison, the sum of five hundred dollars, to be paid to the chaplain, upon the production by him of the proper vouchers for the same, subject to the approval of the comptroller; for building and repairs, five thousand dollars; for dock and basin, five thousand dollars, and for repairing mess-room floor, five hundred dollars.

Auburn State prison. For the Auburn State prison, for building and repairs, two thousand dollars; for purchase of land for burying ground for prison and asylum, five hundred dollars; for slating and repairing roofs, one thousand dollars; for paints and oils, five hundred dollars; for new doors, casements and locks for north wing, ten thousand dollars; and for replenishing the library for the use of the convicts therein, five hundred dollars, and for supplying an additional number of testaments and hymn books, two hundred dollars; these two last items to be expended under the direction of the chaplain of the prison, upon vouchers to be approved by the comptroller.

Asylum for Insane Convicts at Auburn. For the purpose of enlarging the Asylum for Insane Convicts at Auburn, the sum of twenty-five thousand dollars, to be expended by the inspectors of state prisons, and in the construction of said enlargement, said inspectors are required to employ convict labor as far as practicable, and they may take such or, so many convicts, skilled in mechanical labor from any of the prisons of this state, as may be necessary.

Clinton State prison. For the Clinton State prison, for making an inclosure to the prison, two thousand dollars; for repairs to the state plank-roads, one thousand dollars; for finishing the new coal kilns, five hundred dollars; for the prison library, to be expended under the direction of the chaplain of the prison, upon vouchers to be approved by the comptroller, five hundred dollars; for finishing and furnishing the new tailor shop, five hundred dollars; and for the salary of the superintendent of the manufacturing department for one year ending May fifth, eighteen hundred and seventy-two, two thousand dollars.

State prisons. For the support and maintenance of the state prisons, for the residue of the current fiscal year, including expenses of manufacturing at Clinton prison, three hundred and seventy-five thousand dollars.

Rev. Jas. Hasson. For the Reverend James Hasson, for religious and other services rendered to the convicts of Sing Sing prison, nine hundred dollars.

David B. McNeill. For David B. McNeill, for compensation in making up report of inspectors of state prisons, after the expiration of his term of service, one thousand dollars. Hereafter no such compensation shall be paid to any inspector of state prisons. And any failure on the part of said inspectors hereafter to make their annual report to the comptroller, at the time and in the

Failure of inspectors to make report, a

misdemeanor. manner now required by law, shall be a misdemeanor on the part of each of such inspectors, and shall subject each of them to the indictment and punishment now provided by law for misdemeanors. And the comptroller of this state, or such persons as he may appoint in his place, shall have power, at any time that he may deem proper, to make such examination as he may deem necessary into the affairs of the prisons of this state, and for that purpose shall have the powers of a court of record to subpœna witnesses and compel their attendance, to administer oaths and to examine such witnesses under oath, in relation to any matters pertaining to such prisons. The persons whom he may appoint shall also have power to examine all the books, papers and vouchers of said prisons; and it shall be the duty of any and all the officers of said prisons to furnish the persons appointed by said comptroller with all books, papers and vouchers pertaining to said prisons, whenever they shall be demanded by said persons so appointed by said comptroller.

Comptroller may examine into affairs of prisons of this state.

Comptroller to pay moneys to Salmon Wheat on order of Jas. Wheat. For Nelson K. Hopkins, comptroller, sixteen hundred and sixty-eight dollars and seventy-two cents, with interest thereon at six per cent per annum, to be calculated upon balances, at any time in the treasury, of moneys deposited to the credit of James Wheat, a life convict in the state prison at Auburn, to be paid by said comptroller to Salmon Wheat, his father, upon the order of said James Wheat, convict, duly attested by the keeper of the state prison at Auburn, and properly acknowledged before a notary public.

Mary Doheny. For Mary Doheny, to re-imburse her for her costs and expenses incurred by her in defending her title to lands purchased by her grantor from the state, and to refund to her the consideration money paid therefor, and interest thereon, and for taxes paid and improvements made on said lands by her, the sum of four hundred and twenty-two dollars, or so much thereof as shall be certified by the attorney-general and the state engineer and surveyor to be a just and legal claim against the state, in case the state was an individual or corporation.

Frederick Kilian. For Frederick Kilian, for repayment of expenses incurred by him in the case of the contested election for member of assembly for the fifteenth district of the county of New York, as follows, namely: For compensation of counsel, one thousand two hundred and fifty dollars; for traveling expenses and disbursements, one hundred and twenty-five dollars; and for compensation as member of assembly for the period that his seat was held by Alexander Frear, three dollars per day and the allowance for mileage which is made by law to the members of the legislature; but one allowance for mileage for the whole time is to be made to him.

Alexander Frear. For Alexander Frear, for compensation of counsel employed by him in the case of the contested election for member of assembly for the fifteenth district of the county of New York, the sum of fourteen hundred and fifty dollars.

For John H. Reynolds, five hundred dollars for counsel fees for defending the right of the sitting member from the nineteenth assembly district of the county of New York to his seat. John H. Reynolds.

For John J. Blair, for compensation of counsel employed by him in the case of the contested election for member of assembly for the fourth district of the county of New York, the sum of four hundred and seventy-five dollars, and for expenses of witnesses and their traveling expenses, one hundred and eighteen dollars. John J. Blair.

For James Dunphy, for compensation of counsel employed by him in the case of the contested election for member of assembly for the second district of the county of New York, and for his expenses incurred therein, the sum of four hundred and fifty dollars. James Dunphy.

For such persons as the supreme court may, on notice to the attorney-general, pursuant to the statute, decide, are entitled to the same or any part thereof, the sum of thirteen hundred and thirty-three dollars and sixty-six cents, heretofore paid into the treasury of the state by E. A. Roe, treasurer of the county of Queens, as administrator of the estate of Diedrich Schmonsees, deceased, on or about the twenty-eighth day of June, eighteen hundred and seventy-one, to the credit of such estate. Relative to moneys of Diedrich Schmonsees.

The sum of one million dollars is hereby appropriated toward the erection of the new capitol, which shall be paid by the treasurer upon the warrant of the comptroller to the order of the new capitol commissioners as they shall require the same. Whenever there is a deficiency in the treasury of moneys applicable to the payment of this appropriation, the comptroller is hereby authorized and required to borrow, from time to time, such sums as the said commissioners may require, and the money so borrowed shall be refunded from the moneys received from the taxes levied to meet this appropriation. Erection of the new capitol.

For furnishing a statue of George Clinton to be placed in the capitol at Washington, the sum of twelve thousand five hundred dollars, or so much thereof as may be necessary. Statue of George Clinton.

For the Normal School at Fredonia, to be paid to and expended by the local board thereof for improving the heating apparatus of said school, the sum of three thousand dollars. Normal School at Fredonia.

For supplying the Potsdam Normal School building with water, six hundred dollars. At Potsdam.

For the Normal School at Geneseo, to be paid and expended by the local board for repairing and replacing the heating apparatus of said school, the sum of three thousand dollars. At Geneseo.

For the Normal School at Cortland, the sum of one thousand dollars appropriated by chapter four hundred and ninety-two of the laws of eighteen hundred and seventy, for repairs, etc., but not drawn, is hereby re-appropriated to be paid upon the certificate of the superintendent of public instruction as provided in said act. At Cortland.

At Buffalo. For the Normal School at Buffalo, to be exper local board thereof, for repairing of the school b thousand dollars, or so much thereof as may be n

At Brockport. For the Normal School at Brockport, for repai pended by the local board, three thousand dollars, thereof as may be necessary.

National Lincoln Monument Association. For the National Lincoln Monument Associati in the erection of a suitable monument at the gra liam Lincoln, at Springfield, in the state of I particularly for completing the adornment of t for the same; for the flag-stones and walks base of the monument, and for the bronze panels in the memorial hall thereof, the sum of te dollars, to be paid to the treasurer of such assoc evidence shall be furnished to the comptroller that amount of funds has been secured to build the This appropriation is in lieu of a like amount app chapter four hundred and eighty-one of the laws hundred and sixty-seven, and is a re-appropriatio the same purpose.

When to be paid.

Theodore F. Olmstead, treasurer of Livingston county. For Theodore F. Olmstead, treasurer of the co ingston, one thousand eight hundred and four seventy-one cents, that being the amount claime said county pursuant to chapter eight hundred a of the laws of eighteen hundred and sixty-eight, eight hundred and fifty-seven of the laws of eight and sixty-nine, but which it is claimed has not and said sum is hereby re-appropriated and shall the treasury of said county of Livingston upon thereof by the above-mentioned Theodore F. Olmst treasurer, if upon investigation the comptroller sh that the same has not been paid and is due.

Nathan P. Wheeler, treasurer of Chenango county. For Nathan P. Wheeler, county treasurer of th Chenango, the sum of four hundred and eighty and ninety-six cents, and the sum of eight hundre two dollars and sixty-three cents, being the amou to be due said county pursuant to chapter eight h seventeen of the laws of eighteen hundred and sixt chapter eight hundred and fifty-seven of the laws hundred and sixty-nine, respectively, but which not been drawn, and said sums it is claimed* ar appropriated and shall be paid into the treas county of Chenango upon the receipt thereof by mentioned Nathan P. Wheeler, as such treasur investigation the comptroller shall ascertain the sa been paid and are due.

Wm. D. Brennan, treasurer of Franklin county, "as such treasurer." For William D. Brennan, county treasurer of th Franklin, "as such county treasurer," the sum dred and twenty-nine dollars and fifty-five cent amount due said county pursuant to chapter eig and fifty-seven of the laws of eighteen hundred an

---

* So in the original.

but which sum has not been drawn, and said sum is hereby re-appropriated, and shall be paid into the treasury of said county of Franklin, upon the receipt thereof by the above-named William D. Brennan, as such treasurer, if upon investigation the comptroller shall ascertain the same has not been paid and is due.

Treasurer of Herkimer county. For the treasurer of the county of Herkimer, eight hundred and thirty-nine dollars and thirty-seven cents, that being the amount claimed to be due said county, pursuant to chapter eight hundred and fifty-seven, laws of eighteen hundred and sixty-nine, but which said amount it is claimed has not been drawn, and it is hereby re-appropriated, and shall be paid into the treasury of said county of Herkimer, subject to the order of the board of supervisors thereof, if upon investigation the comptroller shall ascertain that the same has not been drawn and is due.

James McDermott. For James McDermott, messenger to the postmaster of the assembly of eighteen hundred and seventy-one, the sum of three hundred and eighty-one dollars and fifty cents, that being alleged to be the amount due him as such messenger, but which it is alleged he has not received, the same to be paid by the comptroller when he is satisfied that the said McDermott was entitled to and has not received his pay.

Treasurer of Otsego county. For the treasurer of the county of Otsego, nine hundred and forty-nine dollars and eighty-one cents, that being the amount claimed to be due said county pursuant to chapter eight hundred and fifty-seven, laws of eighteen hundred and sixty-nine; and nine hundred and sixty-five dollars and fifty cents, that being the amount claimed to be due said county pursuant to chapter seven hundred and four, laws of eighteen hundred and seventy; and the sum of nine hundred and thirty-one dollars and sixty-five cents, that being the amount claimed to be due said county pursuant to chapter eight hundred and sixty-nine, laws of eighteen hundred and seventy-one, but which said amounts, it is claimed, have not been drawn, and they are hereby reappropriated, and shall be paid into the treasury of said county of Otsego, subject to the order of the board of supervisors thereof, if upon investigation the comptroller shall ascertain that the same have not been drawn and are due.

Comptroller may withhold certain appropriations. The comptroller is hereby authorized to withhold payment of any appropriation named in chapter eight hundred and fifty-seven, laws of eighteen hundred and sixty-nine, seven hundred and four, laws of eighteen hundred and seventy, and eight hundred and sixty-nine, laws of eighteen hundred and seventy-one, when possessed of information from any responsible source which in his judgment will justify such action until the objection is removed.

Willard asylum for the insane. For the Willard asylum for the insane, to be expended under the direction of the trustees thereof, for the completion, furnishing, heating, putting in steam, water and gas pipe, and for sewerage of the north wing extension, and for the detached buildings now partially erected, and for finishing and furnishing the same, thirty-five thousand dollars; for enlarging and equipping the laundry thereof, for grading and ornamenting the grounds, and for completing the center buildings and wings, twenty thousand dollars; for the erection and furnishing of two dormitory buildings, to complete the group of detached buildings now in course of erection, thirty-five thousand dollars; for the extension and improvement of piers, dock and harbor, five thousand dollars; for the improvement of the farm, making fences, bridges and roads, and the purchase of stock and implements, ten thousand dollars; for fuel until the first of October, eighteen hundred and seventy-two, six thousand dollars, and after said first of October, eighteen hundred and seventy-two, the necessary fuel shall be included among the expenses of maintaining the patients of said institution; for fire engine and appliances for extinguishing fire, ten thousand dollars; and for furnishing a permanent supply of water, fan and furniture, ten thousand dollars. Section three of chapter three hundred and forty-two of the laws of eighteen hundred and sixty-five, is hereby amended so as to allow the employment of a building superintendent other than one of the board of trustees of said asylum.

Buffalo state asylum for the insane. For the Buffalo state asylum for the insane, for the construction of buildings, to be paid to, and expended by, the trustees thereof, the sum of one hundred and fifty thousand dollars, and the following named persons are hereby appointed managers thereof in addition to those heretofore appointed: Silas H. Fish, Joseph Churchyard, Robert G. Stewart, Orlando Allen, Philip Houck, Alonzo Tanner and Merritt Brooks, whose respective terms of office shall be and continue for five years. Managers.

N. Y. S. Institution for the Blind at Batavia. To the New York State Institution for the Blind at Batavia, for furnishing, repairs, improvement of grounds and other necessary expenses, ten thousand dollars, or so much thereof as may be necessary.

Managers of the Society for the Reformation of Juvenile Delinquents in the city of N. Y. For the managers of the Society for the Reformation of Juvenile Delinquents in the city of New York, commonly called the House of Refuge on Randall's Island, for deficiencies in the support and maintenance of juvenile delinquents therein for the year ending on the first day of January, eighteen hundred and seventy-two, the sum of twelve thousand six hundred and ninety dollars and ninety-eight cents; and to enable the board of managers of said institution to make necessary alterations in the school buildings, kitchen and laundry thereof, and to erect a suitable workshop on the premises for the temporary employment of a class of boys discharged from confinement and awaiting employment elsewhere, the sum of thirty-five thousand dollars.

Chapter 724, laws of 1871, repealed. Chapter seven hundred and twenty-four of the laws of eighteen hundred and seventy-one, entitled "An act to define the powers of the corporation attorney of the city of New York, in suits for fines and penalties," passed April twenty-six, eighteen hundred and seventy-one, is hereby repealed, and section three of chapter thirteen, of the laws of eighteen hundred and Section 3, chapter 13, laws of thirty-nine is hereby re-enacted, so that all license money received by the mayor or other authorities in the city of New York, for permission to exhibit theatrical or equestrian performances within said city, shall be paid over by the officer receiving the same to the treasurer of the Society for the Reformation of Juvenile Delinquents in the city of New York, for the use of said society. 1839, re-enacted.

For the Thomas Asylum, for orphan and destitute Indian children, for the education and maintenance of one hundred children at the rate of eighty-five dollars per capita, eight thousand five hundred dollars. Thomas Asylum, for orphan Indian children.

For the New York Asylum for Idiots at Geddes, Onondaga county, for furniture for the new building, the sum of five thousand dollars. N. Y. Asylum for Idiots at Geddes.

For the Inebriate Asylum at Binghamton, to purchase a certain mortgage upon the property thereof, authorized by the legislature of eighteen hundred and sixty-one, for principal and interest, the sum of sixty-six thousand three hundred dollars; the commissioners of the land office shall take an assignment and transfer of, and hold said mortgage for the benefit of the state. Allen Munroe is hereby appointed a trustee of said asylum in the place of Pierson Mundy, Lotus Ingalls in the place of William W. Gordon, Benjamin F. Bruce in the place of Asher P. Nichols, E. Ely in the place of John G. Orton, and Charles Van Benthuysen in the place of Peter L. Danforth; and the said Pierson Mundy, William W. Gordon, Asher P. Nichols, John G. Orton, and Peter L. Danforth, are hereby removed as such trustees, and the state comptroller is hereby added to the board of trustees of said asylum. Inebriate Asylum at Binghamton, to purchase mortgage. Trustees.

For the completion of the buildings of the Hudson River State Hospital for the Insane, already commenced, for water and sewerage, for stock and improvement of farm and grounds, for furniture, furnishing books and instruments, and for deficiencies in expense account incident upon the opening of the hospital, one hundred and fifty thousand dollars. Hudson River State Hospital for the Insane, for completion of buildings, etc.

For the salaries of officers, eight thousand dollars, or so much thereof as may be necessary. Salaries of officers.

For the New York State Lunatic Asylum at Utica, to reimburse their fund for the support and maintenance for moneys taken therefrom to make additions, alterations and repairs to the buildings thereof, the sum of fifty-two thousand nine hundred and twenty-nine dollars and sixty cents. N. Y. State Lunatic Asylum at Utica.

For the Asylum for Insane Convicts at Auburn, for maintenance for the residue of the current fiscal year, three thousand dollars. Asylum for Insane Convicts at Auburn.

For furniture for the Homœopathic Asylum for the Insane, at Middletown, to be paid when the comptroller is satisfied that the said asylum buildings are ready to receive the same, ten thousand dollars, or so much thereof as may be necessary. Homœopathic Asylum for the Insane at Middletown.

The lands of the State Homœopathic Asylum for the Insane, at Middletown, consisting of about two hundred acres, having been paid for by private donations, and good and sufficient Comptroller to pay unexpended balance of

Appropriation by act ch. 237, laws of 1871. warranty deed, free from all incumbrances, having been obtained for the state, the treasurer is hereby directed to pay, on the warrant of the comptroller, the remainder yet unpaid of the appropriation of one hundred and fifty thousand dollars, made by chapter two hundred and thirty-seven of the laws of eighteen hundred and seventy-one, passed March thirty-one, eighteen hundred and seventy-one, without the conditions prescribed requiring the trustees to raise by private or municipal donations other than from the state an amount equal to one-half of the sum appropriated by the state.

N. Y. Orthopædic Dispensary. For the New York Orthopædic Dispensary, for treatment of spinal and hip-joint diseases, twenty-thousand dollars, to be expended in the erection of a hospital and clinic rooms, whenever a like amount shall have been raised and paid in by private subscription, and whenever it shall be proven to the comptroller that said institution has, during the past year, treated free of charge at least three hundred indigent patients, residents of this state, and on the further condition that said nstitution shall hereafter treat annually, free of charge, all indigent patients, residents of this state, who shall apply for such treatment to the number of five hundred.

Brooklyn City Hospital. For the Brooklyn City Hospital, the sum of nineteen hundred and forty-nine dollars and seventy-eight cents, being the proportionate part of the appropriation of seventy-five thousand dollars, to hospitals in chapter eight hundred and sixty-nine, of the laws of eighteen hundred and seventy-one, due to said Brooklyn City Hospital, but not received by it.

State Reformatory at Elmira. For the purpose of carrying out the provisions of chapter four hundred and twenty-seven, laws of eighteen hundred and seventy, for the erection of the State Reformatory at Elmira, the sum of two hundred thousand dollars is hereby appropriated, and the board of building commissioners thereof shall hereafter consist of nine persons instead of five, as provided in said act; and from and after the passage of this act, William

Commissioners. Dundas, Frank H. Atkinson, Samuel C. Taber, John Davis Baldwin, Stephen T. Arnot, of Elmira: Charles C. B. Walker, of Corning; Charles D. Champlain, of Urbana; Ezra S. Buckbee and Abraham H. Miller, of Owego, shall constitute such commissioners in place of those heretofore appointed under said act, and they shall possess all the powers, and be subject to all the provisions contained in said act, in relation to said building commissioners.

Western House of Refuge. For the Western House of Refuge, for deficiency in the appropriations of last year, and for over drafts for expenses in putting in apparatus for heating, for constructing main and lateral sewers, and for building boiler-house, the sum of twenty thousand dollars.

Widow and heirs of John G. Wasson. The comptroller is authorized to pay six hundred dollars, being six per cent on ten thousand dollars due the widow and heirs at law of John G. Wasson, upon a certificate issued under chapter eight hundred and thirty of the laws of eighteen hundred and sixty-eight, and he is authorized to pay such interest semi-annually until the principal can be paid.

For Peter Allanson, for the construction and erection of cases and shelving in the State Geological Hall for the preservation and care of the Museum of Natural History, pursuant to contract awarded to him by authority of the commissioners of the land office, the sum of two thousand seven hundred dollars, or so much thereof as may be necessary, payable whenever evidence shall be furnished to the comptroller that the work has been performed. Peter Allanson.

For T. W. Stevens, for ink, dies and stamps furnished to the late postmaster of the assembly, twenty-six dollars and fifty cents. T. W. Stevens.

For Thorn and Watson, for the balance due them for iron ore sold and delivered by them to the Clinton state prison authorities in eighteen hundred and sixty-five, eighteen hundred and sixty-six, eighteen hundred and sixty-seven, eighteen hundred and sixty-eight, and eighteen hundred and sixty-nine, including the interest, the sum of three thousand two hundred and twenty-seven dollars and forty-five cents, or so much thereof as may be necessary. Thorn and Watson.

For Henry S. Van Etten, as compensation for services as superintendent in the manufacturing department of Sing Sing prison, the sum of two thousand dollars, which the comptroller is hereby authorized and required to pay to him. Henry S. Van Etten.

For Michael M. O'Sullivan, for balance due him for services as page to the assembly during the session of eighteen hundred and seventy-one, beyond the time for which he was paid, the sum of one hundred and eighteen dollars. Michael O'Sullivan.

For additional compensation for the keeper of Washington's head-quarters, Newburgh, one hundred and fifty dollars. Washington's head-quarters.

For John Graff, for the amount awarded to him by the adjutant-general, inspector-general and quartermaster-general of this state, under and in pursuance of chapter two hundred and seventy of the laws of eighteen hundred and seventy-one, the sum of two thousand dollars, or so much thereof as may be necessary. John Graff.

For Murray and Goodwin, for lithographing, as per resolution of assembly passed February third, eighteen hundred and seventy-one, twenty-five sets diagrams for each member, officer and reporter of the house, and fifty on boards, one thousand seven hundred and fifty-eight dollars and seventy-five cents; and for lithographing, as per resolution of assembly passed March thirty-first, eighteen hundred and, seventy-one, twenty-five sets diagrams for each member, officer and reporter of the house, eight hundred copies in gilt and fifty on boards, one thousand eight hundred and eighteen dollars and seventy-five cents. Murray and Goodwin.

For Banks and Brothers, for law books supplied for the library of the court of appeals at Rochester, the sum of eleven hundred and sixteen dollars and fifty-one cents; for supplying books for the library of the court of appeals at Syracuse, seven hundred and twenty-four dollars and thirty-seven cents; for supplying books for the office of the attorney-general, three hundred and fifty-one dollars and sixty-four cents; for Banks & Brothers.

supplying books for the office of the secretary of state, four hundred and twelve dollars; for books supplied to the regents of the university, two hundred and seventy-seven dollars and fifty cents; for books supplied to the late clerk of the assembly, seventy-six dollars; and for sets of the statutes, reports and digests of the state, sent by the authority and action of the governor, as a gift from this state to the law library of Chicago, one thousand six hundred dollars, or so much thereof as may be necessary, the last item to be paid upon the certificate of the governor; for furnishing for one year for the use of the members of the commission of appeals, a law library, one thousand dollars, and for Hand's reports furnished to the office of the secretary of state, one hundred and sixty-six dollars and fifty cents.

Gift to law library of Chicago.

Law libraries.

For the law libraries of each of the judicial districts of the state, for the purchase of books, one thousand dollars.

Section two of chapter seven hundred and fifteen of the laws of eighteen hundred and seventy-one is hereby amended by striking out the following: "The contract for printing and publishing the reports of the court of appeals shall be extended for five years, provided the secretary of state shall deem it for the interest of the state."

Charles Van Benthuysen & Sons.

For Charles Van Benthuysen and Sons for printing annual report of the superintendent of public instruction, and for interest on their bill for two years, three thousand nine hundred and fifty-eight dollars and seventy-two cents; to be paid only on the certificate of the superintendent of public instruction, both as to the amount and value of services rendered; for printing and binding one thousand copies of the catalogue of the state library for eighteen hundred and seventy-two, in accordance with chapter two hundred and fifty-five, section seven of the laws of eighteen hundred and forty-four, four thousand dollars, or so much thereof as may be necessary. The bill for this last item shall be audited by the secretary of the board of regents, and paid for on his certificate, subject to the revision of the comptroller.

Weed, Parsons & Co.

For Weed, Parsons and Company, for lithographing and printing five thousand six hundred copies title page, and five thousand six hundred copies railroad maps of the state of New York for the state engineer and surveyor's report on railroads for eighteen hundred and seventy-one, to be refunded to the treasury by the several railroad corporations of this state in proportion to their respective gross receipts, pursuant to chapter five hundred and twenty-six of the laws of eighteen hundred and fifty-five, the sum of two thousand and fifty-six dollars; for printing, ruling and binding thirteen thousand five hundred copies school registers for the department of public instruction, the sum of thirteen thousand five hundred dollars; for printing five hundred copies of annual report of the superintendent of the insurance department for eighteen hundred and seventy-one, to be refunded to the treasury by the several insurance companies, associations, persons and agents, pursuant to chapter three hundred and sixty-six of the laws of eighteen hundred and fifty-nine, the sum of fourteen hundred and ninety-one dollars and thirty cents, to be paid upon the certificate of the delivery of the book by the superintendent of the department; for printing for the use of the commissioners to revise the statutes of the state of New York, to be paid upon the certificate of said commissioners that the work has been performed, the sum of four thousand dollars; for printing miscellaneous books, blanks, etcetera, for the adjutant-general's office, the sum of five thousand two hundred and ninety-two dollars and seventy cents; and for publishing the general laws of the state of New York, for the year eighteen hundred and seventy, in the Albany Law Journal, to be paid on the affidavit of the publisher, two thousand seven hundred dollars, and for engraving, printing and coloring lithographic plates for volumes twenty-three and twenty-four of the state cabinet of natural history, seven thousand dollars, or so much thereof as may be necessary, to be paid on the certificate of the state curator of the state cabinet of natural history. Publishing general laws in Albany Law Journal.

For the Argus company, for printing and binding blank forms for reports of horse and steam railroads of the state, and for binding two volumes of original reports of railroads, the sum of one hundred and ninety-six dollars; which said two several sums of eight thousand six hundred and forty dollars* and one hundred and ninety-six dollars, are to be refunded to the treasury of the state by the several railroad corporations of this state in proportion to their respective gross receipts, pursuant to chapter five hundred and twenty-six of the laws of eighteen hundred and fifty-five; on which two sums there has been advanced to the Argus company from the treasury of the state, the sum of five thousand dollars, which is to be refunded to the treasury out of the said fund so to be drawn from the several railroads; for printing calendars, registers, decision books, and other printing and binding for the commission of appeals, from September fifteenth, eighteen hundred and seventy, to November twenty-ninth, eighteen hundred and seventy-one, inclusive, the sum of two thousand and seventy dollars and fifty cents, and for printing and binding four thousand copies "military code," five hundred in paper covers and three thousand five hundred in cloth, with gilt side title, two thousand five hundred and ninety-one dollars. Argus company.

For W. C. Little and company, for law books supplied to the office of the attorney-general, from January seventeen to March twenty-two, eighteen hundred and seventy-two, the sum of three hundred and ninety-five dollars, and for books furnished said office from May first, eighteen hundred and sixty-nine, to March ten, eighteen hundred and seventy, sixty-four dollars. W. C. Little & Co.

For Lyman B. Smith, late assistant clerk of the assembly, for preparing for the use of the legislature a compilation of the majority and minority reports in contested elections to seats in the assembly, under resolution of the assembly passed Lyman B. Smith.

*So in the original.

April eighteenth, eighteen hundred and seventy-one, the sum of two thousand dollars; and for compiling the majority and minority reports of any standing or special committee appointed by the assembly to investigate any breach of privilege, under the same resolution, the sum of one thousand dollars.

C.W. Armstrong. For Cornelius W. Armstrong, for arranging the files of the assembly in such a manner that papers when wanted can be readily found, and for separating and labeling bills passed, and for arranging alphabetically petitions and papers connected with bills, under a resolution of the assembly passed April eighteen, eighteen hundred and seventy-one, the sum of five hundred dollars; for making an index to the papers on file in the assembly, and also an index of bills introduced during the session of eighteen hundred and seventy-one, under a resolution of the assembly passed April eighteen, eighteen hundred and seventy-one, the sum of four hundred dollars; for preparing for the use of the legislature an index of all senate bills printed from eighteen hundred and sixty-two to and including eighteen hundred and seventy-one, under a resolution of the assembly passed April eighteen, eighteen hundred and seventy-one, the sum of one thousand dollars.

Walter A. Cook. For Walter A. Cook, for making index to documents under the direction of the clerk, pursuant to a resolution of the house, the sum of one thousand dollars.

John Paterson. To John Paterson, state superintendent of weights and measures, in accordance with the provisions of section eighteen, chapter one hundred and thirty-four of the laws of eighteen hundred and fifty-one, two hundred dollars.

Edward Danforth. For Edward Danforth, for additional compensation for services as deputy superintendent of public instruction, the sum of nine hundred and seventy-five dollars.

Salt springs at Montezuma. The sum of three thousand dollars is hereby appropriated for the purpose of further developing the salt springs at Montezuma, to be expended by the present commissioners, appointed by chapter four hundred ninety-two of the laws of eighteen hundred and seventy; and the sum of five thousand dollars is hereby appropriated for the purpose of developing the salt springs near the village of Weedsport, in the county of Cayuga, to be expended in boring and sinking wells, under the direction of Harvy C. Beach, Charles S. Gross and Leonard F. Hardy, who are hereby appointed commissioners for that purpose, and who shall account to the comptroller therefor.

Salt springs near Weedsport.

Syracuse Solar Salt Company. For the Syracuse Solar Salt Company, for the removal of seven hundred and fifty-five salt vats from the lands of the state in the third ward of the city of Syracuse, the sum of thirty-seven thousand seven hundred and fifty dollars; to the Onondaga Solar Salt Company, for the removal of eighteen hundred and fifty-six salt vats from the lands of the state in the third ward of the city of Syracuse, the sum of ninety-two thousand eight hundred dollars; to Lyman Stevens and company, for the removal of five hundred and seventeen salt vats from the lands of the state in the third ward of the city of

Onondaga Solar Salt Company.

Lyman Stevens & Co.

Syracuse, the sum of twenty-five thousand eight hundred and fifty dollars; to Chauncey B. Clark, the sum of five thousand two hundred and twenty dollars, and to George F. Comstock and Harvey Stewart, the sum of eight thousand four hundred and sixty dollars, for the purchase-money of lands conveyed by them respectively to the state of New York to supply the deficiency created by the sale by the state of the lands from which salt vats in the third ward of the city of Syracuse had been removed, pursuant to a resolution of the commissioners of the land office, passed December six, eighteen hundred and seventy-one, and chapter two hundred and seventy-nine of the laws of eighteen hundred and seventy, and section seven of article seven of the constitution of this state, together with interest at six per cent per annum upon the several sums above mentioned from the time of the removal of the vats in the several instances aforesaid, or from the date of the delivery of the respective deeds aforesaid, which said several sums are to be re-imbursed to the general fund from the moneys already in the treasury, or from such sums of money as may hereafter be paid therein, arising from the sales of the lands from which said salt vats have been or are ordered to be removed. The balance remaining from the sale of such lands, after the payment of the several amounts hereinbefore mentioned, shall be and remain in the treasury as a part of the general fund.

C. B. Clark. G. F. Comstock and Harvey Stewart.

To John White and company, for the removal of eleven hundred salt vats from the lands of the state in the third ward of the city of Syracuse, to be paid whenever the commissioners of the land office shall cause the same to be removed, and for the purchase of other land whereon to erect a like number of salt vats, pursuant to chapter two hundred and seventy-nine of the laws of eighteen hundred and seventy, the sum of sixty thousand dollars, or so much thereof as may be necessary.

John White & Co.

For the health officer of the port of New York, the sum of four thousand dollars, or so much thereof as may be necessary, to pay the salaries of not exceeding four policemen, at quarantine, on the average, during the year eighteen hundred and seventy-two; such policemen may be appointed and dismissed by him at pleasure, and they shall perform patrol and police duty, under his direction, in connection with the quarantine establishment and upon the waters of the bay of New York; and they shall possess all the powers possessed by policemen in the cities of New York and Brooklyn; and any person arrested by either of said policemen for violating any law relating to quarantine, in said port, may be taken by him before any court of criminal jurisdiction, or any magistrate or police justice, within the county of Richmond, and, thereupon, the court, magistrate or police justice before whom such offender shall be brought, shall have jurisdiction to hear, try and punish the offender for the offense committed by him, in the same manner, and with the like effect, as if the same had been committed within the limits over which such court, magistrate or police justice has jurisdiction to punish for offenses under existing laws.

Health officer of port of New York.

Commissioners of quarantine. For the commissioners of quarantine, for the payment of existing obligations incurred under the authority for fitting up the hospital ship "Illinois," the sum of twenty thousand three hundred and seventy-nine dollars and seven cents; for repairs on steamboats "Andrew Fletcher" and "Governor Fenton," eleven thousand five hundred and sixteen dollars and eighteen cents; and for indebtedness on account of cholera, seventeen thousand eight hundred and forty-nine dollars and sixty-two cents; for the rent and keeping in order of that portion of the quarantine establishment leased under and in pursuance of the provisions of chapter four hundred and ninety-two of the laws of eighteen hundred and seventy, the sum of fifteen thousand dollars; for the care and maintenance of the quarantine establishment, and defraying the necessary expenses of said board in the discharge of the duties imposed upon it by law, the sum of fifty-six thousand dollars; and said commissioners shall also therefrom pay the running expenses of a steamboat for boarding vessels, and transporting the sick and burying the dead.

Site for boarding station for vessels. The commissioners of quarantine are hereby authorized and empowered to select a site to be approved by the health officer, for a boarding station for vessels coming from non-infected ports, including, if practicable, a residence for the health officer and his deputies, and to purchase or enter into a contract for the purchase of the same upon such terms and conditions as shall be approved by the health officer, and the commissioners of the land office. But such site shall not be located on Long Island or Coney Island.

Board of commissioners constituted by act passed April 21, 1866. For the board of commissioners constituted by the act entitled "An act in relation to quarantine, and providing for the construction of the permanent quarantine establishment," passed April twenty-one, eighteen hundred and sixty-six, in addition to existing appropriations, the sum of one hundred and ninety thousand dollars, or such part of said sum as, in the opinion of the health officer, may be required for the following purposes, namely: For the purpose of defraying the necessary expenses of said board in the discharge of the duties imposed upon it by law, and for the erection and equipment of suitable buildings on the island at West Bank, for the reception and care of passengers who may have been exposed to disease, and who may be sent there by the health officer; such buildings shall be erected under a contract to be entered into therefor in the manner prescribed in the fourth section of the aforesaid act, passed April twenty-one, eighteen hundred and sixty-six; except that said board shall award the contract to the lowest responsible bidder; but it may in its discretion reject any bid which it may not deem for the interest of the state to accept; and it may also enter into separate contracts for separate portions of said work; and for the necessary care and preservation of the quarantine establishment structures on West Bank Island; provided that the plans for such buildings and the bids for the construction thereof, shall be approved by the present health officer.

Buildings at West Bank.

"And the lower of the West Bank Islands, built under the direction of Dr. Swinburne, shall hereafter be known and designated as Swinburne Hospital Island." Swinburne Hospital Island.

"For the owners of the lands on Staten Island, conveyed to them by the state, by letters patent, dated January fourteen, eighteen hundred and sixty-nine, the sum of six thousand dollars, or so much thereof as the comptroller shall ascertain and determine to have been paid by them for interest accruing prior to May first, eighteen hundred and seventy-one, on the mortgage executed by the commissioners of emigration on said lands, and for costs and expenses paid by said owners by reason of an action brought to foreclose said mortgage, and for interest on such moneys paid for such interest, costs and expenses of foreclosure from the time of the payment of the same by said owners." Owners of land on Staten Island.

"The time for the corporation, formed under the authority of chapter four hundred and ninety of the laws of eighteen hundred and seventy, for the erection of warehouses for quarantine purposes to commence its operations, is hereby extended for the period of two years from and after the passage of this act, and said corporation shall not be deemed dissolved if it shall commence its operations within that period." Time for erection of warehouses for quarantine extended.

So much of chapter four hundred and ninety-two of the laws of eighteen hundred and seventy, as provides for the exemption from taxation of the premises leased for the residence of the health officer and his deputies, is hereby repealed, and the premises so leased shall be no longer exempt from taxation. Premises occupied by health officer, etc., to be taxed.

For the proprietor of congress hall, for lighting, warming, and taking charge of senate committee rooms, on roads and bridges, on canals and commerce, on municipal affairs, and on internal affairs, and committee rooms for ways and means committee of the assembly, the sum of five hundred dollars. Proprietor of congress hall.

For D. Willers, junior, late deputy secretary of state, for deficiency in compensation as clerk of the commissioners of the land office in the years eighteen hundred and sixty-eight, eighteen hundred and sixty-nine and eighteen hundred and seventy, the sum of seven hundred and fifty dollars. D. Willers, jr., late deputy secretary of state.

For H. H. Hawkins, attorney for the Cayuga Indians residing in western New York, for compensation for paying annuity for eighteen hundred and seventy-one, the sum of twenty-five dollars. H. H. Hawkins.

For Horatio N. Farnham, for compensation as agent of the Cayuga Indians, for disbursing annuities four years, one hundred dollars. H. N. Farnham.

For James I. Hendryx, librarian of the assembly, for labor and clerk hire in preparing statistical list of the officers and members of the assembly, and for the preparing the list of officers and members of the assembly, with their boarding places, fifty dollars. James I. Hendryx.

For the city chamberlain of the city and county of New York, or the official acting as county treasurer of said city and county, for his fees for receiving and paying into the state City chamberlain of city of N. Y.

treasury the state tax levied and collected in said city and county, the sum of five thousand dollars in lieu of all other compensation therefor, and no greater sum shall hereafter be paid or allowed in any one year for such services; such sum to be paid by the treasurer on the warrant of the comptroller on or before the first day of May in each year, providing, the whole of the state tax levied and collected for the preceding year in such city and county shall have then been paid into the state treasury; the officer authorized and required to receive and pay over the state tax levied and collected in the city and county of New York shall, after this year (ending May first, eighteen hundred and seventy-two), on the first day in October in each year, and on the first day of each month thereafter, notify officially the comptroller of the state how much of the state tax has been collected and paid into his hands during the preceding month; whereupon the comptroller shall immediately draw his warrant therefor, payable to the treasurer of the state, who shall proceed to collect and deposit the same in the treasury of the state, and the county treasurer, or other officer acting as such in the city and county of New York, shall pay such warrant immediately upon its presentation and demand for payment.

William J. Walsh. For William J. Walsh, for compensation for services as messenger to the committee on trade and manufactures, on grievances and on militia from the organization of the session of eighteen hundred and seventy-two to the sixteenth day of February, eighteen hundred and seventy-two, the sum of one hundred and thirty-eight dollars.

Commissioners appointed by ch. 715, laws of 1871. The commissioners appointed under and by virtue of the provisions of chapter seven hundred and fifteen of the laws of eighteen hundred and seventy-one, to examine the subject of taxation of lands upon the Buffalo creek, Allegany and Cattaraugus Indian reservations, and to report a plan for the equitable adjustment and settlement of the same, as between the state, the counties and individuals, are hereby authorized to report to the next legislature; and Nelson K. Hopkins is hereby appointed as one of said commissioners, in place of Asher P. Nichols, absent from the state.

Michael Cassidy. For Michael Cassidy, for compensation for additional services imposed on him by the trustees of the capitol, and by the state officers in taking charge of state property and buildings adjoining the capitol, three hundred dollars, and hereafter the salary of the keeper of the capitol shall be twelve hundred dollars, and no allowance shall be made to him for additional compensation.

For cleaning chambers of senate and assembly. For the women employed in cleaning the chambers and rooms adjoining the senate and assembly, for compensation to each of them for every day's service, to be certified by the superintendent of the capitol, two dollars.

Firemen employed about capitol, state hall, etc. For the firemen employed about the Capitol, State Hall and Geological Hall, and for the watchmen employed during the session of the legislature for the year eighteen hundred and seventy-two, for compensation to each of them for every day's service, to be certified by the respective superintendents, three dollars.

Any city or county, in which a hospital duly incorporated is situated, may send to and support, in the same, such sick and disabled indigent persons as require medical or surgical treatment, and when admitted the authorities of such city or county shall pay to the directors of such hospital such sum per week as may be agreed upon or found to be just during the period in which such person shall remain in such hospital. Any city or county may send to incorporated hospital sick indigent persons.

PAYABLE FROM THE UNITED STATES DEPOSIT FUND.

For the city of Binghamton, to be applied as a portion of the common school fund apportioned to said city for the current fiscal year, the sum of eight hundred dollars, payable from the United States deposit fund, which sum was withheld from said city, owing to failure of apportionment. City of Binghamton.

PAYABLE FROM THE GENERAL FUND DEBT SINKING FUND.

For the redemption of state stock issued to the New York and Erie Railroad company, reimbursable May first and July first, eighteen hundred and sixty-one, six thousand dollars. Redemption of state stock

PAYABLE FROM THE CANAL FUND.

For the auditor of the canal department, for addition to his salary for the year eighteen hundred and seventy-two, the sum of fifteen hundred dollars. Auditor of canal department.

For the canal appraisers, for additional compensation for the current fiscal year, to each of them, the sum of three thousand dollars; and from and after the first of October, eighteen hundred and seventy-two, the salary of said officers is hereby fixed at five thousand dollars each, in full of all compensation for their services; and for clerk hire in the office of the canal appraisers, in addition to the amount now allowed by law, the sum of four thousand dollars, or so much thereof as may be found necessary, to be paid by the auditor of the canal department, on the certificate of the chairman of the board of canal appraisers. Canal appraisers. Clerk hire.

For William McGourkey, deputy auditor in the canal department, and Edmund Savage, clerk in that department, for extra labor performed by them in the years eighteen hundred and sixty-nine and eighteen hundred and seventy, in consequence of the change in the system of canal repairs, to each of them five hundred dollars. Wm. McGourkey. Edmund Savage.

For completing the dreding of Cayuga inlet and for rebuilding the pier at the head of Cayuga lake, in accordance with the intention of the law of eighteen hundred and seventy-one, the sum of ten thousand dollars, to be expended under the direction of the canal commissioner in charge of the division. Dredging Cayuga inlet, and pier at head of Cayuga lake.

The comptroller shall not pay out any thing under the provisions of this act to or for the benefit of any asylum or Comptroller not to pay any sum for erecting new buildings, etc., for reformatories or asylums until plans are submitted to and approved by him. reformatory, for the purpose of erecting new buildings or making other permanent improvements, unless the plans thereof and estimates therefor shall be first presented to and approved by him; and in determining whether he will approve such plans he shall require that they shall provide for plain, substantial work that will involve the least possible expense consistent with proper provisions for the treatment, comfort, protection and safe-keeping of the inmates of such asylums and reformatories. And with a view of securing the most careful and economical expenditure of all moneys devoted to asylums or reformatories by this act, the comptroller is authorized at all times to visit any of said asylums or reformatories, and any part of them he may desire; and whenever he shall desire he shall be allowed to examine and take abstracts or copies of any or all papers, accounts, or books of account, of any such asylum or reformatory, in whosoever hands they may be, and he shall have power to subpœna to attend before him any witness that he may think proper to examine as to the affairs of any of said asylums and reformatories, and for such purpose is authorized to administer oaths to and examine such witnesses; and if the comptroller shall, from other official engagements, be unable to make such visitation or examination, he shall appoint, in writing, an examiner for that purpose, who shall be vested with all the power and authority of visitation or examination as to the asylum or asylums or reformatories that the said appointment shall specify, as are hereby conferred upon the comptroller, and such examiner shall, in all cases, report to the comptroller, in writing, what proceedings he has taken, what facts he has collected, the testimony he has taken, and his opinion thereon. Whenever it shall, by the examination herein provided for, or otherwise, be made to appear to the comptroller that any of the moneys by this act appropriated for the benefit of any asylum or reformatory is not being properly and economically used, he shall be authorized to withhold from such asylum or reformatory any unpaid balance of the sum for such asylum or reformatory in this act specified. The expenses of visitation and examination herein authorized shall be paid by the comptroller out of the moneys by this act appropriated to the institution so visited and examined; and the comptroller shall report to the legislature, in detail, all proceedings had, and information collected, as to said asylums and reformatories, under the provisions hereof, with such other information as he can give and such recommendations as he shall think proper to make, that will tend to improve and economize the management of such asylums and reformatories.

Comptroller to visit asylums, etc., and examine books of account, etc.

Comptroller may appoint examiner.

When to withhold unpaid balance of appropriation.

Expenses of visitation, how paid.

§ 3. This act shall take effect immediately.

CHAP. 734.

AN ACT to provide means to pay the canal and general fund deficiencies directed to be paid by the act chapter seven hundred of the laws of eighteen hundred and seventy-two.

PASSED May 15, 1872; three-fifths being present.

The People of the State of New York, represented in Senate and Assembly, do enact as follows:

Tax for 1872.

SECTION 1. There shall be imposed, levied and collected for the fiscal year commencing on the first day of October, eighteen hundred and seventy-two, a tax of three and one-half mills per dollar, upon the assessed value of the real and personal property in the state of New York, or so much thereof as may be necessary to provide for the payment of the canal and general fund deficiencies directed to be paid by the act chapter seven hundred of the laws of eighteen hundred and seventy-two, which tax shall be levied, collected and paid into the state treasury in the same manner that all other taxes are required to be levied, collected and paid.

Comptroller to issue bonds for deficiencies.

§ 2. For the purpose of raising the money required for said canal and general fund deficiencies, whithout delay, the comptroller is authorized to issue bonds in anticipation of the said tax, to such an amount as may be necessary, and in such sums and forms as may be most convenient, at a rate of interest not exceeding seven per cent per annum.

Appropriation for paying deficiencies.

§ 3. The sum of six million six hundred thousand dollars, or so much thereof as may be necessary, is hereby appropriated from any moneys in the treasury not othewise appropriated, for the purpose of paying the aforesaid canal and general fund deficiencies, the principal and interest of the said bonds and the necessary expenses of carrying into effect this act, and also the act chapter seven hundred aforesaid of the laws of eighteen hundred and seventy-two.

Corporations may invest.

§ 4. Any moneyed institution, incorporated under the laws of this state, may invest the moneys held by it in the said bonds, or in the stock of this state, to any extent which it may deem proper, without regard to the amount to which it may have been limited in making such investments by its charter.

Proviso.

§ 5. If the aforesaid act chapter seven hundred of the laws of eighteen hundred and seventy-two shall be approved by the people at the next general election, as therein provided, then the tax imposed by the first section of this act shall not be levied and collected; but the said bonds to be issued by the comptroller, under this act, shall be paid from the proceeds of the stocks authorized by said chapter seven hundred, or shall, at the option of the state, be converted into such stocks, bearing the same rate of interest as the said bonds.

Tax to be omitted, when.

§ 6. If the debt proposed by chapter seven hundred of the laws of eighteen hundred and seventy-two shall be approved by the people at the next general election as therein provided, the comptroller, so soon as such approval shall be known to his satisfaction from the official returns received by him or by either of the state canvassers, shall issue a circular directing the tax herein provided for to be omitted, and shall direct a copy of such circular to the treasurer, and another to the clerk of the board of supervisors of each county.

§ 7. This act shall take effect immediately.

CHAP. 736.

AN ACT to provide ways and means for the support of government.

PASSED May 15, 1872; three-fifths being present.

The People of the State of New York, represented in Senate and Assembly, do enact as follows:

State tax in 1872. SECTION 1. There shall be imposed, for the fiscal year beginning on the first day of October, eighteen hundred and seventy-two, on each dollar of real and personal property of this state subject to taxation, taxes for state purposes hereinafter mentioned, which taxes shall be assessed, levied and collected by the annual assessment and collection of taxes for that year, in the manner prescribed by law, and shall be paid by the several county treasurers into the treasury of this state, to be held by the treasurer for application to the purposes specified, that is to say, for the general fund and for the payment of those claims and demands which shall constitute a lawful charge upon that fund during the fiscal year, commencing October first, eighteen hundred and seventy-two, one mill and one-fourth of one mill; for the free school fund, for the maintenance of common schools in this state, one mill and one-fourth of one mill, pursuant to chapter four hundred and six of the laws of eighteen hundred and sixty-seven; for the payment of the interest and redemption of the principal of the state debt of two and one-half million dollars, as provided in chapter two hundred and seventy-one of the laws of eighteen hundred and fifty-nine, one-eighth of one mill; for the payment of the interest, and to provide for the redemption of the principal of the state bounty debt, pursuant to chapter three hundred and twenty-five of the laws of eighteen hundred and sixty-five, two mills; for the purposes of the new capitol, one-half of one mill; and for the benefit of the academies and academical department of the union schools, pursuant to chapter five hundred and forty one of the laws of eighteen hundred and seventy-two, one sixteenth of one mill.

To be paid in state treasury.

CHAP. 746.

AN ACT relating to the examination of candidates for the degree of doctor of medicine.

PASSED May 16, 1872.

The People of the State of New York, represented in Senate and Assembly, do enact as follows:

SECTION 1. The regents of the university of the state of New York shall appoint one or more boards of examiners in medicine, each board to consist of not less than seven members, who shall have been licensed to practice physic and surgery in this state. Regents of the university to appoint examiners.

§ 2. Such examiners shall faithfully examine all candidates referred to them for that purpose by the chancellor of said university, and furnish him a detailed report in writing of all the questions and answers of each examination, together with a separate written opinion of each examiner as to the acquirements and merits of the candidates in each case. Duty of examiners.

§ 3. Such examinations shall be in anatomy, physiology, materia medica, pathology, histology, clinical medicine, chemistry, surgery, midwifery and in therapeutics, according to each of the systems of practice represented by the several medical societies of this state. Examinations.

§ 4. The said reports of examinations, and the annexed opinions of the examiners, shall forever be a part of the public records of the said university, and the orders of the chancellor addressed to the examiners, together with the action of the regents, in each case shall accompany the same. Report of examiners, etc.

§ 5. Any person over twenty-one years of age, of good moral character and paying not less than thirty-five dollars into the treasury of the university, and on applying to the chancellor for the aforesaid examination shall receive an order to that effect, addressed to one of the boards of examiners, provided he shall adduce proofs satisfactory to the chancellor, that he or she has a competent knowledge of all the branches of learning taught in the common schools of this state, and of the Latin language, and that he has diligently studied medicine not less than three years, under the direction of one or more physicians duly qualified to practice medicine, or has himself been licensed, on examination, by some medical society or college legally empowered to issue licenses or degrees in medicine. Who may be examined. Proofs to be furnished to the chancellor.

§ 6. The regents of the university, on receiving the aforesaid reports of the examiners, and on finding that not less than five members of a board have voted in favor of a candidate, shall issue to him or her a diploma conferring the degree of doctor of medicine of the university of the state of New York, which degree shall be a license to practice physic and surgery. When to issue diplomas.

Fees. § 7. The candidate, on receiving said diploma, shall pay to the university the further sum of not less than ten dollars.

How appropriated. § 8. The moneys paid to the university, as aforesaid, shall be appropriated by the regents for the expenses of executing the provisions of this act.

Rules, etc. § 9. The regents may establish such rules and regulations, from time to time, as they may deem necessary to insure the faithful execution of the provisions of this act.

§ 10. This act shall take effect immediately.

CHAP. 747.

AN ACT for the suppression of the trade in and circulation of obscene literature, illustrations, advertisements and articles of indecent or immoral use, and obscene advertisements of patent medicines, and articles for producing abortion, and to repeal chapter four hundred and thirty of the laws of eighteen hundred and sixty-eight.

Ante, vol. 7, p. 809.

PASSED May 16, 1872; three-fifths being present.

The People of the State of New York, represented in Senate and Assembly, do enact as follows:

Penalty for selling, offering to sell, giving away, offering to give away, etc., any obscene book, etc. SECTION 1. If any person shall sell, or offer to sell, or shall give away, or offer to give away, or have in his or her possession, with or without intent to sell or give away, any obscene and indecent book, pamphlet, paper, drawing, lithograph, engraving, daguerreotype, photograph, stereoscopic picture, model, cast, instrument or article of indecent or immoral use, or medicine for procuring abortion, or shall advertise the same for sale, or write or cause to be written, or print or cause to be printed any circular, handbill, card, book, pamphlet, advertisement or notice of any kind, or shall give information orally, stating when, how or of whom, or by what means any of the said indecent and obscene articles and things hereinbefore mentioned can be purchased or otherwise obtained, or shall manufacture, draw and expose, or draw with intent to sell, or to have sold, or print any such articles, every such person shall, on conviction thereof, be imprisoned in the county jail or state prison not more than six months, or be fined not less than one hundred nor more than one thousand dollars for each offense. One-half of said fine to be paid to the informer upon whose evidence the person so offending shall be convicted, and one-half to the school fund of the county in which the said conviction is obtained, except that in the city and county of New York, if the conviction is in said city and county, one-half shall go to the treasurer of the Homœopathic dispensary, in said city and county, and in the county of Kings one-half shall go the Brooklyn Homœo- (One-half fine to be paid to informer. Balance, how disposed of.)

pathic hospital, when the conviction is in the county of Kings. And in every other county of the state, one-half of the said fine shall go to the treasurer of the orphan asylum of said county, if there be such an institution in the county.

Penalty for depositing or causing to be deposited in any post-office or place in charge of any express company, etc., any obscene book, etc.

§ 2. If any person shall deposit or cause to be deposited in any post-office within this state, or place in charge of any express company, or person connected therewith, or of any common carrier or other person, any of the obscene and indecent articles and things mentioned in the first section of this act, or any circular, handbill, card, advertisement, book, pamphlet, or notice of any kind, or shall give oral information stating where, how or of whom such indecent and obscene articles or things can be purchased or otherwise obtained in any manner, with the intent of having the same conveyed by mail or express, or in any other manner; or if any person shall knowingly or willfully receive the same with intent to carry or convey, or shall carry or convey the same by express, or in any other manner (except in the United States mail); every person so offending shall, on conviction thereof, be subject for each offense to the same fines and penalties as are prescribed in the first section of this act for the offenses therein set forth, and said fine shall be divided and paid in the same manner as therein provided.

Magistrates to issue warrants to search for, obscene books, etc.

§ 3. All magistrates are authorized, on complaint founded on information and belief, supported by oath or affirmation, to issue a warrant, directed to the sheriff of the county within which such complaint shall be made, or to any constable, marshal or police officer within said county (provided, nevertheless, that nothing in this act contained, shall be construed to affect, alter, diminish or extend, or in anywise interfere with the powers and authority of the board of metropolitan police), directing him, them, or any of them, to search for, seize and take possession of such obscene and indecent books, papers, articles and things; and said magistrates shall transmit, inclosed and under seal, specimens thereof to the district attorney of his county, and shall deposit within the county jail of his county, or such other secure place as to him shall seem meet, inclosed and under seal, the remainder thereof, and shall, upon the conviction of the person or persons offending under any of the provisions of this act, forthwith destroy, or cause to be destroyed, the remainder thereof so seized as aforesaid, and shall cause to be entered upon the records of his court the fact of such destruction.

Specimens of same to be sent to district attorney.

Judge to charge grand jury at each term of court, etc., etc.

§ 4. It shall be the duty of the presiding judge of every court of sessions or oyer and terminer within this state, especially to charge the grand jury at each term of said court, to take notice of all offenses committed in violation of any of the provisions of this act; and it shall be the duty of all superintendents of the poor and commissioners of charities and corrections to prosecute and recover the penalties in this act.

§ 5. Chapter four hundred and thirty of the laws of eighteen hundred and sixty-eight is hereby repealed.

§ 6. This act shall take effect immediately.

CHAP. 757.

AN ACT to perfect an amendment to the constitution relative to the court of appeals and for the extension of the service of the commissioners of appeals.

PASSED May 17, 1872; three-fifths being present.

The People of the State of New York, represented in Senate and Assembly, do enact as follows:

Preamble. Whereas, the following amendment to the constitution of this state was agreed to by a majority of all the members elected to each branch of the legislature for the year one thousand eight hundred and seventy-one; and the said amendment was duly entered on the journals of each branch of the legislature, with the yeas and nays taken thereon, and referred to the legislature to be chosen at the next general election of senators; and was duly published for three months previous to the time of making such choice in pursuance of the thirteenth article of the constitution of this state; and whereas, said amendment was also agreed to by a majority of all the members elected to each of the said branches of the legislature for the year one thousand eight hundred and seventy-two, pursuant to the said thirteenth article; which said amendment is in the words following, to wit:

Proposed amendment. "Relative to the court of appeals and for the extension of the term of service of the commissioners of appeals."

Resolved (if the assembly concur), That the sixth article of the constitution of this state be amended, by adding thereto the following section:

§ 28. The court of appeals may order any of the causes, not exceeding five hundred in number, pending in that court at the time of the adoption of this provision, to be heard and determined by the commissioners of appeals, and the legislature may extend the term of service of the commissioners of appeals, for a period not exceeding two years.

Now, therefore, for the purpose of submitting the said proposed amendment to the people of this state:

The People of the State of New York, represented in Senate and Assembly, do enact as follows:

Inspectors to provide box to receive ballots. SECTION 1. The inspectors at each poll in the several towns and wards of this state at the general election to be held in this state on the fifth day of November in the year of our lord one thousand eight hundred and seventy-two, shall provide a box to receive the ballots of the citizens of this state, in relation to the said proposed amendment; and each voter may present a ballot on which shall be written or printed, or partly written and partly printed, one of the following forms, namely:

"For the proposed amendment relative to the court of appeals," or

"Against the proposed amendment relative to the court of appeals."

Form of ballots.

The said ballots shall be indorsed "Proposed amendments relative to the court of appeals," and shall be so folded as to conceal the contents of the ballot and exhibit the indorsement.

How indorsed and folded

And all the citizens of this state entitled to vote for members of assembly in their respective districts shall be entitled to vote on the adoption of the said proposed amendment, during the day of election, in the several election districts in which they reside.

Electors.

§ 2. After finally closing the poll of such election, the inspectors thereof shall count and canvass the ballots given relative to the said proposed amendment, in the same manner as they are required by law to canvass the ballots given for governor, and thereupon shall set down in writing, and in words at full length the whole number of votes given "For the proposed amendment relative to the court of appeals," and the whole number of votes given "Against the proposed amendment relative to the court of appeals," and shall certify and subscribe the same, and cause copies thereof to be made and certified and delivered as prescribed by law in respect to the canvass of votes given at an election for governor.

Ballots, how counted and canvassed.

§ 3. The votes so given shall be canvassed by the board of county canvassers, and statements thereof shall be made, certified and signed, and recorded in the manner required by law, in respect to the canvassing of votes given at an election for governor, and certified copies of the statements and certificates of the county canvassers shall be made, certified, and transmitted by the county clerks, respectively, in the manner provided by law in cases of election for governor. The said certified copies transmitted by the county clerks shall be canvassed by the board of state canvassers, in the like manner as provided by law, in respect to the election of governor, and in like manner they shall make and file a certificate of the result of such canvass, which shall be entered of record by the secretary of state, and shall be published by him in the state paper.

Canvass and statements to be made by county and state canvassers.

To be entered of record and published by secretary of state.

§ 4. This act shall take effect immediately.

CHAP. 761.

AN ACT to amend chapter eighty of the laws of eighteen hundred and seventy, entitled "An act to provide for the enrollment of the militia, for the organization of the National Guard of the state of New York, and for the public defense, and entitled the military code."

PASSED May 17, 1872; three-fifths being present.

The People of the State of New York, represented in Senate and Assembly, do enact as follows:

Clerks to be employed.

SECTION 1. Section one hundred and sixty-nine of chapter eighty of the laws of eighteen hundred and seventy, entitled "An act to provide for the enrollment of the militia, for the organization of the National Guard of the state of New York, and for the public defense, and entitled the military code," is hereby amended so as to read as follows:

Compensation.

§ 169. Such and so many clerks shall be employed in the several departments of the general staff of the state as shall be actually necessary for the public service in the opinion of the commander-in-chief, and they shall receive, for the time they may be actually necessarily employed, such compensation as the commander-in-chief shall prescribe.

Ante, vol. 7, p. 629.

§ 2. This act shall take effect immediately.

CHAP. 765.

AN ACT to legalize payments made by the comptroller to justices of the supreme court in the second judicial district, and to authorize further payments by said comptroller to said justices.

PASSED May 17, 1872; three-fifths being present.

The People of the State of New York, represented in Senate and Assembly, do enact as follows:

Payments by comptroller to justices of supreme court of second district legalized.

SECTION 1. All payments heretofore made by the comptroller of the state to justices of the supreme court of the second judicial district out of moneys received by him under and pursuant to the provisions of an act of the legislature, entitled "An act authorizing the supervisors of the several counties in the second judicial district, not including the county of Kings, to appropriate and pay compensation to justices of the supreme court and to stenographers of said court," passed May nine, eighteen hundred and sixty-eight, are hereby declared to be in all things legal and valid.

§ 2, The said comptroller is hereby authorized and directed to pay to the justices of the supreme court, referred to in the aforesaid act, and in the manner therein specified, all the moneys heretofore received by him for said justices, under the provisions of said act, and now remaining unpaid to said justices, and also all moneys which may hereafter be received for them by him, under the provisions of such act; the said moneys are hereby appropriated to the above purposes. Comptroller to make further payments to said justices.

§ 3. This act shall take effect immediately.

CHAP. 767.

AN ACT to establish the compensation of county judges and surrogates, pursuant to the fifteenth section of the amended sixth article of the constitution.

PASSED May 17, 1872; three-fifths being present.

The People of the State of New York, represented in Senate and Assembly, do enact as follows:

SECTION 1. Pursuant to the fifteenth section of the amended sixth article of the constitution, the annual salaries of county judges and surrogates, in the several counties of this state, except in the county of New York, from and after the first day of January, in the year one thousand eight hundred and seventy-two, are hereby established as follows, viz.: Salaries of county judges and surrogates.

The salary of the county judge of the county of Kings is hereby fixed at the sum of eight thousand dollars. Judges.

The salaries of the county judges of the counties of Albany and Westchester are hereby fixed at the sum of four thousand five hundred dollars each.

The salaries of the county judges of the counties of Erie and Rensselaer are hereby fixed at the sum of five thousand dollars.

The salaries of the county judges of the counties of Onondaga, Oneida and Monroe are hereby fixed at the sum of four thousand dollars each.

The salaries of the counties judges of the counties of Otsego, Saratoga, Ulster, Dutchess, Orange, Clinton, Columbia and Washington are hereby fixed at the sum of three thousand dollars each.

The salaries of the county judges of the counties of Niagara, Jefferson and Queens are hereby fixed at the sum of two thousand five hundred dollars each.

The salaries of the county judges of the counties of St. Lawrence, Oswego, Cayuga and Ontario are hereby fixed at the sum of two thousand dollars each.

The salary of the county judge of the county of Chautauqua is hereby fixed at the sum of one thousand six hundred dollars.

The salary of the county judge of the county of Cattaraugus is hereby fixed at the sum of one thousand five hundred dollars.

Surrogates. § 2. The salary of the surrogate of the county of Kings is hereby fixed at the sum of eight thousand dollars.

The salaries of the surrogates of the counties of Albany, Monroe and Rensselaer are hereby fixed at the sum of four thousand dollars each.

The salary of the surrogate of the county of Onondaga is hereby fixed at the sum of three thousand five hundred dollars.

The salaries of the surrogates of the counties of Queens, Dutchess, Ulster, Orange, Oneida, Columbia and Westchester, are hereby fixed at the sum of three thousand dollars each.

The salaries of the surrogates of the counties of Otsego, Jefferson, Saratoga and Washington, are hereby fixed at the sum of two thousand five hundred dollars each.

The salaries of the surrogates of the counties of Niagara, Cayuga, St. Lawrence and Oswego, are hereby fixed at the sum of two thousand dollars each.

The salary of the surrogate of the county of Chautauqua, is hereby fixed at the sum of one thousand six hundred dollars.

The salaries of the surrogates of the counties of Cattaraugus and Ontario, are hereby fixed at the sum of one thousand five hundred dollars each.

The salary of the surrogate of the county of Erie is hereby fixed at the sum of four thousand five hundred dollars.

The salary of the surrogate of the county of New York shall be the same as that of the judges of the court of common pleas of the city and county of New York.

Judges doing duties of surrogates. § 3. The salaries of the county judges who perform the duties of the office of surrogate are hereby fixed in the counties named, and at the sums stated, as follows:

In the counties of Warren, Franklin, Schenectady, Wayne, Rockland and Lewis, two thousand dollars each.

In the counties of Chenango, Madison, Delaware, Greene, Herkimer, Livingston, Montgomery, Chemung and Broome, three thousand dollars each.

In the counties of Steuben and Richmond, three thousand five hundred dollars each.

In the counties of Schoharie, Cortland, Sullivan, Genesee, Essex, Orleans, Tioga, Tompkins, Wyoming, Suffolk and Seneca, two thousand five hundred dollars each.

In the county of Putnam, one thousand dollars. And in the counties of Yates and Schuyler, one thousand five hundred dollars each.

In the county of Allegany, two thousand seven hundred

and fifty dollars. In the county of Fulton, two thousand two hundred and fifty dollars.

In the county of Hamilton, eight hundred dollars.

Whenever in any county where there is now a separate county judge and surrogate, the supervisors shall decide to have but one officer to act as county judge and surrogate, the salary of such officer shall be five hundred dollars less than the aggregate salary herein allowed to the county judge and surrogate of such county. Salary of county judge in case office of surrogate is abolished.

§ 4. The salaries of the several county judges and surrogates, as hereby established, shall be paid quarterly by the county treasurers of the respective counties. Payable quarterly.

§ 5. Whenever the county judge of one county shall hold the county court, or preside at the court of sessions of any other county, he shall be paid the sum of five dollars per day for his expenses in going to and from, and holding or presiding at any such court, which shall be paid by the county treasurer of such other county on the presentation to him of the certificate of the clerk of such court of the number of days. Compensation for expenses holding court in any other county.

§ 6. Section three of chapter four hundred and sixty-seven of the laws of eighteen hundred and seventy is hereby repealed. Chapter 467, laws of 1870, repealed.

§ 7. This act shall take effect immediately.

CHAP. 772.

AN ACT to authorize the canal commissioners to construct a road-bridge over the Erie canal in the town of Gates, in the county of Monroe.

PASSED May 20, 1872; three-fifths being present.

The People of the State of New York, represented in Senate and Assembly, do enact as follows:

SECTION 1. The canal commissioners are hereby authorized and required to construct, or cause to be constructed and maintained, at the expense of the state, over the Erie canal, in the town of Gates, in the county of Monroe, at a point where said canal is intersected by Emmerson street, in said town, a road-bridge, in such manner as they may deem advisable, and the expense of the same, not exceeding seven thousand dollars, may be paid from any money appropriated, or to be appropriated, for extraordinary repairs of the Erie canal; provided that, after investigation and examination into all the facts in relation thereto, the canal board shall be of opinion that the state is under legal or equitable obligation to build said bridge, the canal commissioners shall require and receive a full and sufficient release legally executed, acknowledged and delivered, free of expense to the state, of all claims for damages in consequence of the construction of said bridge, or Bridge over canal in Gates. Proviso. Release of damages.

of the approaches and embankments of the same, and also a good and sufficient license or permission to the state, duly executed, acknowledged and delivered as aforesaid, to alter, raise or change such bridge approaches or embankments whenever necessary, which necessity is to be determined by the canal commissioners, from all persons whose property, rights or interests may be affected by such bridge approaches or embankments.

§ 2. This act shall take effect immediately.

CHAP. 776.

AN ACT further to amend an act entitled "An act to amend an act to prevent animals from running at large in the public highways," passed April twenty-third, eighteen hundred and sixty-two, passed May ninth, eighteen hundred and sixty-seven, passed April twenty-ninth, eighteen hundred and sixty-nine.

Ante, vol. 3, p. 547, ; vol. 7, pp. 185, 448.

PASSED May 20, 1872; three-fifths being present.

The People of the State of New York, represented in Senate and Assembly, do enact as follows:

SECTION 1. Section one of an act entitled "An act to amend an act to prevent animals from running at large in the public highways," passed April twenty-third, eighteen hundred and sixty-two, and to create a short bar to actions arising under said act, passed May ninth, eighteen hundred and sixty-seven, as amended April twenty-ninth, eighteen hundred and sixty-nine, is hereby amended so as to read as follows:

Cattle, etc. not to run at large in highway. § 1. It shall not be lawful for any cattle, horses, sheep, swine or goats to run at large or to be herded or pastured in any public street, park, place or highway in this state; and Duty of overseer to seize animals so running at large it shall be the duty of every overseer of highways within his road district, and of every street commissioner in any incorporated village, who shall have personal knowledge, or who shall be notified of any violation of this act, to seize and to take into his possession, and to keep until disposed of according to law, any animal so found running at large or being herded or pastured, and any person suffering or permitting any animal to so run at large, or be herded or pastured in violation of this Penalty. section, shall forfeit a penalty of five dollars for every horse, swine or cattle, and one dollar for every sheep or goat so found, to be recovered by civil action, by any inhabitant of the town in his own name, or in the name of the overseer of the poor of the town, or the proceedings hereinafter provided.

§ 2. This act shall take effect immediately.

CHAP. 778.

AN ACT to amend chapter seven hundred and sixty-six of the laws of eighteen hundred and seventy-one, entitled "An act to allow the justices of the supreme court, assigned to hold the general terms thereof in the several judicial departments of this state, to fix the times and places of holding the same," passed April twenty-seven, eighteen hundred and seventy-one.

Ante, p. 202.

PASSED May 20, 1872; three-fifths being present.

The People of the State of New York, represented in Senate and Assembly, do enact as follows:

SECTION 1. The first section of the act entitled "An act to allow the justices of the supreme court, assigned to hold the general terms thereof in the several judicial departments of this state, to fix the times and places of holding the same," passed April twenty-seven, eighteen hundred and seventy-one, is hereby amended so as to read as follows:

§ 1. Within twenty days after the passage of this act, the several justices of the supreme court, who have been assigned to hold the general terms thereof in the several judicial departments of this state, shall, by appointment in writing, designate the times and places for holding the general terms of said court, within their respective judicial departments, for two years from January first, eighteen hundred and seventy-one; provided at least one term in each year shall be designated to be held in each of the judicial districts composing the several judicial departments of this state, and provided further, that at least one of such terms shall be held at Elmira.

Justices of supreme court assigned to hold general terms, when to designate time and place for holding same.

One term to be held at Elmira.

§ 2. Section three of said act is hereby amended so as to read as follows:

§ 3. On or before the first day of December, in the year eighteen hundred and seventy-two, and thereafter every two years, the justices aforesaid shall make appointments for the holding of the general terms of the supreme court, within their respective departments. One term in each year shall be designated to be held in each of the judicial districts composing the several judicial departments of this state, and at least one term shall be designated to be held at Elmira, which appointment shall also, on or before the fifteenth day of December in such year, be filed in the office of the secretary of state, and immediately thereafter be by him published in the state paper for one month.

Terms, where appointed to be held.

§ 3. All acts and parts of acts inconsistent with this act, as hereby amended, are hereby repealed.

§ 4. This act shall take effect immediately.

CHAP. 779.

AN ACT requiring commissioners of highways to act as inspectors of plank-roads and turnpikes.

PASSED May 20, 1872.

The People of the State of New York, represented in Senate and Assembly, do enact as follows:

When complaint is made by three freeholders, commissioners to examine plank-roads.

SECTION 1. Whenever complaint in writing, signed by three freeholders of any town of this state, shall be made to a commissioner of highways of any town through which, or through any part of which, any plank-road or turnpike road has been laid out and constructed, and on which the tolls are charged, that any portion of such road lying within the limits of such town is out of repair, and is not constructed and kept in repair as required by the several laws under and by virtue of which such road has been constructed; it shall be the duty of such highway commissioner, and he is hereby required to immediately proceed to examine and inspect any part of such road in reference to which such complaint has been made, and if upon such examination and inspection he shall deem it necessary for the interest of the town and the traveling public, he shall notify the toll-gatherer nearest to the portion of such road so determined to be out of repair, in writing, stating the fact that such complaint has been made, and as near as may be setting forth the portion of the road deemed by him out of repair; and shall also serve a similar notice upon one of the plank-road inspectors of the county in which such town is situated, who shall, within three days thereafter, proceed to inspect the portion of the road so complained against, and if he shall find the road still out of repair, he shall, by virtue of his office, by a notice, in writing, served on the toll-gatherer, direct that the toll-gate shall be thrown open, and that no tolls shall be charged until such repairs shall be made on such road as in his judgment shall be required by the several laws in relation to plank and turnpike roads.

To notify toll-gatherer, and serve notice on plank-road inspector.

Inspector to inspect road, and if out of repair, to direct toll-gate to be thrown open.

Penalty for neglect of duty.

§ 2 Any inspector of plank and turnpike roads, who shall neglect to fulfill the duties required by the first section of this act, shall be deemed guilty of neglect of his official duty, and shall be liable to a fine of not to exceed twenty-five dollars.

§ 3. This act shall take effect immediately.

CHAP. 780.

AN ACT in relation to plank-roads.

PASSED May 20, 1872.

The People of the State of New York, represented in Senate and Assembly, do enact as follows:

When corporation to be dissolved. In what cases its road bed to be deemed a public highway.

SECTION 1. Any plank-road corporation which, for a period of five consecutive years, shall have heretofore neglected or omitted to exercise its corporate functions shall be deemed dissolved, and, provided its road-bed or right of way shall have been used as a public highway for the said five years, the same shall be deemed and be a public highway to all intents and purposes, and with the same effect as if laid out by the commissioners of highways of towns under the statute, and all laws relating to the erection, repairing and preservation of bridges shall apply to such highway.

§ 2. This act shall take effect immediately.

CHAP. 782.

AN ACT to amend section one hundred and fifty-six of article four of chapter three of title two of part four of the Revised Statutes, in relation to bodies of deceased convicts at Auburn state prison.

PASSED May 20, 1872.

The People of the State of New York, represented in Senate and Assembly, do enact as follows:

SECTION 1. Section one hundred and fifty-six of article four of chapter three of title two of part four of the Revised Statutes is hereby amended so as to read as follows: *

Dead bodies of convicts at Auburn prison, how disposed of.

§ 156. It shall in like manner be the duty of the warden of the Auburn state prison, whenever a convict shall die in that prison, whose body shall not be taken away for interment by his relatives or friends within twenty-four hours after his death, to deliver, on demand, such dead body to the agent of the medical faculty of the University of Buffalo, or to the agent of the college of physicians and surgeons of the Syracuse University, so that one-half of the number of such dead bodies shall be delivered to each institution.

§ 2. This act shall take effect immediately.

* There is no such section in the Revised Statutes. This section probably refers to § 133 of art. IV, title 2, chap. 3, part I. *Ante*, vol. 1, p. 816.

CHAP. 783.

AN ACT to authorize the canal commissioners to construct a road bridge over the Tonawanda creek, western division of the Erie canal, at or near Bush's place, connecting the Bush road with Sawyer's creek road, at Martinsville.

PASSED May 20, 1872; three-fifths being present.

The People of the State of New York, represented in Senate and Assembly, do enact as follows:

Bridge over Tonawanda creek. SECTION 1. The canal commissioners are hereby authorized and directed to construct or cause to be constructed and maintained at the expense of the state, over Tonawanda creek, western division of the Erie canal, at or near Bush's place, a road bridge in such manner as they may deem advisable, at a cost not to exceed sixteen thousand dollars, and the expense of the same may be paid from any money appropriated for the extraordinary repairs of the Erie canal; Proviso. provided, that before proceeding to the construction of any such bridge, the canal commissioners shall require and receive a full and sufficient Release of damages. release, legally executed and acknowledged and delivered free of expense to the state, of all claims for damages in consequence of the construction of said bridge, or of the approaches and embankments of the same, and also a good and sufficient license or permission to the state, duly executed, acknowledged and delivered as aforesaid, to alter, raise or change such bridge, approaches or embankments whenever necessary, which necessity is to be determined by the canal commissioners, from all persons whose property, rights or interests may be affected by such bridge, approaches or embankments.

§ 2. This act shall take effect immediately.

CHAP. 784.

AN ACT to provide for the care and maintenance, by the canal commissioners, of certain bridges over a portion of the Black river used for canal purposes.

PASSED May 20, 1872; three-fifths being present.

The People of the State of New York, represented in Senate and Assembly, do enact as follows:

Bridges over Black river. SECTION 1. The canal commissioners are hereby authorized and directed to maintain and protect the bridge across Black river, between the towns of Lowville and New Bremen, known as the Illingworth bridge; also the bridge between the towns of Lowville and Watson, known as Beach's bridge; that, before proceeding to maintain or protect said bridges, the canal commissioners shall require and receive a full and sufficient release, legally executed, acknowledged and delivered free of expense to the state, of all claims for damages in consequence of the construction of such bridges, or of the approaches or embankments of the same, and also a good and sufficient license or permission to the state, duly executed, acknowledged and delivered as aforesaid, to alter, raise or change such bridge, approaches or embankments whenever necessary, which necessity is to be determined by the canal commissioners, from all persons whose property, rights or interests may be affected by such bridge, approaches or embankments. Release of damages

§ 2. This act shall take effect immediately.

CHAP. 788.

AN ACT to amend part one, chapter eleven, title three, article two, section forty-three of the Revised Statutes in relation to constables.

PASSED May 20, 1872; three-fifths being present.

The People of the State of New York, represented in Senate and Assembly, do enact as follows:

SECTION 1. Section forty-three* of article two of title three of chapter eleven of part one of the Revised Statutes is hereby amended so as to read as follows:

§ 43. Every person chosen or appointed to the office of constable, before he enters on the duties of his office, and within eight days after he shall be notified of his election or appointment, shall take and subscribe the oath of office provided by the constitution, and shall execute, in the presence of the supervisor or town clerk of the town, with at least two sufficient sureties, to be approved of by such supervisor or town clerk, an instrument in writing, by which such constable and his sureties shall jointly and severally agree to pay to each and every person who may be entitled thereto, all such sums of money as the said constable may become liable to pay on account of any execution which shall be delivered to him for collection; and shall also jointly and severally agree and become liable to pay each and every such person for any damages which he may sustain from or by any act or thing done by said constable, by virtue of his office of constable. Every constable so chosen or appointed shall, in good faith, be an actual resident of the town or ward in which he shall be chosen or appointed. Constables to take oath and give bond with two sureties. Condition of bond. Constables must reside in town where appointed.

* There is no such section in the Revised Statues. The section referred to is probably § 21, art. 2 of title 3 of ch. 11 of part 1.

CHAP. 800.

AN ACT making an appropriation for the improvement of the navigation of Peconic river, in the county of Suffolk.

PASSED May 21, 1872; by a two-third vote.

The People of the State of New York, represented in Senate and Assembly, do enact as follows:

Appropriation for improvement of Peconic river.

SECTION 1. The sum of five thousand dollars is hereby appropriated out of any moneys in the treasury belonging to the general fund, not otherwise appropriated, for the purpose of improving the navigation of Peconic river, in the county of Suffolk, in this state, from the village of Riverhead, in said county, to the mouth of the river; which sum of money shall be expended by and under the direction of David F. Vail, Isaac C. Winters and Joshua L. Wells, all of Riverhead, of the county of Suffolk, and the state engineer and surveyor, who are hereby appointed commissioners for that purpose. The said sum of five thousand dollars is to be paid to them upon the presentation, by them, of the proper vouchers to the comptroller.

Commissioners to expend same.

Commissioners to give bonds.

§ 2. The said commissioners, excepting said state engineer and surveyor, before entering upon the duties of their office, shall execute and file in the office of the comptroller, a bond to the people of the state of New York, in the penal sum of ten thousand dollars, conditioned for the faithful performance of their duties, with sufficient sureties to be approved by the comptroller.

How money to be expended.

§ 3. The said commissioners shall expend the said sum of money upon the improvement of the navigation of the said river, between the village of Riverhead in said county and the mouth of the said river, as they shall deem most desirable.

Commissioners to report annually.

§ 4. The said commissioners shall annually report their proceedings hereon, on or before the first day of December in each year, verified by their oath, to the comptroller. The said commissioners shall receive no compensation for their services out of the money hereby appropriated.

Vacancies, how filled.

§ 5. The comptroller shall have power to fill vacancies that may occur in said board of commissioners.

§ 6. This act shall take effect immediately.

CHAP. 801.

AN ACT for the improvement of the main, middle and north branches of Grass river.

PASSED May 21, 1872; by a two-third vote.

The People of the State of New York, represented in Senate and Assembly, do enact as follows:

SECTION 1. The sum of twenty thousand dollars is hereby appropriated out of any moneys in the treasury not otherwise appropriated, ten thousand dollars in the year eighteen hundred and seventy-two, and ten thousand dollars in the year eighteen hundred and seventy-three, for the purpose of improving the main, middle and north branches of Grass river, which moneys shall be expended by and under the direction of Jeremiah Traver, Lucius Moody and the state engineer and surveyor, who are hereby appointed to constitute a board of commissioners to carry into effect the provisions of this act. A majority of said commissioners shall constitute a quorum for the transaction of business. Appropriation for improving Grass river. Commissioners to expend money. Quorum.

§ 2. The said sum of twenty thousand dollars, so appropriated for the purpose aforesaid, shall be expended by said commissioners in clearing and improving the channels of the main, middle and north branches of said river, and in erecting dams, slides, piers, booms and such other erections as said commissioners shall deem most conducive to the improvement of said river for the passage of logs, timber and lumber over and through said channels. How appropriation to be expended.

§ 3. The said commissioners, excepting the said state engineer and surveyor, before entering upon the duties of their said office, shall execute and file in the office of the comptroller of this state, a bond in the penal sum of forty thousand dollars, with sufficient sureties, to be approved by the comptroller, conditioned for the faithful performance of their duties. Commissioners to give bonds.

§ 4. The said commissioners shall receive no compensation for their services out of the moneys hereby appropriated. They shall, between the first and tenth days of December in each of said years, make and file with the comptroller a report under oath of their proceedings, including a detailed statement of all their expenditures under this act, and thereupon the comptroller shall draw his warrant upon the treasurer for the amount of such expenditures, payable to the order of said commissioners, not exceeding the amount hereby appropriated. Not to receive compensation. To report to comptroller.

§ 5. In case of the death, resignation, refusal to serve or removal from the county of all or either of the above commissioners, such vacancy shall be filled by appointment, in writing, to be made by the county judge of St Lawrence Vacancies, how filled.

county, such appointee to be a resident of the town of Canton, and such appointment to take effect so soon as the person or persons so appointed shall file the bail required by the third section of this act, and said appointment be filed in the office of the secretary of state.

§ 6. This act shall take effect immediately.

CHAP. 819.

AN ACT supplemental to an act entitled "An act for the improvement of the navigation of the tributaries of the Great South Bay," passed April twenty-eight, eighteen hundred and seventy-one.

PASSED May 22, 1872, by a two-third vote.

The People of the State of New York, represented in Senate and Assembly, do enact as follows:

Appropriation of $2,500 for improvement of the tributaries of the Great South Bay.

SECTION 1. The sum of two thousand five hundred dollars is hereby appropriated out of any moneys in the treasury belonging to the general fund, not otherwise appropriated, for the purposes mentioned in an act entitled "An act for the improvement of the navigation of the tributaries of the Great South Bay," passed April twenty-eight, eighteen hundred and seventy-one, and to enable the commissioners in said act named to complete the work already begun by them.

§ 2. The comptroller shall draw his warrant upon the treasurer for the said sum of two thousand five hundred dollars in favor of said commissioners, and the treasurer shall pay the same out of the said fund.

Ante, vol. 8, p. 749.

§ 3. This act shall take effect immediately.

CHAP. 820.

AN ACT to authorize the formation of corporations to to provide the members thereof with lots of lands suitable for homesteads.

PASSED May 22, 1872.

The People of the State of New York, represented in Senate and Assembly, do enact as follows:

Number of corporators and corporate object.

SECTION 1. Any number of persons, not less than three, may associate and form themselves into an incorporated company for the purpose of accumulating a fund for the purchase of real estate, paying off incumbrances thereon, the improvement and the subdivision thereof into lots or parcels suitable for homesteads, and the distribution of such lots or parcels among the shareholders.

§ 2. Such persons shall severally subscribe articles of association, in which shall be set forth the name and objects of the association or corporation, the time for which the same is limited to exist, the amount of capital stock and the number of shares into which it is proposed to be divided, the number of directors and officers, their terms of office, and such other regulations as may be necessary to enable the corporation to carry on its business and accomplish its objects, and how amendments thereto may be made. Articles of association.

§ 3. A certificate in writing shall be made, duly signed and acknowledged by three or more of the persons proposing to form such corporation, before some officer competent to take acknowledgment of deeds, in which shall be set forth the corporate name of the association, its principal objects, the amount of the capital stock, the number of shares, the time of its existence, the number of directors who shall manage the concerns of the association, their names, and the name of the city, town or county in which the office or principal place of business is to be located, shall be filed in the office of the county clerk of the county in which the office or principal place of business is intended to be located, and a copy thereof, duly certified under the hand and seal of such county clerk, in the office of the secretary of state of the state of New York, and thereupon the persons who have subscribed the said certificate, and such other persons who have become members of such association, and their successors, shall be a body corporate by the name of the corporation specified in said certificate, and shall possess the powers and privileges specified therein, subject to the provisions contained therein, and no further; and they shall, by their corporate name, be capable in law of purchasing, holding, conveying and improving any personal or real estate or property whatever, which may be necessary to enable said associates to carry on the operations named in said certificate. Certificate to be in writing and duly signed and acknowledged. What to contain. To be filed. Corporate powers.

§ 4. It shall be lawful for the directors to call in and demand from the shareholders, respectively, all such sums of money as they have agreed to pay, and by them subscribed, at such times and in such payments or installments as the articles of association shall prescribe, under the penalty of forfeiture of the shares of stock subscribed for, and all deposits, assessments and previous payments made thereon toward the principal funds of the association, and the property acquired therewith and owned by the association, if payment shall not be made by the stockholder within thirty days after a demand, notice requiring such payment having been sent to the address of the stockholder, as such address had been stated by such stockholder. Payment for stock subscribed.

§ 5. All corporations formed under this act shall have power to borrow money for temporary purposes not inconsistent with the objects of their organization, and to loan to their own members or other persons any moneys belonging to such corporation not needed for immediate use, on approved marketable securities, for which they may pay or receive a com- May borrow money and make loans to members and others.

mission, as shall be agreed in writing by parties thereto, not contrary to law; nor shall such indebtedness exceed at any one time one-half of the aggregate amount of the shares and parts of shares and the income thereof actually paid in and received. Such corporation, however, for the purpose of completing the purchase of land to be subdivided and distributed among the shareholders, may borrow, upon the security of the land so purchased, or the land owned or held by them at the time of making such loan or loans, any sum or sums of money which shall not exceed ninety per cent of the purchase money of such land.

Parents, guardians and executors may take shares in behalf of minor children.

§ 6. Parents, guardians, executors, or other legal representatives may take and hold shares in such association in behalf and for the use of minor children; provided, the cost of such shares, and the amount of deposits and assessments thereon to be paid from the personal earnings of such minor children, or the earnings or money of such parent or representatives for this purpose voluntarily bestowed. Married women may take and hold shares in such association, provided the cost of such shares and the amount of deposits and assessments shall be paid from their personal earnings or money of their children voluntarily bestowed for this purpose, or from property bequeathed or given to them, or given to them by persons other than their husbands.

Married women may take and hold shares.

Dissolution of corporation.

§ 7. Every such corporation shall terminate, except for the purpose of settling its affairs, at the expiration of the time stated in articles of association for its existence, or whenever it is dissolved in the manner provided in the articles of association; but no dividend of the funds belonging to the corporation, or the proceeds of property owned by the corporation, shall be paid to the shareholders upon such dissolution, until all the debts of the association shall have been paid or otherwise sufficiently provided for.

Financial statement to be published.

§ 8. Each association formed under the provisions of this act shall, at the close of its first year's operations, and annually at the same period in each year thereafter, publish, in at least one newspaper of general circulation published in the city, town or county where the principal office or place of business of such corporation is located, a concise statement, verified by the oath of its president and secretary, showing the actual financial condition of the association, and the amount of its property and liabilities, specifying the same particularly.

Liability of stockholders.

§ 9. All shareholders of any association, formed under the provisions of this act, shall be liable to the creditors of such association to an amount equal to the paid-up assessments on the stock held by them respectively, for all debts contracted by such association until the amount to be paid for the shares is fully paid; the directors and officers of every association formed under the provisions of this act shall be personally liable for any fraudulent use, disposition or investment of any money, securities or other property belonging to such association, or for any loss which shall be incurred by any invest-

Of directors and officers.

ment or use made by such directors or officers, other than such as are mentioned in and authorized by the articles of association; but no director or officer of any such association shall be liable, as aforesaid, unless he authorized, sanctioned or approved, or made such fraudulent use, disposition or investment, as aforesaid.

§ 10. No person holding any stock in such corporation as executor, administrator, guardian or trustee, and no person holding such stock as collateral security shall be personally subject to any liability as stockholder of such corporation; but the person pledging such stock shall be considered as holding the same, aad shall be liable as stockholder accordingly; and the estate or funds in the hands of such executor, administrator, guardian or trustee, shall be liable in any like manner, and to the same extent as the testator or intestate, or the ward or person interested in such trust fund, would have been if he, she or they had been living or competent to act, and held the same stock in his, her or their own name or names. Liability of parties who hold stock in trust.

§ 11. Every such executor, administrator, guardian or trustee shall have the right of having the share or shares of stock in hand represented at all meetings of the company, subject to the provisions of the articles of association; and every person who shall pledge stock as aforesaid may, nevertheless, represent the same at all such meetings, and may vote accordingly as a stockholder. Executor, etc., to have stock represented at meetings of stockholders.

§ 12. In case it shall happen at any time that an election of officers shall not be made on the day designated by the by-laws or articles of association of such corporation at the time for holding such election, the corporation shall not for that reason be dissolved; but it shall be lawful on any other day thereafter to hold an election for directors in such manner as may be provided for by said by-laws or articles of association; and all acts of directors or officers shall be valid and binding as against such company until their successors are elected and qualified. Failure to hold election not to dissolve corporation.

§ 13. Any corporation which may be formed under the provisions of this act may increase or diminish its capital stock, by complying with the provisions of this act, to any amount not exceeding one million of dollars, which may be deemed sufficient and proper for the purposes of the corporation; but, before any such corporation shall be entitled to diminish the amount of its capital stock, if the amount of its debts and liabilities shall exceed the amount of capital to which it is proposed to be reduced, such amount of debt and liabilities shall be satisfied and reduced so as not to exceed such diminished amount of capital. Increase of capital stock.

§ 14. Whenever any such corporation shall desire to increase or diminish the amount of its capital stock, it shall be the duty of the directors or trustees to publish a notice, signed by at least a majority of them, in a newspaper of general circulation, published in the city, town or county where the principal office or place of business of such corporation is located, for at Proceedings therefor.

least ten days, and to deposit a written or printed copy thereof in the post-office, addressed to each shareholder, at his business office or usual place of residence, or to the address left at the office of the company in writing, at least ten days previous to the day fixed upon for holding such meeting, calling a meeting of the stockholders, which notice shall specify the object of the meeting, the time and place when and where such meeting shall be held, and the amount to which it shall be proposed to increase or diminish the capital; and a vote of at least two-thirds of all the shares of stock issued shall be necessary to an increase or diminution of the amount of its capital stock.

When meeting to organize, etc.

§ 15. If, at any meeting provided for in the preceding section of this act, stockholders shall appear in person, or by proxy, in numbers representing not less than two-thirds of all the stock issued by the corporation, the meeting shall organize and proceed to a vote of those present in person, or by proxy; and if, on canvassing the votes, it shall appear that a sufficient number of votes has been given in favor of increasing or diminishing the amount of capital, a certificate of the proceedings, showing a compliance with the provisions of this act, the amount of capital actually paid in, the whole amount of debts and liabilities of the corporation, and the amount to which the capital stock shall be increased or diminished, and how the same is to be done, shall be made out, signed and verified by the affidavit of the chairman, and attested by the secretary of the meeting; and such affidavit shall be acknowledged by the chairman, and filed as required by the third section of this act; and, when so filed, the capital stock of such corporation shall be increased or diminished to the amount specified in such certificate.

Certificate to be filed.

Evidence.

§ 16. The copy of any certificate of incorporation filed in pursuance of this act, certified by the county clerk or his deputy to be a true copy of such certificate and the whole thereof, shall be received in all courts and places as presumptive evidence of the facts therein stated.

Loans to members limited.

§ 17. No loan made by any such association to any one of its members may exceed in amount the par value of the capital stock for which such member may have subscribed.

By-laws, etc.

§ 18. The directors of such corporation shall have power to make such prudential by-laws and regulations as they shall deem proper for the management and disposition of the stock and business affairs of such corporation, not inconsistent with the laws of this state or of the articles of the association; and prescribing the duties of directors, officers and servants that may be employed; for the appointment of officers and agents; for the security of the funds of the corporation, and for carrying out the objects and purposes of such corporation.

Saving clause.

§ 19. The legislature may at any time hereafter amend or repeal this act, and such amendment or repeal shall not, nor shall the dissolution of any company, take away or impair any remedy given against such corporation, its stockholders or officers, for any liability which shall have been previously incurred.

§ 20. The shares held by the members of associations incorporated under the provisions of this act, together with any amounts of deposits or assessments made on account thereof, shall be exempt from attachment or sale on execution for debt, to an extent not exceeding one thousand dollars, in such shares, deposits or assessments, at their par value; provided, the person holding such shares is not the owner of a homestead. Shares, etc., exempt from seizure on execution.

§ 5. This act shall take effect immediately.

CHAP. 826.

AN ACT to repeal chapter six hundred and sixty-eight of the laws of eighteen hundred and seventy-one, entitled "An act to provide for the payment of counsel, required to be employed on behalf of the state, in pursuance of the provisions of section two of chapter three hundred and twenty-one of the laws of eighteen hundred and seventy."

PASSED May 22, 1872; three-fifths being present.

The People of the State of New York, represented in Senate and Assembly, do enact as follows:

SECTION 1. Chapter six hundred and sixty-eight, laws of eighteen hundred and seventy-one, entitled "An act to provide for the payment of counsel required to be employed on behalf of the state in pursuance of the provisions of section two of chapter three hundred and twenty-one of the laws of eighteen hundred and seventy," is hereby repealed. Chapter 668, laws of 1871, repealed.

Ante, vol. 7, p. 711.

§ 2. This act shall take effect immediately.

CHAP. 829.

AN ACT in relation to the formation of railroad companies.

PASSED May 22, 1872.

The People of the State of New York, represented in Senate and Assembly, do enact as follows:

SECTION 1. Whenever any number of persons, not less than twenty-five, shall make and sign, or shall before the passage of this act have made and signed, articles of association, con- When persons who have signed articles and who shall thereafter become stockholders, shall be and become a corporation. taining the statements required by section one of an act entitled "An act to authorize the formation of railroad corporations and to regulate the same," passed April second, eighteen hundred and fifty, except the names and places of residence of thirteen directors of the company as therein provided; and thereafter thirteen directors have been chosen at a meeting of subscribers to such articles, and the names and places of residence of such directors so chosen have been inserted in such articles so subscribed, and there has been indorsed thereon the affidavit prescribed by the second section of said act, and said articles have been filed and recorded in the office of secretary of state; thereupon, the persons who have subscribed such articles, and all persons who shall thereafter become stockholders in such company shall be a corporation by the name specified in such articles of association, and have the same powers and privileges, and be subject to the same liabilities, as though such articles had when signed contained the names and places of residence of such directors.

§ 2. This act shall take effect immediately.

CHAP. 838.

AN ACT to amend "An act to secure to creditors a just division of the estates of debtors who convey to assignees for the benefit of creditors," passed April thirteenth, eighteen hundred and sixty.

PASSED May 22, 1872.

The People of the State of New York, represented in Senate and Assembly, do enact as follows:

SECTION 1. Section four of "An act to secure to creditors a just division of the estates of debtors who convey to assignees for the benefit of creditors," passed April thirteen, eighteen hundred and sixty, is hereby amended so as to read as follows:

Ante, vol. 4, p. 485.

When county judge to have power to issue citation. § 4. After the lapse of one year from the date of such assignment, the county judge of the county where such inventory is filed, shall have power to issue a citation or summons compelling such assignee or assignees to appear before him, and show cause why an account of the trust funds arising under any such assignment should not be made, and in case the said When to take accounting. county judge deem the cause, if any shown, not sufficient, he shall have power to proceed and take such accounting, and to decree the payment to any petitioning creditor or creditors their just proportionate share of such fund, or to take a final accounting thereof, and distribute and divide said fund between the claimants and persons entitled thereto. On whose application citation to issue. Such citation or summons may be issued, and such accounting had, on the application of the said assignee, his surety or sureties, or any person interested in said trust estate, which application shall be by petition, duly verified, stating the facts on which it is founded, and showing the relation the petitioners bear to or the interest they have in said trust estate, and stating, as far as the petitioners can, all other persons interested in said trust fund. Such citation must be served and such accounting shall be had and conducted just as citations are served, and as accountings for the estates of deceased persons are had and conducted by surrogates. All laws governing surrogates on such accountings are made applicable as far as may be to proceedings under this act, and the county judge before whom any proceeding is pending shall have all powers granted surrogates therein. He may also examine the parties and all other persons as witnesses in relation to such assignment and accounting and all other matters connected therewith, and shall have the power of the county court in like cases to compel their attendance before himself or any referee whom he may and is hereby authorized, to appoint, to take and report to him such evidence. All orders or decrees in these proceedings shall have the same force and effect and may be entered, docketed, enforced and appealed from the same as like orders or decrees of the county court in an original action brought therein. In case the county judge of the county where such inventory is filed on presentation of the petition is, or he or his successor in office at any time during the pendency of any proceeding shall become for any reason incapacitated to take or continue such accounting, such county judge or his successor shall, by order, transfer such accounting to the county judge of some adjoining county, and thereupon such proceedings shall be transferred to said county judge as in said order stated, and he shall have all the powers and proceed in like manner as the county judge with whom the petition was filed would have done had he not been incapacitated and no order been entered transferring the same; and all subsequent proceedings, orders or decrees made by said county judge to whom such proceeding has been thus transferred shall have the same force and effect as in proceedings where the petition is originally filed with him. In case any assignee has died during any proceeding now pending or undetermined under the act hereby amended, or shall hereafter die during the pendency of any proceeding under this act, his personal representatives or successor in office or both may be brought in and substituted in said proceeding, on such notice of not less than eight days as the county judge before whom said proceeding is pending may order, in all cases and with like force and effect as if said accounting had been an action in any court having jurisdiction thereof, and any decree afterward made in said proceeding shall bind the said parties thus substituted, and the property of the deceased assignee as in such action.

How served, etc.

Laws applicable.

May examine witnesses, etc.

Orders or decrees, effect of.

When proceedings to be transferred to county judge of an adjoining county.

Proceedings in case of death of assignee.

§ 2. This act shall take effect immediately.

CHAP. 843.

AN ACT to amend an act entitled "An act supplementary to the act entitled 'An act to authorize the formation of railroad corporations, and to regulate the same,' passed April second, eighteen hundred and fifty."

PASSED May 23, 1872; three-fifths being present.

The People of the State of New York, represented in Senate and Assembly, do enact as follows:

SECTION 1. Section five of chapter six hundred and ninety-seven of the laws of eighteen hundred and sixty-six, is hereby amended so as to read as follows:

Ante, vol. 6, p. 809; vol. 4, p. 617.

R. R. corporations, how continued beyond time fixed in articles of association.

§ 5. Any railroad corporation now existing or hereafter to be formed under the laws of this state may extend the time for the continuance of such corporation, beyond the time named for that purpose in the original act of incorporation or articles of association of such corporation, by the consent of the holders of two-thirds in amount of the stock of such corporation, in a certificate to be signed and proved, or acknowledged by the stockholders signing the same, so as to entitle it to be recorded in the office of the secretary of state, in the book kept in said office for the record of articles of association of railroad companies; and thereupon the time of the existence of such corporation shall be extended for the period designated in such certificate, and such corporation shall, from time to time during its existence so extended, possess all the rights, privileges and franchises at that time enjoyed or exercised by such corporation.

Certificate to be filed and recorded.

Where portion of lines of two roads embrace same location, companies may provide by agreement for construction of line by one company.

§ 2. Whenever two railroad companies for a portion of their respective lines embrace the same location of line, or whenever their lines connect or are tributary to each other, such companies may by agreement provide for the construction by one of said companies of so much of said line as is common to both or connects with its own line, and for the manner and terms upon which the business thereon shall be performed; and the company so constructing the common and connecting and tributary portion of road shall, if the terms of such agreement so provide, be entitled to have and receive all the town bonds which have been or may be authorized to be issued to either company in aid of the construction thereof, and the towns authorized to issue such bonds are hereby authorized and required to exchange the same for the stock or bonds of the railroad company that shall, under such agreement, construct a railroad upon the line designated therein, to an amount specified in the petition of the tax payers, or remaining unpaid on their subscription to the stock of either of said railroad companies. Nothing in this act contained shall be construed so as

R. R. commissioners

to compel the commissioners of any town that has assented to bond for railroad purposes for any specified line of railroad to surrender the bonds of any such town to any other railroad organization, until the assent of a majority of the tax payers, owning a majority of the property appearing upon the assessment roll of such town, has been first obtained. Not to be compelled to surrender bonds until consent of tax payers is obtained.

§ 3. This act shall take effect immediately.

CHAP. 848.

AN ACT to appoint commissioners of parks for the state of New York.

PASSED May 23, 1872.

The People of the State of New York, represented in Senate and Assembly, do enact as follows:

SECTION 1. A commission of state parks for the state of New York is hereby established. Commission of parks.

§ 2. It shall be the duty of the commissioners to inquire into the expediency of providing for vesting in the state the title to the timbered regions lying within the counties of Lewis, Essex, Clinton, Franklin, St. Lawrence, Herkimer and Hamilton, and converting the same into a public park; such commissioners to report the result of their labors, together with such suggestions as they may have to present, to the legislature at its next session. Duty of commissioners.

§ 3. Horatio Seymour, Patrick H. Agan, William B. Taylor, George H. Raynor, William A. Wheeler, Verplanck Colvin and Franklin B. Hough, are hereby appointed commissioners under this act, to hold office for two years, to act without compensation. Names of commissioners.

§ 4. This act shall take effect immediately.

CHAP. 850.

AN ACT to authorize a tax of seven-tenths of a mill per dollar of valuation of the year eighteen hundred and seventy-two, for the construction of new work upon and extraordinary repairs of the canals of this state.

PASSED May 23, 1872; three-fifths being present.

The People of the State of New York, represented in Senate and Assembly, do enact as follows:

SECTION 1. There shall be imposed for the fiscal year beginning on the first day of October, eighteen hundred and seventy-two, a state tax of seven-tenths of a mill on each dollar of the real and personal property in this state, subject to taxation, Seven-tenths mill tax for new work and extraordinary repairs. which tax shall be assessed, levied and collected by the annual assessment and collection of taxes for that year, in the manner prescribed by law, and shall be paid by the several county treasurers into the treasury of the state, to be held by the treasurer for application to the following purposes, to wit:

EASTERN DIVISION — ERIE CANAL.

Rebuilding lock at junction of Erie and Champlain canals. For rebuilding combined wooden locks (of stone) at the junction of the Erie and Champlain canals, the sum of sixty thousand dollars, or so much thereof as may be necessary, and if any excess of this amount is needed, it shall be paid out of any moneys appropriated for ordinary repairs of the eastern division of the canals, the whole cost thereof not to exceed eighty thousand dollars.

Iron bridge at West Troy. For construction of an iron bridge over Erie canal at West Troy, in pursuance of an act passed in eighteen hundred and seventy-two, the sum of forty-five hundred dollars, or so much as may be necessary, and any excess of this amount shall be paid out of any moneys appropriated for ordinary repairs of the eastern division of the canals.

State shop at Cohoes. For construction of a new state shop at Cohoes, Albany county, the sum of five thousand dollars, or so much thereof as may be necessary.

State shop at Fultonville. For construction of a new state shop at Fultonville, Montgomery county, the sum of three thousand dollars, or so much thereof as may be necessary.

Culvert in Mohawk. For enlarging a culvert in the village of Mohawk, west of lock number forty-two, the sum of four thousand dollars, or so much thereof as may be necessary.

Culvert at Ilion. For constructing culvert under Erie canal at Ilion, Herkimer county, and digging ditches to drain water through said culvert, the sum of five thousand dollars, or so much thereof as may be necessary.

Bridge in Cohoes. For raising approaches to White street bridge, in the city of Cohoes, the sum of two hundred and ten dollars, or so much thereof as may be necessary.

Schuyler street bridge, Utica. For removing embankment and constructing approaches to Schuyler street bridge, in the city of Utica, the sum of three thousand two hundred dollars, or so much thereof as may be necessary.

Bridge, in Port Jackson. For raising and improving approaches to the west bridge, in the village of Port Jackson, Montgomery county, the sum of seventeen hundred dollars, or so much thereof as may be necessary.

To pay E. H. French. For the payment of Edwin H. French the amount as adjusted by the canal board, for work on section five of Erie canal, greater than his contract price, the sum of fifteen thousand dollars.

Bridge at Hulser's farm. For building stone abutments for canal bridge, at Hulser's farm, West Frankfort, authorized by an act passed in eighteen hundred and sixty-six, the sum of two thousand five hundred dollars, or so much thereof as may be necessary.

The sum of one thousand dollars appropriated by chapter seven hundred and eighty-one of the laws of eighteen hundred and seventy-one, for construction of a fishway in the Mohawk river at the upper aqueduct, near the city of Schenectady, is re-appropriated to the same purpose, and to be repaid out of moneys appropriated for extraordinary repairs of the eastern division of the canals. Fishway in the Mohawk river.

The sum of one hundred thousand dollars, which was appropriated by chapter five hundred and seventy-nine of the laws of eighteen hundred and sixty-seven, to build two stone side-cut locks in the village of West Troy as authorized by chapter three hundred and fifty-four of the laws of eighteen hundred and sixty-four, and re-appropriated to the same purpose by chapter eight hundred and seventy-seven of the laws of eighteen hundred and sixty-nine, is again hereby re-appropriated to the same purpose. Side-cut locks in West Troy.

For the construction of a canal bridge over the Erie canal at Madison street, in the city of Rome, the sum of five thousand dollars, or so much thereof as may be necessary. Bridge at Rome.

For raising the road bed and improving the road at the head of Otisco lake in Onondaga county, if, in the opinion of the canal board, the state is legally or equitably liable for this work and that the same is now necessary, the sum of five thousand dollars, or so much thereof as may be necessary. For improving road at head of Otisco lake.

For changing location of canal bridge at the west line of the town of German Flats, raising and widening road-bed, and extending culvert at East Frankfort, the sum of six thousand dollars, or so much thereof as may be necessary. Bridge at German Flats, and culvert at East Frankfort.

For completing the raising of the road from the first ward in Syracuse to the village of Geddes, pursuant to chapter one hundred and forty-two of the laws of eighteen hundred and seventy, the sum of nine thousand seven hundred and fifty dollars, or so much thereof as may be necessary. Raising road from Syracuse to Geddes.

For completion of removal of wall benches and substituting therefor slope and vertical walls under contract between Port Schuyler and the lower Mohawk aqueduct on the Erie canal, the sum of fifty thousand dollars, or so much thereof as may be necessary. Wall benches, etc., between Port Schuyler and lower Mohawk aqueduct.

CHAMPLAIN CANAL.

For raising the road-bed in the town of Kingsbury, Washington county, the sum of one thousand dollars, or so much thereof as may be necessary. Raising road in Kingsbury.

For constructing an iron bridge over Champlain canal at Comstock's landing, Washington county, as authorized by an act passed in eighteen hundred and seventy-two, the sum of five thousand dollars, or so much thereof as may be necessary. Bridge at Comstock's landing.

For constructing a wooden bridge and abutments on the farm of Hiram Cramer, in the town of Saratoga, county of Saratoga, over the Champlain canal, as authorized by an act passed in eighteen hundred and seventy-two, the sum of two thousand dollars, or so much thereof as may be necessary. Bridge on Cramer's farm.

Guard-lock in Wood creek. For rebuilding guard-lock in wood creek, on Champlain canal, the sum of fifteeen thousand dollars, or so much thereof as may be necessary, and any excess of above sum for this work shall be paid out of any moneys appropriated for ordinary repairs of the canals on the eastern division, the whole cost thereof not to exceed twenty thousand dollars.

State shop at Fort Edward. For building new state shop at Fort Edward, Washington county, the sum of three thousand dollars, or so much thereof as may be necessary.

Basin, etc., south of Whitehall. For construction of a basin on the five mile level, south of the village of Whitehall, and improving and deepening the Champlain canal from said basin to Whitehall locks, including cutting down breast-wall of said locks to conform to said deepening, and to be done upon a plan adopted by the commissioner and engineer in charge, and approved by the canal board, the sum of twenty thousand dollars, or so much thereof as may be necessary.

Bridge at Glens Falls. For constructing a wooden road bridge across Glens Falls feeder, in the village of Glens Falls, as authorized by an act passed in eighteen hundred and seventy-two, the sum of two thousand dollars, or so much thereof as may be necessary.

Raising road-bed in Fort Ann. For raising road-bed in the town of Fort Ann, Washington county, pursuant to chapter five hundred and forty-four of the laws of eighteen hundred and seventy, the sum of two thousand dollars, or so much thereof as may be necessary, which work may be done by the canal commissioner in charge through his superintendent or by contract in his discretion.

State dam at Fort Miller bridge. For rebuilding of stone, the state dam now in progress across the Hudson river, near Fort Miller bridge, the sum of sixty thousand dollars; the remainder of the cost shall be charged to any money appropriated for ordinary repairs on eastern division of the canals; the entire cost thereof not to exceed eighty thousand dollars.

Dredging Whitehall basin. For dredging Whitehall basin, under existing contract, and paying retained percentage under said contract as provided by act chapter nine hundred thirty, laws of eighteen hundred and seventy-one, fifteen thousand dollars, or so much thereof as may be necessary.

BLACK RIVER.

Parker's Landing bridge. For completion of Parker's Landing bridge over a portion of Black river used as a canal, the sum of nine thousand dollars, or so much thereof as may be necessary.

Dam across Moose river. For construction of a dam across Moose river at the old Brown's tract forge at foot of Fulton chain of lakes, to raise the water in lakes to supply deficiency on Black river improvement, pursuant to chapter one hundred and eighty-one, laws of eighteen hundred and fifty-one, in dry season, the sum of eighteen thousand dollars, if, in the opinion of the canal board, the state is under equitable obligations to construct such dam, and if, in the opinion of said board, it is, under all the circumstances, expedient to do said work, provided the owners of said (Proviso.) lakes and lands adjoining release to the state all damages for use of said lakes and damages to land to be flowed in consequence of the construction of said dam.

Lock No. 2, Erie canal.

For completing lock number two on the Erie canal, and building vertical wall connected therewith, the sum of seven thousand five hundred dollars, or so much thereof as may be necessary.

Jason street bridge, Utica.

For completion of Jason street bridge, in the city of Utica, the sum of two thousand dollars, or so much thereof as may be necessary.

Bridge in Frankfort.

For enlarging approach ways and widening abutment to canal bridge on the street leading to the cemetery in the village of Frankfort, the sum of fifteen hundred dollars, or so much thereof as may be necessary.

To pay S. N. Payne.

For the payment of Samuel N. Payne, for furnishing piling machine, payment of transportation and other expenses incurred in constructing aqueduct in place of culvert on Champlain canal carried out by break on the thirteenth day of September, eighteen hundred and sixty-eight, the sum of one hundred and seven dollars and ninety-seven cents.

To pay G. Hendricks, T. Abele and E. Husson.

For the payment of certificates of the canal commissioners to George Hendricks, Thomas Abele and Edward Husson for damages awarded them for personal injuries occasioned by the fall of canal bridge in the city of Syracuse in April, eighteen hundred and sixty-nine, the sum of seven thousand eight hundred and nineteen dollars and eight cents.

MISCELLANEOUS.

Iron bridges.

For construction of iron bridge superstructures, made necessary in consequence of change of plan, the sum of forty thousand dollars, or so much thereof as may be necessary.

Bench walls, vertical walls, etc.

For removing bench wall and constructing slope and vertical walls, including completion of removal of wall benches, and construction of vertical wall from starch factory bridge to completed wall near old lime-kiln, in the city of Utica; completion of vertical wall on Glens Falls feeder at Sandy Hill, pursuant to chapter nine hundred and thirty of the laws of eighteen hundred and seventy-one; removing bench wall between locks number forty-two and forty-six on Erie canal; to pay the expenses of constructing a vertical wall along the berme bank of the Erie canal in the village of Canajoharie, commencing three hundred feet east of the aqueduct, thence westwardly through the village of Canajoharie, terminating fifty feet west of the dwelling-house of Samuel Beekman, and elsewhere on said division as may be directed by the canal board, the sum of one hundred and seventeen thousand dollars, or so much thereof as may be necessary.

State engineer to make estimates.

No part or portion of this appropriation shall be expended, nor shall any contract be made involving such expenditure, until the state engineer shall make, or cause to be made, an estimate of the cost of completing and paying for all work now under contract for removing wall benches and substituting slope or vertical wall on said division, and the amount so ascertained to be necessary shall be set apart for and applied to that purpose.

Fishways at Troy and Fort Miller. For construction of fishways in the state dam across the Hudson river at Troy and Fort Miller, pursuant to chapter five hundred and fifty-five, laws of eighteen hundred and seventy, the sum of two thousand dollars, or so much thereof as may be necessary.

Lock and side-cut at Wilber's basin. For construction of a lock and side-cut at Wilber's basin, on the Champlain canal, the sum of ten thousand dollars, or so much thereof as may be necessary, in addition to the amount heretofore appropriated by chapter seven hundred and sixty-seven of the laws of eighteen hundred and seventy, for constructing an aqueduct at the same place, which appropriation is hereby re-appropriated and applied to the construction of this lock, provided the state engineer is satisfied that the cost of the work, when finished, will not exceed forty thousand dollars.

MIDDLE DIVISION — ERIE CANAL.

Miscellaneous. To pay miscellaneous expenses and certain damages which owners of farms and lots have suffered in consequence of leakage in the bottom of the Erie canal recently deepened east of Lodi locks; to construct ditches outside of the blue line by bargain with land owners and to pay for such ditches as have already been constructed, where necessary to do work to protect the canal and to avert claims against the state, the sum of twenty-five thousand dollars, or so much thereof as may be necessary, the said sum being under the control of the canal board, to be appropriated for such purposes, from time to time, as said board shall be satisfied the public interest may require.

Bridge in Syracuse. For the construction of an iron bridge over the Erie canal at Catharine street, in the city of Syracuse, eight thousand dollars, or so much thereof as may be necessary.

To pay C. Snook. For amount of final estimate due to Clark Snook for brush and stone used in the vicinity of Pool's brook, the sum of twenty-four hundred and nineteen dollars and seventy cents.

Cowasel creek. For the improvement of the channel of Cowasel creek in the town of Lenox, county of Madison, the sum of fifteen hundred dollars, or so much thereof as may be necessary.

Repairs at Weedsport. The sum of five thousand dollars appropriated by chapter nine hundred and thirty of the laws of eighteen hundred and seventy-one, for excavation and vertical wall of wood and stone on the berme bank of the Erie canal at Weedsport, is hereby re-appropriated to the same object, and may be paid, or any part thereof, by the commissioners in charge of the Southern Central railroad company, on satisfactory evidence that the said work has been done as well and as cheaply for the state as if the same had been advertised and let to the lowest bidder.

MIDDLE DIVISION — CHENANGO CANAL.

For amount due and to become due for the partial reconstruction of the locks numbers seven and nine on Chenango canal, near Utica, the sum of fifteen thousand dollars, or so much thereof as may be necessary. Locks No. 7 and 9.

ONEIDA LAKE CANAL.

The sum of fifty thousand dollars is hereby appropriated to complete the Oneida Lake canal; but no portion of this sum shall be expended unless the canal commissioner can make a contract within such sum on public notice of letting to the lowest bidder for all the work necessary to make the said canal, and its works and structures safe, and secure good navigation, the modified plan of the work to be determined by the canal commissioner and the state engineer. Completion of Oneida Lake canal.

OSWEGO CANAL.

The provision for the payment of the heirs of George A. Humphrey, in chapter nine hundred and thirty of the laws of eighteen hundred and seventy-one, is amended as follows: For the payment of George W. Humphrey, for work done on the enlargement of the Oswego canal, the sum of fifteen hundred and thirty-three dollars and ninety-six cents, in full of the claim of said Humphrey. Amending chapter 930, Laws of 1871.

For completing the high dam on the Oswego canal, the sum of eighty-eight thousand dollars, or so much thereof as may be necessary. High dam.

For the purpose of extending the east wing of Oswego falls dam at Fulton, on a plan similar to the east wing of Minetto dam, the sum of twenty-five hundred dollars, or so much thereof as may be necessary, and if said sum is insufficient, the balance to be paid out of money appropriated to ordinary repairs of the middle division, not exceeding twenty-five hundred dollars. Oswego falls dam.

CHEMUNG CANAL.

For lengthening the pier and necessary dredging in the harbor at Watkins, the sum of fifteen thousand dollars, or so much thereof as may be necessary under existing contracts for doing the same. Repairs in harbor at Watkins.

For construction of an iron bridge over Chemung canal at Watkins, the sum of forty-five hundred dollars (as authorized by an act passed in eighteen hundred and seventy-two), or so much thereof as may be necessary. Bridge at Watkins.

MISCELLANEOUS.

For changing the plan of bridges on middle division, the sum of twenty-five thousand dollars, or so much thereof as may be necessary. Changing plan of bridges.

Horse dredge on Owasco outlet. For pay of construction of a horse dredge on the Owasco outlet the sum of six hundred dollars, or so much thereof as may be necessary.

Miscellaneous repairs. For removing bench walls and constructing slope pavement and vertical wall, and paying any arrearages due for said work, including the construction of three hundred feet of vertical wall in front of the brewery of Lewis Gross and Company at Weedsport; also one hundred and fifty feet of vertical wall on the tow-path side of Erie canal, adjacent to the factory and lumber yard of Laraway, Butterfield and Peck, in village of Port Byron, also six hundred feet of vertical wall on the landing of the Midland Railroad Company at village of Durhamville, and elsewhere on said division as may be directed by the canal board, the sum of eighty thousand dollars, or so much thereof as may be necessary.

To pay J. Ostrander. For amount due to John Ostrander, for work done on the berme protection on Seneca lake, near Geneva, over and above the amount paid to him under his contract, the sum of six hundred dollars, or so much thereof as may be necessary.

For removing obstructions from Cayuga lake outlet. For removing the obstruction from the outlet of Cayuga lake and the channel of Seneca river, the sum of twenty thousand dollars, or so much thereof as may be necessary, and the sum of thirty thousand dollars appropriated by chapter three hundred and four, laws of eighteen hundred and sixty-eight, is hereby re-appropriated for the same purpose.

WESTERN DIVISION — ERIE CANAL.

Repairing bank along Tonawanda creek. For repairing the north bank of Erie canal along Tonawanda creek in the town of Pendleton, and protection of highway along said canal from injury by being washed by the waters thereof, the sum of two thousand dollars, or so much thereof as may be necessary.

Dredging, etc. For dredging out Black Rock harbor, the sum of ten thousand dollars, under the present contract for doing the same.

Cribs, etc., in Tonawanda. For cribs and vertical walls, in place of pile docking, in Erie canal between military road and state ditch culvert, in the village of Tonawanda, the sum of eighty thousand dollars, or so much thereof as may be necessary.

Doubling locks. For completing the doubling the locks on the western division of Erie canal, the sum of one hundred and twenty-six thousand dollars, or so much thereof as may be necessary.

Deepening Erie canal. For continuing and completing the deepening of the Erie canal, from first lock east of Rochester to Lyell street, the sum of twenty thousand dollars, or so much thereof as may be necessary.

Bridge at Lockville. For setting back berme abutment of, and constructing an iron in place of a wooden bridge at, Lockville, the sum of five thousand dollars, or so much thereof as may be necessary.

Waste-weir at Lock Berlin. For reconstructing waste-weir at lock Berlin, at a new location, the sum of thirty-five hundred dollars, or so much thereof as may be necessary.

For reconstructing culvert on three mile level in Brighton, on change of plan from wood to iron pipe, the sum of eight thousand dollars, or so much thereof as may be necessary. Culvert in Brighton.

For reconstructing protection railing of iron on berme protection wall along South St. Paul street, in the city of Rochester, the sum of one thousand dollars, or so much thereof as may be necessary. Protection railing in Rochester.

For payment of work done, and to be done, to complete the changing line of Erie canal, and protecting the same High Clay bluff, west of Rochester, the sum of one thousand dollars. Changing line at High Clay bluff.

For improving the channel discharge from Rochester weigh-lock, the sum of three thousand dollars, or so much thereof as may be necessary. Channel discharge at Rochester.

For constructing three hundred and sixty feet of vertical wall on berme side of Erie canal, in village of Middleport, along the premises of H. A. Robertson, the sum of eighteen hundred dollars, or so much thereof as may be necessary. Vertical wall in Middleport.

For constructing four hundred feet of dry vertical wall on berme side of Erie canal, in front of the premises of Underhill, Branan and Company of Brockport, extending easterly from berme abutment of Smith street bridge, in said village, the sum of two thousand dollars, or so much thereof as may be necessary. Vertical wall in Brockport.

For constructing two hundred feet of vertical wall on the berme bank of Erie canal, along the premises of Absalom Mesler, in Gasport, Niagara county, the sum of one thousand dollars, or so much thereof as may be necessary. Vertical wall in Gasport.

For constructing three hundred feet of vertical wall, commencing one thousand three hundred and fifty-three feet east of abutment of bridge, and fronting the stone yard of Squire and Phillips on tow-path side of canal, in village of Hulberton, Orleans county, the sum of fifteen hundred dollars, or much thereof as may be necessary. Vertical wall in Hulberton.

For constructing two hundred feet of vertical wall on the berme bank of Erie canal, opposite the quarry of Eugene Sullivan, in Albion, Orleans county, the sum of one thousand dollars, or so much thereof as may be necessary. Vertical wall in Albion.

To pay Thomas Hodge for constructing vertical wall on the berme bank of Erie canal, opposite his stone quarry, near Albion, Orleans county, done under the supervision of canal commissioner and resident engineer, the sum of fifteen hundred dollars, which sum, if accepted, shall be in full payment of said work.

For constructing vertical wall on both sides of Erie canal, at Lockville, in the short reaches between the locks, the sum of twenty-five thousand dollars, or so much thereof as may be necessary. Vertical wall in Lockville.

For constructing two hundred feet of vertical wall, under the existing contract, in village of Fairport, the sum of one thousand dollars, or so much thereof as may be necessary. Vertical wall in Fairport.

For constructing two hundred feet of vertical wall, under Vertical

Wall at Cartersville. the existing contract, at village of Carterville, the sum of one thousand dollars, or so much thereof as may be necessary.

Hamilton street bridge, Buffalo. For re-building Hamilton street bridge of iron, in the city of Buffalo, the sum of thirty-five hundred dollars, or so much thereof as may be necessary, may be paid by the canal commissioner in charge, to the repair contractor for the said iron bridge complete, after deducting the amount said contractor should pay for constructing said bridge.

Division banks, etc., in Black Rock harbor canal. For continuing the work of constructing division bank and widening, deepening and otherwise improving the narrow canal in Black Rock harbor, under existing contract, so far as the prices therein contained are applicable to said work, and *the engineers' estimate prices, for the balance thereof, if, in the opinion of the canal board, it is for the best interest of the state so to do, said engineers' estimated prices being the same as presented in their estimate to the canal board, September fifth, eighteen hundred and seventy-one, when said board adopted the plan of constructing said division bank and widening the canal through the entire length of the harbor, so as to make the canal independent thereof, the sum of one hundred and twenty-five thousand dollars, or so much thereof as may be necessary.

Bridge over Tonawanda creek. For constructing a road bridge over Tonawanda creek, at or near Bush's place, connecting with Sawyer's creek road at Martinsville, the sum of sixteen thousand dollars, or so much thereof as may be necessary.

Erie basin, Buffalo. For dredging Erie basin in the city of Buffalo, the sum of ten thousand dollars, or so much thereof as may be necessary. Of the above amount the canal commissioner in charge may give his draft upon the auditor for the sum of twenty-three hundred and twenty dollars, for dredging done in said basin, during the year eighteen hundred and seventy-one; but before the payment of such draft, the said commissioner shall certify to the auditor that the work was properly done, and the prices for the same were fair and reasonable.

Repairs in Buffalo. For constructing a retaining wall, and piling and sheet piling a dock one hundred and seventy-five feet of dock in front of the premises of Taylor and Crate, on the south side of Ohio basin slip, between Elk street and the Ohio basin, in the city of Buffalo, the sum of two thousand dollars, or so much thereof as may be necessary.

Culvert under Genesee Valley canal in Rochester. For constructing a culvert under the Genesee Valley canal, in the city of Rochester, the sum of fifteen hundred dollars, or so much thereof as may be necessary; provided that said culvert shall be built under the supervision of the canal commissioner in charge, and that the cost thereof shall not exceed the sum appropriated.

Same at Cuylerville. For constructing a culvert under the Genesee Valley canal at Cuylerville, Livingston county, and cleaning out the state ditch, the sum of twenty-five hundred dollars, or so much thereof as may be necessary.

* So in the original.

GENESEE VALLEY CANAL.

Bridge. The sum of six hundred dollars is hereby appropriated to be paid by the commissioner in charge of the western division of canals to the commissioners of highways of the town of West Sparta, Livingston county, toward building a bridge over the Genesee Valley canal, at a point where the road laid out by the commissioners of highways of said town intersects said canal. Such sum to be paid after said bridge has been erected and finished to the satisfaction of said canal commissioner.

Conveying water from Loon lake. For conveying the water from Loon lake by discharging the same through Mill creek into the canal at Dansville for the purpose of supplying water to that branch of the Genesee Valley canal, and as a feeder to the Erie canal at Rochester, ten thousand dollars, or so much thereof as may be necessary.

To pay Lewis Selye. For the payment of Lewis Selye, assignee of Valentine F. Whitman, repair contractor of section number eleven, Erie canal, the amount paid by him to the military and sheriff and his deputies, of the county of Monroe, in suppressing a riot and guarding the works and men during the time of repairing the break at Oxbow embankment in the spring of eighteen hundred and seventy-one, as evidenced by the returns of the same in the canal department, the sum of three thousand three hundred and nine dollars and thirteen cents, or so much thereof as may be justly due him, provided that before the payment of the same such accounts shall be examined and passed by the auditor of the canal department.

To pay drainage commissioners of Lyons. For the payment to the order of John C. Bishop, Joel A. Putnam, and B. P. Van Mastar, commissioners of drainage of the town of Lyons, Wayne county, for constructing a drain and tiling the same, one hundred and seventy-five rods in length, in rear of the tow-path of the Erie canal in the village of Lyons, to carry off the leakage water of the canal, and to preserve the health of that locality, one hundred and seventy-five dollars, or so much thereof as may be necessary.

To complete enlargement maps. For completion of enlargement maps on the western division of the Erie canal, the sum of twenty-five hundred dollars, or so much thereof as may be necessary.

To pay award to R. L. Howard. For the payment of award by the canal board to Rufus L. Howard, November twenty-first, eighteen hundred and seventy-one, under chapter five hundred and eighty-six of the laws of eighteen hundred and seventy-one, the sum of six thousand one hundred dollars, or so much thereof as may be necessary.

MISCELLANEOUS.

Changing plan of bridges. For changing plans of bridges on the western division of the canals, the sum of thirty-five thousand dollars, or so much thereof as may be necessary; this appropriation to be used only on the Erie canal.

Waste-weir at Rochester. For constructing a waste-weir through the north wall of the new canal aqueduct over the Genesee river at Rochester, and a rubble wall in cement across the old canal at the east end of said aqueduct, as authorized by resolution of the canal board, November seventeenth, eighteen hundred and seventy-one, the sum of forty-seven hundred dollars, or so much thereof as may be necessary.

Bridge in Lockport. For completing Transit street bridge over the Erie canal, in the city of Lockport, the sum of two thousand dollars, or so much thereof as may be necessary.

State ditch in Tonawanda. For docking and clearing out State ditch immediately north of Tonawanda creek, in the village of Tonawanda, twenty-five hundred dollars, or so much thereof as may be necessary.

Improvements between Lyons and Lockville. For completing the removal of bench walls and constructing slope walls and pavement between Lyons and Lockville, the sum of ten thousand dollars, or so much thereof as may be necessary.

Miscellaneous expenses. For paying miscellaneous expenditures incident to the western division of canals, the sum of ten thousand dollars; this money to be paid only upon the order of the canal board and upon vouchers, with the items for such expenditures.

Construction of powers of commissioners. In order to remove all doubts in respect to the authority of the canal commissioners to commence the new works for which appropriations are herein made, and no legislative direction is otherwise given by special laws, it is hereby declared that the said canal commissioners are hereby authorized to construct, or cause to be constructed, all such new works for which appropriations are herein made, subject, however, to all restrictions, provisions and conditions contained in this act. Moneys; when to be paid and contracts w en to bdlet. No part or portion of the moneys herein appropriated for new work shall be expended or paid, nor shall any contract involving such expenditure and payment be made on behalf of this state until the maps, plans and estimates for such new work shall have been submitted to and approved by the canal board. Contracts to be let to lowest bidder. All contracts for work or material on any canal (other than ordinary repairs) which shall be directed by the canal board to be advertised and let, shall be made with the person who shall offer to do or provide the same at the lowest price, with adequate security for their performance, which letting shall be under regulations to be made by the board of canal commissioners as to the form, regularity and validity of all bids, securities and contracts. Commissioners may require deposits. And the canal commissioners may require the deposit by the proposer for said work or materials of such a sum in United States bonds or stocks of the state of New York, or money, not exceeding twenty nor less than eight per cent of the aggregate estimate of the work to be let, as they may deem necessary to secure the entering into said contract. And in case the proposer, to whom such work shall be awarded, shall neglect or refuse to enter into such contract, the sum so deposited shall be forfeited to the state, and the commissioners shall pay the same into the state treasury, and it shall become a part of the canal fund. Securities may be held for comple- And upon the entering into said contract, the bonds or stocks or money required by the commissioners as security for the entering into said contract, together with such other additional securities as they may require, may be held as security for the completion of the work, and shall be deposited with the treasurer as a special trust, to be returned by him to the contractor with such further sum as he may have realized for the use thereof, when the commissioner in charge and the state engineer shall certify that the contractor has fully completed his contract, and that the state has no further claim upon such funds. But in case he shall enter into said contract and fail in the performance thereof, the same shall be declared abandoned by said commissioners, pursuant to the terms of the contract, then the bonds or stocks or money so deposited shall be forfeited to the state, and paid into the treasury and become a part of the canal fund. The canal board may, in the resolution authorizing any work to be let, prescribe the length of time of advertising not less than ten days. No more money shall be expended on the works hereinbefore enumerated than is above appropriated; and it shall not be lawful for the officers having in charge the execution of the said works to make any contracts whereby any expenditure in excess of the appropriation will be incurred, or any further appropriation for the same rendered necessary. To meet the appropriations made in this act of the moneys to be collected by and upon the said tax with as little delay as practicable, the commissioners of the canal fund or comptroller may, from time to time, invest in the said tax any surplus moneys of the principal of the sinking fund under article seven of the constitution, a sum or sums not exceeding in all the amount to be realized from said tax hereby authorized; and the moneys so invested shall be applied to pay the appropriation under this act; and so much of the moneys arising from the said tax as may be necessary, when paid into the treasury, is hereby pledged, and shall be applied in the first instance to re-imburse the said sinking fund for the amount invested in said tax, and for the interest on the same at a rate not exceeding six per cent per annum, from the time of investment to the day of payment. The final account for any new work authorized by the provisions of this act or any previous acts, or for which money has been or is hereby appropriated, may be subject to revision by the canal board.

tion of the work. | When deposit to be forfeited. | Canal board may prescribe time to advertise. | No more money to be expended. | Commissioners or comptroller may invest in said tax.

For constructing farm and other bridges and crossings over the Chenango canal extension, between Binghamton and Owego, the sum of fifteen thousand dollars, or so much thereof as may be required to construct bridges over roads and lanes, and make other necessary crossings and connections between parts of farms now divided by said Chenango canal extension, unfinished. The above specified amount to be expended under the supervision and direction of the canal commissioners, but only for the purposes above specified. The canal commissioner in charge is hereby authorized to sell at auction any perishable property being on or connected with said Chenango canal extension, and belonging to the state of New York. For the purpose of paying the counsel and agents employed by the canal commissioners or either of them, and

Crossings between Binghamton and Owego. | Sum, how expended. | Canal commissioner to sell personal property. | To pay counsel and agents. the canal appraisers, for their expenses, disbursements and services incurred, or which may be incurred, in the defense of claims against the state connected with the canals, ten thousand dollars, or so much thereof as shall be necessary; provided, however, that all bills or accounts for such expenses, disbursements or services shall, before payment, be presented to and audited by the canal board; and upon the certificate of said board (or of said officers) the auditor is directed, out of said funds, to pay said bills and accounts. Proviso.

§ 2. This act shall take effect immediately.

CHAP. 873.

AN ACT to establish and maintain an institution for the relief of indigent and disabled soldiers and sailors of the State of New York.

PASSED June 8, 1872; three-fifths being present.

The People of the State of New York, represented in Senate and Assembly, do enact as follows:

SECTION 1. The twenty-one persons named in this section, and their successors, are hereby constituted a body corporate, by the corporate name of The New York Soldiers' Home, and invested with all the powers, rights, functions, duties and liabilities of corporations as the same are declared by the constitution of this state and defined by title third of chapter eighteen of part first of the Revised Statutes, and by this act, to wit: Henry A. Barnum, John C. Robinson, Henry W. Slocum, William Johnson, John Hammond, James McQuade, William F. Rodgers, John B. Murray, James Jourdan, William M. Gregg, John H. Martindale, David C. Stoddard, Clinton D. McDougall, J. B. Kiddoo, Timothy Sullivan, Adolph Nolte, John C. Carmichael, N. M. Curtis, Joseph Forbes, James E. Jones and Edmund L. Cole. Corporate name. Corporators.

§ 2. The above-named persons, when qualified as herein provided, and their duly qualified successors, shall be the trustees of the said corporation, and shall hold office until their successors shall have been duly appointed and qualified. Within ten days after the passage of this act, the above-named persons shall meet in the office of the secretary of state, at Albany, and, in his presence, draw lots for terms of office; three to hold for one year, three for two years, three for three years, three for four years, three for five years, three for six years, and three for seven years, respectively, from the first day of May, eighteen hundred and seventy-two; and if any trustee be absent, the secretary of state shall act as proxy and draw lots for such absentee. After the expiration of such terms of office, respectively, the succeeding full terms shall be seven years. The secretary of state shall file in his office a certificate of the determination of the terms of office by lot, as aforesaid, and furnish to each trustee a copy thereof, and First trustees. To meet and draw lots for terms of office. Secretary of State to draw for absentees. Secretary to file certificate.

each of said trustees shall take and file with the secretary of state the constitutional oath of office, and thereupon they shall become the trustees of said corporation. The governor, attorney-general and comptroller shall be, *ex-officio*, members of said board of trustees.

Ex officio trustees.

§ 3. The governor, by and with the advice and consent of the senate, shall, annually thereafter, appoint three trustees of said corporation to take the places of those whose terms of office shall expire, as provided in section two. He shall also, in like manner, fill any vacancy in the office of trustee of said corporation that may occur, other than by expiration of term of office, and any such appointment, made during the vacation of the senate, shall be held valid until the action of the senate thereon. Any trustee failing to qualify, as herein provided, within one month from notice of his appointment, shall be held to have declined said appointment, and the governor may thereupon appoint another person to fill such vacancy. A trustee removing, permanently, from the state, shall be held to have vacated his said office; and for misconduct, neglect of duty, or any act or acts showing the unfitness of any trustee to fill such office, such trustee may be removed from such office, by the governor, on the written application for such removal of two-thirds of the members of such board, setting forth the grounds of such application for removal; but a copy of such application for removal shall be served on the trustee so recommended for removal, and he shall have reasonable time and opportunity to be heard on his own behalf, before the governor, upon the question of such removal.

Three trustees to be annually appointed by governor and senate.

Vacancies, how filled.

Removals from office.

§ 4. The said trustees shall, from their own number, by a majority ballot or vote, choose one trustee to be president, another to be secretary, and another to be treasurer, and when thus organized, said board shall have the power, and it shall be their duty, to establish, organize, control and manage an institution under the said name of The New York Soldiers' Home, for the relief, maintenance, support and protection of meritorious invalid or disabled persons who served in the army or navy during the war of the rebellion, and were honorably discharged therefrom, and who were enlisted in the state of New York, or, if enlisted elsewhere, shall have been a resident of said state for four months, at the time of such person's application for admission to said institution; the board of trustees to have the discretionary power to decide upon the acceptance of every applicant for admission to the benefits of said institution, and to dismiss for misconduct or other adequate cause, any of the persons admitted to said institution. The treasurer of such corporation shall, before entering upon the duties of the office, execute and file in the office of the comptroller of the state, his bond, with such sureties and in such penalty as shall be approved by the comptroller, with the condition that he shall well and faithfully perform and discharge the duties of treasurer of said corporation, and well and truly account for, pay over and deliver to the persons legally entitled to the same, or to said corporation, all moneys,

Officers of board of trustees.

Trustees to establish an institution for relief, etc., of invalid soldiers and sailors.

Treasurer to give bonds.

securities and property which shall come to his possession or control as such treasurer.

Officers of institution. § 5. The said board of trustees shall appoint a governor, lieutenant-governor, surgeon, chaplain, steward and such supernumeraries as they may deem necessary for the proper internal management of said institution, and may remove these officers and supernumeraries, or any of them, at their discretion. Qualifications of. These officers and supernumeraries shall be persons who served in the army or navy of the United States during the war of the rebellion, and who have been honorably discharged therefrom, preference being given to those who were disabled by wounds or otherwise during their term of service. Rules. The said board of trustees shall establish such rules as they may deem necessary for the government of said institution and the admission of inmates, not inconsistent with the provisions of this act.

Corporate powers. § 6. The corporation hereby created shall have power to receive and disburse funds, and to purchase or take, by gift, deed or devise, bequest or otherwise, any real for personal estate for the uses or purposes of said corporation, and shall have full power to grant, bargain, lease, incumber or dispose of the same or any part thereof; provided, however, that all moneys arising from any such grant, lease, incumbrance or disposal, shall be appropriated to the objects and purposes of said corporation, and all gifts, bequests, donations, purchases, sales, leases or incumbrances, shall be immediately To report to comptroller. reported to the comptroller of the state, and shall be set forth in detail in their annual report; and the title to all real estate acquired by said board of trustees for the said institution shall vest in the state of New York. Donations, etc., how invested. All donations and contributions to the said corporation (except such lands as shall be appropriated as the site for said institution) shall be converted into money, and be invested in the public stocks of the United States, the state of New York, or of any of the cities of the state, and shall form the capital of an endowment fund, to be known as "The New York Soldiers' Home endowment fund," the income of which only may be used and applied to defraying the current expenses of said institution. The board of trustees of said corporation shall be the trustees of said fund, and shall have power to make all necessary agreements and contracts, and to take all necessary and proper legal proceedings to protect and administer said fund for the purposes intended by this act. Comptroller to examine books, etc., of corporation. It shall be the duty of the comptroller of the state, at least four times in each year, and as often as he shall deem proper, to examine, or cause to be examined, the books, accounts, vouchers, correspondence, papers and property of said corporation, and express annually, in his report to the legislature, his opinion upon the management and transactions of said trustees, with such suggestions as shall appear to him to be necessary and proper.

Site for buildings. § 7. The board of trustees may procure, by purchase, lease or donation, an appropriate site for buildings for said institution in a rural, agricultural district, with a proper quantity of land, and may thereon construct, or cause to be constructed, appropriate and commodious buildings, and structures for the institution, and finish and furnish the same ready for use.

§ 8. The board of trustees shall hold regular meetings at least once in three months, and such other meetings by adjournment or upon the call of the president as shall be required for the proper and efficient management of the affairs and business of the corporation; and the president shall, upon the written request of any five of the trustees, call a special meeting of the board, for the purpose of transacting such business only as shall be stated in said written request, a notice of which shall be duly served, in writing, upon every member of said board. Said trustees shall receive no compensation for their services as such trustees, except the actual traveling expenses incurred in attending the meetings of the board, and except a just compensation to one of their number, who shall be selected as treasurer, to whom reasonable compensation may be allowed, to be fixed by the board of trustees. Meetings. Trustees not to receive compensation.

§ 9. The board of trustees shall annually make a report of all the transactions and business of said corporation, including an itemized, fiscal account of all receipts and expenditures for the year ending on the first day of December in each year, which report shall, on or before the fifteenth day of December in each year, be transmitted to the governor, to be by him submitted to the legislature. Annual report.

§ 10. This act shall take effect immediately.

CHAP. 883.

AN ACT to confer jurisdiction upon the supreme court or the judges thereof in proceedings under chapter nine hundred and seven of the laws of eighteen hundred and sixty-nine, entitled "An act to authorize the formation of railroad corporations and to regulate the same, passed April second, eighteen hundred and fifty, so as to permit municipal corporations to aid in the construction of railroads," as amended by chapter nine hundred and twenty-five of the laws of eighteen hundred and seventy-one, and to repeal section ten of said act as thus amended.

PASSED June 15, 1872.

The People of the State of New York, represented in Senate and Assembly, do enact as follows:

SECTION 1. The petition of a majority of the tax payers of any municipal corporation in this state, who are assessed or taxed, or represent a majority of the taxable property of said corporation, as required and provided by section one of chapter nine hundred and seven of the laws of eighteen hundred and sixty-nine, as amended by chapter nine hundred and Petition of tax payers under general railroad bonding acts may be presented to justice of supreme

Court at special term. twenty-five of the laws of eighteen hundred and seventy one, duly verified as therein required, may be presented to any judge of the supreme court, at any special term of said court, and on such presentation, said judge or said court shall have all power and proceed to give notices, hear the parties and proofs and adjudge, decree and determine as to all matters in like manner, and in all respects and with like force and effect as the county judge would have done under the acts hereby amended, had such petition been presented to him. Such court or judge thereof upon the presentation of such petition or at any time thereafter during the pendency of any proceeding are hereby authorized to appoint any proper person as referee to take the evidence, and report thereupon upon any questions pending in such proceedings, and such person thus appointed referee shall have all the powers of referees appointed by the supreme court in actions therein, and shall report the evidence taken by him with his conclusions of fact and law and opinion thereupon to said judge or court appointing him. The said judge or any special term of said court may, on a notice of not less than eight days to all parties appearing on the hearing upon filing the report of said referee, hear, determine and decree as to all matters as though the proofs had been taken without any reference in such proceedings, and with like force and effect as is provided with regard to a county judge under the acts hereby amended. No appeal can be taken from any order or decree under this act, unless on notice to all parties appearing on the hearing and the granting or refusing said appeal, and proceedings thereunder shall be governed by the same rules as govern the granting or refusing a certiorari of proceedings under the acts hereby amended and proceedings under said certiorari if allowed.

Said judge or court may take proofs, etc.

May appoint referee to take evidence, etc.

Powers of referee.

Upon filing report of referee, court or judge, may proceed, etc.

Appeal, how taken.

Section 10, chapter 907, laws of 1869, as amended, repealed.

§ 2. Section ten of chapter nine hundred and seven of the laws of eighteen hundred and sixty-nine, as amended by section three of chapter nine hundred and twenty-five of the laws of eighteen hundred and seventy-one is hereby repealed.

§ 3. This act shall take effect immediately.

Ante, vol. 8, p. 617; vol. 7, p. 517.

CHAP. 884.

AN ACT to provide for a commission to propose amend ments to the constitution.

PASSED June 15, 1872; three-fifths being present.

The People of the State of New York, represented in Senate and Assembly, do enact as follows:

Governor, with the senate, to appoint commissioners, etc.

SECTION 1. The governor by and with the advice and consent of the senate to designate thirty-two persons, four from each judicial district, who shall constitute a commission for the purpose of proposing to the legislature, at its next session, amendments to the constitution; provided that no amendments shall be proposed to the sixth article thereof.

Vacancies, how filled.

§ 2. Every vacancy that may at any time occur among the members of such commission shall be filled by the governor and secretary of state.

Meetings, where to be held.

§ 3. The meetings of such commission shall be held in the city of Albany.

Chairman, clerks, etc.

§ 4. The commission shall have power to choose a chairman, and to appoint so many clerks, messengers and doorkeepers as may be necessary for the transaction of its business, not exceeding ten in number, and to regulate their pay.

Compensation of commissioners.

§ 5. Each member of the commission shall be entitled to receive for his services the sum of ten dollars a day for not exceeding fifty days, and the same mileage as is allowed to members of the legislature.

Bills for printing, audited by comptroller.

§ 6. All bills for printing, stationery, postage and other incidental expenses of such commission, shall be certified by the presiding officer thereof, and audited by the comptroller.

Appropriation for expenses.

§ 7. The sum of twenty-five thousand dollars, or so much thereof as may be necessary, is hereby appropriated out of any money in the treasury not otherwise appropriated, to defray the expenses connected with such commission.

§ 8. This act shall take effect immediately.

CONCURRENT RESOLUTIONS

OF THE

SENATE AND ASSEMBLY.

CONCURRENT RESOLUTIONS relative to the adoption of the Fifteenth Amendment to the Federal Constitution.

WHEREAS, The legislature of the state of New York, at its annual session in eighteen hundred and seventy, adopted a preamble and resolutions in the words and figures following, to wit:

"WHEREAS, At the last session of the legislature of this state, a preamble and concurrent resolution were adopted in the words and figures following, to wit:

"WHEREAS, At the session of the fortieth congress, it was resolved by the senate and house of representatives of the United States of America, in congress assembled, two-thirds of both houses concurring, that the following articles shall be proposed to the legislature of the several states as an amendment to the constitution of the United States, which amendment when it shall have been ratified by three-fourths of the said legislatures, shall be valid to all intents and purposes as a part of the said constitution, namely:

"ARTICLE FIFTEEN.

"1. The right of citizens of the United States to vote shall not be denied or abridged by the United States, or by any state, on account of race, color or previous condition of servitude.

"2. The congress shall have power to enforce this article by appropriate legislation; therefore,

"*Resolved* (if the assembly concur), That the said proposed amendment to the constitution be and the same is hereby ratified by the legislature of the state of New York.

"AND WHEREAS, The proposed fifteenth amendment, above recited, has not been ratified by the legislatures of three-fourths of the several states, and has not become a part of the constitution of the United States;

"AND WHEREAS, The state of New York, represented in the legislature here now assembled, desire to withdraw the consent expressed in the above recited concurrent resolutions; now, therefore, be it

"*Resolved* (if the assembly concur), That the above recited concurrent resolution be and it is hereby repealed, rescinded and annulled; and be it further

Resolved (if the assembly concur), That the legislature of the state of New York refuse to ratify the above recited proposed fifteenth amendment to the constitution of the United States, and withdraw absolutely any expression of consent heretofore given thereto or ratification thereof; be it further

Resolved (if the assembly concur), That the governor be requested to transmit a copy of these resolutions and preamble to the secretary of state of the United States, at Washington, and to every member of the senate and house of representatives of the United States, and the governors of the several states."

AND WHEREAS, The said preamble and resolutions were transmitted to and are now on file in the department of state at Washington, purport to withdraw the assent of the people of the state of New York to the fifteenth amendment to the federal constitution previously given by the legislature of this state to which said amendment had been regularly proposed;

AND WHEREAS, The action of the legislature of eighteen hundred and seventy, in entertaining and adopting the said preamble and resolution, is deemed an unwarranted assumption of authority over a subject-matter not within its prerogatives;

AND WHEREAS, It is desirable that the record of the state of New York shall be clear and unequivocal in favor of the said fifteenth amendment; therefore,

Resolved (if the assembly concur), That the preamble and resolution adopted by the legislature of this state in eighteen hundred and seventy, purporting to withdraw the assent of the people of this state previously given to the fifteenth amendment of the federal constitution, be and the same are hereby rescinded.

Resolved (if the assembly concur), That the secretary of the department of state at Washington be and he is hereby requested (if not inconsistent with the rules and regulations of his department) to return to the governor of this state the preamble and resolutions of the legislature of this state, passed in eighteen hundred and seventy, and now on file in his office, which purport to withdraw the assent of the people of this state to the adoption of the fifteenth amendment of the federal constitution.

Resolved (if the assembly concur), That the governor be and he is hereby requested to transmit a copy of this preamble and the resolutions accompanying the same to the secretary of state of the United States.

STATE OF NEW YORK,
In Senate, *January* 3, 1872.

The foregoing resolutions were duly passed.

JAS. TERWILLIGER, *Clerk*.

STATE OF NEW YORK,
In Assembly, *February* 8, 1872.

The foregoing resolutions were duly passed.

C. S. UNDERWOOD, *Clerk*.

CONCURRENT RESOLUTIONS proposing an amendment to the constitution relative to pay of members of the legislature.

Resolved (if the senate concur), That section six of article three, and section six of article ten of the constitution of this state be amended so as to read as follows:

ARTICLE THREE.

SECTION 6. The members of the legislature shall each receive an annual salary of one thousand dollars for their services, except in proceedings for impeachment, and ten cents for every mile they shall travel in once going to and returning from their place of meeting by the most usual route. The speaker of the assembly shall receive an additional salary of two hundred dollars; but the legislature shall provide, by law, for a deduction from the salary of members for non-attendance.

ARTICLE TEN.

SECTION 6. The political year and legislative term shall begin on the first day of December; and the legislature shall every year assemble on the first Tuesday of December, unless a different day be appointed by law.

Resolved (if the senate concur), That the foregoing amendment be referred to the legislature to be chosen at the next general election of senators, and that, in conformity to section one of article thirteen of the constitution, it be published for three months previous to the time of such election.

STATE OF NEW YORK,
In Assembly, *March* 7, 1872.

The foregoing resolutions were duly passed.

By order.

C. S. UNDERWOOD,
Clerk.

STATE OF NEW YORK,
In Senate, *April* 4, 1872.

The foregoing resolutions were duly passed.
By order.
CHAS. R. DAYTON,
Clerk.

CONCURRENT RESOLUTIONS relative to the pier and bulkhead lines in the harbor of New York.

Resolved (the assembly concurring), That the governor be requested to apply to the president of the United States to appoint three officers in the service of the United States, familiar with harbors, to examine into and revise the exterior pier and bulkhead lines of the harbor of New York, on the Brooklyn side, and report such revised line to the legislature.

STATE OF NEW YORK,
In Senate, *February* 17, 1872.

The foregoing resolution was duly passed.
By order.
CHAS. R. DAYTON,
Clerk.

STATE OF NEW YORK,
In Assembly, *April* 6, 1872.

The foregoing resolution was duly passed.
By order.
C. S. UNDERWOOD,
Clerk.

CONCURRENT RESOLUTION relative to taking regimental flags from Military Bureau for use of Grand Army of Republic.

Resolved (if the assembly concur), That the posts of the Grand Army of the Republic of the city of Albany be allowed the use of regimental flags of Albany regiments, from the Military Bureau, on the thirtieth day of May, eighteen hundred and seventy-two, annual decoration day.

STATE OF NEW YORK,
In Senate, *April* 6, 1872.

The foregoing resolution was duly passed.
By order.
CHAS. R. DAYTON,
Clerk,

STATE OF NEW YORK,
In Assembly, *April* 10, 1872.

The foregoing resolution was duly passed.

By order.

C. S. UNDERWOOD,
Clerk.

CONCURRENT RESOLUTIONS relative to establishing Albany as a port of entry.

Resolved (if the assembly concur), That our senators and representatives in congress from this state be requested to endeavor to secure such legislation as shall establish Albany as a port of entry.

Resolved (if the assembly concur), That his excellecy, the governor, be requested to transmit a copy of the foregoing resolution to each of our senators and representatives in congress from this state.

STATE OF NEW YORK,
In Senate, *February* 5, 1872.

The foregoing resolutions were duly passed.

By order of the senate.

JAS. TERWILLIGER,
Clerk.

STATE OF NEW YORK,
In Assembly, *April* 17, 1872.

The foregoing resolutions were duly passed.

By order of assembly.

C. S. UNDERWOOD,
Clerk.

RESOLUTION that the senate agree to the proposed amendment of the sixth article of the constitution relative to the court of appeals.

WHEREAS, At the last session of the legislature, the following amendment to the constitution was proposed in the senate and assembly, viz.:

That the sixth article of the constitution of this state be amended by adding thereto the following section:

§ 28. The court of appeals may order any of the causes, not exceeding five hundred in number, pending in that court at the time of the adoption of this provision, to be heard and determined by the commissioners of appeals, and the legislature may extend the term of service of the commissioners of appeals, not exceeding two years; and

Whereas, The said proposed amendment was agreed to by a majority of the members elected to each of the two houses of the said legislature, and entered on the journals with the yeas and nays taken thereon, and referred to the legislature, to be chosen at the then next general election of senators; and,

Whereas, Such election has taken place, and said proposed amendment was duly published for three months previous to the time of making such choice, in pursuance of the provisions of section one of article thirteen of the constitution, therefore,

Resolved (if the assembly concur), That the senate do agree to the proposed amendment.

STATE OF NEW YORK,
In Senate, *April* 3, 1872.

The foregoing resolution was duly passed.

CHAS. R. DAYTON,
Clerk.

STATE OF NEW YORK,
In Assembly, *April* 26, 1872.

The foregoing resolution was duly passed.

By order.

C. S. UNDERWOOD,
Clerk.

CONCURRENT RESOLUTION that the senate and assembly agree to the proposed amendment to section two, article two of the constitution, relative to bribery.

WHEREAS, At the last session of the legislature, the following amendment to the constitution was passed in senate and assembly, namely:

That section two of article two of the constitution of this state be amended so that it will read as follows:

Laws may be passed excluding from the right of suffrage all persons who have been or may be convicted of bribery, or larceny, or of any infamous crime, and for depriving every person who shall make or become directly or indirectly interested in any wager depending upon the result of any election, or who shall pay, give, or receive, or promise to pay, or give money, or other property, or valuable consideration, with intent to influence any elector in giving his vote, or to deter any elector from voting, or from the right to vote at such election, or from holding any office voted for at such election.

And Whereas, The said proposed amendment was agreed to by a majority of the members elected to each of the two houses of the said legislature, and entered on the journal, with the yeas and nays taken thereon, and referred to the legislature to be chosen at the then next general election of senators.

And Whereas, Such election has taken place, and said proposed amendment was duly published for three months previous to the time of making such choice, in pursuance of the provisions of section one of article thirteen of the constitution; therefore,

Resolved (if the senate concur), That the assembly agree to the proposed amendment.

STATE OF NEW YORK,
In Assembly, *April* 19, 1872.

The foregoing resolutions were duly passed.

By order of the assembly.

C. S. UNDERWOOD,
Clerk

STATE OF NEW YORK,
In Senate, *May* 2, 1872.

The foregoing resolutions were duly passed.

By order of the senate.

CHAS R. DAYTON,
Clerk

CONCURRENT RESOLUTION proposing an amendment to the constitution relative to state prisons.

Resolved (if the assembly concur), That the following amendment to the constitution be proposed for adoption to people of the state, to wit:

1. There shall be a board of managers of prisons, to consist of five persons, to be appointed by the governor, with the advice and consent of the senate, who shall hold office for ten years, except that the five first appointed shall, in such manner as the legislature may direct, be so classified that the term of one person so appointed shall expire at the end of each two years during the first ten years, and vacancies in the office of manager occurring from expiration of term or otherwise, shall be filled in like manner.

2. Said board shall have the charge and superintendence of the state prisons, and shall possess such powers and perform such duties, in respect to county jails and other penal and reformatory institutions in this state, as the legislature may prescribe.

3. The board shall appoint a secretary, who shall be removable at their pleasure, and who shall perform such duties as the legislature or the board may prescribe, and shall receive a salary to be determined by law.

4. The members of the board shall receive no compensation other than reasonable traveling and other expenses incurred while engaged in the performance of official duty.

5. The board shall appoint a warden or chief officer, physician, chaplain and clerk or financial officer of each state prison, and shall have power to remove them for cause after an opportunity to be heard on written charges. All other officers of each prison shall be appointed by the warden thereof, and be removable at his pleasure.

6. The governor may remove either of the managers for misconduct, incompetency or neglect of duty, after the opportunity to be heard on written charges.

7. This amendment shall go into effect on the first Monday of January after its adoption by the people, from and after which date section four of article five of the constitution shall be null and void.

Resolved (if the assembly concur), That the foregoing amendment be referred to the legislature to be chosen at the next general election of senators; and that in conformity to section one of article thirteen of the constitution, it be published for three months previous to the time of such election.

STATE OF NEW YORK,
In Senate, *April* 3, 1872.

The foregoing resolutions were duly passed.

By order of the senate.

CHAS. R. DAYTON,
Clerk.

STATE OF NEW YORK,
In Assembly, *May* 3, 1872.

The foregoing resolutions were duly passed.

By order of the assembly.

EDW. M. JOHNSON,
Clerk.

CONCURRENT RESOLUTION relative to granting aid to the American Printing House for the Blind in the District of Columbia.

WHEREAS, The central board of trustees of the American Printing House for the Blind and the American University for the Blind has been organized in the District of Columbia, under the name of the Board of Regents of the American Printing House for the Blind and the American University for the Blind.

AND WHEREAS, The objects of said institution are to provide for the blind facilities of instruction not heretofore enjoyed or attainable by them; that is to say, a series of text books, works of general literature, and illustrative apparatus addressed to the sense of touch, with all other methods conducive to the acquisition of thorough and liberal education.

AND WHEREAS, The respective state boards of trustees of said printing house or of said university are entitled to representation in said board of regents.

AND WHEREAS, It is for the benefit of the blind of the the nation, in which those in this state are generally interested and are recipients of said facilities of education.

AND WHEREAS, There is a bill in congress to make an appropriation to said printing house and university for the blind; therefore be it

Resolved (if the assembly concur), That our senators and representatives in congress be requested to favor the granting of aid by an appropriation of money to said institution, and that his excellency the governor be requested to forward a copy of this memorial to our representatives in congress.

STATE OF NEW YORK,
In Senate, *May* 10, 1872.

The foregoing resolution was duly passed.

By order.

CHAS. R. DAYTON,
Clerk

STATE OF NEW YORK,
In Assembly, *May* 10, 1872.

The foregoing resolution was duly passed.

By order.

EDW. M. JOHNSON,
Clerk

TITLES

OF ALL THE

LAWS OF THE STATE OF NEW YORK.

PASSED AT THE

NINETY-SIXTH SESSION OF THE LEGISLATURE.

1873.

[The titles of the acts included in this compilation are in this list printed in italics.]

CHAP. 1. An Act to ratify and confirm the acts of the commissioners in the town of York, in Livingston county, in issuing the bonds of said town in exchange for the stock of the Rochester, Nunda and Pennsylvania Railroad Company. Passed January 30, 1873; three-fifths being present.

CHAP. 2. An Act ratifying and confirming the acts and enlarging the powers of the commissioners of the town of Chili, in the county of Monroe, in receiving the stock of the Rochester, Nunda and Pennsylvania Railroad Company, and in issuing in exchange therefor the bonds of the said town. Passed January 30, 1873; three-fifths being present.

CHAP. 3. *An Act extending the term of the Commission of Appeals pursuant to the amendment of the Constitution, and fixing their salaries. Passed January* 30, 1873*; three-fifths being present.*

CHAP. 4. An Act to authorize the board of supervisors of the county of Albany, to issue bonds to pay bonds of said county that will mature during the year 1873. Passed January 30, 1873; three-fifths being present.

CHAP. 5. *An Act to authorize the extension of the time for the collection of taxes in the several towns of the state. Passed Jauuary* 31, 1873*; three-fifths being present.*

CHAP. 6. *An Act to amend an act entitled "An act to provide for a commission to propose amendments to the constitution." Passed February* 5, 1873*; three-fifths being present.*

CHAP. 7. An act to legalize the acts of Charles W. Woodworth, a justice of the peace of the town of Rushford, Allegany county. Passed February 5, 1873; three-fifths being present.

CHAP. 8. An Act to authorize the Utica Mechanics' Assoc ation to borrow money to pay its floating debt, and to issue bonds and execute a mortgage to secure the payment of the same. Passed February 7, 1873; three-fifths being present.

CHAP. 9. *An Act in relation to the calendar of the Commission of Appeals, authorizing the transfer of causes from the calendar of the Court of Appeals, and the disposition of causes on the calendar of the Commission of Appeals;. Passed February* 7, 1873.

CHAP. 10. An Act to legalize the action of a special town-meeting in the town of Rhinebeck, county of Dutchess, and provide for the completion of the town hall in said town. Passed February 7, 1873; three-fifths being present.

CHAP. 11. An Act in relation to the appointment of inspectors of elections in the connty of Richmond. Passed February 7, 1873; three-fifths being present.

CHAP. 12. *An Act to authorize the board of supervisors of the several counties of the state to levy a tax to pay the three and one-half mills tax for canals and general deficiencies, and to authorize a loan for that purpose, and to satisfy the acts of any board of supervisors in issuing bonds to meet said tax; or in extending any loan to enable said boards of supervisors to pay said tax. Passed February* 10, 1873; *three-fifths being present.*

Chap. 13. An Act to confirm the official acts of Hermance H. Ferris, a justice of the peace, and to enable him to take and file his oath of office. Passed February 11, 1873; three-fifths being present.

Chap. 14. An Act to amend an act entitled "An act to incorporate The Protectives, number one, of the city of Rochester," passed March twenty-eighth, eighteen hundred and sixty-eight. Passed February 12, 1873.

Chap. 15. An Act to abolish the office of Railroad Commissioners of the town of Johnstown, in the county of Fulton, and to authorize the supervisor of said town to discharge the duties now appertaining to said office. Passed February 13, 1873; three-fifths being present.

Chap. 16. An Act to legalize the action of the trustees of the Seneca Woolen Mills, a corporation formerly existing and doing business at Seneca Falls, Seneca county, and to ratify and confirm the conveyance made by said trustees of the real estate and its appurtenances of the said corporation to The Phœnix Company of Seneca Falls, by deed bearing date the twelfth day of May, eighteen hundred and fifty-five, under and in pursuance of an act entitled "An act to apply the provisions of an act entitled 'An act to facilitate the dissolution of manufacturing corporations in the county of Herkimer, and to secure the payment of their debt without preference," passed April sixteenth, eighteen hundred and fifty-two, to the Empire Faced Brick Company of Richmond county, and Seneca Woolen Mills Company at Seneca Falls, Seneca county," passed March ninth, eighteen hundred and fifty-five. Passed February 13, 1873.

Chap. 17. An Act releasing the interests of the state of New York, in certain lands under the waters of the Hudson river, near the lower dock in the village of Peekskill, Westchester county. Passed February 14, 1873; by a two-third vote.

Chap. 18. *An Act to authorize the Commissioners of Quarantine to purchase a steamboat for the use of the quarantine establishment of the Port of New York, and making an appropriation therefor. Passed February* 18, 1873; *three-fifths being present.*

Chap. 19. *An Act to punish the careless use of fire-arms. Passed February* 19, 1873; *three-fifths being present.*

Chap. 20. An Act to amend an act entitled "An act to provide for the incorporation of villages," passed December seventh, eighteen hundred and forty-seven, and acts amendatory thereof, so far as relates to the village of Niagara Falls. Passed February 20, 1873; three-fifths being present.

Chap. 21. An Act to repeal an act entitled "An Act to legalize the action of a special town meeting held in the town of Little Valley, county of Cattaraugus, on the twenty-ninth day of August, eighteen hundred and sixty-four," passed May five, eighteen hundred and sixty-nine. Passed February 20, 1873; three-fifths being present.

Chap. 22. An Act to amend the charter of the village of Lansingburgh. Passed February 20, 1873; three-fifths being present.

Chap. 23. An Act to release the interest of the people of the State of New York in certain real estate, of which Rober Davis, late of Hanover, Chautauqua county, died seized, to Leroy Andrus. Passed February, 1873; three-fifths being present.

Chap. 24. An Act ratifying the consolidation of the Rochester, Nunda and Pennsylvania Railroad Company with the Northern Railroad and Navigation Company. Passed February 22, 1873.

Chap. 25. *An Act to amend sections eleven and thirteen of article one, title one, chapter eight, Part Two of Revised Statutes, entitled "of marriage and of the solemnization and proof thereof." Passed February* 22, 1873; *three-fifths being present.*

Chap. 26. An Act to amend an act entitled "An act to organize and establish a police for the village of West Troy," passed April twenty-eighth, eighteen hundred and seventy, and to amend an act entitled "An act to amend an act entitled 'An act to organize and establish a police for the village of West Troy,'" passed April sixth, eighteen hundred and seventy-one. Passed February 26, 1873; three-fifths being present.

Chap. 27. An Act to amend an act entitled "An act to amend an act entitled 'An act to provide for the establishment of free schools in the village of Newburgh,' passed April sixth, eighteen hundred and fifty-two," passed March seventh, eighteen hundred and sixty-five. Passed February 26, 1873; three-fifths being present.

Chap. 28. An Act to amend the charter of the Arctic Fire Insurance Comany in the city of New York. Passed February 26, 1873.

CHAP. 29. An Act to authorize the construction of a canal or drain from Shinnecock bay into Quanteck bay, in the county of Suffolk. Passed February 26, 1873; three-fifths being present.

CHAP. 30. An Act to create a board of charities in and for the city of Utica. Passed February 28, 1873; three-fifths being present.

CHAP. 31. An Act to incorporate the Albany Safe Deposit Company of the city of Albany. Passed February 28, 1873; three-fifths being present.

CHAP. 32. An Act to regulate the pay of firemen in the city of New York. Passed February 28, 1873; three-fifths being present.

CHAP. 33. An Act to incorporate the Guilderland Mutual Insurance Association, and for other purposes. Passed February 28, 1873.

CHAP. 34. An Act in relation to the division of the town of Yonkers. Passed February 28, 1873; three-fifths being present.

CHAP. 35. An Act to re-enact and amend an act entitled "An act to incorporate the city of Yonkers," passed June first, eighteen hundred and seventy-two. Passed February 28, 1873; three-fifths being present.

CHAP. 36. An Act to provide for a supply of water in the city of Yonkers. Passed February 28, 1873; three-fifths being present.

CHAP. 37. An Act to amend "An act conferring additional corporate powers upon the village of Ellenville," passed May fifth, one thousand eight hundred and sixty-eight. Passed February 28, 1873; three-fifths being present.

CHAP. 38. An Act to authorize the village of Saugerties, in the county of Ulster, to purchase a steam fire engine, and necessary apparatus therefor, and a new engine house and lot, and to sell and convey Rough and Ready engine house and lot and hook and ladder house and lot in said village. Passed February 28, 1873; three-fifths being present.

CHAP. 39. An Act to change the time for the election of village officers in the village of Middletown, in the county of Orange. Passed February 28, 1873; three-fifths being present.

CHAP. 40. An Act to repeal an act entitled "An act to enable the electors of the town of Cornwall, Orange county, to vote by districts for town officers and for other purposes," passed fourth March, one thousand eight hundred and sixty-five. Passed March 4, 1873; three-fifths being present.

CHAP. 41. An Act to amend an act entitled "An act to establish and amend the charter of the village of Deposit," passed March second, eighteen hundred and fifty-eight and the acts amendatory thereto. Passed March 4, 1873; three-fifths being present.

CHAP. 42. An Act to amend an act entitled "An act for the completion of Westchester avenue, in the towns of White Plains, Harrison and Rye, in the county of Westchester," passed May thirteenth, eighteen hundred and seventy-two. Passed March 5, 1873; three-fifths being present.

CHAP. 43. An Act to extend the time for the collection of taxes in the city of Oswego. Passed March 5, 1873; three-fifths being present.

CHAP. 44. An Act to authorize the Buffalo city cemetery to sell and convey certain portions of its real estate not required for burial purposes. Passed March 5, 1873; three-fifths being present.

CHAP. 45. An Act to authorize the village of Middletown to issue bonds. Passed March 5, 1873; three-fifths being present.

CHAP. 46. *An Act to provide for the laying out, improvement and preservation of burial grounds in the several towns of the State. Passed March* 5, 1873; *three-fifths being present.*

CHAP. 47. An Act to amend the charter of the village of Akron, in the county of Erie, and to extend the limits of said village. Passed March 6, 1873; three-fifths being present.

CHAP. 48. An Act to amend the charter of the Harlem River and Port Chester Railroad Company. Passed March 6, 1873; three-fifths being present.

CHAP. 49. An Act to authorize the Common Council of the city of Buffalo to borrow money and purchase additional fire engines and fire apparatus. Passed March 6, 1873 three-fifths being present.

CHAP. 50. An Act to amend an act entitled "An act to incorporate the Lewiston Suspension Bridge Company," passed March twenty-sixth, eighteen hundred and forty-nine. Passed March 6, 1873.

CHAP. 51. An Act to extend the time for the colleotion of taxes in the town of New Baltimore, in the county of Greene. Passed March 6, 1873; three-fifths being present.

CHAP. 52. An Act to extend the time for the collection of taxes in the in the town of Struter, in the county of Greene. Passed March 6, 1873; three-fifths being present.

CHAP. 53. An Act to enable the supervisors of the county of Tioga to convey title of the old county clerk's office, and the land on which it is built, to the school commissioners of the union schools of the village of Owego. Passed March 6, 1873; three-fifths being present.

CHAP. 54. An Act to amend an act entitled "An act to establish a recorder's court in the city of Utica, and for other purposes," passed May seventh, eighteen hundred and forty-four, and acts amendatory thereof. Passed March 6, 1873; three-fifths being present.

CHAP. 55. An Act relating to the Washington Street and State Asylum Railroad Company of the city of Binghamton. Passed March 6, 1873.

CHAP. 56. An Act to extend the time for the collection of assessments for the improvement of Atlantic avenue, in the town of New Lots, Kings county. Passed March 7, 1873; three-fifths being present.

CHAP. 57. An Act to authorize the city of Rome to borrow money. Passed March 7, 1873; three-fifths being present.

CHAP. 58. An Act to authorize the town of Milo, in the county of Yates, to borrow money, and to provide for the repayment of the same. Passed March 8, 1873; three-fifths being present.

CHAP 59. An Act to amend chapter eight hundred and nine of the laws of eighteen hundred and seventy-two, entitled "An act to authorize the construction of a sewer in the county of Kings, from the county buildings at Flatbush, in said county," passed May twenty-first, eighteen hundred and seventy-two. Passed March 8, 1873; three-fifths being present.

CHAP. 60. An Act to amend an act entitled "An act to supply the village of Warren, in the county of Rockland, with pure and wholesome water," passed May tenth, eighteen hundred and seventy-two. Passed March 8, 1873; three-fifths being present.

CHAP. 61. An Act in relation to the city oourt of Yonkers. Passed March 8, 1873; three-fifths being present.

CHAP. 62. An Act to amend an act entitled "An act to amend and consolidate the several acts relative to the city of Schenectady," passed April twenty-first, eighteen hundred and sixty-two, and the several acts amendatory thereof. Passed March 10, 1873; three-fifths being present.

CHAP. 63. *An Act to amend the general highway laws of the state of New York. Passed March* 10, 1873; *three-fifths being present.*

CHAP. 64. An act to supply the village of Cortland with pure and wholesome water. Passed March 10, 1873; three-fifths being present.

CHAP. 65. An Act relative to paving streets and constructing sewers in the village of West Troy. Passed March 10, 1873; three-fifths being present.

CHAP. 66. An Act in relation to the Washington Park of the city of Albany. Passed March 11, 1873; three-fifths being present.

CHAP. 67. An Act to authorize the Lockport and Cambria Plank-road Company to collect certain additional tolls. Passed March 11, 1873.

CHAP. 68. An Act to amend "An act to incorporate the Poughkeepsie fire department of the city of Poughkeepsie," passed March twenty-ninth, eighteen hundred and sixty-six. Passed March 11, 1873; three-fifths being present.

CHAP. 69. *An Act requiring commissioners of highways to give notice of the discontinuance of public highways. Passed March* 11, 1873; *three-fifths being present.*

CHAP. 70. *An Act to authorize writs of mandamus and of prohibition to issue the special term of the supreme court, or to any justice thereof holding such term or sitting at chambers. Passed March* 13. 1873; *three-fifths being present.*

CHAP. 71. An Act to confirm and legalize the official acts of the directors of the Odd Fellows Relief and Benevolent Association of the city of Syracuse, during the years eighteen hundred and seventy-one, eighteen hundred and seventy-two and eighteen hundred and seventy-three, and to transfer the real and personal property of said association to Mutual Benefit Association of Syracuse. Passed March 13, 1873.

CHAP. 72. An Act to extend the time for the collection of taxes in the county of Richmond. Passed March 13, 1873.

CHAP. 73. An Act to authorize the extension of the time for the collection of taxes in the several towns of the county of Livingston in this State. Passed March 13, 1873; three fifths being present.

CHAP. 74. *An Act to continue the Fishing Commission of the State of New York. Passed March* 13, 1873; *three-fifths being present.*

CHAP. 75. An Act to amend the charter of the Mechanics' Savings Bank of Rochester. Passed March 13, 1873.

CHAP. 76. An Act to define and establish the boundaries of school district number five of the town of Flushing, Queens county; to provide for the purchase of a new school-house site and erection of a new school-house thereon, and for the sale of the present school-house and site in said school district. Passed March 13, 1873; three-fifths being present.

CHAP. 77. An Act to equalize representation in the board of supervisors of Fulton county, Passed March 13, 1873; three-fifths being present.

CHAP. 78. An Act to release the interest of the People of the State of New York in certain real estate, to Thomas Shedd, John Shedd and William Shedd. Passed March 13, 1873, by a two-third vote.

CHAP. 79. *An Act to amend the third section of article first, title two, chapter six, part two of the Revised Statutes, entitled "of granting letters testamentary." Passed March* 13, 1873.

CHAP. 80. An Act to confirm and legalize the official acts of the president and board of trustees, and the assessors of the village of Fort Plain, in the county of Montgomery, during the year eighteen hundred and seventy-two, in regard to the assessment and collection of taxes, and disbursement of moneys. Passed March 13, 1873; three-fifths being present.

CHAP. 81. An Act to release the interest of the People of the State of New York in certain surplus money derived from a mortgage foreclosure and sale of certain real estate to Michael Doyle. Passed March 13, 1873; by a two-third vote.

CHAP. 82. An Act to extend the time for the collection of taxes in the towns of North Hempstead, Oyster Bay, and Jamaica, in the county of Queens. Passed March 14, 1873; three-fifths being present.

CHAP. 83. An Act to amend an act entitled "An Act to incorporate the village of Richfield Springs," passed March thirteen, eighteen hundred and sixty-one. Passed March 14, 1873; three-fifths being present.

CHAP. 84. An Act in relation to the village of Brockport. Passed March 14, 1873; three-fifths being present.

CHAP. 85. *An Act to authorize the Private Secretary of the Governor to sign in his behalf certain commissions. Passed March* 14, 1873.

CHAP. 86. An Act to extend the time for the collection of taxes in the city of Elmira. Passed March 14, 1873; three-fifths being present.

CHAP. 87. An Act authorizing the Glens Falls Railroad Company to extend its road to the village of Caldwell. Passed March 14, 1873; three-fifths being present.

CHAP. 88. An Act to incorporate the Faxton Hospital in the city of Utica. Passed March 14, 1873; three-fifths being present.

CHAP. 89. An Act relative to the improvement of the town of Kingsbridge, in the county of Westchester. Passed March 17, 1873; three-fifths being present.

CHAP. 90. An Act to provide for the election of town officers and the transaction of town business in the town of Greenburgh, in the county of Westchester. Passed March 18, 1873; three-fifths being present.

CHAP. 91. An Act to amend an act entitled "An act to authorize Dodge and Stevenson Manufacturing Company to issue preferred stock," passed March fifteenth, eighteen hundred and seventy-two. Passed March 18, 1873.

CHAP. 92. *An Act to amend an act entitled "An act for the incorporation of villages," passed April twentieth, eighteen hundred and seventy. Passed March* 18, 1873*; three-fifths being present.*

CHAP. 93. An Act to amend an act entitled "An act to incorporate the Riverhead Savings Bank," passed April twenty-seven, eighteen hundred and seventy-two. Passed March 18, 1873.

CHAP. 94. An Act to amend an act entitled "An act to incorporate the Rockland Savings Bank," passed April fourteenth, eighteen hundred and seventy-one. Passed March 18, 1873.

CHAP. 95. An Act in relation to taxation in the city of New York for the year eighteen hundred and seventy-three. Passed March 18, 1873; three-fifths being present.

CHAP. 96. An Act for the preservation of timber and stone on the Onondaga Indian Reservation. Passed March 19, 1873; three-fifths being present.

CHAP. 97. An Act to repeal chapter two hundred and seventy-nine of the Laws of eighteen hundred and sixty-two, passed April seventeen, eighteen hundred and sixty-two; and chapter two hundred and eighty-five of the Laws of eighteen hundred and sixty-three, passed April twenty-nine, eighteen hundred and sixty-three, relating to the better improvement of highways, at Rockland Lake and vicinity. Passed March 19, 1873; three-fifths being present.

CHAP. 98. An Act to release the interest of the people of the State in certain real estate to Elizabeth Werner. Passed March 19, 1873; by a two-third vote.

CHAP. 99. An Act to amend an act entitled "An act to amend an act entitled 'An act to authorize the Syracuse Northern Railroad Company to construct and maintain a swing bridge over the Oswego canal, in the first ward of the city of Syracuse,' passed April seventh, eighteen hundred and seventy-one, so as to include the Erie canal, the second, third and other wards of said city," passed April eighteenth, eighteen hundred and seventy-two. Passed March 19, 1873; three-fifths being present.

CHAP. 100. An Act to authorize the Twenty-third Street Railway Company of the city of New York to extend their tracks, and use and operate the same. Passed March 19. 1873.

CHAP. 101. An Act to amend chapter seventy-two of the Laws of eighteen hundred and seventy-two, entitled "An act to amend chapter one hundred and fifty-six of the Laws of eighteen hundred and sixty-six, entitled 'An act to incorporate the village of Greenport, Suffolk county." Passed March 19, 1873; three-fifths being present.

CHAP. 102. An Act in relation to the issue and registry of the bonds of the city of Buffalo. Passed March 19, 1873; three-fifths being present.

CHAP. 103. An Act to amend title seven, entitled "Of the Board of Education," entitled "An act revising the charter of the city of Oswego," passed April sixteen, eighteen hundred and sixty. Passed March 20, 1873; three-fifths being present.

CHAP. 104. An Act to authorize the town of Pelham, in the county of Westchester, to purchase, pay for, acquire title to and maintain the bridge owned by the City Island Bridge Company. Passed March 20, 1873; three-fifths being present.

CHAP. 105. An Act to authorize the Newtown and Maspeth Plank-road Company to abandon their road, and declaring said road a public highway. Passed March 20, 1873.

CHAP. 106. An Act to authorize the city of Buffalo to exchange lands with John C. Lord. Passed March 20, 1873.

CHAP. 107. An Act to establish a board of health in and for the city of Brooklyn. Passed March 20, 1873; three-fifths being present.

CHAP. 108. An Act to incorporate the Albany Board of Underwriters. Passed March 20, 1873.

CHAP. 109. An Act in relation to Mount Albion cemetery. Passed March 20, 1873.

CHAP. 110. An Act authorizing the sale of the town hall at Cold Spring, in the town of Phillipstown, in Putnam county. Passed March 20, 1873; three-fifths being present.

CHAP. 111. An Act to extend the time for the collection of taxes, in the town of Morrisania, in the county of Westchester. Passed March 21, 1873; three-fifths being present.

CHAP. 112. An Act relative to common schools in the city of New York. Passed March 21, 1873; three-fifths being present.

CHAP. 113. An Act to authorize the city of Utica to borrow money, and issue its corporate bonds therefor, for the purchase of a site and erection of a school district library building, and other city purposes. Passed March 21, 1873; three fifths being present.

CHAP. 114. An Act to authorize the common council of the city of Syracuse to pay William Burke for constructing a sewer. Passed March 21, 1873; three-fifths being present.

CHAP. 115. An act to amend an act entitled "An act to amend an act entitled 'An act to amend and consolidate the several acts relative to the village of Ballston Spa,' passed April twelfth, eighteen hundred and fifty-five, as amended by an act to amend an act entitled 'An act to amend and consolidate the several acts relative to the village of Ballston Spa,' passed May ninth, eighteen hundred and sixty-eight, and for the purpose of securing an additional supply of water for the use of said village," passed May ninth, eighteen hundred and seventy-two. Passed March 21, 1873; three-fifths being present.

CHAP. 116. An Act to authorize the board of supervisors of Washington county to purchase for the maintenance of the poor of the county, an additional one hundred acres of land, and to raise, by tax upon the taxable real and personal estate of the inhabitants of the county, the sum of seven thousand dollars, to defray the expense of such purchase. Passed March 22, 1873; three-fifths being present.

CHAP. 117. An Act to reduce the number comprising the board of education of the union school district number two of the town of Ellington, county of Chautauqua. Passed March 22, 1873; three-fifths being present.

CHAP. 118. An Act to provide for the construction and improvement of the road from Piseco lake to Clapflin's tannery, in the county of Hamilton. Passed March 22, 1873; three-fifths being present.

CHAP. 119. *An Act to amend an act entitled "An act to vest in the board of supervisors certain legislative powers, and to prescribe their fees for certain services, passed April third, eighteen hundred and forty-nine." Passed March 22, 1873; three-fifths being present.*

CHAP. 120. *An Act conferring certain additional powers upon the Comptroller. Passed March 22, 1873; three-fifths being present.*

CHAP. 121. An Act to amend an act entitled "An act for the preservation of fish in the waters of Steele's creek and McGowan's creek, in the county of Herkimer," passed May ninth, eighteen hundred and seventy-two. Passed March 22, 1873; three-fifths being present.

CHAP. 122. An Act to amend an act entitled "An act to incorporate the village of Oswego Falls," passed March twenty-second, eighteen hundred and sixty-six. Passed March 22, 1873; three-fifths being present.

CHAP. 123. An act to amend an act entitled "An act to incorporate the Union Hotel Company in the city of Buffalo," passed April twelfth, eighteen hundred and seventy-one. Passed March 24, 1873.

CHAP. 124. An Act to amend an act entitled "An act to amend an act to establish a department of police in the city of Buffalo, and to provide for the government thereof," passed April twenty-sixth, eighteen hundred and seventy one, passed April twenty-third, eighteen hundred and seventy-two. Passed March 24, 1873; three-fifths being present.

CHAP. 125. An Act to amend an act entitled "An Act to provide for the building of iron bridges across the Chemung river, in the city of Elmira, and bonding said city to pay the expenses thereof," passed April twenty-fourth, eighteen hundred and seventy-two. Passed March 24, 1873; three-fifths being present.

CHAP. 126. An Act to organize a board of school commissioners in and for the city of Troy. Passed March 25, 1873; three-fifths being present.

CHAP. 127. An Act to provide for a town hall at Waterford, Saratoga county. Passed March 25, 1873; three-fifths being present.

CHAP. 128. An Act to incorporate the Long Island City and Maspeth Railway Company. Passed March 25, 1873; three-fifths being present.

CHAP. 129. An Act to authorize David S. S. Sammis to establish and continue a ferry across Fire Island or Great South bay, from the village of Babylon to Fire Island beach, in the county of Suffolk. Passed March 25, 1873.

CHAP. 130. An Act to confer additional powers upon the New York and Canada Railroad Company. Passed March 25, 1873; three-fifths being present.

CHAP. 131. An Act to amend an act entitled "An act to consolidate and amend the several acts relating to the village of Peekskill, to alter the bounds and to enlarge the powers of the corporation of said village," passed March twenty-fifth, eighteen hundred and fifty-nine. Passed March 25, 1873; three-fifths being present.

CHAP. 132. An Act to authorize the town of Southold, in the county of Suffolk, to appropriate money from the treasury, and to raise money by tax, if necessary, for the purchase of a site, and for the erection thereon of a town hall. Passed March 25, 1873; three-fifths being present.

CHAP. 133. An Act to amend an act entitled "An Act to annex a part of the town of Clermont to the town of Germantown, in the county of Columbia," passed March second, eighteen hundred and fifty-eight. Passed March 25, 1873; three-fifths being present.

CHAP. 134. An Act to repeal an act passed May sixteenth, one thousand eight hundred and seventy-two entitled "An act to amend 'An act authorizing the confinement of convicts from Dutchess county in the Albany Penitentiary," etc., passed April fifteenth, one thousand eight hundred and fifty-four." Passed March 25, 1873; three-fifths being present.

CHAP. 135. An Act to establish a receiver of taxes and to authorize the sale of lands for non-payment of taxes, and for the collection of unpaid taxes in the town of Jamaica, Queens county. Passed March 26, 1873, three-fifths being present.

CHAP. 136. An Act to amend section one of chapter seven hundred and thirty of the Laws of eighteen hundred and seventy-one, entitled "An act in relation to highways in the the county of Rockland." Passed March 26, 1873; three-fifths being present.

CHAP. 137. An Act for the relief of R. T. Baxter. Passed March 26, 1873; three-fifths being present.

CHAP. 138. An Act to amend an act entitled "An act to revise the charter of the city of Buffalo," passed April twenty-eighth, eighteen hundred and seventy. Passed March 26, 1873; three-fifths being present.

CHAP. 139. An Act to amend an act entitled "An act to authorize the Fall Brook Coal Company, a corporation of the commonwealth of Pennsylvania, to hold real estate, and to lease and operate certain railroads." Passed March 26, 1873.

CHAP. 140. An Act to legalize the acts of Edmund J. Porter as police justice of the village of New Rochelle, in the county of Westchester. Passed March 26, 1873; three-fifths being present.

CHAP. 141. An Act to provide for the purchase of additional fire apparatus for the village of Cooperstown, and for the better equipment of the fire department for said village. Passed March 26, 1873; three-fifths being present.

CHAP. 142. An Act to amend chapter ninety-seven of the Laws of eighteen hundred and sixty-nine, entitled "An act to incorporate the trustees of the Minard fund for the benefit of widows and orphans of deceased preachers of the Genesee Annual Conference." Passed March 26, 1873; three-fifths being present.

CHAP. 143. *An Act to amend an act passed April twenty-first, one thousand eight hundred and seventy, entitled "An act relative to the Union Home and School for the education and maintenance of the children of volunteers." Passed March 27, 1873; three-fifths being present.*

CHAP. 144. An Act to amend chapter five hundred and sixty-seven of the Laws of eighteen hundred and seventy-two, entitled "An act conferring additional powers upon the trustees of the village of Bavaria." Passed March 27, 1873; three-fifths being present.

CHAP. 145. An Act to regulate rates of passenger fare upon the Southern Central Railroad. Passed March 27, 1873.

CHAP. 146. *An Act to amend section one hundred and twelve of chapter two, part three, article seven of the Revised Statutes in relation to justices' courts. Passed March 27, 1873; three-fifths being present.*

CHAP. 147. An Act to amend an act entitled "An act to provide for a supply of water in the city of Poughkeepsie, and for sewers therein, passed April twelfth, eighteen hundred and sixty-seven." Passed March 27, 1873; three-fifths being present.

CHAP. 148. An Act to incorporate the Mechanics' Savings Bank of Cohoes, Albany County, New York. Passed March 27, 1873; three-fifths being present.

CHAP. 149. An Act to incorporate the Cathedral of All Saints in the city and diocese of Albany. Passed March 27, 1873; three-fifths being present.

CHAP. 150. An Act to authorize the Pennsylvania and Sodus Bay railroad, to change its route. Passed March 27, 1873.

CHAP. 151. *An Act for the relief of stockholders of corporations whose certificates of stock have been lost or destroyed. Passed March 27, 1873.*

CHAP. 152. An Act authorizing the Schuyler County Agricultural Society to mortgage its property, and issue bonds thereon, for certain purposes. Passed March 27, 1873; three-fifths being present.

CHAP. 153. An Act to grant certain additional powers to the trustees of the village of North Tonawanda. Passed March 27, 1873; three-fifths being present.

CHAP. 154. An Act to postpone the charter election in Long Island City in the year eighteen hundred and seventy-three. Passed March 27, 1873; three-fifths being present.

CHAP. 155. An Act to provide for the payment of tuition in Cortland academy of academic scholars residing in the village of Homer. Passed March 28, 1873; three-fifths being present.

Chap. 156. An Act to provide for paying the floating debt of the village of Saratoga Springs. Passed March 28, 1873; three-fifths being present.

Chap. 157. An Act to enable the electors of the town of Manchester, Ontario county, to hold their town elections in the separate election districts thereof. Passed March 28, 1873; three-fifths being present.

Chap. 158. An Act to amend an act entitled "An act to amend the charter of the village of Little Falls." Passed March 28, 1873; three-fifths being present.

Chap. 159. An Act authorizing the election of a police justice in the town of Newtown, Queens county, and prescribing his duties and compensation. Passed March 28, 1873; three-fifths being present.

Chap. 160. An Act to authorize the transportation of passengers in the city of New York, by means of street railways, to be constructed through certain streets and avenues therein. Passed March 28, 1873.

Chap. 161. An Act to incorporate the Gloversville Water-works Company. Passed March 28, 1873; three-fifths being present.

Chap. 162. An Act to incorporate the Nyack Water-works Company. Passed March 28, 1873; three-fifths being present.

Chap. 163. An Act to organize and establish a police for the city of Yonkers. Passed March 31, 1873; three-fifths being present.

Chap. 164. An Act to amend an act entitled "An act for the support and relief of the poor, and for the government of the poor department in the county of Erie." Passed April 1, 1873; three-fifths being present.

Chap. 165. An Act to authorize the sheriff of the county of Kings to appoint certain court officers. Passed April 1, 1873; three-fifths being present.

Chap. 166. An Act in reference to the summoning of jurors in the county of Kings, and fixing the compensation of the sheriff therefor. Passed April 1, 1873; three-fifths being present.

Chap. 167. An Act to incorporate the Union Savings Bank of Saratoga Springs. Passed April 1, 1873; three-fifths being present.

Chap. 168. An Act to amend chapter sixteen of the laws of eighteen hundred and sixty-one, entitled "An act to enable the electors of the town of Poughkeepsie to vote by districts for town officers," passed February fourteenth, eighteen hundred and sixty-one. Passed April 1, 1873; three-fifths being present.

Chap. 169. An Act entitled "An act to revise, consolidate and amend the act to incorporate the village of Stillwater," passed April seventeenth, eighteen hundred and sixteen, and the act to amend the same, passed March seventeenth, eighteen hundred and sixty, and the act to amend the same, passed April twenty-seventh, eighteen hundred and sixty-five. Passed April 1, 1873; three-fifths being present.

Chap. 170. An Act to authorize the Board of Supervisors of the county of Greene, to provide for the payment of the principal of a portion of the bounty debt of said county by issuing new bonds. Passed April 1, 1873; three-fifths being present.

Chap. 171. An Act in relation to elections in the village of Akron, Erie county. Passed April 1, 1873; three-fifths being present.

Chap. 172. An Act extending the time for the building of the road of the Buffalo East Side Street Railway Company. Passed April 4, 1872.

Chap. 173. An Act authorizing the comptroller of the city of Buffalo to add to the general tax laws of the city of Buffalo certain unpaid school taxes, and to collect the same as a portion of such general tax. Passed April 4, 1873; three-fifths being present.

Chap. 174. An Act to authorize the sale and conveyance of a portion of the real estate belonging to School District Number One of the town of Lansingburgh. Passed April 4, 1873; three-fifths being present.

Chap. 175. An Act to amend the charter of the Missionary Society of the Methodist Episcopal Church. Passed April 4, 1873.

Chap. 176. An Act in relation to the Schuylerville and Upper Hudson Railroad Company. Passed April 4, 1873.

Chap. 177. An Act to amend an act entitled "An act to provide for the endowment of the Unadilla Academy," passed May third, eighteen hundred and seventy-two. Passed April 4, 1873; three-fifths being present.

CHAP. 178. An Act to authorize the First Congregation of Disciples of Christ, of Brewerton, Onondaga county, to elect trustees. Passed April 4, 1873.

CHAP. 179. An Act in relation to the New York, Housatonic and Northern Railroad Company. Passed April 4, 1873.

CHAP. 180. An Act to authorize the election of a police justice in and for the village of Greenport, Suffolk county, and to prescribe his duties and compensation, and regulating charges in criminal proceedings in said village. Passed April 4, 1873; three-fifths being present.

CHAP. 181. *An Act to amend an act entitled "An act to provide for furnishing two status of eminent deceased citizens of the State, to be placed in the capitol at Washington, in compliance with the invitation of the President of the United States," passed May sixth, eighteen hundred and seventy-two. Passed April 7, 1873; three-fifths being present.*

CHAP. 182. An Act in relation to the justices' courts of the city of Albany. Passed April 8, 1873; three-fifths being present.

CHAP. 183. An Act to drain and improve certain lands of Thomas Hunt lying in the eighth ward of the city of Brooklyn, between the Third avenue and New York bay and Forty-fourth and Forty-ninth streets, and to alter the commissioners' map of said city in conformity thereto. Passed April 8, 1873; three-fifths being present.

CHAP. 184. An Act to release the interest of the People of this State in certain real estate, in the city of Brooklyn, to Charles Ferber. Passed April 8, 1873; by a two-third vote.

CHAP. 185. An Act supplemental to and amendatory of chapter eight hundred and forty-two of the laws of eighteen hundred and sixty-eight, an act entitled "An act to provide for the transmission of letters, packages and merchandise, in the cities of New York and Brooklyn, and across the North and East rivers, by means of pneumatic tubes, to be constructed beneath the surface of the streets, squares, avenues and public places in said cities, and under the waters of said rivers," passed June first, eighteen hundred sixty-eight; and of chapter five hundred and twelve of the laws of eighteen hundred and sixty-nine, entitled "An act supplementary to chapter eight hundred and forty-twe of the laws of eighteen hundred and sixty-eight, in relation to carrying letters, packages and merchandise by means of pneumatic tubes, in New York and Brooklyn, and to provide for the transportation of passengers in said tubes." Passed April 9, 1873.

CHAP. 186. *An Act to provide for the protection of citizens in their civil and public rights. Passed April 9, 1873; three-fifths being present.*

CHAP. 187. An Act to authorize the town of Newport, in Herkimer county, to raise money to build and complete a town-house in the said town of Newport. Passed April 9, 1873; three-fifths being present.

CHAP. 188. An act to amend an act entitled "An act to authorize the town of Owego to purchase the toll-bridge across the Susquehanna river in said village, and to maintain the same as a free bridge," passed May fifth, eighteen hundred and seventy. Passed April 9, 1873; three-fifths being present.

CHAP. 189. An Act relating to the first society of the Free Methodist Church, in the town of Parma. Passed April 9, 1873; three-fifths being present.

CHAP. 190. An Act to facilitate the removal of the remains of bodies interred in an ancient and disused burial plot, at Cornelison Point, Nyack, Rockland county, state of New York. Passed April 9, 1873; three-fifths being present.

CHAP. 191. An Act to amend "An act to amend and consolidate the several acts in relation to the charter of the village of Penn Yan," passed April twenty-first, eighteen hundred and sixty-four. Passed April 9, 1873; three-fifths being present.

CHAP. 192. An Act to amend "An act to authorize the lighting of public streets and avenues in the town of Fishkill, in the county of Dutchess," passed April twenty-third, one thousand eight hundred and seventy-two. Passed April 9, 1873; three-fifths being present.

CHAP. 193. An Act to authorize Union College, known by the corporate name of The Trustees of Union College of the town of Schenectady, in the state of New York, The Albany Medical College, University of Albany, and The Dudley Observatory of the city of Albany, to unite for certain purposes and to form a corporation, to be called The Union University. Passed April 10, 1873; three-fifths being present.

CHAP. 194. An Act to continue in force and amend chapter one hundred and thirty-eight of the laws of eighteen hnndred and fifty-two, entitled "An act to incorporate the firemen of the city of Utica as a benevolent association." Passed April 10, 1873; three-fifths being present.

CHAP. 195. *An Act giving the consent of the State of New York to the acquisition by the United States of certain lands for the purpose of the erection of government buildings at Albany and Utica, New York, and ceding jurisdiction over the same. Passed April* 10, 1873, *by a two-third vote.*

CHAP. 196. An Act to extend and define the jail liberties of the county of Herkimer. Passed April 10, 1873.

CHAP. 197. An Act incorporating the trustees of the Northern New York Conference of the Methodist Episcopal Church. Passed April 10, 1873.

CHAP. 198. An Act to change the corporate name of the Black River Conference Seminary. Passed April 10, 1873.

CHAP. 199. An Act to authorize the Bleecker Street and Fulton Ferry Railroad Company of the city of New York to extend their railroad tracks through certain streets and avenues in the city of New York. Passed April 11, 1873.

CHAP. 200. An Act to amend the charter of the village of Addison, in the county of Steuben, incorporated under chapter four hundred and twenty-six of the laws of eighteen hundred and forty-seven. Passed April 12, 1873; three-fifths being present.

CHAP. 201. An Act to amend an act entitled "An act to amend and consolidate the several acts relating to the village of Hornellsville," passed April ninth, eighteen hundred and sixty-seven. Passed April 12, 1873; three-fifths being present.

CHAP. 202. An Act to amend chapter six hundred and sixty-two of the laws of eighteen hundred and seventy, passed May fifth, eighteen hundred and seventy, entitled "An act to repeal 'An act to provide for the publication of legal notices in the county of Hamilton,' passed April nineteenth, eighteen hundred and sixty-six; also an act amending the same," passed March twenty-sixth, eighteen hundred and sixty-seven. Passed April 12, 1873; three-fifths being present.

CHAP. 203. An Act to change the name of the Albany Iron Manufacturing Company, and to amend its charter in respect to the liability of its stockholders. Passed April 12, 1873; three-fifths being present.

CHAP. 204. An Act to amend an act entitled "An act to prohibit the interment of the dead in the old burial ground, in the village of Heuvelton, St. Lawrence county, and to authorize the removal of the dead from the old to the new cemetery, passed April twenty-one, eighteen hundred and seventy. Passed April 12, 1873; three-fifths being present.

CHAP. 205. An Act to authorize the Oswego Falls Agricultural Society to mortgage its real estate. Passed April 12, 1873.

CHAP. 206. An Act to renew the charter of the State road from the Orange turnpike to Nyack, in the county of Rockland, as passed on the twentieth day of April, eighteen hundred and thirty, renewed June eighteenth, eighteen hundred and fifty-three. Passed April 12, 1873; three-fifths being present.

CHAP. 207. An Act to amend an act entitled "An act to authorize the Ridgefield and New York Railroad to extend their road through the towns of Lewisboro, Poundridge and Rye, in the county of Westchester," passed May sixth, eighteen hundred and seventy-two. Passed April 12, 1873; three-fifths being present.

CHAP. 208. An Act to amend an act entitled "An act to amend an act incorporating the village of Sing Sing, in the county of Westchester, passed April ninth, eighteen hundred and fifty-three, and the act supplementary thereto and amendatory thereof, passed April eighteenth, eighteen hundred and fifty-nine." Passed April 12, 1873; three-fifths being present.

CHAP. 209. An act to provide for the election of superintendent of the poor of Fulton county. Passed April 12, 1873; three-fifths being present.

CHAP. 210. An Act to release the interest of the People of the State of New York in and to certain real estate to Henry Siedenburg. Passed April 12, 1873.

CHAP. 211. *An Act to amend chapter eight hundred and forty-five of the laws of eighteen hundred and sixty-nine, entitled "An act to amend an act entitled 'An act concerning the proof of wills, executors and administrators, guardians and wards, and surrogates' court,"' passed May sixteenth, eighteen hundred and thirty-seven. Passed April* 12, 1873; *three-fifths being present.*

CHAP. 212. An Act in relation to petit jurors in courts of record in the county of Westchester. Passed April 12, 1873; three-fifths being present.

CHAP. 213. An Act to authorize Mary M. J. de Courval, an infant alien, to take and hold certain lands in this State devised to her by her grandfather, Richard Ray, and to release interest of the State therein. Passed April 12, 1873.

CHAP. 214. An Act to constitute the village of Brewerton, in the county of Onondaga, a separate road district. Passed April 12, 1873; three-fifths being present.

CHAP. 215. An Act to enable the Rhinebeck and Connecticut Railroad Company to extend their road. Passed April 15, 1873.

CHAP. 216. An Act authorizing the bonds of the town of Portville, Cattaraugus county, to be issued in aid of the Rochester, Nunda and Pennsylvania Extension Railroad Company, and dispensing with certain conditions heretofore imposed upon the commissioners appointed to issue such bonds in aid of said company. Passed April 15, 1873; three-fifths being present.

CHAP. 217. An Act to change the name of the Board of Foreign Missions of the Reformed Protestant Dutch Church to "Board of Foreign Missions of the Reformed Church in America." Passed April 15, 1873.

CHAP. 218. An Act to amend an act entitled "An act to revise the charter of the city of Oswego, passed April sixteenth, eighteen hundred and sixty," and the acts amendatory thereof and supplementary thereto. Passed April 15, 1873; three-fifths being present.

CHAP. 219. An Act to legalize and confirm the merger and consolidation of the Whitehall and Plattsburgh Railroad Company, The New York and Canada Railroad Company and The Montreal and Plattsburgh Railroad Company into a new corporation called The New York and Canada Railroad Company, and granting and extending thereto the provisions of the act relating to the consolidation of railroad companies, and for the facilitating the construction of The New York and Canada railroad, and the several acts of this State relating to said companies or either of them. Passed April 15, 1873.

CHAP. 220. An Act to authorize the supervisors of the towns of Little Falls, Danube and Manheim, in the county of Herkimer, to borrow money upon the credit of said towns for the purpose of defraying the expenses of completing the bridge across the Mohawk river at Fink's basin, and to issue bonds for the re-payment of the moneys borrowed. Passed April 15, 1873; three-fifths being present.

CHAP. 221. An Act to amend an act entitled "An act relative to common schools in the city of New York," passed March twenty-one, eighteen hundred and seventy-three. Passed April 15, 1873; three-fifths being present.

CHAP. 222. An Act to incorporate the Cathedral Church of St. John the Divine, in the city and diocese of New York. Passed April 16, 1873; three-fifths being present.

CHAP. 223. An Act to incorporate the Lockport Catholic Literary Union of the city of Lockport. Passed April 16, 1873.

CHAP. 224. An Act to amend an act entitled "An act to amend act incorporating the village of Sing Sing, in the county of Westchester," passed April ninth, eighteen hundred and fifty-three, and the act supplementary thereto and amendatory thereof, passed April eighteenth, eighteen hundred and fifty nine, and also the act supplementary thereto and amendatory thereof, passed April nineteenth, eighteen hundred and seventy-one. Passed April 16, 1873; three-fifths being present.

CHAP. 225. *An Act to amend the provisions of the Revised Statutes with regard to the fees of appraisers appointed by surrogates. Passed April 16, 1873; three-fifths being present.*

CHAP. 226. An Act authorizing the city of Troy to borrow money to improve the water, works of said city. Passed April 16, 1873; three-fifths being present.

CHAP. 227. An Act to amend an act entitled "An act to incorporate the Round Lake Camp Meeting Association of the Methodist Episcopal Church of the Troy Conference," passed May fifth, eighteen hundred and sixty-eight. Passed April 16, 1873.

CHAP. 228. An Act entitled "An act to enable the town of Amity, in the county of Allegany, to hold special town meetings for the purpose of raising money to protect the public highways against the encroachments of the Genesee river. Passed April 16, 1873; three-fifths being present.

CHAP. 229. An Act to confirm the official acts of Jonathan C. Fowler, a justice of the peace. Passed April 16, 1873; three-fifths being present.

CHAP. 230. An Act for the relief of the Clarks Mills Company. Passed April 16, 1873.

CHAP. 231. An Act to amend the charter of the West Side German Dispensary in the city of New York. Passed April 16, 1873.

CHAP. 232. An Act to authorize the city of Elmira to purchase lands for cemetery purposes, and to issue the bonds of the city for the payment thereof. Passed April 17, 1873; three-fifths being present.

CHAP. 233. An Act to incorporate the fire department of the village of Peekskill. Passed April 17, 1873; three-fifths being present.

CHAP. 234. An Act to amend an act entitled "An act in relation to common schools in the village of Lockport," passed March thirty-first, eighteen hundred and forty-seven, and the acts amendatory thereof. Passed April 17, 1873; three-fifths being present.

CHAP. 235. An Act to amend an act entitled "An act to establish free schools in school district number four in the town of East Chester, Westchester county," passed June eighth, eighteen hundred and fifty-three. Passed April 17, 1873; three-fifths being present.

CHAP. 236. An Act authorizing the commissioners of highways in the town of Bethlehem, in the county of Albany, to lay out and open a certain highway in said town, of the width of two rods. Passed April 17, 1873; three-fifths being present.

CHAP. 237. An Act to incorporate the Forestville Market-day and Agricultural Association. Passed April 17, 1873.

CHAP. 238. An Act to amend an act entitled "An act providing for the better collection of county taxes in the city of Buffalo, and for the sale, by the treasurer of Erie county, of lands in said city for unpaid taxes," passed April seventh, eighteen hundred and fifty-nine. Passed April 17, 1873; three-fifths being present.

CHAP. 239. An Act extending and defining the civil jurisdiction of the Court of Common Pleas for the city and county of New York, the Superior Court of the city of New York, the Superior Court of Buffalo, and the City Court of Brooklyn, and relating to civil proceedings in those courts. Passed April 17, 1873; three-fifths being present.

CHAP. 240. An Act to authorize the Common Council of the city of Utica to borrow and disburse money for city purposes, and to levy and collect taxes to pay the same. Passed April 19, 1873; three-fifths being present.

CHAP. 241. An Act to incorporate the Kingsborough Water-works Company. Passed April 19, 1873; three-fifths being present.

CHAP. 242. An Act to incorporate the New York Loan and Security Company. Passed April 21, 1873.

CHAP. 243. *An Act further to amend an act entitled "An act to amend title sixteen, chapter eight, part three of the Revised Statutes, relative to the proceedings for the draining of swamps, marshes and other low or wet lands," passed May twelfth, eighteen hundred and sixty-nine. Passed April* 21, 1873; *three-fifths being present.*

CHAP. 244. An Act to confirm the official acts of Joel F. Potter, a justice of the peace, in and for the town of Schroon, Essex county, and to enable him to take and file his oath of office. Passed April 21, 1873; three-fifths being present.

CHAP. 245. An Act to incorporate the McClintock Association. Passed April 21, 1873.

CHAP. 246. An Act to authorize the Board of Supervisors of the county of Schenectady to sell its poor-house farm and buildings, and to remove such poor-house. Passed April 21, 1873; three-fifths being present.

CHAP. 247. An Act authorizing the Supervisor of the town of Johnsburg, in the county of Warren, to sell and convey by deed a lot of land known as the town poor lot. Passed April 21, 1873; three-fifths being present.

CHAP. 248. An Act to release the interest of the people of the State of New York in certain escheated lands to David Curry. Passed April 21, 1873; by a two-third vote.

CHAP. 249. *An Act to amend an act entitled "An act regulating the sale of intoxicating liquors," passed April eleventh, eighteen hundred and seventy. Passed April* 21, 1873; *three-fifths being present.*

CHAP. 250. An Act to enable the electors of the town of Canandaigua, Ontario county, to hold their town elections in the separate election districts thereof. Passed April 21, 1873; three-fifths being present.

CHAP. 251. An Act to provide for the regulation and licensing of scavengers in the city of New York. Passed April 22, 1873; three-fifths being present.

CHAP. 252. An Act making provision for the support of the Cohoes Hospital. Passed April 22, 1873; three-fifths being present.

CHAP. 253. An Act to authorize the city of Syracuse to fund the floating debt of that city. Passed April 22, 1873; three-fifths being present.

CHAP. 254. An Act to repeal an act entitled "An act to incorporate the Grand Commandery of the State of New York," passed April twenty-eighth, eighteen hundred and seventy-one. Passed April 22, 1873; three-fifths being present.

CHAP. 255. An Act to amend an act entitled "An act to amend and consolidate the several acts in relation to the charter of the city of Rochester, chapter one hundred and forty-three of the Laws of New York; passed April eighth, eighteen hundred and sixty-one, and to authorize said city to issue its bonds in payment of the floating debt of said city. Passed April 22, 1873; three-fifths being present.

CHAP. 256. An Act to authorize the Troy and West Troy Bridge Company to increase its capital stock, and to issue bonds of the company. Passed April 22, 1873; three-fifths being present.

CHAP. 257. An Act to extend the time to complete the organization of the Mutual Trust Institution of the city of New York. Passed April 22, 1873.

CHAP. 258. An Act to authorize the Board of Supervisors of the county of Otsego to issue bonds for the benefit of and chargeable to the towns of Cherry Valley and Otsego, whereby to provide means for the payment, and extend the time for levying and collecting, of such sums as should be apportioned upon the property of those towns, respectively, under chapter nine hundred and thirty-eight of the Laws of eighteen hundred and sixty-seven. Passed April 22, 1873; three-fifths being present.

CHAP. 259. An Act to amend an act in relation to common schools in the city of Elmira, passed April fourth, eighteen hundred and fifty-nine. Passed April 22, 1873; three-fifths being present.

CHAP. 260. An Act to incorporate the Gloversville Savings Bank. Passed April 22, 1873.

CHAP. 261. An Act to legalize the acts of the town officers of the town of Seneca, county of Ontario, and State of New York. Passed April 22, 1873; three-fifths being present.

CHAP. 262. An Act confirming the proceedings of the trustees and electors of the village of Clifton Springs had for the purpose of becoming incorporated under the general act for the incorporation of villages. Passed April 22, 1873; three-fifths being present.

CHAP. 263. An Act to amend an act entitled "An act to consolidate and amend the several acts relating to the village of Jamestown, and to enlarge the powers of the corporation," passed April twenty-sixth, eighteen hundred and sixty-nine. Passed April 22, 1873; three-fifths being present.

CHAP. 264. An Act to authorize the North Shore Staten Island Ferry Company to reduce the number of its directors. Passed April 23, 1873.

CHAP. 265. An Act to amend an act entitled "An act to revise and consolidate the laws in relation to the village of Geneva, in the county of Ontario," passed March third, eighteen hundred and seventy-one. Passed April 23, 1873; three-fifths being present.

CHAP. 266. An Act to incorporate the People's Water Transit Company. Passed April 23, 1873.

CHAP. 267. An Act to extend the time for the collection of taxes in the town of Fort Ann, county of Washington. Passed April 23, 1873; three-fifths being present.

CHAP. 268. An Act to release to Margaret Thompson the title of certain lands escheated to the State of New York, formerly belonging to Robert Thompson, deceased. Passed April 23, 1873, by a two-third vote.

CHAP. 269. An Act to amend an act entitled "An act to establish and maintain a police force in the city of Cohoes," passed May sixth, eighteen hundred and seventy. Passed April 23, 1873; three-fifths being present.

CHAP. 270. An Act authorizing Ann Whittam to hold, convey and mortgage real estate. Passed April 23, 1873, by a two-third vote.

CHAP. 271. An Act authorizing Esmeal McNamara to hold, mortgage and convey real estate. Passed April 23, 1873, by a two-third vote.

CHAP. 272. An Act authorizing the canal appraisers to hear and determine the claim of Michael Long, administrator of the goods, chattels and credits of Jane Long deceased, for canal damages. Passed April 23, 1873; three-fifths being present.

CHAP. 273. An Act to supply a deficiency in appropriations for ordinary repairs of the canals. Passed April 23, 1873; three-fifths being present.

CHAP. 274. An Act entitled "An act to amend an act entitled an act to authorize the making and opening of a road or avenue from the intersection of the highway running east of Rockland lake, with the highway running from the lake to Rockland lake landing, in the county of Rockland, to intersect the highway running from

Upper Piermont to Orangeburgh," passed April twenty-one, eighteen hundred and seventy-one, as amended and extended by an act entitled as above, and to extend Highland avenue south to the State line, passed April twenty-four, eighteen hundred and seventy-two. Passed April 23, 1873; three-fifths being present.

CHAP. 275. An Act to extend the time and duties of the commissioners for the laying out of streets, avenues, roads and parks in Long Island City. Passed April 23, 1873; three-fifths being present.

CHAP. 276. An Act to incorporate the Mount Prospect and Carroll Street Railroad Company in the city of Binghamton. Passed April 24, 1873.

CHAP. 277. An Act to amend an act entitled "An act to supply the city of Binghamton with pure and wholesome water," passed April twenty-fifth, eighteen hundred and sixty-seven. Passed April 24, 1873; three-fifths being present.

CHAP. 278. An Act to release the title and interest of the people of the State of New York in and to certain real estate in the village of Waverly, county of Tioga, State of New York, to David Decker, the surviving husband of Sarah Decker, deceased. Passed April 24, 1873, by a two-third vote.

CHAP. 279. An Act to release to Daniel Schoonmaker certain real estate in the city of New York, of which Bridget Schoonmaker, lately his wife, died seized. Passed April 24, 1873, by a two-third vote.

CHAP. 280. An Act to legalize and confirm a patent issued to Ann E. Coe, executrix of and trustee under the last will and testament of Frederick A. Coe, deceased, for lands under water in the city of Yonkers. Passed April 24, 1873, by a two-third vote.

CHAP. 281. An Act to legalize the acts of Shipman L. Griffith, a justice of the peace of the county of Wyoming. Passed April 24, 1873; three-fifths being present.

CHAP. 282. An Act to amend chapter two hundred and fifty-nine of the laws of eighteen hundred and sixty-seven, entitled "An act to incorporate the village of College Point, Queens county." Passed April 24, 1873; three-fifths being present.

CHAP. 283. An Act to enable The Evergreens to acquire and hold a certain piece of land. Passed April 24, 1873.

CHAP. 284. An Act to authorize the Canandaigua, Palmyra and Ontario Railway Company to construct and maintain a draw-bridge over the Erie canal, in or near the village of Palmyra. Passed April 24, 1873; three-fifths being present.

CHAP. 285. An Act to authorize the village of Dansville to create a debt for the purpose of bringing water into said village for the protection against fires, and to amend the charter of said village. Passed April 24, 1873; three-fifths being present.

CHAP. 286. An Act to amend the charter of the village of Clinton. Passed April 23, 1873; three-fifths being present.

CHAP. 287. An Act to amend an act entitled "An act in relation to the debts of the town of Newtown, Queens county," passed May twenty-one, eighteen hundred and seventy-two. Passed April 24, 1873; three-fifths being present.

CHAP. 288. An Act to authorize the Board of Education for the City and County of New York to establish a Nautical School. Passed April 24, 1873; three-fifths being present.

CHAP. 289. An Act to enable the Utica, Clinton and Binghamton Railroad Company to extend its road. Passed April 24, 1873.

CHAP. 290. An Act to amend an act entitled "An act to revise the charter of the city of Auburn," passed April twenty-second, eighteen hundred and sixty-nine. Passed April 24, 1873.

CHAP. 291. An Act to legalize and confirm the acts of the commissioners of the several towns through which the Rochester, Nunda and Pennsylvania railroad is located, appointed in proceedings to bond said towns under the act permitting municipal corporations to aid in the construction of railroads, passed May eighteen, eighteen hundred and sixty-nine, for the purpose of aiding the several railroad companies merged in said Rochester, Nunda and Pennsylvania Railroad Company as consolidated, and authorizing the issuing of bonds by the commissioners in such proceedings in cases where they have not been issued. Passed April 24, 1873; three-fifths being present.

CHAP. 292. An Act to amend the charter of the National Academy of Design. Passed April 24, 1873.

CHAP. 293. An Act to incorporate the Oneonta Savings Bank, located at Oneonta, Otsego county, New York. Passed April 25, 1873.

CHAP. 294. An Act to incorporate the Saratoga Cemetery Association. Passed April 25, 1873.

CHAP. 295. An Act to incorporate the Anglo-Mexican Railway Company. Passed April 25, 1873.

CHAP. 296. An Act to incorporate the New Baltimore Chestnut Lawn Cemetry. Passed April 25, 1873; three-fifths being present.

CHAP. 297. An Act for the benefit of common schools in the county of Richmond. Passed April 25, 1873; three-fifths being present.

CHAP. 298. An Act to amend an act entitled "An act to provide for the improvement of Newtown creek between Maspeth avenue and Metropolitan avenue," passed April twenty-first, eighteen hundred and seventy-one. Passed April 25, 1873; three-fifths being present.

CHAP. 299. *An Act for the relief of sick prisoners confined upon civil process. Passed April 25, 1873; three-fifths being present.*

CHAP. 300. An Act in relation to the Port Richmond and Bergen Point Ferry Company. Passed April 25, 1873; three-fifths being present.

CHAP. 301. An Act to authorize the construction of a railroad in Christopher and certain other streets and avenues in the city of New York. Passed April 25, 1873; three-fifths being present.

CHAP. 302. *An Act to create a Board of Commissioners of Emigration, and to confer certain powers thereon. Passed April 26, 1873; three-fifths being present.*

CHAP. 303. An Act to amend an act entitled "An act to incorporate the village of Warwick," passed April fifteenth, eighteen hundred and sixty-seven. Passed April 26, 1873.

CHAP. 304. An Act to amend an act entitled "An act to amend the act entitled 'An act to amend an act entitled 'An act to revise, amend and consolidate the several acts relating to the village of Whitesborough,' passed February twelve, eighteen hundred and fifty-nine.'" Passed April 26, 1873; three fifths being present.

CHAP. 305. An Act to authorize the board of supervisors of the county of Kings to borrow money for the completion of the contracts for erecting a female prison and for heating the same and the penitentiary of said county. Passed April 26, 1873; three-fifths being present.

CHAP. 306. An Act in relation to highway labor in the village of Sloansville, Schoharie county, to extend its limits and to constitute it a separate road district. Passed April 26, 1873; three-fifths being present.

CHAP. 307. An Act to amend an act entitled "An act to amend the several acts incorporating the village of Fulton, in the county of Oswego," passed March seventeenth, one thousand eight hundred and sixty-two. Passed April 26, 1873; three-fifths being present.

CHAP. 308. An Act to amend the charter of the Buffalo Fine Arts Academy. Passed April 26, 1873.

CHAP. 309. An Act to authorize the alms-house commissioners of the city of Poughkeepsie to build an addition to their alms-house building, and to raise the money therefor. Passed April 26, 1873; three-fifths being present.

CHAP. 310. An Act to enable the trustees of the parochial fund for the diocese of western New York to convey lands situated in the diocese of central New York. Passed April 26, 1873.

CHAP. 311. An Act to amend an act entitled "An act to amend the charter of the village of Ilion," passed April seven, eighteen hundred and sixty-six. Passed April 26, 1873; three-fifths being present.

CHAP. 312. An Act in relation to the Free Academy in the city of Albany. Passed April 26, 1873; three-fifths being present.

CHAP. 313. An Act to amend the charter of the Western New York Life Insurance Company. Passed April 26, 1873.

CHAP. 314. *An Act to provide for submitting to the electors of this State at the general election to be held on the Tuesday following the first Monday of November, eighteen hundred and seventy-three, the question whether the offices of chief judge and associate judge of the Court of Appeals, of justices of the Supreme Court, of the judge of the Superior Court of the city of New York, of the judge of the Court of Common Pleas of the city and county of New York, of the judge of the Superior Coart of Buffalo, of the judge of the City Court of Brooklyn, of the county judge of the several counties of this State, shall be hereafter filled by appointment pursuant to section seventeen, article six, of the Constitution. Passed April* 26, 1873; *three-fifths being present.*

Chap. 315. *An Act to amend the Revised Statutes in relation to laying out public roads, and the alteration thereof. Passed April* 28, 1873.

Chap. 316. An Act to incorporate the Peoples' Savings Bank of Amsterdam. Passed April 28, 1873.

Chap. 317. An Act to authorize the trustees of the village of Kinderhook to borrow money to be expended in the purchase of a lot of ground and the erection thereon of a suitable building adapted to the purposes of a public hall and a room for a fire engine, for the use of said village. Passed April 29, 1873; three-fifths being present.

Chap. 318. An Act to authorize the town of Westfield, in Chautauqua county, to issue bonds for the purpose of building a bridge across Chautauqua creek, in said town. Passed April 29, 1873; three-fifths being present.

Chap. 319. An Act to incorporate the Young Ladies' Christian Association of the city of New York. Passed April 29, 1873.

Chap. 320. An Act to authorize the Mayor, Aldermen and Commonalty of the city of New York to convey certain lands to the United States. Passed April 29, 1873; by a two-third vote.

Chap. 321. An Act to amend an act entitled "An act to incorporate the Eighth Ward Savings Bank of the city of New York," passed March twenty-two, eighteen hundred and seventy-one, and to change its name to Fifth Avenue Savings Bank. Passed April 29, 1873.

Chap. 322. An Act to authorize the town of Colesville to purchase the bridges over the Susquehanna river in said town, and the property and franchises appertaining thereto, of the existing bridge companies or owners of said town, and to maintain the same as free bridges, and to borrow money therefor. Passed April 29, 1873; three-fifths being present.

Chap. 323. *An Act to amend an act entitled "An act to extend the powers of boards of supervisors, except in the counties of New York and Kings," passed May eleventh, eighteen hundred and sixty-nine. Passed April* 29, 1873; *three-fifths being present.*

Chap. 324. An Act to authorize the Common Council of the city of Lockport to raise, by tax, moneys to pay the present indebtedness of the city. Passed April 29, 1873; three-fifths being present.

Chap. 325. An Act making the lower or north bridge across the Wallkill, at Walden, Orange county, a charge upon the village of Walden. Passed April 29, 1873; three-fifths being present.

Chap. 326. An Act to limit in certain respects the effect of certain repealing clauses in a bill which has passed the senate and assembly at the present session, entitled "An act to reorganize the local government of the city of New York," so that such bill shall, as a law, conform to the intent of the legislature. Passed April 29, 1873; three-fifths being present.

Chap. 327. *An act to amend chapter three hundred and twelve of the laws of eighteen hundred and fifty-nine, entitled "An act to equalize the State tax among the several counties in this state." Passed April* 29, 1873; *three-fifths being present.*

Chap. 328. An Act to amend an act entitled "An act to provide for an additional supply of water in the city of Albany," passed March twenty, eighteen hundred and sixty-eight. Passed April 29, 1873; three-fifths being present.

Chap. 329. An Act to amend an act entitled "An act to incorporate the village of Greene," passed April twenty-second, eighteen hundred and forty-two. Passed April 29, 1873; three-fifths being present.

Chap. 330. An Act to amend the charter of the village of Deposit, situated partly in the town of Sanford, Broome county, and partly in the town of Tompkins, Delaware county, and to revise and compile the several acts relative to said village. Passed April 29, 1873; three-fifths being present.

Chap. 331. An Act authorizing the Common Council of the city of Lockport to raise, by tax, the necessary means to repair the Hydrant Hose carriage-house, in the fourth ward of said city. Passed April 29, 1873; three-fifths being present.

Chap. 332. An Act to enable the electors of the town of Kingston, Ulster county, to vote by districts for town officers. Passed April 29, 1873; three-fifths being present.

CHAP. 333. An Act in relation to the compensation of the Commissioner of Public Works in the city of New York. Passed April 29, 1873; three-fifths being present.

CHAP. 334. An Act to change the bulk-head and pier-head lines or line of solid-filling, and the pier-line in a part of the port of New York, in conformity with the map entitled "Map of water-fronts on East river, of Bushwick inlet, Brooklyn, E. D.," made by D. Ross, City Surveyor, which was filed in the office of the Secretary of State, on the fifth day of June, in the year eighteen hundred and sixty-five. Passed April 29, 1873; three-fifths being present.

CHAP. 335. An Act to reorganize the local government of the city of New York. Passed April 30, 1873; three-fifths being present.

CHAP. 336. *An act to amend an act entitled "An act making appropriations for certain expenses of government and for supplying deficiencies in former appropriations," passed May fifteenth, eighteen hundred and seventy-two. Passed April 30, 1873; by a two-third vote.*

CHAP. 337. An Act to incorporate the Fort Edward and Sandy Hill Gas-light Company in the county of Washington. Passed April 30, 1873; three-fifths being present.

CHAP. 338. An Act in reference to the Brooklyn Sunday School Union. Passed April 30, 1873.

CHAP. 339. An Act to incorporate the Suffolk County Camp Meeting Association of the Methodist Episcopal Church. Passed April 30, 1873.

CHAP. 340. An Act to incorporate the Stony Clove Turnpike Road Company. Passed April 30, 1873.

CHAP. 341. An Act to amend chapter eight hundred and seventy-four of the laws of eighteen hundred and seventy-two, in relation to school district number one in the town of Milton, Saratoga county. Passed April 30, 1873; three-fifths being present.

CHAP. 342. An act to authorize the city of Newburg to borrow moneys and issue bonds therefor for the payment of certain certificates of indebtedness given by said city for the grading of South street, in said city, and to provide for the payment of said bonds, and the interest thereon, by levy and collection of taxes. Passed April 30, 1873; three-fifths being present.

CHAP. 343. An Act to fix the compensation of the auditor of the city of Brooklyn. Passed April 30, 1873; three-fifths being present.

CHAP. 344. An Act in relation to the supply of water for the city of New York, to be acquired in Putnam county. Passed April 30, 1873; three-fifths being present.

CHAP. 345. An Act to authorize the county clerk of Livingston county to sign the certificates of record of deeds and mortgages, and other records, or of filing of papers recorded or filed in Livingston county clerk's office, which were not signed by the former clerks of the said county of Livingston. Passed April 30, 1873; three-fifths being present.

CHAP. 346. An Act to incorporate the Free Methodist General Conference of North America. Passed April 30, 1873.

CHAP. 347. An Act to incorporate O. K. Lodge, number six hundred ond seventy-two, Independent Order of Good Templars. Passed April 30, 1873.

CHAP. 348. An Act to exempt the real estate of the Home for Incurables, in the county of Westchester, from taxation. Passed April 30, 1873, by a two-third vote.

CHAP. 349. An Act to incorporate the Machpelah Cemetery Association of Le Roy. Passed April 30, 1873; three-fifths being present.

CHAP. 350. An Act to authorize the city of Newburg to borrow moneys and issue bonds therefor for the payment of certain water bonds of said city heretofore issued, and to provide for the payment of said bonds and the interest thereon by levy and collection of taxes. Passed April 30, 1873; three-fifths being present.

CHAP. 351. An Act to amend the act entitled "An act to incorporate the Saratoga Monument Association," passed eighteen hundred and fifty-nine, chapter four hundred and ninety-eight. Passed April 30, 1873; three-fifths being present.

CHAP. 352. An Act to amend the act entitled "An act authorizing the consolidation of certain railroad companies," passed May twentieth, eighteen hundred and sixty-nine. Passed April 30, 1873.

CHAP. 353. An Act for the protection and preservation of deer and fish in the county of Suffolk. Passed April 30, 1873; three-fifths being present.

CHAP. 354. An Act to close part of the old Bushwick road or avenue, in the city of Brooklyn. Passed April 30, 1873; three-fifths being present.

CHAP. 355. An Act to incorporate the Staten Island and New Jersey Ferry Company. Passed April 30, 1873.

CHAP. 356. An Act to legalize the action of the town meeting of the town of Leyden, Lewis county, held on the eighteenth day of February, eighteen hundred and seventy-three. Passed April 30, 1873; three-fifths being present.

CHAP. 357. *An Act to authorize summary convictions of professional thieves, burglars, pick-pockets, counterfeiters and forgers. Passed April* 30, 1873; *three-fi ths being present.*

CHAP. 358. An Act in relation to the Jewish Theological Seminary and Scientific Institution. Passed April 30, 1873; three-fifths being present.

CHAP. 359. An Act to amend an act passed March twenty-ninth, eighteen hundred and twenty-four, entitled "An act to incorporate the Society for the Reformation of Juvenile Delinquents in the city of New York." Passed April 30, 1873; three-fifths being present.

CHAP. 360. An Act to amend "An act to provide for the improvement of the highways extending from Lansing street, Genesee street and Caroline avenue, in the village of West Troy, to the Loudon road, in the town of Watervliet (highways lying in part in the town of Watervliet and in part in the village of West Troy), and to authorize the board of supervisors of the county of Albany to assess the expense thereof upon the said town," passed April twenty-fourth, eighteen hundred and seventy-two. Passed April 30, 1873; three-fifths being present.

CHAP. 361. *An Act to amend an act entitled "An act authorizing the incorporation of rural cemetery associations," passed April twenty-seventh, eighteen hundred and forty-seven. Passed April* 30, 1873; *three-fifths being present.*

CHAP. 362. An Act to authorize the corporate authorities of the village of Whitesborough, Oneida county, to borrow money for purchasing a steam fire engine and apparatus for the same. Passed May 1, 1873.

CHAP. 363. *An Act to amend an act entitled "An act to secure to creditors a just division of the estate of debtors, who convey to assignees for the benefit of creditors," passed April thirteen, eighteen hundred and sixty. Passed May* 1, 1873.

CHAP. 364. An Act to lay out, open and grade Eighty-sixth street, in the towns of New Utrecht and Gravesend, in the county of Kings. Passed May 1, 1873; three-fifths being present.

CHAP. 365. An Act to amend an act entitled "An act to regulate elections in the city of Brooklyn," passed May seventh, eighteen hundred and seventy-two. Passed May 1, 1873; three-fifths being present.

CHAP. 366. An Act authorizing and requiring the clerk of the county of Cattaraugus to record a deed made and executed on the eighth day of June, eighteen hundred and fifty-eight, by one Daniel Hickok and wife, of Douglas county, territory of Kansas, conveying a piece of land in Hinsdale, Cattaraugus county, to one Parkman Johnson, of the latter place. Passed May 1, 1873.

CHAP. 367. An Act amending an act entitled "An act to establish free schools in district number three in the town of Flushing," passed April sixteenth, eighteen hundred and fifty-seven, enlarging said district and authorizing a greater school tax therein. Passed May 1, 1873; three-fifths being present.

CHAP. 368. An Act to amend the charter of the village of Gouverneur, in the county of St. Lawrence. Passed May 1, 1873; three-fifths being present.

CHAP. 369. An Act to enable the Maple Grove Cemetery Association, in the town of Candor, county of Tioga, to acquire title to lands, and to alter and lay out roads, and to extend its grounds. Passed May 1, 1873; three-fifths being present.

CHAP. 370. An Act to revise and amend an act entitled "An act to incorporate the village of Port Jervis," passed March thirtieth, eighteen hundred and sixty-six, and all acts relating thereto. Passed May 1, 1873; three-fifths being present.

CHAP. 371. An Act to authorize the trustees of the Rushville Cemetery Association, of the town of Gorham, in the county of Ontario, to sell a portion of their real estate. Passed May 1, 1873; three-fifths being present.

CHAP. 372. An Act to legalize the action of the town meeting of the town of Jamaica, Queens county, held April first, eighteen hundred and seventy-three. Passed May 1, 1873; three-fifths being present.

CHAP. 373. An Act to confirm the official acts of Horace B. Lincoln, a justice of the peace in and for the town of Elizabethtown, Essex county, and to enable him to take and file his oath of office. Passed May 1, 1873.

CHAP. 374. An Act to release Eliza Sweezy, widow of Isaac H. Sweezy, deceased the interest of the People of the State of New York in certain surplus moneys arising from the sale of certain lands of which said Isaac H. Sweezy died seized. Passed May 1, 1873; by a two-third vote.

CHAP. 375. An Act to amend chapter two hundred and twenty-four of the laws of eighteen hundred and seventy-three, entitled an act to amend an act entitled "An act to amend act incorporating the village of Sing Sing, in the county of Westchester," passed April ninth, eighteen hundred and fifty-three, and the act supplementary thereto and amendatory thereof, passed April eighteenth, eighteen hundred and fifty-nine, and also the act supplementary thereto and amendatory thereof, passed April nineteenth, eighteen hundred and seventy-one," passed April sixteenth, eighteen hundred and seventy-three. Passed May 1, 1873; three-fifths being present.

CHAP. 376. An Act to provide for the election of a receiver of taxes in the town of Newtown, Queens county. Passed May 1, 1873; three-fifths being present.

CHAP. 377. An Act releasing the interest of the State in certain lands of which Mary Ann Wilcox died possessed. Passed May 1, 1873; three-fifths being present.

CHAP. 378. An Act to legalize and confirm the action of the electors of the town of Colton, in the county of St. Lawrence, and also to provide for the care and custody of the town hall in the said town of Colton. Passed May 1, 1873; three-fifths being present.

CHAP. 379. An Act to confirm the official acts of Justus Barrett, a justice of the peace, and to enable him to take and file his oath of office. Passed May 1, 1873.

CHAP. 380. An Act to authorize the trustees of Pine Wood Cemetery, in the town of Phelps, in the county of Ontario, to dispose of a part of their cemetery lands. Passed May 1, 1873; three-fifths being present.

CHAP. 381. *An Act for the preservation of fish in waters lying within, or bordering upon, the counties of Schuyler, Steuben, Chemung, Seneca, Yates and Ontario. Passed May* 1, 1873; *three-fifths being present.*

CHAP. 382. An Act to legalize the proceedings of the annual town meeting of Whitestown, Oneida county, held March fourth, eighteen hundred and seventy-three, in reference to raising money for highway purposes, and to determine the amount of the official bond of the Commissioner of Highways. Passed May 1, 1873; three-fifths being present.

CHAP. 383. An Act to repeal and annul chapter three hundred and forty-three of the Laws of eighteen hundred and sixty-eight, entitled "An act to incorporate the Union Foundery Company of Troy," and the several acts amendatory thereof, and for the dissolution of the Union Foundery Company of Troy. Passed May 1, 1873.

CHAP. 384. An Act to incorporate the Young Men's Christian Association of the town of New Utrecht. Passed May 1, 1873.

CHAP. 385. An Act to amend an act entitled "An act to incorporate the Commercial Warehouse Company of New York," passed April thirteenth, eighteen hundred and sixty-seven. Passed May 2, 1873; three-fifths being present.

CHAP. 386. An Act to encourage and promote education in the village of Hornellsville. Passed May 2, 1873; three-fifths being present.

CHAP. 387. An Act to amend an act entitled "An act to incorporate the city of Lockport," passed April eleventh, eighteen hundred and sixty-five, and the several acts amendatory thereof. Passed May 2, 1873; three-fifths being present.

CHAP. 388. An Act to confirm the reorganization of the Baptist Society of Russel, New York, and to authorize the trustees of said society to sell and convey real estate. Passed May 2, 1873.

CHAP. 389. An Act to authorize the rector, church wardens and vestrymen of St. Mark's Church, in Malone, Franklin county, to execute a release to James S. Amsden of the property of William F. Amsden, deceased. Passed May 2, 1873.

CHAP. 390. An Act to amend an act entitled "An act to amend and consolidate the charter of the village of Le Roy," passed April six, eighteen hundred and fifty-seven. Passed May 2, 1873; three-fifths being present.

CHAP. 391. An Act to amend the charter of the New York Fire Insurance Company of the city of New York. Passed May 2, 1873; three-fifths being present.

CHAP. 392. An Act for the relief of the Corning Library. Passed May 2, 1873; three-fifths being present.

CHAP. 393. An Act to incorporate the Western New York Agricultural, Mechanical and Driving Park Association of Rochester. Passed May 2, 1873.

CHAP. 394. An Act to amend an act entitled "An act for the protection and improvement of the Tonawanda band of Seneca Indians, residing on the Tonawanda reservation in this State," passed April seventh, one thousand eight hundred and sixty-three. Passed May 2, 1873.

CHAP. 395. *An Act to alter the system of repairing the highways. Passed May 2, 1873; three-fifths being present.*

CHAP. 396. An Act relating to the Mohawk and Ilion and Frankfort and Ilion horse railroad companies. Passed May 2, 1873.

CHAP. 397. *An Act for the incorporation of fire, hose and hook and ladder companies. Passed May 2, 1873.*

CHAP. 398. An Act in relation to the closing up of the affairs of the president, directors and company of the Montgomery County Bank. Passed May 2, 1873.

CHAP. 399. An Act to authorize a part of the records of the counties of Herkimer, Cayuga, Oneida and Onondaga to be transcribed and deposited in the clerk's office of the county of Oswego. Passed May 2, 1873; three-fifths being present.

CHAP. 400. An Act to alter, open and improve the canal in and along the west branch of Newtown creek, within the city of Brooklyn, to construct a bridge over the same, and to alter the commissioners' map of the town of Bushwick in relation thereto. Passed May 2, 1873, by a two-third vote.

CHAP. 401. An Act to enable the town of Pike, Wyoming county, to raise five thousand dollars in aid of an endowment of Pike seminary. Passed May 2, 1873; three-fifths being present.

CHAP. 402. An Act to amend an act entitled "An act to incorporate the Vesuvius Fire-proof Warehousing Company," passed May sixteenth, eighteen hundred and sixty-eight. Passed May 2, 1873.

CHAP. 403. An Act to authorize the Haight Family Cemetery, in Goshen, Orange county, to take and hold personal estate, either by gift or bequest, for the purposes of said cemetery. Passed May 2, 1873; three-fifths being present.

CHAP. 404. An Act for the relief of the inhabitants of union free school district number two, in the town of Newark Valley and the county of Tioga. Passed May 2, 1873; three-fifths being present.

CHAP. 405. An Act to permit the Bath and Hammondsport Railroad Company to use rails of forty pounds weight to the lineal yard in the construction of their road. Passed May 2, 1873.

CHAP. 406. An Act to amend "An act to incorporate the city of Ogdensburg," passed April twenty-seven, eighteen hundred and sixty-eight, and the acts amending the same. Passed May 2, 1873; three-fifths being present.

CHAP. 407. An Act to incorporate the St. Bernard's Young Men's Literary and Benevolent Association of the city of Rochester. Passed May 3, 1873; three-fifths being present.

CHAP. 408. An Act to confirm an assessment for the expense of paving a portion of Genesee street in the city of Utica. Passed May, 5, 1873; three-fifths being present.

CHAP. 409. An Act further to amend the charter of the village of White Plains, in the county of Westchester. Passed May 6, 1873; three-fifths being present.

CHAP. 410. An Act to amend chapter one hundred and thirty of the laws of eighteen hundred and sixty-nine, entitled "An act to prevent injury to the bridge over the Tioughnioga river in the town of Marathon in the county of Cortland," passed April seventh, eighteen hundred and sixty-nine. Passed May 6, 1873; three-fifths being present.

CHAP. 411. An Act to amend chapter one hundred and two of the laws of eighteen hundred and seventy-one entitled "An act to amend an act entitled 'An act to incorporate the village of Oneonta, Otsego county,' passed March fourteenth, eighteen hundred and seventy-one," and to amend the act passed April twentieth, eighteen hundred and seventy. Passed May 6, 1873; three-fifths being present.

CHAP. 412. An Act to amend an act entitled "'An act to authorize the town of Johnstown, in the county of Fulton, to issue town bonds and loan the same to the Fonda, Johnstown and Gloversville Railroad Company, and to regulate the rate of charges for carrying passengers upon said road," passed February first, eighteen hundred and sixty-seven. Passed May 6, 1873; three-fifths being present.

CHAP. 413. An Act to amend chapter four hundred and eighty-six of the laws of eighteen hundred and fifty-five, entitled "An act to amend the charter of the village of Horseheads, in the county of Chemung." Passed May 6, 1873; three-fifths being present.

CHAP. 414. An Act to extend the time for the construction of a railroad in the village of Schoharie, as authorized by chapter two hundred and eighty-one of the Laws of eighteen hundred and seventy-one. Passed May 6, 1873; three-fifths being present.

CHAP. 415. An Act to amend chapter five hundred and ten of the Laws of eighteen hundred and sixty-nine, entitled "An act to amend an act entitled 'An act to incorporate the village of Flushing,' passed April fifteenth, eighteen hundred and thirty-seven, and the several acts amendatory thereof," passed March twenty, eighteen hundred and fifty-seven. Passed May 6, 1873; three-fifths being present.

CHAP. 416. An Act to amend chapter seven hundred and forty-three of the Laws of eighteen hundred and seventy-two, and to reduce the number of directors, and provide for a sale of the stock held by the town of Schoharie, in the Schoharie Valley Railroad Company. Passed May 6, 1873; three-fifths being present.

CHAP. 417. *An Act to enable lodges of the Independent Order of Odd Fellows to take, hold and convey real and personal estate. Passed May* 6, 1873.

CHAP. 418. An Act to enable the excise board of the trustees of the village of Owego to pay twenty-five per cent of the moneys derived from licenses granted in said corporations to the Union School Board, to be expended by them for purpose of maintaining a public library in said village. Passed May 6, 1873; three-fifths being present.

CHAP. 419. An Act to extend the time for commencing the work of construction of tunnel by the New York Tunnel Company. Passed May 6, 1873.

CHAP. 420. An Act to authorize the Board of Education of the city of Brooklyn to elect a superintendent of public instruction and associate superintendents. Passed May 6, 1873; three-fifths being present.

CHAP. 421. An Act for the relief of the Steuben County Agricultural Society, and to incorporate the same. Passed May 6, 1873.

CHAP. 422. An Act to release the interest of the people of this State in certain real estate in the village of Saratoga Springs to Rosa Gormley. Passed May 6, 1873; by a two-third vote.

CHAP. 423. An Act to amend an act entitled "An act to provide for the improvement of a certain highway in the town of Newtown, Queens county, and the city of Brooklyn, Kings county, and for the payment of property taken for such improvement," passed May seventeen, eighteen hundred and seventy-two. Passed May 6, 1873; three-fifths being present.

CHAP. 424. An Act to repeal so much of section three, of chapter seven hundred and sixty-six of the Laws of eighteen hundred and seventy, as amended by chapter seven hundred and thirty-two of the Laws of eighteen hundred and seventy-one, so far as the same appropriates the taxes on the non-resident lands in that part of township number eleven in the old military tract in the town of St. Armand, in Essex county. Passed May 6, 1873; three-fifths being present.

CHAP. 425. *An Act in relation to the improvement of the Racket river, and of the hydraulic power thereon, and to check freshets therein. Passed May* 7, 1873; *three-fifths being present.*

CHAP. 426. An Act to incorporate the Lotus Club. Passed May 7, 1873.

CHAP. 427. *An Act in relation to challenges of jurors. Passed May* 7, 1873.

CHAP. 428. An Act to amend an act entitled "An act to revise the charter of Long Island City." Passed May 7, 1873; three-fifths being present.

CHAP. 429. An Act in relation to armories in the city of New York. Passed May 7, 1873; three-fifths being present.

CHAP. 430. An Act in relation to the Frankfort and Ilion Street Railroad Company, in Herkimer County. Passed May 7, 1873.

CHAP. 431. An Act for providing a site for an armory in the city of New York, for the use of the Seventh Regiment of the National Guard of the State of New York. Passed May 7, 1873; three-fifths being present.

CHAP. 432. *An Act to authorize the use of improved motive power on railroads in any city or county of this State. Passed May* 7, 1873; *three-fifths being present.*

CHAP. 433. An Act to provide for supplying the city of Hudson with pure and wholesome water. Passed May 7, 1873; three-fifths being present.

CHAP. 434. An Act authorizing the formation of a corporate body, to be known as the Fireman's Association of the State of New York. Passed May 7, 1873.

CHAP. 435 *An Act to amend chapter four hundred and thirty-three, Laws of eighteen hundred and seventy-two, entitled "An act to amend chapter seven hundred and twenty-one of the Laws of eighteen hundred and seventy-one, entitled 'An act to amend and consolidate the several acts relating to the preservation of moose, wild deer, birds and fish"' passed April twenty-six, eighteen hundred and seventy-one, also to repeal section thirty of said act. Passed May* 7, 1873; *three-fifths being present.*

CHAP. 436. *An Act to amend an act entitled "An act to amend and consolidate the several acts relating to the preservation of moose, wild deer, birds and fish," passed April twenty-six eighteen hundred and seventy-one. Passed May* 7, 1873; *three-fifths being present.*

CHAP. 437. An Act to provide for the improvement of the southerly portion of Bedford avenue, in the city of Brooklyn. Passed May 7, 1873; three-fifths being present.

CHAP. 438. An Act to incorporate the Ticonderoga Water-works Company. Passed May 8, 1873; three-fifths being present.

CHAP. 439. An Act to amend an act entitled "An act to consolidate and amend the several acts relating to the village of Jamestown, and to enlarge the powers of the corporation," passed April twenty-sixth, eighteen hundred and sixty-nine, as amended by chapter two hundred and sixty-three of the laws of eighteen hundred and seventy-three, passed April twenty-two, eighteen hundred and seventy-three. Passed May 8, 1873; three-fifths being present.

CHAP. 440. *An Act requiring commissioners of highways to act as inspectors of plank-roads and turnpikes. Passed May* 8, 1873; *three-fifths being present.*

CHAP. 441. An Act to provide for the compensation of persons appointed under chapter five hundred and eighty, of the laws of eigheeen hundred and seventy-two, in relation to contracts for improving streets in the city of New York. Passed May 8, 1873; three-fifths being present.

CHAP. 442. An Act to amend an act entitled "An act to amend 'An act to incorporate the Orient Wharf Company, in the county of Suffolk,' passed January twenty-eight, eighteen hundred and fifty-one, passed March seventeen, eighteen hundred and sixty. Passed May 8, 1873.

CHAP. 443. *An act to authorize the trustees of the Willard Asylum for the Insane to appoint a fourth assistant physician. Passed May* 8, 1873; *three-fifths being present.*

CHAP. 444. An Act to incorporate the Central New York Agricultural, Horticultural and Mechanical Association. Passed May 8, 1873.

CHAP. 445. An Act to authorize the Sodus Bay and Corning Railroad Company to construct and maintain a draw-bridge over the Erie canal, near the village of Lyons. Passed May 8, 1873; three-fifths being present.

CHAP. 446. An Act to incorporate the Mount Morris Hospital, in the city of New York. Passed May 8, 1873; three-fifths being present.

CHAP. 447. An Act to release the interest of the State in certain lands of which Catherine Fox died seized or possessed to Catherine Keller and Mary Haley. Passed May 8, 1873; by a two-third vote.

CHAP. 448. *An Act in relation to the duties of commissioners of highways in certain cases. Passed May* 8, 1873; *three-fifths being present.*

CHAP. 449. An Act to amend an act entitled "An act to incorporate an association for the relief of respectable, aged, indigent females in the city of New York," passed March tenth, eighteen hundred and fifteen, and the acts continuing in force and amending the same. Passed May 8, 1873.

CHAP. 450. An Act to increase and make available the water-power of Silver creek, in the county of Chautauqua, by draining the waters of Mud lake into the same. Passed May 8, 1873; three-fifths being present.

CHAP. 451. An Act to amend an act entitled "An act to incorporate the Oneida Park Association for the improvement of the breed of horses and cattle, and to encourage improvements in agriculture and mechanics," passed March twenty-ninth, eighteen and seventy. Passed May 8, 1873; three-fifths being present.

CHAP. 452. *An Act to amend section one of chapter seven hundred and sixty of the Laws of eighteen hundred and seventy, in reference to acquiring title to real estate for burial purposes. Passed May* 8, 1873; *three-fifths being present.*

CHAP. 453. An Act in relation to the Marine Court of the city of New York. Passed May 9, 1873; three-fifths being present.

CHAP. 454. An Act in relation to taxes illegally levied and assessed upon the Buffalo Creek, Allegany and Cattaraugus Indian reservations, under the provisions of chapter two hundred and fifty-four of the Laws of eighteen hundred and forty, and chapter one hundred and sixty-six of the Laws of eighteen hundred and forty-one. Passed May 9, 1873; three-fifths being present.

CHAP. 455. An Act in relation to the Seneca Indians residing on the Cattaraugus and Allegany reservations. Passed May 9, 1873.

CHAP. 456. An Act authorizing the settlement of the claim of the commissioners appointed by virtue of an act passed May twenty-third, eighteen hundred and seventy-one, providing for the laying out, opening and construction of a public highway in the town of Hempstead, Queens county. Passed May 9, 1873; three-fifths being present.

CHAP. 457. An Act to incorporate "The New York Home for Aged and Infirm Hebrews," and to authorize other corporations, incorporated societies or other associations to give and transfer property to, or wholly to consolidate with, the corporation hereby created. Passed May 9, 1873; three-fifths being present.

CHAP. 458. An Act to enable the mayor and common council of Long Island City to borrow money. Passed May 9, 1873; three-fifths being present.

CHAP. 459. An Act to authorize the building of an addition to the court-house at White Plains, Westchester county, and to provide for the issuing of bonds for the purpose of building the same. Passed May 9, 1873; three-fifths being present.

CHAP. 460. An Act to amend an act entitled "An act to authorize the election of a police justice in and for the village of Greenport, Suffolk county, and to prescribe his duties and compensation, and regulating charges in criminal proceedings in said village. Passed May 9. 1873; three-fifths being present.

CHAP. 461. An Act to amend an act entitled "An act to authorize the incorporation of the Iroquois Agricultural Society, among the Iroquois Indians in this State,' passed May five, eighteen hundred and sixty-three. Passed May 9, 1873.

CHAP. 462. An Act to authorize the transfer and investment of the moneys of the accumulated fund of the Mechanics' Library Association of the city of Newburgh. Passed May 9, 1873.

CHAP. 463. An Act to amend section fourteen of chapter seven hundred and forty-four of the Laws of eighteen hundred and sixty-seven, entitled "An act to define the objects of the New York State Institution for the Blind, and to provide for its management." Passed May 9, 1873; three-fifths being present.

CHAP. 464. An Act to amend section two of an act entitled "An act to incorporate the village of Spencerport," passed April twenty-two, eighteen hundred and sixty-seven. Passed May 9, 1873; three-fifths being present.

CHAP. 465. An Act to amend an act entitled "An act to incorporate the city of Binghamton, passed April nine, eighteen hundred and sixty-seven, and the several acts amending the same. Passed May 9, 1873; three-fifths being present.

CHAP. 466. An Act to authorize the city of Binghamton to provide for the deficiency in the assessment of the Court street pavement, and to liquidate the outstanding indebtedness of said city. Passed May 9, 1873; three-fifths being present.

CHAP. 467. *An Act to enable the commissioners appointed to revise the statutes to incorporate in their report the Political and Penal Codes, or so much thereof as they shall deem advisable. Passed May 9, 1873; three-fifths being present.*

CHAP. 468. An Act to incorporate Ringgold Fire Company number one of Pulaski, Oswego county, New York. Passed May 9, 1873.

CHAP. 469. *An Act relative to purchases of the franchises and property of corporations, whose franchises and property shall have been sold by mortgage. Passed May 9, 1873.*

CHAP. 470. An Act to release the interest of the State in certain lands of which Samuel Biggin died seized, to Sarah Ann Biggin, his widow. Passed May 9, 1873.

CHAP. 471. An Act to authorize the erection of street lamps, and lighting the streets in the village of Pine Plains, Dutchess county. Passed May 9, 1873; three-fifths being present.

CHAP. 472. An Act to authorize the Wyoming County Mutual Insurance Company to sell stock and invest the same in the Wyoming County Soldiers' Monument. Passed May 9, 1873.

CHAP. 473. An Act to release the interest of the People of the State of New York in and to certain real estate to Henry Siedenburg. Passed May 9, 1873, by a two-third vote.

CHAP. 474. *An Act requiring county clerks to transmit to the Secretary of State, certified copies of the official county canvass. Passed May* 9, 1873; *three-fifths being present.*

CHAP. 475. An Act to incorporate the Carmel Grove Camp-meeting Association of the Methodist Episcopal Church. Passed May 9, 1873.

CHAP. 476. An Act to amend an act entitled "An act to incorporate the village of Clyde, in the county of Wayne," passed May two, eighteen hundred and thirty-five, and the act amendatory thereof, passed May fourteen, eighteen hundred and forty. Passed May 9, 1873; three-fifths being present.

CHAP. 477. *An Act authorizing the commissioners of highways in the several towns in this State to increase the penalty for riding or driving over bridges faster than a walk. Passed May* 9, 1873; *three-fifths being present.*

CHAP. 478. An Act to repeal an act entitled "An act to amend an act entitled 'An act to revise the charter of the city of Buffalo, passed April twenty-eighth, eighteen hundred and seventy,'" passed March twenty-sixth, eighteen hundred and seventy-three. Passed May 9, 1873; three-fifths being present.

CHAP. 479. *An Act to amend an act entitled "An act to amend and consolidate the several acts relating to the preservation of moose, wild deer, birds and fish," passed April twenty-six, eighteen hundred and seventy-one. Passed May* 9, 1873; *three-fifths being present.*

CHAP. 480. *An Act to amend an act entitled "An act to foster and develop the internal commerce of the State, by inviting and rewarding the practical and profitable introduction upon the canals of steam, caloric, electricity or any motor other than animal power, for the propulsion of boats," passed April twenty-eight, eighteen hundred and seventy-one. Passed May* 9, 1873; *three-fifths being present.*

CHAP. 481. An Act to amend an act entitled "An act to amend and consolidate the several acts relating to the village of Ilion," passed March eight, eighteen hundred and sixty-five. Passed May 10, 1873; three-fifths being present.

CHAP. 482. An Act to amend an act passed May four, eighteen hundred and sixty-four, entitled "An act to amend an act entitled 'An act to provide for the incorporation of villages,' passed the seventh of December, eighteen hundred and forty-seven, so far as relates to the village of Corning, in the county of Steuben." Passed May 10, 1873; three-fifths being present.

CHAP. 483. An Act to authorize the construction of a railroad from, at or near, Bath Ferry, in the town of North Greenbush, to Douw's Point, in the town of East Greenbush, in the county of Rensselaer. Passed May 10, 1873.

CHAP. 484. An Act to amend the charter of the village of Lansingburgh. Passed May 12, 1873; three-fifths being present.

CHAP. 485. An Act to further amend an act entitled "An act to provide for draining swamp lands in the towns of Lima, Livonia and Avon, in the county of Livingston," passed April twentieth, eighteen hundred and sixty-six. Passed May 12, 1873; three-fifths being present.

CHAP. 486. An Act to confirm the proceedings taken by the Common Council of the city of Buffalo, to lay out and extend Genesee street, from its termination at Best street, through to intersect the Buffalo and Batavia plank-road. Passed May 12, 1873; three-fifths being present.

CHAP. 487. An Act to amend chapter eight hundred and seventy-four of the Laws of eighteen hundred and seventy-two, in relation to the boundaries of the school districts therein mentioned. Passed May 12, 1873; three-fifths being present.

CHAP. 488. An Act to amend chapter six hundred and fifteen of the Laws of eighteen hundred and seventy-two, being an act entitled "An act to establish St. Paul's American Protestant Episcopal Church, Rome, Italy, by a board of trustees in New York city." Passed May 12, 1873.

CHAP. 489. *An Act to amend an act entitled "An act for the better security of mechanics and others erecting buildings in the counties of Westchester, Oneida, Cortland, Broome, Putnam, Rockland, Orleans, Niagara, Livingston, Otsego, Lewis, Orange and Dutchess, passed April seventeen, eighteen hundred and fifty-four, and as amended by chapter five hundred and fifty-eight of the Laws of eighteen hundred and sixty-nine, entitled 'An act for the better security of mechanics and others erecting buildings in either of the counties of this State, except the counties of Erie, Kings, Queens, New York and Onondaga.'" Passed May* 12, 1873; *three-fifths being present.*

CHAP. 490. An Act to amend an act entitled "An act to amend an act entitled 'An act to organize a fire department and board of fire commissioners in and for the city of Troy,' passed April thirteenth, eighteen hundred and sixty-one," passed April twenty-four, eighteen hundred and seventy-two. Passed May 12, 1873; three-fifths being present.

CHAP. 491. An Act to incorporate "The Xavier Union of the city of New York." Passed May 12, 1873.

CHAP. 492. An Act relative to local improvements in the city of Brooklyn and to amend an act entitled "An act to restrict the power of the city of Brooklyn to issue bonds or loan its credit for local improvements." Passed May 12, 1873; three-fifths being present.

CHAP. 493. An Act to incorporate the Brooooklyn Industrial Institute Company, and to authorize said company to purchase real estate in the city of Brooklyn, and to erect thereon a building or buildings, which shall be used for the holding of annual industrial exhibitions. Passed May 12, 1873; three-fifths being present.

CHAP. 494. An Act to amend an act entitled "An act to incorporate the city of Cohoes," passed May nineteenth, eighteen hundred and sixty-nine. Passed May 12, 1873; three-fifths being present.

CHAP. 495. An Act to amend an act entitled "An act to amend title twelve of the charter of the city of Albany, entitled the police department," passed March sixteenth, eighteen hundred and seventy; passed April sixth, one thousand eight hundred and seventy-two, and also to amend section nine of title twelve of the charter of the city of Albany, entitled "the police department," passed March sixteenth, eighteen hundred and seventy. Passed May 13, 1873; three-fifths being present.

CHAP. 496. An Act to lay out a public road or highway in the town of Hempstead, Queens county. Passed May 13, 1873; three fifths being present.

CHAP. 497. An Act in relation to the performance of labor upon the highways and bridges in the towns of Oyster Bay, Hempstead and North Hempstead, in the county of Queens. Passed May 13, 1873; three-fifths being present.

CHAP. 498. An Act to amend an act entitled "An act to facilitate the construction of the Southern Central Railroad, and to authorize towns to subscribe to the capital stock thereof," passed April seventh, eighteen hundred and sixty-six, and to authorize the town of Moravia to borrow money to pay its bonds issued in pursuance thereof. Passed May 13, 1873; three-fifths being present.

CHAP. 499. An Act authorizing the city of Kingston to issue bonds for the purpose of creating a fund to pay for the erection of a city hall building. Passed May 13, 1873; three-fifths being present.

CHAP. 500. An Act relative to the establishment, laying out and opening or extension of Lexington avenue, from One hundred and Second street to the Harlem river, in the city of New York. Passed May 13, 1873; three-fifths being present.

CHAP. 501. *An Act to amend an act entitled "An act requiring mortgages of personal property to be filed in the town clerks' and other offices," passed April twenty-nine, eighteen hundred and thirty-three. Passed May* 13, 1873; *three-fifths being present.*

CHAP. 502. An Act to amend section three of chapter five hundred and thirty-three of laws of eighteen hundred and sixty-seven, entitled "An act for the relief of the Van Brunt Street and Erie Basin Railroad Company." Passed May 14, 1873.

CHAP. 503. An Act to amend an act entitled "An act to incorporate the Trustees of the Masonic Hall and Asylum fund," passed April twenty-first, eighteen hundred and sixty-four. Passed May 14, 1873.

CHAP. 504. An Act in relation to a certain highway in the county of Hamilton, appropriating certain non-resident highway moneys thereto, and repealing acts heretofore passed in relation thereto. Passed May 14, 1873; three-fifths being present.

CHAP. 505. An Act to reorganize the village of Gloversville. Passed May 14, 1873; three-fifths being present.

CHAP. 506. An Act to amend an act entitled "An act to authorize the town of Pelham, in the county of Westchester to purchase, pay for, acquire title to and maintain the bridge owned by the City Island Bridge Company," passed March twenty, eighteen hundred and seventy-three. Passed May 14, 1873; three-fifths being present.

CHAP. 507. An Act to amend an act entitled "An act to incorporate the village of New Brighton, in the county of Richmond," passed April twenty-six, eighteen hundred and sixty-six, and the several acts to amend the same, passed April twenty-two, eighteen hundred and seventy-one, and April twenty-seven, eighteen hundred and seventy-one, and March twenty-seven, eighteen hundred and seventy-two. Passed May 14, 1873; three-fifths being present.

CHAP. 508. An Act to incorporate the Long Island Loan and Trust Company. Passed May 14, 1873.

CHAP. 509. An Act to provide for the laying out and opening of a public highway in the towns of North Hempstead and Oyster Bay, in the county of Queens. Passed May 14, 1873; three-fifths being present.

CHAP. 510. An Act to regulate rates of passenger fare upon the Ithaca and Athens Railroad. Passed May 14, 1873.

CHAP. 511. An Act to authorize the County Treasurer of Oneida county to borrow money upon the faith and credit of said county, and issue bonds therefor. Passed May 15, 1873; three-fifths being present.

CHAP. 512. An Act to amend an act entitled "An act to incorporate the Buffalo East Side Street Railway Company," passed May tenth, eighteen hundred and seventy, as the same is amended by chapter three hundred and seventy of the Laws of eighteen hundred and seventy-two, passed April twenty-five, eighteen hundred and seventy-two, and entitled "An act to amend an act entitled 'An act to incorporate the Buffalo East Side Street Railway Company,' passed May tenth, eighteen hundred and seventy." Passed May 15, 1873; three-fifths being present.

CHAP. 513. An Act to amend an act entitled "An act to establish a department of police in the city of Buffalo, and to provide for the government thereof," passed April twenty-six, eighteen hundred and seventy-one. Passed March 15, 1873; three-fifths being present.

CHAP. 514. An Act to authorize the First Reformed Dutch Church in Clarkstown, in the county of Rockland, to apply certain moneys to the payment of the indebtedness incurred in the erection of an edifice for the education of the poor children belonging to said church. Passed May 15, 1873.

CHAP. 515. *An Act to amend chapter seven hundred and sixty-seven of the Laws of eighteen hundred and seventy two, relating to salaries of county judge and surrogate. Passed May* 15, 1873; *three-fifths being present.*

CHAP. 516. An Act in regard to highways and bridges in the towns of Le Ray and Rutland, in the county of Jefferson. Passed May 15, 1873; three-fifths being present.

CHAP. 517. An Act to amend an act entitled "An act to amend an act entitled 'An act to authorize the construction of a railway and tracks in the towns of West Farms and Morrisania,' passed May second, eighteen hundred and sixty-three," passed April twentieth, eighteen hundred and seventy-one. Passed May 15, 1873.

CHAP. 518. An Act to incorporate the Utica Masonic Hall Association. Passed May 15, 1873.

CHAP. 519. An Act to increase the rate of ferriage between the city of Hudson, in the county of Columbia, and the village of Athens, in the county of Greene. Passed May 15, 1873; three-fifths being present.

CHAP. 520. An Act to authorize the town of Mamaroneck, in Westchester county, to issue bonds in payment or renewal of its outstanding town bonds. Passed May 16, 1873; three-fifths being present.

CHAP. 521. An Act to authorize the trustees of the village of Geddes, in the county of Onondaga, to lay out and open a street in the town of Geddes. Passed May 16, 1873; three-fifths being present.

CHAP. 522. An Act to authorize the formation of the East Avenue Omnibus Company. Passed May 16, 1873.

CHAP. 523. An Act to provide an armory in the city of Brooklyn, county of Kings, for the use of the Thirteenth Regiment of the National Guard of the State of New York. Passed May 16, 1873; three-fifths being present.

CHAP. 524. An Act to amend chapter two hundred and fifty-one of the Laws of eighteen hundred and sixty-six, entitled "An act for the preservation of fish in Kinderhook lake, and waters adjacent thereto." Passed May 16, 1873.

CHAP. 525. An Act to amend chapter six hundred and sixty-four, Laws of eighteen hundred and sixty-seven, entitled "An act to enable the supervisors of Montgomery county to refund illegal taxes," passed April twenty-three, eighteen hundred and sixty-seven. Passed May 16, 1873; three-fifths being present.

CHAP. 526. An Act to incorporate the Monticello and White Lake Turnpike Company. Passed May 16, 1873.

CHAP. 527. An Act to incorporate the New York Society for the Suppression of Vice. Passed May 16, 1873; three-fifths being present.

CHAP. 528. An Act to provide for the Eastern Boulevard in the city of New York, and in relation to certain alterations of the map or plan of said city, and certain local improvements in connection therewith to amend chapter six hundred and twenty-six of the Laws of eighteen hundred and seventy. Passed May 16, 1873; three-fifths being present.

CHAP. 529. *An Act to re-appropriate moneys for construction of new work upon, and extraordinary repairs of, the canals of this state. Passed May* 16, 1873; *three-fifths being present.*

CHAP. 530. *An Act to amend section two, title one, chapter thirteen, part one of the Revised Statutes of the State of New York. Passed May* 16, 1873; *three-fifths being present.*

CHAP. 531. An Act to open, lay out and improve Gravesend avenue in the county of Kings, and to authorize the construction of a railroad thereon. Passed May 16, 1873; three-fifths being present.

CHAP. 532. An Act to authorize the Rochester, Nunda and Pennsylvania Railroad Company to construct and operate two branches of its railroad, from a point at or near Angelica, in the county of Allegany, one branch running to a point at or near Scott's Corner's in the town of Hinsdale, Cattaraugus county, and the other to a point on the north line of the State of Pennsylvania, at or near Shongo, in the town of Willing, county of Allegany. Passed May 16, 1873.

CHAP. 533. An Act in relation to the salary of the Recorder of the city of Watertown. Passed May 16, 1873; three-fifths being present.

CHAP. 534. An Act to incorporate the New York Underground Telegraph Company Passed May 16, 1873.

CHAP. 535. An Act to provide for the location and erection of a new city prison, and place for holding certain courts in the city of New York. Passed May 16, 1873; three-fifths being present.

CHAP. 536. An Act to give effect to a deed from the Farmers' Bank of Orwell, to Benjamin Cheney. Passed May 16, 1873.

CHAP. 537. An Act to authorize the Joseph Dixon Crucible Company, a corporation of the State of New Jersey, to hold, mortgage and sell real estate within this State. Passed May 17, 1873.

CHAP. 538. An Act to secure better administration in the police courts of the city of New York. Passed May 17, 1873; three-fifths being present.

CHAP. 539. An Act to repeal an act entitled "An act to authorize the city of Buffalo and the board of supervisors of Erie county to grant and convey certain lands in the city of Buffalo." Passed May 19, 1873; three-fifths being present.

CHAP. 540. An Act to authorize the taking of certain lands in the city of Buffalo, for the purposes of an avenue leading from the Parade park southerly to Seneca street, and for improving and embellishing the same. Passed May 19, 1873; three-fifths being present.

CHAP. 541. An Act for the final settlement of the safety fund Hudson River Bank, with the Banking Department. Passed May 19, 1873; three-fifths being present.

CHAP. 542. An Act relative to lands in the county of Westchester, devised by Joseph Miller, deceased, to William H. Miller, and to provide for the sale and conveyance thereof. Passed May 19, 1873.

CHAP. 543. An Act to amend an act entitled "An act to incorporate the New York Commericial Association," passed April nine, eighteen hundred and sixty-two, amended by a subsequent act passed February thirteen, eighteen hundred and sixty-eight, changing the name of said corporation to New York Produce Exchange. Passed May 19, 1873.

CHAP. 544. An Act to legalize certain assessments ordered by the common council of the city of Buffalo, and contained in certain rolls delivered to the comptroller of said city. Passed May 20, 1873; three-fifths being present.

CHAP. 545. *An Act to provide for the repair, construction and improvement of bridges on the Cattaraugus Indian Reservation in the county of Erie. Passed May* 20, 1873; *by a two-third vote.*

CHAP. 546. An Act to incorporate the Schenectady City Railway Company. Passed May 20, 1873; three-fifths being present.

CHAP. 547. An Act to authorize the supervisor of the town of Oswego to convey, by deed, part of lot number five of the original township of Hannibal, known as the Gospel lot. Passed May 20, 1873; three-fifths being present.

CHAP. 548. An Act to confirm the purchase by the New York and Oswego Midland Railroad Company of a portion of the road-bed and rights of the Lake Ontario, Auburn and New York Railroad, and to authorize said New York and Oswego Midland Railroad Company to construct a railroad from its Auburn branch to, or near, the village of Ithaca. Passed May 20, 1873; three-fifths being present.

CHAP. 549. *An act to amend an act entitled "An act regulating the sale of intoxicating liquors," passed April eleven, eighteen hundred and seventy, and the act entitled "An act to suppress intemperance and to regulate the sale of intoxicating liquors," passed April sixteen, eighteen hundred and fifty-seven. Passed May* 21, 1873; *three-fifths being present.*

CHAP. 550. An Act to extend the time for the completion of the Boston, Hartford and Erie Railroad by the New York and New England Railroad Company. Passed May 21, 1873.

CHAP. 551. *An Act to amend chapter seven hundred and ninety-eight of the Laws of eighteen hundred and sixty-eight, entitled "An act to amend chapter three hundred and sixty-five of the Laws of eighteen hundred and sixty-two, entitled "An act to authorize the discharge of mortgages of record in certain cases," passed May nine, eighteen hundred and sixty-eight. Passed May* 21, 1873; *three-fifths being present.*

CHAP. 552. *An Act in relation to lands of which parties die seized. Passed May* 21, 1873.

CHAP. 553. An Act to amend chapter three hundred and thirty-five of the Laws of eighteen hundred and sixty-nine, entitled "An act to provide a charter for the village of Oneida," passed April twenty-six, eighteen hundred and sixty-nine. Passed May 21, 1873; three-fifths being present.

CHAP. 554. An act amending chapter eight hundred and thirty-seven, Laws of eighteen hundred and sixty-eight, and chapter six hundred and twenty-three, Laws of eighteen hundred and sixty-nine, in reference to the laying out, opening and continuing Bushwick avenue, in the town of New Lots, Kings county. Passed May 21, 1873; three-fifths being present.

CHAP. 555. An Act to amend chapter one hundred and nineteen of the Laws of eighteen hundred and seventy-two, entitled "An act to release Mary Wheleleam the real of which John Wheleleam died seized, in the town of Canandaigua, county of Ontario," passed March twentieth, eighteen hundred and seventy-two. Passed May 21, 1873; by a two-third vote.

CHAP. 556. An Act to legalize the proceedings in relation to the building of a bridge over Dongan's mill-creek, dividing the towns of Castleton and Northfield, in the county of Richmond, and to provide for the raising of money to pay for the expense thereof. Passed May 21, 1873; three-fifths being present.

CHAP. 557. An Act to release the interest of the State in the real estate of which George Johnson, late of the town of Cicero, in the county of Onondaga, died seized, to Matthew Johnson. Passed May 21, 1873, by a two-third vote.

CHAP. 558. An Act to amend the act entitled "An act to incorporate the Genesee Wesleyan Seminary," and also to amend an act entitled 'An act to incorporate the Genesee College." Passed May 21, 1873.

CHAP. 559. An Act to legalize the election for village officers of the village of Brewerton, in the county of Onondaga, held on the third Monday of March, eighteen hundred and seventy-three. Passed May 21, 1873; three-fifths being present.

CHAP. 560. An Act in relation to the Rochester Superphosphate Company and its capital stock. Passed May 21, 1873.

CHAP. 561. *An Act to amend chapter seven hundred and thirty-nine of the Laws of eighteen hundred and fifty-seven, entitled "An act to authorize the formation of town insurance companies." Passed May* 21, 1873.

CHAP. 562. An Act to authorize the town board of the town of Salina, in the county of Onondaga, to raise money to repair and protect a road in said town. Passed May 21, 1873; three-fifths being present.

CHAP. 563. An Act to amend an act entitled "An act to revise, amend and consolidate the several acts in relation to the charter of the city of Hudson," passed May first, eighteen hundred and seventy-two. Passed May 21, 1873; three-fifths being present.

CHAP. 564. An Act to amend an act entitled "An act to amend an act entitled 'An act to incorporate the Bowery savings bank,' passed May first, eighteen hundred and thirty-four," passed March twenty-fifth, eighteen hundred and sixty-nine. Passed May 21, 1873.

CHAP. 565. *An Act making an appropriation to pay the expenses of the collection of tolls, superintendence, ordinary repairs and maintenance of the canals for the fiscal year, commencing on the first day of October, eighteen hundred and seventy-three, and to supply a deficiency in former appropriations. Passed May* 21, 1873; *three-fifths being present.*

CHAP. 566. An Act to authorize the removal of the remains of bodies now buried and remaining on land now owned by Harvey H. Hendon, in the town of Clarkson, Monroe county. Passed May 21, 1873.

CHAP. 567. An Act authorizing the commissioners of the alms-house of the city of Kingston to borrow money for the purpose of erecting an alms-house, and to issue bonds therefor. Passed May 21, 1873; three-fifths being present.

CHAP. 568. An Act to amend an act entitled "An act to establish the office of receiver of taxes and assessments in the town of East Chester, in the county of Westchester, New York," passed March twenty-seventh, eighteen hundred and sixty-five. Passed May 21, 1873; three-fifths being present.

CHAP. 569. An Act to incorporate the Auburn fire department. Passed May 21, 1873; three-fifths being present.

CHAP. 570. An Act to amend an act entitled "An act to amend an act entitled 'An act to provide for the incorporation of villages,' passed December seven, one thousand eight hundred and forty-seven, and the several acts amendatory thereof, so far as the same relate to the village of Mount Vernon, in the county of Westchester, and to declare, enlarge and define the powers and duties of the officers of said village, and to confirm and extend the powers of the corporation of said village," passed May ten, one thousand eight hundred and seventy. Passed May 21, 1873; three-fifths being present.

CHAP. 571. *An Act to further define the powers and duties of the Board of State Commissioners of public charities, and to change the name of the board to The State Board of Charities. Passed May* 21, 1873.

CHAP. 572. An Act to legalize assessments made in pursuance of certain resolutions and ordinances of the common council of the city of Rochester. Passed May 21, 1873; three-fifths being present.

CHAP. 573. An Act to authorize the audit and payment of the claims of James O'Brien, late sheriff of the county of New York. Passed May 22, 1873; three-fifths being present.

CHAP. 574. An Act to amend an act entitled "An act to incorporate the Old Guard of the city of New York," passed April twenty-second, eighteen hundred and sixty-eight. Passed May 22, 1873.

CHAP. 575. An Act to authorize the formation of a mutual insurance company in the town of Hamden, in the county of Delaware. Passed May 22, 1873.

CHAP. 576. An Act to authorize the Church of Martinsburg, in the town of Martinsburg, in the county of Lewis, to sell certain real estate situated in said town. Passed May 22, 1873.

CHAP. 577. *An Act to amend an act entitled "An act to amend an act entitled 'An act to designate the holidays to be observed in the acceptance and payment of bills of exchange and promissory notes,'" passed April twenty-third, eighteen hundred and seventy. Passed May* 22, 1873.

CHAP. 578. An Act to confirm the title of certain lands conveyed to William Taylor, an alien. Passed May 22, 1873; by a two-third vote.

CHAP. 579. An Act to amend an act entitled "An act to protect, improve and keep in repair the west part of the road formerly known as the Buffalo plank-road, in the county of Erie," passed April thirteen, eighteen hundred and seventy-one. Passed May 22, 1873.

CHAP. 580. An Act to amend an act entitled "An act to revise the charter of the city of Auburn," passed April twenty-second, eighteen hundred and sixty-nine. Passed May 22, 1873; three-fifths being present.

CHAP. 581. An Act to amend "An act to incoporate the Albany Safe Deposit Company, in the city of Albany," passed February twenty-eight, eighteen hundred and seventy three. Passed May 22, 1873.

CHAP. 582. An Act to change the name of Central Park avenue in the county of Westchester. Passed May 22, 1873.

CHAP. 583. *An Act to define some of the rights and responsibilities of landlords and tenants. Passed May* 22, 1873.

CHAP. 584. *An act to provide building sites for life-saving stations on the coast of Long Island, State of New York. Passed May* 22, 1873; *by a two-third vote.*

CHAP. 585. *An act to provide for the final closing of incorporated banks. Passed May* 22, 1873.

CHAP. 586. *An act to amend the twenty-third section of article first, title four, chapter two, part four of the Revised Statutes, entitled "of the return and summoning of grand jurors, their powers and duties." Passed May* 22, 1873; *three-fifths being present.*

CHAP. 587. *An Act in relation to the State Lunatic Asylum. Passed May* 22, 1873; *three-fifths being present.*

CHAP. 588. An Act to establish a commission in and for the city and county of New York, to be known and designated as the Commission of Charitable Correction and to define its powers and jurisdiction. Passed May 22, 1873; three-fifths being present.

CHAP. 589. *An act to amend an act in relation to the calendar of the Commission of Appeals, authorizing the transfer of causes from the calendar of the Court of Appeals and the disposition of causes on the calendar of the Commission of Appeals," passed February seven, eighteen hundred and seventy-three. Passed May* 22, 1873.

CHAP. 590. An Act to amend an act entitled "An act to provide for the improvement of Pleasant street in the city of Utica and town of New Hartford, Oneida county, between Oneida street and Seymour avenue," passed May twenty-first, eighteen hundred and seventy-two. Passed May 22, 1873; three-fifths being present.

CHAP. 591. An Act supplemental to an act entitled "An act to provide for the construction of a drain or sewer in Central avenue, Johnson avenue and Knickerbocker avenue and other streets in the city of Brooklyn," passed May third, eighteen hundred and sixty-nine, and to an act amendatory thereof. Passed May 22, 1873; three-fifths being present.

CHAP. 592. An Act supplementary to an act entitled "An act to open and widen portions of Sackett, Douglass and President streets, and otherwise alter the commissioners' map of the city of Brooklyn," passed May sixth, eighteen hundred and sixty-eight. Passed May 22, 1873; three-fifths being present.

CHAP. 593. *An Act to amend an act entitled "An act to establish an Insurance Department," passed April fifteenth, eighteen hundred and fifty-nine. Passed May* 22, 1873; *three-fifths being present.*

CHAP. 594. An Act to incorporate the Rochester and Charlotte Boulevard and Railway Company. Passed May 22, 1873.

CHAP. 595. *An Act relative to certain negotiable corporate bonds and obligations. Passed May* 22, 1873; *three-fifths being present.*

CHAP. 596. An Act to amend section twelve of the act entitled "An act to reduce the several acts relating to the district courts in the city of New York into one act," passed April thirteenth, eighteen hundred and fifty-seven. Passed May 22, 1873; three-fifths being present.

CHAP. 597. An Act in relation to the Saranac River Plank-road Company, and authorizing said company to lay rails upon its road. Passed May 22, 1873.

CHAP. 598. An Act to amend an act entitled "An act in relation to the taxes to be annually raised in the city of Brooklyn and county of Kings," passed April nineteenth, eighteen hundred and seventy-one. Passed May 22, 1873; three-fifths being present.

CHAP. 599. An Act repealing chapter two hundred and twenty-seven of the Laws of eighteen hundred and seventy-two, so far as the same affects lands in the town of Minerva, Essex county. Passed May 23, 1873; three-fifths being present.

CHAP. 600. *An Act relating to the building commissioners for the erection of the State Reformatory at Elmira, Chemung county. Passed May* 23, 1873; *three-fifths being present.*

CHAP. 601. An Act to authorize the city of Buffalo to issue its bonds for the purpose of extending the supply of water to the city and its inhabitants, and to purchase land and to construct a reservoir thereon. Passed May 23, 1873; three-fifths being present.

CHAP. 602. An Act to amend an act entitled "An act to incorporate the village of Havana in the town of Montour, in the county of Schuyler, and to repeal its present charter," passed April eleven, eighteen hundred and sixty-eight. Passed May 23, 1873; three-fifths being present.

CHAP. 603. An Act to define the jail limits in the county of Rensselaer. Passed May 23, 1873; three-fifths being present.

CHAP. 604. An Act to incoporate the Union Hospital of the city of New York. Passed May 23, 1873; three-fifths being present.

CHAP. 605. An Act to amend an act entitled "An act to incorporate the village of Stamford, in the counties of Delaware and Schoharie," and also to amend the title thereof. Passed May 23, 1873; three-fifths being present.

CHAP. 606. An Act to incorporate the Hornellsville Water Company. Passed May 23, 1873; three-fifths being present.

CHAP. 607. An Act to authorize the Ontario County Agricultural Society to sell and convey its real estate. Passed May 23, 1873; three-fifths being present.

CHAP. 608. An Act for the relief of William P. McCormick. Passed May 23, 1873; three-fifths being present.

CHAP. 609. An Act to provide for supplying the village of College Point, Queens county, with pure and wholesome water. Passed May 23, 1873; three-fifths being present.

CHAP. 610. An Act to release the interest of the People of the State of New York in and to certain lands situate in Long Island City, and county of Queens, to Caroline West, and to authorize her to hold and convey the same. Passed May 23, 1873, by a two-third vote.

CHAP. 611. An Act to amend an act entitled "An act to incorporate the Brooklyn Steam Transit Company," passed June second, eighteen hundred and seventy-one. Passed May 23, 1873.

CHAP. 612. An Act in relation to Grace Church, New York. Passed May 23, 1873.

CHAP. 613. An Act to provide for the annexation of the towns of Morrisania, West Farms and Kings Bridge, in the county of Westchester, to the city and county of New York. Passed May 23, 1873; three-fifths being present.

CHAP. 614. *An Act to authorize marine insurance companies to declare extra dividends in certain cases. Passed May* 24, 1873.

CHAP. 615. An Act to authorize the formation of a mutual insurance company in the town of Cairo, in the county of Greene. Passed May 24, 1873.

CHAP. 616. *An act to authorize the consolidation of companies organized under the act entitled "An act to authorize the formation of companies for the erection of buildings," passed April five, eighteen hundred and fifty-three, or any of the acts amendiug or extending the same. Passed May* 24, 1873; *three-fifths being present.*

CHAP. 617. *An Act regulating the deposit of securities by plate glass insurance companies. Passed May* 24, 1873.

CHAP. 618. An Act to legalize and confirm the appointment of collectors of taxes in those parts of the towns of Middletown and Southfield, in the county of Richmond, included in the corporate limits of the village of Edgewater, and the issue of and delivery of the assessment rolls and warrants to them, and to authorize said collectors to proceed with the collection of such taxes. Passed May 24, 1873; three-fifths being present.

CHAP. 619. An Act to incorporate the Staten Island and New Jersey Suspension Bridge and Railroad Company, for the purpose of maintaining and constructing suspension bridges, appurtenances and approaches to the same, over the Kill von Kull, at a point or points between the village of New Brighton, Richmond county, and at a point or points near Constable's Point, in the State of New Jersey, and at a point or points over Arthur Kill or Staten Island Sound, between the town of Westfield, Richmond county, and Middlesex county, in the State of New Jersey, and also for the purpose of constructing and maintaining a railroad over and across said bridges, and to and through the center of Staten Island, Richmond county, to and from the points above named. Passed May 26, 1873; three-fifths being present.

CHAP. 620. An Act to amend the statutes in reference to the collection of taxes in the county of Suffolk. Passed May 27, 1873; three-fifths being present.

CHAP. 621. An Act to amend an act entitled "An act to amend and consolidate the several acts relative to the city of Schenectady, passed April twenty-first, eighteen hundred and sixty-two, and the several acts amendatory thereof. Passed May 27, 1873; three-fifths being present.

CHAP. 622. An Act to release the interest of the People of the State of New York in certain lands to Darius E. King and Lucretia E. King, his wife. Passed May 27, 1873.

CHAP. 623. An Act to amend an act entitled "An act in relation to common schools in the village of Lockport," passed March thirty-one, eighteen hundred and forty-seven, and the acts amendatory thereof. Passed May 27, 1873; three-fifths being present.

CHAP. 624. *An Act to appropriate money for the building of a bridge over the Cayuga inlet, in the village of Ithaca. Passed May 27*, 1873; *three-fifths being present.*

CHAP. 625. *An Act to reorganize the New York State Inebriate Asylum and to provide for the better support and maintenance of the same. Passed May 27*, 1873; *three-fifths being present.*

CHAP. 626. *An Act to declare Marsh Creek in Allegany county a public highway. Passed May* 27, 1873; *three-fifths being present.*

CHAP. 627. An Act to incorporate the Niagara County Fruit Growers' Association. Passed May 27, 1873.

CHAP. 628. An Act further to amend the charter of the Real Estate Trust Company of the city of New York, passed April seventeen, eighteen hundred and seventy-one. Passed May 25, 1873.

CHAP. 629. An Act to incorporate the New York Mortgage and Trust Company. Passed May 28, 1873.

CHAP. 630. *An Act to amend the Revised Statutes. Passed May* 27, 1873; *three-fifths being present.*

CHAP. 631. An Act to make further provisions for the audit and payment of the claims and expenses mentioned in act chapter five hundred and eight of the Laws of eighteen hundred and seventy-two, being the expenses of conducting civil and criminal suits and prosecutions growing out of the frauds upon the treasury of the city and county of New York, which were brought to light in eighteen hundred and seventy-one. Passed May 28, 1873; three-fifths being present.

CHAP. 632. An Act to incorporate The Albany Agricultural and Art Association. Passed May 28, 1873.

CHAP. 633. *An Act to authorize the incorporation of Baptist churches in the State of New York and supplementary to an act entitled "An act to provide for the incorporation of religious societies," passed April fifth, eighteen hundred and thirteen. Passed May* 28, 1873.

CHAP. 634. *An Act to amend article one, title four, of chapter eight, of third part of the Revised Statutes entitled "of proceedings by aud against corporations in courts of law. Passed May* 28, 1873; *three-fifths being present.*

CHAP. 635. An Act to amend an act entitled "An act to provide laying out and improving roads and avenues in the village and town of Saratoga Springs," passed May fifth, eighteen hundred and seventy. Passed May 28, 1873; three-fifths being present.

CHAP. 636. An Act to provide for the appointment of a recorder and collector in the village of Plattsburg, and to provide for the pavement of certain streets in said village. Passed May 28, 1873; three-fifths being present.

CHAP. 637. An Act to amend chapter three hundred and twenty-three of the Laws of eighteen hundred and seventy-two, entitled "An act authorizing the election of a receiver of taxes and assessments for the town and village of Saratoga Springs." Passed May 28, 1873; three-fifths being present.

CHAP. 638. An Act to establish a Rensselaer police district, and to provide for the government thereof. Passed May 29, 1873; three-fifths being present.

CHAP. 639. *An Act to amend an act entitled "An act to amend an act entitled 'An act to amend an act to designate the holidays to be observed in the acceptance and payment of bills of exchange and promissory notes,' passed April twenty-three, eighteen hundred and seventy, passed May twenty-second, eighteen hundred and seventy-three. Passed May*, 29, 1873.

CHAP. 640. An Act to amend chapter five hundred and five of the Laws of eighteen hundred and seventy-three, entitled "An act to reorganize the village of Gloversville." Passed May 29, 1873; three-fifths being present.

CHAP. 641. An Act to legalize the construction of a pier or wharf in the waters of the East river, between Jerolamen street and Atlantic street, in the city of Brooklyn, outside the bulkhead line, and to authorize the continuation, use and repair of the same. Passed May 29, 1873; three-fifths being present.

CHAP. 642. *An Act in relation to academies and academical departments of union schools and the distribution of public funds. Passed May* 29, 1873; *three-fifths being present.*

CHAP. 643. *An Act to provide for the support of government and for other purposes. Passed May* 29, 1873; *three-fifths being present.*

CHAP. 644. *An Act to amend an act entitled "An act to repeal chapter four hundred and ten, passed April fourteen, eighteen hundred and sixty, and chapter three hundred and three, passed April seventeen, eighteen hundred and sixty-one, and to divide the crime of murder into two degrees and to prescribe the punishment of arson," passed April twelve, eighteen hundred and sixty-two. Passed May* 29, 1873; *three-fifths being present.*

CHAP. 645. An Act to alter the map or plan of the city of New York by extending Desbrosses street. Passed May 29, 1873; three-fifths being present.

CHAP. 646. *An Act to suppress intemperance, pauperism and crime. Passed May* 29, 1873; *three-fifths being present.*

CHAP. 647. An Act in relation to the Bleecker Street and Fulton Ferry Railroad Company of the city of New York. Passed May 29, 1873.

CHAP. 648. An Act to legalize the acts of Robert E. Dorchester as notary public. Passed June 6, 1873; three-fifths being present.

CHAP. 649. An act to incorporate the Independent Hose Company Number Three of Elmira, New York. Passed June 6, 1873.

CHAP. 650. An Act for the relief of John W. Shilcock. Passed June 6, 1873; three-fifths being present.

CHAP. 651. An Act to legalize the official acts of Samuel B. Wood, as notary public. Passed June 6, 1873; three-fifths being present.

CHAP. 652 An Act to amend the charter of the North-eastern Homœopathic Medical and Surgical Dispensary in the city of New York. Passed June 6, 1873; three-fifths being present.

CHAP. 653. An Act to amend an act entitled "An act to incorporate the University Railroad Company of Syracuse," passed April fifteenth, eighteen hundred and seventy-one. Passed June 6, 1873.

CHAP. 654. An Act to enable Torekeld Andersen, Kirster Andersdotter and Signe Andersdotter to take and hold real estate, and to release to them the interest and title to land escheated to the State. Passed June 6, 1873; by a two-third vote.

CHAP. 655. An Act to release the title and interest of the people of the State of New York in and to certain real estate of which Louisa Lowrie, late of the city of Brooklyn, in the State of New York, died seized, to William Lowrie, her husband. Passed June 6, 1873; by a two-third vote.

CHAP. 656. An act to amend chapter seven hundred and twenty-nine of the Laws of eighteen hundred and seventy-one, entitled "An act authorizing the Board of Supervisors of the county of Essex to levy and assess certain taxes on certain lands in the town of Minerva, in said county." Passed June 6, 1873; three-fifths being present.

CHAP. 657. *An Act to amend section seven of article one, title two, chapter six, part second of the Revised Statutes, in reference to non-resident executors. Passed June* 6, 1873.

CHAP. 658. An Act to incorporate the Albany Loan and Trust Company. Passed June 6, 1873.

CHAP. 659. An Act to authorize the town of Glenville, Schenectady county, to purchase Mohawk bridge. Passed June 6, 1873; three-fifths being present.

CHAP. 660. An Act to amend an act entitled "An act to amend, consolidate and re-enact an act entitled 'An act to incorporate the village of Edgewater,' passed March twenty-second, eighteen hundred and sixty-six, and an act amending the same, passed April twenty-second, eighteen hundred and sixty-seven, and to extend the powers of the corporation," passed May fifth, eighteen hundred and seventy, and also an act amending the same, passed June eighth, eighteen hundred and seventy-two. Passed June 7, 1873; three-fifths being present.

CHAP. 661. *An Act to provide for the support and care of state paupers. Passed June* 7, 1873; *three-fifths being present.*

CHAP. 662. An Act to dissolve the Cayuga Midland Railroad Company. Passed June 7, 1873.

CHAP. 663. *An Act to amend article second of title first of chapter nine of part third of the Revised Statutes, entitled "Of writs of habeas corpus and certiorari, when issued to inquire into the cause of detention." Passed June* 7, 1873; *three-fifths being present.*

CHAP. 664. An Act to organize the village of Monticello into a separate school district, and to provide for the purchase of a site and erection of a school edifice. Passed June 7, 1873; three-fifths being present.

Chap. 665. *An Act to punish the taking of fish from private ponds. Passed June* 7, 1873; *three-fifths being present.*

Chap. 666. An Act to amend certain acts in relation to common schools in the city of Utica. Passed June 7, 1873; three-fifths being present.

Chap. 667. An Act in relation to a sidewalk from the village of Albion to Mount Albion Cemetery. Passed June 7, 1873; three-fifths being present.

Chap. 668. An Act to amend an act entitled "An act to incorporate the village of Olean, in the county of Cattaraugus, to provide for the election of officers for the same, and to declare the said village a separate road district," passed April first, eighteen hundred and fifty-eight. Passed June 7, 1873; three-fifths being present.

Chap. 669. An Act to amend chapter three hundred and ninety of the Laws of eighteen hundred and seventy-three, entitled "An act to amend an act entitled 'An act to amend and consolidate the charter of the village of Leroy,' passed April six, eighteen hundred and fifty-seven. Passed June 7, 1873; three-fifths being present.

Chap. 670. An Act to amend an act entitled "An act to authorize the construction of sewers in the village and town of Saratoga Springs," passed April twenty-one, eighteen hundred and seventy-one. Passed June 7, 1873; three-fifths being present.

Chap. 671. An Act to establish and maintain union graded schools in the village of Cambridge, Washington county, New York, and constitute said village a single school district. Passed June 7, 1873; three-fifths being present.

Chap. 672. An Act to incorporate the Fire Assurance Agency Company. Passed June 7, 1873.

Chap. 673. An Act to incorporate the Buffalo Safe Deposit Company. Passed June 7, 1873.

Chap. 674. An Act to amend the charter of the German-American Loan and Mortgage Company. Passed June 7, 1873.

Chap. 675. *An Act to provide for the payment of the attendants of the commission of appeals. Passed June* 7, 1873; *three-fifths being present.*

Chap. 676. An Act to authorize the change of the name of the Atlantic Savings Bank of the city of New York, to the Bond Street Savings Bank of the city of New York. Passed June 7, 1873.

Chap. 677. An Act to authorize the apportionment of the indebtedness incurred in the late town of Yonkers by the Board of Commissioners of the Department of Public Parks of the city of New York, under chapter five hundred and thirty-four of the Laws of eighteen hundred and seventy-one, and to provide for the payment thereof. Passed June 7, 1873; three-fifths being present.

Chap. 678. An Act to amend an act entitled "An act to incorporate the Westchester County Trust Company." Passed June 7, 1873.

Chap. 679. *An Act to supply a deficiency in the appropriation for the fiscal year, beginning on the first day of October, eighteen hundred and seventy-three, for clerk hire in the office of the comptroller. Passed June* 7, 1873; *three-fifths being present.*

Chap. 680. An Act to enable the Staten Island Railway Company to have, own and run ferry boats. Passed June 9, 1873.

Chap. 681. An Act to establish communication between Richmond county and New Jersey, incorporating the Tubular Transit Company of Staten Island. Passed June 9, 1873.

Chap. 682. An Act to amend an act entitled "An act to incorporate the city of Elmira," passed April seventh, eighteen hundred and sixty-four, as amended by an act amendatory thereof, passed May seventh, eighteen hundred and seventy. Passed June 9, 1873; three-fifths being present.

Chap. 683. An Act to provide for the extension of the New York, Kingston and Syracuse Railroad. Passed June 9, 1873; three-fifths being present.

Chap. 684. An Act to incorporate the International Exchange and Agency Company of New York. Passed June 9, 1873.

Chap. 685. An Act to amend, extend and continue an act entitled "An act to incorporate the Bankers' Life Insurance and Trust Company of New York," passed May sixth, eighteen hundred and seventy. Passed June 9, 1873.

Chap. 686. An Act to authorize any life or fire insurance, or any trust or loan company, or any savings bank in the county of Westchester, to invest their funds or deposits in the bonds issued pursuant to any law of this state, by the village of Peekskill, Westchester county, for the purpose of constructing water-works. Passed June 10, 1873.

CHAP. 687. An Act to amend an act entitled "An act to consolidate and amend the several acts relating to the village of Peekskill, to alter the bounds and to enlarge the powers of the corporation of said village," passed March twenty-fifth, eighteen hundred and fifty-nine. Passed June 10, 1873; three-fifths being present.

CHAP. 688. *An Act regulating the responsibility of agents of insurance companies. Passed June* 10, 1873.

CHAP. 689. An Act to amend an act entitled "An act authorizing the city of Rochester to issue its bonds to an amount not to exceed seventy-five thousand dollars, for the purpose of building a free academy," passed April third, eighteen hundred and seventy-two. Passed June 10, 1873; three-fifths being present.

CHAP. 690. An Act to release the interest of the State of New York in the real estate of which James Wilde, late of the city of Brooklyn, Kings county, died seized, to Walter Swift. Passed June 10, 1873, by a two-third vote.

CHAP. 691. An act to extend the time for the levying and collection of the tax authorized to be levied and collected by chapter four hundred and seventy-nine of the Laws of eighteen hundred and sixty-nine, entitled "An act to authorize the town of Ellisburgh, in the county of Jefferson, to raise money to build a town-house." Passed June 10, 1873; three-fifths being present.

CHAP. 692. An Act to amend an act entitled "An act to incorporate Cataract Fire Engine Company Number Two, of the town of Castleton, in the county of Richmond," passed July seventeen, eighteen hundred and sixty-seven. Passed June 10, 1873.

CHAP. 693. An Act for the protection and preservation of fish in the county of Cayuga. Passed June 10, 1873; three-fifths being present.

CHAP. 694. An Act to amend an act entitled "An act to incorporate New Brighton Fire Engine Company Number Four, in Richmond county," passed April nineteenth, eighteen hundred and fifty-nine. Passed June 10, 1873.

CHAP. 695. An Act authorizing the Adirondack Company to build a branch railroad to the village of Caldwell. Passed June 10, 1873.

CHAP. 696. An Act to incorporate the Stuyvesant Medical Institute for Diseases of the Lungs and Throat. Passed June 10, 1873.

CHAP. 697. An Act to authorize the Steuben County Bank (of Bath, New York), to reduce its capital stock. Passed June 10, 1873.

CHAP. 698. *An Act to amend the act passed April eleven, eighteen hundred and sixty-five, entitled "An act for the incorporation of societies or clubs for certain social and recreative purposes." Passed June* 10, 1873.

CHAP. 699. *An Act to amend chapter four hundred and forty of the Laws of eighteen hundred and seventy-three, entitled "An act requiring commissioners of highways to act as inspectors of plank-roads and turnpikes." Passed June* 10, 1873; *three-fifths being present.*

CHAP. 700. An Act authorizing the city of Rochester to issue fifteen thousand dollars of bonds for the purpose of erecting a public school building. Passed June 10, 1873; three-fifths being present.

CHAP. 701. An Act to release the interest of the State in certain lands situate in the city of Brooklyn, county of Kings, to William Henry Dinwoodie. Passed June 10, 1873, by a two-third vote.

CHAP. 702. An Act to establish bulkheads and pier lines adjacent to the shores of the port of New York in the county of Kings. Passed June 10, 1873.

CHAP. 703. An Act to authorize the extension of railroad tracks on Buffalo avenue and other streets and avenues in the city of Brooklyn and the county of Kings. Passed June 10, 1873.

CHAP. 704. An Act to authorize the Atlantic Avenue Railroad Company of Brooklyn to extend their tracks through Boerum street and other streets in said city. Passed June 10, 1873.

CHAP. 705. An Act to authorize the construction of a railroad in Butler street and certain other streets in the city of Brooklyn and county of Kings. Passed June 10, 1873.

CHAP. 706. An Act to authorize the drainage of certain low lots in the city of Brooklyn, for the preservation of the public health. Passed June 10, 1873; three-fifths being present.

CHAP. 707. An Act to provide for the laying of certain crosswalks in the Eighth, Tenth and Twenty-second wards, in the city of Brooklyn. Passed June 10, 1873; three-fifths being present.

CHAP. 708. *An Act to authorize a tax of seven-tenths of a mill per dollar of valuation for the payment of the awards of the canal appraisers and expenses attending the same, and of the canal commissioners; to pay certificates on indebtedness on interest now outstanding, and to supply deficiencies in appropriations for new work under act chapter eight hundred and fifty of the Laws of eighteen hundred and seventy-two, and to provide for deficiency in the sinkiug funds under sections one and three of article seven of the Constitution. Passed June* 11, 1873; *three-fifths being present.*

CHAP. 709. An Act to amend an act entitled "An act in relation to the Troy Water-works," passed March nine, eighteen hundred and fifty-five. Passed June 11, 1873; three-fifths being present.

CHAP. 710. *An Act to amend an act entitled "An act to authorize the formation of railroad corporations, and to regulate the same," passed April two, eighteen hundred and fifty. Passed June* 11, 1873.

CHAP. 711. An Act to amend chapter seven hundred and eighty-seven of the Laws of eighteen hundred and seventy-two, authorizing the city of Binghamton to use a portion of the Chenango canal for a public street. Passed June 11, 1873; three-fifths being present.

CHAP. 712. An Act to reimburse the counsel assigned by the court to defend John Stephen Gamelhe for expenses actually incurred in his defense on charge of murder. Passed June 11, 1873; three-fifths being present.

CHAP. 713. *An Act for the improvement of the navigation of the Hudson river, and to make an appropriation therefor. Passed June* 11, 1873; *three-fifths being present.*

CHAP. 714. An Act to authorize the New York Protestant Episcopal Public School to sell a portion of their real estate. Passed June 11, 1873.

CHAP. 715. An Act to authorize the trustees of the North American Mineral Land Company, a corporation formed under the law of February seventeenth, eighteen hundred and forty-eight, and the amendments thereof, to alienate or sell such portion of their real estate or other property as is not needed for the purposes of their incorporation. Passed June 11, 1873.

CHAP. 716. An Act to release the interest of the people of the State of New York in certain real estate to Anna Blenck. Passed June 11, 1873; by a two-third vote.

CHAP. 717. *An Act authorizinng the scle of the State armories at Westport, Ogdensburgh, Canandaigua, Corning and Dunkirk, and the armory lot at Malone. Passed June* 11, 1873; *by a two-third vote.*

CHAP. 718. An Act to legalize the acts of William T. Handlin, a justice of the peace of Wyoming county. Passed June 11, 1873.

CHAP. 719. An Act to confirm the election and acts of James H. Vail, a justice of the peace of the county of Livingston. Passed June 11, 1873; three-fifths being present.

CHAP. 720. *An Act to compel railroad commissioners to give bonds. Passed June* 11, 1873.

CHAP. 721. An Act to authorize the city of Yonkers to issue bonds for the purpose of raising money to construct bridges over water-courses in said city. Passed June 11, 1873; three-fifths being present.

CHAP. 722. *An Act to authorize the electors at elections for town officers to fix by ballot the place for holding town elections in the respective towns of this State. Passed June* 11, 1873; *three-fifths being present.*

CHAP. 723. An Act to legalize the official acts of William Phair as commissioner of deeds. Passed June 11, 1873.

CHAP. 724. An Act in relation to the salary of the messenger in the coroner's office in the city and county of New York. Passed June 11, 1873; three-fifths being present.

CHAP. 725. An Act to incoporate the New York Coal Exchange, and to confer certain powers on it. Passed June 12, 1873.

CHAP. 726. An Act to provide for the more effectual extinguishment of fires in the city of New York. Passed June 12, 1873; three-fifths being present.

CHAP. 727. An Act relative to lands devised by Joseph H. Bininger, deceased. Passed June 12, 1873; three-fifths being present.

CHAP. 728. An Act to incorporate the New York Cotton-press Company. Passed June 12, 1873.

CHAP. 729. An Act to extend the power and authority of the police commissioners and police force of the city of Yonkers over the town of Kingsbridge. Passed June 12, 1873; three fifths being present.

CHAP. 730. An Act to amend an act entitled "An act to revise the charter of the city of Buffalo," passed April twenty-eighth, eighteen hundred and seventy. Passed June 12, 1873; three-fifths being present.

CHAP. 731. An Act to incorporate the New York Real Estate Guaranty Company and to define its powers. Passed June 12, 1873; three-fifths being present.

CHAP. 732. An Act to authorize the trustees of the village of Attica to lay out, open, widen, repair and improve highways, public grounds and parks in said village. Passed June 12, 1873; three-fifths being present.

CHAP. 733. An Act to authorize the town of Liberty, in the county of Sullivan, and the corporate village of Liberty in said county, to loan money and to issue bonds therefor, and to subscribe to the stock of the New York and Oswego Midland Railroad Company. Passed June 12, 1873; three-fifths being present.

CHAP. 734. An Act to release the title of the people of the State of New York in and to certain real estate in the county of Kings to Mary Agnes Foulks. Passed June 12, 1873.

CHAP. 735. An Act to confirm, reduce and levy a certain assessment in the city of Brooklyn. Passed June 12, 1873; three-fifths being present.

CHAP. 736. An Act in relation to the Long Island Schutzen Halle Association, incorporated by chapter forty-five of the Laws of eighteen hundred and seventy, to incorporate the Long Island Schutzen Halle Association, passed March third, eighteen hundred and seventy. Passed June 12, 1873; three-fifths being present.

CHAP. 737. *An Act in relation to the creation and formation of water works companies in towns and villages of the State of New York. Passed June* 12, 1873; *three-fifths being present.*

CHAP. 738. An Act authorizing the construction of a railroad through certain streets in the city of Oswego. Passed June 12, 1873; three-fifths being present.

CHAP. 739. *An Act for the preservation of fish in the River St. Lawrence. Passed June* 12, 1873; *three-fifths being present.*

CHAP. 740. *An Act relating to the preservation of speckled brook trout within the counties of Tioga and Tompkins, State of New York. Passed Jnne* 12, 1873; *three-fifths being present.*

CHAP. 741. An Act to enable the Young Men's Christian Association of Buffalo to take and hold real and personal estate to the amount of two hundred thousand dollars. Passed June 12, 1873; three-fifths being present.

CHAP. 742. An Act to enable Mary McCaffery to take and hold real estate, and to release to her tne interest and title in lands escheated to the State. Passed June 12, 1873.

CHAP. 743. An Act to amend an act entitled "An act to authorize the construction of a street railroad in the city of Auburn." Passed June 12, 1873; three-fifths being present.

CHAP. 744. *An Act authorizing and directing the comptroller of the State of New York to convey certain lands of the Tonawanda reservation, to the trustees of the Tonawanda Reservation Manual Labor School for the purposes of such school, and re-appropriating certain moneys formerly appropriated therefor. Passed June* 13, 1873, *by a two-third vote.*

CHAP. 745. An Act for the relief of George R. Potter. Passed June 13, 1873; three-fifths being present.

CHAP. 746. *An Act making appropriations for the payment of the principal and interest on the canal debt, commencing on the first day of October, eighteen hundred and seventy-three, and to provide for the payment of the debt contracted under section twelve of article seven of the constitution, and further to preserve the credit of the State. Passed June* 13, 1873; *three-fifths being present.*

CHAP. 747. An Act to amend an act entitled "An act to authorize the lighting of public streets and avenues in the town of Fishkill, in the county of Dutchess," passed April nine, eighteen hundred and seventy-three. Passed June 13, 1873; three-fifths being present.

CHAP. 748. An Act to enable Francisco Jose Alvarez Calderon y Kessel, Marquis de Casa Calderon, to take, hold, convey and transmit, by descent or devise, real estate, and to lease to him the interest of this State in certain lands. Passed June 13, 1873, by a two-third vote.

CHAP. 749. An Act to incorporate Kings County Trust Company. Passed June 13, 1873.

CHAP. 750. An Act in relation to assessing the cost of sewers in the city of Brooklyn. Passed June 13, 1873; three-fifths being present.

CHAP. 751. An Act to amend chapter seven hundred and seventy-nine of the Laws of eighteen hundred and seventy, entitled "An act to incoporate the Farmers and Mechanics' Savings Bank of the city of Lockport." Passed June 13, 1873.

CHAP. 752. An Act in relation to the Monroe County Savings Bank. Passed June 13, 1873.

CHAP. 753. An Act authorizing the adjudication and settlement of certain claims, arising out of the defalcation of the late treasurer of Yates county, with this state and the said county. Passed .June 13, 1873; three-fifths being present.

CHAP. 754. An Act to define and restrict the powers of the board of water commissioners of the city of Rochester. Passed June, 13, 1873; three-fifths being present.

CHAP. 755. An Act supplemental to the act entitled "An act to reorganize the local government of the city of New York," passed April thirty, eighteen hundred and seventy-three. Passed June 13, 1873; three-fifths being present.

CHAP 756. An Act to make further provision for the payment of further expenses of the local government of the city of New York. Passed June 13, 1873; three-fifths being present.

CHAP. 757. An Act to amend chapter three hundred and thirty-five of the Laws of eighteen hundred and seventy-three, entitled "An act to reorganize the local government of the city of New York," passed April thirteenth, eighteen hundred and seventy-three. Passed June 13, 1873; three-fifths being present.

CHAP. 758. An Act in relation to the city of New York, Passed June, 13, 1873; three-fifths being present.

CHAP. 759. An Act to provide for the completion of county buildings in the city and county of New York. Passed June 13, 1873; three-fifths being present.

CHAP. 760. *An Act making appropriations for certain expenses of government and supplying deficiencies in former appropriations. Passed June* 13, 1873; *by a two-third vote.*

CHAP. 761. An Act to release to Patrick H. Carey certain real estate in the city of New York, of which his wife Mary Ann Carey died seized. Passed June 13, 1873; by a two-third vote.

CHAP. 762. An Act to release to Caroline A. Lewis all the interest of the people of the State of New York in certan land of which her husband Joseph Lewis died seized. Passed June 13, 1873; by a two-third vote.

CHAP. 763. An Act in relation to supervisors of the county of New York. Passed June 14, 1873; three-fifths being present.

CHAP. 764. An Act to authorize the Old Dominion Steamship Company to increase its number of Directors and for the election thereof. Passed June 14, 1873.

CHAP. 765. *An Act to provide for ways and means for the support of government. Passed June* 14, 1873; *three-fifths being present.*

CHAP. 766. *An Act to authorize a tax of one-half of a mill per dollar of valuation of the year eighteen hundred and seventy-three for the construction of new work upon and extraordinary repairs of the canals of this state. Passed June* 14, 1873; *three-fifths being present.*

CHAP. 767. An Act to amend an act entitled "An act to provide for the collection of taxes in the city of New York," passed April eighteenth, eighteen hundred and forty-three. Passed June 14, 1873; three-fifths being present.

CHAP. 768. An Act to amend an act entitled "An act to incorporate The Oriental Savings Bank of the city of New York," passed May first, eighteen hundred and sixty-nine. Passed June 14, 1873.

CHAP. 769. An Act to incorporate the Bushwick Savings Bank. Passed June 14, 1873; three-fifths being present.

CHAP. 770. An Act to confirm the conveyance of certain real estate to the Andrews Methodist Episcopal Church of Cypress Hills, in the town of New Lots, county of Kings, and to legalize certain acts of said religious society. Passed June 14, 1873; three-fifths being present.

CHAP. 771. An Act to provide for the collection of unpaid assessments which have been laid under an act entitled "An act to provide for widening the Coney Island plank-road in the county of Kings, and for the subsequent management thereof," passed May fifteenth, eighteen hundred and sixty-eight. Passed June 14, 1873; three-fifths being present.

CHAP. 772. An Act to amend an act entitled "An act in relation to the widening of the Coney Island plank-road, in the county of Kings," passed May eleven, eighteen hundred and sixty-nine. Passed June 14, 1873.

CHAP. 773. *An Act to amend the Revised Statutes in relation to laying out public highways. Passed June* 14, 1873; *three-fifths being present.*

CHAP. 774. An Act to incorporate the New York State Retreat for the Blind. Passed June 14, 1873.

CHAP. 775. An Act authorizing the town of Friendship, Allegany county, to issue bonds for the use and benefit of Friendship Academy. Passed June 14, 1873.

CHAP. 776. An Act authorizing the construction of a railroad from the city of Syracuse to the new freight-yard of the New York Central and Hudson River Railroad, in the town of Dewitt, in the county of Onondaga. Passed June 14, 1873.

CHAP. 777. *An Act to amend an act for the suppression of the traffic in and circulation of obscene literature, being chapter seven hundred and forty-seven of the Laws of eighteen hundred and seventy-two. Passed June* 14, 1873; *three-fifths being present.*

CHAP. 778. An Act to change the name of the village of Genesee, in the town of Wellsville, in the county of Allegany, to Wellsville. Passed June 14, 1873.

CHAP. 779. An Act in relation to raising money by taxation in the county of New York, for county purposes. Passed June 14, 1873; three-fifths being present.

CHAP. 780.. An Act to amend chapter four hundred and ninety-two of the Laws of eighteen hundred and seventy-one, entitled "An act relative to courts of civil and criminal jurisdiction in the city of Brooklyn," passed April fourteenth, eighteen hundred and seventy-one. Passed June 14, 1873; three-fifths being present.

CHAP. 781. An Act to amend an act entitled "An act to incorporate the Union Trust Company of New York," passed April twenty-three, eighteen hundred and sixty-four. Passed June 14, 1873.

CHAP. 782. An Act to enable the Syracuse and Chenango Railroad Company to purchase the property and franchises of the Syracuse and Chenango Valley Railroad Company. Passed June 14, 1873.

CHAP. 783. An Act to incorporate the Atlantic Guarantee and Trust Company, Passed June 14, 1873.

CHAP. 784. An Act to amend an act, entitled "An act to incorporate the Industrial Exhibition Company, and to authorize said company to purchase real estate and erect thereon a building or buildings, which shall be used as an industrial exhibition," passed April twenty-first, eighteen hundred and seventy, and the act amendatory thereof; and to authorize the mayor, aldermen and commonalty of the city of New York to make a loan to the said company. Passed June 18, 1873; three-fifths being present.

CHAP. 785. *An Act in relation to further testing a steam dredge for which appropriations were made by chapter seven hundred and sixty-seven, Laws of eighteen hundred and seventy; and chapter seven hundred and fifteen, Laws of eighteen hundred and seventy-one. Passed June* 18, 1873; *three-fifths being present.*

CHAP. 786. An Act to provide for the making and completion of certain highways in the county of Westchester. Passed June 18, 1873; three-fifths being present.

CHAP. 787. An Act to amend chapter eight hundred and sixty-three of the Laws of eighteen hundred and sixty-seven, entitled "An Act to construct a bridge over Tonawanda creek, in the village of Tonawanda, in the counties of Erie and Niagara, and to provide means therefor." Passed June 18, 1873; three-fifths being present.

CHAP. 788. An Act to grant additional privileges to the Broadway Railroad Company, of Brooklyn. Passed June 18, 1873.

CHAP. 789. An Act to provide for the collection of the unpaid assessments which have been laid under an act entitled "An act to lay out and improve a public highway or avenue from Prospect Park, in the city of Brooklyn, toward Coney Island, in the county of Kings," passed May eleventh, eighteen hundred and sixty-nine. Passed June 18, 1873; three-fifths being present.

CHAP. 790. An Act to repeal section four of an act entitled "An act to amend the several acts in relation to the city of Rochester," passed May twentieth, eighteen hundred and seventy-two. Passed June 18, 1873; three-fifths being present.

CHAP. 791. An Act to amend an act passed April twenty-four, eighteen hundred and sixty-eight, entitled "An act for the further extension of Prospect Park in the city of Brooklyn." Passed June 18, 1873; three-fifths being present.

CHAP. 792. An Act to incorporate the East German Conference of the Methodist Episcopal Church. Passed June 18, 1873; three-fifths being present.

CHAP. 793. An Act to authorize the Bruynswick Rural Cemetery Association in the county of Ulster, to sell and convey a portion of their real estate. Passed June 18, 1873.

CHAP. 794. An Act supplemental to an act entitled "An act to provide for the construction of a main and lateral drain or sewer in Navy street, Johnson street and Hudson avenue, and other streets and avenues in the city of Brooklyn," passed April sixth, eighteen hundred and seventy-one. Passed June 18, 1873; three-fifths being present.

CHAP. 795. An Act to amend "An act passed April twenty-third, eighteen hundred and seventy, entitled 'An act to authorize the improvement and sale of certain portions of Prospect Park in the city of Brooklyn.'" Passed June 18, 1873; three-fifths being present.

CHAP. 796. An Act to incorporate the Forest Lake Villa Park Association. Passed June 18, 1873.

CHAP. 797. An Act to amend an act entitled "An act to incorporate the Inebriate Home for Kings county," passed May ninth, eighteen hundred and sixty-seven, and the acts amendatory thereof, passed April thirtieth, eighteen hundred and sixty-eight, and April fifteenth, eighteen hundred and seventy-one. Passed June 18, 1873; three-fifths being present.

CHAP. 798. *An Act dividing the state into congressional districts. Passed June* 18, 1873.

CHAP. 799. An Act to incorporate the Wine and Spirit Traders Society of the United States. Passed June 18, 1873.

CHAP. 800. An Act to authorize the Geneva and Ithaca Railroad Company to extend their road. Passed June 18, 1873.

CHAP. 801. An Act to amend an act entitled "An act to incorporate the New York Underground Telegraph Company," passed May sixteenth, eighteen hundred and seventy-three. Passed June 18, 1873.

CHAP. 802. An Act to release the interest of the people of the State of New York in certain real estate to Nathaniel Edmonds. Passed June 18, 1873, by a two-third vote.

CHAP. 803. An Act to enable Cornelia de G. La Ray Chaumont, Virginie de G. Levin, Maria Caroline de G. de Laureneel, Anna H. Millet, Louisa L. Bredif and Amedee de Gouvello to take, hold and convey real estate. Passed June 18, 1873.

CHAP. 804. An Act to legalize the official acts and proceedings of Hiram F. Birge, deceased, a justice of the peace of the town of Geneseo, in the county of Livingston, at the time of his decease. Passed June 18, 1873; three-fifths being present.

CHAP. 805. An Act to incorporate the New York College of Anæsthesia. Passed June 18, 1873.

CHAP. 806. An Act in relation to the erection of the court-house in third judicial district of the city of New York. Passed June 18, 1873; three-fifths being present.

CHAP. 807. An Act concerning notaries public in the counties of Kings, Queens, Richmond, Westchester and Rockland, and in the city and county of New York, and authorizing them to exercise the functions of their office therein. Passed June 18, 1873.

CHAP. 808. An Act to revise and amend an act entitled "An act to construct a road from Carthage, in Jefferson county, to Lake Champlain, in the county of Essex," passed April fourteen, eighteen hundred and forty-one. Passed June 18, 1873; three-fifths being present.

CHAP. 809. *An Act to amend chapter three hundred and twenty-seven of the laws of eighteen hundred and forty-six, entitled "An act to equalize taxation," passed May thirteenth, eighteen hundred and forty-six. Passed June* 18, 1873; *three-fifths being present.*

CHAP. 810. An Act to amend an act entitled "An act to revise and consolidate the laws in relation to the village of Whitehall," passed March sixteenth, eighteen hundred and fifty, and other acts amendatory thereof. Passed June 18, 1873; three-fifths being present.

CHAP. 811. An Act to legalize the acts of Thomas H. Horton as notary public. Passed June 18, 1873.

CHAP. 812. An Act to extend the powers of the Troy and Lansingburgh Railroad Company. Passed June 19, 1873.

CHAP. 813. An Act to amend an act entitled "An act to amend an act to incorporate the city of Troy," passed April twelfth, eighteen hundred and sixteen, and the several acts amendatory thereto, and also to amend other acts relating to the city of Troy, passed March twenty-third, eighteen hundred and seventy-two. Passed June 19, 1873; three-fifths being present.

CHAP. 814. *An Act to extend the operation and effect of the act passed February seventeen, eighteen hundred and forty-eight, entitled "An act to authorize the formation of corporations for manufacturing, mining, mechanical or chemical purposes." Passed June 19, 1873; three-fifths being present.*

CHAP. 815. An Act entitled "An act to amend chapter six hundred and forty-three of the Laws of eighteen hundred and seventy-two, entitled 'An act to empower the levying of a tax on Union School District Number One, in the town of Clarence, county of Erie, for the purpose of creating a permanent fund for the employment of teachers, and to regulate the investment and management of said fund; also, to create the office of loan commissioner for said district, and to provide for the exemption of said district from taxes for the purpose of teachers' wages,' passed May eleven, eighteen hundred and seventy-two." Passed June 19, 1873; three-fifths being present.

CHAP. 816. An Act authorizing the village of Fort Plain to levy taxes. Passed June 23, 1873; three-fifths being present.

CHAP. 817. An Act to provide for the support of the poor in the county of Jefferson. Passed June 23, 1873; three-fifths being present.

CHAP. 818. An Act to enable the New York Western Midland Railroad Company to construct its road through Tompkins county. Passed June 23, 1873.

CHAP. 819. An Act to authorize Frances Upton Morris Vence to change her name to Frances Upton Morris. Passed June 23, 1873.

CHAP. 820. *An Act to amend an act entitled "An act to suppress intemperance, and to regulate the sale of intoxicating liquors," passed April sixteen, eighteen hundred and fifty-seven. Passed June 23, 1873; three-fifths being present.*

CHAP. 821. *An Act to amend an act entitled "An act to amend an act entitled 'An act to amend an act entitled An act for the benefit of married women in insuring the lives of their husbands,' passed April fourteen, eighteen hundred and fifty-eight, passed April eighteen, eighteen hundred and seventy." Passed June 23, 1873; three-fifths being present.*

CHAP. 822. An Act to incorporate "The Arcadian Club" of the city of New York. Passed June 23, 1873.

CHAP. 823. An Act to amend an act entitled "An act in relation to elections in the city and county of New York, and to provide for ascertaining, by proper proofs, the citizens who shall be entitled to the right of suffrage thereat," passed May fourteen, eighteen hundred and seventy-two. Passed June 23, 1873; three-fifths being present.

CHAP. 824. *An Act to amend section nineteen of chapter five hundred and seventy of the Laws of eighteen hundred and seventy-two, entitled "An act to ascertain by proper proofs the citizens who shall be entitled to the right of suffrage in the State of New York, except in the city and county of New York and the city of Brooklyn, and to repeal chapter five hundred and seventy-two of the Laws of eighteen hundred and seventy-one, entitled 'An act to amend an act entitled an act in relation to elections in the city and county of New York.'" Passed June 23, 1873; three-fifths being present.*

CHAP. 825. An Act to authorize the laying of rails and to run cars thereon for the transportation of passengers in certain streets and avenues in the upper part of the city of New York. Passed June 24, 1873; three-fifths being present.

CHAP. 826. An Act to repeal the charter of the Manhattan Marble Company of Rutland, Vermont. Passed June 24, 1873; three-fifths being present.

CHAP. 827. An Act to amend an act entitled "An act for the construction of a work-house in the county of Monroe," passed May twenty-seventh, eighteen hundred and fifty-three. Passed June 25, 1873; three-fifths being present.

CHAP. 828. An Act to authorize the purchase of a farm for the town poor of the town of Dix, in the county of Schuyler. Passed June 25, 1873; three-fifths being present.

CHAP. 829. An Act to empower the Board of Water Commissioners of the city of Buffalo, together with the common council of said city to establish or designate free public hydrants in said city, and providing for the appointment of water commissioners in said city. Passed June 25, 1873; three-fifths being present.

CHAP. 830. *An Act to legalize the adoption of minor children by adult persons. Passed June 25, 1873.*

CHAP. 831. An Act to allow the persons associated as The Chi Psi Society to incorporate under chapter three hundred and nineteen of the Laws of eighteen hundred and forty-eight, and to take and hold real and personal estate. Passed June 25, 1873.

CHAP. 832. An Act to incorporate the Central Trust Company of New York. Passed June 25, 1873.

CHAP. 833. *An Act to regulate the fees of coroners. Passed June 25*, 1873; *three-fifths being present.*

CHAP. 834. An Act to authorize the Utica, Ithaca and Elmira Railroad Company to extend their road, and for other purposes. Passed June 26, 1873.

CHAP. 835. An Act to authorize the Binghamton, Dushore and Williamsport Railroad Company to lay a railroad track on the tow-path of that part of the Chenango canal extension which lies south of the Susquehanna river. Passed June 26, 1873; three-fifths being present.

CHAP. 836. An Act to authorize and empower the trustees of Yates Union Free School District Number Two of the town of Sullivan, to sell and convey a portion of the school site of said district. Passed June 26, 1873; three-fifths being present.

CHAP. 837. An Act to amend chapter eight hundred and eighty-five, Laws of eighteen hundred and seventy-two, entitled "An act to incorporate the Gilbert Elevated Railroad Company, and to provide a feasible, safe and speedy system of transit through the city of New York," passed June seventeen, eighteen hundred and seventy-two. Passed June 26, 1873.

CHAP. 838. An Act to authorize the New York and Oswego Midland Railroad Company to increase its capital stock, to extend its road and increase the number of its board of directors. Passed June 26, 1873; three-fifths being present.

CHAP. 839. An Act to authorize the board of health of the health department of the city of New York to make a contract to remove the contents of sinks and privies in said city. Passed June 26, 1873; three-fifths being present.

CHAP. 840. An Act to incorporate "The Manhattan Loan and Trust Company" of the city of New York. Passed June 26, 1873.

CHAP. 841. An Act to authorize the construction of a street railroad from the village of Almond, in Allegany county, to the village of Hornellsville, in the county of Steuben. Passed June 27, 1873.

CHAP. 842. An Act to amend an act entitled "An act to establish a board of health and of vital statistics in the county of Richmond, and to define its powers and duties," passed April second, eighteen hundred and seventy-two. Passed June 27, 1873; three-fifths being present.

CHAP. 843. An Act to repeal the charter of the Napanock and Deming Plank-road Company. Passed June 27, 1873; three-fifths being present.

CHAP. 844. An Act to incorporate the Saratoga Safe Deposit and Trust Company. Passed June 27, 1873; three-fifths being present.

CHAP. 845. An Act to amend an act entitled "An act to incorporate the Fire-proof Warehousing Company," passed May ninth, eighteen hundred and sixty-eight, as amended by an act entitled "An act to amend an act entitled 'An act to incorporate the Fire-proof Warehousing Company,' passed March thirtieth, eighteen hundred and seventy." Passed June 27, 1873; three-fifths being present.

CHAP. 846. An Act to enable the trustees of the Trinity Methodist Episcopal Church to assign and convey certain real estate to the New York City Church-Extension and Missionary Society of the Methodist Episcopal Church. Passed June 27, 1873.

CHAP. 847. An Act for the relief of John McCarthy. Passed June 27, 1873; three-fifths being present.

CHAP. 848. An Act to incorporate the Cotton and Produce Exchange Clearing-house Association of the city of New York. Passed June 26, 1873.

CHAP. 849. *An Act to amend chapter* 623 *of the laws of eighteen hundred and sixty-eight, entitled "An act to amend an act entitled 'An act to amend an act entitled 'An act to provide for the incorporation of life and health insurance companies, and in relation to agencies of such companies,' passed June twenty-four, eighteen hundred and fifty-three;' passed April twenty-four, eighteen hundred and sixty-six." Passed June* 28, 1873.

CHAP. 850. An Act in relation to the powers and duties of the department of public parks of the city of New York. Passed June 28, 1873; three-fifths being present.

CHAP. 851. *An Act to amend an act entitled "An act to provide for the incorporation of fire insurance companies, passed June twenty-five, eighteen hundred and fifty-three." Passed June 28, 1873; three-fifths being present.*

CHAP. 852. An Act to create the West-side infirmary for diseases of the eye and throat in the city of New York. Passed June 28, 1873; three-fifths being present.

CHAP. 853. An Act to annex to the city of Brooklyn the town of New Lots, and to provide for its government and control in said city. Passed June 28, 1873; three-fifths being present.

CHAP. 854. An Act to confirm, reduce and levy certain assessments on the city of Brooklyn. Passed June 28, 1873; three-fifths being present.

CHAP. 855. An Act to provide for the relaying, reflagging or repairing of sidewalks in the city of Brooklyn. Passed June 28, 1873; three-fifths being present.

CHAP. 856. An Act in relation to the pay of the officers and members of the fire department of the city of Brooklyn. Passed June 28, 1873; three-fifths being present.

CHAP. 857. An Act in relation to the keeping open of certain public offices in the county of Kings. Passed June 28, 1873.

CHAP. 858. An Act to provide for the improvement of Park avenue from Clinton avenue to Broadway, in the city of Brooklyn, and to repeal an act heretofore passed for the improvement of Park avenue from Clinton avenue to Broadway, and from Hudson avenue to Bridge street, in the city of Brooklyn. Passed June 28, 1873; three-fifths being present.

CHAP. 859. An Act to determine a plan of grades for certain streets and avenues in the town of New Utrecht. Passed June 28, 1873; three-fifths being present.

CHAP. 860. An Act to open a square to be known as Putnam square in the city of Brooklyn, and to improve the square at the junction of Underhill and Washington avenues, with Atlantic avenue and Pacific street in said city, the same to be known as Washington square. Passed June 28, 1873; three-fifths being present.

CHAP. 861. An Act to provide for establishing a municipal government in the county of Kings, and consolidating the city of Brooklyn and the towns of New Lots, Flatbush, Flatlands, New Utrecht and Gravesend under the same. Passed June 28, 1873; three-fifths being present.

CHAP. 862. An Act to provide means for the payment of certain claims against the city of Brooklyn. Passed June 28, 1873; three-fifths being present.

CHAP. 863. An Act to amend the charter of the city of Brooklyn, and the various amendments thereof. Passed June 28, 1873; three-fifths being present.

CHAP. 864. An Act to authorize the opening, grading and paving of Nassau avenue, and certain other streets in the city of Brooklyn, and also to close a portion of Hooper street, in said city. Passed June 28, 1873; three-fifths being present.

CHAP. 865. An Act to extend the distribution of Croton water through the city of New York, and to lay the necessary mains therefor, and to deliver it at higher elevations. Passed June 28, 1873; three-fifths being present.

CHAP. 866. An Act exempting from taxation real estate owned by the House of Rest for Consumptives. Passed June 28, 1873; three-fifths being present.

CHAP. 867. An Act to amend section ten of chapter seven hundred and thirty-nine of the Laws of eighteen hundred and fifty-seven, entitled "An act to authorize the formation of town insurance companies," passed April seventeen, eighteen hundred and fifty-seven, so far as the same may apply to the Claverack Fire Insurance Company. Passed June 28, 1873.

CHAP. 868. An Act for the relief of the Home for Fallen and Friendless Girls in the city of New York. Passed June 28, 1873; three-fifths being present.

CHAP. 869. An Act for the relief of the Woman's Hospital of the State of New York. Passed June 28, 1873; three-fifths being present.

CHAP. 870. *An Act to appropriate two thousand five hundred dollars for the removal of obstructions from and to improve the navigation of Indian river. Passed June 28, 1873; three-fifths being present.*

CHAP. 871. An Act to authorize the consolidation of the Hahnemann Hospital and the New York Medical College and Hospital for Women. Passed June 28, 1873.

CHAP. 872. An Act to divide the town of Seneca and to erect the town of Geneva, in the county of Ontario, passed by the board of supervisors of the county of Ontario the eleventh day of October, eighteen hundred and seventy-two; two-thirds of all the members elected to said board voting in favor thereof.

CHAP. 873. An Act for the division of the town of Yonkers by the erection of a new town from the southerly part thereof.

CHAP. 874. An Act to divide the town of Cornwall, Orange county, into two towns, by the board of supervisors of said county. Passed December 3, 1872.

CONCURRENT RESOLUTIONS.

Relative to Reduction of Canal Tolls.
Passed February 14, 1873.

Appointing Commission to Examine Obstructions in Seneca River.
Passed April 29, 1873.

Directing Superintendent of Insurance Department to Expunge a Portion of the Report for 1872.
Passed April 30, 1873.

Appointing a Select Committee to meet the Committee of United States Senate on Transportation Routes.
Passed May 6, 1873.

Relative to Purchase of Watervliet Arsenal.
Passed May 13, 1873.

For Printing the Game Laws.
Passed May 16, 1873.

Proposing Amendment to Article Seven of the Constitution.
Passed May 21, 1873.

Proposing Amendment to Article 12 of the Constitution.
Passed May 22, 1873.

Proposing Amendment to Article 6 of the Constitution.
Passed May 22, 1873.

Proposing Amendment to Article 8 of the Constitution.
Passed May 22, 1873.

Proposing Amendment to Article 10 of the Constitution.
Passed May 22, 1873.

Proposing Amendment to Article 2 of the Constitution.
Passed May 22, 1873.

Providing for Portrait of President Lincoln.
Passed May 26, 1873.

Proposing Amendment to the Constitution as to Funding the Canal and General Fund Debts.
Passed May 28, 1873.

Proposing Amendment to Article 3 of the Constitution.
Passed May 29, 1873.

Proposing Amendment to Article 4 of the Constitution.
Passed May 29, 1873.

Proposing Amendment to Article 5 of the Constitution.
Passed May 29, 1873.

Proposing two new Articles to Constitution.
Passed May 29, 1873.

Directing an inquiry into the Causes of the increase of Crime, Pauperism and Insanity.
Passed May 29, 1873.

As to publication of Session Laws.
Passed January 31, 1873.

As to College Land Grants.
Passed May 20, 1873.

NAMES CHANGED.

In Erie County — Charles Thom, Jr., to Charles Thompson. November 1, 1872.
George R. Yaw to George Russell Potter. August 20, 1872.
Charlotte Bliss Yaw to Charlotte Bliss Potter. August 31, 1872.
Edward Walden Yaw to Edward Walden Potter. October 1, 1872.
Russell Ambrose Yaw to Russell Ambrose Potter. October 1, 1872.

In Genesee County — Florence Dombey Carpenter to Florence Carpenter Stanley. February 20, 1872.
Ellen D. Doty to Ellen D. Prentice. February 24, 1872.
Mary E. Doty to Mary E. Prentice. February 24, 1872.
Daisy M. Doty to Daisy M. Prentice. February 24, 1872.

In Onondaga County — Ristoria L. Thomas to Ristoria L. West.
Minnie E. Thomas to Minnie E. West.

In St. Lawrence County — Willis Goff to Willis Bristod. May 24, 1873.

In Albany County — The Corning Iron Company to The Jagger Iron Company. July 2, 1873.

In Onondaga County — Sweet, Barnes & Company to George Barnes & Company. June, 1873.

In New York County — Marcus Witowski to Marcus Witmark. February 11, 1872.
Simon Witowski to Simon Witmark. February 11, 1872.
Henry Schlageter to Henry Denner. March 1, 1872.
Oliver Byron Doud to Oliver Doud Byron. March 1, 1872.
Charles Tyler Lasure to Charles Tyler Gage. March 27, 1872.
Claus Docher to Charles Claus Docher. March 31, 1872.
Julia Sheehan to Julia Bradford. April 15, 1872.
August Schimmel to August Shimmel. April 3, 1872.
Charles J. Rosenthal to Charles J. Tilford. April 12, 1872.
John Malony to John Allan Malony. June 1, 1872.
Lucinda Morgan Ely to Lucinda Morgan. June 1, 1872.
Ernest Heber Smith to Ernest Hebersmith. June 2, 1872.
Francis Herbert Palmer to Herbert Francis Palmer. July 31, 1872.
Jacob Jones to Jacob John. September 1, 1872.
Frank Millington Jones to Frank Millington John.
Edward Morgan Jones to Edward Morgan John.
Frederick Jones to Frederick John.
Charles Henry Jones to Charles Frederick John.
Margaret Mercer Jones to Margaret Mercer John. September 14, 1872.

In Kings County — Otto F. H. Sahn to Herman F. Zahn. April 19, 1872.
Horatio Simms to Horatio Ogden. June 29, 1872.
Ellen Victoria Lindblad to Carrie Alice Crandell. October 13, 1872.
Henry Maynard Smith to Henry Smith Munroe.
Charles Frederick Nordstrom to Charles Frederick Norton. October 10, 1872.
Isaac Walter Powers to Henry Walter Bowers. December 2, 1872.
Charles Brown to Conrad Agatius Huet.
Katie Brown to Katie Huet. November 18, 1872.

GENERAL STATUTES

OF THE

STATE OF NEW YORK

PASSED AT THE

96TH SESSION, 1873.

CHAP. 3.

AN ACT extending the term of the commission of appeals pursuant to the amendment of the constitution, and fixing their salaries.

PASSED January 30, 1873; three-fifths being present.

The People of the State of New York, represented in Senate and Assembly, do enact as follows:

SECTION 1. The term of service of the commissioners of appeals is extended to the first day of July, eighteen hundred and seventy-five, unless the causes which have been or may be ordered to be heard by the said commissioners shall be sooner determined, and thereupon the said term shall cease. Terms of service extended.

§ 2. The commissioners of appeals shall receive the same salary and allowances as are given by law to the associate judges of the court of appeals. Salary.

§ 3. This act shall take effect immediately.

CHAP. 5.

AN ACT to authorize the extension of the time for the collection of taxes in the several towns of the State.

PASSED January 31, 1873; three-fifths being present.

The People of the State of New York, represented in Senate and Assembly, do enact as follows:

SECTION 1. If any collector of taxes in any town of this State shall, within fifteen days after the passage of this act, Collector to renew official bond. pay over all moneys collected by him, and shall renew his bond as is herein provided, the time for the collection of taxes and for making return thereof by him, shall be, as is herein provided, extended to a day not later than the fifteenth day of March, eighteen hundred and seventy-three. Such bond shall be renewed with such sureties as in any town shall be approved by the supervisor thereof, or, in case of his inability to act, by the town clerk thereof. The penalty thereof in any case shall be double the amount of the taxes in that case remaining uncollected. The bond shall be approved in writing and filed as required by law, and have all the effect of a collector's bond. A copy of the bond and the approval thereof shall, within fifteen days after the passage of this act, be delivered to the county treasurer of the county in which is said town. The time, not later than the said fifteenth day of March, eighteen hundred and seventy-three, to which the collection of said taxes and the making returns thereof may be extended, shall in any town be fixed and limited in writing, and indorsed on the warrant of the collector by the supervisor of the town, or, in case of his inability to act by the town clerk thereof.

How renewed.

How approved.

Limit of extension.

Secretary of State to distribute copies. § 2. It shall be the duty of the secretary of State at once, after the passage of this act, to cause it to be printed upon slips of paper, and to deliver to each county treasurer a sufficient number thereof to supply one copy to each collector of taxes in said county; and it shall be the duty of said county treasurer to deliver one copy thereof to each collector of taxes in his county.

Not to extend to cities. § 3. This act shall not extend to any of the cities of this State.

§ 4. This act shall take effect immediately.

CHAP. 6.

AN ACT to amend an act entitled "An act to provide for a commission to propose amendments to the constitution."

PASSED February 5, 1873; three-fifths being present.

The People of the State of New York, represented in Senate and Assembly, do enact as follows:

SECTION 1. Section one of chapter eight hundred and eighty-four of the laws of eighteen hundred and seventy-two, entitled "An act to provide for a commission to propose amendments to the constitution," is hereby amended so as to read as follows:

Commissioners to propose amendments to constitution to be appointed. § 1. The governor, by and with the advice and consent of the senate, shall designate thirty-two persons, four from each judicial district, who shall constitute a commission for the purpose of proposing to the legislature, at its next session, amendments to the constitution.

§ 2. This act shall take effect immediately.

Ante, p. 510.

CHAP. 9.

AN ACT in relation to the calendar of the commission of appeals, authorizing the transfer of causes from the calendar of the court of appeals and the disposition of causes on the calendar of the commission of appeals.

PASSED February 7, 1873; three-fifths being present.

The People of the State of New York, represented in Senate and Assembly, do enact as follows:

SECTION 1. All the causes pending in the court of appeals on the first day of January, eighteen hundred and sixty-nine, not on the printed calendar of the commission of appeals for eighteen hundred and seventy-three, and not heretofore disposed of by the commissioners, may be put upon the calendar by their order; and, from time to time, such other causes as, in pursuance of section twenty-eight of the sixth article of the constitution, have been or may be ordered to be heard and determined by said commissioners, may be added to the said calendar without any further notice of hearing; and all such causes, with those now upon the calendar, shall stand for hearing in their order accordingly, and subject to correction by said commissioners.

Causes pending Jan. 1, 1869 may be put on calendar by order.

Causes may be added to calendar.

§ 2. When any such cause shall be called for argument, and no other disposition shall be made thereof at the time of the call, it shall stand dismissed without costs; and an order shall be entered accordingly, which shall be absolute, unless, on the first day of the next term, the cause be submitted by one or more of the parties, on fifteen days' notice to the other parties at the last term for arguments to be held by the commissioners.

When to stand dismissed.

§ 3. This act shall take effect immediately.

CHAP. 12.

AN ACT to authorize the boards of supervisors of the several counties of the state to levy a tax to pay the three and one-half mills tax for canals and general deficiences, and to authorize a loan for that purpose, and to ratify the acts of any board of supervisors in issuing bonds to meet said tax or in extending any loan to enable said boards of supervisors to pay said tax.

PASSED February 10, 1873; three-fifths being present.

The People of the State of New York, represented in Senate and Assembly, do enact as follows:

SECTION 1. The board of supervisors of any county in this state that have not levied the three and one-half mills tax

Boards of supervisors may

levy tax at special meeting. ordered to be levied by the comptroller of the state for canals and general fund deficiencies, are hereby authorized, in their discretion, to levy the same at a special meeting, called for that purpose, in the manner now provided by law for calling special meetings, and all laws relating to the levying and collecting of taxes now in force shall apply to the levying and collecting of the taxes authorized to be levied by this act.

§ 2. The said boards of supervisors are hereby authorized, in their discretion, to issue the bonds of their respective counties, bearing not more than seven per cent interest per annum, and payable at such time or times, not later than March first, one thousand eight hundred and ninety-three, as said boards of supervisors shall designate, sufficient to pay the tax mentioned in the first section of this act; and any bonds authorized by any board of supervisors in pursuance of this act shall be a lawful debt against the county authorizing such loan, and it shall be the duty of the board of supervisors of any county issuing bonds under this act to levy a tax to pay such bonds and the interest thereon as they shall become due.

May issue bonds.

When to be made payable.

Tax to pay bonds.

§ 3. The resolutions of the board of supervisors of any county in this state already passed authorizing the issue of bonds to pay the tax mentioned in the first section of this act, or any resolutions to extend the time of payment of any bonds now due or to become due, with the consent of the holders of such bonds and for the application of any money raised by tax to pay such bonds, for the purpose of paying such tax, are hereby ratified and confirmed.

Resolutions heretofore passed legalized.

§ 4. All bonds issued under and pursuant to this act shall be signed by the chairman and clerk of the board of supervisors, and countersigned by the county treasurer of the county at the time they are issued; such bonds shall be in sums of not less than one hundred nor more than one thousand dollars each, and shall not be disposed of by such county treasurer for less than the par value thereof.

Bonds, how issued.

Not to be sold for less than par

§ 5. This act shall take effect immediately.

CHAP. 18.

AN ACT to authorize the commissioners of quarantine to purchase a steamboat for the use of the quarantine establishment of the port of New York, and making an appropriation therefor.

PASSED February 18, 1878; three-fifths being present.

The People of the State of New York, represented in Senate and Assembly, do enact as follows:

SECTION 1. The commissioners of the quarantine, by and with the approval and under the direction of the health officer of the port of New York, are hereby authorized to purchase or procure a steamboat for the use of the quarantine establishment of the port of New York, to take the place of the steamboat Andrew Fletcher, lately destroyed by fire.

§ 2. The commissioners of the quarantine are hereby authorized and directed to use the wreck or remains of the Andrew Fletcher in the procuring or construction of the steamboat hereby authorized to be procured or purchased for the purpose herein specified, or to convert the same into money by sale, or otherwise, and the proceeds of such disposition or sale shall be paid into the treasury of the state. Wreck of former boat disposed of.

§ 3. The sum of thirty thousand dollars, or so much thereof as may be necessary, is hereby appropriated for the purpose of procuring a steamboat as herein provided, and for the purpose herein designated, and the treasurer is hereby authorized to pay, on the warrant of the comptroller, the said sum of thirty thousand dollars, or so much thereof as is necessary, as herein provided, to the commissioners of quarantine of the port of New York; but the comptroller shall not draw his warrant unless proper vouchers are produced to him, nor unless he is furnished with satisfactory proof that a suitable and proper steamboat for the purposes herein contemplated has been procured or purchased, and is ready for use. Appropriation.

§ 4. This act shall take effect immediately.

CHAP. 19.

AN ACT to punish the careless use of fire-arms.

PASSED February 19, 1873; three-fifths being present.

The People of the State of New York, represented in Senate and Assembly, do enact as follows:

SECTION 1. Any person who shall intentionally, without malice, point or aim any fire-arms at or toward any other person, shall be guilty of a misdemeanor, and shall be subject to a fine of not more than fifty dollars, and not less than five. To point fire-arms at a person a misdemeanor.

§ 2. Any person who shall discharge, without injury to any other person, any fire-arms, while intentionally, without malice, aimed at or toward any person, shall be deemed guilty of a misdemeanor, and shall be liable to a fine of not more than one hundred dollars, or imprisonment in the county jail not to exceed one year, or both, at the discretion of the court. Discharge of, without injury, how punished.

§ 3. Any person who shall maim or injure any other person by the discharge of any fire-arm pointed or aimed intentionally, but without malice, at any such person, shall be deemed guilty of a misdemeanor, and shall be punished by a fine of not less than fifty dollars, or imprisonment in the county jail for a period of not more than two years. In case of injury.

§ 4. Any person maimed or wounded by the discharge of any fire-arms as aforesaid, or the heirs or representatives of any person who may be killed by such discharge, may have Injured party may recover damages.

an action against the party offending to recover damages therefor.

Restrictions. § 5. This act shall not apply to any case where fire-arms shall be used in self-defense, or in the discharge of official duty, or any case of justifiable homicide.

§ 6. This act shall take effect immediately.

CHAP. 25.

AN ACT to amend sections eleven and thirteen of article one, title one, chapter eight, part two of the Revised Statutes, entitled "Of marriage and of the solemnization and proof thereof."

PASSED February 22, 1878; three-fifths being present.

The People of the State of New York, represented in Senate and Assembly, do enact as follows:

SECTION 1. Section eleven of article one of title one of chapter eight of part two of the Revised Statutes is hereby amended so as to read as follows:

Duty of minister or magistrate where parties are not personally known to him. § 11. If either of the parties, between whom the marriage is to be solemnized, shall not be personally known to him, the minister or magistrate shall ascertain from the respective parties their right to contract marriage, and, for that purpose, he may examine the parties, or either of them, or any other person under oath, which he is hereby authorized to administer, which examination shall be reduced to writing and subscribed by the parties; and either of the respective parties making a false statement under this oath shall be deemed guilty of willful and corrupt perjury, and shall be liable therefor.

§ 2. The first subdivision of section thirteen of article one, title one of chapter eight of part two of the Revised Statutes is hereby amended so as to read as follows:

1. The names and places of residence of the parties married, and that they were known to such minister or magistrate, or were satisfactorily proved, by the oath of the parties themselves or a person known to him, that they were the persons described in such certificate, and that they were of sufficient age to contract marriage.

§ 3. This act shall take effect immediately.

Ante, vol. 2, p. 145.

CHAP. 46.

AN ACT to provide for the laying out, improvement and preservation of burial grounds in the several towns of the state.

PASSED March 5, 1873; three-fifths being present.

The People of the State of New York, represented in Senate and Assembly, do enact as follows:

Electors may choose trustees.

SECTION 1. The electors of each town in the state of New York shall have power, at any annual town meeting to choose three or five persons to act as a board of trustees of any burying ground or burying grounds, within the limits of and belonging to the town, as said electors may designate; and to authorize and direct the supervisor of the town to convey by deed to the said board of trustees and their successors in office, for the purposes hereinafter mentioned, the lands already composing such ground or grounds, and also any other lands that may be hereafter acquired for the purpose of enlarging such ground or grounds. The said electors shall also have the power, as aforesaid, to fill any vacancies that may occur in the said board of trustees.

Trustees to lay out grounds and sell lots.

§ 2. The said board of trustees shall lay out into burial lots such ground or grounds, conveyed to them as aforesaid, and likewise any lands that may thereafter be conveyed to them, for the purpose of enlarging such ground or grounds aforesaid; and within one year after the said conveyance to them they shall cause to be recorded in the office of the clerk of the county in which they reside, a plot or plots of the ground or grounds so laid out by them, as aforesaid, which shall clearly indicate the number and location of the several lots, which plot or plots shall be duly certified to under the hands and seals of the chairman and secretary of the board, and acknowledged before an officer authorized to take proof and acknowledgment of deeds. They shall designate and set aside certain lots which shall be free for the interment of the remains of indigent persons, deceased, and shall sell and convey, by direction of a majority of said board, under the hands and seals of its chairman and secretary, burial lots on such terms as may be agreed upon between the parties, and expend the moneys realized from such in improving and preserving the particular burial ground from the sale of whose lots the moneys were received.

Lots to be set aside for free interments.

Not to effect certain burial grounds, etc.

§ 3. Nothing contained in this act shall affect any rural cemetery association, nor any burying ground for which a special act of the legislature has made provisions inconsistent with the provisions of this act.

§ 4. This act shall take effect immediately.

CHAP. 63.

AN ACT to amend the general highway laws of the State of New York.

PASSED March 10, 1873; three-fifths being present.

The People of the State of New York, represented in Senate and Assembly, do enact as follows:

Commissioners may allow water pipes to be laid in highway.

SECTION 1. The commissioners of highways of the several towns of this State are hereby authorized and empowered, upon application in writing of any resident of their district, to permit such applicant to lay and maintain water pipes in the earth within the bounds of the public highway, for the purpose of supplying any dwelling or farm premises with water for household or farming purposes, provided that such laying and maintaining of water pipes shall in no manner interrupt or interfere with the public travel upon such highway, and that such person laying or maintaining such pipes shall replace all earth removed, and leave the highway in all respects in as good condition as before the laying of such pipe. Provided further, that no such pipe shall be laid under the traveled part of such highway, except to cross the same.

Permission to be filed.

§ 2. The permission to lay such water pipes shall be in writing, and shall describe the portion of the highway in which such pipes are to be laid, and such permission shall be signed by a majority of the commissioners of such town, and shall be filed by such applicant in the office of the town clerk of the town in which such highway is situated.

§ 3. This act shall take effect immediately.

CHAP. 69.

AN ACT requiring commissioners of highways to give notice of the discontinuance of public highways.

PASSED March 11, 1873; three-fifths being present.

The People of the State of New York, represented in Senate and Assembly, do enact as follows:

Commissioners to give notice before commencing proceedings.

SECTION 1. Upon application being made to the commissioners of highways of any town, for the discontinuance of a public highway, it shall be the duty of said commissioners to give notice, in writing, to all persons living on such highway of such application, not less than six days before commencing proceedings of the time and place of hearing before said commissioners.

§ 2. This act shall take effect immediately.

CHAP. 70.

AN ACT to authorize writs of mandamus and of prohibition to issue to the special term of the supreme court, or to any justice thereof holding such term or sitting at chambers.

PASSED March 13, 1873; three-fifths being present.

The People of the State of New York, represented in Senate and Assembly, do enact as follows:

SECTION 1. The supreme court, at a general term, may issue writs of mandamus and of prohibition, directed to any special term of said court, or any justice thereof holding such term or sitting at chambers, and may hear, adjudge and determine the same, and enforce such determination in the same manner and with the same effect, in all respects, as in the like proceedings when the writs are directed to inferior courts and judges thereof. Application for such writ shall be made to the general term of the judicial department in which the subject-matter of the proceeding sought to be enforced or prohibited originated, or in case such general term shall not be in session, then to the general term of an adjoining judicial department, and shall be brought on upon an order to show cause or otherwise, according to the present practice in like cases of writs directed to such inferior courts or officers. The writ or order shall be returnable at such time as the said court shall direct, and when placed on the calendar the proceeding may, in the discretion of the court, have a preference over all actions or proceedings, except in criminal cases, and may be moved out of its order on the calendar. General term may issue writs. Application for, where to be made. To have preference.

§ 2. An appeal may be taken to the court of appeals from any order, judgment or final determination of any such general term in any such proceeding; and the practice on such appeal shall be the same in all respects as on appeals to that court in proceedings upon mandamus as now regulated by law or the practice of the court. Such appeal, if the said court shall so order, shall have a preference over all actions or proceedings, except in criminal cases, and may be moved out of its order on the calendar. Appeal to court of appeals.

§ 3. The proceedings on any application for such writ of mandamus or prohibition shall not be stayed or suspended by any other writ or order of any court or officer, other than that of the general term, before which the same is pending; nor shall any appeal from the order, judgment or final determination of such general term stay the proceedings, unless such general term so order, which order may be upon such terms, as to security or otherwise, as may be just. Stay of proceedings.

§ 4. If the application for the writ shall be made to the general term of an adjoining judicial department as provided in the first section of this act, such general term, in its discretion, Where writ returnable.

may make the alternative writ or order to show cause returnable before the general term of the department in which the subject-matter of the proceeding originated, at the next subsequent term thereof, with the same effect, in all respects, as if such alternative writ or order had been made by such general term.

§ 5. This act shall take effect immediately.

CHAP. 74.

AN ACT to continue the fishery commission of the State of New York.

PASSED March 18, 1878; three-fifths being present.

The People of the State of New York, represented in Senate and Assembly, do enact as follows:

Fishery commission continued. SECTION 1. The fishery commission of the State of New York, created by act passed April twenty-second, eighteen hundred and sixty-eight, laws of eighteen hundred and sixty-eight, chapter two hundred and eighty-five, is continued, with Amount to be expended. the powers conferred upon them by the said act. The commissioners to receive no salary, and to expend only such sums as have heretofore been appropriated, or shall hereafter from time to time be appropriated for such purpose.

Ante, vol. 6, pp. 806, 759.

CHAP. 79.

AN ACT to amend the third section of article first, title second, chapter sixth, part second of the Revised Statutes, entitled "Of granting letters testamentary."

PASSED March 18, 1878.

The People of the State of New York, represented in Senate and Assembly, do enact as follows:

SECTION 1. The third section of article first, title second, chapter sixth, part second, of the Revised Statutes, is hereby amended so as to read as follows:

Persons incompetent to serve as executors. § 3. No person shall be deemed competent to serve as an executor who, at the time the will is proved, shall be: First. Incapable in law of making a contract (except married women). Second. Under the age of twenty-one years. Third. An alien not being an inhabitant of this State. Fourth. Who shall have been convicted of an infamous crime. Fifth. Who, upon proof, shall be adjudged by the surrogate to be incompetent to execute the duties of such trust, by reason of drunkenness, dishonesty, improvidence or want of understanding.

If any such person be named as the sole executor in any will, or if all the persons named therein as executors be incompetent, letters of administration (with the will annexed) shall be issued, as hereinafter provided in the case of all the executors renouncing. When letters with the will annexed to issue.

§ 2. This act shall take effect immediately.

Ante, vol. 2, p. 681.

CHAP. 84.

AN ACT to authorize the private secretary of the governor to sign in his behalf certain commissions.

PASSED March 14, 1873.

The People of the State of New York, represented in Senate and Assembly, do enact as follows:

SECTION 1. The private secretary of the governor is hereby authorized to sign, in his behalf, commissions issued to notaries public. All such commissions, so signed, shall have the same force and effect as if signed by the governor.

§ 2. This act shall take effect immediately.

CHAP. 92.

AN ACT to amend an act entitled "An act for the incorporation of villages," passed April twentieth, eighteen hundred and seventy.

PASSED March 18, 1873; three-fifths being present.

The People of the State of New York, represented in Senate and Assembly, do enact as follows:

SECTION 1. Section one of the act entitled "An act for the incorporation of villages," passed April twentieth, eighteen hundred and seventy, as amended by chapter two hundred and ninety-one of the laws of eighteen hundred and seventy-one, and chapter six hundred and eighty-eight of the laws of eighteen hundred and seventy-one, is hereby amended so as to read as follows:

§ 1. Any part of any town or towns, not in any incorporated village, containing a resident population of not less than three hundred persons, and if it shall include in its boundaries a territory of more than one square mile in extent, containing a resident population of not less than three hundred persons in each and every additional square mile of territory included within such boundaries, may be incorporated as a village under the provisions of this act, by complying therewith. When village may be incorporated.

§ 2. This act shall take effect immediately.

Ante, vol. 7 p. 681—ante, p. 120.

CHAP. 96.

AN ACT for the preservation of the timber and stone on the Onondaga Indian reservation.

PASSED March 19, 1878; three-fifths being present.

The People of the State of New York, represented in Senate and Assembly, do enact as follows:

Cutting of wood, etc., prohibited.

SECTION 1. No person other than an Onondaga Indian shall cut upon, or remove from the Onondaga Indian reservation, in the county of Onondaga, any tree, timber, wood, bark or poles, under any pretense whatever, except as provided in the second section of this act.

When Indians may cut for sale, etc.

§ 2. No Indian shall cut any tree, timber wood poles or bark for the purpose of sale, or to be removed from said reservation, nor shall, under any pretense whatever, sell or remove, or cause to be removed, or be in any way instrumental or a party to the removal from said reservation, of any trees, timber, wood, poles or bark, except upon written permission for the same, signed by a majority of the chiefs of said Onondaga Indians, which permit shall particularly specify the quantity and kind of trees, timber, wood, bark or poles so sought to be cut and removed.

Lessee of saw-mill may sell lumber.

§ 3. The lessee of the saw-mill on said reservation may dispose of, to any person, any timber or lumber sawed by and belonging to him at said saw-mill.

§ 4. No individual Indian shall have the right to lease any lands to any person to be used as a stone quarry.

Duty of agent.

§ 5. It shall be the duty of the duly appointed agent for the Onondaga Indians to prosecute any person violating the provisions of this act, in the name of the Onondaga Indian nation, or the chiefs of said nation may prosecute for said offenses.

Penalty.

§ 6. Any person offending against the provisions of this act, shall be deemed guilty of a misdemeanor, and shall be punished by a fine not to exceed two hundred and fifty dollars, or by imprisonment in the penitentiary of Onondaga county for a period not to exceed six months, or by both such fine and imprisonment, and one-half of all such fines, when collected, shall be paid over to the agent of said Onondaga Indians, for the use and benefit of said Onondaga Indians, and the other half shall be paid into the treasury of Onondaga county.

§ 7. This act shall take effect immediately.

CHAP. 119.

AN ACT to amend an act entitled "An act to vest in the board of supervisors certain legislative powers, and to prescribe their fees for certain services," passed April third, eighteen hundred and forty-nine.

PASSED March 22, 1873; three-fifths being present.

The People of the State of New York, represented in Senate and Assembly, do enact as follows:

SECTION 1. Section four of chapter one hundred and ninety-four of the laws of eighteen hundred and forty-nine, being an act to vest in the board of supervisors certain legislative powers, and to prescribe their fees for certain services, passed April third, eighteen hundred and forty-nine, as amended by chapter three hundred and sixty-one of the laws of eighteen hundred and seventy, is hereby further amended by adding as subdivision sixteen of said section the following:

§ 16. To ascertain, fix and determine the amount to which any person, persons or corporation is equitably entitled to receive back from any town or towns for taxes paid while the boundary line between such towns was in dispute, and to levy and assess such amount upon such town or towns, and cause the same to be collected in the same manner that other taxes are levied, assessed and collected. Board to fix amount for taxes paid in case of disputed boundary lines of towns.

Ante, vol. 3, p. 334; vol. 7, p. 716.

CHAP. 120.

AN ACT conferring certain additional powers upon the comptroller.

PASSED March 22, 1873; three-fifths being present.

The People of the State of New York, represented in Senate and Assembly, do enact as follows:

SECTION 1. The comptroller of the State of New York shall have the power to set aside any cancellation of sale made by him under the provisions of chapter four hundred and twenty-seven of the laws of eighteen hundred and fifty-five, entitled "An act in relation to the collection of taxes on lands of non-residents, and to provide for the sale of such lands for unpaid taxes" in either of the following cases: First, Whenever such cancellation was procured by fraud or misrepresentation. Second, Whenever such cancellation was procured by the suppression of any material fact bearing upon the case. Third, Whenever the cancellation was made under a mistake Comptroller may set aside cancellation of sale.

of fact. But the comptroller shall in all cases specify the particular grounds upon which such cancellation is set aside.

§ 2. This act shall take effect immediately.

Ante, vol. 8, p. 857.

CHAP. 143.

AN ACT to amend an act passed April twenty-first, one thousand eight hundred and seventy, entitled "An act relative to the Union Home and School, for the education and maintenance of the children of volunteers."

PASSED March 27, 1873; three-fifths being present.

The People of the State of New York, represented in Senate and Assembly, do enact as follows:

SECTION 1. The first section of the act entitled "An act relative to the Union Home and School, for the education and maintenance of the children of volunteers," passed April twenty-first, one thousand eight hundred and seventy, is hereby amended so as to read as follows:

§ 1. The board of supervisors of each and every county of the state of New York shall levy and collect by tax, in the year one thousand eight hundred and seventy, and every year thereafter, at the same time and in the same manner as the contingent charges and expenses of said county are levied and collected, and shall pay over to the Union Home and School for the education and maintenance of the children of volunteers, the sum of one hundred and fifty dollars per annum, and in like proportion for any fraction of a year, for each and every destitute child received from said county or counties which may be supported and maintained by said institution. But the number of children for whom money is drawn under the provisions of this act shall in no case exceed four hundred in any one year.

Annual tax.

Rate for each child.

Number limited.

§ 2. This act shall take effect immediately.

CHAP. 146.

AN ACT to amend section one hundred and twelve of chapter two, part three, article seven, of the Revised Statutes, in relation to justice's courts.

PASSED March 27, 1873; three-fifths being present.

The People of the State of New York, represented in Senate and Assembly, do enact as follows:

SECTION 1. Section one hundred and twelve of chapter two, part three, article seven, of the Revised Statutes, is hereby amended so as to read as follows:

§ 112. Whenever any person who shall be duly summoned as a juror shall not appear, or appearing shall refuse to serve, the justice before whom the venire is returnable, upon the certificate of the constable that such juror was personally summoned as a juror, may issue an attachment to any constable authorized to summon the juror to bring the person so summoned as a juror at the time to be named in said precept, before the said justice, and if said juror shall not render a reasonable excuse for his default, at the time named in said precept, the said justice may impose a fine upon him in a sum not to exceed ten dollars. And the justice imposing any fine shall make up and enter in his docket a minute of the conviction, and the cause thereof, and the same shall be deemed a judgment in all respects at the suit of the overseers of the poor of the town. Such judgment may be enforced in manner provided in section eighty-eight of article six of this title. In case the constable to whom such attachment was issued shall make a return to the said justice that the person so summoned as a juror, and not appearing, cannot be found, the said justice shall issue an attachment to compel the attendance of the defaulting juror at a future day to be named in said attachment, which shall be not less than two nor more than four days thereafter, and on the appearance of such defaulting juror before such justice, under such attachment, the same proceedings shall be had as hereinbefore provided, and the said justice may issue like attachments from time to time until any or all of said defaulting jurors shall be brought before him.

Proceedings in case jurors fail to appear.

Fine.

Judgment, how enforced.

Attachment to compel attendance.

§ 2. This act shall take effect immediately.

Ante, vol. 2, p. 261.

CHAP. 151.

AN ACT for the relief of stockholders of corporations whose certificates of stock have been lost or destroyed.

PASSED March 27, 1873.

The People of the State of New York, represented in Senate and Assembly, do enact as follows:

SECTION 1. Whenever any company incorporated under the laws of this State shall have refused to issue a new certificate of stock in place of one theretofore issued by it, but which is alleged to have been lost or destroyed, the owner of such lost or destroyed certificate, or his legal representatives, may apply to the supreme court, at any special term thereof appointed to be held in the judicial district where such owner resides, for an order requiring such corporation to show cause why it should not be required to issue a new certificate of stock in place of the one so lost or destroyed. Such application shall be by petition duly verified by the owner, in which shall be stated the name of the corporation, the number and date of

Stockholders may compel corporators to issue duplicate certificates in case of loss.

the certificate, if known, or can be ascertained by the petitioner, the number of shares of stock named therein and to whom issued, and as particular a statement of the circumstances attending such loss or destruction as such petitioner shall be able to give. Upon the presentation of said petition, said court shall make an order requiring said corporation to show cause, at a time and place therein mentioned, why it should not be required to issue a new certificate of stock in place of the one described in said petition. A copy of said petition and of said order shall be served upon the president or other head of such corporation, or on the cashier, secretary or treasurer thereof, personally, at least ten days before the time designated in said order for showing cause.

Court to proceed summarily.

§ 2. At the time and place specified in said order, and on proof of due service thereof, the said court shall proceed in a summary manner and in such mode as it may deem advisable to inquire into the truth of the facts stated in said petition, and shall hear such proofs and allegations as may be offered by or in behalf of said corporation or other party, relative to the subject-matter of said inquiry, and if, upon such inquiry, said court shall be satisfied that such petitioner is the lawful owner of the number of shares of the capital stock, or any part thereof, described in said petition, and that the certificate therefor has been lost or destroyed, and cannot after due diligence be found, and that no sufficient cause has been shown why a new certificate should not be issued in place thereof, it shall make an order requiring said corporation or other party, within such time as shall be therein designated, to issue and deliver to such petitioner a new certificate for the number of shares of the capital stock of said corporation which shall be specified in said order as owned by said petitioner, and the certificate for which shall have been lost or destroyed. In making such order the court shall direct that said petitioner deposit such security, or file such a bond in such form and with such sureties as to the court shall appear sufficient to indemnify any person other than the petitioner who shall thereafter appear to be the lawful owner of such certificate stated to be lost or stolen; and the court may also direct the publication of such notice, either preceding or succeeding the making of such final order, as it shall deem proper. Any person or persons who shall thereafter claim any rights under said certificate so alleged to have been lost or destroyed, shall have recourse to said indemnity, and the said corporation shall be discharged of and from all liability to such person or persons by reason of compliance with the order aforesaid; and obedience to said order may be enforced by said court by attachments against the officer or officers of such corporation, on proof of his or their refusal to comply with the same.

To order that duplicate certificates be issued.

Petitioner to give security.

Obedience to order, how enforced.

§ 3. This act shall take effect immediately.

CHAP. 181.

AN ACT to amend an act entitled "An act to provide for furnishing two statues of eminent deceased citizens of this state, to be placed in the capitol at Washington, in compliance with the invitation of the President of the United States," passed May sixth, eighteen hundred and seventy-two.

PASSED April 7, 1873; three-fifths being present.

The People of the State of New York, represented in Senate and Assembly, do enact as follows:

SECTION 1. Section one of an act entitled "An act to provide for furnishing two statues of eminent deceased citizens of this state to be placed in the capitol at Washington, in compliance with the invitation of the president of the United States," passed May sixth, eighteen hundred and seventy-two, is hereby amended so as to allow the statue of George Clinton to be of bronze instead of marble, as therein required, provided the commissioners therein named can procure the consent of the contractor for said statue to such change. Statue of Clinton to be in bronze.

§ 2. The governor, comptroller and secretary of state are hereby appointed a commission to contract with Erastus D. Palmer, in behalf of the state, for furnishing and delivering a bronze statue of Robert R. Livingston, to be handed over, when completed on the part of the state, to the president of the United States, to be placed in the capitol at Washington. Commission to contract for statue of Livingston.

§ 3. This act shall take effect immediately.

Ante, p. 583.

CHAP. 186.

AN ACT to provide for the protection of citizens in their civil and public rights.

PASSED April 9, 1873; three-fifths being present.

The People of the State of New York, represented in Senate and Assembly, do enact as follows:

SECTION 1. No citizen of this state shall, by reason of race, color or previous condition of servitude, be excepted or excluded from the full and equal enjoyment of any accommodation, advantage, facility or privilege furnished by innkeepers, by common carriers, whether on land or water, by licensed owners, managers or lessees of theatres, or other places of amusement, by trustees, commissioners, superintendents, teachers and other officers of common schools and public institutions of learning, and by cemetery associations. No citizen to be denied any accommodation on account of color, etc.

Penalty. § 2. The violation of any part of the first section of this act shall be deemed a misdemeanor, and the party or parties violating the same shall, upon conviction thereof, be subject to a fine of not less than fifty dollars, or more than five hundred dollars.

§ 3. Discrimination against any citizen on account of color, by the use of the word "white," or any other term in any law, statute, ordinance or regulation now existing in this state, is hereby repealed and annulled.

§ 4. This act shall take effect immediately.

CHAP. 195.

AN ACT granting the consent of the state of New York to the acquisition by the United States of certain lands for the purpose of the erection of government buildings at Albany and Utica, New York, and ceding jurisdiction over the same.

PASSED April 10, 1873, by a two-thirds vote.

The People of the State of New York, represented in Senate and Assembly, do enact as follows:

Consent of state given to acquisition of lands by the United States. SECTION 1. The consent of the state of New York is hereby given to the acquisition by the United States, by purchase, in conformity with the laws of this state, of one or more pieces of land in the city of Albany, not exceeding one acre in quantity; and also of one or more pieces of land in the city of Utica, not exceeding one acre in quantity, on which lands, in each of said cities, said United States may erect a government building, and the said United States shall have, hold, occupy and own the said lands when thus acquired, and exercise jurisdiction and control over the same and every part thereof, subject to the restrictions hereinafter mentioned.

Jurisdiction ceded. § 2. The jurisdiction of the state of New York in and over the said land or lands mentioned in the foregoing section, when acquired by the United States, shall be and the same hereby is ceded to the United States, but the jurisdiction hereby ceded shall continue no longer than the said United States shall own the said lands.

Conditions. § 3. The said consent is given and the said jurisdiction ceded upon the express condition that the state of New York shall retain concurrent jurisdiction with the United States in and over the said land or lands, so far as that all civil process in all cases and such criminal or other process as may issue under the laws or authority of the state of New York, against any person or persons charged with crimes or misdemeanors committed within said state, may be executed therein the same way and manner as if such consent had not been given or jurisdiction ceded, except so far as such process may affect the real or personal property of the United States.

§ 4. The jurisdiction hereby ceded shall not vest until the United States shall have acquired the title to the said land or lands by purchase or by condemnation in conformity with the laws of this state, and so long as the said land or lands shall remain the property of the United States, when acquired as aforesaid, and no longer, the same shall be and continue exonerated from all taxes, assessments and other charges which may be levied or imposed under the authority of this state. Jurisdiction, when to vest.

§ 5. Any malicious, willful, reckless or voluntary injury to or mutilation of the grounds, buildings or appurtenances shall subject the offender or offenders to a fine of not less than twenty dollars, to which may be added, for an aggravated offense, imprisonment not exceeding six months in the county jail or workhouse, to be prosecuted before any court of competent jurisdiction. Penalty for willful injuries.

§ 6. If the United States cannot acquire title to the land above mentioned, or any portion thereof, by purchase, they shall cause application to be made to the supreme court for a writ of inquiry of damages, and such proceedings shall thereupon be had and the damages ascertained and paid in the manner prescribed in the fourth article of title two of chapter nine of the third part of the Revised Statutes. Title, how acquired.

§ 7. This act shall take effect immediately.

CHAP. 211.

AN ACT to amend chapter eight hundred and forty-five of the laws of eighteen hundred and sixty-nine, entitled "An act to amend an act entitled 'An act concerning the proof of wills, executors and administrators, guardians and wards, and surrogates' courts," passed May sixteenth, eighteen hundred and thirty-seven."

PASSED April 12, 1873; three-fifths being present.

The People of the State of New York, represented in Senate and Assembly, do enact as follows:

SECTION 1. Section one of chapter eight hundred and forty-five of the laws of eighteen hundred and sixty-nine is hereby amended so as to read as follows:

§ 1. Section seventy-two of an act entitled "An act concerning the proof of wills, executors and administrators, guardians and wards, surrogates' courts," passed May sixteenth, eighteen hundred and thirty-seven, is hereby amended by adding, at the end of said section, the following words:

But no real estate, the title to which shall have passed out of any heir or devisee of the deceased, by conveyance or otherwise, to a purchaser in good faith and for value, shall be sold by virtue of the provisions of this act, or of title four, What real estate not to be sold.

chapter six, part two of the Revised Statutes, unless letters testamentary or of administration, upon the estate of said deceased, shall have been applied for within four years after his death, nor unless application for such sale shall be made to the surrogate within three years after the granting of such letters testamentary or of administration; provided the surrogate of any county in this state had jurisdiction to grant such letters of administration. And provided, further, that the period during which an action may be pending in favor of any creditor, against any executor or administrator for the recovery of any debt or claim against the testator or intestate, shall not be part of the time limited for making such application to the surrogate for such sale; provided the plaintiff in such action shall file in the clerk's office of the county where the real estate is situated, a notice of the pendency of such action, stating the object thereof, and that the said real estate will be held as security for any judgment obtained in said action. But the court in which such action is pending may, on special motion, after eight days' notice to the plaintiff's attorney, on such terms as the court shall see fit, by order, discharge the said real estate, or a specific portion thereof, to be described in such order, from any lien or incumbrance by reason of such action, and direct an entry to be made by the clerk on such lis pendens, or on the record thereof, that such lien or incumbrance is "discharged as per order of the court, dated ," specifying the date of such order; and thereupon the said real estate, or the specific portion thereof described in said order, shall be discharged from such lien or incumbrance, with the same effect in all respects as if no such action had been commenced.

Proviso.

Court on motion may discharge from lien.

§ 2. This act shall take effect immediately.

Ante, vol. 7, p. 484; vol. 4, p. 500.

CHAP. 225.

AN ACT to amend the provisions of the Revised Statutes with regard to the fees of appraisers appointed by surrogates.

PASSED April 16, 1873; three-fifths being present.

The People of the State of New York, represented in Senate and Assembly, do enact as follows:

SECTION 1. The first section of article one, title three, chapter six of the second part of the Revised Statutes is hereby amended so as to read as follows:

Surrogate to appoint appraisers.

§ 1. Upon the application of an executor or administrator, the surrogate who granted letters testamentary or of administration shall, by writing, appoint two disinterested appraisers, as often as occasion may require, to estimate and appraise the personal property of a deceased person, and such appraisers shall be entitled to receive a reasonable compensation for their services, to be allowed by the surrogate, but not exceeding for each appraiser the sum of five dollars for each day actually employed in making an appraisement or inventory, in addition to his actual expenses necessarily incurred, the number of days' services so rendered and the amount of such expenses to be verified by the affidavit of the appraiser performing such services, to be made and delivered to the executor or administrator before payment of such fees, and to be adjusted by the surrogate. And no clerk or employee in a surrogate's office shall act as appraiser in any matter before such surrogate.

Compensation of.

Surrogate's clerk not to act as appraiser.

§ 2. This act shall take effect immediately.

Ante, vol. 2, p. 83.

CHAP. 243.

AN ACT further to amend an act entitled "An act to amend title sixteen, chapter eight, part three of the Revised Statutes, relative to proceedings for the draining of swamps, marshes, and other low or wet lands," passed May twelve, eighteen hundred and sixty-nine.

PASSED April 21, 1873; three-fifths being present.

The People of the State of New York, represented in Senate and Assembly, do enact as follows:

SECTION 1. In all cases where, either by death, resignation, or otherwise, a vacancy or vacancies shall occur, or has, or have heretofore occurred in the office of commissioners appointed, or hereafter to be appointed, under sections one and two of the act hereby amended, or under that act and the act amending that act, passed April fifth, eighteen hundred and seventy-one (being chapter three hundred and three of the laws of eighteen hundred and seventy-one), such vacancy or vacancies shall, on the application of the commissioner or commissioners then in office, or of any other person or persons interested, be supplied and filled by the county court of the county in which such commissioners were originally appointed, and which application shall be upon such notice as the court, to which the application is made, shall prescribe. The commissioners thus appointed shall possess all the powers, and be subject to all the liabilities of the commissioners, whose office they are appointed to supply.

Vacancies, how filled.

§ 2. All the acts of two commissioners heretofore done and performed under the acts hereby amended, while there was a vacancy in the office of commissioners, are hereby confirmed, and shall be of the same force and effect as if the third commissioner had been in office, and had concurred in the acts so done and performed.

Acts of commissioners confirmed.

§ 3. This act shall take effect immediately.

Ante, vol. 7, p. 585.
Ante, p. 78.

CHAP. 249.

AN ACT to amend an act entitled "An act regulating the sale of intoxicating liquors," passed April eleventh, eighteen hundred and seventy.

PASSED April 21, 1873; three-fifths being present.

The People of the State of New York, represented in Senate and Assembly, do enact as follows:

SECTION 1. Section one of the act entitled "An act regulating the sale of intoxicating liquors," passed April eleventh, eighteen hundred and seventy, is hereby amended so as to read as follows:

Commissioners of excise. In cities. In villages. § 1. There shall be a board of commissioners of excise in each of the cities, incorporated villages and towns of this State. Such boards in cities shall be composed of three members, who shall be appointed as hereinafter provided; in incorporated villages the board shall consist of the president of the board of trustees and two other trustees, to be designated by said board of trustees, and said president of the board of trustees shall be president of said board of commissioners of excise; In towns. and in towns they shall consist of the supervisors and justices of the peace thereof, for the time being, respectively. Any three members shall be competent to execute the powers vested in any town boards, and in case the office of supervisor be vacant, or there be not two justices in the town, then the town clerk shall act in their places respectively. Town commissioners not to grant licenses in villages. No license for the sale of intoxicating liquors shall be granted within the limits of any incorporated village of this state by the commissioners of excise of the town within the limits of which said village is situated in whole or in part; but in any incorporated village licenses for the sale of intoxicating liquors shall be granted by the commissioners of excise of said village only.

§ 2. This act shall take effect immediately.

Ante, vol. 7, p. 666.

CHAP. 299.

AN ACT for the relief of sick prisoners confined upon civil process.

PASSED April 25, 1873; three-fifths being present.

The People of the State of New York, represented in Senate and Assembly, do enact as follows:

Removal of prisoners to hospital. SECTION 1. Part three, chapter seven, title six, article two, section twenty-eight of the Revised Statutes of the state of New York, is hereby amended by adding thereto the following: "And whenever such physicians, or a physician acting as such, in the absence of any regular appointment, and the warden or jailer of such jail shall certify that any prisoner confined therein upon civil process, is in such bodily health as to endanger his life, and to require his removal to a hospital for treatment, the county judge, or if in the city of New York, one of the judges of the court of common pleas shall, upon application, order the removal of such prisoner to such hospital within the county as such judge may select, and if there be no hospital within the county, then to such nearest hospital as the judge may direct, but such order shall not be obeyed, unless it directs that such prisoner be kept in the custody of the warden or official of such hospital, and that when he shall have recovered from such illness, such warden or official shall notify the jailer of such jail, and return said prisoner to said jailer's custody, and such transfer of custody shall not impair the right of arrest of any creditor at whose suit such prisoner was held, and in the event of an escape of such prisoner going to, at or returning from such hospital, the creditor may renew the process and arrest such prisoner, whenever and wherever within this state he may be found.

§ 2. This act shall take effect immediately.

Ante, vol. 2, p. 449.

CHAP. 302.

AN ACT to create a board of commissioners of emigration, and to confer certain powers thereon.

PASSED Apr. 25 1873; three-fifths being present.

The People of the State of New York, represented in Senate and Assembly, do enact as follows:

SECTION 1. It shall be the duty of the governor, by and with the advice and consent of the senate, and within ten days after the passage of this act, to appoint six commissioners of emigration for the state of New York. Two of said commissioners shall be appointed and shall hold their office for two years; two of said commissioners shall be appointed and shall hold their office for four years, and two of said commissioners shall be appointed and shall hold their office for six years. The mayor of the city of New York, the president of the German emigrant society of the city of New York, the president of the Irish emigrant society of the city of New York, shall be additional commissioners of emigration by virtue of their respective offices, but the two last-named commissioners shall not have the right to vote upon the appointment or removal of subordinates. The said commissioners of emigration shall have all the powers and perform all the duties now imposed upon the commissioners of emigration, by virtue of an act entitled "An act concerning passengers in vessels coming to the city of New York," passed May fifth, eighteen hundred and forty-seven, and the various acts supplementary

Appointment of commissioners.

Their powers.

thereto and amendatory thereof. They may elect from their number a president and vice-president, and appoint a secretary and treasurer, and such other officers and employees as may be necessary.

Term of office. § 2. Upon the expiration of the several terms of office of the commissioners appointed as herein provided, their successors shall be appointed by the governor, by and with the advice and consent of the senate, and shall respectively hold their offices for the term of six years, and until their successors shall be appointed in like manner and qualified. In case of Vacancies. a vacancy in the office of any one of said commissioners, the same shall be filled by an appointment to be made by the governor, by and with the advice and consent of the senate, and the appointee shall hold his office for the remainder of the term of the person in whose place he shall be appointed. The commissioners of emigration appointed as herein provided, before entering upon their duties as such commissioners, shall take, subscribe and file in the office of the secretary of state, the oath prescribed by the twelfth article of the constitution of this state.

§ 3. The terms of office of each of the present commissioners of emigration shall cease and determine at the end of five days after the filing of the oath of office of the commissioners of emigration first appointed as herein provided, and all their power and authority, property, rights of property, archives, records and possessions as such commissioners, shall there upon pass to and become vested in the first board of commis sioners of emigration constituted under the provisions of this act, and their successors.

Support. § 4. The commissioners of emigration shall not be required to support any person capable of earning a livelihood for a longer period than two years. This section shall not take effect until the first day of May, eighteen hundred and seventy-three.

Agent. § 5. The commissioners of emigration may appoint an agent in all incorporated cities, at a salary not to exceed three hundred dollars per annum.

§ 6. All acts and parts of acts inconsistent with the provisions of this act are hereby repealed.

§ 7. This act shall take effect immediately.

CHAP. 314.

AN ACT to provide for submitting to the electors of this state, at the general election to be held on the Tuesday following the first Monday of November, eighteen hundred and seventy-three, the question whether the offices of chief judge and associate judge of the court of appeals, of justices of the supreme court, of the judge of the superior court of the city of New York, of the judge of the court of common pleas of the city and county of New York, of the judge of the superior court of Buffalo, of the judge of the city court of Brooklyn, of the county judge of the several counties of this state, shall be hereafter filled by appointment, pursuant to section seventeen, article six, of the constitution.

PASSED April 26, 1873; three-fifths being present.

The People of the State of New York, represented in Senate and Assembly, do enact as follows:

SECTION 1. The question whether the offices of chief judge and associate judge of the court of appeals, the justices of the supreme court, the judges of the superior court of the city of New York, of the court of common pleas of the city and county of New York, of the superior court of Buffalo, of the city court of Brooklyn, and the county judge of the several counties of this state, shall hereafter be filled by appointment, shall be submitted to the electors of this state at the general election to be held on the Tuesday succeeding the first Monday of November next, as provided in section seventeen of article six of the constitution of this state, in the manner hereinafter mentioned. Question of election of judges to be submitted to a vote.

§ 2. The inspectors of election in each election district in the state shall provide two boxes, in which they shall deposit the ballots of the electors upon the question whether the judges and justices of the several courts named in the first section of this act shall hereafter be filled by appointment. One of said boxes shall be labeled "appointment or election of the chief judge and associate judges of the court of appeals and of justices of the supreme court." The other one shall be labeled "appointment or election of judges of city and county courts." Each citizen entitled to vote at such election may vote two ballots, as follows: One of them shall be indorsed "appointment or election of the chief judge and associate judges of the court of appeals, and of the justices of the supreme court," and shall contain on the inside, when folded, the words "shall the offices of chief judge and associate judge of the court of appeals and of the justices of the supreme court be hereafter filled by appointment—Yes," or the words, "Shall the offices of chief judge and associate Ballot boxes. Form of ballots.

judge of the court of appeals and of the justices of the supreme court be hereafter filled by appointment — No;" and all such ballots shall be deposited in the boxes labeled "appointment or election of chief judge and associate judges of the court of appeals and justices of the supreme court." The other of said ballots shall be indorsed, "appointment or election of judges of city and county courts," and on the inside, when folded, shall contain the words, "shall the offices of the judge of the superior court of the city of New York, of the judge of the court of common pleas of the city and county of New York, of the judge of the superior court of Buffalo, of the judge of the city court of Brooklyn, of the county judge of the several counties of this state be hereafter filled by appointment — Yes," or the words "shall the offices of the judge of the superior court of the city of New York, of the judge of the court of common pleas of the city and county of New York, of the judge of the superior court of Buffalo, of the judge of the city court of Brooklyn, of the county judge of the several counties of this state be hereafter filled by appointment — No." And all such ballots shall be deposited in the box labeled "appointment or election of the judges of the city and county courts."

Canvass of votes. § 3. The inspectors of election in each election district, after the closing of the polls of such election, shall count and canvass separately the ballots deposited in each of the said boxes in the manner prescribed by law in reference to other elections, and shall ascertain the whole number of ballots upon each of the questions to be submitted as aforesaid. The inspectors, after having so counted said ballots, shall set down in writing the whole number of such ballots upon each question, and the whole number for and against each of the said questions, and shall certify and make return of the said several votes in the same manner as prescribed by law in reference to other ballots at a general election.

Canvass by boards of county canvassers. § 4. The votes so given shall be canvassed by the several boards of county canvassers at the next meeting thereof after such election, and the aggregate results in the several counties shall be canvassed and certified by the board of state canvassers. The existing laws in reference to a general election shall in all respects, so far as applicable, apply to and regulate the proceedings and duties of the said board of county and state canvassers, and of the county clerks and secretary of state. From the statements made to the board of state canvassers it shall determine whether a majority of the votes upon the questions submitted to the electors of the state as herein provided be in the affirmative or negative. The said board shall make a certificate of such determination and shall deliver the same to the secretary of state, who shall file the same in his office.

In case of a majority vote, the office to be filled by appoint- § 5. If a majority of all the ballots indorsed "Appointment or election of chief judge and associate judges of the court of appeals and of justices of the supreme court" shall be in the affirmative, then the said officers shall not after said election be elective, but, as vacancies occur, they shall be filled by appointment by the governor, by and with the advice and consent of the senate, or if the senate be not in session, by the governor; but in such case, he shall nominate to the senate, when next convened, and such appointment by the governor alone shall expire at the end of that session; but if the majority of said ballots so indorsed be in the negative, then the said officers shall be elective, as heretofore. If a majority of the ballots indorsed "Appointment or election of judges of city and county courts" shall contain on the inside the question as hereinbefore provided, answered in the affirmative, then the said officers mentioned in the said question shall not after said election be elective, but, as vacancies occur, they shall be filled by appointment by the governor, by and with the advice and consent of the senate, or if the senate be not in session, by the governor; but in such case he shall nominate to the senate, when next convened, and such appointment by the governor alone shall expire at the end of that session; but if a majority of the ballots so indorsed shall be answered in the negative, then the said officers shall be elected as heretofore.

ment. Otherwise by election.

§ 6. It shall be the duty of the secretary of state to cause the said questions, together with the forms of the ballots as herein specified, to be published in two or more newspapers in each of the counties of this state, the same number of times prior to the said election as is now required by law to be published of the officers to be elected and the offices to be filled at such election; such newspapers to be designated by the secretary of state in the manner now provided by law for designating newspapers to publish election notices; but no neglect or failure to publish, or informality of publication, shall impair the validity of such election.

Duty of secretary of state.

§ 7. It shall be the duty of the secretary of state to include in and cause to be published with the election notices for the said general election a notice in substance and effect as follows: "Pursuant to section seventeen of article six of the constitution of this state two questions will be submitted to the electors of this state, to be voted upon separate ballots, as follows: 1st. Shall the offices of chief judge and associate judge of the court of appeals, and of justice of the supreme court, be hereafter filled by appointment. 2d. Shall the offices of the judge of the superior court of the city of New York, the court of common pleas of the city and county of New York, the judge of the superior court of Buffalo, the judge of the city court of Brooklyn, and the judge of the county courts of the several counties of this state be hereafter filled by appointment." And at such election each elector will be entitled to vote separately for or against each of said questions, and if a majority of the votes shall be in the affirmative of said questions, then the said judges and justices therein referred to, after said election, as vacancies occur, will be appointed by the governor, as provided by law. No failure or omission to give notice, or any informality in the notice or

To publish the notice in this section.

the giving thereof, shall impair the validity of such notice, or the election herein provided for.

§ 8. This act shall take effect immediately.

CHAP. 315.

AN ACT to amend the Revised Statutes in relation to laying out public roads and the alteration thereof.

PASSED April 28, 1878.

The People of the State of New York, represented in Senate and Assembly, do enact as follows:

SECTION 1. Section seventy-five, article fourth of title one, chapter sixteen (fifth edition) of the first part of the Revised Statutes is amended so as to read as follows:

Ante, vol. 1, p. 472.

Notice to be given to clerk or justice, asking for a jury.

§ 75. In all cases of the alteration of any road, or the laying out of any new road, the person or persons applying for the same shall serve a notice on the town clerk of the town, and on a justice of the peace and the commissioners of highways thereof, asking for a jury to certify to the necessity of the same, and specifying a time not less than ten nor more than twenty days from the time of serving such notice, when such jury will be drawn at the clerk's office of the town by the town clerk thereof.

Jury, how drawn.

§ 2. At the time and place mentioned, the town clerk of such town, having received such notice that such jury is to be drawn, shall, in the presence of a justice of the peace or one of the commissioners of highways of the town, deposit in a box the names of all persons then residents of his town, whose names are on the list filed in said town clerk's office of those selected and returned as jurors, pursuant to article second, title four, chapter seventh, part third of the Revised Statutes, who are not interested in the lands through which such road is to pass or be located, nor of kin to the owner thereof, and shall publicly, in the presence of said justice of the peace or commissioner, draw therefrom the names of twenty-four persons who shall be freeholders of the town, and shall make a certificate of such names and the purposes for which they were drawn, and shall deliver the same to the person asking for the jury; and the applicant for such road shall pay to the said town clerk one dollar for drawing such jury.

Justice shall cause jury to be summoned.

§ 3. The applicant for such road or alteration of a road, on receiving such certificate, shall deliver the same to a justice of the peace of the town wherein the road is to be laid, and it shall be the duty of such justice forthwith to issue a summons to one of the constables of said town, directing him to summon the persons named in said certificate, specifying a time and place in said summons, which shall be the time and place mentioned in the notice at which the persons to be summoned shall meet, which shall be not less than ten nor more than twenty days from the issuing thereof; and if any person so summoned to attend as a juror shall neglect or refuse to attend at the time and place designated in said summons, the person or persons so neglecting or refusing to attend shall be liable to pay a fine of five dollars, to be sued for and recovered by the overseers of the poor of said town, and such fine shall be applied by them to the support of the poor of such town. Neglect to attend as a juror.

§ 4. If twelve or more of the persons whose names have been so drawn not interested in the lands through which the road is to be laid nor of kin to the owner thereof shall appear at the time and place specified in the summons, they shall then be sworn by the justice of the peace who issued such summons, well and truly to examine and certify as to the necessity and propriety of the highway applied for, and if said justice of the peace shall refuse or neglect to attend at the time and place mentioned in said summons, such oath may be administered to such jurors by any other justice of the peace of said county, and the justice of the peace, swearing such jury, shall receive therefor from such applicant two dollars.

§ 5. Such jury shall then personally examine the route of such highway, and shall hear any reasons that may be offered for or against any proposed road or alteration. If thirteen or more of the number thereof shall be of opinion that such highway or alteration of a highway is necessary and proper, they shall make and subscribe a certificate in writing to that effect, which shall be delivered to the commissioners of highways of the town; but if such a number thereof should not certify that such road or alteration is necessary, then no application for such road or alteration shall be made again in one year. Jury to examine route, etc.

§ 6. Every juror shall be entitled to receive for his services as such juror, the sum of fifty cents, to be paid by such applicant, and the constable who may summon such jury shall receive from such applicant therefor ten cents for summoning each juror summoned, and ten cents a mile for each and every mile actually and necessarily traveled in summoning such jury, in going from and returning to his place of residence therefor. Juror's fees.

§ 7. If thirteen of such freeholders shall make a certificate that such highway or alteration is necessary and proper, then the fees of officers and jurors, paid by such applicant, shall be a charge against such town, in favor of such applicant. When to be a town charge.

§ 8. No road or highway which may be laid out and opened, with the consent of the owners of the property through which it passes, shall hereafter be accepted and maintained by the town or towns through which it runs, except in accordance with the provisions of this act.

§ 9. This act shall take effect immediately.

CHAP. 323.

AN ACT to amend an act entitled "An act to extend the powers of boards of supervisors, except in the counties of New York and Kings," passed May eleventh, eighteen hundred and sixty-nine.

*PASSED April 29, 1878; three-fifths being present.

The People of the State of New York, represented in Senate and Assembly, do enact as follows:

SECTION 1. An act to extend the powers of boards of supervisors, except in the counties of New York and Kings, passed May eleventh, eighteen hundred and sixty-nine, is hereby amended by adding thereto, as an additional section, the following:

When consent of trustees must be obtained.

§ 10. In case the road or roads, or bridge or bridges, referred to in the first section of this act shall be wholly or partly within the limits of any incorporated village, the consent of a majority of the trustees of such village shall be necessary for the action of supervisors of towns under said section, in addition to the consent of the commissioner or commissioners of highways, town clerk and justices of the peace of such town.

§ 2. This act shall take effect immediately.

Ante, vol. 7, p. 488.

CHAP. 327.

AN ACT to amend chapter three hundred and twelve of the laws of eighteen hundred and fifty-nine, entitled "An act to equalize the state tax among the several counties in this state."

PASSED April 29, 1878; three-fifths being present.

The People of the State of New York, represented in Senate and Assembly, do enact as follows:

SECTION 1. Chapter three hundred and twelve of the laws of eighteen hundred and fifty-nine, entitled "An act to equalize the state tax among the several counties in the state," is hereby amended by adding thereto the following sections:

When appeal must be made and filed.

§ 14. Any appeal made in pursuance of section thirteen of this act, the determination of which is not made and filed with the clerk of said board of supervisors on or before the commencement of the next succeeding annual session thereof, shall be null and void, and the same shall be deemed as dismissed.

Costs in case appeal is not sustained.

§ 15. Whenever any appeal so made shall not be sustained, the cost and expenses arising therefrom and connected therewith shall be a charge upon the town, city or ward so appealing, which shall be audited by the board of supervisors, and levied upon the taxable property in said town, city or ward.

§ 2. Section fourteen of said act is hereby changed to section sixteen.*

§ 3. This act shall take effect immediately.

Ante, vol. 8, p. 879.

CHAP. 336.

AN ACT to amend an act entitled "An act making appropriations for certain expenses of government, and for supplying deficiencies in former appropriations," passed May fifteenth, eighteen hundred and seventy-two.

PASSED April 30, 1873, by a two-third vote.

The People of the State of New York, represented in Senate and Assembly, do enact as follows:

SECTION 1. The following paragraph in chapter seven hundred and thirty-three, laws of eighteen hundred and seventy-two: Appropriation for dredging of Cayuga inlet, etc.

"For completing the dredging of Cayuga inlet, and for rebuilding the pier at the head of Cayuga lake, in accordance with the intention of the law of eighteen hundred and seventy-one, the sum of ten thousand dollars, to be expended under the direction of the canal commissioner in charge of the division," and which amount is made payable by said act from the canal fund, is hereby so amended that the said sum of ten thousand dollars therein appropriated shall be paid from the general fund by the comptroller, on the drafts of the canal commissioner of the middle division.

§ 2. This act shall take effect immediately.

Ante, p. 429.

CHAP. 357.

AN ACT to authorize summary convictions of professional thieves, burglars, pickpockets, counterfeiters and forgers.

PASSED April 30, 1873; three-fifths being present.

The People of the State of New York, represented in Senate and Assembly, do enact as follows:

SECTION 1. If any person shall be charged on oath or affirmation before any police magistrate or justice of the peace in this state with being a professional thief, burglar, Professional thieves to be

* There is no section 14 to chapter 812 of laws of 1859.

deemed disorderly persons. pickpocket, counterfeiter or forger, or shall have been arrested by the police authorities at any steamboat landing, railroad depot, church, banking institution, brokers' office, place of public amusement, auction room, store, auction sale in private residences, passenger car, hotel or restaurant, or at any other gathering of people, whether few or many, and if it shall be proven to the satisfaction of any such magistrate or justice of the peace, by sufficient testimony, that he or she was frequenting or attending such place or places for an unlawful purpose, and that he or she has at some time been convicted of any of the crimes herein named, he or she shall be deemed a disorderly person, and upon conviction after trial shall be committed by the said magistrate or justice of the peace to the penitentiary, in counties where there is a penitentiary, for a term not exceeding one hundred days, there to be kept at hard labor, and in counties where there is no penitentiary, or where no contract exists with any authorities of any penitentiary in the state, then to the county jail of said county, for a term not exceeding one hundred days, or, in the discretion of any such police magistrate or justice of the peace he or she shall be required to enter security for his or her good behavior for a period not exceeding one year.

Persons aggrieved may apply for habeas corpus. § 2. Any person who may or shall feel aggrieved at any such act, judgment or determination of any such police magistrate or justice of the peace pursuant to the provision of this act, may apply to any judge or justice of any court having the power to issue a writ of habeas corpus for the issuance of said writ, and upon return thereof there shall be a rehearing of the evidence, and the judge or justice may either discharge, modify or confirm the commitment.

§ 3. This act shall take effect immediately.

CHAP. 361.

AN ACT to amend an act entitled "An act authorizing the incorporation of rural cemetery associations," passed April twenty-seventh, eighteen hundred and forty-seven.

PASSED April 30, 1878; three-fifths being present.

The People of the State of New York, represented in Senate and Assembly, do enact as follows:

SECTION 1. The fifth section of the act entitled "An act authorizing the incorporation of rural cemetery associations," passed April twenty-seventh, eighteen hundred and forty-seven, is hereby amended so as to read as follows:

Annual election. § 5. The annual election for trustees to supply the place of those whose term of office expires shall be holden on the day mentioned in the certificate of incorporation, and at such hour and place as the trustees shall direct, at which election shall be chosen such number of trustees as will supply the places of those whose term expires. But the trustees of any corporation, organized under this act, shall have power, by resolution of a majority of all of said trustees, to change the time for the annual election of trustees as fixed in their act of incorporation; but no such resolution shall take effect until sixty days after the same shall have been published six successive weeks, once a week, in some newspaper published in the city or county where the cemetery of the said association is situated, and a copy of said resolution, certified by the president and secretary thereof, shall have been filed in the office of the clerk of the county where their certificate of incorporation is recorded. The trustees chosen at any election, subsequent to the first, shall hold their places for three years, and until others are chosen to succeed them. The election shall be by ballot, and every person of full age who shall be proprietor of a lot or plat in the cemetery of the association containing not less than ninety-six square feet of land, or, if there are more than one proprietor of any such lot or plat, then such one of the proprietors as the majority of joint proprietors shall designate to represent such lot or plat may, either in person or by proxy, give one vote for each plat or lot of the dimensions aforesaid, and the persons receiving a majority of all the votes given at such election shall be trustees to succeed those whose term of office expires. If at any such election one-fifth in number of the said proprietors shall not, in person or by proxy, vote thereat, then the trustees to be chosen shall be elected and chosen by the existing trustees, or a majority of them, and the existing trustees shall, in all cases, hold their places until their successors are elected and qualified. But in all elections after the first, the trustees shall be chosen from among the proprietors of lots or plats, and the trustees shall have power to fill any vacancy in their number occurring during the period for which they hold their office. Public notice of the annual elections shall be given in such manner as the by-laws of the corporation shall prescribe.

Term of office of trustees.

Qualifications of electors.

Qualifications of trustees.

§ 2. This act shall take effect immediately.

Ante, vol. 8, p. 747.

CHAP. 363.

AN ACT to amend an act entitled "An act to secure to creditors a just division of the estate of debtors who convey to assignees for the benefit of creditors," passed April thirteenth, eighteen hundred and sixty.

PASSED May 1, 1873.

The People of the State of New York, represented in Senate and Assembly, do enact as follows:

SECTION 1. The fifth section of the act entitled "An act to secure to creditors a just division of the estate of debtors who convey to assignees for the benefit of creditors," passed April thirteenth, eighteen hundred and sixty, is hereby amended by adding to such section the words:

Court or judge may order bond prosecuted. But in case such assignee or assignees shall have been or shall hereafter be removed from his or their trust as such assignee or assignees, by reason of insolvency or other cause, by any court having jurisdiction to effect such removal, and any other person or persons shall have been or shall hereafter be substituted as trustee or trustees in place of such assignee or assignees, and shall have given the requisite security, such county judge or such court above mentioned may, in case of such omission or refusal, as hereinbefore mentioned, order the bond of such assignee or assignees to be prosecuted by such substituted trustee or trustees, in the name of the people of this state, on the relation of such substituted trustee or trustees; and such substituted trustee or trustees shall apply the moneys collected thereon in satisfaction of the debts of such debtor or debtors, in the same manner as the same ought to have been applied by such assignee or assignees. Moneys—how to be applied.

§ 2. This act shall not apply to any action which may have been commenced prior to the passage thereof.

§ 3. This act shall take effect immediately.

Ante, vol. 4, p. 485.

CHAP. 381.

AN ACT for the preservation of fish in waters lying within or bordering upon the counties of Schuyler, Steuben Chemung, Seneca, Yates and Ontario.

PASSED May 1, 1873; three-fifths being present.

The People of the State of New York, represented in Senate and Assembly, do enact as follows:

Catching of fish except by hook and line prohibited. SECTION 1. No person shall take, procure or catch, or assist in taking, procuring or catching, with or by means of any device whatever, except hook and line, any fish of any kind, except minnows for bait, which may be taken with a small net from the waters of Seneca, Canandaigua or Honeoye lakes, their outlets or inlets, or any canal running into or out of said lake, or from the waters of any other lakes or rivers lying wholly or partly in the counties of Schuyler, Steuben, Seneca, Chemung, Yates or Ontario in this state, or either of them, their outlets or inlets, within ten years from and after the passage of this act; and no person shall take any fish through the ice from said waters in any way whatever.

Penalty. § 2. Upon complaint, made on oath to any justice of the peace, against any person as having violated any of the provisions of this act, said justice of the peace shall issue his warrant for the apprehension of the offender and cause him or her to be brought before such justice for examination. If it shall appear, by the confession of the offender, or by competent testimony, that he or she has violated any of the provisions of this act, the justice shall commit such offender to the county jail, for not more than six months and not less than thirty days, and shall impose a fine upon such offender of one hundred dollars, and the offender shall remain in jail until such fine be paid, but not exceeding thirty days in addition to the time for which he may have been committed by the justice.

§ 3. The fine collected from any offender under the provisions of this act shall be paid by the justice collecting the same, one-half to the county treasurer, to be placed to the credit of the poor fund of the town in which the justice shall reside, and one-half to the person making the complaint. Fines, how disposed of.

§ 4. It shall be the duty of the sheriff of any of the aforesaid counties or any constable of any of the towns in said counties, or the game constable of each town to make the complaint described in this act against any person whom such officer or constable may know to have violated any of the provisions of this act; and it shall be the duty of the said officer or game constable of each town, after trustworthy information, to make such complaint, upon information and belief, against any person of whose violation of any of the provisions of this act he may have been so informed. In case such officer or game constable shall make the complaint upon information derived from another person, he shall pay to such person one-half of the portion of the penalty which he shall have received from the justice. In case of neglect or refusal of any such officer or game constable to make complaint as provided in this act, he shall forfeit the penalty of twenty-five dollars, to be sued for and recovered, with costs of suit, by any person in his own name, before a justice of the peace in the county where such officer or game constable resides. Sheriffs and constables to make complaints. Penalty for neglect.

§ 5. This act shall take effect immediately.

CHAP. 395.

AN ACT to alter the system of repairing the highways.

PASSED May 2, 1873; three-fifths being present.

The People of the State of New York, represented in Senate and Assembly, do enact as follows:

SECTION 1. For such towns in this state as may wish to change the present system of working and repairing the highways and adopt the privileges of this act in the manner herein provided for, article second and article third of chapter sixteen, title one, part one of the Revised Statutes, and all laws amending the same, are hereby repealed.

§ 2. Upon the written request of twenty-five tax payers of any town, it shall be the duty of the justices of the peace or other officers who preside at the town election of any such Question to be submitted to town meeting.

town, to submit to the electors, and the electors of any town may vote at the next regular annual town meeting upon, the question of changing the manner of working the highways. Such vote shall be by ballots, upon which shall be written or printed respectively, "for changing the mode of working the highways," and "against changing the mode of working the highways." The ballots shall be deposited in a separate box by themselves, be counted by the inspectors of election, or other officers presiding at such town election, and if a majority of the electors shall vote in favor of the proposed change, the town voting therefor may avail itself of the privileges of this act, upon causing a minute of its action to be entered by the town clerk in the town records.

Annual tax for highways. § 3. It shall be lawful for any town voting in favor of such change to raise by tax, to be levied and collected the same as any other tax, for the repair of its highways, an annual sum of money, which shall be at least equivalent to the value of the day's work theretofore assessed at the commutation prices, and not to exceed five thousand dollars.

Amount. § 4. The amount of such tax shall be determined by the commissioners of highways, or a majority of them, and shall be delivered to the board of town audit, who shall certify the same to the board of supervisors, the same as any other town charges.

Board of highway commissioners. § 5. The commissioners of highways shall constitute a board to be known as "the board of highway commissioners for the town of ." They shall elect one of their number president, and in the event of their failing so to do, the commissioner longest in office shall be entitled to that position. The president of said board is hereby authorized to receive, and the collector of taxes is directed to pay, the moneys collected for highway purposes. Before receiving such moneys, the said president shall execute to the supervisor of the town a bond with sureties in penalty of double the sum which may come into his hands, conditioned for the faithful accounting of such moneys, the said bond to be approved, both as to its form and sufficiency, by the supervisor of the town.

President to receive money. To give bond.

Powers of board. § 6. The said "board of highway commissioners" shall have full power to do any and all acts necessary to the prompt and effectual repairs to the highway. They may divide or consolidate the road districts in their town; may give out the work to the lowest bidder or contract, or appoint an overseer to do the same. They may contract for the work on some districts, and have that on others done by days' labor, as they think best. Their pay and general duties shall remain the same as now provided by law. If any town has but one highway commissioner, the powers and duties hereby conferred on the board of highway commissioners is hereby conferred on such highway commissioner.

Board to render accounts. § 7. At the annual meeting of the board of town audit, the said commissioners of highways shall render a detailed account of the moneys received, and the manner in which they have been expended, which account must be verified by oath.

§ 8. It shall continue, as heretofore, the duty of said commissioners of highways to lay out the several roads in their town in districts, and in the application of the road money they shall have due regard to the interests of all sections. Commissioners to lay out roads.

§ 9. All acts and parts of acts inconsistent with this act are hereby repealed.

§ 10. This act shall take effect immediately.

CHAP. 397.

AN ACT for the incorporation of fire, hose and hook and ladder companies.

PASSED May 2, 1873.

The People of the State of New York, represented in Senate and Assembly, do enact as follows:

SECTION 1. Any ten or more persons, residents of this state, who shall desire to associate themselves together in a corporate capacity as a fire, hose or hook and ladder company, may make, sign and acknowledge, before any officer authorized to take the acknowledgment of deeds in this state, and file in the office of the secretary of state, and also in the office of the clerk of the county in which the office of the proposed company shall be situate, a certificate in writing, in which shall be stated the name or title by which said company shall be known in law, the particular business and object of said incorporation, the name of the incorporated city or village, or the town in which said company proposes to act, the number of trustees, directors or managers to manage the same, and the names of the trustees, directors or managers for the first year of its existence, and the number of years said company shall exist, not to exceed fifty years, but such certificate shall not be filed unless there shall be annexed thereto a certified copy of a resolution of the board of trustees of the village, or approval of the mayor of the city in which said company is situate, or if said company be not located in an incorporated city or village, then a resolution of the board of town auditors of the town, consenting to such incorporation; provided that such corporations shall only engage in or conduct such business as properly belongs to fire, hose or hook and ladder companies, and only in the incorporated city or village or the town named in the aforesaid certificate; and provided further, that in taking part in the prevention and extinguishment of fires in cities and villages, said corporations shall be under the control and subject to the orders of the city or village authorities or officers, who, by law, have or may have control over the prevention or extinguishment of fires in incorporated cities or villages in which said corporations shall conduct their business. Corporations, how formed.

Upon filing certificate, persons to become a body corporate. § 2. Upon filing a certificate as aforesaid, together with such resolution of approval, the persons who shall have signed and acknowledged such certificate, and their associates and successors, shall thereupon, by virtue of this act, be a body politic and corporate by the name stated in such certificate, and by that name they and their successors shall and may have succession, and shall be capable in law of suing and being sued; and they and their successors by their corporate name shall, in law, be capable of taking, receiving, holding and purchasing real estate for the purposes of their incorporation, and for no other purpose, to an amount not exceeding the sum of fifty thousand dollars in value, and personal estate for like purposes to an amount not exceeding the sum of fifty thousand dollars in value; to make by-laws for the management of its affairs not inconsistent with the constitution and laws of this state or of the United States, to elect and appoint the officers and agents of such company for the management of its business, and to allow them a suitable compensation, and to prescribe the qualifications of membership of said company.

Corporate powers.

Annual election of trustees, etc. § 3. The company so incorporated may annually elect from its members its trustees, directors or managers, at such time and place, and in such manner as may be specified in its by-laws, who shall have the control and management of the affairs and funds of said company, and a majority of whom shall be a quorum for the transaction of business. Whenever any vacancy shall happen among said trustees, directors or managers, by death, resignation or neglect to serve, such vacancy shall be filled in the manner provided in the by-laws of said company.

Failure to hold election. § 4. In case it shall at any time happen that an election of trustees, managers or directors shall not be made on the day designated by the by-laws, said company shall not for that cause be dissolved, but it shall and may be lawful on any other day to hold an election for trustees, directors or managers, in such manner as said company may determine.

May take property by devise, etc. § 5. Any corporation formed under this act may take, hold or receive any property, real or personal, by virtue of any devise or bequest contained in any last will and testament; provided, that no person leaving a wife, child or parent shall devise or bequeath to such corporation more than one-fourth of his or her estate, after payment of all debts existing against said estate, and such devise or bequest shall be valid to the extent of such one-fourth only.

Liability of trustees. § 6. The trustees of any company or corporation organized under the provisions of this act shall be jointly and severally liable for all debts due from said company or corporation, contracted while they are trustees; provided said debts are payable within one year from the time they shall have been contracted; and provided further, that a suit for the collection of the same shall be brought within one year after the debt shall become due and payable.

Certificate and inventory to § 7. It shall be the duty of the trustees, directors or managers of all corporations formed under this act, or a majority of said trustees, directors or managers, on or before the fifteenth day of January in each year, to make and file in the county clerk's office where the certificate of incorporation is filed, a certificate under their hands, stating the names of the trustees and officers of such corporation, with an inventory of the property and effects and liabilities thereof, with an affidavit of said trustees, directors or managers of the truth of such certificate and inventory; and also a like affidavit that such corporation has not been engaged, directly or indirectly, in any other business than such as is set forth in the certificate of incorporation. be annually made and filed.

§ 8. Every corporation formed under this act shall possess the general powers conferred by and be subject to the provisions and restrictions of the third title of the eighteenth chapter of the first part of the Revised Statutes. General powers.

§ 9. The legislature may at any time alter, amend or repeal this act, or any part thereof.

§ 10. This act shall take effect immediately.

CHAP. 417.

AN ACT to enable lodges of the Independent Order of Odd Fellows to take, hold and convey real and personal estate.

PASSED May 6, 1873.

The People of the State of New York, represented in Senate and Assembly, do enact as follows:

SECTION 1. Whenever any lodge of Odd Fellows which is or hereafter may be duly chartered by and installed according to the general rules and regulations of the Grand Lodge of the Independent Order of Odd Fellows of the state of New York shall be desirous of having the benefit of this act it shall and may be lawful for such lodge at any regular communication thereof, held in accordance with the constitution and general regulations of the grand lodge aforesaid, and in conformity to its own by-laws, to elect three trustees for such lodge for the purpose aforesaid, a certificate of which election and purpose shall be made and subscribed by the first three elective officers of such lodge under their hands, and stating therein the time and place of such election, the regularity thereof, the names of said trustees and the terms severally for which they are allotted to serve, and the name of the lodge for which they are elected. The execution of such certificate shall be acknowledged or proved before some officer authorized to take the acknowledgment of deeds, who shall indorse thereon a certificate of such acknowledgment under his hand, and the same shall be filed in the office of the secretary of state. Such trustees and their successors shall thereupon be and become entitled to all the benefits, rights and privileges Election of trustees. Certificate of election.

granted by this act, to and for the use and behoof of said lodge, and a copy of said certificate, certified by the secretary of state or his deputy, shall be evidence of the right of such trustees to exercise all the rights and privileges conferred by this act; and said trustees shall thereupon be authorized to take, hold and convey real and personal estate for the charitable purposes of said lodge, not exceeding the clear annual value of ten thousand dollars.

Trustees to be classified. § 2. The persons so first elected trustees shall be divided by lot, by said officers making said certificate, so that the term of one shall expire on the thirty-first day of December next thereafter, and another in one year, and the third in two years thereafter. One trustee shall annually thereafter, prior to the expiration of the terms of office of said trustees and their successors, be elected by said lodge by ballot, in the same manner and at the same time as the first three officers thereof severally are or shall be elected according to the constitution, by-laws and general regulations aforesaid, and a certificate of said election, under the hands of said officers and the seal of the lodge, if they shall have one, shall be made and shall be evidence of said election, and entitle said person so elected to act as trustee. Vacancy. Said lodge may, at any regular communication, fill any vacancy that may have occurred in said board of trustees, to be certified in like manner and with like effect as at an annual election. The person so elected shall hold his office for and during the term of the trustee whose place he was elected to fill.

§ 3. If any person so elected trustee shall die, resign, demit, or be suspended or expelled from said lodge, remove from the state, or become insane, or otherwise incapacitated for performing the duties of said trust, his office as trustee therefor shall be deemed vacant, and such lodge may thereafter at any regular meeting fill such vacancy in the manner and with the effect stated in the last section.

Trustees to hold temporalities, etc. § 4. The trustees of any such lodge and their successors shall be and are hereby authorized to take, hold and convey, by and under the direction of said lodge, and for the use and benefit thereof, all the temporalities and property belonging thereto, whether consisting of real or personal estate, and whether the same shall have been given, granted or devised directly to such lodge or to any person or persons for their use or in trust for them or their benefit, and also in their individual names, with the addition of their title of trustees aforesaid, to sue and be sued in all courts and places having jurisdiction, and to recover, hold and enjoy in trust and subject as aforesaid, all the debts, demands, rights and privileges, and all Odd Fellows' halls, with the appurtenances, and all other estate and property belonging to such lodges in whatsoever manner the same may have been acquired, or in whose name soever the same may be held, as fully and amply as if the right or title thereto had originally been vested in said trustees, and also to purchase and hold for the purposes and subject as aforesaid, other real and personal estate, and to demise, lease and improve the same; and such lodge shall have power to make rules and regulations not inconsistent with the laws of this state, nor contrary to the constitution or general regulations of the grand body to which it shall be subordinate, for managing the temporal affairs of such lodge, and to dispose of its property and all other temporal concerns and revenue thereof, and the secretary and treasurer of such lodge duly elected and installed according to the constitution and general regulations aforesaid, shall, for the time being, be ex officio the secretary and treasurer of said trustees.

§ 5. Nothing in this act contained shall be construed or taken to give to such trustees of any lodge the power to purchase, sell, convey or dispose of any property, real or personal, of such lodge, nor shall they have such power except by and under the direction of such lodge duly had at a regular or stated communication thereof, according to the constitution and general regulation aforesaid, and said trustees shall at all times obey and abide by the directions, orders and resolutions of said lodge, duly passed at any regular or stated communication or convocation thereof, according to and not contravening the constitution and laws of this state, or of the grand body to which it shall be subordinate, or of the lodge aforesaid. Such trustees shall give such bonds for the faithful performance of their duties as are required by the by-laws of the lodge of which they are trustees. Powers of trustees limited.

§ 6. It shall and may be lawful for any lodge, or the trustees or officers thereof, under the direction of such lodge heretofore incorporated by the laws of this state, or thereby enabled to take and hold real or personal estate, or both, to surrender such act of incorporation, charter or privilege, and to be enabled to take and hold property, with all the rights and subject to all the provisions of this act, on making and filing the certificate in the manner specified in the first section of this act, and therein stating, in addition to what is therein required, the surrender of said act, charter or privilege, referring to and specifying the same, and on such certificate being so made and filed, the lodge making and filing the same shall thereupon be deemed as having fully surrendered such incorporation, charter or right, and its property shall be fully vested in the trustees specified in said certificate, and their successors, with all the rights, powers and privileges, and subject to all the provisions of this act. When lodge may surrender charter, etc.

§ 7. No board of trustees for any lodge filing the certificate aforesaid shall be deemed to be dissolved for any neglect or omission to elect a trustee annually or fill any vacancy or vacancies that may occur or exist at any time in said board, but it shall and may be lawful for said lodge to fill such vacancy or vacancies at any regular communication thereafter to be held, and until a vacancy arising from the expiration of the term of office of a trustee is filled as aforesaid, he shall continue to hold the said office and perform the duties thereof. Failure to elect trustee.

§ 8. This act shall be deemed a public act and shall be benignly construed in all courts and places to effectuate the objects thereof.

§ 9. This act shall take effect immediately.

CHAP. 425.

AN ACT in relation to the improvement of the Racket river, and of the hydraulic power thereon, and to check freshets therein.

PASSED May 7, 1878; three-fifths being present.

The People of the State of New York, represented in Senate and Assembly, do enact as follows:

Time to make and file maps, etc., extended.

SECTION 1. The commissioners appointed under and in pursuance of chapter ninety, laws of eighteen hundred and sixty-nine, being an act entitled "An act to provide for the improvement of the Racket river, and of the hydraulic power thereon, and to check freshets therein," shall have one year, from and after the passage of this act, in which to make and file the surveys and maps contemplated by the sixth section of said act; and in case any part or portion of the river, or of the lakes, ponds or lands mentioned in said sixth section shall be situate outside of the boundaries of St. Lawrence county, then the maps and surveys of such part and portion shall be filed also in the office of the clerk of the county where the same shall be located. Such commissioners shall, within one year after the making and filing of the surveys and maps aforesaid, commence proceedings for acquiring title to lands, as contemplated by section eleven of said act; and the statements, account, schedule and maps shall be thereafter made and filed, and the proceedings had, as provided in sections twelve and thirteen of said act.

Where to be filed.

Proceedings to acquire title, when to be commenced.

Plan of construction not to be changed.

§ 2. The plan of the construction of the dams, erections and other works made or established to create and maintain a reservoir on the Racket river, under or in pursuance of chapter ninety of the laws of eighteen hundred and sixty-nine, and acts amendatory thereof, shall not be essentially changed, enlarged or diminished, except by the consent of the owners of two-thirds in value of water powers on said river liable to be assessed under the acts aforesaid.

Duty of county judge on appeal.

§ 3. Upon the hearing of any appeal authorized or provided for by the act aforesaid, the county judge shall review and examine the matter appealed from, and it shall be his duty to thoroughly examine and review the findings, assessments, schedules and statements, or other matters appealed from, and the principles upon which the same have been made, and to affirm, amend, revise, modify, correct or reconstruct the whole or any portion of any finding, assessment, schedule or statement appealed from, or concerning which the appeal shall have been taken.

§ 4. This act shall take effect immediately.

Ante, vol. 7, p. 416.

CHAP. 427.

AN ACT in relation to challenges of jurors.

PASSED May 7, 1873.

The People of the State of New York, represented in Senate and Assembly, do enact as follows:

SECTION 1. All challenges of jurors, both in civil and criminal cases, shall be tried and determined by the court only. Either party may except to such determination, and, upon a writ of error or certiorari, the court may review any such decision the same as other questions arising upon the trial. Challenges to be tried by the court.

§ 2. On the trial of all felonies and misdemeanors, the prosecution shall be entitled to the same number of peremptory challenges as are or may be by law given to the defense. Peremptory challenges.

§ 3. This act shall take effect immediately.

CHAP. 432.

AN ACT to authorize the use of improved motive power on railroads in any city or county of this state.

PASSED May 7, 1873; three-fifths being present.

The People of the State of New York, represented in Senate and Assembly, do enact as follows:

SECTION 1. The mayor and common council of any city, the board of trustees of any village, and as to streets or roads outside of any such city or village, the board of supervisors of any county of this state are hereby authorized to permit the use of any motive power or motor, for the traction or propelling of cars on any city or street railroad which is or may be constructed and operated by horse power, within their respective jurisdiction, such permission to be subject to such restrictions, regulations and conditions as the said local authorities may impose, and subject to revocation at any time by the authority granting the same, by a two-third vote of its members. Mayor, etc., may allow use of improved motive power on street railroads.

§ 2. Nothing contained in this act shall authorize an increase of the rate of fare, nor allow the transportation of freight in any city, or allow the use of the ordinary dummy or box car engine, or of locomotives of the kind not used for the traction of cars on steam railroads of this state. Nothing in this act contained shall affect any contract in relation to the removal of steam power on any street in any city of this state. Not to authorize increase of fare, etc.

§ 3. This act shall take effect immediately.

CHAP. 435.

AN ACT to amend chapter four hundred and thirty-three, laws of eighteen hundred and seventy-two, entitled "An act to amend chapter seven hundred and twenty-one of the laws of eighteen hundred and seventy-one, entitled 'An act to amend and consolidate the several acts relating to the preservation of moose, wild deer, birds and fish,'" passed April twenty-six, eighteen hundred and seventy-one, also to repeal section thirty of said act.

PASSED May 7, 1873; three-fifths being present.

The People of the State of New York, represented in Senate and Assembly, do enact as follows:

SECTION 1. Section three of chapter four hundred and thirty-three of the laws of eighteen hundred and seventy-two, passed April twenty-ninth, eighteen hundred and seventy-two, entitled "An act to amend chapter seven hundred and twenty-one of the laws of eighteen hundred and seventy-one, entitled 'An act to amend and consolidate the several acts relating to the preservation of moose, wild deer, birds and fish,'" passed April twenty-six, eighteen hundred and seventy-one, also to repeal section thirty of said act, is hereby amended so as to read as follows:

Act not to apply to certain waters. § 3. Nothing in this act contained shall in any manner affect or apply to the waters of the river St. Lawrence, the lakes in Jefferson county, or the waters of Lake Ontario, except Irondequoit bay and Great Sodus bay, Port bay, and East bay in the county of Wayne, and the inlets thereof.

§ 2. Section seven of chapter four hundred and thirty-three of the laws of eighteen hundred and seventy-two is hereby amended so as to read as follows:

Taking fish with nets, etc., prohibited. § 7. No person shall at any time take any fish with a net or trap of any kind, or set any trap, net, weir or pot with intent to catch fish in any of the fresh waters or canals in this state, except as hereinbefore or hereinafter provided; nor shall it be lawful at any time to draw any seine or net for the taking of fish in any portion of Flushing bay or its branches, nor in Lakes Canandaigua, Cayuga, Oneida, Champlain, Great Sodus bay, Port bay and East bay, in the county of Wayne, or the inlets thereof; and any person violating the provisions of this section shall be deemed guilty of a misdemeanor, and shall likewise be liable to a penalty of twenty-five dollars for each offense; but suckers, cat-fish, bull-heads, bony fish or moss-bunkers, eels, white-fish, shad, herring and minnows are exempted from the operation of this section; also pike, in all waters save those lying in Columbia county and Oneida and Cayuga lakes, and their inlets; provided, however, that nothing in this section shall be so construed as to legalize the use of gill-nets in any of the inland waters or canals in this

Penalty.

Exemptions.

state; nor seines or nets of any kind in the waters of Otsego lake, except from the first day of March to the last day of August, and no gill-nets, except during the months of July and August. But no such seine or net shall have meshes less than two inches in size, and in the Hudson river the meshes of all gill-nets shall not be less than four and one-half inches in size each, and those of fykes set in any of the waters surrounding Long Island, Fire Island, Staten Island, and the bays and salt water estuaries and rivers approaching thereto, to be not less than four and one-half inches in size; and any person who shall willfully injure or destroy, by grappling or otherwise, any nets used in the Hudson or East rivers for the purposes of catching shad, shall be liable to a penalty of twenty-five dollars for each offense, and, in default of payment thereof, shall be imprisoned in the county jail of the county within whose jurisdiction the offense may be committed, for not more than thirty days. All drawing of seines in the Susquehanna river is prohibited.

Size of meshes.

Penalty.

§ 3. This act shall take effect immediately.

Ante, p. 369.

CHAP. 436.

AN ACT to amend an act entitled "An act to amend and consolidate the several acts relating to the preservation of moose, wild-deer, birds and fish," passed April twenty-sixth, eighteen hundred and seventy-one.

PASSED May 7, 1873; three-fifths being present.

The People of the State of New York, represented in Senate and Assembly, do enact as follows:

SECTION 1. Section twenty-nine of an act entitled "An act to amend and consolidate the several acts relating to the preservation of moose, wild deer, birds and fish," passed April twenty-sixth, eighteen hundred and seventy-one, is hereby amended so as to read as follows:

§ 29. It shall be unlawful for any person or persons to take, catch or procure in or from Conesus lake, Hemlock lake, and Silver lake, Seneca lake, Canandaigua lake and Honeoye lake, or the inlets or outlets thereof, lying within the counties of Livingston, Ontario, Seneca, Yates and Wyoming, any fish, except minnows, with or by any means or device other than a hook and line. And no person shall, in any manner whatever, take or catch from the waters of said Conesus or Silver lakes, Seneca lake, Canandaigua lake, and Honeoye lake, or the inlets or outlets thereof, any pike, pickerel, muscalonge, salmon-trout, black bass, or rock bass, between the first day of January and the first day of May. No person shall knowingly sell, or offer for sale, any fish caught in or from said

Fishing except with hook and line prohibited.

Sale of fish prohibited.

CHAP. 435.

AN ACT to amend chapter four hundred and thirty-three, laws of eighteen hundred and seventy-two, entitled "An act to amend chapter seven hundred and twenty-one of the laws of eighteen hundred and seventy-one, entitled 'An act to amend and consolidate the several acts relating to the preservation of moose, wild deer, birds and fish,'" passed April twenty-six, eighteen hundred and seventy-one, also to repeal section thirty of said act.

PASSED May 7, 1873; three-fifths being present.

The People of the State of New York, represented in Senate and Assembly, do enact as follows:

SECTION 1. Section three of chapter four hundred and thirty-three of the laws of eighteen hundred and seventy-two, passed April twenty-ninth, eighteen hundred and seventy-two, entitled "An act to amend chapter seven hundred and twenty-one of the laws of eighteen hundred and seventy-one, entitled 'An act to amend and consolidate the several acts relating to the preservation of moose, wild deer, birds and fish,'" passed April twenty-six, eighteen hundred and seventy-one, also to repeal section thirty of said act, is hereby amended so as to read as follows:

Act not to apply to certain waters. § 3. Nothing in this act contained shall in any manner affect or apply to the waters of the river St. Lawrence, the lakes in Jefferson county, or the waters of Lake Ontario, except Irondequoit bay and Great Sodus bay, Port bay, and East bay in the county of Wayne, and the inlets thereof.

§ 2. Section seven of chapter four hundred and thirty-three of the laws of eighteen hundred and seventy-two is hereby amended so as to read as follows:

Taking fish with nets, etc., prohibited. § 7. No person shall at any time take any fish with a net or trap of any kind, or set any trap, net, weir or pot with intent to catch fish in any of the fresh waters or canals in this state, except as hereinbefore or hereinafter provided; nor shall it be lawful at any time to draw any seine or net for the taking of fish in any portion of Flushing bay or its branches, nor in Lakes Canandaigua, Cayuga, Oneida, Champlain, Great Sodus bay, Port bay and East bay, in the county of Wayne, or the inlets thereof; and any person violating the provisions of this Penalty. section shall be deemed guilty of a misdemeanor, and shall likewise be liable to a penalty of twenty-five dollars for each Exemptions. offense; but suckers, cat-fish, bull-heads, bony fish or moss-bunkers, eels, white-fish, shad, herring and minnows are exempted from the operation of this section; also pike, in all waters save those lying in Columbia county and Oneida and Cayuga lakes, and their inlets; provided, however, that nothing in this section shall be so construed as to legalize the use of gill-nets in any of the inland waters or canals in this state; nor seines or nets of any kind in the waters of Otsego lake, except from the first day of March to the last day of August, and no gill-nets, except during the months of July and August. But no such seine or net shall have meshes less than two inches in size, and in the Hudson river the meshes of all gill-nets shall not be less than four and one-half inches in size each, and those of fykes set in any of the waters surrounding Long Island, Fire Island, Staten Island, and the bays and salt water estuaries and rivers approaching thereto, to be not less than four and one-half inches in size; and any person who shall willfully injure or destroy, by grappling or otherwise, any nets used in the Hudson or East rivers for the purposes of catching shad, shall be liable to a penalty of twenty-five dollars for each offense, and, in default of payment thereof, shall be imprisoned in the county jail of the county within whose jurisdiction the offense may be committed, for not more than thirty days. All drawing of seines in the Susquehanna river is prohibited.

Size of meshes.

Penalty.

§ 3. This act shall take effect immediately.

Ante, p. 369.

CHAP. 436.

AN ACT to amend an act entitled "An act to amend and consolidate the several acts relating to the preservation of moose, wild-deer, birds and fish," passed April twenty-sixth, eighteen hundred and seventy-one.

PASSED May 7, 1873; three-fifths being present.

The People of the State of New York, represented in Senate and Assembly, do enact as follows:

SECTION 1. Section twenty-nine of an act entitled "An act to amend and consolidate the several acts relating to the preservation of moose, wild deer, birds and fish," passed April twenty-sixth, eighteen hundred and seventy-one, is hereby amended so as to read as follows:

§ 29. It shall be unlawful for any person or persons to take, catch or procure in or from Conesus lake, Hemlock lake, and Silver lake, Seneca lake, Canandaigua lake and Honeoye lake, or the inlets or outlets thereof, lying within the counties of Livingston, Ontario, Seneca, Yates and Wyoming, any fish, except minnows, with or by any means or device other than a hook and line. And no person shall, in any manner whatever, take or catch from the waters of said Conesus or Silver lakes, Seneca lake, Canandaigua lake, and Honeoye lake, or the inlets or outlets thereof, any pike, pickerel, muscalonge, salmon-trout, black bass, or rock bass, between the first day of January and the first day of May. No person shall knowingly sell, or offer for sale, any fish caught in or from said

Fishing except with hook and line prohibited.

Sale of fish prohibited.

lakes, or the inlets or outlets thereof, contrary to the provisions of this section; and it shall be unlawful for any person knowingly to purchase any fish so taken in or from said lakes, or inlets or outlets. Whoever shall violate any foregoing provisions of this section shall be deemed guilty of a misdemeanor, and shall also be subject to a penalty for each offense of not less than fifteen nor more than fifty dollars, to be recovered in a civil action, with costs, as hereinafter provided. All fines and penalties imposed under the provisions of this section may be recovered with costs of suit by any person or persons, in his or their own names, by an action in the supreme court or any court of record of this state; which action shall be governed by the same rules as other actions in said supreme court or other court of record. On the non-payment of any judgment recovered in pursuance hereof, the defendant shall be committed to the common jail of the county in which such action shall be brought, for the period which shall be computed, at the rate of one day for each dollar of the amount of judgment, not to exceed thirty days. Any penalties, when collected, shall be paid by the court before which recovery shall be had, one-half to the commissioners of fisheries of the state of New York, and the remainder to the plaintiff or plaintiffs.

Penalty.

Imprisonment for non-payment of judgment.

§ 2. This act shall take effect immediately.

Ante, p. 187.

CHAP. 440.

AN ACT requiring commissioners of highways to act as inspectors of plank-roads and turnpikes.

PASSED May 8, 1873; three-fifths being present.

The People of the State of New York, represented in Senate and Assembly, do enact as follows:

SECTION 1. The commissioners of highways of the several towns in this state, and the trustees or other officers in the incorporated cities and villages of this state, who are authorized to perform the duties of commissioners of highways, are hereby constituted inspectors of plank-roads and turnpikes in their respective towns, cities and villages.

Plank-road inspectors.

Powers of. § 2. The said commissioners or officers shall possess the same power, perform the same duties, receive the same compensation, and be subject to the same restrictions, penalties and liabilities, in all respects, as inspectors now are under statute of this state, except as herein provided.

Duties of. § 3. It shall be the duty of said officers to personally inspect the whole of such plank or turnpike roads, or such part thereof as lie within their respective towns, villages or cities, at least once in each month, and in case the same shall be out of repair, or in such condition that the same cannot be conveniently used by the public, to give notice in writing thereof immediately to the toll-gatherer or person attending the gate nearest to each place out of repair or in bad condition, to order the toll-gate or gates upon said road to be immediately thrown open, and such gate or gates shall not be closed until such road shall be fully repaired or be in proper condition, to the satisfaction of said officers or a majority thereof. The notice to said toll-gatherer shall point out the part of such road to which the said officers shall object. The fees of each Fees. of said officers for the service in this section mentioned, shall be two dollars for each day actually employed in such service, to be paid by the corporation or persons whose road shall be so inspected by said officers in case they shall order said toll-gate or gates to be thrown open, but otherwise to be charged, audited and paid in the same manner as the other fees and expenses of commissioners of highways. Any party feeling himself aggrieved by the order of said plank-road inspector may appeal therefrom to the county court of the county in Appeals. which the part of the road embraced in said order is situate, said appeal to be brought within twenty days after the service of said order. The notice of the appeal shall be served upon one of said inspectors, and a copy thereof shall be filed in the county clerk's office. The said court shall proceed to hear said appeal, and after hearing the proofs and allegations of the parties, said judge may affirm, reverse or modify said order. During the pendency of such appeal, said toll-gate or gates shall remain open.

§ 4. All acts or parts of acts inconsistent with this act are hereby repealed.

§ 5. This act shall take effect immediately.

CHAP. 443.

AN ACT to authorize the trustees of The Willard Asylum for the Insane to appoint a fourth assistant physician.

PASSED May 8, 1873; three-fifths being present.

The People of the State of New York, represented in Senate and Assembly, do enact as follows:

SECTION 1. The trustees of The Willard Asylum for the Insane are hereby authorized to appoint a fourth assistant physician for said asylum, whenever in their judgment such assistant is required.

§ 2. This act shall take effect immediately.

CHAP. 467.

AN ACT to enable the commissioners appointed to revise the statutes to incorporate in their report the political and penal Codes, or so much thereof as they shall deem advisable.

PASSED May 9, 1873; three-fifths being present.

The People of the State of New York, represented in Senate and Assembly, do enact as follows:

Commissioners authorized to make Codes part of their revision. SECTION 1. The commissioners appointed to revise the statutes of this state, under and by virtue of chapter thirty-three of the laws of eighteen hundred and seventy, are hereby authorized to incorporate in and make a part of such revision, the Political Code, the Penal Code, the Code of Civil Procedure and the Code of Criminal Procedure, reported to the legislature by commissioners appointed pursuant to chapter two hundred and sixty-six of the laws of eighteen hundred and fifty-seven, or so much and such parts of said codes as the said commissioners for the revision of the statutes may deem advisable, with the same force and effect as though the said codes were now a part of the statutes of this state.

To submit their work in parts to the legislature. § 2. Whenever the said commissioners shall have completed one or more distinct parts or portions of their work, which may, in their opinion, be conveniently enacted into laws, before the completion of the entire work, they may submit the same to the legislature in print, with the appropriate repealing, supplemental or temporary acts also in print, and they may submit in like manner, at any time, such separate acts as they may recommend to be enacted for the purpose of facilitating or simplifying their work during its progress.

§ 3. This act shall take effect immediately.

CHAP. 469.

AN ACT relative to the purchasers of the franchises and property of corporations, whose franchises and property shall have been sold by mortgage.

PASSED May 9, 1873.

The People of the State of New York, represented in Senate and Assembly, do enact as follows:

When purchasers of franchises, sold under mortgage, may become a body corporate. SECTION 1. Whenever the franchises, privileges, easements, rights and liberties of any corporation, created by any act of the legislature of this state, or formed and incorporated under or by virtue of any general act thereof, and empowered by said act to mortgage its property or franchises, and the property, estate and effects of any such corporation, have been heretofore, or may be hereafter, sold by virtue of any mortgage executed by such corporation; and whenever the purchaser or purchasers thereof shall have acquired title to the same, in the manner prescribed by law, such purchaser or purchasers may associate with him or them any number of persons; and upon making and filing articles of association, as prescribed by this act, such purchaser or purchasers and his or their associates, and their successors and assigns, being residents of this state, shall thereupon become and be a body politic and corporate, and may take and receive a conveyance of, and shall thereupon succeed to possess and exercise and enjoy all the rights, powers, franchises, privileges, easements, liberties, property, estate and effects of which the title shall have been acquired and conveyed as aforesaid.

§ 2. In case the said corporation, whose franchises, privileges, easements, rights, powers, liberties, property, estate and effects shall have been so sold as aforesaid, shall have been incorporated under or by virtue of the provisions of any general statute or statutes of this state for the formation of corporations, the certificate so to be made and filed shall be in the form of, and shall state and set forth the particulars which, in and by such statute or statutes, were required to be stated and set forth in the original certificate of incorporation or articles of association of the said corporation. Certificate to state, where corporation was incorporated under general law.

§ 3. In case the corporation whose franchises, privileges, easements, rights, powers, liberties, property, estate and effects shall have been so sold as aforesaid, shall have been created by any special act of incorporation, then, and in that case, said certificates so to be made and filed shall state and set forth the following particulars, namely: Under special act.

1. The name of the body politic and corporate so to be formed as aforesaid.

2. The amount of the capital stock thereof, which shall not exceed the amount of the capital stock of the said former or pre-existing corporation authorized by law at the time of such sale as aforesaid, and the number of shares of which the said stock shall consist.

3. The title and time of the passage of the said original act creating the said former corporation, and any other act or acts relating thereto.

4. The number of the directors who shall manage the concerns of the said body politic and corporate, and the names of the first board of directors thereof, and who shall hold their office for one year and until others are chosen in their places.

§ 4. The said certificate shall be executed in duplicate and acknowledged before some officer competent to take acknowledgment of deeds. One of the said duplicates shall be filed in the office of the secretary of state, and the other thereof shall be filed in the office of the clerk of the county in which the said corporation first mentioned in this act had its principal place of business. And thereupon the said body politic and corporate so formed as aforesaid shall exist for the time, How to be executed.

Powers, etc. and may and shall possess, exercise and enjoy, all the powers, privileges, rights, liberties, easements and franchises possessed by the said former corporation, and in the same manner, and to the same extent, and with the same force and effect as the same could have been exercised by the said former corporation, had not such sale as aforesaid been made.

Evidence. § 5. A copy of any articles of association filed in pursuance of this act, and certified by the secretary of state and county clerk, with whom the same shall have been filed, or their deputies, to be a true copy of such articles and of the whole thereof, shall be received in all courts and places as legal evidence of the incorporation of the said body politic or corporate so to be formed as aforesaid.

§ 6. This act shall take effect immediately.

CHAP. 474.

AN ACT requiring county clerks to transmit to the secretary of state certified copies of the official county canvass.

PASSED May 9, 1878; three-fifths being present.

The People of the State of New York, represented in Senate and Assembly, do enact as follows:

SECTION 1. It shall be the duty of the clerk of each county in the state to transmit by mail to the secretary of state on or before the fifteenth day of December in each year, a certified copy of the official canvass of the votes cast in said county, by election districts, at the then next preceding general election.

CHAP. 477.

AN ACT authorizing the commissioners of highways in the several towns in this state to increase the penalty for riding or driving over bridges faster than a walk.

PASSED May 9, 1878; three-fifths being present.

The People of the State of New York, represented in Senate and Assembly, do enact as follows:

Penalty. SECTION 1. The commissioners of highways in the several towns in the state shall have the power to fix and prescribe the penalty incurred by any person or persons for riding or driving over any bridge in their respective towns faster than a walk. But such penalty shall not be less than one dollar nor more than five dollars.

§ 2. The commissioners of highways may put up and maintain in conspicuous places at each end of any bridge in such town maintained at the public charge, and the length of whose chord is not less than twenty-five feet, a notice in large characters stating the penalty incurred by any person or persons for riding or driving over such bridge faster than a walk. Notice to be put upon bridges.

§ 3. Whoever shall ride or drive faster than a walk over any bridge upon which such notice shall have been placed and shall then be, shall forfeit for every offense the amount fixed by such commissioners and specified in such notice.

§ 4. This act shall take effect immediately.

CHAP. 479.

AN ACT to amend an act entitled "An act to amend and consolidate the several acts relating to the preservation of moose, wild deer, birds and fish," passed April twenty-sixth, eighteen hundred and seventy-one.

PASSED May 9, 1873; three-fifths being present.

The People of the State of New York, represented in Senate and Assembly, do enact as follows:

SECTION 1. The thirty-eighth section of the act entitled "An act to amend and consolidate the several acts relating to the preservation of moose, wild deer, birds and fish," passed April twenty-sixth, eighteen hundred and seventy-one, is hereby amended by adding at the end of said section thirty-eight as follows: Judgments, how to be collected and enforced.

All judgments hereafter recovered by or in the name of any person, in pursuance of the provisions of this act, with the interest thereon, may be collected and the payment thereof enforced by execution; and any person imprisoned upon any such execution shall be so imprisoned for a period of not less than five days, and at the rate of one day for every dollar or fractional part thereof of such judgment and interest when the same exceeds five dollars. And such imprisonment shall not be satisfaction of such judgment. But no person shall be but once imprisoned upon any such judgment or execution. And any execution issued upon any such judgment against the body shall either recite the fact or have an indorsement thereon to the effect that such judgment was recovered for a violation of said act.

§ 2. This act shall take effect immediately

Ante, p. 187.

CHAP. 480.

AN ACT to amend an act entitled "An act to foster and develop the internal commerce of the state, by inviting and rewarding the practical and profitable introduction upon the canals of steam, caloric, electricity, or any motor other than animal power, for the propulsion of boats," passed April twenty-eight, eighteen hundred and seventy-one.

PASSED May 9, 1878; three-fifths being present.

The People of the State of New York, represented in Senate and Assembly, do enact as follows:

Powers of commissioners continued for one year.

SECTION 1. Chapter eight hundred and sixty-eight of the laws of eighteen hundred and seventy-one, entitled "An act to foster and develop the internal commerce of the state, by inviting and rewarding the practical and profitable introduction upon the canals of steam, caloric, electricity, or any motor other than animal power, for the propulsion of boats," is hereby amended so as to continue the powers of the commissioners appointed therein one year beyond the time limited by sections one and seven of said act.

Ante, p. 215.

CHAP. 489.

AN ACT to amend an act entitled "An act for the better security of mechanics and others erecting buildings in the counties of Westchester, Oneida, Cortland, Broome, Putnam, Rockland, Orleans, Niagara, Livingston, Otsego, Lewis, Orange and Dutchess, passed April seventeenth, eighteen hundred and fifty-four," and as amended by chapter five hundred and fifty-eight of the laws of eighteen hundred and sixty-nine, entitled "An act for the better security of mechanics and others erecting buildings in either of the counties of this state, except the counties of Erie, Kings, Queens, New York and Onondaga."

PASSED May 12, 1878; three-fifths being present.

The People of the State of New York, represented in Senate and Assembly, do enact as follows:

SECTION 1. Section one of the act entitled "An act for the better security of mechanics and others erecting buildings in the counties of Westchester, Oneida, Cortland, Broome, Putnam, Rockland, Orleans, Niagara, Livingston, Otsego, Lewis, Orange and Dutchess, passed April seventeenth, eighteen hundred and fifty-four," and as amended by chapter five hundred and fifty-eight of the laws of eighteen hundred and sixty-nine, entitled "An act for the better security of mechanics and others erecting buildings in either of the counties of this state, except the counties of Erie, Kings, Queens, New York and Onondaga," is hereby amended so as to read as follows:

Ante, vol. 4, p. 673; vol. 7, p. 456.

Persons who may have lien.

§ 1. Any person who shall hereafter perform any labor in erecting, altering or repairing any house, building, or the appurtenances to any house or building in either of the counties of this state, except the counties of Erie, Kings, Queens, New York, Onondaga and Rensselaer, or who shall furnish any materials therefor, with the consent of the owner, being such owner as is in this section hereinafter described, shall, on filing with the county clerk of the county in which the property is situate the notice prescribed by the fourth section of this act, have a lien for the value of such labor and materials upon such house, building or appurtenances, and upon the lot, premises, parcel or farm of land upon which the same shall stand, to the extent of the right, title and interest of the owner of the property, whether owner in fee or of a less estate, or whether a lessee for a term of years thereafter, or vendee in possession under a contract existing at the time of the filing of said notice, or any right, title and interest in real estate against which an execution at law may now be issued under the general provisions of the statutes in force in this state, relating to liens of judgment and enforcement thereof.

§ 2. Section two of said act is hereby amended so as to read as follows:

Amount limited.

§ 2. Whenever the labor performed or materials furnished shall be upon the credit of any contractor who shall have made a contract therefor with the owner of the property, or such person interested as aforesaid, whether such contract be oral or in writing, express or implied, or for any specified sum or otherwise, or upon the credit of any subcontract, or the assignee of any contractor, the provisions of this act shall not oblige the owner of the property or other person in interest as aforesaid to pay for or on account of any labor performed or materials furnished for such house, building or appurtenances any greater sum or amount than the price so stipulated and agreed to be paid therefor by said contract, or the value of such labor and materials, except as in the next section provided.

§ 3. Section three of said act is hereby amended to read as follows:

Payments made on contract, by collusion.

§ 3. If the owner, or such person in interest as aforesaid, of any building for or toward the construction, altering or repairing of which, or its appurtenances, labor or materials shall have been furnished by contract, whether oral or written, shall pay to any person any money or other valuable thing on such contract, by collusion, for the purpose of avoiding or with intent to avoid the provisions of this act, when the amount still due or to grow due to the contractor, subcontractor or assignee, after such payment has been made, shall be insufficient to satisfy the demands made, in conformity with the provisions of this act, the owner or other party in interest, as aforesaid, shall be liable to the amount that would have been due and owing to said contractor, subcontractor or assignee, at the time of the filing of the notice in the first section of this act mentioned, in the same manner as if no such payment had been made.

§ 4. Section four of said act is hereby amended to read as follows:

Within what time notice to be filed.

§ 4. Within sixty days after the performance and completion of such labor, or the final furnishing of such materials, the contractor, subcontractor, laborer or person furnishing the same, shall file a notice in writing in the clerk's office in the county where the property is located, specifying the amount of the claim and the person against whom the claim is made, the name of the owner, or of the party in interest, as aforesaid, of the premises, and if in a city or village, the situation of the building by street and number, if the street or number be known. The county clerk shall enter the particulars of such notice in a book to be kept in his office, to be called the "lien docket," which shall be suitably ruled in columns headed "claimants," "against whom claimed," "owners and parties in interest," "buildings," "amount claimed," and the date of the filing of the notice, hour and minute, what proceedings have been had. The names of the owners and parties in interest and other persons against whom the claims are made shall be entered in said book in alphabetical order. A fee of ten cents shall be paid to said clerk on filing such lien, and no lien shall attach to said land, buildings or appurtenances unless such notice shall be filed by said clerk; and such notice when so filed shall thereafter operate as an incumbrance upon said property.

Lien docket.

Clerk's fees.

§ 5. Section five of said act is hereby amended to read as follows:

Evidence to establish lien.

§ 5. Any person performing labor, or furnishing materials, in availing himself of the provisions of this act, shall, upon the trial, or at the assessment of damages, produce evidence to establish the value of such labor or materials; and that the same was performed for or used by the said owner or party in interest as aforesaid, or his agent, original contractor, subcontractor or assignee of such contractor, in or toward the construction, altering or repairing of such house, building or appurtenances.

§ 6. Section six of said act is hereby amended to read as follows:

Action to enforce lien.

§ 6. Any contractor, subcontractor, mechanic, laborer or other person performing any work or furnishing any materials as above provided, or the assignee of any such person or persons, may, after such labor has been performed or materials furnished, and filing of the notice required by the fourth section of this act, bring an action in the supreme court in the county in which the property is situate, or in the county court of said county when the amount exceeds fifty dollars, to enforce such lien, which action shall be commenced by serving a notice containing a statement of the facts constituting the claim and the amount thereof, and any other facts material to the case, on the owner of the property, or such party in interest as aforesaid, or his agent, as well as upon each and every claimant by whom notice of lien shall have been previously filed, as well as upon any contractor, subcontractor or other person having an interest in the subject-matter of said claim, requiring such person or persons to appear in person or by attorney within twenty days after such service and answer the same, and serve a copy of such answer, together with a notice of any set-off or claim that he or they may have, upon the claimant or his attorney, or in default thereof, that the claimant will take judgment against said owner or other person in interest as aforesaid, for the amount claimed to be due for the labor performed or materials furnished, with interest thereon and costs, and the enforcement of said lien; said supreme court and county court shall have full power to adjust and enforce all the rights and equities between all or any of said parties, and enforce or protect the same by any of the remedies usual in said courts.

§ 7. Section seven of said act is hereby amended so as to read as follows:

§ 7. Within twenty days after the service of said notice and a bill of particulars, as hereinafter provided, the defendant or defendants named therein shall personally serve the claimant, or his attorney, with a copy of his or their answer or answers, and notice of set-off, or counter-claim, if any, duly verified by oath, to the effect that the same is in all respects true, or his or their default may be entered and judgment taken and enforced as hereinafter provided. Answer, within what time to be served.

§ 8. Section eight of said act is hereby amended so as to read as follows:

§ 8. When the amount of the lien claimed is two hundred dollars or under, the claimant may commence his action in a justice's court of the town or city in which the premises are located, by serving a notice upon the owner or party in interest as aforesaid, or his or their agent anywhere within this state, requiring him or them to appear before a justice of the town or city in which such premises are located, which notice shall contain a statement of the facts constituting the claim and the amount thereof, and shall require him or them to appear before said justice in person, or by attorney, at a time certain, not less than twenty days after such service, and answer the same, or in default thereof, that the claimant will take judgment against such person or party in interest, for the amount so claimed to be due, with interest thereon and costs. Action in justices' court.

§ 9. Section nine of said act is hereby amended to read as follows:

§ 9. In any case where a notice hereinbefore mentioned can-

Notice, service of. not be served personally on such owner or party in interest, or his or their agent, by reason of absence from the state, or being concealed therein, then such service may be made by leaving a copy of such notice at the last place of residence of such owner or party in interest, and publishing a copy thereof for three weeks in succession, in a newspaper published in the city or county where the property is located; and in case of the service of such notice by publication, then the said twenty days shall commence to run from the date of first publication of said notice.

§ 10. Section ten of said act is hereby amended to read as follows:

Bill of particulars. § 10. At the time of the service of said notice, as hereinbefore directed, a bill of particulars of the amount claimed to be due from such owners or party in interest, his or their contractor or subcontractor, verified by the oath of the claimant, or his attorney, to the effect that the same is true, shall be served as aforesaid upon such owner or party in interest, or his or their agent, and all other persons made parties, if any, except that such bill of particulars need not be published with such notice.

§ 11. Section eleven of said act is hereby amended to read as follows:

When clerk may assess amount of lien. § 11. In case said owner or other party in interest, or the person or persons upon whom such notice shall have been served, as mentioned in section six of this act, shall not appear as required in and by the notice given in pursuance of the sixth and eighth sections of this act, then, on filing with the county clerk, when such action is brought in the supreme court or county court, or with the justice, when the action is before said justice, an affidavit of the service of such notice and bill of particulars, and the failure of the owner or other party in interest, and such person or persons as aforesaid, to appear as therein required, the amount of such claim may be assessed by said county clerk, or by the court or justice, as the case may be; and upon the assessment of damages as aforesaid, judgment shall be entered upon the said assessment, establishing the amount of said lien, with the costs; execution shall thereupon issue for the enforcement and collection (Execution.) of said claim so adjudicated and established, in the same manner as executions upon other judgments in said courts, in actions arising on contract for the recovery of money only, except that the execution shall direct the officer to sell the right, title and interest which the owner, or other person in interest, had in the premises at the time of filing the notice prescribed by the first section of this act.

§ 12. Section twelve of said act is hereby amended to read as follows:

Issue in justice's court, how formed. § 12. On the appearance of both parties before the justice, where an action is brought before a justice of the peace, the owner or other party in interest as aforesaid shall put in an answer in writing duly verified with a bill of particulars, or counter-claim or set-off (if any) annexed, and the issue formed by the service of the notice and bill of particulars on the part of the claimant, and the answer and bill of particulars on the part of the owner or other party in interest, shall be tried and governed by the same rules as other issues in justices' courts; and the judgment thereon shall be enforced, if for the claimant, as hereby provided, and if for the owner or other party in interest, as in other actions arising on contract.

§ 13. Section thirteen of said act is hereby amended to read as follows:

§ 13. When the action is brought in the supreme court or in the county court, the issue shall be formed by the service of the notice and the bill of particulars, on the part of the claimant as before directed; and the answer with a bill of particulars, set-off or counter-claim of the owner or other party in interest, or of any other person who has been made defendant as hereinbefore provided, duly verified. In supreme court.

§ 14. Section fourteen of said act is hereby amended to read as follows:

§ 14. At any time after the issue shall be so joined in the supreme court or county court, and at least fourteen days before the commencement of the court, the same may be noticed for trial and put upon the calendar of said courts by either party furnishing the clerk of the court with a note of issue as now required in other actions; and the action thereafter shall be governed and tried in all respects as upon issues joined and judgment rendered in other actions for relief arising on money demands upon contracts in said courts; and judgment thereupon shall be enforced if for the claimant, as provided by this act, and if for the owner or person or persons in interest, as in other actions arising on contract. Notice of trial.

§ 15. When such action is brought in the supreme court or in the county court, such court shall have power to ascertain and declare the interest of the several claimants, if more than one, in the moneys due or to grow due from the owner or other person or persons interested in said premises, as aforesaid, and the priority and amounts of the respective liens, as well as to adjudge or decree the particular person or persons entitled thereto, and to declare the interest of all parties who have been made parties to the proceedings, and to conclude the whole controversy in one final decision, and for that purpose to render judgment or make such order or decree in favor of or against any one or more of the parties severally or jointly as may be just, leaving the action to proceed against the other party or parties, and may order separate trials between any of the parties in its discretion. When the court to determine interests of the several claimants.

§ 16. When a judgment has been rendered by any justice in favor of a claimant, such justice shall give a transcript thereof, which may be filed and docketed in the office of the clerk of the county where the judgment was rendered. Such transcript shall contain the full name or names of the party or parties, in whose favor or against whom such judgment shall be rendered, and their relation as claimant or owner, debtor or creditor, a specific description of the premises affected thereby, Transcript of judgment to be filed, etc.

the amount for which such judgment is rendered, together with the costs incident thereto. The time of receipt of such transcript by the county clerk shall be noted thereon, and entered on a docket, and thereupon such judgment shall become a judgment of the county court and enforceable in all respects as provided by section eleven of this act.

Reference to take proof. § 17. All or any of the issues in such action (if brought in the supreme court or a county court) or for the purpose of taking proofs therein, may be referred by the written consent of the parties, or where the parties do not consent, the court may, upon the application of any party to such action, direct a reference thereof, in the same manner and to the same effect, in all respects, as specified in section two hundred and seventy-one of the Code of Procedure, and such referee or referees shall have all the powers conferred upon referees by sections two hundred and seventy-two and two hundred and seventy-three of said Code.

§ 18. Section sixteen of said act is hereby amended to read as follows:

Costs, etc. § 16. Costs and disbursements shall be allowed to either party upon the principles and by the same rules in such actions as are now allowed by law in actions for relief arising on contract, and shall be included in the judgment recovered therein, and the expenses incurred in serving said notice by publication may be allowed in justices' courts, and added to the amount of costs now allowed in said courts. When the action is brought in the supreme court or in a county court, such direction shall be made in the discretion of the court, as to the payment of costs, as shall be just and equitable, and the judgment entered shall specify as to whom and by whom the costs are to be paid.

§ 19. Section seventeen of said act is hereby amended so as to read as follows:

Transcript, filing of, etc. § 17. A transcript of every judgment rendered under this act, headed "lien docket," shall be furnished by the clerk of the county where rendered and docketed to the successful party, who may file the same with the county clerk of any other county, and the same shall thereafter be a lien on the real property, in the county where the same is filed and docketed, of every person against whom the same is rendered, if, for twenty-five dollars or upward, exclusive of costs, in like manner and to the same extent as in other actions for the recovery of money arising on contracts, and where the judgment is against the claims, the county clerk shall enter the word "discharged" under the last head in his lien docket, on receiving a transcript from the county clerk or justice that judgment has been rendered against the claimant.

§ 20. Section eighteen of said act is hereby amended so as to read as follows:

Proofs of claims of other claimants. § 18. In case the owner or his agent, or other parties in interest, shall desire to secure proofs of and from persons having claims under the provisions of this act, he may at any time give personal notice to such person or persons, or if, by reason of absence from the state, or being concealed therein, such personal service cannot be made, then such owner or party interested in such property as aforesaid, or his or their agent, may, at any time, give public notice in the same manner as notice is required to be given for sale of real estate by virtue of an execution, to all persons having claims under any of the provisions of this act against such buildings, lands, premises or appurtenances, at the time of the date of publishing such notice, to present the same, with vouchers in support thereof, to any justice of the peace in the city, town or village where such premises are situated, on or before a certain hour or day to be specified in said notice, and to be at least six weeks from the service or the first publication of said notice; and in case of the failure of such person or persons to present his or their claims as required by said notice, each and every person so failing shall forever lose the benefit and be precluded of the said lien.

§ 21. Section nineteen of said act is hereby amended to read as follows:

§ 19. Whenever such owner or party in interest as aforesaid, or his or their agent, shall be proceeded against by a mechanic, contractor or subcontractor, or any other person claiming under the provisions of this act, it shall be lawful for such owner or person in interest, or his or their agent, to give the notice prescribed by the preceding section for the presentation of claims to the court or justice before whom the proceedings all commenced, and present as a set-off, all claims and liens thereupon presented or established, and the justice before whom, or a judge of the court in which, the proceedings shall be commenced, may, upon the request of the owner or his agent, or such person interested in the premises as aforesaid, grant a stay of proceedings, sufficient to enable such notice to be given, and call in all such claims, which said claims, if established and allowed by the justice or the court, shall be adjusted and may be a set-off to such contractor's claim to the amount so allowed, or otherwise, as shall be just, according to priority, and the court may determine and enforce any of the claims so presented, and render judgment thereupon.

Owner to give notice to claimants to present claims.

Stay of proceedings.

§ 22. Section twenty of said act is hereby amended to read as follows:

§ 20. Every lien created under the provisions of this act shall continue until the expiration of one year, unless sooner discharged by the court, or some legal act of the claimant in the proceedings, but if, within such year, proceedings are commenced under this act to enforce or foreclose such lien, then such lien shall continue until judgment is rendered thereon, and for one year thereafter; such lien shall also continue during the pendency of an appeal, and for one year after the determination thereof. When a judgment is rendered as aforesaid, it may be docketed in any county of this state and enforced as if obtained in an action in a court of record.

Limitation.

§ 23. Section twenty-one of said act is hereby amended so as to read as follows:

Appeal. § 21. After a judgment shall have been rendered in pursuance of the provisions of this act, either party may appeal therefrom in the same manner, and within the time appeals may now be taken in actions for the recovery of money arising on contract, and said appeal shall be thereafter heard, governed and determined upon the same principles and by the rules that appeals in said actions are now heard, governed and determined, with like costs and disbursements, and the judgment thereon enforced in the same manner as judgments on appeal are now enforced and collected. Such appeal shall be had and taken only in the proceeding or action wherein judgment shall be given or rendered, but such appeal shall not be operative as a stay of proceedings, or in any manner to affect the foreclosure or action of any other claimant or claimants then pending.

Judgment for deficiency. § 24. When any action is brought in the supreme court or county court, under the provisions of this act, the court shall have power to direct that judgment be entered for any deficiency remaining after the enforcement of the judgment originally rendered in such action against the owner or other party interested in said premises affected thereby, and may issue execution against other property, real or personal, of such owner or party interested as aforesaid.

§ 25. Section twenty-two of said act is hereby amended so as to read as follows:

Priority of payment. § 22. The liens created and established by virtue of the provisions of this act shall be paid and settled according to priority of notice filed with the county clerk, as directed by the fourth section hereof.

§ 26. Section twenty-three of said act is hereby amended so as to read as follows:

Liens, how discharged. § 23. All liens created by this act may be discharged as follows: First. By filing with the county clerk a certificate of the claimant or his successor in interest, acknowledged or proved in the same manner as a conveyance of real estate, stating that the lien has been paid or discharged. Second. By depositing with the justice or clerk of the court a sum of money equal to double the amount claimed, which money shall thereupon be held subject to the determination of the lien; or, Third. By an entry of the county clerk, made in the book of liens, that the proceedings on the part of the claimant have been dismissed by the court in which it is brought, or a judgment rendered against the said claimant; or, Fourth. By an affidavit of the service of a notice from the owner or party in interest, as aforesaid, or his or their agent, attorney, contractor or subcontractor, to the claimant, requiring such claimant to commence an action for the enforcement of his lien, and the failure of said claimant to commence an action as provided by section twenty of this act.

§ 27. Section twenty-four is hereby amended so as to read as follows:

§ 24. All acts heretofore passed for the better security of mechanics and others erecting buildings and furnishing materials, in either of the counties of this state, except the counties of Kings, Queens, Erie, New York, Onondaga and Rensselaer, are hereby repealed; but this act shall not be so construed as to affect, enlarge, invalidate or defeat any lien or right to a lien now existing, or any proceeding to enforce such liens now pending by virtue of the provisions of the acts hereby repealed. Acts repealed.

§ 28. This act to take effect immediately.

CHAP. 501.

AN ACT to amend an act entitled "An act requiring mortgages of personal property to be filed in the town clerk's and other offices," passed April twenty-nine, eighteen hundred and thirty-three.

PASSED May 18, 1873; three-fifths being present.

The People of the State of New York, represented in Senate and Assembly, do enact as follows:

SECTION 1. The third section of the act entitled "An act requiring mortgages of personal property to be filed in the town clerk's and other offices," passed April twenty-ninth, eighteen hundred and thirty-three, is hereby amended so as to read as follows: When mortgage to cease to be a lien as against creditors.

§ 3. Every mortgage filed in pursuance of this act shall cease to be valid as against the creditors of the person making the same, or against subsequent purchasers or mortgagees in good faith, after the expiration of one year from the filing thereof, unless within thirty days next preceding the expiration of each and every term of one year after the filing of such mortgage, a true copy of such mortgage, together with a statement exhibiting the interest of the mortgagee in the property thereby claimed by him by virtue thereof, shall be again filed in the office of the clerk aforesaid, of the town or city where the mortgagor shall then reside.

Ante, vol. 4, p. 435.

CHAP. 515.

AN ACT to amend chapter seven hundred and sixty-seven of the laws of eighteen hundred and seventy-two, relating to salaries of county judge and surrogate.

PASSED May 15, 1873; three-fifths being present.

The People of the State of New York, represented in Senate and Assembly, do enact as follows:

SECTION 1. The ninth paragraph of section one of the act entitled "An act to establish the compensation of county judges and surrogates, pursuant to the fifteenth section of the amended sixth article of the constitution," passed May seventeenth, eighteen hundred and seventy-two, is hereby amended so as to read as follows:

Salaries of county judges. "The salary of the county judge of the county of Chautauqua is hereby fixed at the sum of two thousand dollars."

§ 2. The sixth paragraph of the third section of said act is hereby amended so as to read as follows:

"In the counties of Yates, Schuyler, and Putnam, one thousand five hundred dollars."

§ 3. The second paragraph of section one of said act is hereby amended so as to read as follows:

"The salary of the county judge of the county of Kings is hereby fixed at the sum of ten thousand dollars."

§ 4. The first paragraph of section two of said act is hereby amended so as to read as follows:

Of surrogates. "The salary of the surrogate of the county of Kings is hereby fixed at the sum of ten thousand dollars."

§ 5. The second paragraph of section two of said act is hereby amended so as to read as follows:

"The salaries of the surrogates of the counties of Albany, Monroe, Rensselaer and Westchester are hereby fixed at the sum of four thousand dollars."

§ 6. The third paragraph of section two of said act is hereby amended so as to read as follows:

"The salaries of the surrogates of the counties of Onondaga and Oneida are hereby fixed at the sum of three thousand and five hundred dollars each."

§ 7. The fourth paragraph of section two of said act is hereby amended so as to read as follows:

"The salaries of the surrogates of the counties of Queens, Dutchess, Ulster, Orange and Columbia are hereby fixed at the sum of three thousand dollars each."

Increased salaries, when due and payable. § 8. The increased salaries of the judicial officers whose salaries are changed by this act shall be due and payable to them respectively from and after the first day of January, eighteen hundred and seventy-three.

Ante, p. 478.

CHAP. 529.

AN ACT to re-appropriate moneys for construction of new work upon, and extraordinary repairs of, the canals of this state.

PASSED May 16, 1873; three-fifths being present.

The People of the State of New York, represented in Senate and Assembly, do enact as follows:

SECTION 1. The unexpended balance of seven hundred and seventy-six thousand eight hundred and fifty-five dollars and twenty-eight cents, appropriated by act chapter nine hundred and thirty of the laws of one thousand eight hundred and seventy-one, entitled "An act to authorize a tax of one-third mill of the valuation of the year eighteen hundred and seventy-one, for construction of new work upon, and extraordinary repairs of, the canals of this state," passed May twenty-third, eighteen hundred and seventy-one, being the sum of one hundred and sixty-seven thousand four hundred and nineteen dollars and seventy-three cents, or so much thereof as shall remain unexpended on the twenty-third day of May, eighteen hundred and seventy-three, is hereby re-appropriated to the same objects. Re-appropriation of money for new work, etc.

§ 2. This act shall take effect immediately.

Ante, p. 244.

CHAP. 530.

AN ACT to amend section two, title one, chapter thirteen, part one of the Revised Statutes of the state of New York.

PASSED May 16, 1873; three-fifths being present.

The People of the State of New York, represented in Senate and Assembly, do enact as follows:

SECTION 1. Section two of title one of chapter thirteen of part first of the Revised Statutes of this state is amended so as to read as follows:

§ 2. The term land, as used in this chapter, shall be construed to include the land itself, including land under water, all buildings and other articles erected upon, or affixed to the same, all trees and underwood growing thereon, and all mines, mineral, quarries, and fossils, in and under the same, except mines belonging to the state; and the terms real estate and real property, whenever they occur in this chapter, shall be construed as having the same meaning as the term land thus defined. Term "land" defined.

Ante, vol. 1, p. 360.

CHAP. 545.

AN ACT to provide for the repair, construction and improvement of bridges on the Cattaraugus Indian reservation, in the county of Erie.

PASSED May 20, 1878, by a two-third vote.

The People of the State of New York, represented in Senate and Assembly, do enact as follows:

Appropriation. SECTION 1. The sum of four thousand dollars, or so much thereof as shall be necessary, is hereby appropriated for the purpose of building a bridge across Clear creek, on the old plank-road, on the Cattaraugus Indian reservation, in the town of Collins, Erie county, and the necessary repairs on other bridges on said Indian reservation.

Commissioner. § 2. Asher Wright shall be the commissioner to superintend and direct the construction, repairs and improvement of said bridges, and to properly protect the same, with full power to contract for material and work for the erection and improvement of such bridge or bridges; and said commissioner is hereby authorized and empowered, by himself, his agent or contractor, to enter upon the public domain of said reservation, and take therefrom such timber and stone as may be necessary for the erection, repairs and improvement of said bridges, or the protection thereof.

Vacancy. § 3. In case of the death or refusal to serve of said commissioner, the comptroller shall have power and it shall be his duty to fill such vacancy.

Official bond. § 4. Such commissioner, before entering upon the discharge of his duties, shall execute a bond to the people of the state in the sum of eight thousand dollars, with two or more sureties, to be approved by the comptroller, conditioned for the faithful performance of his duties under this act.

Commissioner to account. § 5. Said commissioner shall account to the comptroller, from time to time, as he shall require, for all moneys received or expended by him under this act, and, within sixty days after the completion of said work, shall make a final report to the comptroller, containing a detailed description of said work and a full account of his expenditures. The said commissioner shall be entitled to receive three dollars for every day he shall devote to the performance of his duties, to be paid by the county of Erie.

Payment. § 6. The treasurer shall pay, on the warrant of the comptroller, the sums hereinbefore appropriated, or so much thereof as shall be necessary, to the said commissioner, on his voucher, in such sums and at such times as the comptroller shall prescribe for the purposes before mentioned.

§ 7. This act shall take effect immediately.

CHAP. 549.

AN ACT to amend an act entitled "An act regulating the sale of intoxicating liquors," passed April eleventh, eighteen hundred and seventy, and the act entitled "An act to suppress intemperance, and to regulate the sale of intoxicating liquors," passed April sixteenth, eighteen hundred and fifty-seven.

PASSED May 21, 1873; three-fifths being present.

The People of the State of New York, represented in Senate and Assembly, do enact as follows:

SECTION 1. Section two of the act entitled "An act regulating the sale of intoxicating liquors," passed April eleventh, eighteen hundred and seventy, is hereby amended by inserting after the words "and shall be paid as other city officers are paid," the words following: Provided that, in the city of New York, the commissioners of excise shall receive a salary not to exceed five thousand dollars a year each, to be fixed by the board of estimate and apportionment of said city, who shall annually fix such amount as may be necessary for hire of employees, rent and other necessary expenses of said board of commissioners, which amount shall be paid out of moneys received for licenses, and said commissioners shall receive no other compensation or emolument for their services as commissioners; and provided, further, that all moneys received for licenses in said city, under this act, shall be paid into the sinking fund for the payment of the principal of the city debt of said city, excepting such amounts as are otherwise appropriated by law.

Salary of commissioners in New York.

Moneys to be paid into sinking fund.

§ 2. Section four of said act is hereby amended so as to read as follows:

§ 4. The board of excise in any city, town or village shall have the power to grant license to any person or persons of good moral character, who shall be approved by them, permitting him or them to sell or dispose of, at any one named place within such city, town or village, strong or spirituous liquors, wines, ales and beer in quantities less than five gallons at a time upon receiving a license fee, to be fixed in their discretion, and which shall not be less than thirty dollars nor more than one hundred and fifty dollars in any town or village, and not less than thirty dollars nor more than two hundred and fifty dollars in any city. Such licenses shall only be granted on written application to the said board, signed by the applicant or applicants, specifying the place for which license is asked, and the name or names of the applicant or applicants, and of every person interested or to be interested in the business to authorize which the license shall be used; and the license shall be kept posted, by the person or persons licensed, in a conspicuous position in the room or place where his or their sales are made, and shall be exhibited at all times

To whom licenses may be granted.

Amount to be paid therefor.

Application for.

License to be posted in room where

sales are made. by the person or persons so licensed, and by all persons acting under such license, on demand, to every sheriff, constable or officer, or member of police. Any omission so to display and exhibit such certificate shall be presumptive evidence that any person or persons so omitting to display and exhibit the same has and have no license. The said board of excise shall keep a complete record of the names of all persons licensed, as herein provided, with a statement of the place licensed, and license fee imposed and paid in each case, which record they shall at all times permit to be seen in a convenient place at their principal office in any city, or at the clerk's office in any town or village. Persons not licensed may keep, and, in quantities not less than five gallons at a time, sell and dispose of strong and spirituous liquors, wines, ale and beer, provided that no part thereof shall be drunk or used in the building, garden or inclosure communicating with, or in any public street or place contiguous to the building in which the same be so kept, disposed of or sold.

Sales in quantities of five gallons and over.

§ 3. Section five of said act is amended so as to read as follows:

No sales to be made between one and five o'clock A. M., etc.,

§ 5. Licenses granted as in this act provided shall not authorize any person or persons to expose for sale, or sell, give away or dispose of any strong or spirituous liquors, wines, ale or beer on any day between the hours of one and five o'clock in the morning. And all places licensed as aforesaid shall be closed and kept closed between the hours aforesaid, and at all other times when such selling is not authorized by law. And it shall be the duty of every sheriff, constable, policeman and officer of police to enforce the observance of the foregoing provisions. Nothing herein contained shall be construed to prevent hotels from receiving and entertaining travelers at any time, subject to the restrictions contained in this act and the act hereby amended.

§ 4. Section eight of said act is hereby amended so as to read as follows:

When license to be forfeited.

§ 8. Any conviction for the violation of any provision of this act, or of the acts hereby amended, by any person or persons licensed, or at any place licensed as herein provided, shall forfeit and annul such license. The board of excise of any city, town or village may, at any time, and upon the complaint of any resident of said city, town or village, shall summon before them any person or persons licensed as aforesaid; and if they shall become satisfied that any such person or persons has or have violated any of the provisions of this act, or of the acts hereby amended, they shall revoke, cancel and annul the license of such person or persons, which they are hereby empowered to do, and where necessary to enter upon the premises and take possession of and cancel such license. Upon an inquiry, the said board, or the party complained of, may summon, and the said board may compel, the attendance of witnesses before them and examine them under oath.

§ 5. Section twenty-one of the act entitled "An act to suppress intemperance and to regulate the sale of intoxicating liquors," passed April fifteenth, eighteen hundred and fifty-seven, is hereby amended so as to read as follows:

§ 21. No inn, tavern or hotel keeper, or other person, shall sell or give away intoxicating liquors or wines on Sunday, or upon any day on which a general or special election or town meeting shall be held, and within one-quarter of a mile from the place where such general or special election or town meeting shall be held, in any of the villages, cities or towns of this state, to any person whatever, as a beverage. In case the election or town meetings shall not be general throughout the state, the provisions of this section, in such case, shall only apply to the city, county, village or town in which such election or town meeting shall be held. Whoever shall offend against the provisions of this section shall be guilty of a misdemeanor, and shall be punished for each offense by a fine not less than thirty dollars nor more than two hundred dollars, or by imprisonment not less than five days nor more than fifty days, or both such fine and imprisonment, at the discretion of the court. Days upon which sales are prohibited.

§ 6. Nothing herein contained shall in any manner apply to any city or town where the majority of voters have voted for, or shall hereafter vote for, local prohibition in accordance with any law providing for such voting, until such city or town shall reverse, by vote, such local prohibition. Not to apply to certain towns, etc.

§ 7. This act shall take effect immediately.

CHAP. 551.

AN ACT to amend chapter seven hundred and ninety-eight of the laws of eighteen hundred and sixty-eight, entitled "An act to amend chapter three hundred and sixty-five of the laws of eighteen hundred and sixty-two, entitled 'An act to authorize the discharge of mortgages of record in certain cases,' passed May ninth, eighteen hundred and sixty-eight."

PASSED May 21, 1873; three-fifths being present.

The People of the State of New York, represented in Senate and Assembly, do enact as follows:

SECTION 1. Section one of an act entitled "An act to authorize the discharge of mortgages of record in certain cases," passed April nineteen, eighteen hundred and sixty-two, is hereby amended by adding at the end thereof the following:

Provided, however, that if such mortgage has been duly assigned by indorsement thereon, or otherwise, but not acknowledged so as to entitle the same to be recorded, then it shall be competent for the court, at any time within the period aforesaid, upon proof that all the matters hereinbefore required to be stated in said petition are true, and that the assignee of Proviso as to mortgages assigned where assignment is not acknowledged.

such mortgage, if living, or his personal representative, if dead, has been paid the amount due thereon, to make an order that such mortgage be discharged of record.

CHAP. 552.

AN ACT in relation to lands of which parties die seized.

PASSED May 21, 1878.

The People of the State of New York, represented in Senate and Assembly, do enact as follows:

SECTION 1. In case of the death of any person intestate, seized in fee of real estate, within the state, it shall be lawful for the heirs at law of such person, or any one of them, to make an affidavit setting forth the fact of such death, the last place of residence of said intestate, the number of heirs, their names, ages and respective places of residence and relationship to the deceased, and, as nearly as possible, describing such real estate, and the respective interests of such heirs therein.

§ 2. Such affidavit, when so made, shall be presented to the surrogate of the county in which such real estate is situate, and said surrogate may, in his discretion, examine any witness or witnesses under oath as to the truth of the matters in such affidavit stated, and upon being satisfied of the truth of all such matters, shall indorse upon such affidavit his certificate thereof, and thereupon the said affidavit thus indorsed, together with the proofs so taken, shall be recorded in the county clerk's office of the county or counties where such lands are situated in the same books and manner as deeds are now recorded; and from the date of such record said affidavit, record and proofs shall be taken and regarded in all courts and legal proceedings in this state, in respect to the succession of such real estate, as presumptive evidence of the facts therein contained, and by this act required to be stated.

CHAP. 561.

AN ACT to amend chapter seven hundred and thirty-nine of the laws of eighteen hundred and fifty-seven, entitled "An act to authorize the formation of town insurance companies."*

PASSED May 21, 1873.

The People of the State of New York, represented in Senate and Assembly, do enact as follows:

SECTION 1. Section four of chapter seven hundred and thirty-nine of the laws of eighteen hundred and fifty-seven, entitled "An act to authorize the formation of town insurance companies," is hereby amended so as to read as follows, and as amended is hereby made applicable to all town insurance companies heretofore formed or organized thereunder:

§ 4. The directors of such company may issue policies, signed by their president and secretary, agreeing, in the name of such company, to pay all damages which may be sustained by fire or lightning, for a term not exceeding five years, by the holders of such policies, not exceeding the sum named in said policy, and which shall not exceed the sum of three thousand dollars in any one risk. Policies.

§ 2. Section ten of said act is hereby amended so as to read as follows:

§ 10. No company formed under this act shall insure any property out of the limits of the town or towns comprised in the formation of the company, nor shall they insure any property other than detached dwellings and their contents, farm buildings and their contents, and such stores, hotels, churches, school-houses and other public buildings, together with their contents, as the directors of any company formed under this act shall deem proper, provided such store, hotel, church, school-house or public building shall be at least one hundred feet from any other building, nor shall they insure any property within the limits of any incorporated city in this state. All acts and parts of acts inconsistent with the provisions of this act are hereby repealed. Property that may be insured.

§ 3. This act shall take effect immediately.

---

* The law of 1857, which authorized the formation of such companies, after being amended in 1858, 1860 and 1861, was repealed in 1862. Hence it was that that act and those amending it were not inserted in the former volumes of this compilation. Two acts were passed afterward, in 1866 and 1867, relating to companies actually organized, but expressly declaring that the act of 1857 was not revived. The act of 1873 would seem to regard the act of 1857 as still in force, and therefore all the acts relating to town insurance companies are now inserted here.

CHAP. 739.

[OF LAWS OF 1857.]

AN ACT to authorize the formation of town insurance companies.

PASSED April 17, 1857.

The People of the State of New York, represented in Senate and Assembly, do enact as follows:

What persons may form corporation. SECTION 1. It shall be lawful for any number of persons, not less than twenty-five, residing in any town in this state, who collectively shall own property of not less than fifty thousand dollars in value, which they desire to have insured, to form themselves into an incorporated company for the purpose of mutual insurance against loss or damage by fire, which corporation shall possess the usual powers and be subject to the usual duties of corporations, and the corporate name whereof shall embrace the name of the town in which the business office of said company shall be located.

Amended in 1858, post, p. 641.

Directors. § 2. Every company so formed shall choose of their number, not less than five nor more than nine directors, to manage the affairs of such company, who shall hold their office for one year and until others are elected, and such directors shall choose one of their number president and one as secretary.

Duties. § 3. The directors of such company shall file their articles of association, together with a copy of their by-laws and the names of the officers of such company, in the clerk's office of the town in which the office of such company is located, and shall keep a record of their proceedings in a book to be kept for that purpose, together with the names of all persons insured, and the amount each person is insured, which record shall be open for the inspection of all the members of such company, from the hours of nine o'clock A. M. to four o'clock P. M. of each secular day, the established holidays excepted.

Policies. § 4. The directors of such company may issue policies, signed by their president and secretary, agreeing, in the name of such company, to pay all damages which may be sustained by fire for a term not exceeding five years, by the holders of such policies, not exceeding the sum named in said policy, and which shall not exceed the sum of two thousand dollars in any one risk.

Amended 1873, ante, p. 637.

Undertakings. § 5. Every person so insured shall give his undertaking, bearing even date with the policy so issued to him, binding himself, his heirs and assigns, to pay his pro rata share to the company of all losses by fire which may be sustained by any member thereof; and every such undertaking shall, within five days after the execution thereof, be filed by the secretary of such company, in the office of the clerk of the town in which the office of said company is located, and shall remain permanently on file in such office, except when required to be produced in court as evidence. He shall also at the time of effecting insurance pay such percentage in cash, and such reasonable sum for a policy as may be required by the rules or by-laws of the company.

Amended 1860, post, p. 641.

§ 6. Every member of such company who may sustain loss or damage by fire, shall immediately notify the president of such company, or in case of his absence, the secretary thereof, who shall forthwith convene the directors of such company, whose duty it shall be when so convened, to appoint a committee of not less than three nor more than five members of such company to ascertain the amount of such loss, and in case of the inability of the parties to agree upon the amount of such damage, the claimant may appeal to the county judge of such county, whose duty it shall be to appoint three disinterested persons as a committee of reference, who shall have full authority to examine witnesses and to determine all matters in dispute; who shall make their award in writing to the president, or in his absence, to the secretary of such company, which award thereon shall be final. The said committee of reference shall each be allowed the sum of two dollars per day for each day's service so rendered, and the sum of four cents for every mile necessarily traveled in the discharge of such duties, which shall be paid by the claimant, unless the award of said committee shall exceed the sum offered by the company in liquidation of such loss or damage, in which case said expenses shall be paid by the company. In case of loss.

§ 7. The companies formed under the provisions of this act may classify the property insured therein at the time of issuing policies thereon under different rates, corresponding as nearly as may be to the greater or less risk from fire and loss, which may attach to each several building insured. Whenever the amount of any loss shall have been ascertained, which exceeds in amount the cash funds of the company, the president shall convene the directors of said company, who shall make an assessment upon all the property insured, to the amount for which each several piece of property is insured, taken in connection with the rate of premium under which it may have been classified. Insured property.

§ 8. It shall be the duty of the president, whenever such assessment shall have been completed, to immediately notify every person composing such company, by letter, sent to his usual post-office address, of the amount of such loss, and the sum due from him as his share thereof, and of the time when and to whom such payment is to be made; but such time shall not be less than sixty nor more than ninety days from the date of such notice, and every person designated to receive such money may demand and receive two per cent in addition to the amount due on each assessment as aforesaid, for his fees in receiving and paying over such money. Duty of president.

§ 9. Suits at law may be brought against any member of such company who shall neglect or refuse to pay any assess- Suits at law.

ment made upon them by the provisions of this act, and the directors of any company so formed who shall willfully refuse or neglect to perform the duties imposed upon them by the foregoing sections of this act, shall be liable in their individual capacity to the person sustaining such loss.

Insurance limits. § 10. No company formed under this act shall insure any property out of the limits of the town in which the office of the company is located, nor shall they insure any property other than detached dwellings and their contents, and farm buildings and their contents, nor shall they insure any property within the limits of any incorporated city of this state.

Amended in 1873, ante, p. 637; in 1858, post, p. 641.

§ 11. The directors of each company so formed shall be chosen by ballot at the annual meeting thereof, which shall be held on the first Tuesday of January in each year, and every person insured shall have one vote for each two hundred and fifty dollars which he may be insured, but no person shall be allowed to vote by proxy at such elections.

Annual statement. § 12. It shall be the duty of the secretary of every company as aforesaid, to prepare a statement showing the condition of such company on the day preceding their annual meeting, which statement shall contain the amount of property insured, the number of policies issued and to whom, and the amount insured by each policy, and all other matters pertaining to the interests of such company, which statement shall be filed in the office of the town clerk in which said company may be located, on or before the fifteenth day of January in each year, and which statement shall also be read to the members of said company at their annual meeting.

Withdrawals. § 13. Any member of such company may withdraw therefrom at any time by giving notice in writing to the president, or in his absence, to the secretary thereof, and paying his share of all claims then existing against said company, and the directors, or a majority thereof, shall have power to annul any policy by giving notice in writing to that effect to the holder thereof.

Amended in 1861, post, p. 642.

Non-residents. § 14. Non-residents of any town in this state owning property therein, may become members of any company founded under this act, and shall be entitled to all rights and privileges appertaining thereto, except that it shall not be lawful for any such non-resident to become a director in said company, unless he be at the time of such membership a resident of a town adjoining the town in which said company has been formed under the provisions of this act.

§ 15. The company so formed may adopt such by-laws for its regulation as are not inconsistent with the provisions of this act, and may therein prescribe the compensation of its officers.

§ 16. No company formed under this act shall continue for a longer period than thirty years.

§ 17. This act shall take effect immediately.

Repealed in 1869, post, p. 643.

CHAP. 285.

[Of Laws of 1858.]

AN ACT to amend an act entitled "An act authorizing the formation of town insurance companies."

Passed April 16, 1858; three-fifths being present.

The People of the State of New York, represented in Senate and Assembly, do enact as follows:

Section 1. The first section of "An act to authorize the formation of town insurance companies," passed April seventeenth, eighteen hundred and fifty-seven, is hereby altered to read as follows:

§ 1. It shall be lawful for any number of persons, not less than twenty-five, residing in any town, or in any two adjoining towns in this state, who collectively shall own property of not less than fifty thousand dollars in value, which they desire to have insured, to form themselves into an incorporated company, for the purpose of mutual insurance against loss or damage by fire, which corporation shall possess the usual powers, and be subject to the usual duties of corporations, and the corporate name whereof shall embrace the name of the town in which the business office of said company is located.

§ 2. Section ten is hereby amended so as to read as follows:

§ 10. No company formed under this act shall insure any property out of the limits of the town or towns comprised in the formation of the company, nor shall they insure any property other than detached dwellings and their contents, and farm buildings and their contents, nor shall they insure any property within the limits of any incorporated city in this state.

§ 3. This act shall take effect immediately.

CHAP. 153.

[Of Laws of 1860.]

AN ACT to amend an act entitled "An act to authorize the formation of town insurance companies," passed April seventeenth, eighteen hundred and fifty-seven.

Passed April 3, 1860.

The People of the State of New York, represented in Senate and Assembly, do enact as follows:

Section 1. So much of section five of the act entitled "An act to authorize the formation of town insurance companies," passed April seventeenth, eighteen hundred and fifty-seven, as relates to the filing of undertakings therein specified, within five days, is hereby amended so as to read as follows:

Every such undertaking shall, within thirty days after the execution thereof, be filed by the secretary of such company in the office of the clerk of the town in which the office of said company is located.

CHAP. 80.

[Of Laws of 1861.]

AN ACT to amend an act authorizing the formation of town insurance companies, passed April seventeenth, eighteen hundred and fifty-seven.

PASSED March 26, 1861; three-fifths being present.

The People of the State of New York, represented in Senate and Assembly, do enact as follows:

SECTION 1. Section thirteen, of an act entitled "An act to authorize the formation of town insurance companies," passed April seventeenth, eighteen hundred and fifty-seven, is hereby amended so as to read as follows:

§ 13. Any member of such company, with the consent of the majority of parties insured, may withdraw therefrom, at any time, by giving notice in writing to the president, or in his absence, to the secretary thereof, and paying his share of all claims then existing against said company; except that no such withdrawal shall be allowed, as to any insurance on property which shall have been damaged or destroyed by fire, and on which the company shall have paid to the insured damages for the loss sustained; but in such case and to the extent of such insurance, the insured shall remain a member of the company and be liable to be assessed for its losses or expenses on the amount so insured, during the term of such insurance. And the directors, or a majority of them, shall have power, subject, however, to the foregoing exceptions, to annul any policy, by giving notice in writing to that effect to the holder thereof.

CHAP. 347.

[Of Laws of 1862.]

AN ACT to repeal chapter seven hundred and thirty-nine of the laws of eighteen hundred and fifty-seven, and chapter two hundred and eighty-five of the laws of eighteen hundred and fifty-eight, in relation to town insurance companies.

PASSED April 19, 1862.

The People of the State of New York, represented in Senate and Assembly, do enact as follows:

SECTION 1. Chapter seven hundred and thirty-nine of the laws of eighteen hundred and fifty-seven, and chapter two hundred and eighty-five of the laws of eighteen hundred and fifty-eight, relating to town insurance companies, are hereby repealed; but nothing in this act contained shall affect any company or companies heretofore formed or organized under said chapters or either of them, or any rights acquired by such company or companies by virtue of such organization or organizations.

CHAP. 441.

[Of Laws of 1867.]

AN ACT to amend the act entitled "An act to authorize the formation of town insurance companies," passed April seventeenth, eighteen hundred and fifty-seven.

PASSED April 19, 1867.

The People of the State of New York, represented in Senate and Assembly, do enact as follows:

SECTION 1. The directors of any insurance company now existing, which was organized under chapter seven hundred and thirty-nine of the laws of eighteen hundred and fifty-seven, may issue policies, signed by their president and secretary, agreeing, in the name of such company, to pay all damages which may be sustained by fire, for a term not exceeding five years, by the holders of such policies, not exceeding the sum named in said policy, and which shall not exceed the sum of four thousand dollars. But nothing in this act contained shall be held or construed to revive or re-enact the said chapter seven hundred and thirty-nine of the laws of eighteen hundred and fifty-seven.

§ 2. This act shall take effect immediately.

CHAP. 828.

[Of Laws of 1866.]

AN ACT in relation to such companies or organizations as have been formed under the act entitled "An act to authorize the formation of town insurance companies," passed April seventeenth, eighteen hundred and fifty-seven.

PASSED April 27, 1866.

The People of the State of New York, represented in Senate and Assembly, do enact as follows:

SECTION 1. The directors of any company or organization formed under the act entitled "An act to authorize the formation of town insurance companies," passed April seventeenth, eighteen hundred and fifty-seven, shall be chosen by ballot at the annual meeting thereof, which shall be held on the second Tuesday in January in each year, and every person insured shall have one vote for each two hundred and fifty dollars which he may be insured, but no person shall be allowed to vote by proxy at such election. It shall be the duty of the secretary of every company as aforesaid, to prepare a statement showing the condition of such company on the day preceding their annual meeting, which statement shall contain the amount of property insured, and the number of policies issued and to whom, and the amount issued by each policy, and all other matters pertaining to the interests of such company, which statement shall be filed in the office of the town clerk in which such company may be located, on or before the twenty-fifth day of January in each year, and which statement shall also be read to the members of said company at their annual meeting.

§ 2. Nothing herein contained shall be held or construed to revive the act mentioned in section one hereof, or to authorize the formation of other companies under what were the provisions thereof before the same was repealed.

§ 3. This act shall take effect immediately.

CHAP. 565.

AN ACT making an appropriation to pay the expenses of the collection of tolls, superintendence, ordinary repairs and maintenance of the canals for the fiscal year commencing on the first day of October, one thousand eight hundred and seventy-three, and to supply a deficiency in former appropriation.

PASSED May 21, 1873; three-fifths being present.

The People of the State of New York, represented in Senate and Assembly, do enact as follows:

Appropriations. SECTION 1. The following sums are hereby appropriated out of the revenues of the state canals for the fiscal year commencing on the first day of October, eighteen hundred and seventy-three: For paying the expenses of the collection of tolls, the superintendence and ordinary repairs of the canals, the salaries, traveling expenses and clerk hire of the canal commissioners, the state engineer and surveyor, the canal appraisers and the incidental charges and expenses of their offices, the salary of the auditor of the canal department, the clerk hire therein and the incidental charges and expenses thereof, the sum of one million four hundred and sixty-five thousand three hundred and twenty-three dollars and seventy-four cents, or so much thereof as may be necessary to be expended during the fiscal year, to be distributed, applied, apportioned and disposed of as follows:

Salaries of commissioners, etc. For salaries, traveling expenses and clerk hire of the canal commissioners, twelve thousand and sixty dollars, and the clerk of the board of canal commissioners, two thousand and twenty-five dollars.

State engineer. For the salary and traveling expenses of the state engineer and surveyor, two thousand seven hundred dollars.

Clerks. For the salaries and clerk hire of the superintendents of repairs of the canals, the sum of seventy thousand dollars, or so much thereof as may be necessary.

Appraisers. For the salaries and traveling expenses of the canal appraisers, and for clerk hire in their office, the sum of twenty-five thousand twenty-five dollars, or so much thereof as may be necessary.

Auditor. For the salary of the auditor of the canal department, two thousand five hundred dollars, and for clerk hire in the said department, the sum of fifteen thousand dollars.

Engineers. For the salaries and compensation of the engineers employed on the ordinary repairs of the canals, including the incidental expenses of such engineers, the sum of twenty-four thousand dollars, or so much thereof as may be necessary.

Collectors, etc. For the salaries and compensation of the collectors of canal tolls and their clerks, and for salaries and compensation of weigh-masters and their assistants, including the incidental expenses of said collectors and weigh-masters, and the compensation of inspectors of boats and their cargoes, the sum of one hundred and ten thousand dollars, or so much thereof as may be necessary.

Miscellaneous expenses. For the payment of such incidental and miscellaneous charges and expenses as are authorized by existing statutes to be paid out of the canal revenues, and charged to the account of the Erie and Champlain canal fund and the canal debt sinking fund, under section one of article seven of the constitution, the sum of sixty thousand dollars, or so much thereof as may be necessary.

Ordinary repairs. For the payment of the expenses of the ordinary repairs of the completed canals of the state, and for the sums that may become due to the contractors for repairs under their contracts, and for no other object and purpose whatever, the sum of one million dollars, or so much thereof as may be necessary, to be distributed, assigned and apportioned, in the first instance, to the three divisions of the canals, as now constituted, as follows:

Eastern division. To the eastern division of the canals, the sum of five hundred thousand dollars.

Middle. To the middle division of the canals, the sum of two hundred and seventy-five thousand dollars.

Western. To the western division of the canals, the sum of two hundred and twenty-five thousand dollars.

Deficiency. The further sum of one hundred thousand dollars is hereby appropriated from the revenues of the canals for the current fiscal year, to supply a deficiency in the appropriation by act chapter three hundred and thirty-four of the laws of eighteen hundred and seventy-two, for payments to superintendents for the ordinary repairs of the eastern division of the canals.

Expenditures limited. The canal commissioners shall not expend any more money on their respective divisions, nor incur any charge against the state for the repairs of the canals during the fiscal year, than is above appropriated and apportioned to the said divisions by this act, unless the canal board, by resolution, to be entered on the minutes of said board, and by the concurring votes of five members thereof, shall otherwise order and direct.

Transfer of appropriations by canal board. And the said canal board, in case of breaks or breaches, or other extraordinary occurrences happening on any one of said divisions, causing or tending to a suspension or interruption of navigation upon such division, shall, and the said board is hereby authorized to direct, in manner above provided, the transfer of such portion of the unexpended balance of one or both the other divisions to the division requiring the same to sustain navigation, and the commissioner in charge of the division to which such transfer of appropriation shall be made, shall expend the same in the amendment and reparation of the canals under his charge, designated in the resolution of the canal board authorizing such transfer.

Auditor to notify amount required to § 2. The auditor of the canal department shall notify the canal commissioners of the sum of money that will be needed to pay the drafts during the fiscal year to the contractors for repairs under their contracts, upon their respective divisions, and he shall reserve such sums out of the appropriations made by this act for the purpose of paying the monthly drafts to contractors, and no part of the sums so reserved shall be paid or applied to any other object or purpose, and no draft shall be drawn on the auditor in favor of the contractors, unless upon a certificate from the canal commissioner in charge, that the contractor has fulfilled his contract during the preceding month. Pay contractors.

§ 3. This act shall take effect immediately.

CHAP. 571.

AN ACT further to define the powers and duties of the board of state commissioners of public charities, and to change the name of the board to The State Board of Charities.

PASSED May 21, 1873.

The People of the State of New York, represented in Senate and Assembly, do enact as follows:

SECTION 1. The commissioners now in office, appointed pursuant to the act entitled "An act to provide for the appointment of a board of commissioners of public charities and defining their duties and powers," passed May twenty-third, eighteen hundred and sixty-seven, and their successors to be hereafter appointed, shall constitute a board to be called "The State Board of Charities," and such board and commissioners shall have the powers conferred by said law and all amendments thereof, together with such further powers and duties as are hereinafter mentioned; and all provisions of said laws not inconsistent herewith shall apply to said board and to the said commissioners respectively. Such a board shall cause a record to be kept of its proceedings by its secretary or other proper officer. It shall have power to make and use an official seal and alter the same at pleasure, and its proceedings and copies of all papers and documents in its possession or custody may be authenticated in the usual form, under its official seal and the signature of its president and secretary, which may be used as evidence in all courts and places in this state, in like manner as similar certificates by the secretary of state or any other public officer. "The State Board of Charities." Record of proceedings. Official seal.

Ante, vol. 7, p. 213.

§ 2. Such board may, by its orders, from time to time, define the duties of its officers, and regulate the discharge of its functions; and shall, also, provide for the holding of, at least, four meetings during each year, which shall be public. Six members of the board, regularly convened, shall constitute a quorum. The failure, on the part of any commissioner appointed as aforesaid, to attend any three successive public Duties of officers, etc. Quorum. Failure to attend meetings a resignation. meetings of the board above provided for, during any calendar year, may be treated by the governor as a resignation by such non-attending commissioner, and the vacancy be filled; and the annual reports of said board shall give the names of each commissioner present at each of the said public meetings of the board.

Residence. § 3. One additional member of said board, who shall reside in the county of Kings, and two who shall reside in the county of New York, shall be appointed for the term of eight years, in the same manner as is provided in respect to the present commissioners.

Visitations. § 4. The said board or any one or more of said commissioners are hereby authorized, whenever they may deem it expedient, to visit and inspect any charitable, eleemosynary, correctional or reformatory institution in this state, excepting prisons, whether receiving state aid or maintained by municipalities or otherwise, and, also, to visit and inspect any incorporated or private asylums, institutions, homes or retreats, licensed for the detention, treatment and care of the insane, or persons of unsound mind, as hereinafter provided for.

Attorney-general to investigate affairs of institutions. § 5. If, in the opinion of said board, or any three members thereof, any matter in regard to the management or affairs of any institution, subject to the visitation of said board, or to any inmate of any such institution, or person in any way connected therewith, requires legal investigation or action of any kind, notice thereof may be given by the board or any three members thereof to the attorney-general; and it shall be his duty thereupon to make inquiry and take such proceedings in the premises as he may deem necessary and proper, and to report his action and the result thereof to the said board without delay.

Information from officers in charge. § 6. Said board shall have authority to require from the managers and from the officers in charge of any institution it is authorized to visit, any information which said board may require in the discharge of its duties, and may prepare regulations according to which and provide blanks upon which such information shall be furnished by any such officer and managers in a clear, uniform and prompt manner, for use by such board.

Statistics. § 7. The said board shall be authorized to collect (and as far as it may think advantageous to embody in its annual reports) such information, both in this state and elsewhere, as it may deem proper, relating to the best manner of dealing with those who require assistance from the public funds, or who receive aid from private charity; and to make such suggestions, from time to time, as to any legislation or action which may be desirable in regard thereto. The said board may also, from time to time, in its reports to the legislature, present such views in regard to the best method of caring for the pauper and destitute children distributed through the various institutions of this state, or are without the instruction and guidance which the public welfare demands; and, also, to furnish in tabulated statements, as nearly as possible, the numbers, sex, age and nativity of those in this state, and in the several counties thereof, which are in any way receiving the aid of public or private organized charity, with any other particulars they may deem proper.

County visitors. § 8. The said board shall have power, by a resolution to be entered on its minutes, subject to such terms and regulations as it may prescribe, to designate three or more suitable persons in any county to act as visitors, in said county, of the several poor-houses and other institutions therein, subject to the visitation of the board, in aid of and as representatives of said board, except such institutions as have a board of managers appointed by the state; and all officers and others in charge of such institutions shall admit to said institutions all such persons so designated, upon a production of a copy of such resolution, certified by the president or secretary of said board, to visit, examine and inspect the grounds and buildings of every institution, and every part thereof, and all its hospital and other arrangements, and to have free access to all its inmates. Penalty for refusal to admit county visitors, etc. Any officer, superintendent or person in charge of any such institution, who shall refuse to admit any person so designated, or shall refuse to give said visitors all requisite facilities for the examination and inspection as herein provided for, shall be subject to a penalty of two hundred and fifty dollars for each such refusal, which penalty may be sued for and recovered in the name of the people of the state, by the attorney-general, and the sum so recovered shall be paid into the treasury of this state.

Asylums, etc., to be licensed. § 9. No person, association or corporation shall establish or keep an asylum, institution, house or retreat for the care, custody or treatment of the insane, or persons of unsound mind, without first obtaining a license therefor from the said state board of charities, provided that all persons, associations or corporations who, at the time of the passage of this act, are engaged in keeping such asylums, institutions, houses or retreats, or in keeping insane persons, or persons of unsound mind, for compensation or hire, shall obtain such license within three months thereafter; and provided further, that this section shall not apply to any state asylum or institution, or any asylum or institution established or conducted by any county, or by any city or municipal corporation chartered by the legislature; and provided, also, that it shall not apply to cases where insane persons, or persons of unsound mind, are detained and treated at the houses of their families or relatives.

Applications for license. § 10. Every application for such license shall be accompanied by a plan of the premises proposed to be occupied, to be drawn on a scale of not less than one-eighth of an inch to a foot, with a description of the situation thereof, and the length, breadth and height of, and a reference by figure or letter to every room and apartment therein, and a statement of the quantity of land not covered by any building annexed to such house and appropriated to the exclusive use, exercise and recreation of the patients proposed to be received therein, and also a statement of the number of patients proposed to be received into such house, and whether the license so applied for is for the reception of male or female patients, or for both, and if for the reception of both, of the number of each sex proposed to be received into such house, and for the means by which the one sex may be kept distinct and apart from the other. And it shall not be lawful for said board to grant any such license without having first, either collectively or by a committee thereof, visited the premises proposed to be licensed, and, being satisfied by such examination that they conform to the description of the application, and are otherwise fit and suitable for the purposes for which they are designed to be used.

When board to grant license.

§ 11. Whenever said state board of charities, upon the application of any person, association or corporation, made as provided by the preceding section of this act, and examination of the building and means employed, or proposed to be employed, to take the care of insane persons, or persons of unsound mind, by such person, association or corporation, shall determine that the same are sufficient and proper for such purpose, the said board is hereby authorized and required to grant such license, and to make such conditions, terms and regulations, in regard thereto, as shall seem meet and proper for the care and protection, health and comfort, and for the inspection and examination of all insane persons, or persons of unsound mind, so lodged, boarded, kept or detained in such asylum or institution, and of all insane persons, or persons of unsound mind, in the charge or keeping of such person, association or corporation; which said license shall be filed in the office of the clerk of the county in which such asylum or institution is situated. The said board may revoke the license of any asylum or institution, issued under the provisions of this act, for reasons deemed satisfactory to said board; but such revocation shall be in writing and filed as aforesaid, and notice thereof given in writing to the person, association or corporation to whom such license was given.

Penalty for maintaining asylum without license.

§ 12. After the expiration of three months from the passage of this act, any person or persons who shall conduct or maintain any private insane asylum or institution, and the officers of any corporation who shall conduct or maintain such private asylum or institution without having obtained a license as herein provided, or for more than thirty days after the revocation of such license, or shall receive any patient after notice of such revocation, shall be guilty of a misdemeanor, and it shall be the duty of the district attorney of the proper county to proceed against such offender as may be provided by law.

State commissioner in lunacy.

§ 13. The governor shall nominate, and by and with the advice and consent of the senate, appoint an experienced and competent physician, to be called the state commissioner in lunacy, who shall hold his office for five years, and receive an annual salary of four thousand dollars, and traveling expenses not to exceed one thousand dollars, to be paid on presentation of vouchers to the comptroller; and who shall ex-officio be a member of the state board of charities, and shall make full report of all his official acts and visitation's to the said board, from time to time, under such regulations as the said board may prescribe. The said board shall furnish such assistance as the said commissioner may, in their opinion, require to aid him in the proper and efficient discharge of the duties of his office.

§ 14. It shall be the duty of such commissioner to examine into and report to said board the condition of the insane and idiotic in this state, and the management and conduct of the asylums and other institutions for their custody. The duties of said commissioner and those of said board in regard to the insane shall be performed, as far as practicable, so as not to prejudice the established and reasonable regulations of such asylums and institutions aforesaid; and it shall be the duty of the officers and others respectively in charge thereof to give the members of said board and such commissioner at all times free access to and full information concerning the insane and their treatment therein. It shall also be the duty of such commissioner, under the direction of said board, to inquire and report, from time to time, as far as he may be able, the results of the treatment of the insane of other states and countries, together with such particulars pertaining thereto as he may deem proper, or the said board may require; and he shall perform such other duties as the board may from time to time prescribe. The authority conferred upon said board and commissioners to issue compulsory process for the attendance of witnesses, administer oaths and to examine persons under oath, is hereby conferred upon said commissioner of lunacy in all cases where there is, in the opinion of the board or said commissioner, from information given to the board or to the said commissioner, or otherwise, reason to believe that any person is unjustly deprived of liberty, or is improperly treated in any asylum, institution or establishment in this state for the custody of the insane, and he shall report the testimony taken in any investigation to the said board with his opinions and conclusions thereon without delay. The said board of commissioners may, in their report, from time to time, to the legislature, suggest any improvements they think desirable for the care and treatment of the insane, with such facts and information pertaining thereto as they may deem expedient and proper, and such report shall be made annually on or before the fifteenth day of January.

Duty of commissioner.

Attendance of witnesses, etc.

§ 15. This act shall take effect immediately.

CHAP. 577.

AN ACT to amend an act entitled "An act to amend an act entitled 'An act to designate the holidays to be observed in the acceptance and payment of bills of exchange and promissory notes,'" passed April twenty-third, eighteen hundred and seventy.

PASSED May 22, 1873.

The People of the State of New York, represented in Senate and Assembly, do enact as follows:

SECTION 1. Section one of an act entitled "An act to amend an act entitled 'An act to designate the holidays to be observed in the acceptance and payment of bills of exchange and promissory notes,'" passed April twenty-third, eighteen hundred and seventy, is hereby amended so as to read as follows:

Holidays. § 1. The following days, namely: the first day of January, commonly called new year's day, the twenty-second day of February, the fourth day of July, the twenty-fifth day of December, any general election day, any day appointed or recommended by the governor of this state or the president of the United States, as a day of thanksgiving, or as a day of fasting or prayer, or other religious observance, the thirtieth day of May, to be known as decoration day, shall, for all purposes whatsoever, as regards the presenting for payment or acceptance, and of the protesting and giving notice of the dishonor of bills of exchange, bank checks and promissory notes, made after the passage of this act, be treated and considered as the first day of the week, commonly called Sunday and as public holidays.

Days to be holidays when days first named fall on Sunday. § 2. Whenever any of the holidays mentioned in the first section of this act shall fall hereafter upon Sunday, the Monday next following shall be deemed and considered as the first day of the week or Sunday, and a public holiday for all or any of the purposes aforesaid; and all bills of exchange, checks and promissory notes which shall, with or without grace, become due and payable on Sunday, or on any of the days mentioned in the preceding section, or on any Monday kept as aforesaid as a public holiday, shall be deemed to be due and payable on the business day next succeeding the day of their maturity.

§ 3. All acts or parts of acts inconsistent with this act are hereby repealed, but such repeal shall not affect any act done, or proceeding or suit instituted prior to the passage of this act.

§ 4. This act shall take effect immediately.

Ante, vol. 7, p. 718.

CHAP. 583.

AN ACT to define some of the rights and responsibilities of landlords and tenants.

PASSED May 22, 1873.

The People of the State of New York, represented in Senate and Assembly, do enact as follows:

SECTION 1. Whenever the lessee or occupant, other than the owner of any building or premises, shall use or occupy the same, or any part thereof, for any illegal trade, manufacture or other business, the lease or agreement for the letting or occupancy of such building or premises shall thereupon become void, and the landlord of such lessee or occupant may enter upon the premises so let or occupied, and shall have the same remedies to recover possession thereof as are given by law in the case of a tenant holding over after the expiration of his lease. When lease to become void.

§ 2. The owner or owners of any building or premises knowingly leasing or giving possession of the same, to be used or occupied, in whole or in part, for any illegal trade, manufacture or business, or knowingly permitting the same to be used for any illegal trade, manufacture or business, shall be jointly and severally liable with the tenant or tenants, occupant or occupants, for any damage that may result by reason of such illegal use, occupancy, trade, manufacture or business. Liability of owner leasing for illegal business.

§ 3. This act shall take effect immediately.

CHAP. 584.

AN ACT to provide building sites for life saving stations on the coast of Long Island, state of New York.

PASSED May 22, 1873, by a two-third vote.

WHEREAS, The congress of the United States has made appropriations for the repairing of the various life saving stations, and the building of additional ones on the coast of Long Island, New York; and as difficulties have, in some instances, arisen in procuring, from the owners of lands, proper sites on which to locate their buildings, and as it is deemed important and necessary in this humane cause that the people of this state should, through their representatives, secure to the United States such sites as the honorable the secretary of the treasury may have selected, or may, from time to time, select for the erection of buildings for this purpose. Therefore, Preamble.

The People of the State of New York, represented in Senate and Assembly, do enact as follows:

SECTION 1. The governor shall appoint three commissioners, with authority to procure for the state, by purchase, the title Commissioners to purchase site. to any land selected by the secretary of the treasury, or his agents, for the purpose of erecting any buildings connected with the life saving stations, and not to exceed one-half acre of land at any one point on the Long Island coast, at such prices as said commissioners, or a majority of them, may deem fair and just, and the title to the same to be taken in the name of the state of New York.

Title how acquired. § 2. In case the said commissioners cannot agree with the owner or owners of such required lands for the purchase thereof, or where by the legal incapacity or absence of such owner or owners no such agreement can be made, the said commissioners shall make, or cause to be made, a survey of the land, for the purpose of ascertaining and determining the value of the same, and assessing the damages, and shall cause ten days' notice of a meeting, and a copy of such particular description of the land to be given in writing to the parties interested, if known and in this state, or if out of this state, such notice to be published in one of the newspapers published in the county where said lands are situate, for a period of at least thirty days prior to the time appointed for such meeting; and the said commissioners shall meet at the time and place so appointed, and proceed to view and examine the said land, and make a just and equitable estimate or appraisement of the same, and assessment of damages;. which report shall be made in writing under the hands and seals of the said commissioners, or any two of them, and filed within ten days thereafter, together with the aforesaid survey and description of the lands, in the clerk's office of the county where said lands are situate, to remain on record therein; which report, or copy thereof certified by the clerk of said county, shall at all times be considered as plenary evidence of the right of the state to have, hold, use, occupy, convey, cede, possess and enjoy the said land; and said commissioners shall, at the said time of filing the said report, pay the amount of the said award to the county court of the said county where the said lands are situate, for the benefit of the owner or owners of the said land, and the state may take the said land upon the payment of the said award into the said court.

Appeal from report of commissioners. § 3. In case the owner or owners of the said land shall be dissatisfied with the report made by the said commissioners, the party so aggrieved may appeal to the county court of the county where the said lands are situate, at the first term after filing of the said report, by proceeding in form of petition to said court, which proceeding shall vest said court with power and right to direct an estimate or appraisement of the value of the land, and assessment of damages by a jury, to be impaneled and sworn as in other cases, and a view of the premises, if desired, and the same to be tried at the next term of the said court to be holden in said county, upon like notice and in the manner as other issues in the said court are tried; and it shall be the duty of the jury to assess the value of the said land and the damages sustained; and if they shall find a greater sum than the commissioners have awarded, then judgment thereon with costs shall be entered, and such excess with the cost shall be immediately paid into the county court for the benefit of the parties interested. But if the jury shall find the same or less sum than the commissioners awarded, then costs shall be paid by the said applicant or applicants, and the payments so made and paid into the county court shall be deemed to be valid and legal payments, and such application shall not prevent the state from taking the said land.

§ 4. The said commissioners shall take and file, in the office of the secretary of state, an oath well, truly and faithfully to perform the duties of their appointment before entering upon said duties. Official oath.

§ 5. The sum of two thousand dollars, or so much thereof as may be necessary, shall be, and the same is hereby, appropriated for the purchase of said land, and for the expenses attending the same, to be paid by the treasurer of this state out of any funds in the treasury, not otherwise appropriated on the warrant of the comptroller under requisition from the said commissioners. And said commissioners shall not contract any obligation nor create any liability on the part of the state beyond what will be paid by said sum of two thousand dollars hereby appropriated. Appropriation.

§ 6. Immediately after the title to the said lands or sites shall have been acquired by purchase or otherwise, the governor of this state is hereby authorized and required to convey the said lands or sites to the United States by good and sufficient conveyances and under the great seal of the state, for building sites, life saving stations, and for no other purpose, and without compensation to be paid by the United States. State to convey lands to the United States

§ 7. This act shall take effect immediately.

CHAP. 585.

AN ACT to provide for the final closing of incorporated banks.

PASSED May 22, 1873.

The People of the State of New York, represented in Senate and Assembly, do enact as follows:

SECTION 1. Any time after six years from the expiration of the charter of any bank, incorporated under the laws of this state, and whenever the trustees or legal representatives thereof shall have redeemed and returned to the bank department, to be canceled, eighty per cent of the circulating notes of said bank outstanding at the expiration of said charter, said trustees may publish in the state paper, and in one or more public newspapers printed in the city or village where When trustees may publish notice to bill holders to present same for redemption.

the said bank is located, or if no paper is printed in such place, then in some public newspaper or newspapers printed in the same county, once in each week successively, for six months, in which notice it shall be stated that the outstanding notes of said bank will be redeemed at par, at some bank in the city of Albany, to be named in such notice, at any time within two years from the first publication of said notice; which notice shall state the day on which said two years will expire, and shall require all persons holding any of said circulating notes to present the same within the said time at the designated bank for redemption, and that any of the notes of such bank not so presented for redemption within the time specified, will cease to be a charge or lien upon the property, funds or effects of such bank in the hands of said trustees, and that all liability of such trustees, for or on account of any notes which may not have been presented for redemption within the time specified in such notice, will cease.

Proof of publication to be filed.

§ 2. A copy of such notice shall be filed in the office of the superintendent of the banking department, at or before the first publication thereof, and also the proof of the due publication of the same, which proof shall be the affidavit of the printer and publisher of the newspapers in which such notice has been printed respectively. And upon the filing of said notice on proof, the superintendent of the banking department shall give to said trustees a certificate under his hand and seal of office, of the filing of such notice and of such proof, which certificate shall be conclusive evidence in all courts and places that such notice and proof of publication were so filed, and presumptive evidence of the publication of said notice in the papers, and for the time and manner in the affidavit of printer and publisher stated respectively.

Evidence.

When remaining effects may be divided.

§ 3. After the expiration of the two years mentioned in said notice, and the payment of all the notes of such bank which may have been presented for redemption, and after the delivery of the redeemed notes to the banking department to be canceled, and the payment of its proportion of the expenses of the bank department, and all other lawful claims and demands against such bank, the trustees or legal representatives who may have given such notice may divide the remaining property or effects of such bank among the stockholders thereof, their representatives or assigns, according to their respective shares or interest therein.

Liability of trustees, etc.

§ 4. In case the trustees or legal representatives of any bank shall neglect or refuse to redeem any of the circulating notes of such bank when presented within the time limited, and at the place mentioned in said notice, such trustees or legal representatives shall be personally liable to the holders of any such notes for the payment of the same after they may have made distribution of the property and effects of such bank among its stockholders; and so they shall be personally liable to the holders of any notes of any such bank when distribution of its property or effects has been made by them, without first giving such notice.

§ 5. All banks incorporated under the laws of this state, or their legal representatives, having an open account for circulation, or otherwise, on the books of the bank department, shall be subject to assessment for expenses of the department in the manner provided by section one, chapter one hundred and sixty-four, laws of eighteen hundred and fifty-one, until they shall have complied with the provisions of this act, or of former acts, relative to the final redemption of their circulating notes, and no bank shall be subject to such assessment after the expiration of the time for such redemption. Banks subject to assessment for expenses.

§ 6. This act shall take effect immediately.

CHAP. 586.

AN ACT to amend the twenty-third section of article first, title four, chapter second, part fourth of the Revised Statutes, entitled "Of the return and summoning of grand juries, their powers and duties."

PASSED May 22, 1873; three-fifths being present.

The People of the State of New York, represented in Senate and Assembly, do enact as follows:

SECTION 1. The twenty-third section of article first, title four, chapter second, part fourth of the Revised Statutes, is hereby amended so as to read as follows:

§ 23. If at any court of oyer and terminer, or court of sessions, there shall not appear at least sixteen persons, duly qualified, to serve as grand jurors, who shall have been summoned for that purpose, or, if the number of grand jurors attending shall be reduced below sixteen, by any of them being discharged, or otherwise, such court shall, by an order to be entered in its minutes, require the clerk of the county to draw, and the sheriff to summon, such additional number of grand jurors as it shall deem necessary, which number shall be specified in said order. The clerk of the county in which such court is held shall forthwith bring into said court the box containing the names of the grand jurors, from which grand jurors from said county are required to be drawn, and the said clerk shall, in the presence of said court, proceed publicly to draw the number of grand jurors specified in said order of such court, and when such drawing is complete, the said clerk shall make two lists of the persons so drawn, each of which shall be certified by him to be a correct list of the names of the persons so drawn by him, one of which he shall file in his office, and the other he shall deliver to the sheriff. The sheriff shall thereupon immediately proceed to summon the persons mentioned in such list to appear in the court in which the order requiring the attendance of such jurors shall have been made, at the time designated in such order, and the persons so summoned shall appear in obedience to such sum- When court to order additional grand jurors to be summoned.

mons, and all the provisions of law relating to the summoning and the swearing in of grand jurors, and their punishment for non-attendance, not inconsistent with this act, shall apply to the swearing in, summoning and punishment of the grand jurors drawn and summoned under this act; and said court is hereby prohibited from completing said grand jury in any way other than under the provisions of this act. But this act shall not apply to the counties of Genesee, Orleans and St. Lawrence.

Counties exempt.

§ 2. This act shall take effect immediately.

Ante, vol. 2, p. 747.

CHAP. 587.

AN ACT in relation to the State Lunatic Asylum.

PASSED May 22, 1873; three-fifths being present.

The People of the State of New York, represented in Senate and Assembly, do enact as follows:

Fourth assistant physician to be appointed.

SECTION 1. The managers of the State Lunatic Asylum are authorized, in their discretion, to appoint, on the nomination of the superintendent of said asylum, a fourth assistant physician, whose salary shall be fixed and paid in the same manner as those of the other resident officers of said asylum.

Annual salaries.

§ 2. The managers shall, from time to time, determine the annual salaries and allowances of the treasurer and resident officers of the asylum, who have been, or may hereafter be, appointed, subject to the approval of the governor of the state, secretary of state and the comptroller; provided that such salaries shall not exceed, in the aggregate, fifteen thousand dollars.

§ 3. This act shall take effect immediately.

CHAP. 589.

AN ACT to amend "An act in relation to the calendar of the commission of appeals, authorizing the transfer of causes from the calendar of the court of appeals and the disposition of causes on the calendar of the commission of appeals," passed February seven, eighteen hundred and seventy-three.

PASSED May 22, 1873.

The People of the State of New York, represented in Senate and Assembly, do enact as follows:

SECTION 1. The second section of the act entitled "An act in relation to the calendar of the commission of appeals, authorizing the transfer of causes from the calendar of the court of appeals and the disposition of causes on the calendar of the commission of appeals," passed February seventh, eighteen hundred and seventy-three, is hereby amended so as to read as follows:

§ 2. Whenever any cause shall be called for argument, and no other disposition shall be made thereof at the time of the call, it shall stand dismissed without costs; and an order shall be entered accordingly, which shall be absolute, unless, on the first day of the next term, the cause be submitted by one or more of the parties, on fifteen days' notice to the other parties. At the last term for arguments to be held by the commissioners, such dismissal may be absolute, unless the cause be submitted at that term. When cause to stand dismissed.

§ 2. This act shall take effect immediately.

Ante, p. 569.

CHAP. 593.

AN ACT to amend an act entitled "An act to establish an insurance department," passed April fifteenth, eighteen hundred and fifty-nine.

PASSED May 22, 1873; three-fifths being present.

The People of the State of New York, represented in Senate and Assembly, do enact as follows:

SECTION 1. The second section of the act entitled "An act to establish an insurance department," passed April fifteenth, eighteen hundred and fifty-nine, shall be and the same is hereby so amended as to read as follows:

§ 2. The chief officer of said department shall be denominated the superintendent of the insurance department. After the expiration of the term of office of the present superintendent, or whenever a vacancy shall occur in such office, such chief officer shall be appointed by the governor by and with the advice and consent of the senate, and shall hold his office for the term of three years. He shall receive an annual salary of seven thousand dollars, to be paid in monthly installments, which salary shall be in full of all services to be performed by said superintendent in any capacity, and all fees and moneys collected by him shall be paid into the state treasury monthly. He shall employ from time to time the necessary clerks to discharge such duty as he shall assign them, whose compensation shall be paid to them monthly on his certificate and upon a warrant of the comptroller. He shall appoint one of the said clerks to be his deputy, who shall possess the power and perform the duties attached by law to the office of principal, during a vacancy in such office and during the absence or inability of his principal. Whenever examinations shall be made of any insurance company by the superintendent or deputy superintendent personally, or by one or more Superintendent. Salary. Clerks. Deputy. Examinations, expense of.

of the regular clerks of said department, no charge shall be made on such examination but for necessary traveling and other actual expenses, and all charges for making examinations of any insurance company, and all charges against any company by any attorney or appraiser of this department, shall be presented in the form of an itemized bill, which shall first be approved by the said superintendent and then audited by the comptroller, and shall be paid on his warrant, drawn in the usual manner upon the state treasurer, to the person or persons making such examination, and the company examined, on receiving a certified copy of said bill of charges, as audited and paid by the comptroller, shall repay the amount of the same to the said superintendent, to be by him paid into the state treasury to replace the money drawn out as above provided for; and no company examined shall either directly or indirectly pay, by way of gift, gratuity or otherwise, any other or further sum to said superintendent or examiners for services, extra services, or for purposes of legislation, or on any other pretense whatever. Said superintendent, examiner or any officer, clerk or other employee of any insurance company, violating the provisions of this section, shall be guilty of a misdemeanor. Within fifteen days from the time of notice of their appointment respectively, the superintendent and his deputy shall take and subscribe the oath of office prescribed by the constitution, and file the same in the office of the secretary of state; and the said officers shall be in all respects subject to the provisions of the sixth title of chapter five of the first part of the Revised Statutes, as far as the same may be applicable; and within the said fifteen days the said superintendent of the insurance department shall give to the people of the state of New of York a bond in the penalty of twenty-five thousand dollars, with two good sureties, to be approved by the comptroller, conditioned for the faithful discharge of the duties of his office; and the said superintendent shall not, either directly or indirectly, be interested in any insurance company except as an ordinary policy holder.

Official oath.

Bond.

Admission to companies to transact business in this state.

§ 2. The said superintendent shall have power to refuse admission to any company, corporation or association, applying to be permitted to transact the business of insurance in this state from any other state or country, whenever, upon examination, the capital stock of such company, corporation or association shall be impaired, and, also, whenever, in his judgment, such refusal to admit shall best promote the interests of the people of this state.

§ 3. This act shall take effect immediately.

Ante, vol. 4, p. 252.

CHAP. 595.

AN ACT relative to certain negotiable corporate bonds and obligations.

PASSED May 22, 1873; three-fifths being present.

The People of the State of New York, represented in Senate and Assembly, do enact as follows:

SECTION 1. The owner or holder of any corporate or municipal bond or obligation (except such as are designed to circulate as currency), payable to bearer, heretofore issued, or which may hereafter be issued, and payable in this state, but not registered in pursuance of any law thereof, may make the same non-negotiable (except as provided in the second section of this act) by subscribing his name to a statement indorsed thereon that such bond or obligation is his property; and thereupon the principal sum therein mentioned shall be payable only to such owner or holder, or his legal representatives or assigns. How owner may make bonds non-negotiable.

§ 2. The bonds and obligations mentioned in the last section, after having been indorsed as therein provided, may be transferred by an indorsement, in blank, or payable to bearer, or to order, with the addition of the assignor's place of residence. How transferred after such indorsement.

§ 3. The provisions of this act shall apply to all interest coupons accompanying any corporate or municipal bond or obligation payable in this state. To apply to interest coupons.

§ 4. So much of chapter eighty-four of the laws of one thousand eight hundred and seventy-one, entitled "An act to authorize the owners and holders of certain railroad mortgage bonds, made payable to bearer, to render the same payable to order only," as is inconsistent with this act, is hereby repealed.

§ 5. This act shall take effect immediately.

Ante, p. 64.

CHAP. 600.

AN ACT relating to the building commissioners for the erection of the state reformatory at Elmira, Chemung county.

PASSED May 23, 1873; three-fifths being present.

The People of the State of New York, represented in Senate and Assembly, do enact as follows:

SECTION 1. The board of building commissioners for the erection of the state reformatory at Elmira, Chemung county, shall hereafter consist of five persons, and the governor shall, Board of building commissioners.

appointment of. by and with the advice and consent of the senate, appoint such commissioners in place of those now in office, whose term of office shall terminate as soon as their successors shall be appointed and shall have qualified.

Powers of new board. § 2. The new board of building commissioners for the erection of such state reformatory, appointed by this act, shall possess all the powers and be subject to all the provisions contained in chapter four hundred and twenty-seven of the laws of eighteen hundred and seventy, in relation to said building commissioners.

§ 3. This act shall take effect immediately.

Ante, vol. 7, p. 787.

CHAP. 614.

AN ACT to authorize marine insurance companies to declare extra dividends in certain cases.

PASSED May 24, 1873.

The People of the State of New York, represented in Senate and Assembly, do enact as follows:

Sums received from the Geneva award, how to be divided. SECTION 1. If any marine insurance company organized under the laws of this state, having paid a loss, shall receive a sum derived from the Geneva award, by way of reimbursement of that loss, it shall be lawful for such company to divide the net amount so received, after deducting the expenses and liabilities relating hereto, among the persons or parties who paid premiums and suffered by the payment of the original loss, or were prevented from receiving so much as they otherwise would have received by occasion of that loss, instead of dividing the same among the more recent scrip holders or dealers with such company; such division to be in the form of an extra dividend, or extra dividends upon the plan contemplated by the charter of such company, subject to all just claims for debts and liabilities, and payable to the same persons or their representatives, and in like manner as the money from which the loss was originally paid would have been payable if the loss had not been borne by the company, and the action of the board of directors or trustees in ascertaining the amount and making such extra dividend or dividends shall have the like force and effect as their action in making and declaring dividends under the charter.

§ 2. This act shall take effect immediately.

CHAP. 616.

AN ACT to authorize the consolidation of companies organized under the act entitled "An act to authorize the formation of companies for the erection of buildings," passed April fifth, eighteen hundred and fifty-three, or any of the acts amending or extending the same.

PASSED May 24, 1873; three-fifths being present.

The People of the State of New York, represented in Senate and Assembly, do enact as follows:

SECTION 1. Any two or more companies heretofore organized, or which shall hereafter be organized, under the act entitled "An act to authorize the formation of companies for the erection of buildings," passed April fifth, eighteen hundred and fifty-three, or any of the acts amending or extending the same, are hereby authorized to consolidate such companies into a single company in manner following: The trustees of any two or more such companies may enter into and make an agreement under their respective corporate seals, for the consolidation of the said companies, prescribing the terms and conditions thereof, the mode of carrying the same into effect, the name of the new company, the number of trustees thereof, the names of the trustees who shall manage the concerns of the new company for the first year and until others shall be elected in their places, the name of the town or towns, county or counties, in which the operations of the new company are to be carried on, the amount of capital and number of shares of the stock into which the same is to be divided (which capital shall not be larger in amount than the aggregate amount of capital of the several companies thus to be consolidated, and shall not be increased or diminished except in accordance with the provisions of the first-mentioned act or the act or acts amending or extending the same), the manner of converting the shares of capital stock in each of said companies into the shares of such new company, with such other particulars as they may deem necessary, not inconsistent with the provisions of the said act entitled "An act to authorize the formation of companies for the erection of buildings," passed April fifth, eighteen hundred and fifty-three, or any of the acts amending or extending the same. Companies may consolidate.

Ante, vol. 3, p. 793.

§ 2. Such agreement of the trustees of the companies so proposing to consolidate shall be submitted to the stockholders of each of said companies respectively, separately, at a meeting thereof to be called upon a notice signed by a majority of the trustees thereof, specifying the time and place of such meeting, and the object thereof, published for at least three successive weeks in the state paper, and in one of the newspapers published in each of the counties in which either of the said companies shall have its place of business, and of Agreement to be submitted to stockholders.

which said notice a written or printed copy shall be deposited in the post-office, post paid, addressed to each stockholder at his last known place of residence, at least three weeks previous to the day fixed upon for holding such meeting, and in case such agreement shall be sanctioned and approved by such stockholders by the vote of at least two-thirds in amount of the stockholders present, at such meetings respectively, voting by ballot in regard to such agreement, either in person or by proxy, each share of such capital stock being entitled to one vote, then the same shall be deemed to be the agreement of the said several companies, and a sworn copy of the proceedings of such meeting, made by the secretaries thereof respectively, and attached to the said agreement, shall be evidence of the holding and of the action of such meetings in the premises. If any stockholder shall, at said meeting of stockholders, or within twenty days thereafter, object to the said consolidation, and demand payment for his stock, such stockholder or said new company may, if said consolidation take effect at any time thereafter, apply to the supreme court, at any special term thereof held in any county in which the said new company may have its place of business, for the appointment of three persons to appraise the value of said stock, and shall designate the time and place of meeting of such appraisers, and give such directions in regard to the proceedings on said appraisement as shall be deemed proper, and shall also direct the manner in which payment for such stock shall be made to such stockholder. The court may fill any vacancy in the board of appraisers occurring by refusal or neglect to serve, or otherwise; the appraisers shall meet at the time and place designated, and they or any two of them, after being duly sworn honestly and faithfully to discharge their duties, shall estimate and certify the value of such stock, at the time of such dissent as aforesaid, and deliver one copy of their appraisal to the said company, and another to the said stockholder, if demanded; the charges and expenses of the appraisers shall be paid by the new company. When the company shall have paid the amount of the appraisal, as directed by the court, such stockholder shall cease to have any interest in the said stock, and in the corporate property of the said company, and the said stock may be held or disposed of by the said company.

In case any stockholder objects to consolidation.

When companies to be merged.

§ 3. Upon the making, sanctioning and approving of the said agreement, in the preceding sections mentioned in the manner therein required, and upon the filing of the duplicates or counterparts thereof, and of the verified copies of the meetings of the stockholders of the several companies showing their action in respect to such proposed consolidation in the office of the clerk of the county or counties in which the operations of said new company is to be carried on, and in the office of the secretary of state, then and immediately thereafter the said companies agreed to be consolidated shall be merged in the new company provided for in the said agreement, to be known by the corporate name therein mentioned, and the details of such agreement shall be carried into effect as provided therein, only such new company shall not have any larger powers than are granted by the said act mentioned in the first section hereof, and the acts amending and extending the same, nor be exempt from the performance of any duty which the said several companies may be liable to perform.

General powers.

§ 4. Such new companies shall possess the general powers and be subject to the general liabilities and restrictions expressed in the third title of the eighteenth chapter of the first part of the Revised Statutes, and to all the liabilities and restrictions to which either of the companies from which it has been formed were subject. It shall also have the general powers and privileges, and be subject to the general liabilities, restrictions, duties and provisions expressed and contained in the said act, entitled "An act to authorize the formation of companies for the erection of buildings," passed April fifth, eighteen hundred and fifty-three, or any of the acts amending or extending the same, so far as the same may be applicable to a company organized for the purposes expressed in the said agreement for consolidation, and for which said new company shall have been organized.

Corporate rights transferred.

§ 5. Upon the consolidation of said companies, and the corporate organization of said new company, as hereinbefore prescribed, all and singular the rights, franchises and interest of the said several companies so consolidated in and to every species of property, real, personal and mixed, and things in action thereunto belonging, shall be deemed to be transferred to and vested in such new company, without any other deed or transfer; and such new company shall hold and enjoy the same, and all rights of property, franchises and interest, in the same manner and to the same extent as if the said several companies so consolidated should have continued to retain the title and transact the business of such companies, and the title and real estate acquired by either of the said companies shall not be deemed to revert or be impaired by means of such act of consolidation or any thing relating thereto.

Rights of creditors, etc.

§ 6. The rights of creditors of any companies that shall be so consolidated shall not in any manner be impaired by any act of consolidation, nor shall any liability or obligation for the payment of any money now due, or hereafter to become due, to any person or persons, or any claim or demand in any manner, or for any cause existing against any such companies, or against any stockholder thereof, be in any manner released or impaired, but such new company is declared to succeed to such obligations and liabilities, and to be held liable to pay and discharge all such debts and liabilities of each of the companies that shall be so consolidated, in the same manner as if such new company had itself incurred the liability or obligation to pay such debt or damages; and the stockholders of the respective companies so entering into such consolidation shall continue subject to all the liabilities, claims and demands existing against them as such, at or before such consolidation; and no suit, action or other proceeding then pending before any court or tribunal, in which any company that may be so consolidated is a party, or in which any such stockholder is a party, shall be deemed to have abated or discontinued by reason of any such consolidation, but the same may be prosecuted to final judgment, in the same manner as if the said company had not entered into the said agreement of consolidation, or the said new company may be substituted as a party in the place of any company so consolidated as aforesaid, with any other company or companies, and forming such new company by order of the court in which such action, suit or proceeding may be pending.

§ 7. This act shall take effect immediately.

CHAP. 617.

AN ACT regulating the deposit of securities by plate-glass insurance companies.

PASSED May 24, 1873.

The People of the State of New York, represented in Senate and Assembly, do enact as follows:

Amount to be deposited by companies. SECTION 1. Any company heretofore or hereafter organized under the laws of this state to make insurance against loss or damage to plate-glass, exclusively, shall be required to deposit with the superintendent of the insurance department, for the benefit of all their policy holders, securities amounting to at least fifty thousand dollars; and no company created by the laws of any other state of the United States, with authority to insure against loss or damage to plate-glass, shall be permitted to transact business in this state without having previously deposited, for the benefit of their policy holders, securities amounting to at least fifty thousand dollars, with the auditor, comptroller, treasurer or chief financial officer of the state by whose laws said company is incorporated. Such deposits shall consist of the same securities in character and description as are required to be made by companies under the act providing for the formation of life and health insurance companies, and in relation to agencies of such companies, passed June twenty-fourth, one thousand eight hundred and fifty-three, and the amendments and additions thereto.

§ 2. This act shall take effect immediately.

CHAP. 624.

AN ACT to appropriate money for the building of a bridge over the Cayuga inlet, in the village of Ithaca.

PASSED May 27, 1873; three-fifths being present.

The People of the State of New York, represented in Senate and Assembly, do enact as follows:

SECTION 1. The sum of five thousand dollars is hereby appropriated out of the general funds of the state in payment for the construction of a swing bridge over Cayuga inlet, at a point where Seneca street, in the village of Ithaca, in the county of Tompkins, crosses the Cayuga inlet. Appropriation.

§ 2. The treasurer shall pay, on the warrant of the comptroller, the said sum of five thousand dollars, or so much thereof as the canal commissioner in charge of the middle division of the canals shall certify has been actually expended upon said bridge, and the comptroller is hereby directed and required to draw his warrant upon the treasurer for such sum as the said canal commissioner shall certify, not exceeding the said sum of five thousand dollars. Payment by treasurer.

§ 3. This act shall take effect immediately.

CHAP. 625.

AN ACT to reorganize the New York State Inebriate Asylum, and to provide for the better support and maintenance of the same.

PASSED May 27, 1873; three-fifths being present.

The People of the State of New York, represented in Senate and Assembly, do enact as follows:

SECTION 1. Within thirty days after the passage of this act, the governor, by and with the consent of the senate, shall appoint nine persons to be managers of the State Inebriate Asylum, three of whom shall hold their offices for one year from the fifteenth day of January, eighteen hundred and seventy-three, three for two years, and three for three years, as indicated by the governor on making the appointments, and until others are appointed in their stead, subject to be removed at any time by the senate, upon the recommendation of the governor. Their successors shall be appointed by the governor, by and with the advice and consent of the senate, and shall hold their office for three years, and until others are appointed in their stead, and subject to be removed in the manner aforesaid. The term of office of the present trustees of said asylum shall terminate on the thirtieth day of June, eighteen hundred and seventy-three, after which the government of said asylum shall be vested in the board of managers Governor to appoint managers. Term of trustees, when to terminate.

appointed under this act, and their successors in office. The said trustees shall make out and file with the said managers, at the time aforesaid, a true and perfect inventory of all the property belonging to the asylum; and the managers shall receipt for and take possession of the same, and thereupon the trustees shall be relieved from liability for the care and custody of such property.

Inventory.

Powers and duties of managers.

§ 2. Said board of managers shall have the general direction and control of all the property and concerns of the institution not otherwise provided for by law, and shall take charge of its general interests, and see that its designs be carried out, and every thing done faithfully according to the requirements of the legislature and the by-laws, rules, and regulations of the asylum.

Superintendent.

§ 3. The managers shall appoint a superintendent, who shall be an educated physician, and a treasurer, who shall reside in the city of Binghamton, and give bonds for the faithful performance of his trust, in such sum and with such sureties as the comptroller of the state shall approve. They shall also appoint, upon the recommendation of the superintendent, a chaplain, a steward, an assistant physician, and other physicians as occasion may require, and a matron, all of whom, and the superintendent himself, shall constantly reside in the asylum, and shall be designated the resident officers thereof.

Chaplain, etc.

Salaries.

§ 4. The managers shall, from time to time, determine the annual salaries and allowances of the treasurer and resident officers of the asylum, subject to the approval of the comptroller, and such salaries and allowances shall not exceed in the aggregate six thousand dollars.

When payable.

§ 5. The salaries of the treasurer and resident officers of the asylum shall be paid on the first day of each month in each year, by the treasurer of the state, on the warrant of the comptroller, to the treasurer of the asylum, on his presenting a bill of particulars signed by the steward and certified by the superintendent.

Official oath.

§ 6. The treasurer and resident officers of the asylum, before entering upon their respective duties, shall severally take the oath prescribed by the first section of the twelfth article of the constitution of the state; and such oath shall be filed with the clerk of the county of Broome.

By-laws, etc.

§ 7. The managers are hereby directed and empowered to establish such by-laws as they may deem necessary and expedient for regulating the appointment and duties of officers, attendants and assistants, for fixing the conditions of admission, support, employment and discharge or expulsion of patients, and for conducting, in a proper manner, the business of the institution; also to ordain and enforce a suitable system of rules and regulations for the internal government, discipline and management of the asylum. They may take and hold in trust for the state any grant or devise of land, or any donation or bequest of money or other personal property, to be applied to the maintenance of patients and the general uses of the asylum. Any person who shall donate or leave

Free beds.

by legacy the sum of five thousand dollars to the New York State Inebriate Asylum, may thereby establish forever a free bed in said asylum. Two thousand five hundred dollars shall provide a free bed in said asylum for six months in each year; twelve hundred and fifty dollars shall provide a free bed in said asylum for three months in each year. The donor or testator may name the patient who shall occupy the said free bed. But, in case the donor or testator shall fail to name a patient to occupy the free bed which said donor or testator shall have endowed, then the trustees of said asylum shall fill the said free bed with a poor patient. The said patients in said free beds shall be provided with medical treatment and board free of charge, and said patients shall be subject to the rules and regulations of said asylum. All legacies and donations given to the "New York State Inebriate Asylum," for the support of free beds in said asylum, shall be deposited with the comptroller of the state of New York forever. The interest of said fund shall be sacredly applied and paid over to the board of trustees of said asylum, for the support of free beds, for which said fund provides.

Duties of the superintendent.

§ 8. The superintendent shall be the chief executive officer of the asylum. He shall have the general superintendence of the buildings, grounds and farm, together with their furniture, fixtures and stock; and the direction and control of all persons therein, subject to the laws and regulations established by the managers. He shall daily ascertain the condition of all the patients and prescribe their treatment, in the manner directed in the by-laws. He shall also have power to appoint, with the managers' approval, such and so many attendants and employees as he may think proper and necessary for the economical and efficient performance of the business of the asylum, and to prescribe their several duties and place, and to fix, with the managers' approval, their compensation, and to discharge any of them at his sole discretion; but in every case of discharge, he shall forthwith record the same, with the reasons, under an appropriate head, in one of the books of the asylum for the information, and subject to the approval of the board of managers. He shall also have the power to suspend, for good and sufficient cause, a resident officer; but in such case he shall forthwith give written notice of the fact, with the causes and circumstances, to one of the managers, whose duty thereupon shall be to call a special meeting of the board to provide for the exigency. He shall also, from time to time, give such orders and instructions as he may judge best calculated to insure good conduct, fidelity and economy in every department of labor and expense; and he is authorized and enjoined to maintain salutary discipline among all who are employed by the institution, and to enforce strict compliance with such instructions and uniform obedience to all the rules and regulations of the asylum. He shall further cause full and fair accounts and records of all his doings and of the entire business and operations of the institution, to be kept regularly from day to day, in books provided for that

Appointment of attendants, etc.

Removals.

Accounts.

purpose, in the manner and to the extent prescribed in the by-laws; and he shall see that all such accounts and records are fully made up to the last day of December in each year, and that the principal facts and results, with his report thereon, be presented to the managers within three days thereafter. The assistant physician shall perform the duties and be subject to the responsibilities of the superintendent, in his sickness or absence.

Assistant physician.

Managers to keep record.

§ 9. The managers shall keep in a bound book, to be provided for that purpose, a fair and full record of all their doings, which shall be open at all times to the inspection of the governor of the state, and of all persons whom he or either house of the legislature may appoint to examine the same.

Inspection

§ 10. The managers shall maintain an effective inspection of the asylum, for which purpose one of them shall visit it every week; two once every month; a majority once every quarter; and the whole board once every year, at the times and in the manner prescribed in the by-laws. The visiting manager or managers shall note in a book kept for that purpose, the date of each visit, the condition of the buildings, surroundings and patients, with remarks of commendation or censure, and all the managers present shall sign the same. The general results of their inspection, with suitable hints, shall be inserted in their annual report, detailing the past year's operations and actual state of the asylum, which the managers shall make to the legislature before the fifteenth day of the month of January, in each year, accompanied with the annual reports of the superintendent and treasurer of the asylum.

Resident officers to admit managers, etc.

§ 11. It shall be the duty of the resident officers to admit any of the managers into every part of the asylum, and to exhibit to him or them on demand, all books, papers, accounts and writings belonging to the institution or pertaining to its business, management, discipline, or government; also to furnish copies, abstracts and reports, whenever required by the managers.

Custody of moneys.

§ 12. The treasurer shall have the custody of all moneys, bonds, notes, mortgages and other securities and obligations belonging to the asylum. He shall open with one of the banks in the city of Binghamton, to be selected with the approbation of the comptroller of the state, an account in his own name as treasurer of the asylum, and he shall deposit all moneys, immediately upon receiving them, in said bank; and shall draw from the same only for the uses of the asylum, and in the manner prescribed in the by-laws, upon the written order of the steward, specifying the object of the payment. He shall keep full and accurate accounts of receipts and payments, and in the manner directed in the by-laws, and such other accounts as the managers shall prescribe. He shall balance all of the accounts on his books annually, on the last day of December, and make a statement of the balance therein, and an abstract of the receipts and payments of the past year, which he shall, in three days thereafter, deliver to

Treasurer's accounts.

the auditing committee of the managers, who shall compare the same with his books and vouchers, and verify the results by a further comparison with the books of the steward, and certify the correctness thereof, within the next five days, to the managers. He shall also render a quarterly statement of his receipts and payments, on the last day of March, June and September, in each year, to the auditing committee, who shall compare and verify the same as aforesaid, and report the results duly certified to the managers, who shall cause the same to be entered in one of the books of the asylum. He shall further render an account of the state of his books, and of the funds and other property of the asylum in his custody whenever required to do so by the managers.

Quarterly statements.

§ 13. The treasurer of the asylum shall be vested with the same powers, rights and authority which are now by law given, either to the superintendents of the poor, or to the overseers of the poor, in any county or town of the state, so far as may be necessary for the indemnity and benefit of the asylum, and for the purpose of compelling a patient, or a relative, or a committee liable for his maintenance, to defray the expense of his support in the asylum, and reimburse actual disbursements for his necessary clothing and traveling expenses, according to the by-laws of the institution; also for the purpose of coercing the payment of similar charges, when due, according to said by-laws, from any town or city or county that is liable for the support of any inebriate in said asylum.

Powers of treasurer.

§ 14. Said treasurer is also authorized to recover, for the uses of the asylum, any a nd all sums which may be due upon any note or bond in his hands, belonging to the asylum; also any and all sums which may be charged and due, according to the by-laws of the asylum, for the support of any patient, or for actual disbursements made on his behalf, for necessary clothing and traveling expenses, in an action to be brought in said treasurer's name, as treasurer of the State Inebriate Asylum, and which shall not abate by his death or removal, against the individual, town, city or county legally liable for the maintenance of said patient, and having neglected to pay the same when demanded by the treasurer, in which action judgment shall be rendered for such sum as shall be found due, with interest from the time of the demand aforesaid. Said treasurer may also, upon the receipt of the money due upon any mortgage in his hands, belonging to the asylum, execute a release, and acknowledge full satisfaction thereof, so that the same may be discharged of record.

To recover moneys due asylum.

§ 15. The steward, under the direction of the superintendent, shall make all purchases for the asylum, and preserve the original bills and receipts thereof, and keep full and accurate accounts of the same, and copies of all orders drawn by himself on the treasurer; he shall also, under like direction, make contracts in the superintendent's name, with the attendants and employees, and keep and settle their accounts; he shall also keep the accounts for the support of patients, and expenses incurred in their behalf, and furnish the treasurer

Steward to make purchases, etc.

every month with copies of such as fall due; he shall make quarterly abstracts of his accounts to the last day of March, June, September and December in each year, for the treasurer and managers; he shall also be accountable for the careful keeping and economical use of all furniture, stores and other articles provided for the asylum, and shall annually, during the first week in January, make out and file with the managers a true and perfect inventory, verified by oath, of all the personal property belonging to the asylum, in and about the premises, with an appraisal thereof, made under oath by himself and some discreet householder in the city of Binghamton, whom the managers shall appoint for that purpose.

Quaterly abstracts.

Number of patients each county entitled to send.

§ 16. As soon as practicable, after entering upon their duties, the managers shall ascertain the number of patients the asylum will properly accommodate, and shall designate in a just and equitable manner, with the approval of the board of state commissioners of public charities, the number of patients each county may be entitled to send to the institution. They shall cause notice thereof to be published for two weeks in the state paper, and sent to the clerk of every county, who shall transmit copies of the same to the county judge, and to the superintendent of the poor of said county, by mail. A circular from the superintendent of the asylum shall accompany said notice to each county clerk, and to the county judge and superintendents of the poor, stating the respective quotas of patients each county may be entitled to send to the asylum, and giving all necessary directions respecting admission and support, according to the by-laws. Upon the completion of the present buildings, and in the event of the erection of other buildings for the purposes of the institution, the managers shall apportion the room thus provided for patients among the several counties in the manner above stated, and shall cause notice thereof to be promulgated as herein provided.

Admission of indigent inebriates.

§ 17. The county superintendents of the poor of the several counties may make application in behalf of any inebriate, in indigent circumstances, to the county judge of the county where he resides, and said judge shall call two respectable physicians, and other credible witnesses, and fully investigate the facts of the case, and, either with or without the verdict of jury, at his discretion, as to his being an inebriate, shall decide the case as to his indigence. And if the judge certifies that satisfactory proof has been adduced, showing him to be an inebriate, and his estate is insufficient to support him and his family (or if he has no family, himself), and that he would probably reform under treatment therein, on his certificate, authenticated by the county clerk and seal of the county courts, he shall be admitted into the asylum and supported there at the expense of said county until he shall be reformed, if such reformation is probably to be effected in one year. The judge in such case shall have requisite power to compel the attendance of witnesses and jurors, and shall file the certificate of the physicians taken under oath, and other papers, with a report of his proceedings and decisions, with the clerk of the county, and report the facts to the supervisors, whose duty it shall be, at their next annual meeting, to raise the money requisite to meet the expense of support accordingly. In counties having no superintendents of the poor, application may be made by the overseer of the poor of any town or city in said county, or other officer charged with the support and relief of indigent persons, and the same proceedings may be conducted, and the inebriate sent to the asylum, as if the application had been made by a county superintendent. In case, however, of persistent indulgence by said inebriate, or of constant disregard of the rules and by-laws of the asylum, or from any other cause or circumstance rendering his case hopeless or incurable, he may be returned to the county from where he came, at the discretion of the superintendent appointed by the managers.

Private patients.

§ 18. Whenever there are vacancies in the asylum the managers may authorize the superintendent to admit, under special agreements, such private patients as may seek admission, who, in his opinion, promise reformation, but preference in all cases shall be given to citizens of this state; or, he may receive public patients from counties in excess of their quotas.

Price to be paid for keeping.

§ 19. The price to be paid for keeping any person in indigent circumstances in the asylum, shall be annually fixed by the managers, so it shall not exceed the actual cost of support and attendance, exclusive of officers' salaries. The managers may, at their discretion, require payments to be made quarterly or semi-annually, in advance.

Expense of clothing, etc.

§ 20. The expense of clothing and maintaining, in the asylum, a patient who has been sent upon the order of any county judge, shall be paid by the county from which he was sent to the asylum. The treasurer of said county is authorized and directed to pay to the treasurer of the asylum the bills for such clothing and maintenance, as they shall become due and payable, according to the by-laws of the asylum, upon the order of the steward; and the supervisors of said county shall annually levy and raise the amount of such bills and such further sums as will probably cover all similar bills for one year in advance. Said county, however, shall have the right to require any town or city, that is legally liable for the support of such patient, to reimburse the amount of said bills, with interest from the day of paying the same.

Expenses of removal.

§ 21. Whenever the managers shall order an indigent person removed from the asylum to the county whence he came, the superintendent of the poor of said county shall audit and pay the actual expense of such removal as part of the contingent expenses for the care of the poor of said county. But if any town or city be legally liable for the support of such patient, the amount of such expense may be recovered for the use of the county, by such superintendent. If such superintendent of the poor neglect or refuse to pay such expense on demand, the treasurer of the asylum may pay the same and charge the amount to the said county, and the treasurer of the said county is authorized to pay the same with interest, after thirty days; and the supervisors of said county shall levy and raise the amount as other county charges.

Managers not to receive compensation.

§ 22. The managers of the State Inebriate Asylum shall receive no compensation for their time or services, but shall receive their actual and necessary traveling and other expenses, to be paid by the state treasurer, on the warrant of the comptroller, on the rendering of their accounts.

Purchases to be for cash.

§ 23. All purchases for the use of the asylum shall be made for cash, and not on credit or time, and the managers shall make all needful rules and regulations to enforce the provisions of this section.

Words defined.

§ 24. The term "inebriate," as used in this act, is applied to "an habitual or periodical drunkard;" the word "oath" includes affirmation; the word "county superintendent" means "superintendent of the poor;" the word "asylum" and "institution" means "State Inebriate Asylum;" a word denoting the singular number is to include one or many; and every word importing the masculine gender only, may extend to and include females.

§ 25. This act shall take effect on the first day of July, eighteen hundred and seventy-three, except so far as it relates to the appointment of the managers of the asylum, which shall take effect immediately.

CHAP. 626.

AN ACT to declare Marsh creek, in Allegany county, a public highway.

PASSED May 27, 1873; three-fifths being present.

The People of the State of New York, represented in Senate and Assembly, do enact as follows:

Marsh creek a public highway. Proviso.

SECTION 1. The stream known as Marsh creek, in the town of Willing, in the county of Allegany, is hereby declared a public highway from the point where it crosses the south line of lot number seventy-four, township one, range one, Willing and Francis tract, Morris reserve, to the point where said creek empties into the Genesee river, on lot number thirty-nine, in the said tract, township and range. Provided that any and all parties, before using said creek as a public highway, shall execute a bond to the supervisor, to be approved by the town board of the said town of Willing, in Allegany county, and deliver the same at the town clerk's office of said town, and to be there filed as a good and sufficient security against any and all damages that may be done to any and all property, public or private, such as bridges, booms, dams, mills, machinery, that are now or may hereafter be erected on said creek, by using it as a public highway.

§ 2. This act shall take effect immediately.

CHAP. 630.

AN ACT to amend the Revised Statutes.

PASSED May 28, 1873; three-fifths being present.

The People of the State of New York, represented in Senate and Assembly, do enact as follows:

SECTION 1. Section thirty-seven of article second, chapter second, part fourth of the fourth title of the Revised Statutes, is hereby amended so as to read as follows:

§ 37. Indictments for murder may be found at any time after the death of the person killed; in all other cases indictments shall be found and filed in the proper court, within five years after the commission of the offense, but the time during which the defendant shall not have been an inhabitant of or usually resident within this state shall not constitute any part of the said limitation of five years. Indictments, within what time to be found.

§ 2. This act shall take effect immediately.

Ante, vol. 2, p. 749.

CHAP. 633.

AN ACT to authorize the incorporation of Baptist churches in the state of New York, and supplementary to an act entitled "An act to provide for the incorporation of religious societies," passed April fifth, eighteen hundred and thirteen.

PASSED May 28, 1873.

The People of the State of New York, represented in Senate and Assembly, do enact as follows:

SECTION 1. It shall be lawful for any Baptist church now existing, or that may hereafter be organized in this state, to be incorporated according to the provisions of this act as follows: Any Baptist church may incorporate under this act.

§ 2. The members of any such church, of full age, may assemble at their place of worship, and, by a majority of the votes of such members, elect any number of persons, not less than three nor more than nine, as trustees, at the time and in the manner provided for in the third section of this act. Members of full age to meet and elect trustees.

§ 3. Public notice shall be given in the congregation of the meeting for the incorporation of such church and the first election of trustees under the provisions of this act, and also for all subsequent meetings for the election of trustees, at least fifteen days previous to the time for such incorporation and election or elections, and on not less than two successive Sabbaths or other days of public service. The object, time and place of such meeting shall be distinctly stated in such notice. Notice of meeting how given.

§ 4. The trustees so elected shall file, under oath, in the office of the clerk or register of the county in which the church is located, a certificate of their election, duly signed by the Certificate of election to be filed.

chairman and secretary of the meeting at which such election took place, and thenceforth said church, organized under the provisions of this act, shall be a body corporate by the name expressed in the certificate of their incorporation. Such trustees shall hold regular meetings for business at such time and place as they may appoint, and special meetings may be called by any three of them; a majority of the whole number shall be a quorum for the transaction of business, and a majority of votes shall decide any question.

Meetings of trustees.

When trustee to vacate his office.

§ 5. Whenever a trustee, by removal or otherwise, ceases to be a member of such church, or, if not a member, ceases to attend or to support its worship, he shall at the same time cease to act as trustee, and his place shall be declared vacant by an official notice of the board of trustees to the church, and a new election shall be ordered to fill such vacancy as provided in section three of this act.

General act to apply.

§ 6. All the provisions of the act entitled "An act for the incorporation of religious societies," and the several acts amendatory thereof, so far as they relate to the term of service and the powers and duties of trustees, shall apply to the trustees of churches which shall be organized or incorporated pursuant to the provisions of this act so far as the same are not in conflict or inconsistent therewith.

§ 7. This act shall take effect immediately.

Ante, vol. 3, p. 687.

CHAP. 634.

AN ACT to amend article first, title four, of chapter eight of third part of Revised Statutes, entitled "Of proceedings, by and against corporations in courts of law."

PASSED May 28, 1878; three-fifths being present.

The People of the State of New York, represented in Senate and Assembly, do enact as follows:

SECTION 1. The second section of article first, title four, of chapter eight of the third part of the Revised Statutes is hereby amended so as to read as follows:

Foreign corporations not to maintain actions in certain cases.

§ 2. But when by the laws of this state any act is forbidden to be done by any corporation or by any association of individuals without express authority by law, and such act shall have been done by a foreign corporation, it shall not be authorized to maintain an action founded upon such act, or upon any liability or obligation, express or implied, arising out of or made or entered into in consideration of such act, provided, however, that whenever any foreign corporation is authorized by its charter, the amendments thereto, or the general laws under which it is created, to hold meetings of its stockholders or its directors within the state of New York, such meetings and the acts done thereat when not in conflict with the law creating such incorporation or the provisions of

Proviso.

its charter, and not in conflict with the laws of the state of New York, shall be valid to the same extent as though such corporation were created by the laws of this state.

§ 2. This act shall take effect immediately.

Ante, vol. 2, p. 477.

CHAP. 639.

AN ACT to amend an act entitled "An act to amend an act entitled 'An act to amend an act entitled an act to designate the holidays to be observed in the acceptance and payment of bills of exchange and promissory notes,' passed April twenty-third, eighteen hundred and seventy," passed May twenty-second, eighteen hundred and seventy-three.

PASSED May 29, 1873.

The People of the State of New York, represented in Senate and Assembly, do enact as follows:

SECTION 1. Section two of chapter five hundred and seventy-seven of the laws of eighteen hundred and seventy-three is hereby amended so as to read as follows:

§ 2. Whenever any of the holidays mentioned in the first section of this act shall fall hereafter upon Sunday, the Monday next following shall be deemed and considered as the first day of the week, or Sunday, and a public holiday for all or any of the purposes aforesaid; and all bills of exchange, checks and promissory notes made on or after the twenty-second day of May, eighteen hundred and seventy-three, which shall, with or without grace, become due and payable on any of the days mentioned in the preceding section, or on any Monday kept as aforesaid as a public holiday, shall be deemed to be due and payable on the business day next succeeding the day of their maturity. When holiday falls on Sunday, following Monday to be a holiday.

§ 2. This act shall take effect immediately.

Ante, vol. 7, p. 718.

CHAP. 642.

AN ACT in relation to academies and academical departments of union schools, and the distribution of public funds.

PASSED May 29, 1873; three-fifths being present.

The People of the State of New York, represented in Senate and Assembly, do enact as follows:

SECTION 1. The sum of one hundred and twenty-five thousand dollars, ordered by chapter five hundred and forty-one Money to be distributed.

of the laws of eighteen hundred and seventy-two, to be levied for each and every year, for the benefit of academies and academical departments of union schools, shall be annually distributed by the regents of the university, for the purposes and in the manner following, that is to say:

For purchase of books. § 2. Three thousand dollars, or so much thereof as may be required, in addition to the annual appropriation of three thousand dollars for the same purpose from the literature fund, for the purchase of books and apparatus, to be annually apportioned and paid in the manner now provided by law.

For instruction of teachers. § 3. Twelve thousand dollars, or so much thereof as may be required, in addition to the annual appropriation of eighteen thousand dollars from the United States deposit fund, for the instruction of common school teachers, the whole sum to be apportioned and paid to the several institutions which may give such instruction as now provided by law, at the rate of fifteen dollars for each scholar instructed in a course prescribed by the said regents, during a term of thirteen weeks, and at the same rate for not less than ten weeks or more than twenty weeks.

Admission to academic examinations. § 4. The said regents shall cause to be admitted to the academic examination, established by them in the academies and academical departments of union schools, any common school, or free school, any scholar from any common school who may apply for such examination, bearing the certificate of the principal teacher, or of any trustee of such school, that, in his judgment, such scholar is qualified to pass the said examination.

Free instruction. § 5. Free instruction in the classics or the higher branches of English education, or both, shall be given in every academy and academical department of a union school, subject to the visitation of the said regents, under such rules and regulations as the said regents may prescribe, to all scholars in any academy and in any free school, or in any common school, who, on any examination held subsequent to the beginning of the present academic year, shall have received the certificate of academic scholarship issued by the said regents to the extent of twelve dollars, and if the condition of the fund will admit not less than twenty dollars tuition, at such rates of tuition as are usually charged for such scholars in such academies and academical departments respectively, and in case the tuition is free to resident pupils, at the rates charged to non-resident pupils, or at such rates, in all cases, as the said regents may deem reasonable; but such free instruction must be obtained by such scholars within two years from the date of their examination respectively.

Premiums for excellence. § 6. The said regents may, in their discretion and under such rules as they may adopt, annually apply a sum not exceeding twenty-five hundred dollars, in book or other premiums, for excellence in scholarship and conduct, as shown in the papers and returns of the academic examination; but the cost of any one premium shall not exceed ten dollars; and the said sum of twenty-five hundred dollars, or such part thereof as may be needed, shall be paid to the said regents out of the amount referred to in the first section of this act, by the treasurer, on the warrant of the comptroller.

§ 7. The balance of the said one hundred and twenty-five thousand dollars remaining after the apportionments described in the preceding sections of this act shall have been made, shall be distributed as the literature fund is now by law directed to be distributed, but no money shall be paid to any school under the control of any religious or denominational sect or society. Balance to be distributed.

§ 8. The said regents of the university are hereby authorized to make such just and equitable regulations as they may deem necessary for the purposes of this act. Regulations.

§ 9. The treasurer shall pay, on the warrant of the comptroller, the several sums to which the said regents may certify any institution to be entitled under the provisions of this act. Payments.

§ 10. Every academy shall make up its annual report for its academic year, and shall transmit the same to the regents on or before the first day of September in each year. Annual reports.

§ 11. This act shall take effect immediately.

CHAP. 643.

AN ACT to provide for the support of government, and for other purposes.

PASSED May 29, 1873; three-fifths being present.

The People of the State of New York, represented in Senate and Assembly, do enact as follows:

SECTION 1. The several amounts named in this act are hereby appointed* and authorized to be paid from the several funds indicated to the respective public officers, and for the several purposes specified for the fiscal year beginning on the first day of October, eighteen hundred and seventy-three, namely: Appropriation for fiscal year.

FROM THE GENERAL FUND — EXECUTIVE DEPARTMENT.

For the governor, for salary, four thousand dollars. Governor.

For the private secretary of the governor, for salary, three thousand five hundred dollars. Secretary.

For the clerks and messengers in the executive department, for compensation, seven thousand seven hundred dollars. Clerks.

For expenses of the house occupied by the governor, five thousand dollars. House.

For the executive department, for furniture, blank and other books necessary for the use of the department, binding, Furniture, etc.

* So in the original.

blanks, printing, stationery, telegraphing and other incidental expenses, two thousand five hundred dollars.

Apprehension of criminals, etc. For the executive department, for the apprehension of criminals pursuant to part one, chapter nine, title one, section fifteen of the Revised Statutes, one thousand dollars; for the apprehension of fugitives from justice, pursuant to part four, chapter two, title seven, section forty-five of the Revised Statutes, one thousand dollars.

For the rent of the governor's house, four thousand dollars.

JUDICIARY — COURT OF APPEALS.

Judges. For judges of the court of appeals, for salaries and expenses, pursuant to chapter two hundred and three of the laws of eighteen hundred and seventy, and chapter seven hundred and eighteen of the laws of eighteen hundred and seventy-one, sixty-three thousand five hundred dollars.

Commissioners. For the commissioners of appeals, for salaries and expenses, pursuant to chapter two hundred and three of the laws of eighteen hundred and seventy, and chapter three of the laws of eighteen hundred and seventy-three, forty-five thousand dollars.

Reporter. For state reporter, for salary, pursuant to chapter six hundred and ninety-eight of the laws of eighteen hundred and sixty-nine, and chapter seven hundred and eighteen of the laws of eighteen hundred and seventy-one, five thousand dollars; and for clerical help to state reporter, two thousand dollars.

Clerk. For the clerk of the court of appeals, for salary, five thousand dollars.

Deputy. For the deputy clerk of the court of appeals, for salary, three thousand dollars.

Messenger. For the messenger to the court of appeals and the state engineer and surveyor (the same messenger), for his annual salary, six hundred dollars.

Clerks. For clerks in the office of the clerk of the court of appeals, for salaries, four thousand five hundred dollars.

Furniture, etc. For furniture, books, binding, printing calendar and other necessary expenses of the office of the clerk of the court of appeals, twenty-five hundred dollars.

Criers. For compensation of criers and attendants for the court of appeals and commissioners of appeals, five thousand dollars.

For the clerk of the commissioners of appeals, for salary, thirty-five hundred dollars.

Assistant clerk and messenger. For compensation of the assistant clerk and messenger and office expenses in the office of the clerk of the commissioners of appeals, twenty-four hundred dollars.

SUPREME COURT.

Justices. For justices of the supreme court, for salaries and expenses, two hundred and thirty-seven thousand six hundred dollars.

Stenographer. For compensation of stenographer, three thousand dollars.

General terms. For the expenses of the general terms of the supreme court, ten thousand dollars.

For the attorney-general, for salary, two thousand dollars. Attorney-general, deputy, etc.

For the deputy attorney-general, for salary, three thousand five hundred dollars.

For clerk and messenger, in the office of attorney-general, for salaries, two thousand dollars.

For furniture, books, binding, blanks, printing and other necessary expenses of the office of the attorney-general, five hundred dollars.

For costs of suits, fees of sheriffs, compensation of witnesses, and for expenses and disbursements by the attorney-general, two thousand dollars. Fees of sheriffs, etc.

For compensation of counsel employed to assist the attorney-general, three thousand dollars. Counsel.

For compensation and expenses of the attorney-general, pursuant to part one, chapter eight, title five, section six of the Revised Statutes, one thousand dollars, or so much thereof as may be proper, the amount to be certified by the governor. All costs adjudged to the people of this state, in actions prosecuted or defended by the attorney-general, may be applied by him, in his discretion, to any of the purposes for which appropriations are hereinbefore made in relation to his office, and the attorney-general shall, at the close of each fiscal year, render to the comptroller an account of such costs received, with vouchers of such expenditures. Expenses of attorney-general, etc.

OFFICE OF THE SECRETARY OF STATE.

For the secretary of state, for salary, two thousand five hundred dollars. Secretary of state.

For the deputy secretary of state, and clerk of the commissioners of the land office, for salary, and for indexing and making marginal notes of the session laws, thirty-five hundred dollars; and no other or further compensation shall hereafter be allowed in the supply bill, or by the commissioners of the land office. Deputy.

For clerks in the office of the secretary of state, for salaries, sixteen thousand five hundred dollars. Clerks.

For messenger in the office of secretary of state, for salary, eight hundred dollars. Messenger.

For furniture, blank and other books, binding, blanks, printing and other necessary expenses of the secretary of state's office, two thousand dollars. Furniture, etc.

COMPTROLLER'S OFFICE.

For the comptroller, for salary, two thousand five hundred dollars. Comptroller.

For the deputy comptroller, for salary, two thousand dollars. Deputy.

For second deputy comptroller, for salary, three thousand five hundred dollars. Second deputy

For clerks in the office of the comptroller, for salaries, three thousand five hundred dollars. Clerks.

Messenger. For messenger in the office of the comptroller, for salary, five hundred dollars.

Furniture, etc. For furniture, books, binding, blanks, printing and other necessary expenses of the office of the comptroller, two thousand dollars.

TREASURER'S OFFICE.

Treasurer. For the treasurer, for salary, one thousand five hundred dollars, and for compensation for countersigning transfers and assignments of securities made in the banking department, to be refunded to the treasury, pursuant to chapter one hundred and three of the laws of eighteen hundred and fifty-seven, one thousand dollars.

Deputy. For the deputy treasurer, for salary, three thousand five hundred dollars.

Clerks. For clerks in the office of the treasurer, for salaries, eight thousand dollars.

Furniture, etc. For furniture, books, binding, printing, extra clerk hire and other necessary expenses of the office of the treasurer, eight hundred dollars.

DEPARTMENT OF PUBLIC INSTRUCTION.

Superintendent. For the superintendent of public instruction, for salary, five thousand dollars.

Deputy. For the deputy superintendent of public instruction, for salary, three thousand dollars.

Clerks. For clerks in the office of superintendent of public instruction, for salaries, eight thousand six hundred and seventy-five dollars.

Furniture, etc. For furniture, books, binding, blanks, printing and other necessary expenses in the office of the superintendent of public instruction, one thousand dollars.

STATE ENGINEER AND SURVEYOR'S OFFICE.

Deputy. For the deputy state engineer and surveyor, for salary, two thousand dollars.

Clerks. For compensation of clerks to assist in the preparation of railroad reports, twenty-two hundred dollars, and for the expenses of printing and binding said reports, five thousand dollars, to be refunded and paid by the several railroad companies in the manner and form provided in chapter five hundred and twenty-six of the laws of eighteen hundred and fifty-five, and the several acts of the legislature in relation thereto, and in case of any default in the payment by the respective railroad companies of the amounts heretofore or hereafter assessed against them respectively, under the acts aforesaid, the comptroller is hereby authorized to issue his warrant for the collection thereof, in the manner provided in said chapter five hundred and twenty-six of the laws of eighteen hundred and fifty-five.

For clerks in the office of the state engineer and surveyor, for salaries, thirty-five hundred dollars.

For furniture, books, binding, blanks, printing and other necessary expenses of the office of the state engineer and surveyor, five hundred dollars. Furniture, etc.

For James Hall, as state geologist, as compensation for authorship, the superintendence of drawings and engravings, for clerk hire and the use of working rooms for the arranging, labeling and distribution of the duplicate fossils and minerals, as fixed by the lieutenant-governor, comptroller and secretary of state, pursuant to chapter seven hundred and fifteen of the laws of eighteen hundred and seventy-one, twenty-five hundred dollars. James Hall as state geologist.

BANKING DEPARTMENT.

For the superintendent of the banking department, for salary, five thousand dollars. Superintendent.

For compensation of deputy, clerk hire, furniture, books, binding, blanks, printing and other necessary expenses of the office of the superintendent of the banking department, twelve thousand dollars. The aforesaid salary, clerk hire and other expenses above indicated shall be refunded to the treasury by the several banks and banking associations of this state, pursuant to chapter one hundred and sixty-four of the laws of eighteen hundred and fifty-one. Deputy, clerks, etc.

INSURANCE DEPARTMENT.

For the superintendent of the insurance department, for salary, seven thousand dollars, pursuant to chapter three hundred and twenty-six of the laws of eighteen hundred and sixty-one, and chapter seven hundred and thirty-two of the laws of eighteen hundred and sixty-eight. Superintendent.

For compensation of deputy, clerk hire, furniture, books, binding, blanks, printing and other necessary expenses of the insurance department, fifty thousand dollars. The aforesaid salary, clerk hire and other expenses above indicated shall be refunded to the treasury by the several insurance companies, associations, persons and agents, pursuant to chapter three hundred and sixty-six of the laws of eighteen hundred and fifty-nine. All fees and perquisites of every name and nature charged, received and collected by the insurance department, or any officer thereof, shall be immediately paid into the treasury. Deputy, clerks, etc.

STATE ASSESSORS.

For the state assessors, for compensation and traveling expenses, pursuant to chapter three hundred and twelve of the laws of eighteen hundred and fifty-nine, the sum of four thousand five hundred dollars. State assessors.

INSPECTORS OF GAS METERS.

For inspector of gas meters, for salary and contingent expenses, pursuant to chapter one hundred and sixteen of the laws of eighteen hundred and sixty, and to the conditions and requirements imposed by chapter one hundred and thirty-five Inspector of gas meters.

of the laws of eighteen hundred and sixty-three, two thousand five hundred dollars, which amount shall be refunded to the treasury by the several gas-light companies, pursuant to chapter three hundred and eleven of the laws of eighteen hundred and fifty-nine, but no payment shall be made by the comptroller upon such salary and expenses till an amount equal to such payment shall be received by him from gas companies, or some of them.

QUARANTINE COMMISSIONERS.

Commissioners of quarantine. For the commissioners of quarantine, for salaries, to each of them, two thousand five hundred dollars, pursuant to chapter three hundred and fifty-eight of the laws of eighteen hundred and sixty-three; and from and after the passage of this act the board of commissioners constituted by chapter seven hundred and fifty-one of the laws of eighteen hundred and sixty-six is hereby abolished, and the powers and duties of said board are hereby devolved upon the health officer of the port of New York; and hereafter no moneys appropriated for the completion of the quarantine establishment shall be used for the payment of any salary or compensation of any officer, but shall be devoted exclusively to the purposes for which it is appropriated; and no salary shall be paid to any officer in connection with the quarantine establishment, except such as is expressly authorized and provided for by law.

AUCTIONEERS' ACCOUNTS.

Agent to examine. For compensation of the agent to examine the accounts of auctioneers, Revised Statutes, volume second, page four hundred and sixty-seven and chapter five hundred and forty-seven of the laws of eighteen hundred and sixty-six, one thousand two hundred dollars.

WEIGHTS AND MEASURES.

Superintendent. For superintendent of weights and measures, for salary, five hundred dollars.

LAND OFFICE.

Expenses of public lands. For assessments and other expenses of public lands, and for the compensation and mileage of the lieutenant-governor and the speaker of the assembly for attendance as commissioners of the land office, two thousand dollars.

PUBLIC OFFICES.

Postage. For postage on official letters, documents and other matter sent by mail, of the governor, secretary of state, comptroller, treasurer, superintendent of public instruction, attorney-general, state engineer and surveyor, adjutant-general, inspector-general, and clerks of the court and commission of appeals, five thousand dollars; and for stationery for the aforesaid public officers and departments (Revised Statutes, volume one, page four hundred and eighty), five thousand dollars.

CAPITOL.

For repairs, cleaning, labor, gas and other necessary expenses of the capitol, ten thousand dollars. Repairs, etc.

For the superintendent of the capitol, for salary, twelve hundred dollars. Superintendent.

STATE HALL.

For repairs, cleaning, labor, gas and other necessary expenses of the state hall, five thousand dollars. Repairs, etc.

For superintendent of state hall, for salary, twelve hundred dollars. Superintendent.

REGENTS OF THE UNIVERSITY.

For secretary of the regents of the university, for salary, two thousand five hundred dollars. Secretary.

For assistant secretary of the regents of the university, for salary, two thousand dollars. Assistant.

For compensation of a botanist, fifteen hundred dollars. Botanist.

For expense of postage, expressage, printing, stationery, visitation, expenses of regents attending meetings of the board and other necessary expenses, two thousand dollars. Postage, etc.

STATE LIBRARY.

For the purchase of books, for the state library, three thousand dollars. Purchase of books, etc.

For binding, lettering and marking books for the state library, one thousand five hundred dollars.

For repairs, cleaning, gas, transportation of books and other necessary expenses of the state library, two thousand dollars. Repairs, etc.

For the salaries of the librarians and assistant and janitor of the state library, six thousand and eight hundred dollars. Salaries.

HALL FOR THE STATE CABINET OF NATURAL HISTORY AND THE AGRICULTURAL MUSEUM.

For the state cabinet of natural history, pursuant to chapter five hundred and fifty-seven of the laws of eighteen hundred and seventy, ten thousand dollars. State cabinet.

For superintendence, repairs, cleaning, labor, gas, fuel and other necessary expenses, including the compensation of the keeper of the hall for the state cabinet of natural history, four thousand five hundred dollars, and from and after the first day of October, eighteen hundred and seventy-three, the hall for the museum shall be placed in the joint care and control of the regents of the university and the executive committee of the State Agricultural Society; and all bills and charges shall be audited and paid only on the certificate of the secretary of the board of regents and the secretary of the State Agricultural Society. Superintendence, etc.

For the persons employed in preparing drawings for the natural history of the state, for compensation, two thousand five hundred dollars. Drawings, etc.

FUEL.

Fuel. For fuel for the capitol, the state hall and the state library, five thousand dollars.

AGRICULTURAL.

Agricultural societies. For donations to the societies in the several counties of the state and to the state society for the promotion of agriculture, twenty thousand dollars.

LEGISLATURE.

Compensation of members, etc. For compensation and mileage of members and officers of the legislature, one hundred and forty-five thousand dollars.

Advances to clerks. For advances by the comptroller to the clerks of the senate and assembly, for contingent expenses of the two houses of the legislature, twenty thousand dollars, or so much thereof as may be necessary.

Postage, etc. For postage, expenses of committees, compensation of witnesses, Legislative Manual, Crosswell's Manual, Clerk's Manual and other contingent expenses of the legislature, eighteen thousand dollars.

STATE PRINTING.

Printing, etc. For the legislative printing for the State, including natural history, binding, mapping, engraving, publication of the official canvass and other official notices, one hundred and seventy-five thousand dollars.

STATE PRISONS, ETC.

Inspectors. For the inspectors of state prisons, for salaries to each of them, one thousand six hundred dollars, and for traveling expenses to each of them, six hundred dollars.

Maintenance. For the support and maintenance of the several state prisons, and for material and expense of manufacturing, eight hundred thousand dollars.

Sheriffs. For compensation of sheriffs for the transportation of convicts to the prisons, asylum for insane convicts, house of refuge and penitentiaries, twenty thousand dollars.

Croton water, etc. For supplying Croton water to the Sing Sing prison, one thousand five hundred dollars.

For supply of water for Auburn prison and asylum for insane convicts, one thousand five hundred dollars.

For the maintenance of convicts sentenced to penitentiaries, ten thousand dollars.

For refunding deposits to prison contractors, one thousand dollars.

ASYLUM FOR INSANE CONVICTS.

Asylum for insane convicts. For the support and maintenance of the asylum for insane convicts, pursuant to chaper one hundred and thirty of the laws of eighteen hundred and fifty-eight, sixteen thousand dollars.

STATE LUNATIC ASYLUM.

For salaries of the officers of the state asylum for lunatics, fifteen thousand dollars. Salaries.

For the support of Mark Jack, an insane Indian at the asylum, two hundred and fifty dollars. Mark Jack.

HUDSON RIVER STATE HOSPITAL FOR THE INSANE.

For salaries of the officers of the Hudson river state hospital for the insane, eight thousand dollars, or so much thereof as may be necessary. Salaries.

INDIAN AFFAIRS.

For the relief of the Onondaga Indians, pursuant to chapter two hundred and six of the laws of eighteen hundred and fifty eight, three hundred dollars. Onondagas.

For compensation of the agent of the Onondaga Indians, two hundred dollars.

For compensation of the agent of the Onondaga Indians, sixty-five dollars (chapter one hundred and seventy-eight, laws of eighteen hundred and forty-seven, and chapter six hundred and thirty-five, laws of eighteen hundred and sixty-nine), or so much thereof as may be necessary.

For compensation of the agent of the Onondaga Indians, on the Allegany and Cattaraugus reservations, one hundred and fifty dollars.

For compensation of the attorney of the St. Regis Indians, one hundred and fifty dollars. St. Regis.

For compensation of the attorney of the Seneca Indians, one hundred and fifty dollars. Senecas.

For compensation of the attorney for the Tonawanda band of Seneca Indians, one hundred and fifty dollars.

For the Willard asylum, for the support of Susan Green, an insane Indian woman, two hundred and fifty dollars. Susan Green.

ONONDAGA SALT SPRINGS.

For salary of the superintendent, compensation of clerks, and other persons employed, and other necessary expenses of the Onondaga salt springs, fifty-two thousand seven hundred dollars. Salaries.

MILITIA OF THE STATE.

For expenses of the national guard of the state of New York, pursuant to chapter eighty of the laws of eighteen hundred and seventy, two hundred and twenty-five thousand dollars. National guard.

For the purchase, under the direction of the governor, of six thousand breech-loading rifles to complete the arming of the national guard, ninety-six thousand dollars, or so much thereof as may be necessary, and for two batteries of Gatling guns, twelve thousand dollars, or as much thereof as may be necessary. Breech loading rifles. Gatling guns.

ROADS.

Payments to commissioners. For payments to commissioners, or moneys received into the treasury for taxes on lands of non-residents, appropriated to the construction of roads, six thousand dollars.

INTEREST ON STATE INDEBTEDNESS.

Interest. For interest on the debt of thirty-six thousand dollars, created for the benefit of the Stockbridge Indians, two thousand one hundred and sixty dollars.

COUNTY TREASURERS.

County treasurers. For advances to county treasurers, on account of taxes on property of non-residents, which may be returned to the comptroller's office, sixty thousand dollars.

TRANSPORTATION.

Transportation. For expenses of transportation of the Session Laws, journals and documents of the legislature, reports, books, etc., and packages by express, for the public offices, and for expenses of boxes, five thousand dollars.

REPAYMENT OF MONEYS.

Repayments to purchasers. For payment of moneys to purchasers, for redemption of land sold for taxes, one hundred thousand dollars.

Erroneous payments, etc. For repayment of money erroneously paid into the treasury for taxes, ten thousand dollars.

For repayment of money in cases of failure of title to lands sold by the state (Revised Statutes, volume one, page five hundred and forty-one), three hundred dollars.

For repayment of moneys paid into the treasury through mistake (Revised Statutes, page four hundred and seventy-nine), five hundred dollars.

FOR ACADEMIES, ETC.

Academies, etc. For the benefit of the academies and the academical departments of the union schools, the sum of one hundred and twenty-five thousand dollars, or so much thereof as may be derived from a tax of one-sixteenth of one mill, upon each dollar of the taxable property of the state, this sum to be divided as the literature fund is now divided, and in accordance with the law passed in eighteen hundred and seventy-two; but no part of this fund shall be distributed in aid of any religious or denominational academy of this state.

MISCELLANEOUS.

Mexico Independent. Radii. For supplying the "Mexico Independent" to the deaf and dumb persons of the state, in the same manner and upon the same terms as the "Radii" was furnished under and pursuant to chapter three hundred and twenty-nine, of the laws of eighteen hundred thirty-nine, six hundred and fifty dollars.

For supplying other states with reports of the court of appeals and of the supreme court, five hundred dollars. Court of appeals' reports, etc.

For expenses of books and stationery for the transfer office at the Manhattan Company, New York, two hundred and fifty dollars.

For compensation of agent in the city of New York, to superintend the issue and transfer of state stock, pursuant to chapter two hundred of the laws of eighteen hundred and sixty-six, seven hundred and fifty dollars.

For the compensation of the keeping of Washington's headquarters, two hundred and fifty dollars. Washington's headquarters, etc.

For the expense of the board of pilot commissioners, New York, forty-five hundred dollars.

For the commissioners to revise the statutes of the state, appointed under chapter thirty-three of the laws of eighteen hundred and seventy, for their services, fifteen thousand dollars, and for their expenditures for clerical services and other incidental matters, six thousand dollars. Commissioners to revise statutes.

INSPECTION OF STEAM BOILERS.

For inspector-in-chief of steam boilers, created by chapter nine hundred and sixty-nine of the laws of eighteen hundred and sixty-seven, for salary of chief and assistants, clerk hire, printing, traveling and contingent expenses, eight thousand dollars. Inspector.

For services and expenses of medical commissioners appointed pursuant to chapter six hundred sixty-six of laws of eighteen hundred and seventy-one, by the governor or courts of oyer and terminer, to inquire into the mental condition of persons under indictment or conviction for offenses, the punishment of which is death, two thousand dollars, the amount to be paid in each case to be certified by the governor. Medical commissioners.

DEAF AND DUMB.

For the support and instruction of three hundred and seventy pupils at the institution for deaf and dumb in New York, pursuant to chapter ninety-seven of the laws of eighteen hundred and fifty-two, or a proportionate amount for a shorter period of time than one year, or for a smaller number of pupils, as shall be duly verified by affidavits of the president and secretary of the institution, one hundred and eleven thousand dollars, and this sum is in full of all demands upon the state in behalf of said institution during the next fiscal year. Support of pupils.

For the support and instruction of thirty pupils, at the institution for the improved instruction of deaf mutes in New York, pursuant to chapter one hundred and eighty of the laws of eighteen hundred and seventy, or a proportionate amount for a shorter period of time than one year, or for a smaller number of pupils, as shall be duly verified by affidavits of the president and secretary of the institution, nine thousand dollars.

For the support and instruction of one hundred and fifty pupils for one year at the institution for the blind, in New

York, or a proportionate amount for a shorter period of time than one year, or for a smaller number of pupils, as shall be duly verified by affidavits of the president and secretary of the institution, forty-five thousand dollars.

JUVENILE DELINQUENTS.

Society for reformation of. For the society for the reformation of juvenile delinquents, in the city of New York, forty thousand dollars.

HOUSE OF REFUGE.

House of refuge. For the house of refuge for western New York, forty thousand dollars.

IDIOT ASYLUM.

State asylum. For the state asylum for idiots, at Syracuse, thirty-two thousand dollars.

WILLARD ASYLUM FOR THE INSANE.

Salaries. For the salaries of officers of the Willard asylum for the insane, ten thousand five hundred dollars, or so much thereof as may be necessary.

INSTITUTION FOR THE BLIND, BATAVIA.

Maintenance. For the maintenance of the institution for the blind, at Batavia, forty thousand dollars.

STATE COMMISSIONERS OF PUBLIC CHARITIES.

Salary of secretary and expenses. For the salary of the secretary of the commissioners of public charities, twenty-five hundred dollars; and for the traveling expenses of the commissioners and the secretary, and for office expenses, clerk hire and contingencies of the state commissioners of public charities, two thousand five hundred dollars.

PAYABLE FROM THE FREE SCHOOL FUND.

State normal school at Albany. For the state normal school at Albany, for its maintenance, eighteen thousand dollars.

Brockport. For the state normal and training school at Brockport, for its maintenance, eighteen thousand dollars.

Buffalo. For the state normal and training school at Buffalo, for its maintenance, eighteen thousand dollars.

Cortland. For the state normal and training school at Cortland, for its maintenance, eighteen thousand dollars.

Fredonia. For the state normal and training school at Fredonia, for its maintenance, eighteen thousand dollars.

Geneseo. For the state normal and training school at Geneseo, for its maintenance, eighteen thousand dollars.

Oswego. For the state normal and training school at Oswego, for its maintenance, eighteen thousand dollars.

Potsdam. For the state normal and training school at Potsdam for its maintenance, eighteen thousand dollars.

For the maintenance of the teachers' institutes, pursuant to chapter five hundred and fifty-five, title eleven, of the laws of eighteen hundred and sixty-four, eighteen thousand dollars. Institutes.

For the support of the common schools of this state, two million six hundred and eleven thousand dollars, or so much thereof as shall remain of the proceeds of the tax of one and one-fourth mills upon each dollar of the taxable property in this state levied for the support of common schools, after deducting from the proceeds of said tax the several sums appropriated in the items above mentioned, payable from the free school fund. Common schools.

PAYABLE FROM THE GENERAL FUND DEBT SINKING FUND.

For interest on the sum of three millions eight hundred and twenty-nine thousand eight hundred and thirty-one dollars and fifty-three cents of the general fund state debt, one hundred and ninety-nine thousand one hundred and ninety dollars and fifty-two cents. Interest.

For the payment of the annuities to the several Indian tribes, viz.: Annuities.

Onondagas, two thousand four hundred and thirty dollars.

Cayugas, two thousand three hundred dollars.

Senecas, five hundred dollars.

St. Regis, two thousand one hundred and thirty-one dollars and sixty-seven cents.

PAYABLE FROM SCHOOL FUND — CAPITAL.

For investment for loans to towns and counties, pursuant to chapter one hundred and ninety-four of the laws of eighteen hundred and forty-nine, fifty thousand dollars, or so much thereof as may be necessary. For investment for loans to towns and counties.

REVENUE.

For dividends to common schools (Revised Statutes, volume one, page five hundred and thirty-eight), one hundred and seventy-thousand dollars. Dividends to common schools.

For support of Indian schools, pursuant to chapter seventy-one of the laws of eighteen hundred and fifty-six, four thousand dollars. Indian schools.

For refunding money paid into the treasury for redemption of lands sold for arrears of consideration, pursuant to chapter four hundred and fifty seven of the laws of eighteen hundred and thirty-six, five hundred dollars. Redemption of lands.

For refunding surplus moneys received on resales of land (Revised Statutes, volume one, page four hundred and ninety-six), five hundred dollars. Surplus moneys.

For expenses of lands (Revised Statutes, volume one, page five hundred and fifty-four), two hundred dollars. Expenses.

PAYABLE FROM THE LITERATURE FUND.

Dividends to academies. For dividends to the academies, twelve thousand dollars.

Text-books, etc. For the purchase of text-books, maps and globes, philosophical and chemical apparatus for the academies (Revised Statutes, volume one, page seventy-two), three thousand dollars.

PAYABLE FROM THE UNITED STATES DEPOSIT FUND — CAPITAL.

U. S. deposit fund. For investment as capital of the United States deposit fund, one hundred thousand dollars, or so much thereof as may be necessary.

REVENUE.

Salaries of school commissioners, etc. For dividends to common schools, including the salaries of the county school commissioners, one hundred and sixty-five thousand dollars.

For dividends to academies, twenty-eight thousand dollars.

For amount to be added to the capital of the school fund (article nine of the constitution), twenty-five thousand dollars.

For instruction of common school teachers in the academies designated by the regents of the university, eighteen thousand dollars.

PAYABLE FROM THE BOUNTY DEBT SINKING FUND.

Contributions to sinking fund, etc. For investment of contributions to the sinking fund, and payment of interest on the state indebtedness, incurred pursuant to chapters two hundred and twenty-six and three hundred and twenty-five of the laws of eighteen hundred and sixty-five, known and designated as the bounty debt, four millions two hundred thousand dollars, or so much thereof as may be necessary.

PAYABLE FROM THE COLLEGE LAND SCRIP FUND REVENUE.

Cornell University. For the Cornell University, thirty-five thousand dollars.

PAYABLE FROM THE CORNELL ENDOWMENT FUND REVENUE.

For the Cornell University, ten thousand dollars.

PAYABLE FROM THE MILITARY RECORD FUND REVENUE.

Bureau of military statistics. For expenses of the bureau of military statistics, three thousand dollars.

PAYABLE FROM THE ELMIRA FEMALE COLLEGE EDUCATIONAL FUND REVENUE.

Elmira Female College. For the Elmira Female College, pursuant to chapter six hundred and forty-three of the laws of eighteen hundred and sixty-seven, three thousand five hundred dollars.

Appropriations, how to be paid. The amounts herein appropriated shall be paid by the treasurer from the respective funds as specified, and the salaries named by this act for the several officers for whom they are designated; but the comptroller shall not draw his warrant for the payment of the several amounts heretofore named, except for salaries, the amounts of which are duly established and fixed by law, till the persons demanding them shall present to him a detailed statement, in items, of the same, and if such account shall be for services it must show when, where and under what authority they were rendered; if for expenditures, when, where and under what authority they were made; if for articles furnished, when, where they were furnished, to whom they were delivered, and under what authority; and if the demand shall be for traveling expenses, the account must also specify the distance traveled, the place of starting and destination, the duty of business and the date and items of expenditures. All accounts must be verified by an affidavit to the effect that the account is true, just and correct, and that no part of it has been paid, but is actually and justly due and owing; on all accounts for transportation, furniture, blank and other books purchased for the use of office, binding, blanks, printing, stationery, postage, cleaning and other necessary and incidental expenses, a bill duly receipted must also be furnished, and it shall be the duty of the treasurer to report annually to the legislature the detail of these several expenditures. Every institution or society entitled under the provisions of this act, or of any future appropriation act, to receive money from the state, shall make an annual report to the legislature, which report shall contain a detail statement of all receipts and expenditures, debts and liabilities of said institution or society during the year for which said report is made, and a full and accurate statement of the financial condition thereof at the date of said report, which report shall be presented to the legislature on or before the fifteenth day of January in each and every year hereafter.

Accounts to be verified.

Institutions to make annual report.

The failure to make the said report to the legislature on or before the fifteenth day of January in each and every year hereafter, by any such institution or society, shall work a forfeiture of the office of every trustee or manager at the time in charge of said institution or society failing to report as aforesaid, and the governor shall thereupon proceed to fill such vacancies by nominations to the senate for its confirmation of other persons to fill said vacancies.

Failure to make report.

A special report of the condition of such institutions or societies may at any time be called for by the comptroller, and shall be made and filed with him within ten days after notice of such call by the comptroller to such institution or society, and no money hereby or hereafter appropriated shall be paid to any institution or society which shall hereafter neglect to make such reports as aforesaid. The comptroller between the first and the tenth days of December in each year shall send, by mail or otherwise, a copy of this section to the officers required to report to the legislature as hereinbefore provided.

Comptroller may call for special report.

§ 2. There shall be imposed for the fiscal year, beginning on the first day of October, eighteen hundred and seventy-three,

Tax of one and one-quarter

on each dollar of real and personal property in this state, subject to taxation, a tax of one mill and one-quarter of a mill per dollar thereof, for the object following, namely, to be paid into the canal fund, which taxes shall be assessed, levied and collected by the annual assessment and collection of taxes for that year in the manner prescribed by law, and shall be paid by the several county treasurers into the treasury of this state, to be held by the treasurer for application to the purposes specified. There shall be imposed for the fiscal year beginning on the first day of October, eighteen hundred and seventy-three, on each dollar of real and personal property in this state, subject to taxation, a tax of two mills and one-quarter of a mill per dollar thereof, for the object following, namely: to be paid into the general fund, which taxes shall be assessed, levied and collected by the annual assessment and collection of taxes for that year in the manner prescribed by law, and shall be paid by the several county treasurers into the treasury of the state, to be held by the treasurer for application to the purposes specified.

Mills to be paid into canal fund.

Tax of two and one-quarter mills to be paid into the general fund

Action of boards of supervisors, etc., legalized, etc.

§ 3. The action of all boards of supervisors, assessors and collectors of taxes, and all other officers of this state, in imposing, levying and collecting taxes, in obedience to what purported to be chapter seven hundred and thirty-four of the laws of eighteen hundred and seventy-two, and in paying over moneys raised thereby, is hereby ratified, confirmed, legalized and made valid the same as if the said chapter had been and was a constitutional and valid act of the legislature; and all moneys paid by any county into the treasury of the state, or by any town or city into the county treasury, in consequence thereof, are hereby declared to be legal, and the amount so paid by any county, city or town shall be held and taken as a satisfaction, in whole or to the extent of such payment, of the amount which said county, city or town would be required to and would raise by tax under the provisions of section two of this act; and said county, city or town to the amount of such payment shall not be compelled or required to raise money by tax in pursuance of section two of this act. But if any of said moneys shall not yet have been paid into the state treasury by any county, the same shall not apply in such satisfaction until the same shall have been paid into the state treasury; and if any of said moneys shall not yet have been paid into the county treasury by any city or town, the same shall not apply in such satisfaction until the same shall have been paid into the county treasury.

Tax to be levied in Kings county.

§ 4. There shall be levied and imposed by the board of supervisors of the county of Kings upon the real and personal property of said county liable to taxation, for the fiscal year, beginning on the first day of October, eighteen hundred and seventy-three, in addition to any and all other taxes levied and collected therein by law, the sum of six hundred and eighty-two thousand nine hundred and eighty-four dollars and twenty-two cents, and when the same shall be paid into the treasury of the state it shall be in satisfaction of the tax to be levied and imposed, and of the money to be raised and collected in said county in pursuance of this act.

Action of supervisors, etc., in borrowing money etc., legalized.

§ 5. The action of any and all boards of supervisors and other public officers of any county or city, who have heretofore borrowed money for their respective counties, or issued bonds thereof, for the purpose of raising money with which to pay to the state treasury the amount required of their respective counties by the comptroller according to said supposed chapter seven hundred and thirty-four, is hereby ratified, legalized, confirmed and made valid. And any board of supervisors, or other public officers of any county or city. may hereafter, in accordance with any law authorizing them to borrow money or issue bonds for the purpose of paying the amount of money required by said supposed chapter, proceed to borrow money or issue bonds under such law to raise the money required of said city or county by this act.

Appropriations out of proceeds of tax for the canal fund.

§ 6. The following amounts of money for the following purposes are hereby appropriated out of the proceeds of the aforesaid tax for the canal fund, namely: For deficiency in the appropriations made by act chapter seven hundred and sixty-eight, laws of eighteen hundred and seventy-four, for payment of the awards made by the canal appraisers during the year eighteen hundred and sixty-eight and eighteen hundred and sixty-nine, the sum of fifty-five thousand eight hundred and one dollars and ninety-five cents. For deficiency in appropriation made by act chapter seven hundred and sixty-seven, laws of eighteen hundred and seventy, for extraordinary repairs of the canals, namely: for the Erie canal, one hundred and seventy-two thousand six hundred and sixty-two dollars and six cents; for the Champlain canal, twenty-eight thousand three hundred and sixty-five dollars and ninety cents; for the Black River canal, eight hundred and sixty-three dollars and thirty-one cents; for the Oswego canal, eleven thousand nine hundred and sixty-three dollars and one cent; for the Cayuga and Seneca canal, thirty-six hundred and ninety-nine dollars and ninety cents; for the Chenango canal, twenty-six thousand eight hundred and eighty-five dollars and ninety-four cents; for the Chemung canal, twelve thousand two hundred and nine dollars and sixty-seven cents; for the Crooked Lake canal, two hundred and forty-six dollars and sixty-six cents; for the Genesee Valley canal, twelve thousand three hundred and thirty-eight dollars and thirty-nine cents.

For deficiency in appropriation by chapter 930, laws of 1871.

For deficiency in appropriation made by act chapter nine hundred and thirty, laws of eighteen hundred and seventy-one, for extraordinary repairs of the canals, namely: for the Erie canal, sixty-six thousand seven hundred and seventy-eight dollars and one cent; for the Champlain canal, ten thousand six hundred and twenty-seven dollars and eighty cents; for the Black River canal, five hundred and thirty dollars and one cent; for the Oswego canal, seventy-seven hundred and ninety-three dollars and seventy-two cents; for the Cayuga and Seneca canals, thirty-eight hundred and ninety-six dollars and eighty-six cents; for the Chenango canal, thirty-eight thousand seven hundred and ninety-one dollars and forty-seven cents; for the Chemung canal, forty-seven hundred and eighty-two dollars and fifty-one cents; for the Oneida Lake canal, forty-four hundred and twenty-eight * and twenty-five cents; for the Crooked Lake canal, five hundred and thirty-one dollars and thirty-nine cents; for the Genesee Valley canal, six thousand one hundred and ninety-nine dollars and fifty-five cents.

To pay certificates of indebtedness, etc. The sum of sixty-five thousand dollars, or so much thereof as may be necessary, to meet and pay the interest on the money borrowed, or certificates of indebtedness issued, to meet the deficiencies enumerated in the three foregoing items of deficiencies.

The sum of three hundred and ninety-three thousand seven hundred and fifty-five dollars and fifty-one cents, for outstanding certificates of awards of canal damages made by and expenses attending cases heard before the canal appraisers in the year eighteen hundred and seventy-one now on interest.

The sum of fifty thousand dollars, or so much thereof as may be necessary, to meet and pay the interest on the certificates in the last foregoing item mentioned.

Eastern division Erie canal. The sum of twenty-five thousand four hundred and thirty-one dollars and ninety-nine cents, the amount of certificates on interest now outstanding for work done on the eastern division of the Erie canal, in excess of any appropriation therefor.

Champlain canal. The sum of sixty-one thousand six hundred and eleven dollars and thirty-one cents, the amount of certificates on interest now outstanding for work done on the Champlain canal improvement, in excess of any appropriation therefor.

Black River canal. The sum of two thousand five hundred and sixty dollars, the amount of certificates on interest now outstanding for work done on the Black River canal, in excess of any appropriation therefor.

Chenango canal extension. The sum of one hundred and twenty thousand dollars, or so much thereof as may be necessary, to pay the amount of certificates on interest now outstanding and for work done on the Chenango canal extension, in excess of any appropriation therefor, a portion of which was specially excepted from payment out of the appropriation of such Chenango canal extension made by chapter nine hundred and thirty of the laws of eighteen hundred and seventy-one.

Work on Oneida Lake canal. The sum of twenty thousand dollars, or so much thereof as may be necessary, and now due and unpaid for work done and performed on the Oneida Lake canal, in excess of any appropriation therefor.

The sum of forty-five thousand dollars, or so much thereof as may be necessary, to meet and pay the interest on the last four foregoing items.

The sum of two hundred and thirty-one thousand four hundred and thirty-four dollars and forty-six cents, to pay the

* So in the original.

sum of awards for damages and extra compensation made by the canal board in the year eighteen hundred and seventy-one.

The sum of seventy-one thousand nine hundred and sixty-four dollars and sixty-eight cents, to pay the sum of awards for damages and extra compensation and expenses attending the same, made by the board of canal commissioners in the year eighteen hundred and seventy-one. Awards for damages, etc.

The sum of twenty-five thousand dollars, or so much thereof as may be necessary, to pay the interest on the last two foregoing items.

The sum of three hundred and fifty-six thousand seven hundred and sixty-six dollars and sixty-five cents, to supply the deficiency in the canal debt sinking fund, to meet the requirements of section three, article seven of the constitution of the state, for interest on the canal debt, which was due September thirtieth, eighteen hundred and seventy-one. Deficiency in canal debt sinking fund, etc.

The sum of five hundred and fifty-seven thousand one hundred dollars, to supply the canal debt sinking fund with means to pay interest on the thirtieth day of September, eighteen hundred and seventy-two, as required by section three, article seven of the constitution of the state.

The sum of one hundred and twenty-four thousand four hundred and fifteen dollars, or so much thereof as may be necessary, due and to be paid on final settlement of contracts for moneys heretofore retained by the state to secure the performance of contracts. Final settlement of contracts.

§ 7. The following amount is hereby appropriated, out of the proceeds of the aforesaid tax, for the general fund: Appropriations out of proceeds of tax for general fund.

The sum of four million fifty-one thousand one hundred and fifty-nine dollars for the deficiency in the general fund on the thirtieth day of September, eighteen hundred and seventy-two.

CHAP. 644.

AN ACT to amend an act entitled "An act to repeal chapter four hundred and ten, passed April fourteenth, eighteen hundred and sixty-six, and chapter three hundred and three, passed April seventeenth, eighteen hundred and sixty-one, and to divide the crime of murder into two degrees, and to prescribe the punishment of arson," passed April twelfth, eighteen hundred and sixty-two.

PASSED May 29, 1873; three-fifths being present.

The People of the State of New York, represented in Senate and Assembly, do enact as follows:

SECTION 1. Section six of the act entitled "An act to repeal chapter four hundred and ten, passed April fourteenth, eighteen hundred and sixty, and chapter three hundred and three, passed April seventeenth, eighteen hundred and sixty one, and to divide the crime of murder into two degrees, and to prescribe the punishment of arson," passed April twelfth, eighteen hundred and sixty-two, is hereby amended so as to read as follows: Section five of said title shall be so altered as to read as follows:

Murder in first degree. § 5. Such killing, unless it be manslaughter or excusable justifiable homicide, as hereinafter provided, shall be murder in the first degree, in the following cases: First, when perpetrated from a deliberate and premeditated design to effect the death of the person killed, or of any human being. Second, when perpetrated by an act imminently dangerous to others, and evincing a depraved mind, regardless of human life, although without any premeditated design to effect the death of any particular individual. Third, when perpetrated without any design to effect death by a person engaged in the commission of any felony. Such killing, unless it be murder in the first degree, or manslaughter, or excusable or justifiable homicide, as hereinafter provided, shall be murder in the second degree when perpetrated intentionally but without deliberation and premeditation.

Murder in second degree.

§ 2. Section seven of said act is hereby amended so as to read as follows:

Punishment. § 7. Add to said title another section in these words: Every person who shall be convicted of murder in the second degree, or of arson in the first degree, as herein defined, shall be punished by imprisonment in a state prison during the period of his natural life.

Not to affect offenses heretofore committed, etc. § 3. No offense committed previous to the time when this statute shall take effect, shall be affected by this act. No prosecution for any offense pending at the time this statute shall take effect shall be affected by this act. The provisions of this act shall only apply to offenses hereinafter committed. And the statutes now in force shall apply to and be and remain in full force as to all offenses committed before this act shall take effect, and to the prosecution and punishment thereof.

§ 4. This act shall take effect immediately.

Ante, vol. 5, p. 148.

CHAP. 646.

AN ACT to suppress intemperance, pauperism and crime.

PASSED May 29, 1873; three-fifths being present.

The People of the State of New York, represented in Senate and Assembly, do enact as follows:

Persons injured may maintain action against seller, etc. SECTION 1. Every husband, wife, child, parent, guardian, employer or other person who shall be injured in person, or property, or means of support, by any intoxicated person, or in consequence of the intoxication, habitual or otherwise, of any person, shall have a right of action in his or her name, against any person or persons who shall, by selling or giving away intoxicating liquors, have caused the intoxication, in whole or in part, of such person or persons, and any person or persons owning or renting or permitting the occupation of any building or premises, and having knowledge that intoxicating liquors are to be sold therein, shall be liable severally, or jointly with the person or persons selling or giving intoxicating liquors aforesaid, for all damages sustained and for exemplary damages; and all damages recovered by a minor under this act shall be paid either to such minor or to his or her parent, guardian or next friend, as the court shall direct; and the unlawful sale or giving away of intoxicating liquors shall work a forfeiture of all rights of the lessee or tenant under any lease or contract of rent upon the premises.

§ 2. In any action arising for violations of the provisions of this act, any justice of the peace in the county where the offense is committed shall have jurisdiction to try and determine the same, providing the amount of damages claimed do not exceed two hundred dollars, in which case and where the damages claimed do not exceed five hundred dollars, the justice of the peace before whom the action is commenced, shall associate with himself any other two justices of the peace in the same county, who shall have jurisdiction to try and determine the same. Jurisdiction of justices of the peace.

§ 3. This act shall take effect immediately.

CHAP. 657.

AN ACT to amend section seven of article one, title two, chapter six, part second of the Revised Statutes, in reference to non-resident executors.

PASSED June 6, 1873.

The People of the State of New York, represented in Senate and Assembly, do enact as follows:

SECTION 1. Section seven of article one, title two, chapter six, part second of the Revised Statutes is hereby amended so as to read as follows:

§ 7. If any person applying for letters testamentary be a non-resident of the state, such letters shall not be granted until the applicant shall give a like bond; provided, however, that such non-resident executor may receive such letters without bonds if the testator, by words in his last testament, has requested that his executor be allowed to act without giving bonds, and if such executor has his usual place of business within this state. When non-residents applying for letters to give bonds.

§ 2. This act shall take effect immediately.

Ante, vol. 2, p. 72.

CHAP. 661.

AN ACT to provide for the support and care of state paupers.

PASSED June 7, 1873; three-fifths being present.

The People of the State of New York, represented in Senate and Assembly, do enact as follows:

State paupers.

SECTION 1. Every poor person who is blind, lame, old, impotent or decrepit, or in any other way disabled or enfeebled, so as to be unable by work to maintain himself, who shall apply for aid to any superintendent or overseer of the poor or other officer charged with the support and relief of indigent persons, and who shall not have resided sixty days in any county of this state within one year preceding the time of such application, shall be deemed to be a state pauper, and shall be maintained as hereinafter provided.

State board of charities to contract for support of.

§ 2. The state board of charities is hereby authorized, from time to time, on behalf of the state, to contract, for such time and on such terms as it may deem proper, with the authorities of not more than five counties or cities of this state, for the reception and support, in the poor-houses or other suitable buildings of such counties or cities respectively, of such paupers as may be committed to such poor-houses as provided by this act. The said board may establish rules and regulations for the discipline, employment, treatment and care of such paupers and for their discharge. Every such contract shall be in writing, and be filed in the office of the said board. The poor-houses or other buildings so contracted for, with the authorities of any county or city, while used for the purposes herein mentioned, shall be appropriately designated by the said board, and shall be known as state alms-houses. The said board may from time to time direct the transfer of any such paupers from one alms-house to another, and may give notice, from time to time, to counties to which alms-house they shall send paupers.

Notice to be given to county clerks of location of alms-houses.

§ 3. The said board shall give notice to the county clerks of the several counties of this state of the location of each of such alms-houses, who thereupon shall cause such notice to be duly promulgated to the superintendents and overseers of the poor and other officers charged with the support and relief of indigent persons in their respective counties. A circular from the secretary of said board shall accompany such notice to each county clerk, giving all necessary information respecting the commitment, support and care of state paupers in such alms-houses, according to the provisions of this act.

Removal of state paupers to state alms-house.

§ 4. The county judge and justices of the peace of the several counties of this state, and all police justices, upon the application of any superintendent or overseer of the poor, or other officer charged with the support and relief of indigent persons, and on satisfactory proof being made that the person applying to such officer for relief is a state pauper, as defined by the first section of this act, shall by warrant directed to such officer, or other suitable person, cause such pauper to be removed or conveyed to the nearest state alms-house, and such pauper shall be maintained therein until duly discharged. The application and all testimony taken in any such proceeding, and the order for the issuing of any warrant for the removal of any such pauper, shall be filed in the office of the clerk of the county in which such proceeding shall be had, and a copy of the same shall be forwarded by mail, within five days thereafter, to the secretary of the state board of charities. A verified statement of the expenses incurred by the officer, or other person, in making such removal, shall be presented to the officer issuing such warrant, who shall examine and audit the same, and allow such expenses as have been actually and necessarily incurred in such removal, a copy of which account and audit shall be filed in the county clerk's office. All such accounts for expenses incurred by counties, cities and towns, by reason of the removal of any such pauper, shall be paid by the treasurer of the county in which such expenses were incurred, who shall render a statement of the same to the comptroller on or before the third Tuesday in October, annually, and which statement shall include all claims for such charges to the first day of said October, and the same shall be reimbursed by the state treasurer, on the warrant of the comptroller, in like manner as other claims of counties against the state are now by law reimbursed, provided that no payment shall be made by the state to any officer or other person for their time or service in making any such removal. The comptroller may require such accounts to be accompanied by such statement of particulars and facts, and substantiated by affidavit, as may to him seem proper. Expenses of removal.

§ 5. The expenses for the support, treatment and care of all persons who shall be sent as state paupers to such alms-houses, shall be paid quarterly on the first days of January, April, July and October in each year, to the treasurer of the county, or proper city officer incurring the same, by the treasurer of the state on the warrant of the comptroller, but no such expenses shall be paid to any county or city until an account of the number of persons thus supported, and the time that each shall have been respectively maintained, shall have been rendered in due form and approved by the state board of charities. Expenses for support.

§ 6. The keeper or principal officer in charge of each and all such alms-houses shall enter the names of all persons received by them under the provisions of this act, with such particulars in reference to each as the said board, from time to time, may prescribe, together with the names of the officer making the complaint, and the judge or justice by whom the commitment was made, in a book to be kept for that purpose. Within three days after the admission of any such person, such keeper or principal officer shall transmit by mail the Duty of keepers of.

name of such person, with the particulars hereinbefore mentioned, to the secretary of said board; and notice of the death, discharge or absconding of any such person shall, in like manner, and within the time above named, be thus sent to said secretary. The secretary of said board shall cause the names of the paupers in each of said alms-houses, furnished as above provided for, to be entered in a book to be kept for that purpose in the office of said board, and he shall verify the correctness thereof by comparison with the books kept in such alms-houses as aforesaid, and by personal examination of the several inmates thereof, and in any other manner the board, from time to time, may direct; and he shall furnish the said board, in tabulated statements, on or before the second Tuesday in January, annually, the number of inmates maintained in each and all of such alms-houses during the preceding year, the number discharged, transferred to other institutions, bound out or removed from the state, and the number who died or left without permission during the year, with such other particulars and information as the board may require.

Secretary to keep record of names.

Visitation of alms-houses.

§ 7. In addition to the visitation of the secretary of said board, as hereinafter provided for, the said board shall cause each of such alms-houses to be visited periodically by some member or members of such board, who shall examine into the condition and management of said alms-houses respectively, and make such report thereof to the said board as may be deemed proper.

By the secretary.

§ 8. It shall be the duty of the secretary of said board to visit and inspect each and all of the said alms-houses at least once in every three months, and as much oftener as in his judgment it may be expedient, or the board may direct. For the purposes of such inspections the said secretary shall possess all the powers of a member of the said board and also such further powers as are hereinafter mentioned. It shall be the duty of the officer in charge of each and every such alms-house to give to the said secretary free access to all parts of the grounds, buildings, hospital and other arrangements connected therewith, and to every inmate thereof, and to extend to him the same facilities for the inspection of such alms-house and its inmates as is required by law to be extended to said board and commissioners, and in default thereof he shall be subject to the same penalty as if access were denied to any member of said board.

Insane paupers.

§ 9. If any inmate of any such alms-house, when admitted, is insane, or thereafter becomes insane or of unsound mind, and the accommodation in said alms-house, in the opinion of said secretary, are not adequate and proper for his treatment and care, the said secretary may cause his removal to the appropriate state asylum for insane, and he shall be received by the officer in charge of such asylum and be maintained therein until duly discharged. The expenses for the support, treatment and care of insane persons or persons of unsound mind, so received in any state asylum, shall be paid to the

Expenses.

treasurer thereof by the treasurer of the state, on the warrant of the comptroller, upon the account being duly rendered and certified to by the secretary of said board; provided, however, that such expenses shall not exceed those charged to counties, cities or towns for the support, treatment and care of insane persons or persons of unsound mind in such asylum.

§ 10. When any child under ten years of age shall be committed to any such alms-house, the said secretary in his discretion may cause the transfer of such child to such orphan asylum in this state as he may deem proper. The expenses for the maintenance and care of such child thereafter, and until otherwise provided for, shall be paid out of the state treasury on the certificate of said secretary, in the same manner as provided in the preceding section as to the maintenance and care of insane persons or persons of unsound mind; provided, that such expenses shall not exceed the cost of maintenance of such child in said alms-house. The said secretary, also, in his discretion, may bind out any orphan or indigent child which may be committed to any such alms-house or may be placed in any orphan asylum as aforesaid, if a male child under twenty-one years, or if a female, under the age of eighteen, to be clerks, apprentices or servants until such child, if a male, be twenty-one years old, or if a female, shall be eighteen years old, which binding shall be as effectual as if such child had bound himself with the consent of his father or other legal guardian.

Transfer of children.

Expenses.

Secretary may bind out indigent children, etc.

§ 11. Any person becoming an inmate of any such alms-house, and expressing a preference to be sent to any state or country where said pauper may have a legal settlement or friends, willing to support or to aid in supporting him, the secretary of said board may cause the removal of such pauper to such state or country; provided, in the judgment of said secretary, the interest of the state and the welfare of the pauper will be promoted thereby; and the said secretary shall report, from time to time, to said board, the names of all persons removed under the provisions of this act, the places whence removed, and the cost of the several removals.

Transfer of paupers to counties.

§ 12. The said secretary of the said state board of charities, before entering upon his duties under this act, shall take and subscribe the constitutional oath of office, which shall be filed in the office of the secretary of state. In addition to the powers hereinbefore conferred upon said secretary, he shall possess and exercise the like powers, and be subject to the like duties as to such state paupers as superintendents of the poor exercise and are subject to in the care and support of county paupers. In case of the illness, absence, or other inability of said secretary, from any cause, to perform his duties, they may be temporarily performed and discharged by any other person or persons to be appointed by said board for such purpose.

Secretary to take official oath.

Powers, etc., of.

§ 13. If any inmate of either of said alms-houses shall leave the same without being duly discharged, and within one year thereafter is found in any city or town of this state soliciting

Punishment for leaving alms-house.

public or private aid, he may be punished by confinement in the county jail of the county in which so found, for a term not exceeding three months, or he may be committed for a like term to any work-house of this state, by any court of competent jurisdiction, and it shall be the duty of every superintendent and overseer of the poor and other officers charged with the support and relief of indigent persons, to cause, as far as may be, the provisions of this section to be enforced.

Terms defined. § 14. The terms "alms-house" and "state alms-house," as used in this act, are to be applied to the county or city poor-houses or other buildings in which state paupers are being maintained, as herein provided for; the words "superintendent" and "county superintendent" mean county superintendent of the poor; and the words "overseer" and "overseers of the poor" mean town and city overseers of the poor.

Appropriation. § 15. The sum of twenty-five thousand dollars, or so much thereof as may be necessary, is hereby appropriated to be paid for the purposes of this act, out of any moneys in the state treasury not otherwise appropriated, for the removal of paupers and their maintenance and care as herein provided for, and for the contingent and miscellaneous expenses attending the execution of this act, to be certified and allowed by the said state board of charities.

§ 16. This act shall take effect immediately.

CHAP. 663.

AN ACT to amend article second of title first of chapter nine of part third of the Revised Statutes, entitled, of writs of habeas corpus and certiorari when issued to inquire into the cause of detention.

PASSED June 7, 1878; three-fifths being present.

The People of the State of New York, represented in Senate and Assembly, do enact as follows:

SECTION 1. The second article of the first title of the ninth chapter of the third part of the Revised Statutes is hereby amended by adding an additional section, as follows:

When proceedings are removed into supreme court, etc. § 90. Whenever any proceedings commenced under this article shall be removed by the prisoner into the supreme court, to be there examined and corrected, or whenever any prisoner shall appeal to the court of appeals from any decision refusing his discharge, and the offense with which such prisoner stands charged is one for which such prisoner may be admitted to bail by the laws of this state, the court or officer so refusing such discharge shall, on the demand of such prisoner, or his counsel, at or any time after the time of rendering its decision, fix the amount in which such prisoner may be admitted to bail, and thereupon, if such prisoner shall

Court to fix amount of bail.

serve on such officer, or on the clerk of such court, and on the district attorney of the county in which such proceedings are had, a notice of his intention to remove said proceedings into the supreme court, to be examined and corrected, or of his appeal to the court of appeals, as the case may be, and enter into recognizance in the amount so fixed in manner and form, and with such surety or sureties, as shall be approved by such officer or court, or by a justice of the supreme court, or the county judge of the county in which such proceedings shall be had, conditioned that the said prisoner will appear at a time and place to be stated in such recognizance, to abide by and perform the judgment or order of the court into which said proceedings may have been removed, in case the proceedings so removed are intended to be removed, shall be affirmed by the supreme court or the court of appeal, then such prisoner shall be discharged from custody until the said supreme court shall hear and decide the matters so removed into it, or until the court of appeals shall hear and decide such appeal, or until such proceedings or appeal be dismissed; and such prisoner shall remain in the custody of the sheriff of the county in which he may then be until he give bail as aforesaid, or if he do not give bail, then until the supreme court or the court of appeals shall hear and decide the matters so removed into it, or the appeal so be taken, or until said proceedings or appeal shall be dismissed.

§ 2. This act shall take effect immediately.

Ante, vol. 3, p. 594.

CHAP. 665.

AN ACT to punish the taking of fish from private ponds.

PASSED June 7, 1873; three-fifths being present

The People of the State of New York, represented in Senate and Assembly, do enact as follows:

SECTION 1. Every person who shall be convicted of wrongfully and willfully taking any fish from any private pond without the consent of the owner thereof, shall be adjudged guilty of malicious trespass and shall be liable to a penalty of three times the value of the fish taken, and shall also be liable to indictment for a misdemeanor, and, on conviction, shall be punished by imprisonment in a county jail not exceeding thirty days, or by a fine not exceeding two hundred and fifty dollars, or by both fine and imprisonment. Wrongfully taking fish from private ponds.

§ 2. Every person who shall willfully place any poison, or other substance injurious to the health of fish, in private pond or stream used for propagating or preserving fish, with intent to capture or harm any fish, shall, upon conviction, be punished by imprisonment in a county jail not to exceed six months, or by a fine not exceeding two hundred and fifty dollars, or by both fine and imprisonment. Poisoning fish.

Wrongfully letting water out. § 3. Every person who shall wrongfully and willfully let the water out of any such pond in any way, with intent to take fish from such pond, or to do harm to such fish, shall be guilty of a misdemeanor, and upon conviction be punished by imprisonment in a county jail not exceeding six months, or by a fine not exceeding two hundred and fifty dollars, or by both fine and imprisonment. The penalties provided for in this act shall be posted in two of the most conspicuous places upon the borders of every such pond.

§ 4. This act shall take effect immediately.

CHAP. 675.

AN ACT to provide for the payment of the attendants of the commission of appeals.

PASSED June 7, 1878; three-fifths being present.

The People of the State of New York, represented in Senate and Assembly, do enact as follows:

Per diem of attendants. SECTION 1. From and after the passage of this act, the attendants of the commission of appeals shall each receive five dollars for each and every day of their attendance on said commission, to be paid, upon the certificate of the clerk of said commission of the number of days' attendance, by the comptroller, upon the presentation of such certificate.

§ 2. All acts or parts of acts inconsistent with this act are hereby repealed.

§ 3. This act shall take effect immediately.

CHAP. 679.

AN ACT to supply a deficiency in the appropriation for the fiscal year beginning on the first day of October, eighteen hundred and seventy-three, for clerk hire in the office of the comptroller.

PASSED June 7, 1878; three-fifths being present.

The People of the State of New York, represented in Senate and Assembly, do enact as follows:

Appropriation for clerk hire. SECTION 1. The sum of twenty thousand dollars is hereby appropriated for deficiency in the appropriation clerk hire in the comptroller's office for the fiscal year beginning on the first day of October, eighteen hundred and seventy-three, in addition to the sum appropriated by chapter six hundred and forty-three of the laws of eighteen hundred and seventy-three, passed May twenty-nine, eighteen hundred and seventy-three.

CHAP. 688.

AN ACT regulating the responsibility of agents of insurance companies.

PASSED June 10, 1873.

The People of the State of New York, represented in Senate and Assembly, do enact as follows:

Agents receiving money liable in a fiduciary capacity.

SECTION 1. Any person who shall be appointed, or who shall act as agent for any insurance company within this state, or who shall as such agent solicit applications, issue policies or renewals, and collect premiums, either for original insurances or renewals, or who shall receive or collect moneys from any source or any account whatsoever, as such agent, for any insurance company doing business in this state, whether such company be organized under the laws of this state or any other state of the union, such person shall be held responsible, in a trust or fiduciary capacity, to such companies for any moneys received by him for such company.

Taking moneys, with intent to embezzle, larceny.

§ 2. Any such agent or person who shall embezzle or convert to his own use, or shall take or secrete or otherwise dispose of, with intent to embezzle or use, or who shall fraudulently withhold or appropriate, invest, loan or otherwise fraudulently apply or make use of, without the consent of such company, or contrary to its instructions, any money belonging to such company which shall have come into his possession, or shall be under his care, by reason of such agency, he shall be deemed by so doing to have committed the crime of larceny, and upon conviction shall be punished for such crime.

CHAP. 698.

AN ACT to amend the act passed April eleven, eighteen hundred and sixty-five, entitled "An act for the incorporation of societies or clubs for certain social and recreative purposes."

PASSED June 10, 1873.

The People of the State of New York, represented in Senate and Assembly, do enact as follows:

SECTION 1. The third section of the act entitled "An act for the incorporation of societies or clubs for certain social and recreative purposes," is hereby amended by adding at the conclusion of said section, as follows:

Increase of trustees, etc.

The number of trustees in any corporation organized under this act may be increased to not more than thirteen or diminished to not less than three, as follows: The existing trustees of any such corporation, or a majority of them, shall make and sign a certificate declaring how many trustees the corporation shall thereafter have, and stating the names of such trustees for the present time, which certificate shall be acknowledged by the trustees signing the same or proved by a subscribing witness, and shall be filed in the office of the clerk of the county where the original certificate of incorporation was filed, and a duplicate or transcript thereof duly certified under the official seal of such clerk, filed in the office of the secretary of state; and from and after the filing of such certificate and duplicate or transcript, the trustees of such corporation shall be deemed increased to the number therein stated, and the persons so named therein shall be trustees until a new election of trustees shall be had according to the said act, and the constitution, by-laws or regulations of such corporation.

§ 2. This act shall take effect immediately.

Ante, vol. 6, p. 479.

CHAP. 699.

AN ACT to amend chapter four hundred and forty of the laws of eighteen hundred and seventy-three, entitled "An act requiring commissioners of highways to act as inspectors of plank-roads and turnpikes," passed May eighth, eighteen hundred and seventy-three.

PASSED June 10, 1878; three-fifths being present.

The People of the State of New York, represented in Senate and Assembly, do enact as follows:

County of Cortland exempted from chapter 440, laws of 1873.

SECTION 1. The county of Cortland is hereby exempted from the operation of chapter four hundred and forty of the laws of eighteen hundred and seventy-three, entitled "An act to require commissioners of highways to act as inspectors of plank-roads and turnpikes," passed May eighth, eighteen hundred and seventy-three.

§ 2. This act shall take effect immediately.

Ante, p. 612.

CHAP. 708.

AN ACT to authorize a tax of seven-tenths of a mill per dollar of valuation for the payment of the awards of the canal appraisers and expenses attending the same, and of the canal commissioners; to pay certificates of indebtedness on interest now outstanding, and to supply deficiencies in appropriations for new work under act chapter eight hundred and fifty of the laws of eighteen hundred and seventy-two; and to provide for deficiency in the sinking funds under sections one and three of article seven of the constitution.

PASSED June 11, 1873; three-fifths being present.

The People of the State of New York, represented in Senate and Assembly, do enact as follows:

SECTION 1. There shall be imposed for the fiscal year, beginning on the first day of October, one thousand eight hundred and seventy-three, a state tax of seven-tenths of a mill on each dollar of the valuation of the real and personal property in this state subject to taxation, which tax shall be assessed, levied and collected by the annual assessment and collection of taxes for that year, in the manner prescribed by law, and shall be paid by the several county treasurers into the treasury of this state, to be held by the treasurer for appropriation to the purposes designated in this act. Seven-tenths of a mill tax.

For the payment of the awards of the canal appraisers for the year one thousand eight hundred and seventy-two, and on interest now outstanding, the sum of five hundred and seventy-nine thousand one hundred and sixty-four dollars and seventy-two cents. Awards of canal appraisers.

For paying the counsel and agents employed by the canal commissioners, or either of them, and the canal appraisers, for their services, disbursements and expenses incurred in the defense of claims against the state connected with the canals, the sum of twelve thousand dollars or so much thereof as may be necessary; provided, however, that all bills or accounts for such services, disbursements or expenses shall, before payment, be presented to and audited by the canal board. Counsel and agents. Proviso.

For the payment of awards for damages made by the canal commissioners, the sum of twenty-one thousand six hundred and twelve dollars and thirty-seven cents. Awards by canal commissioners.

For the payment of the amount of certificates on interest now outstanding for work done on the Chenango canal extension, in excess of any appropriation therefor, the sum of four thousand two hundred and eighteen dollars and eighty-three cents. Chenango canal extension.

To meet the deficiency of the appropriations made by act chapter eight hundred and fifty of the laws of eighteen hun- Deficiency.

dred and seventy-two, the sum of forty-four thousand seven hundred and sixty-six dollars and forty-three cents.

Purchase of coin. For the purchase of coin to pay the principal of the canal debt under section one of article seven of the constitution, which matures on the first day of January, one thousand eight hundred and seventy-four, and for which the sinking fund has been provided, the sum of one hundred and ninety-five thousand dollars, or so much thereof as said sinking fund may be deficient.

Canal debt sinking fund. The sum of five hundred and seventy-five thousand three hundred and thirty-nine dollars and sixty-nine cents, to supply the canal debt sinking fund with means to pay interest on the thirtieth day of September, eighteen hundred and seventy-three, as required by section three of article seven of the constitution.

Surplus moneys of canal sinking fund to be invested. § 2. To meet the appropriations made in this act of the moneys to be collected by and upon said tax with as little delay as practicable, the commissioners of the canal fund, or the comptroller, shall, from time to time, invest in the said tax any surplus moneys of the principal of the sinking funds, under article seven of the constitution, a sum or sums not exceeding in all the amount to be realized from said tax hereby authorized, and the moneys so invested shall be applied to pay the appropriations under this act; and so much of the moneys arising from the said tax as may be necessary, when paid into the treasury, is hereby pledged and shall be applied in the first instance to reimburse the said sinking funds for the amount invested in said tax and for the interest on the same, at a rate not exceeding six per cent per annum from the time of investment to the day of payment.

§ 3. This act shall take effect immediately.

CHAP. 710.

AN ACT to amend an act entitled "An act to authorize the formation of railroad corporations and to regulate the same," passed April second, eighteen hundred and fifty.

PASSED June 11, 1873.

The People of the State of New York, represented in Senate and Assembly, do enact as follows:

Purchasers may associate with any number of persons and make and file articles, etc. SECTION 1. The fifth section of an act entitled "An act to authorize the formation of railroad corporations and to regulate the same," passed April second, eighteen hundred and fifty, is hereby amended by adding thereto the following: The purchaser or purchasers, or the grantee or grantees of any purchaser or purchasers of the real estate, tracks and fixtures of any railroad corporation, which has heretofore been sold, or may be hereafter sold by virtue of any mortgage, or by virtue of any judgment, decree or order of any court having jurisdiction in the premises, may associate with him or them any number of persons and make and acknowledge and file articles of association as prescribed by the first section of this act, such articles shall be entitled to be filed when there is indorsed thereon an affidavit made by at least three of the directors named in said articles, that it is intended in good faith to maintain and operate the road mentioned in such articles, and upon the filing thereof, so indorsed, the parties making such articles of association, and their associates, shall thereupon be a corporation with all the powers, privileges and franchises, and subject to all the provisions of this act. Nothing herein contained shall be construed to authorize any company organized under this act to charge any greater rate of fare than they were authorized by law to charge previous to such reorganization. Not to authorize increase of fare.

§ 2. This act shall take effect immediately.

Ante, vol. 8, p. 617.

CHAP. 713.

AN ACT for the improvement of the navigation of the Hudson river, and to make an appropriation therefor.

PASSED June 11, 1873; three-fifths being present.

The People of the State of New York, represented in Senate and Assembly, do enact as follows:

SECTION 1. The sum of fifty thousand dollars is hereby appropriated out of any moneys in the treasury not otherwise appropriated, for the purpose of removing any obstructions in, and improving the navigation of, the Hudson river, between the city of Troy and the town of Coxsackie, and for dredging, deepening and widening the channel of said river where it is necessary, between the said city of Troy and the said town of Coxsackie. Appropriation.

§ 2. The state engineer and surveyor, Samuel Schuyler; John W. Harcourt, of Albany; Alfred Van Santford, of Albany; J. L. Blanchard, of Troy, are hereby appointed commissioners, and are hereby authorized and empowered to superintend and control the expenditure of the said sum so appropriated by the first section of this act. Commissioners.

§ 3. The commissioners appointed by this act shall, before they are authorized to draw upon the comptroller for any of the moneys appropriated by this act, execute to the people of the state of New York a bond in the penal sum of fifty thousand dollars, with satisfactory sureties, conditioned that they will faithfully discharge their duties as such commissioners, and truly account to the comptroller of this state for the expenditure of all moneys received by them under this act, which bond shall be approved by the comptroller and the treasurer of this state. Official bond of.

§ 4. The comptroller of the state is hereby authorized to draw his warrant on the treasury of this state for the pay- Comptroller to draw warrant.

ment of any money expended by the said commissioners, not exceeding the amount appropriated by this act, by a draft drawn by the treasurer of said commissioners. But the comptroller shall not draw such warrant, nor pay over to the said commissioners any portion of the money hereby appropriated, except for work that has been already done, and, upon proper vouchers having been presented therefor, specifying the items for which the payment is asked, which vouchers shall be properly verified, by oath or otherwise, as the said comptroller may direct; and provided, further, that the said commissioners shall receive no compensation for their services in the discharge of the duties created by this act, beyond their actual expenses.

Rules, etc., for dumping earth, etc.

§ 5. The commissioners hereby appointed shall also have the power to prescribe rules and regulations relative to the dumping of earth, stone, gravel, cinders, mud or any other materials, in or near the said river, which, in their opinion, would have a tendency to obstruct navigation; and any person or persons who shall, by themselves or their agents, violate such rules and regulations, shall be deemed guilty of a misdemeanor, and also liable to a penalty of one hundred dollars, to be recovered in any court of competent jurisdiction in the name of said commissioners, or any one of them; and they shall have the further power to remove any and all obstructions to navigation in the Hudson river, between the said city of Troy and the said town of Coxsackie, or to lighter, or cause to be lightered, any boat or vessel which may be aground by reason of drawing a greater depth of water than the channel affords, or which, from any other cause whatever, may be obstructing the navigation of said river; and they, or either of them, or their agents are hereby authorized to remove such boat or vessel so aground and obstructing the navigation as aforesaid, and to assess the expense of such lightering or removing on such vessel and cargo, and said expenses so incurred shall be a lien on such cargo, boat or vessel as aforesaid, and shall be enforced and collected as hereinbefore provided.

Penalty.

Commissioners not to be interested in work.

§ 6. The said commissioners shall not be directly or indirectly interested in any contract made under this act, and shall spend fifteen thousand dollars of the money hereby appropriated, or so much thereof as may be necessary, for work done in said river, between the city of Albany and the city of Troy.

§ 7. All acts and parts of acts inconsistent with this act are hereby repealed.

§ 8. This act shall take effect immediately.

CHAP. 717.

AN ACT authorizing the sale of the state armories at Westport, Ogdensburgh, Canandaigua, Corning and Dunkirk, and the armory lot at Malone.

PASSED June 11, 1873, by a two-third vote.

The People of the State of New York, represented in Senate and Assembly, do enact as follows:

SECTION 1. The commissioners of the land office are hereby authorized to sell, in the manner provided by law for the sale of state lands, at public auction, the armories belonging to the state at Westport, Ogdensburgh, Canandaigua, Corning and Dunkirk, and also the lots purchased by the state as a site for the erection of an armory in the village of Malone, the proceeds of said sales to be paid into the treasury of the state; provided, nevertheless, that said sale shall not take place until the certificate of the adjutant-general shall be procured that said property is not required for military purposes. Provided further, that the proceeds of the sale of armory site in the village of Malone shall be paid over to the trustees of said village, to be expended by them in securing and fencing the state grounds in said village, and said proceeds are hereby appropriated for that purpose. Commissioners of the land office to sell state armories.

§ 2. The state armory at Schoharie being a revolutionary land-mark is hereby donated to the county of Schoharie, to be by said county preserved for public purposes without expense to the state. The commissioners of the land office are hereby directed to pay to the village of Dunkirk and city of Ogdensburgh, out of the proceeds of the sale of the armories in said village and city, such sums of money as the said village and city paid for the sites on which said armories are located. Armory at Schoharie donated to Schoharie county.

§ 3. This act shall take effect immediately.

CHAP. 720.

AN ACT to compel railroad commissioners to give bonds.

PASSED June 11, 1873.

The People of the State of New York, represented in Senate and Assembly, do enact as follows:

SECTION 1. The commissioners referred to in section three of the act entitled "An act to amend an act entitled 'An act to authorize the formation of railroad corporations, and to regulate the same,' passed April second, eighteen hundred and fifty, so as to permit municipal corporations to aid in the construction of railroads," passed May eighteen, eighteen Commissioners to give bonds.

hundred and sixty-nine, are hereby required in all cases of future appointment, within ten days after entering upon the duties of their office, and before receiving any funds belonging to the town in said section three referred to, to make and deliver to the clerk thereof a bond in such penalty and with such sureties as the board of auditors for such town shall prescribe, conditioned for the faithful discharge of their official duties, and that they will well and truly keep and pay over and account for all moneys belonging to such town and coming into their hands as such commissioners. And in all cases where such commissioners have entered upon the duties of their offices without executing such bond, it shall be their duty to make and file the same within twenty days after the passage of this act, and within ten days after notice thereof from the supervising officer of said municipal corporation. Failure to give bonds to vacate office. Such office of commissioner shall be and become vacated on failing or refusal to file the bond as herein required.

§ 2. No railroad commissioner of a town shall hereafter be eligible to the office of supervisor thereof.

§ 3. This act shall take effect immediately.

Ante, vol. 8, p. 617; vol. 7, p. 517.

CHAP. 722.

AN ACT to authorize the electors at elections for town officers to fix by ballot the place for holding town elections in the respective towns of this state.

PASSED June 11, 1878; three-fifths being present.

The People of the State of New York, represented in Senate and Assembly, do enact as follows:

Whenever fifteen electors file request clerk to prepare box, etc. SECTION 1. Whenever fifteen electors of any town in this state shall ten days before any annual town election, file a request in writing with the town clerk of such town that they desire to have the question as to where the next annual town election in such town shall be held, submitted to a vote of the electors at the then next annual town election, then it shall be the duty of such clerk to prepare and have at such election, a box in which shall be deposited the ballot of each elector Ballots. offering to vote thereon, which ballot shall be written or printed, or both, and shall designate the place in such town where the elector voting the same shall desire the next town election to be held, and on the canvass of such ballots by the board holding such town election, that place for which the most ballots shall appear shall be the place at which the next annual town election shall be held in such town, and if the electors of any town shall fail at any annual town election, to designate the place where the next annual town election shall be held, then the same shall be held at the place where the last annual town election in said town was held.

§ 2. This act shall not apply to any town in which the election for town officers shall be held by election districts, and all special town elections shall be held at the place in such town designated for holding the annual town elections. Not to apply to certain towns.

§ 3. This act shall take effect immediately.

CHAP. 737.

AN ACT in relation to the creation and formation of water-works companies in towns and villages of the state of New York.

PASSED June 12, 1873; three-fifths being present.

The People of the State of New York, represented in Senate and Assembly, do enact as follows:

SECTION 1. Any number of persons not less than seven may hereafter organize in any town or village of this state a water-works company, under the provisions of this act.

§ 2. Whenever any persons to the number of seven or more shall organize for the purpose of forming a water-works company in any of the towns or villages in this state, they shall present to the town or village authorities an application, setting forth the persons who propose to form said company, the proposed capital stock thereof, the proposed number and character of the shares of such capital stock, and the name or names of the streams, ponds, springs, lakes or other sources and their location, from which water is to be supplied. Such applications shall be signed by the persons who propose to form said company, and shall contain a request that the said town or village authorities shall consider the application of said company to supply said town or village of this state, or the inhabitants thereof, with pure and wholesome water. Upon the presentation of such application, the authorities of any town or village, which authorities are for the purposes of this act defined to consist for incorporate villages and towns, the board of trustees and supervisor, and for all other towns, the supervisor, justices of the peace, town clerk and commissioner of highways. Said authorities shall within thirty days of the presentation of such application determine by a vote of a majority of the authorities of said town or village, whether said application shall be granted; and the authorities of any town or village in this state are hereby authorized and empowered to make such determination, and when the same shall be made, to sign a certificate to that effect, and immediately transmit the same to the persons making such application or either of them. Duplicate certificates of such determination shall be filed in the office of the clerk of said town or village, and in the office of the county clerk of the county in which said town or village granting such application shall be situated. The persons named in such application shall thereupon meet and organize as a water-works com- Companies how formed. Authorities to decide on application.

Certificate to be filed. What to contain, etc. pany under such corporate name as they may select. They shall file in the office of the secretary of state a certificate of such organization. Said certificate shall contain the name of the corporation, the names of the members of said corporation and their residences, the amount of capital stock, the location of the office of said company. Such certificate shall be subscribed and sworn to by the president of said corporation, and shall be attested by the secretary thereof. Upon the filing of said certificate, said water-works company shall be known and deemed a body corporate, and shall be capable of suing and being sued by the corporate name which they shall have selected, in any of the courts of this state. Capital stock. The capital stock of said company shall be paid in in the manner and within the time provided by the "Act to authorize the formation of corporations for manufacturing, mechanical and chemical purposes," passed February seventeenth, eighteen hundred and forty-eight, and the several amendments thereto, and the stockholders of said companies shall be personally liable for the debts of said companies in the same manner and to the same extent as is provided by said act and the amendments thereto.

Corporate powers. § 3. Said corporation shall have power to take and hold real estate for the purpose of their corporation, and may have, hold and occupy any of the waters of this state; provided, however, that nothing herein contained shall be deemed to infringe upon any private right which shall not have been the subject of an agreement and lease or purchase by said corporation. Provided, that said companies shall have no power to take or use water from any of the canals of this state or any canal reservoirs as feeders or any streams which have been taken by the state for the purpose of supplying the canals with waters.

§ 4. Any corporation organized under the provisions of this act may, and they are hereby authorized and empowered to lay their water pipes in any streets or avenues or public places, in any streets or avenues of an adjoining town or village, to the town or village where their application shall have been granted.

§ 5. Said corporations are authorized and empowered to supply the authorities or inhabitants of any town or village where they may have organized, with pure and wholesome water, at such rates and costs to consumers as they shall agree upon.

Injuries to works how punished. § 6. Any person who shall maliciously or willfully destroy or injure any of the works or property of said company, or who shall maliciously or willfully do any act which shall injuriously affect or tend to affect the water of said company, shall be guilty of a misdemeanor, and may be punished by a fine or imprisonment, or by both fine and imprisonment, in the discretion of the court, and shall also forfeit and pay to the company treble damages sustained thereby, to be recovered in any court having cognizance thereof, with costs.

CHAP. 739.

AN ACT for the preservation of fish in the River St. Lawrence.

PASSED June 12, 1873; three-fifths being present.

The People of the State of New York, represented in Senate and Assembly, do enact as follows:

SECTION 1. No person shall, at any time, take any fish with net, weir or trap of any kind, or set any trap, net, weir or pot, with intent to catch fish in the waters of the River St. Lawrence, from the town line between the towns of Cape Vincent and Clayton on the main shore, down the river in the American waters to the Canada line, below the city of Ogdensburg. And any person violating the provisions of this section shall be deemed guilty of a misdemeanor, and shall likewise be liable to a penalty of twenty-five dollars for each offense, and ten dollars for each fish so taken. But the taking of herring and minnows are exempted from the operation of this act; the penalty to be recovered as already provided for in chapter seven hundred and twenty-one of the laws of eighteen hundred and seventy-one. Fishing with nets prohibited.

§ 2. All acts or parts of acts, the provisions of which are inconsistent with this act, are hereby repealed.

§ 3. This act shall take effect July first, eighteen hundred and seventy-three.

CHAP. 740.

AN ACT relating to the preservation of speckled brook trout within the counties of Tioga and Tompkins, state of New York.

PASSED June 12, 1873; three-fifths being present.

The People of the State of New York, represented in Senate and Assembly, do enact as follows:

SECTION 1. No person shall, at any time within three years from the passage of this act, fish for, nor catch with intent so to do, either with hook or line, or any other means, trap or device whatsoever, any speckled brook trout, in any of the streams, ponds or other waters within the limits of the county of Tioga or county of Tompkins, in the state of New York; nor shall any person kill or have or retain in his possession any such trout caught or taken from any such waters. Catching of trout prohibited.

§ 2. Any person violating the provisions of this act shall be deemed guilty of a misdemeanor, and shall likewise be liable to a penalty of fifty dollars for each offense; and it shall be the duty of all sheriffs, police officers and the constables of each and every town in said county to see that these provisions are enforced. Penalty.

How recovered. § 3. All penalties imposed by the provisions of this act may be recovered, with costs of suit, by any person or persons, in his or their own names, before any justice of the peace in said counties of Tioga or Tompkins, and every such penalty, when collected, shall be paid by the justice before whom recovery was had, one-half to the overseers of the poor of the town in which such recovery was had, for the benefit of the poor in such town, and the remainder to the person or persons in whose name the prosecution was conducted; and the same process and means for the collection of the penalties given by this act may be issued and had as are now allowed by law for the collection of damages in actions of tort.

Not to apply to "Newark Valley trout ponds." § 4. None of the provisions of this act shall apply to or affect the streams or waters upon the premises now occupied by N. K. Waring, in the town of Newark Valley, in said county, and known as "Newark Valley trout ponds," nor to any fish taken therefrom.

§ 5. This act shall take effect immediately.

CHAP. 744.

AN ACT authorizing and directing the comptroller of the state of New York to convey certain lands of the Tonawanda reservation of the trustees of the Tonawanda Reservation Manual Labor School for the purposes of such school, and reappropriating certain moneys formerly appropriated therefor.

PASSED June 13, 1873, by a two-third vote.

The People of the State of New York, represented in Senate and Assembly, do enact as follows:

When comptroller to convey certain lands to trustees of the Tonawanda Reservation Manual Labor School. SECTION 1. Whenever the Tonawanda band of Senecas shall pay or cause to be paid to the "Trustees of the Tonawanda Reservation Manual Labor School" the sum of three thousand dollars, in pursuance of chapter six hundred and fifty-one of the laws of eighteen hundred and sixty-nine, entitled "An act to provide for the erection of school buildings and the maintenance of a manual labor school upon the Tonawanda reservation," passed May six, eighteen hundred and sixty-nine, the comptroller of the state of New York shall convey and deed to the said trustees of the Tonawanda Reservation Manual Labor School in said trust eighty acres of land to be selected by said trustees upon said reservation, for the purposes of such school, said money to be used in erecting school-house buildings and appurtenances on said land, as provided for in the act above mentioned, and the treasurer of said state shall pay upon the warrant of the comptroller to the trustees of said Tonawanda Reservation Manual Labor School the sum of three thousand dollars, to be also used by said trustees in erecting upon said eighty acres of land the necessary buildings and appurtenances for a manual labor school for the children of the Tonawanda band of the Senecas, which sum was appropriated by said act, but remains unpaid and is hereby reappropriated therefor.

§ 2. The sum of one thousand five hundred dollars named in section two of chapter six hundred and forty-seven of the laws of eighteen hundred and seventy-one, entitled "An act confirming former appropriations made in relation to the Manual Labor School upon the Tonawanda reservation, and to require the trustees of the Tonawanda Manual Labor School to give additional security," passed April twenty, eighteen hundred and seventy-one, which was appropriated by said section two, but which remains unpaid, is hereby reappropriated for the purchase of domestic animals, wagons, agricultural implements and seeds, required for the use of said Tonawanda Reservation Manual Labor School and farm. And the treasurer shall pay the same on the warrant of the comptroller, to the said trustees, in one sum or in installments, as required by said trustees, on a statement duly verified that such payments are necessary, and such trustees shall expend such moneys for the purposes aforesaid, and in the manner directed by section two of said act. Reappropriation.

§ 3. All acts and parts of acts, so far as the same are inconsistent with the provisions of this act, are hereby repealed.

§ 4. This act shall take effect immediately.

CHAP. 746.

AN ACT making appropriations for the payment of the principal and interest on the canal debt, commencing on the first day of October, one thousand eight hundred and seventy-three; to provide for the payment of the debt contracted under section twelve of article seven of the constitution, and further to preserve the credit of the state.

PASSED June 18, 1873; three-fifths being present.

The People of the State of New York, represented in Senate and Assembly, do enact as follows:

SECTION 1. The following sums are hereby appropriated out of the revenues of the state canals for the fiscal year commencing on the first day of October, one thousand eight hundred and seventy-three. Appropriations.

For payment toward the sinking fund for the extinguishment of the general fund debt, the sum of fifteen hundred thousand dollars, or so much thereof as may be necessary to make a final contribution to said fund. Sinking fund of general fund debt.

For the payment of the interest, in coin, and reimbursement of the principal of the loans made under the constitution for Interest in coin, etc.

the enlargement and completion of the canals, the sum of two millions three hundred and forty thousand dollars, or so much thereof as may be necessary.

Expenses of state government. To pay the general fund to defray the necessary expenses of the state government, the sum of two hundred thousand dollars.

§ 2. The sum of one million one hundred and twenty-two thousand three hundred and twenty-four dollars and seventy-nine cents, or so much thereof as may be necessary, is hereby appropriated from the sinking fund under section one of article seven of the constitution for the payment of the interest, in coin, and the reimbursement of the principal of the canal debt for which said sinking fund has been provided.

From proceeds of tax under act of 1859 to pay principal, etc., of loan. § 3. The following sums are hereby appropriated out of the proceeds of any tax to be levied and collected under the provisions of the act (chapter two hundred and seventy-one of the laws of eighteen hundred and fifty-nine), to pay the interest and reimburse the principal of the loan of two millions five hundred thousand dollars to provide for the payment of the floating debt of the state.

Interest in coin. To pay the interest, in coin, on said loan for the fiscal year commencing on the first day of October next, sixty thousand dollars, or so much thereof as may be necessary.

For sinking fund. To provide for the sinking fund to pay the principal of said loan, one hundred and thirty-eight thousand eight hundred and eighty-eight dollars, being for one year's contribution to said fund, as provided for by the act aforesaid.

CHAP. 760.

AN ACT making appropriations for certain expenses of government and supplying deficiencies in former appropriations.

PASSED June 18, 1878, by a two-third vote.

The People of the State of New York, represented in Senate and Assembly, do enact as follows:

Payments by treasurer. SECTION 1. The treasurer shall pay on the warrant of the comptroller, from the several funds specified, to the persons indicated in this act, the amounts named, or such parts of those amounts as shall be sufficient to accomplish in full the purposes designated by the appropriations; but no warrant shall be issued, except in cases of salaries or extra compensation for official services, until the amounts claimed shall have been audited and allowed by the comptroller, who is hereby authorized to determine the same. The persons demanding payment shall present to him a detailed statement in items, verified by affidavit, and if such account shall be for services, it must show when, where and under what authority they were rendered; if for expenditures, when, where and under what authority they were made; if for articles furnished,

Comptroller to audit claims.

Accounts to be made out in items, etc.

when and where they were furnished, to whom they were delivered, and under what authority; and if the demand shall be for traveling expenses, the account must also specify the distance traveled, the places of starting and destination, the duty or business, the date and items of expenditure on all accounts for transportation, furniture, blank and other books furnished for use of office, binding, blanks, printing, stationery and postage; a bill duly certified must also be furnished; but whenever an appropriation shall have been made for the same purpose, or the amount shall have been provided otherwise, the sum herein directed to be paid shall not be considered as an addition to such appropriation, unless it shall be expressly so declared in this act. For the purpose of a full and perfect examination into the items of any bill herein allowed, the comptroller is further authorized to examine under oath, to be administered by him, any person applying for any appropriation herein named.

§ 2. The following amounts are hereby appropriated for the several objects specified, namely: Appropriations.

FROM THE GENERAL FUND.

For the clergymen officiating as chaplains of the senate and assembly during the present session of the legislature, for compensation, to be paid one-half to the clerk of the senate and one-half to the clerk of the assembly, for distribution by them to those clergymen at the rate of three dollars for every day of attendance, six hundred dollars. For chaplains of the legislature.

For the clerk of the assembly, for revising, mailing and sending to the members of the assembly previous to the organization of the next house the Clerk's Manual, the sum of two hundred and fifty dollars. Clerk of the assembly.

For the clerk of the senate, five hundred dollars, and for the clerk of the assembly, seven hundred and fifty dollars, for indexing the journals, bills and documents of the senate and assembly; for the clerk of the senate, four hundred dollars, and for the clerk of the assembly, seven hundred and fifty dollars, for compensation for extra clerical services and engrossing; and for the clerk and journal clerk of the sub-committee of the whole of the senate, three hundred dollars to each of them, and to the clerk and journal clerk of the sub-committee of the whole of the assembly, five hundred dollars to each of them. Clerk of the senate.

For the clerks, the journal clerks, assistant clerks and deputy clerks, and stenographers of the senate and assembly, and the clerks of the president of the senate and speaker of the assembly, for services from and after the sixteenth day of April, until the close of the present session, to each of them the same per diem compensation respectively as their respective salaries as now established by law would give per day for a session of one hundred days, provided that the salary, and the per diem compensation of the deputy clerk acting as clerk of the committee on engrossed bills of the assembly Clerks, etc.

shall be the same as the salary and per diem compensation of the other deputy clerks, and he shall be paid for the entire session accordingly.

Journal clerks. To the journal clerk of the senate and to the journal clerk of the assembly, to each of them, five hundred dollars, in addition thereto.

Clerks of president and speaker. And to the clerks of the president of the senate and speaker of the assembly, and the clerk of the committees on engrossed bills of the senate, to each of them six dollars per day for services from and after the sixteenth day of April until the close of the present session, such service to be certified by the presiding officers of the respective houses of the legislature.

George Morris. For George Morris, for services as superintendent of the expressing and mailing department of senate post-office, which service was rendered necessary by virtue of resolution of the senate imposing additional labor upon the post-office department, five dollars per day for each day of the session, from January seventeenth, eighteen hundred and seventy-three.

Clerks of committees. To the clerks of the committees on finance of the senate, and ways and means of the assembly, for additional compensation to each of them, five hundred dollars; to the clerks of the committees on the affairs of cities of the senate and assembly, to each of them, and to the clerks of the committees on judiciary of the senate and assembly, to each of them, for additional compensation, three hundred dollars; and to the clerks of the committees on railroads, on commerce and navigation, and on canals, of the senate and assembly, to each of them for additional compensation, one hundred and fifty dollars; and to the clerks of the committees on insurance of the senate and assembly, to each of them, for additional compensation, one hundred dollars; and to E. S. Jones, for compensation for services performed as a general messenger of the assembly during the present session, the sum of three hundred dollars.

Clerk of the senate. To the clerk of the senate for the repayment of moneys necessarily advanced by him to Levi Hurlburt, door-keeper, J. W. Hannan, superintendent of documents, and S. C. Curran, bank messenger, officers of the court for the trial of impeachment, not provided for in the rules of said court, four hundred and eighty-four dollars.

James I. Hart. To James I. Hart, as messenger to the sergeant-at-arms of the senate, three dollars per day from the commencement of the session to the close.

Assistant clerk, etc. To the assistant clerk, journal clerk, librarian, assistant sergeant-at-arms, door-keeper, superintendent of documents, clerks and bank messenger, messengers and pages of the senate who served at the extra session of the senate in eighteen hundred and seventy-two, and to each of them, compensation for thirty days, at the same rate per diem, respectively, as is paid for like services during the regular session.

To Robert Stafford and George W. P. Scholefield, as pages of the senate from March seventh to the end of the session, two dollars each per day. Pages.

The sum of one hundred and four dollars is hereby reappropriated for the payment of the salary due Matthew L. Brennan, as general messenger of the house in eighteen hundred and sixty-eight. General messenger.

For the expenses of the joint committee of the legislature on the memorial services to the Hon. William H. Seward, to be audited and paid by the comptroller, twenty-seven hundred and thirty-six dollars and forty-three cents, or so much thereof as may be necessary. Seward memorial services.

To De Forest N. Parker, for services as assistant librarian during the extra session in eighteen hundred and seventy-two, fifty dollars. Assistant librarian.

To Helen M. Scholefield, for engrossing for the legislature of eighteen hundred and seventy-two, the sum of one hundred dollars. Helen M. Scholefield.

For Daniel S. Lamont, for services as clerk to committee on banks, of the assembly, from January twelfth to February second, eighteen hundred and seventy-two, twenty-two days, one hundred and ten dollars, to be paid on the certificate of the speaker of the assembly of eighteen hundred and seventy-two, and the chairman of said committee, that such services were actually rendered. Daniel S. Lamont.

The accounts of counsel and stenographers employed on the part of the state by the committees of investigation of the senate and assembly during the present session of the legislature, shall be audited by the comptroller and paid by him out of any funds appropriated for the payment of legislative expenses. Counsel, etc.

To O. C. Bently, for services as clerk of the special committee appointed to investigate the subject of legislative postage, during the session of eighteen hundred and seventy-two, one hundred dollars. O. C. Bently.

For compensation of the members and officers of the senate, convened in extra session during the year eighteen hundred and seventy-two, pay of witnesses and other expenses necessarily incurred, fifteen thousand dollars, or so much thereof as may be necessary. Compensation for officers, etc., of senate.

For expenses necessarily incurred by the court of impeachment, or its authorized officers, including printing, the sum of five thousand dollars, or so much as may be required. Court of impeachment.

For James I. Hart, for services and expenses in carrying manuscript copy of the evidence taken before the court for the trial of impeachment in the case of George G. Barnard, from Saratoga to Albany, during the trial, thirty-eight days, one hundred and fourteen dollars. James I. Hart.

For William H. Johnson, for services as janitor during the extra session of the senate in eighteen hundred and seventy-two, thirty-eight days, one hundred and ninety dollars. Wm. H. Johnson.

L. L. Chaffee. For L. L. Chaffee, for ten days' services as door-keeper during the extra session of the senate for the trial of Judge Curtis, the sum of fifty dollars.

Edmund Kingsland. For Edmund Kingsland, for payment of judgment against John Parkhurst, agent and warden of Clinton state prison, obtained February twenty-eighth, eighteen hundred and sixty-five, with interest thereon to date, one hundred and ninety-one dollars and seventy-one cents, to be paid to Robert S. Hale, attorney, the lawful holder and owner of said judgment.

Kingsland & Scribner. For Jacob D. Kingsland and Levi S. Scribner, for payment of judgment against John Parkhurst, agent and warden of Clinton state prison, obtained January thirtieth, eighteen hundred and seventy-one, with interest thereon to date, one hundred and twenty-eight dollars and nineteen cents, to be paid to Hale and Smith, attorneys, as the lawful holders and owners of said judgment.

Women cleaning rooms. For the women employed in cleaning the chambers and rooms adjoining the senate and assembly, for compensation to each of them for every day's service, to be certified by the superintendent of the capitol, two dollars per day in lieu of all other compensation.

W. W. Wright. For William W. Wright, late canal commissioner, for his compensation in making his final report and expenses of clerical assistance after the expiration of his term of office, the sum of five hundred dollars.

Robert D. Evans. For Robert D. Evans, for wrapping, mailing and sending, by express, Red Books to senators and officers of the senate during the summer of eighteen hundred and seventy-one, under the direction of the clerk of the senate, the sum of one hundred and fifty dollars.

Lewis H. Clark. For Lewis H. Clark, librarian of the assembly, for labor in preparing a statistical list of the officers and members of the assembly, with their boarding places, the sum of fifty dollars.

John Laidlow. For John Laidlow, for preparing a statistical list of the officers and members of the senate, with their boarding places, the sum of twenty-five dollars.

Members of legislature. For the members of the legislature of eighteen hundred and seventy-two, for salary for fourteen days' service in proceedings for impeachment, the sum of sixty-eight hundred dollars, or so much thereof as may be necessary; and the president of the senate and speaker of the assembly of the year eighteen hundred and seventy-two are hereby authorized to sign the certificates of service of the members of the senate and assembly respectively, with the same force and effect as if said certificates had been signed by them during their respective official terms.

Edward M. Johnson. For Edward M. Johnson, for services as clerk of the assembly for the year eighteen hnndred and seventy-two, after the death of Cornelius S. Underwood, clerk of the assembly for the year eighteen hundred and seventy-two, for arranging and placing the papers of the session of eighteen hundred and seventy-two on the files of the assembly; for assorting and placing in charge of the regents of the university the papers on the files of the assembly, proper to be placed in their charge, and for all other official services rendered by him as clerk, after the death of said Underwood, twelve hundred dollars.

O. T. Atwood. For O. T. Atwood, for compensation for duties performed as clerk to the judiciary committee of the assembly, for ten days, ending February fourth, eighteen hundred and seventy-three, the sum of fifty dollars. And for George C. Storrs, for services as clerk of the judiciary committee of the assembly for eight days, ending January twenty-second, eighteen hundred and seventy-three, the sum of forty dollars.

Darius A. Ogden. For Darius A. Ogden, for compensation for services as building superintendent of Willard Asylum, the sum of fifteen hundred dollars in lieu of all other compensation, payable out of the appropriation for the construction of Willard Asylum, the same being for one year's salary. Thereafter the said building superintendent shall be paid for his services monthly, at the rate of one hundred and twenty-five dollars per month, and necessary expenses, according to the provisions of chapter three hundred and forty-two of the laws of eighteen hundred and sixty-five.

James S. Browne. For James S. Browne, for services in reporting testimony for the assembly committee on public health during the session of eighteen hundred and seventy-two, the sum of thirty dollars.

William Sniffen. For William Sniffen, for compensation for services on dock, at Sing Sing prison in the year eighteen hundred and sixty-eight, and for money paid his son, George Sniffen, for similar labor for the state of New York, the sum of seventy-four dollars.

E. B. O'Callaghan. For E. B. O'Callaghan, for services from the first to the twenty-second of October, eighteen hundred and seventy-two, in translating into English, Dutch manuscript records in the office of the secretary of state, the sum of one hundred and twenty-six dollars and fifty-six cents.

Ellen J. Calvert. For Ellen J. Calvert, widow of Samuel Calvert, who was killed while in the discharge of his duty, as keeper of the house of refuge on Randall's Island, March seventeenth, eighteen hundred and seventy-two, the sum of one thousand dollars is hereby appropriated, to be paid out of any moneys to be appropriated to said house of refuge.

Wm. H. Bodwell. For William H. Bodwell, as representative of the Journeymen Printers' Co-operative Association of the city of New York, for printing done and material furnished upon the order of the judiciary committee of the assembly, in the winter of eighteen hundred and seventy-two, the sum of two hundred and fifteen dollars and sixty cents.

Cornell University. For Cornell University, for premium on the interest of New York state stocks held by said institution, and for which the comptroller paid currency instead of coin, as was paid to other holders of similar stocks, from the time coin interest was first paid to January first, eighteen hundred and seventy-three, the sum of three thousand four hundred and five dollars and thirty-one cents.

Rent of governor's house. For rent of the house occupied by the governor, from January first to October first, eighteen hundred and seventy-three, the sum of three thousand dollars.

Monument over grave of Col. Ellsworth. For aiding in the erection of a granite monument over the grave of the late Colonel Elmer E. Ellsworth, at Mechanicville, Saratoga county, which sum shall be paid to the committee having the erection of said monument in charge, the sum of two thousand dollars.

Gen. W. B. Burnett. For General Ward B. Burnett, for services and disbursements from June first to December thirty-first, eighteen hundred and sixty-three, under orders from the adjutant-general of this state, of May twelfth, eighteen hundred and sixty-three, in perfecting various regimental organizations in the city of New York, the sum of two thousand four hundred and fifty-six dollars and sixty-five cents, or so much thereof as the comptroller and adjutant-general of the state, after investigation, shall decide to be justly due to said Ward B. Burnett, from the state of New York, to be refunded to the state by the general government; this appropriation to be in full of all claims for services and disbursements.

Wm. D. Ferguson. For William D. Ferguson, of twenty-fourth regiment New York state volunteers, for money expended by him for board of his company on their route from Oswego county to Elmira, in eighteen hundred and sixty-one, the sum of eighty-five dollars and fifty-five cents, or so much thereof as the comptroller and adjutant-general of the state, after investigation, shall decide to be justly dne to said William D. Ferguson, from the state of New York, to be refunded to the state by the general government; this appropriation to be in full of all claims for services and disbursements.

Francis C. Upton. For Francis C. Upton, inspector-in-chief of steam boilers, for salary for the fiscal year ending October first, eighteen hundred and seventy-three, and expenses of the office, including pay of assistant, clerk hire, traveling, stationery, printing, apparatus and repairs to the same, to be paid upon bills presented to the comptroller, properly verified, the sum of eight thousand dollars.

Seth Wiley, Jessie Parks and Samuel Lewis. To reimburse the following named persons for loss sustained by reason of failure of title to lands derived from the state: To Seth Wiley, the sum of two thousand and nine hundred and eighty-five dollars; to Jessie Parks, the sum of two thousand four hundred and twelve dollars; and to Samuel Lewis, the sum of two thousand and seventy-seven dollars.

Henry Robinson. For Henry Robinson, for compensation for services in attending to the assembly closets at the capitol, the sum of three hundred dollars.

Representatives of Hon. Eleazer Jones. For the legal representatives of the Hon. Eleazer Jones, deceased, late a member of the assembly, the sum of two hundred and twenty-five dollars, for the balance of his per diem allowance during the present session of the legislature.

For Thomas Ackerson, for services as postmaster of the assembly for fourteen days after the adjournment of the legislature of eighteen hundred and seventy-one, in compliance, with a resolution of the assembly, the sum of eighty-four dollars. Thomas Ackerson.

For the compensation of sheriffs, for transportation of persons indicted for capital offenses who have been or may be delivered to the superintendent of the State lunatic asylum for insane convicts at Auburn, in pursuance of chapter six hundred and sixty-six of the laws of eighteen hundred and seventy-one, the sum of five hundred dollars, or so much thereof as may be necessary. Sheriffs.

To Henry L. Arnold, sheriff of Livingston county, for transporting Maria Patridge, convict from Geneseo, in said county, to Sing Sing prison, one hundred and thirty-two dollars and twenty-five cents. Henry L. Arnold.

For the board of commissions on steam navigation on the canals, appointed under chapter eight hundred and sixty-eight of the laws of eighteen hundred and seventy-one, as a compensation for their reasonable expenses in the discharge of their duty, the sum of five thousand dollars, or so much thereof as may be necessary, to be determined by said board of commissioners. Commissioners on steam navigation on the canals.

For the legislature, for advances for contingent expenses of the clerk of the senate and the clerk of the assembly, the sum of six thousand dollars; and for postage, expenses of committees, compensation of witnesses, the legislative manual, the clerk's and Croswell's manual, and other contingent expenditures, the sum of eight thousand dollars, or so much thereof as may be necessary. Contingent expenses of the legislature.

For Samuel P. Allen, assistant clerk of the assembly, for additional salary, the sum of five hundred dollars. S. P. Allen.

For the commissioners of fisheries, to be expended as they deem proper, upon vouchers approved by the comptroller, for the purpose of replenishing the lakes and rivers of this state with fish, the sum of fifteen thousand dollars.

For Gustavus A. Scroggs, in full for compensation for services during the years eighteen hundred and sixty-one and eighteen hundred and sixty-two, in recruiting volunteers for the United States army, and which were applied upon the quota of the state of New York, the sum of four thousand three hundred and thirty-six dollars and ninety-five cents, and the additional sum of nine hundred and sixty-nine dollars and fifty-one cents, to reimburse him for money expended by him in the above-named service, or so much of said two sums, or either of them, as the comptroller and adjutant-general of the state, after investigation, shall decide to be justly due to said Gustavus A. Scroggs from the state of New York, to be refunded to the state by the general government; the appropriation to be in full of all claims for services and disbursements. G. A. Scroggs.

For William S. Fullerton, in full, for compensation for his services during the year eighteen hundred and sixty-two, in Wm. S. Fullerton.

recruiting volunteers for the United States army, the sum of one thousand dollars, to reimburse him for money expended by him in the above-named service, or so much of said sum as the comptroller and adjutant-general of the state, after investigation, shall decide to be justly due to said William S. Fullerton, from the state of New York, to be refunded to the state by the general government; this appropriation to be in full of all claims for services and disbursements.

Franklin B. Hough. The sum of fifteen hundred dollars, being part of an appropriation made by chapter seven hundred and fifteen of the laws of eighteen hundred and seventy-one, is hereby re-appropriated to be paid to Franklin B. Hough in full for the balance of his claims against the state, for compiling and superintending the printing of meteorological observations at New York academies, from eighteen hundred and fifty to eighteen hundred and sixty-three, inclusive.

John Gibhard. For John Gibhard, for expenses incurred by him in furnishing boxes, packing the collection of minerals and fossils purchased of him by the state, cash paid assistants, transportation to Albany, and cash paid to truckman and laborers in delivering the collection in the basement of the geological rooms at Albany, the sum of two hundred dollars.

Law libraries. For the law libraries of each of the judicial districts of the state, the sum of one thousand dollars each.

Congress Hall. For the proprietor of Congress Hall for lighting, warming and taking charge of senate committee rooms on roads and bridges, on canals and commerce, on municipal affairs, and committee rooms for ways and means committee of the assembly, the sum of five hundred dollars.

C. A. Stevens. For C. A. Stevens, for compensation for rent of rooms occupied by the assembly judiciary and canal committees from the first of February, eighteen hundred and seventy-three, to the following May, the sum of five hundred dollars, to be paid to J. M. F. Lightbody, of number four hundred and eighty Broadway, Albany, to whom the same is assigned.

Eliza O'Sullivan. For Eliza O'Sullivan, daughter of Michael O'Sullivan, deceased, the sum of one hundred and fifty dollars, being his compensation as clerk in the office of the secretary of state for the month of February, eighteen hundred and seventy-three.

Expenses of joint committee. For the expenses of the joint committee of the senate and assembly appointed to meet the committee of the senate of the United States, on transportation routes to the sea board, within or partially within this state, with a view of examining such routes, the sum of five thousand dollars, or so much thereof as may be necessary; such expenses to be audited by the comptroller.

A. B. Le Clure. For A. B. Le Clure, for expenses incurred as a witness appearing before the committee on state prisons of the assembly of the session of eighteen hundred and seventy-three, the sum of fifty dollars, or so much thereof as may be necessary.

Bank messengers. The salary of the bank messengers of the senate and assembly is hereby fixed at five dollars per day from the beginning of the present session; and the sum of six hundred dollars, or so much thereof as may be necessary, is hereby appropriated to pay William R. Marks and S. C. Curran deficiency of such salary; and to George Mingay, messenger of the assembly library, for services as acting assistant librarian in the absence of the assistant librarian, the sum of one hundred dollars.

Jesse L. Parker.

For Jesse L. Parker, for compensation for services performed as page of the assembly during the present session, the sum of two hundred dollars.

M. M. Lindenstein.

For M. M. Lindenstein, for compensation for services as superintendent of the pages of the assembly, and overlooking the arrangement of the files in the assembly chamber, the sum of one hundred and fifty dollars.

E. J. Dayton.

To E. J. Dayton, for extra services as clerk's messenger during the session of the assembly of eighteen hundred and seventy-three, the sum of one hundred and fifty dollars.

Hun, Smith & Spencer.

For Hun, Smith and Spencer, for chairs and upholstering for use of pages in the assembly, pursuant to resolution, the sum of sixty-six dollars and seventy cents.

Joseph Jennings.

For Joseph Jennings, for expenses while accompanying the committee on privileges and elections to New York for eighteen hundred and seventy-three, the sum of seventy-six dollars.

Clinton L. Baxter.

For Clinton L. Baxter, for services as messenger on sub-committee, from the fourteenth day of January until the first day of March, eighteen hundred and seventy-three, the sum of one hundred and thirty-five dollars.

Employees of assembly attending at opening of session.

For the employees of the assembly who attended from the opening of the present session, until the regular officers were appointed, the same per diem allowance, for the time they performed duty, as is allowed by law for such services to the said officers so appointed, the sum of one thousand dollars, or so much thereof as may be necessary, to be paid upon the certificate of the speaker and clerk that they were present and performed the work for which they are to receive pay; provided, however, that no officer or other person who came here under a resolution of the assembly shall be included in the number hereby paid, if other provision has been made for their payment, and provided further, that the amount due to A. S. Burdick be paid to his son to defray funeral expenses incurred by him.

George McEwing.

For George McEwing, number sixty-eight Clinton avenue, Albany, New York, for compensation for services performed as page of the assembly, for the session of eighteen hundred and seventy-three, from the opening of the session to the fifteenth day of February, the sum of sixty dollars.

Simeon Dillingham.

For Simeon Dillingham, for compensation for services as assistant doorkeeper of the assembly, from January fourteenth to January thirtieth, eighteen hundred and seventy-three, the sum of seventy-five dollars, to be paid on the certificate of the speaker and clerk that the services were rendered.

Austin K. Hoyt. For Austin K. Hoyt, for services and expenditures as acting secretary for the board of managers, during the trial of the impeachment of Judge Barnard, the sum of ninety-six dollars and eighty cents.

Robert S. Kelsey. For Robert S. Kelsey, for fourteen days' services as postmaster of the assembly of eighteen hundred and seventy-two, after the adjournment of the legislature, pursuant to resolution of the assembly, the sum of eighty-four dollars.

Chas. D. Lane. For Charles D. Lane, for services as messenger in assembly post-office for fourteen days after the adjournment of the legislature of eighteen hundred and seventy-two, pursuant to resolution of the assembly, the sum of forty-two dollars.

Support of pupils at institution for deaf mutes. For the support and instruction of twenty-six pupils at the institution for the improved instruction of deaf mutes, pursuant to chapter one hundred and eighty, laws of eighteen hundred and seventy, during the fiscal year commencing on the first day of October, eighteen hundred and seventy-two, or a proportionate amount for a shorter period of time than for one year, or for a smaller number of pupils, as shall be duly verified by affidavits of the president and secretary of the institution, seven thousand five hundred dollars, which sum shall be in full of all demands upon the state to the first day of October, eighteen hundred and seventy-three.

At the Le Couteulx St. Mary's institution. For the support and instruction of twenty-nine pupils at the Le Couteulx St. Mary's institution for the improved instruction of deaf mutes at Buffalo, New York, pursuant to the provisions of chapter six hundred and seventy of the laws of eighteen hundred and seventy-two, and sections nine and ten of title one, chapter five hundred and fifty-five of the laws of eighteen hundred and sixty-four, the sum of thirty-four hundred and ninety-five dollars, to be paid by the comptroller upon the certificate and oath of the president and secretary of the said institution, approved by the superintendent of public instruction; and this sum shall be in full of all demands upon the state up to the first day of January, eighteen hundred and seventy-three, and for the same institution for the instruction of twenty-nine pupils from January first to October first, eighteen hundred and seventy-three, the further sum of six thousand five hundred and twenty-five dollars, or a proportionate amount for a shorter period of time than nine months, or for a smaller number of pupils, as shall be duly verified by affidavits of the president and secretary of the institution, and this sum is in full of all demands upon the state, in behalf of said institution, to the first day of October, eighteen hundred and seventy-three.

Society for reformation of juvenile delinquents. For the managers of the society for the reformation of juvenile delinquents, commonly called the house of refuge, on Randall's Island, for deficiencies in the support and maintenance of juvenile delinquents therein, for the year ending on the first day of January, eighteen hundred and seventy-three, the sum of twelve thousand five hundred and twenty-five dollars and forty-four cents; and to enable the board of managers of said institution to make necessary repairs, improvements and additions in and to the buildings thereof, and to the furniture in, and interior arrangements of, said buildings, the said board are hereby authorized to use for the same the special appropriation heretofore made to them for the erection of a new workshop and for other purposes, so far as said purposes shall require and said appropriation remains unused.

To the New York institution for the instruction of the deaf and dumb, for the support and education for one year, from the first of September, eighteen hundred and seventy-two, of Victor Axtel Bergguist, an uneducated deaf mute, who has passed the age under which provision can be made for his education under existing laws, three hundred dollars. N. Y. institution for deaf and dumb.

For the New York Infant Asylum, thirty thousand dollars, to be expended in the erection of an asylum building, whenever a like amount shall have been raised and paid in by private subscription or donation, and on the further condition that said institution shall furnish accommodations for, and receive, provide and care for, free of charge, every year hereafter, at least sixty state patients, which said sum of thirty thousand dollars the comptroller of the city of New York is hereby directed to pay out of the excise fund of said city to said institution. N. Y. Infant asylum.

For the New York Orthopædic Dispensary, for treatment of spinal and hip-joint diseases, five thousand dollars to assist in furnishing and equipping their new hospital, payable whenever it shall be proven to the comptroller that said institution has, during the past year, treated, free of charge, all indigent patients applying to the number of not over five hundred residents of this state, and on the further condition that said institution shall hereafter treat annually, free of charge, all indigent patients, residents of this state, who shall apply for such treatment, to the number of five hundred, which said sum of five thousand dollars the comptroller of the city of New York is hereby directed to pay to said institution out of the excise fund of the said city. N. Y. Orthopædic dispensary.

For the Willard Asylum for the insane, for completing, warming, gas and water pipes and fittings for two of the group erected last year, and for furnishing the same ready for use; for two inside flights of iron stairs, as fire-proof escapes; repairing damages by fire to gas-house, and works since annual report for eighteen hundred and seventy-two; mangle and other small machines and implements for laundry; wringer, washing machine, shafting and pulleys, pipes and labor for putting up and fitting up the same, and belting, deepening and raising embankments of reservoir; for riprapping sides and grouting bottom of reservoir; eight thousand feet of iron pipe for connecting upper and lower reservoirs, freight and cartage, digging ditch, leading and laying pipe; replacing embankment of upper reservoirs recently carried away by flood; widening and strengthening remaining old embankment, and constructing spillway culverts to protect north wing from abrasure from water; constructing brick culvert, between lake and main building; changing entrance of street Willard asylum.

culvert into the lake so as to prevent filling up of harbor; grading drains at detached building; building one hundred rods of high, tight board fence, at branch and main building; shade and fruit trees; ice-house and cool rooms for meat, sixty thousand dollars.

Prison association. To aid the prison association of New York to maintain the system of guidance, employment and aid of discharged prisoners as now established, five thousand dollars, said association being hereby required to maintain agencies for said purposes at Auburn, Plattsburgh, Dannemora, Sing Sing and New York, and to report annually to the legislature the results of said system of aid or the expenditures for its support.

N. Y. Inebriate asylum. For the New York Inebriate Asylum, for cost of water-works, changing and repairing heating apparatus, changing sewers, and for other purposes, the sum of ten thousand dollars.

State lunatic asylum. For the State Lunatic Asylum at Utica, to refund advances made from the ordinary current funds for improvement and repairs of the asylum buildings, sixteen thousand two hundred and seven dollars and thirty-one cents, and to refund the amount advanced for laying four thousand five hundred feet of cast-iron water pipe from the fifth lock of the Chenango canal to the asylum, and the pumps and necessary connections with the water tanks in the asylum buildings, seven thousand two hundred and eighty-five dollars and forty-seven cents; for constructing a hospital building for the women's department, seven thousand two hundred dollars, and for enlarging six dining rooms in women's department, three thousand five hundred dollars, and for salaries of increased number of physicians and expenses authorized by law passed by the legislature of eighteen hundred and seventy-three, four thousand dollars.

Western house of refuge. For the Western House of Refuge for deficiencies in former appropriations, sixteen thousand dollars.

Hudson River State hospital. For the Hudson River State Hospital for the insane at Poughkeepsie, for deficiency in the maintenance account and liabilities incurred for material and labor, and for completion of building already commenced, two hundred thousand dollars; the further construction of such building shall be under the charge and supervision of a competent superintendent, to be appointed by the governor.

Trustees N. Y. State Institution for the blind. The Trustees of the New York State Institution for the Blind, at Batavia, are hereby authorized, in their discretion, to expend for maintenance or repairs, or to purchase furniture or books, or for the improvement of the grounds of the institution or other necessary expenses, any money which said board have received or may receive from any source, except the treasury of the state.

Buffalo State asylum. For the Buffalo State Asylum for the Insane, for the construction of buildings, to be paid to and expended by the trustees thereof, on that portion of the building now in process of construction, the sum of two hundred thousand dollars.

For the New York State Asylum for Idiots, for the completion of the north wing thereof, repairs of and addition to laundry, painting and other necessary expenses, the sum of six thousand dollars. N. Y. State Asylum for Idiots.

For the Thomas Asylum for Orphan and Destitute Indian Children, for the education and maintenance of one hundred children, at the rate of eighty-five dollars per capita, the sum of eight thousand five hundred dollars. Thomas Asylum for Orphan children.

For John P. Hendricks, representative of the Stockbridge Indians, for expenses incurred in presenting unsettled claims of said Indians, against the state of New York, two hundred dollars. John P. Hendricks.

To the New York State Institution for the Blind, at Batavia, for painting, repairs, furniture, books, improvement of grounds, and other necessary expenses, the sum of ten thousand dollars. N. Y. State Institution for the blind.

For the support and maintenance of the asylum for insane convicts, at Auburn, for the residue of the current fiscal year, the sum of two thousand five hundred dollars. Insane convicts.

The appropriation of two hundred and fifty dollars to the county of Niagara, per chapter five hundred and forty-one of the laws of eighteen hundred and seventy-two, for the support and maintenance of Susan Green, an insane Indian woman, is hereby reappropriated to the Willard asylum for the insane, for the support of the said Susan Green. Susan Green, support of.

For the Homœopathic asylum for the insane, at Middletown, the sum of one hundred and fifty thousand dollars. Homœopathic Asylum for insane.

For the widow of Oliver A. Tilton, of the first regiment of New York volunteers engaged in the war with Mexico, pursuant to chapter five hundred and eight, laws of eighteen hundred and fifty-one, the sum of one hundred and twenty-one dollars and eighty cents, or so much thereof as may be necessary to pay the amount due Oliver A. Tilton when he was killed; the amount to be determined by the comptroller of the state of New York. Widow of Oliver A. Tilton.

For the comptroller to pay claims of surviving members of the first regiment of New York volunteers, who served in the war with Mexico, presented since the apportionment of the appropriations, per chapter seven hundred and eighty of the laws of eighteen hundred and seventy, and chapter seven hundred and twenty-five of the laws of eighteen hundred and seventy-one, the sum of five hundred dollars, or so much thereof as may be necessary. Surviving members of first regiment of N. Y. volunteers.

For services and expenses in the preparation and prosecution of the war claims of the state against the United States, eleven thousand four hundred and fifty-six dollars and seventy cents, or so much thereof as in the judgment of the adjutant-general may be necessary, to be paid on the certificate of the governor of the state; provided that such allowance shall not exceed in all two per cent upon the amount which has been allowed, and passed to the credit of the state since January first, eighteen hundred and seventy-two. War claims, expense of prosecution of.

Walter M. Dallman. To Walter M. Dallman, the late assistant paymaster-general, eighteen hundred dollars, for services in preparing the papers and proofs in reference to the war claims of this state against the United States during the years eighteen hundred and sixty-six, eighteen hundred and sixty-seven and eighteen hundred and sixty-eight, provided that amount does not exceed two per cent of the moneys received and paid into the state treasury from such source during said time.

Repairs of arsenals, etc. For the repairs of arsenals and armories belonging to the state, the sum of seven thousand dollars, or so much thereof as may be necessary.

R. P. Cormack. For R. P. Cormack, for overhauling, rearranging and labeling senate library, over the sergeant-at-arms' room, during the recess of the legislature in eighteen hundred and seventy-one, pursuant to instructions of the clerk of the last senate, one hundred dollars.

R. G. Milks. For R. G. Milks, for additional services in matters of the deficiency of seven thousand dollars in the late treasurer's accounts, examining books for four years previous to January first, eighteen hundred and seventy-two, the sum of three hundred dollars.

Annesley & Vint. For Annesley and Vint, for framing resolutions passed by the legislature of eighteen hundred and seventy-two in relation to the death of the late honorable Peter G. Peck, and for framing resolutions passed by the legislature of eighteen hundred and seventy-two upon the death of the late Professor Morse, the sum of ninety-seven dollars, or so much thereof as shall be audited by the comptroller.

Co. E, 54th regiment N. Y. National Guard. For company E, fifty-fourth regiment New York state national guard, for compensation for services in protecting state property on state work during the strike on Erie canal at the Ox Bow break in May, eighteen hundred and seventy-two, the sum of one thousand dollars.

Assessment on state arsenal, etc. For payment of assessment on state arsenal, corner Seventh avenue and Thirty-fifth street, New York city, the sum of twenty-five hundred dollars, and for repairing Portland avenue, in front of the state arsenal, Brooklyn, the sum of four hundred and twenty-nine dollars and forty-five cents, or so much thereof as may be necessary.

Myers, Wines & Fencer. To Michael S. Myers, E. C. Wines and Thomas Fencer, commissioners appointed under a joint resolution of the legislature of eighteen hundred and seventy, to investigate the question of prison labor in its relation with free labor, to reimburse them for moneys by them paid for eighty-six days' services of a stenographer in reporting testimony, at the rate of six dollars per day, the sum of five hundred and sixteen dollars.

Wm. V. Peacon. To William V. Peacon, for engrossing resolutions passed by the senate December sixth, eighteen hundred and seventy-two, complimentary to Lieutenant-governor Allen C. Beach, the sum of five hundred dollars; and to Sherk Brothers, for framing the same, one hundred and ninety-five dollars, or so much thereof as shall be necessary.

Sherk Brothers.

For completing the state armory at Auburn, the sum of fifteen thousand dollars; for completing the state armory at Oswego, the sum of five thousand dollars; and for completing the state armory at Schenectady, the sum of two thousand dollars, subject to the approval of the adjutant-general. State armory at Auburn.

The sum of twenty thousand dollars is hereby appropriated out of any moneys in the treasury not otherwise appropriated, for the purpose of completing the state armory at Syracuse for the use of the twenty-fourth brigade, national guard, and for the erection of a drill-room to be attached thereto, to be expended under the direction of the commission appointed under chapter seven hundred and thirty-three of the laws of eighteen hundred and seventy-two, for the expenditure of certain funds therein appropriated for the said armory; and the governor of this state is hereby authorized to appoint one commissioner, being a resident of Syracuse, to serve upon said commission, in place of General John A. Green, deceased, who shall execute and give to the people of this state a bond, in such penal sum as the comptroller of this state shall require, conditioned for the faithful discharge of his duties as such commissioner. All vouchers for expenditures under this appropriation shall be subject to the approval of the comptroller. State armory at Syracuse.

For H. E. Barnard, district attorney of Clinton county, for compensation for labor and disbursements in the examination of the charges against the sheriff of Clinton county, ordered by the governor, the sum of one thousand dollars, or so much thereof as may be necessary, the account to be audited, approved and certified by the governor; and five hundred dollars, or so much as may be certified by the governor, for printing the evidence and for compensation to George M. Beckwith, Clinton county judge, for taking and certifying the evidence in said matter, provided the comptroller shall decide the same to be a legal charge against the state. H. E. Barnard.

For the office of the comptroller, for furniture, blank and other books necessary for the use of the office, binding, blanks, printing and other necessary expenses, the sum of one thousand dollars. Office of comptroller.

For the office of the attorney-general, for furniture, blank and other books necessary for the use of the office, blanks, printing and other necessary expenses, the sum of one thousand seven hundred and sixty-three dollars and forty-four cents. Of attorney-general.

For the land office, for compensation and mileage of the lieutenant-governor and speaker of the assembly for their attendance at the meetings of the commissioners of the land office, and for assessments and other expenses of public lands, the sum of one thousand dollars. Land office.

For the hall of the state cabinet of natural history and the agricultural museum, for repairs, cleaning, labor, gas, fuel, compensation of keeper, and other necessary expenses, the sum of three thousand dollars. Cabinet of natural history.

For the special increase of the zoological collection of the state museum, one thousand dollars.

For books already purchased, and for others necessary for the library of the state museum of natural history, three hundred and fifty dollars.

For the state hall, for expenses for repairs, cleaning, labor, gas and other necessary expenses, the sum of six thousand dollars.

For the capitol, for expenses for repairs, cleaning, labor, gas and other necessary expenses, the sum of eleven thousand dollars.

Office of state engineer. For the office of the state engineer and surveyor, for furniture, blank and other books necessary for the use of the office, binding, blanks, printing and other necessary expenses, the sum of five hundred dollars.

Legislative printing. For printing for the legislature, including wrapping, binding and engraving, also for the publication of the official canvass and other official notices, for printing and binding the session laws, and for printing the natural history of the state, the sum of fifty thousand dollars.

Criers and attendants. For the criers and attendants of the court of appeals and commission of appeals, as provided by law, the sum of five hundred dollars.

Purchase of coin. For the purchase of coin for the payment of the interest on the general fund debt, including the Indian annuities, the sum of eight thousand five hnndred dollars.

Annuities to Stockbridge Indians. For the comptroller, to pay balance of annuities to the heirs of two Stockbridge Indians, the sum of one hundred and forty-two dollars, with interest at six per centum per annum, being a reappropriation of this amount in supply bill of eighteen hundred and seventy-two, to correct error in same.

State prison. For the support and maintenance of the state prisons for the residue of the current fiscal year, including the expenses of manufacturing at Clinton, and carrying on the lime works at Sing Sing, the sum of two hundred and fifty thousand dollars.

John Parkhurst. For John Parkhurst, for three months and twelve days' service as superintendent of the manufacturing department of Clinton prison, in eighteen hundred and seventy-two and eighteen hundred and seventy-three, five hundred and sixty-four dollars and forty-four cents.

George Moore. For George Moore, for compensation as foreman in the iron business at Clinton prison, in pursuance of an agreement with the agent and warden of that prison in eighteen hundred and seventy-two, four hundred and twenty-five dollars, or so much thereof as the comptroller shall find, on investigation, to be his due.

James Hasson. For the Rev. James Hasson, for religious and other services rendered to the convicts at Sing Sing, the sum of nine hundred dollars.

Executive department, etc. For the executive department, for furniture, blank and other books necessary for the use of the department, binding, blanks, printing, stationery, telegraphing and other incidental expenses, the sum of one thousand dollars; and for the military secretary of the governor, for extra compensation, the sum of one thousand dollars.

For John Hyland, as superintendent of labor on farm at Sing Sing prison for year eighteen hundred and sixty-nine, the sum of two hundred dollars. John Hyland.

For compensation to the private secretary of the governor, for nine months, from the first of January to the first of October of the current year, seven hundred and fifty dollars, or so much thereof as shall be necessary, to make his salary equal to thirty-five hundred dollars per annum, as now fixed by law. Private secretary of governor.

For the executive department, for deficiency in the appropriations for clerks and messengers therein, for compensation, six hundred dollars. Clerks, etc., in executive department.

For James C. Brown, to make his compensation for services in the department of public instruction, in the year eighteen hundred and seventy-one, the same as that received by him for similar services in that department in each of the two previous years, the sum of seven hundred and fifty dollars. James C. Brown.

For John L. Dintruff, sheriff of the county of Yates, for expenses in executing a certain requisition issued by John A. Dix, governor of the state of New York, upon the governor of the state of California, for the arrest of James Burns, a fugitive from justice, the sum of eight hundred and eighty-seven dollars and seventy cents; and for his legal fees in serving the above process, the sum of six hundred and sixty dollars, the above amount to be paid by the comptroller, if, upon investigation, he shall find the same to be a just and legal claim against the state of New York. Sheriff of Yates county.

For carpets and furniture, fixtures and repairs for the executive mansion, three thousand dollars, or so much thereof as may be necessary. Carpets, etc., for executive mansion.

For Alfred H. Taylor, for compensation for extra services performed in indexing the military code of the state of New York, the sum of five hundred dollars. A. H. Taylor.

For books and stationery expenses for the transfer office at the Manhattan company, New York, the sum of two hundred dollars. Books, etc. transfer office.

For compensation and mileage of officers of the legislature, in pursuance of chapters twelve and four hundred and eighty-five of the laws of eighteen hundred and seventy-two, the sum of fifty-five thousand dollars, in addition to the appropriation of ninety thousand dollars per chapter five hundred and forty-one of the laws of eighteen hundred and seventy-two. Mileage, etc., of members of the legislature.

For James Hogan, for additional compensation as assistant doorkeeper for the present session, for services in acting as doorkeeper, the sum of one hundred dollars. James Hogan.

For the comptroller, to make good the deficiency in the revenue of the United States deposit fund to September thirtieth, eighteen hundred and seventy-two, the sum of thirteen thousand and fifty-one dollars and seventy-seven cents, and in addition the sum of eight hundred dollars in payment of appropriation to the city of Binghamton from said fund by chapter seven hundred and thirty-three of the laws of eighteen hundred and seventy-two. Revenue of U. S. deposit fund.

City of Binghamton. Payable from the United States deposit fund for the city of Binghamton, to be applied as a portion of the common school fund apportioned to said city for the current fiscal year the sum of eight hundred dollars, which sum was withheld from said city owing to failure of apportionment.

John Palmer. For John Palmer, for painting done for the state museum of natural history, by order of Professor Hall, curator, the sum of thirty-nine dollars and seventy-five cents.

For John Palmer, for painting cases at geological hall, the sum of three hundred and ninety-five dollars and fifty cents.

A. B. Van Gaasbeck & Co. For A. B. Van Gaasbeck & Company, for carpets and work done in the senate and assembly chambers, the sum of two thousand six hundred and two dollars and eighteen cents; and for carpets and work done in the judiciary and canal committee rooms of the assembly, for the year eighteen hundred and seventy-three, the sum of two hundred and fifteen dollars and thirty-five cents.

Palmer and others. For the payment of the bills of John W. Palmer, C. C. Nichols, Robert K. Oliver, J. D. Walsh, James A. Shattuck and Tucker & Crawford, and H. R. Watson, for expenses of alterations, repairs, painting and decorating of the senate chamber, and for upholstering and chandeliers for the same, six thousand and seventy-two dollars and seventy-nine cents, or so much thereof as shall be necessary. All bills for the same to be audited and paid by the comptroller.

Awards to Morton and others. To pay the awards to Robert Morton, La Fayette and Mehitable Burdick and Daniel B. Paddock, made by the commissioners appointed by the supreme court, in pursuance of the provisions of chapter three hundred and forty-six of the laws of eighteen hundred and fifty-nine and the acts amendatory thereof, dated January twenty, eighteen hundred and seventy-three, for damages caused by the appropriation of the waters of the Nine Mile creek, for the purpose of working the state pumps on the salt springs reservation, during the period of suspended navigation of the Erie canal, as follows: to Robert Morton, twenty-five hundred dollars; to La Fayette and Mehitable Burdick, nine thousand dollars; and to Daniel B. Paddock, one hundred dollars. Said awards shall be paid from the surplus revenues derived from salt duties in the year eighteen hundred and seventy-three.

Place college. To the comptroller, to adjust and pay the claim of the Place college for the rent of certain premises, Binghamton, Broome county, owned by said college, and leased to the officers of the state, which property was held or possessed by the commissioners of the land office, the sum of three thousand one hundred and fifty-five dollars and thirty-four cents, in pursuance of chapter four hundred and nine of the laws of eighteen hundred and seventy-one, being the amount ascertained to be due said college, on the computation required to be made by said act.

Medina academy. For the trustees of Medina academy, the sum of two hundred dollars and fifty-five cents, being the amount of a share of said academy in a distribution of forty thousand dollars from the income of the literature fund made by the regents of the university on the tenth day of January, eighteen hundred and sixty-eight, and which has never been claimed by or paid to the said academy; the amount to be paid upon the order of the treasurer of said academy by the comptroller, in case he shall find the above amount was set apart for said academy, and has not since been paid to it.

For the office of the clerk of commission of appeals for deficiency in the appropriation for clerk hire for the current fiscal year, four hundred dollars. Clerk of commission of appeals for clerk hire.

For the purpose of repairing state roads running through the St. Regis Indian reservations in Franklin county, the sum of two thousand five hundred dollars, to be expended under the supervision and direction of Samuel Barlow, James W. Weld and Z. N. Falsom; said commissioners to receive no compensation for their services. State roads.

From the surplus revenues derived from salt duties in the years eighteen hundred and seventy-three and eighteen hundred and seventy-four, for new salt wells on the Onondaga salt springs reservation, to take the place of the old wells that have failed, the sum of ten thousand dollars in each of those years; the work of furnishing the tubing and boring the wells to be done by contract and let to the lowest bidder, by the superintendent of the Onondaga salt springs, and no part of the money hereby appropriated shall be used for any purpose, except to furnish an increased supply of brine. New salt wells.

For compensation of Henry H. Hawkins, attorney of the Cayuga Indians, for distributing the annuity from the state to said Indians, the sum of twenty-five dollars. Henry M. Hawkins.

For the crier and attendants of the court of appeals, for additional expenses for the March term of the court of appeals, held in the city of New York March twenty-fourth, eighteen hundred and seventy-three, the sum of one hundred dollars, or so much thereof as may be necessary. Crier and attendants of court of appeals.

For the clerk of the court of appeals, for expenses of an extra clerk and book-keeper, required to make the report to the assembly, called for by the resolution passed February twenty-fourth, eighteen hundred and seventy-three, the sum of three hundred dollars, or so much thereof as may be necessary. Clerk of court of appeals for clerks, etc.

For the clerk of the court appeals, for amount of actual personal expenses incurred by him while attending the court of appeals at its session at Saratoga in July and August. eighteen hundred and seventy-two, the sum of one hundred and fifty dollars. Expenses of.

For Samuel Hand, to repay him moneys disbursed by him as state reporter for assistance in the double work of reporting for the court of appeals and commission of appeals, the sum of fifteen hundred dollars in full of all claims. Samuel Hand.

For compensation of the state assessors, in addition to the sum now provided by law, the further sum of fifteen hundred dollars; and the salary of each of said assessors is hereby fixed and established at the sum of two thousand dollars a year. State assessors.

Banks & Brothers. For Banks and Brothers, for books furnished the secretary of state for distribution to the judges, the sum of six hundred and sixty-six dollars, and for furnishing for one year for use of the members of the commission of appeals a law library, the sum of one thousand dollars.

W. C. Little & Co. For W. C. Little and Company, for books furnished the secretary of state, most of which were distributions to new towns, pursuant to sections fourteen, fifteen and sixteen, title two, chapter eight, part first of the Revised Statutes, the sum of one hundred and eighty-four dollars and twenty-five cents.

Purchasers of state lands where title has failed. For refunding to purchasers of lands from the state, in case the patents have been canceled by the commissioners of the land office, the sum of five hundred dollars, or so much thereof as may be necessary, to be paid on the order of said commissioners and audited by the comptroller.

Verplanck Colvin. For Verplanck Colvin, to complete topographical survey and exploration of the Adirondack wilderness, and to render available for mapping the work already done, four thousand two hundred and fifty dollars.

State library. For the state library, for repairs, cleaning, gas, transportation of books, and other necessary expenses, the sum of one thousand dollars.

Treasurer of Cortland county. For the treasurer of the county of Cortland, the sum of two hundred and eighty-five dollars and eighty-eight cents, that being the amount claimed to be due said county, pursuant to chapter eight hundred and seventeen, laws of eighteen hundred and sixty-eight, but which said amount it is claimed has not been drawn, and it is hereby reappropriated and shall be paid into the treasury of said county of Cortland on the order of the treasurer of said county, if upon investigation the comptroller shall ascertain that the same has not been drawn, and is due.

Treasurer of Yates county. For the treasurer of the county of Yates, the sum of six hundred and twenty-nine dollars and sixty-one cents is hereby reappropriated, that being the amount apportioned to said county in pursuance of chapter eight hundred and fifty-seven of the laws of eighteen hundred and sixty-nine; the above amount shall be paid into the treasury of the said county of Yates, subject to the order of the board of supervisors thereof, if upon investigation the comptroller shall ascertain that the same has not been drawn, and is due.

Cope, Sanders & Co. For Cope, Sanders and Company, for amount due them upon the circulating notes of the Lewis county bank, the sum of eighty-one dollars, being the amount of sixty-per cent upon the circulating notes of said bank, held by Corning and Company, and by them assigned to the said Cope, Sanders and Company, the certificate for the payment of which had not been presented for payment during the time allowed by law, and the money paid into the treasury of the state of New York, to the credit of the banking department; said sum to be charged to account of the expenses of the banking department and paid from the appropriation for said expenses, to be repaid to the treasury pursuant to chapter one hundred and sixty-four, laws of eighteen hundred and fifty-one.

To supply deficiency in appropriation for messenger in the office of the attorney-general, the sum of three hundred dollars. Messenger of attorney-general.

For the normal school at Albany, for deficiency in appropriation caused by expenses of replacing furnaces and repair of damages by fire, and other extraordinary repairs, two thousand dollars. Normal school at Albany.

For the normal school at Fredonia, the sum of two thousand seven hundred and forty-four dollars and twenty-eight cents, being the unexpended balance of the appropriation made by chapter seven hundred and fifteen of the laws of eighteen hundred and seventy-one, is hereby reappropriated for the purposes for which it was originally appropriated. Fredonia.

For the state normal school at Brockport, five thousand one hundred and sixty-nine dollars and thirteen cents, to pay deficiency caused by an erroneous credit to that institution on the books of the comptroller in eighteen hundred and sixty-seven, said appropriation to be used for no other purpose. Brockport.

For Jacob H. Ten Eyck, for services rendered in conveying the mails between the assembly post-office and the Albany post-office, during the present session, the sum of one hundred dollars. Jacob H. Ten Eyck.

The sum of ten thousand dollars is hereby appropriated to supply a deficiency in the amount of the appropriation in the fifth item of appropriation in section one, chapter seven hundred of the laws of eighteen hundred and seventy-two, or so much thereof as may be necessary to pay such deficiency and interest, provided that no such awards as involve the payments to contractors for work and material on the canals, of any sum in excess of contract prices, be paid. Deficiency.

The sum of thirty thousand dollars for removing obstructions in the outlet of Cayuga lake, and the channel of Seneca river, reappropriated by act chapter eight hundred and fifty, laws of eighteen hundred and seventy-two, but which proved unavailable for this purpose, shall be paid by the comptroller from the general fund on the drafts of the canal commissioner for the middle division. Obstructions in outlet of Cayuga lake, etc.

For the Central Railroad Company of New Jersey, to pay a judgment for costs recovered against the people in a suit begun in eighteen hundred and sixty-five, to procure the removal of piers and docks at Jersey City, the sum of three thousand three hundred and twenty-four dollars and forty-seven cents. Central R. R. Co. of New Jersey.

For Sterling G. Hadley, for services as attorney and counselor for canal commissioner William W. Wright, and canal superintendent John Haggerty, in their defense on charges preferred against them before the canal committee of the assembly of eighteen hundred and seventy-two, the sum of two hundred dollars. S. G. Hadley.

A. P. Lanning. For A. P. Lanning, in full for services rendered upon the retainer in the capital cases of the People versus Montgomery, the sum of one thousand dollars.

M. B. Anderson and others. For M. B. Anderson, of Rochester, Thomas Hun, of Albany, and Francis C. Barlow, a commission, acting under an order from the governor of the state of New York, for examining the lunatic asylums of the state, for compensation for services and expenses at the rate of one thousand dollars for each, the sum of three thousand dollars, and for stenographers attending said commissioners, the sum of six hundred and thirty-nine dollars and forty cents.

Amasa J. Parker. For Amasa J. Parker, for compensation for his services as counsel on request of the late board of canal appraisers in defending them against eleven suits of mandamus brought to compel them to file nineteen different claims for damages after the expiration of the time fixed by statute for filing the same, including services rendered before the supreme court at Herkimer and Utica, and in preparing and arguing two appeals before the general term of the supreme court at Rochester, and two appeals before the court of appeals, and including expenses incurred and paid, the sum of nine hundred and forty-seven dollars, or so much thereof as shall be audited by the canal board.

Amasa J. Parker, Jr. For Amasa J. Parker, junior, for his taxable costs in the cases last above mentioned, the sum of four hundred and forty-seven dollars and thirty-five cents.

Daniel C. Springsteen. For Daniel C. Springsteen, sheriff of the county of Rockland, for services and expenses in the suit of the People versus James Eckerson and others, the sum of ten hundred and seventy-four dollars and ninety-six cents, or so much thereof as the attorney-general shall certify to be just; and the board of supervisors of said county at its next annual session is hereby authorized and required to raise the money hereby appropriated, and to pay the same into the treasury of the state.

Awards of commissioners on claims of Rankin and Livingston to be retried. The determination and award of the commissioners appointed by the supreme court on the claims of Henry Rankin and Henry Livingston, against the state, is hereby directed to be retried and redetermined by and before the three commissioners to be appointed by the governor. The time and place of hearing of said claim shall be fixed by the said commissioners, and such retrial shall be had before them on the usual notice of trial prescribed by the rules and practice of the supreme court, either by the attorney-general or the claimants, and the attorney-general is hereby required and directed to attend said retrial and protect the interests of the state, and the sum of fifty thousand dollars, or so much thereof as may be necessary, is hereby appropriated out of any money in the treasury not otherwise appropriated to pay to the said claimants respectively, as the said com missioners may award, and the expenses of said award and the compensation of said commissioners at the rate of ten dollars per day and the necessary expenses incurred by them in hearing said claim. The governor is hereby authorized to appoint the commissioners as herein provided.

Claims of Lawton, Bailey & Crocker. The comptroller is hereby authorized to audit and pay the claims of Israel Lawton, John M. Bailey and L. L. Crocker, commissioners appointed by chapter six hundred and ninety of laws of eighteen hundred and seventy-one, to investigate the claims of Henry Rankin and Henry Livingstone, against the state of New York, and for the purpose of such payment the sum of twelve hundred dollars, or so much thereof as may be necessary, is hereby appropriated.

Asa Fitch. The sum of fifteen hundred dollars is hereby appropriated to be paid to Asa Fitch, for revising and completing for publication his survey of the noxious and other insects of the state, the state to have the right to publish at all times any number of copies of said work for its own use without further payment.

Commissioners under chapter 715, laws of 1871. To Albert Haight, Marshall B. Champlain, Homer A. Nelson, Nelson B. Hopkins and Norman M. Allen, for disbursements and services rendered as commissioners under the provisions of chapter seven hundred and fifteen of the laws of eighteen hundred and seventy-one, and chapter seven hundred and thirty-three of the laws of eighteen hundred and seventy-two, in relation to the illegal assessment and collection of taxes upon the Buffalo creek, Allegany and Cattaraugus Indian reservations, two thousand dollars, of which sum there shall be paid to Marshall B. Champlain, the sum of five hundred dollars; to Albert Haight, five hundred dollars; to Norman M. Allen, five hundred dollars; to Nelson K. Hopkins, two hundred and fifty dollars, and to Homer A. Nelson, two hundred and fifty dollars.

To investigate college land grant. For expenses of commission to investigate the college land grant, so called, the sum of four thousand dollars, or so much thereof as shall be necessary.

To ascertain number of Cayuga Indians, etc. The comptroller, on a written application of a majority of the adult male Indians of the Cayuga tribe or nation of Indians, residing upon the Cattaraugus Indian reservation, shall appoint one or more commissioners to proceed to the state of Kansas, or other western states and territories, and ascertain the number of Cayuga Indians, residing off the said Cattaraugus reservation, who are entitled to share in the annuities paid by the state under treaty stipulations made by the state with said Cayuga Indians, and the expenses, disbursements and compensation of the commissioner or commissioners so appointed shall be audited, fixed and allowed by the comptroller, and by him paid out of the annuities payable to said Cayuga Indians by the state, and the person or persons so appointed shall report to the comptroller the result of their investigations.

Deficiency chapter 341, laws of 1872. To supply the deficiency in appropriation made by act chapter three hundred and forty-one of the laws of eighteen hundred and seventy-two, for the payment of counsel assigned to assist district attorneys in capital cases, under part first, chapter eighth, title five, section six of the Revised Statutes, and the laws amendatory thereof, the sum of two thousand dollars.

Commission to investigate charges against district attorney of Kings county. To pay the expenses of the commission and stenographer and other necessary expenses in investigation of charges against the district attorney of the county of Kings, the sum of fifteen hundred dollars, or so much thereof as shall be necessary, to be paid on the certificate of the governor; and the board of supervisors of said county are hereby directed to raise said sum so paid by taxation at their next annual meeting, and to pay the same into the treasury of the state.

Expenses of revising harbor lines. For the expenses of the officers of the United States service, appointed by the president of the United States to revise the exterior lines of the harbor of New York, to be paid upon vouchers to be furnished to and audited by the comptroller, the sum of seven thousand dollars, or so much thereof as shall be necessary.

Commissioners to confer with New Jersey. For the commissioners appointed to confer with the state of New Jersey in regard to quarantine jurisdiction and boundary lines pursuant to section seven, chapter six hundred and thirteen of the laws of eighteen hundred and sixty-five, for compensation and expenses, one thousand dollars each.

Survey of Quarantine Island. For labor and expenses incurred by the state engineer and surveyor in making survey and estimate of Quarantine Island number two, in the lower bay of New York, pursuant to resolution of the assembly, passed May seventh, eighteen hundred and seventy-two, the sum of eleven hundred and fifty dollars.

Investigation of building ninth district court-house. The expenses of the investigation as to building of ninth district court-house in the city of New York, and into the affairs of the department of buildings in said city, by the investigating committee of the senate, authorized at its last session, shall be audited by the comptroller and paid by him out of the fund appropriated for legislative expenses, and the amount so audited and paid shall be charged against the city of New York, and shall be refunded to the treasury of the state by the comptroller of the city of New York upon demand of the comptroller of the state.

Money to be expended by attorney-general. The sum of three thousand dollars is appropriated, to be expended by the attorney-general, with the approval of the governor, in relation to the decision of the supreme court of the United States, in the suit of Whitman versus Thompson, now in that court, in which is involved a question of title between New York and New Jersey to the main ship channel at Sandy Hook, made by act chapter five hundred and ninety-eight of the laws of eighteen hundred and sixty-five, and for the further purpose of paying the legal, necessary expenses, and the expense of surveying and other necessary expenses to determine the title as between New York and Connecticut to certain oyster beds on Long Island sound, off the harbor of Bridgeport and to Norwalk islands, and other points in said sound below low-water marks, there being now pending a dispute between said states on that point.

James B. Craig and others. For James B. Craig, three hundred dollars; to John E. Burrell, six hundred dollars; to Samuel Hand, three hundred dollars; to Hiram E. Sickles, seven hundred and sixteen dollars and fifty cents, for counsel fees, professional services rendered and disbursements made at the request of the governor and the late attorney-general, in the suit of the people on the relation of Edward F. Underhill against Edward S. Darrel, or so much thereof as the comptroller, upon investigation, shall decide to be due.

For Enoch L. Fancher, for expenses incurred in employing counsel in the supreme court, and in the court of appeals, to defend a suit brought by the attorney-general to test his right to office of justice of the supreme court, under the appointment to such office by the governor of this state, such a sum as the comptroller shall ascertain to be just and reasonable, not exceeding twelve hundred and fifty dollars. Enoch L. Fancher.

For Mary Doheney, to reimburse her for her costs and expenses incurred by her in defending her title to lands purchased by her grantor from the state, and interest thereon, and for taxes paid and improvements made on said lands by her, the sum of four hundred and twenty-two dollars, or so much thereof as may be necessary, in full of all claims, the same a reappropriation from eighteen hundred and seventy-two. Mary Doheney.

For Joshua M. Van Cott, for services as counsel and expenses in prosecuting against George G. Barnard, a judge of the supreme court in the city of New York, before the trial of impeachment, the sum of six thousand dollars; and for Daniel Pratt and John E. Parsons, for services as counsel and expenses in the same trial, to each of them the sum of three thousand dollars. Joshua M. Van Cott.

For the expenses of the prosecution of Horace G. Prindle, judge and surrogate of Chenango county, upon the charges preferred against him before the senate, namely: To Robert A. Stanton, for services and expenses, seventeen hundred and fifty-nine dollars; to Peckham and Tremain, for services and expenses, fifteen hundred dollars. Expense of prosecution of Horace G. Prindle.

To Horace G. Prindle, judge and surrogate of Chenango county, in full for the payment of counsel fees of Henry R. Mygatt, James W. Glover and E. H. Prindle, and all other expenses incurred by him in defending himself against the charges preferred against him before the senate, three thousand two hundred and fifty-nine dollars. Horace G. Prindle.

For Hudson C. Tanner, for stenographic services of him and assistant stenographers, and of amanuenses in reporting the proceedings in the trial of Judge McCunn, before the senate, seventeen hundred and thirty-two dollars and fifty-eight cents, and for like services in reporting the proceedings in the trial of Judge Curtis before the senate, twenty-two hundred and seventeen dollars and sixty cents, and also for like services, expenses and disbursements in the trial of Judge Prindle before the senate, thirty-five hundred and eighty-seven dollars and eighty-five cents. Hudson C. Tanner.

For the expenses of the prosecution of George M. Curtis, justice of the marine court of the city of New York, upon Geo. M. Curtis.

charges preferred against him before the senate; to Martin L. Townsend, John A. Beale and Peter B. Olney in full for services and expenses, as counsel on said trial, the sum of two thousand dollars, whose accounts shall be presented to the comptroller and audited and paid by him.

Henry Smith and others. To Henry Smith, Robert Cochrane and H. C. Dennison, counsel appearing on the part of the defendant on said trial, in full for services and expenses, two thousand dollars, whose accounts shall be presented to the comptroller and audited and paid by him.

Daniel J. Pratt. For Daniel J. Pratt for labor in the preparation of the annals of public education in the state of New York, for the colonial period, from sixteen hundred and twenty-six to seventeen hundred and forty-six, as ordered by the senate on the twenty-ninth day of March, eighteen hundred and seventy-one, two hundred and fifty dollars.

James M. Oakley. For James M. Oakley, for counsel fees in defending his right to his seat as member of assembly for the second district of Queens county, including the services of counsel in the preparation of his defense, the sum of twelve hundred and fifty dollars.

Theodore J. Cogswell. For Theodore J. Cogswell, for expenses incurred by him in the case of the contested election for member of assembly for the second district of the county of Queens, as follows, namely: For compensation of counsel, the sum of six hundred dollars; for traveling expenses and disbursements, the sum of five hundred and ninety-seven dollars.

Gaylord B. Hubbell. For Gaylord B. Hubbell, as compensation for services as superintendent of the manufacturing department at the Sing Sing prison for the year eighteen hundred and seventy-three, the sum of two thousand dollars.

Lewis E. Carpenter. For Lewis E. Carpenter, agent and warden of the state prison at Auburn, one thousand dollars in addition to the salary now allowed by law; and the salary of the agent and warden of said prison is hereby established at three thousand dollars per annum.

Office of secretary of state. Of treasurer. For deficiency in amount appropriated for salaries of clerks in the office of secretary of state, the sum of two thousand five hundred dollars; and for deficiency in amount appropriated for salaries of clerks in the treasurer's office, the sum of two thousand five hundred and fifty-three dollars and six cents.

State arsenal at Buffalo. For heating apparatus for the state arsenal at Buffalo, and for repairing roof, and for plastering rooms thereof, the sum of twenty-five hundred dollars, or so much thereof as may be necessary, to be expended under the direction of the chief of ordnance.

State library. For the state library, for boxes for British patents, the sum of two hundred dollars, and for the purchase of books, one thousand dollars.

General fund. The sum of six hundred and thirty-nine thousand six hundred and one dollars and ten cents is hereby appropriated for the general fund, and for the payment of those claims and demands which shall constitute a lawful charge upon that fund, being the amount of the three and one-half mill deficiency tax levied in pursuance to chapter seven hundred and thirty-four of the laws of eighteen hundred and seventy-two, in excess of the appropriation of said tax enumerated in chapter seven hundred of the laws of eighteen hundred and seventy-two.

For an assistant in the work of arranging and labeling the duplicate fossils and minerals for distribution, payable on the certificate of the secretary of the board of regents of the university, fifteen hundred dollars. Labeling fossils, etc.

For William N. Lombard, night watchman at the capitol, from the first day of October, eighteen hundred and seventy-two, to the first day of January, eighteen hundred and seventy-three, the sum of ninety-two dollars. Wm. N. Lombard.

For William Turner, junior, for services as superintendent of the expressing and mailing department of assembly post-office, which service was rendered necessary by virtue of resolution of the assembly, imposing additional labor upon the post-office department, five dollars per day for each day of the session, from January seventeenth, eighteen hundred and seventy-three. William Turner.

For Auburn prison, for new doors, casements and locks to continue improvement of north wing as per existing contract, forty-two thousand eight hundred and five dollars and forty cents; for new boiler for cooking and heating, stack and pipe, five thousand dollars; for library, testaments and hymn books, five hundred dollars, or so much thereof as may be necessary. Auburn prison.

For convict insane asylum at Auburn, for finishing the new enlargement of said asylum, fifteen thousand dollars, to be expended under the direction of the inspectors of state prisons; for new boiler and heating apparatus for cooking and heating, two thousand five hundred dollars; for coping for outer walls to preserve the same, one thousand dollars; and for the library, the sum of one hundred dollars, or so much thereof as may be necessary. Convict insane asylum.

For Clinton prison, for finishing prison inclosure, for new plank for roads and repairs to same; for five new coal-kilns to furnish sufficient coal for the iron works; for opening new mines, and reaching ores; for the library, for testaments and hymn books, the sum of fifteen thousand three hundred dollars, or so much thereof as the comptroller on investigation shall decide to be necessary; and for Stephen Moffatt, agent and warden of said prison, for his services as superintendent of the iron manufacturing department, the sum of two thousand dollars. Clinton prison.

For state prison at Sing Sing, for the support of the quarry and lime works, to be paid from the moneys received from the income of said works, seven thousand dollars per month, and all receipts from said quarry works shall be reported monthly to the comptroller, and the moneys derived therefrom shall be paid into the treasury monthly; for purchase Sing Sing prison.

of prison library; for testaments and hymn books, five hundred dollars; for new iron galleries in place of present wooden ones, twelve thousand dollars; for erection and alteration of shops, to enable prison authorities to let new contracts and carry out existing ones, fifteen thousand dollars; and for sheds for stone cutters, two thousand dollars, or so much thereof as the comptroller on investigation shall decide to be necessary.

Inspectors of state prisons. For the inspectors of state prisons, for traveling expenses in addition to the amount provided by law for the last fiscal year, to each of them, the sum of eight hundred dollars, and for the current fiscal year the sum of eight hundred dollars.

Thomas Hamilton. The comptroller is authorized to pay the claim of Thomas Hamilton for wood and lumber delivered to the Sing Sing state prison, and to pay out of the moneys appropriated for the support of the prisons such sums as he shall find justly due said Hamilton.

Onondaga county. To reimburse the county of Onondaga for maintaining state prisoners confined in the penitentiary at Syracuse, in pursuance of act chapter one hundred and fifty-eight of the laws of eighteen hundred and fifty-six, at the rate of one dollar and fifty cents per week, the sum of seven thousand dollars, or so much thereof as may be necessary.

John K. Porter. For John K. Porter, retained by the late attorney-general as associate counsel in the case of William Barnes, superintendent of the insurance department, impleaded with the British Commercial Insurance Company, and for subsequent professional services in the same case, one thousand dollars.

Weed, Parsons & Co., for printing, etc. For Weed, Parsons and Company, for furnishing to the office of the adjutant-general five hundred general order books, five hundred letter books, five hundred enlistment books, five hundred roster and descriptive books for companies, five hundred roster and descriptive books for regiments, and for boxing and shipping the same by express, the sum of nine thousand one hundred and sixty-five dollars and fifty cents; for furnishing the office of the secretary of state seven thousand five hundred copies of the canal laws of eighteen hundred and seventy-two, and four thousand copies of chapter five hundred and seventy, an act relative to suffrage, passed in eighteen hundred and seventy-two, the sum of five hundred and sixty-four dollars and twenty cents; for furnishing thirteen thousand five hundred school registers to the department of public instruction, for the year eighteen hundred and seventy-two, the sum of eight thousand one hundred dollars, and for balance due on school registers furnished the department of public instruction in the year eighteen hundred and seventy-one, the sum of three thousand five hundred dollars; for one thousand two hundred and twenty-five copies of the Civil List of eighteen hundred and seventy-one, pursuant to resolution of assembly, April eighteenth, eighteen hundred and seventy-one, at the rate of three dollars per copy, the sum of three thousand six hundred and seventy-five dollars; for fifteen thousand and thirty-five manuals for the breech loading Remington rifle, for the office of the adjutant-general, the sum of six hundred and one dollars and forty cents; for furnishing the state engineer and surveyor two thousand four hundred lithographic railroad maps, and two thousand four hundred lithographic title pages, and three thousand seven hundred railroad maps, and three thousand seven hundred lithographic title pages for the edition of the state, the sum of two thousand two hundred dollars, the same to be refunded to the state by an equitable assessment on railroads, by the comptroller; for printing three thousand two hundred state engineer and surveyor's reports on railroads, made in eighteen hundred and seventy-two, the sum of nine thousand six hundred and four dollars, the same to be refunded to the state by an equitable assessment on railroads, by the comptroller; for printing for the commissioners to revise the statutes, the sum of seven thousand dollars; for furnishing fifty-seven copies of the Legislative Manual of eighteen hundred and seventy-two, to the senate, per resolution passed January seventh, eighteen hundred and seventy-three, the sum of fifty-seven dollars; for one hundred and twenty-eight copies of Legislative Manual for eighteen hundred and seventy-two, pursuant to resolution of the assembly, January seventeenth, eighteen hundred and seventy-three, the sum of one hundred and twenty-eight dollars, and for one hundred Legislative Manuals of eighteen hundred and seventy-one, furnished to new members of the assembly of eighteen hundred and seventy-two, pursuant to resolution January thirty-first, eighteen hundred and seventy-two, the sum of one hundred dollars; for balance for printing meteorological observations, made by Franklin B. Hough, from January, eighteen hundred and fifty, to eighteen hundred and sixty-three, inclusive, under resolution of the assembly, April first, eighteen hundred and seventy, the sum of eight hundred and eighteen dollars and sixty-eight cents; for eleven thousand copies constitutional commission documents number one, statement of the public indebtedness of the state, furnished pursuant to resolution of the senate, March nineteenth, eighteen hundred and seventy-three, and of the assembly, March nineteenth, eighteen hundred and seventy-three, the sum of one thousand one hundred dollars; for setting up and electrotyping life insurance calculation tables, three millions four hundred and thirty-four thousand four hundred and sixty-four ems, rule and figure work, calculated as plain matter at two dollars per one thousand ems, and binding forty copies of life insurance calculation tables, at three dollars and fifty cents per copy, the sum of five thousand six hundred and seventy-eight dollars and nineteen cents, to be reimbursed to the treasury by the several insurance companies of the state, pursuant to law. The appropriation in the supply bill of eighteen hundred and seventy-one is hereby renewed for two thousand five hundred and twenty-five volumes of Barnes' condensed New York insurance reports, pursuant to resolution of assembly, passed April sixteenth, eighteen hundred and seventy, the sum of fourteen thousand nine hundred and twenty dollars, to be paid on the certificate of the secretary of state of the delivery of the work at the secretary's office, or so much as may be certified by the superintendent of the insurance department to be the value thereof, such sums to be reimbursed to the treasury out of the insurance fund.

Argus company for printing, etc.

For the Argus Company, for printing messages, charges and articles of impeachment for the trials of Judge McCunn, Judge Curtis, Judge Barnard and Judge Prindle, the sum of eight hundred and sixty-nine dollars and ten cents. For printing proceedings and testimony, court of impeachment, trial of Judge George M. Curtis, three hundred copies, seven hundred and four pages, the sum of one thousand four hundred and forty-nine dollars and sixty-seven cents. For printing proceedings and testimony, court of impeachment, trial of Judge John H. McCunn, seven hundred and fifty copies, five hundred and fifty pages, the sum of thirteen hundred and eighty-two dollars and fifty-seven cents. For printing proceedings and testimony, court of impeachment, trial of Judge Horace G. Prindle, two hundred copies, ten hundred and fifty-eight pages, the sum of two thousand and seventy-two dollars and eight cents. For printing eight hundred copies of journal of the extra session of the senate, held in eighteen hundred and seventy-two, the sum of one hundred and fifty-five dollars and seventy-eight cents, and for printing four hundred copies of the annual report of the auditor of the canal department upon tolls, trade and tonnage of the canals of this state, for the year eighteen hundred and seventy-two; and for binding seventy-nine copies of the same in cloth, the sum of three hundred and twenty-eight dollars and sixty cents; and for printing, binding and advertising for the museum of natural history of the state of New York, the sum of ninety dollars; and for printing and advertising for the geological hall of the state of New York, the sum of fourteen dollars and eighty cents. For printing and binding classified index of bills introduced into the assembly, pursuant to resolution passed April eighteenth, eighteen hundred and seventy-one, the sum of two hundred and twenty-one dollars and ninety-two cents; and for printing and binding, pursuant to resolution passed April twentieth, eighteen hundred and seventy-one, five hundred copies of the catalogue of petitions and papers presented to the senate, the sum of one hundred and sixty-nine dollars and seventeen cents; for printing and binding, in pursuance of a resolution passed April, eighteen hundred and seventy-one, eight hundred copies of the catalogue of petitions and papers on file in the assembly, the sum of two hundred and ninety-four dollars and eighty-nine cents; for printing and binding five hundred copies of the index to senate bills (four hundred and fifty bound in cloth and fifty in full sheep), in pursuance of resolution passed April, eighteen hundred and seventy-one, the sum of one thousand and fourteen dollars and thirty-three cents; for printing and binding, in pursuance of resolution passed March fifteenth, eighteen hundred and seventy-one, two thousand copies of report of the board of commissioners of the department of parks in the city of New York, including the engraving and printing of two maps (two thousand copies of each), fifteen hundred and fifty-six dollars and thirty-four cents; for printing and binding in full sheep, five hundred copies of the cases of contested elections to seats in the assembly from seventeen hundred and seventy-one to eighteen hundred and seventy-one, with an appendix of the election laws, in pursuance of resolution passed April eighteenth, eighteen hundred and seventy-one, the sum of eighteen hundred and sixty-six dollars and sixty-seven cents; for printing and binding, in full sheep, five hundred copies of the index to documents, in pursuance of resolutions passed April eighteenth, eighteen hundred and seventy-one, the sum of two thousand one hundred and twenty-nine dollars and twenty-one cents; for printing and binding, in full sheep, five hundred copies of the compilation of cases of breaches of privilege of the house, pursuant to resolution passed April eighteen, eighteen hundred and seventy-one, the sum of nine hundred and fifty dollars and six cents; for printing and binding, in cloth, with engraved title pages, in pursuance of resolution passed February fifth, eighteen hundred and sixty-nine, two thousand copies of volume third of the adjutant-general's report for eighteen hundred and sixty-eight, the sum of four thousand and two hundred and one dollars and thirteen cents; for balance due for printing on fine paper, and binding in cloth, in addition to the regular legis* number, forty-eight hundred copies of the report of the state engineer and surveyor on railroads, for eighteen hundred and seventy, four thousand one hundred and four dollars and fifty-two cents, and for printing and binding blank forms for reports by steam and horse railroad companies to the state engineer and surveyor, and for binding two volumes of original reports of railroad companies, the sum of two hundred and nine dollars and seventy-two cents; the said last two sums to be refunded by the several railroad companies, pursuant to chapter five hundred and twenty-six of the laws of eighteen hundred and fifty-five.

For the commissioners of quarantine, for the payment of rent and keeping in order of that portion of the quarantine establishment leased under and in pursuance of the provisions of chapter four hundred and ninety-two of the laws of eighteen hundred and seventy, the sum of fifteen thousand dollars, or so much thereof as may be necessary for the care and maintenance of the quarantine establishment and defraying the necessary expenses of said board (including a clerk whose salary shall not exceed two thousand dollars a year) in discharge of the duties imposed upon it by law, the sum of sixty thousand dollars, and said commissioners shall also pay therefrom the running expenses of a steamboat for boarding vessels, and transporting the sick and burying the dead; also the taxes

Commissioners of quarantine.

* So in the original.

which have accrued or may accrue during the present lease of the property. The sum of thirty thousand dollars, or such parts of said sum as in the opinion of said comptroller may be required in addition to the balance of appropriation of one hundred and forty-three thousand one hundred and fifty-four dollars and forty-five cents, by chapter seven hundred and thirty-three of the laws of eighteen hundred and seventy-two, to the commissioners constituted by the act entitled "An act in relation to quarantine and providing for the construction of a permanent quarantine establishment," passed April twenty-first, eighteen hundred and sixty-six, which amount is hereby re-appropriated, to be expended by said health officer of the port of New York in carrying out the object and purpose of the original appropriation and for the following expenses: For constructing on Hoffman's Island, cisterns, sewers, water closets, and the general fitting up wards three, four and five, now in process of construction, and for engineer services and expenses, and also to keep in repair the structure and hospital at Swinburne Island.

Health officer of the port of New York. For the health officer of the port of New York, the sum of four thousand dollars, or so much thereof as may be necessary to pay the salaries of not exceeding four policemen at quarantine, on the average, during the year eighteen hundred and seventy-three; such policemen may be appointed and dismissed by him at pleasure, and they shall perform patrol and police duty under his direction in connection with the quarantine establishment and upon the waters of the bay of New York; and they shall possess all the powers possessed by policemen in the cities of New York and Brooklyn; and any person arrested by either of said policemen for violating any law or regulation relating to quarantine, in said port, may be taken by him before any court of criminal jurisdiction, or any magistrate or police justice within the county of Richmond, and thereupon the court, magistrate or police justice, before whom such offender shall be brought, shall have jurisdiction to hear, try and punish the offender for the offense committed by him in the same manner, and with the like effect, as if the same had been committed within the limits over which such court, magistrate or police justice has jurisdiction to punish offenses under existing laws; for the payment of the existing obligations incurred under the authority and direction contained in chapter seven hundred and thirty-three of the laws of eighteen hundred and seventy-two, to enter into the contract for purchasing a site for a boarding station for vessels coming from non-infected ports, and buildings included therein, these amounts to be expended under the direction and with the approval of the governor, health officer of the port of New York, and the board of commissioners, the sum of sixty thousand dollars; to fulfill the contract heretofore made for the boarding station and buildings included aforesaid for the erection of bulk-head, piers and dock, and for obtaining fresh water for steamboat, for grading, for necessary repairs to existing building, the further sum of sixty

Powers of policemen.

thousand dollars, or so much thereof as may be necessary. The warehouses, docks and wharves authorized to be constructed for quarantine purpose by the corporation, formed under the authority of chapter four hundred and ninety-two of the laws of eighteen hundred and seventy, may be erected at such point or points in the harbor or bay of the port of New York, as shall be designated, and upon such plans as shall be approved by the governor, state engineer and surveyor, and health officer of the port of New York, whose duty it shall be to make such designation within four months after the passage of this act, and said corporation shall not be deemed dissolved if it shall commence its operation within two years after the passage of this act. Location of warehouses, etc.

For the purchase of ten repeating rifles for Clinton prison, four hundred and fifty dollars, or so much thereof as may be necessary, to be purchased by the chief of ordnance of the state of New York. Repeating rifles for Clinton prison.

For Thomas Hyde, the sum of one hundred dollars in addition to the amount paid him by the comptroller for repairing roof of state library. Thomas Hyde.

The sum of nine hundred and thirty-three dollars and thirty-eight cents, being the unexpended balance of appropriation of twelve thousand nine hundred and seventy-six dollars per chapter seven hundred and fifteen of the laws of eighteen hundred and seventy-one, to the state lunatic asylum at Utica, for grading, paving and laying sidewalks in front of the asylum grounds on Court and York streets, is hereby reappropriated to the same object. State lunatic asylum at Utica.

To the city of Utica, for improving and paving road-bed of Whitesboro street, fronting on New York State Lunatic Asylum grounds, said frontage being three hundred and ninety feet, twelve hundred and sixty-seven dollars and thirty-six cents. City of Utica.

All that part of section one of chapter six hundred and seventy of the laws of eighteen hundred and sixty-seven, in the following words, to wit: "And all taxes due from the city and county of New York, remaining unpaid on the first day of December in each year, shall be subject to the payment of interest to the state from that date, at the rate authorized to be charged other counties by section five of chapter three hundred and ninety-three of the laws of eighteen hundred and sixty-three," is hereby repealed. Part of section 1, chapter 670, laws of 1867, repealed.

And every county shall pay its quota of state taxes into the state treasury, the one-half on or before the fifteenth day of April, and the other half on or before the first day of May in each and every year thereafter. When counties to pay state taxes.

In the fiscal year beginning on the first day of October, eighteen hundred and seventy-three, the board of supervisors of each and every county which did not, in the fiscal year beginning on the first day of October, eighteen hundred and seventy-two, pay into the treasury of the state the amount which would have been required from said county in pursuance of what purported to be chapter seven hundred and Counties that did not pay amount required by chapter 734, laws of 1873, to pay same with interest.

thirty-four of the laws of eighteen hundred and seventy-two, had the said chapter been a valid act of the legislature, shall pay into the treasury of the state, according to law, a sum which shall be equal, when paid, to the legal interest upon the amount which would thus have been required from said county, from the day on which the same would have been, in accord with laws, due and payable from the said county to the treasury of the state, until the day when the money to be paid in pursuance of this section shall be paid by the said county into the state treasury, and the said interest, and the amount thereof, is hereby declared to be and the same is a debt due and owing from the said county to this state, to be provided for, raised and paid over by the said board of supervisors and said county in the same manner as other debts and moneys for which said county is at any time and for any purpose liable to the state.

County treasurers to pay into state treasury amount levied and raised under chapter 734, laws of 1873.

Whenever in any county the board of supervisors thereof has levied and imposed a tax upon the taxable property thereof, to carry out the provisions of the said supposed chapter seven hundred and thirty-four of the laws of eighteen hundred and seventy-two, and the collector of taxes of any town has received and collected moneys for said tax, and has paid over the same to the county treasurer thereof, and the said county treasurer has not paid the same or any part thereof to the treasurer of the state, he, the said county treasurer, shall pay over the said moneys so paid to him, or such part thereof as he has not yet so paid to the treasurer of the state, on or before the first day of July, eighteen hundred and seventy-three, or in default thereof the comptroller of the state may require and collect the same of and from such county treasurer, and may compel the payment thereof by him, in the same manner in which the said comptroller may have, demand and compel from any county treasurer the payment into the treasury of the state, of the amount of any state tax lawfully imposed, levied and collected.

New capitol.

The sum of one million dollars is hereby appropriated toward the erection of the new capitol, which shall be paid by the treasurer upon the warrant of the comptroller, to the order of the new capitol commissioners, as they shall require the same; whenever there is a deficiency in the treasury of moneys applicable to the payment of this appropriation the comptroller is hereby authorized and required to borrow, from time to time, such sums as the said commissioners may require, and the money so borrowed shall be refunded from the moneys received from taxes levied to meet this appropriation. The new capitol commissioners are hereby authorized to remove that part of the dining-room of Congress Hall projecting west of the main building to some other part of said hall, and to make provision to secure the new capitol building against damage from fire, either by means of a blank wall or by iron shutters upon the rear windows of Congress Hall.

For John Palmer, for painting, glazing and labor upon the capitol, pursuant to order of the superintendent, and approved by two members of the trustees of the capitol, the sum of seven hundred and five dollars and eighty-five cents. John Palmer.

The sum of two thousand and fifty-five dollars and eight cents, or so much thereof as may be necessary, is hereby appropriated to pay Robert K. Oliver, carpenter and builder, of Albany, for work done and material furnished upon the capitol since January first, eighteen hundred and seventy-three, the accounts to be audited and paid by the comptroller. Robert K. Oliver.

The sum of two hundred and fifty-one dollars and fifty cents, or so much thereof as may be necessary, is hereby appropriated to pay John Palmer, painter, of Albany, for work done and material furnished upon the capitol since January, eighteen hundred and seventy-three; also for Van Allen and Purdy, for work done and material furnished upon the capitol, the sum of seventy-six dollars, the accounts to be audited and paid by the comptroller. John Palmer. Van Allen and Purdy.

For the Mechanics and Farmers' Bank of Albany, New York, the sum of thirteen thousand dollars, or so much thereof as may be necessary for interest due on money advanced for the ordinary repairs of the canal, under resolutions of the commissioners of the canal fund, adopted July first, September sixth and October sixth, in the year eighteen hundred and seventy, said interest to be paid out of the sum of sixty-five thousand dollars appropriated by act chapter seven hundred of the laws of eighteen hundred and seventy-two, to pay interest on deficiencies, being the fourth item appropriated in this act. Mechanics and Farmers' Bank of Albany.

For the canal fund, for the payment of interest on deferred payments of the state tax levied for canal purposes in the years eighteen hundred and seventy-one and eighteen hundred and seventy-two, the sum of thirty-three thousand six hundred and forty-six dollars and twenty-seven cents, or so much thereof as may be necessary. Canal fund.

For George W. Chapman, for his services and disbursements up to this date in compiling and preparing for publication a manual of canal laws and regulations now in force, and an index of statutes relating to the canals of this state, for the use of canal officers, the sum of twenty-five hundred dollars, and a further sum of three hundred dollars to be hereafter paid for his services and disbursements in compiling and incorporating therein the laws of this session relating to canals, and for preparing and completing a full index to the said manual after the same shall be printed. Geo. W. Chapman.

For the purchase of coin to pay the principal of the canal debt, under section one of article seven of the constitution, which matures on the first day of January, eighteen hundred and seventy-four, the sum of one hundred and sixty-five thousand dollars, or so much thereof as said sinking fund may be deficient. Purchase of coin.

FROM THE CANAL FUND.

Deficiency in salaries of canal appraisers. For deficiency in the appropriation for salaries of canal appraisers for the fiscal year ending September thirty, eighteen hundred and seventy-three, the sum of nine thousand dollars.

In appropriation for clerk hire. For deficiency in the appropriation for clerk hire in the office of the canal appraisers, the sum of four thousand dollars, or so much thereof as shall be found necessary, to be paid by the auditor of the canal department on the certificate of the chairman of the board of canal appraisers, the same to be paid from the canal fund.

Furniture, etc. For furniture, stationery and other incidental expenses in the office of canal appraisers for the fiscal year commencing October first, eighteen hundred and seventy-two, the sum of seven hundred dollars, to be paid by the auditor of the canal department, on the certificate of the chairman of the board of such canal appraisers, the same to be paid from the canal fund.

Auditor of canal department. For the auditor of the canal department for addition to his salary for the year eighteen hundred and seventy-three, the sum of fifteen hundred dollars.

Canal commissioners. To each of the canal commissioners for deficiency for traveling expenses for quarter ending March third, eighteen hundred and seventy-three, the sum of one hundred dollars.

There shall be paid to each of the canal commissioners, in full for all traveling expenses incurred by them in the discharge of their official duties, the sum of eight hundred dollars per annum, payable quarterly by the auditor of the canal department. All acts and parts of acts conflicting with or inconsistent with this provision are hereby repealed.

Nathan Ackley. For Nathan Ackley, clerk of the late contracting board and of the board of canal commissioners, to repay him moneys disbursed by him for travel and expenses necessarily incurred in the performance of his duties as such clerk, and for which no appropriation has previously been made, the sum of twenty-four hundred and thirty dollars.

Office of auditor of canal department. For the office of the auditor of the canal department, to defray the expenses incurred in the preparation of statistics for the commission to revise and amend the constitution, and in making the reports to the assembly called for by the resolution passed January twenty-fourth and March seventeenth, the sum of twelve hundred dollars.

FROM THE FREE SCHOOL FUND.

National Commercial Bank of Albany. For the National Commercial Bank of Albany, for interest upon overdrafts on the free school fund up to July first, eighteen hundred and seventy-two, the sum of eighteen hundred and thirty-three dollars and fifty-eight cents, or so much thereof as may be necessary.

Printing bills to be audited. No money hereby appropriated for payment of printing bills shall be paid until the items of each bill have been audited by the comptroller, and the work shall have been done pursuant to some proper and legal authority, and if the work is not included within a contract, shall be paid for only at prices usually paid by the state for similar services.

Plans, etc., of asylums, etc., to be submitted to comptroller.

The comptroller shall not pay out any thing under the provisions of this act to or for the benefit of any asylum or reformatory for the purpose of erecting new buildings or making other permanent improvements, unless the plans thereof and estimates therefor shall be first presented to and approved by him; and in determining whether he will approve such plans, he shall require that they shall provide for plain, substantial work, that will involve the least possible expense consistent with proper provisions for the treatment, comfort, protection and safe-keeping of the inmates of such asylums and reformatories, and with a view of securing the most careful and economical expenditure of all moneys devoted to asylums and reformatories by this act. The comptroller is authorized at all times to visit any of said asylums or reformatories, and any part of them he may desire, and whenever he shall desire he shall be allowed to examine and take abstracts or copies of any or all papers, accounts or books of account of any such asylum or reformatory, in whosesoever hands they may be, and he shall have power to subpœna to attend before him any witness that he may think proper to examine as to the affairs of any of said asylums and reformatories, and for such purpose is authorized to administer oaths to and examine such witnesses; and if the comptroller shall, from other official engagements, be unable to make such visitation or examination, he shall appoint, in writing, an examiner for that purpose, who shall be vested with all the power and authority of visitation or examination as to the asylum or asylums or reformatories that the said appointment shall specify, as are hereby conferred upon the comptroller, and such examiner shall, in all cases, report to the comptroller, in writing, what proceeding he has taken, what facts he has collected, the testimony he has taken, and his opinion thereon. Whenever it shall, by the examination herein provided for, or otherwise, be made to appear to the comptroller that any of the moneys by this act appropriated for the benefit of any asylum or reformatory is not being properly and economically used, he shall be authorized to withhold from such asylum or reformatory any unpaid balance of the sum for such asylum or reformatory in this act specified.

Comptroller to visit asylums, etc.

Comptroller may withhold appropriations.

Expenses of visitation.

The expenses of visitation and examination herein authorized shall be paid by the comptroller out of the moneys by this act appropriated to the institution so visited and examined; and the comptroller shall report to the legislature, in detail, all proceedings had and information collected as to said asylums and reformatories, under the provisions hereof, with such other information as he can give, and such other recommendation as he shall think proper to make, that will tend to improve and economize the management of such asylums and reformatories.

Comptroller to report to legislature.

§ 3. This act shall take effect immediately.

CHAP. 765.

AN ACT to provide ways and means for the support of government.

PASSED June 14, 1873; three-fifths being present.

The People of the State of New York, represented in Senate and Assembly, do enact as follows:

Tax. SECTION 1. There shall be imposed, for the fiscal year beginning on the first day of October, eighteen hundred and seventy-three, on each dollar of real and personal property of this state subject to taxation, taxes for state purposes, hereinafter mentioned, which taxes shall be assessed, levied and collected by the annual assessment and collection of taxes for that year, in the manner prescribed by law, and shall be paid by the several county treasurers into the treasury of this state, to be held by the treasurer for application to the purposes specified, that is to say, for the general fund, and for the payment of those claims and demands which shall constitute a lawful charge upon that fund during the fiscal year, commencing October first, eighteen hundred and seventy-three, one and one-half mills for the free school fund, for the maintenance of common schools in this state, one mill and one-fourth of one mill, pursuant to chapter four hundred and six of the laws of eighteen hundred and sixty-seven; for the payment of the interest and redemption of the principal of the state debt of two and one-half million dollars, as provided in chapter two hundred and seventy-one of the laws of eighteen hundred and fifty-nine, one-eighth of one mill; for the payment of the interest, and to provide for the redemption of the state bounty debt, pursuant to chapter three hundred and twenty-five of the laws of eighteen hundred and sixty-five, two mills; for the purposes of the new capitol, one-half of one mill; and for the benefit of the academies and academical department of the union school, pursuant to chapter five hundred and forty-one of the laws of eighteen hundred and seventy-two, one-sixteenth of one mill; for continuing the erection of the asylums and reformatories now in process of construction, five-sixteenths of one mill.

(Margin notes: For general fund. Common schools. State debt. State bounty debt. New capitol. Academies. Asylums, etc.)

§ 2. This act shall take effect immediately.

CHAP. 766.

AN ACT to authorize a tax of one-half of a mill per dollar of valuation of the year one thousand eight hundred and seventy-three for the construction of new work upon and extraordinary repairs of the canals of this state.

PASSED June 14, 1873; three-fifths being present.

The People of the State of New York, represented in Senate and Assembly, do enact as follows:

SECTION 1. There shall be imposed for the fiscal year beginning on the first day of October, eighteen hundred and seventy-three, a state tax of one-half of a mill on each dollar of real and personal property in this state subject to taxation, which stock shall be assessed, levied and collected by the annual assessment and collection of taxes for that year in the manner prescribed by law, and shall be paid by the several county treasurers into the treasury of the state, to be held by the treasurer, and is hereby appropriated and applied to the objects and purposes hereinafter specified, to wit: Tax of one-half mill for canals. Appropriation.

EASTERN DIVISION — ERIE CANAL.

For completing iron road bridge over the Erie canal at Ilion, Herkimer county, the sum of thirty-five hundred dollars, or so much thereof as may be necessary. Bridge at Ilion.

For completing iron chord road bridge over the Erie canal at Crescent, Saratoga county, the sum of fifteen hundred dollars, or so much thereof as may be necessary. At Crescent.

For completing wood frame bridge over the Erie canal at Sprakers, Montgomery county, the sum of one thousand dollars. At Sprakers.

For completing iron road bridge over the Erie canal at Columbia street, in the city of Cohoes, the sum of twenty-five hundred dollars, or so much thereof as may be necessary. In Cohoes.

For completing iron change bridge over the Erie canal at West Troy, the sum of three thousand dollars, or so much thereof as may be necessary. At West Troy.

For repairing bottom and banks of the Erie canal along the premises of Stillman A. Fields, in the town of Canajoharie, so as to prevent leakage upon the premises of said Field, and for constructing a waste ditch along the premises of Samuel Beekman in said town, so as to carry off the leach-waters of the Erie canal, the sum of five hundred dollars, or so much thereof as may be necessary. Repairing canal in Canajoharie.

For constructing one hundred feet of vertical wall on the berme bank of the Erie canal at the east end of the aqueduct over the Canajoharie creek, in the village of Canajoharie, the sum of five hundred dollars, or so much thereof as may be necessary. Vertical wall in.

Iron bridges, eastern division. For constructing iron bridge superstructures, on the eastern division, made necessary in consequence of change of plan, the sum of twenty-five thousand dollars, or so much thereof as may be necessary.

Vertical wall in Port Jackson. For constructing one hundred feet of vertical wall on the berme bank of the Erie canal in the village of Port Jackson, to be located by the canal commissioner in charge, as the commerce of the canal shall require, the sum of five hundred dollars.

Rebuilding lock at Glen's Falls. For rebuilding wooden lock of stone on the Glen's Falls feeder, the sum of thirty thousand dollars, or so much thereof as may be necessary.

Bridge, etc., Champlain canal. For constructing a wooden bridge and abutments over the Champlain canal, on the farm of Hiram Cramer, at Coveville, Saratoga county, the sum of two thousand dollars, or so much thereof as may be necessary.

Rebuilding wall. For rebuilding protection wall on highway at Fort Edward, Washington county, carried away by break in canal in the month of April, eighteen hundred and sixty-nine, the sum of fifteen hundred dollars, or so much thereof as may be necessary.

Vertical wall. For constructing one hundred feet of vertical wall at Norris' lime kiln, near Fort Ann, and one hundred feet of vertical wall at Keenan's lime kiln, near Smith's basin, the sum of one thousand dollars, or so much thereof as may be necessary.

Bridge, Fort Edward. For completing bridge over Fort Edward feeder, the sum of five hundred dollars, or so much thereof as may be necessary.

Rocky Rift feeder dam. For raising the Rocky Rift feeder dam, the sum of seven thousand seven hundred dollars.

Farm bridge. For the construction of a farm bridge over the Rocky Rift feeder, on the lands of John H. Keyser, in the county of Montgomery, the sum of two hundred and fifty dollars, or so much thereof as may be necessary.

Saratoga dam. For the completion of the Saratoga dam, the sum of fifty-three thousand dollars, or so much thereof as may be necessary.

New piers, etc., at Cohoes. The sum of twenty-five thousand two hundred dollars, or so much thereof as may be necessary, is hereby appropriated, to pay for the cost of building new piers, snubbing posts, wire cable approaches, embankments and towing-path connected with the bridge over the Mohawk river, for the purposes of the Champlain canal at Cohoes.

Parapet wall, Port Jackson. For parapet wall in the village of Port Jackson, along the approaches to canal bridge in said village, the sum of eight hundred dollars.

Wilbur's basin. For constructing a lock at Wilbur's basin on the Champlain canal, in addition to the amount heretofore appropriated by chapter eight hundred and fifty, laws of eighteen hundred and seventy-two, the sum of ten thousand dollars.

Bridge in Watervliet. For constructing and maintaining a highway bridge over the Erie canal, in the town of Watervliet, in the county of Albany, from the Ireland Corners road, on the west of said canal, to Island park, on the east of said canal, the sum of six thousand and five hundred dollars.

For constructing two locks at Three Locks, just north of the village of Waterford, Saratoga county, the sum of twenty thousand dollars, that sum having been taken out of the appropriation of forty thousand dollars, provided for by chapter nine hundred and thirty, laws of eighteen hundred and seventy-one, by virtue of chapter one hundred and sixty-four, laws of eighteen hundred and seventy-two. Two locks at Three Locks, north of Waterford.

For raising iron bridge superstructure on Genesee street, Utica, to the height required, and adopting approaches to the same, the sum of four thousand five hundred dollars. Raising iron bridge in Utica.

For the construction of a Whipple's patent draw bridge over the Erie canal in Hotel street, in the city of Utica, the sum of ten thousand dollars, and the canal commissioners are hereby authorized to contract with Squire Whipple for the construction of said bridge, at an aggregate cost not exceeding the sum above mentioned. Patent draw bridge.

For removing wall benches and constructing slope walls on the towing-path side of the Erie canal, between the east line of the city of Utica and lock number forty-five, at Frankfort, and between lock number forty-six and Whitesboro' street bridge, in the city of Utica, the sum of fifty-four thousand dollars; and between lock number thirty-three and section number seventy-five, the sum of three thousand dollars. Removing wall benches, etc.

For removing wall benches and constructing slope walls elsewhere on the eastern division of the Erie canal, under direction of the canal board, the sum of one hundred thousand dollars.

For reconstructing the wood bridge of iron, with single road track and sidewalk over the Erie canal at Alexander street, in the city of Cohoes, county of Albany, the sum of six thousand dollars, or so much thereof as may be necessary. Bridge in Cohoes.

For constructing blind drains on section number one hundred and eleven, west of lock number forty-six, the sum of eighteen hundred dollars. Blind drains.

For the payment of George H. Taylor's account for rebuilding waste-weir on the Fort Edward feeder, on the Champlain canal, which was done under the direction of the late canal commissioner, Bascom, the sum of fifteen hundred and fifty-six dollars and eighty-nine cents, the same to be audited by the auditor of the canal department. George H. Taylor.

For constructing a sewer at Mansion street, in the village of West Troy, extending from the Watervliet turnpike, on the west side of the Erie canal, under said canal, so as to discharge into the Hudson river, the sum of three thousand five hundred dollars, or so much thereof as may be necessary. Sewer in West Troy.

For completing the rebuilding of guard lock in Wood creek, on Champlain canal, the sum of ten thousand four hundred dollars. Guard lock in Wood creek.

For completing the two stone side-cut locks in the village of West Troy, authorized by act chapter three hundred and Stone side-cut locks, West Troy.

fifty-four, laws of eighteen hundred and sixty-four, the sum of twenty-five thousand dollars.

Highway, Fort Ann. For repairing highway in the town of Fort Ann, pursuant to chapter five hundred and forty-four, laws of eighteen hundred and seventy, which work may be done by the canal commissioner in charge, through his superintendent, or by contract, in his discretion, the sum of eight hundred dollars, or so much thereof as may be necessary.

Schuylerville aqueduct. For the completion of Schuylerville aqueduct, on enlargement of Champlain canal, the sum of twenty-three thousand dollars, or so much thereof as may be necessary.

MIDDLE DIVISION — ERIE CANAL.

Relaying vertical walls in Syracuse, etc. For taking down dry vertical walls and relaying the same in cement, in order to avert claims against the state, in consequence of leakage from the Erie canal into the cellars of adjoining property owners in the city of Syracuse; and for removing bench walls and constructing vertical walls, where necessary, on the Syracuse level of the Erie canal, the sum of ten thousand dollars, or so much thereof as may be necessary, provided that the canal commissioner in charge shall, before expending any of said sums of money, procure a release of all damages on account of such leakage, free of charge to the state.

Removal of bench walls, etc. For removing bench walls and substituting slope walls, upon the towing-path, Jordan level and Long level of the Erie canal, and for constructing two hundred lineal feet of vertical wall opposite the marble works of McCarty and Paul and the malt-house of Adam Miller and Company in the village of Weedsport, the sum of forty thousand dollars, or so much thereof as may be necessary.

Jamesville reservoir. For completing Jamesville reservoir on the Butternut creek, for the purpose of furnishing additional water to the Rome level of the Erie canal, authorized by act chapter three hundred and forty-three of the laws of eighteen hundred and seventy-two, to be expended as provided in said act, the sum of thirty thousand dollars, or so much thereof as may be necessary.

Removal of bench walls, etc. For the removal of wall benches on the towing-path side of the Erie canal in city of Rome, between James and Washington streets, and constructing vertical walls, the sum of two thousand five hundred dollars.

Bridge abutments at Hulser's farm. The sum of five hundred dollars, appropriated by chapter eight hundred and fifty, laws of eighteen hundred and seventy-two, for building stone abutments for canal bridge at Hulser's farm in West Frankfort, is hereby reappropriated, to build stone abutments at Myers' bridge, in the village of Mohawk, which work may be done by the commissioner in charge or by contract, in his discretion.

East Frankfort. For extending abutments, raising and widening approaches to highway bridges at East Frankfort, the sum of fifteen hundred dollars, or so much thereof as may be necessary.

For rebuilding broken culverts at Oswego, and repairing docking and improving side-cuts at Salina, building vertical wall at necessary points on the Liverpool level, and such other improvements of the Oswego canal as shall be directed by the canal commissioners, the sum of ten thousand dollars, or so much thereof as may be necessary. Culverts at Oswego, etc.

For repairing the state piers in the harbor at Geneva, the sum of seven thousand five hundred dollars, or so much thereof as may be necessary, to be expended under the direction of the canal commissioner in charge. For constructing vertical wall on the berme side of the Cayuga and Seneca canal, near the junction with the Erie canal, in the village of Montezuma, the sum of five hundred dollars. State piers in Geneva. Vertical wall Cayuga and Seneca canal.

For constructing a dam at Waterloo, which shall be constructed during the year eighteen hundred and seventy-three, the sum of fifteen thousand dollars, which was appropriated for the construction of said dam by act chapter three hundred and forty-three, laws of eighteen hundred and seventy-two, and the further sum of twenty-five thousand dollars hereby appropriated shall be applied to the construction of a permanent tight dam in the Seneca river, at or near the site of the present state dam at Waterloo, and to the extension of the same across the raceways on the south bank of said river. The permanent waste or spill-way of said dam to be the same height as the present one, except across the raceways on the south side of the river, where the waste shall be three feet below the top of the main dam, with ample flood-gates therein, to discharge the surplus water into the main channel of said river, and such fixture shall be constructed on top of said spill-way as can be readily removed to give free vent to floods, and which shall be closed, and no water permitted to waste over said dam after the water in said lake shall have subsided to the original natural height thereof. When deemed necessary by the canal board, breast walls or weirs of the same height at the spill-ways on the south side of the river shall be constructed in front of all raceways drawing water from said level, so that thereafter no water can be drained from the Cayuga and Seneca canal, or from the Seneca river, where used for such canal for hydraulic purposes, except over the top of such weirs, and shall be built of solid masonry without apertures therein, and of such height as is necessary to maintain seven feet depth of water in the canal. The balance of the foregoing appropriations not required to construct said dams shall be applied in deepening the prism of the canal as contemplated by act chapter four hundred and seventy-nine, laws of eighteen hundred and fifty-seven. Dam at Waterloo. In Seneca river. Breast walls, etc.

For completing the high dam on the Oswego river, now under contract, the sum of sixty thousand dollars, or so much thereof as may be necessary. High dam, Oswego river.

For the completion of the Oneida lake canal the sum of twenty-five thousand dollars, or so much thereof as may be necessary. Oneida lake canal.

Iron bridges. For constructing iron bridge superstructures, on the middle division of the Erie canal, made necessary in consequence of the change of plan, the sum of fifteen thousand dollars.

Pier at Watkins. For repairing pier at entrance of the Chemung canal, in the harbor of Watkins, at the head of Seneca lake, the sum of four thousand dollars, or so much thereof as may be necessary.

WESTERN DIVISION — ERIE CANAL.

Deepening canal in Buffalo, etc. For deepening and improving the canal between slip number three and York street in the city of Buffalo, as authorized by the canal board August sixth, eighteen hundred and seventy-two, and for completing division bank and other work connected therewith in Black Rock harbor, so as to separate the canal from and make it independent of said harbor, the sum of one hundred and seventy thousand dollars. For protecting canal against encroachments against Lake Erie, between Erie basin break-water and Black Rock pier, and thus furnish additional facilities for transhipment of property, the sum of twenty-five thousand dollars. Canal board may cancel existing contracts. The canal board is hereby authorized to cancel the existing contracts upon condition that the contractor shall release all claims for damages relating thereto, and relet the work on such plan as the state engineer and surveyor shall approve.

Bridge in Syracuse. For a wrought iron foot bridge over the Erie canal at Franklin street, in the city of Syracuse, the sum of twenty-five hundred dollars, or so much thereof as may be necessary.

Vertical wall in Port Byron. For building one hundred and fifty feet of vertical wall on Erie canal, in the village of Port Byron, in front of the property of the Thompson Patent Paper Manufacturing Company, the sum of seven hundred and fifty dollars, or so much thereof as may be necessary.

Betz and Nester. For the payment of Betz and Nester, for work on the middle division of the Erie canal, the sum of twelve hundred and two dollars. No part of said sum shall be paid until it is proven to the satisfaction of the auditor of the canal department that there is that amount due to said Betz and Nester for work and material furnished the state upon the canals, and that such work was done by direction of the commissioner in charge.

Heath's plan of tumble gates. For payment for introducing Heath's plan of tumble gates in the old poor-house and lower Macedon locks, as per estimate of J. F. Behee, division engineer, adopted and authorized by the canal board December fifth, eighteen hundred and seventy-two, the sum of forty-five hundred dollars.

Removing bench walls, etc. For completing the removal of bench walls and constructing slope walls, and removing about one hundred and fifty feet of slope wall, and substituting vertical wall therefor, in front of the premises of Nelson McCormack, about one mile east of the canal collector's office, in the village of Medina, in the Erie canal, if in the judgment of the canal commissioner in charge it shall be deemed necessary for commercial purposes, and for other works under contract on the western division not sufficiently provided for, the sum of ten thousand dollars.

For cleaning out, improving and deepening the canal an average of six inches below established grade between Thomas creek culvert and Macedon locks, the sum of ten thousand dollars. Deepening canals, etc. Road bridge in Rochester.

For constructing and maintaining a road bridge over the Erie canal, connecting Averill and Munger streets, in the city of Rochester, the sum of ten thousand dollars.

For constructing one hundred feet of vertical wall on the Erie canal, in the village of Fairport, Monroe county, on the towning-path side and adjoining the Winnie bridge, commencing at the warehouse property now owned by W. K. Goodrich and A.. Briggs, the sum of five hundred dollars. Vertical wall in Fairport.

For building seventy feet of vertical wall on the Erie canal, in the village of Gasport, three hundred and fifty dollars, or so much thereof as may be necessary; to be located by the canal commissioner in charge. In Gasport.

For rebuilding three bridges over the State ditch at Adams, Broad and Morgan streets, in the village of Tonawanda, Erie county, the sum of three thousand dollars. Bridges over State ditch in Tonawanda.

For additional roadway track to change bridge, over the Erie canal, in the village of Tonawanda, on the road leading to Grand Island ferry, the sum of four thousand dollars, or so much thereof as may be necessary. Roadway track to change bridge.

For aiding in constructing a bridge over the Tonawanda creek, according to the provisions made in chapter eight hundred and sixty-three of the laws of eighteen hundred and sixty-seven, the sum of eight thousand dollars. Bridge over Tonawanda creek.

For constructing one hundred and twenty-five feet of vertical wall on the berme side of the Erie canal, in front of the premises of J. W. Parker and others, in the village of Port Gibson, Ontario county, the sum of six hundred and twenty-five dollars. Vertical wall in Port Gibson.

For deepening Erie basin, Buffalo harbor, the sum of eight thousand dollars. Deepening Erie basin.

For dredging and excavating in Black rock harbor, the sum of eight thousand dollars. Dredging Black Rock harbor.

For dredging and excavating in the Ohio basin and slip, the sum of ten thousand dollars. Ohio basin and slip.

For constructing about two hundred feet of vertical wall in front of the premises of Whitmore, Rathbon and Brady, about one mile east of the collector's office, in Albion, in Erie canal, one thousand dollars. Vertical wall east of Albion.

For constructing about one hundred and fifty feet of vertical wall on the berme side of the Erie canal, in front of the premises of Isaac Holloway, east of Bidwell's bridge, and three miles east of Albion, the sum of seven hundred and fifty dollars.

For building one hundred and fifty feet of vertical wall on the berme bank of the Erie canal, at Macedon, east of the bridge, commencing at the easterly end of the present wall, provided that parties interested in said wall shall, without At Macedon.

expense to the state, make all necessary excavations, and place the banks of the canal in a suitable condition for said wall, as the canal commissioner in charge shall direct, the sum of four hundred and fifty dollars, or so much thereof as may be necessary.

At Spencerport. For building two hundred and seventy-five feet of vertical wall in the Erie canal, in the village of Spencerport, Monroe county, to be located in said village by the canal commissioner in charge, as the interests of the local commerce of the canal shall require, the sum of thirteen hundred and seventy-five dollars.

At Adams' basin. For building one hundred feet of vertical wall on the berme bank of the Erie canal at Adams' basin, in the county of Monroe, commencing at the west end of J. Cady and Son's warehouse and extending west one hundred feet, the sum of five hundred dollars.

Approaches to bridge. For constructing protection wall and repairing approaches to a bridge near lot ninety-seven of Niagara river reservation, the sum of two hundred and fifty dollars, or so much thereof as may be necessary.

New bridge at Woodville. For a new bridge over the Dansville branch of the Genesee Valley canal at Woodville, in the town of West Sparta, Livingston county, on the site of the old bridge where the east and west road crosses said canal, the sum of eight hundred dollars, or so much thereof as may be necessary.

Iron bridges. For constructing iron bridge superstructures on the western division of the Erie canal, made necessary in consequence of change of plan, the sum of fifteen thousand dollars.

Draw bridges in Rochester. The sum of twenty thousand dollars appropriated by act chapter nine hundred and thirty, laws of eighteen hundred and seventy-one, for the construction of a swing or draw-bridge over the Erie canal in Buffalo street in the city of Rochester, is hereby re-appropriated for such purpose, or the state engineer and surveyor may erect a Whipple elevating bridge at said street in lieu of a swing bridge, if in his judgment said Whipple bridge shall be more economical and practicable than a swing bridge.

S. P. and S. R. R. Co. to build a vertical wall, appropriation for. The Sodus Point and Southern Railroad Company is hereby authorized to construct three hundred and fifty feet of vertical wall on the berme bank of the Erie canal in the village of Newark, Wayne county, about two hundred feet westerly from the point where the iron bridge of said road crosses the canal; and the sum of fifteen hundred dollars is hereby appropriated and shall be paid to said railroad company by the canal commissioner in charge of said division, whenever said three hundred and fifty feet of vertical wall shall be completed and accepted by said commissioner.

Removing state dam, etc. For removing the remains of state dam on Scajaquadays creek, and the bars in said creek adjacent thereto, the sum of twelve hundred and fifty dollars, or so much thereof as may be necessary.

For the removal, replacement and repair of the bridge on Ohio street, over the Clark and Skinner canal, the sum of nine hundred dollars, or so much thereof as may be necessary. Bridge over Clark and Skinner canal.

For repair and reconstruction of docking on the Clark and Skinner canal, the sum of seven thousand dollars, or so much thereof as may be necessary. The action of the canal board, at a meeting thereof held on the eighth day of November, eighteen hundred and seventy-two, in adjusting the rent due the state from the holders of leases of surplus waters of the Erie canal at Black Rock, is legalized and confirmed, and the four thousand and eight hundred dollars paid by the owners of such lease in pursuance of such settlement, are accepted in full payment and settlement of the rent due on account of all leases of surplus waters of the Erie canal at Black Rock, up to and including the year eighteen hundred and seventy-two; but the owners of such leases shall not, by virtue of any thing herein contained, be released from the payment of rent accruing by virtue of the terms of their leases, on and after the year eighteen hundred and seventy-two. Docking on same.

For the payment of J. B. Griffin and Company, the sum of one thousand nine hundred and twenty-two dollars, for money expended by them in the construction of a bridge over the Erie canal at Mill street, in Black Rock, provided the canal commissioner in charge of the western division of the canals is satisfied that the said sum was expended by said firm in the construction of said bridge. J. B. Griffin and Co.

For aiding in the construction of a bridge over the Genesee river at Mount Morris, used as tow-path of the canal, three thousand dollars, or so much thereof as may be necessary, the bridge to be built by the towns of Mount Morris and Leicester, said towns to pay two-thirds of the expenses of said bridge and the state one-third thereof; the one-third of the cost of said bridge, not exceeding three thousand dollars, shall be paid to the commissioners of highways of the two towns, after the work is completed and accepted by the canal commissioner in charge. Bridge at Mount Morris.

To pay to the town of Pittsford four hundred dollars, and the town of Brighton six hundred dollars, or so much thereof as may be necessary, for damages caused by water flowing from the side-cuts in the Erie canal, during the freshets of the spring of eighteen hundred and seventy-three, and the canal commissioner of the western division is hereby authorized to settle with the road commissioners of either of said towns, providing said road commissioners, and each and every person claiming to be damaged thereby, will receipt in full for said damages for such sums as shall be agreed upon, not exceeding the sums named above. Towns of Pittsford and Brighton.

For constructing one hundred feet of vertical wall on the berme side of the Erie canal, in the village of Pittsford, in front of Eckler's warehouse, coal and lumber yard, commencing at the east end of the vertical wall already built, the sum of five hundred dollars, or so much thereof as may be Vertical wall in Pittsford.

Releases to be procured before constructing bridges.

necessary; the canal commissioner shall in each instance, before proceeding to the construction of the bridges provided for in this act, require and receive from all persons, whose property, rights or interests may be affected by such bridge, approaches or embankments, a full and sufficient release, legally executed and acknowledged, free of all expense to the state, of all claims for damages in consequence of the construction of said bridge, or of the approaches or embankments of the same, and also a good and sufficient license or permission to the state, duly executed and acknowledged, to alter, change and raise such bridge, approaches or embankment, wherever necessary, which necessity is to be determined by the canal commissioners.

Canal commissioners to commence new works.

In order to remove all doubts in respect to the authority of the canal commissioners to commence the new works for which appropriations are herein made, and no legislative direction is otherwise given by special laws, it is hereby declared that the said canal commissioners are hereby authorized to construct, or cause to be constructed, all such new works for which appropriations are herein made, subject, however, to all restrictions, provisions and conditions contained in this act. No part or portion of the moneys herein appropriated for new work shall be expended or paid, nor shall any contract involving such expenditures and payment be made on behalf of this state until the maps, plans and estimates for such new work shall have been submitted to and approved by the canal board. All contracts for work and material on any canal (other than ordinary repairs) which shall be directed by the canal board to be advertised and let, shall be made with the person who shall offer to do or provide the same at the lowest price, with adequate security for their performance, which letting shall be under regulations to be made by the board of canal commissioners, as to the form, regularity and validity of all bids, securities and contracts. And the canal commissioners shall require the deposit by the proposer for said work or materials of such a sum, in United States bonds or stocks of state of New York, or money, not exceeding twenty and not less than eight per cent of the aggregate estimate of the work to be let, as they may deem necessary to secure the entering into said contract. And in case the proposer to whom such work shall be awarded shall neglect or refuse to enter into such contract, the sum so deposited shall be forfeited to the state, and the commissioners shall pay the same into the state treasury, and it shall become a part of the canal fund. And upon entering into said contract, the bonds or stocks, or money required by the commissioners as security for the entering into said contract, together with such additional securities as they may require, may be held as security for the completion of the work, and shall be deposited with the treasurer as a special trust, to be returned by him to the contractor with such further sum as he may have realized for the use thereof, when the commissioner in charge and the state engineer shall certify that the contractor has fully completed

Maps, etc., to be approved by canal board.

Contracts, letting of.

Deposit by proposer.

When sum deposited to be forfeited.

Bonds, etc., to be deposited.

his contract, and that the state has no further claim upon such funds. But in case he shall enter into said contract and fail in the performance thereof, the same shall be declared abandoned by said commissioners, pursuant to the terms of the contract, then the bonds or stocks or money so deposited shall be forfeited to the state and paid into the treasury and become a part of the canal fund. The canal board may, in the resolution authorizing any work to be let, prescribe the length of time of advertising, not less than ten days.

When bonds, etc., to be forfeited to state.

Time of advertising.

No more money shall be expended on the work hereinbefore enumerated than is appropriated; and it shall not be lawful for the officers having in charge the execution of the said works to make any contracts whereby any expenditure in excess of the appropriation will be incurred, or any further appropriation for the same rendered necessary.

Expenditures.

In order to meet the appropriations, made in this act, of the moneys to be collected by and upon the said tax with as little delay as practicable, the commissioners of the canal fund or comptroller may, from time to time, invest in the said tax any surplus moneys of the principal of the sinking funds under article seven of the constitution, a sum or sums not exceeding in all the amount to be realized from said tax hereby authorized; and the moneys so invested shall be applied to pay the appropriation under this act, and so much of the moneys arising from the said tax as may be necessary when paid into the treasury, is hereby pledged and shall be applied in the first instance to re-imburse the said sinking funds for the amount invested in said tax and for the interest on the same at a rate not exceeding six per cent per annum, from the time of investment to the day of payment.

Surplus moneys of sinking fund may be invested in tax.

CHAP. 773.

AN ACT to amend the Revised Statutes, in relation to laying out public highways.

PASSED June 14, 1873; three-fifths being present.

The People of the State of New York, represented in Senate and Assembly, do enact as follows:

SECTION 1. Section fifty-seven of article four, of title one, of chapter sixteen of part one of the Revised Statutes is hereby amended by adding at the end thereof the following:

Unless the commissioners of highways shall, on application duly made, after five days' notice to the owner, or if he be a non-resident of the town, to the occupant of said premises, certify to the county judge that the public interest will be greatly promoted by the laying out and opening of such road, the commissioners shall serve on the owner, or if he be a non-resident of said town, on the occupant of said land, a notice of five days, to appear before the county judge to attend the hearing of said matter; if the county judge shall affirm the

When commissioners to serve notice on owner or occupant to attend hearing before county judge.

Proceedings in

case of affirmance of order. decision of said commissioners, they shall present the order of the county judge for confirmation at the supreme court, at a general term, in the judicial department in which such premises are situated, upon the usual notice of motion in said court to the owner, or if he be a non-resident of the town, to the occupant of the premises; if said court shall confirm the said order, it shall then be the duty of the commissioners to proceed and lay out and open said road, as in other cases.

§ 2. This act shall take effect immediately.

Ante, vol. 1, p. 478.

CHAP. 777.

AN ACT to amend an act for the suppression of the traffic in and circulation of obscene literature, being chapter seven hundred and forty-seven of the laws of eighteen hundred and seventy-two.

PASSED June 14, 1873; three-fifths being present.

The People of the State of New York, represented in Senate and Assembly, do enact as follows:

SECTION 1. The first section of the act for the suppression of the traffic in and circulation of obscene literature, being chapter seven hundred and forty-seven of the laws of eighteen hundred and seventy-two, is hereby amended so as to read as follows.

Penalty for selling or offering to sell, giving away, etc., any obscene book, picture, etc., or having same in possession. § 1. If any person shall sell, or lend, or give away, or in any manner exhibit, or shall offer to sell, or to lend, or to give away, or in any manner to exhibit, or shall otherwise publish or offer to publish in any manner, or shall have in his possession, for any such purpose or purposes, any obscene book, pamphlet, paper, writing, advertisement, circular, print, picture, drawing or other representation, figure or image on or of paper, or other material, or any cast, instrument, or other articles of an indecent or immoral nature or use, or any drug or medicine, or any article whatever, for the prevention of conception, or for causing unlawful abortion, or shall advertise the same for sale, or shall write or print, or cause to be written or printed, any card, circular, book, pamphlet, advertisement or notice of any kind whatsoever, stating when, where, how, or of whom, or by what means, any of the articles in this section hereinbefore mentioned can be purchased or obtained, or shall manufacture, draw or print, or in anywise make any of such articles, every such person if of twenty-one years of age or over, shall, on conviction thereof, be imprisoned at hard labor for not less than three months or more than two years, and be fined not less than one hundred dollars or more than five thousand dollars for each offense; but if under twenty-one years of age, shall be imprisoned not more than three months and be fined not more than five hundred dollars, in the discretion of the court, for each offense; one-half of said fine shall be paid to the orphan asylum of the county, and one-half to the school fund of the county in which said conviction is obtained, except that in the city and county of New York, one-half shall go to the Female Guardian Society in said city and the other half to the Prison Association of New York.

§ 2. All articles of raw materials found in the possession of any person or persons intending to manufacture the same into the articles or things described in the first section of this act, and also all tools, machinery, implements, instruments and personal property found in the place or building where the articles described in the first section of this act are found or seized, and used or intended to be used in the manufacture of such articles or things, may be seized and shall be forfeited; and the proceedings to enforce such forfeiture shall be in the nature of a proceeding in rem before the court or record of criminal jurisdiction having jurisdiction of the crime specified in the first section of this act in the city or county wherein the arrest or seizure was made. Raw materials, tools, etc., to be forfeited.

§ 3. Nothing in this act shall be construed as repealing section one of the act to which this is amendatory or as affecting any indictments heretofore found for offenses against the same, and such indictments may be prosecuted to judgment and sentence passed upon persons convicted and punishments inflicted as if this act had not been enacted. Act, how to be construed.

§ 4. Section three of said act is hereby amended so as to read as follows:

§ 3. All magistrates are authorized, on due complaint, supported by oath or affirmation, to issue a warrant directed to the sheriff of the county within which such complaint shall be made, or to any constable, marshal, or police officer within said county, directing him, them, or any of them, to search for, seize and take possession of such obscene and indecent books, papers, articles and things, and said magistrate shall transmit, inclosed and under seal, specimens thereof, to the district attorney of his county, and shall deposit within the county jail of his county or such other secure place as to him shall seem meet, inclosed and under seal, the remainder thereof, and shall upon the conviction of the person or persons offending under any of the provisions of this act, forthwith, in the presence of the person or persons upon whose complaint the said seizure or arrest was made, if he or they shall after notice thereof elect to be present, destroy or cause to be destroyed the remainder thereof so seized as aforesaid, and shall cause to be entered upon the records of his court the fact of such destruction. Warrants to search and seize obscene books, etc.

§ 5. The words in this act in section one, "articles of indecent or immoral nature or use," shall not be construed as applying to articles or instruments which are used or applied for the cure or prevention of disease.

§ 6. This act shall take effect immediately.

Ante, p. 468.

CHAP. 785.

AN ACT in relation to further testing a steam dredge for which appropriations were made by chapter seven hundred and sixty-seven, laws of eighteen hundred and seventy, and chapter seven hundred and fifteen, laws of eighteen hundred and seventy-one.

PASSED June 18, 1873; three-fifths being present.

The People of the State of New York, represented in Senate and Assembly, do enact as follows:

Canal commissioners may deliver possession of state dredge.

SECTION 1. The canal commissioners may, if they shall deem it for the best interests of the state, deliver possession to B. Hughes, the inventor thereof, the steam dredge now in said commissioners' possession, for constructing which appropriations were made by act chapter seven hundred and sixty-seven, laws of eighteen hundred and seventy, and act chapter seven hundred and fifteen, laws of eighteen hundred and seventy-one, said Hughes to give good and sufficient bonds for the return of the same to the state, or payment therefor as hereinafter provided.

May enter into contract for the use of dredge, etc.

§ 2. The board of canal commissioners may, if they shall deem it for the best interests of the state, enter into a contract with said Hughes, for a term not exceeding three years, for the use of said dredge in clearing out deposits in the Erie canal, at such points as the said commissioners may elect, at a price to be fixed by the canal commissioner and division engineer of the division on which said dredge shall be employed, reserving therefrom ten per cent, to be applied in the purchase of said dredge until said dredge is paid for, and the canal commissioner for the western division and the division engineer for said division shall make an estimate of the value of said dredge, which estimate shall be the price which said Hughes shall pay the state for said dredge, to be paid for out of its earnings as aforesaid; and in case said Hughes shall neglect or fail to diligently work with said dredge at prices fixed as aforesaid, and pay over to the canal commissioners the per cent named as aforesaid, then and in that case the canal commissioners shall take possession of said dredge, and all interest of said Hughes therein shall thereupon case.* When said Hughes shall fully pay for said dredge he shall own the same.

§ 3. This act shall take effect immediately.

Ante, p. 186.

* So in the original.

CHAP. 798.

AN ACT dividing the state into congressional districts.

PASSED June 18, 1873.

The People of the State of New York, represented in Senate and Assembly, do enact as follows:

SECTION 1. For the election of representatives in congress of the United States, this state shall be and is hereby divided into thirty-three districts, namely: State divided into congressional districts.

First district. — The counties of Suffolk, Queens and Richmond shall compose the first district. First.

Second district. — The first, second, fifth, sixth, eighth, tenth, twelfth and twenty-second wards of the city of Brooklyn shall compose the second district. Second.

Third district. — The third, fourth, seventh, eleventh, thirteenth, nineteenth and twentieth wards of the city of Brooklyn and the twenty-first ward of said city as bounded by section two of chapter eight hundred and fourteen of the laws of eighteen hundred and sixty-eight, shall compose the third district. Third.

Fourth district. — The ninth ward of the city of Brooklyn as bounded by section one of chapter eight hundred and fourteen of the laws of eighteen hundred and sixty-eight, the fourteenth, fifteenth, sixteenth, seventeenth and eighteenth wards of said city, and the towns of Flatbush, Flatlands, Gravesend, New Lots and New Utrecht in the county of Kings, shall compose the fourth district. Fourth.

Fifth district. — The first, second, third, fourth, fifth, sixth, eighth and fourteenth wards of the city of New York, Bedloe's Island, Ellis Island and Governor's Island shall compose the fifth district. Fifth.

Sixth district. — The seventh, eleventh and thirteenth wards of said city shall compose the sixth district. Sixth.

Seventh district. — The tenth and seventeenth wards of said city shall compose the seventh district. Seventh.

Eighth district. — The ninth, fifteenth and sixteenth wards, and that portion of the eighteenth ward lying within Fourteenth street, Twenty-sixth street, and Fourth and Sixth avenues, shall compose the eighth district. Eighth.

Ninth district. — So much of the twentieth ward as lies within Twenty-sixth street, Fortieth street, Seventh avenue and the Hudson river, and so much of the twelfth and twenty-second wards as lies within Fortieth street, Spuyten Duyvel creek, Eighth avenue and Hudson river, shall compose the ninth district. Ninth.

Tenth district. — So much of the eighteenth ward as is east of Fourth avenue, and so much of the nineteenth and twenty-first wards of said city as is east of Third avenue and Blackwell's Island, shall compose the tenth district. Tenth.

Eleventh. Eleventh district. — So much of the twentieth ward as lies within Twenty-sixth street, Fortieth street, Sixth and Seventh avenues, and so much of the twelfth and twenty-second wards as is east of Eighth avenue, and so much of nineteenth and twenty-first wards of said city as lies west of Third avenue and Ward's and Randall's Island, shall compose the eleventh district.

Twelfth. Twelfth district.— The county of Westchester shall compose the twelfth district.

Thirteenth. Thirteenth district.— The counties of Putnam, Dutchess and Columbia shall compose the thirteenth district.

Fourteenth. Fourteenth district.— The counties of Rockland, Orange and Sullivan shall compose the fourteenth district.

Fifteenth. Fifteenth district.— The counties of Ulster, Greene and Schoharie shall compose the fifteenth district.

Sixteenth. Sixteenth district.— The county of Albany shall compose the sixteenth district.

Seventeenth. Seventeenth district.— The counties of Rensselaer and Washington shall compose the seventeenth district.

Eighteenth. Eighteenth district.— The counties of Warren, Essex and Clinton shall compose the eighteenth district.

Nineteenth. Nineteenth district.— The counties of St. Lawrence and Franklin shall compose the nineteenth district.

Twentieth. Twentieth district.— The counties of Fulton, Hamilton, Montgomery, Saratoga and Schenectady shall compose the twentieth district.

Twenty-first. Twenty-first district.— The counties of Delaware, Otsego and Chenango shall compose the twenty-first district.

Twenty-second. Twenty-second district.— The counties of Jefferson, Lewis and Herkimer shall compose the twenty-second district.

Twenty-third. Twenty-third district.— The county of Oneida shall compose the twenty-third district.

Twenty-fourth. Twenty-fourth district.— The counties of Madison and Oswego shall compose the twenty-fourth district.

Twenty-fifth. Twenty-fifth district.— The counties of Onondaga and Cortland shall compose the twenty-fifth district.

Twenty-sixth. Twenty-sixth district.— The counties of Cayuga, Wayne and Seneca shall compose the twenty-sixth district.

Twenty-seventh. Twenty-seventh district.— The counties of Ontario, Livingston and Yates shall compose the twenty-seventh district.

Twenty-eighth. Twenty-eighth district.— The counties of Tioga, Tompkins, Broome and Schuyler shall compose the twenty-eighth district.

Twenty-ninth. Twenty-ninth district.— The counties of Chemung, Steuben and Allegany shall compose the twenty-ninth district.

Thirtieth. Thirtieth district.— The counties of Monroe and Orleans shall compose the thirtieth district.

Thirty-first. Thirty-first district.— The counties of Niagara, Genesee and Wyoming shall compose the thirty-first district.

Thirty-second. Thirty-second district.— The county of Erie shall compose the thirty-second district.

Thirty-third. Thirty-third district.— The counties of Chautauqua and Cattaraugus shall compose the thirty-third district.

CHAP. 809.

AN ACT to amend chapter three hundred and twenty-seven of the laws of eighteen hundred and forty-six, entitled "An act to equalize taxation," passed May thirteen, eighteen hundred and forty-six.

PASSED June 18, 1873; three-fifths being present.

The People of the State of New York, represented in Senate and Assembly, do enact as follows:

SECTION 1. Section one of chapter three hundred and twenty-seven of the laws of eighteen hundred and forty-six is amended so as to read as follows:

§ 1. It shall be the duty of the assessors of each town and ward, while engaged in ascertaining the taxable property therein, by diligent inquiry, to ascertain the amount of rents reserved in any leases in fee, or for one or more lives, or for a term of years exceeding twenty-one years, and chargeable upon lands within such town or ward, which rent shall be assessed to the person or persons entitled to receive the same as personal estate, which it is hereby declared to be, for the purpose of taxation under this act, at a principal sum, the interest of which at the legal rate per annum shall produce a sum equal to such annual rents; and in case such rents are payable in any other thing except money, the value of such annual rents in money shall be ascertained by the assessors, and the same shall be assessed in manner aforesaid. And in case the name or names of the person or persons entitled to receive the rent reserved upon any lot or parcel of land on which any rent is reserved, as provided in this section, cannot be ascertained by the assessors, then the same shall be assessed against the tenant or tenants in possession of said lot as rents reserved.

Assessors to ascertain amount of reserved rents in leases, in fee, etc.

Amount of assessment

When to be assessed against tenant.

§ 2. Section two of said act is hereby amended so as to read as follows:

§ 2. The board of supervisors in each county shall assess the taxes to be raised for town, county and state purposes upon the person or persons entitled to receive such rents within the town or ward where the lands upon which such rents are reserved and situated, in the same manner, and to the same extent, as any personal estate of the inhabitants of such town. And in case the name or names of the person or persons entitled to receive the rents upon any lot or parcel of land has not been ascertained by the assessor, then the board of supervisors shall assess the tax authorized by the act hereby amended to be levied and collected of the tenant or tenants in possession of the lands upon which said rent is reserved; said tenant to be reimbursed for the tax upon the rent reserved so collected of him, in the manner provided in section three of this act.

To be assessed at same rate and extent as personal estate.

§ 3. Section three of chapter three hundred and twenty-seven of the laws of eighteen hundred and forty-six is hereby amended so as to read as follows:

Collection of tax. § 3. If such tax shall not be paid the collector or the person authorized by law to receive said tax shall levy the same by distress and sale of the goods and chattels of the person against whom the same is assessed within the town or ward of such collector, in the same manner as if such person was an inhabitant of such town or ward. And if no sufficient goods or chattels belonging to the person against whom the same is assessed can be found in said town or ward, then in that case it shall be the duty of the collector to levy and collect the same by distress and sale of the goods and chattels of the tenant or lessee in possession of the demised premises on which said rent is reserved; and the tenant, lessee in possession, or person in possession of said premises, may abate from the amount of any rent reserved upon said premises either due or to grow due thereon, the amount of tax so paid by or collected of him upon the rents so reserved, with interest on the amount so paid from the time of the payment of said tax; and the warrant for the collection of said tax, issued by the board of supervisors to the collector of any town in which said tax shall be assessed, shall direct the collection of the same in accordance with the provisions of this section.

Ante, vol. 7, p. 848.

CHAP. 814.

AN ACT to extend the operation and effect of the act passed February seventeen, eighteen hundred and forty-eight, entitled "An act to authorize the formation of corporations for manufacturing, mining, mechanical or chemical purposes."

PASSED June 19, 1878; three-fifths being present.

The People of the State of New York, represented in Senate and Assembly, do enact as follows:

Number of corporators. SECTION 1. Any nine or more persons may organize themselves into a corporation, in the manner specified and required in and by the act entitled "An act to authorize the formation of corporations for manufacturing, mining, mechanical or chemical purposes," passed February seventeen, eighteen Purposes. hundred and forty-eight, for the purposes of building, manufacturing, owning, furnishing, letting, selling and maintaining locomotive engines, cars, rolling stock and machinery to be used or operated upon railways, or any one or more of such purposes.

Benefits and privileges. § 2. Every corporation so formed shall be entitled to all the benefits and privileges conferred by the before-mentioned act, and may contract and transact its business with any railway company or other person engaged in the operation of any railway in the United States or Canada, but shall otherwise be subject to all the provisions, duties and obligations in the said act contained.

§ 3. This act shall take effect immediately.

Ante, vol. 8, p. 788.

CHAP. 820.

AN ACT to amend an act entitled "An act to suppress intemperance, and to regulate the sale of intoxicating liquors," passed April sixteenth, eighteen hundred and fifty-seven.

PASSED June 28, 1873; three-fifths being present.

The People of the State of New York, represented in Senate and Assembly, do enact as follows:

SECTION 1. Section twenty-two of the "Act to suppress intemperance, and to regulate the sale of intoxicating liquors," passed April sixteenth, eighteen hundred and fifty-seven, is hereby amended so as to read as follows: Penalties, how to be sued for.

§ 22. The penalties imposed by this act, except those provided for by sections fifteen and nineteen, shall be sued for and recovered in a civil action in a manner provided by law for the recovery of penalties, by and in the name of the overseers of the poor of the town in which the alleged penalty was incurred, and the amount so recovered, when collected, together with all the costs of the proceedings for such recovery and collection, shall, within thirty days after such collection, be paid by the officer or party receiving the same to the county treasurer of the county, for the support of the poor of such county, except as is otherwise provided by law. Who may prosecute.

§ 2. Section thirty of the said act is hereby amended so as to read as follows:

§ 30. In case the parties or persons whose duty it is to prosecute for any penalty imposed for any violation of the provisions of this act shall, for the period of ten days after complaint to them that any person has incurred such penalty, accompanied with reasonable proof of the same, neglect or refuse to prosecute for such penalty, any other person may prosecute therefor, in the name of the overseers of the poor of the town in which such alleged penalty was incurred, and in the manner provided by section twenty-two of this act, as the same isamended by section one of this chapter.

Ante, vol. 4, pp. 53, 54.

CHAP. 821.

AN ACT to amend an act entitled "An act to amend an act entitled 'An act to amend an act entitled 'An act for the benefit of married women in insuring the lives of their husbands,' passed April fourteenth, eighteen hundred and. fifty-eight,' passed April eighteenth, eighteen hundred and seventy."

PASSED June 23, 1873; three-fifths being present.

The People of the State of New York, represented in Senate and Assembly, do enact as follows:

SECTION 1. The second section of the act entitled "An act to amend an act entitled 'An act to amend an act entitled "An act for the benefit of married women in insuring the lives of their husbands," passed April fourteenth, eighteen hundred and fifty-eight,' passed April eighteenth, eighteen hundred and seventy," is hereby amended so as to read as follows:

How policies may be surrendered.

§ 2. Any policy in favor of a married woman, or of her and her children, or assigned in her, or in her and their favor, on written request of said married woman, duly acknowledged before a commissioner of deeds, or other officer authorized to take acknowledgments of deeds, in the same manner as required by law, to pass her dower right in lands of her husband, and on the written request of the policy holder may be surrendered to and purchased by the company issuing the same in the same manner as any other policy. And such married woman may, in case she has no child or children born of her body, or any issue of any child or children born of her body, dispose of such policy in and by a last will and testament, or any instrument in the nature of a last will and testament, or by deed duly executed and acknowledged before an officer authorized to take acknowledgments of deeds, in the same manner as required by law to pass her dower right in lands of her husband, which disposition lawfully made shall invest the person or persons to whom such policy shall have been so bequeathed, or granted and conveyed, with the same rights in respect thereto as such married woman would have had in case she survived the person on whose life such policy was issued, and such legatee or grantee shall have the same right to dispose of such policy as herein conferred on such married woman.

May be disposed of by last will.

§ 2. This act shall take effect immediately.

Ante, vol 4, p. 515; vol. 6, p. 790; vol. 7, p. 677.

CHAP. 824.

AN ACT to amend section nineteen of chapter five hundred and seventy of the laws of eighteen hundred and seventy-two, entitled "An act to ascertain by proper proofs the citizens who shall be entitled to the right of suffrage in the state of New York, except in the city and county of New York and the city of Brooklyn, and to repeal chapter five hundred and seventy-two of the laws of eighteen hundred and seventy-one, entitled 'An act to amend an act entitled an act in relation to elections in the city and and county of New York.'"

PASSED June 28, 1873; three-fifths being present.

The People of the State of New York, represented in Senate and Assembly, do enact as follows:

SECTION 1. Section nineteen of chapter five hundred and seventy of the laws of eighteen hundred and seventy-two, entitled "An act to ascertain by proper proofs the citizens who shall be entitled to the right of suffrage in the state of New York, except in the city and county of New York, and the city of Brooklyn, and to repeal chapter five hundred and seventy-two of the laws of eighteen hundred and seventy-one, entitled 'An act to amend an act entitled an act in relation to elections in the city and county of New York,'" is hereby amended so as to read as follows: This act shall apply to all the incorporated cities in this state, except New York and Brooklyn, and in all incorporated villages containing over ten thousand inhabitants, as determined by the last census. Act extended to other places.

§ 2. This act shall take effect immediately.

CHAP. 830.

AN ACT to legalize the adoption of minor children by adult persons.

PASSED June 25, 1873.

The People of the State of New York, represented in Senate and Assembly, do enact as follows:

SECTION 1. Adoption, as provided for in this act, as the legal act whereby an adult person takes a minor into the relation of child, and thereby acquires the rights and incurs the responsibilities of parent in respect to such minor. "Adoption" defined.

§ 2. Any minor child may be adopted by any adult, in the cases and subject to the rules prescribed in this act. Any minor child may be adopted.

§ 3. A married man, not lawfully separated from his wife, cannot adopt a child without the consent of his wife; and a married woman, not lawfully separated from her husband, cannot adopt a child without the consent of her husband. Who may adopt.

Consent of child. § 4. The consent of a child, if over the age of twelve years, is necessary to its adoption.

Consent of parents. § 5. Except in the cases provided for in the next section, a legitimate child cannot be adopted without the consent of its parents, if living, or the survivor, if one is dead; nor an illegitimate child without the consent of its mother, if she is living.

When not necessary. § 6. The consent provided for by this last section is not necessary from a father or mother deprived of civil rights, or adjudged guilty of adultery or cruelty, and who is from either cause divorced; or is adjudged to be an insane person or an habitual drunkard, or is judicially deprived of the custody of the child on account of cruelty or neglect.

Consent of person having custody. § 7. When the child to be adopted has neither father nor mother living, or whose consent, if living, is made unnecessary by the provisions of the last section, such consent shall be gi en by an adult person having the lawful custody of the childv

Proceedings before county judge. § 8. The person adopting a child, and the child adopted, and the other persons whose consent is necessary, shall appear before the county judge of the county in which the person adopting resides, and the necessary consent shall thereupon be signed, and an agreement be executed by the person adopting, to the effect that the child shall be adopted and treated, in all respects, as his own lawful child should be treated.

Examination of persons. § 9. The judge shall examine all persons appearing before him pursuant to the last section, each separately, and if satisfied that the moral and temporal interests of the child will be promoted by the adoption, he shall make an order in which shall be set forth, at length, the reasons for such order, directing that the child shall thenceforth be regarded and treated, in all respects, as the child of the person adopting.

Name of child, etc. § 10. A child, when adopted, shall take the name of the person adopting, and the two thenceforth shall sustain toward each other the legal relation of parent and child, and have all the rights and be subject to all the duties of that relation, excepting the right of inheritance, except that as respects the passing and limitations over of real and personal property, under and by deeds, conveyances, wills, devises and trusts, and said child adopted shall not be deemed to sustain the legal relation of child to the person so adopting.

When parent to forfeit claims. § 11. Whenever a parent has abandoned or shall abandon an infant child such parent shall be deemed to have forfeited all claim that he or she would otherwise have, as to the custody of said child or otherwise, against any person who has taken, adopted and assumed the maintenance of such child; and in such case the person so adopting, taking and assuming the maintenance of such child may adopt it under the provisions of this act, with the same effect as if the consent of such parents had been obtained. In all cases of abandonment after this act takes effect the person adopting shall proceed under the provisions of this act within six months after he or she has assumed the maintenance of such child; in such case of abandonment, the county judge may make the order provided for in this act without the consent of such parent or parents.

§ 12. The parents of an adopted child are, from the time of adoption, relieved from all parental duties toward, and of all responsibility for, the child so adopted, and have no rights over it. After adoption parents relieved from care, etc.

§ 13. Nothing herein contained shall prevent proof of the adoption of any child, heretofore made according to any method practiced in this state, from being received in evidence, nor such adoption from having the effect of an adoption hereunder; but no child shall hereafter be adopted except under the provisions of this act, nor shall any child that has been adopted be deprived of the rights of adoption, except upon a proceeding for that purpose, with the like sanction and consent as is required for an act of adoption under the eighth section hereof; and any agreement and consent in respect to such adoption, or abrogation thereof hereafter to be made, shall be in writing, signed by such county judge or a judge of the supreme court, and the same, or a duplicate thereof, shall be filed with the clerk of the county and recorded in the book of miscellaneous records, wherein the same shall be made, and a copy of the same, certified by such clerk, may be used in evidence in all legal proceedings; but nothing in this act contained in regard to such adopted child inheriting from the person adopting shall apply to any devise or trust now made or already created, nor shall this act in any manner change, alter or interfere with such will, devise, or said trust or trusts, and as to any such will, devise or trust said adopted child shall not be deemed an heir so as to alter estates, or trusts, or devises in wills already made or trusts already created. Not to affect proof of adoption heretofore made by any method practiced in this state. Evidence.

CHAP. 833.

AN ACT to regulate the fees of coroners.

PASSED June 25, 1873; three-fifths being present.

The People of the State of New York, represented in Senate and Assembly, do enact as follows:

SECTION 1. The coroners in and for the state of New York, except in the counties of New York and Kings, shall be entitled to and receive the following compensation for services performed: Coroner's fees.

Mileage to the place of inquest and return, ten cents per mile.

Summoning and attendance upon jury, three dollars.

Viewing body, five dollars.

Serving of subpœna, ten cents per mile traveled.

Swearing each witness, fifteen cents.

Drawing inquisition for jurors to sign, one dollar.

Copying inquisition for record, per folio, twenty-five cents, but such officers shall receive pay for one copy only.

For making and transmitting statement to board of supervisors, each inquisition, fifty cents.

For warrant of commitment, one dollar.

For arrest and examination of offenders, fees shall be the same as justices of the peace in like cases.

When performing duties of sheriff. When required to do the duties of a sheriff, shall be entitled to and receive the same fees as sheriffs for the performance of like duties.

Shall be re-imbursed for all moneys paid out actually and necessarily by him in the discharge of official duties.

Shall receive for each and every day and fractional parts thereof spent in taking inquisition (except for one day's service), three dollars.

For performing the requirements of law in regard to wrecked vessels, shall receive three dollars per day and fractional parts thereof, and a reasonable compensation for all official acts performed, and mileage to and from such wrecked vessel, ten cents per mile.

For taking ante-mortem statement, shall be entitled to the same rates of mileage as before mentioned, and three dollars per day and fractional parts thereof, and for taking deposition of injured person in extremis, one dollar.

Power to employ surgeons. § 2. A coroner shall have power, when necessary, to employ not more than two competent surgeons to make post-mortem examinations and dissections, and to testify to same, and fix their compensation, the same to be a county charge.

Fees, when required to attend as a witness. § 3. Whenever, in consequence of the performance of his official duties, a coroner becomes a witness, he shall be entitled to receive mileage to and from his place of residence, ten cents per mile, and three dollars per day for each day or fractional parts thereof actually detained as such witness.

§ 4. All items of coroners' compensation shall be a county charge, to be audited and allowed by board of supervisors.

§ 5. All acts and parts of acts inconsistent with this act are hereby repealed.

§ 6. This act shall take effect immediately.

CHAP. 849.

AN ACT to amend chapter six hundred and twenty-three of the laws of eighteen hundred and sixty-eight, entitled "An act to amend an act entitled 'An act to amend an act entitled an act to provide for the incorporation of life and health insurance companies, and in relation to agencies of such companies, passed June twenty-fourth, eighteen hundred and fifty-three;' passed April twenty-fourth, eighteen hundred and sixty-six."

PASSED June 28, 1873.

The People of the State of New York, represented in Senate and Assembly, do enact as follows:

SECTION 1. Section one of chapter six hundred and twenty-three of the laws of eighteen hundred and sixty-eight, entitled "An act to amend an act entitled 'An act to amend an act entitled an act to provide for the incorporation of life and health insurance companies, and in relation to agencies of such companies, passed June twenty-fourth, eighteen hundred and fifty-three;' passed April twenty-fourth, eighteen hundred and sixty-six," is hereby amended by adding to the end thereof the following:

When superintendent may accept valuation of insurance department of other states.

The superintendent may, in his discretion, accept the valuation of the department of insurance of any other state in place of the valuation required in this act, provided the insurance officer of such state does not refuse to accept, as sufficient and valid for all purposes, the certificate of valuation of the insurance department of this state.

§ 2. This act shall take effect immediately.

Ante, vol. 7, p. 322; vol. 6, p. 832; vol. 4, p. 220.

CHAP. 851.

AN ACT to amend an act entitled "An act to provide for the incorporation of fire insurance companies," passed June twenty-five, eighteen hundred and fifty-three.

PASSED June 28, 1873; three-fifths being present.

The People of the State of New York, represented in Senate and Assembly, do enact as follows:

SECTION 1. The third section of the act entitled "An act to provide for the incorporation of fire insurance companies," passed June twenty-five, eighteen hundred and fifty-three, is hereby amended so as to read as follows:

Declaration to be filed.

§ 3. Such persons shall file in the office of the superintendent of the insurance department a declaration signed by all the corporators, expressing their intention to form a company for the purpose of transacting the business of insurance, as expressed in the first section of this act, which declaration shall also comprise a copy of the charter proposed to be adopted by them, and shall publish a notice of their intention in a public newspaper, in the county in which such insurance company is proposed to be located, for at least two weeks successively.

Examinations to be made. § 2. It shall be the duty of the superintendent of the insurance department to make the examination into the affairs of any fire insurance company doing business in this state, in the manner authorized by section twenty-four of the act of which this is amendatory, whenever any stockholder or creditor of any such company shall, by a declaration subscribed and sworn to by him, notify the said superintendent that, from facts within the knowledge of the person making such declaration, he believes that the condition of such insurance company does not justify its continuance in business. Such examination may also be made without any such declaration, whenever the said superintendent shall deem it expedient, Supreme court to have power to appoint a receiver. and the supreme court shall have power, after any such examination shall have been made in either of the cases mentioned in said section twenty-four, to appoint a receiver of its property and effects, and no stockholder or creditor, unless with the consent of such company, by a vote of its board of directors, at a meeting called for the purpose, shall have the right to maintain an action for the dissolution of any such company, or to apply for the appointment of a receiver of its property and effects until after notification to the said superintendent by such creditor or stockholder as hereinbefore provided, the said superintendent of the insurance department shall have refused or neglected, for the space of ten days from the filing of such notice, to make the examination authorized by said section twenty-four of the act of which this is amendatory.

§ 3. This act shall take effect immediately.

Ante, vol. 4, p. 226.

CHAP. 870.

AN ACT to appropriate two thousand five hundred dollars for the removal of obstructions from, and to improve the navigation of the Indian river.

PASSED June 28, 1873; three-fifths being present.

The People of the State of New York, represented in Senate and Assembly, do enact as follows:

Appropriation. SECTION 1. The sum of two thousand five hundred dollars, returned to the treasury of this state by the commissioners appointed by chapter eight hundred and thirty-six of the laws of eighteen hundred and seventy-one, is hereby appropriated out of any moneys in the treasury belonging to the general fund not otherwise appropriated, for the purpose of completing the removal of obstructions from, and improving the navigation of Indian river, between the village of Rossie, in the county of St. Lawrence, and the village of Theresa, in the county of Jefferson. The moneys so appropriated shall be expended for the purposes aforesaid, by and under the direction of Rodney Simons, George E. Yost and Leeman W. Tyler, commissioners, and the state engineer and surveyor, who shall proceed in the manner provided in said chapter. Commissioners.

§ 2. The said commissioners, except the state engineer and surveyor, before entering upon the duties of their office, shall execute and file in the office of the comptroller a bond, with sufficient sureties to be approved of by the comptroller, in the penal sum of five thousand dollars, for the faithful performance of their duties. Official oath and bond.

§ 3. The commissioners aforesaid shall perform the duties required by this act and shall report their proceedings on or before the first day of December next after the passage of this act, verified by their oath, to the comptroller. Report.

§ 4. The comptroller shall have power to fill vacancies that may occur in said board of commissioners. Vacancies.

§ 5. This act shall take effect immediately.

CONCURRENT RESOLUTIONS

OF THE

SENATE AND ASSEMBLY.

CONCURRENT RESOLUTION relative to the reduction of canal tolls.

Resolved (if the assembly concur), That the legislature do concur in the recommendation of the canal board and assent to the reduction of canal tolls to such an extent during the ensuing season of navigation, not exceeding fifty per cent below the rates prescribed by the toll-sheet of eighteen hundred and fifty-two, as the canal board shall, in its discretion, think expedient, and as the exigencies of trade shall demand, and to change the same from time to time as circumstances shall, in the judgment of the board, require.

STATE OF NEW YORK,
In Senate, *January* 29, 1873.

The foregoing resolution was duly passed.

By order.

CHAS. R. DAYTON,
Clerk.

STATE OF NEW YORK,
In Assembly, *February* 14, 1873.

The foregoing resolution was duly passed.

By order.

J. O'DONNELL,
Clerk.

CONCURRENT RESOLUTION appointing commission to examine obstructions in the Seneca river.

Resolved (if the senate concur), That a commission consisting of the Hon. Josiah B. Williams, of Tompkins county, Hon. George Geddes, of Onondaga county, Hon. Sterling G. Hadley, of Seneca county, Thomas Smith of Clyde, Wayne county, and Henry Stokes, of Cayuga county, be appointed to proceed at once to the Seneca river and examine, without expense to the state, and report upon the condition of the same; the crossings over it consisting of the New York Central railroad bridge (old route); the Seneca Towing-path bridge; the aqueduct; the New York Central railroad bridge (direct route), and such other obstructions as they may find to the full, free and natural flow of the water through the said Seneca river and the outlets of the Seneca lake, Crooked lake, the Cayuga lake, and the Canandaigua and Clyde rivers.

Said committee to report to the next legislature.

STATE OF NEW YORK,
In Assembly, *April* 29, 1873.

The foregoing resolution was duly passed.

By order of the assembly.

J. O'DONNELL,
Clerk.

STATE OF NEW YORK,
In Senate, *April* 21, 1873.

The foregoing resolution was duly passed.

By order of the senate.

CHAS. R. DAYTON,
Clerk.

CONCURRENT RESOLUTIONS directing the superintendent of the insurance department to expunge a certain portion of the report of his department for eighteen hundred and seventy-two.

WHEREAS, The assembly, after a full investigation as to the official conduct of George W. Miller, as superintendent of the insurance department, did, on the seventh day of May, eighteen hundred and seventy-two, pass a resolution that the said Miller be removed from that office, and send the same to the senate for its concurrence; and,

WHEREAS, The said Miller did, while said resolution was pending in the senate, and on the thirteenth day of May, eighteen hundred and seventy-two, resign his said office; and,

WHEREAS, It is required by law that the annual report of the insurance department shall be made by the first day of April, in each year, and the said Miller did make what purported to be the annual report of that department, on the first day of April of that year; nevertheless, he has, after his forced resignation, composed and been permitted by that department, to have printed and published, as a part of said annual report, matter that was not in fact a part of it; but which relates to proceedings that transpired after the making of said report, devoting over fifty printed pages thereof to an attempt to justify himself, and to personal attacks upon others, to a direct charge of intentional injustice perpetrated by the assembly, and avowed to be intended by the senate; to a charge that the speaker of the assembly permitted a man, who was seeking his removal, to control the appointment of the committee on insurance, and to succeed in "packing a committee to suit his purpose," and to a charge in the most offensive language against the integrity and intelligence of the committee on insurance; and,

WHEREAS, Such publication was wholly unauthorized and illegal, and it is believed to be untruthful and unjust; therefore,

Resolved (if the senate concur), That all of the matter introduced in said report, in relation to occurrences and proceedings after the first day of April, eighteen hundred and seventy-two, and printed therein, entitled "Thirteenth annual report of the superintendent of the insurance department, State of New York, part one, Life and Casualty Insurance," from page twenty to thirty-nine inclusive, under head of "Superintendent's Reports, part one, Life and Casualty Insurance," from pages twenty to thirty-nine inclusive," under head of "Superintendent's Reports, part one, Life Insurance," and appendix to same, under title of "Appendix Life Insurance," from page two hundred and ninety-two to three hundred and nine inclusive, be expunged from all such reports hereafter printed or circulated, and that no parts of said printed report thus expunged, or which relates to transactions after the first day of April, eighteen hundred and seventy-two, shall hereafter be published or distributed by the insurance department, or any officer of the state having charge thereof.

Resolved, That the several matters referred to in the preamble hereof relating to the legislature of eighteen hundred and seventy-two, or either branch thereof, or to any officer or committee thereof, are believed to be untrue, unjust, and, under any circumstances, in that report, and as to personal attacks upon individuals, are improper matter to appear as the report of a state officer.

Resolved, That these resolutions, with the preamble, be transmitted to the superintendent of the insurance department, and that he be instructed to print and publish the same in connection with his next annual report, and that a copy of the same be immediately printed by the superintendent, and pasted in the preface of "part two, Superintendent's Report, Life Insurance," one in each volume now published, and which may be hereafter circulated from the insurance department.

STATE OF NEW YORK,
In Assembly, *February* 5, 1873.

The foregoing resolution was duly passed.

By order of assembly.

J. O'DONNELL,
Clerk.

STATE OF NEW YORK,
In Senate, *April* 30, 1873.

The foregoing resolution was duly passed.
By order of the senate.
CHAS. R. DAYTON,
Clerk.

CONCURRENT RESOLUTION appointing a select committee to meet the committee of the senate of the United States on transportation routes to the seaboard on its visit to the city of New York.

WHEREAS, The senate of the United States, in conformity to the recommendation of the president, has appointed a select committee on "transportation routes to the seaboard," with power to sit during the recess of congress, and to investigate and report upon the subject of transportation between the interior and the seaboard; and,

WHEREAS, Said committee has decided upon the plan of investigation, which embraces inquiries regarding four great water routes from the western states to the Atlantic, of which that by the St. Lawrence river and that by the Erie canal are two; and,

WHEREAS, It is proper and desirable that full information relating to all the routes wholly or partially within the state of New York, should be furnished to said committee, the advantages of such routes as compared with the proposed routes from the Ohio and the Tennessee be properly set forth, and the interests generally of the state in this connection, be presented before said senate committee; therefore,

Resolved (if the senate concur), That a joint committee be appointed, consisting of five members of the senate and nine members of the assembly, to meet the committee of the senate of the United States on "transportation routes to the seaboard," on its visit to the city of New York, and to present to the attention of that committee such facts as may appear proper regarding the transportation routes to the seaboard, within, or partially within, the state of New York, and generally to represent before said senate committee the interests of this state, said joint committee to have power to act after the adjournment of the legislature, but without expense to the state.

STATE OF NEW YORK,
In Assembly, *May* 5, 1873.

The foregoing resolution was duly passed.
By order of the assembly.
JOHN O'DONNELL,
Clerk.

STATE OF NEW YORK,
In Senate, *May* 6, 1873.

The foregoing resolution was duly passed.
By order of the senate.
CHAS. R. DAYTON,
Clerk.

CONCURRENT RESOLUTION authorizing the governor to correspond with the president of the United States for the purchase of the war relics at the Watervliet arsenal.

Resolved (if the senate concur), That the governor be and is hereby authorized and requested to correspond with the president and other officers of the United States government, with reference to the alleged proposed sale of certain condemned pieces of ordnance now at the Watervliet arsenal, having historical interest and value, and to secure, by purchase or otherwise, such of them as he may think proper to be preserved by the state of New York, as trophies or relics of the war of independence, or of our foreign wars previous or subsequent thereto.

STATE OF NEW YORK,
In Assembly, *May* 13, 1873.

The foregoing resolution was duly passed.
By order.
JOHN O'DONNELL,
Clerk.

STATE OF NEW YORK,
In Senate, *May* 13, 1873.

The foregoing resolution was duly passed.
By order.
CHAS. R. DAYTON,
Clerk.

CONCURRENT RESOLUTION directing the secretary of state to cause the game laws now in force to be printed in pamphlet form.

Resolved (if the senate concur), That the secretary of state cause the game laws of this state, which are now in force, to be printed in pamphlet form in sufficient number to furnish each sheriff and game constable in the state with a copy, and cause the same to be distributed to them through the several county clerks.

STATE OF NEW YORK,
In Assembly, *May* 16, 1873.

The foregoing resolution was duly passed.
By order.

JOHN O'DONNELL,
Clerk.

STATE OF NEW YORK,
In Senate, *May* 16, 1873.

The foregoing resolution was duly passed.
By order.

CHAS. R. DAYTON,
Clerk.

CONCURRENT RESOLUTION proposing an amendment to article seven of the constitution.

Resolved (if the assembly concur), That sections three and six of article seven be amended as follows:

Section three to be amended by adding at the end of the section the following:

No extra compensation shall be made to any contractor, but if, from any unforeseen cause, the terms of any contract shall prove to be unjust and oppressive, the canal board may, upon the application of the contractor, cancel such contract.

§ 6. The legislature shall not sell, lease or otherwise dispose of the Erie canal, the Oswego canal, the Champlain canal, the Black River canal or the Cayuga and Seneca canal; but they shall remain the property of the state, and under its management forever. Hereafter the expenditures for collections, superintendence, ordinary or extraordinary repairs on the canals named in this section, shall not exceed, in any year, their gross receipts for the previous year. All funds that may be derived from any lease, sale or other disposition of any canal, shall be applied in payment of the debt for which the canal revenues are pledged.

That the following be added as sections thirteen and fourteen, in place of sections thirteen and fourteen of this article, which have been transferred and inserted as sections twenty-one and twenty-two of article three.

§ 13. The sinking funds provided for the payment of interest and the extinguishment of the principal of the debts of the state, shall be separately kept and safely invested, and neither of them shall be appropriated or used in any manner, other than for the specific purpose for which it shall have been provided.

§ 14. Neither the legislature, canal board, canal appraisers, nor any person or persons acting in behalf of the state, shall audit, allow, or pay any claim, which, as between citizens of the state, would be barred by lapse of time. The limitation of existing claims shall begin to run from the adoption of this section; but this provision shall not be construed to revive claims already barred by existing statutes, nor to repeal any statute fixing the time within which claims shall be presented or allowed, nor shall it extend to any claims duly presented within the time allowed by law, and prosecuted with due diligence from the time of such presentment. But if the claimant shall be under legal disability, the claim may be presented within two years after such disability is removed.

Resolved (if the assembly concur), That the foregoing amendment be referred to the legislature to be chosen at the next general election of senators, and that, in conformity to section one, article thirteen of the constitution, it be published for three months previous to the time of such election.

STATE OF NEW YORK,
In Senate, *May* 21, 1873.

The foregoing resolutions were duly passed.

By order.

CHAS. R. DAYTON,
Clerk.

STATE OF NEW YORK,
In Assembly, *May* 21, 1873.

The foregoing resolutions were duly passed.

By order.

J. O'DONNELL,
Clerk.

CONCURRENT RESOLUTION proposing an amendment to article twelve of the constitution.

Resolved (if the assembly concur), That article twelve of the constitution be amended so as to read as follows:

ARTICLE XII.

§ 1. Members of the legislature (and all officers, executive and judicial, except such inferior officers as shall be by law exempted), shall, before they enter upon the duties of their respective offices, take and subscribe the following oath or affirmation: "I do solemnly swear (or affirm) that I will support the constitution of the United States, and the constitution of the State of New York, and that I will faithfully discharge the duties of the office of , according to the best of my ability;" and all such officers who shall have been chosen at any election shall, before they enter on the duties of their respective offices, take and subscribe the oath or affirmation above prescribed, together with the following addition thereto, as part thereof: "And I do further solemnly swear (or affirm) that I have not directly or indirectly paid, offered or promised to pay, contributed or offered or promised to contribute, any money or other valuable thing as a consideration or reward for the giving or withholding a vote at the election at which I was elected to said office, and have not made any promise to influence the giving or withholding any such vote," and no other oath, declaration or test shall be required as a qualification for any office of public trust.

Resolved (if the assembly concur), That the foregoing amendment be referred to the legislature to be chosen at the next general election of senators, and that in conformity to section one of article thirteen of the constitution, it is published for three months previous to the time of said election.

STATE OF NEW YORK,
In Senate, *May* 21, 1873.

The foregoing resolutions were duly passed.

By order.
CHAS. R. DAYTON,
Clerk.

STATE OF NEW YORK,
In Assembly, *May* 22, 1873.

The foregoing resolutions were duly passed.

By order.
J. O'DONNELL,
Clerk.

CONCURRENT RESOLUTIONS proposing amendments to article six of the constitution.

Resolved (if the assembly concur), That section eighteen of article six of the constitution be amended so as to read as follows:

§ 18. The electors of the several towns shall, at their annual town meeting and in such a manner as the legislature may direct, elect justices of the peace, whose term of office shall be four years. In case of an election to fill a vacancy occurring before the expiration of a full term, they shall hold for the residue of the unexpired term. Their number and classification may be regulated by law. Justices of the peace and judges or justices of inferior courts, not of record, and their clerks, may be removed after due notice and an opportunity of being heard by such courts as may be prescribed by law for causes to be assigned in the order of removal. Judicial officers of courts not of record, in the several cities of the state having a population of not less than three hundred thousand, shall be appointed by the governor, with the consent of the senate, for the term of four years, and shall be subject to removal after due notice, and an opportunity of being heard, by such courts as may be prescribed by law, for causes to be assigned in the order of removal. All other judicial officers in cities, whose election or appointment is not otherwise provided for in this article, shall be chosen by the electors of cities or appointed by some local authorities thereof.

Resolved (if the assembly concur), That the foregoing amendment be referred to the legislature to be chosen at the next general election of senators, and that, in conformity to section one of article thirteen of the constitution, it be published for three months previous to time of such election.

STATE OF NEW YORK,
In Senate, *May* 21, 1873.

The foregoing resolutions were duly passed.

By order.

CHAS. R. DAYTON,
Clerk.

STATE OF NEW YORK,
In Assembly, *May* 22, 1873.

The foregoing resolutions were duly passed.

By order.

J. O'DONNELL,
Clerk.

CONCURRENT RESOLUTION proposing an amendment to article eight of the constitution.

Resolved (if the assembly concur), That article eight of the constitution be amended, by amending section four thereof, so as to read as follows:

§ 4. The legislature shall, by general law, conform all charters of savings banks, or institutions for savings, to a uniformity of powers, rights and liabilities, and all charters hereafter granted for such corporations shall be made to conform to such general law, and to such amendments as may be made thereto. And no such corporation shall have any capital stock, or shall be trustees thereof, or any of them have any interest whatever, direct or indirect, in the profits of such corporation; and no director or trustee of any such bank or institution shall be interested in any loan or use of any money or property of such bank or institution for savings. The legislature shall have no power to pass any act granting any special charter for banking purposes; but corporations or associations may be formed for such purposes under general laws.

And further, by adding thereto additional sections to be known as sections ten and eleven, as follows:

§ 10. Neither the credit nor the money of the state shall be given or loaned to or in aid of any association, corporation or private undertaking. This section shall not, however, prevent the legislature from making such provision for the education and support of the blind, the deaf and dumb, and juvenile delinquents, as to it may seem proper. Nor shall it apply to any fund or property now held or which may hereafter be held by the state for educational purposes.

§ 11. No county, city, town or village shall, hereafter, give any money or property, or loan its money or credit, to or in aid of any individual, association, or corporation, or become, directly or indirectly, the owner of stock in or bonds of any association or corporation, nor shall any such county, city, town or village be allowed to incur any indebtedness, except for county, city, town or village purposes. This section shall not prevent such county, city, town or village from making such provision for the aid and support of its poor as may be authorized by law.

Resolved (if the assembly concur), That the foregoing amendment be referred to the legislature to be chosen at the next general election of senators, and that, in conformity to section one of article thirteen of the constitution, it be published for three months previous to the time of such election.

STATE OF NEW YORK,
In Senate, *May* 21, 1873.

The foregoing resolutions were duly passed.
By order.

CHAS. R. DAYTON,
Clerk.

STATE OF NEW YORK,
In Assembly, *May* 22, 1873.

The foregoing resolutions were duly passed.
By order.

J. O'DONNELL,
Clerk.

CONCURRENT RESOLUTION proposing an amendment to article ten of the constitution.

Resolved (if the assembly concur), That article ten of the constitution be amended, by adding at the end thereof an additional section, as follows:

§ 9. No officer whose salary is fixed by the constitution shall receive any additional compensation. Each of the other state officers, named in the constitution, shall, during his continuance in office, receive a compensation, to be fixed by law, which shall not be increased or diminished during the term for which he shall have been elected or appointed; nor shall he receive to his use any fees or perquisites of office, or other compensation.

Resolved (if the assembly concur), That the foregoing amendments be referred to the legislature to be chosen at the next general election of senators, and that, in conformity to section one of article thirteen of the constitution, it be published for three months previous to the time of such election.

STATE OF NEW YORK,
In Senate, *May* 21, 1873.

The foregoing resolutions were duly passed.
By order.

CHAS. R. DAYTON,
Clerk.

STATE OF NEW YORK,
In Assembly, *May* 22, 1873.

The foregoing resolutions were duly passed.
By order.

J. O'DONNELL,
Clerk.

CONCURRENT RESOLUTION proposing amendments to article two of the constitution.

Resolved (if the assembly concur), That sections one and two of article two of the constitution be amended so as to read as follows:

§ 1. Every male citizen of the age of twenty-one years who shall have been a citizen for ten days and an inhabitant of this state one year next preceding an election, and for the last four months a resident of the county, and for the last thirty days a resident of the election district in which he may offer his vote, shall be entitled to vote at such election in the election district of which he shall at the time be a resident, and not elsewhere, for all officers that now are or hereafter may be elective by the people, and upon all questions which may be submitted to the vote of the people, provided that, in time of war, no elector in the actual military service of the state, or of the United States, in the army or navy thereof, shall be deprived of his vote by reason of his absence from such election district; and the legislature shall have the power to provide the manner in which and the time and place at which such absent electors may vote, and for the return and canvass of their votes in the election districts in which they respectively reside.

§ 2. No person who shall receive, expect or offer to receive, or pay, offer or promise to pay, contribute, offer or promise to contribute to another, to be paid or used, any money or other valuable thing as a compensation or reward for the giving or withholding a vote at an election, or who shall make any promise to influence the giving or withholding any such vote, or who shall make or become directly or indirectly interested in any bet or wager depending upon the result of any election, shall vote at such election; and upon challenge for such cause, the person so challenged, before the officers authorized for that purpose shall receive his vote, shall swear or affirm before such officers that he has not received or offered, does not expect to receive, has not paid, offered or promised to pay, contributed, offered or promised to contribute to another, to be paid or used, any money or other valuable thing as a compensation or reward for the giving or withholding a vote at such election, and has not made any promise to influence the giving or withholding of any such vote, nor made or become directly or indirectly interested in any bet or wager depending upon the result of such election. The legislature, at the session thereof next after the adoption of this section, shall, and from time to time thereafter may, enact laws excluding from the right of suffrage all persons convicted of bribery or of any infamous crime.

Resolved (if the assembly concur), That the foregoing amendment be referred to the legislature to be chosen at the next general election of senators, and that, in conformity to section one of article thirteen of the constitution, it be published for three months previous to the time of such election.

STATE OF NEW YORK,
In Senate, *May* 21, 1873.

The foregoing resolutions were duly passed.
By order.

CHAS. R. DAYTON,
Clerk.

STATE OF NEW YORK,
In Assembly, *May* 22, 1873.

The foregoing resolutions were duly passed.
By order

J. O'DONNELL,
Clerk.

CONCURRENT RESOLUTION authorizing the lieutenant-governor and speaker of the assembly to contract with F. B. Carpenter, of New York, for a full length portrait of Abraham Lincoln, for the governor's room.

Resolved (if the senate concur), That the lieutenant-governor and speaker of the assembly be and they are hereby authorized to contract with Mr. F. B. Carpenter, of New York city, for a whole length portrait of Abraham Lincoln, to be placed in the governor's room of the capitol, at an expense not to exceed the sum of three thousand dollars.

STATE OF NEW YORK,
In Assembly, *May* 9, 1873.

The foregoing resolution was duly passed.
By order.
JOHN O'DONNELL,
Clerk.

STATE OF NEW YORK,
In Senate, *May* 26, 1873.

The foregoing resolution was duly passed.
By order.
CHAS. R. DAYTON,
Clerk.

CONCURRENT RESOLUTIONS proposing an amendment to the constitution relative to funding the canal and general fund debts now charged on the canals.

Resolved (if the assembly concur), That the following amendment to the constitution be proposed for adoption to the people of the state, viz.:

Article . The commissioners of the canal fund shall borrow, on the credit of the state, such sums as may be necessary for paying the canal and general fund debts now charged on the canals, as the same shall fall due, by the issue and sale of bonds, or certificates of stock, having forty years to run from their date, bearing interest at the rate of five per cent per annum, payable semi-annually, for the payment of the principal whereof at maturity a sinking fund of one per cent per annum shall be established, and the tolls of the canals shall be fixed from time to time by the canal board at rates sufficing, as near as may be, to provide only for said sinking fund the interest on the debt so created, the expenses of collection, superintendence and keeping the canals in repair; and the contribution so created for said sinking fund shall be invested annually by the comptroller in the bonds or certificates of stock authorized by this article, or in the stocks or bonds of the state of New York or of the United States, which shall be held for the redemption and payment of the bonds or certificates herein authorized to be issued and sacredly applied to that purpose; all of said debt and interest shall be paid from the revenues of the canals, and no direct tax shall ever be levied or collected for canal purposes, either for current expenses or repairs, ordinary or extraordinary.

Resolved (if the assembly concur), That the foregoing amendment be referred to the legislature to be chosen at the next general election of senators, and that in conformity to section one of article thirteen of the constitution, it be published for three months previous to time of such election.

STATE OF NEW YORK,
In Senate, *May* 1, 1873.

The foregoing resolutions were duly passed.
By order of the senate.
CHAS. R. DAYTON,
Clerk.

STATE OF NEW YORK,
In Assembly, *May* 28, 1873.

The foregoing resolutions were duly passed.
By order of the assembly.
JOHN O'DONNELL,
Clerk.

CONCURRENT RESOLUTION proposing amendments to article three of the constitution.

Resolved (if the assembly concur), That sections one, four, five, six, seven and eight of article three of the constitution be amended so as to read as follows:

ARTICLE III.

SECTION 1. The legislative power of this state shall be vested in a senate and an assembly.

§ 4. An enumeration of the inhabitants of the state shall be made under the direction of the legislature, in the year one thousand eight hundred and seventy-five, and in every tenth year thereafter.

§ 5. The assembly shall consist of one hundred and twenty-eight members, elected for one year. The members of assembly shall be apportioned among the several counties of the state, by the legislature, as nearly as may be, according to the number of their respective inhabitants, excluding aliens, and shall be chosen by single districts. The assembly districts shall remain as at present organized, until after the enumeration of the inhabitants of the state, in the year eighteen hundred and seventy-five. The legislature, at its first session, after the return of every enumeration, shall apportion the members of assembly among the several counties of the state, in the manner aforesaid, and the board of supervisors in such counties as may be entitled under such apportionment, to more than one member, except the city and county of New York, and in said city and county the board of aldermen of said city shall assemble at such time as the legislature, making such apportionment, shall prescribe, and divide their respective counties into assembly districts, each of which districts shall consist of convenient and contiguous territory, equal to the number of members of assembly to which such counties shall be entitled, and shall cause to be filed in the offices of the secretary of state and the clerks of their respective counties, a description of such districts, specifying the number of each district and the population thereof, according to the last preceding enumeration, as near as can be ascertained, and the apportionment and districts shall remain unaltered until another enumeration shall be made as herein provided. No town shall be divided in the formation of assembly districts. Every county heretofore established and separately organized, except the county of Hamilton, shall always be entitled to one member of the assembly, and no new county shall be hereafter erected, unless its population shall entitle it to a member. The county of Hamilton shall elect with the county of Fulton, until the population of the county of Hamilton shall, according to the ratio, be entitled to a member. But the legislature may abolish the said county of Hamilton, and annex the territory thereof to some other county or counties. Nothing in this section shall prevent division at any time of counties and towns, and the erection of new towns and counties by the legislature.

§ 6. Each member of the legislature shall receive for his services an annual salary of one thousand five hundred dollars. The members of either house shall also receive the sum of one dollar for every ten miles they shall travel, in going to and returning from their place of meeting, once in each session, on the most usual route. Senators, when the senate alone is convened in extraordinary session, or when serving as members of the court for the trial of impeachments, and such members of the assembly, not exceeding nine in number, as shall be appointed managers of an impeachment, shall receive an additional allowance of ten dollars a day.

§ 7. No member of the legislature shall receive any civil appointment within this state, or the senate of the United States, from the governor, the governor and senate, or from the legislature, or from any city government during the time for which he shall have been elected; and all such appointments and such votes given for any such member, for any such office or appointment, shall be void.

§ 8. No person shall be eligible to the legislature, who, at the time of his election is, or within one hundred days previous thereto, has been a member of congress, a civil or military officer under the United States, or an officer under any city government. And if any person shall, after his election as a member of the legislature, be elected to congress, or appointed to any office, civil or military, under the government of the United States, or under any city government, his acceptance thereof shall vacate his seat.

And that the following additional sections be added to said article three of the constitution:

§ 17. No act shall be passed which shall provide that any existing law, or any part thereof, shall be made or deemed a part of said act, or which shall enact that any existing law, or any part thereof, shall be applicable, except by inserting it in such act.

§ 18. The legislature shall not pass a private or local bill in any of the following cases:

Changing the names of persons.

Laying out, opening, altering, working or discontinuing roads, highways or alleys, or for draining swamps or other low lands.

Locating or changing county seats.

Providing or changing of venue in civil or criminal cases.

Incorporating villages.

Providing for election of members of boards of supervisors.

Selecting, drawing, summoning or impaneling grand or petit jurors.

Regulating the interest on money.

The opening and conducting of elections or designating places of voting.

Creating, increasing or decreasing fees, percentage or allowances of public officers, during the term for which said officers are elected or appointed.

Granting to any corporation, association or individual, the right to lay down railroad tracks.

Granting to any private corporation, association or individual, any exclusive privilege, immunity or franchise whatever.

Providing for building bridges, and chartering companies for such purposes, except on the Hudson river, below Waterford, and on the East river, or over the waters forming a part of the boundaries of the state.

The legislature shall pass general laws providing for the cases enumerated in this section, and for all other cases which, in its judgment, may be provided for by general laws. But no law shall authorize the construction or operation of a street railroad, except upon the condition that the consent of the owners of one-half in value of the property bounded on, and the consent also of the local authorities having the control of that portion of a street or highway upon which it is proposed to construct or operate such railroad be first obtained, or in case the consent of such property owners cannot be obtained, the general term of the supreme court in the district in which it is proposed to be constructed, may, upon application, appoint three commissioners who shall determine, after a hearing of all parties interested, whether such railroad ought to be constructed or operated, and their determination, confirmed by the court, may be taken in lieu of the consent of the property owners.

§ 19. The legislature shall neither audit nor allow any private claim or account against the state, but may appropriate money to pay such claims as shall have been audited and allowed according to law.

§ 20. Every law which imposes, continues or revives a tax shall distinctly state the tax and the object to which it is to be applied, and it shall not be sufficient to refer to any other law to fix such tax or object.

§ 21. On the final passage, in either house of the legislature, of any act which imposes, continues or revives a tax or creates a debt or charge, or makes, continues or revives any appropriation of public or trust money or property, or releases, discharges or commutes any claim or demand of the state, the question shall be taken by yeas and nays, which shall be duly entered upon the journals, and three-fifths of all the members elected to either house shall, in all such cases, be necessary to constitute a quorum therein.

§ 22. There shall be in the several counties, except in cities whose boundaries are the same as those of the county, a board of supervisors, to be composed of such members, and elected in such manner, and for such period, as is, and may be, provided by law. In any such city the duties and powers of a board of supervisors may be devolved upon the common council or board of aldermen thereof.

Section seventeen of said article is hereby made section twenty-three of the proposed amendment, and is amended so as to read as follows:

§ 23. The legislature shall, by general laws, confer upon the boards of supervisors of the several counties of the state such further powers of local legislation and administration as the legislature may from time to time deem expedient.

§ 24. The legislature shall not, nor shall the common council of any city, nor any board of supervisors, grant any extra compensation to any public officer, servant, agent or contractor.

§ 25. Sections seventeen and eighteen of this article shall not apply to any bill or the amendments of any bill, which shall be reported to the legislature by commissioners, who have been appointed pursuant to law to revise the statutes.

Resolved (if the assembly concur), That the foregoing amendment be referred to the legislature to be chosen at the next general election of senators, and that, in conformity to section one of article thirteen of the constitution, it be published for three months previous to the time of such election.

STATE OF NEW YORK,
In Senate, *May* 29, 1873.

The foregoing resolutions were duly passed.

By order.

CHAS. R. DAYTON,
Clerk.

STATE OF NEW YORK,
In Assembly, *May* 29, 1873.

The foregoing resolutions were duly passed.

By order.

J. O'DONNELL,
Clerk.

CONCURRENT RESOLUTIONS proposing amendments to article four of the constitution.

Resolved (if the assembly concur), That sections one, two, four, eight and nine of article four of the constitution be amended so as to read as follows:

SECTION 1. The executive power shall be vested in a governor who shall hold his office for three years; a lieutenant-governor shall be chosen at the same time, and for the same term. The governor and the lieutenant-governor elected next preceding the time when this section shall take effect, shall hold office during the term for which they were elected.

§ 2. No person shall be eligible to the office of governor or lieutenant-governor, except a citizen of the United States, of the age of not less than thirty years, and who shall have been five years next preceding his election a resident of this state.

§ 4. The governor shall be commander-in chief of the military and naval forces of the state. He shall have power to convene the legislature (or the senate only) on extraordinary occasions. At extraordinary sessions no subject shall be acted upon, except such as the governor may recommend for consideration. He shall communicate by message to the legislature at every session the condition of the state, and recommend such matters to them as he shall judge expedient. He shall transact all necessary business with the officers of the government, civil and military. He shall expedite all such measures as may be resolved upon by the legislature, and shall take care that the laws are faithfully executed. He shall receive for his services an annual salary of ten thousand dollars, and there shall be provided for his use a suitable and furnished executive residence.

§ 8. The lieutenant-governor shall receive for his services an annual salary of five thousand dollars, and shall not receive or be entitled to any other compensation, fee or perquisite, for any duty or service he may be required to perform by the constitution or by law.

§ 9. Every bill which shall have passed the senate and assembly shall, before it becomes a law, be presented to the governor; if he approve, he shall sign it; but if not, he shall return it with his objections to the house in which it shall have originated, which shall enter the objections at large on the journal, and proceed to reconsider it. If, after such reconsideration, two-thirds of the members elected to that house shall agree to pass the bill, it shall be sent together with the objections to the other house, by which it shall likewise be reconsidered; and if approved by two-thirds of the members elected to that house, it shall become a law notwithstanding the objections of the governor. In all such cases, the votes in both houses shall be determined by the yeas and nays, and the names of the members voting shall be entered on the journal of each house respectively. If any bill shall not be returned by the governor within ten days (Sundays excepted) after it shall have been presented to him, the same shall be a law in like manner as if he had signed it, unless the legislature shall, by their adjournment, prevent its return; in which case it shall not become a law without the approval of the governor. No bill shall become a law after the final adjournment of the legislature, unless approved by the governor within thirty days after such adjournment. If any bill presented to the governor contain several items of appropriation of money, he may object to one or more of such items, while approving of the other portion of the bill. In such case, he shall append to the bill, at the time of signing it, a statement of the items to which he objects; and the appropriation so objected to shall not take effect. If the legislature be in session, he shall transmit to the house in which the bill originated a copy of such statement, and the items objected to shall be separately reconsidered. If, on reconsideration, one or more of such items be approved by two-thirds of the members elected to each house, the same shall be part of the law, notwithstanding the objections of the governor. All the provisions of this section, in relation to bills not approved by the governor, shall apply in cases in which he shall withhold his approval from any item or items contained in a bill appropriating money.

Resolved (if the assembly concur), That the foregoing amendment be referred to the legislature to be chosen at the next general election of senators, and that, in conformity to section one, article thirteen of the constitution, it be published for three months previous to the time of such election.

STATE OF NEW YORK.
In Senate, *May* 29, 1873.

The foregoing resolutions were duly passed.

By order.
CHAS. R. DAYTON,
Clerk.

STATE OF NEW YORK.
In Assembly, *May* 29, 1873.

The foregoing resolutions were duly passed.

By order.
J. O'DONNELL,
Clerk.

CONCURRENT RESOLUTIONS proposing amendments to article five of the constitution.

Resolved (if the assembly concur), That article five of the constitution be amended so as to read as follows:

§ 1. The comptroller and secretary of state shall be chosen at the same general election, and for the same term, as the governor. The persons holding the offices at the time when this section shall take effect shall continue to hold the same until the first day of January next succeeding the first election of comptroller and secretary of state, pursuant to the provisions hereof, and shall each receive a salary to be fixed by law, for such time as they may hold such offices beyond the term for which they shall have been elected.

§ 2. The attorney-general and state engineer and surveyor shall be appointed by the governor, with the consent of the senate, and hold their offices until the end of the term of the governor by whom they shall be nominated, and until their successors are appointed. No person shall be appointed state engineer and surveyor who is not a practical engineer.

§ 3. A superintendent of state prisons shall be appointed by the governor, with the consent of the senate, and hold his office for five years, unless sooner removed; he shall give security in such amount, and with such sureties, as shall be required by law for the faithful discharge of his duties; he shall have the superintendence, management and control of the state prisons, subject to such laws as now exist or may hereafter be enacted; he shall appoint the agents, wardens, physicians and chaplains of the prisons. The agent and warden of each prison shall appoint all other officers of such prison, except the clerk, subject to the approval of the same by the superintendent. The comptroller shall appoint the clerks of the prisons. The superintendent shall have all the powers and perform all the duties, not inconsistent herewith, which have heretofore been had and performed by the inspectors of state prisons; and from and after the time when such superintendent of state prisons shall have been appointed and qualified, the office of inspector of state prisons shall be and is hereby abolished. The governor may remove the superintendent for cause at any time, giving to him a copy of the charges against him, and an opportunity to be heard in his defense.

§ 4. The treasurer shall be chosen by the senate and assembly in joint ballot, and hold his office for three years, and until his successor shall be chosen and qualified. He shall, before entering upon the duties of his office, give such security as may be required by law. He may be suspended from office by the governor during the recess of the legislature, and until thirty days after the commencement of the next session of the legislature, whenever it shall appear to him that such treasurer has, in any particular, violated his duty. The governor shall appoint a competent person to discharge the duties of the office during such suspension of the treasurer.

§ 5. The lieutenant-governor, comptroller, secretary of state, attorney-general, treasurer and state engineer and surveyor shall be the commissioners of the land office. The office of the commissioner of the canal fund is abolished, and all the powers and duties heretofore had or performed by the commissioners of the canal fund shall hereafter be had and performed by the comptroller. The canal board shall consist of the lieutenant-governor, secretary of state, treasurer, attorney-general, state engineer and surveyor, and superintendent of public works.

§ 6. A superintendent of public works shall be appointed by the governor, with the consent of the senate, and to hold his office until the end of the term of the governor by whom he was nominated and until his successor is appointed. He shall receive for his services a compensation to be fixed by law. He shall be required by law to give security for the faithful execution of his office, before entering upon the duties thereof. He shall be charged with the execution of all laws relating to the repair and navigation of the canals; and also those relating to the construction and improvement of the canals, except so far as the execution of the laws relating to such construction or improvement shall be confided to the state engineer and surveyor. Subject to the control of the legislature, he shall make the rules and regulations for the navigation or use of the canals. He may be suspended or removed from office by the governor, whenever in his judgment the public interest shall so require; but in case of removal of such superintendent of public works from office, the governor shall file with the secretary of state a statement of the cause of such removal, and shall report such removal and the cause thereof, to the legislature at its next session.

§ 7. The superintendent of public works shall appoint not more than three assistant superintendents, whose duties shall be prescribed by him, subject to modification by the legislature, and who shall receive for their services a compensation to be fixed by law. They shall hold their office for three years, subject to suspension or removal by the superintendent of public works, whenever in his judgment the public interest shall so require. Any vacancy in the office of any such assistant superintendent shall be filled, for the remainder of the term for which he was appointed, by the superintendent of public works; but in case of the suspension or removal of any such assistant superintendent by him, he shall at once report to the governor, in writing, the cause of such removal. All other persons employed in the care and management of the canals, except collectors of tolls, and those in the department of the state engineer and surveyor, shall be appointed by the superintendent of public works, and be subject to suspension or removal by him.

§ 8. The office of canal commissioner is abolished from and after the appointment and qualification of the superintendent of public works, until which time the canal commissioners shall continue to discharge their duties as now provided by law. The superintendent of public works shall perform all the duties of the canal commissioners, and board of canal commissioners as now declared by law, until otherwise provided by the legislature.

§ 9. The governor, by and with the consent of the senate, shall have power to fill vacancies in the offices in this article named except as herein otherwise provided; or, if the senate be not in session, he may grant commissions, which shall expire at the end of the next succeeding session of the senate.

§ 10. The attorney-general, state engineer and surveyor and treasurer, in office at the time this article shall take effect, shall hold their offices until their successors are appointed.

§ 11. The powers and duties of the respective boards, and of the several officers in this article named, shall, except as herein otherwise provided, be such as now are or hereafter may be prescribed by law.

§ 12. All offices for the weighing, gauging, measuring, culling or inspecting any merchandise, produce, manufacture or commodity whatever, are hereby abolished, and no such office shall hereafter be created by law; but nothing in this section contained shall abrogate any office created for the purpose of protecting the public health or the interest of the state in its property, revenue, tolls or purchases, or of supplying the people with correct standards of weights and measures, or shall prevent the creation of any office for such purposes hereafter.

Resolved (if the assembly concur), That the foregoing amendment be referred to the legislature to be chosen at the next general election of senators, and that in conformity to section one of article thirteen of the constitution, it be published for three months previous to the time of such election.

STATE OF NEW YORK,
In Senate, *May* 29, 1873.

The foregoing resolutions were duly passed.
By order.

CHAS. R. DAYTON,
Clerk.

STATE OF NEW YORK,
In Assembly, *May* 29, 1873.

The foregoing resolutions were duly passed.
By order.

J. O'DONNELL,
Clerk.

CONCURRENT RESOLUTION proposing an amendment to the constitution by additional articles thereto, to be known as articles fifteen and sixteen.

Resolved (if the assembly concur), That the constitution of this state be amended by adding additional articles thereto, to be known as articles fifteen and sixteen, as follows:

ARTICLE XV.

SECTION 1. Any person holding office under the laws of this state, who, except in payment of his legal salary, fees or perquisites, shall receive or consent to receive, directly or indirectly, any thing of value or of personal advantage, or the promise thereof, for performing or omitting to perform any official act, or with the express or implied understanding that his official action or omission to act is to be in any degree influenced thereby, shall be deemed guilty of a felony. This section shall not affect the validity of any existing statutes in relation to the offense of bribery.

§ 2. Any person who shall offer or promise a bribe to an officer, if it shall be received, shall be deemed guilty of a felony and liable to punishment, except as herein provided. No person offering a bribe shall, upon any prosecution of the officer for receiving such bribe, be privileged from testifying in relation thereto, and he shall not be liable to civil or criminal prosecution therefor, if he shall testify to the giving or offering of such bribe. Any person who shall offer or promise a bribe, if it be rejected by the officer to whom it is tendered, shall be deemed guilty of an attempt to bribe, which is hereby declared to be a felony.

§ 3. Any person charged with receiving a bribe, or with offering or promising a bribe, shall be permitted to testify in his own behalf in any civil or criminal prosecution therefor.

§ 4. Any district attorney who shall fail faithfully to prosecute a person charged with the violation in his county of any provision of this article which may come to his knowledge, shall be removed from office by the governor, after due notice and an opportunity of being heard in his defense. The expenses which shall be incurred by any county, in investigating and prosecuting any charge of bribery, or attempting to bribe any person holding office under the laws of this state, within such county, or of receiving bribes by any such person in said county, shall be a charge against the state, and their payment by the state shall be provided for by law.

ARTICLE XVI.

Section 1. All amendments to the constitution shall be in force from and including the first day of January succeeding the election at which the same were adopted, except when otherwise provided by such amendments.

Resolved (if the assembly concur), That the foregoing amendment be referred to the legislature to be chosen at the next general election of senators, and that, in conformity to section one of article thirteen of the constitution, it be published for three months previous to the time of such election.

State of New York, }
In Senate, *May* 21, 1873. }

The foregoing resolutions were duly passed.

By order.

CHAS. R. DAYTON,
Clerk.

STATE OF NEW YORK,
In Assembly, *May* 29, 1873.

The foregoing resolutions were duly passed.
By order.

J. O'DONNELL,
Clerk.

CONCURRENT RESOLUTION directing the board of state commissioners of public charities to examine into the causes of the increase of crime, pauperism and insanity.

WHEREAS, It is well known that there is a vast increase of crime and pauperism in this state; and

WHEREAS, It is desirable to have statistics in concise form which shall show the various influences that are producing these effects; and

WHEREAS, It is important to the tax payers of the state that they be in possession of said information; therefore,

Resolved (if the senate concur), That the board of state commissioners of public charities be directed to examine into the causes of the increase of crime, pauperism and insanity, with power to examine the records of all public institutions, and institute inquiries; and for this purpose are authorized to employ such clerical aid as may be necessary for that purpose, and submit their report to the next legislature; and without additional expense to the state, except for services of a stenographer, who shall perform the duties of both stenographer and clerk at the usual compensation.

STATE OF NEW YORK,
In Assembly, *May* 27, 1873.

The foregoing resolutions were duly passed.
By order of the assembly.

JOHN O'DONNELL,
Clerk.

STATE OF NEW YORK,
In Senate, *May* 29, 1873.

The foregoing resolutions were duly passed.
By order of the senate.

CHAS. R. DAYTON,
Clerk.

CONCURRENT RESOLUTIONS in relation to the publication of the session laws.

Resolved (if the assembly concur), That the secretary of state be and he hereby is authorized to cause the session laws to be printed and published upon paper of the same size, and type similar to that of Edmonds' Statutes at large; and that such session laws be published in one volume, if it can be done without making it inconveniently bulky, and if published in two volumes, there be an index of the session laws in both volumes.

STATE OF NEW YORK,
In Senate, *January* 24, 1873.

The foregoing resolution was duly passed.
By order.

CHAS. R. DAYTON,
Clerk.

STATE OF NEW YORK,
In Assembly, *January* 31, 1873.

The foregoing resolutions were duly passed.
By order.

J. O'DONNELL,
Clerk.

CONCURRENT RESOLUTION for the appointment of a commission to inquire into the condition of the college land grant.

Resolved (if the assembly concur), That the governor be requested, and he is hereby authorized, to appoint three citizens of this state, as a commission to inquire into and ascertain the condition of the college land grant, so called, and that they particularly inquire into and ascertain:

First. Whether the act of congress, chapter one hundred and thirty, laws of eighteen hundred and sixty-two, and the act of the legislature of this state, chapter four* and sixty of the laws of eighteen hundred and sixty-three, have been complied with in the sale and disposition of college lands.

Second. Also to inquire into and ascertain what security or securities the state is obligated to receive for the sale of said lands; also, whether the state has the securities required by the aforesaid enactments, and whether securities other than those therein mentioned, can be taken or received by the state.

Third. That they inquire into and ascertain the quantity of land sold by Ezra Cornell under his contract with the state, of date August fourth, eighteen hundred and sixty-six, as well as a contract prior to that date, the prices for which he sold said lands, the amount received by him, the amount unpaid of the purchase-money, and how the payments of the same is secured, and how much of the purchase-money he has paid into the treasury of the state.

Fourth. Also to inquire into the value of certain timbered lands located in the states of Wisconsin, Minnesota and Kansas, said to contain about four hundred thousand acres, and

---

* So in the original.

whether said Cornell has made any contracts with any person or persons for the sale of said last-mentioned lands; if so, to whom, and the contract prices, and how such contract prices compare with the real value of the lands.

Fifth. That they also inquire into the amount of charges of said Ezra Cornell upon the sales of said lands (that is, the whole quantity embraced in his contract with the state), for the costs and expenses attending the location, management and sale of said lands, and the taxes assessed and paid thereon. Also whether such charges can, under the aforesaid act of congress, be lawfully deducted from the proceeds of sales.

Sixth. That they inquire into and ascertain whether agriculture and mechanic arts are the leading studies taught at Cornell University, or whether the leading object of said university is to teach branches of learning as are related to agriculture and the mechanic arts, as required by the fourth section of chapter one hundred and thirty of the laws of the congress of the United States, passed in eighteen hundred and sixty-two, and approved July two, eighteen hundred and sixty-two. Also to inquire into and report upon the present condition of said university in all its departments.

And, lastly, to inquire into all matters and things connected with said lands, the management and disposition thereof, their present situation and value, and report to the governor for transmission to the next legislature, with a recommendation what legislation is necessary to properly secure said funds in compliance with the act of congress, with power to send for persons and papers.

STATE OF NEW YORK,
In Senate, *May* 16, 1873.

The foregoing resolutions were duly passed.
By order.

CHAS. R. DAYTON,
Clerk.

STATE OF NEW YORK,
In Assembly, *May* 20, 1873.

The foregoing resolutions were duly passed.
By order.

JOHN O'DONNELL,
Clerk.

TITLES

OF ALL THE

LAWS OF THE STATE OF NEW YORK,

PASSED AT THE

NINETY-SEVENTH SESSION OF THE LEGISLATURE.

1874.

[The titles of the acts included in this compilation are in this list printed in italics.]

CHAP. 1. An Act to extend the time for the collection of city taxes in the city of Auburn. Passed January 16, 1874; three-fifths being present.

CHAP. 2. An Act to authorize the common council of the city of Utica to borrow and disburse money for city purposes, and to levy and collect taxes to pay the same. Passed January 29, 1874; three-fifths being present.

CHAP. 3. An Act amendatory of an act providing for the improvement of certain highways in the town of Watervliet. Passed January 30, 1874; three-fifths being present.

CHAP. 4. An Act to authorize the extension of the time for the collection of taxes in the several towns and certain cities of the state. Passed January 30, 1874; three-fifths being present.

CHAP. 5. An Act authorizing the board of supervisors of the county of Albany to issue bonds to pay a portion of the bonds of said county that will mature during the year eighteen hundred and seventy-four. Passed February 2, 1874; three-fifths being present.

CHAP. 6. An Act authorizing the commissioners of highways of the town of Russia, in the county of Herkimer, to build a bridge across the West Canada creek, at a place called the "Ledge." Passed February 3, 1874; three-fifths being present.

CHAP. 7. An Act for the relief of John George Milburn. Passed February 4, 1874.

CHAP. 8. An Act to authorize the city of Utica to borrow and disburse money to pay for fire apparatus and to levy and collect a tax to pay the same. Passed February 4, 1874; three-fifths being present.

CHAP. 9. *An Act to amend chapter seventy-four of the laws of eighteen hundred and seventy, in reference to the records of surrogates' courts. Passed February* 6, 1874.

CHAP. 10. An Act to amend the charter of the village of Lansingburgh. Passed February 9, 1874; three-fifths being present.

CHAP. 11. An Act to provide for the completion of the rebuilding of stone the combined wooden locks at Cohoes, Champlain canal. Passed February 10, 1874; three-fifths being present.

CHAP. 12. *An Act relating to animals. Passed February* 12, 1874; *three-fifths being present.*

CHAP. 13. An Act to amend an act entitled "An Act to incorporate the village of Spencerport, in the county of Monroe," passed April twenty-second, eighteen hundred and sixty-seven. Passed February 12, 1874; three-fifths being present.

CHAP. 14. An Act to release the interest of the people of the state of New York in certain real estate to Ann Smith, George Smith, and others, being the widow and heirs at law of Thomas Smith, deceased. Passed February 12, 1874, by a two-thirds vote.

CHAP. 15. *An Act to amend section ten of chapter two hundred and fifty-four of the laws of eighteen hundred and forty-seven, entitled "An act concerning the laws, journals and documents of the legislature." Passed February* 13, 1874; *three-fifths being present.*

CHAP. 16. An Act to authorize the town auditors of the town of Waterford to issue bonds for the completion of and furnishing the town hall at Waterford, and for the purchase of a bell and town clock. Passed February 13, 1874; three-fifths being present.

CHAP. 17. An Act to provide for the payment of the indebtedness of Amsterdam village, Montgomery county, in the state of New York, and to regulate the incurring of future liability by the board of trustees of said village. Passed February 14, 1874; three-fifths being present.

CHAP. 18. An Act to amend chapter four hundred and thirty-five of the laws of eighteen hundred and sixty-eight, entitled "An act to incorporate the village of Hamilton, in the town of Hamilton, in the county of Madison, and to repeal its present charter." Passed February 18, 1874; three-fifths being present.

CHAP. 19. An Act to confirm the official acts of Sidney P. Morse, a justice of the peace in and for the town of Friendship, Allegany county, and to enable him to take and file his oath of office. Passed February 19, 1874; three-fifths being present.

CHAP. 20. An Act authorizing Union Free School District Number One, of the town of Athens, to issue bonds and to borrow money for the purpose of erecting school buildings and purchasing a site. Passed February 20, 1874; three-fifths being present.

CHAP. 21. An Act to amend the charter of Hobart (late Geneva) College. Passed February 20, 1874; three-fifths being present.

CHAP. 22. *An Act to repeal chapter five hundred and ninety-eight of the laws of eighteen hundred and seventy-two, entitled "An act for the better preservation of horse records." Passed February* 20, 1874; *three-fifths being present.*

CHAP. 23. An Act to amend an act entitled "An act to establish communication between Richmond county and New Jersey, incorporating the Tubular Transit Company of Staten Island," passed June ninth, eighteen hundred and seventy-three. Passed February 20, 1874.

CHAP. 24. An Act to confirm the official acts of John Meredith Read, Jr., a commissioner of deeds for the state of New York, at Paris, in the Republic of France. Passed February 20, 1874.

CHAP. 25. An Act to authorize the trustees of "The Clyde High School" district, in the town of Galen, Wayne county, New York, to borrow money and issue bonds or certificates of indebtedness therefor, for the purpose of purchasing site and building and repairing school-house in said district, and furnishing the same. Passed February 20, 1874; three-fifths being present.

CHAP. 26. *An Act authorizing the formation of corporations to secure camp grounds, and other property connected therewith, for the use of the Methodist Episcopal Church. Passed February* 20, 1874; *three-fifths being present.*

CHAP. 27. An Act for the relief of Sarah Ann Whaites, formerly widow and devisee of John Playfair, deceased. Passed February 20, 1874, by a two-thirds vote.

CHAP. 28. An Act relative to the salary of the recorder of the city of Utica. Passed February 20, 1874; three-fifths being present.

CHAP. 29. An Act to authorize the city of Rochester to issue the last installment of its bonds in aid of the Rochester and State Line Railway Company in advance of the terms and conditions specified in the act entitled "An act to authorize the city of Rochester to issue its bonds in aid of the Rochester and State Line Railway, and to take bonds of that company therefor," passed April sixth, eighteen hundred and seventy-two. Passed February 24, 1874; three-fifths being present.

CHAP. 30. An Act to authorize the city of Rochester to levy a tax for the purpose of erecting and completing a public school building known as the "Genesee" school building, and also for furnishing the same, and the "Madison Park" school building. Passed February 26, 1874; three-fifths being present.

CHAP. 31. An Act to incorporate the McCoy fund. Passed February 26, 1874.

CHAP. 32. An Act to provide for a deficiency in moneys applicable to the repair and building of roads and bridges in the town of Geneva, for the year eighteen hundred and seventy-three; to legalize the acts of the commissioners of highways and the collector of said town, and for the relief of said commissioners. Passed February 26, 1874; three-fifths being present.

CHAP. 33. An Act to amend section one of chapter three hundred and eighty-one of the laws of eighteen hundred and seventy-three, entitled "An act for the preservation of fish in waters lying within or bordering upon the counties of Schuyler, Steuben, Chemung, Seneca, Yates and Ontario," passed May first, eighteen hundred and seventy-three. Passed February 27, 1874; three-fifths being present.

CHAP. 34. An Act to repeal an act entitled "An act to provide for the location and erection of a new city prison and place for holding certain courts in the city of New York," being chapter five hundred and thirty-five of the laws of eighteen hundred and seventy-three. Passed February 27, 1874; three-fifths being present.

CHAP. 35. *An Act to amend chapter three hundred and sixty-eight of the laws of eighteen hundred and sixty-five, entitled "An act for the incorporation of societies or clubs for certain social and recreative purposes." Passed February* 27, 1874.

CHAP. 36. An Act relative to the village of Ballston Spa, to provide for completing the water-works and paying all indebtedness incurred on account thereof. Passed February 27, 1874; three-fifths being present.

CHAP. 37. *An Act supplementary to an act entitled "An act to provide for the incorporation of religious societies," passed April fifth, eighteen hundred and thirteen, and the several acts amendatory thereof. Passed February* 27, 1874.

CHAP. 38. An Act for the disposition of excise moneys and fines for intoxication, within the village of Monticello. Passed February 27, 1874.

CHAP. 39. An Act to reorganize the village of Medina. Passed February 28, 1874; three-fifths being present.

CHAP. 40. An Act to incorporate the Citizens' Savings Bank of Hornellsville. Passed March 2, 1874.

CHAP. 41. An Act to amend an act entitled "An act to continue in force and amend chapter one hundred and thirty-eight of the laws of eighteen hundred and fifty-two, entitled 'An act to incorporate the firemen of the city of Utica, as a benevolent association,'" passed April tenth, eighteen hundred and seventy-three. Passed March 2, 1874; three-fifths being present.

CHAP. 42. An Act to amend chapter one hundred and twenty-one of laws of eighteen hundred and sixty-seven, entitled "An act authorizing the assessment of highway labor upon the Jeffersonville and Monticello turnpike road," passed March twenty-third, eighteen hundred and sixty-seven. Passed March 3, 1874; three-fifths being present.

CHAP. 43. An Act to confirm, reduce and levy a certain assessment in the city of Brooklyn. Passed March 3, 1874; three-fifths being present.

CHAP. 44. An Act to regulate the salaries of the president, trustees and other officers of the village of Dunkirk. Passed March 3, 1874; three-fifths being present.

CHAP. 45. An Act to amend an act entitled "An act to revise and consolidate the general acts relating to public instruction," passed May second, eighteen hundred and sixty-four, so far as relates to the school commissioner districts in and for the county of Steuben. Passed March 3, 1874.

CHAP. 46. An Act to authorize the board of education of Union Free School District Number One of the town of Ovid, in the county of Seneca, state of New York, to sell and convey a portion of the land occupied as a site for the school-house of said district. Passed March 5, 1874; three-fifths being present.

CHAP. 47. An Act to amend an act entitled "An act to amend and consolidate the several acts in relation to the charter of the city of Rochester," passed April eighth, eighteen hundred and sixty-one. Passed March 6, 1874; three-fifths being present.

CHAP. 48. An Act to authorize the common council of the city of Binghamton to erect a bell-tower over Academy street. Passed March 6, 1874; three-fifths being present.

CHAP. 49. *An Act ceding to the United States of America jurisdiction over certain lands in this state for light-house purposes, and exempting the same from taxation. Passed March* 6, 1874, *by a two-thirds vote.*

CHAP. 50. An Act to authorize the city of Binghamton to provide for the payment of the Ruloff reward and expenses. Passed March 6, 1874; three-fifths being present.

CHAP. 51. An Act to extend the time for the collection of taxes in the town of Hunter, in the county of Greene. Passed March 6, 1874; three-fifths being present.

CHAP. 52. *An Act authorizing county courts and courts of sessions to summon additional petit jurors, same as circuit courts of oyer and terminer. Passed March* 6, 1874; *three-fifths being present.*

CHAP. 53. *An Act to prevent persons from obtaining employment in positions of trust upon forged and false papers. Passed March* 6, 1874; *three-fifths being present.*

CHAP. 54. An Act to authorize the district attorney of Livingston county to discharge the duties of surrogate of said county, during the inability of the county judge and surrogate thereof, on account of sickness. Passed March 9, 1874; three-fifths being present.

CHAP. 55. An Act in relation to the Brooklyn Trust Company. Passed March 10, 1874.

CHAP. 56. An Act to amend chapter two hundred and seven of the laws of eighteen hundred and fifty-two, entitled "An act to incorporate the Cayuga Asylum for Destitute Children," passed April ten, eighteen hundred and fifty-two. Passed March 11, 1874; three-fifths being present.

CHAP. 57. An Act to empower the judges of the superior court of Buffalo to employ a stenographer. Passed March 11, 1874; three-fifths being present.

CHAP. 58. An Act to extend the time for the collection of taxes in the city of Oswego. Passed March 11, 1874; three-fifths being present.

CHAP. 59. An Act supplementary to chapter seventy-six of the laws of eighteen hundred and seventy-three, entitled "An act to define and establish the boundaries of school district number five of the town of Flushing, Queens county; to provide for the purchase of a new school-house site and erection of a new school-house thereon, and for the sale of the present school-house and site in said school district." Passed March 11, 1874; three-fifths being present.

CHAP. 60. An Act to regulate the fare upon the Gloversville and Kingsboro' Street Railroad, and the weight of rails to be used thereon. Passed March 11, 1874.

CHAP. 61. An Act granting certain rights and privileges to the Gloversville and Northville Railroad Company. Passed March 11, 1874; three-fifths being present.

CHAP. 62. An Act to provide for the election or appointment of a police justice in the village of Northville, Fulton county, and for other purposes in relation to the excise moneys in said village. Passed March 13, 1874; three-fifths being present.

CHAP. 63. An Act to amend an act entitled "An act to incorporate the village of Port Richmond, in the county of Richmond," passed April twenty-fourth, eighteen hundred and sixty-six, and the act amendatory thereof, passed April twenty-fifth, eighteen hundred and sixty-seven. Passed March 14, 1874; three-fifths being present.

CHAP. 64. *An Act to amend section one of chapter seven hundred and sixty-seven of the laws of eighteen hundred and seventy-two, entitled "An act to establish the compensation of county judges and surrogates, pursuant to the fifteenth section of the amended sixth article of the constitution." Passed March* 14, 1874; *three-fifths being present.*

CHAP. 65. An Act establishing a ferry from the farm of Clark P. Ives, of the county of Essex, across Lake Champlain. Passed March 17, 1874.

CHAP. 66. An Act extending the time in which the Canandaigua, Palmyra and Ontario Railway Company shall expend ten per cent of its capital in the construction of its road, and in which to finish the same and to put it in operation. Passed March 17, 1874.

CHAP. 67. An Act in relation to town meetings in the town of Cortland, in the county of Westchester. Passed March 17, 1874; three-fifths being present.

CHAP. 68. An Act to repeal part of chapter four hundred and ninety-five, relating to the building of a new bridge over Chambers' creek, and "making the present toll-bridge over Murderer's creek, in the town of New Windsor (in Orange county), free," passed May fifth, eighteen hundred and sixty-three, and for other purposes. Passed March 17, 1874; three-fifths being present.

CHAP. 69. An Act to amend an act entitled "An act to amend the Revised Statutes in relation to laying out public roads, and of public roads, and of the alteration thereof, in the town of Greenburgh," passed April fifteenth, eighteen hundred and fifty-four. Passed March 17, 1874; three-fifths being present.

CHAP. 70. An Act to authorize the election of town auditors, in the several towns of the county of Westchester, and to prescribe their powers and duties. Passed March 17, 1874; three-fifths being present.

CHAP. 71. An Act to amend an act passed April twenty-sixth, eighteen hundred and sixty-nine, entitled "An act for the election of a receiver of taxes and assessments for the town of Cortlandt and village of Peekskill." Passed March 17, 1874; three-fifths being present.

CHAP. 72. An Act authorizing and empowering the board of directors of the village of Saugerties, in the county of Ulster, to assess, levy and collect the sum of four thousand six hundred dollars, for the purpose of liquidating and discharging the indebtedness of said village. Passed March 18, 1874; three-fifths being present.

CHAP. 73. An Act to authorize the sale of certain lands and premises situate in the city of New York, belonging to Nehemiah Denton and his issue. Passed March 20, 1874; three-fifths being present.

CHAP. 74. An Act to authorize the city of Elmira to purchase lands for cemetery purposes and to issue the bonds of the city in payment thereof. Passed March 23, 1874; three-fifths being present.

CHAP. 75. An Act to extend the time for the collection of taxes in the counties of Livingston and Richmond. Passed March 24, 1874; three-fifths being present.

CHAP. 76 *An Act to amend an act entitled "An act to authorize corporations to change their names," passed April twenty-first, eighteen hundred and seventy. Passed March 24*, 1874.

CHAP. 77. An Act to authorize the commissioners of the town of Plainfield, in the county of Otsego, appointed under and by virtue of chapter three hundred and sixty-four of the laws of eighteen hundred and sixty-six, to issue bonds, and with the proceeds thereof to pay the bonds heretofore issued by said town under and by virtue of said act, and now due. Passed March 24, 1874; three-fifths being present.

CHAP. 78. *An Act to amend chapter two hundred and ninety-one of the laws of eighteen hundred and seventy, entitled "An act for the incorporation of villages." Passed March* 25, 1874; *three-fifths being present.*

CHAP. 79. An Act to legalize and confirm the proceedings of the annual town meeting of the town of Huntington, Suffolk county, held April first, one thousand eight hundred and seventy-three, authorizing the supervisors of said town to offer a certain reward, and to provide for the payment of the same. Passed March 25, 1874; three-fifths being present.

CHAP. 80. An Act to authorize a tax for fire purposes in the village of Greene, Chenango county. Passed March 25, 1874; three-fifths being present.

CHAP. 81. An Act to authorize the board of education of the city of Ogdensburg to borrow money for school purposes. Passed March 25, 1874; three-fifths being present.

CHAP. 82. An Act to repeal chapter five hundred and eighty-eight, laws of eighteen hundred and seventy-three, "An act to establish a commission in and for the city and county of New York, to be known and designated as the commission of charitable correction, and to define its powers and jurisdiction," passed May twenty-two, eighteen hundred and seventy-three. Passed March 25, 1874; three-fifths being present.

CHAP. 83. An Act to amend an act entitled "An act authorizing the town of Leicester, in the county of Livingston, to purchase additional land to enlarge their burying-ground near the village of Moscow," passed April twenty-seven, eighteen hundred and sixty-nine. Passed March 25, 1874; three-fifths being present.

CHAP. 84. An Act to extend the powers of the Ellenville Glass Works, and to authorize the said glass works to borrow money and to secure the same by a mortgage upon all their property, real and personal. Passed March 27, 1874; three-fifths being present.

CHAP. 85. An Act to consolidate the corporations known as the Congregation Anshi Chesed and the Temple Adas Jeshurun into one corporation, to be known as "The Temple Beth-El." Passed March 27, 1874.

CHAP. 86. An Act to incorporate The Butter and Cheese Exchange of New York. Passed March 27, 1874.

CHAP. 87. An Act to amend an act passed March twenty-eighth, eighteen hundred and sixty-eight, entitled "An act to amend the charter of the National Travelers' Insurance Company, and also to amend an act entitled 'An act to authorize the National Travelers' Insurance Company to effect insurance upon the lives of individuals,'" passed April ninth, eighteen hundred and sixty-seven. Passed March 27, 1874.

CHAP. 88. An Act to enable Long Island City to sell real estate. Passed March 27, 1874; three-fifths being present.

CHAP. 89. An Act to amend chapter seventy-one of the laws of eighteen hundred and seventy-four, entitled "An act to amend an act passed April twenty-sixth, eighteen hundred and sixty-nine, entitled 'An act for the election of a receiver of taxes and assessments for the town of Cortland and village of Peekskill.'" Passed March 27, 1874; three-fifths being present.

CHAP. 90. An Act relating to the court of general sessions in and for the city and county of New York. Passed March 27, 1874; three-fifths being present.

CHAP. 91. An Act for the protection of fish in Queechy lake, in Canaan, Columbia county. Passed March 27, 1874; three-fifths being present.

CHAP. 92. An Act to authorize the village of Jordan to borrow money upon its corporation notes or bonds; to purchase a steam fire-engine and necessary fire apparatus for the use of said village, and to levy and collect a tax for the payment of the same. Passed March 27, 1874; three-fifths being present.

CHAP. 93. An Act to extend the time for the collection of taxes in the town of Catskill, in the county of Greene. Passed March 27, 1874; three-fifths being present.

CHAP. 94. An Act to enable Maria Pauss, widow of Frederick Pauss, to take and hold real estate, and to release to her the interest and title to land escheated to the state. Passed March 27, 1874, by a two-thirds vote.

CHAP. 95. An Act to extend the time for the collection of taxes in the towns of North Hempstead and Oyster Bay, in the county of Queens. Passed March 27, 1874; three-fifths being present.

CHAP. 96. An Act to incorporate the Farmers and Mechanics' Savings Bank of the village of Medina, county of Orleans. Passed March 28, 1874.

CHAP. 97. An Act to authorize the change of the name of the "Sixpenny Savings Bank of the city of New York," to "The City Savings Bank of New York." Passed March 28, 1874; three-fifths being present.

CHAP. 98. An Act to amend "An act supplementary to and amendatory of an act in relation to a public park in the city of Albany," passed February sixteen, eighteen hundred and seventy-two, and the "Act in relation to the Washington park of the city of Albany," passed March eleven, eighteen hundred and seventy-three. Passed March 28, 1874; three-fifths being present.

CHAP. 99. An Act to amend an act entitled "An act to amend and consolidate the several acts relating to the public schools of the city of Auburn," passed March fourth, eighteen hundred and seventy-one. Passed March 31, 1874; three-fifths being present.

CHAP. 100. *An Act providing for the appointment of additional notaries public. Passed March 31, 1874; three-fifths being present.*

CHAP. 101. An Act in relation to the village of Hempstead, in the county of Queens. Passed March 31, 1874; three-fifths being present.

CHAP. 102. An Act to amend an act entitled "An act to provide for the appointment of commissioners of deeds in the village of Waterford." Passed March 31, 1874; three-fifths being present.

CHAP. 103. An Act to incorporate the Evangelical Lutheran Ministerium of the state of New York and adjacent states and countries. Passed March 31, 1874; three-fifths being present.

CHAP. 104. An Act to amend an act entitled "An act to establish a department of police in the city of Buffalo, and to provide for the government thereof," passed April twenty-six, eighteen hundred and seventy-one. Passed March 31, 1874; three-fifths being present.

CHAP. 105. An Act to amend an act entitled "An act to authorize the city and town of Binghamton, to purchase the two toll-bridges across the Susquehanna river at Binghamton, and to maintain them as free bridges," passed April fifteenth, eighteen hundred and sixty-nine. Passed March 31, 1874; three-fifths being present.

CHAP. 106. An Act to amend an act entitled "An act to authorize the trustees of the village of Kinderhook to borrow money, to be expended in the purchase of a lot of ground and the erection thereon of a suitable building, adapted to the purposes of a public hall, and a room for a fire-engine, for the use of said village," passed April twenty-ninth, eighteen hundred and seventy-three. Passed April 1, 1874; three-fifths being present.

CHAP. 107. An Act to amend the charter of the village of Potsdam. Passed April 2 1874; three-fifths being present.

CHAP. 108. An Act to authorize the canal commissioners to construct a bridge over the Erie canal at Austin street, in the city of Buffalo, and to provide for the payment thereof. Passed April 2, 1874; three-fifths being present.

CHAP. 109. An Act to release the right, title and interest of the people of the state of New York of, in and to certain real estate of which Anthony O'Carroll died seized, to Georgianna O'Carroll, his widow. Passed April 2, 1874, by a two-thirds vote.

CHAP. 110. An Act to confirm the official acts of John P. Bennett, as a notary public of Wayne county. Passed April 2, 1874; three-fifths being present.

CHAP. 111. An Act to confirm the official acts of Cicero W. Barber, as a notary public in and for the county of Washington, done from March thirtieth, eighteen hundred and seventy-three, to and including February eighteenth, eighteen hundred and seventy-four. Passed April 2, 1874; three-fifths being present.

CHAP. 112. An Act to authorize the board of supervisors of the county of Suffolk to erect a building for the offices of the county clerk and the surrogate of the said county, and to raise or borrow money for the same, and to provide for the payment thereof, and to remove the county clerk's office in said county to such building. Passed April 2, 1874; three-fifths being present.

CHAP. 113. An Act to amend chapter ninety of the laws of eighteen hundred and seventy-three, entitled "An act to provide for the election of town officers, and the transaction of town business, in the town of Greenburgh, in the county of Westchester," passed March eighteenth, eighteen hundred and seventy-three. Passed April 2, 1874; three-fifths being present.

CHAP. 114. An Act to amend an act entitled "An act to provide for the relief and support of the poor of the county of Kings, and to change the name of the office of the superintendents of the poor therein to the office of the commissioners of charities of the county of Kings," passed April fourteenth, eighteen hundred and seventy-one. Passed April 2, 1874; three-fifths being present.

CHAP. 115. An Act to authorize the common council of "the city of Albany" to borrow money for certain purposes, to issue obligations therefor, and to provide for the payment thereof. Passed April 2, 1874; three-fifths being present.

CHAP. 116. *An Act in relation to mendicant and vagrant children. Passed April* 3, 1874; *three-fifths being present.*

CHAP. 117. An Act to provide for the election and appointment of registers and inspectors of elections and poll clerks in Long Island City. Passed April 3, 1874; three-fifths being present.

CHAP. 118. An Act for the relief of the Plank Road Railroad Company, passed April twenty-first, eighteen hundred and sixty-six, and amended April twenty-fifth, eighteen hundred and seventy-one. Passed April 3, 1874; three-fifths being present.

CHAP. 119. An Act to increase the capital stock of the Jamaica and Brooklyn Plank-road Company. Passed April 3, 1874.

CHAP. 120. An Act to amend an act entitled "An act to amend and consolidate the several acts in relation to the charter of the city of Rochester," and the several acts amendatory thereof. Passed April 3, 1874; three-fifths being present.

CHAP. 121. An Act to incorporate the Western New York Conference of the Methodist Episcopal Church. Passed April 3, 1874; three-fifths being present.

CHAP. 122. An Act to provide for the payment of the salaries of the teachers and janitors formerly employed under the board of education of school district number one of the town of West Farms, as the same was constituted prior to the first day of January, eighteen hundred and seventy-four, and the other creditors of said board. Passed April 3, 1874; three-fifths being present.

CHAP. 123. An Act to amend the charter of Hudson Suspension Bridge and New England Railway Company. Passed April 4, 1874.

CHAP. 124. An Act for the relief of the "Peekskill Manufacturing Company." Passed April 4, 1874.

CHAP. 125. An Act to provide for the establishment of a system of graded schools in the village of Ithaca. Passed April 4, 1874; three-fifths being present.

CHAP. 126. *An Act to amend an act entitled "An act to authorize the business of banking," passed April eighteenth, eighteen hundred and thirty-eight. Passed April* 6, 1874.

CHAP. 127. *An Act to amend an act entitled "An act in relation to lands of which parties die seized," passed May twenty-first, eighteen hundred and seventy-three. Passed April* 6, 1874; *three-fifths being present.*

CHAP. 128. An Act to authorize the common council of the city of Binghamton to purchase lands for a cemetery and a public park in or outside of the limits of the city of Binghamton, and to lay out the same. Passed April 6, 1874; three-fifths being present.

CHAP. 129. An Act to legalize the acts of John H. Mattice, as justice of the peace of the town of Broome, in the county of Schoharie. Passed April 6, 1874; three-fifths being present.

CHAP. 130. An Act authorizing the supervisor of the town of Kiantone, in the county of Chautauqua, to convey to the Maple Grove Cemetery Association the lands now held by the said town, and used for cemetery purposes. Passed April 6, 1874; three-fifths being present.

CHAP. 131. An Act to ratify and confirm the proceedings to incorporate the religious society known as "The Rector, Churchwardens and Vestrymen of the Church of the Heavenly Rest," in the city and county of New York, and to legalize and confirm its acts. Passed April 6, 1874; three-fifths being present.

CHAP. 132. An Act to confirm and validate the agreement heretofore made between "The Society of the Church of the Puritans," and "The Second Presbyterian Church of Harlem," to become one organization. Passed April 7, 1874.

CHAP. 133. An Act to authorize the village of Albion to raise money by tax to complete the new village hall. Passed April 7, 1874; three-fifths being present.

CHAP. 134. An Act to provide for a lease of land to the Samaritan Home for the Aged of the city of New York. Passed April 8, 1874; three-fifths being present.

CHAP. 135. An Act to amend the charter of the village of Fairport, in the county of Monroe. Passed April 8, 1874; three-fifths being present.

CHAP. 136. An Act to incorporate "The Herkimer and Middleville Stone Road." Passed April 8, 1874.

CHAP. 137. An Act to authorize the laying out of public highways upon and across the Onondaga Indian Reservation, in the county of Onondaga. Passed April 8, 1874; three-fifths being present.

CHAP. 138. An Act to incorporate the fire department of the village of Saugerties. Passed April 8, 1874; three-fifths being present.

CHAP. 139. An Act to authorize the trustees of "The Bay Side Cemetery Association, of the town of Potsdam," to purchase and convey land formerly owned by Liberty Knowles, situate in the village and town of Potsdam, St. Lawrence county, and state of New York, and, also, other lands owned by Noble S. Elderkin, situate in the said village, and to remove the remains of bodies now interred therein. Passed April 8, 1874; three-fifths being present.

CHAP. 140. An Act to amend an act entitled "An act authorizing the construction of a bridge across the Hudson river, at the city of Troy," passed April twenty-third, eighteen hundred and seventy-two. Passed April 8, 1874; three-fifths being present.

CHAP. 141. An Act to amend the charter of the village of Little Falls, New York. Passed April 8, 1874; three-fifths being present.

CHAP. 142. An Act to extend the limits of Union Free School District, No. 1, of the town of Ovid, in the county of Seneca, and to dissolve school districts numbers three and four, in the town of Romulus, in said county. Passed April 9, 1874; three-fifths being present.

CHAP. 143. *An Act to authorize the formation of corporations for the erection and keeping of hotels. Passed April* 9, 1874.

CHAP. 144. An Act to regulate the sale of illuminating gas manufactured by the Equity Gas Light Company, of the eastern district of the city of Brooklyn, and to authorize the laying of mains and conductors in certain wards of said city. Passed April 9, 1874; three-fifths being present.

CHAP. 145. An Act legalizing the conveyance of the trustees of joint school district number nine, of the towns of Plattsburgh and Peru, Clinton county. Passed April 9, 1874; three-fifths being present.

CHAP. 146. An Act to facilitate the removal of the remains of bodies interred in ancient and disused burial plots in the town of Springwater, county of Livingston, and town of Canadice, in the county of Ontario. Passed April 9, 1874.

CHAP. 147. An Act to provide for the payment of the quota of state taxes imposed upon the city and county of New York. Passed April 9, 1874; three-fifths being present.

CHAP. 148. An Act to authorize the Oneonta Manufacturing Company, of Oneonta, Otsego county, New York, to issue preferred stock. Passed April 10, 1874; three-fifths being present.

CHAP. 149. *An Act to amend the act passed April twenty-seventh, eighteen hundred and seventy-two, entitled "An act to amend chapter six hundred and fifty-seven of the laws of eighteen hundred and seventy-one, entitled 'An act to amend the act passed February seventeen, eighteen hundred and forty-eight, entitled 'An act to authorize the formation of corporations for manufacturing, mining, mechanical or chemical purposes,'" passed April twentieth, eighteen hundred and seventy-one. Passed April* 10, 1874.

CHAP. 150. An Act to authorize the trustees of the First Presbyterian Church in Catlin, in the town of Dix, Schuyler county, state of New York, to remove the bodies buried in the burial ground belonging to said church, to the burial ground of the Moreland Cemetery-Association, and to empower said trustees to sell and convey the title of said burial ground, and the old church lot adjoining, after the bodies have been removed. Passed April 10, 1874.

CHAP. 151. An Act to release to Elizabeth Buerkel the real estate of which Henry Buerkel died seized. Passed April 10, 1874, by a two-thirds vote.

CHAP. 152. An Act to confirm the title of certain real estate in Esther Young, the widow of Joseph Young, late of the county of Clinton, an alien, deceased. Passed April 10, 1874, by a two-thirds vote.

CHAP. 153. An Act to release the interest of the people of the state of New York, in certain real estate in the town of Dunkirk, to Jane Errington. Passed April 10, 1874, by a two-thirds vote.

CHAP. 154. An Act to extend the time for the collection of taxes in the city of Elmira. Passed April 10, 1874; three-fifths being present.

CHAP. 155. An Act to legalize and confirm the official acts of Isaac Carpenter, a justice of the peace in the town of Shodack, in the county of Rensselaer, and to enable him to take and file his oath of office. Passed April 10, 1874; three-fifths being present.

CHAP. 156. *An Act in regard to serving citations upon minors and special guardians. Passed April* 10, 1874.

CHAP. 157. An Act to authorize the city of Rochester to levy a tax for the purpose of completing public school buildings. Passed April 10, 1874; three-fifths being present.

CHAP. 158. An Act to amend the charter of the village of Akron, in the county of Erie. Passed April 10, 1874; three-fifths being present.

CHAP. 159. An Act to legalize and confirm all laws, ordinances and resolutions heretofore passed by the common council of the city of Albany, and approved by the mayor thereof, directing or authorizing the constructing or building of any drain or sewer, together with the contracts made or entered into thereunder by said common council or the board of contract and apportionment of said city, to provide for the taking and acquiring of real estate and appurtenances for the purpose of constructing, building (or) maintaining any drain or sewer, built or to be built or constructed, assessing the damages and recompense of the owner or owners thereof, and for the apportionment and assessment of such damages and recompense, and expense of building and constructing such drain or sewer, with the incidental expenses attending the same, and for the enforcing and collecting of such apportionments and assessments. Passed April 10, 1874; three-fifths being present.

CHAP. 160. An Act to extend the time for the collection of taxes in the town of Wallkill in the county of New York.* Passed April 10, 1874; three-fifths being present.

CHAP. 161. An Act in relation to the Herkimer and Mohawk Street Railroad Company. Passed April 10, 1874; three-fifths being present.

CHAP. 162. An Act authorizing the Dry Dock Savings Institution of the city of New York to change its location. Passed April 11, 1874.

CHAP. 163. An Act for the relief of Thomas O'Brine. Passed April 11, 1874; three-fifths being present.

CHAP. 164. An Act to legalize and confirm a sale of real estate, by the supervisor and town clerk of the town of Jamaica, Queens county, Long Island, to Sally Ann Carpenter and her heirs and assigns. Passed April 11, 1874; three-fifths being present.

CHAP. 165. An Act to extend the time for the organization of the Mutual Trust Institution of the city of New York. Passed April 11, 1874.

*So in original.

CHAP. 166. An Act to incorporate the Maritime Association of the Port of New York. Passed April 11, 1874.

CHAP. 167. An Act to amend the charter of the Sunday School Union of the Methodist Episcopal Church, and the acts amendatory thereof Passed April 11, 1874.

CHAP. 168. An Act to amend chapter two hundred and thirty-five of the laws of eighteen hundred and sixty-seven, entitled "An act to amend an act entitled 'An act to consolidate road districts eighteen and nineteen, in the town of Ledyard, in the county of Cayuga, and to provide for the election of path-master in said district,'" providing for the appointment of an overseer of highways in said district. Passed April 11, 1874; three-fifths being present.

CHAP. 169. *An Act to amend chapter three hundred and ninety-five of the laws of eighteen hundred and seventy-three, entitled "An act to alter the system of repairing the highways," passed May second, eighteen hundred and seventy-three. Passed April 13, 1874; three-fifths being present.*

CHAP. 170. An Act to amend chapter five hundred and twenty-six of the laws of eighteen hundred and seventy-three, entitled "An act to incorporate the Monticello and White Lake Turnpike Company," passed May sixteenth, eighteen hundred and seventy-three. Passed April 13, 1874; three-fifths being present.

CHAP. 171. An Act to amend an act entitled "An act in relation to the city court of Yonkers," passed March eighth, eighteen hundred and seventy-three. Passed April 14, 1874; three-fifths being present.

CHAP. 172. *An Act to amend an act entitled "An act requiring canal superintendents to publish monthly abstracts of their official disbursements," passed March twenty-fifth, eighteen hundred and fifty-three. Passed March 14, 1874; three-fifths being present.*

CHAP. 173. *An Act to fix the time for transacting the business of the town at the annual town meeting for election of town officers. Passed April 14, 1874.*

CHAP. 174. An Act to enable the trustees of the village of Batavia, in the county of Genesee, in this state, to raise money by a special tax to pay the existing debt of said village. Passed April 14, 1874; three-fifths being present.

CHAP. 175. An Act to amend an act entitled "An act to amend and consolidate the charter of the village of Le Roy," passed April sixth, eighteen hundred and fifty-seven, and of the acts amendatory thereof. Passed April 14, 1874; three-fifths being present.

CHAP. 176. An Act to incorporate the Utica and Fair Ground Railroad Company. Passed April 14, 1874.

CHAP. 177. An Act to change the name of the village of Warren, in Rockland county, state of New York, to "Haverstraw." Passed April 14, 1874; three-fifths being present.

CHAP. 178. An Act to facilitate the construction of the New York and Canada Railroad, and re-appropriating certain moneys to aid in the construction of said road. Passed April 15, 1874; three-fifths being present.

CHAP. 179. An Act to improve Fourth street, in the city of Brooklyn. Passed April 15, 1874; three-fifths being present.

CHAP. 180. An Act to repeal an act entitled "An act to amend chapter six hundred and sixty-four, laws of eighteen hundred and sixty-seven, entitled 'An act to enable the supervisors of Montgomery county to refund illegal taxes,' passed April twenty-three, eighteen hundred and sixty-seven," passed May sixteenth, eighteen hundred and seventy-three. Passed April 15, 1874; three-fifths being present.

CHAP. 181. An Act to authorize the construction of a street railroad in the village of Catskill. Passed April 16, 1874.

CHAP. 182. An Act to establish the Evangelical Italian Orphans' Asylum. Passed April 16, 1874.

CHAP. 183. An Act to authorize the Buffalo Street Railroad Company to make certain contracts with the Buffalo East Side Railway Company. Passed April 16, 1874.

CHAP. 184. An Act to release the interest of the people of the state of New York in and to certain land situate in the town of Hamburg, Erie county, to George Irensterter Passed April 16, 1874, by a two-thirds vote.

CHAP. 185. An Act to authorize the board of supervisors of the county of Putnam to issue bonds to pay its indebtedness to the state. Passed April 16, 1874; three-fifths being present.

CHAP. 186. An Act for the relief of the president, directors and company of the Schoharie Kill Bridge Company. Passed April 16, 1874.

CHAP. 187. An Act supplementary to "An act to amend an act to incorporate the city of Ogdensburg, passed April twenty-seventh, eighteen hundred and sixty-eight, and the acts amending the same." Passed April 16, 1874; three-fifths being present.

CHAP. 188. An Act to provide a board of water commissioners for the village of Plattsburgh, and to prescribe and regulate their duties, and amend chapter two hundred and seventy-five of the laws of eighteen hundred and fifty-nine, relating to the incorporation of said village. Passed April 16, 1874; three-fifths being present.

CHAP. 189. *An Act to provide security against extraordinary conflagrations, and for the creation of safety funds by fire insurance companies. Passed April* 16, 1874; *three-fifths being present.*

CHAP. 190. An Act to legalize the action of the board of supervisors of Wayne county, designating persons to serve as grand jurors in said county, and for other purposes. Passed April 16, 1874; three-fifths being present.

CHAP. 191. An act to enable the commissioners of highways of the several towns through which the Mohawk turnpike passes to contract. Passed April 17, 1874; three-fifths being present.

CHAP. 192. An Act to amend the act entitled "An act in relation to the fees of the sheriff of the city and county of New York, and to the fees of referees in sales in partition cases," passed May fourth, eighteen hundred and sixty-nine. Passed April 17, 1874; three-fifths being present.

CHAP. 193. An Act to amend an act entitled "An act to revise and consolidate the laws in relation to the village of Ithaca in the county of Tompkins," passed April twenty-first, eighteen hundred and sixty-four. Passed April 17, 1874; three-fifths being present.

CHAP. 194. An Act to prevent extortion by gas companies in the counties of New York and Kings. Passed April 17, 1874.

CHAP. 195. An Act for the relief of Amariah Holbrook. Passed April 17, 1874; three-fifths being present.

CHAP. 196. An Act to incorporate the Orinoco Navigation Company. Passed April 17, 1874.

CHAP. 197. An Act in relation to the management of the bridge crossing the Mohawk river, between the city of Schenectady and town of Glenville, in the county of Schenectady. Passed April 18, 1874; three-fifths being present.

CHAP. 198. An Act to prevent encroachments and obstructions to the navigation of the water front of the city of Yonkers, and to authorize their removal and sale. Passed April 18, 1874; three-fifths being present.

CHAP. 199. An Act to amend and supplementary to chapter one hundred and ninety-nine of the laws of eighteen hundred and sixty-nine, entitled "An act to incorporate the village of Whitestone, in Queens county." Passed April 18, 1874; three-fifths being present.

CHAP. 200. An Act to authorize the appraisal and sale of leased fine salt lots, on the Onondaga salt springs reservation, by the commissioners of the land office. Passed April 18, 1874; three-fifths being present.

CHAP. 201. An Act to amend chapter one hundred and thirty-three of the laws of eighteen hundred and forty-seven, entitled "An act authorizing the incorporation of Rural Cemetery Associations," passed April twenty-seventh, eighteen hundred and forty-seven, so far as it applies to or affects "The United German and French Roman Catholic Cemetery Association of the city of Buffalo." Passed April 18, 1874; three-fifths being present.

CHAP. 202. An Act to amend an act entitled "An act to incorporate the city of Binghamton," passed April ninth, eighteen hundred and sixty-seven, and the several acts amending the same. Passed April 18, 1874; three-fifths being present.

CHAP. 203. An Act to amend an act entitled "An act to incorporate the city of Binghamton," passed April ninth, eighteen hundred and sixty-seven, and the several acts amending the same. Passed April 18, 1874; three-fifths being present.

CHAP. 204. An Act to provide for the erection of a school-house in school district number three of the town of Flatlands, in the county of Kings. Passed April 18, 1874; three-fifths being present.

CHAP. 205. An Act to authorize the village of Dunkirk to purchase certain real estate in said village, known as the "armory," for a city hall, and to issue the bonds of said village in payment thereof and for other purposes. Passed April 18, 1874; three-fifths being present.

CHAP. 206. An Act to incorporate the Seneca county Savings Bank of Waterloo, Seneca county, New York. Passed April 18, 1874.

CHAP. 207. *An Act to amend the Revised Statutes relating to embezzlements by clerks, servants, officers, agents and other persons. Passed April 18, 1874; three-fifths being present.*

CHAP. 208. *An Act to amend article two of title ten of chapter eight of part three of the Revised Statutes relating to summary proceedings to recover the possession of land. Passed April 18, 1874; three-fifths being present.*

CHAP. 209. *An Act to amend an act passed April eighteenth, eighteen hundred and fifty-nine, entitled "An act to extend the provisions of an act authorizing the imprisonment of persons convicted of certain crimes, in the counties of Montgomery and Oneida, in the Albany county penitentiary," passed April twelfth, eighteen hundred and fifty-eight, to all the counties in this state. Passed April 18, 1874; three-fifths being present.*

CHAP. 210. An Act to amend the charter of the village of Horseheads, Chemung county. Passed April 18, 1874; three-fifths being present.

CHAP. 211. An Act to authorize the city of Utica to provide a building for fire department purposes, and borrow and disburse money to pay for the same. Passed April 18, 1874; three-fifths being present.

CHAP. 212. *An Act to extend the time to complete the revision of the statutes by the commissioners appointed for that purpose. Passed April 18, 1874; three-fifths being present.*

CHAP. 213. An Act to amend chapter one hundred and sixty of the laws of eighteen hundred and seventy-four. Passed April 18, 1874; three-fifths being present.

CHAP. 214. *An Act making appropriations for the payment of the principal and interest on the canal debt for the fiscal year commencing on the first day of October, one thousand eight hundred and seventy-four, and to provide for the payment of the debt contracted under section twelve of article seven of the constitution. Passed April 20, 1874; three-fifths being present.*

CHAP. 215. An Act to amend the charter of the Tract Society of the Methodist church. Passed April 20, 1874.

CHAP. 216. An Act to incorporate the Albany County Savings Bank. Passed April 20, 1874.

CHAP. 217. An Act to enable the common council of the city of Yonkers to construct a police station-house. Passed April 20, 1874; three-fifths being present.

CHAP. 218. An Act to amend, revise and consolidate the laws in relation to the village of Seneca Falls, in the county of Seneca. Passed April 20, 1874; three-fifths being present.

CHAP. 219. An Act authorizing Erminda O. Goodwin to continue a ferry across Seneca lake. Passed April 21, 1874; three-fifths being present.

CHAP. 220. An Act to amend an act entitled "An act authorizing and providing for the election of a police justice and a police constable in the village of Addison, in the county of Steuben, and for the erection of a jail or lock-up therein," passed March second, eighteen hundred and sixty-eight. Passed April 1, 1874; three-fifths being present.

CHAP. 221. An Act to authorize the construction and use of a railroad from the Thirty-fourth street ferry to the Ninety-second street ferry, in Long Island City, and through certain streets and avenues in the fourth ward of said city. Passed April 21, 1874.

CHAP. 222. An Act to amend "An act to authorize the trustees of the village of Flushing to issue bonds and raise money for the purchase of a steam fire-engine, and for the mapping and establishment of lines and grades for the streets and public places in said village," passed April eighteenth, eighteen hundred and seventy-two. Passed April 21, 1874; three-fifths being present.

CHAP. 223. An Act for the removal of certain old burial grounds in the village of Amsterdam, Montgomery county. Passed April 21, 1874; three-fifths being present.

CHAP. 224. An Act to repeal chapter four hundred and forty of the laws of eighteen hundred and seventy-three, entitled "An act requiring commissioners of highways to act as inspectors of plank-roads and turnpikes," so far as the same relates to the counties of Clinton, Chenango, Seneca, Queens, Orange, Essex, Cayuga, Madison and Steuben. Passed April 21, 1874; three-fifths being present.

CHAP. 225. An Act in relation to the police court and police justice of the sixth police district of the city of New York. Passed April 21, 1874; three-fifths being present.

CHAP. 226. An Act in relation to the New York Institution for the Blind. Passed April 21, 1874; three-fifths being present.

CHAP. 227. An Act to provide for the purchase of a new school-house site and erection to a new school-house thereon, and for the sale of the present school-houses and sites in school district number two of the town of Kinderhook, county of Columbia. Passed April 21, 1874; three-fifths being present.

CHAP. 228. An Act to release the interest of the people of the state of New York in and to certain land situate in the city of Buffalo, to Gertrude Theile. Passed April 21, 1874, by a two-thirds vote.

CHAP. 229. An Act to confirm the official acts of Philander H. Wellman, a justice of the peace of the town of Harmony, in the county of Chautauqua. Passed April 21, 1874; three-fifths being present.

CHAP. 230. An Act to amend an act entitled "An act supplementary to the act entitled 'An act to incorporate the Hebrew Benevolent Society of the city of New York,' passed February second, eighteen hundred and thirty-two," passed April twelfth, eighteen hundred and sixty. Passed April 21, 1874.

CHAP. 231. An Act for the protection and preservation of fish in that portion of the Wallkill river in the counties of Ulster and Orange. Passed April 21, 1874; three-fifths being present.

CHAP. 232. An Act in relation to the superior court of Buffalo. Passed April 21, 1874; three-fifths being present.

CHAP. 233. An Act to authorize the corporate authorities of the village of Hornellsville to borrow money for purchasing a steam fire-engine and apparatus for the same, and to secure a supply of water therefor. Passed April 22, 1874; three-fifths being present.

CHAP. 234. An Act to amend an act entitled "An act for providing a site for an armory in the city of New York for the use of the seventh regiment of the national guard of the state of New York." Passed April 22, 1874; three-fifths being present.

CHAP. 235. An Act to authorize the town of Oswegatchie to raise money to build a bridge over the Oswegatchie river, above the mill-dam, in the city of Ogdensburg, appointing commissioners for that purpose and providing means for payment. Passed April 23, 1874; three-fifths being present.

CHAP. 236. An Act to incorporate the Metropolitan Safe Deposit Company of the city of New York. Passed April 23, 1874.

CHAP. 237. An Act to incorporate the Kingston Savings Bank. Passed April 23, 1874.

CHAP. 238. An Act to amend an act incorporating the village of Phœnix, in the county of Oswego. Passed April 23, 1874; three-fifths being present.

CHAP. 239. An Act to amend chapter three hundred and twenty of the laws of eighteen hundred and sixty, entitled "An act to incorporate the Schoharie Valley Stock Growers' Association." Passed April 23, 1874.

CHAP. 240. *An Act to further amend an act passed April twentieth, eighteen hundred and sixty-six, entitled "An act supplementary to the act entitled 'An act to authorize the formation of railroad corporations, and to regulate the same,'" passed April second, eighteen hundred and fifty. Passed April 23, 1874; three-fifths being present.*

CHAP. 241. An Act to authorize the Pennsylvania and Sodus Bay Railroad to construct a branch of its railroad from near Newfield, in the county of Tompkins, to a point at or near the state line at Waverly, in the county of Tioga. Passed April 23, 1874.

CHAP. 242. An Act to amend section two of chapter eight hundred and ninety of the laws of eighteen hundred and sixty-eight, entitled "An act to authorize Lewis Runyon to establish a ferry across the Seneca lake at Lodi Landing." Passed April 23, 1874; three-fifths being present.

CHAP. 243. An Act to enable John Shaw to take, hold, convey and transmit by descent or devise, real estate, and to release to him the interest of the state in certain lands. Passed April 24, 1874, by a two-thirds vote.

CHAP. 244. An Act to authorize the canal commissioners in charge of the middle division of the Erie canal to widen and deepen the Stroud, Chapman, Olcott and Douglass ditches, so called, in Cowasselon swamp, and to dig and construct such new ditches as may be necessary to drain said swamp and lowlands of the surplus waters of the Erie canal. Passed April 24, 1874; three-fifths being present.

CHAP. 245. *An Act to amend an act entitled "An act authorizing the incorporation of rural cemetery associations," passed April twenty-seventh, eighteen hundred and forty-seven, and the acts amendatory thereof. Passed April* 24, 1874; *three fifths being present.*

CHAP. 246. An Act relative to the powers of the Buffalo East Side Street Railway Company. Passed April 24, 1874.

CHAP. 247. An Act to provide for the maintenance of certain convicts in the penitentiaries of Onondaga and Kings counties. Passed April 24, 1874; three-fifths being present.

CHAP. 248. An Act to authorize the city of Rochester to issue the last three installments of its bonds in aid of the Rochester, Nunda and Pennsylvania Railroad Company in advance of the terms and conditions specified in the act entitled "An Act to authorize the city of Rochester to issue its bonds in aid of the Rochester, Nunda and Pennsylvania Railroad Company, and to take the bonds of the company therefor," passed April sixth, eighteen hundred and seventy-two. Passed April 24, 1874; three-fifths being present.

CHAP. 249. An Act in relation to the city of Troy and the charter thereof. Passed April 24, 1874; three-fifths being present.

CHAP. 250. An Act to legalize the acts and proceedings of the Union Village and Johnsonville Railroad Company, done in the name of the Greenwich and Johnsonville Railroad Company. Passed April 24, 1874.

CHAP. 251. An Act for the relief of "The Hebrew Benevolent and Orphan Asylum Society of the city of New York," and to authorize changes in conditions of leases to said society. Passed April 25, 1874; three-fifths being present.

CHAP. 252. An Act to provide for supplying the village of Owego, in the county of Tioga, with water. Passed April 25, 1874; three-fifths being present.

CHAP. 253. *An Act relative to the care and education of deaf-mutes. Passed April* 25, 1874.

CHAP. 254. An Act to authorize the Genesee and Water Street Railroad Company to extend its track in the city of Syracuse. Passed April 25, 1874.

CHAP. 255. An Act in relation to the Johnstown, Gloversville and Kingsboro Horse-Railroad Company, to regulate the weight of rails to be laid, the amount of fare to be charged, and to release the amount of capital stock requisite to authorize said company to acquire a right of way. Passed April 25, 1874; three-fifths being present.

CHAP. 256. An Act to amend an act entitled "An act to provide for laying out and improving roads and avenues in the village and town of Saratoga Springs," passed May fifth, eighteen hundred and seventy. Passed April 27, 1874; three-fifths being present.

CHAP. 257. An Act to amend the charter of the village of Saratoga Springs, so as to provide for the appointment of a superintendent of public works of the village of Saratoga Springs, and abolishing the office of superintendents of the village and of water-works of said village. Passed April 27, 1874; three-fifths being present.

CHAP. 258. *An Act to amend an act entitled "An act to authorize the sale of real estate, in which a widow is or shall be entitled to dower, in satisfaction and discharge thereof," passed May sixth, eighteen hundred and seventy. Passed April* 27, 1874; *three-fifths being present.*

CHAP. 259. An Act to extend the time for organization and the terms of office and powers of the incorporators and board of directors of the Troy, Lansingburgh and Cohoes Bridge Company, and to amend chapter three hundred and twenty-one of the laws of the state of New York, entitled "An act to incorporate the Troy, Lansingburgh and Cohoes Bridge Company, for the purpose of constructing and maintaining a bridge, appurtenances and approaches to the same, over the Hudson river, from some point on Van Schaick's Island, in the city of Cohoes, to some point in the village of Lansingburgh, south of Bolton's brewery, on said river," passed April twenty-third, eighteen hundred and seventy-two. Passed April 27, 1874; three-fifths being present.

CHAP. 260. *An Act to amend an act entitled "An act to extend the powers of boards of supervisors, except in the counties of New York and Kings," passed May eleventh, eighteen hundred and sixty-nine. Passed April* 27, 1874; *three-fifths being present.*

CHAP. 261. *An Act to amend an act entitled "An act to enable resident aliens to hold and convey real estate, and for other purposes," passed April thirty, eighteen hundred and forty-five. Passed April* 27, 1874, *by a two-thirds vote.*

CHAP. 262. *An Act for the further protection of private property. Passed April* 27, 1874; *three-fifths being present.*

CHAP. 263. An Act to amend an act entitled "An act in relation to the location and erection of public buildings for the use of Erie county and the city of Buffalo," passed April twenty-first, eighteen hundred and seventy-one. Passed April 27, 1874; three-fifths being present.

CHAP. 264. An Act to amend an act entitled "An act to open, lay out and improve Gravesend avenue, in the county of Kings, and to authorize the construction of a railroad thereon," passed May sixteenth, eighteen hundred and seventy-three. Passed April 27, 1874; three-fifths being present.

CHAP. 265. An Act to release the interest of the people of the state of New York in ceartin real estate to Lucelia Willis. Passed April 27, 1874, by a two-thirds vote.

CHAP. 266. An Act to extend the time for the exercise and discharge of the official duties, and for the completion of the work of the commissioners of streets, roads, avenues and parks in Long Island City. Passed April 27, 1874; three-fifths being present.

CHAP. 267. *An Act to amend an act entitled "An act concerning the proof of wills, executors and administrators, guardians and wards, and surrogates' courts," passed May sixteenth, one thousand eight hundred and thirty-seven. Passed April* 27, 1874; *three-fifths being present.*

CHAP. 268. *An Act for the promotion of rifle practice in the national guards. Passed April* 27, 1874; *three-fifths being present.*

CHAP. 269. An Act in relation to the improvement of Racket river. Passed April 28, 1874; three-fifths being present.

CHAP. 270. An Act for the improvement of Worth street and parts of the streets intersecting Worth street, between Broadway and Chatham street, in the city of New York. Passed April 28, 1874; three-fifths being present.

CHAP. 271. An Act to amend an act entitled "An act to authorize the construction of sewers in the village and town of Saratoga Springs." Passed April 28, 1874; three-fifths being present.

CHAP. 272. An Act to authorize the common council of the city of Oswego to borrow money, and to raise by tax upon the real and personal property of said city, in the year eighteen hundred and seventy-four, a sum sufficient to repay the same. Passed April 28, 1874; three-fifths being present.

CHAP. 273. An Act to enable the Edwin Forest Home, a corporation existing under the laws of Pennsylvania, to take, hold and convey real estate, and releasing to said corporation the interest of this state in certain lands. Passed April 28, 1874, by a two-thirds vote.

CHAP. 274. An Act to authorize the executors and trustees named in the will of Edwin Forest, deceased, to compromise with Catherine N. Forest, his widow, for her dower right in the whole estate of which the said Edwin Forest died seized. Passed April 28, 1874.

CHAP. 275. An Act supplementary to chapter eight hundred and eighty-five of the laws of eighteen hundred and seventy-two, entitled "An act to incorporate the Gilbert Elevated Railway Company, and to provide a feasible, safe and speedy system of transit through the city of New York," passed June seventeenth, eighteen hundred and seventy-two. Passed April 28, 1874.

CHAP. 276. An Act to lay out, open and grade Twenty-second avenue, in the towns of New Utrecht and Gravesend, in the county of Kings. Passed April 28, 1874; three-fifths being present.

CHAP. 277. An Act to close part of Tenth street, in Long Island City. Passed April 28, 1874; three-fifths being present.

CHAP. 278. *An Act to amend chapter two hundred and fifty-one of the laws of eighteen hundred and sixty-one, and to provide for the arbitration of mercantile disputes in the port of New York. Passed April* 29, 1874; *three-fifths being present.*

CHAP. 279. An Act in relation to the compensation for the consumption of gas, and lighting and maintaining street lamps, in such portion of the twenty-fourth ward of the city of New York, as formerly constituted the town of West Farms, Westchester county. Passed April 29, 1874; three-fifths being present.

CHAP. 280. An Act to amend the several acts in relation to the Industrial Exhibition Company, and to authorize the issuing of bonds for the purposes of its organization. Passed April 29, 1874; three-fifths being present.

CHAP. 281. An Act to amend an act entitled "An act to amend an act entitled 'An act to legalize the state and county taxes in the county of Rensselaer, for the year eighteen hundred and fifty-nine, and to provide for the collection thereof, and to authorize the sale of lands in the city of Troy for unpaid state and county taxes, passed April tenth, eighteen hundred and sixty,' and to provide for all lands returned for non-payment of taxes by collectors of the several towns in said county of Rensselaer, shall be sold by the county treasurer in the city of Troy, and be subject to redemption and conveyance," passed April second, eighteen hundred and sixty-six. Passed April 29, 1874; three-fifths being present.

CHAP. 282. An Act to release to Samuel McCracken the real estate of which Robert McCracken died seized, in the town of Lewiston, in the county of Niagara. Passed April 29, 1874, by a two-thirds vote.

CHAP. 283. An Act for the relief of Christian A. Nauert. Passed April 29, 1874; three-fifths being present.

CHAP. 284. An Act to authorize the town of Glenville, Schenectady county, to purchase the bridge belonging to the Schenectady Bridge Company. Passed April 29, 1874; three-fifths being present.

CHAP. 285. An Act in reference to the cemetery in the village of Herkimer. Passed April 29, 1874; three-fifths being present.

CHAP. 286. An Act to authorize the town of Clifton Park, Saratoga county, to purchase the bridge belonging to the Rexford Flats Bridge Company. Passed April 29, 1874; three-fifths being present.

CHAP. 287. An Act to provide for opening Front street, in Long Island City, Queens county. Passed April 29, 1874; three-fifths being present.

CHAP. 288. *An Act to incorporate societies for the improvement of poultry, small birds and domestic animals and fish culture. Passed April* 29, 1874.

CHAP. 289. An Act to release the interest of the state of New York in and to certain real estate of which George H. Hausen died seized or possessed. Passed April 29, 1874, by a two-thirds vote.

CHAP. 290. An Act requiring the town collector of the town of Poughkeepsie to publish the times and places at which he will attend to receive taxes. Passed April 29, 1874; three-fifths being present.

CHAP. 291. An Act to amend an act to revise, amend and consolidate the laws in relation to the village of Norwich, in the county of Chenango, passed March twenty-third, eighteen hundred and fifty-seven. Passed April 29, 1874; three-fifths being present.

CHAP. 292. An Act to amend an act entitled "An act to incorporate the Sag Harbor Wharf Company," passed April nineteenth, eighteen hundred and thirty-three. Passed April 29, 1874.

CHAP. 293. An Act to enable the supervisor of the town of East Hampton, Suffolk county, to purchase landing places for said town. Passed April 29, 1874; three-fifths being present.

CHAP. 294. An Act in relation to the Mohawk and Ilion Horse Railroad Company, in Herkimer county. Passed April 29, 1874.

CHAP. 295. An Act to release the right, title and interest of the people of the state of New York to John B. Thomas, in and to certain lands in the city of Rochester, of which Charlotte Thomas died seized. Passed April 29, 1874, by a two-thirds vote.

CHAP. 296. An Act to subject the real and personal property of the New York and Oswego Midland Railroad Company, to taxation, and to appropriate the amount of the county taxes thereon to certain town bonds. Passed April 29, 1874, by a two-thirds vote.

CHAP. 297. An Act releasing the interest of the people of the state of New York in certain real estate owned by John Kirkland, now deceased, in the town of Cicero, Onondaga county, to Adaline Kirkland, his widow. Passed April 29, 1874, by a two-thirds vote.

CHAP. 298. An Act to enable the clerk of Lewis county to discharge of record a certain mortgage. Passed April 30, 1874; three-fifths being present.

CHAP. 299. An Act making an appropriation to pay the expenses of the collection of tolls, superintendence, ordinary repairs and maintenance of the canals for the fiscal year commencing on the first day of October, one thousand eight hundred and seventy-four, and to supply deficiencies in former appropriations. Passed April 30, 1874; three-fifths being present.

Chap. 300. An Act to amend chapter three hundred and thirty-five of the laws of eighteen hundred and seventy-three, entitled "An act to reorganize the local government of the city of New York," passed April thirty, eighteen hundred and seventy-three, and the acts amendatory thereof. Passed April 30, 1874; three-fifths being present.

Chap. 301. An Act to extend the time for the collection of taxes in the county of Richmond. Passed April 30, 1874; three-fifths being present.

Chap. 302. An Act supplementary to an act, entitled "An act to provide an armory in the city of Brooklyn, county of Kings, for the use of the thirteenth regiment of the national guard of the state of New York," passed May sixteen, eighteen hundred and seventy-three. Passed April 30, 1874; three-fifths being present.

Chap. 303. An Act in relation to the estimates and apportionment for the support of the government of the county of New York. Passed April 30, 1874; three-fifths being present.

Chap. 304. An Act to consolidate the government of the city and county of New York, and further to regulate the same. Passed April 30, 1874; three-fifths being present.

Chap. 305. An Act explanatory of an act to consolidate the government of the city and county of New York, and further to regulate the same. Passed April 30, 1874; three-fifths being present.

Chap. 306. An Act to amend the charter of the Central Trust Company of New York. Passed April 30, 1874.

Chap. 307. An Act for the relief of the Greenwood and Coney Island Railroad Company in Kings county, and to authorize the extension of its tracks through certain streets and avenues in the city of Brooklyn. Passed May 1, 1874; three-fifths being present.

Chap. 308. An Act in relation to the estimates and apportionments for the support of the government of the city of New York. Passed May 1, 1874; three-fifths being present.

Chap. 309. An Act to amend an act entitled "An act to incorporate the United States Trust Company of New York," passed April twelfth, eighteen hundred and fifty-three and the act amendatory thereof, passed March thirty-first, eighteen hundred and sixty-three. Passed May 1, 1874.

Chap. 310. An Act to amend the charter of the village of Edgewater. Passed May 1, 1874; three-fifths being present.

Chap. 311. An Act to allow the New York and South Side Railroad Company of Long Island to purchase the South Side Railroad of Long Island, and its franchises. Passed May 1, 1874.

Chap. 312. An Act in relation to taxes and assessments in the city of New York, and the collection and vacation thereof. Passed May 2, 1874; three-fifths being present.

Chap. 313. An Act to amend an act entitled "An act in relation to certain local improvements in the city of New York," passed May seventh, eighteen hundred and seventy-two. Passed May 2, 1874; three-fifths being present.

Chap. 314. An Act to establish a board of police and fire commissioners of the city of Utica. Passed May 2, 1874; three-fifths being present.

Chap. 315. An Act to enable the mayor and common council of Long Island City to borrow money. Passed May 2, 1874; three-fifths being present.

Chap. 316. An Act to amend an act entitled "An act to incorporate the city of Cohoes," passed May nineteenth, eighteen hundred and sixty-nine. Passed May 2, 1874; three-fifths being present.

Chap. 317. An Act to amend an act entitled "An act to amend the charter of the village of Dunkirk," passed April twentieth, eighteen hundred and sixty-seven. Passed May 2, 1874; three-fifths being present.

Chap. 318. An Act to repeal chapter one hundred and eighty-two of the laws of eighteen hundred and seventy-two, entitled "An act to authorize the city of Rochester to issue its bonds in aid of the Lake Ontario Shore Railroad Company, and to take the bonds or stock of that company therefor." Passed May 2, 1874; three-fifths being present.

Chap. 319. An Act to amend an act entitled "An act to consolidate and amend the several acts relating to the village of Watkins, and to enlarge the powers of the corporation of said village," passed April third, eighteen hundred and sixty-one. Passed May 2, 1874; three-fifths being present.

Chap. 320. An Act to authorize the Geneva and Southwestern Railway Company to acquire title to certain real estate for the purposes of said railway. Passed May 2, 1874; three-fifths being present.

CHAP. 321. *An Act to amend section twenty-seven, title seventeen of chapter eight of part third of the Revised Statutes, entitled "General miscellaneous provisions concerning suits and proceedings in civil cases." Passed May 2, 1874; three-fifths being present.*

CHAP. 322. *An Act to amend chapter three hundred and seventy-nine of the laws of eighteen hundred and forty-eight, entitled "An act to simplify and abridge the practice, pleadings and proceedings of the courts of this state," passed April twelfth, eighteen hundred and forty-eight. Passed May 2, 1874.*

CHAP. 323. An Act making appropriations for certain expenses of government, and supplying deficiencies in former appropriations. Passed May 5, 1874; three-fifths being present.

CHAP. 324. *An Act relative to moneyed corporations, other than banks, institutions for savings and insurance companies. Passed May 5, 1874.*

CHAP. 325. An Act to incorporate the village of Bath-on-the-Hudson, Rensselaer county, New York. Passed May 5, 1874; three-fifths being present.

CHAP. 326. An Act to provide for improvements in and adjoining the first ward of Long Island City. Passed May 5, 1874; three-fifths being present.

CHAP. 327. An Act to suppress intemperance and to regulate the sale of intoxicating liquors in the county of Westchester. Passed May 6, 1874; three-fifths being present.

CHAP. 328. An Act authorizing the recording of a certain indenture made between Thomas Mesnard and Simon Schermerhorn of the city of New York. Passed May 6, 1874; three-fifths being present.

CHAP. 329. An Act to re-enact and amend an act entitled "An act to provide for the annexation of the towns of Morrisania, West Farms and Kingsbridge, in the county of Westchester, to the city and county of New York," passed May twenty-third, eighteen hundred and seventy-three. Passed May 6, 1874; three-fifths being present.

CHAP. 330. *An Act to provide for submitting amendments to the constitution to the electors of the state. Passed May 6, 1874; three-fifths being present.*

CHAP. 331. *An Act to amend an act entitled "An act to amend an act entitled 'An act to provide for the incorporation of fire insurance companies,' passed June twenty-fifth, eighteen hundred and fifty-three," passed April nineteenth, eighteen hundred and sixty-two. Passed May 6, 1874.*

CHAP. 332. An Act to amend the general plank-road law, and chapter four hundred and eighty-seven of the laws of eighteen hundred and fifty-one, relative to plank-roads in the town of Chesterfield, in the county of Essex, so far as it relates to plank-roads between the villages of Keeseville and Port Kent. Passed May 6, 1874; three-fifths being present.

CHAP. 333. An Act to incorporate the Cotton Exchange Trust Company. Passed May 6, 1874.

CHAP. 334. An Act to incorporate "The Home for Christian Care." Passed May 6, 1874; three-fifths being present.

CHAP. 335. An Act in relation to taxes in the city of Syracuse. Passed May 6, 1874; three-fifths being present.

CHAP. 336. An Act relating to the preservation of fish within the county of Cortland, state of New York. Passed May 6, 1874; three-fifths being present.

CHAP. 337. An Act to authorize the Corning, Cowanesque and Antrim Railway Company to extend their road and to acquire lands for the purpose of straightening their tracks. Passed May 6, 1874.

CHAP. 338. An Act to release the right, title and interest of the people of the state of New York in and to certain real estate, of which Dennis Minihan died seized, to Ellen Minihan, widow of said Dennis Minihan. Passed May 6, 1874, by a two-thirds vote.

CHAP. 339. An Act to legalize the acts of the commissioners of public works of the city of Rochester, and assessments made in pursuance thereof. Passed May 6, 1874; three-fifths being present.

CHAP. 340. *An Act to punish persons personating members of police in the several cities of the state. Passed May 6, 1874; three-fifths being present.*

CHAP. 341. An Act to authorize the county clerk of Erie county to sign the record of deeds, mortgages and other record of papers recorded in Erie county clerk's office, which were not signed by the former clerks of said county of Erie, and providing compensation for his services in that respect. Passed May 6, 1874; three-fifths being present.

CHAP. 342. An Act to authorize the railroad commissioners of the town of Unadilla, in the county of Otsego, to borrow money and issue bonds to redeem and pay the outstanding bonds of the said town. Passed May 6, 1874; three-fifths being present.

CHAP. 343. An Act to authorize the Cary Cemetery Association to acquire additional lands for cemetery purposes. Passed May 6, 1874.

CHAP. 344. An Act to legalize the official acts of William R. Tanner, as notary public. Passed May 6, 1874.

CHAP. 345. *An Act in regard to publishing the accounts of incorporated villages in this state. Passed May* 6, 1874; *three-fifths being present.*

CHAP. 346. An Act to confirm the title of certain lands in the town of Newtown, Long Island, to the Newtown Young Men's Christian Association, and to release any claim of the state therein. Passed May 7, 1874, by a two-thirds vote.

CHAP. 347. An Act to provide for the recording of certain deeds and mortgages in Queens county. Passed May 7, 1874; three-fifths being present.

CHAP. 348. An Act supplementary to an act entitled "An act to provide for the improvement of a certain highway in the town of Newtown, Queens county, and the city of Brooklyn, Kings county, and for the payment of property taken for such improvement," passed May seventeenth, eighteen hundred and seventy-two, and the acts amendatory thereof, passed May sixth, eighteen hundred and seventy-three. Passed May 7, 1874; three-fifths being present.

CHAP. 349. An Act to amend an act, entitled "An act to incorporate the New York Floating Dry Dock Company," passed April eighteenth, eighteen hundred and forty-three. Passed May 7, 1874.

CHAP. 350. An Act further to provide for the payment of certain certificates issued to the militia of the state, for services in the war of eighteen hundred and twelve. Passed May 7, 1874; three-fifths being present.

CHAP. 351. *An Act to amend chapter three hundred and twelve of the laws of eighteen hundred and fifty-nine, entitled "An act to equalize the state tax among the several counties in this state," and to amend chapter three hundred and twenty-seven of the laws of eighteen hundred and seventy-three, amendatory thereof. Passed May* 7, 1874; *three-fifths being present.*

CHAP. 352. An Act to amend an act entitled "An act relating to the preservation of speckled brook-trout within the counties of Tioga and Tompkins, state of New York," passed June twelfth, eighteen hundred and seventy-three. Passed May 7, 1874; three-fifths being present.

CHAP. 353. An Act to authorize the inhabitants of the village of Willink to vote on a question of a change of name. Passed May 7, 1874; three-fifths being present.

CHAP. 354. An Act authorizing the city of Albany to close a part of Exchange street, in said city. Passed May 7, 1874; three-fifths being present.

CHAP. 355. An Act to release the interest of the people of the state of New York, in certain real estate to Charles Durring. Passed May 7, 1874, by a two-thirds vote.

CHAP. 356. An Act in relation to the redemption of real estate sold for the non-payment of assessments in the city of Albany. Passed May 7, 1874; three-fifths being present.

CHAP. 357. An Act to amend chapter two hundred and forty-nine of the laws of eighteen hundred and sixty-four, entitled "An act to amend an act entitled 'An act to provide for the incorporation of villages,' passed December seventh, eighteen hundred and forty-seven, and the several acts amendatory thereof, so far as the same relates to the village of New Rochelle, in the county of Westchester." Passed May 7, 1874; three-fifths being present.

CHAP. 358. An Act to amend section six of chapter seventy-six of the laws of eighteen hundred and fifty, entitled "An act to revise and consolidate the laws in relation to the village of Whitehall," passed March sixteen, eighteen hundred and fifty. Passed May 7, 1874; three-fifths being present.

CHAP. 359. An Act to make further provisions for the audit and payment of the claims and expenses mentioned in chapter five hundred and eight of the laws of eighteen hundred and seventy-two, being the expenses of conducting civil and criminal suits and proceedings growing out of the frauds upon the treasury of the city and county of New York. Passed May 7, 1874; three-fifths being present.

CHAP. 360. An Act to authorize the paving of Bank street, between West street and Thirteenth avenue, in the city of New York, with Belgian or trap block pavement. Passed May 7, 1874; three-fifths being present.

CHAP. 361. An Act to enable the town of Hume, in the county of Allegany, to pay off its bonds before their maturity. Passed May 7, 1874; three-fifths being present.

CHAP. 362. An Act to authorize the village of Mount Vernon to take, hold and convey certain lands. Passed May 7, 1874; three-fifths being present.

CHAP. 363. An Act to amend an act entitled "An act to facilitate the construction of the New York and Oswego Midland Railroad," passed April fifth, one thousand eight hundred and sixty-six. Passed May 7, 1874; three-fifths being present.

CHAP. 364. An Act to authorize the town of Caldwell, in the county of Warren, to issue bonds to raise money to aid in building a court-house and other county buildings, and to provide for the payment thereof. Passed May 7, 1874; three-fifths being present.

CHAP. 365. An Act to regulate the quality, supply and price of illuminating gas in the city of Poughkeepsie, and for the protection of manufacturers and consumers thereof. Passed May 7, 1874; three-fifths being present.

CHAP. 366. An Act to confirm the election of officers for the village of Phelps, Ontario county. Passed May 7, 1874; three-fifths being present.

CHAP. 367. An Act to extend the time for the building and completion of the Watkins and Havana Street Railway. Passed May 7, 1874.

CHAP. 368. An Act to extend the time for the completion of the railroad of the North Shore Railroad Company. Passed May 7, 1874.

CHAP. 369. An Act to authorize the construction of a railroad in and through certain streets and avenues in the counties of Madison and Oneida. Passed May 7, 1874.

CHAP. 370. An Act to release the interest of the people of the state of New York in certain real estate owned by John McKay, now deceased, in the county of Genesee, to Agnes Spark and Robert McKay. Passed May 7, 1874, by a two-thirds vote.

CHAP. 371. An Act authorizing the supervisor of the town of Pitcher to receive, collect and use certain moneys belonging to said town. Passed May 7, 1874; three-fifths being present.

CHAP. 372. An Act to regulate fare on the Lansingburgh and Troy Steam Railroad. Passed May 7, 1874.

CHAP. 373. An Act requiring the board of supervisors of the county of Chenango to levy and assess upon the town of Pharsalia such sum, not exceeding three hundred dollars and interest thereon, as such town shall vote to be raised, to be paid to Charles D. Geer, a volunteer. Passed May 7, 1874; three-fifths being present.

CHAP. 374. An Act in relation to the Iroquois Agricultural Society. Passed May 8, 1874; three-fifths being present.

CHAP. 375. An Act to regulate the fare upon the Amsterdam Street Railroad, and the weight of rails to be used by them. Passed May 8, 1874.

CHAP. 376. An Act to amend "An act to revise, amend and consolidate the several acts in relation to the village of Salem, in the county of Washington," passed April seventeen, eighteen hundred and fifty-one, and the several acts amendatory thereof. Passed May 8, 1874; three-fifths being present.

CHAP. 377. An Act in relation to the Wallabout improvement in the city of Brooklyn. Passed May 8, 1874; three-fifths being present.

CHAP. 378. An Act to legalize and authorize the town of Westchester, in the county of Westchester, to raise money to alter and improve their fire-engine. Passed May 8, 1874; three-fifths being present.

CHAP. 379. An Act regulating the payment of accounts, by the county treasurer of the county of Rensselaer, audited by the board of supervisors of said county. Passed May 8, 1874; three-fifths being present.

CHAP. 380. An Act in relation to the High School in the city of Poughkeepsie. Passed May 8, 1874; three-fifths being present.

CHAP. 381. An Act to authorize the canal commissioners to construct a swing, hoist, or turn-table bridge over the Erie canal, on Salina street, in the city of Syracuse, and to use the materials of the old bridge in constructing a bridge over said canal, to connect University avenue, heretofore called Walnut street, with Canal street in said city. Passed May 8, 1874; three-fifths being present.

CHAP. 382. An Act to authorise the canal commissioners to construct a swing, hoist or turn-table bridge over the Oswego canal on Salina street, at its junction with Bridge street, in the city of Syracuse, and to use the materials of the old bridge in constructing a bridge over said canal to connect Danforth and Marsh streets in said city. Passed May 8, 1874; three-fifths being present.

CHAP. 383. An Act to amend an act entitled "An act to provide for the appointment of a police justice of the village of Saratoga Springs," passed May fourteenth, eighteen hundred and forty-five, and the acts amendatory thereof, passed March twenty-seventh, eighteen hundred and fifty-seven, and May sixth, eighteen hundred and sixty-eight. Passed May 8, 1874; three-fifths being present.

CHAP. 384. An Act to amend an act entitled "An act to incorporate the New York Coal Exchange, and to confer certain powers upon it." Passed June twelfth, eighteen hundred and seventy-three. Passed May 8, 1874.

CHAP. 385. An Act to authorize the Royalton Mountain Ridge Cemetery Association to purchase and convey certain lands in the town of Royalton, Niagara county. Passed May 8, 1874; three-fifths being present.

CHAP. 386. *An Act to amend an act entitled "An act to provide for the enrollment of the militia for the organization of the national guard of the state of New York, and for the public defense, and entitled the Military Code." Passed May 9, 1874; three-fifths being present.*

CHAP. 387. An Act relating to certain assessment proceedings in the city of Brooklyn, and providing for the payment of work done thereunder. Passed May 8, 1874; three-fifths being present.

CHAP. 388. An Act to incorporate the South American Trading Company. Passed May 9, 1874; three-fifths being present.

CHAP. 389. An Act to amend and supplementary to an act to incorporate the New York Eye Infirmary, passed March twenty-ninth, one thousand eight hundred and twenty-two, and the act amendatory thereof, passed April thirtieth, eighteen hundred and sixty-four. Passed May 9, 1874; three-fifths being present.

CHAP. 390. *An Act to amend an act entitled "An act to amend and consolidate the several acts relating to the preservation of moose, wild deer, birds and fish," passed April twenty-sixth, eighteen hundred and seventy-one. Passed May 9, 1874; three-fifths being present.*

CHAP. 391. An Act extending the time for collecting taxes in the village of Whitney's Point, in the county of Broome. Passed May 9, 1874; three-fifths being present.

CHAP. 392. An Act to reappropriate moneys for construction of new work upon and extraordinary repairs of the canals of this state, and for payments of awards made by the canal appraisers. Passed May 9, 1874; three-fifths being present.

CHAP. 393. An Act to extend the time to complete the organization of the Atlantic Guaranty and Trust Company. Passed May 9, 1874.

CHAP. 394. An Act to prevent the taking of fish from certain parts of the waters of the Esopus creek with any net, weir or trap of any kind, or set any trap, net, weir or pot in said part of the waters of the Esopus creek with intent to catch fish. Passed May 9, 1874; three-fifths being present.

CHAP. 395. An Act to amend an act entitled "An act to authorize the making and opening of a road or avenue from the intersection of the highway running east of Rockland lake, with the highway running from the lake to Rockland Lake Landing, in the county of Rockland, to intersect the highway running from upper Piermont to Orangeburg," passed April twenty-first, A. D. eighteen hundred and seventy-one, as amended and extended by an act entitled as above, and "to extend Highland avenue south to the state line," passed April twenty-fourth, A. D. eighteen hundred and seventy-two, and to enlarge, confirm and extend the powers of the commissioners appointed by said act for the laying out, opening and constructing of said avenue. Passed May 9, 1874; three-fifths being present.

CHAP. 396. An Act to release the interest of the people of the state of New York in and to certain land situate in the county of Queens to Alexander B. C. Cranston, and confirming certain conveyances made to him. Passed May 9, 1874, by a two-thirds vote.

CHAP. 397. An Act to release the interest of the people of the state of New York in certain real estate to John Waters and Catharine Waters. Passed May 9, 1874, by a two-thirds vote.

CHAP. 398. An Act to provide for the support of government and for other purposes. Passed May 9, 1874; three-fifths being present.

CHAP. 399. An Act to authorize a tax of seven-eighths of a mill per dollar of valuation of the year one thousand eight hundred and seventy-four, for the construction of new work upon and extraordinary repairs of the canals of this state. Passed May 9, 1874; three-fifths being present.

CHAP. 400. An Act to provide for the transmission of letters, parcels, packages, mails, messages, merchandise and property between the city of New York and the villages, towns and cities in the vicinity thereof. Passed May 9, 1874.

CHAP. 401. An Act to legalize the official acts of James H. Stevens, as notary public. Passed May 9, 1874; three-fifths being present.

CHAP. 402. An Act to confirm the official acts of Aikins Foster, as justice of the peace of the town of Colton, St. Lawrence county. Passed May 9, 1874.

CHAP. 403. An Act to confirm and validate the consolidation of the corporation known as the Congregation Bikur Cholim Ukadisha and the Congregation Chaari Zedek of New York, and incorporating the Chaari Zedek Cemetery Association. Passed May 9, 1874; three-fifths being present.

CHAP. 404. An Act to release the title and interest of the people of this state, in the real estate in this state, of which Mary Ann Reilly, late of the city of Buffalo, died seized or had an interest in at the time of her death. Passed May 9, 1874, by a two-thirds vote.

CHAP. 405. An Act in relation to the tolls upon the Western Plank-road Company's roads, in the counties of Franklin and Clinton. Passed May 9, 1874.

CHAP. 406. An Act to amend an act entitled "An act to authorize the lighting of public streets and avenues in the town of Fishkill, in the county of Dutchess," passed April ninth, eighteen hundred and seventy-three. Passed May 9, 1874; three-fifths being present.

CHAP. 407. An Act to legalize the acts of William H. Gardner, as notary public. Passed May 9, 1874.

CHAP. 408. An Act to legalize and confirm the official acts of Ira Tifft, as notary public, in the town of Stephentown, in the county of Rensselaer. Passed May 9, 1874.

CHAP. 409. *An Act to amend chapter four hundred and thirty-three of the laws of eighteen hundred and seventy-two, entitled "An act to amend chapter seven hundred and twenty-one of the laws of eighteen hundred and seventy-one, entitled 'An act to amend and consolidate the several acts relating to the preservation of moose, wild deer, birds and fish,' passed April twenty-sixth, eighteen hundred and seventy-one; also to repeal section thirty of said act," passed April twenty-ninth, eighteen hundred and seventy-two. Passed May 9, 1874; three-fifths being present.*

CHAP. 410. *An Act to authorize towns and villages to provide a sinking fund for the payment of their bonded indebtedness. Passed May 11, 1874; three-fifths being present.*

CHAP. 411. An Act to authorize the county of Essex to borrow money for the purpose of enlarging, repairing and improving its county poor-house, and to authorize the issue of bonds and provide for the payment thereof. Passed May 11, 1874; three-fifths being present.

CHAP. 412. An Act to confirm the election and proceedings of the trustees of Friends academy. Passed May 11, 1874.

CHAP. 413. An Act to authorize the trustees of the village of Jamestown to raise, by tax upon the village, a sum of money for the purpose of laying water-pipe in certain streets in said village. Passed May 11, 1874; three-fifths being present.

CHAP. 414. *An Act relating to the commitment of indigent and pauper insane persons to the State Homœopathic Asylum for Insane, at Middletown. Passed May 11, 1874; three-fifths being present.*

CHAP. 415. An Act to legalize the acts of Ralph Beach, junior, a justice of the peace of the county of Lewis. Passed May 11, 1874.

CHAP. 416. *An Act further to amend section six of chapter two hundred and eighty of the laws of eighteen hundred and forty-five, entitled "An act for the publication of the session laws in two newspapers in each county of this state," passed May fourteenth, eighteen hundred and forty-five. Passed May 11, 1874; three-fifths being present.*

CHAP. 417. An Act to provide ways and means for the support of government. Passed May 11, 1874; three-fifths being present.

CHAP. 418. An Act to provide for the building of a town house in the town of Bombay, in the county of Franklin. Passed May 11, 1874; three-fifths being present.

CHAP. 419. An Act to enable the town of Sardinia, Erie county, to raise money to build a town hall. Passed May 11, 1874; three-fifths being present.

CHAP. 420. An Act re-appropriating certain moneys for the improvement of the navigation of Peconic river, in the county of Suffolk. Passed May 11, 1874, by a two-thirds vote.

CHAP. 421. *An Act to secure the children to benefits of elementary education. Passed May* 11, 1874; *three-fifths being present.*

CHAP. 422. An Act to further amend the charter of the Union Theological Seminary in the city of New York. Passed May 11, 1874.

CHAP. 423. An Act to amend an act entitled "An act to incorporate the Union League Club, of the city of New York," passed February sixteenth, eighteen hundred and sixty-five, and the act amendatory thereof, passed March twenty-sixth, eighteen hundred and sixty-seven. Passed May 11, 1874.

CHAP. 424. An Act prohibiting the killing of quail within the counties of Orleans and Genesee, for the period of three years from the passage of said act. Passed May 11, 1874; three-fifths being present.

CHAP. 425. An Act to release and convey to Sarah E. Morel all the interest of the people of the state of New York, in certain real estate situate in the city of Brooklyn, county of Kings. Passed May 11, 1874, by a two-thirds vote.

CHAP. 426. An Act to provide for the care of the lands and buildings known as Washington's Head-quarters, in the city of Newburgh, and the property connected therewith. Passed May 11, 1874; three-fifths being present.

CHAP. 427. An Act to amend an act entitled "An act providing for the opening and improvement of new roads and avenues and closing old highways in the town of Flatbush, in Kings county," passed April nineteenth, eighteen hundred and seventy-one. Passed May 11, 1874.

CHAP. 428. An Act in relation to highways in the town of Flatbush, in Kings county. Passed May 11, 1874; three-fifths being present

CHAP. 429. An Act to amend an act entitled "An act to determine a plan of grades for certain streets and avenues in the town of New Utrecht," passed June twenty-eighth, eighteen hundred and seventy-three. Passed May 11, 1874; three-fifths being present.

CHAP. 430. *An Act to facilitate the reorganization of railroads sold under mortgage, and providing for the formation of new companies in such cases. Passed May* 11, 1874.

CHAP. 431. An Act to incorporate the Buenaventura and Cauca Valley Railroad Company. Passed May 11, 1874.

CHAP. 432. *An Act ceding jurisdiction over certain upland and sub-marine sites in the state of New York, for light-house purposes of the United States. Passed May* 11, 1874, *by a two-thirds vote.*

CHAP. 433. An Act relative to the Metropolitan Drawing-room Car Company. Passed May 11, 1874.

CHAP. 434. An Act to incorporate the Yonkers Ferry Company. Passed May 11, 1874.

CHAP. 435. An Act to amend an act entitled "An act to amend an act entitled 'An act to authorize the sale of lands for non-payment of taxes, and for the collection of unpaid taxes in the county of Westchester,' passed April sixteenth, eighteen hundred and sixty, and the acts amendatory thereof, passed March twenty-sixth, eighteen hundred and sixty-one, and May fifth, eighteen hundred and sixty-three, and April seventeenth, eighteen hundred and sixty-eight, so that all of said acts shall apply to the county of Richmond, as well as for the county of Westchester," passed April twenty-first, eighteen hundred and seventy. Passed May 11, 1874; three-fifths being present.

CHAP. 436. *An Act to regulate the practice of medicine and surgery in the state of New York. Passed May* 11, 1874.

CHAP. 437. *An Act in relation to publication of notices and publications. Passed May* 11, 1874; *three-fifths being present.*

CHAP. 438. An Act to authorize the Utica, Chenango and Cortland Railroad Company to extend their road, and for other purposes. Passed May 11, 1874.

CHAP. 439. An Act to authorize the sentencing of certain convicts and criminals convicted in Greene county, to hard labor and their employment at such labor. Passed May 11, 1874; three-fifths being present.

CHAP. 440. *An Act to declare the publication and dissemination of false news a crime, and to provide for its punishment. Passed May* 11, 1874; *three-fifths being present.*

CHAP. 441. An Act to incorporate the Rome Street Railroad Company in the city of Rome. Passed May 11, 1874.

CHAP. 442. An Act to enable the town of Amity, in the county of Allegany, to pay its railroad bonds before they become due. Passed May 11, 1874; three-fifths being present.

CHAP. 443. An Act to extend the time for beginning the construction of the road of New York and Highland Suspension Bridge Company. Passed May 11, 1874.

CHAP. 444. *An Act to create a board of excise in the several towns of this state. Passed May 4, 1874; three-fifths being present.*

CHAP. 445. An Act for the relief of the Nassau Drawing-room Car Company. Passed May 12, 1874.

CHAP. 446. *An Act to revise and consolidate the statutes of the state relating to the care and custody of the insane, the management of the asylums for their treatment and safe-keeping, and the duties of the state commissioner in lunacy. Passed May 12, 1874; three-fifths being present.*

CHAP. 447. An Act to further amend an act entitled "An act to incorporate the Real Estate Trust Company of the city of New York," passed April fourteenth, one thousand eight hundred and seventy-one, passed May twenty-first, one thousand eight hundred and seventy-two, passed May twenty-eighth, one thousand eight hundred and seventy-three. Passed May 12, 1874.

CHAP. 448. An Act for the relief of the Park Avenue Railroad Company in the city of Brooklyn, and to authorize the extension of its tracks through certain streets and avenues in said city. Passed May 12, 1874.

CHAP. 449. An Act to provide for the extension of Ocean avenue, in the county of Kings, to the Atlantic ocean. Passed May 12, 1874; three-fifths being present.

CHAP. 450. An Act to provide for the collection of money expended for the improvement of Gowanus canal in the city of Brooklyn, and to confirm certain assessments heretofore laid therefor. Passed May 12, 1874; three-fifths being present.

CHAP. 451. *An Act to amend the several acts in relation to state prisons. Passed May 12, 1874; three-fifths being present.*

CHAP. 452. An Act reappropriating certain moneys to the State Homœopathic Asylum for the Insane at Middletown, New York. Passed May 12, 1874; three-fifths being present.

CHAP. 453. An Act authorizing the town clerk of the town of Andes, in Delaware county, to call a special town meeting, and authorizing the voters of said town to decide by ballot, whether they will authorize the railroad commissioners of said town to sell and convey the town stock owned by said town in the Delhi and Middletown Railroad. Passed May 12, 1874; three-fifths being present.

CHAP. 454. An Act to authorize the board of supervisors of Erie county to regulate the publishing of election notices in said county. Passed May 12, 1874; three-fifths being present.

CHAP. 455. An Act to protect the fisheries of "Cross lake," in the county of Onondaga, state of New York; also of Clyde and Seneca rivers, in the counties of Wayne and Cayuga. Passed May 12, 1874; three-fifths being present.

CHAP. 456. *An Act enlarging the powers of clerks to surrogates' courts. Passed May 12, 1874; three-fifths being present.*

CHAP. 457. An Act to authorize the Westchester Villa Company to increase its capital stock. Passed May 12, 1874.

CHAP. 458. An Act relating to the police justice in the village of Charlotte, county of Monroe. Passed May 12, 1874; three-fifths being present.

CHAP. 459. An Act to authorize the Grand Trunk Railway Company of Canada to purchase and hold real estate in the city of Buffalo. Passed May 12, 1874; three-fifths being present.

CHAP. 460. An Act to amend an act entitled "An act in relation to jurors in the city and county of New York," passed May second, eighteen hundred and seventy. Passed May 13, 1874; three-fifths being present.

CHAP. 461. An Act in relation to the Croton aqueduct in the city of New York. Passed May 13, 1874.

CHAP. 462. An Act to authorize a tax of seven thirty-seconds of a mill per dollar of valuation for the payment of the awards of the canal appraisers and of the canal board, and to pay certain certificates of indebtedness on interest now outstanding. Passed May 13, 1874; three-fifths being present.

CHAP. 463 An Act to provide for the maintenance of prisoners sent to Monroe county penitentiary from the several towns and the city of Rochester, in the county of Monroe. Passed May 18, 1874; three-fifths being present.

CHAP. 464. *An Act to amend an act entitled "An act to provide for the support and care of state paupers," passed June seventh, eighteen hundred and seventy-three. Passed May* 18, 1874; *three-fifths being present.*

CHAP. 465. An Act providing for the purchase of a site for and the erection of a town hall in the town of Flatbush, in the county of Kings. Passed May 18, 1874; three-fifths being present.

CHAP. 466. An Act to amend an act entitled "An act in relation to the Firemen's Benevolent Association of Buffalo, and to regulate the number of trustees thereof," passed April thirteenth, eighteen hundred and sixty-nine. Passed May 18, 1874; three-fifths being present.

CHAP. 467. An Act to amend an act entitled "An act to incorporate the village of Port Richmond, in the county of Richmond," passed April twenty-fourth, eighteen hundred and sixty-six, and the act amendatory thereof, passed April twenty-fifth, eighteen hundred and sixty-seven. Passed May 18, 1874; three-fifths being present.

CHAP. 468. An Act to extend and continue and amend the act entitled "An act to create a special highway district in the town of Elizabethtown, Essex county," passed May twelfth, eighteen hundred and sixty-nine. Passed May 18, 1874; three-fifths being present.

CHAP. 469. *An act to amend the Revised Statutes, relating to guardians and wards. Passed May* 18, 1874.

CHAP. 470. *An Act to amend section nine, title three, chapter six, part two of the Revised Statutes. Passed May* 15, 1874; *three-fifths being present.*

CHAP. 471. *An Act to amend section twenty-eight, of article two, of title ten, of chapter eight, of part three of the Revised Statutes, in relation to summary proceedings to recover the possession of land. Passed May* 18, 1874.

CHAP. 472. An Act supplementary to and amending section three, chapter seven hundred and seventy-five, laws of eighteen hundred and seventy-three, being an act to authorize the town of Friendship, in the county of Allegany, to issue its bonds for the aid and benefit of Friendship Academy. Passed May 18, 1874; three-fifths being present.

CHAP. 473. An Act to amend an act entitled "An act to incorporate the city of Rome," passed February twenty-third, eighteen hundred and seventy. Passed May 18, 1874; three-fifths being present.

CHAP. 474. An Act to amend an act entitled "An act for the incorporation of villages," passed April twentieth, eighteen hundred and seventy, and the acts amendatory thereof, so far as the same relate to the village of Port Henry, in the county of Essex, and state of New York. Passed May 18, 1874; three-fifths being present.

CHAP. 475. An Act for the relief of the Glendale and East River Railroad Company. Passed May 19, 1874.

CHAP. 476. An Act in relation to the assessment for repaving Taylor street from Kent avenue to Wallabout basin, in the city of Brooklyn. Passed May 19, 1874; three-fifths being present.

CHAP. 477. An Act to amend an act entitled "An act for the improvement of First street and Franklin street in the city of Brooklyn," passed May twenty-first, eighteen hundred and seventy-two, and to improve Kent avenue. Passed May 19, 1874; three-fifths being present.

CHAP. 478. An Act to require the Eighth Avenue Railroad Company to extend its railroad route in the city of New York, and to regulate the use and operation of the railroad of said company. Passed May 19, 1874.

CHAP. 479. An Act to authorize the construction and use of a railroad in the city of Brooklyn and county of Kings, and the towns of Newtown and Jamaica in the county of Queens. Passed May 19, 1874; three-fifths being present.

CHAP. 480. An Act for the relief of certain hospitals and dispensaries in the city of Brooklyn. Passed May 19, 1874; three-fifths being present.

CHAP. 481. An Act to incorporate the Brooklyn Guaranty and Indemnity Company. Passed May 19, 1874; three-fifths being present.

CHAP. 482. An Act to amend the charter of the city of Rochester, and to extend its boundaries. Passed May 19, 1874; three-fifths being present.

CHAP. 483. An Act to authorize the city of Elmira to acquire, by purchase, lands for the purpose of widening the eastern approach to the Lake street bridge across the Chemung river, and to issue the bonds of the city in payment thereof. Passed May 20, 1874; three-fifths being present.

CHAP. 484. An Act to authorize the construction of a bridge over the Tioga river, in the town of Erwin, county of Steuben. Passed May 20, 1874; three-fifths being present.

CHAP. 485. An Act to amend an act entitled "An act to provide for the construction of a swing bridge over city ship canal in the city of Buffalo," passed May second, eighteen hundred and seventy-one. Passed May 20, 1874; three-fifths being present.

CHAP. 486. An Act to amend "An act to incorporate the United States Loan and Security Company." Passed May 20, 1874.

CHAP. 487. An Act to incorporate the Rosendale Savings Bank. Passed May 20, 1874.

CHAP. 488. An Act authorizing the establishment of a ferry across the Genesee river near Charlotteville, and incorporating a company for that purpose. Passed May 20, 1874; three-fifths being present.

CHAP. 489. An Act to amend an act passed April seventeenth, eighteen hundred and sixty-one, entitled "An act authorizing the establishment of the House of Refuge for Juvenile Delinquents in western New York." Passed May 20, 1874; three-fifths being present.

CHAP. 490. An Act to amend chapter five hundred and four of the laws of eighteen hundred and seventy-three, entitled "An act in relation to a certain highway in the county of Hamilton, appropriating certain non-resident highway moneys thereto, and repealing acts heretofore passed in relation thereto, passed May fourteenth, eighteen hundred and seventy-three." Passed May 20, 1874; three-fifths being present.

CHAP. 491. An Act to amend chapter one hundred and ninety-five of the laws of eighteen hundred and sixty-eight, entitled "An act to provide for the draining of certain swamp lands, in the town of New Rochelle, in the county of Westchester." Passed May 20, 1874; three-fifths being present.

CHAP. 492. An Act to incorporate The Home for the Friendless in northern New York. Passed May 20, 1874; three-fifths being present.

CHAP. 493. An Act to extend the time for the completion of the New York and Albany Railroad Company. Passed May 20, 1874.

CHAP. 494. An Act to amend an act entitled "An act to incorporate the city of Rome," passed February twenty-third, eighteen hundred and seventy. Passed May 20, 1874; three-fifths being present.

CHAP. 495. An Act in relation to certain assessments for sewers in the city of Brooklyn. Passed May 20, 1874; three-fifths being present.

CHAP. 496. An Act relative to filling in certain low lands in the city of Brooklyn. Passed May 20, 1874; three-fifths being present.

CHAP. 497. An Act to amend the charter of the city of Poughkeepsie, and to consolidate with it other acts relating to said city. Passed May 20, 1874; three-fifths being present.

CHAP. 498. An Act to legalize the acts of Coe Mullock, a justice of the peace of the county of Tioga. Passed May 20, 1874.*

CHAP. 499. An Act to incorporate the Farmers and Mechanics' Savings Bank of Palmyra. Passed May 20, 1874.

CHAP. 500. *An Act to amend chapter three hundred and fifty-eight of the laws of eighteen hundred and forty, entitled "An act concerning payment of interest by railroad companies on loans of the state credit, and for other purposes," passed May fourteenth, eighteen hundred and forty. Passed May* 20, 1874.

CHAP. 501. An Act to amend the charter of the Universal Life Insurance Company. Passed May 20, 1874.

*Certified by the presiding officer of the senate as having passed the senate; "three-fifths being present."

CHAP. 502 *An Act to amend chapter six hundred and ninety-six, laws of eighteen hundred and sixty-six, entitled "An act to amend section eighteen, article two, title two, chapter twelve, part one of the Revised Statutes, entitled 'Of the county treasurer,' and to require an additional bond from county treasurers to the state." Passed May* 20, 1874; *three-fifths being present.*

CHAP. 503. An Act changing the name of the "Beach Pneumatic Transit Company" to the "Broadway Underground Railway Company," and extending its powers. Passed May 20, 1874.

CHAP. 504. An Act in relation to the fees of stenographers in the district courts of the city of New York. Passed May 20, 1874.

CHAP. 505. An Act to provide for the construction and maintenance of four additional public baths in the city of New York. Passed May 20, 1874; three-fifths being present.

CHAP. 506. *An Act conferring certain powers on the Children's Fold, of the city of New York. Passed May* 20, 1874; *three-fifths being present.*

CHAP. 507. An Act for the relief of Isaac Orr, of the city of Brooklyn. Passed May 20, 1874; three-fifths being present.

CHAP. 508. An Act to authorize the construction of a railway from Vesey street, through certain streets in the city of New York, to the south ferry. Passed May 20, 1874.

CHAP. 509. An Act to authorize the board of supervisors of the county of Kings to borrow money for the purpose of paying certain bonds and certificates of indebtedness which mature in the year one thousand eight hundred and seventy-five, and to defray the county expenses between the first day of August in each year, and the confirmation of the tax levy. Passed May 20, 1874; three-fifths being present.

CHAP. 510. An Act to confirm the official acts of the highway commissioners of the town of Fine, St. Lawrence county. Passed May 20, 1874.

CHAP. 511. *An Act to amend chapter seven hundred and twenty-one, of the laws of eighteen hundred and seventy-one, entitled "An act to amend and consolidate the several acts relating to the preservation of moose, wild deer, birds and fish." Passed May* 20, 1874; *three-fifths being present.*

CHAP. 512. An Act in relation to the Ausable River Plank-road Company, and authorizing said company to lay rails upon its road. Passed May 21, 1874; three-fifths being present.

CHAP. 513. An Act in relation to school commissioners' districts and school commissioners in the county of Cayuga. Passed May 21, 1874; three-fifths being present.

CHAP. 514. *An Act to amend an act entitled "An act to revise and consolidate the general acts relating to public instruction," passed May second, eighteen hundred and sixty-four. Passed May* 21, 1874; *three-fifths being present.*

CHAP. 515. An Act to amend an act entitled "An act to reorganize the local government of the city of New York," passed April thirtieth, eighteen hundred and seventy-three. Passed May 21, 1874; three-fifths being present.

CHAP. 516. An Act to authorize the construction of a road owned by the state near Chazy lake to Chateaugay lake. Passed May 21, 1874; three-fifths being present.

CHAP. 517. An Act to authorize the city of Buffalo to issue its bonds for the purpose of perfecting the extended system of water supply to the city and its inhabitants. Passed May 21, 1874; three-fifths being present.

CHAP. 518. An Act to repeal an act entitled "An act to incorporate the Buffalo and Hamburg Turnpike Company," passed April thirteenth, eighteen hundred and twenty-six, and all acts in addition to and amendatory thereof. Passed May 21, 1874; three-fifths being present.

CHAP. 519. An Act authorizing the trustees of the Evangelical Lutheran Church of St. James, of Guilderland, to grant and convey a portion of their real estate for cemetery purposes. Passed May 21, 1874.*

CHAP. 520. An Act to incorporate "The Association of the Alumni of Columbia College." Passed May 21, 1874.

CHAP. 521. An Act to incorporate the St. John's Savings Bank of Fordham, of the city of New York. Passed May 21, 1874.

---

* Certified by the presiding officer of the assembly as having passed the assembly, "three-fifths being present."

CHAP. 522. An Act relating to the grade of that portion of Water street, in the city of Auburn, in front of the new armory in said city. Passed May 21, 1874; three-fifths being present.

CHAP. 523. An Act to increase the number comprising the board of education of the union free school district number one, of the town of Fort Edward, county of Washington. Passed May 21, 1874.

CHAP. 524. *An Act in relation to county treasurers. Passed May 21, 1874; three-fifths being present.*

CHAP. 525. An Act to provide for the incorporation of the New York State Grange of the Patrons of Husbandry, and councils and granges subordinate thereto. Passed May 21, 1874.

CHAP. 526. An Act to amend an act entitled "An act to incorporate the Anglo-Mexican Railway Company." Passed May 21, 1874.

CHAP. 527. An Act to authorize the city of Oswego to convey by deed a part of lot number ninety-seven, Van Buren tract, in said city. Passed May 21, 1874; three-fifths being present.

CHAP. 528, An Act in relation to free union school district number one of the town of Plattsburgh. Passed May 21, 1874; three-fifths being present.

CHAP. 529. An Act to provide increased facilities for the fire department in the town of New Lots, Kings county. Passed May 21, 1874; three-fifths being present.

CHAP. 530. An Act to provide for the opening, regulating and improving of Fulton avenue, in the town of New Lots, Kings county. Passed May 21, 1874; three-fifths being present.

CHAP. 531. An Act to amend an act entitled "An act to empower the board of water commissioners of the city of Buffalo, together with the common council of said city, to establish or designate public hydrants in said city, and providing for the appointment of water commissioners in said city," passed June twenty-fifth, eighteen hundred and seventy-three. Passed May 22, 1874; three-fifths being present.

CHAP. 532. *An Act to amend act chapter two hundred and seventy-six of the laws of eighteen hundred and sixty-four, entitled "An act in relation to the sale, use and disposition of butts, hogsheads, barrels, casks or kegs used by the manufacturers of malt liquors." Passed May 22, 1874; three-fifths being present.*

CHAP. 533. An Act authorizing the supervisor of the town of Poland, in the county of Chautauqua, to convey to the Levant Cemetery Association the lands now held by said town for said cemetery. Passed May 22, 1874.

CHAP. 534. An Act authorizing the supervisor of the town of Poland, in the county of Chautauqua, to convey to the Kennedy Cemetery Association the land now held by said town in the village of Kennedy and used for cemetery purposes. Passed May 22, 1874; three-fifths being present.

CHAP. 535. *An Act to amend chapter eight hundred and thirty-three of the laws of eighteen hundred and seventy-three, entitled "An act to regulate the fees of coroners." Passed May 22, 1874; three-fifths being present.*

CHAP. 536. An Act to amend the charter of the village of Weedsport, in the county of Cayuga. Passed May 22, 1874; three-fifths being present.

CHAP. 537. An Act to repeal an act passed May eleventh, eighteen hundred and seventy-two, entitled "An act to amend an act entitled 'An act to provide for the drainage of swamp, bog and other low and wet lands in the village of White Plains, and adjacent thereto,' passed May second, eighteen hundred and seventy-one," so far as the same relates to that portion of the town of Greenburgh lying without the limits of the village of White Plains. Passed May 22, 1874; three-fifths being present.

CHAP. 538. An Act to amend an act entitled "An act in relation to the keeping open of certain public offices in the county of Kings," passed June twenty-eighth, eighteen hundred and seventy-three. Passed May 22, 1874; three-fifths being present.

CHAP. 539. An Act to incorporate the state council of the Order of United American Mechanics of the state of New York. Passed May 22, 1874.

CHAP. 540. An Act to amend "An act to provide for supplying the village of Flushing, Queens county, with pure and wholesome water," passed February fifteenth, eighteen hundred and seventy-two. Passed May 22, 1874; three-fifths being present.

CHAP. 541. An Act to amend an act entitled "An act in relation to the location and erection of public buildings for the use of the city of Rochester," passed April twelfth, eighteen hundred and seventy-two. Passed May 22, 1874; three-fifths being present.

CHAP. 542. An Act to amend an act entitled "An act to revise the charter of the city of Buffalo," passed April twenty-eighth, eighteen hundred and seventy, as amended January twelfth, eighteen hundred and seventy-two. Passed May 22, 1874; three-fifths being present.

CHAP. 543. *An Act to amend chapter eleven, part one, title three, article three, section thirty-one of the Revised Statutes. Passed May 22, 1874; three-fifths being present.*

CHAP. 544. An Act to authorize the election of town auditors in the town of Saratoga Springs in the county of Saratoga, and to prescribe their powers and duties. Passed May 22, 1874; three-fifths being present.

CHAP. 545. An Act in relation to the marine court of the city of New York. Passed May 22, 1874; three-fifths being present.

CHAP. 546. An Act to provide for the safe-keeping of the money raised for the payment of town expenses in the city of Utica. Passed May 22, 1874; three-fifths being present.

CHAP. 547. An Act to amend an act entitled "An act to amend and reduce to one act the several acts relating to buildings in the city of New York, passed May fourth, eighteen hundred and sixty-six, May seventeenth, eighteen hundred and sixty-seven, and May sixth, eighteen hundred and sixty-eight," passed April twentieth, eighteen hundred and seventy-one. Passed May 22, 1874; three-fifths being present.

CHAP. 548. An Act to amend an act entitled "An act to incorporate the New York and Canada Bridge and Tunnel Company," passed May fourth, eighteen hundred and seventy-two. Passed May 22, 1874.

CHAP. 549. An Act to provide for the planting and protection of oysters in those portions of the Great South bay, lying in the town of Islip, Suffolk county, wherein the taking of clams cannot be profitably followed as a business. Passed May 22, 1874; three-fifths being present.

CHAP. 550. An Act to amend an act entitled "An act to create a separate road district in the town of Middletown, county of Richmond," passed April twenty-fifth, eighteen hundred and sixty-six. Passed May 22, 1874; three-fifths being present.

CHAP. 551. An Act to extend the provisions of chapter four hundred and eighty-nine, of the laws of eighteen hundred and seventy-three, amending certain acts for the better security of mechanics and others erecting buildings in certain counties of this state, to the county of Erie, except the city of Buffalo. Passed May 22, 1874.*

CHAP. 552. An Act to rectify and correct certain boundaries of the first, second, third and fourth wards of Long Island City, so as to adjust and conform such boundaries to streets and avenues laid down on the commissioners' map of said city. Passed May 22, 1874; three-fifths being present.

CHAP. 553. An Act to amend an act entitled "An act to authorize the construction of a railway and tracks in the towns of West Farms and Morrisania," passed May second, eighteen hundred and sixty-three. Passed May 22, 1874.*

CHAP. 554. An Act to amend section one of "An act to amend an act entitled 'An act to establish a department of police in the city of Buffalo, and to provide for the government thereof,'" passed April twenty-sixth, eighteen hundred and seventy-one, passed March fifteenth, eighteen hundred and seventy-three. Passed May 22, 1874; three-fifths being present.

CHAP. 555. An Act to amend an act entitled "An act to incorporate the Evangelical Lutheran St. John's Orphans' Home in the city of Buffalo," passed April fourteenth, eighteen hundred and sixty-five. Passed May 22, 1874.

CHAP. 556. An Act to enable the towns of East Chester and Pelham, in the county of Westchester, to purchase and obtain lands for the improvement of East Chester creek. Passed May 22, 1874; three-fifths being present.

CHAP. 557. An Act to amend an act entitled "An act to provide for a supply of water in the city of Yonkers," passed February twenty-eighth, eighteen hundred and seventy-three. Passed May 22, 1874; three-fifths being present.

CHAP. 558. An Act to incorporate the Niagara River Transit Company, and to authorize said company to construct a bridge or tunnel. Passed May 22, 1874; three-fifths being present.

* Certified by the presiding officer of the assembly as having passed the assembly, "three-fifths being present."

CHAP. 559. An Act to incorporate the Niagara Grand Island Bridge Company. Passed May 22, 1874.

CHAP. 560. *An Act to amend an act entitled "An act to authorize the formation of town insurance companies," passed April seventeenth, eighteen hundred and fifty-seven, and an act to amend the same, passed May twenty-first, eighteen hundred and seventy-three. Passed May 22, 1874.*

CHAP. 561. An Act to amend chapter four hundred of the laws of eighteen hundred and seventy-two, entitled "An act to incorporate the Oswegatchie Bridge Company." Passed May 22, 1874.

CHAP. 562. An Act to amend chapter five hundred and five of the laws of eighteen hundred and sixty-five, entitled "An act to provide for the improvement of the navigation of the Oswegatchie river, and of the hydraulic powers thereon, and to check freshets therein." Passed May 23, 1874; three-fifths being present.

CHAP. 563. An Act to amend an act entitled "An act to amend the act entitled 'An act to amend the act to combine into one act the several acts relating to the city of Albany, passed April twelfth, eighteen hundred and forty-two, and the several acts amendatory thereof; and also to repeal the act establishing a capital police district, and to provide for the government thereof, passed April twenty-second, eighteen hundred and sixty-five, and the several acts amendatory thereof, in so far as they relate to the city of Albany,' passed March sixteenth, eighteen hundred and seventy," passed April fifteenth, eighteen hundred and seventy-one. Passed May 23, 1874; three-fifths being present.

CHAP. 564. An Act to amend an act entitled "An act to incorporate the village of Green Island, and for other purposes," passed May twelfth, eighteen hundred and sixty-nine. Passed May 23, 1874; three-fifths being present.

CHAP. 565. An Act to amend an act entitled "An act to reorganize the fire department of the city of Albany," passed March twenty-ninth, eighteen hundred and sixty-seven. Passed May 23, 1874; three-fifths being present.

CHAP. 566. An Act in relation to the general interpreter of the criminal courts of the county of New York. Passed May 23, 1874; three-fifths being present.

CHAP. 567. An Act to provide for grading and macadamizing the highway known as Broadway, in the town of Flushing, Queens county, and for keeping the same in repair. Passed May 23, 1874; three-fifths being present.

CHAP. 568. An Act to amend an act entitled "An act to condense and amend the several acts incorporating or relating to the village of Skaneateles," passed April sixteenth, eighteen hundred and fifty-seven. Passed May 23, 1874; three-fifths being present.*

CHAP. 569. An Act to amend the charter of the city of Buffalo.* Passed May 23, 1874; three-fifths being present.

CHAP. 570. *An Act to amend chapter ninety-three of the laws of eighteen hundred and sixty-three, entitled "An act to authorize the making of sidewalks and planting shade trees along highways of this state, other than in cities and incorporated villages," passed April seventh, eighteen hundred and sixty-three. Passed May 23, 1874; three-fifths being present.*

CHAP. 571. An Act to amend the charter of the International Exchange and Agency Company of New York, incorporated by chapter six hundred and eighty-four of the laws of eighteen hundred and seventy-three. Passed May 25, 1874.

CHAP. 572. An Act to amend an act entitled "An act to provide for the improvement of the Coney Island plank-road, as recently widened, passed May three, eighteen hundred and seventy-two." Passed May 25, 1874; three-fifths being present.

CHAP. 573. An Act to amend an act entitled "An act to provide for the improvement of Park avenue, from Clinton avenue to Broadway, in the city of Brooklyn, and to repeal an act heretofore passed for the improvement of Park avenue, from Clinton avenue to Broadway, and from Hudson avenue to Bridge street, in the city of Brooklyn," passed June twenty-eight, eighteen hundred and seventy-three. Passed May 25, 1874; three-fifths being present.

CHAP. 574. An Act authorizing the Brooklyn Cross-town Railroad Company to extend its tracks through certain streets in the city of Brooklyn. Passed May 25, 1874.*

CHAP. 575. An Act in relation to the Brooklyn, Winfield and Newtown Railway Company. Passed May 25, 1874.

---

* Certified by the presiding officer of the assembly as having passed the assembly, "three-fifths being present."

CHAP. 576. An Act in relation to Second avenue in the town of New Utrecht. Passed May 25, 1874.*

CHAP. 577. An Act to confirm, reduce and levy a certain assessment in the city of Brooklyn. Passed May 25, 1874; three-fifths being present.

CHAP. 578. An Act to authorize the city of Poughkeepsie to pay certain deficencies and liabilities and to issue bonds for that purpose. Passed May 25, 1874; three-fifths being present.

CHAP. 579. An Act requiring the commissioners appointed by the county judge of Madison county, under the act to aid the construction of the New York and Oswego Midland Railroad, for the purpose of bonding the village of Oneida, in said county, in aid of said railroad, to pay over the balance of money in their hands to the treasurer of said village, for the redemption of certain bonds of said village. Passed May 25, 1874; three-fifths being present.

CHAP. 580. An Act to provide for the payment of certain money by the supervisor of the town of New Utrecht to the commissioners for grading Bay Ridge avenue in said town, and for the liquidation of a portion of the assessment due upon certain lands and premises of Charles Meyers on said avenne. Passed May 25, 1874; three-fifths being present.

CHAP. 581. An Act in relation to the town survey commissioners of Kings county, and for the preservation of the maps and monuments prepared and established by them. Passed May 25, 1874; three-fifths being present.

CHAP. 582. An Act to authorize the Bushwick Railroad Company to extend their tracks. Passed May 25, 1874.

CHAP. 583. An Act to lay out and improve a public highway or avenue and concourse in a continuation of a public highway or avenue heretofore laid out from Prospect park, in the city of Brooklyn, toward Coney Island, in the county of Kings. Passed May 25, 1874; three-fifths being present.

CHAP. 584. An Act to incorporate the Newtown Savings Bank. Passed May 26, 1874.

CHAP. 585. An Act to incorporate the Brooklyn Elevated Silent Safety Railway, for the purposes of providing rapid transit through the city of Brooklyn, Kings county, to Wood Haven, in the town of Jamaica, in the county of Queens, and state of New York, and to provide for constructing and operating a railway therefor. Passed May 26, 1874; three-fifths being present.

CHAP. 586. An Act to repeal chapter one hundred and sixty of the laws of eighteen hundred and seventy-two, entitled "An act to establish a board of health and of vital statistics in the county of Richmond, and to define its powers and duties." Passed May 29, 1874; three-fifths being present.

CHAP. 587. An Act to amend an act entitled "An act to provide a charter for the village of Oneida," passed April twenty-six, eighteen hundred and sixty-nine. Passed June 1, 1874; three-fifths being present.

CHAP. 588. An Act to provide for the completion and improvement of Sackett, Douglass and Degraw streets, in the city of Brooklyn, and also for the collection and payment of all moneys expended or indebtedness incurred by said city on account of the improvement of such streets by the Brooklyn park commissioners. Passed June 1, 1874; three-fifths being present.

CHAP. 589. An Act to amend "An act to amend the charter of the city of Brooklyn, and the various amendments thereof," passed June twenty-eighth, eighteen hundred and seventy-three, and to further amend the charter of the city of Brooklyn. Passed June 1, 1874; three-fifths being present.

CHAP. 590. An Act to amend an act entitled "An act in relation to Orphan Asylum societies at Brooklyn," passed March seventh, eighteen hundred and forty-eight. Passed June 1, 1874; three-fifths being present.

CHAP. 591. An Act to authorize the Utica Park Association to convey and mortgage its property and to issue its corporate bonds. Passed June 1, 1874; three-fifths being present.

CHAP. 592. An Act to incorporate the Merchants' Loan Company. Passed June 1, 1874.

CHAP. 593. An Act to amend an act entitled "An act to incorporate the Westchester County Trust Company," passed April sixth, eighteen hundred and seventy-one. Passed June 1, 1874.†

---

* Certified by the presiding officer of the senate as having passed the senate, three-fifths being present.

† Certified by the presiding officer of the assembly as having passed the assembly, three-fifths being present.

CHAP. 594. An Act to incorporate the Harlem Safe Deposit Company. Passed June 1, 1874; three-fifths being present.

CHAP. 595. An Act legalizing and confirming the vote taken at the annual town meeting of the town of Olean, in the county of Cattaraugus, the twenty-fourth day of February, eighteen hundred and seventy-four, to assess and raise money to build the foundation for a bridge over Olean creek, at Martin's Mills. Passed June 1, 1874; three-fifths being present.

CHAP. 596. An Act to incorporate the Manhattan Mortgage Company. Passed June 1, 1874; three-fifths being present.

CHAP. 597. An Act to amend section nine of chapter five hundred and eight of the laws of eighteen hundred and seventy-three, entitled "An act to incorporate the Long Island Loan and Trust Company." Passed June 1, 1874.*

CHAP. 598. An Act authorizing the electors of the town of Olean, Cattaraugus county, at the next annual town meeting, to vote a special tax for the building of a bridge over Olean creek, at Martin's Mills. Passed June 1, 1874; three-fifths being present.

CHAP. 599. An Act to amend an act entitled "An act to authorize the town of Ellisburgh, in the county of Jefferson, to raise money to build a town house," passed May first, eighteen hundred and sixty-nine. Passed June 4, 1874; three-fifths being present.

CHAP. 600. *An Act to amend an act entitled "An act to convey to creditors a just division of the estates of debtors who convey to assignees for the benefit of creditors," passed April thirteenth, eighteen hundred and sixty. Passed June 4, 1874.*

CHAP. 601. An Act to amend an act entitled "An act to incorporate the New York Bridge Company, for the purpose of constructing and maintaining a bridge over the East river, between the cities of New York and Brooklyn, passed April sixteenth, eighteen hundred and sixty-seven, and to provide for the speedy construction of said bridge." Passed June 5, 1874; three-fifths being present.

CHAP. 602. An Act to provide for the liquidation, funding and payment of the debts of the town of Newtown, in Queens county, as apportioned between Long Island City and the town of Newtown. Passed June 5, 1874; three-fifths being present.

CHAP. 603. *An Act to repeal chapter three hundred and forty-six of the laws of eighteen hundred and sixty-five, entitled "An act authorizing the election of chiefs and clerk of St. Regis Indians, and defining their powers," passed April tenth, eighteen hundred and sixty-five. Passed June 5, 1874.*

CHAP. 604. An Act to provide for the surveying, laying out and monumenting of certain portions of the city and county of New York, and to provide means therefor. Passed June 5, 1874; three-fifths being present.

CHAP. 605. An Act to authorize canal commissioners to build a road or street bridge over the Erie canal on Goodman street, at the east boundary line of the city of Rochester. Passed June 5, 1874; three-fifths being present.

CHAP. 606. An Act to authorize the canal commissioners to construct a road bridge over the Erie canal in the town of Gates, in the county of Monroe. Passed June 5, 1874; three-fifths being present.

CHAP. 607. An Act to provide for the protection of the guard-lock on the Chenango canal extension and South Water street, and to prevent the inundation of South street in the city of Binghamton. Passed June 6, 1874; three-fifths being present.

CHAP. 608. An Act to enable the trustees of the village of Greenbush to raise, by tax, the sum of eighteen thousand dollars, wherewith to pay the outstanding adjusted claims against said village. Passed June 6, 1874; three-fifths being present.

CHAP. 609. An Act to amend an act entitled "An act for the relief of the Co-operative Iron Founders' Association of Troy," passed April twenty-third, eighteen hundred and sixty-seven. Passed June 6, 1874.

CHAP. 610. An Act to authorize the sale of lands for non-payment of taxes and for the collection of unpaid taxes in the several towns of the county of Westchester. Passed June 6, 1874; three-fifths being present.

---

* Certified by the presiding officer of the senate as having passed the senate, three-fifths being present.

CHAP. 611. An Act to amend an act entitled "An act to amend an act entitled 'An act to provide for the incorporation of villages,' passed December seventh, one thousand eight hundred and forty-seven, and the several acts amendatory thereof, so far as the same relate to the village of Mount Vernon, in the county of Westchester, and to declare, enlarge and define the powers and duties of the officers of said village, and to confirm and extend the powers of the corporation of said village," passed May tenth, eighteen hundred and seventy. Passed June 6, 1874; three-fifths being present.

CHAP. 612. An Act to amend an act entitled "An act to provide for the incorporation of villages," passed December seventh, eighteen hundred and forty-seven, and the several acts amendatory thereof, so far as relates to the village of Niagara City, in the county of Niagara. Passed June 6, 1874; three-fifths being present.

CHAP. 613. *An Act to amend an act entitled "An act to amend the Revised Statutes in relation to laying out public roads and the alteration thereof," passed April twenty-eighth, eighteen hundred and seventy-three. Passed June* 8, 1874; *three-fifths being present.*

CHAP. 614. *An Act to amend an act entitled "An act to confer additional powers upon the metropolitan police, relating to the inspection of steam boilers," passed April ninth, eighteen hundred and sixty-two, also to amend an act entitled "An act in relation to the inspection of steam boilers except in the metropolitan district," passed June twenty-second, eighteen hundred and sixty-seven. Passed June* 8, 1874; *three-fifths being present.*

CHAP. 615. An Act to incorporate the Oneonta Waterworks Company, and to authorize the trustees of the village of Oneonta to take and lease lands and water for the purposes of said company. Passed June 8, 1874; three-fifths being present.

CHAP. 616. An Act to supply the village of Gloversville with pure and wholesome water. Passed June 8, 1874; three-fifths being present.

CHAP. 617. An Act to incorporate the Lewiston Waterworks Company. Passed June 8, 1874; three-fifths being present.

CHAP. 618. An Act for the relief of William Baxter, David P. Dobbins and Theodore Davis. Passed June 8, 1874, by a two-thirds vote.

CHAP. 619. An Act to amend an act entitled "An act authorizing the construction of a railroad through certain streets in the city of Poughkeepsie, and through certain streets or roads in the town of Poughkeepsie, in the county of Dutchess," passed April fourth, eighteen hundred and sixty-six. Passed June 8, 1874; three-fifths being present.

CHAP. 620. An Act to amend chapter three hundred and ninety-six of the laws of eighteen hundred and seventy-two, entitled "An act to incorporate the Mamaroneck and Rye Neck Fire Department," passed April twenty-sixth, eighteen hundred and seventy-two. Passed June 8, 1874; three-fifths being present.

CHAP. 621. An Act to amend an act entitled "An act in relation to elections in the city and county of New York, and to provide for ascertaining by proper proof the citizens who shall be entitled to the right of suffrage thereat," passed May fourteenth, eighteen hundred and seventy-two, being chapter six hundred and seventy-five of the laws of eighteen hundred and seventy-two, and the act or acts amendatory thereof or supplementary thereto. Passed June 8, 1874; three-fifths being present.

CHAP. 622. An Act to authorize the Cameron street Baptist church in the city of New York to sell certain lands in the city of Brooklyn, formerly used for cemetery purposes, and to perfect titles in the purchasers thereof. Passed June 8, 1874.

CHAP. 623. An Act to amend an act entitled "An act to revise and consolidate the laws in relation to the village of Geneva, in the county of Ontario," passed March third, eighteen hundred and seventy-one. Passed June 9, 1874; three-fifths being present.

CHAP. 624. An Act to amend the several acts incorporating the village of Oswego Falls. Passed June 9, 1874.

CHAP. 625. An Act to amend an act entitled "An act to incorporate the village of Oneonta, Otsego county, New York," passed April twentieth, eighteen hundred and seventy. Passed June 9, 1874; three-fifths being present.

CHAP. 626. An Act to amend an act entitled "An act to incorporate the city of Newburgh," passed April twenty-second, eighteen hundred and sixty-five, and the several acts amendatory thereof. Passed June 9, 1874; three-fifths being present.

CHAP. 627. An Act to amend an act entitled "An act to amend the charter of the village of Johnstown," passed March thirtieth, eighteen hundred and sixty-seven. Passed June 9, 1874; three-fifths being present.

CHAP. 628. *An Act to amend an act entitled "An act for the incorporation of villages," passed April twentieth, eighteen hundred and seventy. Passed June 9, 1874; three-fifths being present.*

CHAP. 629. An Act to amend an act entitled "An act to incorporate The Buffalo Safe Deposit Company," passed June seventh, eighteen hundred and seventy-three. Passed June 10, 1874.

CHAP. 630. An Act to incorporate the Teutonia Savings Bank of Brooklyn. Passed June 10, 1874.

CHAP. 631. An Act to authorize the construction of a foot-bridge over the Erie canal, on Mohawk street, in the city of Utica, New York. Passed June 10, 1874; three-fifths being present.

CHAP. 632. An Act to amend an act entitled "An act to organize and establish a police for the city of Schenectady," passed April fifteenth, eighteen hundred and seventy. Passed June 12, 1874; three-fifths being present.

CHAP. 633. An Act to amend an act entitled "An act to amend an act entitled 'An act to regulate elections in the city of Brooklyn,' passed May seventh, eighteen hundred and seventy-two," passed May first, eighteen hundred and seventy-three. Passed June 12, 1874; three-fifths being present.

CHAP. 634. An Act to amend an act entitled "An act to authorize the construction of a railroad from, at or near Bath ferry, in the town of North Greenbush, to Douw's Point, in the town of East Greenbush, in the county of Rensselaer," passed May tenth, eighteen hundred and seventy-three. Passed June 12, 1874; three-fifths being present.

CHAP. 635. An Act to secure effective vaccination in the city of New York, and the collection of pure vaccine lymph or virus. Passed June 15, 1874; three-fifths being present.

CHAP. 636. An Act relating to the board of health of the health department of the city of New York; to the commissioners of health and the officers of the said department, their duties and powers, and the expenses of said department. Passed June 15, 1874; three-fifths being present.

CHAP. 637. An Act to provide for the opening and improvement of a portion of Grand street, in the city of Brooklyn, and the extension of the same, and improvement of such extension, in Queens county, and to provide for the payment therefor. Passed June 16, 1874; three-fifths being present.

CHAP. 638. An Act to ratify and confirm certain orders and acts of the county judge of the county of Steuben, appointing commissioners to issue bonds and invest the same in the stock of the Rochester, Hornellsville and Pine Creek Railroad Company, and to legalize all proceedings under and pursuant to such orders and acts. Passed June 16, 1874; three-fifths being present.

CHAP. 639. An Act for the relief and protection of Martha Howell as purchaser of the real estate of David O. Howell, deceased, in proceedings by the administrators of said deceased, for the sale of said lands to pay his debts, and to confirm the acts of said administrators, and of the surrogate of the county of Livingston, in said proceedings. Passed June 17, 1874; three-fifths being present.

CHAP. 640. An Act relating to evidence as to the passage of an act to release the interest of the people of this state to Alicia C. O'Brien, passed May twentieth, eighteen hundred and seventy-two. Passed June 17, 1874.

CHAP. 641. An Act to amend an act passed May first, eighteen hundred and seventy-three, entitled "An act to lay out, open and grade Eighty-sixth street, in the towns of New Utrecht and Gravesend, in the county of Kings. Passed June 23, 1874; three-fifths being present.

CHAP. 642. *An Act declaratory of, and to amend chapter five hundred and forty-nine of the laws of eighteen hundred and seventy-three, entitled "An act to amend an act entitled 'An act regulating the sale of intoxicating liquors,'" passed April eleventh, eighteen hundred and seventy, and the act entitled "An act to suppress intemperance, and to regulate the sale of intoxicating liquors," passed April sixteenth, eighteen hundred and fifty-seven. Passed June 23, 1874; three-fifths being present.*

CHAP. 643. An Act to amend an act entitled "An act in relation to the Nursery and Child's Hospital of the city of New York," passed April seventeenth, eighteen hundred and sixty-six, and amended by act chapter three hundred and sixty-six of the laws of eighteen hundred and sixty-nine. Passed June 23, 1874; three-fifths being present.

CHAP. 644. An Act to amend the charter of the Foundling Asylum of the Sisters of Charity, in the city of New York. Passed June 23, 1874; three-fifths being present.

CHAP. 645. An Act to make further provision for the payment of further expenses of the local government of the city of New York. Passed June 25, 1874; three-fifths being present.

CHAP. 646. An Act telegalize* the acts of John G. Safford, a justice of the peace of Washington county. Passed June 25, 1874.

CHAP. 647. An Act to amend an act entitled "An act to authorize the selection and location of certain grounds for public parks, in the city of Buffalo, and to provide for the maintenance and embellishment thereof," passed April fourteenth, eighteen hundred and sixty-nine. Passed June 26, 1874; three-fifths being present.

CHAP. 648. An Act to provide for the building of a bridge over the Boston and Albany railroad in the town of East Greenbush, Rensselaer county. Passed June 26, 1874.

CHAP. 649. An Act to amend several acts in relation to the city of Rochester. Passed June 26, 1874; three-fifths being present.

CHAP. 650. An Act to amend an act entitled "An act exempting from taxation real estate owned by the House of Rest for Consumptives," passed June twenty-eighth, eighteen hundred and seventy-three. Passed June 30, 1874; three-fifths being present.

CHAP. 651. An Act to confirm the apportionment of the indebtedness incurred in the late town of Yonkers, under chapter five hundred and thirty-four of the laws of eighteen hundred and seventy-one, by the board of commissioners of the department of public parks of the city of New York, and to provide for the payment thereof. Passed July 3, 1874; three-fifths being present.

CHAP. 652. An Act to provide for the improvement of the hydraulic powers of the Chateaugay river. Passed July 3, 1874; three-fifths being present.

CHAP. 653. An Act to authorize the construction of fishways in the Mohawk river. Passed July 11, 1874; three-fifths being present.

CONCURRENT RESOLUTIONS.

Proposing amendments to Article 2 of the Constitution.

Proposing amendments to Article 3 of the Constitution.

Proposing amendments to Article 4 of the Constitution.

Proposing amendments to Article 7 of the Constitution.

Proposing amendments to Article 8 of the Constitution.

Proposing amendment to Article 10 of the Constitution.

Proposing amendment to Article 12 of the Constitution.

Proposing an amendment to the Constitution, to be known as Articles 15 and 16.

Relative to a message from the governor on the inflation of the currency of the United States.

In relation to the completion of the work of removing the obstructions at Hell Gate.

Relative to the dam on the Owasco river, in the city of Auburn.

Authorizing the governor to appoint commissioners to represent the state at the Centennial Exhibition.

Directing the board of commissioners of the department of docks of the city of New York to cause to be made the necessary surveys, surroundings, and other examination of the water-front of that part of Westchester county, recently annexed to said city.

NAMES CHANGED.

In Cortland county — Elizabeth Garner to Kitty Elizabeth Simms. November 7, 1872.

In Columbia county — De Witt C. Van Valkenburgh Lyon to De Witt C. Van Valkenburgh.
Helen V. N. Humphrey to Helen Van Ness.
Herbert Humphrey to Herbert Van Ness.
Lester Humphrey to Lester Van Ness.

* So in original.

In Kings county — Elsie Ann Morris to Elsie Ann Murray. June 15, 1873.

Lars Anders Mortensen to Lars Anders Morton. November 25, 1873.

Charlotte Sidney Hickok to Charlotte Sidney Thomas. February 1, 1874.

The Rector, Church Wardens and Vestrymen of Zion Church, in the city of Brooklyn, county of Kings, and State of New York, to The Rector, Church Wardens and Vestrymen of Saint Barnabus Church, in the city of Brooklyn, county of Kings, and State of New York. May 24, 1873.

Rector, Church Wardens and Vestrymen of Guion Church, in the city of Brooklyn, to Rector, Church Wardens and Vestrymen of St. George Church, in the city of Brooklyn. October 8, 1873.

In County of New York. — C. H. Achilles Weidner to Achilles Rose. March 1, 1873.

Michael James Lowe to James Michael Lowe. February 26, 1873.

Jacob Hassendeuble to Jacob Hasse. February 26, 1873.

Otto Hassendeuble to Otto Hasse. February 26, 1873.

Frederick Hassendeuble to Frederick Hasse. February 26, 1873.

Carrie Thompson to Carrie Foster. March 15, 1873.

John Smith Magonagle to John Smith Magonagle Hill. April 4, 1873.

Charles H. Weed to Charles Reed. May 10, 1873.

Anna J. Weed to Anna J. Reed. May 10, 1873.

Maurice G. Weed to Maurice G. Reed. May 10, 1873.

Marie G. Weed to Marie G. Reed. May 10, 1873.

Sextus L. Weed to Sextus L. Reed. May 10, 1873.

Edward H. Coburn to Edward H. Cockburn. June 1, 1873.

Martha A. Coburn to Martha A Cockburn. June 1, 1873.

Martha A. Coburn, Jr., to Martha A. Cockburn, Jr. June 1. 1873.

Edward H. Coburn, Jr., to Edward H. Cockburn, Jr. June 1, 1873.

Emma J. Coburn to Emma J. Cockburn. June 1, 1873.

Robert A. Coburn to Robert A. Cockburn. June 1, 1873.

Ada Elizabeth Coburn to Ada Elizabeth Cockburn. June 1, 1873.

Amy F. Coburn to Amy F. Cockburn. June 1, 1873.

Walter J. Coburn to Walter J. Cockburn. June 1, 1873.

Annie Irene Callahan to Annie Irene Temple. August 1, 1873.

Adolph Schitter to Adolph Schiller. September 21, 1873.

Katrina Schitter to Katrina Schiller. September 21, 1873.

Louis Schitter to Louis Schiller. September 21, 1873.

Charles Adolph Rindskopf to Charles Adolph Risdorf. December 25, 1873.

Adolph Morris Gotosky to Adolph Morris Morris. December 15, 1873.

David Wilkowski to David Witmark. December 15, 1873.

GENERAL STATUTES

OF THE

STATE OF NEW YORK,

PASSED AT THE

97TH SESSION, 1874.

CHAP. 9.

AN ACT to amend chapter seventy-four of the laws of eighteen hundred and seventy, in reference to the records of surrogates' courts.

PASSED February 6, 1874.

The People of the State of New York, represented in Senate and Assembly, do enact as follows:

SECTION 1. Section two of chapter seventy-four of the laws of eighteen hundred and seventy is hereby amended so as to read as follows:

§ 2. For greater certainty and to avoid all doubt, it is hereby declared to be lawful for any surrogate or officer acting as such, hereafter, in like manner and under like circumstances, in his own name, to sign, certify and complete all unfinished records of wills, and of proofs and examinations taken by and before his predecessor in office; also all records of letters testamentary, administration or guardianship, adding to his signature the date of so doing, and which shall have the like effect as if such predecessor had signed the same.

Surrogates may complete unfinished records of predecessors.

§ 2. This act shall take effect immediately.

CHAP. 12.

AN ACT relating to animals.

PASSED February 11, 1874; three-fifths being present.

The People of the State of New York, represented in Senate and Assembly, do enact as follows:

Animals, any act of cruelty to, a misdemeanor.

SECTION 1. Every person who shall willfully set on foot, or instigate, or move to or carry on, or promote, or engage in, or do any act toward the furtherance of any act of cruelty to any animal shall be guilty of a misdemeanor.

Society for prevention of cruelty to animals, powers of officers of.

§ 2. All agents of the American Society for the Prevention of Cruelty to Animals shall have all the powers now conferred on them by law. Any person who shall falsely represent or personate an officer, agent or member of said society shall be guilty of a misdemeanor.

Interference a misdemeanor.

§ 3. Any officer, agent or member of said society may lawfully interfere to prevent the perpetration of any act of cruelty upon any animal in his presence. Any person who shall interfere with or obstruct any such officer, agent or member in the discharge of his duty shall be guilty of a misdemeanor.

Any agent of, may destroy abandoned or diseased animals.

§ 4. Any agent or officer of said society may lawfully destroy, or cause to be destroyed, any animal found to be abandoned and not properly cared for, appearing, in the judgment of two reputable citizens called by him to view the same in his presence, to be glandered, injured or diseased past recovery for any useful purpose.

Agent may take charge of animals when person in charge of arrested.

§ 5. When any person arrested is at the time of such arrest in charge of any vehicle drawn by or containing any animal, any agent of such society may take charge of such animal, and of such vehicle and its contents, and deposit the same in a safe place of custody, or deliver the same into the possession of the police or sheriff of the county or place wherein such arrest was made, who shall thereupon assume the custody thereof.

Fines to inure to society.

§ 6. All fines, penalties and forfeitures imposed and collected in any county in this state under the provisions of every act passed, or which may be passed relating to or in anywise affecting animals, except where otherwise provided, shall inure to said society in aid of the purpose for which it was incorporated. And no injunction shall be granted against said society, or any of its officers or agents, except upon motion, after due notice and hearing thereof.

No injunction against.

Warrant to issue.

§ 7. Upon complaint under oath or affirmation to any magistrate authorized to issue warrants in criminal cases that the complainant has just and reasonable cause to suspect that any of the provisions of law relating to or in anywise affecting animals are being, or are about to be violated in any particular building or place, such magistrate shall immediately issue and deliver a warrant to any person authorized by law to make arrests for such offenses, authorizing him to enter and search such building or place, and to arrest any person there present found violating any of said laws, and to bring such person before the nearest magistrate of competent jurisdiction, to be dealt with according to law.

§ 8. In this act, and in every law of this state passed, or which may be passed, relating to or affecting animals, the singular shall include the plural; the words "animal" or "dumb animal" shall be held to include every living creature; the words "torture," "torment," or "cruelty" shall be held to include every act, omission or neglect whereby unjustifiable pain, suffering or death is caused or permitted; and the words "owner" and "person" shall be held to include corporations as well as individuals. But nothing in this act shall be construed as prohibiting the shooting of birds for the purposes of human food.

The words torture, torment and cruelty defined.

§ 9. This act shall take effect immediately.

Ante, vol. 6, p. 796; vol. 7, p. 86.
"The Stage Horse cases," 15 Abb. Pr. (N. S.) 51.
People v. Tinsdale, 10 Abb. Pr. (N. S.) 374.

CHAP. 15.

AN ACT to amend section ten of chapter two hundred and fifty-four of the laws of eighteen hundred and forty-seven, entitled "An act concerning the laws, journals and documents of the legislature."

PASSED February 13, 1874; three-fifths being present.

The People of the State of New York, represented in Senate and Assembly, do enact as follows:

SECTION 1. The fourth subdivision of section ten of chapter two hundred and fifty-four of the laws of eighteen hundred and forty-seven, entitled "An act concerning the laws, journals and documents of the legislature," is hereby amended so as to read as follows:

4. To each of the following officers, namely, town clerks, for the use of their respective towns, district attorneys, to be delivered to their successors in office, supervisors' clerks, for the use of the board of supervisors, and surrogates, for the use of the surrogates' courts, and to the mayors of the several cities, for the use of said cities, one copy of the laws without the journals.

Distribution of session laws extended to surrogates and mayors of cities.

§ 2. This act shall take effect immediately.

Ante, vol. 3, p. 61.

CHAP. 22.

AN ACT to repeal chapter five hundred and ninety-eight of the laws of eighteen hundred and seventy-two, entitled "An act for the better preservation of horse records."

PASSED February 20, 1874; three-fifths being present.

The People of the State of New York, represented in Senate and Assembly, do enact as follows:

SECTION 1. Chapter five hundred and ninety-eight of the laws of eighteen hundred and seventy-two, entitled "An act for the better preservation of horse records," passed May eighth, eighteen hundred and seventy-two, is hereby repealed.

§ 2. This act shall take effect immediately.

CHAP. 26.

AN ACT authorizing the formation of corporations to secure camp grounds and other property connected therewith, for the use of the Methodist Episcopal Church.

PASSED February 20, 1874; three-fifths being present.

The People of the State of New York, represented in Senate and Assembly, do enact as follows:

Presiding elder and district stewards to make certificate. SECTION 1. The presiding elder of any district, or the presiding elders of any number of districts, and a majority of the district stewards of any district or districts, appointed according to the discipline of the Methodist Episcopal church, residing in any ecclesiastical district or districts in this state erected by an annual conference of said church as a presiding elder's district or districts, may make, sign and acknowledge, before some officer competent to take the acknowledgment of deeds, and file in the office of the clerk of any county in such district or districts, and a duplicate thereof in the office of the secretary of state, a certificate in writing, in which shall be stated the corporate name of said corporation; the names, residence and official relation to the district of the person signing such certificate, the number of trustees, not less than three nor more than nine, who shall manage the property and affairs of said corporation for the first year, and their names; and in which certificate it shall be further stated, in substance, that the object of such corporation is to secure the benefits of this act.

Certificate, where filed. What to contain. Trustees, number of.

Trustees, how appointed, etc. § 2. The district stewards of any presiding elder's district, at their annual meeting, may appoint, from time to time, trustees for any such corporation within their district, to supply the places of those whose terms of office shall expire, and to fill any vacancies in the number of such trustees. And when two or more districts join in such corporation, then the district stewards of each district, at their annual meeting, may appoint their equal portion of said trustees; but in case the number of trustees cannot be equally divided between the districts, then the district in which the camp ground is located may appoint such trustee.

§ 3. When such certificate shall be filed, as aforesaid, the persons who shall have made, signed and acknowledged the same, and their successors shall be and become a body politic and corporate, by the name stated in such certificate; and such corporation shall have succession, and possess the general powers conferred on corporations by the eighteenth chapter of the first part of the Revised Statutes of this state; and shall also have power to take, by gift, grant or purchase, any estate, real or personal, the annual income of which shall not exceed twenty-five thousand dollars, for the use of the authorities of the Methodist Episcopal church, representing said district or districts, as a camp ground for camp meeting purposes; and from time to time to sell and convey the same, and to reinvest the proceeds thereof for a like purpose, as the trustees of such corporation, with the approval of the annual conference having jurisdiction over the district or districts, may direct. And all the provisions of article seven, title eight, chapter twenty, part first of the Revised Statutes of this state, entitled "of the disturbance of religious meetings," shall apply to religious meetings held in pursuance of this act, in accordance with the usages of said Methodist Episcopal church. And the trustees of any such camp ground appointed according to the provisions of this act, and for the purpose named in this act, and their successors in office, are hereby clothed with the same powers as are conferred upon peace officers in and by said article seven.

Powers of the corporation.

Religious meetings, disturbance of.

§ 4. Any real estate heretofore conveyed for camp meeting purposes may be conveyed, by the trustees holding the title thereof, to a corporation formed as aforesaid, whereupon the title thereto shall vest in such corporation for the purpose defined in this act.

Real estate may be conveyed.

§ 5. Districts may unite with such corporation by conforming to this act and appending their certificates to the original ones.

§ 6. This act shall take effect immediately.

CHAP. 35.

AN ACT to amend chapter three hundred and sixty-eight of the laws of eighteen hundred and sixty-five, entitled "An act for the incorporation of societies or clubs for certain social and recreative purposes."

PASSED February 27, 1874.

The People of the State of New York, represented in Senate and Assembly, do enact as follows:

SECTION 1. The second section of chapter three hundred and sixty-eight of the laws of eighteen hundred and sixty-five, entitled "An act for the incorporation of societies or clubs for certain social and recreative purposes," is hereby amended so as to read as follows:

Corporation, when perfected. § 2. Upon filing a certificate, as aforesaid, the persons who shall have signed and acknowledged such certificate, and their associates and successors, shall thereupon, by virtue of this act, be a body politic and corporate, by the name stated in such certificate, and by that name they and their successors shall have succession, and shall be persons in law capable of suing and being sued; and they and their successors may have and use a common seal, and the same may be altered and changed at pleasure; and they and their successors, by their corporate name, shall, in law, be capable of taking, receiving, purchasing and holding real estate, for the purposes of their incorporation, and for no other purpose, to an amount not exceeding the sum of five hundred thousand dollars in value, and personal estate for like purposes to an amount not exceeding the sum of one hundred and fifty thousand dollars in value; but the clear annual income of such real and personal estate shall not exceed the sum of fifty thousand dollars; to make by-laws for the management of its affairs, not inconsistent with the constitution and laws of this state or of the United States; to elect and appoint the officers and agents of such society, for the management of its business, and to allow them a suitable compensation.

Seal may be changed.

May hold real estate.

Annual income limited.

By-laws.

Agents.

§ 3. This act shall take effect immediately.

CHAP. 37.

AN ACT supplementary to an act entitled "An act to provide for the incorporation of religious societies," passed April fifth, eighteen hundred and thirteen, and the several acts amendatory thereof.

PASSED February 27, 1874.

The People of the State of New York, represented in Senate and Assembly, do enact as follows:

Religious corporations may consolidate. SECTION 1. Any two religious corporations incorporated under the provisions of the third section of the act entitled "An act to provide for the incorporation of religious societies," passed April fifth, eighteen hundred and thirteen, and the several acts amendatory thereof or supplemental thereto, are hereby authorized to unite and consolidate themselves into a single corporation in the manner following:

Agreement. § 2. The said two corporations may enter into an agreement under their respective corporate seals for the union and consolidation of the said corporations, setting forth the terms and conditions thereof, the name of the proposed new corporation, the names of the persons who shall be its church wardens and vestrymen, ministers, elders, and deacons or trustees, or other

What to contain.

officers, as the case may be, until the first annual election of the proposed new corporation, and fixing the day of its annual election.

§ 3. Each of the said corporations may make its separate petition to the supreme court for an order for such union and consoldation, setting forth in such petition the reasons for such union and consolidation, the agreement made pursuant to the second section of this act, all its property, real and personal, all its debts and liabilities, and the amount and source of its annual income. *Petition to supreme court, what to contain.*

§ 4. A meeting of each of said two corporations to consider and act upon the proposed union and consolidation, and the agreement and petition therefor, shall be called by a notice given in the same manner and for the same length of time, as is provided for notices of election of trustees in the said third section of the act hereby amended; and in case the proposed union and consolidation, and the agreement and petition therefor shall receive the approval of three-fourths of the persons entitled to vote at an election of trustees of each of the two corporations, assembled at such meeting, or at an adjourned meeting, or a subsequent meeting called in like manner, then, and not otherwise, the proposed union and consolidation may be proceeded with and the petition presented to the court. *Meeting, notice of.* *Proposed union, how approved.*

§ 5. Upon such petitions from each of such corporations so proposing to be united and consolidated, and upon the said agreement, and the proceedings of the meetings prescribed in the fourth section, satisfactorily proved or certified, the supreme court may, in case it shall deem it proper, make an order for the union and consolidation of such corporations, determining all the terms, conditions and provisions thereof. All parties interested therein may be heard on such petition. *Supreme court may make an order for consolidation.*

§ 6. When such order is made and entered, according to the practice of the court, the said two corporations shall be united and consolidated into one corporation by the name designated by the order, and it shall have all the rights and powers, and be subject to all the obligations of religious corporations under the act to which this is supplementary, and the acts amendatory thereof and supplementary thereto. *Consolidation, when perfected.* *Rights and powers of new corporation.*

§ 7. And thereupon all the estate, rights and property of whatsoever nature belonging to either of said two corporations shall, without further act or deed, be vested and transferred to the new corporation as effectually as they were vested in or belonged to the former corporations, and the said new corporation shall be liable for all the debts and liabilities of the former corporations, in the same manner and as effectually as if said debts or liabilities had been contracted or incurred by it. *Property transferred to new corporation.*

§ 8. This act shall take effect immediately.

Ante, vol. 3, p. 687; vol. 6, p. 733; vol. 8, p. 697.

CHAP. 49.

AN ACT ceding to the United States of America jurisdiction over certain lands in this state for light-house purposes, and exempting the same from taxation.

PASSED March 6, 1874, by a two-thirds vote.

WHEREAS, The United States propose to establish a light-house at Thirty Mile Point, on the south shore of lake Ontario, in the town of Somerset, in the county of Niagara, and state of New York, for the purpose of aiding navigation; therefore,

The People of the State of New York, represented in Senate and Assembly, do enact as follows:

Jurisdiction ceded. SECTION 1. The jurisdiction of the lands and their appurtenances, that have been or may be purchased for the establishment of a light-house in aid of navigation on Lake Ontario, in the town of Somerset, in the county of Niagara, is hereby ceded to the United States of America; provided, however, (Proviso.) that all civil and criminal process issued under the authority of the state of New York, or any officer thereof, may be executed on said lands, and in the buildings that may be erected thereon, in the same way and manner as if jurisdiction had not been ceded as aforesaid.

Exemption from taxation. § 2. The lands above described, with their appurtenances and all buildings and other property that may be placed thereon, shall forever hereafter be exempted from all state, county and municipal taxation and assessments whatsoever, so long as the same shall remain the property of the said United States.

§ 3. This act shall take effect immediately.

CHAP. 52.

AN ACT authorizing county courts and courts of sessions to summon additional petit jurors same as *circuit courts of oyer and terminer.**

PASSED March 6, 1874; three-fifths being present.

The People of the State of New York, represented in Senate and Assembly, do enact as follows:

County courts and courts of sessions may summon additional jurors. SECTION 1. All statutes now in force authorizing circuit courts and courts of oyer and terminer to summon additional jurors to serve in said courts, shall apply to the county courts and courts of sessions in this state.

§ 2. This act shall take effect immediately.

Ante, vol. 7, p. 782.

* So in original.

CHAP. 53.

AN ACT to prevent persons from obtaining employment in positions of trust upon forged and false papers.

PASSED March 6, 1874; three-fifths being present.

The People of the State of New York, represented in Senate and Assembly, do enact as follows:

SECTION 1. Any person who shall present any forged letter or forged certificate of recommendation, or make any false statement in writing as to his or her name or residence or previous employments, and thereupon shall obtain appointment to any position of trust, the duties of which are wholly or in part to collect, or receive, or disburse money, shall, upon conviction thereof, be deemed guilty of a misdemeanor, and be punished by imprisonment in the county jail, not to exceed one year, or by fine not to exceed the sum of two hundred and fifty dollars, or by both such fine and imprisonment. Misdemeanor. Punishment.

§ 2. This act shall take effect immediately.

CHAP. 64.

AN ACT to amend chapter seven hundred and sixty-seven of the laws of eighteen hundred and seventy-two, entitled "An act to establish the compensation of county judges and surrogates, pursuant to the fifteenth section of the amended sixth article of the constitution."

PASSED March 14, 1874; three-fifths being present.

The People of the State of New York, represented in Senate and Assembly, do enact as follows:

SECTION 1. Section five of chapter seven hundred and sixty-seven of the laws of eighteen hundred and seventy-two, entitled "An act to establish the compensation of county judges and surrogates, pursuant to the fifteenth section of the amended sixth article of the constitution," is hereby amended so as to read as follows:

§ 5. Whenever the county judge of one county shall hold the county court, or preside at the court of sessions in any other county, he shall be paid the sum of five dollars per day for his expenses in going to and from, and holding or presiding at any such court, which shall be paid by the county treasurer of such other county on the presentation to him of the certificate of the clerk of such court of the number of days, provided, that such compensation shall be paid only in case of the sickness or disability of the county judge of the county in which such court is held. Expenses of county judges to be paid. By whom paid. Proviso.

CHAP. 76.

AN ACT to amend an act entitled "An act to authorize corporations to change their names," passed April twenty-first, eighteen hundred and seventy.

PASSED March 24, 1874.

The People of the State of New York, represented in Senate and Assembly, do enact as follows:

SECTION 1. Section one of "An act to authorize corporations to change their names," passed April twenty-first, eighteen hundred and seventy, is hereby amended so as to read as follows:

Corporations may change their names. § 1. Any incorporation, incorporated company, society or association, organized under the laws of this state, excepting banks, banking associations, trust companies, life, health, accident, marine and fire insurance companies and railroad companies, may apply at any special term of the supreme court sitting in the county in which shall be situated its chief business office, for an order to authorize it to assume another corporate name.

§ 2. This act shall take effect immediately.

Ante, vol. 7, page 712. *McGary* v. *People*, 45 N. Y. 153.

CHAP. 78.

AN ACT to amend chapter two hundred and ninety-one of the laws of eighteen hundred and seventy, entitled "An act for the incorporation of villages."

PASSED March 25, 1874; three-fifths being present.

The People of the State of New York, represented in Senate and Assembly, do enact as follows:

SECTION 1. The twenty-second and twenty-fifth subdivisions of section one, title three of the act entitled "An act for the incorporation of villages," passed April twentieth, in the year one thousand eight hundred and seventy, are hereby amended so as to read as follows:

Powers of trustees defined. 22. To restrain and prevent hawking and peddling in the streets; to regulate, restrain or prohibit sales by auction, and grant licenses to auctioneers; to regulate the use and running of all hacks, public carriages or vehicles for the conveyance of passengers, baggage or movables of any kind, for hire; to designate their places of waiting, and to grant licenses to the owners or proprietors thereof.

Trustees, their powers to repair roads, buildings, etc. 25. To keep the roads, avenues, streets, lanes, public buildings and public places of the village in good order and repair and condition; to construct culverts and drains; to make and repair all bridges which may be necessary within the bounds of the village; to regulate and prescribe the width, line and grade of streets, avenues, lanes and sidewalks; to pave, plank or flag roads, crosswalks or sidewalks; lay out and open new roads and streets; to widen, alter and change the grade or otherwise improve roads, avenues, streets, lanes and sidewalks; to drain stagnant waters, and to raise or fill up low grounds, if nuisance, and assess the expense thereof on the porperty benefited, in proportion to the amount of such benefit, and to regulate the water-courses, ponds and watering-places in the village; to cause all necessary sewers to be built, and assess the expense thereof upon the property benefited, in proportion to the amount of such benefit. The amount of the benefit in any case where the same is made the basis of assessment under this section, shall be determined by the president and trustees; provided, however, that no property beyond the limit of one hundred and seventy-five feet from the line terminus of any such sewer shall be liable to assessment for the expense of building the same; and provided, also, that no sewer shall be constructed under the provisions hereof, except upon a written petition, signed by a majority of the persons whose property shall be liable to assessment for the said expense. All assessments for the drainage of stagnant waters, the raising or filling up of low grounds, or the building of sewers under the provisions of this section, shall be enforced and collected in the same manner as assessments for the annual village tax.

Improvement of roads, avenues etc.

Assessment of expenses.

Proviso.

Assessments for drainage, etc., how enforced.

§ 2. Subdivision thirteen of section three of said chapter is hereby amended so as to read as follows:

13. To construct and maintain reservoirs and cisterns, and supply them with water for use at fires; to protect and preserve property at fires; to establish fire limits within the corporate bounds, by resolution of the board of trustees, describing the same by metes and boundaries, which resolution shall be filed in the office of the village clerk, and be posted in three public places within the corporate bounds, to prevent fires and provide for their extinguishment.

Further powers of trustees.

§ 3. This act shall take effect immediately.

Ante, vol. 7, p. 681.

CHAP. 100.

AN ACT providing for the appointment of additional notaries public.

PASSED March 31, 1874; three-fifths being present.

The People of the State of New York, represented in Senate and Assembly, do enact as follows:

SECTION 1. The governor is hereby authorized and empowered, by and with the consent of the senate, to appoint in each county, notaries public equal to ten for each assembly district, in addition to the number now provided by law; provided, however, that in each county which is a single assembly district, the additional number of notaries public shall be fifteen.

§ 2. This act shall take effect immediately.

CHAP. 116.

AN ACT in relation to mendicant and vagrant children.

PASSED April 3, 1874; three-fifths being present.

The People of the State of New York, represented in Senate and Assembly, do enact as follows:

SECTION 1. Any person, whether as parent, relative, guardian, employer or otherwise, having in his care, custody or control, any child under the age of sixteen years, who shall sell, apprentice, give away, let out or otherwise dispose of any such child to any person, under any name, title or pretense, for the vocation, use, occupation, calling, service or purpose of singing, playing on musical instruments, rope walking, dancing, begging or peddling in any public street or highway, or in any mendicant or wandering business whatsoever; and any person who shall take, receive, hire, employ, use or have in custody any such child for such purposes or either of them, shall be deemed to be guilty of a misdemeanor, and, upon conviction thereof before any court of special sessions, or other competent tribunal, shall be fined in a sum not less than fifty nor more than two hundred and fifty dollars, or suffer imprisonment in a county jail for a period not less than thirty days nor more than one year, or both such fine or imprisonment, in the discretion of the court.

§ 2. This act shall take effect immediately.

CHAP. 126.

AN ACT to amend an act entitled "An act to authorize the business of banking," passed April eighteenth, eighteen hundred and thirty-eight.

PASSED April 6, 1874.

The People of the State of New York, represented in Senate and Assembly, do enact as follows:

SECTION 1. The fifteenth section of the act entitled "An act to authorize the business of banking," passed April eighteenth, eighteen hundred and thirty-eight, is hereby amended so as to read as follows:

Offices of discount, etc., may be established.

§ 15. Any number of persons may associate to establish offices of discount, deposit and circulation, upon the terms and conditions, and subject to the liabilities prescribed in this act, and the acts amendatory thereof; but the aggregate amount of the capital stock of any such association or bank shall not be less than one hundred thousand dollars; provided, however, that banks with a capital of not less than fifty thousand dollars may, with the consent and approval of the superintendent of the banking department, be organized in any village or place, the population of which does not exceed six thousand inhabitants. Amount of capital.

§ 2. This act shall take effect immediately.

Ante, vol. 4, p. 127; 33 Barb. 620; 29 id. 243; 24 Wend. 345; 17 How. 110; 15 N. Y. 9, 171; 19 id. 245; 10 id. 550; 5 id. 389; 25 Barb. 413.

CHAP. 127.

AN ACT to amend an act entitled "An act in relation to lands of which parties die seized," passed May twenty-first, eighteen hundred and seventy-three.

PASSED April 6, 1874; three-fifths being present.

The People of the State of New York, represented in Senate and Assembly, do enact as follows:

SECTION 1. Section two of an act entitled "An act in relation to lands of which parties die seized," passed May twenty-first, eighteen hundred and seventy-three, is hereby amended so as to read as follows:

§ 2. Such affidavit, when so made, shall be presented to the surrogate of the county in which such real estate is situated, and said surrogate may, in his discretion, examine any witness or witnesses, under oath, as to the truth of the matters in such affidavit stated, and, upon being satisfied of the truth of all such matters, shall indorse upon such affidavit his certificate thereof, and thereupon the said affidavit thus indorsed, together with the proof so taken, shall be recorded in the county clerk's office of the county or counties where such lands are situated, unless there be a register's office in such county, in which case the same shall be recorded in such register's office in the same book and manner as deeds are now recorded; and from the date of such record, said affidavit, record and proof shall be taken and regarded in all courts and legal proceedings in this state, in respect to the succession of such real estate, as presumptive evidence of the facts therein contained, and by this act required to be stated. Affidavit of heirs at law to be presented to surrogate. Certificate to be indorsed. Affidavits and certificates to be recorded. Evidence.

§ 2. This act shall take effect immediately.

Ante, page 636.

CHAP. 143.

AN ACT to authorize the formation of corporations for the erection and keeping of hotels.

PASSED April 9, 1874.

The People of the State of New York, represented in Senate and Assembly, do enact as follows:

Certificate of incorporation. SECTION 1. At any time hereafter any five or more persons who may desire to form a company for the business of erecting buildings for hotel purposes or keeping hotels, or for either or both of such purposes, may make, sign and acknowledge, before some officer competent to take the acknowledgment of deeds, and file in the office of the clerk of the county in which (Where to be filed.) the business of the company shall be carried on, and a duplicate thereof in the office of the secretary of state, a certificate in writing, in which shall be stated the corporate name of the (Contents of certificate.) said company and the object for which the company shall be formed; the amount of the capital stock of the said company, (Amount of capital.) which shall not be less than ten thousand dollars nor exceeding one million dollars; the term of its existence not to exceed fifty years; the number of shares which the stock shall consist; the number of trustees and their names, who shall manage (Trustees.) the concerns of the said company for the first year, and the name of the place in which the operations of the said company are to be carried on.

Corporation, when perfected. § 2. When the certificate shall have been filed, as aforesaid, the persons who shall have signed and acknowledged the same, and their successors, shall be a body politic and corporate, in fact and in name, by the name stated in such certificate, and by that name have succession, and shall be capable (Capacity and powers of corporation.) of suing and being sued in any of the courts of this state; and they and their successors may have a common seal, and may make and alter the same at pleasure; and they shall, by their corporate name, be capable in law of purchasing, holding, leasing and conveying any real and personal estate whatever, which may be necessary to enable the said company to carry on its operations named in such certificate.

Trustees, their number, etc. § 3. The stock, property and concerns of such company shall be managed by not less than three nor more than nine trustees, who shall respectively be stockholders in such company and citizens of the United States, and a majority of whom shall be citizens of this state, who shall, except the first year, be annually elected, by the stockholders, at such time and place as shall be directed by the by-laws of the company; and public notice of the time and place of holding such election (Election notice, how given.) shall be published, not less than ten days previous thereto, in a newspaper printed in the town or city in which or nearest to the place where the operations of the said company shall (Stockholders may vote in person or by proxy.) be carried on, and the election shall be made by such of the stockholders as shall attend for that purpose, either in person or by proxy. All elections shall be by ballot, and each stockholder shall be entitled to as many votes as he owns shares of stock in the said company, and the persons receiving the greatest number of votes shall be trustees; and when any vacancy shall happen among the trustees, by death, resignation or otherwise, it shall be filled by the remainder of the year in such manner as may be provided for by the by-laws of the said company.

Vacancies, how filled.

§ 4. In case it shall happen at any time that an election of trustees shall not be made on the day designated by the by-laws of said company, when it ought to have been made, the company for that reason shall not be dissolved, but it shall be lawful on any other day to hold an election for trustees in such manner as shall be provided for by the said by-laws; and all acts of trustees shall be valid and binding as against such company, until their successors shall be elected.

Failure to elect trustees not to dissolve corporation.

§ 5. There shall be a president of the company, who shall be designated from the number of the trustees, and also such subordinate officer as the company by its by-laws may designate, who may be elected or appointed, and required to give such security for the faithful performance of the duties of their office as the company by its by-laws may require.

Officers. Security may be required.

§ 6. It shall be lawful for the trustees to call in and demand from the stockholders respectively, all such sums of money by them subscribed, at such times and in such payments or installments as the trustees shall deem proper, under the penalty of forfeiting the shares of stock subscribed for and all previous payments made thereon, if payment shall not be made by the stockholder within sixty days after a personal demand of the same or notice requiring such payment shall have been published for six successive weeks, in a newspaper printed in a city or town in which or nearest to the place where the business of the company shall be carried on as aforesaid.

Trustees may call in subscription of stock. Forfeiture for non-payment.

§ 7. The trustees of such company shall have power to make such prudential by-laws as they shall deem proper for the management and disposition of the stock and business affairs of such company, not inconsistent with the laws of this State, and prescribing the duties of officers, artificers and servants that may be employed, for the appointment of all officers, and for carrying on all kinds of business within the object and purposes of said company.

By-laws.

§ 8. The stock of such company shall be deemed personal estate, and shall be transferable in such manner as shall be prescribed by the by-laws of the company; but no share shall be transferable until all previous calls thereon shall have been fully paid in, or shall have been declared forfeited for the non-payment of calls thereon. And it shall not be lawful for such company to use any of its funds in the purchase of any stock in any other corporation, or to hold the same, except as collateral security to a prior indebtedness.

Stock deemed personal estate. Not to purchase stock in another corporation.

§ 9. The copy of any certificate of incorporation filed in pursuance of this act, certified by the county clerk under his official seal to be a true copy, and of the whole of such certifi-

Evidence.

cate, shall be received in all courts and places as presumptive legal evidence of the facts herein stated.

Personal liability exemption from. § 10. No person holding stock in any such company, as executor, administrator, guardian or trustee, and no person holding such stock as collateral security, shall be personally subject to any liability as stockholder of such company; Pledge of stock, effect of. but the person pledging such stock shall be considered as holding the same, and shall be liable as stockholder, Trust estate, how far liable. accordingly; and the estate and funds in the hands of such executor, administrator, guardian or trustee, shall be liable in like manner and to the same extent as the testator or intestate, or the ward or person interested in such trust fund, would have been if he had been living and competent to act and hold the same stock in his own name.

Trustee, etc., may vote as stockholder. § 11. Every such executor, administrator, guardian or trustee shall represent the share of stock in his hands at all meetings of the company, and may vote accordingly as a stockholder; and every person who shall pledge his stock as aforesaid may, nevertheless, represent the same at all such meetings, and may vote accordingly as a stockholder.

Liability of company to guests. § 12. The said company shall be subject to the same liabilities as natural persons for all the purposes of this act; and shall be liable in the same manner and to the same extent as the proprietors of other hotels are liable, for loss, injury or destruction of the property of guests, except as may be otherwise provided by special written contract; but this section shall not be construed so as to make said company liable as hotel keepers in case said company shall have leased said hotel.

Stockholder liable for debts of company to amount of his stock. § 13. Each stockholder of said company shall be jointly, severally and individually liable to the creditors of, or those holding claims against, said company, to an amount equal to the amount of stock held by him or her in said company, for all the debts and liabilities of the company, but shall not be liable to an action therefor before an execution shall be returned unsatisfied, in whole or in part, against the company, and then the amount due on such execution shall be the amount recoverable, with costs, against such stockholders.

Book to be kept. § 14. It shall be the duty of the trustees of every such corporation or company to cause a book to be kept by the treasurer or clerk thereof, containing the names of all persons, Its contents. alphabetically arranged, who are or shall within six years have been stockholders of such company, and showing their places of residence, the number of shares of stock held by them respectively, and the time when they respectively became the owners of such shares, and the amount of stock actually paid in; which book shall, during the usual business hours Book to be open to inspection of stockholders and judgment creditors. of the day, on every day except Sunday, and the thirtieth day of May, the fourth day of July, the twenty-fifth day of December and the first day of January, be open for the inspection of stockholders and creditors of the company, who have obtained judgment upon their claims, upon which execution has been returned unsatisfied in whole or in part, and their personal representatives, at the office or principal place of business of such company, in the county where its business operations shall be located; and any and every such stock-holder, creditor or representative shall have a right to make extracts from such book; and no transfer of such stock shall be valid for any purpose whatever, except to render the person to whom it shall be transferred liable for the debts of the company according to the provisions of this act, until it shall have been entered therein, as required by this section, by an entry showing to and from whom transferred. Such book shall be presumptive evidence of the facts therein stated in favor of the plaintiff in any suit or proceeding against such company or against any one or more stockholders. Every officer or agent of any such company who shall neglect to make any proper entry in such book, or shall refuse or neglect to exhibit the same or allow the same to be inspected and extracts to be taken therefrom, as provided by this section, shall be deemed a misdemeanor, and the company shall forfeit and pay to the party injured a penalty of fifty dollars for every such neglect or refusal, and all the damages resulting therefrom; and every company that shall neglect to keep such book open for inspection as aforesaid shall forfeit to the people the sum of fifty dollars for every day it shall so neglect, to be sued for and recovered in the name of the people by the district attorney of the county in which the business of such corporation shall be located; and when so recovered, the amount shall be paid into the treasury of such county for the use thereof.

Books, where to be kept.

Transfers of stock to be entered therein.

Book to be evidence.

Misdemeanors.

Penalties therefor.

District attorney to sue for penalties.

§ 15. Every corporation created under this act shall possess the general powers and privileges, and be subject to the liabilities and restrictions contained in title third of chapter eighteen of the first part of the Revised Statutes.

Provisions of Revised Statutes applicable to.

§ 16. After the passage of this act it shall not be lawful to organize any corporation under chapter three hundred and seventy-one of the laws of eighteen hundred and sixty-six, or the acts passed supplementary thereto or amendatory thereof.

Not to organize hereafter under manufacturing act.

CHAP. 149.

AN ACT to amend the act passed April twenty-seventh, eighteen hundred and seventy-two, entitled "An act to amend chapter six hundred and fifty-seven of the laws of eighteen hundred and seventy-one, entitled 'An act to amend the act passed February seventeen, eighteen hundred and forty-eight, entitled 'An act to authorize the formation of corporations for manufacturing, mining, mechanical or chemical purposes,'" passed April twentieth, eighteen hundred and seventy-one.

PASSED April 10, 1874.

The People of the State of New York, represented in Senate and Assembly, do enact as follows:

Amendment. SECTION 1. The first section of the act entitled "An act to authorize the formation of corporations for manufacturing, mining, mechanical or chemical purposes," passed February seventeenth, eighteen hundred and forty-eight, as amended by chapter two hundred and sixty-two of the laws of eighteen hundred and fifty-seven, as amended by section two of chapter six hundred and fifty-seven of the laws of eighteen hundred and seventy-one, as amended by chapter four hundred and twenty-six of the laws of eighteen hundred and seventy-two, is hereby amended so as to read as follows:

For what purposes corporations may be formed. § 1. At any time hereafter, any three or more persons who may desire to form a company for the purpose of carrying on any kind of manufacturing, mining, mechanical or chemical business, or the business of printing and publishing books, pamphlets and newspapers, or the business of preserving and dealing in meats, or the business of making butter, cheese, concentrated or condensed milk, or any other products of the dairy, or the business of erecting buildings for church sheds or laundry purposes, and the carrying on of laundry business, or the business of slaughtering animals, may make, sign and acknowledge, before some officer competent to take the acknowledgment of deeds, and file in the office of the clerk of the county in which the business of the company shall be carried on, and a duplicate thereof in the office of the secretary of state, a certificate in writing, in which shall be stated the corporate name of the said company, and the objects for which the company shall be formed, the amount of the capital stock of the said company, the term of its existence (not to exceed fifty years), the number of shares of which the said stock shall consist, the number of trustees and their names, who shall manage the concerns of said company for the first year, and the names of the town and county in which the operations of the said company are to be carried on.

Certificate to be made, signed, acknowledged and filed.

Its contents.

Liability of stockholders. § 2. The stockholders of any corporation hereafter formed under the act hereby amended, or any act amendatory thereof or supplementary thereto, or extending the operation and effect thereof, shall, in addition to the liabilities provided for in said acts, be individually responsible, equally and ratably, in an amount to the extent of their respective shares of stock in such corporation. The term stockholder, as used in this section, shall apply not only to such persons as appear by the books of the corporation or association to be such, but also to every equitable owner of stock, although the same may appear on such books in the name of another person; and also to every person who shall have advanced the installments or purchase-money of any stock in the name of any person under twenty-one years of age, and while such person remains a minor, to the extent of such advance; and also to every guardian or other trustee who shall voluntarily invest any trust funds in such stock; and no trust funds in the hands of such guardian or trustee shall be in any way liable under the provisions of this act and the acts aforesaid, by reason of any such investment, nor shall the person for whose benefit any such investment may be made be responsible in respect to such stock until thirty days after the time when such persons, respectively, become competent and able to control and dispose of the same; but the guardian or other trustee making such investment as aforesaid shall continue responsible as a stockholder until such responsibility devolves upon the person beneficially interested therein; and in respect to stock held by a guardian or other trustee under a transfer of the same by a third person, or under positive directions by a third person for such investment, the person making such transfer or giving such directions, and his executors and administrators shall, for the purposes of this act and the acts aforesaid, be deemed a stockholder, and the estate of such person, if he be deceased, shall be responsible for the debts and liabilities chargeable on such stock, according to the provisions of this act.

Term stockholder defined.

Trust fund, not liable, nor person interested therein, while incompetent.

Responsibility of guardian, or other trustee.

Term stockholder, further defined.

CHAP. 156.

AN ACT in regard to serving citations upon minors and special guardians.

PASSED April 10, 1874.

The People of the State of New York, represented in Senate and Assembly, do enact as follows:

SECTION 1. In proceedings of administrators and executors, on final settlements of their accounts, minors shall be served with citations, and special guardians appointed, in the same manner as citations are required to be served, and special guardians appointed on the proof of wills, and in no other way.

§ 2. This act shall take effect immediately.

CHAP. 169.

AN ACT to amend chapter three hundred and ninety-five of the laws of eighteen hundred and seventy-three, entitled "An act to alter the sytem of repairing the highways," passed May second, eighteen hundred and seventy-three.

PASSED April 18, 1874; three-fifths being present.

The People of the State of New York, represented in Senate and Assembly, do enact as follows:

SECTION 1. Section three of chapter three hundred and ninety-five of the laws of eighteen hundred and seventy-three, entitled "An act to alter the system of repairing the highways," passed May second, eighteen hundred and seventy-three, is hereby amended so as to read as follows:

Annual tax for highways. § 3. It shall be lawful for any town voting in favor of such change to raise by tax, to be levied and collected the same as any other tax, for the repair of its highways, an annual sum of money, which shall be at least equivalent to the value of the days' work theretofore assessed at the commutation prices.

§ 2. This act shall take effect immediately.

CHAP. 172.

AN ACT to amend an act entitled "An act requiring canal superintendents to publish monthly abstracts of their official disbursements," passed March twenty-fifth, eighteen hundred and fifty-three.

PASSED April 14, 1874; three-fifths being present.

The People of the State of New York, represented in Senate and Assembly, do enact as follows:

SECTION 1. Section one of chapter fifty-two of the laws of eighteen hundred and fifty-three, entitled "An act requiring canal superintendents to publish monthly abstracts of their official disbursements," passed March twenty-fifth, eighteen hundred and fifty-three, is hereby amended so as to read as follows:

Monthly abstract of disbursements to be published. § 1. It shall be the duty of each canal superintendent of this state, or of the officer upon whom the duties of superintendent shall be devolved, on or before the twentieth day of each month, to publish in some newspaper printed in any county through which any part of the section of canal in his charge shall pass (giving preference to a newspaper published in a city and town located on the line of the section of canal in his charge, or in the county of his residence when possible), an abstract of his official disbursements during the preceding calendar month, stating therein the name and residence of every

Contents of abstract.

person to whom he has paid money, and the amount paid to each; if for labor, the number of days and the amount per day; if for material, the kind, quantity and price; also a similar statement of all tools and implements purchased, which abstract, verified by the oath of such superintendent, shall be published in the entire weekly edition of such newspaper, and said superintendent shall also make and file a duplicate thereof in the office of the county clerk in the county in which such superintendent shall reside. The expense of publication herein provided for, at not exceeding the legal rates now allowed by law for the publication of Session Laws, shall be included from time to time in the monthly abstracts of the superintendent, and the amount thereof shall be paid in like manner, and upon like vouchers, as other disbursements and expenditures of the said superintendent are audited and paid; the said publication to be made in such form and manner as may be prescribed by the auditor, and the expense for publication shall be determined and approved by him.

Verification.

Expense of publication.

§ 2. Section two of said act is hereby repealed.

§ 3. This act shall take effect immediately.

CHAP. 173.

AN ACT to fix the time for transacting the business of the town at the annual town meeting for election of town officers.

PASSED April 14, 1874.

The People of the State of New York, represented in Senate and Assembly, do enact as follows:

SECTION 1. The time for transacting the business of the towns in the state of New York, which requires a vote of the people thereof, shall be and is hereby fixed at twelve o'clock, M., of the day of the annual town meeting for the election of town officers and continue without adjournment until finished, excepting the balloting for town officers and the duties connected therewith.

Time for transaction of business.

§ 2. No question involving the expenditure of money shall be introduced after two o'clock, P. M., of the same day.

§ 3. This act shall not apply to any town in this state, wherein the manner of holding town meetings is regulated by special act.

Not applicable to certain towns.

§ 4. This act shall take effect immediately.

CHAP. 189.

AN ACT to provide security against extraordinary conflagrations, and for the creation of safety funds by fire insurance companies.

PASSED April 16, 1874; three-fifths being present.

The People of the State of New York, represented in Senate and Assembly, do enact as follows:

Guaranty and special reserve funds. SECTION 1. Hereafter it shall be lawful for any fire insurance company, organized under the laws of this state, to create the funds herein provided for, to be known and designated as the guaranty surplus fund and the special reserve fund, and to avail itself of the provisions of this act upon complying with the requirements thereof.

How created. § 2. Any fire insurance company desiring to create such funds shall be and it is hereby authorized to do so, upon the adoption of a resolution by its board of directors at a regular meeting thereof, and filing with the superintendent of the insurance department a copy thereof, declaring the desire and intention of such company to create such funds and to do business under the provisions of this act; and as soon after the filing of such copy of the resolution as convenient, the superintendent shall make, or cause to be made, an examination of such company, and he shall make a certificate of the result thereof, which shall particularly set forth the amount of surplus funds held by such company at the date of such examination, which under the provisions of this act, are to and may be equally divided between and be set apart to constitute said guaranty surplus and special reserve funds, which certificate shall be recorded in the insurance department; and from and after the date of the recording of such certificate, all the policies and renewals of policies issued by such company shall have printed thereon, by such company, a notice that the same are issued under and in pursuance of this act, referring to the same by its chapter, date and title; and such policies and renewals shall be deemed to have been issued and received, subject to the provisions of this act.

Examination of company by superintendent.

Notice on policies.

Dividends. § 3. After the date mentioned in any such resolution so passed and filed, it shall not be lawful for such company to make, declare or pay, in any form, any dividend upon its capital stock, exceeding seven per centum per annum thereupon and upon the surplus funds to be formed hereunder, until after its guaranty surplus fund and its special reserve fund shall have together accumulated to an amount equal to its said capital stock, and the entire surplus profits of such company above such annual dividend of seven per cent shall be equally divided between and be set aside to constitute the said guaranty surplus fund and the said special reserve fund, which said funds shall be held and used as hereinafter provided and not otherwise; and any company doing business

Surplus profits to be set part to constitute fund.

under this act, which shall declare or pay any dividend contrary to the provisions herein contained, shall be liable to be proceeded against by the attorney-general for its dissolution.

§ 4. Said guaranty surplus fund shall be held and invested by such company the same as its capital stock and surplus accumulations; and shall be liable and applicable in the same manner as the capital stock to the payment generally of the losses of such money. Guaranty fund, how to be invested.

§ 5. Said special reserve fund shall be invested according to existing laws relating to investments of capital by fire insurance companies, and shall be deposited from time to time, as the same shall accumulate and be invested, with the superintendent of the insurance department, who shall permit the company depositing the same to change such deposits by substituting for those withdrawn others of equal amount and value, and to collect and receive the interests or dividends upon such securities as the same may accrue; and such special reserve fund shall be deemed a fund contributed by the stockholders to protect such company and its policy-holders other than claimants for losses already existing or then incurred, in case of such extraordinary conflagration or conflagrations as hereinafter mentioned; and said fund shall not be regarded as any part or portion of the assets in possession of said company, so as to be or render the same liable for any claim or claims for losses, by fire or otherwise, except as herein provided. Special reserve fund, how to be invested. Fund, not assets.

§ 6. In estimating the profit of any such company, for the purpose of making a division thereof, between such guaranty surplus fund and such special reserve fund, there shall be deducted from the gross assets of the company, including for this purpose the amount of the special reserve fund, the sum of the following items: First, the amount of all outstanding claims; second, an amount sufficient to meet the liability of such company for the unearned premiums upon its unexpired policies, which amount shall be at least equal to one-half of the premiums received on policies having less than one year to run from date of policy, and a pro-rata proportion of the premiums received on policies having more than one year to run from date of policy, and shall be known as the reinsurance liability; third, the amount of its guaranty surplus fund and of its special reserve fund; fourth, the amount of the capital of the company; and fifth, interest at the rate of seven per cent per annum upon the amount of the capital and of the said funds, for whatever time shall have elapsed since the last preceding cash dividend; and the balance shall constitute the net surplus of the company, subject to an equal division between the said funds, as herein provided. Profit, how to be estimated. Surplus for division.

§ 7. In the event of any extensive conflagration or conflagrations, whereby the claims upon such company shall exceed the amount of the capital stock, and of the guaranty surplus fund provided for by this act, the said company shall notify the said superintendent of the fact, who shall then make or cause to be made an examination of said company, and shall issue his When surplus reserve fund shall be held for protection of policy-holders.

certificate of the result, showing the amounts of capital, of guaranty surplus fund, of special reserve fund, of re-insurance liability and of other assets; and upon his issuing such certificate in duplicate, one copy to be given the company and one to be recorded in the insurance department, the said special reserve fund shall be immediately held to protect all policy-holders of such company other than such as are claimants upon it at the time, or such as become such claimants in consequence of such conflagration or conflagrations, and the amount of said special reserve fund, and an amount equal to the unearned premiums of such company, to be ascertained as hereinbefore provided, shall constitute the capital and assets of such company for the protection of policy-holders other than such claimants, and for the further conduct of its business; and such official certificate of the superintendent shall be binding and conclusive upon all parties interested in such company, whether as stockholders, creditors or policy-holders; and upon the payment to the claimants for losses or otherwise, existing at the time of, or caused by, such general conflagration or conflagrations, of the amount to which they are respectively entitled, in proportion to their several claims, of the full sum of the capital of such company and of its guaranty surplus fund, and of its assets, excepting only such special reserve fund and an amount of its assets equal to the liability of the company for unearned premiums, as so certified by such superintendent, such company shall be forever discharged from any and all further liability to such claimants, and to each of them. And the said superintendent shall, after issuing his said certificate, upon the demand of such company, transfer to it all such securities as shall have been deposited with him by such company as such special reserve fund; and if the amount of such special reserve fund be less than fifty per cent of the full amount of the capital of the company, a requisition shall be issued by the said superintendent upon the stockholders, to make up such capital to that proportion of its full amount, in the manner now provided by law, in the case of companies with impaired capitals; and, provided further, that any capital so impaired shall be made up to at least the sum of two hundred thousand dollars. And in case said company, after such requisition, shall fail to make up its capital to at least said amount of two hundred thousand dollars, as therein directed, said special reserve fund shall still be held as security, and liable for any and all losses occurring upon policies of such company after such conflagration or conflagrations. Such company shall, in its annual statement to the insurance department of this state, set forth the amount of such special reserve fund, and of its guaranty surplus fund.

Company discharged from liability, when.

Transfer of securities.

Requisition upon stockholders.

Proviso.

Annual statement.

Impairment of capital, how to be made up.

§ 8. If, at any time after such special reserve fund shall have been accumulated by any company, it shall appear, upon examination by the said superintendent, that the capital of such company has, in the absence of any such extensive conflagration, become impaired so as to cause him to order a call upon the stockholders to make up such impairment, the board of directors of such company may either comply with such order and require the necessary payment by the stockholders, or at their option they may apply for that purpose so much of said special reserve fund as will make such impairment good. No company doing business under this act shall insure any larger amount upon any single risk than is permitted by law to a company possessing the same amount of capital, irrespective of the funds hereby provided for.

§ 9. This act shall take effect immediately.

CHAP. 207.

AN ACT to amend the Revised Statutes relating to embezzlements by clerks, servants, officers, agents and other persons.

PASSED April 18, 1874; three-fifths being present.

The People of the State of New York, represented in Senate and Assembly, do enact as follows:

SECTION 1. Section fifty-nine, article five, title three, chapter one, of the fourth part of the Revised Statutes, is hereby amended so as to read as follows:

§ 59. If any clerk or servant of a private person or a copartnership (except apprentices and persons under the age of eighteen years), or if any officer, agent, clerk or servant of a municipal or other corporation, or of a joint-stock company or association, or any director, trustee or manager of such corporation, joint-stock company or association, converts to his own use, or, without the consent of his master or employer, takes, makes way with or secretes with intent to convert to his own use or to the use of another, or withholds or appropriates or otherwise fraudulently applies or makes use of any money, goods, rights in action or other valuable securities or effects belonging to another and which may have come into his possession, or under his care, by virtue of such employment or office, he shall be judged guilty of embezzlement, and shall, upon conviction, be punished in the manner prescribed by law for feloniously stealing property of the value of the article so embezzled.

Embezzlement, what acts by a clerk officer, etc., shall constitute.

Punishment.

§ 2. Nothing herein contained shall affect crimes committed before the passage of this act.

Not to have retrospective effect.

§ 3. This act shall take effect immediately.

Ante, vol. 2, p. 678; vol. 1, R. L., pp. 112 and 412; Laws of 1819, p. p. 314; 22 N. Y. 245; 17 id. 114; 2 Barb. 429; 5 Denio, 76; 8 Hill, 195; 15 Wend. 147 and 582; 10 id. 299; 6 How. Pr. 59; 41 id. 298.

CHAP. 208.

AN ACT to amend article two of title ten of chapter eight of part three of the Revised Statutes, relating to summary proceedings to recover the possession of land.

PASSED April 18, 1874; three-fifths being present.

The People of the State of New York, represented in Senate and Assembly, do enact as follows:

SECTION 1. Subdivision four of section twenty-eight of article two of title ten of chapter eight of part three of the Revised Statutes is hereby amended so as to read as follows:

Summary proceedings. 4. When any person shall hold over and continue in possession of any real estate which shall have been sold pursuant to the foreclosure of a mortgage thereon, or by virtue of an execution against such person, after a title under such sale shall have been perfected.

§ 2. This act shall take effect immediately.

Ante, 21 How. Pr. 108; 16 N. Y. 567; 13 Wend. 29; 17 id. 464; 20 id. 22.

CHAP. 209.

AN ACT to amend an act, passed April eighteenth, eighteen hundred and fifty-nine, entitled "An act to extend the provisions of an act authorizing the imprisonment of persons convicted of certain crimes in the counties of Montgomery and Oneida, in the Albany county penitentiary," passed April twelfth, eighteen hundred and fifty-eight, to all the counties in this state.

PASSED April 18, 1874; three-fifths being present.

The People of the State of New York, represented in Senate and Assembly, do enact as follows:

SECTION 1. The act entitled "An act to extend the provisions of an act authorizing the imprisonment of persons convicted of certain crimes in the counties of Montgomery and Oneida, in the Albany county penitentiary, passed April twelfth, eighteen hundred and fifty-eight, to all the counties in this state," is hereby amended so as to read as follows:

Agreement by boards of supervisors for keeping prisoners. § 1. It shall be lawful for the several boards of supervisors in the several counties in this state to enter into an agreement with the board of supervisors of any county having a penitentiary therein, or with any person in their behalf by them appointed to receive and keep in the said penitentiary any person or persons who may be sentenced to confinement therein by any court or magistrate in any of the said several counties in this state, for any term not less than sixty days. Whenever such agreement shall have been made, it shall be the duty of the said several boards of supervisors of the several counties aforesaid, to give public notice thereof, specifying in such notice the period of the continuance of such agreement, which said notice shall be published in such newspapers, printed in said several counties, not less than two, and for such period of time not less than four weeks, as the several boards of supervisors of said several counties shall direct. Notice thereof to be given.

§ 2. It shall be the duty of every court, police justice, justice of the peace, or other magistrate, by whom any person may be sentenced, in the several counties in this state, for any term not less than sixty days, for any crime or misdemeanor not punishable by imprisonment in the state prison during the continuance of the agreement mentioned in the first section of this act, to sentence such person to imprisonment in the penitentiary in the county with the board of supervisors of which the said agreement is made, there to be received, kept and employed in the manner prescribed by law, and the rules and discipline of said penitentiary; and it shall be the duty of such court, justice or magistrate, by a warrant, duly signed by the presiding judge or justice of such court, or by such justice or other magistrate so giving such sentence, to cause such person so sentenced, to be forthwith and by the most direct route conveyed by some proper officer to the county jail of the county in which he is so sentenced, and to be thereupon conveyed by the sheriff of such county to said penitentiary. Duty of courts, etc., as to sentence. Warrant.

§ 3. It shall be the duty of the constables in and for the several counties of this state, to whom any warrant or commitment for that purpose may be directed, by any court or magistrate in this act mentioned, to convey such person so sentenced, to the county jail of the county in which he is so sentenced, and of the sheriff of said county forthwith to convey such person to the penitentiary referred to in the second section of this act, and there deliver such person to the keeper of said penitentiary, whose duty it shall be to receive such persons, so sentenced, during the continuance of said agreement, authorized by the first section of this act, to be there safely kept and employed, according to the rules and discipline of said penitentiary; and the officers thus conveying such convicts, so sentenced, shall be paid such fees and expenses therefor, as the several boards of supervisors of the several counties of this state shall prescribe and allow. Constables and sheriffs. Fees.

§ 4. This act shall take effect immediately.

CHAP. 212.

AN ACT to extend the time to complete the revision of the Statutes by the commissioners appointed for that purpose.

PASSED April 18, 1874; three-fifths being present.

The People of the State of New York, represented in Senate and Assembly, do enact as follows:

SECTION 1. The time to complete the work of revising the statutes of the state, and the term of office of each of the commissioners appointed to make such revision, is hereby extended two years.

CHAP. 214.

AN ACT making appropriations for the payment of the principal and interest on the canal debt for the fiscal year commencing on the first day of October, one thousand eight hundred and seventy-four, and to provide for the payment of the debt contracted under section twelve of article seven of the constitution.

PASSED April 20, 1874; three-fifths being present.

The People of the State of New York, represented in Senate and Assembly, do enact as follows:

SECTION 1. The following sums are hereby appropriated out of the canal revenues for the fiscal year commencing on the first day of October, one thousand eight hundred and seventy-four:

For the payment of the interest in coin on the loans made under section three of article seven of the constitution, the sum of six hundred and thirty thousand dollars, or so much thereof as may be necessary.

To provide for the sinking fund for the extinguishment of the principal of the loans made under section three of article seven of the constitution, the sum of three hundred and fifty thousand dollars.

After complying with the foregoing provisions, if there shall be any remainder of the surplus revenues, the sum of six hundred thousand dollars, or so much thereof as shall remain of said surplus, is hereby appropriated to the sinking fund for the payment of the loans under section three of article seven of the constitution.

§ 2. The sum of two million three hundred and sixty-one thousand three hundred and seventy-five dollars, or so much thereof as may be necessary, is hereby appropriated from the sinking fund under section three of article seven of the constitution, or from the proceeds of any deficiency loan on account of said sinking fund, to pay the principal in coin of the enlargement debt maturing on the first day of October, one thousand eight hundred and seventy-four.

§ 3. The following sums are hereby appropriated out of the proceeds of any tax to be levied and collected under the provisions of the act chapter two hundred and seventy-one of the laws of eighteen hundred and fifty-nine, to pay the interest and reimburse the principal of the loan of two million five hundred thousand dollars, to provide for the payment of the floating debt of the state:

To pay the interest in coin on said loan for the fiscal year, commencing on the first day of October, one thousand eight hundred and seventy-four, sixty thousand dollars, or so much thereof as may be necessary.

To provide for the sinking fund to pay the principal of said loan, one hundred and thirty-eight thousand eight hundred and eighty-eight dollars, being for one year's contribution to said fund, as provided for by the act aforesaid.

CHAP. 240.

AN ACT to further amend an act, passed April twentieth, eighteen hundred and sixty-six, entitled "An act supplementary to the act entitled 'An act to authorize the formation of railroad corporations, and to regulate the same,'" passed April second, eighteen hundred and fifty.

PASSED April 23, 1874; three-fifths being present.

The People of the State of New York, represented in Senate and Assembly, do enact as follows:

SECTION 1. Section five of chapter six hundred and ninety-seven of the laws of eighteen hundred and sixty-six, entitled "An act supplementary to the act entitled 'An act to authorize the formation of railroad corporations, and to regulate the same,'" passed April second, eighteen hundred and fifty, is hereby amended so as to read as follows:

§ 5. The continuance of any railroad corporation now existing, or hereafter to be formed under the laws of this state, may be extended beyond the time named for that purpose in its act or acts of incorporation, or in the articles of association of such corporation, by the filing in the office of the secretary of state a certificate of consent to such extension, signed by the holders of two-thirds in amount of the stock held by the stockholders of such corporation, and in every case where such consent has been or shall be so filed, the term of existence of such corporation is hereby extended and declared to be extended for the period designated in such certificate, and each such corporation shall, during the period named in such certificate, possess and enjoy all the rights, privileges and franchises enjoyed or exercised by such corporation at the time such certificate was or shall be so filed. Each such certificate shall be proved or acknowledged by the individuals signing

Extension of corporate existence, how effected.

the same, before some officer authorized by law to take acknowledgments of deeds, and whenever such stock shall be owned or held by firms or copartnerships the execution of such certificate shall be acknowledged by one or more of such copartners; and it shall be the duty of the secretary of state to record such certificate in the book kept in his office for the record of articles of association of railroad companies. A copy of such certificate and of the acknowledgment thereof, certified by the secretary of state, shall be presumptive evidence of the truth of the facts therein stated.

Firms.

Certified copy of certificate evidence.

§ 2. This act shall take effect immediately.

CHAP. 245.

AN ACT to amend an act entitled "An act authorizing the incorporation of rural cemetery associations," passed April twenty-seventh, eighteen hundred and forty-seven, and the acts amendatory thereof.

PASSED April 24, 1874; three-fifths being present.

The People of the State of New York, represented in Senate and Assembly, do enact as follows:

SECTION 1. Section four of chapter one hundred and thirty-three of the laws of eighteen hundred and forty-seven is hereby amended so as to read as follows:

Corporation may take by purchase, etc.

§ 4. Any association incorporated under this act may take by purchase or devise, and hold, within the county in which the certificate of their incorporation is recorded, not exceeding two hundred acres of land, or such further quantity as the legislature has prescribed or may prescribe, to be held and occupied exclusively for a cemetery for the burial of the dead. Such lands or such parts thereof as may from time to time be required for that purpose shall be surveyed and subdivided into lots or plats of such size as the trustees may direct, with such avenues, paths, alleys and walks as the trustees may deem proper, and a map or maps of such surveys shall be filed and kept in the office of the associations, open to the inspection of the lot owners. The trustees may sell and convey the lots or plats and parts of lots or plats designated on such maps upon such terms as shall be agreed and subject to such conditions and restrictions as may be imposed upon the use of such lots or plats by rules and regulations now adopted or hereafter to be adopted by the trustees of such association. The conveyances shall be executed under the common seal of the association and signed by the president or vice-president and the treasurer of the association. Any association incorporated under this act may hold personal property to an amount not exceeding five thousand dollars, or such further amount as the legislature has prescribed or may prescribe, besides what may arise from the sale of lots or plats.

Survey.

Maps.

Trustees may sell lots.

Conveyances, how to be executed.

Personal property.

§ 2. Section seven of said act is hereby amended so as to read as follows:

§ 7. All lots or parts of lots or plats which shall be conveyed by the association as a separate lot or plat, shall be indivisible, but may be held and owned in undivided shares; but any lots or plats and parts of lots or plats remaining unsold, and in which there shall have been no interment, may, by order of the trustees, be resurveyed, enlarged, subdivided or altered in shape or size, and designated by numbers or otherwise on any map or maps which may be filed and kept pursuant to the fourth section of the act hereby amended; one-half at least of the proceeds of all sales of lots or plats shall be first appropriated to the payment of the purchase-money of the lands acquired by the association until the purchase-money shall be paid, and the residue thereof to preserving, improving and embellishing the said cemetery grounds and the avenues or roads leading thereto, and to defray the incidental expenses of the cemetery establishment, and after the payment of the purchase-money and the debts contracted therefor, and for surveying and laying out the land, the proceeds of all future sales shall be applied to the improvement, embellishment and preservation of such cemetery and for incidental expenses, and to no other purpose or object.

Lots, indivisible.

May be enlarged or subdivided.

Proceeds of sales, how to be applied.

§ 3. Section eleven of said act is hereby amended by adding thereto at the end thereof:

"And provided further, that in case all bodies interred upon any lot, or part of a lot, shall be lawfully removed therefrom, the owner or owners may apply to any court of record held in any county in which said courts are situated, for leave to sell the same; upon such application, the court shall require such notice of the hearing of the application, as it shall prescribe to be given to all parties interested, including said cemetery association, and may, for proper cause shown, authorize the sale of the same.

Application to court of record for sale of lots.

§ 4. Every association incorporated under the act hereby amended may, from time to time, by its trustees, make such rules and regulations as it shall deem proper for the care, management and protection of the cemetery lands and property; for the use, care and protection of all lots and plats and parts of lots therein; the conduct of persons while within the cemetery grounds; to exclude improper persons therefrom and improper assemblages therein; to regulate the dividing marks between the various lots and plats and parts of lots and plats, and their size, shape and location; to regulate the size of erections, and to forbid the erection of structures upon such lots or plats and parts of lots or plats; to prevent the burial within the cemetery of persons executed for crime; to prevent the burial on any lot or plat or part of any lot or plat of any person not entitled to such burial by section eleven of said act of April twenty-seventh, eighteen hundred and forty-seven, hereby amended; to regulate and prevent disinterments; to prevent improper monuments, effigies, structures and inscriptions within the cemetery grounds, and to remove

Rules and regulations.

the same; and to regulate the introduction and growth of plants, trees and shrubs within the cemetery grounds. Such rules and regulations, when adopted, shall be binding upon all lot owners and persons visiting said cemetery grounds, and shall apply to all lots and parts of lots sold or hereafter to be sold. Such rules and regulations, when adopted, shall be plainly printed and publicly posted in the principal office of the association, and in such places upon the cemetery grounds as the trustees of the association shall by resolution prescribe.

Rules, etc., binding.

To be posted.

§ 5. This act shall take effect immediately.

CHAP. 253.

AN ACT relative to the care and education of deaf mutes.

PASSED April 25, 1874.

The People of the State of New York, represented in Senate and Assembly, do enact as follows:

Application by parent, guardian, etc.

SECTION 1. Any parent, guardian or friend of any deaf mute child within this state, over the age of six years and under the age of twelve years, may make application to the supervisor of the town or city where such child may be, for a permit or order to place such child in the New York Institution for the Deaf and Dumb or in the Institution for the Improved Instruction of Deaf Mutes, or in any of the deaf mute institutions of this state, and it shall be the duty of such supervisor, if in his judgment the means of the child, or the parents or parent of such child, will not enable them to defray the expense in a public institution, to grant such permit or order and to cause said child to be received and placed in such one of the institutions of this state for the education of deaf mutes, as the said supervisor shall select.

Duty of supervisor.

CHAP. 258.

AN ACT to amend an act entitled "An act to authorize the sale of real estate, in which a widow is or shall be entitled to dower in satisfaction and discharge thereof," passed May six, eighteen hundred and seventy.

PASSED April 27, 1874; three-fifths being present.

The People of the State of New York, represented in Senate and Assembly, do enact as follows:

SECTION 1. Section two of an act entitled "An act to authorize the sale of real estate, in which a widow is or shall be entitled to dower in satisfaction and discharge thereof," passed May sixth, eighteen hundred and seventy, is hereby amended so as to read as follows:

Court may direct

§ 2. The court in any such action shall also have authority to direct that all taxes, assessments and water-rates which are liens upon the real estate so adjudged to be sold, at the time of the sale thereof, be paid out of the proceeds of such sale, and to direct that the sheriff or referee making the sale, with and out of such proceeds of sale, redeem such real estate from all sales thereof for unpaid taxes, assessments or water-rates. The plaintiff in any such action, if a sale of real estate shall be adjudged therein, shall be entitled to recover her costs and disbursements of such action, to be paid out of the proceeds of such sale. It shall not be necessary to make any creditor having a lien on the premises in question, or upon any part thereof, or upon the undivided share or interest of any party to the action by judgment, decree, mortgage or otherwise, a party to such action, nor if any part of such premises shall be actually admeasured or assigned to the the plaintiff in satisfaction of her dower, shall the lien of such creditor be altered, impaired or affected thereby so far as regards the remainder of said premises not set apart or assigned to such plaintiff, but such lien shall be a charge on the remainder of such premises or of such undivided interest therein, and in case the court shall deem that a sale of such real estate is for the best interest of the parties to said action, and shall so adjudge them, all subsequent proceedings in said action shall be concluded in accordance with the provisions of title three of chapter five of the third part of the Revised Statutes, entitled "Of the partition of lands owned by several persons," as amended, altered or modified by the several acts passed subsequent thereto, and the provision of said title as so amended, altered and modified for the purposes of such sale and the distribution of the proceeds thereof are made applicable to the proceedings in such action.

Taxes, etc. to be paid. Costs. Creditor not a necessary party. Liens, how affected. Provisions of R. S. made applicable.

§ 2. This act shall take effect immediately.

CHAP. 260.

AN ACT to amend an act entitled "An act to extend the powers of boards of supervisors, except in the counties of New York and Kings," passed May eleventh, eighteen hundred and sixty-nine.

PASSED April 27, 1874; three-fifths being present.

The People of the State of New York, represented in Senate and Assembly, do enact as follows:

SECTION 1. Section one of an act entitled "An act to extend the powers of boards of supervisors, except in the counties of New York and Kings," passed May eleventh, eighteen hundred and sixty-nine, is hereby amended so as to read as follows:

§ 1. The boards of supervisors of each county in this state, except New York and Kings, shall have power, at their annual meeting, or at any other regular meeting, to authorize

Money may be borrowed for highway pur

poses in any towns. the supervisor of any town in said county, by and with the consent of the commissioner or commissioners of highways, town clerk and justices of the peace of such town, to borrow such sum of money, for and on the credit of each town, not exceeding, however, in any year, the amount of one-half of one per cent on the assessed valuation of the taxable property of the town for such year, as the said town officers may deem necessary to build or repair any road or roads, or bridge or bridges in such town, or which shall be partly in such town and partly in an adjoining town, or to pay any existing debt incurred in good faith by or on behalf of such town for such purpose, before the passage of this act; and the said board of supervisors shall have power to prescribe the form of obligation to be issued on any such loan, and the time and place of payment, the time not to exceed ten years from the date of such obligation, and the rate of interest thereon not exceeding seven per cent per annum. And the said board of supervisors shall have power, and it shall be their duty, from time to time, as the said obligations shall become due and payable, to impose upon the taxable property of such town sufficient tax to pay the said principal and interest of such obligations according to the terms and conditions thereof.

Board of supervisors to prescribe form of obligation.

Tax.

Town officers to meet annually to determine amounts, etc.

The town officers hereinbefore mentioned shall meet at the town clerk's office in the town for which they are elected or appointed, on the first Monday of September in each year, at ten o'clock in the morning, to determine what amount, if any, shall be borrowed on the credit of such town for the purposes contained in the first section of the act hereby amended, and for what roads or bridges such amount shall be borrowed or appropriated; and such meeting may be adjourned from time to time, either for want of a quorum or in default of any final determination of any question arising concerning such appropriation, but no such meeting shall be held subsequent to the first Monday of October in each year.

Certificate to be indorsed on bonds.

The bonds authorized by this act shall have indorsed thereon a certificate signed by the town clerk of the town for which they are issued, to the effect that such bonds are issued with the consent of the town officers herein mentioned, at a meeting the date of which shall be mentioned in such certificate.

Town clerk to keep record of bonds.

The town clerk of any town on account of which such bonds are issued shall keep a record showing the date and amount of such bonds, the time and place when the same are made payable, and the rate of interest thereon.

Bonds to be delivered to supervisor.

Such bonds shall be delivered to the supervisor of the town, who shall dispose of the same for not less than the par value thereof, and pay the proceeds thereof to the commissioner or commissioners of highways of such town, to be used by him or them for the purposes for which the same were appropriated; but not more than five hundred dollars of such proceeds shall be expended upon any one road or bridge except under and in pursuance of a contract to be made by the contractor with the commissioner or a majority of the commissioners of highways of such town for the construction or repair

Proceeds, how to be applied.

of such road or bridge, which contract shall be approved by a majority of the town auditors of such town, neither of whom shall be interested in such contract.

Excess, how to be applied. Any amount borrowed and appropriated, pursuant to the provisions of this act, for the repair or construction of any road or bridge in any town, and which it shall not be necessary to use for such purpose, shall be applied by the commissioner or commissioners of highways to the repair of any other road or bridge in such town.

§ 2. This act shall take effect immediately.

CHAP. 261.

AN ACT to amend an act entitled "An act to enable resident aliens to hold and convey real estate, and for other purposes," passed April thirty, eighteen hundred and forty-five.

PASSED April 27, 1874, by a two-thirds vote.

The People of the State of New York, represented in Senate and Assembly, do enact as follows:

SECTION 1. Section four of chapter one hundred and fifteen of the laws of eighteen hundred and forty-five, entitled "An act to enable resident aliens to hold and convey real estate, and for other purposes," passed April thirty, eighteen hundred and forty-five, is hereby amended so as to read as follows, to wit:

Aliens may take as heirs in certain cases. If any alien, resident of this state, or any naturalized or native citizen of the United States, who has purchased and taken, or hereafter shall purchase and take, a conveyance of real estate, within this state, has died, or shall hereafter die, leaving persons who, according to the statutes of this state, would answer the description of heirs of such deceased person, such persons so answering the description of heirs of such deceased person, whether they are citizens or aliens, are hereby declared and made capable of taking and holding, and may take and hold as heirs of such deceased person, as if they were citizens of the United States, the lands and real estate owned and held by such deceased alien or citizen at the time of his decease. But if any of the persons so answering the description of heirs of such deceased person are males of full age, they shall not hold the real estate hereby made descendible to them as against the state unless they are citizens of the United States; or in case they are aliens, unless they make and file in the office of the secretary of state the deposition or affirmation mentioned in the first section of this act. Deposition of aliens.

Repeal. § 2. All acts or parts of acts inconsistent with or repugnant to the provisions of this act are hereby repealed; provided, however, that nothing herein contained shall be taken or construed to affect any grant of land heretofore made by this state; and provided, further, that nothing in this act contained shall be taken or construed to affect the title to any Proviso.

land or lands which may have been heretofore derived through any devise, grant, gift or purchase prior to the passage of this act, or to give any person not heretofore entitled thereto under the laws of this state any right, title or interest as against any such devisee, grantee or purchaser, or any right to impeach or in any manner call in question the validity of any will of the person so dying seized as aforesaid, and it is hereby declared that the record of any such will in the office of the surrogate of any county in this state shall be conclusive evidence of its validity against any and all persons claiming or to claim under this act.

Record of will, its effect.

§ 3. This act shall take effect immediately.

CHAP. 262.

AN ACT for the further protection of private property.

PASSED April 27, 1874; three-fifths being present.

The People of the State of New York, represented in Senate and Assembly, do enact as follows:

Misdemeanor.

SECTION 1. Any person or persons who shall designedly, willfully and maliciously mark, obliterate, alter, deface, paste over, destroy or in any way injure any bill board, bills, notices or printed matter thereon relating to theatrical or other lawful business, shall be deemed guilty of a misdemeanor, and, upon conviction thereof, shall be punished for each offense by imprisonment in the county jail not more than ten days, or by fine, not exceeding fifty dollars, or by both such fine and imprisonment.

Punishment.

§ 2. This act shall take effect immediately.

CHAP. 267.

AN ACT to amend an act entitled "An act concerning the proof of wills, executors and administrators, guardians and wards and surrogates' courts," passed May sixteenth, one thousand eight hundred and thirty-seven.

PASSED April 27, 1874; three-fifths being present.

The People of the State of New York, represented in Senate and Assembly, do enact as follows:

SECTION 1. Section forty of an act entitled "An act concerning the proofs of wills, executors and administrators, guardians and wards, and surrogates' courts," passed the sixteenth day of May, one thousand eight hundred and thirty-seven, is hereby amended so as to read as follows:

When executor or administrator may apply

§ 40. Executors or administrators may apply to the surrogate, pursuant to the fourth title of chapter six of the second part of the Revised Statutes, for authority to mortgage, lease or sell the real estate of their testator or intestate, and for the sale of the interest of such testator or intestate in any land held under a contract for the purchase thereof, whenever they shall discover that the personal estate of the testator or intestate is insufficient to pay his debts and funeral expenses, subject, however, to the provisions of the first section of said title, as the same has been amended. And the word "debts," in said title, shall be construed as including funeral expenses, except that the charges for funeral expenses shall be a preferred debt, and be paid out of the proceeds of such sale before the general distribution to creditors shall be made.

to surrogate for authority to mortgage, etc., real estate.

Funeral expenses a preferred debt.

§ 2. This act shall take effect immediately.

CHAP. 268.

AN ACT for the promotion of rifle practice in the national guard.

PASSED April 27, 1874; three-fifths being present.

The People of the State of New York, represented in Senate and Assembly, do enact as follows:

SECTION 1. There shall be in the inspector-general's department an assistant inspector-general, with the rank of colonel, in addition to those now prescribed by law, to be known as general inspector of rifle practice, who shall be appointed by the commander-in-chief and whose commission shall expire with the time for which the governor may have been elected.

General inspector of rifle practice to be appointed.

§ 2. There shall also be in each division a division inspector of rifle practice with the rank of lieutenant-colonel, in each brigade a brigade inspector of rifle practice with the rank of captain, who shall be appointed and hold their commissions in the manner prescribed by law for division and brigade staff officers.

Division inspector to be appointed.

§ 3. It shall be the duty of the general inspector of rifle practice to exercise general supervision over the rifle practice of the national guard; to inspect or cause to be inspected, from time to time, all armories, ranges and practice grounds, and see that the prescribed regulations for rifle practice are carried out by the national guard and that proper returns thereof are made, and to report direct to general head-quarters, from time to time, the improvement in marksmanship, among the uniformed forces, together with all other matters appertaining to his duties.

Duties of general inspectors.

§ 4. Commandants of divisions, brigades, regiments or companies, shall furnish to the general inspector of rifle practice such information as he shall require in regard to the rifle practice of their commands, and as to the number and condition of all targets or other military property of the state issued to their respective commands for use in rifle practice; and if, at the conclusion of his inspection of any armory, range, or practice ground, he shall find any property appertaining to

Commandants of divisions, etc., to furnish information.

Report.

rifle practice, which ought to be kept therein, missing, injured, unfit for use, or deficient in any respect, or that such range or practice ground is dangerous, he shall forthwith report the facts in respect thereto to general head-quarters. He may, from time to time, examine the officers upon the theory and practice of marksmanship, and upon the system of instruction in rifle practice.

Further duties of general inspectors. § 5. It shall also be his duty to attend the annual competition for the "state prize," and, as far as practicable, all other general competitions in marksmanship among the national guard, and see that such competitions are conducted with fairness, and according to prescribed regulations. He shall make an annual report to general head-quarters, in which he shall state the result of all competitions in marksmanship for any prizes offered by the state, with the names of the winners, together with such suggestions as he may see fit.

Division and brigade inspectors. § 6. The division and brigade inspectors of rifle practice shall have supervision of all matters appertaining to rifle practice within the limits of their respective commands, under the directions of the commandants of such organizations, respectively, as above prescribed for the general inspector of rifle practice; they shall report to such general inspector of rifle practice, whenever required by him, the condition of rifle practice in their respective divisions, brigades or regiments, and what practice of that description has been carried on during any period, and shall also, at his request, report to him upon any matter relating to rifle practice which may require examination, within their respective division or brigade districts. To attend competitions, etc. They shall attend the competitions for any prizes that may be offered by the state to the command to which they are attached, and see that the same are conducted with fairness and according to the prescribed regulations, and report to the adjutant-general the result of all such competitions, with the names of the winners, together with such suggestions as they may see fit to make.

§ 7. No avenue, street or public highway shall be laid out, extended into, or opened through, the grounds of the National Rifle Association at Creedmoor.

Bonds to secure care of property. § 8. Before any targets or appurtenances are furnished by the state, a certified copy of the by-laws and other regulations of the associations to which they may be issued shall be filed with the adjutant-general, and approved by him, and bonds in such sum as shall be required by the commissary-general of ordnance shall be given to him to secure the care and custody of such property.

Ex officio members of board of directors. § 9. The general inspector of rifle practice and the brigadier-general of the district in which a range is located must be constituted permanent ex-officio members of the board of directors of the association having control of such range, and the commanding officers of the third and fifth divisions, the inspector-general of the state, and the commissary-general and chief of ordnance, permanent ex-officio members of the board of directors of the National Rifle Association, before such association or the National Rifle Association shall receive any of the benefits of this act; and such brigadier-general shall have the same authority to direct the use of any range within his district by any of the organizations of his command, without compensation, as is now given to the commanding officers of the first and second divisions, with reference to the ranges of the National Rifle Association; provided that not less than one-fourth of the targets of such associations and of the National Rifle Association shall be at all times reserved for the use of members. Proviso.

§ 10. For the purpose of preserving the property of the state and of the rifle associations, and of preventing accidents and maintaining order upon such ranges, the officers and employees of such associations and of the National Rifle Association are hereby vested with the powers of constables when in the performance of their duty and wearing such badge of office as shall be prescribed by the National Rifle Association, and all persons trespassing upon such ranges, or injuring any of the targets or other property situate thereon, or willfully violating thereon any of the regulations established to maintain order, preserve property, or prevent accidents, shall be guilty of a misdemeanor. Officers and employees vested with the powers of constables. Misdemeanor.

§ 11. The range of the National Rifle Association at Creedmoor, or any grounds hereafter acquired by that or any other rifle association for rifle practice, and toward the purchase of which the state has contributed, shall not be sold, mortgaged or otherwise alienated from use in rifle practice without the written consent of at least two-thirds of the board of directors of such association, including a majority of the ex-officio members of said board, and without the written consent of the adjutant-general of the state. Grounds not to be sold or mortgaged without, etc.

§ 12. Section five, chapter six hundred and ninety-nine, laws of eighteen hundred and seventy-two, is hereby amended to read as follows:

§ 5. It shall also be the duty of the treasurer of the National Rifle Association, and the treasurer of all other rifle associations authorized by this act, to file with said comptroller and with adjutant-general of the state, within twenty days after the first days of January and July in each year, a detailed account of all receipts and expenditures of such associations during the previous six months, verified by such treasurers under oath; it shall also be the duty of the presidents of such rifle associations to file in the adjutant-general's office, within twenty days after the first day of January in each year, a return in detail of the property and its condition, and the directors of the National Rifle Association hereafter elected shall be chosen from and elected by the life members of such association. Treasurers, their duties. Presidents, their duties.

§ 13. This act shall take effect immediately.

CHAP. 278.

AN ACT to amend chapter two hundred and fifty-one of the laws of eighteen hundred and sixty-one, and to provide for the arbitration of mercantile disputes in the port of New York.

PASSED April 29, 1874; three-fifths being present.

The People of the State of New York, represented in Senate and Assembly, do enact as follows:

Powers of chamber of commerce. SECTION 1. From and after the passage of this act, the legal powers conferred upon the "chamber of commerce of the state of New York" by chapter two hundred and fifty-one of the laws of eighteen hundred and sixty-one, shall be exercised in the manner in this act provided.

Summons for settlement of dispute. § 2. Any party or parties having a controversy, dispute or matter of difference upon any mercantile or commercial subject, may summon the opposite party or parties to appear before the chamber of commerce of the state of New York for the settlement of such controversy, dispute or matter of difference, on a day and hour named in such summons, which shall not be less than two or more than five days after the personal service of such summons upon such opposite party or one of two or more parties jointly interested in the subject-matter of the controversy; Proviso. provided, all the parties are regularly-elected members of said chamber of commerce, and parties (whether Voluntary appearance. members of such chamber or not) to any controversy, dispute or matter of difference arising or within the port of New York, or relating to a subject-matter situate or coming within said port, as the collection district of said port is established and limited by the act of congress of the United States of America, approved March second, seventeen hundred and ninety-nine, may voluntarily appear before and submit the same to the chamber of commerce, and such chamber shall thereupon entertain jurisdiction of such controversy, dispute or matter of difference, and of the parties thereto.

Filing of summons, etc. § 3. At the time mentioned in such summons, the party or parties serving such summons shall file such summons, with proof of service, with the arbitration clerk hereinafter provided for, and either party may file with him a written declaration, Objection to jurisdiction may be filed. duly acknowledged, objecting to the jurisdiction of the chamber of commerce of the state of New York in the matter mentioned in such summons; and upon the filing of such written objection, such matter shall be dismissed and no further proceedings shall be had therein under the provisions of this act; Effect thereof. and if, at the time mentioned in such summons, the party or parties named therein, or either of them, do not file such written objection, they and each and every one of them shall If no objection be filed jurisdiction is conferred. be deemed and held to have fully submitted to the jurisdiction of said chamber in such matter, and to the arbitration hereinafter provided, and the further proceedings therein shall be in accordance with the provisions of this act; and it shall be competent for any member of a firm to file such objection on behalf of himself and his copartners, and for any agent or attorney, in fact, or other representative, to do so on behalf of his principal. A copy of this section of this act shall be served with, and in the same manner, as the summons. Who may file objection.

§ 4. Upon the chamber of commerce of the state of New York acquiring jurisdiction, as aforesaid, of any matter pursuant to the provisions of this act, such matter shall be proceeded upon with dispatch to a settlement, by the arbitrator or board of arbitration provided for by this act; the respective parties to such matter shall each be entitled, at the time of submitting to such jurisdiction as herein provided, to nominate and appoint in writing one person to sit with the arbitrator whose appointment by the governor is hereinafter provided for, to hear and determine the matter; and the award made by them, or the majority of them, shall be deemed and held to be the award therein; and if the said parties refuse or neglect to nominate and appoint each one person, as aforesaid, then they shall be deemed and held to have waived their right to do so, and the matter shall proceed before the arbitrator whose appointment is hereinafter provided for, as sole arbitrator to hear and determine said matter. Adjournments may be had upon reasonable cause shown; but if any person named by either party shall fail to appear at the time set for the hearing of the matter, without good reason shown for such failure to the satisfaction of the arbitrator appointed by the governor, and that the same is only of a temporary nature, his nomination and appointment shall thereupon be declared and held to be vacated, and the same party shall forthwith nominate and appoint another person to act in his place, and upon failure to do so, the arbitrator hereinafter provided for shall appoint a disinterested person, not of kin to either party, to act in his place; and upon any failure of one party to nominate a person to sit with the arbitrator when the opposing party has nominated such a person, then the arbitrator hereinafter provided for shall appoint a disinterested person, not of kin to either party, and not nominated by the opposing party, to sit as a member of the board of arbitration; and the matter shall proceed as if such party had appointed such person to act. The persons appointed by or for the respective parties shall be duly sworn before the arbitrator, honestly, truly, and fairly to hear and determine the matter thus submitted to them; and their oaths, subscribed by them respectively, shall be filed with the award in such matter; and the arbitrator hereinafter provided for, shall make and subscribe an oath faithfully and truly to perform the duties of arbitrator according to the provisions of this act, which oath shall be filed in the office of the secretary of state at Albany, and he need not be separately sworn in each matter; and he shall have full power to administer oaths and affirmations, and to take the proof and acknowledgment of all charter parties, marine protests, contracts and other written instruments, and to issue

Proceedings when jurisdiction is obtained. Person to sit with arbitrator. Award. Waiver, effect of. Adjournments. Failure to appear. Another person may be appointed. Arbitrator may appoint. Persons appointed to be sworn. Oath of arbitrator. His power to administer oaths, etc.

subpœnas for witnesses to appear and testify, with like effect and penalties as subpœnas issued by courts of justice. All willful false swearing in any proceeding under the provisions of this act shall be deemed and held to be willful perjury, and indictable and punishable as such. After the allegations and proofs of the respective parties have been heard, the arbitrator shall have power, upon notice to both parties, to summon any person to give testimony before the arbitrator or the board, if he or they shall deem such additional testimony necessary to enable them to do justice between the parties. After the final hearing, the arbitrator or board, or a majority thereof, shall make an award in writing, under his or their hands, stating the settlement of the controversy, dispute or matter of difference heard and determined by him or them, and file the same, within five days after such final hearing, with the arbitration clerk hereinafter provided for; and if the said award shall construe any contract, or require either party or both parties to do or forbear doing a particular act or acts, or to pay a sum of money, the arbitrator hereinafter mentioned shall, at the request of either party, make an order to that effect, and otherwise to carry out the provisions of the award, which order shall, at the instance of either party, be filed by such party in the office of the clerk of the county of New York; and it shall be the duty of such county clerk, upon being paid his fees therefor, to docket such order. If such order shall require the payment of a sum of money, or the delivery of any property, any party may enter up, in the manner now prescribed by law for entering judgments of the supreme court, a judgment against the party or parties required to pay such sum of money, or deliver any property, and in favor of the party or parties to whom it should be paid or delivered, and execution may thereupon be issued and enforced thereon as and with like effect and validity as on a judgment of the supreme court docketed in said office; and the said judgment shall in other respects conform to said orders, and when so entered, have the same force and effect as a judgment of the supreme court of similar purport, and shall be enforced in the same methods and by the same processes and officers, upon the payment of the fees now allowed by law; and in case any such order shall be filed and judgment entered thereon, as aforesaid, the same may be satisfied of record and discharged in the same manner as judgments of the supreme court are or may be satisfied and discharged. Judgments entered in conformity with these provisions shall not be subject to be removed, reversed, modified, or in any manner appealed from by the parties thereto, except for frauds, collusion or corruption of said arbitrator, or board, or either of them.

Subpœnas. Perjury. Arbitrator may summon any person to testify. Award to be in writing. To be filed. Order. Order. Judgment may be entered thereon. Judgment, effect of and how enforced. How discharged. No appeal except for fraud, etc.

§ 5. The award of the arbitrator, or board, as provided for in this act, shall be binding and conclusive upon all parties thereto, and shall be, effect and secure a final settlement of the matter submitted under the provisions of this act for his or their decision and award, and shall be upheld and sus-

Award, final.

tained in all the courts of this state; but the arbitrator here inafter provided for shall have power, for good cause shown, upon notice to, and hearing the parties, to suspend and defer making the order for carrying out the provisions of the award, and to order that the cause be heard again before the same or other persons to be nominated and appointed as allowed by this act in the case of first hearing. But the party applying for such rehearing shall stipulate to pay all the costs and expenses of the other party or parties incident to such rehearing, and shall give security therefor, and for the payment or performance of any award which shall be rendered against such applying party, or judgment which shall be entered thereon, in such amount and form as shall be approved by the said arbitrator. Upon such rehearing, similar proceedings shall be had as in the case of the first hearing, and all the provisions of this act applying to the first hearing, the award, the order and the subsequent proceedings thereon, shall apply similarly in and to all cases of rehearing. On the first hearing no costs shall be allowed to either party.

Arbitrator may order a rehearing.

Stipulation.

Proceedings on rehearing.

Costs.

§ 6. The governor shall nominate, and by and with the consent of the senate appoint, an experienced, suitable and competent person as arbitrator, to be known as the arbitrator of the chamber of commerce of the state of New York, to have and perform the functions, duties and powers provided for in this act, in connection with his said office; and the salary of said arbitrator shall be fixed and paid by the said chamber of commerce. The governor shall appoint and commission such person as may be elected by the chamber of commerce of the state of New York to be arbitration clerk of the said chamber, and such person shall take and subscribe an oath faithfully to perform his duties under this act, which oath shall be filed in the office of the secretary of state, at Albany. The said clerk shall safely and correctly keep all the minutes, documents, records, books and other papers and effects of the arbitrator and of the board provided in this act, and relating to the arbitrations which may be had hereunder; and the sittings and business of the said arbitrator and board shall be had and conducted, and the office of the said clerk shall be in a building or room provided by the said chamber of commerce, at its own proper expense and charges, and the salary of said clerk shall be fixed and paid by the said chamber of commerce at its own proper expense and charges, and he shall be subject to removal by said chamber, whereupon they shall elect his successor, who shall be commissioned as aforesaid. The arbitrator shall devise and adopt a seal which shall be the seal of his office, and be used to authenticate all awards and orders made pursuant to this act, and copies and certifications thereof, and in all courts and places any instrument sealed with such seal and signed by the said arbitrator, shall be received as prima facie evidence of the existence of such award or order, and of the contents thereof, and shall have the same force and effect as the original thereof. Upon the application of the parties interested, or their representa-

Arbitrator, his appointment.

Salary.

Arbitration clerk.

Official oath.

His duties.

Salary of clerk.

Arbitrator's seal, etc.

Construction of contracts.

tives, the said arbitrator shall interpret and construe any parol or written contract pertaining to any matter which might be the subject of arbitration under the provisions of this act.

Forms and rules of proceedings. § 7. The said arbitrator, appointed by the governor, shall adopt short and simple forms and rules to be observed in proceedings under this act, and shall have power to do and order whatever may be necessary to carry out its provisions. Immediate hearing. In all cases where an immediate hearing is desired by both parties, or is practicable, it shall be had. Arbitrator, his term of office. The arbitrator appointed by this act, and his successors, shall hold office during good behavior, and shall be removed by the governor if, upon due notice and after a hearing, he shall be found guilty by the governor of malfeasance, misfeasance, or continued nonfeasance in office; Removal. in case of the removal or death of any arbitrator, his successor shall be nominated and appointed in the same manner as the first arbitrator. Stealing, mutilating, etc., of books, etc. The same punishment shall be inflicted upon any person convicted of stealing, mutilating or altering the books, records or papers herein directed to be filed with or kept by the clerk of arbitration, as are or may hereafter be, by law, annexed to similar acts in regard to records in the office of the clerk of New York county. Construction as to jurisdiction. Nothing in this act shall be construed to give any jurisdiction to the chamber of commerce of the state of New York, to the arbitrator, or board, except upon the voluntary submission and election of the parties, as provided for in this act; Cause not to be removed to any court, except, etc. nor shall any minor, married woman, or person of unsound mind, nor any matter pertaining to a fee or life tenancy in real estate, be brought before such arbitrator or arbitrators; nor shall any cause or matter submitted to the arbitrator, or board, as provided in this act, be subject to removal by or to the jurisdiction of any of the courts of this state, except as herein provided; nor shall this act apply to any cause or matter which shall be pending in any of the courts of this state, or before any arbitration committee established by law, previous to the service of the summons, as provided in this act. Submission need not be in writing, except, etc. The voluntary submission to arbitration of the particular cases contemplated in this act, and in the method herein provided, need not be in writing, otherwise than as herein provided. This act shall not be held to repeal the existing statutes in relation to arbitration. Commissions, how to be issued. Commissions to take testimony allowed by the arbitrator may be issued in the same manner and with the same effect as in courts of record, and witnesses shall be entitled to the same fees as in said courts.

§ 8. This act shall take effect immediately.

CHAP. 288.

AN ACT to incorporate societies for the improvement of poultry, small birds and domestic animals, and fish culture.

PASSED April 29, 1874.

The People of the State of New York, represented in Senate and Assembly, do enact as follows:

SECTION 1. Any number of persons, not less than thirteen, may form a company for the purpose of importing and improving poultry and small birds and domestic animals, and fish culture, and collecting and disseminating useful knowledge concerning them, by holding fairs, distributing awards and premiums, and by publishing debates and transactions, and by such other lawful means as the members of the society may deem expedient. Company may be formed. Objects.

§ 2. Such societies shall have power to elect a president, one or more vice-presidents, secretaries and a treasurer, and may make a constitution and by-laws for their government, and may hold real estate or other property to the value of twenty thousand dollars. Powers.

§ 3. Societies organized under this act shall possess the powers and be subject to the restrictions and liabilities of title three, of chapter eighteen, of part one of the Revised Statutes. General powers.

§ 4. The stockholders of any corporation hereafter formed under this act, or any act amendatory hereof, or supplementary hereto, or extending the operation and effect hereof, shall, in addition to the liabilities provided for in said acts, be individually responsible, equally and ratably, in an amount to the extent of their respective shares of stock in such corporation. Liability of stockholders. The term stockholder, as used in this section, shall apply, not only to such persons as appear by the books of the corporation or association to be such, but also to every equitable owner of stock although the same may appear on such books in the name of another person; and also to every person who shall have advanced the installments or purchase-money of any stock in the name of any person under twenty-one years of age, and while such person remains a minor, to the extent of such advance; and also to every guardian, or other trustee, who shall voluntarily invest any trust funds in such stock; Term stockholder, to whom to apply. and no trust funds in the hands of such guardian or trustee shall be in any way liable under the provisions of this act, and the acts aforesaid, by reason of any such investment, Trust fund not liable. nor shall the person for whose benefit any such investment may be made, be responsible in respect to such stock until thirty days after the time when such persons, respectively, become competent and able to control and dispose of the same; Beneficiaries, when not liable. but the guardian or other trustee making such investment as aforesaid, shall continue responsible as a stockholder, until such responsibility devolves upon the person beneficially interested therein; and, in respect to stock held by a guardian or other trustee under a transfer of the same by a third person, or under positive directions by a third person for such investment, the person making such transfer, or giving such directions, and his executors and administrators shall, for the purpose of this act, and the acts aforesaid, be deemed a stockholder; and the estate of such person, if he be deceased, shall be responsible for the debts and liabilities chargeable on such stock, according to the provisions of this act.

Estate of deceased person, when liable.

§ 5. This act shall take effect immediately.

CHAP. 321.

AN ACT to amend section twenty-seven, title seventeen of chapter eight of part third of the Revised Statutes, entitled "General miscellaneous provisions concerning suits and proceedings in civil cases."

PASSED May 2, 1874; three-fifths being present.

The People of the State of New York, represented in Senate and Assembly, do enact as follows:

SECTION 1. Section twenty-seven of the seventeenth title of chapter eight of the third part of the Revised Statutes is hereby amended so as to read as follows:

Majority may act.

§ 27. Whenever any power, authority or duty is confided by law to three or more persons, and whenever three or more persons or officers are authorized or required by law to perform any act, such act may be done and such power, authority or duty may be exercised and performed by a majority of such persons or officers upon a meeting of all the persons or officers so intrusted or empowered, unless special provision is otherwise made, and whenever a duty has been or shall be enjoined by law upon three or more persons or officers, and one or more of them shall have died, or have become mentally incapacitated to act, or shall refuse or neglect to attend a meeting of such persons upon reasonable personal notice thereof, then the action of a majority of the whole number appointed shall be binding and effective for all the purposes for which they were appointed, unless special provision is otherwise made in existing laws.

Proviso.

Ante, vol. 2, p. 555; 20 N. Y. 178; 12 id. 156, 190; 11 id. 571; 2 id. 376; 16 id. 294; 30 Barb. 347; 23 id. 179, 310; 22 id. 139, 400. 4 Denio, 126; 21 Wend. 178, 211; 14 How. Pr. 308; 25 N. Y. 228; 7 Cow. 526; 6 Johns. 39.

CHAP. 322.

AN ACT to amend chapter three hundred and seventy-nine of the laws of eighteen hundred and forty-eight, entitled "An act to simplify and abridge the practice, pleadings and proceedings of the courts of this state," passed April twelfth, eighteen hundred and forty-eight.

PASSED May 2, 1874.

The People of the State of New York, represented in Senate and Assembly, do enact as follows:

SECTION 1. Section eleven of chapter three hundred and seventy-nine of the laws of eighteen hundred and forty-eight, entitled "An act to simplify and abridge the practice, pleadings and proceedings of the courts of this state," passed twelfth April, eighteen hundred and forty-eight, as the same has been since then amended, is hereby further amended by adding at the end thereof the following:

Appeal to court of appeals.

No appeal shall be hereafter taken to the court of appeals from any judgment or order granting or refusing a new trial where the amount of the judgment or subject-matter in controversy in the action or proceedings does not exceed five hundred dollars, exclusive of the costs therein, unless the general term of the court, from whose decision or determination such appeal shall be taken, shall, by an order to be entered in its minutes, state that there is involved some question of law which ought to be reviewed in the court of appeals. In actions not founded upon contract where the judgment appealed from is for the defendant the amount claimed in the complaint shall be deemed the amount of the subject-matter of the controversy. But nothing in this provision contained shall apply to actions or proceedings affecting the title to real estate, or an interest therein.

CHAP. 324.

AN ACT relative to moneyed corporations, other than banks, institutions for savings, and insurance companies.

PASSED May 5, 1874.

The People of the State of New York, represented in Senate and Assembly, do enact as follows:

Trust, loan, etc., companies to make semi-annual report to su-

SECTION 1. Every trust, loan, mortgage security, guaranty or indemnity company or association, and every corporation or association having the power and receiving money on deposit, existing or incorporated under any law of this state, or any corporation or association not incorporated under the laws

perintendent of banking department. of this state, which receive deposits of money, or assume obligations in this state (other than banks, institutions for savings and insurance companies), shall semi-annually make a full report in writing of the affairs and conditions of such corporation, at the close of business, on the last business days of June and December in each year, to the superintendent of the banking department, verified by oath, in such form and by such officers of the said corporation as the superintendent may designate, which report shall be in place of any report which any such corporation may now be required to make to the supreme court, the comptroller, or otherwise. Every such report shall be made within twenty days after the day to which it relates, and shall be in such form, and contain such statements, returns and information, as to the affairs, business, condition and resources of such corporation, as the said superintendent may from time to time prescribe or require. And the said superintendent may, if he be of opinion that it is desirable, require that a like report, either wholly or in part, as to the particulars aforesaid, be made to him at any time, by any such corporation aforesaid, within such period as he may designate.

To be in place of report to supreme court.

When to be made, and what to contain.

Superintendent may require report at any time.

Superintendent may publish report. § 2. The said superintendent may at any time, if he deem it to be expedient, cause any such statement, or any statement or report which may be made to him under the provisions of this act, or any part or any abstract thereof, to be published in the state paper for at least three times, the expense of which shall be paid by the corporation to whose affairs such report may relate.

Superintendent to visit and examine said corporations. § 3. It shall be the duty of the said superintendent yearly, either personally or by some competent person or persons, to be appointed by him, to visit and examine every corporation required by this act to report as aforesaid. The said superintendent and every such examiner shall have power to administer an oath to any person whose testimony may be required on any such examination, and to compel the appearance and attendance of any such person for the purpose of such examination, by summons, subpœna or attachment, in the manner now authorized in respect to the attendance of persons as witnesses in the courts of record of this state; and all books and papers which it may be deemed necessary to examine by the superintendent or the examiner or examiners so appointed shall be produced, and their production may be compelled in the like manner. The expenses of every such examination shall be paid by the corporation examined to such amount as the superintendent shall determine. Whenever such examination shall be made by the superintendent personally, or by one or more of the regular clerks in his department, no charge shall be made on such examination, but for necessary traveling and other actual expenses.

May administer oaths.

May compel attendance of witnesses.

Books, etc., to be produced.

Expenses.

No charge except actual expenses.

What inquiry to be made. § 4. On every such examination inquiry shall be made as to the condition and resources of the corporation generally, the mode of conducting and managing its affairs, the action of its directors or trustees, the investment of its funds, the safety and prudence of its management, the security afforded to those by whom its engagements are held, and whether the requirements of its charter and of law have been complied with in the administration of its affairs.

§ 5. If it shall appear to the said superintendent, from any examination made by him, or from the report of any examination made to him, that any corporation has committed a violation of its charter or of law, or is conducting business in an unsafe or unauthorized manner, he shall, by an order under his hand and seal of office, addressed to such corporation, direct the discontinuance of such illegal or unsafe practices, and conformity with the requirements of its charter and of law, and with safety and security in its transactions; and whenever any corporation shall refuse or neglect to make such report as is hereinbefore required, or to comply with any such order as aforesaid; or whenever it shall appear to the superintendent that it is unsafe or inexpedient for any corporation to continue to transact business, he shall communicate the facts to the attorney-general, who shall thereupon be authorized to institute such proceedings against any such corporation as are now or may hereafter be provided for by laws in the case of insolvent corporations, or such other proceedings as the nature of the case may require.

Superintendent may order the discontinuance of illegal or unsafe practices, etc.

To report facts to attorney-general.

§ 6. Every corporation, whether chartered by this state, or any other state or county, engaged in receiving deposits of money in trust in this state, and required to make a report as to its affairs under this act, in case it shall not have already done so, shall, within six months from the passage of this act, and from time to time thereafter, if need be, transfer and assign to the said superintendent registered public stocks of the United States, or of the state of New York, or of any incorporated city of this state authorized by the legislature, to the amount in value (and to be at all times so maintained by said corporation) or ten per cent on the paid-up capital stock of said corporation, now or at any time hereafter, but not less in any case than fifty thousand dollars, which stocks must be registered in the name of the said superintendent officially, as held in trust under and pursuant to this act, and the same shall be held by the said superintendent in trust, as security for the depositors with, and creditors of, said corporation, and subject to sale and transfer, and to the disposal of the proceeds by the said superintendent, only on the order of any court of competent jurisdiction, and until the order of such court authorizing such sale, or transfer, or otherwise, to the contrary, the said superintendent shall pay over to such corporation the interest which may be received on the said securities, or he may authorize the said corporation to collect and receive the same for its own benefit. Should any company at any time have deposited with the superintendent more than the amount hereby required, such excess may be refunded. With the approval of the superintendent such deposit may be made by any company, either wholly or in part, in bonds and mortgages, satisfactory to the said superintendent, on improved

Corporation receiving deposits in trust to assign stocks to superintendent.

Amount thereof.

How registered.

How to be held.

Interest thereon.

Deposit may be of bonds and mortgages.

unincumbered productive real estate in this state, worth at least twice the amount loaned thereon; and all the provisions of this section shall apply to such deposit.

If foreign corporation does not make deposit fact to be reported to attorney-general.

§ 7. In case any corporation doing business in this state not chartered under the authority of this state, shall refuse or neglect to make the deposit with the said superintendent, hereinbefore required, the fact shall be reported by the said superintendent to the attorney-general, who shall thereupon without delay take such proceedings as may be necessary to enjoin and restrain such corporation from transacting any business in this state, and the court to which such application shall be made shall be authorized to make such order or decree and to issue such process in the premises to enforce compliance by such corporation with the provisions of this statute, or to restrain the transaction of business by such corporation in this state, as it may deem proper.

Assessment to be made.

§ 8. Every corporation, subject to the provisions of this act shall be assessed by the said superintendent to pay its proper proportion of the expenses of conducting the business of the banking department, as provided for by the seventh section of the act entitled "An act to organize the bank department," passed April twelfth, eighteen hundred and fifty-one, and shall be considered in all respects as embraced within the provisions of the said section.

Amount of deposits limited.

§ 9. The amount of money which any such corporation shall have on deposit or loan at any time shall not exceed ten times the amount of its paid-up capital and surplus, and its outstanding loans shall not at any time exceed said amount; but

Court deposits.

any such corporation authorized to receive court deposits may at any time receive on deposit and loan out any money which may be deposited with it by any of the courts of this state, including the surrogates' courts, notwithstanding such limitation.

§ 10. This act shall take effect immediately.

CHAP. 330.

AN ACT to provide for submitting amendments to the constitution to the electors of the state.

PASSED May 6, 1874; three-fifths being present.

The People of the State of New York, represented in Senate and Assembly, do enact as follows:

Inspectors of election to provide box for ballots in relation to constitutional amendments.

SECTION 1. The inspectors at each poll in the several towns and wards of this state, at the general election to be held in this state on the third day of November, one thousand eight hundred and seventy-four, shall provide a box to receive the ballots of the citizens of this state in relation to the amendments proposed to the constitution as hereinafter mentioned, and each voter may present a ballot on which shall be written or printed, or partly written or partly printed in the form following, namely:

For all propositions on this ballot which are not canceled with ink or pencil; and against all which are so canceled. Form of ballot.

For the proposed amendments to article two "relative to suffrage and bribery."

For the proposed amendment to article three, part first, "Legislature and its organization," section one to eight inclusive.

For the proposed amendment to article three, part two, "powers and forms of legislature," being sections seventeen to twenty-five, inclusive.

For the proposed amendments to article four, "the governor and lieutenant-governor, their powers and duties."

For the proposed amendments to article seven, "finance and canals."

For the proposed amendments to article eight, part one, being sections four and eleven, "relating to corporations, local liabilities and appropriations."

For the proposed amendments to article eight, part two, section ten, "State appropriations."

For the proposed amendment to section nine of article ten, being section "relative to compensation of certain officers."

For the proposed amendment to article twelve, "oath of office."

For the proposed amendment to add a new article to be known as article fifteen, "relating to official corruption."

For the proposed amendment to add a new article to be known as article sixteen, "time for amendment to take effect."

Each of said ballots shall be counted as a vote cast for each proposition thereon not canceled with ink or pencil, and against each proposition so canceled; and returns thereof shall be made accordingly by inspectors of election and canvassers. Each ballot how to be counted

The said ballot shall be indorsed "Constitutional Amendments." Indorsement.

And all the citizens of this state, entitled to vote for members of assembly in their respective districts, shall be entitled to vote on the adoption of the said proposed amendments during the day of election in the several election districts in which they reside. Who may vote on proposed amendments.

§ 2. After finally closing the poll of such election, the inspectors thereof shall count and canvass the ballots given relative to the said proposed amendments in the same manner as they are required by law to canvass the ballots given for governor, and thereupon shall set down in writing the whole number of votes given for each of the said proposed amendments, in the words in which said amendment is hereinbefore given, and the whole number of votes given against each of the said proposed amendments, in the words in which said amendment is hereinbefore given, and shall certify and subscribe the same, and cause copies thereof to be made and certified and delivered as prescribed by law in respect to the canvass of votes given at an election for governor. Ballots, how canvassed. Certificate and copies thereof.

§ 3. The votes so given shall be canvassed by the board of Votes, how to be canvassed by county canvassers. county canvassers, and statements thereof shall be made, certified and signed, and recorded in the manner required by law in respect to the canvassing of votes given at an election for governor, and certified copies of the statements and certificates of the county canvassers shall be made, certified and transmitted by the county clerks respectively, in the manner provided by law in cases of election for governor. The said certified copies transmitted by the county clerks shall be canvassed by the board of state canvassers in the like manner as provided by law in respect to the election of governor, and in like manner they shall make and file a certificate of the result of such canvass, which shall be entered of record by the secretary of state, and shall be published by him in the state paper, and in the papers designated by the several boards of supervisors to publish the session laws, or which may be designated by said board to publish said certificates, and in any county in which such designation is not made for the present year in one paper published in each assembly district of such county to be designated by the secretary of state.

Certificates to be transmitted to county clerks, etc.

To be canvassed by state canvassers.

Certificate of result to be entered of record in office of secretary of state, and published.

Secretary of state to publish amendments and forms of ballot. § 4. It shall be the duty of the secretary of state to cause the said proposed amendments to the constitution, together with the form of the ballot as herein specified, to be published in the manner provided for the publication of the certificate of the result of the canvass as provided by section three hereof. at least prior to such election; but no neglect or failure to publish shall impair the validity of such election.

CHAP. 331.

AN ACT to amend an act entitled "An act to amend an act entitled 'An act to provide for the incorporation of fire insurance companies,' passed June twenty-fifth, eighteen hundred and fifty-three," passed April nineteenth, eighteen hundred and sixty-two.

PASSED May 6, 1874.

The People of the State of New York, represented in Senate and Assembly, do enact as follows:

SECTION 1. The twenty-third section of the act entitled "An act to provide for the incorporation of fire insurance companies," passed June twenty-fifth, eighteen hundred and fifty-three, as amended by an act entitled "An act to amend an act entitled 'An act to provide for the incorporation of fire insurance companies,'" passed April nineteenth, eighteen hundred and sixty-two, is hereby amended by adding at the end of said section twenty-three the following:

Insurance company of the Dominion of Canada may deposit stocks. Any insurance company incorporated by or organized under the laws of the Dominion of Canada, for the transaction of the business of fire and inland navigation insurance, may deposit with the superintendent of the insurance department, for the benefit and security of policy-holders residing in the United States, a sum not less than two hundred thousand dollars, in stocks or bonds of the Dominion of Canada, or in stocks or bonds of the United States or of the state of New York. If any securities other than those above named are offered as a deposit they may be accepted at such valuation and on such conditions as the superintendent of the insurance department may direct; and if the market value of any of the securities which have been deposited by any company shall decline below that at which they were deposited, the superintendent of the insurance department may call upon the company to make a further deposit so that the market value of all the securities deposited by any company shall be equal to the amount which it is required to deposit. But such company shall in all other respects be subject to and comply with all the provisions of existing laws of this state relative to insurance companies incorporated by or organized under any foreign government transacting the business of fire and inland navigation insurance within this state.

Other securities may be accepted by superintendent of insurance department.

Subject to existing laws in other respects.

§ 2. This act shall take effect immediately.

CHAP. 340.

AN ACT to punish persons personating members of police in the several cities of the states.

PASSED May 6, 1874; three-fifths being present.

The People of the State of New York, represented in Senate and Assembly, do enact as follows:

SECTION 1. Any person other than the members of the police department of any city in this state, who, with fraudulent design upon persons or property, shall, at any time, have, use, wear or display the uniform, or any part thereof, or any of the emblems, signs, signals or devices adopted and used by any such police department or force, or falsely representing himself as being such a member, shall be deemed guilty of a misdemeanor, and shall be punished by a fine of not less than two hundred and fifty dollars, or by imprisonment for a term not exceeding six months.

To personate members of the police a misdemeanor.

Punishment.

§ 2. This act shall take effect immediately.

CHAP. 345.

AN ACT in regard to publishing the account* of incorporated villages in this state.

PASSED May 6, 1874; three-fifths being present.

The People of the State of New York, represented in Senate and Assembly, do enact as follows:

Trustees of incorporated villages to publish annually detailed account of moneys received and expended.

SECTION 1. It shall be the duty of the board of trustees of each of the incorporated villages of this state to cause to be published, once in each year, and twenty days next before the annual meeting in at least one public newspaper printed in such village, a full and detailed account of all money received by them, or the treasurer of said village, for the account and use thereof, and of all money expended therefor, giving the items of expenditure in full. Should there be no paper published in said village, they shall be required to publish the same by notice to the tax-payers, by posting in five public places in said incorporated limits.

Debt.

§ 2. Said annual report shall also state the funded and floating or temporary debt of said village.

§ 3. This act shall take effect immediately.

CHAP. 351.

AN ACT to amend chapter three hundred and twelve of the laws of eighteen hundred and fifty-nine, entitled "An act to equalize the state tax among the several counties in this state," and to amend chapter three hundred and twenty-seven of the laws of eighteen hundred and seventy-three amendatory thereof.

PASSED May 7, 1874; three-fifths being present.

The People of the State of New York, represented in Senate and Assembly, do enact as follows:

SECTION 1. Section fifteen of chapter three hundred and twelve of the laws of eighteen hundred and fifty-nine, entitled "An act to equalize the state tax among the several counties in the state," being a section added to said act by chapter three hundred and twenty-seven of the laws of eighteen hundred and seventy-three, is hereby amended so as to read as follows:

Appeal, costs thereof.

§ 15. Whenever any appeal so made shall not be sustained, the costs and expenses arising therefrom and connected therewith shall be a charge upon the town, city or ward so appealing, which shall be audited by the board of supervisors, and levied upon the taxable property of said town, city or ward; and whenever any appeal so made shall be sustained, the comptroller shall certify the reasonable costs and expenses

* So in the original.

arising therefrom and connected therewith on the part of the appellant, and such amount shall be audited by the board of supervisors, and levied upon and collected from the towns and cities of the county other than those by which the determination of the appeal are accredited, by means of an excess of valuation.

Amendment applicable to former appeals.

§ 2. This amendment shall apply to all appeals under the act aforesaid that have been decided by the comptroller since said chapter three hundred and twenty-seven of the laws of eighteen hundred and seventy-three took effect, and the amount of costs and expenses that shall be certified under this amendment shall be audited and levied by the board of supervisors at the next annual meeting thereof after such costs and expenses shall be so certified.

§ 3. Section nine of said act is hereby amended so as to read as follows:

Amount of state tax as fixed by the comptroller to be assessed, etc.

§ 9. The amount of state tax which each county is to pay, so fixed and stated by the comptroller, as aforesaid, shall be assessed by the supervisors or other officers authorized to make the assessment of state taxes in the tax roll for the calendar year, in and for which the same shall have been ascertained and stated by the comptroller, as aforesaid, and shall be included in and collected by the annual collection of taxes in the several counties in the manner prescribed by law; and if the board of supervisors or other officers authorized to make such assessment shall neglect or refuse to include and assess such tax, or any part thereof, in said assessment roll, then the comptroller of the state may immediately proceed by mandamus before any court having jurisdiction to compel the board of supervisors or other officers required to make such assessment to do the same or make a new assessment for the same, which shall be collected as provided for the collection of other taxes.

Mandamus in case of neglect or refusal.

§ 4. Section ten of said chapter three hundred and twelve of the laws of eighteen hundred and fifty-nine is hereby amended so as to read as follows:

Salary of state assessors.

§ 10. The said state assessors shall receive an annual salary of two thousand five hundred dollars each, and not to exceed five hundred dollars each for other expenses, while engaged in the discharge of their official duties.

All appeals to be to state assessors.

§ 5. All appeals that shall be hereafter brought under the provisions of the acts hereby amended shall be to the state assessors instead of the comptroller, and as to such and all appeals pending under said act upon the hearing of which the comptroller has not entered, the state assessors are vested with and shall exercise all the powers, and discharge all the duties, that by said act and the amendments thereof are vested in or imposed upon the comptroller, in lieu of said comptroller, and when any appeal shall hereafter be brought, a notice of such appeal shall be served on the state assessors by filing the same in the office of the secretary of state within the same time that it is now required to be filed with the county clerk.

Notice thereof.

§ 6. This act shall take effect immediately.

CHAP. 386.

AN ACT to amend an act entitled "An act to provide for the enrollment of the militia for the organization of the national guard of the state of New York, and for the public defense, and entitled the Military Code."

PASSED May 8, 1874; three-fifths being present.

The People of the State of New York, represented in Senate and Assembly, do enact as follows:

SECTION 1. Sections twenty-five, one hundred and sixty-seven and one hundred and ninety-six of chapter eighty of the laws of eighteen hundred and seventy, entitled "*An act to amend an act entitled** An act to provide for the enrollment of the militia, for the organization of the national guard of the state of New York, and for the public defense, and entitled the Military Code" are hereby amended so as to read as follows:

Adjutant-general and assistant, etc. § 25. The adjutant-general shall have the rank of major-general, and in the corps of adjutants-general there shall be an assistant adjutant-general, with the rank of brigadier-general, and such acting assistant as shall be required may be appointed by the adjutant-general, with the approval of the commander-in-chief; and to each division an assistant adjutant-general, with the rank of colonel, to be chief of staff; to each brigade an assistant adjutant-general, with the rank of lieutenant-colonel, to be chief of staff; and to each regiment an adjutant, with the rank of first lieutenant.

Salaries, compensation and expenses. § 167. The staff of the commander-in-chief (except the adjutant-general, who shall be paid an annual salary of three thousand dollars and his necessary expenses), and the assistants in the several departments (except the assistant adjutant-general, whose salary shall be fixed by the commander-in-chief at such sum as he may deem proper, and not to exceed thirty-five hundred dollars per annum), in lieu of all compensation and allowances heretofore provided by law, in time of peace, when upon actual duty under the provisions of this act, either at drills, parades, encampments, lake and sea coast defense duty, or otherwise, shall be paid such reasonable and just compensation, not exceeding the full pay and allowances of officers of the same rank in the army of the United States, as the commander-in-chief shall deem proper, and in no event to exceed the sum of twenty-five hundred dollars per annum, together with their necessary expenses and those of their departments, to be paid by the state upon the certificate of the commander-in-chief, showing a detailed statement of such services and expenses.

Regimental or battalion court martial. § 196. For the trial of non-commissioned officers, musicians and privates, the commandant of each brigade may, at any time, appoint a regimental or battalion court-martial for any

* So in the original.

regiment or battalion in his brigade, which court shall consist of the brigade judge advocate, except as provided in section one hundred and ninety-seven of this act.

§ 2. Section one hundred and ninety-seven of said act is hereby amended by adding at the end thereof the following words: "Which vacancy shall be filled by, or new court consist of, an officer of the brigade staff whose rank is not below that of a captain." Vacancy.

§ 3. This act shall take effect immediately.

Ante, vol. 7, pp. 112, 325, 478; vol. 6, pp. 152, 255, 540, 841; vol. 8, p. 246.

CHAP. 490.

AN ACT to amend an act entitled "An act to amend and consolidate the several acts relating to the preservation of moose, wild deer, birds and fish," passed April twenty-sixth, eighteen hundred and seventy-one.

PASSED May 9, 1874; three-fifths being present.

The People of the State of New York, represented in Senate and Assembly, do enact as follows:

SECTION 1. Section one of the act entitled "An act to amend and consolidate the several acts relating to the preservation of moose, wild deer, birds and fish," passed April twenty-sixth, eighteen hundred and seventy-one, as amended April twenty-ninth, eighteen hundred and seventy-two, is hereby amended so as to read as follows:

§ 1. No person shall kill or chase any moose or wild deer in any part of the state save only during the months of September, October and November in any year. No person shall sell, expose for sale, transport, or have in his or her possession in this state after the same has been killed, any moose, wild deer or fresh venison, save only during the months of September, October, November, December and January. No person shall, at any time, in this state, kill any fawn during the time when it is in its spotted coat, or have in his or her possession the carcass or fresh skin of such fawn after the same shall have been killed. No person shall, in any part of this state, set any trap, spring gun or other device at any artificial salt lick or other place, for the purpose of trapping and killing any moose or deer. It shall not be lawful to pursue deer with hounds in the county of Steuben. It shall not be lawful for any person to kill or cause to be killed any wild deer in the county of Suffolk, except from the first day of November until the fifteenth day of November in each year. It shall not be lawful for any person, at any time, to kill or cause to be killed any wild deer while standing, walking, running, swimming or laying down in any of the waters, ponds or streams of the county of suffolk. Any person offending against any of the preceding provisions of this section shall be deemed guilty of a misdemeanor, and in addition, shall be

No person to kill moose or deer, except in certain months. Fawns not to be killed at certain times, etc. Use of traps, etc. Pursuing with hounds. In county of Suffolk.

liable to a penalty of fifty dollars for each moose or wild deer or fawn so killed or pursued or trapped, and for every spring gun so set, or moose or wild deer or fawn skin or fresh venison had in his or her possession, and may be proceeded against therefor in any county of the state in which the offender or prosecutor may reside.

§ 2. Section two of the act entitled "An act to amend and consolidate the several acts relating to the preservation of moose, wild deer, birds and fish," passed April twenty-sixth, eighteen hundred and seventy-one, as amended April twenty-ninth, eighteen hundred and seventy-two, is hereby amended so as to read as follows:

Wild ducks, geese, etc. § 2. No person shall kill or expose for sale, or have in his or her possession after the same has been killed, any wild duck, goose or brant, between the first day of May and the first day of September, nor any wood duck between the first day of January and the first day of September, under a penalty of twenty-five dollars for each one killed or had in possession.

§ 3. This act shall take effect immediately.

CHAP. 409.

AN ACT to amend chapter four hundred and thirty-three of the laws of eighteen hundred and seventy-two, entitled "An act to amend chapter seven hundred and twenty-one of the laws of eighteen hundred and seventy-one, entitled 'An act to amend and consolidate the several acts relating to the preservation of moose, wild deer, birds and fish,' passed April twenty-sixth, eighteen hundred and seventy-one; also to repeal section thirty of said act," passed April twenty-ninth, eighteen hundred and seventy-two.

PASSED May 9, 1874; three-fifths being present.

The People of the State of New York, represented in Senate and Assembly, do enact as follows:

SECTION 1. Section seven of chapter four hundred and thirty-three of the laws of eighteen hundred and seventy-two, entitled "An act to amend chapter seven hundred and twenty-one of the laws of eighteen hundred and seventy-one, entitled 'An act to amend and consolidate the several acts relating to the preservation of moose, wild deer, birds and fish,' passed April twenty-sixth, eighteen hundred and seventy-one," is hereby amended by striking out the word "and" between the words "July and August" at the end of the following sentence in said section, to wit: "Nor seines or nets of any kind in the waters of Otsego lake, except from the first day of March to the last day of August, and no gill-nets, except during the months of July and August," and adding to said sentence, after the word "August," the words "and September."

Time for fishing with gill-nets extended.

§ 2. This act shall take effect immediately.

CHAP. 410.

AN ACT to authorize towns and villages to provide a sinking fund for the payment of their bonded indebtedness.

PASSED May 11, 1874; three-fifths being present.

The People of the State of New York, represented in Senate and Assembly, do enact as follows:

SECTION 1. Any town or incorporated village in the state of New York, having issued its bonds, or that may hereafter issue its bonds, under the provisions of law, and said bonds being a valid debt of said town or village to mature or become due in a specified period of time, may by a vote of a majority of the electors present, and voting at any annual town meeting or charter election of said village, raise by tax levied upon the taxable property of said town or village, such sum as may be specified by said vote in the manner hereinafter provided, for the purpose of buying and canceling said bonds, or the purpose of providing a sinking fund for the ultimate payment of said bonds. Tax may be levied for buying bonds or providing sinking fund.

§ 2. The town board consisting of the supervisor, town clerk and justices of the peace in towns, or the village trustees in villages, shall meet at least twenty days before the annual town meeting or the annual village election, and shall determine by a majority of said board what amount shall be annually raised for the purpose as described in section one of this act, and the form of the ballot and the manner of voting, and shall give notice of such voting by posting at least five notices in public places in said town or village setting forth the time of such voting, the amount to be raised, and the purpose for which the same is raised, and the result of such vote shall be operative until the same shall be changed by a vote of said electors taken in a similar manner at a subsequent election. Amount to be determined by town board or village trustees. Notice, how given.

§ 3. The money so raised shall be used to buy and cancel the said bonds provided the same can be purchased at their par value, or in case said bonds cannot be so purchased, said money shall be paid over to the county treasurer of the county, who shall loan the same at seven per cert per annum interest, secured by mortgage on unincumbered real estate for a period of time equal to the time said bonds have to run, or invest the same in bonds of the state of New York or of the United States, and at the maturity of said town or village bonds said money shall be applied to the payment of said bonds, and the supervisor of such town or president of the trustees of said village shall be charged with the duty of receiving said money from said county treasurer, giving security for the same in double the amount received; and of purchasing or paying said bonds, and of canceling the same in the presence of the said town board or village trustees as the case may be. Money raised, how to be disposed of. Duty of supervisor of town or village president.

CHAP. 414.

AN ACT relating to the commitment of indigent and pauper insane persons to the State Homœopathic asylum for the insane at Middletown.

PASSED May 11, 1874; three-fifths being present.

The People of the State of New York, represented in Senate and Assembly, do enact as follows:

Indigent insane persons may be committed to State Homœopathic Asylum.

SECTION 1. County judges and superintendents of the poor in any of the counties of this state, and all county or other officers having authority to commit insane persons to any of the state lunatic asylums in this state, are hereby authorized to commit indigent and pauper insane persons for whom homœopathic treatment may be desired, to the State Homœopathic asylum for the insane at Middletown, in the same manner and on the same terms and conditions as are now required or may hereafter be required by law for the commitment of indigent or pauper insane persons to any of the other state lunatic asylums in this state, provided the number, in the aggregate, of such patients shall not exceed the accommodations at the disposal of the superintendent in said asylum.

§ 2. This act shall take effect immediately.

CHAP. 416.

AN ACT further to amend section six of chapter two hundred and eighty of the laws of eighteen hundred and forty-five, entitled "An act for the publication of the session laws in two newspapers in each county of this state," passed May fourteenth, eighteen hundred and forty-five.

PASSED May 11, 1874; three-fifths being present.

The People of the State of New York, represented in Senate and Assembly, do enact as follows:

SECTION 1. Section six of chapter two hundred and eighty of the laws of eighteen hundred and forty-five, entitled "An act for the publication of the session laws in two newspapers in each county of this state," is hereby amended so as to read as follows:

Rate per folio.

§ 6. The publisher of each of the papers so designated as aforesaid, shall be entitled to receive for such publication of all the laws above specified, a sum not exceeding fifty cents for each folio, such amount to be determined by the board of supervisors in each county.

§ 2. This act shall take effect immediately.

CHAP. 421.

AN ACT to secure to children the benefits of elementary education.

PASSED May 11, 1874; three-fifths being present.

The People of the State of New York, represented in Senate and Assembly, do enact as follows:

SECTION 1. All parents and those who have the care of children shall instruct them, or cause them to be instructed, in spelling, reading, writing, English grammar, geography and arithmetic. And every parent, guardian or other person having control and charge of any child between the ages of eight and fourteen years shall cause such child to attend some public or private day school at least fourteen weeks in each year, eight weeks at least of which attendance shall be consecutive, or to be instructed regularly at home at least fourteen weeks in each year in spelling, reading, writing, English grammar, geography and arithmetic, unless the physical or mental condition of the child is such as to render such attendance or instruction inexpedient or impracticable.

Children to be instructed.

To attend school at least 14 weeks a year.

§ 2. No child under the age of fourteen years shall be employed by any person to labor in any business whatever during the school hours of any school day of the school term of the public school in the school district or the city where such child is, unless such child shall have attended some public or private day school where instruction was given by a teacher qualified to instruct in spelling, reading, writing, geography, English grammar and arithmetic, or shall have been regularly instructed at home in said branches, by some person qualified to instruct in the same, at least fourteen weeks of the fifty-two weeks next preceding any and every year in which such child shall be employed, and shall, at the time of such employment, deliver to the employer a certificate in writing, signed by the teacher, or a school trustee of the district or of a school, certifying to such attendance or instruction; and any person who shall employ any child contrary to the provisions of this section, shall, for each offense, forfeit and pay a penalty of fifty dollars to the treasurer or chief fiscal officer of the city or supervisor of the town in which such offense shall occur, the said sum or penalty, when so paid, to be added to the public school money of the school district in which the offense occurred.

No child to be employed to labor, unless, etc.

Certificate.

Penalty.

§ 3. It shall be the duty of the trustee or trustees of every school district, or public school, or union school, in every town and city, in the months of September and of February of each year to examine into the situation of the children employed in all manufacturing establishments in such school district; and, in case any town or city is not divided into school districts, it shall, for the purposes of the examination provided for in this section, be divided by the school authorities thereof

School trustees to examine into situation of children employed in manufacturing establishments.

Towns and cities to be districted. Violations to be reported.

into districts, and the said trustees notified of their respective districts, on or before the first day of January of each year; and the said trustee or trustees shall ascertain whether all the provisions of this act are duly observed, and report all violations thereof to the treasurer or chief fiscal officer of said city or supervisor of said town. On such examination, the proprietor, superintendent or manager of said establishment shall, on demand, exhibit to said examining trustee, a correct list of all children between the ages of eight and fourteen years employed in said establishment with the said certificates of attendance on school, or of instruction.

Parent or guardian to send child to school, etc.

§ 4. Every parent, guardian or other person having control and charge of any child between the ages of eight and fourteen years, who has been temporarily discharged from employment in any business, in order to be afforded an opportunity to receive instruction or schooling, shall send such child to some public or private school, or shall cause such child to be regularly instructed as aforesaid at home for the period for which such child may have been so discharged, to the extent of at least fourteen weeks in all in each year, unless the physical or mental condition of the child is such as to render such an attendance or instruction inexpedient or impracticable.

Trustees to see that certain provisions of this act are enforced. Penalties. Penalties to be added to school money.

§ 5. The trustee or trustees of any school district or public school, or the president of any union school, or in case there is no such officer, then such officer as the board of education of said city or town may designate, is hereby authorized and empowered to see that sections one, two, three, four and five of this act are enforced, and to report in writing all violations thereof, to the treasurer or chief fiscal officer of his city or to the supervisor of his town; any person who shall violate any provision of sections one, three and four of this act shall, on written notice of such violation, from one of the school officers above named, forfeit, for the first offense, and pay to the treasurer or chief fiscal officer of the city, or to the supervisor of the town in which he resides, or such offense has occurred, the sum of one dollar, and after such first offense, shall, for each succeeding offense in the same year, forfeit and pay to the treasurer of said city or supervisor of said town the sum of five dollars for each and every week, not exceeding thirteen weeks in any one year during which he, after written notice from said school officer, shall have failed to comply with any of said provisions; the said penalties, when paid, to be added to the public school money of said school district in which the offense occurred.

If parent or guardian is unable to furnish text-books trustees to furnish them.

§ 6. In every case arising under this act where the parent, guardian, or other person having the control of any child between the said ages of eight and fifteen* years, is unable to provide such child for said fourteen weeks with the text-books required to be furnished to enable such child to attend school for said period, and shall so state in writing to the said trustee, the said trustee shall provide said text-books for said four-

* So in the original.

teen weeks at the public school for the use of such child, and the expense of the same shall be paid by the treasurer of said city or the supervisor of said town on the certificate of the said trustee, specifying the items furnished for the use of such child.

Habitual truants.

§ 7. In case any person having the control of any child between the ages of eight and fourteen years, is uable* to induce said child to attend school for the said fourteen weeks in each year, and shall so state in writing to said trustee, the said child shall, from and after the date of the delivery to said trustee of said statement in writing, be deemed and dealt with as an habitual truant, and said person shall be relived* of all penalties incurred for said year after said date, under sections one, four and five of this act, as to such child.

Boards of education or trustees to make needful rules and regulations concerning truants.

§ 8. The board of education or public instruction, by whatever name it may be called in each city, and the trustees of the school districts and union school in each town, by an affirmative vote of a majority of said trustees at a meeting or meetings to be called for this purpose, on ten days' notice in writing to each trustee, said notice to be given by the town clerk, are for each of their respective cities and towns hereby authorized and empowered and directed on or before the first day of January, eighteen hundred and seventy-five, to make all needful provisions, arrangements, rules and regulations concerning habitual truants and children between said ages of eight and fourteen years of age, who may be found wandering about the streets or public places of such city or town during the school hours of the school day of the term of the public school of said city or town, having no lawful occupation or business, and growing up in ignorance, and said provisions, arrangements, rules and regulations shall be such as shall, in their judgment, be most conducive to the welfare of such children, and to the good order of such city or town; and shall provide suitable places for the discipline and instruction and confinement, when necessary, of such children, and may require the aid of the police of cities and constables of towns to enforce their said rules and regulations; provided, however, that such provisions, arrangements, rules and regulations, shall not go into effect as laws for said several cities and towns until they shall have been approved, in writing, by a justice of the supreme court for the judicial district in which said city or town is situated, and when so approved he shall file the same with the clerk of said city or town, who shall print the same and furnish ten copies thereof to each trustee of each school district or public or union school of said city or town. The said trustees shall keep one copy thereof posted in a conspicuous place in or upon each school-house in his charge during the school terms each year. In like manner, the same, in each city or town may be amended or revised annually in the month of December.

To provide suitable places for discipline, etc.

Rules, etc., to be approved by a justice of supreme court.

To be filed and printed.

Copy to be posted in or upon school-house.

Justices of the peace.

§ 9. Justices of the peace, civil justices and police justices shall

* So in the original

etc., to have jurisdiction. have jurisdiction, within their respectives towns and cities, of all offenses and of all actions for penalties or fines described in this act, or that may be described in provisions, arrangements, rules and regulations, authorized by section eight of this act. All actions for fines and penalties under this act shall be brought in the name of the treasurer or chief fiscal officer of the city or supervisor of the town to whom the same is payable, but shall be brought by and under the direction of the said trustee or trustees, or said officer designated by the board of education.

Actions, by whom brought.

Evening schools. § 10. Two weeks' attendance at a half-time or evening school shall for all purposes of this act be counted as one week at a day school.

§ 11. This act shall take effect on the first day of January, eighteen hundred and seventy-five.

CHAP. 430.

AN ACT to facilitate the reorganization of railroads sold under mortgage, and providing for the formation of new companies in such cases.

PASSED May 11, 1874.

The People of the State of New York, represented in Senate and Assembly, do enact as follows:

Purchasers, etc., to become a body politic and corporate by making and filing certificate. SECTION 1. In case the railroad and property connected therewith, and the rights, privileges and franchises of any corporation created under the general railroad law of this state, or existing under any special act of the legislature thereof, shall be sold under or pursuant to the judgment or decree of any court of competent jurisdiction made to execute the provisions or enforce the lien of any deed or deeds of trust, or mortgage theretofore executed by such company, the purchasers of such railroad property and franchises, their grantees or assigns, or a majority of them, may become a body politic and corporate, with all the franchises, rights, powers, privileges and immunities which were possessed before such sale by the corporation whose property shall have been sold as aforesaid, by filing in the office of the secretary of state a certificate, duly executed under their hands and seals, and acknowledged before an officer authorized to take the acknowledgment of deeds, in which certificate the said persons shall describe by name and reference to the act or acts of the legislature of this state under which it was organized, the corporation whose property and franchises they shall have acquired as aforesaid, and also the court by authority of which such sale shall have been made, giving the date of the judgment or decree thereof, authorizing or directing the same, together with a brief description of the property sold, and shall also set forth the following particulars:

Contents of certificate.

Name of new corporation. 1. The name of the new corporation intended to be formed by the filing of such certificate.

2. The maximum amount of its capital stock, and the number of shares into which the same is to be divided. Capital stock.

3. The number of directors by whom the affairs of the said new corporation are to be managed, and the names and residences of the persons selected to act as directors for the first year after its organization. Number of directors.

And upon the due execution of such certificate and the filing of the same in the office of the secretary of state, the persons executing such certificate and who shall have acquired the title to the property and franchises sold as aforesaid, their associates, successors and assigns, shall become and be a body politic and corporate by the name specified in such certificate, and shall become and be vested with, and entitled to exercise and enjoy, all the rights, privileges and franchises which, at the time of such sale, belonged to or were vested in the corporation formerly owning the property so sold, and shall be subject to all the duties and liabilities imposed by the provisions of the act entitled "An act to authorize the formation of railroad corporations and to regulate the same," passed April second, eighteen hundred and fifty, and of the acts amendatory thereof, except so far as may be inconsistent herewith; and a copy of the said certificate, by the secretary of state or his deputy, shall be presumptive evidence of the due formation of the new corporation therein mentioned; provided, always, that a majority of said persons shall be citizens and residents of this state. Execution and filing of certificate, effect thereof. Copy of certificate evidence. Proviso.

§ 2. In case the persons organizing the new corporation to be formed, as provided in the first section of this act, shall have acquired title to the railroad property and franchises which may have been sold as in said section mentioned, pursuant to any plan or agreement for the re-adjustment of the respective interests therein of the mortgage creditors and stockholders of the company owning such property and franchises at the time of any such sale, and for the representation of such interests of such creditors and stockholders in the bonds or stock of the new corporation to be formed, as mentioned in said section, the said new corporation shall be authorized and have the power to issue its bonds and stock in conformity with the provisions of such plan or agreement; and the said new corporation may, at any time within six months after its organization, compromise, settle or assume the payment of any debt, claim or liability of the former company, upon such terms as may be approved by a majority of the agents or trustees intrusted with the carrying out of the plan or agreement of re-organization aforesaid; and for the purposes of such plans and of such settlements, the said new corporation may and shall be authorized to establish preferences in respect to the payment of dividends in favor of any portion of its said capital stock, and to divide such stock into classes; provided, nevertheless, that nothing herein contained shall be held to authorize the issue of capital stock by the said new company to an aggregate amount exceeding the maximum amount of such stock mentioned in its certificate of incorporation. When new corporation may issue bonds and stock. When it may compromise, etc., debt of former company. Preference in dividends. Proviso.

Stockholder of company has the right to assent to plans of re-adjustment.

§ 3. Every stockholder in any company, the franchises and property whereof shall have been sold as aforesaid, shall have the right to assent to the plan of re-adjustment and reorganization of interests pursuant to which such franchise and property shall have been purchased as aforesaid, at any time within six months after the organization of said new company, and by complying with the terms and conditions of such plan become entitled to his *pro rata* benefits therein according to its terms.

Railroad commissioners of any city, etc., may assent to plan of reorganization.

§ 4. Full power is hereby given to the railroad commissioners, corporate authorities or proper officials of any city, town or village, who may hold stock in any corporation, the property and franchises whereof shall be liable to be sold, as mentioned in the first section of this act, to assent to any plan or agreement of reorganization which provides for the formation of a new company, in conformity with this act, and the issue of stock therein to the proper authorities or officials of said cities, towns or villages, in exchange for the stock of the old or former company by them respectively held at par, subject to the foregoing provisions of this act. And such railroad commissioners, corporate authorities or other proper officials, may assign, transfer or surrender the stock so held by them in the manner required by any such plan and accept in lieu thereof the stock issued by said new corporation in conformity therewith.

Issue of stock in exchange for stock of former company.

May assign, etc., stock held by them.

§ 5. This act shall take effect immediately.

CHAP. 432.

AN ACT ceding jurisdiction over certain upland and submarine sites in the state of New York for light-house purposes in the United States.

PASSED May 11, 1874, by a two-third vote.

The People of the State of New York, represented in Senate and Assembly, do enact as follows:

Jurisdiction ceded to the United States.

SECTION 1. Jurisdiction is hereby ceded to the United States over so much land as from time to time has been deeded to and occupied by them for the construction and maintenance of light-houses and keepers' dwellings within this state, sketches and descriptions of which, by metes and bounds, have been filed in the office of the secretary of state on the twentieth of April, eighteen hundred and seventy-four, viz.:

Description of land ceded

No. 1. Split Rock, Lake Champlain, Essex county, New York, containing five acres, two quarters and six perches, conveyed to the United States by deed dated the fifteenth day of July, in the year one thousand eight hundred and thirty-seven.

No. 2. Stuyvesant, county of Columbia, New York, containing five acres, conveyed to the United States by deed dated

August thirteenth, in the year one thousand eight hundred and twenty-eight.

No. 3. Coxsackie, county of Greene, New York, containing five acres, conveyed to the United States by deed dated the third day of August, in the year one thousand eight hundred and twenty-eight.

No. 4. Four-Mile Point, town of Coxsackie, county of Greene, New York, containing two acres, two roods and twenty-five rods, conveyed to the United States by deed dated the twelfth day of February, in the year one thousand eight* and thirty-one.

No. 5. Cedar Island light, Gardiner's bay, town of East-hampton, county of Suffolk, New York, conveyed to the United States by deed dated the twentieth of August, in the year one thousand eight hundred and thirty-eight.

Also, for the lands lying under water, and known as sub-marine sites, sketches and maps of which by metes and bounds have been furnished by the United States were filed in the office of secretary of state on the twentieth day of April, in the year one thousand eight hundred and seventy-four, viz.:

No. 6. Hart's Island, situated in Long Island sound, West-chester county, New York, at the south end of Hart Island, under water and beyond low-water mark, containing three acres and seventy-five hundredths of an acre.

No. 7. Execution Rocks, Long Island sound, one hundred feet in diameter, containing less than an acre, situated seven-eighths of one mile north of Sands Point light, and five miles to the north-east of Fort Schuyler.

No. 8. Robin's Reef, New York harbor, containing an area of less than one acre.

No. 9. Long-beach bar, entrance to Greenport harbor, Long Island, Suffolk county, New York, containing an area of less than one acre.

Stratford shoal, Long Island sound, New York, containing an area of less than one acre.

No. 11. Race Rock, off Fisher's Island point, at the western entrance to Fisher's Island sound, Suffolk county, New York, containing an area of less than one acre.

No. 12. Hudson city, middle ground, Hudson river, opposite the city of Hudson, county of Columbia, New York, containing an area of less than one acre.

No. 13. Saugerties, on the mud flat on the north side of entrance to Saugerties creek, county of Ulster, New York, containing an area of less than one acre.

No. 14. Roah Hook, on the west side of Hudson river, behind the angle of the dyke, south of Roah Hook, New York, containing an area of less than one acre.

Parada Hook, on point of rocks, lower end of dyke, on west side of the Hudson river, New York, containing an area of less than one acre.

---

* So in the original.

No. 16. Nine-mile tree, Castleton, behind the center of dyke, on the east side of the Hudson river, New York, containing an area of less than one acre.

No. 17. Cross-over dyke, on north end of stone dyke below Albany, on the west side of the Hudson river, New York, containing an area of less than one acre.

No. 18. Cuyler's dyke, on the east side of the Hudson river, on the lower or south end of dyke, near Albany, New York, containing an area of less than one acre.

No. 19. Van Wie's point, on the south end of the stone dyke, below Albany, New York, on the west side of the Hudson river, containing an area of less than one acre.

No. 20. Potter's, or Sea-flower reef, Fisher's Island sound, Suffolk county, New York, about one and a half miles north of Fisher's Island, containing an area of less than one acre.

No. 21. Sand spit, entrance to Sag Harbor, Suffolk county, Long Island sound, New York, containing an area of less than one acre.

No. 22. Branford reef, abreast of Branford harbor, Long Island sound, New York, containing an area of less than one acre.

No. 23. Romer Shoal, off Sandy Hook, entrance to New York harbor, containing an area of less than one acre.

No. 24. Oyster-pond point, plum gut entrance to Gardiner's bay, Long Island sound, Suffolk county, New York, containing an area of less than one acre.

No. 25. The Stepping Stones, about one mile south of Hart Island, Long Island sound, New York, containing an area of less than one acre.

No. 26. Mill reef, opposite New Brighton, in the Kill von Kull, Richmond county, New York, containing an area of less than one acre.

How far the state of New York retains concurrent jurisdiction.

§ 2. The said jurisdiction is ceded upon the express condition that the state of New York shall retain a concurrent jurisdiction with the United States, in and over the property aforesaid, so far as that all civil and criminal process which may issue under the laws or authority of the state of New York may be executed thereon in the same way and manner as if such jurisdiction had not been ceded, except so far as such process may affect the real or personal property of the United States.

Exemption from taxation.

§ 3. The said property shall be and continue forever thereafter exonerated and discharged from all taxes, assessments and other charges which may be levied or imposed under the authority of this state; but the jurisdiction hereby ceded, and the exemption from taxation hereby granted shall continue in respect to said property so long as the same shall remain the property of the United States, and be used for public purposes and no longer.

§ 4. This act shall take effect immediately.

CHAP. 436.

AN ACT to regulate the practice of medicine and surgery in the state of New York.

PASSED May 11, 1874.

The People of the State of New York, represented in Senate and Assembly, do enact as follows:

Practitioners of medicine or surgery to obtain certificate.

SECTION 1. Every practitioner of medicine or surgery in this state, excepting licentiates or graduates of some medical society or chartered school, shall be required, and they are hereby commanded, to obtain a certificate from the censors of some one of the several medical societies of this state, either from the county, district, or state society; which certificate shall set forth that said censors have found the person to whom it was issued qualified to practice all of the branches of the medical art mentioned in it. And such certificate must be recorded in a book provided and kept for the purpose by the county clerk of each county in the state.

What certificate shall set forth. **To be recorded.** **Censors to notify practitioners, etc.**

§ 2. The censors of each medical society aforesaid shall notify all practitioners of medicine and surgery of the terms and requirements of this act, and shall request such persons, so notified, to comply with those requirements within thirty days after such notification; and if such persons shall not, within the time specified in the notice, or within such further time as may be allowed by special arrangement with said censors, not exceeding ninety days, comply with the requirements herein made of physicians or surgeons, as the case may be, such persons shall thereafter be subject to all the provisions and penalties prescribed by this act for any violation of the same, and the president of the society making such request shall and he is hereby required to at once commence the proceedings authorized by this act against such person.

Consequences of non-compliance. **A misdemeanor to practice without license or diploma.**

§ 3. It is hereby delared a misdemeanor for any person to practice medicine or surgery in this state, unless authorized so to do by a license or diploma from some chartered school, state board of medical examiners, or medical society; or who shall practice under cover of a medical diploma illegally obtained; and any person found guilty of such a misdemeanor shall for the first offense be fined not less than fifty nor more than two hundred dollars. For any subsequent offense not less than one hundred nor more than five hundred dollars, or by imprisonment not less than thirty days, or by both imprisonment and fine; and all such fines shall go into the county treasury of the county bringing such action.

Penalties.

CHAP. 437.

AN ACT in relation to publication of notices and publications.

PASSED May 11, 1874; three-fifths being present.

The People of the State of New York, represented in Senate and Assembly, do enact as follows:

Publication of citations issued by surrogates.

SECTION 1. All notices and citations issued by surrogates, except in the counties of New York and Kings, and now required by law to be published in the state paper, shall hereafter be published in a newspaper printed in the county in which the surrogate issuing such notices or citations shall reside, instead of the state paper, in case there is a newspaper printed therein, and if not, then in the state paper; and such publication shall be for the same time and with the same effect as if published in the state paper; provided, that in all cases where any of the parties interested reside out of the county, such notice or citation, if the property of the deceased exceed two thousand dollars in value, shall also be published in the state paper; but that, if the property of the deceased shall not exceed two thousand dollars in value, the publication in the state paper shall be at the discretion of the surrogate, and free of expense and without charge for such publication.

When to be published in the state paper.

§ 2. All acts and parts of acts inconsistent with this act are hereby repealed.

§ 3. This act shall take effect immediately.

CHAP. 440.

AN ACT to declare the publication and dissemination of false news a crime, and to provide for its punishment.

PASSED May 11, 1874; three-fifths being present.

The People of the State of New York, represented in Senate and Assembly, do enact as follows:

A misdemeanor to circulate false intelligence with intent of affecting price of funds, etc.

SECTION 1. Every person who shall knowingly circulate false intelligence with the intent of depreciating or advancing the market price of the public funds of the United States, or of any state or territory thereof, or of any foreign country or government, or the stocks, bonds or evidence of debt of any corporation, or association, or the market price of any merchandise or commodity whatever, shall be deemed guilty of a misdemeanor, and shall be punished, upon conviction thereof, by a fine of not exceeding five thousand dollars, and imprisonment for a period not exceeding three years, or either.

Punishment.

Forgery of name to

§ 2. Every person who shall forge the name of any person or of the officer of any corporation to any letter, message or paper whatever, with intent to advance or depreciate the market price of the public funds of the United States, or of any state or territory thereof, or of any foreign country or government, or the market price of bonds or stock or other evidence of debt issued by any corporation or association, or the market price of gold or silver coin or bullion, or of any merchandise or commodity whatever, shall, upon conviction, be adjudged guilty of forgery in the third degree, and shall be punished by imprisonment in a state prison for a term not exceeding five years.

Letter, message, etc., with intent to affect price of public funds, etc.

Punishment.

CHAP. 444.*

AN ACT to create a board of excise in the several towns of this state.

PASSED May 4, 1874; three-fifths being present.

The People of the State of New York, represented in Senate and Assembly, do enact as follows:

Commissioners of excise to be elected.

SECTION 1. At the annual town meetings in the several towns in this state, held next after the passage of this act, there shall be elected in the same manner as other town officers are elected, three commissioners of excise, who, while acting as such commissioners, shall not hold either of the offices of supervisor, justice of the peace, or town clerk, the office of president or trustee of any incorporated village, and who shall compose the board of excise of their respective towns, and discharge the duties imposed upon the supervisor and justices of the peace of towns, and the president and trustees of incorporated villages thereof, by chapter one hundred and seventy-five of the laws of eighteen hundred and seventy, and laws amendatory thereof and supplementary thereto; and shall be entitled to receive compensation at the rate of three dollars per day, while in session, as a board of excise, which shall be a town charge; except in the counties where the moneys received by said board are paid into the county treasury as hereinafter provided, when it shall be a county charge. The commissioners first elected under this act shall be classified by lot, under the superintendence of the supervisor, the justice of the peace having the shortest time to serve, and the town clerk, or a majority of such officers, who shall meet at the office of the town clerk of their respective towns, for such purpose, within ten days after such town meeting, and the persons drawing for one, two and three years shall serve for such terms respectively; and annually thereafter one commissioner of excise shall be elected for a term of three years. Vacancies occurring in said boards, from any cause, shall be filled by appointment by the supervisor and justice of the peace of said town, or a majority of them, until the next annual town meeting, when such vacancy shall be filled by election.

Their duties.

Compensation.

Commissioners first elected to be classified.

One commissioner to be elected annually.

Vacancies.

---

* Chapter assigned to this act at the executive chamber, and act received at and deposited in the office of the secretary of state, May 18, 1874.

Separate ballots. § 2. The said commissioners shall be voted for upon a separate ballot, which shall be deposited in a separate box, marked "excise," and before entering upon the duties of their offices, shall take and subscribe the constitutional oath of office and file the same with the town clerk, and shall execute a bond to the supervisor thereof, to be approved by him in double the amount of the excise moneys of the preceding year, conditioned for paying over to him or his immediate successors in office, within thirty days after the receipt thereof, all moneys received by them as such excise commissioners. Said moneys shall be disposed of as directed by the town board, except in those counties where the support of the poor is a county charge where such excise money shall be paid into the county treasury, subject to the control of the board of supervisors.

Oath of office and bond.

Excise moneys, how disposed of.

§ 3. Nothing in this act shall affect the provisions of any special act in so far as the same provides for any special disposition of excise moneys or fines.

§ 4. This act shall take effect immediately.

CHAP. 446.

AN ACT to revise and consolidate the statutes of the state relating to the care and custody of the insane; the management of the asylums for their treatment and safe keeping, and the duties of the State Commissioner in Lunacy.

PASSED May 12, 1874; three-fifths being present.

The People of the State of New York, represented in Senate and Assembly, do enact as follows:

TITLE FIRST.

GENERAL PROVISIONS.

ARTICLE I.

Commitment of the Insane.

Certificate of physicians. SECTION 1. No person shall be committed to or confined as a patient in any asylum, public or private, or in any institution, home or retreat for the care and treatment of the insane, except upon the certificate of two physicians, under oath, setting forth the insanity of such person. But no person shall be held in confinement in any such asylum for more than five days, unless within that time such certificate be approved by a judge or justice of a court of record of the county or district in which the alleged lunatic resides, and said judge or justice may institute inquiry and take proofs as to any alleged lunacy before approving or disapproving of such certificate, and said judge or justice may, in his discretion, call a jury in each case to determine the question of lunacy.

Approval thereof by a judge of a court of record.

Judges may take proofs, etc.

§ 2. It shall not be lawful for any physician to certify to the insanity of any person for the purpose of securing his commitment to an asylum, unless said physician be of reputable character, a graduate of some incorporated medical college, a permanent resident of the state, and shall have been in the actual practice of his profession for at least three years, and such qualifications shall be certified to by a judge of any court of record. No certificate of insanity shall be made except after a personal examination of the party alleged to be insane, and according to forms prescribed by the State Commissioner in Lunacy, and every such certificate shall bear date of not more than ten days prior to such commitment.

Qualification of physician certifying. To be certified by a judge. Personal examination.

§ 3. It shall not be lawful for any physician to certify to the insanity of any person for the purpose of committing him to an asylum of which the said physician is either the superintendent, proprietor, an officer or a regular professional student therein.

When physician may not certify.

§ 4. Every superintendent of a state asylum or public or private asylum, institution, home or retreat for the care and treatment of the insane, shall, within three days after the reception of any patient, make or cause to be made, a descriptive entry of such case in a book exclusively set apart for that purpose. He shall also make entries from time to time of the mental state, bodily condition and medical treatment of such patient, together with the forms of restraint employed, during the time such patient remains under his care, and in the event of the discharge or death of such patient, the superintendent aforesaid shall state in such case-book the circumstances appertaining thereto.

Descriptive entry of case to be made. Mental state, etc., entries of.

§ 5. The county superintendents of the poor of any county or town, to which any person shall be chargeable, who shall be or shall become a lunatic, may send any such person to any state lunatic asylum by an order under their hands, and in compliance with the provisions of this act.

County superintendents of the poor, power of, over pauper insane.

§ 6. In case of the refusal or neglect of any committee or guardian of any lunatic, or his relatives, to confine and maintain him, or where there is no such committee, guardian or relative of sufficient ability to do so, it shall be the duty of the overseer of the poor, or constables of the city or town where any lunatic shall be found, to report the same forthwith to the superintendent of the poor, who shall apply to the county judge, special county judge or surrogate, who, upon being satisfied upon examination that it would be dangerous to permit such lunatic to go at large, shall issue his warrant, directed to the constables and overseers of the poor of such city or town, commanding them to cause such lunatic to be apprehended, and to be sent within the next ten days to some state lunatic asylum, or to such public or private asylum as may be approved by any standing order or resolution of the supervisors of the county, to be there kept and maintained until discharged by law.

Overseers of the poor or constables to report to superintendent of the poor. His duty thereupon. County judge to issue warrant. Order of supervisors.

§ 7. It shall be the duty of the overseers of the poor or constables to whom such warrant shall be directed, to procure a suitable place for the confinement of such lunatic as therein

Lunatic not to be confined more than ten days,

except in asylum. directed pursuant to the preceding section, but in no case shall any lunatic be confined in any other place than a state lunatic asylum or public or private asylum duly approved as aforesaid, for a longer period than ten days.

Not to be confined as disorderly persons, etc. § 8. No person, who, by reason of lunacy or otherwise, is so far disordered in his mind, as to be dangerous to himself or others shall be committed as a disorderly person to any prison, jail, house of correction, or confined therein unless an agreement shall have been made for that purpose with the keeper thereof; and no such lunatic or person disordered in his mind shall be confined in the same room with any person charged with or convicted of any crime, nor shall such lunatic be confined in any prison, jail or house of correction for more than ten days. Nor with criminals.

Person committed as dangerous lunatic, to be sent to asylum. § 9. If any person being of disordered mind and committed as a dangerous lunatic to any prison, jail or house of correction as set forth in the preceding section shall continue to be insane at the expiration of ten days, he shall be sent forthwith to some state lunatic asylum or to such public or private asylum as may be approved as aforesaid.

To confine lunatic in other place or manner than herein prescribed, a misdemeanor. § 10. Any overseer of the poor, constable, keeper of a jail or other person who shall confine any lunatic in any other manner or in any other place than such as are herein specified, shall be deemed guilty of a misdemeanor, and on conviction thereof shall be liable to a fine not exceeding two hundred and fifty dollars or to imprisonment not exceeding one year, or to both, at the discretion of the court before which the conviction shall be had.

Appeal. § 11. If any lunatic, committed under the provisions of this article, or any friend in his behalf, be dissatisfied with any final decision or order of a county judge, special county judge, surrogate, judge of the superior court or court of common pleas of a city, or police magistrate, he may, within three days after such order or decision, appeal therefrom to a justice of the supreme court, who shall, thereupon, stay his being sent out of the county, and forthwith call a jury to decide upon the fact of lunacy. After a full and fair investigation, aided by the testimony of at least two respectable physicians, if such jury find him sane, the justice shall forthwith discharge him, or otherwise he shall confirm the order for his being sent immediately to an asylum. In case any county judge, special county judge, surrogate, judge of the superior court or common pleas of a city, or police magistrate, refuses to make an order for the confinement of any insane person, proved to be dangerous to himself or others if at large, he shall state his reasons for such refusal in writing, so that any person aggrieved may appeal therefrom to a justice of the supreme court, who shall hear and determine the matter in a summary way or call a jury as he may think most fit and proper. Proceedings upon. If judge refuse order for confinement, he must state his reasons in writing. Appeal therefrom.

When relatives are to provide place for confinement, etc. § 12. If such lunatic is not possessed of sufficient property to maintain himself, it shall be the duty of the father, mother, or children of such lunatic, if of sufficient ability, to provide a suitable place for his confinement, and to confine and maintain him in such manner as shall be agreeable to the provisions of this act. But in case his relatives are not of sufficient ability to maintain him, then the superintendent of the poor of the county shall, upon his order, send such pauper-lunatic to any state asylum, or to such public or private asylum as may be approved by a standing order or resolution of the supervisors, within ten days.

In case of inability, superintendent of poor to send lunatic to asylum.

§ 13. The overseers and superintendents of the poor shall have the same remedies to compel such relatives to confine and maintain such lunatic, and to collect the costs and charges of his confinement, as are given by law in the case of poor and impotent persons becoming chargeable to any town.

Remedies to compel relatives to maintain, etc.

§ 14. When a person in indigent circumstances, not a pauper, becomes insane, application may be made in his behalf to any county judge, special county judge, judge of a superior court or common pleas of the county where he resides, and said judge shall fully investigate the facts of the case, both as to the question of his indigence as well as that of his insanity. And if the judge certifies that satisfactory proof of his insanity has been adduced, and that such person has become insane within one year next prior to the granting of the order of admission, and that his estate is insufficient to support him and his family (or, if he has no family, himself), while under the visitation of insanity, then it shall be the duty of any judge before whom an application for that purpose is made, to cause reasonable notice thereof, and of the time and place of hearing the same, to be given to one of the superintendents of the poor of the county chargeable with the expense of supporting such person in a state asylum, if admitted, and he shall than proceed to ascertain when such person became insane, and shall state in his certificate that satisfactory proof has been adduced before him that such person became insane within a year next prior to the date of such certificate. On granting such certificate the judge may, in his discretion, require the friends of the patient to give security to the superintendent of the poor of the county to remove the patient from the asylum at the end of the two years, in case he does not sooner recover. When a patient who is admitted into an asylum on the certificate of any judge given as hereinbefore recited has remained in such asylum two years and has not recovered, the superintendent of the asylum shall send a written notice to the county judge of the county from which he was sent, that such patient has remained in the asylum two years and has not recovered, and that, in case he is not removed therefrom, the expense of his support will be chargeable to the county until he is so removed, and such expense shall be chargeable to the county accordingly. But in every case where a patient, admitted into an asylum as hereinbefore provided, shall have remained there two years and has not recovered, the managers of the asylum may, in their discretion, cause such person to be returned to the county whence he came, and charge the expense of such removal to the county. The judge granting said order of indigence shall file all papers belong-

Indigent insane person not a pauper.

Judge to investigate facts.

Notice of hearing.

Judge may require security.

If patient has not recovered, superintendent to give notice to county judge.

Patient may be returned to county.

Judge to file papers, etc., and to report.

ing to such proceedings, together with his decision, with the clerk of the county and report the facts to the supervisors whose duty it shall be, at their next annual meeting, to raise the money requisite to meet the expenses of support of such indigent lunatic.

When supervisors to raise money to defray expenses at asylum.

§ 15. When an insane person in indigent circumstances, not a pauper, shall have been sent to any state asylum by his friends, who have paid his bills therein for six months, if the superintendent shall certify that he is a fit patient and likely to be benefited by remaining in the institution, the supervisors of the county of his residence are authorized and required, upon an application under oath in his behalf, to raise a sum of money sufficient to defray the expenses of his remaining there another year, and to pay the same to the treasurer of the asylum. And they shall repeat the same for one year more upon like application and the production of a new certificate of like import from the superintendent of such asylum.

Repetition thereof.

Expenses to be defrayed by county or town.

§ 16. The expense of sending any lunatic to a state asylum, and of supporting him there, shall be defrayed by the county or town to which he may be chargeable. If chargeable to a county, or to any town whose poor moneys are required to be paid into the county treasury, such expense shall be paid by the county treasurer out of the funds appropriated to the support of the poor belonging to such county or town, after being allowed and certified by the county superintendents. If such lunatic be chargeable to a town whose poor moneys are not required to be paid into the county treasury, such expense shall be paid by the overseers of the poor thereof.

When to be paid by county treasurer.

When by overseer of poor.

Remedies to compel committee or guardian to maintain, etc.

§ 17. The overseers of the poor of any city or town shall have the same remedies to compel the committee or guardian of the estate of any lunatic to confine and maintain such lunatic, and to collect of such committee the cost and charges of his confinement and support, as are given in the preceding sections against the relatives of such lunatic. And the court of general sessions of the peace of the city or county shall make orders against such committee personally and enforce them in the same manner as against the relatives of any poor person, so long as such committee has any property in his hands, for the support of such lunatic.

Court of sessions to make orders.

Powers of court not abridged.

§ 18. None of the foregoing provisions shall be deemed to restrain or abridge the power and authority of the supreme court, the superior court and the court of common pleas of the city and county of New York, or the county courts, concerning the safe-keeping of any lunatics, or the charge of their persons or estates.

Powers of county superintendents.

§ 19. The county superintendents of the poor shall have all the powers and authority herein given to overseers of the poor of any town.

ARTICLE SECOND.

Commitment of the insane by criminal process.

Person indicted for arson, murder, etc., and appearing to be insane, court may inquire into his mental condition.

§ 20. If any person in confinement under indictment for the crime of arson, murder or attempt at murder or highway robbery, shall appear to be insane, the court of oyer and terminer in which such indictment is pending shall have power, with the concurrence of the presiding judge of such court, summarily to inquire into the sanity of such person and the degree of mental capacity possessed by him, and for that purpose may appoint a commission to examine such person and inquire into the facts of his case and report thereon to the court, and if the said court shall find such person insane, or not of sufficient mental capacity to undertake his defense, they may by order remand such person to such state lunatic asylum, as in their judgment shall be meet, there to remain until restored to his right mind, when he shall be remanded to prison and criminal proceedings be resumed, or otherwise discharged according to law.

If insane, may remand him to lunatic asylum.

§ 21. The governor shall possess the same powers conferred upon courts of oyer and terminer, in the case of persons confined under conviction for offenses for which the punishment is death.

Powers of governor.

§ 22. When a person accused of the crime of arson or murder, or attempt at murder, shall have escaped indictment, or shall have been acquitted upon trial upon the ground of insanity, the court, being certified by the jury or otherwise of the fact, shall carefully inquire and ascertain whether the insanity in any degree continues, and if it does, shall order such person into safe custody, and to be sent to one of the state lunatic asylums, or to the state lunatic asylum for insane criminals at Auburn, at the discretion of the court. If any person in confinement under indictment for the crime of arson or murder, or attempt at murder, shall appear to be insane, the county judge of the county where he is confined shall institute a careful investigation, call two or more respectable physicians and other credible witnesses, invite the district attorney to aid in the examination, and, if it be deemed necessary, call a jury, and for that purpose is fully empowered to compel the attendance of witnesses and jurors; and if it is satisfactorily proved that such person is insane, said judge may discharge such person from imprisonment, and order his safe custody and removal to one of the state lunatic asylums, or to the state lunatic asylum for insane criminals, at the discretion of such judge, where such person shall remain until restored to his right mind, and then, if the said judge shall have so directed, the superintendent of said asylum shall inform the said judge and the district attorney of the county thereof, so that the person so confined may, within sixty days thereafter, be remanded to prison, and criminal proceedings be resumed or otherwise discharged. If any such person be sent to either of said asylums, the county from which he is sent shall defray all expenses of such person while at the asylum, and the

When a person accused of murder or arson escapes indictment, court to ascertain whether insanity continues, and if so, to send accused to asylum.

County judge, when to institute investigation, etc.

am'd 653 laws 1875

When he may order person sent to asylum.

Superintendent to notify judge and district attorney of recovery.

County to defray expenses.

May recover the same.

expense of returning him to such county; but the county may recover the amount so paid from his own estate, if he have any, or from any relative, town, city or county that would have been bound by existing laws, to provide for and maintain him elsewhere.

Removal to asylum for insane criminals.

§ 23. Any person now or hereafter confined in either of the state lunatic asylums upon the charge of arson or murder, or attempt at murder, or highway robbery, under the provisions of this act or any former act, may, upon the application of any superintendent of an asylum, be brought before a justice of the supreme court, who may order his removal to the state lunatic asylum for insane criminals at Auburn. The provision of the preceding section, requiring the county to defray the expenses of a person sent to either asylum, shall be equally applicable to similar expenses arising under this section.

Expenses thereof.

Transfer from penitentiary to asylum for insane criminals.

§ 24. Any person who is now, or shall be hereafter, confined in any penitentiary, and who shall appear to be insane, may, on application of the superintendent thereof, be transferred to the State Lunatic Asylum for Insane Criminals at Auburn, under an order of any justice of the supreme court, or the county judge of the county in which such penitentiary is located, upon satisfactory evidence that such person is insane; and the judge shall thereupon order his removal forthwith to said asylum, where he shall remain until recovered or otherwise discharged, according to law.

Expenses of care and maintenance.

§ 25. The penitentiary from which such convict shall have been transferred shall be liable for the expenses of his care and maintenance during the time he shall remain in said asylum, provided that he is removed therefrom before the expiration of his sentence. If he shall continue insane after the expiration of the time for which he was sentenced, then the county from which he was sent to said penitentiary shall pay his expenses, as is hereinbefore provided in section twenty-two of this act.

Person in confinement under other than civil process, appearing to be insane, county judge to institute investigation.

§ 26. If any person in confinement under indictment or under sentence of imprisonment, or under a criminal charge, or for want of bail for good behavior, or for keeping the peace, or for appearing as a witness, or in consequence of any summary conviction, or by order of any justice, or under any other than civil process, shall appear to be insane, the county judge of the county where he is confined shall institute a careful investigation, call two respectable physicians and other credible witnesses, invite the district attorney to aid in the examination (and, if he deem it necessary, call a jury, and for that purpose is fully empowered to compel the attendance of witnesses and jurors), and if it be satisfactorily proved that he is insane, said judge may discharge him from imprisonment and order his safe custody and removal to a state asylum, where he shall remain until restored to his right mind; and then the superintendent shall inform the said judge and district attorney, so that the person so confined may, within sixty days thereafter, be remanded to prison and criminal proceedings be resumed or otherwise discharged, or if the

When judge may discharge or order removal to asylum.

Person to be remanded or

period of his imprisonment shall have expired, he shall be discharged. When such person is sent to an asylum, the county from which he is sent shall defray all his expenses while there, and of sending him back if returned, but the county may recover the amount so paid from his own estate, if he have any, or from any relative, town, city or county that would have been bound to provide for and maintain him elsewhere.

Discharged. County to pay expenses. May recover amount paid.

§ 27. If a person imprisoned on attachment, or any civil process, or for the non-payment of a militia fine, becomes insane, one of the judges mentioned in the last preceding section of this act shall institute like proceedings in his case as are required in the case provided for in said section; but notice shall be given, by mail or otherwise, to the plaintiff or his attorney, if in the state; and if it shall be proved to the satisfaction of said judge that the prisoner is insane, he may discharge him from imprisonment and order him into safe custody and to be sent to a state asylum. The provisions of the last preceding section, requiring the county to defray the expenses of a patient sent to a state asylum, shall be equally applicable to similar expenses arising under this section.

Proceedings in case of insane person imprisoned on civil process.

Expenses.

§ 28. Persons charged with misdemeanor and acquitted on the ground of insanity may be kept in custody and sent to a state asylum, in the same way as persons charged with crime, and their expenses shall be paid in the like manner.

Persons acquitted on ground of insanity.

§ 29. The boards of supervisors in the respective counties of this state are hereby empowered, and it shall be their duty, annually to fix and determine the compensation to be allowed and paid to officers for the conveyance of juvenile delinquents to the house of refuge, and of lunatics to the insane asylums, and no other or greater amount than that so fixed and determined shall be allowed and paid for such service.

Compensation of officers to be fixed by board of supervisors.

§ 30. Whenever any person in confinement under indictment for the crime of arson, murder or attempt at murder, or highway robbery, desires to offer the plea of insanity as a general traverse and his whole defense to such indictment, he shall present such plea at the time of his arraignment, and at no other stage of the trial but this, shall such plea or defense be received or entertained by the court; and the court before whom such trial is pending shall have power, with the concurrence of the presiding judge thereof, to appoint a commission to examine such person and to inquire and report to the court aforesaid, upon the fact of his mental sanity at the date of the offense with which he stands charged. The commission aforesaid shall institute a careful investigation, call such wit nesses as may be necessary, and for that purpose is fully empowered to compel the attendance of witnesses.

Defense of insanity, when it must be plead.

Commission to examine and report.

Upon the report of said commission, if the court before whom such indictment is pending shall find that such person was insane and irresponsible at the date of the offense with which he stands charged, the court aforesaid shall order his removal to some state lunatic asylum, there to remain for observation and treatment, until such time as, in the opinion

If found insane, accused to be removed to a state lunatic asylum.

of a justice of the supreme court, it is safe, legal and right to discharge him.

Special verdict in case of acquittal upon ground of insanity.

Accused to be committed to a lunatic asylum.

§ 31. Whenever any person accused of the crime of arson, murder or attempt at murder, or highway robbery, shall have been acquitted upon trial, upon the ground of insanity, the jury shall bring in a special verdict to that effect and so state it in their finding; and the court before whom such trial is had, shall order such person to be committed to some state lunatic asylum, there to remain for observation and care until such time as, in the judgment of a judge of the supreme court, founded upon satisfactory evidence, it is safe, legal and right to discharge him.

Expenses to be paid by county when insane person under indictment shall be committed to asylum.

§ 32. Whenever any insane person in confinement under indictment shall be committed, as hereinbefore recited, to any state lunatic asylum, the county from which he is sent shall defray all the expenses of such person, while at such asylum, and the expense of returning him to such county; but the county may recover the amount so paid from his own estate, or from any relative, town, city or county that would have been bound by existing laws, to provide for and maintain him elsewhere.

Notice of recovery.

§ 33. Whenever any insane person in confinement under indictment for arson, murder, or attempt at murder, or highway robbery, or who has been acquitted thereof on the ground of insanity, and has been committed to some state lunatic asylum, pursuant to the provisions of the preceding sections, shall be restored to his right mind, it shall be the duty of the superintendent of such asylum to send a written notice of the same to a justice of the supreme court of the district in which such asylum is situated, in order that proceedings may be instituted to determine whether it is safe, legal and right that such party in confinement as aforesaid should be discharged.

Object thereof.

No insane person to be discharged from poor-house or county asylum without order from a judge.

§ 34. No insane person confined in any county poor-house or county asylum shall be discharged therefrom by any keeper of such establishment, by any superintendent of the poor, or by any other county authority, without an order from a county judge or judge of the supreme court, founded upon satisfactory evidence that it is safe, legal and right to make such discharge, as regards the individual and the public. The violation of this provision shall be deemed a misdemeanor, and be punishable by a fine not exceeding five hundred dollars nor less than one hundred dollars, in the discretion of the court.

Not applicable to New York and Kings counties.

This section shall not apply to the counties of New York and Kings; but no insane person shall be discharged from either of the lunatic asylums of the said counties, without the certificate, in writing, of the physician thereof, which certificate shall be filed and kept in said asylum, starting* that such discharge is safe and proper.

Policemen may be appointed.

§ 35. The boards of managers of state lunatic asylums are hereby authorized to appoint two or more of the attendants

---

* So in the original.

and employees of said asylums as policemen, whose duty it shall be, under the orders of the superintendent, to arrest and return to the asylum insane persons who may escape therefrom.

§ 36. The resident officers of all state lunatic asylums, and all attendants and assistants actually employed therein shall, during the time of such employment, be exempt from serving on juries, and in time of peace from service in the militia, and the certificate of the superintendent shall be evidence of the fact of such employment. Officers, etc., exempt from jury service, etc.

ARTICLE THIRD.

Maintenance of the insane.

§ 37. Whenever any person who is possessed of sufficient property to maintain himself becomes, by lunacy or otherwise, so far disordered in his senses as to endanger his own person or the person or property of others, it shall be the duty of the committee of his person and estate to provide a suitable place for his confinement, and to confine and maintain him in such manner as shall be approved by the proper legal authority; and in every case of lunacy hereafter occurring, the lunatic shall be sent within ten days to some state lunatic asylum, or to such public or private asylum as may be approved by a standing order or resolution of the supervisors of the county. The superintendents and overseers of the poor are severally enjoined to see that this provision be carried into effect in the most humane and speedy manner, as well in case the lunatic or his relatives are of sufficient ability to defray the expenses, as in case of a pauper. Duty of committee to maintain, etc. Lunatic to be sent to a state or private asylum. Superintendents and overseers of the poor, their duties.

§ 38. When the personal property and the rents, profits and income of the real estate of any idiot, lunatic or person of unsound mind shall be insufficient for his maintenance, or that of his family, or for the education of his children, it shall be the duty of the committee of his estate to apply, by petition, to the supreme court, or to the court having jurisdiction, for authority to mortgage or sell the whole, or so much of the real estate as shall be necessary for that purpose; upon which the same reference and proceedings shall be had, and a like order shall be entered, as directed in section nine of title second of this act, and the court shall direct the manner in which the proceeds of such sale shall be secured, and the income or produce thereof appropriated. Sale of real estate of lunatic, etc.

TITLE SECOND.

CARE OF THE ESTATES OF INSANE PERSONS.

SECTION 1. The supreme court shall have the care and custody of all idiots, lunatics, persons of unsound mind and persons who shall be incapable of conducting their own affairs in consequence of habitual drunkenness, and of their real and personal estates, so that the same shall not be wasted or destroyed, and shall provide for their safe-keeping and maintenance, and for the maintenance of their families and the Supreme court to have custody of idiots, lunatics, etc., and of their estates.

education of their children out of their personal estates and the rents and profits of their real estates respectively. And the county court shall have a similar jurisdiction in the care and custody of the person and estate of a lunatic or person of unsound mind or an habitual drunkard resident within the county.

Jurisdiction of county court.

Commission of lunacy, issue therein.

§ 2. In every commission of lunacy appointed to inquire into the mental sanity of any party, the inquiry or issue shall be confined to the question, whether or not the person who is the subject of the inquiry is at the time of such inquiry of unsound mind and incompetent to manage himself or his affairs; and no evidence as to any thing said or done by such person, or as to his demeanor or state of mind at any time being more than two years before the time of such commission or inquiry, shall be receivable in proof of insanity on any such inquiry, unless the court shall otherwise direct.

Evidence.

Committee of estate to file an inventory.

§ 3. Every committee or guardian of the estate of any idiot, lunatic, or other person of unsound mind, as hereinbefore specified, shall, within six months after their appointment, file in the office of the clerk of the court which appointed such committee or guardian, a just and true inventory of the whole real and personal estate of such idiot, lunatic or other person, stating the income and profits thereof, and the debts credits and effects, so far as the same shall have come to the knowledge of such committee or guardian. He shall also file in the office of the clerk of the court aforesaid, a semiannual account, thereafter under oath, and of the disposition made of the income of such estate; and whenever any property belonging to such estate shall be discovered after the filing of any inventory, it shall be the duty of such committee or guardian to file as aforesaid, a just and true account of the same, from time to time, as the same shall be discovered.

Contents thereof.

Semi-annual account, etc.

Verification of inventory.

§ 4. Such inventories shall be verified by the oath of the committee or guardian, to be taken before a judge of any court of record. And the filing of such inventories may be compelled by the order and process usual in such cases of the court which appointed the committee or guardian.

Filing thereof, how compelled.

Committees, etc., may sue in their own name.

§ 5. Receivers and committees of lunatics and habitual drunkards appointed by any order or decree of any court of competent jurisdiction may sue in their own names for any debt, claim or demand transferred to them, or to the possession and control of which they are entitled as such receiver or committee, and when ordered or authorized to sell such demands the purchaser thereof may sue and recover therefor in his own name, but shall give such security for costs to the defendant as the court in which such suit is brought may direct.

Sale of demand.

Security for costs.

Sale of real estate.

§ 6. Any idiot, lunatic or person of unsound mind, seized of any real estate, or entitled to any term for years in lands, may, by committee duly appointed, apply to the supreme court for the sale or disposition of the same, in the manner hereinafter directed.

See p. 407 Laws 1875

Additional

§ 7. On such application said committee shall give a bond

to such idiot, lunatic or person of unsound mind, in addition to the bond given on appointment as such committee, to be filed with the clerk of said court, in such penalty, with such sureties, in such forms as the court shall direct, conditioned for the faithful performance of the trust reposed, for the paying over, investing and accounting for all moneys that shall be received by such committee, according to the order of any court having authority to give directions in the premises, and for the observance of the orders and directions of the court in relation to the trust. Bond to be given.

§ 8. Upon the filing of such bond the court may proceed in a summary manner by reference to a referee, to inquire into the merits of such application, and if such bond be forfeited, the court shall direct it to be prosecuted for the benefit of the party injured. Mode of proceeding. Prosecution of bond.

§ 9. Whenever it shall appear satisfactorily that a disposition of any part of the real estate of such idiot, lunatic or person of unsound mind, or of any interest in any term for years, is necessary and proper either for the support and maintenance of such idiot, lunatic or person of unsound mind, or for his or her education, or that the interest of such idiot, lunatic or person of unsound mind requires, or will be substantially promoted by such disposition, on account of any part of such property being exposed to waste and dilapidation, or on account of its being wholly unproductive, or when the same has been contracted to be sold and a conveyance thereof cannot be made by reason of such lunacy or unsoundness of mind, or for any other peculiar reason or circumstances, the court may order the letting for a term or years or the sale or other disposition of such real estate or interest to be made by such committee or guardian in such manner and with such restrictions as shall be deemed expedient, or may order the fulfillment of said contract by conveyance by such committee or guardian according to the terms of the contract. Grounds for leasing or sale of real estate.

§ 10. But no real estate, or term for years, or any interest in real estate hereinbefore named, shall be sold, leased or disposed of in any manner against the provisions of any last will, or of any conveyance by which such estate or term or interest was devised or granted to such idiot, lunatic or person of unsound mind. No sale can be made contrary to the provisions of a will, etc.

§ 11. Upon an agreement for the sale, leasing or other disposition of such property being made, or upon any conveyance in fulfillment of a contract being executed in pursuance of such order, the same shall be reported to the court on the oath of the committee making or executing the same, and except in the case of a conveyance to fill a contract, if the report be confirmed, a conveyance shall be executed under the directions of the court. Report. Confirmation.

§ 12. All sales, leases, dispositions and conveyances made in good faith by such committee in pursuance of such orders shall be as valid and effectual as if made by such lunatic when of sound mind. Validity of sales, etc.

Disposition of proceeds and investment of surplus.

§ 13. The court shall make order for the application and disposition of the proceeds of such property, and for the investment of the surplus belonging to such idiot, lunatic or person of unsound mind, and shall ascertain the value of any dower or right of dower, or inchoate right of dower, and shall direct a return of such investment and disposition to be made on oath as soon as may be, and shall require accounts to be rendered periodically by any committee or other person who may be intrusted with the disposition of the income of such proceeds.

Return to be made on oath, accounts, etc.

Proceeds of sale to be deemed real estate.

§ 14. No sale made, as aforesaid, of the real estate or interest therein of any idiot, lunatic or person of unsound mind, shall give to such persons aforesaid any other or greater interest or estate in the proceeds of such sale than such idiot, lunatic or person of unsound mind had in the estate so sold; but the said proceeds shall be deemed real estate of the same nature as the property sold, or the interest therein of the said idiot, lunatic or person of unsound mind, and the court shall make order for the preservation of the same.

Dower or other life estate, how it may be treated.

§ 15. If the real estate of any idiot, lunatic or person of unsound mind, or any part of it, shall be subject to dower or other life estate, and the person entitled thereto shall consent in writing to accept a gross sum in lieu of such dower or other life estate or the permanent investment of a reasonable sum, in such manner as that the interest thereof be made payable to the person entitled to such dower or life estate during life, the court may direct the payment of such sum in gross or the investment of such sum as shall be deemed reasonable, and shall be acceptable to the person entitled to the said dower or other life estate or right therein, actual or contingent, in manner aforesaid.

Release.

§ 16. Before any such sum shall be paid or such investment made, the court shall be satisfied that an effectual release of such right of dower or other life estate, actual or contingent, has been executed.

When it shall be duty of committee to apply for authority to mortgage, lease or sell.

§ 17. Whenever the personal estate of any such idiot, lunatic or person of unsound mind shall not be sufficient for the discharge of his debts, it shall be the duty of the committee of his estate to apply by petition to the court by which they were appointed for authority to mortgage, lease or sell so much of the real estate of such idiot, lunatic or person of unsound mind, as shall be necessary for the payment of such debts. The said petition shall set forth the particulars and amount of the estate, real and personal, of such idiot, lunatic or person of unsound mind, the application which may have been made of any personal estate, and an account of the debts and demands existing against such estate.

What petition shall set forth.

Reference.

§ 18. On the presenting of such petition it shall be referred to a referee, or to the clerk of the court, to inquire into and report upon the matters therein contained; whose duty it shall be to examine into the truth of the representations made, to hear all parties interested in such real estate, and to report thereon with all convenient speed.

Report and order thereon.

§ 19. If, upon the coming in of the report and an examination of the matter, it shall appear to the court that the personal estate of the idiot, lunatic or person of unsound mind is not sufficient for the payment of his debts, and that the same has been applied to that purpose, as far as the circumstances of the case rendered proper, an order shall be entered directing the mortgage, leasing or sale of the whole or such part of the said real estate as may be necessary to discharge the said debts.

Additional security may be required.

§ 20. The court may require any additional security to be given by such committee as may seem necessary to secure a more faithful application of, and accounting for the proceeds of such mortgage, lease or sale, and shall require an account thereof to be rendered from time to time.

Debt, how paid.

§ 21. In the application of any moneys raised by any such mortgage, lease or sale, the committee shall pay all debts in an equal proportion, without giving any preference to such as have a legal priority.

Conveyance, when to be made.

§ 22. The court shall give such orders respecting the time and manner of any sale herein authorized, as shall be deemed proper; and no conveyance in pursuance of any such sale shall be executed until the sale shall have been reported on the oath of the committee, and confirmed by the court directing the same.

Committee may apply for authority to convey trust estate, etc.

§ 23. Whenever any idiot, lunatic or person of unsound mind shall be seized or possessed of any real estate by way of mortgage, or as a trustee for others, in any manner, his committee may apply to the supreme court for authority to convey and assure such real estate to any other person or persons entitled to such conveyance or assurance, in such manner as the said court shall direct, upon which a reference and the like proceedings shall be had, as in the case of an application to sell real estate as aforesaid, and the court, upon hearing all the parties interested, may order such conveyance or assurance to be made.

Proceedings thereon.

Committee may be compelled to execute conveyance.

§ 24. On the application of any person entitled to such conveyance or assurance by action or petition, the committee may be compelled by the supreme court, on a hearing of all parties interested, to execute such conveyance or assurance.

Validity of conveyance, etc.

§ 25. Every conveyance, mortgage, lease and assurance made under the order of the supreme court, or of any court, pursuant to the provisions of this act, shall be as valid and effectual as if the same had been executed by such idiot, lunatic or person of unsound mind when of sound memory and understanding.

Specific performance.

§ 26. The supreme court shall have authority to decree and compel the specific performance of any bargain, contract or agreement which may have been made by any lunatic or person of unsound mind while such person aforesaid was of sound memory and understanding, and to direct the committee of such person to do and execute all necessary conveyances and acts for that purpose.

Term of lease.

§ 27. The real estate of any idiot, lunatic or person of

unsound mind, or person incapable of conducting his own affairs in consequence of habitual drunkenness, shall not be leased for more than five years or mortgaged or aliened or disposed of otherwise than is hereinbefore directed.

Restoration of estate.

§ 28. In case any lunatic or person of unsound mind shall be restored to his right mind and become capable of conducting his own affairs, his real and personal estate shall be restored to him.

On the death of lunatic, powers of committee cease.

Descent of real and distribution of personal estate.

§ 29. In case of the death of any idiot, lunatic or person of unsound mind, or person incapable of conducting his own affairs during such state of incapacity, the power of any committee appointed under this act shall cease and the real estate of such idiot, lunatic or person of unsound mind, or person incapable of conducting his own affairs, shall descend to his heirs, and his personal estate be distributed according to law, in the same way as if he had been of sound mind and memory, and capable of conducting his own affairs. But nothing herein contained shall be held to affect the provisions of any last will and testament duly made, and which shall be duly admitted to probate.

TITLE THIRD.

OF THE STATE LUNATIC ASYLUM AT UTICA.

Managers.

Their term of office, etc.

Successors, how appointed, their term of office.

SECTION 1. There is established at the city of Utica, the State Lunatic Asylum under the control of nine managers who shall hold their offices for three years, and until others are appointed in their stead, subject to being removed at any time by the senate, upon the recommendation of the governor. Their successors shall be appointed by the senate upon the nomination of the governor, and shall hold their offices for three years and until others are appointed in their stead, and subject to be removed in the manner aforesaid. The government of the State Lunatic Asylum shall be vested in said board of managers, a majority of whom shall reside within five miles of said asylum.

Board of managers, their powers and duties.

§ 2. Said board shall have the general direction and control of all the property and concerns of the institution not otherwise provided for by law, and shall take charge of its general interests, and see that its great design be carried into effect, and every thing done faithfully according to the requirements of the legislature, and the by-laws, rules and regulations of the asylum.

Appointment of superintendent and other officers.

Steward, assistant physician and matron.

§ 3. The managers shall appoint a superintendent, who shall be a well-educated physician of experience in the treatment of the insane, and a treasurer, who shall give bonds for the faithful performance of his trust, in such sum and with such sureties as the comptroller of the state shall approve. They shall also appoint, upon the nomination of the superintendent, a steward, four assistant physicians and a matron, all of whom, and the superintendent himself, shall constantly reside in the asylum, and shall be designated the resident officers thereof.

Special pathologist, his salary.

§ 4. The managers of said asylum shall have the power, on the nomination of the superintendent of said asylum, to appoint a special pathologist to said asylum, whose salary shall be determined and paid in the same manner as provided by law in relation to the other officers of said asylum.

Annual salaries.

§ 5. The managers shall, from time to time, determine the annual salaries and allowances of the treasurer and resident officers of the asylum, who have been or may hereafter be appointed, subject to the approval of the governor, secretary of state and the comptroller, provided that such salaries do not exceed in the aggregate fifteen thousand dollars for one year.

Proviso.

Salaries payable quarterly.

§ 6. The salaries of the treasurer and resident officers of the asylum shall be paid quarterly, on the first days of January, April, July and October in each year, by the treasurer of the state, on the warrant of the comptroller, out of any moneys in the treasury not otherwise appropriated, to the treasurer of the asylum on his presenting a bill of particulars, signed by the steward and certified by the superintendent.

Warrant of comptroller.

Managers may take by devise or bequest.

§ 7. The managers may take and hold in trust for the state any grant or devise of land, or any donation or bequest of money or other personal property, to be applied to the maintenance of insane persons and the general use of the State Lunatic Asylum.

Official oath.

§ 8. The superintendent, treasurer and steward of the asylum, before entering upon their respective duties, shall severally take the oath prescribed in the first section of the sixth* article of the constitution of the state; and such oaths shall be filed with the clerk of the county of Oneida.

By-laws, rules and regulations.

§ 9. The managers are hereby directed and empowered to establish such by-laws as they may deem necessary and expedient for regulating the appointment and duties of officers, attendants and assistants, for fixing the conditions of admission, support and discharge of patients, and for conducting in a proper manner the business of the institution; also to ordain and enforce a suitable system of rules and regulations for the internal government, discipline and management of the asylum.

Superintendent, his powers and duties.

§ 10. The superintendent shall be the chief executive officer of the asylum. He shall have the general superintendence of the buildings, grounds and farm, together with their furniture, fixtures and stock; and the direction and control of all persons therein, subject to the laws and regulations established by the managers. He shall daily ascertain the condition of all the patients and prescribe their treatment in the manner directed in the by-laws. He shall have the nomination of his co-resident officers, with power to assign them their respective duties, subject to the by-laws; also to appoint, with the managers' approval, such, and so many other officers, assistants and attendants as he may think proper and necessary for the economical and efficient performance of the business of the asylum, and to prescribe their several duties and places, and

---

* So in original.

to fix, with the managers' approval, their compensation, and to discharge any of them at his sole direction; but in every case of discharge he shall forthwith record the same, with the reasons, under an appropriate head in one of the books of the asylum. He shall also have power to suspend until the next meeting of the managers, for good and sufficient cause, a resident officer; but in such case he shall forthwith give written notice of the fact, with its causes and circumstances, to one of the managers, whose duty thereupon shall be to call a special meeting of the board to provide for the exigency. He shall also, from time to time, give such orders and instructions as he may judge best calculated to insure good conduct, fidelity and economy in every department of labor and expense; and he is authorized and enjoined to maintain salutary discipline among all who are employed by the institution, and to enforce strict compliance with such instructions, and uniform obedience to all the rules and regulations of the asylum. He shall further cause full and fair accounts and records of all his doings, and of the entire business and operations of the institution, to be kept regularly from day to day, in books provided for that purpose, in the manner and to the extent prescribed in the by-laws; and he shall see that all such accounts and records are fully made up to the last day of November in each year, and that the principal facts and results, with his report thereon, be presented to the managers within thirty days thereafter. The first assistant physician shall perform the duties and be subject to the responsibilities of the superintendent in his sickness or absence.

Report.

Assistant physician.

Exemption from jury services, etc.

§ 11. The resident officers of the State Lunatic Asylums, and all attendants and assistants actually employed therein during the time of such employment, shall be exempt from serving on juries, from all assessments for labor on the highways, and in time of peace from all service in the militia; and the certificate of the superintendent shall be evidence of the fact of such employment.

Record of the doings of managers.

§ 12. The managers shall keep in a bound book to be provided for that purpose, a fair and full record of their doings, which shall be open at all times to the inspection of the governor of the state, and of all persons whom he or either house of the legislature may appoint to examine the same.

Inspection and visitation by managers.

§ 13. The managers shall maintain an effective inspection of the asylum, for which purpose they shall make frequent visitations, a majority of them once every quarter, and the whole board once a year, at the times and in the manner prescribed in the by-laws. In a book kept by the managers for this purpose, the visiting manager or managers shall note the date of each visit, the condition of the house, patients, with remarks of commendation or censure, and all the managers present shall sign the same. The general results of the inspections, with suitable hints, shall be inserted in the annual report, detailing the past year's operations and actual state of the asylum, which the managers shall make to the legislature in

Note of visits etc.

To be inserted in annual report.

the month of January in each year, accompanied with the annual reports of the superintendent and treasurer.

§ 14. It shall be the duty of the resident officers to admit any of the managers into every part of the asylum, and to exhibit to him or them, on demand, all the books, papers, accounts and writings belonging to the institution, or pertaining to its business, management, discipline or government; also to furnish copies, abstracts and reports whenever required by the managers.

Resident officers to admit managers and exhibit books, etc.

§ 15. The treasurer shall have the custody of all moneys, bonds, notes, mortgages and other securities and obligations belonging to the asylum. He shall open with one of the banks of Utica, to be selected with the approbation of the comptroller of the state, an account in his own name, as treasurer of the asylum; and he shall deposit all moneys, immediately upon receiving them, in said bank, and shall draw for the same only for the uses of the asylum and in the manner prescribed in the by-laws, upon the written order of the steward, specifying the object of the payment. He shall keep full and accurate accounts of receipts and payments in the manner directed in the by-laws, and such other accounts as the managers shall prescribe. He shall balance all the accounts on his books annually, on the last day of November, and make a statement of the balances thereon, and an abstract of the receipts and payments of the past year; which he shall within three days deliver to the auditing committee of the managers, who shall compare the same with his books and vouchers, and verify the results by further comparison with the books of the steward, and certify the correctness thereof within the next five days to the managers. He shall further render a quarterly statement of his receipts and payments on the first day of March, June and September in each year to the auditing committee, who shall compare and verify the same as aforesaid, and report the results, duly certified, to the managers, who shall cause the same to be recorded in one of the books of the asylum. He shall further render an account of the state of his books, and of the funds and other property in his custody, whenever required so to do by the managers.

Treasurer, his powers and duties.

§ 16. The treasurer of the State Lunatic Asylum shall be vested with the same powers, rights and authority which are now by law given either to the superintendents of the poor or to the overseers of the poor in any county or town of the state, so far as may be necessary for the indemnity and benefit of the asylum, and for the purpose of compelling a relative or committee to defray the expenses of a lunatic's support in the asylum, and re-imburse actual disbursements for his necessary clothing and traveling expenses, according to the by-laws of the institution; also for the purpose of coercing the payment of similar charges when due according to said by-laws, from any town, or city, or county that is liable for the support of any lunatic in said asylum.

Treasurer, his powers, etc., to compel relative or committee to defray expenses

§ 17. Said treasurer is also authorized to recover for the use of the asylum, any and all sums which may be due upon any

May recover moneys

due to the asylum in an action in his official name.

note or bond in his hands belonging to the asylum; also any and all sums which may be charged and due according to the by-laws of the asylum, for the support of any patient therein, or for actual disbursements made in his behalf for necessary clothing and traveling expenses, in an action to be brought in said treasurer's name, as treasurer of the State Lunatic Asylum, and which shall not abate by his death or removal, against the individual town, city or county legally liable for the maintenance of said patient, and having neglected to pay the same when demanded by the treasurer; in which action the declaration may be in a general *indebitatus assumpsit;* and judgment shall be rendered for such sum as shall be found due, with interest from the time of the demand made as aforesaid. Said treasurer may also, upon the receipt of the money due upon any mortgage in his hands belonging to the asylum, execute a release and acknowledge full satisfaction thereof, so that the same may be discharged of record.

Action, not to abate by death or removal.

May execute satisfaction of mortgage.

Steward, his duties.

§ 18. The steward, under the direction of the superintendent, shall make all purchases for the asylum, and preserve the original bills and receipts thereof, and keep full and accurate accounts of the same, and copies of all orders drawn by himself upon the treasurer; he shall also, under like direction, make contracts in the superintendent's name with the attendants and assistants, and keep and settle their accounts; he shall also keep the accounts for the support of patients and expenses incurred in their behalf, and furnish the treasurer every month with copies of such as fall due; he shall make quarterly abstracts of all accounts to the last day of every February, May, August and November, for the treasurer and managers; he shall also be accountable for the careful keeping and economical use of all furniture, stores and other articles provided for the asylum.

Notice of readiness to receive patients.

§ 19. As soon as the asylum shall be ready for the admission of patients, the managers shall cause notice thereof to be published for two weeks in the state paper and sent to the clerk of every county, who shall transmit copies thereof to the superintendents of the poor of said county by mail. A circular from the superintendent shall accompany said notice to each county clerk and to the superintendents of the poor, designating different days for the counties severally to send to the asylum their respective quotas of patients, and giving all necessary directions respecting admission and support according to the by-laws.

Circular from superintendent, its contents.

Superintendent to make minutes of name, residence, etc., of patient.

§ 20. The superintendent shall make, in a book kept for the purpose, at the time of reception, a minute, with date, of the name, residence, office and occupation of the person by whom and by whose authority each insane person is brought to the asylum, and have all the orders, warrants, requests, certificates, and other papers accompanying him, forthwith copied into the same.

Period of admission.

§ 21. No patient shall be admitted into the asylum for a shorter period than six months, except in special cases, as specified in the by-laws.

§ 22. Whenever there are vacancies in the asylum, the managers may authorize the superintendent to admit, under special agreements, such recent cases as may seek admission under peculiarly afflictive circumstances, or which, in his opinion, promise speedy recovery. Patients admitted under special agreement.

§ 23. All town and county officers sending a patient to the asylum shall, before sending him, see that he is in a state of perfect bodily cleanliness, and is comfortably clothed and provided with suitable changes of raiment, as prescribed in the by-laws. Condition of patient as to cleanliness, etc.

§ 24. The managers, upon the superintendent's certificate of complete recovery, may discharge any patient, except one under a criminal charge or liable to be remanded to prison; and they may discharge any patient admitted as "dangerous," or any patient sent to the asylum by the superintendent or overseer of the poor, or by the (first) judge of a county, upon the superintendent's certificate that he or she is harmless and will probably continue so, and not likely to be improved by the further treatment in the asylum, or when the asylum is full, upon a like certificate that he or she is manifestly incurable and can probably be rendered comfortable at the poorhouse; so that the preference may be given, in the admission of patients, to recent cases, or cases of insanity of not over one year's duration. They may discharge and deliver any patient, except one under criminal charge as aforesaid, to his relatives or friends, who will undertake with good and approved sureties for his peaceable behavior, safe custody and comfortable maintenance, without further public charge. And the bond of such sureties shall be approved by the county judge of the county from which said patient was sent, and filed in the county clerk's office of said county. Upon the presentation of a certified copy thereof, the managers may discharge such patient. Discharge of patient. Security from relatives.

§ 25. A patient of the criminal class may be discharged by order of one of the justices of the supreme court, or a circuit judge, if, upon due investigation, it shall appear safe, legal and right to make such order. Discharges of patient of criminal class.

§ 26. No patient shall be discharged without suitable clothing; and, if it cannot be otherwise obtained, the steward shall, upon the order of two managers, furnish it, also money not exceeding twenty dollars, to defray his necessary expenses until he reaches his friends, or can find a chance to earn his subsistence. Clothing and money to be furnished discharged patients.

§ 27. The managers of the State Lunatic Asylum shall receive no compensation for their services, but shall receive their actual and reasonable traveling and other expenses, to be paid on the warrant of the comptroller on the rendering of their accounts. No compensation to managers.

§ 28. All the purchases for the use of the asylum shall be made for cash, and not on credit or time; every voucher shall be taken, duly filled up at the time it is taken; with every abstract of vouchers for money paid shall be proof on oath that the voucher was filled up and the money paid therefor at Purchases, vouchers, etc.

the time the voucher was taken; and the managers shall make all the needful rules and regulations to enforce the provisions of this section.

Price for keeping the poor or indigent.

§ 29. The price to be paid for keeping the poor, or any person in indigent circumstances, in the asylum, shall be annually fixed by the managers, and shall not exceed the actual cost of support and attendance, exclusive of officers' salaries. The managers may, at their discretion, require payments made quarterly or semi-annually in advance.

Liability of patient for his maintenance.

§ 30. Every insane person supported in the asylum shall be personally liable for his maintenance therein, and for all necessary expenses incurred by the institution in his behalf. And the committee, relative, town, city or county, that would have been bound by law to provide for and support him if he had not been sent to the asylum, shall be liable to pay the expense of his clothing and maintenance in the asylum, and actual and necessary expenses to and from the same.

Liability of committee, relative, etc.

County to pay expenses, in certain cases.

§ 31. The expenses of clothing and maintaining in the asylum a patient who has been received upon the order of any court or officer, shall be paid by the county from which he was sent to the asylum. The treasurer of said county is authorized and directed to pay to the treasurer of the asylum the bills for such clothing and maintenance as they shall become due and payable according to the by-laws of the asylum, upon the order of the steward; and the supervisors of said county shall annually levy and raise the amount of such bills, and such further sum as will pro ably cover all similar bills for one year in advance. Said county, however, shall have the right to require any individual, town, city or county, that is legally liable for the support of such patient, to reimburse the amount of said bills with interest from the day of paying the same.

County treasurer to pay to treasurer of asylum.

Supervisors to levy amount, etc.

County may be reimbursed.

When superintendent of the poor to pay expenses of removal.

§ 32. Whenever the managers shall order a patient removed from the asylum to the poor-house of the county whence he came, the superintendents of the poor of said county shall audit and pay the actual and reasonable expenses of such removal as part of the contingent expenses of said poor-house. But, if any town or person be legally liable for the support of such patient, the amount of such expenses may be recovered for the use of the county by such superintendents. If such superintendents of the poor neglect or refuse to pay such expenses on demand, the treasurer of the asylum may pay the same and charge the amount to the said county; and the treasurer of the said county is authorized to pay the same with interest, after thirty days; and the supervisors of the said county shall levy and raise the amount as other county charges.

If superintendents of poor neglect to pay such expenses, treasurer may do so.

Rights and remedies of town and county paying for support.

§ 33. Every town or county paying for the support of a lunatic in the asylum, or for his expenses in going to or from the same, shall have the like rights and remedies to recover the amount of such payments, with interest from the time of paying each bill, as if such expenses had been incurred for the support of the same at other places under existing laws

§ 34. None of the provisions of this act shall restrain or abridge the power and authority of the supreme court of the state over the persons and property of the insane. Power of supreme court.

§ 35. The managers of the said asylum are authorized, under the direction and subject at all times to the control of the acting canal commissioner having charge of the Chenango canal, to use the surplus water discharged around or through the fifth lock on said canal, to operate a pump to supply said asylum with water from said canal or from Nail creek, in case the said commissioner shall be of opinion that the same can be done without detriment to the navigation of said canal. Supply of water.

§ 36. The managers of the said asylum shall have control of the water in the levels of the Chenango canal from the fifth to the tenth locks of said canal, both inclusive, and of the water discharged from said levels and locks, for the purpose of supplying said asylum with water and ice; and it shall be the duty of all officers having charge of said canal, and of the persons employed by them, to do all things necessary, and which may be required by said managers, for the supply of said asylum with water and ice as aforesaid; provided always that the said managers in all their acts in reference to said levels, and locks, and water, shall be at all times subject to the direction and control of the acting commissioner having charge of said canal; and that nothing shall be done or permitted by said managers which shall obstruct or interfere with the navigation of said canal, or which shall not first receive the sanction of the commissioners in charge; and all persons, except such as are in the employ of the state, and such as are engaged in the navigation of the canals, are hereby prohibited from preventing, obstructing or in any way interfering with the said levels, locks and water of the canal, so as to prevent the free and full use thereof by the said asylum, and from doing any thing to injure the quality of said water for said use; and any person who shall in any way willfully violate this prohibition shall be guilty of a misdemeanor. Managers to have control of water in certain portions of Chenango canal for supply of water and ice. Sanction of canal commissioners. Misdemeanor.

§ 37. The terms "lunacy," "lunatic" and "insane," as used in this act, shall include every species of insanity and extend to every deranged person, and to all unsound mind other than idiots. The word "oath" includes "affirmation," the word "overseer" means "overseer of the poor," and "county superintendent" means "superintendent of the poor;" the word "asylum" and "institution" means "any state lunatic asylum;" a word denoting the singular number is to include one or many; and every word importing the masculine gender only may extend to and include females. Certain words and terms used in this act, defined.

TITLE FOURTH.

THE WILLARD ASYLUM FOR THE INSANE.

Trustees.

SECTION 1. There is established in the town of Ovid and county of Seneca, the Williard Asylum for the Insane, under the control of eight trustees. The term of office of said trustees is eight years. The said trustees and their successors shall be appointed by the governor, by and with the consent of the senate.

Their rights, privileges, powers and duties. *Rate of board.* *Counties from which the insane may be sent.*

§ 2. Said trustees shall have all the rights, privileges and powers, and be subject to the same duties, in said asylum, as are now possessed by and imposed upon the board of managers of the State Lunatic Asylum at Utica, and shall be subject to removal at any time by the senate upon recommendation of the governor. Said trustees shall also fix the rate per week, not exceeding the actual cost of support and attendance, exclusive of officers' salaries, for the board of patients. It shall further be the duty of said trustees, as portions of said asylum are completed and ready for the reception of the insane, to designate, in a just and equitable manner, and with the approval of the governor, the counties from which the chronic pauper insane shall be sent to said asylum, as parts of the room shall be ready, from time to time, for the reception of patients, except as hereinafter provided.

Trustee to appoint superintendent and treasurer. *Trustees may appoint steward, matron and four assistant physicians, etc.* *Salaries.*

§ 3. The managers shall appoint a medical superintendent who shall be a well-educated physician of experience in the treatment of the insane, and a treasurer, who shall give bonds for the faithful performance of his trust, in such sum and with such sureties as the comptroller shall approve. They shall also appoint, in their discretion, and upon the nomination of the medical superintendent, a steward and matron, and four assistant physicians, all of whom and the medical superintendent shall constantly reside in the asylum, or on the premises, and such other officers and assistants as may now be allowed by law. They shall also, from time to time, with the approval of the governor, comptroller and secretary of state, determine the annual salary and allowances of the before-named officials, the aggregate amount of such salaries not to exceed the sum of ten thousand five hundred dollars in any year.

Rights, powers and duties of superintendents, etc.

§ 4. The superintendent, resident officers and treasurer shall be subject to the same duties, and shall have the same rights and powers as are possessed by, and imposed upon, the superintendent, resident officers and treasurer of the State Lunatic Asylum at Utica.

Town and county officers to see that patient is well clothed, etc.

§ 5. All town and county officers sending a patient to the asylum shall, before sending him, see that he is in a state of perfect bodily cleanliness, and is comfortably clothed, and provided with suitable changes of raiment as prescribed in the by-laws.

Expenses of clothing, etc., to be paid by county.

§ 6. The expenses of clothing and maintaining, in the asylum, a patient who has been received upon the order of any court, or officer, shall be paid by the county from which he was sent to the asylum. The treasurer of said county is authorized and directed to pay to the treasurer of the asylum the bills for such clothing and maintenance, as they shall become due and payable, according to the by-laws of the asylum, upon the order of the steward; and the supervisors of said county shall, annually, levy and raise the amount of such bills, and such further sums as will probably cover all similar bills for one year in advance. Said county, however, shall have the right to require any individual, town, city or county that is legally liable for the support of such patient, to reimburse the amount of said bills, with interest from the day of paying the same. County treasurer to pay to treasurer of asylum bills for clothing, etc. County to be reimbursed.

§ 7. Every town or county paying for the support of a lunatic in the asylum, or his expenses in going to or from the same, shall have the like rights and remedies to recover the amount of such payments, with interest from the time of paying each bill, as if such expenses had been incurred for the support of the same, at other places, under existing laws. Towns and counties, rights and remedies of.

§ 8. The managers shall receive no compensation for their services, but shall receive their actual and reasonable traveling and other expenses, to be paid on the warrant of the comptroller on rendering their accounts. Trustees to receive compensation.

§ 9. In all purchases for the use of the asylum every voucher shall be taken, duly filled up, at the time it is taken, with every abstract of vouchers for money paid, and shall be proof on oath that the voucher was filled up and the money paid therefor at the time the voucher was taken; and the managers shall make all needful rules and regulations to enforce the provisions of this section. Vouchers to be verified, etc.

§ 10. The chronic pauper insane from the poor-houses of the counties that shall be designated, as provided in section two of this article, shall be sent to the said asylum by the county superintendents of the poor, and all the chronic insane pauper patients who may be discharged not recovered from state lunatic asylums, and who continue a public charge, shall be sent to the asylum for the insane hereby created; and all such patients shall be a charge upon the respective counties from which they are sent. And all the chronic insane paupers of the several counties of the state shall be sent to said asylum by the superintendents of the poor, except from those counties having asylums for the insane, to which they are now authorized to send such insane patients by special legislative enactments, or such counties as have been, or may hereafter be, exempted by the state board of charities. Chronic insane paupers. A charge upon their respective counties. am See chap 655 of laws of 1875

TITLE FIFTH.

HUDSON RIVER STATE HOSPITAL FOR THE INSANE.

SECTION 1. There is established near the city of Poughkeepsie, the Hudson River State Hospital for the Insane, under the control of nine managers, who are appointed by the senate upon the nomination of the governor, and hold their Managers, number and mode of appointment of.

offices for six years and until others are appointed in their stead, and subject to be removed at any time by the senate upon the recommendation of the governor, and a majority of the said managers shall reside within the county of Dutchess.

Residence. Rights, powers and duties. Organization and government.

§ 2. The said managers have the rights and powers, and are subject to the same duties, as now possessed by and imposed upon the managers of the State Lunatic Asylum at Utica; and the Hudson River State Hospital for the Insane is organized and governed under the laws organizing and governing the state asylum at Utica, except as may be herein otherwise provided.

Managers to appoint medical superintendent and treasurer.

§ 3. The managers shall appoint a medical superintendent who shall be a well-educated physician of experience in the treatment of the insane, and a treasurer, who shall reside in the city of Poughkeepsie, and give bonds for the faithful performance of his trust in such sum and with such sureties as the comptroller of the state shall approve. *Other appointments.* They shall also appoint, at their discretion, and upon the nomination of the medical superintendent, a steward and a matron, and such assistant physicians as the necessity of the hospital shall from time to time require, all of whom and the medical superintendent shall constantly reside in the hospital or on the premises and shall be designated as the "resident officers."

Salaries.

§ 4. The managers shall, from time to time, with the approval of the governor, comptroller and secretary of the state, determine the annual salaries and allowances to the treasurer and resident officers, the aggregate amount of said salaries not to exceed the sum of twelve thousand dollars for any one year.

Notice of readiness to receive patients.

§ 5. As soon as portions of the hospital shall be prepared for the reception of patients, the managers shall cause notice thereof to be published in the state paper and sent to the county clerk, county judge and superintendents of the poor of the following counties: Clinton, Essex, Franklin, Warren, Washington, Saratoga, Albany, Rensselaer, Greene, Columbia, Ulster, Dutchess, Orange, Sullivan, Putnam, Rockland, Westchester, New York, Kings, Queens, Suffolk and Richmond. *Circular from medical superintendent.* A circular from the medical superintendent shall accompany said notice to each county clerk, county judge and superintendent of the poor, designating the number and class of patients to be received; *Transfer of patients from Utica asylum.* and when the hospital shall be completed, due notice shall be given as above, so that all patients who may then be in the State Lunatic Asylum at Utica, chargeable to the above-mentioned counties, shall be transferred to the Hudson River State Hospital for the Insane.

Hudson River State Hospital district.

§ 6. The counties enumerated in the last section shall constitute the Hudson River State Hospital district, and the hospital shall be designated the Hudson River State Hospital.

Managers and officers not to have interest in contracts.

§ 7. The managers and other officers shall have no interest, direct or indirect, in the furnishing of any building materials, or in any contracts for the same, or in any contracts for labor in the erection of said hospital.

Report of managers.

§ 8. It shall be the duty of the managers to make a detailed report of all the moneys received by them, and of the progress which shall have been made in the erection of said buildings, to the legislature in January of each year, and also to the comptroller, as often and in such manner as the comptroller shall or may, from time to time, require.

§ 9. The plans and specifications for said hospital shall be upon the basis of accommodating not exceeding five hundred patients at any one time, and shall be approved by the governor, comptroller and secretary of state. Plans, etc., approval of.

TITLE SIXTH.

THE BUFFALO STATE ASYLUM FOR THE INSANE.

SECTION 1. There is established, in the city of Buffalo, the Buffalo State Asylum for the Insane, under the control of ten managers appointed by the governor, by and with the consent of the senate. Managers, number and appointment of.

§ 2. They shall be subject to be removed at any time by the senate, upon the recommendation of the governor. Their successors shall be appointed by the governor, and shall hold their office for six years, and until others are appointed in their stead, and subject to be removed in the manner aforesaid; and, in case of a vacancy in said board, the governor shall appoint, in manner aforesaid, to fill the unexpired term. Vacancy, how filled.

§ 3. The said managers have all the rights and powers and are subject to the same duties, as are now possessed by and imposed upon the managers of the State Lunatic Asylum at Utica; and the Buffalo State Asylum for the Insane shall be organized and governed under the laws organizing and governing the state asylum at Utica, except as may be herein otherwise provided. Managers, their rights, powers and duties.

§ 4. The managers shall appoint a medical superintendent, who shall be a well-educated physician of experience in the treatment of the insane, and a treasurer, who shall reside in the city of Buffalo, and give bonds for the faithful performance of his trust, in such sum and with such sureties as the comptroller of the state shall approve. They shall also appoint, at their discretion and upon the nomination of the medical superintendent, a steward and a matron, and one or more assistant physicians, as the necessities of the hospital shall, from time to time, require, all of whom, and the medical superintendent, shall constantly reside in the hospital, or on the premises, and shall be designated the resident officers. Managers to appoint medical superintendent and treasurer. Other appointments. Officers to reside in the hospital.

§ 5. The managers shall, from time to time, determine the annual salaries and allowances of the treasurer and resident officers, subject to the approval of the governor of the state, secretary of state and the comptroller; provided that such salaries shall not exceed, in the aggregate, ten thousand dollars for any one year. Salaries.

§ 6. The managers shall procure plans, drawings and specifications for the construction of the hospital and other buildings, and the improvement of the grounds, and shall contract for the erection of the buildings in accordance with such plans and specifications, and on such terms as they may deem proper; provided such plans, drawings, specifications, contracts, and Plans, drawings, contracts, etc.

Approval. the terms thereof, shall be approved by the governor, state engineer and comptroller; and further provided, that the managers shall not adopt any plans for the hospital or other buildings, nor alter or change the plans adopted, without the assent of the state officers aforesaid.

Managers and officers not to have an interest in contracts. § 7. The managers and other officers shall have no interest direct or indirect, in the furnishing of any building materials or in any contracts for the same, or in any contracts for labor in the erection of said hospital.

Report of managers. § 8. It shall be the duty of the managers to make a detailed report of all the moneys received by them, and the progress which shall have been made in the erection of said buildings to the legislature in January of each year, and also to the comptroller, as often and in such manner as the comptroller shall or may from time to time require.

Basis of plans, etc. § 9. The plans and specifications for said hospital shall be upon the basis of accommodating not exceeding five hundred patients at any one time.

TITLE SEVENTH.

THE STATE HOMŒOPATHIC ASYLUM FOR THE INSANE AT MIDDLETOWN.

Section 1. There is established at Middletown, in the county of Orange, a state lunatic asylum for the care and treatment of the insane upon the principles of medicine known as the homœopathic; by the name of "The State Homœopathic Asylum for the Insane, at Middletown," under the control of *Trustees, number and mode of appointment of.* twenty-one trustees appointed by the governor, by and with the consent of the senate, and shall be adherents of homœopathy. The trustees shall be subject to removal for cause by the senate, upon the recommendation of the governor. The term of office of said trustees is seven years.

Trustees not to deal, etc. § 2. The said trustees shall not, for their own private advantage or gain, directly or indirectly, deal or trade in buying or selling any goods, wares, merchandise or other property whatsoever, belonging to, or to be used for, the said corporation.

To have direction of business. § 3. The financial and other business concerns of said asylum are under the direction of said board of trustees, who shall elect from their number at each annual meeting, a president, a vice-*To appoint a president, etc.* president, a secretary and a treasurer, who shall hold their offices for one year, or until their successors shall be elected. Seven of said trustees shall constitute a quorum for the transaction *Quorum.* of business, and a majority of the number present at a meeting shall be requisite to make any order in the management of the asylum. All other duties, rights and powers of said trustees *Other duties, etc., of trustees.* shall be the same as those imposed upon the managers of the State Lunatic Asylum at Utica.

When trustee deemed to have vacated his office. § 4. Any trustee failing to attend the regular meetings of the board for one year may thereupon, at the option of said board, be deemed to have vacated his office, and a successor may be appointed to fill the same.

§ 5. The trustees shall hold their annual meeting on the third

Thursday in June, at the asylum, to receive reports of their officers as to the business and affairs of said corporation, and to transact such other business as may be deemed necessary. Annual meeting of trustees.

§ 6. The board of trustees of said asylum shall have power to make, constitute, ordain and establish, from time to time, such by-laws, rules and regulations as they shall deem proper for transacting, managing and directing the affairs of said asylum; provided, that such by-laws, rules and regulations do not conflict with this act, or with the constitution and laws of this state or of the United States. By-laws, etc. Proviso.

§ 7. The board of trustees may appoint a superintending homœopathic physician and assistant physicians, and such other officers and agents of the said corporation as they shall deem necessary, who shall respectively hold and perform the duties pertaining to their offices and agencies during the pleasure of said board, and the said board shall, from time to time, fix the salaries of such superintending physicians, assistant physicians, officers and agents. But the annual salaries of the superintendent, assistant physicians, treasurer, steward and matron shall be approved by the governor, secretary of state and comptroller; provided that such salaries shall not exceed in the aggregate eight thousand dollars for any one year. Board of trustees may appoint superintending physician, etc. Salaries. Approval thereof.

§ 8. The charges to be made by the said asylum for the care and treatment of patients shall be such sum only as shall, in the aggregate, be sufficient to defray the current expenses of said asylum. Charges for care, etc., of patients.

§ 9. The expenditure of all money appropriated by the state for the erection of said asylum, together with all amounts derived or received from other sources, shall be fully and duly accounted for to the comptroller.

§ 10. The treasurer of said asylum shall give bonds for the faithful performance of his trust in such and with such sureties as the comptroller of the state shall approve. Bond of treasurer.

TITLE EIGHTH.

THE STATE LUNATIC ASYLUM FOR INSANE CRIMINALS.

SECTION 1. The building erected on the prison grounds at Auburn for an asylum, is known and designated as the State Lunatic Asylum for Insane Criminals at Auburn. Location.

§ 2. The inspectors of the state prisons shall appoint a medical superintendent for said asylum, who shall be a well-educated physician of experience in the treatment of the insane, who shall, under the direction of the said inspectors, have charge of said asylum, and shall make all the purchases for the support of said asylum, and shall account for all moneys coming to his hand in the same manner as the agent and warden of any of the state prisons are now required by law to account. Inspectors of state prisons to appoint medical superintendent.

§ 3. The said medical superintendent shall reside in the building, and shall devote all the time necessary to the care To reside in the building.

and treatment of those confined therein for treatment. He shall receive a salary of one thousand dollars per annum, payable monthly, and shall be allowed rations for himself and family, and all necessary fuel and lights for warming and lighting his rooms in said building.

His salary.

Other officers, how appointed.

§ 4. The other officers of said asylum shall be an assistant superintendent, and not exceeding ten attendants for the male department, and four female attendants for the female department, who shall be recommended by the medical superintendent, and, if approved of by the board of inspectors of state prisons, shall be appointed as such by said board of inspectors, and shall be paid as follows: The assistant superintendent shall receive thirty dollars per month, payable monthly, and shall also be boarded in and at the expense of said asylum; and the said attendants shall each receive twenty dollars per month and be boarded in said asylum.

Compensation.

Insane female convicts at Sing Sing to be removed, etc.

§ 5. The inspectors of state prisons shall cause any female convict in the state prison at Sing Sing, who now is or may hereafter become insane, to be removed to and retained in the female department of the State Lunatic Asylum for Insane Criminals in the manner provided, and subject to the provisions of the above-mentioned act. And all the provisions of said act shall apply to the cases of convicts so removed, except that whenever any such female convict shall have become restored to reason she shall be transferred to and again received into the female state prison at Sing Sing.

Bond of medical superintendent.

§ 6. The medical superintendent shall file in the office of the comptroller of this state a bond, in the penal sum of ten thousand dollars, conditioned for the faithful performance of his duty as such, which bond, before it shall be filed, shall be approved by the board of inspectors; and no such medical superintendent shall enter upon the discharge of the duties of said office till such bond so approved shall have been duly filed as aforesaid.

Superintendent to make monthly estimates.

§ 7. The superintendent shall estimate monthly, as is now provided by law, and subject to the same restrictions and conditions as in the case of agents and wardens of the state prisons, for all the moneys necessary for the support and maintenance of said asylum; which estimate shall be submitted to and carefully examined by the inspector in charge of said Auburn prison, who, if he is satisfied that the said estimate is correct, and that the articles named in said estimate are actually needed for the support and maintenance of said asylum, shall certify the same; and on the production of said estimate, so certified, to the comptroller, he shall draw his warrant on the treasurer for the amount of said estimate, and the treasurer shall pay the amount of said warrant out of any money in the treasury appropriated for the support of the state prisons.

Inspectors to examine and certify same.

Comptroller's warrant.

Rules and regulations.

§ 8. The inspector of state prisons shall adopt such rules and regulations, from time to time, as they shall deem proper, for the control and management of the said asylum, and shall have power to remove any and all the officers in said asylum for cause, and shall enter such cause in full on the minutes of their proceedings at the asylum. And no officer removed by the said inspectors, for cause, shall be re-appointed to any position in said asylum.

When inspectors to examine into condition of convicts.

§ 9. Whenever the physician of either of the state prisons of this state shall certify to the board of inspectors, or to the inspector in charge, that any convict therein is insane, it shall be the duty of such board, or such inspector in charge, to make, immediately, a full examination into the condition of such convict, and if satisfied that he is insane, the board of inspectors, or inspector in charge, may order the agent or warden of the prison where such convict is confined forthwith to convey such convict to the State Lunatic Asylum for Insane Criminals, and to deliver him to the superintendent thereof, who is hereby required to receive him into the said asylum and retain him there until legally discharged.

May order convicts to be conveyed to asylum.

Disposition of convicts remaining insane at the expiration of sentence.

§ 10. Whenever any convict in the State Lunatic Asylum for Insane Criminals, under and by virtue of the provisions of this act, shall continue to be insane at the expiration of that term for which he was sentenced, the board of inspectors, upon the superintendent's certificate that he is harmless and will probably continue so, and that he is not likely to be improved by further treatment in the asylum, or upon a like certificate that he is manifestly incurable, and can probably be rendered comfortable at the county alms-house, may cause such insane convict to be removed, at the expense of the state, from said asylum, to the county wherein he was convicted, or to the county of his former residence, and delivered to and placed under the care of the superintendent of the poor of such county, and the said superintendent is hereby required to receive such insane convict under his charge; they may also discharge and deliver any convict whose sentence has expired, and who is still insane, to his relatives or friends, who will undertake with good sureties, to be approved by said superintendent of the State Lunatic Asylum for Insane Criminals, for his peaceful behavior, safe custody and comfortable maintenance without further public charge; and no convict shall be retained in the said State Lunatic Asylum for Insane Criminals after the expiration of his sentence to the state prison, unless by the order of the county judge of the county in which said asylum is situated; and the said county judge, upon the application of the said superintendent, shall proceed to investigate the question of the insanity of such convict, and shall cause two respectable physicians, to be designated by him, to examine said convict, and upon their evidence, under oath, and upon such other testimony as he shall require, shall decide the case as to his insanity; and, if he is satisfied that such convict is insane, shall make an order that the said convict shall be retained in the said asylum until he is recovered of his insanity, or is otherwise discharged according to law, and the fees of such physicians and witnesses shall be audited by the state prison inspector in charge and shall be a charge against the state, to

Convict not to remain at asylum after expiration of sentence, unless by order of county judge.

Fees for physicians and witnesses.

be paid by the comptroller out of the general fund; but such fees shall not in any one case exceed the sum of ten dollars.

When convict to be transferred to state prisons. § 11. Whenever any convict, who shall have been confined in the said asylum as a lunatic, shall have become restored to reason, and the medical superintendent of said asylum shall so certify in writing, he shall be forthwith transferred to the Auburn state prison, and the agent and warden of said prison shall receive said convict into the said prison, and shall, in all respects, treat such convict as if he had been originally sentenced to imprisonment in said prison, though said convict may have been conveyed to the said asylum from either of the other prisons of this state.

Certificate of conviction. § 12. Whenever the inspector of state prisons shall order any convict to be transferred to the Asylum for Insane Criminals, the agent and warden of the prison from which such convict is transferred shall cause a correct copy of the original certificate of conviction of said convict to be filed in his office, and shall deliver the original certificate to the superintendent of the asylum; and when any such convict shall be transferred to the Auburn prison from such asylum, as hereinbefore provided, the said superintendent shall deliver to the agent and warden of said prison such original certificate, which shall be filed in the clerk's office in said prison.

Pay of physician. § 13. The physician who shall attend any meeting of the board of inspectors of state prisons, or who shall make any examination of any convict, as hereinbefore provided, shall be paid his actual and reasonable traveling expenses in going to and returning from such examination or meeting, on the certificate of the president of the board of inspectors of state prisons that he has attended such meeting or examination.

Superintendent may recover for support in action in his official name. § 14. The superintendent is hereby authorized to recover for the support of any patient therein chargeable under the law to either counties or penitentiaries, in an action to be brought in said superintendent's name as superintendent of the State Lunatic Asylum for Insane Criminals, and which shall not abate by his death or removal, against the county or penitentiary for the maintenance of the said patient, and in which action Complaint. the complaint may be in a general *indebitatus assumpsit*; and judgment shall be rendered for such sum as shall be found Interest. due, with interest from the time of the demand made.

TITLE NINTH.

LICENSES FOR PRIVATE ASYLUMS.

No private asylum to be established without license therefor. SECTION 1. No person or association shall establish or keep an asylum, institution, house or retreat for the care, custody or treatment of the insane or persons of unsound mind, for compensation or hire, without first obtaining a license therefor from the state commissioner in lunacy; provided that this section shall not apply to any state asylum or institution, or any asylum or institution established or conducted by any Proviso. county; and provided, also, that it shall not apply to cases where an insane person or person of unsound mind is detained and treated at his own house or that of some relative.

§ 2. Every application for such license shall be accompanied by a plan of the premises proposed to be occupied, describing the capacities of the buildings for the uses intended, the extent and location of grounds appurtenant thereto, and the number of patients of either sex proposed to be received therein; and it shall not be lawful for said commissioner to grant any such license without having first visited the premises proposed to be licensed, and being satisfied by such examination that they are as described, and are otherwise fit and suitable for the purposes for which they are designed to be used. Application for license. Commissioner to resist premises before granting license, etc.

TITLE TENTH.

STATE COMMISSIONER IN LUNACY.

SECTION 1. The governor shall nominate, and by and with the advice and consent of the senate, appoint an experienced and competent physician, who shall be designated as the state commissioner in lunacy, who shall hold his office for five years and receive an annual salary of four thousand dollars, and traveling and other incidental expenses not to exceed one thousand dollars, to be paid on presentation of vouchers to the comptroller. State commissioner in lunacy.

§ 2. It shall be the duty of such commissioner to examine into and report annually to the legislature on or before the fifth day of January, the condition of the insane and idiotic in this state and the management and conduct of the asylums, public and private, and other institutions for their care and treatment. The duties of said commissioner in regard to the insane shall be performed so as not to prejudice the established and reasonable regulations of such asylums and institutions aforesaid; and it shall be the duty of the officers and others respectively in charge thereof, to give such commissioner, at all times, free access to and full information concerning the insane, and their treatment therein. It shall also be the duty of such commissioner to inquire and report, from time to time, as far as he may be able, the results of the treatment of the insane of other states and countries, together with such particulars pertaining thereto as he may deem proper. His duties. How performed. To report result of treatment.

am See page 658 of laws of 1885

§ 3. The said commissioner shall have power to make and use an official seal, and all copies of papers and documents in his possession and custody may be authenticated in the usual form under his official seal and signature, and used as evidence in all courts and places in this state, in like manner as similar certificates emanating from any other public officer. Official seal. Copies of papers, etc., how authenticated.

§ 4. The said commissioner is hereby empowered to issue compulsory process for the attendance of witnesses and the production of papers, to administer oaths and to examine persons under oath, in all cases where, from evidence laid before him, there is reason to believe that any person is wrongfully deprived of his liberty, or is cruelly, negligently or improperly treated in any asylum, institution or establish- His powers and duties in cases where person is wrongfully deprived of his liberty, etc.

am See page 689 laws of 1871

In any asylum.

ment, public or private, for the custody of the insane; and if the same shall be proved to his satisfaction, it shall be his duty to report the facts, together with his conclusions thereon, to a justice of the supreme court, who shall thereupon grant the necessary relief.

Keepers of county poor-houses, etc., report annually to commissioner of lunacy.

§ 5. The superintendent or keeper of every county poor-house, city alms-house or other asylum where insane paupers are kept, shall, on or before the fifteenth day of November in each and every year, report to the state commissioner in lunacy the numbers of male and female insane, idiots and epileptics in his custody on the first day of November last past, together with a statistical exhibit of the number of admissions, discharges and deaths that may have occurred within the past year among that class of persons, and the average weekly cost of their maintenance. He shall also state the actual condition of those discharged and the causes of death in those dying within the institution.

Penalty for neglect.

§ 6. Any superintendent or keeper of a county poor-house, city alms-house or other asylum where insane paupers are kept, who shall neglect to report as above recited, shall be guilty of a misdemeanor, and on conviction, be subject to a fine of not less than fifty dollars nor more than two hundred and fifty dollars, and it shall be the duty of the district attorney of the proper county to proceed against such offenders according to law.

TITLE ELEVENTH.

GENERAL PROVISIONS.

Term or tenure of office not affected.

SECTION 1. Nothing in this act shall be construed to *effect either the term or tenure of office of any manager or boards of managers, or any superintendent or resident officers of any state asylum, who may now be in office.

Repeal.

§ 2. All laws, or parts of laws inconsistent with or repugnant to the provisions of this act are hereby repealed.

§ 3. This act shall take effect immediately.

*So in the original.

CHAP. 451.

AN ACT to amend the several acts in relation to state prisons.

PASSED May 12, 1874; three-fifths being present.

The People of the State of New York, represented in Senate aud Assembly, do enact as follows:

SECTION 1. Subdivision one of section thirty-four of chapter four hundred and sixty of the laws of eighteen hundred and forty-seven is hereby amended so as to read as follows:

1. To visit jointly each of the state prisons that now are or may hereafter be established in this state, at least three times in each year, and in addition the president of the board of inspectors shall call a joint meeting whenever requested to do so by two of the inspectors, at such prison or prisons as they may designate. Inspectors to visit jointly each of the state prisons.

§ 2. Subdivision fifteen of section thirty-four of chapter four hundred and sixty of the laws of eighteen hundred and forty-seven is hereby amended so as to read as follows:

15. At either of the prisons where manufacturing is carried on by the state, the inspectors shall appoint, as far as possible, keepers qualified to teach the convicts in the trades and manufactures thus prosecuted in such prisons, and to be inclusive with the number of keepers such prison may be entitled to by existing laws. Appointment of teachers.

§ 3. Subdivision ten of section forty-eight of chapter four hundred and sixty of the laws of eighteen hundred and forty-seven is hereby amended so as to read as follows:

10. To furnish to each convict who shall be discharged from prison, by pardon or otherwise, necessary clothing, not exceeding twelve dollars in value (between the first day of November and the first day of April, clothing not to exceed eighteen dollars may be given), and a sum of money not exceeding upon an average over five dollars, as the agents and wardens may deem proper and necessary, at each of said prisons, and the sum of four cents for each mile for which it may be necessary for such convict to travel to reach the place of his residence, and if he has no residence within this state, to the place of his conviction; but at Clinton prison the mileage shall be five cents per mile as aforesaid. Discharged convicts to be furnished with clothing and money.

§ 4. Section sixty-one of the same chapter is hereby amended so as to read as follows:

§ 61. Four instructors shall be employed by the inspectors for each of the prisons at Sing Sing and Auburn, and two for the Clinton prison; it shall be the duty of such instructors, in conjunction with, and under the supervision of the chaplain and inspector in charge, to give instruction in the usual branches of an English education, to such convicts as in the judgment of the chaplain may require the same and be benefited thereby; such instruction shall be given for not less than Instructors for prisons, their duties.

one hour and a half daily (Sundays excepted), between the hours of six and nine in the evening, in such room or rooms as may be provided for that purpose.

§ 5. Section sixty-nine of same chapter is hereby amended so as to read as follows:

Agents, etc., to support themselves, and not to receive perquisites, etc. § 69. The agents and wardens and other officers, and the guards of the respective prisons, shall support themselves from their own salaries and resources, and shall not receive any perquisites or emoluments for their services other than the compensation provided for by law, except that the agents and wardens, physicians and chaplains shall keep their offices at the respective prisons, and that the agent and warden shall reside therein; they shall all be furnished with the fuel for their offices, and lights, and the house for the agent and warden shall be furnished with household furniture and provided with the necessary fuel and lights for themselves and families; and from the stock provided for the prison, the agent and warden shall furnish fuel for the barracks of the guards.

Fuel and lights. House for agent and wardens to be furnished, etc.

§ 6. Section seventy-four of the same chapter is hereby amended so as to read as follows:

Inspector, agent, etc., not to employ labor of convict, etc. § 74. No inspector, agent and warden, matron, or other officer of either of the prisons of this state, shall employ the labor of any convict or other person employed in such prison, or any work in which such inspector, agent and warden, matron or other officer shall be interested, except that the agent and warden of each prison and the matron of the female prison shall each be entitled to two convict servants and a convict gardener, and to be fed from rations drawn from prisons stores, but of the same quality and quantity as is allowed to other convicts in their respective prisons.

Exceptions.

§ 7. Section twelve of chapter three hundred and ninety-nine of the laws of eighteen hundred and sixty is hereby amended so as to read as follows:

§ 12. Section nine of chapter two hundred and forty of the laws of eighteen hundred and fifty-four is hereby amended so as to read as follows:

Contract for labor of convicts for term of more than one year' resolutions of the board upon the subject. § 9. Whenever the board of inspectors shall deem it expedient and proper for the agent and warden of either of the prisons to enter into any contract for the labor and services of convicts for a term of more than one year, it shall be the duty of said board to pass a resolution to that effect, specifying the number of convicts whose labor and services are to be let; the prison in which they are confined; the business at which they are to be employed; the number of years for which their labor and services are to be let; the time the contracts shall commence; the shop-room, store-room, hydraulic or steam power, machinery and other facilities, if any there be, for the business, which will be furnished with the labor and services to be let; directing the warden to advertise for sealed proposals in the state paper, in one newspaper published in the county where said prison is located, and in one newspaper published in not to exceed eight of the cities of this state. Upon the passage of any such resolution and serving a copy thereof upon

Direction to advertise. Warden, his duties.

the agent and warden, that officer shall proceed at once to execute it, by preparing and publishing for the period of twenty days next preceding the time fixed for opening such proposals, the notice required in the manner above provided, and by preparing a duplicate form of the contract to be entered into, with the date, amount of compensation per day, and names of contractors and their sureties, in blank, to be approved by the inspectors or a majority of them, a copy whereof shall be deposited with the clerk of the prison at which such convict labor is to be let, for the inspection of all persons desirous of proposing therefor, for at least the period of twenty days prior to the time fixed in such notice for opening such proposals. The agent and warden shall receive and preserve unopened all the sealed proposals for the said labor and services, which shall be delivered to or received by him up to the day and hour mentioned in his published notice and no longer, and shall thereupon, as soon thereafter as the board of inspectors shall convene, lay said proposals before the board of inspectors, who shall proceed publicly at once to open and canvass such of them as shall be substantially in the form prescribed in the published notice of the agent and warden, and as shall be accompanied by an offer to enter into the contract for the labor of such convicts, prepared as aforesaid with the names of the bidders and the price per day for the labor and services of the convicts which he or they propose to pay, with the names also of at least two sufficient sureties, accompanied by their written consent to become sureties in such contract, and shall award the contract for such labor and services to the person or persons who shall be found to be, by said canvass, the highest bidder or bidders therefor. The board shall thereupon direct the agent and warden to fill up the blanks in such contract pursuant to such proposal, and execute the same with such bidder or bidders, which contract, when so filled up and signed, and approved by the inspectors or a majority of them as to the sufficiency of the sureties therein, shall be a valid contract in law between the parties thereto and their sureties; provided, however, that no such contract shall be executed by said agent and warden of either prison, which shall contain any stipulation on the part of the agent and warden to accept any less than full contract price (which shall be the price per day only) for the labor and services of any of the contracts referred to in said contract, or that the said convicts shall execute any specific amount of labor per day, per month or year, or that they shall have or possess any particular degree of skill in the trade or business at which they are to be employed, or that the contractor or contractors shall have any accommodations or facilities for business or privileges which were not specified in the contract so prepared as aforesaid, or that the agent and warden shall maintain any particular kind, standard or quality of discipline in said prison over said convicts during the time that they shall be employed under said contract; and provided, further, that no such contract shall be awarded by the agent or warden or

Notice. Sealed proposals. Award of contract. Execution of contract. Approval. Proviso. Further proviso.

be valid in law if it run for a longer time than five years from the time when it is by its terms to commence, and if it shall not contain a stipulation on the part of the contractor or contractors to pay the contract price for the labor and services therein specified, monthly, on the first day of each month, to the agent and warden, at his office at the prison, and that the agent and warden may, by and with the consent of the board of inspectors or a majority of them, annul the said contract and declare it void, if said contractor or contractors shall at any time neglect or refuse to make the monthly payments within ten days from the time they shall respectively fall due; and every such contract shall likewise contain a stipulation that the state will not be held responsible for any loss sustained by fire on the part of any contractor or contractors. In case any bidder or bidders to whom any contract may be awarded shall refuse, or shall, for twenty-four hours after any such award shall be made to him or them, neglect to execute such contract, with at least two sufficient sureties, to be approved by said inspectors or a majority of them; and every bidder to whom such contract shall be so awarded, and who shall refuse or neglect as aforesaid to execute such contract, shall pay to the agent and warden, and his successor in office, as stipulated damages for such refusal or neglect, a sum equal to the difference between the aggregate of earnings of the number of convicts specified in such contract, at the price per day named in the proposal of such bidder, for the term of such contract, and the aggregate of earnings of such number of convicts at the price per day at which the same shall be finally awarded: and such agent and warden shall have an immediate right of action against such bidder so neglecting or refusing, and his proposed sureties, for the recovery of such damages, and unless the same shall be paid within thirty days after personal demand thereof of such bidder, the agent and warden shall forthwith bring suit for the recovery thereof. If, upon opening such proposals, the said inspectors, with the assent of the agent, shall deem it for the interest of the state not to award said contract to any such bidders, they may reject all of said proposals and re-advertise the same; and if, after awarding such contract to any bidder or bidders who shall have refused or neglected to enter into any such contract, the said inspectors shall not deem it for the interest of the state to award the same to any person bidding a lower rate of compensation. they may reject all lower bids and re-advertise; and any bidder whose proposal shall have been accepted by the inspectors, and who shall have refused to enter into such contract, shall be liable to said agent and warden for the expenses of such re-advertisements, in addition to the damages by reason of such refusal or neglect, to be computed as hereinbefore provided. To every proposal for convict labor shall be annexed a justification of the sureties in an amount in the aggregate not less than the sum of five thousand dollars over and above all debts and liabilities, and properly exempt from levy and sale on execution.

Stipulation as to loss by fire.

Damages for refusal to execute contract.

Right of action against bidders.

Inspectors may reject proposals and readvertise. Expense of re-advertising.

Justification of sureties.

§ 8. Section nine of said chapter is hereby amended so as to read as follows:

Officers for each prison to be appointed by inspectors.

§ 9. The inspectors shall appoint to each of the state prisons the following officers: An agent and warden, a principal keeper, a chaplain, a clerk, a physician and surgeon, and a yard keeper; a matron for the female prison at Sing Sing, who shall be a widow or unmarried woman; a store-keeper for each of the prisons at Sing Sing and Auburn, and one kitchen-keeper at each prison, and who at Clinton prison shall perform the duties of store-keeper; and so many keepers at Sing Sing as not to exceed the proportion of one to twenty-seven convicts, exclusive of the yard-keeper for the male prison, and assistant matrons, not to exceed the proportion of one to twenty-five convicts; at Auburn prison, the number of keepers shall not exceed the proportion of one to twenty-eight convicts; at Clinton prison, the number of keepers shall not exceed the proportion of one to every thirty convicts.

§ 9. Section sixty-four of chapter four hundred and sixty of the laws of eighteen hundred and forty-seven, is hereby amended so as to read as follows:

Guards at each prison.

§ 64. There shall be continued to be maintained at each state prison a guard, to be appointed by the inspectors, to consist of one sergeant and so many privates as the inspectors may from time to time direct, but the guard at Sing Sing, including the sergeant, shall not exceed forty-two in number; the guard at Auburn, including the sergeant, shall not exceed the number of twenty-two; and at Clinton, between the first day of November and the first day of April, shall not exceed the number of twenty-eight, and from the first day of April until November, the number shall not exceed twenty-nine; but at each prison the sergeant of the guard shall be included in the number.

Escape of convicts.

§ 10. Section seven of chapter three hundred and ninety-nine of the laws of eighteen hundred and sixty is hereby amended by adding thereto the following: Any convict escaping from any state prison or penitentiary of this state, and afterward arrested, shall serve out the full balance of his then sentence, notwithstanding the time may have expired, as if he had remained in prison, and shall lose all the benefits of the commutation he may have earned by good conduct prior to said escape, unless pardoned by the governor previous to, or after his re-arrest.

Removal of convicts.

§ 11. In addition to the power now granted to the board of inspectors of state prisons authorizing them to remove convicts from one state prison to another, the said board are authorized to remove any convict or convicts from the prison where he or they are confined to either of the other prisons, when in the judgment of said board the interests of the state or the health or improvement of the convict or convicts demand it, or when it is otherwise material, or in furtherance of justice.

Hours of labor.

§ 12. It shall be the duty of the agent and warden of the several state prisons of this state to require of all able-bodied convicts therein an equal number of faithful hours' labor during such hours as the inspector shall designate, and each convict in good faith performing such day's work and being in all respects obedient to the rules and regulations of the prison, or if not able to work, but is faithful and obedient, each shall be allowed "two months" on each of the first two years; "four months" on each succeeding year to the fifth year, and "five months" to each remaining year of the term of his imprisonment; and provided further, commutation of time earned by a convict for good conduct shall be wholly forfeited up to the time he commits any of the offenses mentioned in section two of chapter four hundred and fifteen of the laws of eighteen hundred and sixty-three, or commits any other act that would amount by law to a misdemeanor; and the name of no convict who has escaped or attempted to escape shall be sent to the governor for the commutation of any part of his sentence by prison officials.

Commutation of time.

Forfeiture thereof.

Repeal. § 13. All acts and parts of acts inconsistent with this act are hereby repealed.

§ 14. This act shall take effect immediately.

CHAP. 456.

AN ACT enlarging the powers of clerks to surrogates' courts.

PASSED May 12, 1874; three-fifths being present.

The People of the State of New York, represented in Senate and Assembly, do enact as follows:

Surrogate's clerk may take affidavits, acknowledgments, etc.

SECTION 1. The clerk to any surrogate or surrogate's court in this state, appointed according to law, shall, in addition to the powers now possessed by such clerk, have power and authority to take and certify affidavits, oaths and acknowledgments to any petition, bond, inventory or other paper or instrument, authorized or required to be used, made or filed in any matter, case or proceeding in any surrogate's court, or before any surrogate of, or to which he is clerk; to administer oaths and affirmations in any and all matters, cases and proceedings which shall or may be pending or instituted before said surrogate or surrogate's court; and in the absence of the surrogate, or in case of his sickness or inability to perform the duties appertaining to said court, to adjourn any matter, case, hearing or proceeding which may or shall be pending before such surrogate or before or in said surrogate's court, to some convenient time, but said clerk shall not adjourn any such matter, case, hearing or proceeding more than thirty days at any one time.

When he may adjourn any proceeding pending in surrogate's court.

§ 2. This act shall take effect immediately.

CHAP. 464.

AN ACT to amend an act entitled "An act to provide for the support and care of state paupers," passed June seventh, eighteen hundred and seventy-three.

PASSED May 18, 1874; three-fifths being present.

The People of the State of New York, represented in Senate and Assembly, do enact as follows:

SECTION 1. Section two of the act entitled "An act to provide for the support and care of state paupers," passed June seventh, eighteen hundred and seventy-three, is hereby amended so as to read as follows:

§ 2. The state board of charities is hereby authorized, from time to time, on behalf of the state, to contract, for such time and on such terms as it may deem proper, with the authorities of not more than fifteen counties or cities of this state, for the reception and support, in the poor-houses or other suitable buildings of such counties or cities respectively, of such paupers as may be committed to such poor-houses, as provided for by this act. The said board may establish rules and regulations for the discipline, employment, treatment and care of such paupers and for their discharge. Every such contract shall be in writing, and be filed in the office of said board. The poor-house or other buildings so contracted for with the authorities of any county or city, while used for the purposes herein mentioned, shall be appropriately designated by the said board and shall be known as state alms-houses. The said board may from time to time direct the transfer of any such paupers from one alms-house to another, and may give notice from time to time to counties to which alms-houses they shall send paupers.

State board of charities to contract.

Rules and regulations.

Transfer of paupers.

§ 2. The fifteenth section of the said act, passed June seventh, eighteen hundred and seventy-three, is amended by adding thereto as follows: And also for clerk hire, and the compensation of an assistant secretary for said board to be certified and allowed in like manner. The assistant secretary shall discharge such duties as the board may designate, and in case of a vacancy in the office of secretary of said board, or in his absence or illness, the duties of the office of secretary in the meantime may be discharged by such assistant secretary.

Clerk hire.

Assistant secretary, his duties.

§ 3. This act shall take effect immediately.

CHAP. 469.

AN ACT to amend the Revised Statutes relating to guardians and wards.

PASSED May 18, 1874.

The People of the State of New York, represented in Senate and Assembly, do enact as follows:

SECTION 1. The fourteenth section of the third title of the eighth chapter of the second part of the Revised Statutes is hereby amended so as to read as follows:

Guardian, general or testamentary may be cited by surrogate to show cause why he should not be removed.

§ 14. On the application of any ward, or of any relative in his behalf, or of the surety of a guardian, to the surrogate who appointed any guardian or to the surrogate before whom any last will and testament containing an appointment of a guardian, shall be or shall have been proved, complaining of the incompetency of such guardian or of his wasting the real or personal estate of his ward, or of any misconduct in relation to his duties as guardian, the surrogate, upon being satisfied by the proof of the probable truth of such complaint, shall issue a citation to such guardian to appear before him at the day and place therein specified, to show cause why he should not be removed from his guardianship.

§ 2. This act shall take effect immediately.

Ante, vol. 2, page 158.

CHAP. 470.

AN ACT to amend section nine, title three, chapter six, part two of the Revised Statutes.

PASSED May 18, 1874; three-fifths being present.

The People of the State of New York, represented in Senate and Assembly, do enact as follows:

SECTION 1. Section nine, title third, chapter six, part two of the Revised Statutes is hereby amended so as to read as follows:

Articles to be included in inventory, but not appraised.

§ 9. Where a man having a family shall die, leaving a widow or a minor child, or children, the following articles shall not be deemed assets, but shall be included and stated in the inventory of the estate, without being appraised:

Enumeration.

1. All spinning-wheels, weaving-looms, one knitting machine, one sewing-machine, and stoves put up or kept for use by his family.

Same.

2. The family bible, family pictures, and school-books, used by or in the family of such deceased person, and books not exceeding in value fifty dollars, which were kept and used as part of the family library before the decease of such person.

Same.

3. All sheep to the number of ten, with their fleeces, and the yarn and cloth manufactured from the same, one cow, two

swine and the pork of such swine, and necessary food for such swine, sheep or cow for sixty days, and all necessary provisions and fuel for such widow or child or children for sixty days, after the death of such deceased person.

4. All necessary wearing apparel, beds, bedsteads and bedding, necessary cooking utensils, the clothing of the family, the clothes of the widow and her ornaments proper for her station; one table, six chairs; twelve knives and forks, twelve plates, twelve tea-cups and saucers, one sugar dish, one milk pot, one tea-pot and twelve spoons, and also other household furniture which shall not exceed one hundred and fifty dollars in value. Same.

§ 2. This act shall take effect immediately.

Ante, vol. 2, p. 85.

CHAP. 471.

AN ACT to amend section twenty-eight of article two of title ten of chapter eight of part three of the Revised Statutes in relation to summary proceedings to recover the possession of land.

PASSED May 18, 1874.

The People of the State of New York, represented in Senate and Assembly, do enact as follows:

SECTION 1. Section twenty-eight of article two of title ten of chapter eight of part three of the Revised Statutes is hereby amended by adding thereto the following subdivision:

5. When any person shall hold over and continue in possession of any real estate occupied or held by him under an agreement with the owner to occupy and cultivate the same upon shares or for a share of the crops, after the expiration of the time fixed in the agreement for such occupancy, without the permission of the other party to said agreement, his heirs or assigns. Summary proceedings, cropper may be removed by.

CHAP. 500.

AN ACT to amend chapter three hundred and fifty-eight of the laws of eighteen hundred and forty, entitled "An act concerning payment of interest by railroad companies on loans of the state credit and other purposes," passed May fourteenth, eighteen hundred and forty.

PASSED May 20, 1874.

The People of the State of New York, represented in Senate and Assembly, do enact as follows:

SECTION 1. Section two of the act entitled an act concerning payment of interest by railroad companies on loans of the state credit and for other purposes, passed May fourteenth, eighteen hundred and forty, is hereby amended so as to read as follows:

Canal board may designate banking associations, etc., to receive deposits of tolls.

§ 2. The canal board may designate any banking association, individual or private banker or bankers to receive the deposits of tolls or other canal moneys, provided such association, individual or private banker or bankers shall carry on its or their business in a place convenient for such deposits, and shall comply with such terms as may be prescribed by the board. All the provisions of former acts in relation to the deposits of such moneys in banks shall extend and apply to such deposits and bankers and banking associations.

Vide 8 G. S. 104.

CHAP. 502.

AN ACT to amend chapter six hundred and ninety-six, laws of eighteen hundred and sixty-six, entitled "An act to amend section eighteen, article two, title two, chapter twelve, part one of the Revised Statutes, entitled 'Of the county treasurer,' and to require an additional bond from county treasurers to the state."

PASSED May 20, 1874; three-fifths being present.

The People of the State of New York, represented in Senate and Assembly, do enact as follows:

SECTION 1. Chapter six hundred and ninety-six, laws of eighteen hundred and sixty-six, amending section eighteen, article second, chapter twelfth, part first of the Revised Statutes, entitled "Of the county treasurer," is hereby amended so as to read as follows:

Treasurer's bond.

§ 18. Every person appointed or elected to the office of county treasurer, before he enters upon the duties of his office, shall give a bond to the supervisors of the county, with three or more sufficient sureties, to be approved by the board of supervisors, and in such sum as they shall direct, conditioned that such person shall faithfully execute the duties of his office, and shall pay over, according to law, all moneys which shall have come, or which shall thereafter come, to his hands as treasurer, and render a just and true account thereof to the board of supervisors when thereunto required. Whenever, in the opinion of said board, or a majority of them, the moneys intrusted to such person as treasurer shall be deemed unsafe, or the surety insufficient, such board may require from said treasurer a new and further bond, with like conditions as aforesaid, and in such penalty and with such surety as such board shall deem requisite and proper; and in case said county treasurer shall fail to renew said bond, as required, within twenty days after he shall be notified by said board of such requirement, such omission shall work a forfeiture of his office.

New bond may be required.

Forfeiture of office.

and the same shall become vacant. Every person appointed or elected to the office of county treasurer, within twenty days from the time he shall receive notice of his election or appointment, and before he enters upon the duties of his office, shall, in addition to the bond hereinbefore mentioned, to be given to the supervisors of the county, give a bond to the people of the state of New York, with two or more sureties, to be approved by the comptroller, in such penalty as the comptroller shall direct, conditioned that such person shall faithfully execute the duties of his office, and shall pay over to the state treasury, according to law, all moneys belonging to the state which shall have come, or which shall thereafter come, into his hands as county treasurer, and render a just and true account thereof to the comptroller of the state, which bond shall be filed with the comptroller. At any time when in the opinion of the comptroller the moneys intrusted to such person as treasurer shall be deemed unsafe, or the surety insufficient, the comptroller may require a new and further bond, with like conditions as the first, and in such penalty and with such sureties as the comptroller may deem requisite and proper. Should default be made in the giving and filing of the bond to the people of this state, as herein provided for, within the time limited herein, or should the said county treasurer neglect to renew his bond, as last hereinbefore provided for, the comptroller shall cause a written notice to be served on the person so in default, requiring him to furnish such bond or such renewal, as the case may be, within ten days from the day of service of such notice, whereupon, if such treasurer shall still be in default, he shall be deemed to have vacated his office, and the governor shall appoint a proper person to fill such vacancy.

Bond to state.

Neglect to give bonds vacates office.

§ 2. This act shall take effect immediately.

CHAP. 506.

AN ACT conferring certain powers on "The Children's Fold" of the city of New York.

PASSED May 20, 1874; three-fifths being present.

The People of the State of New York, represented in Senate and Assembly, do enact as follows:

SECTION 1. The trustees of "The Children's Fold," an orphan asylum, located in the city of New York, are hereby authorized and empowered to adopt into families, any orphan, half-orphan or destitute child who may have been in their care and charge for the space of one year, in case said children be under ten years of age, or six months, in case of children over ten years old.

Adopting into families.

§ 2. The board of supervisors of the city and county of New York shall levy and collect by tax in the year one thousand eight hundred and seventy-four, and every year thereafter, at

Board of supervisors to levy annual tax.

the same time and in the same manner as the contingent charges and expenses of the city and county are levied and collected, and shall pay over to "The Children's Fold," of the city of New York, the sum of two dollars per week for each and every orphan, half-orphan and destitute child received and supported by said institution, the expense of whose support is not paid by private parties.

§ 3. This act shall take effect immediately.

CHAP. 511.

AN ACT to amend chapter seven hundred and twenty-one of the laws of eighteen hundred and seventy-one, entitled "An act to amend and consolidate the several acts relating to the preservation of moose, wild deer, birds and fish."

PASSED May 20, 1874; three-fifths being present.

The People of the State of New York, represented in Senate and Assembly, do enact as follows:

SECTION 1. The tenth section of chapter seven hundred and twenty-one of the laws of eighteen hundred and seventy-one, entitled "An act to amend and consolidate the several acts relating to the preservation of moose, wild deer, birds and fish," is hereby amended so as to read as follows:

Killing of birds prohibited. § 10. No person shall kill or expose for sale, or have in his possession after the same has been killed, any robin, brown thrasher, meadow lark or starling, save only during the months of August, September, October, November and December, Penalty. under a penalty of five dollars for each bird; and in the counties of Kings, Queens, Putnam and Suffolk, no person shall kill or expose for sale, or have in his possession after the same has been killed, any of said birds, except meadow larks, in this section named, except during the months of October, November and December, under a penalty of five dollars for each bird.

§ 2. The nineteenth section of said act is hereby amended to read as follows:

Catching fish except with hook and line prohibited. § 19. No person shall at any time catch any speckled trout with any device save with a hooked line, except for the purpose of propagation hereinafter provided, or place any set lines in waters inhabited by them, under a penalty of fifty dollars for each offense; and no person shall at any time, except for the purpose of propagation as aforesaid, catch any kind of fish in Lake Saratoga, in the county of Saratoga, or in Onondaga or Oneida lakes, tributaries or outlets, except minnows, with any device, save with hook and line. And no person shall at any time use more than three lines with hooks attached; and any hook and line unattended by the fisherman Set lines, nets, etc. in person, and all set lines, nets, traps and devices other than fair angling as aforesaid, are hereby prohibited on said lakes and their tributaries and outlets, or within one mile of the lakes, and when found in use or operation, are hereby declared forfeit and contraband, and any person finding such set lines, nets or traps in said waters is hereby authorized to destroy the same, and any person fishing with such prohibited means or devices shall be liable to a penalty of not less than ten nor exceeding one hundred dollars. And no person shall take or catch any black or Oswego bass, in the waters of Lake George, except from the twentieth day of July to the first day of January, under a penalty of ten dollars for each fish so taken. Bass in Lake George.

§ 3. Section twenty-five of said act is hereby amended so as to read as follows:

§ 25. No person shall kill or catch any fish in the Mohawk or Clyde rivers, Irondequoit bay, Braddocks bay, Little pond, Round pond, Cranberry pond, Buck pond and Long pond, in the county of Monroe, or in the inlets thereof, or the lakes in the counties of Westchester, Rockland, Wyoming, Columbia, Ulster, Genesee, Orange, Putnam, Herkimer, Rensselaer, Sullivan, Tioga, Cortland, Broome and Livingston, by any trap, dam, weir, net, seine, or by any device whatever, other than that of angling with hook and line or with a spear, under a penalty of twenty-five dollars for each offense. All fishing in the aforesaid Braddocks bay, Little pond, Round pond, Cranberry pond, Buck pond and Long pond in the county of Monroe, in the months of January, February and March, or either, is hereby forbidden and prohibited. Catching fish by trap, dam, etc., prohibited. Penalty.

§ 4. It shall not be lawful between the first day of December and the fifteenth day of April in any year, to take with hook and line, trap, net or any device whatsoever, any fish from Rockland lake, in the county of Rockland. Any person violating any of the provisions of this section shall be deemed guilty of a misdemeanor, and upon conviction thereof shall pay a penalty of not less than five dollars, nor more than fifteen dollars, or be confined in the county jail not less than five days nor more than fifteen days, in the discretion of the court. When fish may not be taken from Rockland lake. Penalty.

§ 5. This act shall take effect immediately.

CHAP. 514.

AN ACT to amend an act entitled "An act to revise and consolidate the general acts relating to public instruction," passed May second, eighteen hundred and sixty-four.

PASSED May 21, 1874; three-fifths being present.

The People of the State of New York, represented in Senate and Assembly, do enact as follows:

SECTION 1. The tenth section of title thirteen of chapter five hundred and fifty-five of the laws of eighteen hundred and sixty-four, entitled "An act to revise and consolidate the general acts relating to public instruction," passed May second, eighteen hundred and sixty-four, is hereby amended so as to read as follows:

Account of trustees or other officers for costs, etc., incurred in litigations, county judge to decide whether it should be charged upon district. § 10. Upon the appearance of parties, or upon due proof of service of the notice and copy of the account, the county judge shall examine into the matter and hear the proofs and allegations propounded by the parties, and decide by order whether or no the account, or any and what portion thereof, ought justly to be charged upon the district, with costs and disbursements to such officer or officers, in his discretion, which costs and disbursements shall not exceed the sum of thirty dollars, and the decision of the county judge shall be final; but no portion of such account shall be so ordered to be paid which shall appear to such judge to have arisen from the willful neglect or misconduct of the claimant. Verified accounts prima facie evidence. The account, with the oath of the party claiming the same, shall be prima facie evidence of the correctness thereof. The county judge may adjourn the hearing from time to time, as justice shall seem to require.

§ 2. This act shall take effect immediately.

CHAP. 524.

AN ACT in relation to county treasurers.

PASSED May 21, 1874; three-fifths being present.

The People of the State of New York, represented in Senate and Assembly, do enact as follows:

When court may direct an action to be brought on official bond. SECTION 1. Whenever any county treasurer shall, after service on him personally, or by leaving it at his office in his absence with some person having charge thereof, or if such service cannot be made, by leaving with some person of suitable age and discretion at his place of residence, or at his last place of residence in the county, if he has departed therefrom, of a certified copy of an order of the court, directing the payment or delivery of any money or securities held by him pursuant to order of the court, to any person or persons, shall fail or neglect so to do, the court may, by order, direct that an action be brought upon the official bond of such treasurer, against him and his sureties, to recover the amount of the money or securities so directed to be paid or delivered, for the benefit of the person or persons in whose behalf the direction shall have been by such order given, and whose name or names appear therein; and thereupon such action may be brought for such purpose.

County to be protected against costs. § 2. The person or persons for whose benefit any action provided for by the first section of this act may be brought shall protect the county from liability for costs and expenses thereof, and will be entitled to any costs recovered against the defendants therein; Security. and in the order directing the bringing of any such action, the court may direct that security be given in such form, and approved in such manner, as the court may thereby direct, to indemnify the county against such liability. Any judgment which may be recovered in any such action shall not be a bar to another action upon the bond mentioned in the first section of this act, to recover for any other or further default of the same county treasurer. And the provisions of this act shall not be construed to create or increase liability upon the bond of any treasurer. Judgment not a bar.

§ 3. This act shall take effect immediately.

CHAP. 532.

AN ACT to amend chapter two hundred and seventy-six of the laws of eighteen hundred and sixty-four, entitled "An act in relation to the sale, use and disposition of butts, hogsheads, barrels, casks or kegs used by the manufacturers of malt liquors."

PASSED May 22, 1874; three-fifths being present.

The People of the State of New York, represented in Senate and Assembly, do enact as follows:

SECTION 1. Section four of the act chapter two hundred and seventy-six of the laws of eighteen hundred and sixty-four, entitled "An act in relation to the sale, use and disposition of butts, hogsheads, barrels, casks or kegs used by the manufacturers of malt liquors," which section reads as follows: "The provisions of this act shall apply only to the cities of New York, city and county of Albany, and the county of Kings," is hereby stricken out of said law and repealed.

§ 2. This act shall take effect immediately.

CHAP. 535.

AN ACT to amend chapter eight hundred and thirty-three of the laws of eighteen hundred and seventy-three, entitled "An act to regulate the fees of coroners."

PASSED May 22, 1874; three-fifths being present.

The People of the State of New York, represented in Senate and Assembly, do enact as follows:

SECTION 1. The thirteenth paragraph of section one, chapter eight hundred and thirty-three of the laws of eighteen hundred and seventy-three, entitled "An act to regulate the fees of coroners," is hereby amended by adding thereto the words, "as shall be allowed by the board of supervisors," so that said paragraph shall read as follows:

"Shall be reimbursed for all moneys paid out, actually and necessarily, by him in the discharge of official duties as shall be allowed by the board of supervisors." Reimbursement.

§ 2. Section two of said act is hereby amended so as to read as follows:

Coroner may employ surgeons.

§ 2. A coroner shall have power, when necessary, to employ not more than two competent surgeons to make post-mortem examinations and dissections and to testify to the same, the compensation therefor to be a county charge.

§ 3. Section three of said act is hereby amended so as to read as follows:

Fees as witness.

§ 3. Whenever, in consequence of the performance of his official duties, a coroner becomes a witness in a criminal proceeding, he shall be entitled to receive mileage to and from his place of residence, ten cents per mile, and three dollars per day for each day, or fractional parts thereof, actually detained as such witness.

CHAP. 543.

AN ACT to amend chapter eleven, part one, title three, article three, section thirty-one, of the Revised Statutes.

PASSED May 22, 1874; three-fifths being present.

The People of the State of New York, represented in Senate and Assembly, do enact as follows:

SECTION 1. Chapter eleven, part one, title three, article three, section thirty-one, of the Revised Statutes, is hereby amended so as to read as follows:

If proper officers are not chosen at town meeting, justices of the peace may appoint.

§ 31. If any town shall omit or neglect at its annual town meeting to choose its proper town officers or any of them, it shall be lawful for any three justices of the peace of said town, by a warrant under their hands and seals, within five days after such town meeting, to appoint such officer or officers, and the person or persons so appointed shall hold their respective offices until others are chosen or appointed in their places, and shall have the same powers and be subject to the same duties and penalties as if they had been duly chosen by the electors; but if the justices of the peace fail to so appoint, it shall be the duty of the town clerk, within thirty days thereafter, to call a special town meeting for the purpose of electing such officer or officers.

Special town meeting.

§ 2. This act shall take effect immediately.

CHAP. 560.

AN ACT to amend an act entitled "An act to authorize the formation of town insurance companies," passed April seventeenth, eighteen hundred and fifty-seven, and the act to amend the same, passed May twenty-first, eighteen hundred and seventy-three.

PASSED May 22, 1874.

The People of the State of New York, represented in Senate and Assembly, do enact as follows:

SECTION 1. Section four of the act entitled "An act to authorize the formation of town insurance companies," passed April seventeenth, eighteen hundred and fifty-seven, and the act to amend the same, passed May twenty-first, eighteen hundred and seventy-three, is hereby amended so as to read as follows, and as amended is made applicable to all town insurance companies heretofore formed or organized thereunder.

§ 4. The directors of such company may issue policies, signed by their president and secretary, agreeing, in the name of such company, to pay all damages which may be sustained by fire or lightning, for a term not exceeding five years, by the holders of such policies, not exceeding the sum named in the policy, and which shall not exceed the sum of three thousand dollars in any one risk, excepting upon detached buildings upon farms, upon which such risk shall not exceed five thousand dollars. Policies.

§ 2. This act to take effect immediately.

CHAP. 570.

AN ACT to amend chapter ninety-three of the laws of eighteen hundred and sixty-three, entitled "An act to authorize the making of sidewalks and planting shade trees along highways of this state, other than in cities and incorporated villages," passed April seventh, eighteen hundred and sixty-three.

PASSED May 23, 1874; three-fifths being present.

The People of the State of New York, represented in Senate and Assembly, do enact as follows:

SECTION 1. Section one, chapter ninety-three of the laws of eighteen hundred and sixty-three is hereby amended so as to read as follows:

§ 1. All persons owning lands fronting upon any highway (except in cities and incorporated villages) may make and have sidewalks along such land in the highway, and may plant and have shade trees along the road side of such sidewalks; such sidewalks, with shade trees, shall not extend Sidewalks and shade trees along highways.

more than six feet in width from the outward line of such highway to the line of the center of such shade trees; provided such highway is not more than three rods wide. In all cases where the highway is more than three rods wide the central line of such shade trees may be extended into the highway, from its outward line, a distance equal to one-fifth part of the width of such highway; provided such central line shall, in no case, exceed eleven feet from the said outward line of such highway; and for the protection of such walks or trees they may also construct a railing of one bar, of not more than three and a-half feet in height, with posts and with openings at convenient distances, so as in nowise to prevent foot passengers from using such walks, upon the road side adjacent and within two and a-half feet of such trees, or, if there are no trees, then upon the road side of such sidewalks, on the same line on which trees may be planted as hereinabove provided. But no trees of the kinds named in chapter three hundred and twenty-two of the laws of eighteen hundred and sixty-nine shall be planted nearer together than is therein provided.

Railing.

Proviso.

Injury to trees, etc., a misdemeanor.

§ 2. Any person or persons driving any team, vehicle, cattle, sheep, horses or swine, or racing or driving any horse, willfully upon any such sidewalk, or who shall cut, mar, injure or destroy any shade tree, shall be deemed guilty of a misdemeanor, and upon conviction before any justice of the peace or other court having jurisdiction, upon complaint of the owner or any other person, shall be fined not exceeding fifty dollars or imprisonment in the county jail not exceeding thirty days, or both, for every such offense.

Punishment.

§ 3. This act shall take effect immediately.

CHAP. 600.

AN ACT to amend an act entitled "An act to convey to creditors a just division of the estate of debtors who convey to assignees for the benefit of creditors," passed April thirteenth, eighteen hundred and sixty.

PASSED June 4, 1874.

The People of the State of New York, represented in Senate and Assembly, do enact as follows:

SECTION 1. Section two of chapter three hundred and forty-eight of the laws of one thousand eight hundred and sixty, is hereby amended by adding at the end thereof as follows:

Assignment not made invalid by refusal of assignor to deliver inventory.

8. But in case such debtor or debtors shall omit or refuse to make and deliver such inventory or schedule and affidavit as above specified, the assignment shall not for such reasons become invalid or be ineffectual; but in such case the assignee or assignees named in such assigment may, within six months after the date thereof, cause to be made and file in the clerk's office of the county where such debtor or debtors resided or conducted their business at the date of such assignment, an

Assignee may make

inventory or schedule of all the property of such debtor or debtors which he or they may be able to find; and for that purpose the county judge of such county may, at any time, compel such delinquent debtor or debtors to disclose any knowledge or information he may have relative to the matters hereinbefore mentioned in the manner prescribed in the fourth section of this act.

and file inventory.

Debtor may be compelled to disclose.

9. Such county judge may, by an order to be entered in the county clerk's office of such county, authorize such assignee or assignees to advertise for creditors to present to him or them their claims, with the vouchers duly verified, on or before a day to be specified in such advertisement or notice, not less three months from the date of the first publication of such notice, which advertisement shall be by publication once in each week for four successive weeks in such newspapers printed in the county where such assignment was made, as the county judge shall designate in the order authorizing such publication, and if the assignee have reason to believe that any creditor entitled to share in the distribution of such trust estate resides out of this state, he shall also cause such notice to be published once in each week for six successive weeks in the official newspaper of this state, and the assignee or assignees of such debtor or debtors shall, by the order or decree of the said county judge made on the final accounting of such assignee, be protected against any claim or demand not presented in compliance with such notice before such accounting shall be had.

Assignee may advertise for claims.

Assignee protected.

§ 2. The provisions of section one of this act shall apply to all cases of assignments heretofore made under any of the provisions of chapter three hundred and forty-eight of the laws of one thousand eight hundred and sixty and its amendments which are now pending unsettled.

Provisions of section one applied to existing cases.

§ 3. This act shall take effect immediately.

CHAP. 603.

AN ACT to repeal chapter three hundred and forty-six of the laws of eighteen hundred and sixty-five, entitled "An act authorizing the election of chiefs and clerk of the St. Regis Indians and defining their powers," passed April tenth, eighteen hundred and sixty-five.

PASSED June 5, 1874.

The People of the State of New York, represented in Senate and Assembly, do enact as follows:

SECTION 1. Chapter three hundred and forty-six of the laws of eighteen hundred and sixty-five, entitled "An act authorizing the election of chiefs and clerk of the St. Regis Indians and defining their powers," passed April tenth, eighteen hundred and sixty-five, is hereby repealed.

Repeal.

§ 2. This act shall take effect immediately.

Vide 6 G. S. 478.

and after their becoming so incorporated, shall cease to be operative as to such village, except as controlled by the provisions of this act.

§ 2. Section three of title two of the act entitled "An act for the incorporation of villages," passed April twentieth, one thousand eight hundred and seventy, is hereby amended so as to read as follows:

Officers to be elected annually. § 3. The president, treasurer, collector and one-half of the trustees, if an even number, shall be elected annually by the electors of the village, and if an odd number the smallest majority of them shall be so elected at one annual election, and the largest minority of them shall be so elected at the next annual election. At the annual election in the year one thousand eight hundred and seventy-five, the ballots shall designate which of the trustees therein named shall hold office for one year, and which for two years. The clerk and street commissioner shall be appointed annually by the board of trustees.

Ballots.

Officers to be appointed.

§ 3. Section five of title two of the said act is hereby amended so as to read as follows:

Term of office. § 5. All officers elected or appointed under this act shall hold their respective offices one year, except the trustees elected for two years, who shall hold their offices for two years; and the said officers shall so hold for the respective terms aforesaid unless sooner removed or disqualified, and until their successors shall be elected or appointed and qualified.

§ 4. This act shall take effect immediately.

CHAP. 642.

AN ACT declaratory of and to amend chapter five hundred and forty-nine of the laws of eighteen hundred and seventy-three, entitled "An act to amend an act entitled 'An act regulating the sale of intoxicating liquors,'" passed April eleventh, eighteen hundred and seventy, and the act entitled "An act to suppress intemperance, and to regulate the sale of intoxicating liquors," passed April sixteenth, eighteen hundred and fifty-seven.

PASSED June 23, 1874; three-fifths being present.

The People of the State of New York, represented in Senate and Assembly, do enact as follows:

SECTION 1. Section one of the act entitled "An act to amend an act entitled 'An act regulating the sale of intoxicating liquors,'" passed April eleventh, eighteen hundred and seventy, and the act entitled "An act to suppress intemperance, and to regulate the sale of intoxicating liquors," passed April sixteenth, eighteen hundred and fifty-seven, is hereby amended so as to read as follows:

§ 1. Section two of the act entitled "An act to regulate the sale of intoxicating liquors," passed April eleventh, eighteen hundred and seventy, is hereby amended by inserting after the words "and shall be paid as other city officers are paid," the words following: Provided that in the city of New York the commissioners of excise shall receive a salary not to exceed five thousand dollars a year each, to be fixed by the board of estimate and apportionment of said city, who shall annually fix such amount as may be necessary for hire of employees, rent and other necessary expenses of said board of commissioners, which amount shall be paid out of the moneys received for licenses, and said commissioners shall receive no other compensation or emolument for services as commissioners; and provided further, that all excise moneys hereafter derived from licenses for the sale of intoxicating liquors by said commissioners, except as above provided, shall, from time to time, and in sums according to their discretion, be appropriated by the board of apportionment and estimate of said city by resolution of the said board to whatever benevolent, charitable or humane institutions may seem to such board deserving or proper, but no such resolution shall be valid unless adopted by the vote of a majority of said board, and the comptroller of said city is hereby authorized and directed to draw his warrants in favor of the corporations, societies or charitable institutions respectively mentioned in such resolutions according to the tenor thereof, and the chamberlain of said city shall pay such warrants out of the said moneys received for licenses, which are hereby directed to be deposited with and paid over to him within thirty days after it is received.

Salary of commissioners of excise in New York city.

Expenses.

Excise moneys, how disposed of.

§ 2. This act shall take effect immediately.

CONCURRENT RESOLUTIONS

OF THE

SENATE AND ASSEMBLY.

CONCURRENT RESOLUTIONS proposing amendments to article two of the constitution.

WHEREAS, At the last session of the legislature, the following amendment was proposed in the senate and assembly, namely:

That sections one and two of article two of the constitution be amended so as to read as follows:

SECTION 1. Every male citizen of the age of twenty-one years who shall have been a citizen for ten days and an inhabitant of this state one year next preceding an election, and for the last four months a resident of the county and for the last thirty days a resident of the election district in which he may offer his vote, shall be entitled to vote at such election in the election district of which he shall at the time be a resident, and not elsewhere, for all officers that now are or hereafter may be elected by the people, and upon all questions which may be submitted to the vote of the people, provided that in time of war no elector in the actual military service of the state, or of the United States, in the army or navy thereof, shall be deprived of his vote by reason of his absence from such election district; and the legislature shall have power to provide the manner in which and the time and place at which such absent electors may vote, and for the return and canvass of their votes in the election districts in which they respectively reside.

§ 2. No person who shall receive, expect or offer to receive, or pay, offer or promise to pay, contribute, offer or promise to contribute to another, to be paid or used, any money or other valuable thing as a compensation or reward for the giving or withholding a vote at an election, or who shall make any promise to influence the giving or withholding any such vote, or who shall make or become directly or indirectly interested in any bet or wager depending upon the result of any election, shall vote at such election; and upon challenge for such cause, the person so challenged, before the officers authorized for that purpose shall receive his vote, shall swear or affirm before such officers that he has not received or offered, does not expect to receive, has not paid, offered or promised to pay, contributed, offered or promised to contribute to another, to be paid or used, any money or other valuable thing as a compensation or reward for the giving or withholding a vote at such election, and has not made any promise to influence the giving or withholding of any such vote, nor made or became directly or indirectly interested in any bet or wager depending upon the result of such election. The legislature, at the session thereof next after the adoption of this section, shall, and from time to time thereafter may enact laws excluding from the right of suffrage all persons convicted of bribery or of any infamous crime.

AND WHEREAS, The said proposed amendment was agreed to by a majority of the members elected to each of the two houses of the said legislature, entered on their journals, with the yeas and nays taken thereon, and referred to the legislature to be chosen at the then next general election of senators.

AND WHEREAS, Such election has taken place, and said proposed amendment was duly published for three months previous to the time of making such choice, in pursuance of the provisions of section one of article thirteen of the constitution; therefore,

Resolved (if the senate concur), That the assembly do agree to the proposed amendment.

STATE OF NEW YORK,
In Assembly, *January* 23, 1874.

The foregoing resolutions were duly passed.
By order of the assembly.
J. O'DONNELL,
Clerk.

STATE OF NEW YORK,
In Senate, *April* 10, 1874.

The foregoing resolutions were duly passed.
By order of the senate.
HENRY A. GLIDDEN,
Clerk.

CONCURRENT RESOLUTIONS proposing amendments to article three of the constitution.

WHEREAS, At the last session of the legislature, the following amendment was proposed in the senate and assembly, viz.:

That sections one, five, six, seven and eight of article three of the constitution be amended so as to read as follows:

ARTICLE III.

SECTION 1. The legislative power of this state shall be vested in a senate and assembly.

§ 5. The assembly shall consist of one hundred and twenty-eight members, elected for one year. The members of assembly shall be apportioned among the several counties of the state by the legislature, as nearly as may be, according to the number of their respective inhabitants, excluding aliens, and shall be chosen by single districts. The assembly districts shall remain as at present organized, until after the enumeration of the inhabitants of the state, in the year eighteen hundred and seventy-five. The legislature, at its first session after the return of every enumeration, shall apportion the members of assembly among the several counties of the state, in manner aforesaid, and the board of supervisors in such counties as may be entitled under such apportionment to more than one member, except the city and county of New York, and in said city and county the board of aldermen of said city shall assemble at such time as the legislature, making such apportionment, shall prescribe, and divide their respective counties into assembly districts, each of which districts shall consist of convenient and contiguous territory, equal to the number of members of assembly to which such counties shall be entitled, and shall cause to be filed in the offices of the secretary of state and the clerks of their respective counties, a description of such districts, specifying the number of each district and the population thereof, according to the last preceding enumeration as near as can be ascertained, and the apportionment and districts shall remain unaltered until another enumeration shall be made as herein provided. No town shall be divided in the formation of assembly districts. Every county heretofore established and separately organized, except the county of Hamilton, shall always be entitled to one member of the assembly, and no new county shall be hereafter erected, unless its population shall entitle it to a member. The county of Hamilton shall elect with the county of Fulton, until the population of the county of Hamilton shall, according to the ratio, be entitled to a member. But the legislature may abolish the said county of Hamilton, and annex the territory thereof to some other county or counties. Nothing in this section shall prevent division at any time of counties and towns, and the erection of new towns and counties by the legislature.

§ 6. Each member of the legislature shall receive for his services an annual salary of one thousand five hundred dollars. The members of either house shall also receive the sum of one dollar for every ten miles they shall travel, in going to and returning from their place of meeting, once in each session, on the most usual route. Senators, when the senate alone is convened in extraordinary session, or when serving as members of the Court for the Trial of Impeachments, and such members of the assembly, not exceeding nine in number, as shall be appointed managers of an impeachment, shall receive an additional allowance of ten dollars a day.

§ 7. No member of the legislature shall receive any civil appointment within this state, or the senate of the United States, from the governor, the governor and senate, or from the legislature, or from any city government during the time for which he shall have been elected; and all such appointments, and all votes given for any such member for any such office or appointment, shall be void.

§ 8. No person shall be eligible to the legislature who, at the time of his election, is, or within one hundred days previous thereto has been a member of congress, a civil or military officer under the United States, or an officer under any city government. And if any person shall, after his election as a member of the legislature, be elected to congress, or appointed to any office, civil or military, under the government of the United States, or, under any city government, his acceptance thereof shall vacate his seat.

And that the following additional sections be added to said article three of the constitution:

§ 17. No act shall be passed which shall provide that any existing law, or any part thereof, shall be made or deemed a part of said act, or which shall enact that any existing law, or any part thereof, shall be applicable, except by inserting it in such act.

§ 18. The legislature shall not pass a private or local bill in any of the following cases:

Changing the names of persons.

Laying out, opening, altering, working or discontinuing roads, highways or alleys, or for draining swamps or other low lands.

Locating or changing county seats.

Providing for changes of venue in civil or criminal cases.

Incorporating villages.

Providing for election of members of boards of supervisors.

Selecting, drawing, summoning or impaneling grand or petit jurors.

Regulating the rate of interest on money.

The opening and conducting of elections or designating places of voting.

Creating, increasing or decreasing fees, percentage or allowances of public officers, during the term for which said officers are elected or appointed.

Granting to any corporation, association or individual the right to lay down railroad tracks.

Granting to any private corporation, association or individual any exclusive privilege, immunity or franchise whatever.

Providing for building bridges, and chartering companies for such purposes, except on the Hudson river below Waterford, and on the East river, or over the waters forming a part of the boundaries of the state.

The legislature shall pass general laws providing for the cases enumerated in this section, and for all other cases which in its judgment may be provided for by general laws. But no law shall authorize the construction or operation of a street railroad, except upon the condition that the consent of the owners of one-half in value the property bounded on, and the consent also of the local authorities having the control of that portion of a street or highway upon which it is proposed to construct or operate such railroad be first obtained, or in case the consent of such property owners cannot be obtained, the general term of the supreme court, in the district in which it is proposed to be constructed, may, upon application, appoint three commissioners who shall determine, after a hearing of all parties interested, whether such railroad ought to be constructed or operated, and their determination, confirmed by the court may be taken in lieu of the consent of the property owners

§ 19. The legislature shall neither audit nor allow any private claim or account against the state, but may appropriate money to pay such claims as shall have been audited and allowed according to law.

§ 20. Every law which imposes, continues or revives a tax shall distinctly state the tax and the object to which it is to be applied, and it shall not be sufficient to refer to any other law to fix such tax or object.

§ 21. On the final passage, in either house of the legislature, of any act which imposes, continues or revives a tax, or creates a debt or charge, or makes, continues or revives any appropriation of public or trust money or property, or releases, discharges or commutes any claim or demand of the state, the question shall be taken by yeas and nays, which shall be duly entered upon the journals, and three-fifths of all the members elected to either house shall, in all such cases, be necessary to constitute a quorum therein.

§ 22. There shall be in the several counties, except in cities whose boundaries are the same as those of the county, a board of supervisors, to be composed of such members, and elected in such manner, and for such period, as is or may be provided by law. In any such city the duties and powers of a board of supervisors may be devolved upon the common council or board of aldermen thereof.

Section seventeen of said article is hereby made section twenty-three of the proposed amendment, and is amended so as to read as follows:

§ 23. The legislature shall, by general laws, confer upon the boards of supervisors of the several counties of the state such further powers of local legislation and administration as the legislature may from time to time deem expedient.

§ 24. The legislature shall not, nor shall the common council of any city nor any board of supervisors, grant any extra compensation to any public officer, servant, agent or contractor.

§ 25. Sections seventeen and eighteen of this article shall not apply to any bill, or the amendments to any bill, which shall be reported to the legislature by commissioners who have been appointed pursuant to law to revise the statutes.

AND WHEREAS, The said proposed amendment was agreed to by a majority of the members elected to each of the two houses of the said legislature, entered on their journals, with the yeas and nays taken thereon, and referred to the legislature to be chosen at the then next general election of senators.

AND WHEREAS, Such election has taken place, and said

proposed amendments were duly published for three months previous to the time of making such choice, in pursuance of the provisions of section one of article thirteen of the constitution; therefore,

Resolved (if the assembly concur), That the senate do agree to the proposed amendments.

STATE OF NEW YORK,
In Senate, *January* 27, 1874.

The foregoing resolution was duly passed.
By order of the senate.
HENRY A. GLIDDEN,
Clerk.

STATE OF NEW YORK,
In Assembly, *March* 19, 1874.

The foregoing resolutions were duly passed.
By order of the assembly.
JOHN O'DONNELL,
Clerk.

CONCURRENT RESOLUTION proposing amendments to article four of the constitution.

WHEREAS, At the last session of the legislature, the following amendment was proposed in senate and assembly, namely:

That sections one, two, four, eight and nine of article four of the constitution be amended so as to read as follows:

SECTION 1. The executive power shall be vested in a governor, who shall hold his office for three years; a lieutenant-governor shall be chosen at the same time, and for the same term. The governor and lieutenant-governor elected next preceding the time when this section shall take effect shall hold office during the term for which they were elected.

§ 2. No person shall be eligible to the office of governor or lieutenant-governor, except a citizen of the United States, of the age of not less than thirty years, and who shall have been five years, next preceding his election, a resident of this state.

§ 4. The governor shall be commander-in-chief of the military and naval forces of the state. He shall have power to convene the legislature (or the senate only) on extraordinary occasions. At extraordinary sessions no subject shall be acted upon, except such as the governor may recommend for consideration. He shall communicate by message to the legislature, at every session, the condition of the state, and recommend such matters to them as he shall judge expedient. He shall transact all necessary business with the officers of government, civil and military. He shall expedite all such measures as may be resolved upon by the legislature, and shall take care that the laws are faithfully executed. He shall receive for his services an annual salary of ten thousand dollars, and there shall be provided for his use a suitable and furnished executive residence.

struct or operate such railroad be first obtained, or in case the consent of such property owners cannot be obtained, the general term of the supreme court, in the district in which it is proposed to be constructed, may, upon application, appoint three commissioners who shall determine, after a hearing of all parties interested, whether such railroad ought to be constructed or operated, and their determination, confirmed by the court, may be taken in lieu of the consent of the property owners.

§ 19. The legislature shall neither audit nor allow any private claim or account against the state, but may appropriate money to pay such claims as shall have been audited and allowed according to law.

§ 20. Every law which imposes, continues or revives a tax shall distinctly state the tax and the object to which it is to be applied, and it shall not be sufficient to refer to any other law to fix such tax or object.

§ 21. On the final passage, in either house of the legislature, of any act which imposes, continues or revives a tax, or creates a debt or charge, or makes, continues or revives any appropriation of public or trust money or property, or releases, discharges or commutes any claim or demand of the state, the question shall be taken by yeas and nays, which shall be duly entered upon the journals, and three-fifths of all the members elected to either house shall, in all such cases, be necessary to constitute a quorum therein.

§ 22. There shall be in the several counties, except in cities whose boundaries are the same as those of the county, a board of supervisors, to be composed of such members, and elected in such manner, and for such period, as is or may be provided by law. In any such city the duties and powers of a board of supervisors may be devolved upon the common council or board of aldermen thereof.

Section seventeen of said article is hereby made section twenty-three of the proposed amendment, and is amended so as to read as follows:

§ 23. The legislature shall, by general laws, confer upon the boards of supervisors of the several counties of the state such further powers of local legislation and administration as the legislature may from time to time deem expedient.

§ 24. The legislature shall not, nor shall the common council of any city nor any board of supervisors, grant any extra compensation to any public officer, servant, agent or contractor.

§ 25. Sections seventeen and eighteen of this article shall not apply to any bill, or the amendments to any bill, which shall be reported to the legislature by commissioners who have been appointed pursuant to law to revise the statutes.

AND WHEREAS, The said proposed amendment was agreed to by a majority of the members elected to each of the two houses of the said legislature, entered on their journals, with the yeas and nays taken thereon, and referred to the legislature to be chosen at the then next general election of senators;

AND WHEREAS, Such election has taken place, and said

Resolved (if the senate concur), That the assembly do agree to the proposed amendment.

STATE OF NEW YORK,
In Assembly, *January* 23, 1874.

The foregoing resolutions were duly passed.
By order of the assembly.
J. O'DONNELL,
Clerk.

STATE OF NEW YORK,
In Senate, *April* 10, 1874.

The foregoing resolutions were duly passed.
By order of the senate.
HENRY A. GLIDDEN,
Clerk.

CONCURRENT RESOLUTION proposing amendments to article seven of the constitution.

WHEREAS, At the last session of the legislature, the following amendment was proposed in the senate and assembly, viz.:

That sections three and six of article seven be amended as follows:

Section three to be amended by adding at the end of the section the following:

No extra compensation shall be made to any contractor, but if, from any unforeseen cause, the terms of any contract shall prove to be unjust and oppressive, the canal board may, upon the application of the contractor, cancel such contract.

SECTION 6. The legislature shall not sell, lease or otherwise dispose of the Erie canal, the Oswego canal, the Champlain canal or the Cayuga and Seneca canal; but they shall remain the property of the state, and under its management forever. Hereafter the expenditures for collections, superintendence, ordinary and extraordinary repairs on the canals named in this section, shall not exceed, in any year, their gross receipts for the previous year. All funds that may be derived from any lease, sale or other disposition of any canal, shall be applied in payment of the debt for which the canal revenues are pledged.

That the following be added as sections thirteen and fourteen in place of sections thirteen and fourteen of this article, which have been transferred and inserted as sections twenty-one and twenty-two of article three.

§ 13. The sinking fund provided for the payment of interest and the extinguishment of the principal of the debts of the state shall be separately kept and safely invested, and neither of them shall be appropriated or used in any manner other than for the specific purpose for which it shall have been provided.

§ 14. Neither the legislature, canal board, canal appraisers, nor any person or persons acting in behalf of the state, shall

§ 8. The lieutenant-governor shall receive for his services an annual salary of five thousand dollars, and shall not receive or be entitled to any other compensation, fee or perquisite, for any duty or service he may be required to perform by the constitution or by-law.

§ 9. Every bill which shall have passed the senate and assembly shall, before it becomes a law, be presented to the governor; if he approve, he shall sign it; but if not, he shall return it with his objections to the house in which it shall have originated, which shall enter the objections at large on the journal, and proceed to reconsider it. If, after such reconsideration, two-thirds of the members elected to that house agree to pass the bill it shall be sent, together with the objections, to the other house, by which it shall likewise be considered; and if approved by two-thirds of the members elected to that house, it shall become a law notwithstanding the objections of the governor. In all such cases, the votes in both houses shall be determined by yeas and nays, and the names of the members voting shall be entered on the journal of each house respectively. If any bill shall not be returned by the governor within ten days (Sundays excepted) after it shall have been presented to him, the same shall be a law in like manner as if he had signed it, unless the legislature shall, by their adjournment, prevent its return, in which case it shall not become a law without the approval of the governor. No bill shall become a law after the final adjournment of the legislature, unless approved by the governor within thirty days after such adjournment. If any bill presented to the governor contain several items of appropriation of money, he may object to one or more of such items while approving of the other portion of the bill. In such case, he shall append to the bill, at the time of signing it, a statement of the items to which he objects; and the appropriation so objected to shall not take effect. If the legislature be in session, he shall transmit to the house in which the bill originated a copy of such statement, and the items objected to shall be separately reconsidered. If, on reconsideration, one or more of such items be approved by two-thirds of the members elected to each house, the same shall be part of the law, notwithstanding the objections of the governor. All the provisions of this section, in relation to bills not approved by the governor, shall apply in cases in which he shall withhold his approval from any item or items contained in a bill appropriating money.

And whereas, The said proposed amendment was agreed to by a majority of the members elected to each of the two houses of the said legislature, entered on their journals, with the yeas and nays taken thereon, and referred to the legislature to be chosen at the then next general election of senators;

And whereas, Such election has taken place, and said proposed amendment was duly published for three months previous to the time of making such choice in pursuance of the provisions of section one of article thirteen of the constitution; therefore,

Resolved (if the senate concur), That the assembly do agree to the proposed amendment.

STATE OF NEW YORK,
In Assembly, *January* 23, 1874.

The foregoing resolutions were duly passed.
By order of the assembly.
J. O'DONNELL,
Clerk.

STATE OF NEW YORK,
In Senate, *April* 10, 1874.

The foregoing resolutions were duly passed.
By order of the senate.
HENRY A. GLIDDEN,
Clerk.

CONCURRENT RESOLUTION proposing amendments to article seven of the constitution.

WHEREAS, At the last session of the legislature, the following amendment was proposed in the senate and assembly, viz.:

That sections three and six of article seven be amended as follows:

Section three to be amended by adding at the end of the section the following:

No extra compensation shall be made to any contractor, but if, from any unforeseen cause, the terms of any contract shall prove to be unjust and oppressive, the canal board may, upon the application of the contractor, cancel such contract.

SECTION 6. The legislature shall not sell, lease or otherwise dispose of the Erie canal, the Oswego canal, the Champlain canal or the Cayuga and Seneca canal; but they shall remain the property of the state, and under its management forever. Hereafter the expenditures for collections, superintendence, ordinary and extraordinary repairs on the canals named in this section, shall not exceed, in any year, their gross receipts for the previous year. All funds that may be derived from any lease, sale or other disposition of any canal, shall be applied in payment of the debt for which the canal revenues are pledged.

That the following be added as sections thirteen and fourteen in place of sections thirteen and fourteen of this article, which have been transferred and inserted as sections twenty-one and twenty-two of article three.

§ 13. The sinking fund provided for the payment of interest and the extinguishment of the principal of the debts of the state shall be separately kept and safely invested, and neither of them shall be appropriated or used in any manner other than for the specific purpose for which it shall have been provided.

§ 14. Neither the legislature, canal board, canal appraisers, nor any person or persons acting in behalf of the state, shall audit, allow, or pay any claim which, as between citizens of the state, would be barred by lapse of time. The limitation of existing claims shall begin to run from the adoption of this section; but this provision shall not be construed to revive claims already barred by existing statutes, nor to repeal any statute fixing the time within which claims shall be presented or allowed, nor shall it extend to any claims duly presented within the time allowed by law, and prosecuted with due diligence from the time of such presentment. But if the claimant shall be under legal disability, the claim may be presented within two years after such disability is removed.

AND WHEREAS, The said proposed amendment was agreed to by a majority of the members elected to each of the two houses of the said legislature, entered on their journals, with the yeas and nays taken thereon, and referred to the legislature to be chosen at the next general election of senators;

AND WHEREAS, Such election has taken place, and said proposed amendment was duly published for three months previous to the time of making such choice, in pursuance of the provisions of section one of article thirteen of the constitution; therefore,

Resolved (if the assembly concur), That the senate do agree to the proposed amendment.

STATE OF NEW YORK,
In Senate, *January* 27, 1874.

The foregoing resolution was duly passed.
By order of the senate.
HENRY A. GLIDDEN,
Clerk.

STATE OF NEW YORK,
In Assembly, *March* 19, 1874.

The foregoing resolution was duly passed.
By order of the assembly.
J. O'DONNELL,
Clerk.

CONCURRENT RESOLUTION proposing amendments to article eight of the constitution.

WHEREAS, At the last session of the legislature, the following amendment was proposed in the senate and assembly, viz.:

That article eight of the constitution be amended, by amending section four thereof, so as to read as follows:

§ 4. The legislature shall, by general law, conform all charters of savings banks, or institutions for savings, to a uniformity of powers, rights and liabilities, and all charters hereafter granted for such corporations shall be made to conform to such general law and to such amendments as may be made thereto. And no such corporation shall have any capital stock, nor shall the trustees thereof, or any of them, have any interest whatever, direct or indirect, in the profits of such corporation; and no director or trustee of any such bank or institution shall be interested in any loan or use of any money or property of such bank or institution for savings. The legislature shall have no power to pass any act granting any special charter for banking purposes; but corporations or associations may be formed for purposes under general laws.

And further, by adding thereto additional sections to be known as sections ten and eleven, as follows:

§ 10. Neither the credit nor the money of the state shall be given or loaned to or in aid of any association, corporation or private undertaking. This section shall not, however, prevent the legislature from making such provision for the education and support of the blind, the deaf and dumb, and juvenile delinquents, as to it may seem proper. Nor shall it apply to any fund or property now held, or which may hereafter be held by the state for educational purposes.

§ 11. No county, city, town or village shall hereafter give any money or property, or loan its money or credit, to or in aid of any individual, association or corporation, or become, directly or indirectly, the owner of stock in or bonds of any association or corporation, nor shall any such county, city, town or village be allowed to incur any indebtedness, except for county, city, town or village purposes. This section shall not prevent such county, city, town or village from making such provision for the aid or support of its poor as may be authorized by law.

AND WHEREAS, The said proposed amendment was agreed to by a majority of the members elected to each of the two houses of the said legislature, entered on their journals, with the yeas and nays taken thereon, and referred to the legislature to be chosen at the then next general election of senators;

AND WHEREAS, Such election has taken place, and said proposed amendment was duly published for three months previous to the time of making such choice, in pursuance of the provisions of section one of article thirteen of the constitution; therefore,

Resolved (if the assembly concur), That the senate do agree to the proposed amendment.

STATE OF NEW YORK,
In Senate, *January* 27, 1874.

The foregoing resolution was duly passed.
By order of the senate.
HENRY A. GLIDDEN,
Clerk.

STATE OF NEW YORK,
In Assembly, *April* 15, 1874.

The foregoing resolution was duly passed.
By order of the assembly.
J. O'DONNELL,
Clerk.

CONCURRENT RESOLUTION proposing amendment to article ten of the constitution.

WHEREAS, At the late session of the legislature, the following amendment was proposed in the senate and assembly, viz.:

That article ten of the constitution be amended, by adding at the end thereof an additional section as follows:

§ 9. No officer whose salary is fixed by the constitution shall receive any additional compensation. Each of the other state officers named in the constitution shall, during his continuance in office, receive a compensation, to be fixed by law, which shall not be increased or diminished during the term for which he shall have been elected or appointed; nor shall he receive to his use any fees or perquisites of office or other compensation.

AND WHEREAS, The said proposed amendment was agreed to by a majority of the members elected to each of the two houses of the said legislature, entered on their journals, with the yeas and nays taken thereon, and referred to the legislature to be chosen at the then next general election of senators:

AND WHEREAS, Such election has taken place, and said proposed amendment was duly published, for three months previous to the time of making such choice, in pursuance of the provisions of section one of article thirteen of the constitution; therefore,

Resolved (if the assembly concur), That the senate do agree to the proposed amendment.

STATE OF NEW YORK,
In Senate, *January* 27, 1874.

The foregoing resolution was duly passed.
By order of the senate.
HENRY A. GLIDDEN,
Clerk.

STATE OF NEW YORK,
In Assembly, *February* 4, 1874.

The foregoing resolution was duly passed.
By order of the assembly.
J. O'DONNELL,
Clerk.

CONCURRENT RESOLUTION proposing amendment to article twelve of the constitution.

WHEREAS, At the last session of the legislature, the following amendment was proposed in the senate and assembly, viz.:

That article twelve of the constitution be amended so as to read as follows:

ARTICLE XII.

SECTION 1. Members of the legislature (and all officers, executive and judicial, except such inferior officers as shall be by law exempted), shall, before they enter on the duties of their respective offices, take and subscribe the following oath or affirmation: "I do solemnly swear (or affirm) that I will support the constitution of the United States and the constitution of the state of New York, and that I will faithfully discharge the duties of the office of , according to the best of my ability;" and all such officers who shall have been chosen at any election shall, before they enter on the duties of their respective offices, take and subscribe the oath or affirmation above prescribed, together with the following addition thereto as part thereof:

"And I do further solemnly swear (or affirm) that I have not directly or indirectly paid, offered or promised to pay, contributed, or offered or promised to contribute, any money or other valuable thing as a consideration or reward for the giving or withholding a vote at the election at which I was elected to said office, and have not made any promise to influence the giving or withholding any such vote," and no other oath, declaration or test, shall be required as a qualification for any office of public trust.

AND WHEREAS, The said proposed amendment was agreed to by a majority of the members elected to each of the two houses of the said legislature, entered on their journals, with the yeas and nays taken thereon, and referred to the legislature to be chosen at the then next general election of senators;

AND WHEREAS, Such election has taken place, and said proposed amendment was duly published for three months previous to the time of making such choice, in pursuance of the provisions of section one of article thirteen of the constitution; therefore,

Resolved (if the assembly concur), That the senate do agree to the proposed amendment.

STATE OF NEW YORK.
In Senate, *January* 27, 1874.

The foregoing resolution was duly passed.
By order of the senate,
HENRY A. GLIDDEN,
Clerk.

STATE OF NEW YORK,
In Assembly, *February* 4, 1874.

The foregoing resolution was duly passed.
By order of the assembly.
JOHN O'DONNELL,
Clerk.

CONCURRENT RESOLUTION proposing an amendment to the constitution, to be known as articles fifteen and sixteen.

WHEREAS, At the last session of the legislature, the following amendment was proposed in the senate and assembly, viz.: That the constitution of this state be amended by adding additional articles thereto, to be known as articles fifteen and sixteen, as follows:

ARTICLE XV.

SECTION 1. Any person holding office under the laws of this state, who, except in payment of his legal salary, fees or perquisites, shall receive or consent to receive, directly or indirectly, any thing of value or of personal advantage, or the promise thereof, for performing or omitting to perform any official act, or with the express or implied understanding that his official action or omission to act is to be in any degree influenced thereby, shall be deemed guilty of a felony. This section shall not affect the validity of any existing statute in relation to the offense of bribery.

§ 2. Any person who shall offer or promise a bribe to an officer, if it shall be received, shall be deemed guilty of a felony and liable to punishment, except as herein provided. No person offering a bribe shall, upon any prosecution of the officer for receiving such bribe, be privileged from testifying in relation thereto, and he shall not be liable to civil or criminal prosecution therefor, if he shall testify to the giving or offering of such bribe. Any person who shall offer or promise a bribe, if it be rejected by the officer to whom it is tendered, shall be deemed guilty of an attempt to bribe, which is hereby declared to be a felony.

§ 3. Any person charged with receiving a bribe, or with offering or promising a bribe, shall be permitted to testify in his own behalf in any civil or criminal prosecution therefor.

§ 4. Any district attorney who shall fail faithfully to prosecute a person charged with the violation in his county of any provision of this article which may come to his knowledge, shall be removed from office by the governor, after due notice and an opportunity of being heard in his defense. The expenses which shall be incurred by any county, in investigating and prosecuting any charge of bribery, or attempt to bribe any person holding office under the laws of this state, within such county, or of receiving bribes by any such person in said county, shall be a charge against the state, and their payment by the state shall be provided for by law.

ARTICLE XVI.

SECTION 1. All amendments to the constitution shall be in force from and including the first day of January succeeding the election at which the same were adopted, except when otherwise provided by such amendments.

AND WHEREAS, The said proposed amendment was agreed to by a majority of the members elected to each of the two houses of the said legislature, entered on their journals with the yeas and nays taken thereon, and referred to the legislature to be chosen at the then next general election of senators;

AND WHEREAS, Such election has taken place, and said proposed amendment was duly published for three months previous to the time of making such choice, in pursuance of the provisions of section one of article thirteen of the constitution; therefore,

Resolved (if the assembly concur), That the senate do agree to the proposed amendment.

STATE OF NEW YORK,
In Senate, *January* 27, 1874.

The foregoing resolution was duly passed.
By order of the senate.
HENRY A. GLIDDEN,
Clerk.

STATE OF NEW YORK,
In Assembly, *February* 4, 1874.

The foregoing resolution was duly passed.
By order of the assembly.
JOHN O'DONNELL,
Clerk.

STATE OF NEW YORK,
Albany, *April* 7, 1874.

We certify that a joint convention of the senate and assembly, held in the assembly chamber, on the seventh day of April, one thousand eight hundred and seventy-four, pursuant to law, and a concurrent resolution of both houses, Neil Gilmour of the county of Saratoga, having received a majority of all the votes cast, was duly elected superintendent of public instruction, for the term of three years, from the first Tuesday of April, one thousand eight hundred and seventy-four.

Witness our hands and seals of the senate and assembly this seventh day of April, one thousand eight hundred and seventy-four.

[L. S.] JOHN C. ROBINSON,
President of the Senate.
HENRY A. GLIDDEN,
Clerk of the Senate.

[L. S.] JAMES W. HUSTED,
Speaker of the Assembly.
JOHN O'DONNELL,
Clerk of the Assembly.

CONCURRENT RESOLUTIONS relative to message from the governor on the inflation of the currency of the United States.

WHEREAS, His excellency the governor of the state of New York has this day transmitted to both houses of the legislature a special message relating to the inflation of the currency by the general government, calling attention to the disastrous effect of such action upon the welfare and prosperity of the country, therefore be it

Resolved (if the assembly concur), That we fully affirm and heartily indorse the sentiments expressed in such message, and in view thereof, and of the act of congress, approved March, eighteen hundred and sixty-nine, which affirmed that the pledge of the United States was solemnly pledged to the payment in coin, of all the obligations of the United States not bearing interest (known as United States notes), and that "the United States also solemnly pledged its faith to make provision at the earliest practicable period for the redemption of the United States notes in coin," and as this pledge has been repeatedly given; it is the judgment of the legislature of the state of New York, that it is the duty of the administration of the general government at Washington and of congress to stay the pernicious and ruinous policy of increasing the volume of irredeemable paper currency; and be it further

Resolved (if the assembly concur), That our senators and representatives in congress be and they are hereby requested to resist, by all efforts in their power, any inflation of the currency, through the further issue of circulating notes by the government or by the national banks, and that they be and they are also hereby requested respectively to promote by all proper measures an early return to specie payment; and be it further

Resolved (if the assembly concur), That his excellency the governor be requested to transmit these resolutions, with a copy of his message appended, to the president of the United States, and to each of our senators and representatives in congress.

STATE OF NEW YORK,
In Senate, *April* 7, 1874.

The foregoing resolutions were duly passed.
By order.

HENRY A. GLIDDEN,
Clerk.

STATE OF NEW YORK,
In Assembly, *April* 7, 1874.

The foregoing resolutions were duly passed.
By order.

JOHN O'DONNELL,
Clerk.

CONCURRENT RESOLUTION in relation to the completion of the work of removing the obstructions at Hell Gate.

WHEREAS, The commercial interests of the whole country, and especially of the city and state of New York, demand the early completion of the work of removing the obstructions at Hell Gate; and

WHEREAS, The work has now been suspended for four months for the want of funds for its prosecution, and the engineer in charge, General Newton, estimates that six hundred thousand dollars will be required for its completion; therefore

Resolved (if the senate concur), That our senators and representatives in congress be requested to use their influence for an early appropriation of the amount required.

STATE OF NEW YORK,
In Assembly, *April* 11, 1874.

The foregoing resolution was duly passed.
By order.

J. O'DONNELL,
Clerk.

STATE OF NEW YORK,
In Senate, *April* 14, 1874.

The foregoing resolution was duly passed.
By order.

HENRY A. GLIDDEN,
Clerk.

STATE OF NEW YORK,
In Senate, Albany, *April* 22, 1874.

Resolved, (if the assembly concur), That the legislature do concur in the recommendation of the canal board, and assent to the adoption of the toll sheet of 1873, by the said board, for the year 1874.

By order.

H. A. GLIDDEN,
Clerk.

IN ASSEMBLY,
April 24, 1874.

Concurred in without amendment.
By order.

J. O'DONNELL,
Clerk.

CONCURRENT RESOLUTION relative to the dam on the Owasco river, in the city of Auburn.

WHEREAS, Grave doubts exist as to the height at which the state should maintain the dam on the Owasco river, in the city of Auburn, known as the prison dam, for the purpose of supplying water to the said prison; and

WHEREAS, Much litigation has heretofore arisen, and suits are now pending and undetermined for damages alleged to have been sustained by reason of the maintenance of flush boards upon said dam; and which flush boards are alleged to have been so maintained under the directions of the officers of the state in charge of said prison; it is, therefore,

Resolved (if the assembly concur), That the governor be and hereby is authorized to appoint three commissioners, one of which commissioners shall be the state engineer and surveyor, whose duty it shall be with all convenient diligence to examine and determine

1st. The height to which such dam, with or without flush boards, may be lawfully maintained by the officers of the state, for the purpose of supplying water to the Auburn prison.

2d. Whether the maintenance of such dam at the height at which the same may now be legally maintained, will supply sufficient water and water power for the necessary uses of the state in connection with the Auburn prison.

3d. If the maintenance of such dam, at the height to which the same may now be legally maintained, is insufficient for the supply of the water and water power necessary for the state, in connection with the Auburn prison, that then and in that case said commissioners shall determine the height at which such dam shall hereafter be maintained, and the permanent damages caused thereby shall be fixed and determined by commissioners to be hereafter appointed for that purpose in the manner provided by the constitution and laws of the state.

4th. That upon a written stipulation being filed with said commissioners by the parties respectively to the suits now pending and undetermined for temporary damages, alleged to have been sustained by reason of the unlawful maintenance of flush boards upon said dam, by or under the direction of the officers of the state in connection with said Auburn prison, to submit all matters of difference in said actions to the final award and arbitration of said commissioners; it shall be the duty of said commissioners to hear, arbitrate and determine said actions, and to make such award and determination thereof as they may deem equitable and just; and for that purpose, the said commissioners are authorized to examine said parties and each of them, and such witnesses as may be presented by said parties, or either of them, under oath; and to enforce the attendance of said parties, and each of them, and of witnesses by subpœna and attachment in the same manner as such attendance may be enforced in the supreme court. And either of said commissioners is hereby authorized to administer any oath or affirmation requisite upon such hearing. All of said commissioners shall meet together upon all proceedings under this act,* but a majority of said commissioners may determine any question which may arise upon any proceeding under the same, and may make a final award and determination of all matters submitted to them.

STATE OF NEW YORK,
In Senate, *April* 21, 1874.

The foregoing resolution was duly passed.
By order of the senate.
HENRY A. GLIDDEN,
Clerk.

STATE OF NEW YORK,
In Assembly, *April* 29, 1874.

The foregoing resolution was duly passed.
By order of the assembly.
JOHN O'DONNELL,
Clerk.

CONCURRENT RESOLUTION authorizing the governor to appoint commissionersto represent the state at the Centennial Exhibition.

WHEREAS, His excellency, the governor, recommends in his annual message the appointment of a board of commissioners to represent this state, and its industrial and other interests, in the Centennial Exhibition, soon to be held in the city of Philadelphia; and

WHEREAS, The managers of said exhibition advise that each state shall select a commission, not exceeding five in number, for the purpose of organizing their respective states and securing a suitable representation of the same in the exhibition; therefore be it

Resolved (if the senate concur), That the governor be and he is hereby authorized to appoint five citizens to be commissioners, who shall represent the state of New York in all matters connected with or pertaining to the Centennial Exhibition. The said commissioners to receive no compensation for their services or expenses. In addition to the commissioners herein provided, the commissioners and alternates appointed by the president of the United States for the state at large shall be included in the commission herewith created.

---

* So in the original.

STATE OF NEW YORK,
In Assembly, *February* 18, 1874.

The foregoing resolutions were duly passed.
By order.

J. O'DONNELL,
Clerk.

STATE OF NEW YORK,
In Senate, *April* 30, 1874.

The foregoing resolutions were duly passed.
By order.

HENRY A. GLIDDEN,
Clerk.

CONCURRENT RESOLUTION directing the board of commissioners of the department of docks of the city of New York to cause to be made the necessary surveys, soundings, and other examination of the water front of that part of Westchester county recently annexed to said city.

Resolved (if the senate concur), That the board of commissioners of the department of docks of the city of New York are hereby directed to cause to be made the necessary surveys, soundings and other examination of the water front of all that part of Westchester county recently annexed to said city, from the easterly terminus of said water front at the mouth of the Bronx river, as already determined, and thence following the East river bank and the Harlem river, Spuyten Duyvil creek and Hudson river to the northern terminus of said water front on the Hudson river, as already determined, and to ascertain the capacities and requirements of said water front for adaptation to commercial uses, in like manner as the said board has already caused to be surveyed and examined the previously recorded water front of said city.

STATE OF NEW YORK,
In Assembly, *April* 17, 1874.

The foregoing resolutions were duly passed.
By order.

JOHN O'DONNELL,
Clerk.

STATE OF NEW YORK,
In Senate, *April* 30, 1874.

The foregoing resolutions were duly passed.
By order.

HENRY A. GLIDDEN,
Clerk.

STATE OF NEW YORK,
Senate Chamber, Albany, *April* 30, 1874.

Resolved (if the assembly concur), That three thousand copies of the bill codifying and amending the laws relating to the commitment and care of lunatics and organization of asylums be printed, and copies be distributed by the secretary of state to the officers and persons designated to carry out the provisions of the law.

By order.

H. A. GLIDDEN,
Clerk.

IN ASSEMBLY, *April* 30, 1874.

Concurred in.

By order.

J. O'DONNELL,
Clerk.

THE

CONSTITUTION

OF THE

STATE OF NEW YORK

AS AMENDED AND IN FORCE JANUARY 1, 1875.

INDEX

TO THE

CONSTITUTION OF THE STATE OF NEW YORK.

THE

CONSTITUTION

OF THE

STATE OF NEW YORK.

Adopted November 3, 1846.

AS AMENDED AND IN FORCE JANUARY 1, 1875.

ARTICLE I.

SECTION 1. No person to be disfranchised.
SEC. 2. Trial by Jury.
SEC. 3. Religious liberty.
SEC. 4. Writ of *habeas corpus*.
SEC. 5. Bail, fines.
SEC. 6. Grand Jury.
SEC. 7. Private property — Private roads.
SEC. 8. Freedom of speech and of the press.
SEC. 9. Two-third bills.
SEC. 10. Right of petition — Divorces — Lotteries.
SEC. 11. Right of property in lands — Escheats.
SEC. 12. Feudal tenures abolished.
SEC. 13. Allodial tenure.
SEC. 14. Certain leases invalid.
SEC. 15. Fines and quarter sales abolished.
SEC. 16. Sale of lands.
SEC. 17. Old colony laws and acts of the legislature — Common law — Commissioners to be appointed — their duties.
SEC. 18. Grants of land since 1775 — Prior grants.

ARTICLE II.

SECTION 1. Qualification of voters.
SEC. 2. Persons excluded from right of suffrage — Challenge — Laws to be passed excluding from right of suffrage.
SEC. 3. Certain employments not to affect residence of voters.
SEC. 4. Laws to be passed.
SEC. 5. Election to be by ballot.

ARTICLE III.

ARTICLE IV.

days—After adjournment, bills must be approved in thirty days, else cannot become law—Governor may object to items of appropriation in any bill.

ARTICLE V.

SECTION 1. State officers, how elected and terms of office.

SEC. 2. State Engineer and Surveyor, how chosen and term of office.

SEC. 3. Canal Commissioners, how chosen and terms of office.

SEC. 4. Inspectors of State Prisons, how elected and terms of office.

SEC. 5. Commissioners of the Land Office—Commissioners of the Canal Fund—Canal Board.

SEC. 6. Powers and duties of Boards, etc.

SEC. 7. Treasurer may be suspended by Governor.

SEC. 8. Certain offices abolished.

ARTICLE VI.

SECTION 1. Impeachment—Assembly has power of—Effect of judgment.

SEC. 2. Court of Appeals—Judges how chosen—Appointment of clerk.

SEC. 3. Vacancies in office of judge of Court of Appeals, how filled.

SEC. 4. Causes pending in Court of Appeals to be referred to Commissioners of Appeals.

SEC. 5. Commissioners of Appeals—Vacancies how filled—Chief Commissioner to be appointed.

SEC. 6. Supreme Court—Jurisdiction—Justices—Judicial Districts, number of justices in; may be altered without increasing number.

SEC. 7. Terms of Supreme Court.

SEC. 8. Judge or Justice may not set in review of decisions made by him, etc.

SEC. 9. Vacancy in office of Justice of Supreme court, how filled.

SEC. 10. Judges of Court of Appeals, or Justices of Supreme Court, to hold no other office.

SEC. 11. Removals—Proceedings in relation to.

SEC. 12. City Courts.

SEC. 13. Justice of Supreme Court or Judges of City Courts, how chosen—Term of office—Restriction as to age.

SEC. 14. Compensation of Judges or Justices—Not to be diminished during term of office.

SEC. 15. County Courts.

SEC. 16. Local judicial officers.

SEC. 17. Judge of Court of Appeals, or Justice of Supreme Court, election or appointment of—Question to be submitted to people.

SEC. 18. Justices of the Peace.

SEC. 19. Inferior local courts.

SEC. 20. Clerks of Supreme Court and Court of Appeals.

SEC. 21. No judicial officer, except Justice of the Peace, to receive fees.

SEC. 22. Judgments, etc., may be ordered directly to Court of Appeals for review.

SEC. 23. Publication of Statutes to be provided for—To be free to all.

SEC. 24. Judges, first election of—When to enter upon duties.

SEC. 25. Local judicial officers—Term of office of present incumbents.

SEC. 26. Courts of Special Sessions.

SEC. 27. Surrogates' Courts.

SEC. 28. Court of Appeals may order causes to be heard by Commission of Appeals.

ARTICLE VII.

SECTION 1. Canal debt — Sinking Fund — June 1, 1846, $1,300,000 — June 1, 1855, $1,700,000.

SEC. 2. General Fund Debt — Sinking Fund, $350,000; after certain period, $1,500,000.

SEC. 3. $200,000 of the surplus canal revenues annually appropriated to General Fund, and the remainder to specific public works — Certain deficiencies in the revenues not exceeding $2,250,000, annually to be supplied from the revenues of the canals — Contractors, no extra compensation to be made to.

SEC. 4. Loans to incorporated companies not to be released or compromised.

SEC. 5. Legislatures shall, by equitable taxes, increase the revenues of the Sinking Fund in certain cases.

SEC. 6. Certain Canals of the State not to be leased or sold — Expenditures, for collections and repairs, limited — Funds from leases or sale, how applied.

SEC. 7. Salt springs.

SEC. 8. Appropriation bills.

SEC. 9. State credit not to be loaned.

SEC. 10. Power to contract debts limited.

SEC. 11. Debts to repel invasion, etc., may be contracted.

SEC. 12. Limitation of the legislative power in the creation of debts.

SEC 13. Sinking funds to be separately kept and safely invested.

SEC. 14. Claims barred by lapse of time — Limitation of existing claims.

ARTICLE VIII.

SECTION 1. Corporations, how created.

SEC. 2. Debts of corporations.

SEC. 3. "Corporations" defined.

SEC. 4. Charters for savings banks and banking purposes.

SEC. 5. Specie payments.

SEC. 6. Registry of bills or notes.

SEC. 7. Individual responsibility of stockholders.

SEC. 8. Insolvency of banks, preference.

SEC. 9. Legislature to provide for the incorporation of cities and villages, and to define powers thereof in certain cases.

SEC. 10. The credit or money of the State not to be given or loaned.

SEC. 11. Counties, cities, towns and villages not to give money or property or loan their money or credit — Their power to contract debts limited.

ARTICLE IX.

SECTION 1. Common School, Literature and United States Deposit Funds.

ARTICLE X.

SECTION 1. Sheriffs, Clerks of counties, Register and Clerk of New York, Coroners and District Attorneys — Governor may remove.

ARTICLE XI.

ARTICLE XII.

ARTICLE XIII.

ARTICLE XIV.

ARTICLE XV.

ARTICLE XVI.

SECTION 1. Amendments, when to take effect.

WE THE PEOPLE of the State of New York, grateful to Almighty God for our Freedom, in order to secure its blessings, DO ESTABLISH THIS CONSTITUTION.

ARTICLE I.

No person to be disfranchised. SECTION 1. No member of this State shall be disfranchised, or deprived of any of the rights or privileges secured to any citizens thereof, unless by the law of the land, or the judgment of his peers.

Trial by jury. SEC. 2. The trial by jury in all cases in which it has been heretofore used, shall remain inviolate forever; but a jury trial may be waived by the parties in all civil cases in the manner to be prescribed by law.

Religious liberty. SEC. 3. The free exercise and enjoyment of religious profession and worship, without discrimination or preference, shall forever be allowed in this State to all mankind; and no person shall be rendered incompetent to be a witness on account of his opinions on matters of religious belief; but the liberty of conscience hereby secured shall not be so construed as to excuse acts of licentiousness, or justify practices inconsistent with the peace or safety of this State.

Writ of habeas corpus. SEC. 4. The privilege of the writ of *habeas corpus* shall not be suspended, unless, when in cases of rebellion or invasion, the public safety may require its suspension.

Bail, fines. SEC. 5. Excessive bail shall not be required nor excessive fines imposed, nor shall cruel and unusual punishments be inflicted, nor shall witnesses be unreasonably detained.

Grand jury. SEC. 6. No person shall be held to answer for a capital or otherwise infamous crime (except in cases of impeachment, and in cases of militia when in actual service; and the land and naval forces in time of war, or which this State may keep, with the consent of Congress in time of peace; and in cases of petit larceny, under the regulation of the Legislature,) unless on presentment or indictment of a grand jury; and in any trial in any court whatever the party accused shall be allowed to appear and defend in person and with counsel as in civil actions. No person shall be subject to be twice put in jeopardy for the same offense; nor shall he be compelled in any criminal case to be a witness against himself; nor be deprived of life, liberty or property without due process of law; nor shall private property be taken for public use, without just compensation.

Private property, private roads.

SEC. 7. When private property shall be taken for any public use the compensation to be made therefor, when such compensation is not made by the State, shall be ascertained by a jury or by not less than three commissioners appointed by a court of record, as shall be prescribed by law. Private roads may be opened in the manner to be prescribed by law; but in every case, the necessity of the road, and the amount of all damage to be sustained by the opening thereof, shall be first determined by a jury of freeholders, and such amount, together with the expense of the proceeding, shall be paid by the person to be benefited.

Freedom of speech and of the press.

SEC. 8. Every citizen may freely speak, write and publish his sentiments on all subjects, being responsible for the abuse of that right; and no law shall be passed to restrain or abridge the liberty of speech or of the press. In all criminal prosecutions or indictments for libels, the truth may be given in evidence to the jury; and if it shall appear to the jury, that the matter charged as libelous is true, and was published with good motives, and for justifiable ends, the party shall be acquitted; and the jury shall have the right to determine the law and the fact.

Two-third bills.

SEC. 9. The assent of two-thirds of the members elected to each branch of the Legislature shall be requisite to every bill appropriating the public moneys or property for local or private purposes.

Right of petition. Divorce. Lotteries.

SEC. 10. No law shall be passed abridging the right of the people peaceably to assemble and to petition the government, or any department thereof, nor shall any divorce be granted, otherwise than by due judicial proceedings; nor shall any lottery hereafter be authorized or any sale of lottery tickets allowed within this State.

Right of property in lands. Escheats.

SEC. 11. The people of this State, in their right of sovereignty are deemed to possess the original and ultimate property in and to all lands within the jurisdiction of the State; and all lands the title to which shall fail, from a defect of heirs, shall revert, or escheat to the people.

Feudal tenures abolished.

SEC. 12. All feudal tenures of every description, with all their incidents are declared to be abolished, saving however all rents and services certain which at any time heretofore have been lawfully created or reserved.

Allodial tenures.

SEC. 13. All lands within this State are declared to be allodial, so that, subject only to the liability to escheat, the entire and absolute property is vested in the owners, according to the nature of their respective estates.

Certain leases invalid.

SEC. 14. No lease or grant of agricultural land, for a longer period than twelve years, hereafter made, in which shall be reserved any rent or service of any kind, shall be valid.

Fines and quarter sales abolished.

SEC. 15. All fines, quarter sales, or other like restraints upon alienation, reserved in any grant of land, hereafter to be made, shall be void.

Sale of lands.

SEC. 16. No purchase or contract for the sale of lands in this State made since the fourteenth day of October, one thousand seven hundred and seventy-five; or which may hereafter be made, of, or with the Indians, shall be valid, unless made under the authority, and with the consent of the Legislature.

Old Colony laws and acts of the legislature.

SEC. 17. Such parts of the common law, and of the acts of the Legislature of the Colony of New York, as together did form the law of the said Colony, on the nineteenth day of April, one thousand seven hundred and seventy-five, and the resolutions of the Congress of the said Colony, and of the convention of the State of New York, in force on the twentieth day of April, one thousand seven hundred and seventy-seven, which have not since expired, or been repealed or altered; and such acts of the Legislature of this State as are now in force, shall be and continue the law of this State, subject to such alterations as the Legislature shall make concerning the same. But all such parts of the common law, and such of the said acts, or parts thereof, as are repugnant to this Constitution, are hereby abrogated; and the Legislature, at its first session after the adoption of this Constitution, shall appoint three commissioners, whose duty it shall be to reduce into a written and systematic code the whole body of the law of this State, or so much and such parts thereof, as to the said commissioners shall seem practicable and expedient. And the said commissioners shall specify such alterations and amendments therein as they shall deem proper, and they shall at all times make reports of their proceedings to the Legislature, when called upon to do so; and the Legislature shall pass laws regulating the tenure of office, the filling of vacancies therein, and the compensation of the said commissioners, and shall also provide for the publication of the said code, prior to its being presented to the Legislature for adoption.

Common law.

Commissioners to be appointed.

Their duties.

SEC. 18. All grants of land within this State, made by the king of Great Britain, or persons acting under his authority, after the fourteenth day of October, one thousand seven hundred and seventy-five, shall be null and void; but nothing contained in this Constitution shall affect any grants of land within this State, made by the authority of the said king or his predecessors, or shall annul any charters to bodies politic and corporate, by him or them made, before that day; or shall affect any such grants or charters since made by this State, or by persons acting under its authority; or shall impair the obligation of any debts contracted by the State, or individuals, or bodies corporate, or any other rights of property, or any suits, actions, rights of action, or other proceedings in courts of justice.

Grants of lands since 1775.

Prior grants.

ARTICLE II.

*SECTION 1. Every male citizen of the age of twenty-one years who shall have been a citizen for ten days and an inhabitant of this State one year next preceding an

Qualifications of voters.

*As amended by vote of the people, Nov. 3, 1874.

election, and for the last four months a resident of the county and for the last thirty days a resident of the election district in which he may offer his vote, shall be entitled to vote at such election in the election district of which he shall at the time be a resident, and not elsewhere, for all officers that now are or hereafter may be elective by the people, and upon all questions which may be submitted to the vote of the people, provided that in time of war no elector in the actual military service of the State, or of the United States, in the army or navy thereof, shall be deprived of his vote by reason of his absence from such election district; and the Legislature shall have power to provide the manner in which and the time and place at which such absent electors may vote, and for the return and canvass of their votes in the election districts in which they respectively reside.

Persons excluded from right of suffrage. *SEC. 2. No person who shall receive, expect or offer to receive, or pay, offer or promise to pay, contribute, offer or promise to contribute to another, to be paid or used, any money or other valuable thing as a compensation or reward for the giving or withholding a vote at an election, or who shall make any promise to influence the giving or withholding any such vote, or who shall make or become directly or indirectly interested in any bet or wager depending upon the result of any election, shall vote at such election; and upon challenge for such cause, the person so challenged, before the officers authorized for that purpose shall receive his vote, shall swear or affirm before such officers that he has not received or offered, does not expect to receive, has not paid, offered or promised to pay, contributed, offered or promised to contribute to another, to be paid or used, any money or other valuable thing as a compensation or reward for the giving or withholding a vote at such election, and has not made any promise to influence the giving or withholding of any such vote, nor made or become directly or indirectly interested in any bet or wager depending upon the result of such election. The Legislature, at the session thereof next after the adoption of this section, shall, and

Challenge.

Laws to be passed, ex-

*As amended by vote of the people, Nov. 3, 1874.

from time to time thereafter may, enact laws excluding from the right of suffrage all persons convicted of bribery or of any infamous crime.

cluding from right of suffrage.

SEC. 3. For the purpose of voting, no person shall be deemed to have gained or lost a residence, by reason of his presence or absence, while employed in the service of the United States; nor while engaged in the navigation of the waters of this State, or of the United States, or of the high seas; nor while a student of any seminary of learning; nor while kept at any alms-house, or other asylum, at public expense; nor while confined in any public prison.

Certain employments not to affect residence of voters.

SEC. 4. Laws shall be made for ascertaining by proper proofs the citizens who shall be entitled to the right of suffrage hereby established.

Laws to be passed.

SEC. 5. All elections by the citizens shall be by ballot, except for such town officers as may by law be directed to be otherwise chosen.

Election to be by ballot.

ARTICLE III.

SECTION 1. The legislative power of this State shall be vested in a Senate and Assembly.

Legislative powers.

SEC. 2. The Senate shall consist of thirty-two members, and the Senators shall be chosen for two years. The Assembly shall consist of one hundred and twenty-eight members, who shall be annually elected.

Senate, number of Assembly, number of.

SEC. 3. The State shall be divided into thirty-two districts, to be called Senate districts, each of which shall choose one Senator. The districts shall be numbered from one to thirty-two inclusive.*

State divided into thirty-two Senatorial districts.

District number One (1) shall consist of the counties of Suffolk, Richmond and Queens.

Boundaries thereof.

District number Two (2) shall consist of the county of Kings.

District number Three (3), number Four (4), number Five (5), and number Six (6) shall consist of the city and county of New York. And the Board of supervisors of said city and county shall, on or before the first day of May, one thousand eight hundred and forty-seven, divide the said city and county into the number of Senate dis-

Board of Supervisors of the city of New York to divide the county into four Senate districts.

*For existing Senate districts, see chapter 805, Laws of 1866.

tricts, to which it is entitled, as near as may be of an equal number of inhabitants, excluding aliens and persons of color not taxed, and consisting of convenient and contiguous territory; and no Assembly district shall be divided in the formation of a Senate district. The board of supervisors, when they shall have completed such division, shall cause certificates thereof, stating the number and boundaries of each district and the population thereof, to be filed in the office of the Secretary of State, and of the clerk of said city and county.

Certificate, etc., to be filed.

District number Seven (7) shall consist of the counties of Westchester, Putnam and Rockland.

District number Eight (8) shall consist of the counties of Dutchess and Columbia.

District number Nine (9) shall consist of the counties of Orange and Sullivan.

District number Ten (10) shall consist of the counties of Ulster and Greene.

District number Eleven (11) shall consist of the counties of Albany and Schenectady.

District number Twelve (12) shall consist of the county of Rensselaer.

District number Thirteen (13) shall consist of the counties of Washington and Saratoga.

District number Fourteen (14) shall consist of the counties of Warren, Essex and Clinton.

District number Fifteen (15) shall consist of the counties of St. Lawrence and Franklin.

District number Sixteen (16) shall consist of the counties of Herkimer, Hamilton, Fulton and Montgomery.

District number Seventeen (17) shall consist of the counties of Schoharie and Delaware.

District number Eighteen (18) shall consist of the counties of Otsego and Chenango.

District number Nineteen (19) shall consist of the county of Oneida.

District number twenty (20) shall consist of the counties of Madison and Oswego.

District number Twenty-one (21) shall consist of the counties of Jefferson and Lewis.

District number Twenty-two (22) shall consist of the county of Onondaga.

District number Twenty-three (23) shall consist of the counties of Cortland, Broome and Tioga.

District number Twenty-four (24) shall consist of the counties of Cayuga and Wayne.

District number Twenty-five (25) shall consist of the counties of Tompkins, Seneca and Yates.

District number Twenty-six (26) shall consist of the counties of Steuben and Chemung.

District number Twenty-seven (27) shall consist of the county of Monroe.

District number Twenty-eight (28) shall consist of the counties of Orleans, Genesee and Niagara.

District number Twenty-nine (29) shall consist of the counties of Ontario and Livingston.

District number Thirty (30) shall consist of the counties of Allegany and Wyoming.

District number Thirty-one (31) shall consist of the county of Erie.

District number Thirty-two (32) shall consist of the counties of Chautauqua and Cattaraugus.

SEC. 4. An enumeration of the inhabitants of the State shall be taken, under the direction of the Legislature, in the year one thousand eight hundred and fifty-five, and at the end of every ten years thereafter; and the said districts shall be so altered by the Legislature, at the first session after the return of every enumeration, that each Senate district shall contain, as nearly as may be, an equal number of inhabitants, excluding aliens, and persons of color not taxed; and shall remain unaltered until the return of another enumeration, and shall at all times consist of contiguous territory; and no county shall be divided in the formation of a Senate district, except such county shall be equitably entitled to two or more senators.

Census to be taken in 1855, and every ten years.

Senate districts, how altered.

*SEC. 5. The Assembly shall consist of one hundred and twenty-eight members, elected for one year. The members of Assembly shall be apportioned among the several counties of the State, by the Legislature, as nearly as may be, according to the number of their respective inhabitants, excluding aliens, and shall be chosen by

Members of Assembly, number of, and how apportioned and chosen.

*As amended by vote of the people, November 3, 1874.

single districts.* The Assembly districts shall remain as at present organized, until after the enumeration of the inhabitants of the State, in the year eighteen hundred and seventy-five. The Legislature, at its first session after the return of every enumeration, shall apportion the members of Assembly among the several counties of the State, in manner aforesaid, and the board of supervisors in such counties as may be entitled under such apportionment to more than one member, except the city and county of New York, and in said city and county the board of aldermen of said city, shall assemble at such time as the Legislature making such apportionment shall prescribe, and divide their respective counties into Assembly districts, each of which districts shall consist of convenient and contiguous territory, equal to the number of members of Assembly to which such counties shall be entitled, and shall cause to be filed in the offices of the Secretary of State and the clerks of their respective counties a description of such districts, specifying the number of each district and the population thereof, according to the last preceding enumeration as near as can be ascertained, and the apportionment and districts shall remain unaltered until another enumeration shall be made as herein provided. No town shall be divided in the formation of Assembly districts. Every county heretofore established and separately organized, except the county of Hamilton, shall always be entitled to one member of the Assembly, and no new county shall be hereafter erected unless its population shall entitle it to a member. The county of Hamilton shall elect with the county of Fulton, until the population of the county of Hamilton shall, according to the ratio, be entitled to a member. But the Legislature may abolish the said county of Hamilton, and annex the territory thereof to some other county or counties. Nothing in this section shall prevent division at any time of counties and towns, and the erection of new towns and counties by the Legislature.

Board of supervisors in certain counties, and board of aldermen in New York city to divide the same into Assembly districts.

Description of Assembly districts to be filed.

Contents of Assembly districts.

Legislature to reapportion members of Assembly.

Each county entitled to one member.

Hamilton county.

Counties and towns may be divided and new ones erected.

Pay of members.

†SEC. 6. Each member of the Legislature shall receive for his services an annual salary of one thousand five

*For existing Assembly Districts, see chapter 607, Laws of 1866.
†As amended by vote of the people, November 3, 1874.

hundred dollars. The members of either house shall also receive the sum of one dollar for every ten miles they shall travel, in going to and returning from their place of meeting, once in each session, on the most usual route. Senators, when the Senate alone is convened in extraordinary session, or when serving as members of the Court for the Trial of Impeachments, and such members of the Assembly, not exceeding nine in number, as shall be appointed managers of an impeachment, shall receive an additional allowance of ten dollars a day.

*SEC. 7. No member of the Legislature shall receive any civil appointment within this State, or the Senate of the United States, from the Governor, the Governor and Senate, or from the Legislature, or from any city government during the time for which he shall have been elected; and all such appointments and all votes given for any such member for any such office or appointment shall be void. No member to receive an appointment.

*SEC. 8. No person shall be eligible to the Legislature who, at the time of his election, is, or within one hundred days previous thereto, has been a member of Congress, a civil or military officer under the United States, or an officer under any city government; and if any person shall, after his election as a member of the Legislature, be elected to Congress, or appointed to any office, civil or military, under the government of the United States, or under any city government, his acceptance thereof shall vacate his seat. Persons disqualified from being members.

SEC. 9. The elections of Senators and members of Assembly, pursuant to the provisions of this Constitution, shall be held on the Tuesday succeeding the first Monday of November, unless otherwise directed by the Legislature. Time of election fixed.

SEC. 10. A majority of each house shall constitute a quorum to do business. Each house shall determine the rules of its own proceedings, and be the judge of the elections, returns and qualifications of its own members, shall choose its own officers; and the Senate shall choose a temporary president, when the Lieutenant-Governor shall not attend as president, or shall act as Governor. Powers of each house.

*As amended by vote of the people, Nov. 3, 1874.

Journals to be kept.

SEC. 11. Each house shall keep a journal of its proceedings, and publish the same, except such parts as may require secrecy. The doors of each house shall be kept open, except when the public welfare shall require secrecy. Neither house shall, without the consent of the other, adjourn for more than two days.

No member to be questioned, etc.

SEC. 12. For any speech or debate in either house of the Legislature, the members shall not be questioned in any other place.

Bills may originate in either house.

SEC. 13. Any bill may originate in either house of the Legislature, and all bills passed by one house may be amended by the other.

Enacting clause of bills.

SEC. 14. The enacting clause of all bills shall be, "The People of the State of New York, represented in Senate and Assembly, do enact as follows," and no law shall be enacted except by bill.

Assent of a majority of all the members required, etc.

SEC. 15. No bill shall be passed unless by the assent of a majority of all the members elected to each branch of the Legislature, and the question upon the final passage shall be taken immediately upon its last reading, and the yeas and nays entered on the journal.

Restriction as to private and local bills.

SEC. 16. No private or local bill, which may be passed by the Legislature, shall embrace more than one subject, and that shall be expressed in the title.

Existing law not to be made a part of an act except by inserting it therein.

*SEC. 17. No act shall be passed which shall provide that any existing law, or any part thereof, shall be made or deemed a part of said act, or which shall enact that any existing law, or any part thereof, shall be applicable, except by inserting it in such act.

Private and local bills, in what cases they may not be passed.

SEC. 18. The Legislature shall not pass a private or local bill in any of the following cases:

Changing the names of persons.

Laying out, opening, altering, working or discontinuing roads, highways or alleys, or for draining swamps or other low lands.

Locating or changing county seats.

Providing for changes of venue in civil or criminal cases.

Incorporating villages.

*Sections 17 to 25, both inclusive, added by vote of the people, Nov. 3, 1874.

Providing for election of members of boards of supervisors.

Selecting, drawing, summoning or impaneling grand or petit jurors.

Regulating the rate of interest on money.

The opening and conducting of elections, or designating places of voting.

Creating, increasing or decreasing fees, percentage or allowances of public officers, during the term for which said officers are elected or appointed.

Granting to any corporation, association or individual the right to lay down railroad tracks.

Granting to any private corporation, association or individual any exclusive privilege, immunity or franchise whatever.

Providing for public bridges, and chartering companies for such purposes, except on the Hudson river below Waterford, and on the East river, or over the waters forming a part of the boundaries of the State.

General laws to be passed.

The Legislature shall pass general laws providing for the cases enumerated in this section, and for all other cases which in its judgment may be provided for by general laws. But no law shall authorize the construction or operation of a street railroad, except upon the condition that the consent of the owners of one-half in value of the property bounded on, and the consent also of the local authorities having the control of that portion of a street or highway upon which it is proposed to construct or operate such railroad be first obtained, or in case the consent of such property owners cannot be obtained, the general term of the supreme court, in the district in which it is proposed to be constructed, may, upon application, appoint three commissioners who shall determine, after a hearing of all parties interested, whether such railroad ought to be constructed or operated, and their determination, confirmed by the court, may be taken in lieu of the consent of the property owners.

Street railroads, condition upon which they may be authorized.

The Legislature not to audit or allow any private claims.

SEC. 19. The Legislature shall neither audit nor allow any private claim or account against the State, but may appropriate money to pay such claims as shall have been audited and allowed according to law.

Bill imposing a tax, manner of passing.

SEC. 20. Every law which imposes, continues or revives a tax shall distinctly state the tax and the object to which it is to be applied, and it shall not be sufficient to refer to any other law to fix such tax or object.

Same subject.

SEC. 21. On the final passage in either house of the Legislature, of any act which imposes, continues or revives a tax, or creates a debt or charge, or makes, continues or revives any appropriation of public or trust money or property, or releases, discharges or commutes any claim or demand of the State, the question shall be taken by yeas and nays, which shall be duly entered upon the journals, and three-fifths of all the members elected to either house shall, in all such cases, be necessary to constitute a quorum therein.

Board of supervisors.

SEC. 22. There shall be in the several counties, except in cities whose boundaries are the same as those of the county, a board of supervisors, to be composed of such members, and elected in such manner, and for such period, as is or may be provided by law. In any such city the duties and powers of a board of supervisors may be devolved upon the common council or board of aldermen thereof.

Local legislative powers conferred on boards of supervisors.

SEC. 23. The Legislature shall, by general laws, confer upon the boards of supervisors of the several counties of the State such further powers of local legislation and administration as the Legislature may from time to time deem expedient.

No extra compensation to be granted to a public officer, servant, agent or contractor.

SEC. 24. The Legislature shall not, nor shall the common council of any city nor any board of supervisors, grant any extra compensation to any public officer, servant, agent or contractor.

Sections seventeen and eighteen not to apply to certain bills.

SEC. 25. Sections seventeen and eighteen of this article shall not apply to any bill, or the amendments to any bill, which shall be reported to the Legislature by Commissioners who have been appointed pursuant to law to revise the Statutes.

ARTICLE IV.

Executive power, how vested.

*SECTION 1. The executive power shall be vested in a Governor, who shall hold his office for three years; a

* As amended by vote of the people, Nov. 3, 1874.

Lieutenant-Governor shall be chosen at the same time, and for the same term. The Governor and Lieutenant-Governor elected next preceding the time when this section shall take effect shall hold office during the term for which they were elected.

*SEC. 2. No person shall be eligible to the office of Governor or Lieutenant-Governor, except a citizen of the United States, of the age of not less than thirty years, and who shall have been five years, next preceding his election, a resident of this State. Requisite qualifications of Governor.

SEC. 3. The Governor and Lieutenant-Governor shall be elected at the times and places of choosing members of the Assembly. The persons respectively having the highest number of votes for Governor and Lieutenant-Governor shall be elected; but in case two or more shall have an equal and the highest number of votes for Governor, or for Lieutenant-Governor, the two houses of the Legislature, at its next annual session, shall, forthwith, by joint ballot, choose one of the said persons so having an equal and the highest number of votes for Governor or Lieutenant-Governor. Time and manner of electing Governor and Lieutenant-Governor.

*SEC. 4. The Governor shall be Commander-in-Chief of the military and naval forces of the State. He shall have power to convene the Legislature (or the Senate only) on extraordinary occasions. At extraordinary sessions no subject shall be acted upon, except such as the Governor may recommend for consideration. He shall communicate by message to the Legislature at every session the condition of the State, and recommend such matters to them as he shall judge expedient. He shall transact all necessary business with the officers of government, civil and military. He shall expedite all such measures as may be resolved upon by the Legislature, and shall take care that the laws are faithfully executed. He shall receive for his services an annual salary of ten thousand dollars, and there shall be provided for his use a suitable and furnished executive residence. Duties and power of Governor. His compensation.

SEC. 5. The Governor shall have the power to grant reprieves, commutations and pardons after conviction, for Pardoning power vested in the Governor.

---

* As amended by vote of the people Nov. 3, 1874.

all offenses except treason and cases of impeachment upon such conditions, and with such restrictions and limitations, as he may think proper, subject to such regulation as may be provided by law relative to the manner of applying for pardons. Upon conviction for treason, he shall have power to suspend the execution of the sentence, until the case shall be reported to the Legislature at its next meeting, when the Legislature shall either pardon, or commute the sentence, direct the execution of the sentence, or grant a further reprieve. He shall annually communicate to the Legislature each case of reprieve, commutation or pardon granted; stating the name of the convict, the crime of which he was convicted, the sentence and its date, and the date of the commutation, pardon or reprieve.

Power of Governor to devolve on Lieutenant-Governor.

SEC. 6. In case of the impeachment of the Governor, or his removal from office, death, inability to discharge the powers and duties of the said office, resignation, or absence from the State, the powers and duties of the office shall devolve upon the Lieutenant-Governor for the residue of the term, or until the disability shall cease. But when the Governor shall, with the consent of the Legislature, be out of the State in time of war, at the head of a military force thereof, he shall continue Commander-in-Chief of all the military force of the State.

Requisite qualifications of Lieutenant-Governor. To be President of the Senate and to act as Governor in certain cases.

SEC. 7. The Lieutenant-Governor shall possess the same qualifications of eligibility for office as the Governor. He shall be president of the Senate, but shall have only a casting vote therein. If during a vacancy of the office of Governor, the Lieutenant-Governor shall be impeached, displaced, resign, die, or become incapable of performing the duties of his office, or be absent from the State, the President of the Senate shall act as Governor until the vacancy be filled, or the disability shall cease.

Compensation of Lieutenant-Governor.

*SEC. 8. The Lieutenant-Governor shall receive for his services an annual salary of five thousand dollars, and shall not receive or be entitled to any other compensation, fee or perquisite for any duty or service he may be required to perform by the Constitution or by law.

*As amended by vote of the people, Nov. 3, 1874.

*SEC. 9. Every bill which shall have passed the Senate and Assembly shall, before it becomes a law, be presented to the Governor; if he approve, he shall sign it; but if not, he shall return it with his objections to the house in which it shall have originated, which shall enter the objections at large on the journal, and proceed to reconsider it. If, after such reconsideration, two-thirds of the members elected to that house shall agree to pass the bill, it shall be sent, together with the objections, to the other house by which it shall likewise be reconsidered; and if approved by two-thirds of the members elected to that house, it shall become a law notwithstanding the objections of the Governor. In all such cases, the votes in both houses shall be determined by yeas and nays, and the names of the members voting shall be entered on the journal of each house respectively. If any bill shall not be returned by the Governor within ten days (Sundays excepted) after it shall have been presented to him, the same shall be a law in like manner as if he had signed it, unless the Legislature shall, by their adjournment, prevent its return, in which case it shall not become a law without the approval of the Governor. No bill shall become a law after the final adjournment of the Legislature, unless approved by the Governor within thirty days after such adjournment. If any bill presented to the Governor contain several items of appropriation of money, he may object to one or more of such items while approving of the other portion of the bill. In such case, he shall append to the bill, at the time of signing it, a statement of the items to which he objects; and the appropriation so objected to shall not take effect. If the Legislature be in session, he shall transmit to the house in which the bill originated a copy of such statement, and the items objected to shall be separately reconsidered. If, on reconsideration, one or more of such items be approved by two-thirds of the members elected to each house, the same shall be part of the law, notwithstanding the objections of the Governor. All the provisions of this section, in relation to bills not approved by the Gov-

Bills to be presented to the Governor for signature.

If returned by him with objections how disposed of.

Bills to be returned within ten days.

After adjournment bills must be approved in thirty days else cannot become law.

Governor may object to items of appropriation in any bill.

*As amended by vote of the people Nov. 3, 1874.

ernor, shall apply in cases in which he shall withhold his approval from any item or items contained in a bill appropriating money.

ARTICLE V.

State officers, how elected, and term of office.

SECTION 1. The Secretary of State, Comptroller, Treasurer and Attorney-General shall be chosen at a general election, and shall hold their offices for two years. Each of the officers in this article named (except the Speaker of the Assembly) shall, at stated times during his continuance in office, receive for his services, a compensation, which shall not be increased or diminished during the term for which he shall have been elected; nor shall he receive, to his use, any fees or perquisites of office, or other compensation.

State Engineer and Surveyor, how chosen and term of office.

SEC. 2. A State Engineer and Surveyor shall be chosen at a general election, and shall hold his office two years, but no person shall be elected to said office who is not a practical engineer.

Canal Commissioners, how chosen and terms of office.

SEC. 3. Three Canal Commissioners shall be chosen at the general election which shall be held next after the adoption of this Constitution, one of whom shall hold his office for one year, one for two years, and one for three years. The Commissioners of the Canal Fund shall meet at the Capitol on the first Monday of January, next after such election, and determine by lot which of said Commissioners shall hold his office for one year, which for two, and which for three years; and there shall be elected annually, thereafter, one Canal Commissioner, who shall hold his office for three years.

Inspectors of State Prisons, how elected and terms of office.

SEC. 4. Three inspectors of State Prisons shall be elected at the general election which shall be held next after the adoption of this Constitution, one of whom shall hold his office for one year, one for two years, and one for three years. The Governor, Secretary of State, and Comptroller, shall meet at the Capitol on the first Monday of January next succeeding such election, and determine by lot which of said inspectors shall hold his office for one year, which for two, and which for three years; and there shall be elected annually thereafter, one inspector of State Prisons, who shall hold his office for three years; said inspectors shall have the charge and superintendence of the State Prisons, and shall appoint all the officers therein. All vacancies in the office of such inspector shall be filled by the Governor, till the next election.

Commissioners of the Land Office.

SEC. 5. The Lieutenant-Governor, Speaker of the Assembly, Secretary of State, Comptroller, Treasurer, Attorney-General, and State Engineer and Surveyor, shall be the Commissioners of the Land Office. The Lieutenant-Governor, Secretary of State, Comptroller, Treasurer, and Attorney-General, shall be the Commissioners of the Canal Fund. The Canal Board shall consist of the Commissioners of the Canal Fund, the State Engineer and Surveyor, and the Canal Commissioners.

Commissioners of the Canal Fund. Canal Board.

Powers and duties of Boards, etc.

SEC. 6. The powers and duties of the respective Boards, and of the several officers in this article mentioned, shall be such as now are or hereafter may be prescribed by law.

Treasurer may be suspended by Governor.

SEC. 7. The Treasurer may be suspended from office by the Governor, during the recess of the Legislature, and until thirty days after the commencement of the next session of the Legislature, whenever it shall appear to him that such Treasurer has, in any particular, violated his duty. The Governor shall appoint a competent person to discharge the duties of the office, during such suspension of the Treasurer.

Certain offices abolished.

SEC. 8. All offices for the weighing, gauging, measuring, culling or inspecting any merchandise, produce, manufacture or commodity whatever, are hereby abolished, and no such office shall hereafter be created by law; but nothing in this section contained shall abrogate any office created for the purpose of protecting the public health or the interests of the State in its property, revenue, tolls, or purchases, or of supplying the people with correct standards of weights and measures, or shall prevent the creation of any office for such purposes hereafter.

ARTICLE VI.

[Article 6 of the Constitution (except section 28) was framed by delegates elected April 23, 1867, under chapter 194, Laws of 1867, to a Constitutional Convention (convened pursuant to section 2 of article 13 of the Constitution, by vote of the people at the general election held Nov. 6, 1866), which convention met in the city of Albany, June 4, 1867, and adjourned February 28, 1868.

Article 6 (except section 28) was submitted separately to the people, pursuant to chapter 318, Laws of 1869, at the general election held November 2, 1869, and declared ratified and adopted by the Board of State Canvassers, by certificate of determination, dated December 6, 1869, the official vote thereon, as declared, standing, "for the amended judiciary article," 247,240 votes, and "against the amended judiciary article," 240,442 votes.]

Impeachment. Assembly has power of.

SECTION 1. The Assembly shall have the power of impeachment, by a vote of a majority of all the members elected. The court for the trial of impeachments shall be composed of the President of the Senate, the Senators, or a major part of them, and the Judges of the Court of Appeals, or the major part of them. On the trial of an impeachment against the Governor, the Lieutenant-Governor shall not act as a member of the court. No judicial officer shall exercise his office, after articles of impeachment against him shall have been preferred to the Senate, until he shall have been acquitted. Before the trial of an impeachment, the members of the court shall take an oath or affirmation, truly and impartially to try the impeachment, according to evidence; and no person shall be convicted without the concurrence of two-thirds of the members present.

Effect of judgment.

Judgment in cases of impeachment shall not extend further than to removal from office, or removal from office and disqualification to hold and enjoy any office of honor, trust, or profit, under this State; but the party impeached shall be liable to indictment and punishment according to law.

Court of Appeals. Judges, how chosen.

SEC. 2. There shall be a Court of Appeals, composed of a Chief Judge and six associate Judges, who shall be chosen by the electors of the State, and shall hold their office for the term of fourteen years from and including the first day of January next after their election. At the first election of Judges, under this Constitution, every elector may vote for the Chief and only four of the associate Judges. Any five members of the court shall form a quorum, and the concurrence of four shall be necessary to a decision. The court shall have the appointment, with the power of removal, of its reporter and clerk, and of such attendants as may be necessary. Appointment of clerk.

SEC. 3. When a vacancy shall occur, otherwise than by expiration of term, in the office of Chief or Associate Judge of the Court of Appeals, the same shall be filled, for a full term, at the next general election happening not less than three months after such vacancy occurs; and until the vacancy shall be so filled, the Governor by and with the advice and consent of the Senate, if the Senate shall be in session, or if not, the Governor alone, may appoint to fill such vacancy. If any such appointment of Chief Judge shall be made from among the associate judges, a temporary appointment of associate judge shall be made in like manner; but in such case, the person appointed Chief Judge shall not be deemed to vacate his office of associate judge any longer than until the expiration of his appointment as Chief Judge. The powers and jurisdiction of the court shall not be suspended for want of appointment or election, when the number of judges is sufficient to constitute a quorum. All appointments under this section shall continue until and including the last day of December next after the election at which the vacancy shall be filled. Vacancies in office of judges of Court of Appeals, how filled.

SEC. 4. Upon the organization of the Court of Appeals, under this article, the causes then pending in the present Court of Appeals shall become vested in the Court of Appeals hereby established. Such of said causes as are pending on the first day of January, eighteen hundred and sixty-nine, shall be heard and determined by a Commission, to be composed of five Commissioners of Appeals, four of whom shall be necessary to constitute a quorum; but the Court of Appeals hereby established may order any of said causes to be heard therein. Such Commission shall be composed of the Judges of the present Court of Appeals, elected or appointed thereto, and a fifth Commissioner who shall be appointed by the Governor by and with the advice and consent of the Senate; or, if the Senate be not in session, by the Governor; but Cause pending in Court of Appeals to be referred to Commissioners of Appeals.

in such case, the appointment shall expire at the end of the next session.

Commissioners of Appeals: vacancies, how filled.

SEC. 5. If any vacancy shall occur in the office of the said Commissioners, it shall be filled by appointment by the Governor by and with the advice and consent of the Senate; or if the Senate is not in session, by the Governor; but in such case, the appointment shall expire at the end of the next session. The Commissioners shall appoint, from their number, a Chief Commissioner; and may appoint and remove such attendants as may be necessary. The reporter of the Court of Appeals shall be the reporter of said Commission. The decisions of the Commission shall be certified to, and entered and enforced, as the judgments of the Court of Appeals. The Commission shall continue until the causes committed to it are determined, but not exceeding three years; and all causes then undetermined shall be heard by the Court of Appeals.

Chief Commissioner to be appointed.

Supreme Court. Jurisdiction. Justices.

SEC. 6. There shall be the existing Supreme Court, with general jurisdiction in law and equity, subject to such appellate jurisdiction of the Court of Appeals as now is or may be prescribed by law; and it shall be composed of the justices now in office, who shall be continued during their respective terms, and of their successors. The existing judicial districts of the State are continued until changed pursuant to this section.* Five of the justices shall reside in the district in which is the city of New York, and four in each of the other districts. The Legislature may alter the districts, without increasing the number, once after every enumeration, under this Constitution, of the inhabitants of the State.

Judicial districts. Number of justices in.

May be altered without increasing number.

Terms of the Supreme Court.

SEC. 7. At the first session of the Legislature, after the adoption of this article, and from time to time thereafter as may be necessary, but no oftener than once in five years, provisions shall be made for organizing, in the Supreme Court, not more than four general terms thereof, each to be composed of a presiding justice, and not more than three other justices, who shall be designated, according to law, from the whole number of justices. Each pre-

* See chapter 241, Laws of 1847, and chapter 485, Laws of 1857, for existing Judicial Districts.

siding justice shall continue to act as such during his term of office. Provision shall be made by law for holding the general terms in each judicial district. Any justice of the Supreme Court may hold special terms and Circuit Courts, and may preside in Courts of Oyer and Terminer, in any county.

SEC. 8. No judge or justice shall sit, at a general term of any court, or in the Court of Appeals, in review of a decision made by him, or by any court of which he was at the time a sitting member. The testimony in equity cases shall be taken in like manner as in cases at law; and except as herein otherwise provided, the Legislature shall have the same power to alter and regulate the juris diction and proceedings in law and equity that they have heretofore exercised. Judge or justice may not sit in review of decisions made by him, etc.

SEC. 9. When a vacancy shall occur, otherwise than by expiration of term, in the office of Justice of the Supreme Court, the same shall be filled, for a full term, at the next general election happening not less than three months after such vacancy occurs; and until any vacancy shall be so filled, the Governor by and with the advice and consent of the Senate, if the Senate shall be in session, or if not in session, the Governor may appoint to fill such vacancy. Any such appointment shall continue until and including the last day of December next after the election at which the vacancy shall be filled. Vacancy in office of justice of Supreme Court, how filled.

SEC. 10. The Judges of the Court of Appeals, and the Justices of the Supreme Court, shall not hold any other office or public trust. All votes for any of them, for any other than a judicial office, given by the Legislature or the people, shall be void. Judges of Court of Appeals, or justices of Supreme Court to hold no other office.

SEC. 11. Judges of the Court of Appeals, and Justices of the Supreme Court, may be removed by concurrent resolution of both houses of the Legislature, if two-thirds of all the members elected to each house concur therein. All judicial officers, except those mentioned in this section, and except Justices of the Peace and Judges and Justices of inferior courts not of record, may be removed by the Senate, on the recommendation of the Governor, if two-thirds of all the members elected to the Senate concur therein. But no removal Removals. Proceedings in relation to.

shall be made, by virtue of this section, unless the cause thereof be entered on the journals, nor unless the party complained of shall have been served with a copy of the charges against him, and shall have had an opportunity of being heard. On the question of removal, the yeas and nays shall be entered on the journal.

City courts.

SEC. 12. The Superior Court of the city of New York, the Court of Common Pleas for the city and county of New York, the Superior Court of Buffalo, and the City Court of Brooklyn, are continued with the powers and jurisdiction they now severally have, and such further civil and criminal jurisdiction as may be conferred by law. The Superior Court of New York shall be composed of the six judges in office at the adoption of this article, and their successors; the Court of Common Pleas of New York, of the three judges then in office, and their successors, and three additional judges; the Superior Court of Buffalo, of the judges now in office and their successors; and the City Court of Brooklyn, of such number of judges, not exceeding three, as may be provided by law. The Judges of said Courts, in office at the adoption of this article, are continued until the expiration of their terms. A Chief Judge shall be appointed by the judges of each of said courts, from their own number, who shall act as such during his official term. Vacancies in the office of the judges named in this section, occurring otherwise than by expiration of term, shall be filled in the same manner as vacancies in the Supreme Court. The Legislature may provide for detailing judges of the Superior Court and Court of Common Pleas of New York, to hold circuits or special terms of the Supreme Court in that city, as the public interest may require.

Justices of Supreme Court or Judges of City courts, how chosen.

SEC. 13. Justices of the Supreme Court shall be chosen by the electors of their respective judicial districts. Judges of all the courts mentioned in the last preceding section shall be chosen by the electors of the cities respectively in which the said courts are instituted. The official terms of the said justices and judges who shall be elected after the adoption of this article shall be fourteen years from and including the first day of January next after

Terms of office.

their election. But no person shall hold the office of justice or judge of any court longer than until and including the last day of December next after he shall be seventy years of age. Restriction. as to age.

SEC. 14. The judges and justices hereinbefore mentioned shall receive for their services a compensation to be established by law, which shall not be diminished during their official terms. Except the Judges of the Court of Appeals and the Justices of the Supreme Court, they shall be paid, and the expenses of their courts defrayed, by the cities or counties in which such courts are instituted, as shall be provided by law. Compensation of judges or justices not to be diminished during term of office.

SEC. 15. The existing county courts are continued, and the judges thereof in office at the adoption of this article, shall hold their offices until the expiration of their respective terms. Their successors shall be chosen by the electors of the counties, for the term of six years. The County Courts shall have the powers and jurisdiction they now possess, until altered by the Legislature. They shall also have original jurisdiction in all cases where the defendants reside in the county and in which the damages claimed shall not exceed one thousand dollars; and also such appellate jurisdiction as shall be provided by law, subject, however, to such provision as shall be made by law for the removal of causes into the Supreme Court. They shall also have such other original jurisdiction as shall, from time to time, be conferred upon them by the Legislature. The County Judge, with two Justices of the Peace, to be designated according to law, may hold Courts of Sessions, with such criminal jurisdiction as the Legislature shall prescribe, and he shall perform such other duties as may be required by law. His salary, and the salary of the Surrogate when elected as a separate officer, shall be established by law, payable out of the County Treasury, and shall not be diminished during his term of office. The Justices of the Peace shall be paid, for services in Courts of Sessions, a per diem allowance out of the County Treasury. The County Judge shall also be Surrogate of his county; but in counties having a population exceeding forty thousand, the Legislature may provide for the election of a separate County courts.

officer to be Surrogate, whose term of office shall be the same as that of the County Judge. The County Judge of any county may preside at Courts of Sessions, or hold County Courts, in any other County, except New York and Kings, when requested by the judge of such other county.

Local judicial officers.

SEC. 16. The Legislature may, on application of the board of supervisors, provide for the election of local officers, not to exceed two in any county, to discharge the duties of County Judge and of Surrogate, in cases of their inability, or of a vacancy, and to exercise such other powers in special cases as may be provided by law.

Judge of Court of Appeals, or justice of Supreme Court, election or appointment of. Question to be submitted to people.

SEC. 17. The Legislature shall provide for submitting to the electors of the State, at the general election in the year eighteen hundred and seventy-three, two questions to be voted upon on separate ballots, as follows: First, "Shall the offices of Chief Judge and Associate Judge of the Court of Appeals, and of Justice of the Supreme Court, be hereafter filled by appointment?"* If a majority of the votes upon the question shall be in the affirmative, the said officers shall not thereafter be elective, but, as vacancies occur, they shall be filled by appointment by the Governor by and with the advice and consent of the Senate; or if the Senate be not in session, by the Governor; but in such case, he shall nominate to the Senate when next convened, and such appointment by the Governor alone shall expire at the end of that session. Second, "Shall the offices of the judges mentioned in sections twelve and fifteen of article six of the Constitution, be hereafter filled by appointment?"* If a majority of the votes upon the question shall be in the affirmative, the said officers shall not thereafter be elective, but as vacancies occur, they shall be filled in the manner in this section above provided.

Justices of the Peace.

SEC. 18. The electors of the several towns shall, at their annual town meeting, and in such manner as the Legislature may direct, elect Justices of the Peace, whose term of office shall be four years. In case of an election to fill

* Submitted to vote of the people, Nov. 4, 1873—pursuant to chap. 314, Laws of 1873—and determined in the negative.

a vacancy occurring before the expiration of a full term, they shall hold for the residue of the unexpired term. Their number and classification may be regulated by law. Justices of the Peace and Judges or Justices of inferior courts not of record, and their clerks, may be removed, after due notice and an opportunity of being heard by such courts as may be prescribed by law, for causes to be assigned in the order of removal. Justices of the Peace and district court justices shall be elected in the different cities of this State, in such manner, and with such powers, and for such terms, respectively, as shall be prescribed by law; all other judicial officers in cities, whose election or appointment is not otherwise provided for in this article, shall be chosen by the electors of cities, or appointed by some local authorities thereof.

SEC. 19. Inferior local courts of civil and criminal jurisdiction may be established by the Legislature; and, except as herein otherwise provided, all judicial officers shall be elected or appointed at such times, and in such manner as the Legislature may direct. *Inferior local courts.*

SEC. 20. Clerks of the several counties shall be Clerks of the Supreme Court, with such powers and duties as shall be prescribed by law. The Clerk of the Court of Appeals shall keep his office at the seat of government. His compensation shall be fixed by law, and paid out of the public treasury. *Clerks of Supreme Court and Court of Appeals.*

SEC. 21. No judicial officer, except Justices of the Peace, shall receive to his own use any fees or perquisites of office; nor shall any Judge of the Court of Appeals, Justice of the Supreme Court, or Judge of a Court of Record in the cities of New York, Brooklyn or Buffalo, practice as an attorney or counselor in any court of record in this State, or act as referee. *No judicial officer, except Justice of the Peace, to receive fees.*

SEC. 22. The Legislature may authorize the judgments, decrees and decisions of any court of record of original civil jurisdiction, established in a city, to be removed for review, directly into the Court of Appeals. *Judgments, etc., may be ordered directly to Court of Appeals for review.*

SEC. 23. The Legislature shall provide for the speedy publication of all Statutes, and also for the appointment by the Justices of the Supreme Court designated to hold general terms of a reporter of the decisions of that court. *Publication of statutes to be provided for.*

To be free to all.

All laws and judicial decisions shall be free for publication by any person.

Judges, first election of.

SEC. 24. The first election of judges of the Court of Appeals, and of the three additional judges of the Court of Common Pleas for the city and county of New York, shall take place on such day, between the first Tuesday of April and the second Tuesday in June next after the adoption of this article, as may be provided by law. The Court of Appeals, the Commissioners of Appeals, and the additional judges of the said Court of Common Pleas, shall respectively enter upon their duties on the first Monday of July thereafter.

When to enter upon duties.

Local judicial officers. Term of office of present incumbents.

SEC. 25. Surrogates, Justices of the Peace, and local judicial officers provided for in section sixteen, in office when this article shall take effect, shall hold their respective offices until the expiration of their terms.

Courts of special sessions.

SEC. 26. Courts of special sessions shall have such jurisdiction of offenses of the grade of misdemeanors as may be prescribed by law.

Surrogates' Courts.

SEC. 27. For the relief of Surrogates' Courts, the Legislature may confer upon Courts of Record, in any county having a population exceeding four hundred thousand, the powers and jurisdiction of surrogates, with authority to try issues of fact by jury in probate causes.

Court of Appeals may order causes to be heard by Commission of Appeals.

*SEC. 28. The Court of Appeals may order any of the causes, not exceeding five hundred in number, pending in that court at the time of the adoption of this provision, to be heard and determined by the Commissioners of Appeals, and the Legislature may extend the term of service of the Commissioner of Appeals, not exceeding two years.†

ARTICLE VII.

Canal debt. Sinking fund.

SECTION 1. After paying the expenses of collection, superintendence and ordinary repairs, there shall be appropriated and set apart in each fiscal year out of the revenues of the State canals, in each year, commencing on the first day of June, one thousand eight hundred and forty-six, the sum of one million and three hundred thou

June 1, 1846, $1,-300,000.

*Section 28, added by vote of the people, November 5, 1872.

†Term of service of Commissioners of Appeals extended to July 1, 1875, by chap. 3, Laws of 1873.

sand dollars until the first day of June, one thousand eight hundred and fifty-five, and from that time the sum of one million and seven hundred thousand dollars in each fiscal year, as a sinking fund to pay the interest and redeem the principal of that part of the State debt called the Canal debt, as it existed at the time first aforesaid, and including three hundred thousand dollars then to be borrowed, until the same shall be wholly paid; and the principal and income of the said sinking fund shall be sacredly applied to that purpose. June 1. 1855, $1,-700,000.

SEC. 2. After complying with the provisions of the first section of this article, there shall be appropriated and set apart out of the surplus revenues of the State canals, in each fiscal year, commencing on the first day of June, one thousand eight hundred and forty-six, the sum of three hundred and fifty thousand dollars, until the time when a sufficient sum shall have been appropriated and set apart, under the said first section, to pay the interest and extinguish the entire principal of the Canal debt; and after that period, then the sum of one million and five hundred thousand dollars in each fiscal year, as a sinking fund, to pay the interest and redeem the principal of that part of the State debt called the General Fund Debt, including the debt for loans of the State credit to railroad companies which have failed to pay the interest thereon, and also the contingent debt on State stocks loaned to incorporated companies which have hitherto paid the interest thereon, whenever and as far as any part thereof may become a charge on the Treasury or General Fund, until the same shall be wholly paid; and the principal and income of the said last mentioned sinking fund shall be sacredly applied to the purpose aforesaid; and if the payment of any part of the moneys to the said sinking fund shall at any time be deferred, by reason of the priority recognized in the first section of this article, the sum so deferred, with quarterly interest thereon, at the then current rate, shall be paid to the last mentioned sinking fund, as soon as it can be done consistently with the just rights of the creditors holding said Canal Debt. General fund debt sinking fund, $350,000. After certain period, $1,-500,000.

$200,000 of the surplus canal revenue annually appropriated to General Fund, and the remainder to specific public works.

*SEC. 3. After paying the said expenses of collection, superintendence and repairs of the Canals, and the sums appropriated by the first and second sections of this article, there shall be appropriated and set apart in each fiscal year, out of the surplus revenues of the Canals, as a sinking fund, a sum sufficient to pay the interest as it falls due, and extinguish the principal within eighteen years of any loan made under this section, and if the said sinking fund shall not be sufficient to redeem any part of the principal at the stipulated times of payment, or to pay any part of the interest of such loans as stipulated, the means to satisfy any such deficiency shall be procured on the credit of the said sinking fund. After complying with the foregoing provisions, there shall be paid annually out of the said revenues into the Treasury of the State two hundred thousand dollars, to defray the necessary expenses of government. The remainder shall, in each fiscal year, be applied to meet appropriations for the enlargement and completion of the Canals mentioned in this section, until the said Canals shall be completed. In each fiscal year thereafter the remainder shall be disposed of in such manner as the Legislature may direct, but shall at no time be anticipated or pledged for more than one year in advance. The Legislature shall annually, during the next four years, appropriate to the enlargement of the Erie, the Oswego, the Cayuga and Seneca canals, and to the completion of the Black River and Genesee Valley canals, and for the enlargement of the locks of the Champlain canal, whenever, from dilapidation or decay, it shall be necessary to rebuild them, a sum not exceeding two millions two hundred and fifty thousand dollars. The remainder of the revenues of the Canals for the current fiscal year in which such appropriation is made, shall be applied to meet such appriation; and if the same shall be deemed insufficient, the Legislature shall at the same session provide for the deficiency by loan. The Legislature shall also borrow one million and five hundred thousand dollars to refund to the holders of the Canal revenue certificates issued under the provisions of chapter four hundred and eighty-

Certain deficiencies in the revenues not exceeding $2,500,000, annually to be supplied from the revenues of the canals.

* Section 3, as amended by vote of the people, Feb. 15, 1854, and Nov. 3, 1874.

five of the Laws of the year one thousand eight hundred and fifty-one, the amount received into the Treasury thereon. But no interest to accrue after July first, one thousand eight hundred and fifty-five, shall be paid on such certificates. The provisions of section twelve of this article requiring every law for borrowing money to be submitted to the people, shall not apply to the loans authorized by this section. No part of the revenues of the Canals or of the funds borrowed under this section, shall be paid or applied upon or in consequence of any alleged contract made under chapter four hundred and eighty-five of the Laws of the year one thousand eight hundred and fifty-one, except to pay for work done or materials furnished prior to the first day of June, one thousand eight hundred and fifty-two. The rates of toll on persons and property transported on the Canals shall not be reduced below those for the year one thousand eight hundred and fifty-two, except by the Canal Board, with the concurrence of the Legislature. All contracts for work or materials on any Canal shall be made with the person who shall offer to do or provide the same at the lowest price, with adequate security for their performance. **Contracts.**

* No extra compensation shall be made to any contractor, but if, from any unforeseen cause, the terms of any contract shall prove to be unjust and oppressive, the Canal Board may, upon the application of the contractor, cancel such contract. **No extra compensation to be made to.**

SEC. 4. The claims of the State against any incorporated company to pay the interest and redeem the principal of the stock of the State loaned or advanced to such company, shall be fairly enforced, and not released or compromised; and the moneys arising from such claim shall be set apart, and applied as part of the sinking fund provided in the second section of this article. But the time limited for the fulfillment of any condition of any release or compromise heretofore made or provided for, may be extended by law. **Loans to incorporated companies not to be released or compromised.**

* Last paragraph added by vote of the people, November 3, 1874.

Legislature shall, by equitable taxes, increase the revenues of the sinking fund in certain cases.

SEC. 5. If the sinking funds, or either of them provided in this article, shall prove insufficient to enable the State, on the credit of such fund, to procure the means, to satisfy the claims of the creditors of the State as they become payable, the Legislature shall, by equitable taxes, so increase the revenues of the said funds as to make them, respectively, sufficient perfectly to preserve the public faith. Every contribution or advance to the canals, or their debt, from any source, other than their direct revenues, shall, with quarterly interest, at the rates then current, be repaid into the Treasury, for the use of the State, out of the Canal revenues as soon as it can be done consistently with the just rights of the creditors holding the said Canal debt.

Certain canals of the State not to be leased or sold.

* SEC. 6. The Legislature shall not sell, lease or otherwise dispose of the Erie canal, the Oswego canal, the Champlain canal or the Cayuga and Seneca canal; but they shall remain the property of the State, and under its management forever. Hereafter the expenditures for collections, superintendence, ordinary and extraordinary repairs on the canals named in this section, shall not exceed, in any year, their gross receipts for the previous year. All funds that may be derived from any lease, sale or other disposition of any canal, shall be applied in payment of the debt for which the canal revenues are pledged.

Expenditures, for collections and repairs limited.

Funds from lease or sale, how applied.

Salt springs.

SEC. 7. The Legislature shall never sell or dispose of the Salt Springs, belonging to this State. The lands contiguous thereto and which may be necessary and convenient for the use of the Salt Springs, may be sold by authority of law and under the direction of the Commissioners of the Land Office, for the purpose of investing the moneys arising therefrom in other lands alike convenient; but by such sale and purchase the aggregate quantity of these lands shall not be diminished.

Appropriation bills.

SEC. 8. No moneys shall ever be paid out of the Treasury of this State, or any of its funds, or any of the funds under its management, except in pursuance of an appro-

* As amended, by vote of the people, November 3, 1874.

priation by law; nor unless such payment be made within two years next after the passage of such appropriation act; and every such law making a new appropriation, or continuing or reviving an appropriation, shall distinctly specify the sum appropriated, and the object to which it is to be applied; and it shall not be sufficient for such law to refer to any other law to fix such sum.

SEC. 9. The credit of the State shall not, in any manner, be given or loaned to, or in aid of any individual, association or corporation. State credit not to be loaned.

SEC. 10. The State may, to meet casual deficits or failures in revenues, or for expenses not provided for, contract debts, but such debts, direct and contingent, singly or in the aggregate, shall not, at any time, exceed one million of dollars; and the moneys arising from the loans creating such debts shall be applied to the purpose for which they were obtained, or to repay the debt so contracted, and to no other purpose whatever. Power to contract debts limited.

SEC. 11. In addition to the above limited power to contract debts, the State may contract debts to repel invasion, suppress insurrection, or defend the State in war; but the money arising from the contracting of such debts shall be applied to the purpose for which it was raised, or to repay such debts, and to no other purpose whatever. Debts to repel invasion, etc., may be contracted.

SEC. 12. Except the debts specified in the tenth and eleventh sections of this article, no debts shall be hereafter contracted by or on behalf of the State, unless such debt shall be authorized by a law, for some single work or object, to be distinctly specified therein; and such law shall impose and provide for the collection of a direct annual tax to pay, and sufficient to pay the interest on such debt as it falls due and also to pay and discharge the principal of such debt within eighteen years from the time of the contracting thereof. No such law shall take effect until it shall, at a general election, have been submitted to the people, and have received a majority of all the votes cast for and against it, at such election. On the final passage of such bill in either house of the Legislature, the question shall be taken by ayes and noes, to be duly entered on the journals thereof, and shall be: "Shall Limitation of the legislative power in the creation of debts.

this bill pass, and ought the same to receive the sanction of the people?"

The Legislature may at any time, after the approval of such law by the people, if no debt shall have been contracted in pursuance thereof, repeal the same; and may at any time, by law, forbid the contracting of any further debt or liability under such law; but the tax imposed by such act, in proportion to the debt and liability which may have been contracted, in pursuance of such law, shall remain in force and be irrepealable, and be annually collected, until the proceeds thereof shall have made the provision hereinbefore specified to pay and discharge the interest and principal of such debt and liability. The money arising from any loan or stock creating such debt or liability shall be applied to the work or object specified in the act authorizing such debt or liability, or for the repayment of such debt or liability, and for no other purpose whatever. No such law shall be submitted to be voted on, within three months after its passage, or at any general election, when any other law, or any bill, or any amendment to the Constitution shall be submitted to be voted for or against.

Sinking funds to be separately kept and safely invested.

* SEC. 13. The sinking funds provided for the payment of interest and the extinguishment of the principal of the debts of the State shall be separately kept and safely invested, and neither of them shall be appropriated or used in any manner other than for the specific purpose for which it shall have been provided.

Claims barred by lapse of time.

* SEC. 14. Neither the Legislature, Canal Board, Canal Appraisers, nor any person or persons acting in behalf of the State, shall audit, allow, or pay any claim which, as between citizens of the State, would be barred by lapse of time. The limitation of existing claims shall begin to run from the adoption of this section; but this provision shall not be construed to revive claims already barred by existing statutes, nor to repeal any statute fixing the time within which claims shall be presented or allowed, nor shall it extend to any claims duly presented within the time allowed by law, and prosecuted with due diligence

Limitation of existing claims.

* As amended, by vote of the people, November 3, 1874.

from the time of such presentment. But if the claimant shall be under legal disability, the claim may be presented within two years after such disability is removed.

ARTICLE VIII.

SECTION 1. Corporations may be formed under general laws; but shall not be created by special act, except for municipal purposes, and in cases where, in the judgment of the Legislature, the objects of the corporation cannot be attained under general laws. All general laws and special acts passed pursuant to this section, may be altered from time to time or repealed. Corporations, how created.

SEC. 2. Dues from corporations shall be secured by such individual liability of the corporators and other means as may be prescribed by law. Debts of corporations.

SEC. 3. The term, "corporations," as used in this article shall be construed to include all associations and joint-stock companies having any of the powers or privileges of corporations not possessed by individuals or partnerships. And all corporations shall have the right to sue and shall be subject to be sued in all courts in like cases as natural persons. "Corporations" defined.

* SEC. 4. The Legislature shall, by general law, conform all charters of savings banks, or institutions for savings, to a uniformity of powers, rights and liabilities, and all charters hereafter granted for such corporations shall be made to conform to such general law, and to such amendments as may be made thereto. And no such corporation shall have any capital stock, nor shall the trustees thereof, or any of them, have any interest whatever, direct or indirect, in the profits of such corporation; and no director or trustee of any such bank or institution shall be interested in any loan or use of any money or property of such bank or institution for savings. The Legislature shall have no power to pass any act granting any special charter for banking purposes; but corporations or associations may be formed for such purposes under general laws. Charters for savings banks and banking purposes.

* As amended, by vote of the people, November 3, 1874.

Specie payments. SEC. 5. The Legislature shall have no power to pass any law sanctioning in any manner, directly or indirectly, the suspension of specie payments, by any person, association or corporation issuing bank notes of any description.

Registry of bills or notes. SEC. 6. The Legislature shall provide by law for the registry of all bills or notes, issued or put in circulation as money, and shall require ample security for the redemption of the same in specie.

Individual responsibility of stockholders. SEC. 7. The stockholders in every corporation and joint-stock association for banking purposes issuing bank notes or any kind of paper credits to circulate as money, after the first day of January, one thousand eight hundred and fifty, shall be individually responsible to the amount of their respective share or shares of stock in any such corporation or association, for all its debts and liabilities of every kind, contracted after the said first day of January, one thousand eight hundred and fifty.

Insolvency of banks, preference. SEC. 8. In case of the insolvency of any bank or banking association, the billholders thereof shall be entitled to preference in payment, over all other creditors of such bank or association.

Legislature to provide for the incorporation of cities, etc., and to define powers thereof in certain cases. SEC. 9. It shall be the duty of the Legislature to provide for the organization of cities and incorporated villages, and to restrict their power of taxation, assessment, borrowing money, contracting debts, and loaning their credit, so as to prevent abuses in assessments, and in contracting debt by such municipal corporations.

The credit in money of the State not to be given or loaned. * SEC. 10. Neither the credit nor the money of the State shall be given or loaned to or in aid of any association, corporation or private undertaking. This section shall not however prevent the Legislature from making such provision for the education and support of the blind, the deaf and dumb, and juvenile delinquents, as to it may seem proper. Nor shall it apply to any fund or property now held, or which may hereafter be held by the State for educational purposes.

Counties, cities, towns, etc. * SEC. 11. No county, city, town or village shall hereafter give any money or property, or loan its money or

* Sections 10 and 11 added by vote of the people, November 3, 1874.

credit, to or in aid of any individual, association or corporation, or become, directly or indirectly, the owner of stock in or bonds of any association or corporation, nor shall any such county, city, town or village be allowed to incur any indebtedness, except for county, city, town or village purposes. This section shall not prevent such county, city, town or village from making such provision for the aid or support of its poor, as may be authorized by law. not to give money or property or loan the r money or credit. Their power to contract debts limited.

ARTICLE IX.

SECTION 1. The capital of the common school fund, the capital of the literature fund, and the capital of the United States deposit fund, shall be respectively preserved inviolate. The revenue of the said common school fund shall be applied to the support of common schools; the revenue of the said literature fund shall be applied to the support of academies, and the sum of twenty-five thousand dollars of the revenues of the United States deposit fund shall each year be appropriated to and made part of the capital of the said common school fund. Common school, literature and United States deposit funds.

ARTICLE X.

SECTION 1. Sheriffs, clerks of counties, including the Register and Clerk of the city and county of New York, Coroners, and District Attorneys, shall be chosen, by the electors of the respective counties, once in every three years and as often as vacancies shall happen. Sheriffs shall hold no other office, and be ineligible for the next three years after the termination of their offices. They may be required by law to renew their security, from time to time; and in default of giving such new security, their offices shall be deemed vacant. But the county shall never be made responsible for the acts of the Sheriff. The Governor may remove any officer, in this section mentioned, within the term for which he shall have been elected; giving to such officer a copy of the charges against him, and an opportunity of being heard in his defense. Sheriffs, clerks of counties, register and clerk of New York, coroners and district attorneys. Governor may remove.

Officers, how chosen or appointed. SEC. 2. All county officers whose election or appointment is not provided for, by this Constitution, shall be elected by the electors of the respective counties or appointed by the Board of Supervisors, or other county authorities, as the Legislature shall direct. All city, town and village officers, whose election or appointment is not provided for by this Constitution, shall be elected by the electors of such cities, towns and villages, or of some division thereof, or appointed by such authorities thereof, as the Legislature shall designate for that purpose. All other officers, whose election or appointment is not provided for by this Constitution, and all officers whose offices may hereafter be created by law, shall be elected by the people, or appointed, as the Legislature may direct.

Duration of office. SEC. 3. When the duration of any office is not provided by this Constitution, it may be declared by law, and if not so declared, such office shall be held during the pleasure of the authority making the appointment.

Time of election. SEC. 4. The time of electing all officers named in this article shall be prescribed by law.

Vacancies in office, how filled. SEC. 5. The Legislature shall provide for filling vacancies in office, and in case of elective officers, no person appointed to fill a vacancy shall hold his office by virtue of such appointment longer than the commencement of the political year next succeeding the first annual election after the happening of the vacancy.

Political year. SEC. 6. The political year and legislative term shall begin on the first day of January; and the Legislature shall, every year, assemble on the first Tuesday in January, unless a different day shall be appointed by law.

Removal from office. SEC. 7. Provision shall be made by law for the removal for misconduct or malversation in office of all officers (except judicial) whose powers and duties are not local or legislative and who shall be elected at general elections, and also for supplying vacancies created by such removal.

When office deemed vacant. SEC. 8. The Legislature may declare the cases in which any office shall be deemed vacant when no provision is made for that purpose in this Constitution.

* SEC. 9. No officer whose salary is fixed by the Constitution shall receive any additional compensation. Each of the other State officers named in the Constitution shall, during his continuance in office, receive a compensation, to be fixed by law, which shall not be increased or diminished during the term for which he shall have been elected or appointed; nor shall he receive to his use, any fees or perquisites of office or other compensation. Compensation of certain officers.

ARTICLE XI.

SECTION 1. The militia of this State shall, at all times hereafter, be armed and disciplined and in readiness for service; but all such inhabitants of this State of any religious denomination whatever as from scruples of conscience may be averse to bearing arms, shall be excused therefrom upon such conditions as shall be prescribed by law. Militia.

SEC. 2. Militia officers shall be chosen or appointed as follows: Captains, subalterns, and non-commissioned officers shall be chosen by the written votes of the members of their respective companies. Field officers of regiments and separate battalions by the written votes of the commissioned officers of the respective regiments and separate battalions; Brigadier-Generals and brigade inspectors by the field officers of their respective brigades; Major-Generals, Brigadier-Generals and commanding officers of regiments or separate battalions, shall appoint the staff officers to their respective divisions, brigades, regiments or separate battalions. Manner of choosing or appointing militia officers.

SEC. 3. The Governor shall nominate, and with the consent of the Senate, appoint all Major-Generals and the Commissary-General. The Adjutant-General and other chiefs of staff departments, and the Aides-de-camp of the Commander-in-Chief, shall be appointed by the Governor, and their commissions shall expire with the time for which the Governor shall have been elected. The Commissary-General shall hold his office for two years. He shall give security for the faithful execution of the Officers to be appointed by Governor and Senate. Commissary-general.

* Section 9 added by vote of the people, November 3, 1874.

duties of his office in such manner and amount as shall be prescribed by law.

Election of militia officers. SEC. 4. The Legislature shall, by law, direct the time and manner of electing militia officers, and of certifying their elections to the Governor.

Officers, how commissioned. SEC. 5. The commissioned officers of the militia shall be commissioned by the Governor; and no commissioned officer shall be removed from office, unless by the Senate on the recommendation of the Governor, stating the grounds on which such removal is recommended, or by the decision of a court-martial pursuant to law. The present officers of the militia shall hold their commissions subject to removal, as before provided.

Election of militia officers may be abolished. SEC. 6. In case the mode of election and appointment of militia officers hereby directed, shall not be found conducive to the improvement of the militia, the Legislature may abolish the same, and provide by law for their appointment and removal, if two-thirds of the members present in each house shall concur therein.

*ARTICLE XII.

Oath of office prescribed. SECTION 1. Members of the Legislature (and all officers, executive and judicial, except such inferior officers as shall be by law exempted), shall, before they enter on the duties of their respective offices, take and subscribe the following oath or affirmation: "I do solemnly swear (or affirm) that I will support the Constitution of the United States, and the Constitution of the State of New York, and that I will faithfully discharge the duties of the office of   , according to the best of my ability;" and all such officers who shall have been chosen at any election shall, before they enter on the duties of their respective offices, take and subscribe the oath or affirmation above prescribed, together with the following addition thereto, as part thereof:

"And I do further solemnly swear (or affirm) that I have not directly or indirectly paid, offered or promised to pay, contributed, or offered or promised to contribute,

*As amended by vote of the people, November 3, 1874.

any money or other valuable thing as a consideration or reward for the giving or withholding a vote at the election at which I was elected to said office, and have not made any promise to influence the giving or withholding any such vote," and no other oath, declaration or test, shall be required as a qualification for any office of public trust.

ARTICLE XIII.

SECTION 1. Any amendment or amendments to this Constitution may be proposed in the Senate and Assembly; and if the same shall be agreed to by a majority of the members elected to each of the two houses, such proposed amendment or amendments shall be entered on their journals with the yeas and nays taken thereon, and referred to the Legislature to be chosen at the next general election of Senators, and shall be published for three months previous to the time of making such choice, and if in the Legislature so next chosen, as aforesaid, such proposed amendment or amendments shall be agreed to by a majority of all the members elected to each house, then it shall be the duty of the Legislature to submit such proposed amendment or amendments to the people, in such manner and at such time as the Legislature shall prescribe; and if the people shall approve and ratify such amendment or amendments, by a majority of the electors qualified to vote for members of the Legislature, voting thereon, such amendment or amendments shall become part of the Constitution. Amendments.

SEC. 2. At the general election to be held in the year eighteen hundred and sixty-six, and in each twentieth year thereafter, and also at such time as the Legislature may by law provide, the question, "Shall there be a convention to revise the Constitution, and amend the same?"* shall be decided by the electors qualified to vote for members of the Legislature; and in case a majority of the electors so qualified, voting at such election, shall Future conventions, how called.

* A convention, held in 1867, pursuant hereto, proposed a new Constitution, which was voted upon in parts, in November, 1869, and rejected, except article six (sections 1 to 27, inclusive).

decide in favor of a convention for such purpose, the Legislature at its next session shall provide by law for the election of delegates to such convention.

ARTICLE XIV.

Election.

SECTION 1. The first election of Senators and Members of the Assembly, pursuant to the provisions of this Constitution, shall be held on the Tuesday succeeding the first Monday of November, one thousand eight hundred and forty-seven. The Senators and Members of Assembly who may be in office on the first day of January, one thousand eight hundred and forty-seven, shall hold their offices until and including the thirty-first day of December following, and no longer.

Term of office of Senators and members of Assembly.

First election of Governor and Lieut. Governor.

SEC. 2. The first election of Governor and Lieutenant-Governor under this Constitution shall be held on the Tuesday succeeding the first Monday of November, one thousand eight hundred and forty-eight; and the Governor and Lieutenant-Governor in office when this Constitution shall take effect, shall hold their respective offices until and including the thirty-first day of December of that year.

State officers and others to remain in office till December 31, 1847.

SEC. 3. The Secretary of State, Comptroller, Treasurer, Attorney-General, District Attorneys, Surveyor-General, Canal Commissioners and Inspectors of State Prisons, in office when this Constitution shall take effect, shall hold their respective offices until and including the thirty-first day of December, one thousand eight hundred and forty-seven, and no longer.

First election of Judicial officers, when.

SEC. 4. The first election of Judges and Clerk of the Court of Appeals, Justices of the Supreme Court, and County Judges, shall take place at such time between the first Tuesday of April and the second Tuesday of June, one thousand eight hundred and forty-seven, as may be prescribed by law. The said courts shall respectively enter upon their duties on the first Monday of July next thereafter; but the term of office of said Judges, Clerk and Justices, as declared by this Constitution, shall be deemed to commence on the first day of January, one thousand eight hundred and forty-eight.

SEC. 5. On the first Monday of July, one thousand eight hundred and forty-seven, jurisdiction of all suits and proceedings then pending in the present Supreme Court and Court of Chancery, and all suits and proceedings originally commenced and then pending in any Court of Common Pleas (except in the city and county of New York), shall become vested in the Supreme Court hereby established. Proceedings pending in Courts of Common Pleas, and in suits originally commenced in Justices' Courts, shall be transferred to the County Courts provided for in this Constitution, in such manner and form and under such regulations as shall be provided by law. The Courts of Oyer and Terminer hereby established shall in their respective counties have jurisdiction on and after the day last mentioned of all indictments and proceedings then pending in the present Courts of Oyer and Terminer, and also of all indictments and proceedings then pending in the present Courts of General Sessions of the Peace, except in the city of New York and except in cases of which the Courts of Sessions hereby established may lawfully take cognizance; and of such indictments and proceedings the Courts of Sessions hereby established shall have jurisdiction on and after the day last mentioned. Jurisdiction of pending suits.

SEC. 6. The Chancellor and the present Supreme Court shall, respectively, have power to hear and determine any of such suits and proceedings ready on the first Monday of July, one thousand eight hundred and forty-seven, for hearing or decision, and shall, for their services therein, be entitled to their present rates of compensation until the first day of July, one thousand eight hundred and forty-eight, or until all such suits and proceedings shall be sooner heard and determined. Masters in Chancery may continue to exercise the functions of their office in the Court of Chancery, so long as the Chancellor shall continue to exercise the functions of his office under the provisions of this Constitution. And the Supreme Court hereby established shall also have power to hear and determine such of said suits and proceedings as may be prescribed by law. Chancellor and Supreme Court. Masters in Chancery.

Vacancy in office of Chancellor or Justice of supr'me Court, how filled.

SEC. 7. In case any vacancy shall occur in the office of Chancellor or Justice of the present Supreme Court, previously to the first day of July, one thousand eight hundred and forty-eight, the Governor may nominate, and by and with the advice and consent of the Senate, appoint a proper person to fill such vacancy. Any Judge of the Court of Appeals or Justice of the Supreme Court, elected under this Constitution, may receive and hold such appointment.

Offices abolished.

SEC. 8. The offices of Chancellor, Justice of the existing Supreme Court, Circuit Judge, Vice-Chancellor, Assistant Vice-Chancellor, Judge of the existing County Courts of each county, Supreme Court Commissioner, Master in Chancery, Examiner in Chancery, and Surrogate (except as herein otherwise provided), are abolished from and after the first Monday of July, one thousand eight hundred and forty-seven. (1847.)

Chancellor and Justices of present Supreme Court, eligible.

SEC. 9. The Chancellor, the Justices of the present Supreme Court, and the Circuit Judges, are hereby declared to be severally eligible to any office at the first election under this Constitution.

Officers to hold until expiration of term.

SEC. 10. Sheriffs, Clerks of Counties (including the Register and Clerk of the city and county of New York), and Justices of the Peace and Coroners, in office when this Constitution shall take effect, shall hold their respective offices until the expiration of the term for which they were respectively elected.

Judicial officers may receive fees.

SEC. 11. Judicial officers in office when this Constitution shall take effect may continue to receive such fees and perquisites of office as are now authorized by law, until the first day of July, one thousand eight hundred and forty-seven, notwithstanding the provisions of the twentieth section of the sixth article of this Constitution.

Local courts to remain, etc.

SEC. 12. All local courts established in any city or village, including the Superior Court, Common Pleas, Sessions and Surrogates' Courts of the city and county of New York, shall remain, until otherwise directed by the Legislature, with their present powers and jurisdictions; and the Judges of such courts and any clerks thereof in office on the first day of January, one thousand eight hundred and forty-seven, shall continue in office until the expiration of their terms of office, or until the Legislature shall otherwise direct.

SEC. 13. This Constitution shall be in force from and including the first day of January, one thousand eight hundred and forty-seven, except as is herein otherwise provided. When Constitution goes into operation.

* ARTICLE XV.

SECTION 1. Any person holding office under the laws of this State, who, except in payment of his legal salary, fees or perquisites, shall receive or consent to receive, directly or indirectly, any thing of value or of personal advantage, or the promise thereof, for performing or omitting to perform any official act, or with the express or implied understanding that his official action or omission to act is to be in any degree influenced thereby, shall be deemed guilty of a felony. This section shall not affect the validity of any existing statute in relation to the offense of bribery. Bribery and official corruption.

SEC. 2. Any person who shall offer or promise a bribe to an officer, if it shall be received, shall be deemed guilty of a felony and liable to punishment, except as herein provided. No person offering a bribe shall, upon any prosecution of the officer for receiving such bribe, be privileged from testifying in relation thereto, and he shall not be liable to civil or criminal prosecution therefor, if he shall testify to the giving or offering of such bribe. Any person who shall offer or promise a bribe, if it be rejected by the officer to whom it is tendered, shall be deemed guilty of an attempt to bribe, which is hereby declared to be a felony. The same subject.

SEC. 3. Any person charged with receiving a bribe, or with offering or promising a bribe, shall be permitted to testify in his own behalf in any civil or criminal prosecution therefor. Persons offering or receiving bribe may be witness.

SEC. 4. Any district attorney who shall fail faithfully to prosecute a person charged with the violation in his county of any provision of this article which may come to his knowledge, shall be removed from office by the District attorney may be removed for failure to prosecute violation.

* Article 15, added by vote of the people, November 3, 1874.

Expenses of prosecution, how chargeable.

Governor, after due notice and an opportunity of being heard in his defense. The expenses which shall be incurred by any county, in investigating and prosecuting any charge of bribery or attempting to bribe any person holding office under the laws of this State, within such county, or of receiving bribes by any such person in said county, shall be a charge against the State, and their payment by the State shall be provided for by law.

* ARTICLE XVI.

Amendments, when to take effect.

SECTION 1. All amendments to the Constitution shall be in force from and including the first day of January succeeding the election at which the same were adopted, except when otherwise provided by such amendments.

Done, in Convention, at the Capitol in the city of Albany, the ninth day of October in the year one thousand eight hundred and forty-six, and of the Independence of the United States of America the seventy-first.

In witness whereof, we have hereunto subscribed our names.

JOHN TRACY, *President,*
and Delegate from the County of Chenango.

JAMES F. STARBUCK,
H. W. STRONG,
FR. SEGER,
Secretaries.

* Article 16, added by vote of the people, November 3, 1846.

INDEX

TO THE MATTERS CONTAINED IN THE EIGHTH VOLUME.

Lightning Source UK Ltd.
Milton Keynes UK
UKHW020620221218
334411UK00006B/909/P